THE
WARD LOCK
ENCYCLOPEDIA
OF
Practical
Gardening

THE
WARD LOCK
ENCYCLOPEDIA
OF
Practical
Gardening

ANITA PEREIRE

Photographs by A. Descat

WARD LOCK

A WARD LOCK BOOK

First published in the UK 1995
by Ward Lock
Wellington House
125 Strand
LONDON WC2R 0BB

First paperback edition 1997
Reprinted 1999

A Cassell Imprint

Original title *Encyclopédie Pratique du Jardin*
Written by Anita Pereire
Illustrated by Arnaud Descat
Published by Hachette Littérature Générale
(Livres Pratiques) 1994

Distributed in the United States
by Sterling Publishing Co. Inc.,
387 Park Avenue South, New York,
NY 10016–8810

A British Library Cataloguing in Publication Data
block for this book may be obtained from the
British Library

ISBN 0 7063 7639 0

Illustrations: Ferdinand Dhoska
Additional photographs: Philippe Ferret,
Valerie Finnis, Philippe Perdereau,
Alain Meilland, Clive Nichols (pps 2, 3–4, 7, 8, 9),
Ernest Turc

Cover photographs
Front (clockwise): Jerry Harpur (strawberries);
Andrew Lawson (*Osteospermum jucundum*); Fabbri
Publishing/Robert Harding Syndication (trowel);
Jerry Harpur (*Dahlia* 'Conway'); Jerry Harpur
(Bourton House); Andrew Lawson (*Malus* 'Golden
Hornet'); Andrew Lawson (*Macleaya microcarpa*
'Kelway's Coral Plume'); Jerry Harpur (*Meconopsis
betonicifolia*); Fabbri Publishing/Robert Harding
Syndication (shears)
Back (clockwise): Fabbri Publishing/Robert
Harding Syndication (hanging basket); Jerry
Harpur (*Rosa* 'Gertrude Jekyll'); Fabbri
Publishing/Robert Harding Syndication
(primrose cultivar); Andrew Lawson (*Lilium*
'Jetfire')

Typeset by Keystroke, Wolverhampton
Printed in Singapore by Tien Wah Press (Pte.) Ltd.

Photograph on page 2: A dramatic border including
artemisias, linums and a stipa.

Foreword

THERE is nothing more rewarding than turning a piece of previously bare or untamed earth into a garden, and there is no enthusiasm more infectious than that of someone who has been involved in the transformation. But we all need help, in the form of advice and encouragement. This Encyclopedia will give you all the help you need.

It will tell you about the basics of design and prevent you from rushing headlong into disaster. There are chapters on how to build your own garden features and how to propagate plants – both of which can save you money. That's one of the great things about gardening: it need not be an expensive pursuit. From one plant you can usually obtain many more by skill rather than financial outlay.

In recent years gardeners have become more demanding in their quest for plants. They grow a wider range each year, and what they need is a book which shows them the range of treasures on offer. *The Ward Lock Encyclopedia of Practical Gardening* does just that. It contains comprehensive sections on garden flowers, trees, shrubs, climbers and fruit, with details of cultivation and superb photographs.

People tend to develop an enthusiasm for gardening when they realize its full potential. Early on it is all too easy to think of gardening as a chore: all you seem to be doing is pulling up weeds. The plants you want to grow seem reluctant to thrive, and the ones you are discouraging grow like . . . well, weeds! But then you turn the corner. Either a particular plant does well for you, or else you realize that half the fun of gardening is just being there.

As life gets faster and more stressful the garden can offer solace, calmness and an escape from the rat race. It need not amount to stately acres, or be buried deep in the country. Provided it is filled with the kinds of plants you like, it will fulfil your needs rather than anybody else's. Don't be frightened of being an individualist. Grow the flowers you like in the colours that appeal to you.

The biggest secret of success is learning how to enjoy your garden. This may sound simple, but it is amazing how many people fail to achieve it. I hope this book will be instrumental in helping you to achieve that state of mind. It is hard to find one comprehensive volume which can act as a gardener's 'inquire within', but this Encyclopedia by Anita Pereire will go a long way to providing you with the information, enthusiasm and encouragement you need to turn your bit of earth into something that gives you endless pleasure.

Above: An effective container planting of helichrysums, pelargoniums and an agave.

C o n

I

FLOWERS

Acaena to Zinnia
14

This section of the Encyclopedia describes over 2 000 flower species and varieties to help you in your choice of plants, and gives detailed advice on their cultivation, soil requirements and ideal position in the garden

II

TREES & SHRUBS

Abelia to Zenobia
254

Over 2 000 of the most attractive and ornamental trees and shrubs are described here, with advice on how best to use them in the garden

CLIMBERS
Abutilon to Wisteria
448

The best climbing pants for walls, pergolas and other garden features are listed in this section

FRUIT
Actinidia to Vine
480

This part of the book lists the best varieties of all the most popular fruits for the home gardener

tents

Preface

*L*ET *no one tell you that gardening is easy and that all you need are green fingers and an annual trip to the garden centre. Like any creative activity, gardening needs knowledge, patience, and some degree of skill. Perhaps green fingers help – I don't really know, because in a long professional career I haven't found that flowers grow more readily for me than for anyone else. But you certainly need some basic knowledge, and all good gardeners acquire their knowledge gradually over a lifetime, learning from their mistakes (I speak for myself here) and, of course, from the rich fund of experience passed on by other gardeners.*

I believe one of the most reliable and accessible sources of this gardening experience is the gardening encyclopedia. It gathers together in easily assimilated form the many thousands of facts and techniques the modern gardener has at his or her disposal. It also gathers in a volume the accumulated experience of a great number of gardeners and botanists, past and present, who have categorized plants and trees, noted their habits, their virtues and limitations, described their appearance, and described how to grow them to best advantage according to the soil, climate and topography of the garden that you, the gardener, have at your disposal.

Gardening is the most completely satisfying of activities. It involves all five senses and a range of skills: artistic, because you are creating beauty; calling for manual dexterity when you prune and graft; and physical, as you'll soon find out when you pick up a spade. Personally, I am deterred by lengthy instructions and so I avoid writing them. What I try to do here is simply help you to put the right plant in the right place at the right time of year, to create features that will make your garden more attractive, and to deal with any problems you might encounter.

The striking flowers of *Aster* 'King George'.

Right: This stunning white border includes hostas, tulips and a lunaria.

Above: A beautiful combination of sedums, chrysanthemums and anemones.

Overleaf: A superb red border planted with dahlias, gazanias and a sunflower.

I hope you find this volume really useful. In the early pages I describe how best to use it, and towards the end I have tried to simplify all the many considerations which go to make a successful garden into a set of tables for easy reference. Of course, you'll know that tables and charts are not to be followed slavishly. You'll know that things that grow, just like people, have their little ways. So I suggest you treat my tables as nothing more than a general time-saving guide. And as your gardening skills develop, don't be afraid to try your hand at unusual choices of plants and planting schemes.

This Encyclopedia presents some of my own experience of gardening and garden-making in a form which you will find friendly and helpful and free of gardening jargon.

I wish you many hours of happy and successful gardening.

anita Pereire

Achillea

YARROW

Compositae

These superb perennials are unbeatable for their brilliant flowers and for the ease with which they can be grown. On top of that, they bloom for three or four months continuously. Usually yellow but occasionally red or white, they are the queens of the summer garden.

Useful hints

— In a rich soil, don't forget to stake the larger varieties and, in particular, *Achillea filipendulina*.

— Where possible, plant in the spring, especially if your soil is wet and heavy.

— With the exception of *A. tomentosa*, the achilleas are very hardy. Nevertheless, they do require a healthy well-drained soil.

Recommended

— As far as the yellows are concerned, *A. tomentosa* and *A. filipendulina* lead the field.

— For a white flower, the choice falls on *A. ptarmica*. Here, 'The Pearl' grows quickly and makes a good cut flower.

— *A. millefolium* is often a parent of the many hybrids now available. They are frequently noted for their delightful pastel shades, which are so easy to blend.

— Those recommended include: 'Apfelblüte' (pale pink); 'Fanal' (bright red); 'Hoffnung' (sulphur); 'Lachsschönheit' (salmon-pink); 'Summer Pastels' (mixed); 'Wesersandstein' (deep salmon-pink to creamy yellow). Of the *A. millefolium* varieties, 'Red Beauty' grows vigorously and produces rich red umbels, and 'Cerise Queen' has vivid pink flowers.

Height: 130 cm (50 in) for *A. filipendulina*, 80 cm (32 in) for *A. ptarmica*, 45 cm (18 in) for *A. tomentosa* and *A. millefolium*.
Spacing and planting distance: 50 cm (20 in) *A. filipendulina* and 30–40 cm (12–16) in for the other varieties.
Soil: any, even poor, provided that it is well-drained.
Aspect: full sun.
Propagation: by division in the spring.
Flowering season: summer to autumn.
Type: perennial.

◁ *Achillea filipendulina*

Acidanthera bicolor 'Murielae' △

Aconitum

MONKSHOOD

Ranunculaceae

If they weren't so poisonous, the aconites would find a home in every garden. They are robust and their elegant palmate foliage is among the finest of the perennials. The blue of the flowers is of a rare intensity, but unfortunately the sap is extremely toxic. For this reason, it is too dangerous to keep in gardens where children are around and, even for adults, strict precautions must be taken when handling the plant or cutting flowers.

Useful hints

— Plant in autumn or spring in a rich soil that remains moist in summer. Mulch the soil in spring with lawn-cuttings or peat.

— Water once a month with liquid manure.

— When fewer flowers are forthcoming, divide the clumps with an edging spade and replant only cuttings that have at least two or three shoots.

— Wash your hands well each time you handle this plant.

▽ *Aconitum napellus*

Acidanthera (syn. *Gladiolus*)

ETHIOPIAN GLADIOLUS, PEACOCK-ORCHID

Iridaceae

Each bulb of *Acidanthera bicolor* 'Murielae' (syn. *Gladiolus callianthus* 'Murielae') will yield a miniature 'gladiolus', the white flowers bearing a brown spot in the centre. As these open one by one, they have a noticeable perfume that is easily recognized even at about two metres away. Since they are not exactly the most graceful plant, place them next to a plant with a compact outline, e.g. pelargonium.

Useful hints

— Plant in late spring after the frosts are over. The bulbs should be at a depth of about 10 cm (4 in) and are best suited to a light soil.

— To extend the flowering season, water once a week and give liquid manure every fortnight. The appearance of a second spike is by no means uncommon.

— Once the foliage has dried, but before the hard frosts of autumn, dig up the bulbs and store them e.g. in a cellar out of the cold. To protect against parasites, remove leaves and clean before putting away to dry.

Height: 40–80 cm (16–32 in).
Spacing and planting distance: 15 cm (6 in).
Soil: well-drained.
Aspect: full sun.
Propagation: from offsets.
Flowering season: a good month during summer.
Type: bulb.

Recommended

— The best-known aconites are those that flower at the end of spring, especially *Aconitum napellus*, 'Blue Sceptre' (purplish blue) and 'Bicolor' (blue and white). White flowers are also to be found.

— Though as yet relatively unknown, the autumn aconites are very valuable since they flower at the same time as the asters. *A. carmichaelii* 'Arendsii', dark blue, in late autumn, and *A. carmichaelii* Wilsonii Group, amethyst-blue and slightly earlier, reach heights of up to around 180 cm (72 in).

— *A.* 'Ivorine' has more slender white flowers and heavily ribbed foliage.

Height: 100–180 cm (40–72 in).
Spacing and planting distance: 40 cm (16 in).
Soil: rich and moist.
Aspect: full sun.
Propagation: by division as growing starts.
Flowering season: late spring to late autumn, according to species.
Type: perennial.

Actaea

BANEBERRY, COHOSH

Ranunculaceae

Some plants are a treat in themselves and this is the case with *Actaea rubra*. Though the flowering spikes do not last long, the tallish stature and elegant foliage make it a favourite for the wilder corners. The red berries which appear in autumn are beautiful but highly toxic.

Useful hints

— Plant from pots at any time but otherwise in autumn. Dig the ground over well as the roots go deep. Mulch the soil at the end of spring. Water thoroughly during the first year and in periods of great heat.

— Propagate by division as soon as you notice the plants becoming less vigorous, but change their location as they exhaust the soil.

Recommended

— The white berries of *A. alba* shine like porcelain on fleshy, scarlet stalks.

Height: 100–200 cm (40–80 in).
Spacing and planting distance: 60 cm (24 in).
Soil: ordinary, preferably slightly moist in summer.
Aspect: semi-shade.
Propagation: by division in autumn.
Flowering season: summer.
Type: perennial.

Adiantum

MAIDENHAIR, MAIDENHAIR FERN

Adiantaceae

With its shiny mahogany stems and tapered undulating fronds, *Adiantum pedatum* is a charming little fern that should be found more often in the undergrowth of natural gardens. Being hardy, it flourishes in cool shady gardens to which it adds a rare touch of refinement. In more formal settings, it can be placed alongside helxine and the most elegant of decorative mosses.

Useful hints

— Plant in mid- or late spring. Choose a shady bed and enrich the soil with two shovelfuls of leaf-mould or peat per square metre.

— When the clumps have grown to a good size after four years, divide them and plant in shady parts of the garden.

— This little fern loses its leaves in winter so don't worry if they suddenly turn brown.

Height: 15–30 cm (6–12 in).
Spacing and planting distance: 30 cm (12 in).
Soil: rich in humus.
Aspect: semi-shade.
Propagation: by division.
Type: perennial.

Adiantum pedatum ▷
▽ *Actaea rubra*

Adonis

PHEASANT'S EYE

Ranunculaceae

The cheerful yellow flowers of this little plant are one of the earliest signs of life returning to the garden. The finely divided almost feathery foliage is a delight to see. Intersperse the plant with early bulbs such as crocus or scilla for a charming scene. Alternatively, to obtain continuity, plant some hostas which will flower in the space that is left during summer when the foliage of the adonis has died.

Useful hints

— Plant at the beginning of autumn in the semi-shade at the foot of a deciduous tree. Mark the position with twigs as there are no leaves for a good part of the year.

— Mulch the soil in late winter, using pine needles, leaf-mould or peat.

Recommended

— While *Adonis amurensis* comes from Manchuria in north-east China, it also has a well-known European cousin, *A. vernalis*, also with foliage finely divided.

Height: 20–30 cm (8–12 in).
Spacing and planting distance: 20 cm (8 in).
Soil: ordinary; add a little leaf-mould.
Aspect: needs sun for the flowers to open.
Propagation: by division at the end of summer or from fresh seed in early summer (they take a year to germinate).
Flowering season: spring.
Type: bulb.

Aethionema

STONECRESS

Cruciferae

If you need to fill a dry corner of a wall, you can rely on aethionema, a plant close to the alyssums which likes a sunny well-drained position. Given the right conditions, a single pot will produce a clump of spectacular grey-green foliage that remains covered with deep pink flowers for more than six weeks. They blend happily with tulips or, better still, with white decorative alliums.

Useful hints

— If possible, plant in autumn so that it becomes well-established before the

◁ *Adonis amurensis*

△ *Aethionema* 'Warley Rose'

Agapanthus Headbourne Hybrids △

worst of the cold. Place a handful of gravel around the neck to keep it dry.

— Prune after flowering in summer to avoid seed formation.

Recommended

— While the hybrid 'Warley Rose' is the best-known, *Aethionema grandiflorum* may also be found in catalogues. Its flowers are lighter.

Height: 15–20 cm (6–8 in).
Spacing and planting distance: 20 cm (8 in).
Soil: light; leaf-mould and coarse sand.
Aspect: full sun.
Propagation: relatively difficult, from root cuttings or seed in spring.
Flowering season: summer.
Type: perennial.

Agapanthus

AFRICAN LILY, LILY OF THE NILE

Liliaceae

Once a familiar sight, agapanthus has now all but disappeared from our gardens and is more commonly seen in pots. The different varieties keep their fine strap-like foliage from one end of the year to the other except for *Agapanthus campanulatus*, which tends to be deciduous.

Useful hints

— Plant the large tuberous roots of *A. praecox* ssp. *orientalis* in spring, placing them in pots with a diameter of 30 cm (12 in) filled with a mixture composed half of leaf-mould and half of compost.

This species does not tolerate frost and in this way you can bring them in for the winter.

— Place *A. campanulatus* in pots with a diameter of 20 cm (8 in) or directly in the ground. In the latter case, don't forget to protect them in winter with peat or leaves. Avoid moving this variety otherwise it may not flower.

Recommended

— *A. praecox* ssp. *orientalis* has china-blue umbels which go very well with the fine dark blue of the hardy Headbourne Hybrids.

— *A. campanulatus* is a superb blue and is ideal for bordering a gravel path or brightening a shady corner.

— *A. campanulatus* 'Albus' is a very pretty white variety. 'Isis', on the other hand, has a subtle, lavender-blue flower which is slightly larger than that of the species.

— The Bressingham Hybrids have smaller flower heads, but their vigorous clumps produce many blooms.

Height: 50–70 cm (20–28 in).
Spacing and planting distance: 30 cm (12 in).
Soil: rich and light (*A. umbellatus*), ordinary and well-drained (*A. campanulatus*).
Aspect: sun or semi-shade.
Propagation: by division.
Flowering season: late summer (*A. umbellatus*), summer to autumn (*A. campanulatus*).
Type: bulb.

Agathaea coelestis

see *Felicia amelloides*

Agave

CENTURY PLANT

Agavaceae

The agave is found only in warm climates. Suitable as a bedding plant in summer, at around fifty years it begins to flower in enormous stems with the strangest inflorescences, flat and round, rising one above another.

Useful hints

— Away from warm and temperate climates, the agave is more usually to be found in glasshouses although it is rather hardier than you might expect.

— To propagate, remove the young rosettes and leave to dry for three or four days before replanting in any ordinary soil. It goes without saying that these sun-loving plants are not too fond of cold, moist soils.

Recommended

— *Agave americana* is the most common variety. 'Variegata' has large, bluish leaves with cream margins.

— Much more modestly proportioned than its American cousin, *A. victoriae-reginae* has a height and circumference of some 15–20 cm (6–8 in). This is also a more elegant plant, with pointed white-edged leaves.

Height: 15–120 cm (6–48 in).
Spacing and planting distance: 50 cm (20 in).
Soil: ordinary.
Aspect: sun.
Propagation: by division of rosettes.
Flowering season: summer.
Type: perennial.

Ageratum

FLOSSFLOWER

Compositae

Though somewhat out of fashion, *Ageratum houstonianum* is really quite indispensable in a summer garden, its soft violet counter-balancing the loud yellow and orange of marigolds and carnations. Though seeding can be a problem because of the need for a little heat, the growing stage is easy. A few bunches placed around the edge of your beds will add a certain country vicarage charm to your garden.

Useful hints

— Seeding should take place out of the cold in spring. Transplant once before finally planting after the frosts are over. If you buy the plants, nip the shoots to strengthen growth.

— Watering at least once a week will help to get rid of the mites which swarm in hot weather and cause severe loss of moisture. Feed with liquid manure every fortnight.

Recommended

— All the F[1] hybrids are good. They come in a range of colours, the soft shades of pink being particularly attractive. Beware of white, however, which fades very rapidly and is always disappointing.

Height: 15–25 cm (6–10 in).
Spacing and planting distance: 15 cm (6 in).
Soil: ordinary, enriched with a little peat or compost.
Aspect: full sun.
Propagation: from seed, indoors in spring.
Flowering season: throughout summer and early autumn.
Type: annual.

Ajuga

BUGLE, BUGLEWEED

Labiatae

This is one of the best plants of all for ground cover. *Ajuga reptans* is ideal for the foot of shrubs or the front of flower beds. The plant is very robust and its stolons spread rapidly. It flowers in summer with small blue spikes and the brilliant foliage stays all through the year, including winter.

Useful hints

— Don't plant too close together: four or five laid down in the spring will be more than enough to yield a good carpet by the end of the year.

— Propagation by division is very easy and can be done at any time of year.

— A covering of peat spread between the young clumps at the time of planting will help the stolons to take root.

Recommended

— The most soberly coloured is *A. reptans* 'Atropurpurea', which has deep purple foliage. The most striking is *A. reptans* 'Multicolor' with leaves mottled pink, bronze and yellow. *A. reptans* 'Purple Torch', has a great abundance of pink flowers. *A. reptans* 'Burgundy Glow' has pink and white mottled leaves and must be cut back regularly.

Height: 15 cm (6 in).
Spacing and planting distance: 30–40 cm (12–16 in).
Soil: moist in summer.
Aspect: preferably shade or semi-shade (also in sun if the soil is moist).
Propagation: by division at any time of year.
Flowering season: summer.
Type: perennial.

Ageratum houstonianum △

◁ *Agave americana*

Ajuga reptans ▽

Alcea

see *Althaea*

Alchemilla

LADY'S MANTLE

Rosaceae

There is room in every garden for this little plant with its dew-spangled foliage. Lady's mantle gives excellent ground cover both in shade and semi-shade. The elegant foliage is soft to the touch and, in summer, the yellowish green calyx blends harmoniously with roses, lilies and many other perennials. Nothing can compare with alchemilla to soften the line of a new path and, as it grows in very little soil, it will flourish among stone flags or in walls and steps.

Useful hints

— Alchemilla enjoys semi-shade, where its foliage develops best.

— Ideally, soil should be moist at all times. If it's not possible to water, spread peat or grass cuttings around plants at the beginning of summer.

— Twigs may be needed for support.

Recommended

— The best-known is *Alchemilla mollis*, which forms well-rounded clumps. Less common is *A. alpina*, which has bluish foliage and is less invasive. It is sometimes confused with *A. conjuncta*, which has dark green leaves divided into seven lobes that are rimmed with silver. The base of the shoots of *A. erythropoda* are a characteristic red colour. It is an ideal rock garden plant.

Height: 15–40 cm (6–16 in).
Spacing and planting distance: 30 cm (12 in).
Soil: ordinary, preferably moist.
Aspect: semi-shade; avoid direct sun.
Propagation: by division or from seed in spring.
Flowering season: summer.
Type: perennial.

◁ *Alchemilla mollis*

Allium

DECORATIVE ONION, ORNAMENTAL GARLIC

Liliaceae

The onion has lost none of the charm of a wild plant. Compared to many other bulbs, onions have elegant foliage, though, if you don't like the smell of onion, you should avoid bruising it. They make very fine cut flowers.

Useful hints

— Alliums should be planted in autumn after digging over the bed thoroughly. Add a barrow-load of compost if it is a thin soil. The small bulbs should be planted at a depth of 5 cm (2 in) by hand while large bulbs should be planted at 15–20 cm (6–8 in), using a dibble so as not to damage them.

— Check that the bulbs are in good condition by removing the outer skin. If there is any trace of rot, treat them with a fungicide powder.

— Water regularly from spring onwards to build up strength for later in the year and to avoid yellowing of the foliage.

— Most of the decorative onions/ ornamental garlics can be left in the ground from one year to another and, indeed, this is how the best clumps are formed. It is not uncommon for seedlings to appear naturally under trees and this is especially the case with *Allium ursinum*.

— Dwarf species (*A. moly*, *A. karataviense*, *A. cirrhosum* and *A. oreophilum*) can be grown very successfully in pots.

Recommended

— *A. christophii* flowers in summer with balls of blossom some 25 cm (10 in) in diameter on stems that rise 40–50 cm (16–20 in).

— *A. caeruleum* is a smaller plant that produces brilliant, almost electric, blue flowers in summer.

— *A. neapolitanum* has larger, pure white flowers that are scented and somewhat less densely packed. Under glass, it can be made to flower in spring.

— *A. flavum*, with its golden yellow flowers, thrives in dry, stony soil where it self-seeds readily.

— *A. giganteum* is appropriately named, growing to a height of 150 cm (60 in) and producing heads that are around 20 cm (8 in) in diameter. They can be grown together with a shrub artemisia (*Artemisia arborescens*) which will serve as a support.

— *A. moly* reaches a height of almost 20 cm (8 in) and so is almost a miniature compared to the preceding example. The bright yellow flowers are not dense, but the clumps develop very rapidly and guarantee cover after a few years. Ideal for the wilder corners of a garden or for the edges of permanent beds.

— *A. oreophilum*, which is still sold as *A. ostrowskianum*, produces a bright pink flower at the same time as the preceding example (early summer) and similarly grows to about 20 cm (8 in). The two go very well together and blend in perfectly with myosotis.

— *A. schoenoprasum* is better known as chives, which, apart from providing flowering borders in summer, is also the essential ingredient for any vinaigrette. They can be planted in herb gardens, rockeries or even a window-box.

— *A. schubertii* is expensive but impressive. The clump is relatively short with a rather elevated umbel. The metallic-red blooms are borne on 15 cm (6 in) stems and they are well worth keeping for arrangements of dried flowers.

— *A. sphaerocephalon* grows to a height of 80 cm (32 in). Its slender stems bear dense umbels of tiny, pinkish purple flowers in summer.

— *A. ursinum* has broad, shiny leaves and white flowers that add a touch of colour under shrubs in summer.

Height: 15–150 cm (6–60 in), depending on variety.
Spacing and planting distance: 20 cm (8 in).
Soil: ordinary.
Aspect: sun.
Propagation: by separating bulblets in autumn.
Flowering season: spring to summer, depending on variety.
Type: bulb.

Allium neapolitanum ▽

△ *Allium caeruleum*
◁ *Allium moly*
▽ *Allium christophii*

27

Alstroemeria aurea 'Orange King' △

Alstroemeria

PERUVIAN LILY

Liliaceae/Alstroemeriaceae

The alstroemerias are very temperamental plants that can either spring up like weeds or show no progress at all for years. The fleshy root is very sensitive to transplantation.

Useful hints

— Planting should be very shallow and should take place preferably in spring. The soil should be deep and light.

— Water as the foliage develops. As the stems are delicate, they can be either supported with canes or allowed to grow through clumps of lavender or rosemary.

— When the foliage disappears in early or mid-autumn, note the position of the clumps and cover them with a handful of straw or coarse pine bark.

Recommended

— *Alstroemeria aurea* spreads rapidly once it is established. The flowers range from pure yellow to orange, the best-known varieties being 'Dover Orange' and 'Orange King'.

— The Ligtu Hybrids are slightly less hardy. They are often sold as cut flowers for bouquets. The flowers are pink, lilac or white and are streaked with purple.

Height: 40–90 cm (16–36 in).
Spacing and planting distance: 30 cm (12 in).
Soil: well-drained in winter. Add sand if necessary.
Aspect: fully exposed to the sun but sheltered from dry spring winds.
Propagation: from seed *in situ* or by division.
Flowering season: summer.
Type: bulb.

Althaea (syn. Alcea)

HOLLYHOCK

Malvaceae

These should be placed at the back of a border, slightly in the shade. Though often considered to be perennial, they flourish in some regions only as biennials. Their charm and grace is to be admired in many gardens of note.

Useful hints

— When sowing, space the seeds well and use a rich soil. Once their leaves are touching, replant them about 15 cm (6 in) apart.

— They should be planted out in their final positions in mid-autumn, and should then be watered a few times to help them to take.

— In spring, water from time to time and make sure that they are treated against rust every month.

Recommended

— Although the single flower is very attractive it is more and more the case that *Althaea rosea* (syn. *Alcea rosea*) seeds are doubles or semi-doubles. Chater's Double Group, with powder-puff flowers, is very popular. The reddish brown, almost black flowers of *A. rosea* 'Nigra' are an unusual colour.

— *A. ficifolia* (syn. *Alcea ficifolia*) is vigorous and has greater resistance to mildew than *A. rosea*.

Height: 150–200 cm (60–80 in).
Spacing and planting distance: 30–50 cm (12–20 in).
Soil: rich and fairly moist.
Aspect: sun or semi-shade.
Propagation: from seed in spring or by division in winter.
Flowering season: summer.
Type: perennial or biennial.

△ *Alyssum saxatile*

Alyssum

ROCK ALYSSUM, MADWORT

Cruciferae

In spring, the grey-green carpet of this alyssum suddenly blazes bright yellow, flowering at the same time as the tulips and only just after the forsythias. It is also very easy to grow: a clump the size of a fist planted in autumn will be larger than a dinner plate within six months. Be careful, however, or they will soon take over.

◁ *Althaea rosea*

Useful hints

— Protect the young plants against slugs and snails, though they are so vigorous that this is not necessary for long.

— Grow from seed in trays and then plant out in a sunny spot. The only soil requirement is good drainage.

Recommended

— *Alyssum saxatile* (syn. *Aurinia saxatilis*) 'Compacta' and 'Citrinum' are two good varieties. The former has bright yellow flowers, the latter an acid yellow that goes well with tulips. The double flowers of *A. saxatile* 'Flore Pleno' make it appear even more brightly coloured. *A. murale* also has bright yellow flowers with grey-green leaves.

— *A. montanum* covers low walls with a mat of silver-grey foliage. It is denser and more compact in its growth than *A. murale*.

Height: 15–30 cm (6–12 in).
Spacing and planting distance: 15 cm (6 in).
Soil: ordinary.
Aspect: sun.
Propagation: from seed or cuttings.
Flowering season: spring to summer.
Type: perennial.

Amaranthus

AMARANTH, LOVE-LIES-BLEEDING

Amaranthaceae

Amaranthus caudatus produces a fountain of blossom. At the end of the summer, its drooping crimson tassels reach almost to the ground and provide fine decoration for a terrace. They can be combined with field daisies to form large bouquets.

Useful hints

— The seeds germinate easily and it is best to wait till late spring before sowing.

— Transplant the young growths at least once in a pot or forcing frame to get the roots to spread.

— Select the best and place them in a sunny spot. Water well at least once a fortnight during the summer. The addition of special flower nutrient in high summer will produce truly enormous blooms.

— Just before the frosts come, root out and burn the plants to prevent an invasion of self-sown seeds in the following year.

Recommended

— Love-lies-bleeding comes in two colours, the classical crimson and a greenish white variety. They mix well with rudbeckias and tobacco plants.

Height: 100–200 cm (40–80 in).
Spacing and planting distance: 60–80 cm (24–32 in).
Soil: ordinary, rather rich.
Aspect: sun.
Propagation: from seed in spring.
Flowering season: mid-summer to first frosts.
Type: annual.

Amaryllis

AMARYLLIS

Liliaceae/Amaryllidaceae

When *Amaryllis belladonna* puts out great clusters of pink, scented, trumpet-like flowers in late summer, the effect is so splendid that it is easy not to notice the absence of the foliage which does not appear until later. Because of this unusual feature, it's a good idea to plant three or four together as they will compose fine clumps from the very first year.

Useful hints

— Amaryllis should be planted by the beginning of autumn: any later and they

△ *Amaranthus caudatus*

may refuse to display any leaves at all for a year. It is preferable to choose a southerly aspect, as they like the sun.

— Provide a covering of leaves to protect them against heavy frosts.

Height: 70 cm (28 in).
Spacing and planting distance: 20 cm (8 in).
Soil: rich and deep.
Aspect: sun.
Propagation: from seed or by division of bulbs.
Flowering season: late summer to autumn.
Type: bulb.

Anacyclus

ANACYCLUS

Compositae

This little daisy-like plant is free-flowering over several weeks in spring and is an adornment for any rock

△ *Amaryllis belladonna*

garden. The stems are covered with grey leaves and terminate in white flowers with pink on the outside of the ray florets. *Anacyclus pyrethrum* var. *depressus* can be recommended as a pot plant, as it looks good close up.

Useful hints

— Plant in autumn with a handful of round gravel to protect the collar from any winter rot.

— If you decide to have it as a pot plant, choose a container that is more wide than tall, covering the soil with gravel to set off the foliage.

Height: 10 cm (4 in).
Spacing and planting distance: 15–20 cm (6–8 in).
Soil: leaf-mould and coarse sand.
Aspect: full sun.
Propagation: from cuttings in summer or from seed in spring.
Flowering season: spring to summer.
Type: perennial.

Anacyclus pyrethrum **var.** *depressus* △
Anagallis monellii ▷

Anagallis

**ANAGALLIS, SCARLET
PIMPERNEL, POOR MAN'S
WEATHERGLASS**

Primulaceae

A cousin of scarlet pimpernel, *Anagallis monellii* has bright blue flowers with a purplish reverse side. They make an eye-catching decoration for containers in summer.

Useful hints

— In warm and temperate climates anagallis is perennial, but further north it must be treated as an annual since it does not tolerate frosts.

Height: 20 cm (8 in).
Spacing and planting distance: 20 cm (8 in).
Soil: ordinary.
Aspect: sun.
Propagation: from seed.
Flowering season: summer to autumn.
Type: annual.

△ *Anaphalis triplinervis*

Anaphalis

PEARL EVERLASTING, PEARLY EVERLASTING

Compositae

This little perennial is a must, above all for white gardens. The display lasts for nearly nine months, beginning with the silvery grey of the new foliage in spring. The plant gradually fills out and then in late summer takes on a covering of innumerable, creamy white heads. They are commonly used in floral arrangements.

Useful hints

— Like other silvery foliage plants, *Anaphalis triplinervis* cannot stand the water-logged soils of winter. Make sure that it is placed in a well-drained bed.

— To set pearl everlasting off to the best effect, it should be planted in groups of about 180 cm (72 in) surrounded by bright red or blue flowers.

Recommended

— *A. margaritacea* likes the same conditions as *A. triplinervis*, but its tall slender clumps are better suited to background planting.

Height: 30 cm (12 in).
Spacing and planting distance: 30–40 cm (12–16 in).
Soil: any, even poor, provided that it is well-drained.
Aspect: sun or semi-shade in dry soil.
Propagation: by division in spring.
Flowering season: late summer to autumn.
Type: perennial.

Anchusa

BUGLOSS, ALKANET

Boraginaceae

The tiny flowers of anchusa are a dazzling blue but they are more commonly seen in the country than in town gardens. Like wild borage, a distant relation, it is easy to grow. Similarly, it likes a heavy soil in which it will spread rapidly, forming large clumps that, unfortunately, do not last for many years. They are best associated with other undemanding plants such as phlox, sweet william or solidago (golden rod).

Useful hints

— Place in a sunny bed.

— Any reasonable garden soil will do but it should not be loose.

— Because it spreads so rapidly, it should be divided every three years in the autumn.

— To ensure flowering throughout the summer, any withered stems should be removed.

Recommended

— The blues are dazzling whether pure, as with *Anchusa azurea* 'Loddon Royalist', or tending more towards violet, as with *A. azurea* 'Dropmore'. The variety *A. azurea* 'Opal' has paler blue flowers.

Anchusa azurea 'Loddon Royalist' ▷

Height: 100–120 cm (40–48 in).
Spacing and planting distance: 5 cm (2 in).
Soil: ordinary.
Aspect: sun.
Propagation: by division.
Flowering season: summer to autumn.
Type: perennial.

Androsace

ANDROSACE, ROCK JASMINE

Primulaceae

The androsace is a firm favourite of lovers of alpine plants but it is far from easy to manage. A cushion-forming plant of the high mountain screes, it requires a soil that is moist but never water-logged. It needs to be exposed but at the same time needs protection against winter damp, a condition to which it is never exposed in its native habitat. Nevertheless, when success comes, the proliferation of tiny vivid flowers makes it all worthwhile.

Useful hints

— Plant in spring, either directly or, better still, in well-drained pots filled with a humus-rich mixture: e.g. leaf-mould and light-brown peat with lime-stone chippings.

— For the first winter, keep them under shelter in a frame and then bring them out to the chosen spot in the rock garden some time in spring. Take great care not to damage the root clump.

— Cover the soil in the pots with gravel to facilitate drainage.

— Trim the clumps after flowering and keep some of the fruit to have enough seed for future sowing.

— Put the new seeds into a pan which should be left outside for the fresh air to stimulate germination. Lift in the following spring and after transplanting protect against winter damp.

Recommended

— *Androsace carnea* is one of the easiest. It flowers at the beginning of spring, producing very fine shades of pink. A northerly aspect is required.

— *A. sarmentosa* (previously known as *A. primuloides*) can grow to a good size but mostly remains about the diameter of a dinner-plate. In winter, it shrinks in the dry cold and appears greyer because of the 'hair' that covers its leaves. Flowering comes a little earlier than with the previous example but again the colour is pink.

Height: 5–10 cm (2–4 in).
Spacing and planting distance: 20–40 cm (8–16 in).
Soil: rich and light.
Aspect: north side of a rock.
Propagation: from fresh seed.
Flowering season: spring to summer.
Type: perennial.

Anemone

WINDFLOWER

Ranunculaceae

For the connoisseur of perennials, the anemone offers a wealth of variety. The year opens with the little *Anemone nemorosa*, whose pure white flower shines out from beneath the trees. This is soon followed by the blue, pink and mauve of *A. blanda*. Neither of these species grows to over 15 cm (6 in). Twice as big, *A. coronaria* blossoms in mid-spring, blue, pink, white and sometimes even scarlet. Finally, at the end of the year, it is the turn of *A. hupehensis* (Japanese anemone), whose elegant pink flowers can easily reach a height of 120 cm (48 in).

Useful hints

— With the exception of *A. coronaria*, which prefers direct sunlight, all anemones are most at home in the cool of semi-shade. The small varieties of early spring, in particular, need the cover of deciduous trees and shrubs.

— In a mild climate, *A. coronaria* can be made to flower throughout the year if planted at three-month intervals.

Recommended

— Woodland varieties: *A. nemorosa* 'Robinsoniana' has marvellous blue flowers although the species has white.

— Species for direct sunlight: *A. coronaria* De Caen Group and St Brigid Group are recommended for their bright colours.

— Late-flowering species: *A. hupehensis* 'Praecox' flowers in late summer. *A. hupehensis* 'September Charm' has large,

△ *Anemone coronaria* De Caen Group
▽ *Anemone blanda*
Anemone nemorosa ▽

pale pink flowers; *A. × hybrida* 'Honorine Jobert' is a more free-flowering variety with pure white flowers; 'Königin Charlotte' has mauve-pink flowers; 'Prinz Heinrich' is an attractive double variety with slender, deep pink petals.

Height: 15 cm (6 in) (*A. blanda* and *A. nemorosa*), 30 cm (12 in) (*A. coronaria*), 120 cm (48 in) (*A. hupehensis*).
Spacing and planting distance: 40–50 cm (16–20 in).
Soil: well-drained and, if possible, moist.
Aspect: semi-shade (direct sun for *A. coronaria*).
Propagation: by division in spring.
Flowering season: early to mid-spring (*A. blanda* and *A. nemorosa*), late spring (*A. coronaria*) and late summer to autumn (*A. hupehensis*).
Type: bulb, perennial.

△ *Angelica archangelica*

Angelica

ANGELICA

Umbelliferae

Angelica is incomparable for wet ground, where it will quickly develop into large and impressive clumps. The roots can be used as tonics or aids to digestion. *Angelica archangelica* is a magnificent plant, yielding a smooth odour from all its parts. It develops best when cultivated as a biennial, i.e. the seedlings that appear naturally during the summer are taken for replanting in autumn and will be ready to flower the next summer. Massed on either side of a doorway, angelica can look spectacular.

Useful hints

— Sow the seeds in spring and transplant carefully twice before finally planting in rich moist soil in autumn.

— Water the plants regularly as soon as it starts to get hot, adding liquid manure or a handful of dried blood every month.

— If the clumps do not seem to be well developed, remove the floral spikes as soon as they appear to force the plant to produce more leaves. The following year, they will flower abundantly and then wither away.

Height: up to 300 cm (120 in).
Spacing and planting distance: 60–80 cm (24–32 in).
Soil: very rich and moist at all times.
Aspect: full sun.
Propagation: from seed in spring.
Flowering season: summer.
Type: biennial or perennial.

Antennaria

CAT'S FOOT, PUSSY-TOES

Compositae

Taking the common name 'cat's foot' because of the shape of its inflorescence, *Antennaria dioica* is one of the easiest alpine plants to grow. It quickly forms a dense ground cover adorned with pink flowers through a good part of the spring. It serves well to conceal the joints between paving slabs or to cover the soil in tubs around the foot of a shrub. Regular watering is important as the grey foliage does not, in this case, indicate resistance to dry conditions.

Useful hints

— Always buy in pots, preferably in the spring. When planting, be careful not to bury the collar which, as with many tussock-forming plants, is prone to rot.

— Add a layer of coarse sand to the surface every spring and then pat down the foliage to help with rooting.

Recommended

— *A. dioica* var. *hyperborea* forms a downy, silver mat.

— The broader, oval, greyish green leaves of *A. parvifolia* make very good ground cover.

Height: 5–10 cm (2–4 in).
Spacing and planting distance: 15 cm (6 in).
Soil: leaf-mould and sand.
Aspect: sun.
Propagation: by division in spring.
Flowering season: late spring.
Type: perennial.

Antennaria dioica ▷

Anthemis

ANTHEMIS, CHAMOMILE, DOG FENNEL

Compositae

The *Anthemis* genus contains a hundred species which are to be found in all kinds of beds and borders, rockeries and cut flower gardens.

Useful hints

— *Anthemis punctata* ssp. *cupaniana* can be grown in any soil, even chalk, provided that it is well-drained. It must be planted out early in spring.

— To ensure a rapid take-off, add half a shovelful of compost to the soil on planting. When the plants have reached a height of 20 cm (8 in) nip off a few centimetres from the ends to get them to fill out.

— During the first year, remember to water regularly.

— If faded flowers are removed, new flowers will return all the more vigorously.

— The only requirement for *A. tinctoria* (golden marguerite) is for a good well-drained garden soil (a heavy soil would choke it in winter).

— Though often considered to be perennial, it is safer to treat *A. tinctoria* as a biennial since, like antirrhinum and sweet william, it loses vitality after a couple of years.

Recommended

— *A. nobilis* (syn. *Chamaemelum nobile*) (common chamomile) is a dwarf variety with white daisy-like flowers and finely divided aromatic foliage. It is a hardy plant that will grow on any exposed ground and is useful for covering slopes.

— *A. nobilis* 'Treneague' is also good for ground cover. It doesn't flower but forms a soft aromatic carpet of tiny leaves.

— *A. punctata* ssp. *cupaniana* has charming silvery grey foliage that is velvety and finely divided. This delicately scented plant forms large rounded tussocks in dry mountainous country and these go well on a terrace, steps or the bends of paths in steeply sloping gardens. As it prefers sunshine and a dry climate, it makes an ideal plant for rock gardens and, once it is established, makes few demands.

◁ **Antirrhinum punctata** ssp. *cupaniana*

— *A. tinctoria* (ox-eye chamomile) is as easy to grow as common chamomile and is covered with yellow daisy-like flowers throughout the summer. It goes well with grey foliage plants and other perennials such as old roses.

— *A. tinctoria* 'Kelwayi' is lemon-yellow and bushy. *A. tinctoria* 'E. C. Buxton' and 'Sauce Hollandaise' have dark green leaves and paler yellow flowers.

Height: 25 cm (10 in) (*A. punctata* ssp. *cupaniana*), 15 cm (6 in) (*A. nobilis*), 60 cm (24 in) (*A. tinctoria*).
Spacing and planting distance: 15 cm (6 in).
Soil: ordinary, well-drained.
Aspect: sun.
Propagation: A. punctata ssp. *cupaniana* by division in spring, *A. nobilis* from seed or cuttings, *A. tinctoria* from cuttings.
Flowering season: summer to early autumn.
Type: perennial.

Antirrhinum

SNAPDRAGON

Scrophulariaceae

Familar to all of us from childhood memories, the snapdragon with its velvety snout and soft perfume is a flower that everyone, even the beginner, has to grow. Whether they are annual or perennial depends very much on the soil and the region. In northern Europe and in heavy soils they are annual. Whatever the case, they flower endlessly

△ **Antirrhinum majus**

from summer to autumn year after year. There is a great variety of size and colour, except for blue, so that they can be used in any part of a border.

Useful hints

— It is best to sow in a frame in early spring, providing a good rich soil that is light and in a sunny position.

— When the plants have reached about 5–6 cm (2 in), nip the shoots to strengthen growth.

— If they are stopped from running to seed, they will flower for several years.

— In autumn, cut off the bare stems and then cover with dead leaves.

Recommended

— Traditional varieties like *Antirrhinum majus* 'Maximum' have a good smell but the F[1] hybrids such as 'Rocket' or 'Madame Butterfly' are better for cut flowers. 'Black Prince' has delightful deep red flowers and crimson leaves. The dazzlingly coloured 'Floral Carpet' hybrids are only 15 cm (6 in) high.

Height: 25 cm (10 in) for the dwarf varieties; up to 100 cm (40 in) for the giants.
Spacing and planting distance: 20 cm (8 in).
Soil: ordinary.
Aspect: sun.
Propagation: from seed.
Flowering season: summer to early autumn.
Type: annual or perennial.

Aponogeton

WATER HAWTHORN, CAPE PONDWEED

Aponogetonaceae

This water plant deserves to be better known as it is one of the few that will flourish in the shade where water-lilies will produce no more than leaves. The white flowers of *Aponogeton distachyos* are strongly perfumed.

Useful hints

— Wait until late spring before planting either directly in the bottom of the pond if it is not cemented and has at least 20 cm (8 in) of good soil or in perforated baskets filled with heavy soil.

— In regions where the water does not freeze over in winter, aponogeton is hardy, but elsewhere it should be kept in a greenhouse. Problems usually occur if the pond is too shallow, a minimum of 30 cm (12 in) being recommended.

— Plant in semi-shade if possible.

Height: 15 cm (6 in) above the surface of the water, 30–60 cm (12–24 in) below.
Spacing and planting distance: 40–60 cm (16–24 in).
Soil: clay soil with fertilizer granules.
Aspect: semi-shade.
Propagation: by division in late spring.
Flowering season: all summer and sometimes even to mid-winter.
Type: perennial.

Aquilegia

COLUMBINE

Ranunculaceae

The columbines are great favourites, coming in singles and doubles, plain or bicolours and a great range of attractive tones.

Useful hints

— If *Aquilegia vulgaris* is sown in early spring, it will flower the following spring.

— *A. flabellata* should be planted in leaf-mould with a north-westerly aspect. It should be kept out of direct sunlight but needs light to flower.

— *A. vulgaris* likes a moist soil and can tolerate both shade and direct sun.

Recommended

— The dark-blue hoods of *A. vulgaris* are a common sight in country gardens,

◁ *Aponogeton distachyos*

△ *Aquilegia flabellata*

△ *Arabis caucasica*

where the deeply divided blue-green leaves are elegant until the frosts arrive.

— *A. flabellata*, with similarly rounded foliage and tiny flowers, has traditionally been classified with the alpine plants. It makes a pretty sight in a rock garden together with primula and heathers.

— *A. flabellata* var. *pumila* is a dwarf variety, reaching barely 12 cm (5 in). Its light magenta is tinged with soft yellow.

— The hybrids are more free-flowering. Some – like *A.* 'Yellow Queen' or the multi-coloured McKana hybrids – have long spurs. The short-spurred varieties are reminiscent of the columbines grown by our grandmothers: the multi-coloured 'Biedermeier' and the Music Series hybrids, sold according to colour. The flower heads of 'Adelaide Addison' (blue and white) and 'Nora Barlow' (red and cream) look more like tousled powder-puffs. 'Dragonfly' is a dwarf variety.

Height: 50 cm (20 in) *A. vulgaris*, 15 cm (6 in) *A. flabellata*.
Spacing and planting distance: 20 cm (8 in) (*A. vulgaris*), 15 cm (6 in) (*A. flabellata*).
Soil: any (*A. vulgaris*), rich leaf-mould (*A. flabellata*).
Aspect: any (*A. vulgaris*), semi-shade (*A. flabellata*).
Propagation: from seed or by division.
Flowering season: late spring to summer.
Type: perennial.

Arabis

ROCK CRESS

Cruciferae

Arabis can be used to adorn walls or as an excellent source of ground cover, capable of carpeting large areas within a few years and keeping out weeds. Though too invasive for most rock gardens, it goes well at the foot of shrubs or hedges where the only other competition is moss. The downy carpet of rock cress flowers every year at the same time as tulips.

Useful hints

— Plant in any season, though preferably in spring or autumn, in semi-shade and well-drained soil, and water regularly.

— If sowing takes place in spring, a large number of plants will normally be produced.

— After flowering, trim with shears to get them to spread and fill out.

Recommended

— *Arabis caucasica* (syn. *A. albida*) and *A. c.* 'Variegata', which has very decorative mottled-white foliage. Apart from these, the double *A. c.* 'Flore Pleno', which has flowers like lily of the valley. The shiny, bright green leaves of *A. procurrens* form a regularly shaped mat about 5 cm (2 in) high.

Height: 5–20 cm (2–8 in).
Spacing and planting distance: 20–30 cm (8–12 in).
Soil: any, even poor.
Aspect: sun and semi-shade (in the shade it will grow but will not flower).
Propagation: from seed or by division in any season.
Flowering season: late spring.
Type: perennial.

39

Arctotis × *hybrida* △

Arctotis

AFRICAN DAISY

Compositae

If a dry slope exposed to the sun is causing a problem, *Arctotis* × *hybrida* could be the solution. Even in very high temperatures, it will flower all through the summer. The only difficulty will be in finding seed or a few plants, as arctotis seems to be in an undeserved limbo.

Useful hints

— Sow the seeds in early spring, in a frame or in a sheltered spot. Put out the young plants in individual pots and keep them sheltered until after the frosts, when they can be planted out in their final position.

— A month after planting, nip the stems about half-way up to force them to spread. In a warm and temperate climate, the plant will last for years and end up as a shrub.

— The flowers can be used in bouquets but they close at night.

Recommended

— There are many different coloured hybrids with names such as 'Apricot', 'Champagne', and 'Mahogany'.

Height: 30–50 cm (12–20 in).
Spacing and planting distance: 30 cm (12 in).
Soil: light, add sand if necessary.
Aspect: full sun.
Propagation: from seed or, in warm and temperate climates, by division.
Flowering season: mid-summer to first frosts.
Type: annual or perennial.

Arctotis × *hybrida* △

Arenaria

SANDWORT

Caryophyllaceae

Arenaria balearica, a relation of pearlwort, came originally from Corsica and the Balearic Islands. It rapidly forms a carpet that is used to best effect on paving or to conceal the bare soil in rock gardens. Though they cannot withstand hard winters, it is easy to keep a small quantity on hand under a frame.

Useful hints

— Plant in mid-spring between the cracks of paving or in tubs at the foot of a shrub. Place a handful of sand around the plant to help it to take root.

— Every winter, take a clump and keep under a frame even without heat. Divide into dozens of plants in early spring, placing them in a sandy soil in a pan. Rooting takes place quickly and the new growths can be planted out after the frosts.

— Little bulbs (squill, pushkinia, muscaris etc.) can be planted in autumn to produce a fine effect in spring.

Recommended

— The frost-hardy *A. montana* grows to 5 cm (2 in) and is covered in large white flowers at the end of spring.

Height: 2–5 cm (¾–2 in).
Spacing and planting distance: 20 cm (8 in).
Soil: ordinary, not too heavy.
Aspect: any.
Propagation: from seed and by division in spring.
Flowering season: spring to summer.
Type: perennial.

Arenaria caespitosa aurea
(syn. *Sagina subulata* 'Aurea') ▷

Argemone mexicana △

Argemone

PRICKLY POPPY

Papaveraceae

Argemone mexicana is perfect for dry sunny gardens. The foliage, silvery with a milky tinge, is divided like that of eryngium. The flowers are large and silky like the red poppy but scented and with yellows and orange as well as red. The one problem is finding a nursery that stocks it.

Useful hints

— Plant in spring, either directly or from pot plants. This must be done with care as most members of the Papaveraceae are sensitive to transplantation.

— Place in a dry light soil in direct sunlight.

Height: 70 cm (28 in).
Spacing and planting distance: 40 cm (16 in).
Soil: light.
Aspect: sun.
Propagation: from seed.
Flowering season: summer.
Type: perennial.

41

Arisaema candidissimum △

Argyranthemum

see *Chrysanthemum*

Arisaema

JACK-IN-THE-PULPIT, DRAGON ROOT

Araceae

Like all the Araceae, the arisaema has a delicate trumpet, the corolla pink and striated like convolvulus and the spathe veined pink and green. A plant of the semi-shade, it has shiny foliage like that of the arums. It is unlikely to appear before the beginning of summer.

Useful hints

— Plant in the semi-shade in a bed of leaf-mould under shrubs or in a fresh, shady area. The soil must remain moist until the beginning of the flowering season, and must not be allowed to dry out thereafter.

— Bulbs bought over the counter often take a long time to flower. This is because they are from the Far East and need time to adjust.

Recommended

— *Arisaema sikokianum* is purplish brown and delicately veined with white. The cream-coloured spadix is curiously flattened, like a golf club.

— *A. candidissimum* is striped white, green and pink and slightly perfumed.

Height: 40 cm (16 in).
Spacing and planting distance: 30 cm (12 in).
Soil: rich moist leaf-mould.
Aspect: semi-shade.
Propagation: by division.
Flowering season: mid-summer.
Type: perennial.

Armeria

THRIFT, SEA PINK

Plumbaginaceae

This hardy little plant scarcely needs introduction as, with the garden pink, it is the most popular inhabitant of borders. And with good reason, as it is very easy to cultivate and seems to flower forever. The foliage is as fine as that of grasses and the compact tuffets stay green even in winter.

Useful hints

— After flowering, cut back the faded cushions with shears. This shock treatment will give renewed vigour to the foliage through the winter.

Recommended

— *Armeria maritima* has pink flowers. Some may prefer the white of 'Alba' or the deep red of 'Splendens'. 'Düsseldorfer Stolz' has the darkest-coloured (deep red) flowers.

Height: 15–25 cm (6–10 in).
Spacing and planting distance: 30 cm (12 in).
Soil: good, well-drained garden soil.
Aspect: sun.
Propagation: by division in spring.
Flowering season: spring to summer.
Type: perennial.

△ *Armeria maritima*

△ *Artemisia* 'Lambrook Silver'

Artemisia

ARTEMISIA, ABSINTHE, WORMWOOD, MUGWORT

Compositae

This is a plant for connoisseurs and the garden of tomorrow. The flowers are of little interest and the beauty of this plant lies in the blue-green and warm grey aromatic foliage that brings interest to 'white' gardens. Ranging in size and form from tiny cushions to magnificent shrubs, they cater for every taste and the foliage is almost always aromatic.

Useful hint

— Have no qualms about cutting back the flowers as it is only the foliage that is decorative.

Recommended

— *Artemisia dracunculus* (tarragon), with its aromatic green leaves, is widely known but there should also be greater recognition for *A. absinthium* 'Lambrook Silver' (silvery grey) and *A. ludoviciana* (off-white). The best of all is probably the finely spun silver of *A. schmidtiana* 'Nana'.

— *A. abrotanum* is more of a shrub, with slender, dark green, aromatic leaves. Height 130 cm (50 in).

— *A. armeniaca* has finely cut silver leaves, while the stems of *A. pontica* are covered with feathery grey foliage. Height 50 cm (20 in) and 80 cm (32 in) respectively.

— *A. lactiflora* needs cool, moist soil to produce its feathery white flower heads. The purple foliage of 'Guizho' sets off its cream-coloured flowers. Height 150 cm (60 in).

— *A. ludoviciana*. 'Silver Queen' is more vigorous and forms beautiful, dense clumps with broad, lance-shaped leaves.

— *A.* 'Powis Castle' is much hardier and keeps its silvery grey foliage all year round.

— The white-haired, silver leaves of *A. stelleriana*, the whitest of the artemisias, turn orange or pink in autumn.

Height: 130–150 cm (50–60 in) (*A. abrotanum* and *A. lactiflora*), 70–100 cm (28–40 in) (*A. absinthium* 'Lambrook Silver' and *A. ludoviciana*), 50 cm (20 in) (*A. dracunculus*), 5–10 cm (2–4 in) (*A. schmidtiana* 'Nana').
Spacing and planting distance: 30–40 cm (12–16 in).
Soil: light and well-drained.
Aspect: full sun.
Propagation: from cuttings in a cold frame at the end of spring and in summer.
Flowering season: summer.
Type: perennial.

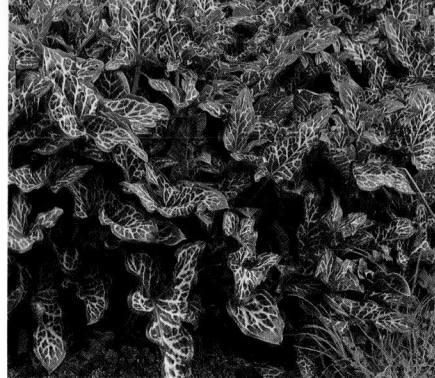

△ *Arum italicum* 'Pictum'

Arum

ARUM, CUCKOO PINT

Araceae

This is by far the most decorative of the genuinely hardy arums, a relative of the lords-and-ladies whose tiny red fruit brightens our undergrowth. The foliage is a finely marbled white. As the leaves appear in autumn and last until the end of spring, *Arum italicum* 'Pictum' is an ideal plant to enliven the garden during the dead season.

Useful hints

— The fruit which ripens in summer after the leaves have gone is very poisonous and should be removed if you have young children.

— The leaves are particularly fine in winter and are useful in bouquets.

Height: 30–40 cm (12–16 in).
Spacing and planting distance: 40 cm (16 in).
Soil: any.
Aspect: sun in winter, shade in summer (e.g. under deciduous trees).
Propagation: by division of tubers at the end of summer.
Flowering season: spring, but the flowers are insignificant.
Type: perennial.

Aruncus sylvester ▷

Aruncus

GOATSBEARD

Rosaceae

Aruncus dioicus has different forms for the male and female: the male is more beautiful than the female, though it is the latter which is most commonly sold by specialists. A mass of feathery foliage is formed rather like that of ferns and in summer this is covered with creamy white plumes. As they grow to over 200 cm (80 in) and occupy a lot of ground, they are suitable for anyone with plenty of space and a small budget.

Useful hints

— Plant in spring and mulch the soil well in early summer with pine bark and grass cuttings.

— Propagation, which is by division in spring, is simple to carry out.

— Put together with the large *Fuchsia magellanica* and Japanese primulas to create a magnificent display. They are, however, very thirsty so do not forget to water regularly in the summer.

Recommended

— *A. dioicus* 'Kneiffii' has a lower habit and is less free-flowering. Its charm lies in its deeply cut, feathery leaves. Height 70 cm (28 in).

— The rounded cushions of *A. aethusifolius* grow to a height of about 40 cm (16 in). It is rather like a small astilbe and is a good rock garden plant.

Height: 40–200 cm (16–80 in).
Spacing and planting distance: 50 cm (20 in).
Soil: rich in humus and very moist in summer.
Aspect: any, even in shade.
Propagation: by division in spring.
Flowering season: summer to early autumn.
Type: perennial.

Asarum caudatum △
Asarum europaeum ▷

Asarum

SNAKEROOT, WILD GINGER

Aristolochiaceae

Originally a native of Canada, this little creeper gives off a strong scent of ginger from its large fleshy tubers. Though it can be situated in borders, it comes into its own as a ground-cover plant in moist and shady parts of the garden. The flowers are a fine deep red but even more important are the silky leaves that cover the soil throughout the year, even in winter.

Useful hint

— *Asarum canadense* dislikes dry conditions so take care in summer.

Height: 10 cm (4 in).
Spacing and planting distance: 30 cm (12 in).
Soil: any, provided that it is kept moist in summer.
Aspect: shade or semi-shade.
Propagation: by division in spring.
Flowering season: spring.
Type: perennial.

45

— Apart from *A. syriaca*, an attractive species is *A. tuberosa*, which has umbels of pale orange flowers and long, lance-shaped leaves.

— *A. incarnata* has red, vanilla-scented flowers and prefers moist soil.

— *A. curassavica* is a splendid evergreen plant for the greenhouse or conservatory, with deep purplish red flowers and narrow oval leaves.

Height: 100–120 cm (40–48 in).
Spacing and planting distance: 40 cm (16 in).
Soil: ordinary.
Aspect: sun.
Propagation: from seed.
Flowering season: summer.
Type: perennial.

◁ *Asclepias curassavica*
▽ *Asperula odorata*

▽ *Asclepias tuberosa*

Asclepias

MILKWEED, SILKWEED

Asclepiadaceae

Asclepias syriaca is commonly termed swallow-wort. It produces bunches of pink to mauve flowers on long stems. Hardy in warm and temperate climates, Asclepias is a perennial that goes well with hollyhocks, tobacco plants and phlox.

Useful hints

— Gather the pods when they are ripe in autumn and remove the seeds the following spring, stripping away their silky covering before planting. Usually, they grow very easily and flower the next summer. They should, however, be supported.

— In colder areas, protect the plants in winter by covering them with leaves or straw.

Asperula (syn. *Galium*)

ASPERULA, WOODRUFF

Rubiaceae

As an alternative to moss under trees and between shrubs, *Asperula odorata* (syn. *Galium odoratum*) will solve the problem. Even in the shade of trees as difficult as the beeches, it will prosper, forming cushions of tender, green leaves that are finely divided. At the end of spring, asperula produces thousands of white flowers. These are odourless until dried when, in Germany, they are used to give a bouquet to white wines. Asperula are divided into three species: alpine, annual and herbaceous.

Useful hints

— If possible plant in autumn and mark the spot, as the foliage disappears in winter. Intersperse with some spring-flowering bulbs such as jonquils or *Tulipa sylvestris*.

— To keep the soil moist in summer, mulch with peat, rotted compost or dead leaves.

— Do not bother to dig up to divide. Simply separate the rooted portions and plant out immediately.

Height: 15–20 cm (6–8 in).
Spacing and planting distance: 20 cm (8 in).
Soil: ordinary.
Aspect: shade.
Propagation: by division.
Flowering season: late spring.
Type: perennial.

Asphodeline lutea ▷

Asphodeline

ASPHODELINE, JACOB'S ROD

Liliaceae

Rather ungainly in its appearance, the asphodeline flourishes on stony sun-drenched slopes. The erect leafy stems with their gold-flecked flowers sit well among cistus, rosemary and thyme. Like them, asphodelines can withstand the worst drought but can be killed off with one cold wet winter.

Useful hints

— Plant asphodelines in autumn so the roots are well set before winter comes.

A rosette of leaves will develop flush with the ground.

— Cut the floral spikes after flowering to prevent the formation of seed pods which weaken growth.

— For use as dried flowers, cut right at the end of the flowering season.

Recommended

— *Asphodeline lutea* (yellow asphodel or Jacob's staff) is the best known. A smaller species, also yellow, is *A. liburnica*, a native of the Mediterranean.

Height: 90–120 cm (36–48 in).
Spacing and planting distance: 20 cm (8 in).
Soil: ordinary, slightly stony and well-drained.
Aspect: sun.
Propagation: by division in early autumn or from seed in spring.
Flowering season: summer.
Type: perennial.

△ *Asplenium trichomanes*

Asplenium (see also *Phyllitis*)

ASPLENIUM, SPLEENWORT, RUSTY-BACK FERN

Aspleniaceae

These undemanding ferns are often to be seen growing on dry stone walls. In the garden, they are well-suited to paved areas or to some shady corner of a rock garden. They can withstand ordinary frosts, suffering only a temporary drying of their foliage.

Useful hints

— Plant in spring, providing a pocket of good soil between two stones. The spot must be well-drained.

— Plant masses of them around your shrubs where the soil tends to be sandy. They will provide good support for your dwarf rhododendrons and kalmias.

Recommended

— *Asplenium adiantum-nigrum* is like a dwarf female fern and is most often found in dry places.

— Easily recognized from the round scales edging its lizard-tail fronds, *A. trichomanes* is a regular sight in wells and on mossy north-facing walls.

Height: 10–20 cm (4–8 in).
Spacing and planting distance: 20 cm (8 in).
Soil: leaf-mould and sand.
Aspect: shade.
Propagation: by division in spring.
Type: perennial.

Aster

MICHAELMAS DAISY

Compositae

The colourful shades of autumn would not be the same without the asters and it is hard to imagine a garden without their violet star-shaped flowers in the border. It is all too easily forgotten that they begin to bloom at the beginning of summer and last until winter. All of them, moreover, are robust and can adapt to poor soils.

Useful hints

— Plant in spring or autumn and do not worry if the plants seem small in their pots. Keep an average distance of 30 cm (12 in) between them in all directions as they grow very rapidly.

— Mulch the soil in summer and water in hot weather. This will help to prevent attacks of oidium which show up as a felty white on the leaves and should be sprayed with triforine.

— Divide every three years or flowering will suffer. Do not replant the cuttings in the same place but give them a good rich soil.

Recommended

— Asters deriving from mountain regions are the earliest. *Aster alpinus*, for example, grows to no more than 25 cm (10 in), the blooms being violet blue ('Triumph'), bright pink ('Happy End') or white (var. *albus*). *A. farreri* is another, this time with a yellow heart.

— These are followed in summer by *A. tongolensis* which is generally violet with an orange heart. Examples are 'Berggarten', 'Wartburgstern', and 'Napsbury', the latter a bright heliotrope blue.

— Towards the end of summer, it is the turn of *A. amellus* which has very fine flowers. The best are 'Lac de Genève', 'Blue King', and 'Rudolf Goethe' for the blues, 'Nocturne' for the mauves. *A. cordifolius* 'Ideal' grows in well-ordered clumps and produces myriads of tiny blue flower heads. Although very similar, the hybrid *A.* × *frikartii* 'Wunder von Stäfa' flowers much more luxuriantly.

— Autumn is on its way when hybrid asters start to bloom. These are usually divided into *A. novae-angliae* and the slightly later *A. novi-belgii*.

— Among the dwarf *novi-belgii* varieties, those recommended are 'Alice Haslam', cherry-red; 'Lady in Blue', violet-blue; 'Marjorie', pink; 'Rosebud', cool pink; 'Professor A. Kippenberg', blue, semi-

△ *Aster amellus* 'King George'

double; and 'Snow Sprite', pure white. Good varieties of *A. novae-angliae* are 'Andenken an Alma Pötschke', cherry-red; 'Harrington's Pink', soft pink; 'September Ruby', vermilion-red.

— Of the *A. novi-belgii*: 'Patricia Ballard', luminous pink; 'Julia', pinky white with strong development and rather late flowering; 'White Ladies', white, semi-double; 'Winston S. Churchill', plain red; 'Fellowship', pink, the large flowers making excellent bouquets; 'Royal Ruby', bright red.

— A final group consists of the botanical asters. *A. laterifolius* 'Horizontalis' flowers at the same time as the chrysanthemums, in the form of a little pinky white bush. *Aster ericoides* and *A. tradescantii* form clouds of tiny white flowers, somewhat reminiscent of gypsophila.

Height: 20–150 cm (8–60 in).
Spacing and planting distance: 30 cm (12 in).
Soil: ordinary, somewhat rich and remaining moist in summer.
Aspect: full sun.
Propagation: by division in spring.
Flowering season: summer to winter, depending on variety, but predominantly autumn.
Type: perennial.

Astilbe × arendsii

ASTILBE

Saxifragaceae

It is useless to try to plant astilbes in dry or even ordinary soil. They need plenty of water and, beside a pond or stream, they flower sumptuously with bright plumes like ostrich feathers rising from a fernlike foliage.

Useful hints

— If possible, plant in autumn, having first added lots of peat to the soil to hold water through the year.

— Water abundantly and regularly, especially at the beginning of the flowering season.

— Divide the plants every three years since, with age, they produce fewer flowers.

Recommended

— Among the many hybrids, frequently of German origin, the best are: 'Koblenz', 'Rheinland' and 'Cattleya' for the pinks; 'Fanal' and 'Amethyst' for the reds; 'Gladstone' and 'Bergkristall' for the whites.

— *Astilbe chinensis* is much more tolerant of dry soil. The dense mat of *A.c.* var 'Pumila' grows to a height of about 30 cm (12 in), while the hybrid 'Purpurlanze' – a veritable purple candle – reaches heights of 120 cm (48 in). Another hybrid, 'Sprite', is a delightful dwarf plant, with pale pink flowers, which forms a dense cushion 40 cm (16 in) high.

Astilbe hybrid ▽ ▷

— *A. thunbergii* has produced some beautiful, tall hybrids such as 'Straussenfeder' with its full, feathery, salmon-pink panicles of flowers.

Height: 30–120 cm (12–48 in).
Spacing and planting distance: 30 cm (12 in).
Soil: rich in organic matter, moist at all times.
Aspect: semi-shade (the colours fade in the sun).
Propagation: by division in autumn or spring. Divisions should be provided with shade during hot weather and liberally watered when dry.
Flowering season: summer.
Type: perennial.

Astrantia

MASTERWORT

Umbelliferae

Like borage, mountain primrose, pheasant's eye and other native wild flowers, *Astrantia major* has such natural charm that it has become very popular with gardeners. Its pink tinged with green will blend perfectly with the pastels in your flower beds. It flowers from midsummer in any situation except for deep shade.

Useful hints

— Very little work is needed: it will flourish wherever you put it, whatever the soil.

— Propagate by division of roots in autumn or early spring, or gather the seeds to sow in spring.

— Astrantias last well as cut flowers, which is an additional bonus.

Recommended

— For those who prefer something a little more exotic, a variety with multi-coloured leaves, 'Sunningdale Variegated', has been introduced. Its green leaves are marked with yellow and cream.

— The leaves of *A. maxima* are similar to those of the hellebore, while its flowers are like big pink powder puffs. It grows to 60 cm (24 in).

Height: 30–60 cm (12–24 in).
Spacing and planting distance: 20 cm (8 in).
Soil: ordinary.
Aspect: sun or semi-shade.
Propagation: by root division or from seed.
Flowering season: mid-summer.
Type: perennial.

Athyrium

LADY FERN

Dryopteridaceae

Athyriums can be found in woods everywhere and make ideal companions, in shady spots, for conifers, fuchsias and hydrangeas. Clumps form from a central point which makes it easy to distinguish athyriums from their invasive cousin, bracken.

Useful hints

— Plant athyriums at any time of year, having first watered the soil thoroughly. The foliage withers from late autumn onwards but must not be cut as it protects the root.

— Every five years, divide clumps where they have grown too dense and replant at 30 cm (12 in) intervals in all directions.

Recommended

— *Athyrium filix-femina*, the true lady fern, includes a number of varieties with foliage more finely divided than the species type but they are difficult to buy. The male fern is a dryopteris.

— *A. nipponicum* 'Pictum', the painted lady fern, is less hardy and needs to be kept under a bell-glass or brought in under a frame. Its mottled silver makes it a good pot plant for the terrace.

Height: 30 cm (12 in) (*A. nipponicum* 'Pictum'), up to 100 cm (40 in) (*A. filix-femina*).
Spacing and planting distance: 30 cm (12 in).
Soil: preferably rich in humus (leaf-mould).
Aspect: shade or semi-shade.
Propagation: by division in spring.
Type: perennial.

Aubrieta

AUBRIETIA, PURPLE ROCK CRESS

Cruciferae

The aubrietas are often to be seen cascading from walls or bordering steps and no rock garden should be without *Aubrieta* × *cultorum*. Though some gardeners consider them vulgar or strident, this is only true of certain seed plants and cannot be said of the beautiful blues and violets of selected varieties. To obtain the best effect, they should be scattered here and there with tulips of pastel shade. Avoid clashes with yellow alyssums.

Useful hints

— Plant in winter with a handful of sand around the collar to avoid rot.

— After flowering, cut off all the dead heads with shears to force the foliage to thicken out. In this way, it is possible to obtain superb trails of soft grey-green leaves. Spray the foliage from time to time in summer.

Recommended

— The range of colours runs through the spectrum from red to purple, starting with 'Royal Red' and passing from 'Leichtlinii', 'Purple Cascade', and 'Dr Mules' to 'Magician'. Pale blue is represented by 'Church Knowle', deep blue by 'Greencourt Purple' and 'Royal Blue', and mauve by 'Joy'. For these varieties

△ *Astrantia major*

△ *Athyrium filix-femina*

the only satisfactory means of propagation is by division.

Height: 10–15 cm (4–6 in).
Spacing and planting distance: 30 cm (12 in).
Soil: ordinary but not water-logged in winter.
Aspect: sun (it flowers less in the shade).
Propagation: from seed or by division in spring.
Flowering season: spring.
Type: perennial.

Aurinia

see *Alyssum*

Aubrieta cultorum ▷

51

Ballota

BALLOTA

Labiatae

Perfectly at home in stony ground and hot sun, *Ballota pseudodictamnus* produces one of the best of all silver-grey foliages. It is best used to set off other plants, especially bulbs with thin foliage, such as the dieramas and crocosmias or other perennials like penstemons, the pasque-flower or *Delphinium nudicaule.* To keep the profile of the clumps it is necessary to cut the purple and white flowers, but these are not really suitable for display.

Useful hints

— Plant in spring, preferably in a thin to stony soil. Water for the first year but after that they can be left. Prune every spring to remove shoots that have been frost-damaged.

— Propagate by taking the tips of the stems from summer to autumn. During the first winter, keep the young plants inside under a cold frame.

Height: 60–80 cm (24–32 in).
Spacing and planting distance: 40 cm (16 in).
Soil: very light.
Aspect: full sun.
Propagation: from cuttings, in summer to autumn.
Flowering season: summer to autumn.
Type: perennial.

▽ *Ballota pseudodictamnus*

Baptisia

BAPTISIA, WILD INDIGO

Leguminosae

Having kept the elegance of a wild plant, *Baptisia australis* is ideal for bringing colour to a grassy patch where it will emerge every spring to display fine lupin-like flowers.

Useful hints

— Plant in the middle of a bed of perennials or in a lawn after cutting out a 30 cm (12 in) square.

— Set up a triangle of bamboo canes or hazel twigs to stake the plants.

— Strip the foliage in mid-summer to encourage new growth and to avoid the formation of seed.

Height: 60–100 cm (24–40 in).
Spacing and planting distance: 30 cm (12 in).
Soil: ordinary, preferably a little chalky and remaining moist in summer.
Aspect: full sun.
Propagation: by division in spring or autumn.
Flowering season: early summer.
Type: perennial.

Bassia

see *Kochia*

Begonia

BEGONIA

Begoniaceae

Three groups of begonias are of interest to the gardener: the annuals obtained from seed in winter for flowering in beds the next summer; the tuberous begonias which are grown like dahlias and are excellent for shaded areas; and, finally, the perennial begonias which, though few in number, are very useful for those parts of the garden that are in semi-shade.

Useful hints

— Sow annual begonias (*Begonia semperflorens*) in late winter, using a pan placed on a radiator. Prick out twice in pots and finally plant out after the frosts are over. Alternatively, you can buy them in pots and plant them out at the same

time after pinching the flowers to force new growth. Water at least once a week and trim the clumps in late summer with hedging shears to induce new vigour.

— To get the tuberous begonias into growth, set them hollow upwards in individual pots in early spring. Do not plant out until late spring when the soil has warmed up. Mulch the soil with peat or peat substitute. Water once a week and add liquid fertilizer once a month. In late autumn, pull up the clumps and leave them to dry in a warm place. Remove the tubers and keep in a warm dry place until spring.

— Plant perennial begonias in spring in the semi-shade. Put down anti-slug pellets and water well throughout the summer. Once the first frosts have come, the foliage will fall. Cover the stems with 15 cm (6 in) of straw or dead leaves until spring when you can propagate by division.

Recommended

— **Annual begonias** are grouped together under the name *B. semperflorens* and they include a large number of F[1] hybrids that have dust-like seeds. The varieties are forever changing but, at the present time, 'Olympia Red', 'Olympia Pink', 'Olympia White' and 'Devon Venus' (mixed) are all enjoying well-deserved success and are easily available.

— The **tuberous begonias** are divided into two groups: varieties with large flowers (doubles, like pinks, 'Nonstop'); and varieties with small flowers, including the superb pendulous 'Chanson'. The 'Bertini' variety is reasonably successful in the sun. The most widely known tuberous begonia is *B. grandis* var. *evansiana*, which produces pink flowers for a good part of the summer.

Height: 15–30 cm (6–12 in).
Spacing and planting distance: 15 cm (6 in) for dwarf varieties, 25 cm (10 in) for tuberous varieties.
Soil: rich and moisture-retaining.
Aspect: full sun for the annuals, shade or semi-shade for the rest.
Propagation: from seed for the annuals, by separating tubers for tuberous varieties, and by division for perennials.
Flowering season: all summer, to first frosts.
Type: annual, tuber, perennial.

◁ Tuberous *Begonia*

Bergenia

BERGENIA

Saxifragaceae

Borders of bergenias have become so common that the sight of their large leathery leaves and ruby flowers is not always a joy to the eye. For the gardener, however, there is the consolation that they will grow where many others will not and will keep their appearance throughout the year if tended.

Useful hints

— Plant at any season after first digging over the ground thoroughly. Enrich the soil with leaf-mould or peat.

— In spring, remove dead leaves to allow new growth and to make way for the flowers that are beginning to show. Plant botanic tulips and ferns around them so that there will be some colour and foliage all year round.

Recommended

— *Bergenia cordifolia* is the most common, whether in red or bright pink. *B. cordifolia* 'Purpurea' has large red leaves tinted purple in winter.

— The best for borders is *B.* 'Ballawley', which produces a fuchsia-red flower and has relatively tight foliage that turns dark red in winter.

◁ *Bellis perennis*
◁ *Bellis perennis* 'Pomponnette'

Bergenia 'Ballawley' ▽

Bellis

DAISY, ENGLISH DAISY

Compositae

The unsophisticated charm of *Bellis perennis* is apparent in all varieties from the simple meadow daisy on the lawn to the pink and red pompons of large display plants.

Useful hints

— Plant in late autumn or at the beginning of spring. They are very resistant to cold but it is worth while watering them after long periods of frost.

— They can also be sown in summer in a shaded spot and then transplanted about two months later. In fact, the daisy is more truly a biennial rather than a perennial, especially in varieties with large flowers.

Recommended

— The most outstanding are the 'Pomponette' doubles which form a magnificent carpet under tulips and among myosotis. Lovers of the unusual can sow 'Monstrosa', with very large red flowers, though this can look rather stark in display beds.

Height: 5–20 cm (2–8 in).
Spacing and planting distance: 15 cm (6 in).
Soil: ordinary, preferably clay.
Aspect: sun.
Propagation: from seed in spring and summer and by division in autumn.
Flowering season: from spring to autumn but mainly spring.
Type: biennial, perennial.

— *B. stracheyi* has given rise to some popular hybrids. 'Abendglut' has leaves that are bronze-red in winter and fiery red flowers. 'Silberlicht' marries white with pink in flowers that stand out well above the foliage.

— Still relatively unknown is *B. ciliata*, one of the few varieties to have deciduous foliage. The leaves are similar to those of the saintpaulias but larger while the soft pink flowers are the finest of the whole genus.

Height: 30 cm (12 in).
Spacing and planting distance: 30 cm (12 in).
Soil: rich in humus.
Aspect: semi-shade.
Propagation: by division after flowering or in autumn.
Flowering season: spring.
Type: perennial.

Beta vulgaris

SWISS CHARD, LEAF BEET

Chenopodiaceae

It may seem strange to include a vegetable among the flowers but the beet 'Rhubarb Chard' is well worth it, producing red stems to compare with many blooms. It is easy to grow and comes into its own during the autumn when the rest of the garden is beginning to look a little drab. It is also edible.

Useful hints

— Do not sow too early: the best time is mid- to late spring. Put three or four seeds in a pot and place directly in the ground at the spot of your choice. They can be transplanted a month later.

— Water once a week in the hot weather and mulch the soil. Liquid manure or dried blood are welcome additions.

— The chards can be cut in autumn for eating. When cooked, they lose their colour.

Recommended

— The best of all is 'Rhubarb Chard', which is usually found in catalogues under leaf beet.

Height: 100–120 cm (40–48 in).
Spacing and planting distance: 40 cm (16 in).
Soil: as rich as possible.
Aspect: full sun.
Propagation: from seed at the end of spring.
Flowering season: summer of the second year but uninteresting.
Type: annual, biennial.

Beta vulgaris 'Rubricaulis' ▷

Bletilla

BLETILLA

Orchidaceae

Bletilla striata grows so easily and so vigorously that it is hard to remember that this is an orchid. The delicacy of the flowers and the elegant pink are certainly a reminder but otherwise it is more comparable to the tulip. The foliage is identical to that of gladioli.

Useful hints

— Plant the bulbs in spring in ordinary well-drained soil.

— Cover with a thick layer of dead leaves or ferns and this will preserve them through the coldest of winters.

— Every three years, dig them up and divide, preferably at the end of summer.

Height: 30 cm (12 in).
Spacing and planting distance: 15 cm (6 in).
Soil: ordinary, even a little limy.
Aspect: semi-shade.
Propagation: by division at the end of the summer or in spring.
Flowering season: late spring to summer.
Type: bulb.

Borago officinalis ▷
Bletilla striata ▽

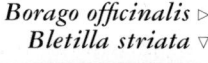

Bocconia

see *Macleaya*

Borago officinalis

BORAGE, TALEWORT

Boraginaceae

Borage is more often to be found in kitchen and herb gardens than in the flower bed. However, it is easy to grow from seed and will produce masses of azure flowers in summer. It seeds itself with equal ease and soon becomes the established neighbour of your rose bushes.

Useful hints

— Sow in spring, placing three seeds in shallow holes spaced at 20 cm (8 in) intervals.

— Water well during the hot weather or cover the soil with a mulch of grass cuttings.

— After flowering, cut the stems back flush with the ground. Remove all the old foliage and put it on your compost heap or you will have lots more borage seedlings appearing in the same place next year.

Height: 40–80 cm (16–32 in).
Spacing and planting distance: 20 cm (8 in).

Soil: ordinary, even poor and dry.
Aspect: sun.
Propagation: from seed in spring.
Flowering season: 3 months after sowing.
Type: annual.

Brachyglottis

see *Senecio*

Brachyscome

BRACHYCOME, SWAN RIVER DAISY

Compositae

Originally from Australia, these flowers are now very popular for the balcony or window-box. *Brachyscome iberidifolia* forms magnificent cushions of blooms throughout the summer. At one time, they were only available in blues but now there are also dazzling yellows.

Useful hints

— Plant immediately after the frosts are over in a mixture of leaf-mould and peat. Although they are fond of the heat, they need to have plenty of water. If the pot is too small, they will fade during the day and only recover at night. In mid-summer, water regularly, at least once a day.

— Every fortnight, cut off the dead heads with scissors to prevent seed formation. Keep cuttings or roots on your verandah or under glass. You can also sow the seeds in early spring in a warm greenhouse.

Height: 30–45 cm (12–18 in).
Spacing and planting distance: 25 cm (10 in).
Soil: leaf-mould and light peat.
Aspect: sun.
Propagation: from seed in spring.
Flowering season: summer to first frosts.
Type: annual, perennial.

57

△ *Browallia speciosa*
◁ *Briza maxima*
Brunnera macrophylla ▷

Briza

QUAKING GRASS

Gramineae

A favourite for displays of dried flowers, this annual grass has hanging spicules that quiver in the least breath of air. *Briza maxima* should be sown in a corner of the herb garden together with everlasting flowers. They also go well in flower beds to soften the outline of zinnias or dahlias.

Useful hints

— Sow in spring and then transplant the surplus a month later. Water regularly until the first spikelets appear and then leave to ripen.

— Briza should be cut in summer when the ears have formed but have not yet opened. Hang in bunches in a cool place for the rest of the summer.

Recommended

— Perennial varieties include *B. media*, with its shorter, heart-shaped spikelets. It grows to 60 cm (24 in).

Height: 20–60 cm (8–24 in).
Spacing and planting distance: 15 cm (6 in).
Soil: ordinary.
Aspect: sun.
Propagation: from seed in spring.
Flowering season: summer.
Type: annual

Browallia

BROWALLIA, BUSH VIOLET

Solanaceae

Frequently on sale at florists from mid-summer onwards, *Browallia speciosa* looks delightful in the living room or on a balcony and also in a sunny flower bed, where its soft blue will persist for weeks on end.

Useful hints

— Sow inside in early spring and then transplant into individual pots. The final planting out should be in late spring. Pinch the stems half-way up to get them to spread.

— Water once a week in summer, adding liquid manure once a month.

Recommended

— 'Blue Troll' does not exceed 30 cm (12 in) and spreads gracefully. 'White Troll' is also stylish.

Height: 30–40 cm (12–16 in).
Spacing and planting distance: 15–20 cm (6–8 in).
Soil: rich (leaf-mould and peat).
Aspect: full sun.
Propagation: from seed, inside, in early spring.
Flowering season: all summer.
Type: annual, perennial.

Brunnera

BRUNNERA, SIBERIAN BUGLOSS

Boraginaceae

Brunnera macrophylla (heart-leaf brunnera) is a sad sight in winter, the foliage black and apparently dead. Nevertheless, do not remove the leaves as they protect the stem from the cold. If you are patient and wait until spring, you will be rewarded two months later with an abundance of myosotis-like flowers. It flourishes in the shade, where it reseeds naturally.

Useful hints

— Plant in autumn if possible. Mulch the soil with pine bark or peat. Water only in the hottest weather.

— Plant with the small-flowered narcissus or the yellow botanic crocus. Epimediums flourish in the same conditions and are set off by the blue of the brunneras.

Recommended

— *B. macrophylla.* 'Hadspen Cream' is more brightly coloured, with variegated creamy foliage. The leaves of 'Langtrees' are decorated with a 'necklace' of tiny silver spots.

Height: 40 cm (16 in).
Spacing and planting distance: 30 cm (12 in).
Soil: ordinary.
Aspect: best in shade, though will cope with sun provided soil does not dry out.
Propagation season: by division in autumn.
Flowering: late spring to summer.
Type: perennial.

Calamintha

CALAMINTHA, CALAMINT

Labiatae

Calamintha forms a tight little bush about 30 cm (12 in) high, covered with soft lavender flowers. It will survive in the semi-shade but prefers the sun and a soil which is not too rich. It should be planted around rose beds.

Useful hints

— Plant in spring if possible, mulching the soil with pine bark or grass cuttings.

— Shortly before the worst frosts, cut the foliage and leave it where it lies to protect the root-stock.

Recommended

— A good variety for rock gardens is *Calamintha alpina* (syn. *Acinos alpinus*) which grows to only 15 cm (6 in) and has mauve-blue flowers.

— A favourite with cats is *C. nepeta* ssp. *nepeta*, which flowers for a good part of the summer.

— *C. grandiflora* likes a warm, sunny spot that isn't too dry. Its reddish tubular flowers give a good display throughout the summer. Height 30 cm (12 in).

Height: 15–30 cm (6–12 in).
Spacing and planting distance: 20 cm (8 in).
Soil: ordinary.
Aspect: full sun.
Propagation: by division in spring.
Flowering season: summer to autumn.
Type: perennial.

▽ *Calamintha alpina*

Calendrinia umbellata △

Calandrinia

CALANDRINIA, ROCK PURSLANE

Portulacaceae

Originally from Peru, *Calandrinia umbellata* is like our purslanes and thrives in the sun. It forms sturdy clumps that are entirely covered with flowers throughout the summer. The silky magenta-crimson blooms open in sunshine.

Useful hints

— In a warm and temperate climate, they should be sown in mid-spring, either in pots or directly into the ground. The seeds should be sown very shallowly and covered with sand.

— Transplant in late spring or thin out the seedlings. They go well in borders, in rock gardens or on dry stone walls.

Height: 15 cm (6 in).
Spacing and planting distance: 15 cm (6 in).
Soil: ordinary.
Aspect: needs full sun for the flowers to open.
Propagation: from seed in mid-spring.
Flowering season: all summer.
Type: annual or perennial.

△ *Calceolaria* Herbeohybrida Group
◁ *Calceolaria darwinii*

△ *Calendula officinalis*

Calceolaria

CALCEOLARIA, SLIPPERWORT, POCKETBOOK FLOWER

Scrophulariaceae

Calceolaria is a wonderful genus. Some species, with their yellows and pouch-like flowers, go well in beds or rock gardens.

Useful hints

— In a warm and temperate climate they are hardy, but elsewhere it is best to wait until spring before planting. Keeping them under a cold frame over the winter is a wise precaution.

— Give them a raised position and do not hesitate to pinch out stems that are too thin to encourage stronger growths.

— If there is any yellowing of the foliage, this could come either from asphyxiation caused by excessive watering or from greenfly swarming under the leaves. In the latter case, treat with a systemic insecticide.

Recommended

— The hardiest of the calceolarias is *Calceolaria darwinii*, which is the jewel of any rock garden. It must be protected from slugs which consider it a delicacy.

— The hybrid calceolarias (*C.* Herbeohybrida Group) are very decorative with spots and mottling. These are better suited to the patio. They are grown as biennials from seed in summer and are kept in a cold frame over the winter.

— *C. integrifolia* is the calceolaria that is to be seen in public parks, a single stem creating the effect of a small mimosa bush. Propagate from cuttings taken in summer and kept under shelter through the winter. They can also be grown from seed and make good pot plants.

Height: 15–60 cm (6–24 in).
Spacing and planting distance: 25 cm (10 in).
Soil: rich and well-drained.
Aspect: full sun.
Propagation: from seed at the beginning of summer or from cuttings in late summer.
Flowering season: summer to autumn.
Type: annual, biennial, perennial.

Calendula

MARIGOLD

Compositae

One of the most engaging of the annuals, the marigold produces large seeds that are easily grown, turning into robust plants that flower throughout the summer provided the faded blooms are regularly removed. It also seeds itself without the least trouble.

Useful hints

— Sow *Calendula officinalis* in a cold frame in early spring or in position in mid- to late spring. Transplant a month later or thin out the seedlings to leave a spacing of 20 cm (8 in). Plant some in the kitchen garden as well, since they cleanse the soil and can also be used for cut flowers.

— Water once a week, at the same time removing faded heads to prolong the flowering season. If a woolly white outbreak should appear on the leaves, spray with triforine.

Recommended

— For cut flowers, the best varieties are the large ones. The smaller ones, 'Fiesta Gitana' and 'Yellow Gitana', are perfect for beds and borders.

Height: 30–60 cm (12–24 in).
Spacing and planting distance: 20 cm (8 in).
Soil: ordinary, preferably moist in summer.
Aspect: full sun.
Propagation: from seed in spring.
Flowering season: late spring to first frosts.
Type: annual.

△ *Callistephus chinensis*

△ *Callistephus chinensis*

Callistephus

CHINA ASTER

Compositae

The china aster, *C. chinensis*, is not as popular as it once was and has become a less common sight in gardens but, even as a source of cut flowers for the end of the summer, it is well worth planting. Unfortunately, though, the plants have become susceptible to a disease that can cut them down overnight even during flowering. For this reason, never grow them in the same place for two years running.

Useful hints

— Sow from mid- to late spring when the ground has warmed up again and cover the seed with 1 cm (½ in) of sand.

— A month later, thin out the seedlings to leave 15 cm (6 in) between them and transplant the surplus with the same spacing in your flower beds. Pinch them half-way up to strengthen growth.

— Treat once with fungicide.

Recommended

— The single-flowered varieties remain firm favourites and include the elegant tall-growing Audrella Series. The dwarf varieties are like tiny cushions: the Milady Series, Lilliput Series, and 'Pinocchio'. To create a little hedge around your kitchen garden, choose the double-flowered giants which will grow to 100 cm (40 in) if staked: Duchess Series, Ostrich Plume Series, and Princess Series. They are good as cut flowers.

Height: 20–100 cm (8–40 in).
Spacing and planting distance: 15–30 cm (6–12 in).
Soil: rich, add compost if necessary.
Aspect: sun.
Propagation: from seed in spring.
Flowering season: 2–3 months after sowing.
Type: annual.

Calluna

HEATHER, LING, SCOTCH HEATHER

Ericaceae

A common plant in clearings, this heather can be recognized from the vertical spikes that appear from the end of summer to the beginning of winter. It creates a perfect scene when planted with grasses, dwarf conifers and other heathers at the foot of birches.

Useful hints

— Plant at any time of year in an acid soil, a mixture of sand, heath soil and peat being ideal. Mulch with pine bark.

— After flowering, the withered blooms remain decorative and should not be removed till spring to keep the plants tightly bunched.

Recommended

— There are many: 'Alba Plena', white, 'Goldsworth Crimson', deep red, and 'H. E. Beale', silvery red, being among the best. 'Beoley Gold', 'Blazeaway', 'Golden Feather' and some others have golden foliage but are often less vigorous.

— *Calluna vulgaris* 'County Wicklow', double pink flowers; 'Elsie Purnell', deep pink buds developing into silvery pink, double flowers; 'J.H. Hamilton', very compact and early flowering with large, double pink flowers; 'Tib', an abundance of deep red, double flowers. 'Wickwar Flame' combines mauve-pink flowers with the yellow and orange tones of its foliage, which turns coppery in winter.

Height: 15–60 cm (6–24 in).
Spacing and planting distance: 25–30 cm (10–12 in).
Soil: acid.
Aspect: sun; semi-shade for the golden varieties.
Propagation: by division in spring.
Flowering season: late summer to autumn.
Type: perennial.

Caltha palustris ▷
▽ *Calluna vulgaris*

Caltha

MARSH MARIGOLD, KINGCUP

Ranunculaceae

Nothing is prettier than a clump of *Caltha palustris* covered with pure yellow flowers at the end of spring. They transform the damper regions of the garden before the arrival of the water-lilies. One variety, *C. palustris* 'Pleno', has double flowers that are almost round. The glossy leathery foliage disappears in winter.

Useful hints

— Plant in spring, into pockets of rich soil just at the edge of the water or even slightly below the surface.

— Divide in spring, keeping one bud per cutting, and replant immediately.

Recommended

— *C. palustris* var. *alba* is even brighter. Its flowers have five pure white petals.

Height: 30–40 cm (12–16 in).
Spacing and planting distance: 30 cm (12 in).
Soil: rich in humus and moist at all times.
Aspect: sun.
Propagation: by division in spring.
Flowering season: late spring, early and sometimes late summer.
Type: perennial

△ *Camassia cusickii*

Camassia

CAMASSIA, QUAMASH

Liliaceae

If you do not like bulbs that have little foliage, why not try the camassias. Within a few years, these robust plants will have formed solid bunches and they will have foliage that remains decorative up to the end of summer. They flower in all shades of blue and go perfectly with pink peonies and yellow roses.

Useful hints

— Plant as early as possible in autumn. Put down anti-slug pellets in spring.

— Leave for at least four years before dividing. Continue watering right up until they wither.

— Remove dead flower heads unless seeds are required.

Recommended

— *Camassia cusickii* grows to an impressive size, up to 100 cm (40 in) once well-installed. The flowers are lavender-blue.

— *C. leichtlinii* has white or blue floral spikes that rise well above the foliage and they do not require staking.

— *C. quamash* was once rooted up by North American Indians for food. Now, as a garden plant, it provides us with a rich variety of shades from white to violet-blue.

Height: 60–100 cm (24–40 in).
Spacing and planting distance: 30 cm (12 in).
Soil: ordinary, rather rich and remaining moist in summer.
Aspect: sun.
Propagation: by separating offsets from bulbs in autumn.
Flowering season: summer.
Type: bulb.

△ *Campanula latifolia*

Campanula

BELLFLOWER, BLUEBELL, HAREBELL, BLUEBELL OF SCOTLAND

Campanulaceae

This is a vast family, ranging from dwarfs of barely 10 cm (4 in) to the large herbaceous varieties which can easily exceed 200 cm (80 in). The basic colour is blue but they incline also towards white and cool pink. Some favour dry soils, other moist. Some prefer the sun, others the shade. There is something here for everyone.

Useful hints

— Plant campanulas in the spring if possible, when roots are beginning to stir again, or in autumn, to give them time to get started before the frosts.

— Water regularly during the first summer and mulch the soil with peat or pine bark.

— Pinch out the faded stems to prevent seeding. This is one way to make the large campanulas flower again but it is necessary to pinch each flower one by one as the new blooms appear at the axilla of the previous ones.

— Divide just before flowering in spring. It is also possible to grow from seed, with flowering occurring, for the most part, in the second year, and this is the only way to propagate the large-flowered bellflower.

Recommended

— *Campanula alliariifolia* is very attractive in shape, the species type with its creamy white flowers in early summer being preferable to the larger flowered but less elegant 'Ivory Bells'.

— *C. carpatica* is often used to border rose beds, the flowers being so broad and numerous that they hide the foliage in mid-summer. The variety *turbinata*, also blue and white, is somewhat more compact.

△ *Campanula medium*
▽ *Campanula fragilis*

Campanula poscharskyana ▽ ▷

△ *Campanula mollis*

— *C. cochlearifolia* produces its tiny blue and white flowers in late summer and is a favourite for rock gardens and paved areas.

— *C. glomerata* is easily recognized from the tight clusters of flowers that appear at the beginning of summer. The 'Joan Elliott' and *dahurica* varieties are both of a very rich violet-blue.

— The great bellflower, *C. latifolia*, flowers in late summer, providing good company for marshmallow, loosestrife and yellow pimpernel in wilder parts of the garden.

— The large-flowered bellflower, *C. medium*, the Canterbury bell, is more biennial than perennial. Sowing in early summer will produce plants with plenty of flowers a year later.

— *C. muralis*, lamentably rechristened *C. portenschlagiana*, brings a vivid blue to late spring and early summer which can be used as wall cover or in borders. A more vigorous variety is *C. poscharskyana* which is ideal for paved areas. 'Birch Hybrid' is an older variety which flowers even more abundantly.

— *C. lactiflora* 'Loddon Anna' has dusty-pink, bell-shaped flowers in summer and prefers cool, humus-rich soil. 'Prichard's Variety' has a profusion of violet-blue flowers. Height 150 cm (60 in).

— A variety that is always reliable is the peach-leaved bellflower, *C. persicifolia*, which often self-seeds in a wonderful mixture of blue and white. The stems of *C. persicifolia* ssp. *sessiliflora* (syn. *C. latiloba*) are even more robust and are covered with large rosette-forming flower heads.

— *C. sarmatica*, with its grey foliage and blue bell-shaped flowers, is one of the more remarkable campanulas that thrive in dry soil. Height 50 cm (18 in).

— With its creeping roots, *C. takesimana* makes very good ground cover, but keep an eye on more fragile neighbours! Its huge, pinkish white, bell-shaped flowers are tinged with red in 'Elizabeth'. Height 60 cm (24 in).

— Unlike the preceding examples, the pyramid bellflower (*C. pyramidalis*) attains a height close to 200 cm (80 in)

Campanula barbata △

and its mid-summer flowering is a spectacular sight. Unfortunately, it can only be relied on for one year.

— *C. trachelium*, which at a distance could be mistaken for a nettle, is often to be found growing wild along lanes. It produces long clusters of mauve-blue flowers in mid-summer and grows well on the poorest soils.

Height: 10–200 cm (4–80 in).
Spacing and planting distance: 15–30 cm (6–12 in).
Soil: ordinary, well-drained in winter.
Aspect: sun or semi-shade.
Propagation: from seed or by division.
Flowering season: spring to autumn, depending on variety.
Type: annual, biennial, perennial.

▽ *Campanula carpatica*

△ *Canna* 'Lucifer'
▽ *Canna* hybrid

— Green foliage: 'Centurion', bright orange; 'En Avant', yellow with red spots; 'Oiseau de Feu', scarlet; 'Soleil d'Or', majestic yellow; 'Talisman', golden yellow with a red heart.

— Purple foliage: 'Angèle Martin', soft salmon-pink; 'Assaut', bright scarlet; 'La Glorie', carmine-pink; 'Peau Rouge', copper-red; 'Semaphore', orange-yellow.

— Dwarf varieties: 'Cléopatre', bright orange with a golden edge; 'Lucifer', blood-red with a yellow edge; 'Mistral', pink; 'Petit Pocuet', yellow with red spots; 'Puck', yellow. It should be said that some of these varieties may not be available everywhere.

Height: 30–120 cm (12–48 in).
Spacing and planting distance: 30 cm (12 in).
Soil: as rich as possible.
Aspect: sun.
Propagation: by separating rhizomes just before planting.
Flowering season: mid-summer to first frosts.
Type: bulb.

Cardiocrinum

GIANT LILY

Liliaceae

There are few plants as impressive as *Cardiocrinum giganteum*, the stems of which can reach up to 300 cm (120 in), each bearing a score or more of fragrant trumpet-shaped flowers. The sad thing is that the plant dies after flowering leaving behind offsets that take another six years before coming into bloom.

Useful hints

— A woodland plant, the giant lily appreciates rich soil and a shaded position.

— Plant as soon as you get them since the bulb must not be allowed to dry out. If the weather is still too cold, place the bulb in a pot of leaf-mould with just the tip showing.

— Put down anti-slug pellets immediately since that garden pest will devour the leaves and even the bulb.

— Straight after flowering, dig up the bulblets that appear around the principal stem and replant immediately at a suitable distance.

Height: 150–300 cm (60–120 in).
Spacing and planting distance: 40 cm (16 in).
Soil: pure leaf-mould.
Aspect: semi-shade.
Propagation: by separating offsets.
Flowering season: summer.
Type: bulb.

Canna

CANNA, CANNA LILY, INDIAN SHOT

Cannaceae

Though sometimes despised because of their over-use, often with discordant colours, in public parks, the cannas may well provide a touch of piquancy to your flower beds. They can, moreover, be grown by anyone.

Useful hints

— Start the rhizomes by placing them in individual pots over a radiator in spring. Let them adjust gradually and then plant out after the frosts are over.

— Water at least once a week, adding liquid manure every second time. Dig up the tubers in autumn and allow to dry in a warm place.

△ *Cardiocrinum giganteum*

△ *Catananche caerulea*

△ *Catharanthus roseus*

Catananche

CATANANCHE, BLUE CUPIDONE, CUPID'S DART

Compositae

Catananche caerulea enjoys a somewhat dry position and is good company for grey foliage plants and at the front of a border. The paper-like bracts keep well if dried. In moist conditions, they tend to be short-lived but, just as often, they reseed spontaneously in another part of the garden.

Useful hints

— If possible, plant in spring or early in autumn, taking the precaution of placing a few handfuls of coarse sand around the plant as a protection against winter rot.

— Propagate by dividing the fleshy roots in winter or, better still, from seed in spring. The plants will flower by the following year. The white variety, however, is not reliable grown from seed.

Height: 50–70 cm (20–28 in).
Spacing and planting distance: 30 cm (12 in).
Soil: sandy, well-drained in winter.
Aspect: sun.
Propagation: by root division or from seed.
Flowering season: summer.
Type: perennial.

Catharanthus

MADAGASCAR PERIWINKLE

Apocynaceae

Catharanthus roseus (syn. *Vinca rosea*) is very different from our woodland periwinkles and its reputation has been based more on its medicinal properties than its beauty. It is, nevertheless, an excellent plant for the flower bed, easily sown in a hot frame and producing flowers throughout the year.

Useful hints

— Sow in spring in pans placed either in the soil or on a radiator. Transplant into pots a month later and finally plant out when there is no likelihood of frost as the slightest touch is fatal.

— Remove the withered flowers once a fortnight. Water frequently, adding liquid manure every three weeks.

— The plant can be kept for a further year by bringing it inside in a pot but it quickly loses its foliage from the base upwards and the result is hardly pretty.

Height: 30–60 cm (12–24 in).
Spacing and planting distance: 25–30 cm (10–12 in).
Soil: somewhat rich, add leaf-mould if necessary.

△ *Catharanthus roseus* hybrid

Aspect: sun.
Propagation: from seed in hothouse, in early spring.
Flowering season: summer to first frosts.
Type: annual, perennial.

Celosia cockscomb type △

Celosia

CELOSIA, WOOLFLOWER, COCKSCOMB

Amaranthaceae

With their tiny flowers forming plumes or velvety caps and with their glowing colours, the celosias are the stuff of a gardener's dreams. However, they are very demanding and require a great deal of expertise if they are to give of their best. Because of their unusual appearance, it is also no easy task to match them with other plants. They do well in deep window-boxes and form excellent bouquets.

Useful hints

— The seeds, which are very fine, should be sown in spring in a tray of leaf-mould kept in the warm. Prick out three weeks later and finally plant out after the frosts.

— Add plenty of fertilizer and well-rotted manure to the soil. Water regularly, adding liquid manure every second time.

— To get long-lasting bouquets, cut the stems as soon as the first flowers open. To dry them, hang them upside down in a dark room for two months.

Recommended

— The cockscomb type has an enormous head that is full of dense curls. Popular are 'Jewel Box', mixed, tall, and the dwarf 'Fairy Fountain'.

— The plumed celosias explode in every colour, 'Apricot Brandy' being a soft orange. The Century, Fairy Fountains, Geisha and Kewpie Series are well-known and include red and yellow shades.

Height: 25–80 cm (10–32 in).
Spacing and planting distance: 20–30 cm (8–12 in).
Soil: very rich and always moist.
Aspect: sun.
Propagation: from seed, in hothouse, in spring.
Flowering season: summer to first frosts.
Type: annual.

Centaurea cyanus ▷

Centaurea

KNAPWEED, CORNFLOWER, BACHELOR'S BUTTON

Compositae

Centaureas provide a delightful splash of colour in any flower bed. Of the 600 or so species, the best-known is the cornflower (*Centaurea cyanus*), which brings rustic charm to city gardens. They combine well with nepeta and echinops.

Useful hints

— Sow the annuals in position either in autumn or at the beginning of spring. Those planted in autumn need protection during the winter.

— Sow the perennials in a cold frame in mid-spring. Prick out into trays and plant out at the beginning of autumn.

— If the withered flowers are removed, there is a good chance that they will flower again.

— Divide the perennials every four years or so.

Recommended

— The best-known annuals are the cornflowers (*C. cyanus*), whose petals look as if they had been cut out of crêpe paper. Among the vivid colours available are striking blues and pinks. 'Frosty Mixed' comes in a wide range of colours and 'Blue Diadem' is a deep blue.

— Among the perennials *C. dealbata* is worth noting. It reaches a height of 60 cm (24 in) and has foliage that is grey-green above and silvery on the underside. The large pink flowers have white hearts and appear from late spring to late summer. *C. hypoleuca* 'John Coutts' has a yellow heart.

— The dense clumps of *C. macrocephala* bear huge yellow flower heads, while *C. montana* spreads in loosely formed clumps and produces large, purple-blue cornflowers.

— The rose-pink flowers of *C. pulcherrima* blend well with its deeply cut, silvery foliage.

Height: 25–60 cm (10–24 in).
Spacing and planting distance: 10 cm (4 in).
Soil: ordinary, preferably light, even dry.
Aspect: sun.
Propagation: from seed or division.
Flowering season: late spring to autumn.
Type: annual, perennial.

△ *Centaurea dealbata* 'Steenbergii'

▽ *Centaurea montana*

Centaurea macrocephala △
Centaurea cyanus hybrid ▷
Centaurea cuneifolia ▽

△ *Centranthus ruber*

Centranthus

VALERIAN, JUPITER'S BEARD

Valerianaceae

An often uninvited but always welcome guest, valerian can transform garden walls, where it will flourish and bloom for a good three months during the summer. Whether white or purplish pink, as in the standard variety, the clusters of flowers are perfectly set off by the abundant, slightly bluish foliage.

Useful hints

— Any packet of seeds will provide you with more than enough young growths that should be planted out in autumn. They are then guaranteed to flower the next summer.

— Clean up the old valerians in spring to let new vigorous growths come through.

— If the soil is acid, add a little chalk or slaked lime before planting. Water only during prolonged hot weather.

Height: 40–60 cm (16–24 in).
Spacing and planting distance: 25 cm (10 in).
Soil: ordinary, preferably limy.
Aspect: full sun.
Propagation: from seed in spring.
Flowering season: progressively through the summer.
Type: perennial.

△ *Cerastium tomentosum*

Cerastium

MOUSE-EAR CHICKWEED, SNOW-IN-SUMMER

Carophyllaceae

Though virtually a weed, cerastium is an attractive sight and a single root-stock will provide a mat almost 100 cm (40 in) in diameter within a month. The fine silvery foliage of *Cerastium tomentosum* is covered with thousands of tiny white stars at the end of spring. As it is somewhat invasive, it should not be placed in company with fragile plants. It provides excellent ground cover under conifers and rose bushes or can be grown in large patches interspersed with irises.

Useful hints

— If possible, plant in autumn to give it time to get established before the arrival of winter frosts. Space widely as the plants spread rapidly.

— Cut back to a height of 5 cm (2 in) in spring, using shears or even a mower.

— Plant botanic tulips among cerastium to obtain a pretty effect in spring.

Recommended

— *C. tomentosum* spreads vigorously, forming a thick, even mat of grey foliage covered in flowers in late spring.

— *C. tomentosum* var. *columnae* produces a low mat of almost white foliage which thrives in dry, stony soil.

Height: 10 cm (4 in).
Spacing and planting distance: 30 cm (12 in).
Soil: any, even poor.
Aspect: any, except dense shade.
Propagation: from cuttings or by division.
Flowering season: late spring to summer.
Type: perennial.

Ceratostigma

PLUMBAGO, CHINESE PLUMBAGO

Plumbaginaceae

Ceratostigma plumbaginoïdes is not a name that trips lightly off the tongue but it is a first-class ground cover plant which, contrary to popular legend, is perfectly hardy and will add colour to the garden at a time when few flowers are in evidence. The sky-blue flowers begin to appear in autumn just before the foliage, which thrives in the cold, turning fiery red. It combines well with sternbergias and white colchicums.

Useful hints

— Plant in spring, having first added a little peat and compost to the soil. Mulch the ground in early summer and water regularly until established. Every spring, add a little peat to encourage new root production.

— It is possible to leave the plant intact for up to ten years but division and replanting can also be carried out in spring. Beware of couch-grass, which will try to insinuate its way into the densely packed mass.

Height: 25 cm (10 in).
Spacing and planting distance: 30 cm (12 in).
Soil: ordinary, preferably well-drained.
Aspect: full sun.
Propagation: by natural layering or by division in spring.
Flowering season: autumn.
Type: shrub.

Cheiranthus cheiri ▷

Cheiranthus (syn. *Erysimum*)

WALLFLOWER

Cruciferae

Though somewhat stiff in appearance, *Cheiranthus cheiri* (syn. *Erysimum cheiri*) possesses an irresistible fragrance and, for that reason, it should be planted close to the house. Bees swarm to it to enjoy the first nectar of the season. In warm climates, the wallflower may become perennial.

Useful hints

— Sow in late spring, spacing the seeds out well and barely covering them with peat or compost. At this time of year, a simple unprotected seeding tray will be quite sufficient.

— When the young plants have reached 8–10 cm (3–4 in), they can be transplanted but care must be taken not to damage the sparse root system. Once the stems have reached 20 cm (8 in), pinch them half-way up.

— If the autumn is dry, water them and fill in the gaps that invariably occur.

— When the flowers fade, cut off the whole floral stem to encourage the appearance of new ones.

Recommended

— Dwarf varieties like 'Tom Thumb' are common and very effective on walls or in rock gardens. The taller yellow varieties such as 'Cloth of Gold' are worth trying, not to mention the violet and carmine shades and the blends of pastel colours which contain soft beige.

Height: 30–60 cm (12–24 in).
Spacing and planting distance: 20–40 cm (8–16 in).
Soil: ordinary.
Aspect: sun.
Propagation: from seed in late spring.
Flowering season: spring to summer.
Type: biennial.

△ *Ceratostigma willmottianum*
Cheiranthus cheiri variety ▽

Chelone

TURTLEHEAD, SNAKEHEAD

Scrophulariaceae

Chelone obliqua is perfect to cover the transition between the summer flowers and the asters. A cousin of the penstemons, it blooms at the end of the summer, opening out in flowers that are like miniature foxgloves. The colours range from pink to white.

Useful hints·

— Plant in autumn or spring and, as chelones make great demands, the soil must be dug over deeply and enriched with leaf-mould.

— Mulch the soil in early summer so that there is no danger of drying out later.

— Leave the dead stems where they are during the winter and do not remove until spring. Divide every three years when the growths become too dense.

— Chelones may need twiggy sticks for support in exposed positions.

Height: 50–60 cm (20–24 in).
Spacing and planting distance: 20 cm (8 in).
Soil: rich and moist in summer.
Aspect: sun or shade.
Propagation: by division in spring.
Flowering season: late summer to autumn.
Type: perennial.

△ *Chelone obliqua*
▽ *Chionodoxa luciliae*

△ *Chionodoxa luciliae* Gigantea Group

Chionodoxa

CHIONODOXA, GLORY OF THE SNOW

Liliaceae

Chionodoxas are very easy to cultivate and deserve to be more widely appreciated. As with the crocus and the snowdrop, the flowering season, two weeks in mid-spring, is short but the light or luminous blue star-like flowers are worth the trouble. They can be grown in short grass, at the front of borders or on rock gardens.

Useful hints

— Plant the tiny bulbs in groups of from five to seven into a rich light garden soil. For window-boxes, use a rich mixture of garden soil and compost.

— They combine perfectly with horned violets and pansies.

Recommended

There are several species: *Chionodoxa luciliae* Gigantea Group is bright blue and fairly tall (30 cm / 12 in); *C. luciliae* is a lighter shade. *C. sardensis* has blue flowers with white centres.

Height: 20–30 cm (8–12 in).
Spacing and planting distance: 10 cm (4 in).
Soil: preferably rich and light.
Aspect: sun.
Propagation: by division.
Flowering season: mid-spring.
Type: bulb.

Chrysanthemum

CHRYSANTHEMUM

Compositae

Chrysanthemums, ever popular with gardeners, are available in a vast range of brightly coloured annuals and perennials (the latter now included in *Dendranthema* and other genera).

Useful hints

— Sow the annuals in spring either in a cold frame or directly into the ground. Prick out or thin out a month later, leaving intervals of 30 cm (12 in). At the same time, pinch the main stem. Water regularly and position a few hazel branches to give support. Extend the flowering by removing dead heads from time to time.

— Plant the perennials in spring or even in summer if they have been in pots waiting for their turn to come. Water a few times to help them to get started. Once the stems have reached a height of 40 cm (16 in), pinch them half-way up. Should white patches appear on the foliage, treat with a triforine-based fungicide. When the foliage dies in winter, protect the roots with a few armfuls of straw which can then be removed in spring. The white Shasta daisy is perfectly hardy.

— Chrysanthemums are suitable for growing as pot plants outside, in the greenhouse or in the home, on rock gardens or amongst mixed borders.

Recommended

— **Annuals**: Carinatum hybrids, which have flowers in the form of concentric circles of contrasting colours, the Tricolor Series being popular at the moment. *C. coronarium* varieties have single and double flowers. Also of note are the small *Chrysanthemum paludosum* (syn. *Leucanthemum paludosum*), which is white with a yellow heart, and its cousin, *C. multicaule*, which is pure yellow. These go particularly well in borders.

— **Summer-flowering perennials**: feverfew (*C. parthenium*, syn. *Tanacetum parthenium*), which is better for bouquets than the flower bed; and the Shasta daisy (*C. maximum*, syn. *Leucanthemum × superbum*). Cultivars include: 'Wirral Supreme', with very large double flowers; 'Little Silver Princess', which is only 30 cm (12 in) high; 'Esther Read', an old favourite that is still in fashion; *C. haradjanii* (syn. *Tanacetum haradjanii*), with fern-like silvery grey foliage; and finally, *C. coccineum* (syn.

△ *Chrysanthemum frutescens*
◁ *Chrysanthemum* hybrid
▽ Annual chrysanthemums

Florist's chrysanthemum △
Chrysanthemum frutescens ▽

△ *Chrysanthemum maximum*
◁ *Chrysanthemum* hybrid
◁ *Chrysanthemum uliginosum*
Chrysanthemum carinatum ▽

74

△ *Chrysanthemum* hybrid

Tanacetum coccineum), popularly known as pyrethrum, whose flowers are excellent for cutting.

— **Autumn-flowering perennials** (all now included under *Dendranthema*): the Rubellum chrysanthemums form whole cushions of flowers: 'Clara Curtis', pink; 'Lady Brockett', apricot; 'Mary Stoker', soft yellow. The Korean chrysanthemums are slightly later and come in many colours. Varieties include 'White Gloss', 'Mauve Gem', 'Ruby Mound', and 'Yellow Starlet'. Also noteworthy is *C. uliginosum* (syn. *Leucanthemella serotina*) which grows to over 200 cm (80 in), forming a cloud of white flowers. Then there are the large-flowered hybrids so often seen in cemeteries, but that's another story . . . Some anemone-flowered and finely petalled florist's types are worth lifting in late autumn and replanting the following year. The florist's varieties need to be grown in a frame but it is difficult to force them to flower outside their normal autumn season.

— The superb *C. arcticum* (syn. *Arctanthemum*) is still a little-known variety in spite of its beautiful, regular cushions which literally disappear beneath the pinkish white flowers of 'Roseum' or the pale sulphur blooms of 'Schwefelglanz'.

— *C. leucanthemum* (syn. *Leucanthemum vulgare*) 'Reine de Mai' – the earliest variety – flowers in spring.

Height: 20–200 cm (8–80 in)
Spacing and planting distance: 20–50 cm (8–20 in).
Soil: rich and moist.
Aspect: sun.
Propagation: in spring from seed or cuttings, or by division.
Flowering season: summer to winter.
Type: annual, perennial.

Cimicifuga
BUGBANE, RATTLETOP
Ranunculaceae

The cimicifuga flourishes in the wilder parts of the garden. Its flowers are reminiscent of the astilbes but are always pure white. Planted together with fuchsias, hydrangeas and ferns, they create an atmosphere of freshness.

Useful hints
— Plant widely spaced in spring.
— Mulch the soil at the beginning of summer with grass cuttings or well-rotted dead leaves.
— Divide every five years when the growths become too large.

Recommended
— *Cimicifuga dahurica* flowers at the beginning of autumn with long thin spikes.
— *C. racemosa* is somewhat larger than the previous example and the fuller plumes bend gracefully. The odour is somewhat unpleasant.
— The branching flower heads of *C. simplex* 'White Pearl' bear short spikes covered with milky white flowers.

Height: 80–150 cm (32–60 in).
Spacing and planting distance: 40–50 cm (16–20 in).
Soil: deep and moist in summer.
Aspect: semi-shade, sun if the soil is moist.
Propagation: by division in spring.
Flowering season: summer to autumn.
Type: perennial.

Cimicifuga dahurica ▷
Cimicifuga racemosa ▽

Clarkia

CLARKIA, GODETIA

Onagraceae

Direct sowing produces masses of flowers. Each plant forms a little pyramid terminating in silky spikes of pink, white or red. *Clarkia unguiculata* are magnificent in combination but, as they do not last for very long, they need to be mixed with earlier plants like oriental poppy and later ones such as aster.

Useful hints

— Sow directly in spring, having first loosened up the soil and spread a 2 cm (1 in) layer of good compost. Tap down the soil with the back of a rake just after sowing.

— Thin out a month later, leaving 20 cm (8 in) intervals and transplant any surplus growths into another bed.

— They can also be sown in autumn, with the plants being kept in a frame over the winter period. When planted out in spring, they will flower a month earlier than the others.

Height: 40–50 cm (16–20 in).
Spacing and planting distance: 20 cm (8 in).
Soil: ordinary.
Aspect: sun.
Propagation: from seed in spring or autumn.
Flowering season: summer.
Type: annual.

Clarkia unguiculata hybrid ▷
Cleome hassleriana ▽

Cleome

SPIDER FLOWER

Capparidaceae/Capparaceae

One of the most beautiful of the annuals, *Cleome hassleriana* has prominent flower heads crowned in mid-summer with flowers in every shade of pink. It has a slightly disagreeable smell but this should not prevent its use in combination with decorative tobacco plants and old-fashioned varieties of rose.

Useful hints

— Sow under cover in trays in early spring, using a light compost. Transplant the young growths after the frosts are over.

— Water regularly during the hot weather.

Height: 70 cm (28 in).
Spacing and planting distance: 20 cm (8 in).
Soil: ordinary.
Aspect: sun.
Propagation: from seed.
Flowering season: early summer to early autumn.
Type: annual

Clivia

CLIVIA, KAFFIR LILY

Amaryllidaceae

With lustrous green foliage, the bearing of a giant leek and spectacular flowers, the clivia is extremely decorative. It flowers very early in spring and requires only little attention. *Clivia miniata* needs a milder climate to survive in the garden and so, as with the agapanthus, is generally best kept as a pot plant.

Useful hints

— Plant in good garden soil to which two spadefuls of well-rotted compost have been added per plant.

— Water well during the hot weather but not at all in winter. This is the secret for successful flowering every year.

Height: 40 cm (16 in).
Spacing and planting distance: 30 cm (12 in).
Soil: ordinary.
Aspect: sun.
Propagation: by division.
Flowering season: spring.
Type: perennial.

▽ *Clivia miniata*

Cobaea

COBAEA, CUP-AND-SAUCER VINE

Polemoniaceae

Although *Cobaea scandens* has fine colours and forms, germinates easily and grows vigorously over everything within reach, it is in some ways a disappointment. Rare indeed are the occasions when it is in full bloom and, even then, the flowers start off green and do not open until just before the frosts that will sound their death knell. As a conservatory plant, however, they are first rate. The white variety is not recommended as the flowers do not stand out against the foliage.

Useful hints

— Sow in spring in pots and then plant out after the frosts, taking care not to damage the roots.

— Water regularly in summer. Add a little liquid manure but not too much as cobaeas do not require too rich a nourishment.

— Once fully grown, the plant is supported on its own tendrils. Up to a height of 50 cm (20 in) or so, however, it should be staked.

— As a conservatory plant, it should be pruned every spring to renew the foliage. Better still, however, is to regrow the plant from seed each year as it prospers better when cultivated as an annual.

Height: up to 6 m (20 ft).
Spacing and planting distance: 100 cm (40 in) or in pots of 30 cm (12 in) diameter.
Soil: moist in summer.
Aspect: sun (will grow in the shade but not flower).
Propagation: from seed in spring.
Flowering season: end of summer.
Type: annual.

Cobaea scandens ▷

Codonopsis

CODONOPSIS, BONNET BELLFLOWER

Campanulaceae

To see inside the tiny bells of this flower, you really need to get down to ground level. The creamy background is splashed with violet like certain types of Chinese porcelain. Unfortunately, the foliage of *Codonopsis clematidea* gives off a foxy odour if bruised.

Useful hints

— Plant in spring if possible, marking the spot carefully with a durable label. If not, there is a danger that this late starter will fall victim to a misplaced stroke of the hoe.

— Every year, add a handful of good compost to the root area. Water in hot weather. As it is a semi-creeper, codonopsis likes to entwine itself in other plants such as lavender, santolina or even a dwarf rose bush.

Height: 60–80 cm (24–32 in).
Spacing and planting distance: 20 cm (8 in).
Soil: leaf-mould and coarse sand.
Aspect: semi-shade.
Propagation: by division in spring.
Flowering season: summer.
Type: perennial.

Colchicum 'Waterlily' ▷
Colchicum autumnale ▷
▽ *Codonopsis clematidea*

78

Colchicum

COLCHICUM, AUTUMN CROCUS, MEADOW SAFFRON

Liliaceae

Plants of lawn and meadow, colchicums flower in the autumn. As all varieties are very poisonous, they are not recommended for growers with children.

Useful hints

— They will grow in any good garden soil but much prefer moist ground.

— Plant in spring for autumn flowering.

Recommended

— *Colchicum autumnale* is a native of our water meadows and it exists in lilac-pink and white varieties. *C. byzantinum* originates from Turkey and produces more flowers per bulb. *C. cilicicum*, also from Turkey, has a darker colouring.

— The hybrids are numerous: 'Lilac Wonder', very late amethyst flowers; 'The Giant', with appropriately large flowers; 'Violet Queen', bright violet; 'Waterlily', with soft pink double flowers like those of the nympheas.

— Among its many peculiarities, *C. luteum* is the only yellow colchicum and the only one to flower in spring. People usually prefer to grow it in pots as it is not reliably hardy. It is, however, a valuable rarity.

Height: 15 cm (6 in).
Spacing and planting distance: 20 cm (8 in).
Soil: ordinary but moist.
Aspect: sun.
Propagation: by separating offsets.
Flowering season: autumn.
Type: bulb.

▽ *Colchicum speciosum* 'Album'

△ *Colchicum* 'Lilac Wonder'
▽ *Convallaria majalis*

Convallaria

LILY OF THE VALLEY

Liliaceae

Convallaria majalis is most at home in deep, moist, slightly clayey soils, forming easily managed displays together with columbines, peonies and snowdrops.

Useful hints

— To be sure of flowering by mid-spring, plant fist-sized clumps in flower pots filled with well-rotted compost and then water regularly.

— Every three years, divide the growths which otherwise are too invasive.

Height: 20 cm (8 in).
Spacing and planting distance: 20 cm (8 in).
Soil: ordinary, tending to clay.
Aspect: semi-shade.
Propagation: by separating rhizomes.
Flowering season: spring.
Type: perennial.

Convolvulus sabatius △

Convolvulus cneorum △

Coreopsis basalis △

Convolvulus

BINDWEED, MORNING GLORY

Convolvulaceae

There is a vast difference between the common bindweed and the marvellous *Convolvulus cneorum* and *C. sabatius*. The former develops into a small grey bush studded with white flowers throughout the summer while the latter is a ground creeper that dons a mantle of sky-blue flowers. Being semi-hardy, they need protection from winter rains.

Useful hints

— Plant in spring into a pocket of good well-drained soil to which sand may be added.

— Water once a week through the summer, stopping in autumn to slow down their metabolism.

— Cuttings taken in summer and rooted in sand take off very quickly and can easily be kept in a frame through the winter.

Recommended

Morning glory (*C. tricolor*) can be grown by any beginner, generally as an annual. The large seeds grow rapidly to form clumps that are covered with flowers arranged in contrasting concentric rings, opening in the morning and closing in the afternoon. All varieties have a yellow throat. If possible install with a south-westerly aspect.

— *C. cantabrica* likes a sunny spot on the rock garden where it will form a mat studded with pink flowers.

Height: 50 cm (20 in) for *C. cneorum*, 15 cm (6 in) for *C. sabatius*; climbers up to 300 cm (10 ft).
Spacing and planting distance: 25 cm (10 in).
Soil: light and well-drained.
Aspect: needs direct full sun for the flowers to open.
Propagation: from cuttings in summer.
Flowering season: summer to first frosts.
Type: perennial.

Coreopsis

COREOPSIS, TICKSEED

Compositae

For anyone who likes pure yellow, the coreopsis are indispensable. Some are annuals (*Coreopsis tinctoria* and *C. basalis*) while others are perennial (*C. grandiflora* and *C. verticillata*). The former are delicate and short-lived while the latter are more robust. All varieties appreciate deep soils that remain moist in summer.

Useful hints

— Annuals: sow in spring either directly in place or in a pan for planting out a month later. Pinch the young plants half-way up the stem to strengthen growth. Remove the dead flowers, as the large seeds will soon drain the plant of all vigour.

— Perennials: plant in spring after enriching the soil with leaf-mould. Leave the dead foliage during the winter and do not remove until the following spring.

Recommended

— *C. basalis* has given rise to some interesting varieties, including 'Couronne d'Or' which has a maroon heart.

— The most elegant is *C. tinctoria*, which carries its flowers very high on fine stems and can be dispersed in beds to lighten the general effect.

— *C. grandiflora*, though well-known, is somewhat disappointing, producing so many flowers that they die off very quickly towards the end of summer. Do not use with a soil too rich in humus or the leaves will be disproportionately large. *C.g.* 'Badengold', 80 cm (30 in); *C.g.* 'Sonnenkind', 40 cm (16 in) and the double-flowered *C.g.* 'Sunray', 40 cm (16 in) are highly recommended.

— Among the best varieties of *C. lanceolata* – often more compact and prolific in the extreme – are the yellow and brown 'Rotkehlchen' and the two-toned and slightly taller 'Sterntaler'.

— Unlike the other varieties, *C. tripteris* likes cool soil where it reaches heights of 200 cm (80 in).

— *C. verticillata* has none of the disadvantages of the previous examples and should find a place in any garden. Even without flowers, it has a pleasing aspect though this period is itself short since few plants bloom so abundantly. *C.v.* 'Zagreb' does not grow above 25 cm (9–10 in). While most varieties are bright yellow, 'Moonbeam' has soft, buttery yellow flowers beautifully set off by its dark green foliage.

Height: 40–200 cm (16–80 in).
Spacing and planting distance: 30 cm (12 in).
Soil: ordinary to fairly rich.
Aspect: full sun.
Propagation: from seed in spring for the annuals and by division at the same time for perennials.
Flowering season: summer to first frosts.
Type: annual, perennial.

Cortaderia

PAMPAS GRASS

Gramineae

The creamy plumes of pampas grass have now been popular in gardens for over three decades. Make any decision carefully, because once installed, it is there to stay.

Useful hints

— It is not fussy about soil or climate and will flourish in any garden.

— After three years, use a sharp spade to divide the growths which will otherwise grow too large.

— Cut the plumes in autumn to make bouquets that will keep for a long time in a cool room.

— Cover the root-stock with a sheet of plastic in autumn, having first pruned the stems. Remove in spring.

Recommended

— *Cortaderia selloana*. There are various lesser-known forms which are just as invasive: 'Aureolineata', whose leaves have yellow margins, and 'Roi des Roses' with its large pink plumes.

Height: 150 cm (60 in).
Spacing and planting distance: 150 cm (60 in).
Soil: ordinary.
Aspect: any.
Propagation: by division of root-stock.
Flowering season: summer to autumn.
Type: perennial.

Corydalis

CORYDALIS, FUMEWORT

Papaveraceae

A few handfuls of soil in some crevice of a dry stone wall or flight of steps will be enough for most varieties of fumewort. The yellow is almost a weed but its cousin, *Corydalis cashmeriana*, is a jewel that requires endless effort.

Useful hints

— Take up a few roots of yellow corydalis during the summer and then replant carefully, watering regularly. Spontaneous reseeding will occur, the seedlings then being planted out as required. Take care, however, as they are very invasive.

— *C. cashmeriana* should be planted in spring in the semi-shade and provided with a pocket of good sandy soil. During winter, protect with a pane of glass or a plastic sheet. As a precaution, take some seed that can be sown in autumn and left in a cold frame through the winter. The plants can then be lifted in spring and planted out in spring.

Recommended

— *C. lutea* flowers for nine months out of twelve in successive waves and the blooms are beautifully set off by fine blue-green foliage.

— *C. cheilanthifolia* has long, delicate, fernlike leaves.

△ *Corydalis lutea*

△ *Corydalis cashmeriana*

— *C. solida* has purplish red flower spikes in spring.

— The blue flowers of *C. cashmeriana* can only be described in superlatives and are a rarity that marks the grower as an expert.

— *C. flexuosa* is a delightful new variety with deep blue flowers.

Height: 15–20 cm (6–8 in).
Spacing and planting distance: 20 cm (8 in).
Soil: well-drained.
Aspect: sun and semi-shade.
Propagation: from seed.
Flowering season: spring to winter.
Type: perennial.

Cortaderia selloana 'Pumila' ▽

Cosmos bipinnatus △

Recommended

— The best-known is *Cosmos bipinnatus* of which 'Sensation Mixed' displays a single line of petals while 'Sunset' has deep red semi-double flowers. The tubular, strap-shaped petals of 'Seashell' are all the more surprising for their very soft, pastel shades and form an eye-catching display.

— Shades of yellow and orange are to be found among the flower colours of *C. sulphureus*, which is more open and less hardy than the previous examples. The semi-doubles 'Bright Lights' and 'Klondyke' are the most popular.

— Becoming better known is *C. atrosanguineus*, which looks more like a single-flowered dahlia than a cosmos. The brownish flowers smell of chocolate. They have to be cultivated like dahlias, i.e. the tuberous roots must be brought inside during the winter.

Height: 60–140 cm (24–55 in).
Spacing and planting distance: 30 cm (12 in).
Soil: ordinary.
Aspect: sun.
Propagation: from seed or by separating rhizomes (*C. atrosanguineus*).
Flowering season: summer to first frosts.
Type: annual and perennial.

Cosmos

COSMEA, COSMOS

Compositae

This is a summer-flowering annual whose plumed foliage sets off flowers in primary colours from purple to pure white. The delicate fragrance comes from the foliage. As almost nothing can go wrong, it is a good flower for beginners.

Useful hints

— Sowing is easy because the seeds are so large – space them a few centimetres apart as growth is rapid. Sow in spring using either a frame or a windowsill. Prick out a month later either in pots or directly in place into ordinary soil that has been well dug over. Water plentifully and remove any dead leaves to promote healthy growth.

— Yellow cosmos is more tricky, needing a little heat at the moment of sowing or requiring a wait until late spring to sow directly in place. Thin out a month later, pinching the stems half-way up to get the plants to fill out.

Crambe cordifolia ▷
Cosmos atrosanguineus ▽

Crambe

CRAMBE, COLEWORT

Cruciferae

A rare and spectacular plant, *Crambe cordifolia* brings a cloud of thousands of tiny delicate flowers to any bed of perennials. Though difficult to find in nurseries, it is by no means difficult to grow. Despite its height, crambe needs no staking but stands solidly on its own stem. It is ideal for use as a specimen plant, or ringed by much smaller plants.

Useful hints

— It needs a sunny situation and is ideal for seaside gardens.

— Place in a well-drained bed enriched with well-rotted compost. A sandy soil is almost certain to succeed.

— As it can also tolerate limy ground, any soil type will do provided that it is light.

— In a small garden, it is spectacular enough to be given the place of honour. Otherwise, ensure that the bed or border is at least 100 cm (40 in) wide.

Height: 120 cm (48 in).
Spacing and planting distance: 100 cm (40 in).
Soil: ordinary.
Aspect: sun.
Propagation: by division.
Flowering season: summer.
Type: perennial.

Crepis

HAWK'S BEARD

Compositae

Looking rather like a weed, *Crepis aurea* may well be relegated to some dry corner where the soil is poor. However, it is there that it will flourish and, if the flowers resemble small orange dandelions, they are still a better sight than bare earth.

Useful hints

— Dig over the ground before planting in spring to allow the roots to go deep.

— In summer, cut back flush with the ground to force new stems to emerge. At this time, cover with straw and well-rotted compost, this mixture removing the chore of watering.

— Beware of self-seeding, as crepis is very invasive.

Recommended

— *C. incana* also thrives in dry, stony soil and has lovely pale pink flowers,

△ *Crepis incana*

whereas the flowers of *C. aurea* are a beautiful coppery orange colour.

Height: 15–35 cm (6–14 in).
Spacing and planting distance: 20 cm (8 in).
Soil: any, rather poor but well-drained.
Aspect: sun.
Propagation: by division or from seed in spring.
Flowering season: summer.
Type: perennial.

Crinum × powellii

CRINUM, SPIDER LILY

Amaryllidaceae

Like agapanthus and clivia, crinum loves mild climates. It will, however, survive the winter if covered with an armful of dead leaves in autumn. Crinum will provide good company for climbing roses, ceanothus and a number of perennials since its delicately scented flowers are a delight, with clusters of trumpets like tiny pink lilies.

Useful hints

— Plant at least 15 cm (6 in) under a good garden soil enriched with two spadefuls of leaf-mould.

— Protect in autumn by covering with dead leaves and placing a plank on top.

Height: 30 cm (12 in).
Spacing and planting distance: 30 cm (12 in).
Soil: ordinary, rich.
Aspect: sun.
Propagation: by separating bulbs.
Flowering season: summer.
Type: bulb.

▽ *Crinum × powellii*

Crocosmia

CROCOSMIA, MONTBRETIA

Iridaceae

Crocosmia has become naturalized in mild climates. The flowers are a gaudy orange or red and the plant spreads with great rapidity. Crocosmias are particularly good for use as cut flowers.

Useful hints

— Plant the bulbs, which resemble a miniature gladiolus, in autumn, giving them a good, preferably sandy, garden soil.

— For the first year, protect them with a layer of dead leaves.

— Plant in groups of ten to twelve for a spectacular effect.

Recommended

The best-known is *Crocosmia × crocosmiiflora*, which has orange or sometimes yellow flowers.

— A more imposing species is *C. masonorum*, which is reddish orange.

— Nurseries are now producing even more brightly coloured hybrids: 'Emberglow' (orange-red); 'Firebird' (red streaked with orange); 'Norwich Canary' (yellow); 'Solfatare' (canary-yellow flowers on bronze foliage); 'Lucifer' (deep rich red flowers).

Height: 60 cm (24 in).
Spacing and planting distance: 15 cm (6 in).
Soil: light and well-drained.
Aspect: sun.
Propagation: by separating bulbs.
Flowering season: summer to autumn.
Type: bulb.

▽ *Crocosmia*

Crocus

CROCUS

Iridaceae

Everyone is familiar with the spring crocus, which breaks the monotony of winter and heralds the return of life. A place must also be reserved, however, for the autumn crocuses, which are an even deeper mauve than the colchicums with which they are sometimes confused. Plant them by the dozen, as they require massing to show up to good effect. They are perfect company for *Iris reticulata*, primulas and the small botanic narcissi.

Useful hints

— Plant in good ordinary garden soil that has been enriched with a handful of general purpose fertilizer per square metre. Place the bulbs gently at a depth of 5 cm (2 in) and at intervals of 10 cm (4 in). This must be done before the end of mid-winter which is when their growth begins. Crocuses bought later than this are often hollow.

— Autumn crocuses are planted in summer for flowering in the same year. Water the soil the night before to loosen it. During the summer, the crocus is at rest and loses its foliage entirely. They can be placed to good effect in rock gardens or among spring flowers such as spreading phlox, for example.

— Allow crocuses to become well established, not dividing the patches unless flowering appears to weaken.

Recommended

— **Spring crocuses**: there are three main groups: *Crocus chrysanthus* blooms very early with small flowers and is resistant to bad weather. 'Advance' (cream and violet), 'Blue Pearl' (blue and silver) 'Zwanenburg Bronze' (golden yellow and brown) are good varieties. The second group, *C. vernus*, is more popular, having larger flowers. Good varieties include: 'Yellow Giant', 'Pickwick' (white with a blue stripe) and 'Vanguard' (light blue) which opens at the same time as 'Yellow Giant' and combines well with it. The third group includes many botanic species (i.e. ones that have retained their natural characteristics). The flowers are generally average to small while the colours are bright. They are often sold in mixtures.

— **Autumn crocuses**: the flowering season is from autumn to mid-winter. The best-known species include *C. ochroleucus* (creamy white), *C. pulchellus*

Crocus sativus △
Crocus hybrid ▷

'Zephyr' (white tinged with pearly grey) and *C. sativus* (pinky white to pale lilac), the pistils of which are used to produce the spice saffron. The most delightful is undoubtedly *C. speciosus*, with its distinctive sky-blue petals.

Height: 10–15 cm (4–6 in).
Spacing and planting distance: 10 cm (4 in).
Soil: ordinary, preferably well-drained.
Aspect: full sun.
Propagation: by separating corms in summer.
Flowering season: autumn to spring.
Type: corm.

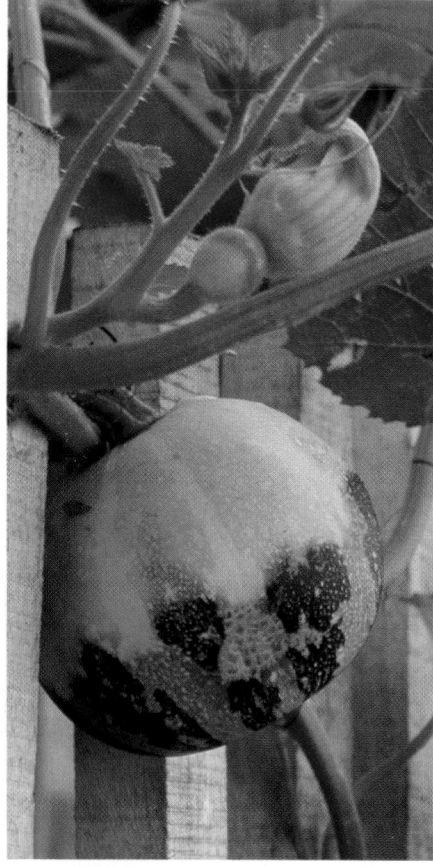

△ Cucurbita pepo

Cucurbita pepo
ORNAMENTAL GOURD

Cucurbitaceae

These annuals are so easy that children will enjoy growing them. Like its cousins, squash and pumpkin, the ornamental gourds need only sunshine and a good rich soil to produce large and curiously striped or bossed fruit.

Useful hints

— Sow in late spring in a tray of compost shielded with a pane of glass. Transplant a month later into a pocket of well-rotted manure next to a trellis or railing in some sunny spot. Water thoroughly during the summer.

— Gather the ripe fruit and leave to dry in a cool dark place. They can be waxed to make interesting compositions.

Height: 200 cm (80 in).
Spacing and planting distance: 50 cm (20 in).
Soil: rich.
Aspect: sun.
Propagation: from seed.
Flowering season: autumn.
Type: annual.

Cuphea
CUPHEA, CIGAR FLOWER

Lythraceae

Though still relatively unknown, *Cuphea cyanea* makes a splendid summer-flowering addition to the garden with its tubular-shaped blooms a mixture of scarlet and violet-blue. It can be used to good effect in window-boxes.

Useful hints

— Plant in late spring when there is no longer any danger of frost. A rich light soil (half sand, half leaf-mould) is required.

— Add liquid manure every three weeks and remove the dead flowers regularly.

— During the summer, take cuttings from the base of the stem and place in sand. They can be kept over winter in a warm well-lit place. This is more effective than bringing in the parent plants which quickly degenerate.

Recommended

— The curious *C. ignea* (cigar flower) is covered with tiny tubular red flowers which have a double – black and white – band at the mouth.
Height: 30–40 cm (12–16 in).
Spacing and planting distance: 25 cm (10 in).
Soil: light and fertile.
Aspect: full sun.
Propagation: from cuttings in summer.
Flowering season: all summer.
Type: annual, hardy in warm and temperate climates.

◁ Cuphea cyanea

Cyclamen
CYCLAMEN, SOWBREAD

Primulaceae

For ground cover in semi-shade there is nothing better than the star-like foliage of cyclamen, which is often edged with silver. With a careful choice of varieties, there will be something to see from spring to autumn. The flowers are as light as butterflies and their fragrance bears a hint of violet. This should be some consolation for the long months when there is nothing to be seen above ground but dead foliage and the bare spires from the base of the flowers. Combine white-flowered periwinkles and lamiums with your cyclamen to make the best use of space.

Useful hints

— Plant in a soil enriched with leaf-mould and perhaps two spadefuls of well-rotted compost per square metre. Leave them for years without hoeing, as spontaneous seeding is common. If the carpet becomes too thick, remove a few bulbs while they are at rest and replant elsewhere in the garden. The curved face of the tuber should be facing downwards.

— Sowing is possible with fresh seed, the first flowers appearing after two years.

Recommended

— Cyclamen flower, for the most part, at the beginning of autumn. *Cyclamen hederifolium* and *C. purpurascens*, however, both flower from summer to autumn in pale pink or carmine against foliage like that of the splashed ivies. Their tubers may grow to the size of a plate. *C. hederifolium* and *C. cilicium* both naturalize very easily.

— Less well-known than the previous examples are the spring cyclamen, which are the rivals of the violet. Here, the most common are *C. coum* and *C. repandum*. The source of all the florist's cyclamen, *C. persicum* has larger leaves than the others and these are often slightly silvery. Their fragrance recalls that of the lily of the valley.

— In warm and temperate climates, miniature cyclamen can be grown outside in pots. They are very close to the botanic cyclamen and bear numerous tiny flowers. The seeds, however, are

△ *Cyclamen repandum*
▽ *Cyclamen coum*

very expensive and take two years to come to bloom.

Height: 10–40 cm (4–16 in).
Spacing and planting distance: 20 cm (8 in).
Soil: rich in humus.
Aspect: semi-shade.
Propagation: from seed in autumn.
Flowering season: in every season if full range of species is grown.
Type: tuber.

△ *Cynara cardunculus*

Cynara cardunculus

CARDOON

Compositae

The cardoon or edible thistle makes a fine plant as well as a traditional meal. They can be planted at the back of a bed or even in front of a hedge, where the almost metallic foliage will show off to good effect. The flowers are like those of the artichoke and go well in bouquets of both fresh and dried flowers. The soil must be rich and well-drained in a sunny and sheltered position. A pretty combination is a mixture of cardoon and 'Queen Elizabeth' roses.

Useful hints

— In spring, sow the seed in fives in a warm place. Transplant a month after shoots appear or leave in place and get rid of any sickly plants. Protect from the cold by earthing up in autumn.

— Water in hot weather and treat against greenfly.

Height: 150–200 cm (60–80 in).
Spacing and planting distance: 100 cm (40 in).
Soil: very rich, dry in winter.
Aspect: sun, foot of a south-facing wall.
Propagation: from seed or by division in spring.
Flowering season: summer to autumn.
Type: perennial.

△ *Cynoglossum*

Cynoglossum

HOUND'S TONGUE, CHINESE FORGET-ME-NOT

Boraginaceae

Cynoglossum is very like a giant myoso-tis, having the same slightly rough leaves and the same china-blue colour. The only difference is the larger size and a later flowering, right at the beginning of summer. This timing allows some excellent combinations, notably with montbretias.

Useful hints

— Plant *Cynoglossum nervosum* in autumn or spring, preferably in the semi-shade. Place a dozen together to form a solid patch.

— After flowering, cut back with lawn shears to encourage new foliage.

— In autumn, divide any growths that are too large and replant the excess elsewhere.

Height: 40–60 cm (16–24 in).
Spacing and planting distance: 25 cm (10 in).
Soil: humus-rich and moist in summer.
Aspect: semi-shade.
Propagation: by division in autumn.
Flowering season: summer.
Type: perennial.

Cyperus

PAPYRUS, GALINGALE, UMBRELLA PLANT

Cyperaceae

At the water's edge, cyperus produces long supple stems that are green and topped with radiating leaves. In warm climates, it is the perfect companion for Siberian iris, arums and bamboo. In colder regions, it must be kept inside during the winter if it is to survive.

Useful hints

— Although cyperus grows readily from cuttings, a leaf cut off flush with the stem will take root in a glass of water. It is recommended, however, to propagate by division which is easy and much quicker.

Recommended

— Though there are over 550 species of cyperus, few are hardy enough to last through moderate northern winters. One example is *Cyperus eragrostis*, which looks very like the popular indoor 'papyrus' (*C. involucratus*) so beloved of cats. *C. longus* forms dense metre-high (40 in) colonies with reddish brown flowers and dangerously sharp leaves.

Height: 60–120 cm (24–48 in).
Spacing and planting distance: 30 cm (12 in).
Soil: ordinary, wet.
Aspect: sun.
Propagation: from cuttings and by division.
Flowering season: summer to autumn.
Type: perennial.

◁ *Cyperus*
▽ *Cypripedium calceolus*

Cypripedium

LADY'S SLIPPER, MOCCASIN FLOWER

Orchidaceae

Lady's slipper is customarily the sign of refinement in a garden, since growing it requires care and assiduity. Unless, of course, conditions are ideal and then they can be quite invasive. In this case, you will be enchanted every spring by the sight of these slipper-like flowers with their strange waxy texture.

Useful hints

— Buy only plants raised in pots and not those with bare roots. Plant out in spring, as soon as the first shoots appear. Provide a humus-rich soil, pure leaf-mould if possible.

— Put down anti-slug pellets in spring.

— Water at least once a fortnight in summer and allow the dead flowers to seed.

— After a few years when the growths have become very thick, they should be divided carefully in spring.

Best varieties

— *Cypripedium calceolus*, a native plant facing extinction, is a mixture of yellow and brown. It appreciates a slightly limy soil and can tolerate a sunny position.

— *C. reginae* originally came from North America and it prefers acid woodland soils that are a reminder of its native forests. It can reach and, indeed, exceed 60 cm (24 in).

Height: 30–60 cm (12–24 in).
Spacing and planting distance: 15–20 cm (6–8 in).
Soil: rich in humus.
Aspect: semi-shade under deciduous trees.
Propagation: by division in spring.
Flowering season: summer.
Type: perennial.

Cypripedium reginae ▽

Daboecia

ST DABEOC'S HEATH, IRISH HEATH

Ericaceae

The daboecias are related to the heathers differing chiefly in terms of their flowers, which are like little rugby balls in varying shades from white to violet. Not quite hardy, they need a maritime climate to flourish. Give them a good covering of dead leaves or coarse pine bark to protect the root.

Useful hints

— Plant in autumn or spring and water regularly during the first year. Put down a 5 cm (2 in) layer of peat before the mid-summer hot weather.

— Every spring, clean up the plants by removing withered stems.

— Combine the daboecias with other autumn-flowering heathers.

Height: 40–60 cm (16–24 in).
Spacing and planting distance: 30 cm (12 in).
Soil: rich in humus and without lime.
Aspect: sun.
Propagation: tricky, from cuttings in winter.
Flowering season: late spring to autumn in successive waves.
Type: perennial.

Daboecia cantabrica ▽

Dahlia

DAHLIA

Compositae

There is a patronizing attitude to dahlias in some quarters, but what other plant can boast such a variety of forms and flowers with such a robust constitution? They should be given a place not only in principal beds to balance the effect of gauras and cleomes but also in the kitchen garden where, in good soil and in the company of vegetables, they stand out like giants.

Useful hints

— Start them in early spring, placed in pots over a radiator and in direct light. Otherwise, wait until after the frosts before planting according to the orientation of the buds. Dahlias are not worth buying after this because they seldom prosper. Check that there are living buds on the remaining parts of the previous year's stems.

— Mulch the soil in summer and water well, putting down anti-slug pellets from time to time. The addition of liquid manure will help to promote generous flowering.

— When the foliage turns colour after the first frost, dig up the root together with a little soil and leave to dry in the cellar until the next spring. If you have sown seed of single-flowered dahlias you can save the tubers of the colours that are the most pleasing. Sowing takes place in spring in a warm place.

Recommended

— Dahlias are classified according to form and flower.

— **Decorative dahlias**: The flowers are flat, double and often very large. Our choices are: 'Lady Linda', yellow; 'Orange Robin', orange; 'Chorus Girl', pink; 'Cherry Wine', red; 'Angora', white; 'Hamari Gold'; and 'Edinburgh', white and purple.

— **Cactus dahlias**: The flowers end in points. The small-flowered varieties are best for garden display and include: 'Cryfield Max', yellow; 'Dana Iris', red; 'Klankstad Kerkrade', sulphur-yellow; and 'Shy Princess', white. The Princess Series is also worthy of note with very light flowers on a fairly small plant. 'Park Princess' is bright and pink and there are also reds and oranges.

— **Pompon dahlias**: These are superb for bouquets and will last for a week if the water is changed every day. Among the best are: 'Moor Place',

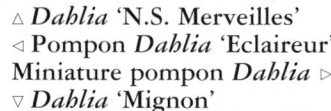

△ *Dahlia* 'N.S. Merveilles'
◁ Pompon *Dahlia* 'Eclaireur'
Miniature pompon *Dahlia* ▷
▽ *Dahlia* 'Mignon'

Dwarf *Dahlia* △

purple; 'Willo's Flecks', yellow and red; 'Small World', white; 'Pensford Marion', dark pink; and 'Kochelsee', scarlet.

— **Double-flowered dwarf dahlias**: These are lighter than the decorative types and the flowers are similar to those of the rudbeckia doubles. Examples are: 'Dwarf Double Redskin', many colours; and 'Dwarf Border Mixed'.

— **Single-flowered dwarf dahlias**: As flowering continues over several months, they are indispensable for display beds. Good varieties are: 'Coltness Gem', various colours; 'Mignon', mixed colours; 'Nellie Geerlings', red; 'Rigoletto', mixed; 'Redskin', yellow and orange; and 'Yellow Hammer', yellow.

— **Anemone-flowered dahlias**: The heart is tightly ruched. The most common in the catalogues are: 'Comet', scarlet; 'Honey', a mix of pink, bronze and yellow; and 'Scarlet Comet', bright red.

— The 'Topmix' dahlias are robust and, as they are available in all the main colours, can be used to good effect in window-boxes or at the edge of beds.

— There is an almost endless list of other varieties with such names as: camellia-flowered dahlia, water-lily dahlia, giraffe-dahlia and even orchid-dahlia. In general, their appearance is disappointing.

Height: 30–160 cm (12–64 in).
Spacing and planting distance: 20–50 cm (8–20 in).
Soil: rich and moist at all times.
Aspect: sun.
Propagation: from seed or by division in spring.
Flowering season: summer to first frosts.
Type: annual, bulb.

Datura metel △

Delphinium 'Cliveden Beauty' △

Darmera

see *Peltiphyllum*

Datura

DATURA, THORN APPLE

Solanaceae

The exotic perfume and vast trumpets of the datura evoke the tropical jungles which were its original home. There are shrubby varieties but we will look only at the annuals and one near perennial. In the garden, they can be displayed in large earthenware pots or placed together with banana and castor-oil plants. One note of caution: the foliage is extremely poisonous.

Useful hints

— Daturas should be sown, like tomatoes, in a heated greenhouse in spring. Let them adjust to the outside temperatures gradually and avoid planting out until after the frosts. They need a very rich soil with frequent watering and liberal additions of liquid manure.

— As soon as the flowers have faded, cut the prickly fruit unless they are wanted for displays of dried flowers.

Recommended

— The so-called Egyptian datura (*Datura metel*) in fact comes from China. It will readily grow to 120 cm (48 in) in a season and bears creamy white flowers that are nearly 20 cm (8 in) across. More common is the double-flowered 'Fastuosa' which has a strong scent and purple on the underside of the petals.

— *D. innoxia* is almost hardy and will flower from the root-stock in spring if it has been covered with 20 cm (8 in) of straw and a plastic sheet. It reseeds freely in the surrounding area. The flowers are white with a suggestion of pink and they remain for much of the summer.

Height: 60–120 cm (24–48 in).
Spacing and planting distance: 30 cm (12 in).
Soil: rich in humus and always moist.

Aspect: sun.
Propagation: from seed in spring, under glass.
Flowering season: summer to autumn.
Type: annual.

Delphinium

DELPHINIUM, LARKSPUR

Ranunculaceae

The highly characteristic silhouette of the delphinium brings substance to any flower bed. The annuals make delightful cut flowers reminiscent of bouquets composed with wild plants. The perennials, on the other hand, are more majestic and can be used to create settings in company with various rosebushes. The beauty, however, has to be earned as they are relatively demanding plants to grow.

Useful hints

— Annuals: Also called larkspur, they should be sown directly in position in spring. Thin out the seedlings a month later, ensuring that they are always well

△ *Delphinium* 'Tessa'

△ *Delphinium cardinale*

△ *Delphinium semibarbatum*
◁ *Delphinium* Pacific Series
▽ *Delphinium* hybrid
Delphinium 'Summer Skies' ▽

watered. Flowering begins in summer and lasts for six weeks. Sowing is also possible in autumn, at the foot of a wall exposed to the sun. The young plants will tolerate moderate frosts.

— Perennials: Plant in autumn or spring. Raise for a year in the kitchen garden until they are sufficiently developed to be bedded out. Put down anti-slug pellets regularly during spring, but after that they have nothing to fear. Cut the floral spikes at the end of their season to avoid exhausting the plant.

— The best means of propagation is by division in spring. They can be grown from seed in the same months but the colours cannot be guaranteed. Flowering occurs after a year.

Recommended

— **Annuals**: The hyacinth-flowered doubles, generally dwarf, are good. 'Giant Imperial' makes an interesting cut flower with varieties like 'Blue Spire' (deep blue) and 'Blue Bell' (azure). The flowers are simple but adorned with an upturned spur like that of the columbine.

— **Perennials**: Best of all is the Pacific Series, bearing the names of figures from the Round Table: 'Black Knight', deep blue; 'Guinevere', mauve-pink; 'Galahad', pure white; 'King Arthur', violet . . . All of these examples are over 150 cm (60 in) whereas the Fountains Series offers the same range of colours in plants under that height.

— **Hybrids**: The Belladonna range are more graceful and do not require staking. The slender spikes, moreover, continue to be produced right up to the end of summer. The most common are: 'Lamartine', violet-blue; 'Cliveden Beauty', light blue; 'Casa Blanca', white.

— Unlike the preceding examples, the red delphiniums are fussy and do not enjoy sandy soils. They tend to be short-lived. *Delphinium nudicaule* and *D. cardinale* barely reach 60 cm (24 in). *D. semibarbatum* is a beautiful soft yellow but it also does not last for long. The finest of the blues is *D. grandiflorum* (or *D. chinense*). It is a wise precaution to save seed in case the plant dies. 'Blue Butterfly' is a dwarf variety which grows to 30 cm (12 in).

Height: 30–180 cm (12–72 in).
Spacing and planting distance: 20–50 cm (8–20 in).
Soil: rich and well-drained.
Aspect: full sun.
Propagation: from seed or by division in spring.
Flowering season: late spring to autumn.
Type: annual, perennial.

△ *Dianthus gratianopolitanus*

Dendranthema

see *Chrysanthemum*

Dianthus

PINK, CARNATION

Carophyllaceae

The pinks seem to have nothing but virtues: bright colours, a rich spicy scent, attractive blue-green foliage and a robust constitution that means they can be grown by beginners. A border of garden pinks alongside some peonies and old roses brings back to mind the gardens of yesteryear.

Useful hints

— Sow in spring. The annuals will flower immediately but the perennials will often need a whole year to bloom. Sweet william is sown in early or even late summer as this gives better resistance to frosts.

— Garden pinks are best sown in autumn unless the soil is very wet in winter in which case they are best sown in spring. Every spring, bank up the earth around them by adding a few handfuls of compost which helps stems to root. Immediately after flowering is over, propagate from these rooted stems or from tip cuttings placed in a sandy mix.

— To produce carnations, remove the lateral buds leaving only the terminal. Stake the stems and water regularly.

△ *Dianthus*

Recommended

— **Annuals**: Indian pinks form a carpet of dazzling colours but are completely odourless. Preferable to these are the selected multi-coloured Chabaud carnations or, better still, the classic Marguerite pinks whose flowers do not go too quickly. Sweet william is a biennial rather than an annual. The doubles last a little longer than the singles. Superb bouquets can be made from the large 'Robustus'.

— **Perennials**: The best-known are the garden pinks (*Dianthus plumarius*), which are available both as singles and as doubles, the fragrant flowers ranging through all shades of red, pink and even bright orange ('Glory'). The most free-flowering of the many hybrids obtained from this species include: 'Desmond' (deep red, double flowers); 'Haytor White' (large, double white flowers); 'Helen' (bright pink, double flowers); 'London Delight' (double white flowers laced with purple); 'Laced Joy' (double flowers, laced with red, with a purple centre). The maiden pink (*D. deltoides*) is slightly later and does not exceed 20 cm (8 in), making an excellent border plant of an intense red well exemplified by 'Flashing Light'. Catalogues still suggest rockery pinks such as: *D. gratianopolitanus*, light pink; *D. alpinus*, pink with carmine centre; *D. arenarius*, white; *D. knappii*, sulphur-yellow. Another that is worth noting is *D. superbus*, still fairly common in meadows, with flowers that are slashed with bright pink.

Height: 15–70 cm (6–28 in).
Spacing and planting distance: 15–30 cm (6–12 in).
Soil: well-drained and somewhat limy.
Aspect: sun.
Propagation: from seed cuttings or by division.
Flowering season: spring to summer.
Type: annual, perennial.

Dianthus plumarius △
Dianthus alpinus ▷
Dianthus deltoides ▽

Diascia cordata △

Diascia

DIASCIA, TWINSPUR

Scrophulariaceae

Diascias are becoming more readily available from nurseries specializing in perennials and they are splendid in rock gardens and on paved areas. It is a pity that they are not hardy enough to be used everywhere.

Useful hints

— Plant in spring if possible in company with campanulas. The soil should be enriched with peat.

— After the first flowering, cut back to allow a second some two months later.

— Protect from the cold with a pane of glass and a few handfuls of coarse pine bark or leaf-mould. To be on the safe side, put aside a few cuttings taken in summer and keep in a frame over the winter.

Recommended

Diascia cordata has been eclipsed by 'Ruby Field', a hybrid obtained from itself and *D. barberae*. The colour is a very warm pink.

— *D. fetcaniensis*, with its pink flowers turning to red at the throat, and *D. vigilis*, with its paler pink flowers, are probably the most hardy and vigorous varieties.

Height: 15–20 cm (6–8 in).
Spacing and planting distance: 25 cm (10 in).
Soil: ordinary, fairly well-drained.
Aspect: sun if possible, or semi-shade.
Propagation: from cuttings in summer.
Flowering season: spring to end of summer.
Type: perennial.

Dianthus 'Waithman Beauty' ▽

Diascia rigescens ▽

△ Dicentra spectabilis

Dicentra

BLEEDING HEART

Fumariceae

Together with the peony, bellflower and myosotis, bleeding heart (*Dicentra spectabilis*) belongs to that indispensable group of plants that is both graceful and uncomplicated. They either like your garden or they don't and there are no two ways about it. They are ideal plants for borders, and the smaller species are good for rock gardens.

Useful hints

— For real success, the soil should be rich in humus and fairly moist though exposed to the sun for at least half the day.

— Plant either early in autumn or early in spring and then leave them undisturbed.

Recommended

— As well as the very popular *D. spectabilis*, which is pink, we would also suggest the early-flowering variant, *D. spectabilis* 'Alba'.

— *D. eximia* varieties are also worth trying. The pink or white flowers appear in mid-summer on plants that reach about 20–30 cm (8–12 in).

— *D. formosa* is very similar, but its blue-tinged foliage highlights the creamy white flowers marked with brownish red in *D.* 'Langtrees' and deep red in *D.* 'Bountiful'.

— *D.* 'Stuart Boothman' has sprays of carmine flowers and grey-green foliage.

Height: 20–60 cm (8–24 in).
Spacing and planting distance: 30 cm (12 in).
Soil: rich and light.
Aspect: sun.
Propagation: by division.
Flowering season: early to late summer, depending on the species.
Type: perennial.

Dichelostemma

FIRECRACKER FLOWER

Liliaceae

Dichelostemma ida-maia deserves to be more widely publicized. Hardy in warm and temperate climates, it produces very elegant flowers clustered on the end of long spikes and these make fine and unusual bouquets. For the garden, they should be placed among low grey foliage plants such as lavender or wormwood.

Useful hints

— Plant in autumn and mark the spot carefully so that it can later be covered with a 10 cm (4 in) layer of crushed pine bark. This should be topped with a cloche or simply a sheet of transparent plastic to avoid excess water. The covering is removed in spring.

— Water regularly until late summer and then let the foliage dry out naturally.

Height: 60 cm (24 in).
Spacing and planting distance: 15 cm (6 in).
Soil: light and sandy.
Aspect: sun.
Propagation: by separating bulbs in autumn.
Flowering season: summer.
Type: bulb.

Dictamnus

BURNING BUSH, DITTANY

Rutaceae

Though dictamnus is sometimes a slow starter in the first year, it very quickly forms solid growth crowned with pink flowers on spikes. The whole plant secretes an essence that will give an explosive crack if approach with a flame. This is harmless and may amuse children. Dictamnus is a good candidate for long-term residence in gardens that are somewhat wild or even dry.

Useful hints

— Plant in spring after digging over the soil thoroughly to allow for the deep roots. Add a little lime if the soil is acid.

— Cover the ground with a thick layer of straw or grass cuttings to retain moisture. Mark the position of the plants carefully to avoid accidental damage while hoeing in spring.

— Every five years, divide growths that have become too dense and replant immediately.

Recommended

— The usual burning bush (*Dictamnus albus*) is white, but the variety *D. albus* var. *purpureus* has purplish pink flowers.
Height: 50–100 cm (20–40 in).
Spacing and planting distance: 40 cm (16 in).
Soil: fairly compact, well-drained and preferably chalky.
Aspect: sun.
Propagation: from seed or by division in spring.
Flowering season: summer.
Type: perennial.

◁ *Dichelostemma ida-maia*

Dictamnus albus var. *purpureus* △

Dierama

DIERAMA, WANDFLOWER

Iridaceae

Dierama is the pride of the garden, with its long grassy leaves and slender arching stems from which hang bells of pink or white or purple. It must, however, be carefully protected against frost and should be grown in a sheltered position.

Useful hints

— Plant in autumn into pockets of rich leaf-mould.

— The plants are very sensitive to transplantation and should be moved as little as possible.

— Every year, in autumn, cut the stems flush with the ground and protect the root-stock with two spadefuls of dead leaves.

Recommended

— Apart from wand flower (*Dierama pulcherrimum*), you can also choose *D.*

△ *Dierama pulcherrimum*

pendulum but this is less hardy. The plant grows to about 40 cm (16 in) and its flowers are mauve or white.

— *D. pumilum* has flowers in shades of pink and violet on wiry stems.

— *D.* 'Blackbird' has cascades of violet flowers.
Height: 40–90 cm (16–36 in).
Spacing and planting distance: 30 cm (12 in).
Soil: rich and light.
Aspect: sun.
Propagation: by division.
Flowering season: summer to autumn.
Type: bulb.

△ *Dionaea muscipula*
◁ *Digitalis purpurea*

△ *Dodecatheon meadia*

Digitalis

FOXGLOVE

Scrophulariaceae

When foxgloves (*Digitalis purpurea*) appear suddenly in summer, the shade under chestnut trees is transformed into a delightful woodland scene. The first flower to re-emerge after undergrowth has been cleared, the foxglove is ideally suited to gardens with a moist, slightly acid soil. They blend well with ferns, columbine, meadow-rue and bleeding heart.

Useful hints

— Plant in autumn for flowering in the following spring.

— If they are prevented from running to seed, they will survive for many years. Otherwise, they are exhausted after two seasons.

Recommended

— The foxgloves are better cultivated as biennials. The purple foxglove (*D. purpurea*) has been improved to give horizontal rather than hanging flowers. The most common are the Excelsior Hybrids Group.

— Not quite hardy, *D. grandiflora* (syn. *D. ambigua*) produces yellow flowers on somewhat small plants of 60–100 cm (24–40 in). It is wise to take precautions against sudden death of the plants by keeping seed in reserve. *D. ferruginea* is copper-coloured and reaches a height of 90 cm (36 in). *D. × mertonensis* has a strawberry-pink flower that will delight the connoisseur, while the milky white flowers of *D. lanata* have a fine ochre tracery on the inside.

Height: 60–130 cm (24–50 in).
Spacing and planting distance: 20 cm (8 in).
Soil: ordinary, moist.
Aspect: sun or semi-shade.
Propagation: from seed.
Flowering season: summer.
Type: biennial, perennial.

Dimorphotheca

see *Osteospermum*

Dionaea

VENUS'S FLYTRAP

Droseraceae

Everyone must have been tempted at one time to try growing this insect-eating plant. However, though dionaeas can last for years, there may be disappointments unless certain precautions are taken.

Useful hints

— Buy a well-developed plant and not some leafless starter. The best time for replanting is between mid-spring and late summer, using pure light peat and a pot that is wider than it is tall. Water thoroughly and place the pot on a saucer that will be kept filled with water from spring to winter.

— Place the dionaea in the open, directly in the sun. Water once a week without adding fertilizer. If a fly lands or is placed on a leaf, it will close up and the prey will be digested in the course of a week.

— When winter approaches, empty the saucer and place the pot in a corner or in a cold frame. Dionaeas can survive temperatures of −5°C (23°F) or even lower. Flowering is usually the sign that the plant is about to die, so gather the seed and germinate in peat from the pot.

Height: 20 cm (8 in).
Spacing and planting distance: 20 cm (8 in).
Soil: pure peat moss.
Aspect: full sun.
Propagation: from seed.
Flowering season: summer, not spectacular.
Type: perennial.

Dodecatheon

SHOOTING STAR, AMERICAN COWSLIP

Primulaceae

A dodecatheon in bloom is a spectacular sight. The shape of the flowers, their subtle colours, the way in which they nod on the end of their long stalks, all adds to the effect, but there are problems involved in cultivating them. Their life cycle is very short, often less than three months from when the first shoots appear. This is a plant for passionate, experienced gardeners, but be warned, it dies off completely in winter.

Useful hints

— Before planting, enrich the soil with peat and leaf-mould. The soil must be capable of holding enough water to feed the plant right through the spring.

— Plant in early autumn and spring. Let clumps fill out before dividing them.

— Sowing fresh seeds can give good results: the plants will shoot in spring.

Recommended

— It's easy to lose your way among the different species of dodecatheon. The best one is *D. meadia*, sometimes listed as *D. pauciflorum*.

Height: 45 cm (18 in).
Spacing and planting distance: 20 cm (8 in).
Soil: rich in organic matter.
Aspect: semi-shade.
Propagation: from seed or by division in early autumn.
Flowering season: late spring to early summer.
Type: perennial.

Doronicum

LEOPARD'S BANE

Compositae

It looks like the first shafts of sunlight in spring. Devotees of marguerites owe it to themselves to include spring-flowering leopard's bane in their gardens. Combined with tulips and myosotis, it brightens up the slopes by its lightness and the brilliance of its colours. In summer, create lovely carpets around your bushes and trees with this hardy plant, which likes the shade.

Useful hints

— Best planted in autumn, turning over the soil a little. Make up the soil with a little peat if it is too light.

— Water from mid-spring onwards if the rain is late in coming: this plant likes a certain amount of moisture.

— Cut the plants to ground level in autumn.

— Divide the clumps every four years to preserve their strength. Replant the roots immediately.

— Watch out for snails.

Recommended

— The most widespread is *Doronicum orientale* or Caucasian leopard's bane: the variety 'Finesse' has very elegant yellow flowers.

— More lavish, *D. plantagineum* 'Excelsum' quickly forms wide clumps 80 cm (32 in) high and has golden yellow flowers. The hybrid 'Miss Mason' has striking bright yellow flowers, which look good as cut flowers for the home.

Height: 50–80 cm (20–32 in).
Spacing and planting distance: 30–40 cm (12–16 in).
Soil: quite deep, moist even in summer.
Aspect: semi-shade or gentle sun.
Propagation: by division at the end of summer.
Flowering season: spring.
Type: perennial.

▽ **Doronicum orientale**

Draba

WHITLOW GRASS

Cruciferae

In spring, this yellow flower is often found at seed merchants' stalls. It owes its charm to its appearance, reminiscent of the mosses of the forest, and to its yellow flowers. It's tricky to keep in good condition for long, though, since it wilts quickly. A well-drained corner of your rock garden would be ideal for *Draba aizoïdes*.

Useful tips

— Plant the flowering pots in spring in a pocket of sandy soil. Cut down the stems after flowering to prevent seeds forming, and sprinkle the clumps with a little handful of sand at the end of winter to help surface rooting.

— You can also cultivate drabas in pots, along with early bulbs like crocus or *Iris reticulata*.

Height: 5–10 cm (2–4 in).
Spacing and planting distance: 15 cm (6 in).
Soil: well-drained, very sandy.
Aspect: full sun.
Propagation: by division after flowering or from seed in spring.
Flowering season: spring.
Type: perennial.

▽ **Draba**

Dryas

MOUNTAIN AVENS

Rosaceae

This native of the tundra is not bothered by the cold. In your rock garden, it will be one of the few flowers able to brighten up north-facing slopes, forming a deep green carpet dotted with white flowers in summer. *Dryas octopetala* goes well with small conifers, heather and early spring bulbs, which will find it easy to grow through its foliage.

Useful hints

— Plant preferably in autumn or just after the first cold spells, in sandy pockets of peaty soil. Water regularly for the first year.

— Add some sand to the centre of the clumps at the start of each winter to avoid standing moisture. Don't cut off flowers once they have wilted, because the fluffy seed heads are very decorative.

— At the end of winter, take cuttings and let them root right through the winter under a cold frame. Prick them out permanently in spring.

Height: 10 cm (4 in).
Spacing and planting distance: 30–50 cm (12–20 in).
Soil: acid, sandy (heath soil).
Aspect: anywhere, even north-facing.
Propagation: from cuttings at the end of winter.
Flowering season: summer.
Type: perennial.

▽ **Dryas octopetala**

Dryopteris

BUCKLER FERN, SHIELD FERN

Polypodiaceae

You will often have seen this in damp undergrowth, cascading down embankments along forest paths. It's an ideal plant for rapidly filling out new gardens, since it thrives on very little and keeps its foliage well. It makes an ideal companion for helxine, eucomis, hostas, hydrangeas and fuchsias. In winter, its leaves cut down and laid on the ground will protect delicate plants.

Useful hints

— Plant it in spring, in moist soil rich in leaf-mould. It particularly likes damp corners.

— Cut away faded fronds in spring.

Recommended

— Everyone knows buckler/shield ferns from the woods. In some places, they are very common, but equally – and surprisingly – they are absent from entire regions. Their light, semi-evergreen fronds are a pretty light green. They are completely separate from the female fern, which is an athyrium.

— *Dryopteris dilatata* (or *D. austriaca*) has almost triangular fronds with very few incisions.

— Very finely sculptured, the foliage of *D. cristata* is reminiscent of Japanese paper cutouts. It loves damp places and goes marvellously with candelabra primroses and astilbes.

— *D. affinis* has large, elegant fronds which are more hardy than those of the buckler (or shield) ferns. The golden fronds of 'Cristata The King' have short, crested segments.

— The vigorous clumps of *D. carthusiana* will tolerate a wide variety of conditions but prefer cool, damp soil.

— *D. erythrosora* has unusual copper-coloured foliage.

— *D. filix-mas* is a common sight in the undergrowth, often appearing unexpectedly as its spores are spread by the wind. Varieties worth noting include 'Crispa' whose fronds have crested segments and 'Linearis Polydactyla' with its almost threadlike segments.

Height: 40 cm (16 in).
Spacing and planting distance: 30 cm (12 in).
Soil: ordinary, moist.
Aspect: semi-shade.
Propagation: from seed.
Type: perennial.

△ *Dryopteris filix-mas*

Eccremocarpus

CHILEAN GLORY FLOWER

Bignoniaceae

Few climbing plants can boast such a glorious red. Indeed, from mid-summer to mid-autumn, this pretty annual creeper offers you tubular flowers in stunning coral, pink, red and yellow, with a little touch of gold at the edge of the throat. But it's not easy to grow. Like the cobaea, *Eccremocarpus scaber* has a capricious streak, and has been known to drive the most patient gardener to despair. Perhaps that's why

◁ *Eccremocarpus scaber*

it's so popular! Try to bring your plant under glass at the end of summer: it will be bound to do well, since it is frost which kills it.

Useful hints

— To get all possible luck on your side, sow it in early spring under glass.

— Make up a rich porous mulch from peat, ripe compost and leaf compost in equal proportions.

— Once the plants are 10 cm (4 in) high, towards mid-spring, plant them out in good, ordinary, well-exposed soil.

— As this is a spreading plant which puts out tendrils, provide it with a trellis or light stakes for support.

Height: 200 cm (80 in)
Spacing and planting distance: 80 cm (32 in).
Soil: ordinary, well-drained.
Aspect: sun.
Propagation: from seed.
Flowering season: summer to autumn.
Type: annual.

Echinacea

CONEFLOWER

Compositae

It's not long since this big pink rudbeckia changed its name, and some people still call it *Rudbeckia purpurea grandiflora*. This is one of the most familiar plants of our older gardens, which it decorates in autumn with its somewhat wistful pink stems crowned with 'daisy heads'. Brighten *Echinacea purpurea* up by planting it by your asters or heleniums, and don't let it take over – it is remarkably vigorous.

Useful hints

— Plant the echinacea during autumn or spring, in good common garden soil.

— Give it a well-shaped slope to show the flowers off to best advantage.

— Divide the clumps every three years.

Height: 100–150 cm (40–60 in).
Spacing and planting distance: 40 cm (16 in).
Soil: ordinary.
Aspect: sun.
Propagation: by division.
Flowering season: summer to autumn.
Type: perennial.

Echinops

GLOBE THISTLE

Compositae

Echinops is only really beautiful in large numbers, next to red campions (lychnis) in a harmony of rather daring minor colours or, more classically, combined with phlox or shrub roses such as 'Cornelia' or 'Penelope'. These false thistles (thistles are in fact *Eryngium*, and therefore members of the Umbelliferae) show both a freedom of movement and an evident rigidity in their dense clumps of flowers. This is one of the best summer flowers for low-maintenance gardens.

Useful hints

— Plant in autumn or spring, in any well-drained soil. Cut off faded stems in autumn.

— Don't overfeed, since the plants will bolt, without losing their spikes or getting more flowers.

Recommended

— *Echinops ritro* is a violet-blue, and forms clumps 60 cm (24 in) high. The 'Veitch's Blue' variety is hardier, and its heads are a darker steel blue.

— *E. bannaticus* 'Blue Globe' has large, pale to mid-blue, spherical flower heads.

— *E. sphaerocephalus* gives a very decorative grey flower at the end of summer. It is a good idea to stake it, since it often grows over 150 cm (60 in) high and may be flattened by storms. *E. niveus* is noted for its white flower heads.

— *E.* 'Taplow Blue' has powder-blue flowers and grey-green foliage.

Height: 60–160 cm (24–64 in).
Spacing and planting distance: 30 cm (12 in).
Soil: ordinary, but must be well-drained.
Aspect: sun.
Propagation: from seed or by division in spring.
Flowering season: summer to autumn.
Type: biennial, perennial.

△ *Echinops ritro*
◁ *Echinacea purpurea*

Echium candicans △

Echium

VIPER'S BUGLOSS

Boraginaceae

On sunny roads or rocky paths, pushing up between the stones, you will find the pretty spikes of *Echium vulgare* speckled with an overwhelming pink; it is a little cousin of *E. candicans* which is such a feature of Mediterranean gardens. It goes well in dry, shady gardens, next to verbascums and agaves. But beware of winter: these pretty plants should only be used on warm slopes and rock gardens.

Useful hints

— Plant in the spring, in rich soil, on a very sunny slope.

— Each year, reseed with the natural seeds which will appear on the slopes, because these plants don't live very long and are often biennial.

— Sow in spring: the plants will flower the following year.

Recommended

— As well as *E. vulgare* and *E. candicans*, *E. plantagineum* will seduce you with its white, red or purple spikes like those of 'Blue Bedder'. It is an annual.

Height: 30–100 cm (12–40 in).
Spacing and planting distance: 30–70 cm (12–28 in).
Soil: ordinary, rich.
Aspect: sun.
Propagation: from seed.
Flowering season: summer.
Type: annual, perennial.

△ *Epilobium angustifolium*

Epilobium
WILLOWHERB, FIREWEED
Onagraceae

Rarely offered in catalogues, although very decorative and a native of our countryside, willowherb works wonders in the slightly wilder corners of the garden, in large spreads next to groups of foxgloves. Its common name suggests a definite preference for moist locations. The common variety is a purple-pink colour, but there is also a very pretty white.

Useful hints

— Plant shoots in autumn or spring. Clumps can easily be separated from new plants. If in flower, don't hesitate to prune it to one-third of its height to make up for its losing its roots and to help it 'take'.

— Watch out for it spreading sometimes further than you would like. Cut back the rhizomes running along the ground with a spade.

Recommended

— Some varieties – such as *Epilobium dodonaei* – are less invasive and ideal for a rock garden.

— *E. fleischeri* likes the cool conditions between the stones of low walls or under paving.
Height: 150 cm (60 in).
Spacing and planting distance: 50 cm (20 in).
Soil: any, but must stay moist in summer.
Aspect: sun or semi-shade.
Propagation: by division in spring or after flowering.
Flowering season: late summer to autumn.
Type: perennial.

Epimedium
BARRENWORT
Berberidaceae

It's strange that barrenwort should still be so little known, since it is probably the best answer to unpromising situations. It prospers in the shade of trees just as well as ivy, and repays the investment in it many times over in its foliage which changes colour over the seasons and also offers a graceful bloom in early spring.

Useful hints

— Plant at any time of year, but don't forget to water it throughout the first year. It grows very slowly at first, then the clumps fill out. By dividing them every three years, you will soon have a veritable carpet of several square metres from a single plant.

— At the end of winter, cut away the old growth to accentuate the blooms. Use this opportunity to add a well-rotted peat or compost mulch.

Recommended

— *Epimedium grandiflorum* has flowers of different colours, as large as (and looking like) columbines.

— The leaves of *E. rubrum* take on magnificent colours in spring and autumn.

— *E. × versicolor* 'Sulphureum' has finely toothed leaves and ravishing pale yellow flowers.

— If you are looking for good ground cover, *E. × perralchicum* 'Fröhnleiten' is by far the most vigorous evergreen variety.

— There are two varieties of the very graceful *E. × youngianum*: 'Niveum' (white) and 'Roseum' (lilac-pink).
Height: 20–30 cm (8–12 in).
Spacing and planting distance: 20 cm (8 in).
Soil: ordinary, preferably rich in humus.
Aspect: shade.
Propagation: by division in autumn.
Flowering season: spring.
Type: perennial.

***Eremurus stenophyllus*
ssp. *stenophyllus* ▷**

△ *Eranthis hyemalis*

Eranthis
WINTER ACONITE
Ranunculaceae

Of a stunning yellow, *Eranthis hyemalis* blooms while the snow is still on the ground. Just like the snowdrop, this is a little plant which should never be picked, since it is only happy in the garden, a rockery or a rich soil slope.

Useful hints

— Plant in autumn, in little groups of seven or eight, in humus-rich but very well-drained soil.

— These plants take easily: use them as undergrowth, in sparse clumps.
Height: 10–15 cm (4–6 in).
Spacing and planting distance: 15 cm (6 in).
Soil: rich and light.
Aspect: sun or semi-shade.
Propagation: by division or from seed.
Flowering season: winter to spring.
Type: bulb.

△ *Eremurus robustus*
Eremurus himalaicus △

Eremurus

FOXTAIL LILY, DESERT CANDLE

Liliaceae

This is undoubtedly one of the most stunning plants in summer. Give it the rich, deep soil that it likes, and the eremurus will think nothing of growing 200 cm (80 in) high. Plant it close to foxgloves, delphiniums and heracleum.

Useful hints

— Plant large clumps in autumn, in pockets of light soil on a shady slope.

— Each autumn, cut away the dry stems and cover the roots with 10 cm (4 in) of mulch to protect them.

— Avoid planting eremurus in windy gardens, or be ready to use stakes.

Recommended

— The best-known and most graceful is *Eremurus stenophyllus* ssp. *stenophyllus*, with its fine yellow flowers; it is not too overwhelming at 100 cm (40 in) high. This has been used to create numerous hybrids, such as the Ruiter Hybrids or 'Oasis' (pink) or 'Romance' (salmon).

— The giant *E. himalaicus* reaches 120 cm (48 in), and is pure white, while the even larger *E. robustus* at 300 cm (120 in) is a lovely peach-yellow.

— The *E.* × *isabellinus* Shelford Hybrids are predominantly yellow and orange.

Height: 100–300 cm (40–120 in).
Spacing and planting distance: 50 cm (20 in).
Soil: rich, well-drained.
Aspect: sun or semi-shade.
Propagation: from seed.
Flowering season: summer.
Type: perennial.

Erica

HEATHER, HEATH

Ericaceae

Heather is something you either love or hate. Its supporters love its soft colours and natural appearance, its detractors denigrate its squat profile and gloom in winter. We can reunite the two camps by finding it a little spot in company with a few grasses to lighten it. Avoid large, monotonous groups and shady corners.

Useful hints

— Plant in autumn or spring in a low-lime soil which keeps slightly moist even in summer.

— Trim off the dead flowers with a pair of hedging shears just after flowering. This will make the clumps much more dense and long-lasting.

— Keep the soil clear for the first few years, making sure above all to weed out couch-grass. Once in place, heather will stop weeds from growing.

Recommended

— *Erica carnea* (winter heather) braves bad weather to present us with its bells. Amongst the prettiest are 'Cecilia M. Beale' (white), 'Praecox Rubra' (pink), 'Springwood White' and 'Springwood Pink' (colour as names) and 'Winter Beauty' (carmine-pink). The last is one of the heathers best able to tolerate lime soils. 'Aurea', a variety with golden leaves and pink flowers, does not always thrive in them. 'Foxhollow' has golden yellow foliage and pale pink flowers, while 'King George' has deep rose-pink flowers with dark green foliage.

— *E. cinerea* (bell heather) is common on our heaths and clearings. Its loose racemes of flowers on the end of its stems herald the end of the summer. The prettiest are 'C. D. Eason' (dark pink), 'Cevennes' (a curious lavender colour), 'Pallida' (light pink with many flowers), 'Atrosanguinea' (deep red) and 'Stephen Davis' (brilliant red flowers).

— *E.* × *darleyensis* is the result of a cross between the winter heather and a Mediterranean species. It tolerates lime relatively well, but flowers a little later. There are several highly prized varieties: 'Arthur Johnson', with long magenta spikes; 'Furzey', deep pink and very free-flowering; 'Silberschmelze', scented white flowers.

— *E. tetralix* is easily recognized by its large umbels of distinctively shaped flowers (like tiny rugby balls). It flowers

△ *Erica vagans*

in early summer, after *E.* × *darleyensis*. The most common varieties are 'Rosea' (pink) and 'Con Underwood' (dark red).

— Linking these and the winter heathers, *E. vagans* (Cornish heath) quickly forms a dense carpet. The stems are sometimes split by hard frosts but soon resprout from the base. 'Mrs D. F. Maxwell' (red) and 'Saint Keverne' (cerise) are well worth trying.

▽ *Erica cinerea*

Height: 30–50 cm (12–20 in).
Spacing and planting distance: 30 cm (12 in).
Soil: acid, sandy.
Aspect: sun or semi-shade.
Propagation: by division after flowering.
Flowering season: all year, depending on species.
Type: perennial.

Erigeron

FLEABANE

Compositae

Aster lovers should like these: they are very similar, and have the advantage of flowering in summer when the prettiest asters aren't around. Use them to edge borders and low walls and don't forget to divide them each spring or autumn, as this makes them produce more flowers. They go well with *Viola cornuta*, cerastium and alyssums.

Useful hints

— Best time for planting is late spring: young plants often prove vulnerable to heavy frosts.

— Divide clumps regularly in autumn to prevent them ageing and fading and prune the clumps down to ground level.

Recommended

— The earliest fleabanes are *Erigeron aurianticus*, whose orange flowers open in early summer, and *E. leiomerus*, pink and a prolific flowerer.

— The vast majority of fleabanes bloom from summer to autumn. These are the famous *E. speciosus* hybrids. The best are 'Foerster's Liebling', double and deep pink, 'Rosa Triumph', brilliant red, or even 'Violetta', a very dark violet, one of the predominant fleabane colours taken to its limit. *E.* 'Rotes Meer' is deep pink.

— As for the others, *E. karvinskianus* is in flower in the frosts. Its very delicate daisies range from pink to white and give a dainty impression on low walls, which it colonizes readily. Protect in winter.

Height: 15–45 cm (6–18 in).
Spacing and planting distance: 15–30 cm (6–12 in).
Soil: ordinary, light, moist.
Aspect: sun.
Propagation: from seed or by division.
Flowering season: summer to autumn.
Type: annual, biennial, perennial.

Erigeron speciosus **hybrid** ▷

△ *Erinus alpinus*

Erinus alpinus

FAIRY FOXGLOVE

Scrophulariaceae

Ideal for starting a rock garden, this slides into the smallest crevices, reseeding itself as required, and forms dark green cushions which literally vanish under flowers for a good part of spring and summer. Its only drawback: it doesn't live very long.

Useful hints

— Plant in autumn or spring in crevices in low walls or paving.

— Prune the clumps after flowering, leaving a few fruit to ripen and produce seeds. Sow these in a dish and leave them under glass over the winter. They will germinate the next spring.

Recommended

— There aren't many *Erinus alpinus* varieties in the catalogues. The best-known varieties are 'Caeruleus' (blue) and 'Dr Hähnle' (carmine-red).

Height: 10 cm (4 in).
Spacing and planting distance: 25 cm (10 in).
Soil: pebbly, on the dry side.
Aspect: gentle sun.
Propagation: from seed or by division in autumn.
Flowering season: late spring to summer.
Type: perennial.

Erodium

STORKSBILL, HERONSBILL

Geraniaceae

Not really easy to cultivate, the erodiums are the mountain equivalent of our hardy geraniums: the same healthy foliage in dense clumps and the same flowers with very simple petals. They are less hardy, however, due to their dislike of too much water in winter.

Useful hints

— Plant in spring, preferably after having let them winter under glass away from too much rain. Give them a sunny spot and well-drained, even pebbly, soil.

— Water regularly until the flowers appear. Once they have passed, prune the clumps to make way for new foliage.

— They are propagated by taking cuttings in autumn.

Recommended

— *Erodium reichardii*, with its slightly sad white and pink flowers, is the most widely grown although not the hardiest.

— Much more vigorous, *E. manescavii* forms a good clump of foliage which peaks at 45 cm (18 in). Its purple flowers can be seen from a distance.

Height: 5 cm (2 in) (*E. reichardii*) to 45 cm (18 in) (*E. manescavii*).
Spacing and planting distance: 25 cm (10 in).
Soil: pebbly, rather poor.
Aspect: full sun.
Propagation: from cuttings.
Flowering season: summer.
Type: perennial.

▽ *Erodium reichardii*

105

Eryngium
SEA HOLLY, ERYNGO
Umbelliferae

Thistles: people love them or hate them, depending on whether they are already in their clutches or looking at them from a distance. In the former case, their formidable spines make us swear to root them out of our gardens mercilessly. The rest of the time, we can only admire their armour, worthy of the knights of old. The majestic sweep of their flowery stems is an unforgettable sight, and you cannot help looking each morning to see if their flowers have opened. Their steel-blue colour harmonizes well with many other plants.

Useful hints

— Plant in spring, away from the edge of slopes. Combine them with some gramineas and yellow summer marguerites to give a vibrant display seen from afar. Cut off faded flowers to prevent seeds spreading over the entire garden. New young shoots are often found at the foot of the old plants.

— For drying under ideal conditions, cut the inflorescences when they are barely opened. Hang them head down in a dry, shady place for two months.

Recommended

— Although *Eryngium agavifolium* has very full rosettes of pink leaves and a flowering stem over 150 cm (60 in) high, its relatively small violet-blue flowers are a little disappointing.

— Hailing from the mountains, *E. alpinum* has much larger flowers in a magnificent steel-blue in summer.

— *E. bourgatii* is smaller, but deserves to be cultivated just for its white- and silver-veined leaves. It is rarely more than 60 cm (24 in) high, and comes from the Pyrenees.

— *E. maritimum*, still common on some beaches, and *E.* × *oliverianum* are some of the best flowers for dried bouquets.

— The branching stems of *E. planum* – with their masses of tiny round blue flower heads – blend well in borders.

— In spite of its exotic-looking blue foliage, *E. yuccifolium* prefers cool conditions.

— *E.* × *zabelii* has almost completely disappeared from our gardens, in spite of its magnificent purplish blue colour.

◁ *Eryngium bromeliifolium*

—Very different in appearance, *E. variifolium* has long-lasting white-veined leaves with few prickles. Its flowers are smaller, but come in extraordinary clusters, so heavy that the plant has to be supported to prevent it collapsing in the first storm. Mix with rosemary, cistus and euphorbia to give a Mediterranean appearance.

Height: 60–150 cm (24–60 in).
Spacing and planting distance: 20–50 cm (8–20 in).
Soil: ordinary, well-drained, even pebbly.
Aspect: sun.
Propagation: from seed when ripe or by division in spring.
Flowering season: summer to autumn.
Type: perennial.

△ *Erysimum* 'Bowles Mauve'

Erysimum (see also *Cheiranthus*)

WALLFLOWER

Cruciferae

A great lover of walls, the erysimum delights owners of dry gardens. Indeed, this hardy plant with pretty yellow flowers is only happy in dry soils, like its cousin cheiranthus. Less fragrant than the latter, it can still offer a gentle scent. Its splendid colour thrives in the company of myosotis and late tulips, especially dark colours such as those of black parrot tulips.

Useful hints

— Sow in a seed bed in autumn, then plant out in early spring. The first flowers will appear the following spring. You can also sow in late spring and plant out in autumn, and so see the plants flower late the following spring.

— Renew beds every other year: although hardy in sunny gardens with light soil, these plants lose their beauty from their second year onwards.

Recommended

— The cushions of *Erysimum hieraciifolium* look wonderful on low walls and between paving stones. The orange clusters of this well-known biennial, known as the Siberian wallflower, are a familiar sight in spring.

— Hybrid erysimums have extended the colour range considerably: 'Butterscotch' (orange-yellow); 'Constant Cheer' (dusty pink, verging on salmon); 'Jacob's Jacket' (with a touch of purplish blue); 'Chelsea Jacket' (soft orange maturing

to pale mauve); 'Moonlight' (pale lemon-yellow).

Height: 30 cm (12 in).
Spacing and planting distance: 30 cm (12 in).
Soil: ordinary.
Aspect: sun.
Propagation: from seed.
Flowering season: late spring to early summer.
Type: biennial, perennial.

Erythronium

DOG'S-TOOTH VIOLET, FAWN LILY

Liliaceae

With their pale flowers, sometimes pink, sometimes yellow, and their cream- or brown-splashed foliage, erythroniums look good in the spring, especially planted in light, humus-rich undergrowth in clusters of five or six.

Useful hints

— Plant moist bulbs in early autumn in good humus-rich earth. They grow best in leaf mould.

— Watch out for fieldmice and frosts. In the first year, protect the bulbs you have planted 10 cm (4 in) underground with a 5 cm (2 in) coat of leaves.

Recommended

— *Erythronium dens-canis* (dog's tooth violet), with its pink flowers, is the best-known. The double variety, 'Flore Pleno', is as yet grown only by experts. More readily available are 'Niveum' (white) and 'Purple King' (cyclamen with pale brown markings).

△ *Erythronium revolutum* 'White Beauty'

— *E. tuolumnense*, with its beautiful lacquered yellow flowers and glistening leaves, is the most graceful.

— *E. revolutum*, with its ivory flowers, is favoured by those with 'white' gardens.

Height: 10–25 cm (4–10 in).
Spacing and planting distance: 15 cm (6 in).
Soil: humus-rich.
Aspect: semi-shade.
Propagation: by separating bulbs.
Flowering season: spring.
Type: bulb.

107

Eschscholzia californica △
Eucomis comosa ▽

Eschscholzia

CALIFORNIA POPPY

Papaveraceae

Owners of dry gardens despairing of ever seeing them produce flowers, and reluctant gardeners whose main aim is to avoid spending their weekends doing a thousand and one little jobs, should discover the California poppy (*Eschscholzia californica*). Give it a minimum of soil and a maximum of sun, and not only will it flower incessantly from early summer until the frosts come, but it will also reseed itself. Plant it with eryngium and marigolds for company and your garden will be a feast for your eyes.

Useful hints

— Sow directly on site in late spring, choosing sunny banks if possible.

— Thin out plants after a little rain if too tightly packed and try pricking out the surplus, watering well.

—Gather the seed pods in dry weather in autumn.

— Spontaneous seedings will revert to their original colour after some years.

Recommended

— There are singles and doubles, but our vote goes to the classic California poppy with its simple flowers, sold in a mixture of colours; it runs through all the yellows and orange.

Height: 20 cm (8 in).
Spacing and planting distance: 15 cm (6 in).
Soil: ordinary.
Aspect: sun.
Propagation: from seed.
Flowering season: summer to autumn.
Type: annual.

108

△ *Eupatorium purpureum*
◁ *Eschscholzia* (mixed)

Eucomis

PINEAPPLE LILY

Liliaceae

For those lucky enough to have a well-watered garden in full sun, and those who worry that their garden is too sunny, the eucomis is a godsend worth investigating. With its unusual delicate green violet-speckled inflorescence, resembling a pineapple, and its long ribbon leaves, it is not lacking in appearance. Other tender bulbs and perennials can keep it company, and, as the seasons pass, you will see it fill out and bloom lavishly.

Useful hints

— Plant the large bulbs, resembling those of hyacinths, in spring, in deep moist soil, 10 cm (4 in) down.

— Where winter is likely to be harsh, mulch the clumps and protect them under a cloche.

— In heavy soil, plant in pockets filled with a very sandy mulch mixture.

Recommended

— There are two species, very similar: *Eucomis bicolor*, which grows to 30 cm (12 in) and has light green petals with purple edges, and the fragrant *E. comosa*, taller at 50 cm (20 in) and with garnet-spotted stems.

Height: 30–50 cm (12–20 in).
Spacing and planting distance: 20 cm (8 in).
Soil: ordinary, moist.
Aspect: full sun.
Propagation: from seed or by separating bulbs.
Flowering season: summer.
Type: bulb.

Eupatorium

BONESET, JOE PYE WEED, THOROUGHWORT, WHITE SNAKEROOT

Compositae

The eupatoriums come mainly from the eastern USA. They are tall and stately perennials and have no equals when it comes to natural decoration for the moister, wilder corners of the garden.

Useful hints

— Plant in spring or autumn, first turning over the soil well and feeding it with peat to help it hold moisture.

— Water regularly and well for the first year. Mulch the soil with turf or lawn cuttings.

— When the flowers on the clumps dwindle, divide them just after they flower.

Recommended

— Perfectly at home among shrubs, the purple eupatorium (*Eupatorium purpureum*) reaches the peak of its beauty in August, when its powerful stems are crowned with hundreds of purple-pink flowers.

— Not quite so tall, but forming larger clumps, *E. rugosum* looks like an enormous ageratum with its feathery white flowers.

Height: 100–200 cm (40–80 in).
Spacing and planting distance: 50 cm (20 in).
Soil: rich, moist even in summer.
Aspect: sun or semi-shade.
Propagation: by division in autumn.
Flowering season: late summer, early autumn.
Type: perennial.

Euphorbia

EUPHORBIA, SPURGE

Euphorbiaceae

There is a euphorbia suited to every nook of the garden, from shade to sun and dry to moist. Some are among the best space-fillers, while others have a majestic enough silhouette to allow them to stand alone at a turn in an avenue. Although most are hardy, there are even easily sown annuals. The choice is really overwhelming.

Useful hints

— Plant euphorbias in spring or early autumn, as this will allow them to put down good roots before winter. A light soil is what suits them best.

— Mulch the soil with peat at the end of winter. Lawn clippings or pine bark are suitable. This will prevent clumps being stripped by rain, exposing the main roots.

— Divide clumps every three years, cutting the fleshy roots cleanly. Plant them out in a mixture of sand and peat and let them spend their first winter under cold glass.

Recommended

— Very spectacular, *Euphorbia characias* grows over 100 cm (40 in) high. Its bluish-leaved stems terminate in spikes of remarkably sulphur-yellow waxen flowers. It blooms at the same time as late tulips, at the end of the spring.

— *E. characias* ssp. *wulfenii* looks very similar, but just a little bigger, and flowers a month later. Plant in a sheltered position.

— Pointed, often red-veined leaves, flowers in bunches with red bracts playing a starring role: this is *E. griffithii*, whose variety 'Fireglow' has the most brilliant shades of orange.

— *E. marginata* (snow on the mountain) is an annual and often used as foliage in dainty bouquets. To seal the cuts and prevent the latex escaping, just soak the ends of the stems in hot water. Sow under glass in spring, or directly into the vegetable garden after the frosts.

— Very unusual, with geometrical interwoven leaves all the way up its trailing stems, *E. myrsinites* works wonders in rock gardens, low walls and dry stone steps. It blooms in mid-spring.

— The evergreen *E. amygdaloïdes* 'Purpurea', with its purple flowers, is one of the most beautiful of the euphorbias.

— *E. cyparissias* spreads in cushions of

△ *Euphorbia characias*

soft, light foliage and thrives in dry soil.

— The chocolate-coloured foliage of *E. dulcis* 'Chameleon' makes it one of the most beautiful of recent introductions.

— *E. × martinii* is a beautiful evergreen which combines the vigour of *E. characias* with the colour of *E. amygdaloïdes*.

— The shrubby but not very hardy *E. mellifera* should be grown only in warmer regions.

— *E. palustris* (marsh euphorbia) produces magnificent rounded clumps. In spring, acid-yellow flowers appear above yellowish green leaves.

— One of our favourites is *E. polychroma*, whose stunning green leaves terminate in pale yellow flowers in spring. Mix with white tulips for a really charming picture. Prune in summer to ensure the new foliage will be perfect. Some nurseries have recently introduced the striking purple variety, 'Purpurea'.

— *E. seguieriana* ssp. *niciciana*, characterized by its wealth of slender stems and tiny, bronze-washed leaves, is a creeping variety which thrives in poor, thin soil.

— *E. robbiae* is the queen of dry, shady spots. Its tough, dark green leaves are in themselves a guarantee of hardiness. It forms beautiful carpets, even at the foot of a weeping willow, and flowers at the end of spring in that green chartreuse colour which is such a feature of the euphorbias.

Height: 10–120 cm (4–60 in), depending on species and variety.
Spacing and planting distance: 20–40 cm (8–16 in).
Soil: ordinary.
Aspect: full sun to shade, depending on variety.
Propagation: by division after flowering.
Flowering season: spring.
Type: annual, perennial.

△ *Euphorbia myrsinites*

▽ *Euphorbia marginata*

△ *Euphorbia griffithii* 'Fireglow'

Euphorbia mellifera ▷

Euphorbia griffithii 'Dixter' ▽

▽ *Euphorbia polychroma*

Euryops acraeus △

Euryops

EURYOPS

Compositae

Its origins in the Drakensberg mountains of South Africa are no doubt the reason why *Euryops acraeus* can withstand average winters. Give it a sunny, well-drained corner in your rock garden, and you will be rewarded with a cushion of delicate grey adorned with bright yellow flowers at the start of summer. You can also put it in large tubs in company with a dark-leaved conifer, such as a yew or a mountain pine, or use it as the background for another delicate plant, the fabulous rhodohypoxis, itself a South African exile.

Useful hints

— Euryops is best planted in spring, to save it having to go through a winter without good roots. Put it in a pocket of well-drained soil and cover the soil with a layer of fine gravel to keep the neck out of reach of moisture.

— Each spring, add a little leaf-mould to the heart of the clumps to help the twigs root. Cuttings taken in summer will also take root well in sand, but must be allowed to winter under glass.

Recommended

— The finely cut, deep green foliage of the shrub-like *E. abrotanifolius* is similar to that of *Artemisia abrotanum*.

Height: 25 cm (10 in).
Spacing and planting distance: 30 cm (12 in).
Soil: very well-drained.
Aspect: sun.
Propagation: from cuttings.
Flowering season: summer.
Type: perennial.

Felicia amelloïdes △
Festuca glauca ▷

Felicia

FELICIA, BLUE MARGUERITE

Compositae

Anyone who likes cacti, the succulent echeverias, agaves and sedums will like this little plant. There is the added advantage that *Felicia amelloïdes* (syn. *Agathaea coelestis*) flowers each year without fail and multiplies with ease. Its only shortcoming is its lack of hardiness except in warm and temperate climates, although it makes a good conservatory plant elsewhere.

Useful hints

— Plant *F. amelloïdes* in spring in a sunny corner of the garden or in tubs to decorate walls and paths.

— It is not very fussy, and will be happy with a good ordinary soil.

— Flowering abundantly, it propagates easily from seed, and is fun for children to try their hand at growing.

Recommended

— *F. amelloïdes.* Among the more abundantly flowering varieties, with their large, brightly coloured flower heads, are 'Astrid Thomas' (deep blue) and 'Variegata' (leaves mottled with white).

Height: 30–40 cm (12–16 in).
Spacing and planting distance: 30 cm (12 in).
Soil: ordinary.
Aspect: sun.
Propagation: from seed or cuttings.
Flowering season: summer to autumn.
Type: perennial.

Festuca

FESTUCA, FESCUE

Gramineae

This pretty blue grass is unusual in that it forms very dense round clumps and also in that it doesn't get everywhere. It is ideal for more subdued borders or for introducing a touch of calm in borders full of colour. Mix it with spring bulbs and wild flowers to create a natural little corner.

Useful hints

— Plant *Festuca glauca* in autumn or spring, first turning over the soil thoroughly. It's a very frugal plant, which even thrives on a little deprivation.

— Avoid soil which holds water in winter. Prune clumps at the end of summer when the flowers are no longer decorative.

— Festuca is easy to propagate, either by dividing the clumps in spring or sowing at the same time. The clumps look good from the second year onwards.

Height: 20–30 cm (8–12 in).
Spacing and planting distance: 20 cm (8 in).
Soil: ordinary, not too rich, but well-drained.
Aspect: sun or semi-shade.
Propagation: from seed or by division in spring.
Flowering season: summer.
Type: perennial.

▽ *Filipendula rubra* 'Venusta'

Filipendula

MEADOWSWEET

Rosaceae

A godsend to gardeners with little time to spare who would prefer to keep their corner of a meadow as a wild garden rather than put the finishing touches to their borders, filipendula needs no care whatsoever. Whether the queen of the meadows (*Filipendula ulmaria*) or other members of this large family, these are plants which are happy with a moist, lightly shaded soil and which, combined with lysimachias, macleayas, rodgersias and ferns, make banks that are as delightful as they are easy to maintain.

Useful hints

— Plant filipendulas in spring or autumn, in clean, moist soil, preferably in semi-shade.

— Create pleasant splashes of colour by planting at least five or six plants side by side.

— Every three years, divide up clumps which are threatening to overrun.

Recommended

— As well as the deliciously scented queen of the meadows, *F. vulgaris*, with its pale rose blooms and incised leaves like those of a fern, and *F. rubra* 'Venusta' (deep pink) give the best effects.

— *F. purpurea* has large, almost red panicles.

— *F. ulmaria* 'Aurea' – the golden-leaved variety of the 'queen of the meadows' – adds a splash of colour to a shady corner. 'Plena' is the double form.

Height: 60–90 cm (24–36 in).
Spacing and planting distance: 30 cm (12 in).
Soil: ordinary.
Aspect: sun or semi-shade.
Propagation: by division.
Flowering season: summer to autumn.
Type: perennial.

Foeniculum

FENNEL

Umbelliferae

The advantages of fennel are a very imposing bearing, thanks to its soaring silhouette, its cloud of very fine green leaves and graceful flowers of a very sweet chartreuse-yellow, and the typical scent of aniseed which it releases at the slightest brush. Use it in abundance, in company with old-fashioned varieties of rose or to lighten over-heavy borders.

△ *Foeniculum vulgare*

The stems, leaves and seeds of fennel can be used as a flavouring in cooking.

Useful hints

— Plant in spring, putting a little pocket of sand around its base. Stake the main stem at the end of spring to help it stand up to gusts of wind.

— Let the flowers go to seed, collect the seeds and sow them all at once at random. Some will come up and you will have the benefit of having seedlings without having to prick them out. Since fennel takes up little room in terms of width, you can leave plants right at the edges of banks.

Recommended

— There is a version with bronze leaves (i.e. a sort of reddish brown) known as *Foeniculum vulgare* 'Purpureum'. It stays true to type.

Height: 150–180 cm (60–72 in).
Spacing and planting distance: 30 cm (12 in).
Soil: ordinary, even dry.
Aspect: full sun.
Propagation: from seed in autumn or spring.
Flowering season: summer.
Type: perennial.

Freesia hybrid △

Freesia

FREESIA

Iridaceae

In summer, the hybrid freesias are in bloom in sunny borders and in jardinières, since they are quite happy to grow in pots. Spreading brilliantly coloured flowers along their delicate stems, they bring the surrounding area alive. It is when combined with eschscholzias, oriental poppies and cerastiums, which, like them, love the sun, that they make the most brilliant borders, leaving gardeners on holiday to enjoy their summer rest, since the freesias need little care to thrive.

Useful hints

— In warm and temperate climates they can be planted in autumn to accelerate flowering. In areas where there is a risk of frost, plant them as early as possible in spring.

— Put your freesias in sandy soil. If your soil is heavy, plant them in 20 cm (8 in) pockets filled with a mixture of peat and sand in equal parts.

Height: 20 cm (8 in).
Spacing and planting distance: 10 cm (4 in).
Soil: sandy.
Aspect: sun.
Propagation: by separating corms.
Flowering season: summer.
Type: corm.

Fritillaria

FRITILLARY, SNAKE'S-HEAD

Liliaceae

Two fritillaries are familiar to all: *Fritillaria imperialis* (crown imperial), with its crown of bright yellow or orange bells, and *Fritillaria meleagris* (snake's-head), a denizen of moist meadows. The latter species owes its common name to the mauve criss-cross markings on its wine-coloured, pink or white blooms. Both fritillaries are stars of spring. Plant them in company with pretty ferns, delicate-leaved arums, golden lady's mantle, and you will have enchanting spring flower beds.

▽ *Fritillaria imperialis*

▽ *Fritillaria meleagris*

Useful hints

— Plant your fritillaries in early autumn. The bulbs *must* be fresh, otherwise you'll never see a single flower.

— Give them a humus-rich but well-drained soil (stagnant moisture in heavy soils kills them off in winter).

— Don't plant crown imperials too close to the house, because of their unpleasant smell.

Recommended

— As well as the two species mentioned, why not try *F. persica* (Persian fritillary), with its marvellous black flowers? This is a rare species to which it is worth giving pride of place.

Height: 20–50 cm (8–20 in).
Spacing and planting distance: 30 cm (12 in).
Soil: permeable, humus-rich.
Aspect: sun or semi-shade.
Propagation: by separating bulbs.
Flowering season: spring.
Type: bulb.

Fuchsia

FUCHSIA

Onagraceae

Where would our shady garden nooks be without fuchsias and their charming, back-turned bells? In company with hostas and ferns, they bring colour to places where few other flowers would survive. You can also cultivate them in hanging baskets, giving preference to varieties with a trailing habit or by cultivating them as bushes, i.e. selecting a stem which you then prune at 50 cm (20 in). Do this several times over two years and this method will give you superb-looking bushy plants.

Useful hints

— Don't plant them outside before all chance of frost is over. Water regularly during heatwaves and mulch the soil with peat or pine needles. Give them soluble fertilizer every month. If tiny white flies are in evidence, treat with a systemic insecticide.

— In late autumn, shelter the plants in a cold greenhouse, just out of reach of the frost. Some fuchsias can stay outside providing they are covered with a good bed of straw and plastic sheeting to prevent them rotting. As a precaution, and to avoid overloading your greenhouse, take cuttings in summer and keep them in little pots for the winter.

△ *Fuchsia boliviana*
▽ *Fuchsia* 'Swing Time'

Fuchsia magellanica var. *gracilis* △
Fuchsia 'Ting-a-ling' ▷
Fuchsia 'Leonora' ▽

Recommended

— There isn't enough room to mention all the interesting hybrids. Just ask your grower how they stand: upright, trailing or prostrate. That will give you an idea of how to use them: on banks or in tubs.

— The only really hardy fuchsia is *Fuchsia magellanica*, which forms wonderful hedges if a particularly hard winter doesn't raze them to the ground. If that does happen, they just bounce back even

better in the spring and before you know it the clumps will be over 150 cm (60 in) high. Best varieties are 'Riccartonii', whose thousands of dainty flowers stir in the slightest breeze; 'Alba', not white in fact but a pale pink – this fuchsia, with its very green tender leaves, does not suffer frost damage, and is one of the hardiest around; 'Versicolor', a handsome fuchsia with leaves a mixed pink and cream, which looks like a mist of all different colours from a distance. It has no equal

when it comes to giving a sense of lightness to shady borders and looks good grown with *Thalictrum dipterocarpum* and hostas.

Height: 30–180 cm (12–72 in).
Spacing and planting distance: 30 cm (12 in).
Soil: rich in humus and always moist.
Aspect: shade or semi-shade.
Propagation: from cuttings in summer.
Flowering season: early summer to first frosts.
Type: annual, perennial.

Gaillardia

BLANKET FLOWER, FIREWHEEL, INDIAN BLANKET

Compositae

With their large brown, red or golden yellow daisy-like flowers, always outlined in brown or a lighter shade, gaillardias are essential summer flowers. Just like marguerites, ornamental tobacco plants, zinnias and gauras, they bloom all summer, filling the garden with colour.

Useful hints

— Sow the annual varieties in spring in a cold frame filled with good light soil, and then prick them out on a sunny slope after the frosts are over.

— Sow the perennial varieties in a nursery bed in summer, and prick them out in autumn on sunny slopes. They will then flower the following summer.

Recommended

— The short-lived perennial gaillardia, *Gaillardia aristata*, is especially pretty in yellow with red centres to the flowers.

— As far as the annual *G. pulchella* is concerned, choose a mixture and then decide on which colours you like.

Height: 30 cm (12 in).
Spacing and planting distance: 20 cm (8 in).
Soil: ordinary.
Aspect: sun.
Propagation: from seed.
Flowering season: summer to autumn.
Type: annual, perennial.

Galanthus

SNOWDROP

Amaryllidaceae

Each year, it's the same: when it's time to buy them, snowdrops are the last thing on your mind, and then, when spring comes, you go wild over those that appear in the garden next door. One year, at least, get some bulbs and plant them near the house so you can have the pleasure of looking at them without freezing.

Useful hints

— Buy several dozen to give a mass effect. Plant before mid-winter in soil to which some peat has been added, since they like a certain amount of moisture.

— Snowdrops settle in easily. Rather than waiting for their leaves to fade before dividing them when they get too tightly packed, do it just after they flower.

Recommended

— The best-known snowdrop is *Galanthus nivalis*: a double-flowered version of this exists. It looks very good under deciduous trees, with its flowers breaking through the dead leaves.

— Slightly larger, *G. elwesii* has lovely bluish green leaves. In the light soils it likes, it can almost become a weed.

Height: 15–20 cm (6–8 in).
Spacing and planting distance: 10 cm (4 in).
Soil: ordinary.
Aspect: under deciduous trees or in sun.
Propagation: by division in spring.
Flowering season: early spring.
Type: bulb.

Galega

GOAT'S RUE

Leguminosae

Galega flowers exuberantly, and must be staked. It owes its common name, goat's rue, to its leaves, which have the same properties as those of rue and are much liked by goats. It does well in ordinary soils, and flowers for a long time. In ornamental gardens, its tendency to spread is not always welcome, but it is very good as a space-filler in less well-tended areas.

Useful hints

— Sow in springtime, first soaking the seeds in water overnight. As soon as three leaves appear, prick out into pots before finally planting in place at the end of summer.

— Cut down the stems at the start of winter, then mark the location of the plants to avoid damaging them in spring.

— The leaves are an excellent raw material for compost or even for sheltering other plants from the cold.

Recommended

— The English cultivars, such as 'Lady Wilson' or 'Her Majesty', are more manageable than the species.

Height: 100–150 cm (40–60 in).
Spacing and planting distance: 50 cm (20 in).
Soil: ordinary, moist even in summer.
Aspect: sun.
Propagation: from seed in spring or by division in winter.
Flowering season: summer.
Type: perennial.

Galium

see *Asperula*

△ *Gaillardia aristata*
▽ *Galanthus nivalis*

Galtonia

SUMMER HYACINTH

Liliaceae

Few bulb flowers bloom in summer other than the gladioli. Also natives of South Africa, *Galtonia candicans* shares this feature. It comes in very handy in brightening up borders of perennial flowers which are a little dull at that time of year and is very effective combined with small-flowered fuchsias or phlox.

Useful hints

— Plant in spring in deep, fairly rich soil which stays moist in summer. Put the bulbs at least 15 cm (6 in) down, since the stem will later grow to over 100 cm (40 in) high: they need to be well secured to stand up to storms.

— Cut the flowering stems in autumn to prevent them going to seed. Seedlings sometimes appear nonetheless, but the young plants must always be pricked out into rich soil if they are to grow at any speed.

— The simplest method of propagation consists of stripping the bulblets from around the main bulb and replanting them in a corner of the kitchen garden. They will flower in two to three years.

— In autumn, pull out the clumps with a little earth and let them dry in a cellar. Then clean the bulbs and store in a temperate place over the winter.

Height: 120–150 cm (48–60 in).
Spacing and planting distance: 20 cm (8 in).
Soil: ordinary, rich in compost.
Aspect: full sun.
Propagation: from seed or by separating young bulbs.
Flowering season: summer to autumn.
Type: bulb.

▽ *Galega officinalis*

△ *Gaultheria procumbens*
▽ *Galtonia candicans*

Gaultheria

PARTRIDGEBERRY, LEMONLEAF, WINTERGREEN

Ericaceae

Partridgeberry, lemonleaf or wintergreen, this is a plant with some pretty names. With its little round leaves and its pretty red berries, this space-filler which never grows higher than 20 cm (8 in) is not short of attractive features. It's also a ground cover plant which makes beautiful carpets in carefully tended clearings, and makes good company for filipendulas and rodgersias.

Useful hints

— Plant in early autumn or spring, in humus-rich, moist, slightly acid soil.

— Divide the roots every three years.

Recommended

— *Gaultheria procumbens*, the most popular (the one most often called partridgeberry), has white or pink flowers.

— *G. shallon*, less well-known, reaches 120 cm (48 in) and flowers equally in pink or white before producing black berries.

Height: 15 cm–120 cm (6–48 in).
Spacing and planting distance: 30–90 cm (12–36 in).
Soil: humus-rich, acid.
Aspect: semi-shade.
Propagation: by division.
Flowering season: summer.
Type: shrub.

117

Gaura

GAURA, WHITE GAURA

Onagraceae

Little known, but very hardy, *Gaura lindheimeri* rapidly becomes an essential plant. It forms very graceful clumps, since each very fine stem carries just a few delicate leaves. Flowers appear along these stems throughout the summer, catching the eye by their resemblance to white butterflies. White with the merest wash of carmine-pink, they flower in succession and are excellent flowers for quality bouquets.

Useful hints

— Plant in spring in any kind of soil, but preferably well-drained. Its place is the second row of mixed borders. You can also combine it with semi-dwarf dahlias or cosmos.

— Mulch the soil to help it stay moist in summer. Collect some seeds in autumn – the little seeds dotted around the stems – and sow them in spring under a cold frame. They germinate rapidly and the plants will flower the first summer.

Height: 90–120 cm (36–48 in).
Spacing and planting distance: 30 cm (12 in).
Soil: ordinary, on the light side.
Aspect: full sun.
Propagation: from cuttings in summer and from seed in spring.
Flowering season: all summer.
Type: perennial.

Gazania

GAZANIA, TREASURE FLOWER

Compositae

With its pretty silver-backed leaves, this is an ideal plant for beginners. Whether you treat it with care and sow it early in spring under glass or just scatter the seeds a little later, in mid-spring or in autumn in a corner of a seed bed, you're bound to succeed. And if you like the idea of yellow leaves crowned in brown, intense yellow, rust or red, don't delay. Gazania brightens up the garden right through summer. All it needs is watering – and there you are. It waits until the sun is right overhead before unfurling its petals, but closes up as soon as the sun goes in.

Useful hints

— From sowing to flowering, all it needs is heat and sunlight. Don't plant gazanias in the shade, as they will not thrive there.

△ *Gaura lindheimeri*
▽ *Gazania* 'Sunbeam'

— Gazania can be grown in open ground, in any soil as long as it is well-drained, as well as in pots. In these conditions the plants frequently last for several years.

Height: 30 cm (12 in).
Spacing and planting distance: 15 cm (6 in).
Soil: ordinary.
Aspect: sun.
Propagation: from seed or cuttings.
Flowering season: summer to autumn.
Type: annual, perennial in warm and temperate climates.

Gentiana

GENTIAN

Gentianaceae

Gentians form an enormous group with a wealth of very beautiful flowers. The only problem is sorting out the varieties which will not thrive in anything but an upland climate from those which are happily at home in rock gardens anywhere.

Useful hints

— Plant gentians in early autumn or spring, in fresh but well-drained soil. The addition of peat and coarse sand is recommended.

▽ *Gentiana septemfida*

◁ *Gentiana acaulis*
Gentiana sino-ornata ▷
▽ *Gentiana verna*

— Since these plants suffer in winter from excess moisture, which can lead to disastrous rot, surround their base with a layer of gravel at least 2 cm (¾ in) thick.

— Gentians can be grown from seed if the seed is fresh; they are sown in autumn and left to winter outside to undergo the effects of the cold and alternate frosts and thaws. Prick the young plants out in the spring.

Recommended

— *Gentiana acaulis*, the stemless gentian, is a little gem which flourishes in fresh, sunny, humus-rich surroundings. Its stunning blue flowers are reminiscent of the azure-blue of mountain skies. The species has a number of different varieties, of which *G. acaulis* 'Dinarica' (*G. dinarica*) is the easiest to cultivate in the open, with larger, later flowers which appear in late spring and summer instead of spring.

— Completely different, with its tall stems and willow-like leaves, the willow gentian (*G. asclepiadea*) can reach 60 cm (24 in). It can be used in mixed borders but is undoubtedly prettier in slightly wild undergrowth.

— Farrer's gentian (*G. farreri*) comes to us from China, and could easily take over from *G. acaulis* in our gardens. Its sky-blue flowers, open wide against the clouds, are superbly enhanced by the stripes on the petals. It is late flowering, usually in autumn.

— The great yellow gentian (*G. lutea*) certainly lives up to its name – it may reach over 200 cm (80 in) tall if it likes the soil. It flowers in late summer, even if grown in the open. Its roots are used in making a well-known aperitif.

— Of all the dwarf gentians, *G. septemfida* is the easiest to grow. It crawls across the soil with bunches of flowers on stems barely 15 cm (6 in) tall.

— You may sometimes have to wait until mid-autumn to admire *G. sino-ornata* in flower. Its flowers, a stunning blue often with violet streaks, are one of the final flings of the rock garden. It is relatively easy to grow in peaty, slightly sandy soil.

Height: 10–200 cm (4–80 in), depending on variety.
Spacing and planting distance: 15–30 cm (6–12 in).
Soil: fresh *and* well-drained.
Aspect: sun or semi-shade.
Propagation: by cold sowing or division.
Flowering season: spring to autumn, depending on variety.
Type: perennial.

Geranium

GERANIUM, CRANESBILL

Geraniaceae

These hardy perennials, which must not be confused with the 'geraniums' at the florist's (which are in fact pelargoniums), are a real boon to lovers of mixed borders and gardeners in general. They quickly form large clumps of flowers, usually in shades of pink, mauve or blue. Nor does their attraction end with their flowering, since they have very elegant, downy leaves running the whole gamut of green in nature. They are ideal for use with columbines, poppies, lupins and even ferns, since they grow in semi-shade.

Useful hints

— Plant early in spring, in fresh, humus-rich soil. Water regularly to help the clumps take. Cut away faded flowers to avoid sapping the plants' strength unnecessarily.

— Every three years, split the clumps into a dozen new specimens and replant immediately. Some, like *Geranium psilostemon*, form very dense roots. Split the clumps with a very sharp knife, preferably in autumn, and plant the shoots in sand enriched with peat. Bring in under cold glass in the first winter. Each specimen must have a shoot if it is to survive.

◁ *Geranium platypetalum*
▽ *Geranium renardii*

120

Recommended

— Spring geraniums open the proceedings from late in the season onwards: *G. macrorrhizum* is an excellent ground cover, with its downy leaves and their rich autumn colours, particularly in the 'Spessart' variety; but don't overlook its delicate pink flowers either. *G. renardii* is ideal for rock gardens, since it never grows over 30 cm (12 in) tall. Its white flowers with their streaks of violet are very delicate seen close up, and are set off to perfection by silvery green leaves. It contrasts well with *G. cinereum* var. *subcaulescens*, with stunning purple-red flowers. The dense mats of *G.* × *cantabrigiense* are tinged with red in autumn. The pure strain is pink, while 'Biokovo' is pinkish white. *G. cinereum* 'Ballerina' will carpet the rock garden with its large, purple-veined pink flowers. *G.c.* var. *subcaulescens* has dark-veined, deep pink petals which are white at the base. *G. dalmaticum* is an ideal rock garden or border plant with its delightful pink flowers and reddish autumn foliage.

— Early summer sees most geraniums flowering in profusion, such as *G. endressii*, mauve-pink in the pure strain and pure pink (one of the prettiest in spring) in 'Wargrave Pink'. The real stars are *G. pratense* and its numerous hybrids, among them 'Johnson's Blue', a very delicate mauve-blue, very much like the blue of *G. platypetalum*. *G. pratense* 'Mrs Kendall Clark' has even paler, white-veined flowers. Hybrid geranium genealogy is a highly complex subject, and the frequent changes of name mean that you would be well advised to consult your grower about the nature of the plants he is selling you. Species are often interbred. *G. endressii* and *G. pratense* are often crossed with each other and with *G.* × *magnificum* or *G. ibericum*. 'Ann Folkard' is a hybrid with a spreading habit whose magenta flowers have a black centre and black veins. *G. himalayense* thrives in light soil. It has cup-shaped, violet-blue flowers with a white centre, and the double variety, 'Plenum', is also violet. *G. nodosum* is always found in a cool, shady part of the garden where its adds a splash of colour with its metallic blue, purple-veined flowers. *G. orientalitibeticum*, with its large, pink flowers and marbled leaves, likes to spread across cool rock gardens. The hardy, vigorous *G.* × *oxonianum* forms a large, greyish green cushion and produces remarkable silvery pink flowers. *G.* × *oxonianum* 'Claridge Druce' has become a standard variety. *G. phaeum* is brownish violet, mauve or white, depending on the

△ *Geranium ibericum*

variety, and is ideal for those shady corners, as well as making very good ground cover.

— The geraniums which follow bloom in a succession of waves over most of the summer: these include the very pretty hybrid 'Russell Prichard', which never grows over 20 cm (8 in) high but forms dense carpets covered in vivid magenta flowers from early summer until the frosts. *G.* × *riversleaianum* is also available in a pink form, 'Mavis Simpson', and both need a sheltered position. *G. sanguineum* is a purple-red, but is also available in white. *G. pylzowianum* is similar, but has tubular rhizomes and tends to spread more vigorously. But the undoubted star of them all is *G. psilostemon* (formerly *G. armenum*), which from early summer onwards forms a majestic dome 120 cm (48 in) high and the same across, with so many magenta-purple black-centred flowers that even its abundant foliage almost disappears. The more compact *G. sanguineum* var. *striatum* has red-veined, white flowers, while *G. wallichianum* 'Buxton's Variety' has brown-flecked leaves and large cup-shaped blue flowers with white centres.

Height: 15–120 cm (6–48 in).
Spacing and planting distance: 20–50 cm (18–20 in).
Soil: ordinary, humus-rich.
Aspect: sun or semi-shade.
Propagation: by division after flowering or in spring.
Flowering season: spring to autumn.
Type: perennial.

△ *Geranium pratense* 'Mrs Kendall Clark'
▽ *Geranium maculatum albiflorum*
Geranium cinereum var. *subcaulescens* ▽

▽ *Geranium endressii*
Geranium argenteum ▽

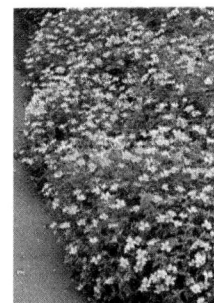

▽ *Geranium sanguineum*

Gerbera

GERBERA, BARBERTON DAISY

Compositae

After gaining acceptance with our florists, *Gerbera jamesonii* is now making minor forays into our gardens. It has to be admitted, however, that its squat silhouette does not make it a good plant for slopes. The dwarf varieties, on the other hand, are ideal for tubs in temperate climates: they tolerate the coldest temperatures without complaining and flower throughout the summer.

Useful hints

— Plant your gerberas in spring, in equal amounts of leaf-mould and good garden soil. Water regularly, adding soluble fertilizer every month, or less often if the leaves turn yellow.

— Bring the pots inside in autumn: they will go on flowering most of the winter in a barely heated conservatory.

— Divide the clumps each spring: this will revive them.

Height: 30 cm (12 in).
Spacing and planting distance: 30 cm (12 in).
Soil: rich.
Aspect: full sun.
Propagation: by sowing in the warm in late winter or by division in spring.
Flowering season: summer to autumn.
Type: annual, perennial.

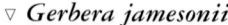

▽ ***Gerbera jamesonii***

△ ***Geum* 'Borisii'**

Geum

AVENS

Rosaceae

Avens were very familiar plants to our grandparents. Their downy delicate green leaves, their vivid, almost enamelled flowers and their highly decorative fruit made them a popular choice. They are worth rediscovering for their resilience and simplicity.

Useful hints

— While at home in any type of soil, they prefer a well-drained soil slightly enriched with leaf-mould.

— Plant in autumn or spring. No protection needed in winter. Let the fruit develop, since it is usually pretty.

Recommended

— There are few summer hardy perennials which can rival *Geum* 'Borisii' for length of flowering – from late spring to autumn, but admittedly only if well watered. Its large flowers are an attractive orange colour.

— Originally from Chile, *G. chiloense* has given rise to some excellent hybrids, of which the best-known are 'Lady Stratheden' (bright yellow), 'Mrs J. Bradshaw' (scarlet), 'Fire Opal' (flame red), 'Georgenberg' (orange-yellow) and 'Princess Juliana' (orange).

— *G. rivale* 'Leonard's Variety' (pink, bell-shaped flowers) and 'Album' (white) are ideal for moist areas of the garden.

Height: 30–60 cm (12–24 in).
Spacing and planting distance: 25 cm (10 in).
Soil: ordinary, enriched with a little peat.
Aspect: sun.
Propagation: from seed or by division in spring.
Flowering season: late spring to autumn.
Type: perennial.

Gilia tricolor ▷
***Geum chiloense* 'Mrs Bradshaw'** ▽

Gilia capitata △

Gilia

GILIA

Polemoniaceae

We won't be far wrong in predicting a great future for gilias in weekend gardens: all you need to do is sow them, and success is assured. Nor is it unusual for them to reappear the following year, so well do they reseed themselves.

Useful hints

— Sow in spring in warm, crumbly soil. Thin out the seedlings after a month, leaving 15–20 cm (6–8 in) between plants. Pinch off the main stems a little later.

— Water once a week in summer, adding a little soluble fertilizer every third watering.

Recommended

— The delicate feathery green leaves of *Gilia capitata* make an excellent background for its dense heads of violet-blue flowers. Sow generously to fill the space at the foot of old rose bushes or to go with gladioli or white nicotiana.

— The flowers of *G. tricolor*, with their purple heart bordered in white which end in a delicate violet, give off a vanilla-like scent reminiscent of chocolate. They flower in succession over a number of weeks. Sow around the edges of beds or on both sides of a gravel path.

Height: 30–40 cm (12–16 in).
Spacing and planting distance: 15–20 cm (6–8 in).
Soil: ordinary, fairly cool in summer.
Aspect: full sun.
Propagation: from seed in spring.
Flowering season: early summer to first frosts.
Type: annual.

Gladiolus (see also *Acidanthera*)

GLADIOLI, SWORD LILY, CORN FLAG

Iridaceae

Everyone knows gladioli, with their long scapes of sometimes slightly outrageous-coloured flowers. While superb in bouquets, it is a different matter in the garden, where their slender silhouette needs the company of plants with generous foliage if it is not to look a little out of place. So plant them in groups on slopes of sage, tobacco, loosestrife or monardas to create wide swathes of colour; and, especially, don't forget the charming spring gladioli, which were once found in the wild and have retained an entirely natural grace.

Useful hints

— Plant spring gladioli in autumn in soil lightened with sand, scattering them among stocks and myosotis.

— Classical gladioli are planted in spring, 10 cm (4 in) down with the point of the shoot upwards. If arranging in groups of three to five, train them inconspicuously with bamboo stakes.

— In the kitchen garden, if growing gladioli for bouquets, plant in rows, earth up in summer and train by tying them to twine strung horizontally between two stakes.

— Water regularly, adding fertilizer once a fortnight. Cut the floral scapes when the first floret opens; the bulbs will usually be exhausted afterwards.

Recommended

— There is a real surfeit of choice among the large-flowered species. Follow your seed merchant's advice and buy only the best quality to ensure good results. There are gladioli in almost every colour, even green, not to mention the 'butterfly' or 'fantasy' varieties. These, however, are not to everyone's taste.

— *Gladiolus primulinus* flowers at the same time as those above, and offers less tightly packed flowers on scapes which are shorter and hence less vulnerable to wind. 'Anitra' is bright red, 'White City' is white and 'Yellow Special' a golden amber.

— The spring-flowering gladioli are less well-known, the commonest being *G. communis* ssp. *byzantinus*, with its purple-red flowers, which spreads if it likes the

◁ *Gladiolus* hybrid

△ *Gladiolus* hybrid

△ *Gladiolus* hybrid

Gladiolus hybrid ▷

soil, and *G. × colvillei*, which never exceeds 60 cm (24 in) in height and flowers in a variety of colours, usually marked by a handsome pink or red throat.

Height: 60–140 cm (24–55 in).
Spacing and planting distance: 15 cm (6 in).
Soil: any.

Aspect: sun.
Propagation: by separating new corms in late autumn.
Flowering season: between spring and autumn, depending on species and when planted.
Type: corm.

125

Glaucium flavum △

Glaucium

HORNED POPPY

Papaveraceae

If you like walking in the countryside in summer, you may have admired the flowers of the horned poppy. Linked firmly to the soil by a massive root system, it unfurls a new flower each day, rather like its cousins the corn poppies. *Glaucium flavum* is a little gem, grown like a biennial or hardy perennial.

Useful hints

— Plant in autumn, in a pocket of sand or gravel, or wait until spring if your soil is heavy in winter.

— They can also be sown in late spring, in which case they will flower the following year. The main problem is finding seeds, so let your first specimens go to seed and harvest them at the end of the year.

Height: 30 cm (12 in).
Spacing and planting distance: 30 cm (12 in).
Soil: rather poor but well-drained in winter.
Aspect: full sun.
Propagation: from seed in late spring.
Flowering season: summer to autumn.
Type: annual, biennial, perennial.

126

Gloriosa

GLORIOSA, CLIMBING LILY

Liliaceae

From mid-summer onwards, *Gloriosa superba* 'Rothschildiana' bursts into a host of scarlet and yellow butterflies, swarming up the slightest support if on a sunny wall. Grow them near your grey-leaved hardy perennials, such as sage or *Stachys byzantina*, to temper the brilliance of their colour a little.

Useful hints

— Plant in autumn, in large tubs filled with leaf-mould mixed with compost in areas where the winters are cold; plant them out in their chosen positions in spring. In places where the climate is mild, plant in the open along a sunny wall in pockets filled with the same compost.

— Protect the roots with a cover of dead leaves each autumn.

Height: 200–300 cm (80–120 in).
Spacing and planting distance: 50 cm (20 in).
Soil: rich in humus.
Aspect: sun.
Propagation: by separating tubers in spring.
Flowering season: summer to autumn.
Type: tuber.

◁ *Gloriosa superba* 'Rothschildiana'
▽ *Godetia amoena* ssp. *whitneyi*

Godetia (syn. *Clarkia*)

GODETIA

Onageaceae

There aren't many annuals with the spectacular colours of *Godetia amoena* (syn. *Clarkia amoena*), the satin flower: delicate pinks, subtle mauves, never-jarring reds … Each plant is a bouquet in itself, since the flowers all unfurl at the same time. This firework lasts only three weeks, but what a beauty!

Useful hints

— Sow directly on the spot in spring, once the soil has warmed up, first mixing the fairly fine seeds with sand to give a better distribution. Thin out the seedlings two weeks later, leaving one plant every 20 cm (8 in).

— Pinch the plants off half-way up a month later. Water regularly, adding a little soluble fertilizer every other time.

Recommended

The subspecies *whitneyi* often has single flowers on semi-dwarf plants. The double 'Azalea-flowered' Series is better known, and is more compact – 35 cm (14 in) on average. Some seed merchants sell colours separately, enabling you to paint a magnificent canvas.

Height: 35–45 cm (14–18 in).
Spacing and planting distance: 20 cm (8 in).
Soil: on the rich, fresh side.
Aspect: full sun.
Propagation: from seed in spring.
Flowering season: summer, for 3 weeks.
Type: annual.

Gomphrena

GLOBE AMARANTH

Amaranthaceae

Gomphrena globosa has funny globulous inflorescences ranging from purple and carmine to charming pink. These plants look good in a bed of hardy perennials, lending it a hint of nostalgia at the end of summer.

Useful hints

— Sow in a sheltered spot in early spring, in a mixture of equal parts of peat and fresh earth, then prick out in place in late spring. The plants will flower from summer to autumn.

— Best grown in the sun, but needs generous watering.

— Very suitable for dried flower arrangements.

△ *Gomphrena globosa*

Height: 30 cm (12 in).
Spacing and planting distance: 20 cm (8 in).
Soil: ordinary.
Aspect: sun.
Propagation: from seed in early spring.
Flowering season: summer to autumn.
Type: annual, biennial, perennial.

Goniolimon

see *Limonium*

Gunnera

GUNNERA

Gunneraceae

Gunnera manicata is an ideal plant for filling out a wild corner of the garden in style, especially if it is crossed by a stream or is in a cool spot. Its enormous leaves usually unfurl some time between mid- and late spring, and then grow to a stunning size. The plant sometimes flowers in summer, in funny caviar-coloured heads. It belongs with the larger Caucasian heracleums, ornamental rhubarbs, water irises and arums.

Useful hints

— Plant in spring by a body of water in well-enriched soil. Allow four spadefuls of manure compost per square metre.

— Protect the roots each autumn with a cover of straw, since a cold winter may harm them.

— Plants are best bought bare-rooted, but should be planted immediately.

Gunnera manicata ▽

Height: 150 cm (60 in).
Spacing and planting distance: 250 cm (100 in).
Soil: rich, humid.
Aspect: sun or semi-shade.
Propagation: by division.
Flowering season: summer.
Type: perennial.

Gypsophila 'Rosenschleier' △
Gypsophila elegans ▷

Gypsophila

GYPSOPHILA, BABY'S BREATH

Caryophyllaceae

Also known as 'mist' because of its extraordinarily light flowers, it belongs on sunny, light-soiled, well-exposed slopes with salvias, old roses and robust perennials such as the oriental poppy or gaura. It will flower throughout the summer, and can be used in dried flower arrangements.

Useful hints

— Sow both annuals and perennials in spring under cover. When pricked out on to sunny slopes, the annuals will flower the same summer and the perennials the following one.

— Always plant gypsophila in light, humus-rich soil: it hates cold, damp clay soil.

Recommended

— One annual species, *Gypsophila elegans*, with flowers 1 cm (½ in) across, lightens up borders.

— Two perennials, *G. paniculata*, with its tiny sometimes double flowers, and *G. repens*, are marvellous in rock gardens.

— *G. paniculata*: 'Bristol Fairy' is a fully double variety with small, pompon-like flowers, 'Flamingo' is a semi-double with pink flowers, while 'Virgo', propagated from seed, produces both double and single flowers. 'Rosenschleier' is a hybrid with a lower habit and very abundant flowers.

Height: 10–60 cm (4–24 in).
Spacing and planting distance: 20 cm (8 in).
Soil: light, humus-rich.
Aspect: sun.
Propagation: from seed and by division in spring.
Flowering season: summer to autumn.
Type: annual, perennial.

△ *Haberlea rhodopensis*

Haberlea

HABERLEA

Gesneriaceae

Your main problem will be resisting the temptation to tear these plants away from their wonderful surroundings in the wild. You may have to join a rock plant club to see them, but it'll be worth it, since you'll then discover one of the joys of European flora. Looking somewhat like a miniature gloxinia, this plant forms a cushion of embossed leaves, with some rosettes of flowers in the spring. The buds unfurl into orchid-pink flowers with a yellow throat. It is certainly worth going to some trouble to obtain it.

Useful hints

— Plant in spring in a corner exposed to the north and shelter under a pane of glass through the winter.

— Put down anti-slug pellets and keep the soil moist through the summer. If mosses appear around the edges, that's a good sign. Collect the seeds and sow them nearby. They will come up the following year and you can prick out the young plants after a year.

Height: 15–20 cm (6–8 in).
Spacing and planting distance: 15 cm (6 in).
Soil: peat and sand.
Aspect: sheltered, north-facing.
Propagation: from seed.
Flowering season: late spring.
Type: perennial.

Hedysarum

SAINFOIN, SWEET VETCH

Leguminosae

These plants are at their best on sunny banks or surrounded by borders of hardy perennials, their compact flowers combining well with achilleas or chrysanthemums.

Useful hints

— Sow direct in autumn or spring. Alternatively, layer long shoots in early autumn, leaving the top 10 cm (4 in) above ground. Separate the new plant from the old a year later.

— Once established, don't disturb, but train if necessary.

— Cut the stems 5 cm (2 in) from the ground in late autumn.

Recommended

— *Hedysarum coronarium* (sainfoin) can be used as a biennial or perennial, in which case its life will be short (three to four years). The flowers are red and scented.

Height: 100 cm (40 in).
Spacing and planting distance: 50 cm (20 in).
Soil: ordinary, well-drained.
Aspect: sun.
Propagation: from seed or by layering.
Flowering season: summer to autumn.
Type: annual, perennial, shrub.

▽ *Hedysarum multijugum*

Helenium autumnale
'Chipperfield Orange' △

Helenium

HELENIUM, SNEEZEWEED

Compositae

Heleniums belong in borders of perennials along with felty-leaved plants such as stachys, sage and autumn-flowering plants such as asters, chrysanthemums or rudbeckias. They make delightful patches of warm colours which go superbly with the mauves, pinks and greys of their companions.

Useful hints

— Give *Helenium autumnale* a rich but well-drained soil, planting in 20 cm (8 in) wide pockets of sandy loam.

— Sow in a seed bed in spring and prick out in autumn or even the spring after sowing: they will flower in the summer after the one in which they are planted.

Recommended

Most are hybrids, like 'Coppelia' (toffee-coloured), 'Moerheim Beauty' (bronze to crimson), 'Pumilum Magnificum' (golden yellow, richer in colour than the true varieties).

— *H. hoopesii* produces large, orange-yellow daisies at the end of spring.

— Hybrids: 'Bruno' (brownish red); 'Kanaria' (yellow); 'The Bishop' (golden yellow, lower-growing); 'Waldtraut' (yellow with brown markings).

Height: 60–80 cm (24–32 in).
Spacing and planting distance: 30 cm (12 in).
Soil: rich, light.
Aspect: sun.
Propagation: in spring, from seed or by division.
Flowering season: late summer to autumn.
Type: annual, perennial.

Helianthemum

ROCK ROSE, SUN ROSE

Cistaceae

Helianthemums are ideal for carpeting rock gardens or the dry slopes often found bordering hillside gardens. *Helianthemum nummularium* and hybrids insist on sunlight and very hot, dry soils, and go well with alpine marigolds.

Useful hints

— Helianthemums should preferably be planted in spring to save the young plants from the summer rains, in ordinary warm soil.

— Cut away shrivelled flowers to encourage new ones to appear.

— Divide major clumps every three years.

Recommended

— Among the many varieties are 'Amy Baring' (yellow, golden bud); 'Ben Afflick' (delicate orange); 'The Bride' (white); 'Wisley Pink' (pink).

— Hybrids: 'Ben Fhada' (yellow with an orange centre); 'Ben Hecla' (copper-coloured with a red centre); 'Elfen-beinglanz' (white with a yellow centre); 'Lawrenson's Pink' (pink with a copper-coloured centre); 'Raspberry Ripple' (unusual white and deep pink markings); 'Rhodanthe Carneum' (large yellow flowers).

Height: 20–30 cm (8–12 in).
Spacing and planting distance: 50 cm (20 in).
Soil: dry.
Aspect: sun.
Propagation: in spring, from seed or by division.
Flowering season: summer to autumn.
Type: perennial.

Helianthus

SUNFLOWER, COMMON SUNFLOWER, MIRASOL

Compositae

Use sunflowers as a temporary hedge to screen off a new garden, or in imposing groups to light up a dull corner. But don't plant any of this family in your flower beds, because their greed is equal only to their thirst, and neighbouring flowers will suffer.

Useful hints

— Sow annual sunflowers directly on site in pockets of three seeds; later, space them out 30 cm (12 in) apart.

— Plant the perennials in spring.

— These plants prefer a rich soil – in fresh, dry soil, they will be somewhat stunted (although some would say a reasonable size!).

Recommended

— As well as the classic sunflower, *Helianthus annuus*, there are several perennial species, including *H. salicifolius*, with long fringed leaves like a willow, which reaches 200 cm (80 in) high before unveiling its yellow flowers; *H. decapetalus* is a large double sunflower. *H.* 'Capenoch Star' produces round, yellow flowers which are ideal for cutting. *H. decapetalus* 'Flore Pleno' is a double variety.

— *H.* 'Gullick's Variety' produces many flowers but must be protected from severe frosts. *H. microcephalus* adds a natural touch to less formal borders.

Height: 100–250 cm (40–100 in).
Spacing and planting distance: 30 cm (12 in).
Soil: rich.
Aspect: sun.
Propagation: from seed or by division.
Flowering season: summer.
Type: annual, perennial.

Helianthus decapetalus ▽

△ *Helichrysum italicum*

△ *Helichrysum bracteatum*

Helichrysum

EVERLASTING FLOWER, STRAWFLOWER, IMMORTELLE

Compositae

There are many helichrysums to choose from – annuals, which we know as 'everlasting', semi-wild varieties, and even shrubs. Their common characteristics are their stars of flowers and their incredible ability to withstand even the hottest ground. Sometimes they are enhanced by grey leaves, which play an important role in their decorative effect. They are usually excellent for growing in pots and window-boxes, since they thrive on very little soil.

Useful hints

— Sow everlastings in the warm in early spring, under cold frames in mid-spring or directly in the ground in late spring, in a corner of your kitchen garden to give you dried flowers all year round.

— The only care needed is a little hoeing and watering. Tie the stems to prevent them collapsing in violent storms.

— Harvest them in late summer to autumn, when the flowers are well open but their hearts have not yet faded. Dry head-down in a dark place for two months.

— Little helichrysums for decorating slopes and window-boxes are planted in mid- to late spring in a rich, sandy soil. Pinch them out several times to give dwarf plants. Take cuttings in summer and keep them out of the cold in winter in a greenhouse or in a heated frame.

— The hardiest varieties can stay where they are, provided you protect the base with straw or leaf-mould then cover the whole with plastic film.

Recommended

— 'Bracted' everlastings (*Helichrysum bracteatum*) are often sold mixed, which is a pity, since you can use specific varieties to greater effect. The Bikini Series variety is most often available in fiery red, and is slightly shorter at 35 cm (14 in).

— Also known as the curry plant, *H. italicum* is one of the wildest of the shrubby helichrysums. All its silvery-grey foliage gives off a very pronounced curry odour. It flowers in late summer in a strong yellow.

— *H.* 'Sulphur Light' will enchant anyone who loves grey foliage. Its very soft mimosa-yellow flowers are exactly what is needed to set off the blue of caryopteris or lavender.

— *H. petiolare* is still popular for growing in containers. It threads its way easily among more distinguished foliage like that of the pelargoniums and sets it off perfectly with its grey leaves. The variety known as 'Limelight' will look quite startling in conjunction with yellow primulas.

Height: 30–120 cm (12–48 in).
Spacing and planting distance: 30 cm (12 in).
Soil: ordinary, even a little on the dry side.
Aspect: full sun.
Propagation: from seed in spring or cuttings in summer.
Flowering season: summer.
Type: annual, perennial, shrub.

131

△ *Heliopsis helianthoïdes* var. *scabra*

Heliopsis

HELIOPSIS, OX-EYE

Compositae

With its double, warmly coloured flowers like large pompons, some gold, some yellow, *Heliopsis helianthoides* var. *scabra* is like a ray of sunshine bringing magic into a garden. It leaves you in no doubt that it's a hardy perennial: sometimes it even threatens to take over. Watch out for your less robust plants! Plant it only in company with other outstandingly robust varieties such as tansies, heleniums, asters or even Chinese lanterns (physalis).

Useful hints

— Sow in late spring in a seed bed and then prick out in autumn or the following spring in a well-exposed site.

— Any good garden soil will do.

Recommended

— There are giants such as 'Golden Plume', golden-yellow doubles which reach 120 cm (48 in), and smaller varieties such as 'Summer Sun', only 50 cm (20 in) tall but semi-double and butter-yellow colour.

— *H. helianthoïdes*. The most beautiful varieties are seldom grown, as they cannot be propagated from seed. They are plants of German origin such as 'Goldgrünherz' (yellow with a green centre), 'Hohlspiegel' and 'Spitzentänzerin', with their long, shaggy petals.

Height: 50–120 cm (20–48 in).
Spacing and planting distance: 30 cm (12 in).
Soil: ordinary.
Aspect: sun.
Propagation: by seed in spring or division in autumn.
Flowering season: summer to autumn.
Type: perennial.

Heliotropium

HELIOTROPE, CHERRY PIE

Boraginaceae

Heliotropes have long been popular, both for their flowers, which come in shades ranging from mauve to blue with a few bursts of white and stand out well from their embossed, slightly coarse foliage, and, above all, for their scent, unique and captivating. It seems that over the years the heliotropes have lost this enchanting scent, and those we grow now just smell of vanilla. They grow into little shrubs in warm climates.

Useful hints

— Sow in early to mid-spring in little boxes filled with rich, light soil, sheltered under glass. Prick out on site in late spring.

— Outside warm and temperate areas, protect in winter or, better still, grow them in tubs which you can take indoors in winter.

Height: 30–50 cm (12–20 in).
Spacing and planting distance: 30 cm (12 in).
Soil: rich, well-drained.
Aspect: sun.
Propagation: from seed or cuttings in early to mid-spring.
Flowering season: summer to autumn.
Type: annual, perennial.

△ *Helipterum manglesii*

△ *Heliotropium* hybrid

Helipterum

EVERLASTING STRAWFLOWER

Compositae

These are the prettiest of the everlasting flowers. Each plant forms a bouquet of charming seersucker flowers in delicate colours. Very easy to grow in a corner of a kitchen garden, *Helipterum manglesii* (syn. *Rhodanthe manglesii*) can also be used to decorate sunlit slopes where they will show to good effect for most of the year.

Useful hints

— Sow seeds on the spot in mid-spring, first adding a little sand if the earth is heavy. Thin the seedlings out in late spring, leaving just one plant every 20 cm (8 in). Water regularly, but don't add any fertilizer.

— Flowers can be harvested in autumn. Cut the whole stems and hang them head down in a dry, shady room for two months.

Recommended

— *H. roseum* (syn. *Acroclinium roseum*) produces a myriad of tiny, delicately coloured flower heads.

Height: 30 cm (12 in).
Spacing and planting distance: 20 cm (8 in).
Soil: any, preferably sandy.
Aspect: full sun.
Propagation: from seed in spring.
Flowering season: summer to autumn.
Type: annual.

△ *Helleborus lividus*
▽ *Helleborus orientalis*

△ *Helleborus lividus*
Helleborus × sternii △
◁ *Helleborus niger*

Helleborus

HELLEBORE, CHRISTMAS ROSE

Ranunculaceae

Plants with a great future, hellebores combine beauty of flowers and an imposing silhouette. These are very robust plants which fit just as well in the slightly wilder corners of the garden as in the most formal beds. As if this were not enough, they also tend to flower in mid-winter, when there aren't many flowers around.

Useful hints

— Plant in autumn to give them time to settle in before the frosts. If planting in pots, put the pots under cold frames since the roots are somewhat prone to freezing.

— Mulch the soil with pine bark or peat from late spring onwards. Let the fruit ripen, since this will give you a lot of natural seeds. In very hot weather, water now and again and watch out for swarms of greenfly on the ends of young stems.

— Every three or four years, rejuvenate by dividing them, preferably in autumn. Water generously to encourage the plants to take.

— *Helleborus foetidus* will do much better in a shady position.

Recommended

— The best-known hellebore is undoubtedly the Christmas rose (*H. niger*). The flowers sometimes appear in mid-winter, but more often wait until late winter or even early spring. They are relatively large, white with a hint of green.

— If you like purple flowers, pick *H. atrorubens*, which is similar in habit to *H. niger*.

— Taller and often darker, *H. orientalis* varieties are truly fascinating. The colours vary widely, so we recommend buying them as flowering plants to avoid washed-out shades.

— Even if you're put off by the name stinking hellebore, leave room for *H. foetidus*. Its handsome palmate leaves and its bouquets of a stunning pale yellow make it the star of winter. It is a lovely sight growing wild in the countryside. Its main stem droops sadly when the cold winds blow but it perks up as soon as it thaws. The Wester Flisk Group has distinctive red stems and leaf stalks.

— The undisputed queen, the Corsican hellebore (*H. argutifolius*), is very similar, but taller and with finely toothed leaves. Its lime-green flowers go superbly with mahonias, narcissi or golden-variegated ivy.

Height: 20–70 cm (8–28 in).
Spacing and planting distance: 25–30 cm (10–12 in).
Soil: very rich in humus (leaf-mould or peat).
Aspect: semi-shade.
Propagation: from seed or by division in autumn.
Flowering season: winter to late spring.
Type: perennial.

Helxine (syn. *Soleirolia*)

MIND YOUR OWN BUSINESS, BABY'S TEARS

Urticaceae

What could be prettier or more delicate than helxine, a godsend to dark, damp gardens, a member of the same family as the stinging nettle? Plant it in a town garden, in a window-box in the shade or a pot, and it will always survive. Hide a few snowdrop, crocus or cyclamen bulbs in the soil beneath it to give a charming, ever-changing display through the seasons.

Useful hints

— Helxine is best planted in spring: water generously.

— Watch out for frost in winter. It isn't very fragile, but droops sadly once the temperature falls towards −10°C (14°F). Don't water so much at this time of year, but remember to keep the earth a bit moist if growing it inside.

Height: 5–10 cm (2–4 in).
Spacing and planting distance: 10 cm (4 in).
Soil: light, rich in humus.
Aspect: shade or semi-shade.
Propagation: by division in spring.
Type: perennial.

Hemerocallis

DAY LILY

Liliaceae

The Americans go wild over day lilies (they even have their own shows), but they are used less in Europe despite their astonishing hardiness. With their flowers like little lilies running the gamut of yellows, oranges, pinks and reds, they have a lot of charm and ought to belong in all perennial beds. When they feel at home, they quickly form impressive clumps covered in flowers from summer to autumn. But don't use them in flower arrangements, since they wilt very quickly. New flowers appear each day.

Useful hints

— Best planted in spring in good, ordinary soil on sunny slopes.

— Every three years, divide any clumps which have become invasive in spring.

Recommended

— *Hemerocallis citrina* has little star-shaped flowers of lemon-yellow with a delicate perfume.

△ *Helxine soleirolii*

Hemerocallis hybrid ▷

— *H. fulva*, very hardy and common, has orange flowers.

— As well as these two charming species, a great many hybrids with large waxen flowers have appeared, such as 'Autumn Red', 'Pink Prelude' and 'Bonanza'.

— Also worthy of mention are 'Art Festival', mauve with a cream throat; 'Corky', which produces a myriad of tiny yellow flowers; 'Stella de Oro', large, pale yellow flowers; and 'Toyland', with its clusters of miniature, melon-coloured flowers.

Height: 40 cm (16 in).
Spacing and planting distance: 40 cm (16 in).
Soil: ordinary.
Aspect: sun or light shade.
Propagation: by division in spring.
Flowering season: summer to autumn.
Type: perennial.

Hemerocallis fulva ▽

134

△ *Hepatica nobilis*
◁ *Hemerocallis citrina*

Hepatica

HEPATICA, LIVERLEAF

Ranunculaceae

Looking a lot like a blue wood anemone, *Hepatica nobilis* is charming in spring alongside early bulbs such as eranthis, crocus or *Iris reticulata*. It is also at home as ground cover or in shady corners of rock gardens and makes delightful edges to borders.

Useful hints

— Plant at any time of year, in groups of at least six to give a feeling of size. Mulch the soil with pine bark to show the flowers off better against a neutral background.

— Divide clumps every three years just after flowering, and water regularly to help them take. They are often self-seeding.

Recommended

— *H. nobilis.* As well as the standard variety, there are also violet-blue, white and pink forms which are, unfortunately, all too rare.

Height: 10 cm (4 in).
Spacing and planting distance: 15 cm (6 in).
Soil: ordinary, fairly rich in humus.
Aspect: shade.
Propagation: by division in spring.
Flowering season: spring.
Type: perennial.

Heracleum mantegazzianum △
Hesperis matronalis ▷

Heracleum

GIANT HOGWEED, CARTWHEEL FLOWER

Umbelliferae

Looking for an imposing, fast-growing plant to hide an unpleasant view or put life into a newly planted garden? Then look no further, this is the one you need. Just over 300 cm (120 in), heracleum will produce increasingly impressive thickets as the years go by. Its only fault is that its leaves can cause terrible itching in people who are sensitive to it.

Useful hints

— Plant in autumn in well-turned-over soil with some peat and leaf-mould added. Water frequently and generously once the warm weather arrives. Use this period to add soluble fertilizer once a month.

— Once flowering is over, cut off a lot of the stems to avoid being invaded by self-sown seedlings (use gloves).

— You can cut the last seed heads in autumn and dry them to give spectacular flower arrangements.

Height: 200–300 cm (80–120 in).
Spacing and planting distance: 150 cm (60 in).
Soil: rich, cool in summer.
Aspect: sun or semi-shade.
Propagation: by division in spring.
Flowering season: summer.
Type: perennial.

Hesperis

SWEET ROCKET, DAMES' VIOLET

Cruciferae

One of the old favourites, sweet rocket enchants us with its delicate violet flowers and its bewitching scent of stocks in spring, especially in the evenings. *Hesperis matronalis* seeds itself with ease everywhere, looks delightful with narcissi or tulips, and at the same time gives depth to slopes, since it grows just over 100 cm (40 in) tall. There is a smaller white variety which flowers longer, and is not uncommonly found in bloom in summer. It grows in the artist Monet's famous garden at Giverny.

Useful hints

— Plant in autumn, preferably away

△ *Heuchera × brizoides*

from the front of your beds, since this hides its inelegant foliage near the ground. Train the stems carefully in spring to stop them collapsing in sudden showers.

— Gather the seeds which appear in summer and sow them at leisure. Generally speaking, the stems which flower profusely quickly wilt. The white variety is hardier.

Recommended

— *H. matronalis candida* 'Alba Plena' (white) and 'Lilacina Flore Pleno' (lilac) are two double varieties which are ideal for cut flowers.

Height: 60–100 cm (24–40 in).
Spacing and planting distance: 30 cm (12 in).
Soil: ordinary, on the rich, heavy side: likes chalk.
Aspect: sun.
Propagation: from seed in summer.
Flowering season: early to mid-summer.
Type: perennial.

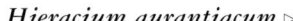

Recommended

The hybrids include Bressingham Hybrids and 'Red Spangles'. 'Pluie de Feu' is an older, red variety which is still very popular. The more recent 'Snow Storm' has purple-red flowers set off by marbled foliage.

— *H. cylindrica* 'Greenfinch' produces large green bell-shaped flowers at the end of vigorous stems.

— The tiny white flowers of *H. micrantha* var. *diversifolia* 'Palace Purple' seem to float above its purple foliage.

Height: 30 cm (12 in).
Spacing and planting distance: 20 cm (8 in).
Soil: ordinary.
Aspect: sun or semi-shade.
Propagation: by division in spring.
Flowering season: summer.
Type: perennial.

Hieracium

HAWKWEED

Compositae

The genus *Hieracium* includes a lot of weeds, some medicinal plants such as hawkweed and some very decorative plants, especially for the slightly wilder corners. They go well with Siberian iris, geum and *Sedum spectabilis*.

Useful hints

— Plant at any time of year, even if in flower, but water them well afterwards. Weed the clumps carefully each spring and build them up with 2–3 cm (1 in) of leaf-mould or well-rotted compost.

— Every three years, divide the clumps and replant immediately, preferably in early spring.

Recommended

— *Hieracium aurantiacum* (syn. *Pilosella aurantiaca*) is a lively orange-red. This creeping plant forms borders resistant even to invasive plants.

— *H. pilosella* (syn. *Pilosella officinarum*), the hawkweed, has lemon-yellow flowers. The leaves and flowers are used in herbal teas for the liver and for fevers.

Height: 10–30 cm (4–12 in).
Spacing and planting distance: 20 cm (8 in).
Soil: any, on the light side.
Aspect: full sun.
Propagation: by division in spring.
Flowering season: summer to autumn.
Type: perennial.

Heuchera

ALUM ROOT, CORAL BELLS

Saxifragaceae

A native of village gardens where it is often found in company with violets, marigolds, bergenias and columbines, *Heuchera sanguinea* needs no care since it grows in any soil, fills out over the years and flowers faithfully each year. It can also be grown in pots, in a shady courtyard where its delicate foliage and strands of coral flowers will look wonderful, as edging in borders or as ground cover underneath deciduous trees. The modern hybrids and varieties are more attractive than the species.

Useful hints

— Plant in early spring or autumn in good garden soil, in semi-shade or in sunlight. Heavy clay soils should be avoided.

— Every three years, divide the clumps in spring and use this opportunity to enrich the soil with four spadefuls of compost per square metre.

Hosta

PLANTAIN LILY

Liliaceae

Hostas prefer cool, shady gardens, where they show at their best, unfurling their sculptural, deeply veined, lacquered leaves, sometimes with splashes of cream or delicate edges of silver. In town, they can be used to good effect in gardens using just the outline of their leaves and the range of greens and whites. Put them with helxines, ferns and primulas: the result will be elegant, surprising and will need no tending.

Useful hints

— Plant in spring, in humus-rich soil.

— Divide the clumps every third or fourth spring.

— Plant varieties with interesting flowers such as *Hosta plantaginea*, *H. fortunei*, *H. lancifolia* and *H. ventricosa* in semishade to make them flower better.

Recommended

— The most beautiful is *H. plantaginea*, for its white lily flowers and its scent. *H. fortunei* and *H. lancifolia* have mauve flowers and *H. ventricosa* violet ones. *H. sieboldiana* foliage is the most seductive, since it is a waxy blue-green. The foliage of *H. fortunei* var. *albopicta*, almost entirely yellow when it appears in spring, gradually turns green. The leaves of *H.f.* var. *aureomarginata* retain their yellow margin throughout the season.

— The big, heart-shaped leaves of *H. crispula* have a narrow white margin.

— The range has been considerably extended by the arrival of new (mainly American) hybrids: 'August Moon' (golden yellow); 'Big Daddy' (velvety blue); 'Krossa Regal' (large, erect, silvergrey leaves); 'Shade Fanfare' (corrugated leaves with cream margins); 'Sum and Substance' (golden, veined leaves); 'Zounds' (large, golden, heavily puckered leaves). *H. montana* is a robust, clump-forming species. In summer, its blue-tinged leaves are surmounted by clusters of lavender flowers.

▽ *Hosta fortunei*

— *H.* 'Frances Williams' has a distinctive irregular, gold margin. The highly prized *H. sieboldiana* var. *elegans* has large, rounded, heavily puckered, blue leaves. Most of the plants sold under this name bear little resemblance to their namesake.

— Among the hybrids sharing the leaf texture and silver-blue colour of *H.* × *tardiana* are: 'Blue Moon', 'Hadspen Blue' and 'Halcyon'.

— The wavy leaves of *H. undulata* var. *univittata* are still very popular. Their white centres look like patches of light falling on the leaves.

— *H. ventricosa* var. *aureomaculata*, with its cream margins, deserves to be much more widely used.

Height: 30 cm (12 in).
Spacing and planting distance: 30 cm (12 in).
Soil: humus-rich.
Aspect: semi-shade.
Propagation: by division in spring.
Flowering season: summer.
Type: perennial.

▽ *Hosta sieboldiana*

Houttuynia cordata △

Hosta △

Houstonia

BLUETS

Rubiaceae

Very little known, *Houstonia caerulea* is a charming little American plant that looks like chickweed and forms a dense cushion of bright green leaves barely 15 cm (6 in) high, with flowers that start off pale blue and then turn white. Give it room in your rock garden in a sheltered corner away from the cold, which can kill it. Its flowers, which stay in bloom for several months, last longer if the earth is cool. Combine with *Phlox subulata*, which has very similar coloured flowers and is the same height.

Useful hints

— Plant in spring in a patch of good, humus-rich soil enriched with peat. Water regularly throughout the year. When winter draws near, cover with glass to keep off excess rainwater.

— Collect some seeds and sow them before winter. They will come up in spring. Or propagate by division.

Height: 12 cm (5 in).
Spacing and planting distance: 15 cm (6 in).
Soil: cool, humus-rich.
Aspect: semi-shade.
Propagation: from seed when ripe or by division in spring.
Flowering season: spring to summer.
Type: perennial.

Houttuynia

HOUTTUYNIA

Saururaceae

Often invasive in gardens with cool soil, *Houttuynia cordata* puts out new mahogany shoots every year before unfurling large, lacquered, leaden-green leaves with red-tinted margins. In early summer, white flowers appear, giving off a unique piquant scent. It is at home with *Arum italicum*, bamboo and water iris, rapidly forming great carpets of colour. There is a variety with leaves that are splashed with red, cream and deep green – it's called 'Chameleon'.

Useful hints

— Plant clumps in a moist soil or by a pond.

— Divide plants every three years to stop them growing too much.

— Plant young rooted shoots in shallow earth about 5 cm (2 in) down. In ponds, plant in a container with the soil just breaking the surface.

— Cut back if it becomes invasive.

Height: 30 cm (12 in).
Spacing and planting distance: 30 cm (12 in).
Soil: clay, moist.
Aspect: any.
Propagation: by division in spring.
Flowering season: summer.
Type: perennial.

△ *Hyacinthoides hispanica*
▽ *Hyacinthoides non-scripta*

Hyacinthoides

BLUEBELL

Liliaceae

In mid-spring, just when the broom is in flower, the bluebell, *Hyacinthoides non-scripta*, spreads in large dark blue sheets in the shelter of the undergrowth or along cool banks. Whether the undergrowth is sparse or entangled with brushwood letting little light in, it appears each spring. Plant the bulbs in large beds at the foot of your flowering cherry trees to give magnificent results at little cost.

Useful hints

— Plant the bulbs as soon as the flowers have faded, burying them 20 cm (8 in) deep in good, moist, humus-rich soil – then leave them alone.

— When your pick the flowers, leave the leaves to allow the plants to go on drawing nourishment and, above all, don't try to uproot them with your bare hands: they are so deeply rooted that you'll spoil them to no avail.

Recommended

— While *H. non-scripta* has a pleasant scent, and mainly blue flowers, with the very occasional white, the Spanish hyacinth, *H. hispanica*, is a pale blue and has no scent at all.

Height: 20–40 cm (8–16 in).
Spacing and planting distance: 15 cm (6 in).
Soil: cool and deep.
Aspect: any.
Propagation: by separating bulbs after foliage fades.
Flowering season: spring.
Type: bulb.

Hyacinthus

HYACINTH

Liliaceae

The common hyacinth, *Hyacinthus orientalis*, is hardly ever grown now, which is a pity, because it was a treat for the eyes, blue and slight, growing even taller than its little hybrid sisters. Growers have bred so many varieties that you can now have hyacinths in flower from mid-winter to mid-spring. They grow happily outside and brighten up the first days of spring.

Useful hints

— Plant the bulbs in pots in a mixture of equal parts of peat and garden soil.

— Plant them in beds in large holes filled with porous compost.

— They withstand cold well, but in heavy earth they do better if you grow them in pockets of permeable soil.

— To make the bulbs in your pots flower again, put them in compost as soon as the flowers have gone, spreading their roots out well and watering them regularly until the leaves turn yellow.

Recommended

— 'White Pearl' (pure white); 'Anna-Marie' and 'Lady Derby' (pale pink); 'Amethyst' (dark mauve); 'Ostara', dark porcelain-blue; 'City of Haarlem' (cream).

Height: 10–20 cm (4–8 in).
Spacing and planting distance: 10 cm (4 in).
Soil: rich and light.
Aspect: sun.
Propagation: by separating bulbils in summer.
Flowering season: mid-winter to spring.
Type: bulb.

Hypericum

ST JOHN'S WORT, AARON'S BEARD, ROSE OF SHARON

Guttiferae

It is difficult to decide the boundary between hardy perennial and shrub varieties, since the latter are often creeping. Their bright yellow flowers brighten up rock gardens and dry stone walls. They used to be mashed in olive oil to make a sovereign remedy for wounds and burns.

△ *Hypericum olympicum*
◁ *Hyacinthus orientalis*
Hyssopus officinalis ▷

Useful hints

— Plant in autumn or spring in a pocket of good soil. Water regularly in the first summer: then let the clumps spread as they will but watch they don't invade less robust plants.

— Remove old leaves in spring to give well-shaped clumps.

Recommended

— While *Hypericum calycinum* is popular for banks, which it decorates with its tough foliage, it's difficult to get rid of it if you tire of its rather hundrum yellow.

— *H. olympicum*, yellow and dense, its variety 'Citrinum', a lemon-yellow, *H. patulum*, a golden yellow with deep green leaves, and *H. olympicum*, golden yellow with bluish leaves, are much to be preferred in rock gardens since their clumps spread relatively slowly.

Height: 15–30 cm (6–12 in).
Spacing and planting distance: 20 cm (8 in).
Soil: on the light side.
Aspect: sun or semi-shade.
Propagation: by division in spring.
Flowering season: summer to autumn.
Type: perennial, shrub.

Hyssopus
HYSSOP
Labiatae

For planting in stony areas where there is very little soil, hyssop is ideal. It does not merely tolerate these conditions – this is where it reaches the peak of its beauty and scent. It would be impossible not to mention the impact of its violet-blue flowers or their delicious scent, a mixture of thyme and camphor. They can be used to make delicious infusions for use against stomach or throat problems.

Useful hints

— Plant in spring. It will be quite at home in poor soil if it is well-drained. Place it where it can trail down gracefully. Its flowers will attract lots of bees and butterflies.

— As winter draws near, cover the clumps with plastic foil or glass to keep rainwater off. Hyssop is more vulnerable to excessive moisture than to cold, and needs protection from damp.

Height: 40 cm (16 in).
Spacing and planting distance: 60 cm (24 in).
Soil: poor and dry.
Aspect: full sun.
Propagation: from seed in autumn or cuttings in spring.
Flowering season: summer to autumn.
Type: perennial.

△ *Iberis umbellata*
Iberis sempervirens △

△ *Impatiens* hybrid
Impatiens balsamina ▷
▽ *Impatiens balfourii*

Iberis

CANDYTUFT

Cruciferae

A very attractive little plant in a garden or terrace, since it keeps its foliage in winter. Planted in a tub or low wall border, iberis makes a pretty trailing clump.

Useful hints

— Sow seeds in early spring or take cuttings in late spring in a mixture of equal parts of sand and peat. Plant out in autumn.

— Dead-head the stems with a pair of scissors.

— For dense, sturdy plants, cut back the young shoots by 2–3 cm (1 in) in mid-spring.

— To rejuvenate old plants and force new shoots, prune to 10 cm (4 in) above ground in spring.

Recommended

Iberis amara flowers in white and the whole range of reds and pinks. Its leaves can be used in salads.

— *I. sempervirens*, a hardy perennial, has white flowers and there are numerous varieties.

— *I. sempervirens* 'Snowflake' spreads in a thick mat, covered in luminous, pure white flowers. 'Weisser Zwerg' has a more restrained habit.

Height: 40 cm (16 in).
Spacing and planting distance: 20 cm (8 in).
Soil: ordinary.
Aspect: sun or semi-shade.
Propagation: from seed in early spring or cuttings in late spring.
Flowering season: summer to autumn.
Type: annual, perennial.

Impatiens

BUSY LIZZIE, BALSAM

Balsaminaceae

The busy lizzie has become extremely popular for summer bedding and containers in recent decades: it is difficult to imagine what our grandparents planted in the shade, where its little flowers work wonders. It has proved to be a marvellous garden plant, even tolerating the sun provided it is watered regularly, which it must be at least once a day during a heatwave.

Useful hints

— Sow in spring in the warm on a radiator shelf. They need light to germinate. Don't bury the seeds, but cover the seed trough with a layer of compost for the first two weeks. If you sow a mixture of colours, prick out all your plants, including those that aren't thriving so well, since this will give you a wider selection of colours. Don't water too much, or the plants will die: and they must be aired regularly.

— Plant out after the frosts are over. Enrich the soil with peat or leaf-mould. Add soluble fertilizer once a fortnight when you water them.

— They can be taken indoors in autumn, where they will continue to flower, but then it is better to grow them in pots since no good ever comes of transplanting adult plants.

Recommended

— Growers are always producing new varieties. The fashion is for very dwarf varieties such as the Novette Series, Super Elfin Series and Tom Thumb Series. The New Guinea impatiens are taller and generally have variegated leaves. They are grown for pots but do very well outdoors in shady beds.

— The garden balsam (*Impatiens balsamina*) has a different appearance, the flowers being shaped like a Greek helmet, or a cockade when double. They are a grand sight, with leaves arranged like a little palm tree. They will give your garden a very marked turn-of-the-century look.

— There are also two almost wild species. *I. balfourii* will undoubtedly already have attracted your eye, since its gaudy two-tone purple and white flowers are a common sight in ditches. Their long fruit bursts open at the slightest touch (hence the name impatiens), spreading the seeds far and wide. Gather them and sow before winter: the plants will come up next year and reappear annually.

— The second wild species, *I. glandulifera*, the Himalayan balsam, is nearly 150 cm (60 in) tall, and the pale or dark pink flowers (or white in rare instances) smell of plums. Sown among macleaya and leycesteria they make a grand show.

Height: 15–150 cm (6–60 in).
Spacing and planting distance: 15–50 cm (6–20 in).
Soil: cool and rich in humus.
Aspect: shade or semi-shade.
Propagation: from seed in spring.
Flowering season: summer to first frosts.
Type: annual.

Incarvillea

INCARVILLEA, TRUMPET FLOWER

Bignoniaceae

Bringing a touch of the exotic to a garden is child's play, thanks to the incarvillea. The pink foxglove-like flowers and delicate leaves of this genus are in fact the perennial cousins of many tropical flowers. Use them in the second row of your herbaceous beds, since they will flower for only about five weeks and then just take up space.

Useful hints

— Plant in spring in humus-rich soil, well turned over since the carrot-shaped roots go down deep. Watch out for slugs or greenfly which often swarm on the young stalks in summer.

— When the clumps are dense, separate the secondary roots with shoots at the start of autumn and replant immediately.

— You can also sow the seeds under glass in spring, in which case they will flower the following year.

Recommended

— *Incarvillea delavayi* is the most common, with its divided leaves which develop after the brilliant purple-pink flowers with pink throat that unfurl at the start of summer. *I. mairei* (or its variety *grandiflora*) is smaller, with undivided leaves. Its flowers are brighter, some even crimson.

Height: 30–60 cm (12–24 in).
Spacing and planting distance: 30 cm (12 in).
Soil: humus-rich.
Aspect: sun or semi-shade.
Propagation: by division or from seed in spring.
Flowering season: spring to summer.
Type: perennial.

Inula

INULA

Compositae

Inula ensifolia will please those who like wild flowers. It has retained the elegance and harmony of roadside plants: no overgrown flowers, no weighed-down stems which collapse at the first gust of wind, no perennially infected or insect-ridden leaves – it can withstand anything.

Useful hints

— Plant in autumn or spring in well-turned-over soil, since the roots go very deep.

— Mulch the soil in spring with leaf-mould, pine bark or lawn trimmings.

— Divide the clumps every three years and cut down plants once they have flowered.

— Mix with eryngiums, pulsatillas and ornamental grasses to give a very natural appearance to the garden.

Recommended

The smallest species is *Inula ensifolia*, which is rarely more than 40 cm (16 in) high and flowers in early summer. *I. orientalis* and *I. hookeri* reach 80 cm (32 in). *I. magnifica* and *I. helenium* reach 200 cm (80 in) by the end of summer.

Height: 40–200 cm (16–80 in).
Spacing and planting distance: 30–60 cm (12–24 in).
Soil: ordinary, deep, retaining some moisture in summer.
Aspect: sun.
Propagation: by division in spring or autumn.
Flowering season: summer to first frosts.
Type: perennial.

△ *Inula magnifica*

◁ *Inula ensifolia*
▽ *Inula*

△ *Ipheion uniflorum*

Ipheion uniflorum

IPHEION, SPRING STARFLOWER

Liliaceae

Although a little sparse in early years, *Ipheion uniflorum* in time gives dense clumps with leaves exactly like grass. The surprise comes in spring, when the flowers appear, one to a stem, a very pale violet-blue. Scatter them over your rock garden or use them to make very decorative tubs in a sheltered place.

Useful hints

— Plant the bulbs in autumn 5 cm (2 in) deep in relatively light soil. In tubs, mix with some yellow crocuses or *Iris danfordiae*.

— Protect the clumps from severe cold by covering with a layer of dead leaves in winter.

— Divide the clumps every three years and replant the bulbs about 10 cm (4 in) apart. Do this when the leaves have died back and replant straight away if possible, or store the bulbs in a cool place.

Height: 15 cm (6 in).
Spacing and planting distance: 10 cm (4 in).
Soil: ordinary, lightened with a little sand or peat.
Aspect: sun.
Propagation: by separating bulbils in summer.
Flowering season: spring.
Type: bulb.

Ipomoea tricolor ▷

Ipomoea

MORNING GLORY, BLUE DAWN FLOWER

Convolvulaceae

Ipomoeas have no rivals when it comes to decorating an old tree or wire fence and covering it with flowers in a variety of colours. One wire is all they need to climb several metres in just a few weeks. It is easy to create a tunnel with them.

Useful hints

— Soak the seeds overnight to soften the very tough coating, then make light incisions with a knife before soaking them again in lukewarm water. They will then double in volume and the first roots will appear very quickly. You can sow them either under cold glass in mid-spring or directly on site after the frosts are over.

— If cold, the leaves will turn yellow.

Recommended

— *Ipomoea purpurea* has red, white or purple flowers which fade after a few hours. The trumpets are around 8 cm (3 in) across.

— The flowers of *I. tricolor* (syn. *I. rubro-caerula*) grow to 10 cm (4 in) across and have a yellow heart. They open in the morning and close in the afternoon.

Height: 200–300 cm (80–120 in).
Spacing and planting distance: 30 cm (12 in).
Soil: rich, staying moist in summer.
Aspect: sun.
Propagation: from seed in spring.
Flowering season: summer to autumn.
Type: annual.

145

Iris

IRIS, FLAG

Iridaceae

The beautiful flowers of the iris can be enjoyed all year round. The Algerian iris (*Iris unguicularis*) flowers right through the winter, and is then followed by *I. reticulata*, Dutch and English irises. Once summer has arrived, there are the Siberian irises, the innumerable *I. germanica* varieties and the Louisiana Hybrids, and *I. spuria*, not forgetting the new remontant hybrids which flower in late summer. However, they don't all like the same conditions, so be careful when choosing and planting.

Useful hints

— Plant rhizomatous irises in mid-summer. They like well-drained soil and sun, except *I. laevigata*, *I. pseudacorus*, *I. kaempferi*, *I. ensata* and *I. versicolor*, which prefer moist soils. Cut the flowers once they have faded, to avoid beds looking dreary.

— Plant bulbous irises in autumn in a well-drained soil and watch out for fieldmice, who will eat the bulbs if they are not planted deep enough. Enrich the soil with well-rotted compost, five shovelfuls for each square metre. *I. bucharica* must be allowed to dry out in summer.

Recommended

— **Bulbous irises**: *I. danfordiae* and *I. reticulata* are the dwarfs here, since they are scarcely 15 cm (6 in) high. The former flowers in early spring and is bright yellow, while the latter is slightly later and often blue or mauve. Both have a pleasant scent – if you bend down to smell them. Grow them in pots and take them indoors when they flower.

— The English iris (*I. latifolia*) and the Dutch iris (*I. xiphium*) are frequently confused. The former's deep rich blue flowers appear from late winter onwards, and don't have the yellow tinge, while the second appears later and flowers in all colours including yellow and claret. They are the same shape and size, about 60 cm (24 in), and are excellent in flower arrangements. The leaves of *I. latifolia* do not overwinter.

— *I. bucharica* is still the easiest of this range to grow. Its leaves appear in spring, curiously folded and waxed. The flowers bloom from the axil of the leaves, a sort of marriage of white and yellow which is very pretty. It grows wonderfully in rock gardens, since it spreads rapidly when it feels at home.

△ *Iris spuria* 'Premier'

△ *Iris xiphium* 'Wedgwood'

△ *Iris latifolia*
◁ *Iris kaempferi*
◁ *Iris bucharica*
▽ *Iris pseudacorus*

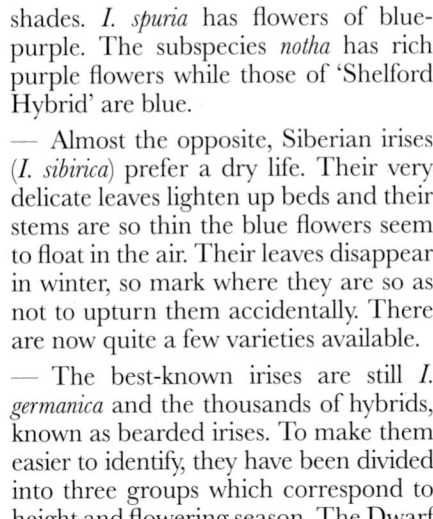

shades. *I. spuria* has flowers of blue-purple. The subspecies *notha* has rich purple flowers while those of 'Shelford Hybrid' are blue.

— Almost the opposite, Siberian irises (*I. sibirica*) prefer a dry life. Their very delicate leaves lighten up beds and their stems are so thin the blue flowers seem to float in the air. Their leaves disappear in winter, so mark where they are so as not to upturn them accidentally. There are now quite a few varieties available.

— The best-known irises are still *I. germanica* and the thousands of hybrids, known as bearded irises. To make them easier to identify, they have been divided into three groups which correspond to height and flowering season. The Dwarf Bearded group contains the miniature irises which flower early. They are followed by Intermediate Bearded, which are followed by Tall Bearded. They run the whole gamut of colours from white to an almost black purple, and from yellow to pink, with only pure red missing. Often undulating and marked with rich patterns, their flowers follow in early summer at the same time as gloxinia, old roses and poppies. They are one of the stars of the garden. Grow them in large groups or mixtures, they are pretty either way. In large numbers, they give off a delightful violet scent. Note that there are now new remontant hybrids, but they will not flower well a second time in autumn if the summer is too hot.

— *I. japonica* 'Ledger's Variety' has clusters of fringed, orchid-like flowers. It prefers damp conditions.

— The Algerian iris (*I. unguicularis*) flowers during the winter in lavender-blue or lilac. Allow it time to settle in, and it will reward you with dozens of flowers over most of the winter. It takes a very severe frost indeed to kill its leaves, and even then it will still be back the next spring. Flowers taken for indoor decoration should be pulled gently at the bud stage. Once indoors, they will open in a matter of minutes.

Height: 10–120 cm (4–48 in).
Spacing and planting distance: 10–40 cm (4–16 in).
Soil: depends on species.
Aspect: sun.
Propagation: by dividing clumps or separating new bulbs a little while after flowering.
Flowering season: all year round, depending on variety.
Type: bulb, perennial.

— **Rhizomatous irises**: The striking gladwyn (*I. foetidissima*) is rarely seen flowering *en masse* in nature and it is its curious half-open fruits and bright red seeds which draw our attention in dried flower arrangements. Its delicate mauve flowers appear discreetly in summer but its elegant leaves make it worth placing by water along with marsh irises with yellow flowers (*I. pseudacorus*).

Iris danfordiae ▽

— Another star of damp corners is the Japanese iris (*I. ensata*, and also *I. laevigata* which is very close). It prefers drier conditions in the winter, as found in its homeland. There are numerous varieties, including 'Geisha Hiskiki' (deep purple), 'Gracieuse' (blue with white centres), 'Comtesse de Paris' (pure white, and with some variations in pink, blue and purple on generally flat flowers), 'Snowdrift' (double, white), and 'Variegata', which has white and green leaves. Perhaps better known are the Higo Hybrids.

— Staying with moisture-loving irises, we come to the Louisiana Hybrids and *I. spuria*, taller than those above since they grow to over 100 cm (40 in) high. The former are only hardy to a limited extent in cooler climates. Their very varied colours include delightful pastel

△ *Ixia*

Ixia

IXIA, CORN LILY

Iridaceae

The best thing you can do with ixias is grow them in pots to make sure of not losing them: these bulbous plants from South Africa are not very hardy. They can also be used in flower arrangements, since the colours of their flattish flowers are very delicate.

Useful hints

— Plant the bulbs in autumn in groups of eight or ten in 15 cm (6 in) diameter pots filled with a crumbly mixture of sand and leaf-mould with one-third of peat. Put them under cold glass to keep the winter rains off. As soon as the shoots appear, put the pots in a light, cool room where the stems can unfurl.

— In warm and temperate climates, you can also plant ixias outside in a sunlit corner in late autumn. Keep the cold off with a cover of leaf-mould through the winter.

Height: 60 cm (24 in).
Spacing and planting distance: 5–10 cm (2–4 in).
Soil: light.
Aspect: full sun.
Propagation: by separating bulbils.
Flowering season: summer (outside), spring (inside).
Type: bulb.

Jasione

SHEEP'S-BIT

Campanulaceae

It would take a botanist's eye to tell that this plant was a cousin of the campanulas. In your mixed borders, *Jasione laevis* will add a dash of blue in mid-summer. It makes pretty borders in front of your pink remontant rose bushes, or an excellent rock garden plant.

Useful hints

— Plant in spring or autumn, adding a little peat. This plant does not like heavy, chalky soils.

— Trim the leaves in spring, but leave them on the clump all winter to protect the plant.

Height: 30–40 cm (12–16 in).
Spacing and planting distance: 30 cm (12 in).
Soil: ordinary.
Aspect: full sun.
Propagation: from seed or by division in spring.
Flowering season: summer to autumn.
Type: perennial.

▽ *Jasione heldreichii*

△ *Kniphofia* hybrid

Kniphofia

TORCH LILY, RED HOT POKER, POKER PLANT

Liliaceae

This plant was very popular around twenty years ago, when it was known by the botanical name *Tritoma* and its curious orange spikes were to be seen in virtually every garden. Since then, possibly as a result of its new and unpronounceable name, only relatively few gardeners have discovered that it also comes in attractive yellow, pink and cream varieties. Yet this is a sturdy plant, evergreen in some species, which causes few problems. It is ideal for poor soils and rough places.

Useful hints

— This plant will grow in any type of garden soil. When planting, to give a good start, allow one spadeful of compost per plant.

— Plant relatively deep, at a depth of 20 cm (8 in).

— To encourage flowering, avoid moving the plants if possible.

Recommended

— *Kniphofia galpinii* is a most attractive orange-yellow species. Some delightful hybrids are 'Bees Yellow' (yellow); 'Bressingham Torch' (flame-orange); 'Little Maid' (ivory); 'Royal Standard' (yellow and vermilion).

Height: 60 cm (24 in).
Spacing and planting distance: 40 cm (16 in).
Soil: ordinary.
Aspect: sun.
Propagation: by division in spring.
Flowering season: summer.
Type: perennial.

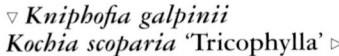

▽ **Kniphofia galpinii**
Kochia scoparia 'Tricophylla' ▷

Kochia

FALSE CYPRESS, SUMMER CYPRESS, BURNING BUSH

Chenopodiaceae

If you are an impatient gardener, looking forward to a garden punctuated with carefully trimmed bushes and tired of waiting for your *Lonicera nitida* to fill out, sow some *Kochia scoparia* (syn. *Bassia scoparia*). In just three months, you will have delightful 'bushes' of pale green, fluffy foliage. In autumn they will turn purplish red, then bright red, before the first frosts finally tinge them with beige. They only last one season, but what a picture they make!

Useful hints

— Sow in early spring, in boxes filled with light compost. Plant out after the frosts, preferably in soil that has been well fertilized over the winter, and in a sunny position. Support in windy locations.

— Plant out in rows, spaced 50 cm (20 in) apart, to imitate French-style gardens, or in groups of three to five.

— When planted in rich soil in a sunny position, kochias will often seed themselves. Collect the seeds by shaking the plants on to a sheet of newspaper in autumn.

Height: 30–60 cm (12–24 in).
Spacing and planting distance: 50 cm (20 in).
Soil: ordinary.
Aspect: sun.
Propagation: from seed in spring.
Flowering season: insignificant flowers.
Type: annual.

Lagurus

HARE'S TAIL GRASS

Gramineae

Rarely has a plant been so aptly named. When you see the fluffy, rounded heads of this variety of grass, it is easy to imagine how it acquired its name. Grown mainly for dried flower arrangements, *Lagurus ovatus* gives attractive relief in a flower bed. Its slightly glaucous shade tones in beautifully with old roses, clarkias or agrostemmas.

Useful hints

— Sow in spring, or better still in autumn, when farmers are sowing their wheat. It will remain quite small over winter, forming large tufts in spring, before producing ears. Prick out the seedlings, leaving 15 cm (6 in) between stems, and plant clarkias, echiums and godetias in between. You could also plant a few wild gladioli, such as *Gladiolus byzantinus*.

— Cut the flowering stalks in summer and dry them, heads down, in a dry, well-ventilated area.

Height: 30 cm (12 in).
Spacing and planting distance: 15 cm (6 in).
Soil: ordinary, even clay.
Aspect: sun.
Propagation: from seed in spring or autumn.
Flowering season: summer.
Type: annual, biennial.

▽ *Lagurus ovatus*

Lamium

DEAD NETTLE, HENBIT

Labiatae

Few ground cover plants have as many qualities as dead nettles – to the extent that they have perhaps been over-used as uniform carpeting. They make a more interesting picture when mixed with other shade-loving plants, such as hostas, peonies or arum lilies, producing some very effective greenery patterns.

Useful hints

— Plant from autumn to spring. Add a little peat, and cover the soil with pine bark to suppress weeds until the dead nettles have provided full cover.

— Propagate by separating rooted stems in spring: plant out immediately.

Recommended

— The most elegant of the lamiums is *Lamium maculatum*, its leaves marked with white in the case of 'Beacon Silver', or silvery green in the case of 'Chequers'. It has pink flowers. *L. maculatum* 'White Nancy' has white flowers and silvery leaves with green margins, while *L.m.* 'Pink Pewter' has white markings on its leaves and pale pink flowers.

— *L. galeobdolon*, which is extremely common, sometimes suffers from a bad reputation, as it tends to spread rampantly. The 'Florentinum', 'Hermann's Pride' and 'Silver Carpet' varieties are rather less guilty of this. Both are plumed, with white flowers. 'Hermann's Pride' forms large rounded cushions.

Height: 20–25 cm (8–10 in).
Spacing and planting distance: 25 cm (10 in).
Soil: ordinary, preferably rich in humus.
Aspect: shade.
Propagation: by division in spring.
Flowering season: spring to summer.
Type: perennial.

△ *Lamium maculatum*
Lantana montevidensis ▷

▽ *Lamium galeobdolon*

Lantana

LANTANA, SHRUB VERBENA

Verbenaceae

With the effective insecticides now available against whitefly, we can once again savour the charms of the lantanas. These tender plants, which should be grown in the same way as fuchsias, flower incessantly throughout the summer, and their domed flower heads, which frequently change colour as they age, are delightful to look at.

Useful hints

— Plant lantanas in relatively large pots, 30 cm (12 in) in diameter, filled with rich, well-drained soil (half compost, half peat, enriched with fertilizer). Do not remove from the pots until late spring. Pinch out the main shoots at half height to encourage side shoots. Remove dead flower heads and water frequently. It is useful to stake the plants.

— Apply preventive treatment against whitefly in the form of a systemic insecticide which is used as soon as the pest is noticed.

— Take cuttings from the ends of shoots in late summer and over-winter in a cool, light room.

Recommended

— *Lantana camara*. Some nurseries are producing remarkably coloured hybrids: 'Arlequin' (deep pink and yellow); 'Avalanche' (white); 'Brasier' (flame-red); 'Cochenille' (raspberry-pink); 'Prof. Raoux' (scarlet and orange).

Height: 150 cm (60 in).
Spacing and planting distance: 50 cm (20 in).
Soil: rich, cool in summer.
Aspect: full sun.
Propagation: from cuttings in summer.
Flowering season: summer to first frosts.
Type: perennial.

▽ **Lantana camara**

Lathyrus hybrid △

△ *Lathyrus grandiflorus*
▽ *Lathyrus latifolius*

Lathyrus

SWEET PEA, EVERLASTING PEA

Leguminosae

The sweet pea is invaluable for providing attractive bunches of flowers, and is just as charming when it is grown in groups, its stalks using other plants as climbing supports, unless it is a true ground-cover variety, which the perennial types become after a few years.

Useful hints

— Sow annual sweet peas in early spring under a cold frame, or in mid-spring directly in the ground. Soak the seeds the night before sowing to soften.

— Plant perennial varieties in spring or autumn and mark the sowing position. The best supports are hazel twigs with side branches, or bean netting.

Recommended

— Among the **annual** varieties (*Lathyrus odoratus*), the most decorative for cut-ting still remain the 'Spencer' varieties, with large, often highly fragrant flowers, or 'Cuthbertson', an earlier-flowering variety. For growing in clumps: the semi-dwarf 'Knee-hi' varieties; 'Bijou', extremely free-flowering; 'Patio', com-pact, and 'Continental Mixed', which reaches a height of 60 cm (24 in).

— Of the **perennial** sweet peas, *L. grandiflorus* and *L. latifolius* differ only in the size of their flowers, which are larger in the former, and the variety of shades, which is greater in the latter, offering purplish reds as well as classic purplish pink, and more especially a magnificent white. *L. vernus* is an earlier variety, begin-ning to flower in mid- to late spring. It is short-lived, and virtually non-climbing.

Height: 30–60 cm (12–24 in) (non-climbers).
Spacing and planting distance: 20 cm (8 in).
Soil: ordinary.
Aspect: sun.
Propagation: from seed in spring.
Flowering season: spring to autumn.
Type: annual, perennial.

152

△ *Lathyrus odoratus*
▽ *Lathyrus* hybrid

▽ *Lathyrus vernus*

△ *Lavandula*
Lavatera trimestris ▷

Lavandula

LAVENDER

Labiatae

Lavender is a very familiar garden plant. Perfect for dry gardens, for covering barren slopes with a frizz of silvery clumps, or for a border to a sunny path, lavender has the added virtue of providing fragrant bouquets of flowers that will leave a delicate scent in your linen cupboard.

Useful hints

— This is a southern plant, a lover of sun and well-drained soils. Avoid planting in the shade or in clay; compact soil will cause it to suffer in winter.

— Plant small clumps in spring in good, perfectly drained garden soil.

— Remove dead flowers immediately to keep the clumps nicely rounded. Where necessary, cut back in mid-spring.

Recommended

— *Lavandula angustifolia* is the prettiest, with its violet-blue, subtly fragrant, long-lasting flowers. Try the 'Hidcote' variety, in a darker blue, white 'Alba Nana' or pink 'Hidcote Pink'.

— *L. × intermedia* Dutch Group are less fragrant but much hardier and do not turn black in damp conditions.

— *L. lanata* is a little shrub with white woolly stems and violet flowers.

— *L. stoechas* has a strange tousled outline, and is less fragrant.

— *L. stoechas* ssp. *pedunculata*, the so-called 'butterfly' lavender, is the most common variety. It should be given a sheltered position.

Height: 30–80 cm (12–32 in).
Spacing and planting distance: 50 cm (20 in).
Soil: ordinary, well-drained.
Aspect: sun.
Propagation: from cuttings in summer.
Flowering season: summer.
Type: shrub.

Lavatera

MALLOW

Malvaceae

A single packet of *Lavatera trimestris* seeds will provide plenty of decoration, as each develops into a little bush covered with flowers throughout the summer. But beware: if you apply too much high nitrogen fertilizer, you will have more foliage than flowers! The colours of lavatera, which are always very fresh, bring beauty to the garden.

Useful hints

— Sow the large seeds in seed trays or pots under cover in mid-spring. Thin out one month later, or sow them directly into the ground like beans in late spring, provided your soil is crumbly, clean and on the dry side, as lavateras dislike excessive moisture.

— Pinch back the main stems to approximately half their height when they have reached 20 cm (8 in), to encourage them to send out side shoots.

— Keep well watered when in flower.

Recommended

The classic varieties such as 'Loveliness' have been superseded by two hybrids, 'Silver Cup' and 'Mont Blanc', which are pink and white respectively and have very much larger flowers.

Height: 60–120 cm (24–48 in).
Spacing and planting distance: 40 cm (16 in).
Soil: rich and cool in summer.
Aspect: sun.
Propagation: from seed in spring.
Flowering season: throughout the summer.
Type: annual.

△ *Leucojum aestivum*

Lewisia cotyledon ▷

△ *Leontopodium alpinum*

Leontopodium

EDELWEISS

Compositae

No rock garden is complete without an edelweiss. This symbol of the high mountains is rarely as silvery in colour as on its native scree, unless you choose 'Mignon', a smaller, pure white variety.

You will have a succession of flower heads all summer long, provided that there is plenty of sun.

Useful hints

— Wait for spring before planting in a hollow between two rocks. A crumbly, slightly chalky soil is ideal. Water regularly throughout the first summer to encourage the plant to become well established. In very rainy areas, protect in winter under a glass cloche.

— Sowing in a cold frame in spring is quite successful. Transfer the young plants into small pots and keep under cover for their first winter before planting them out the next spring.

Height: 10–20 cm (4–8 in).
Spacing and planting distance: 20 cm (8 in).
Soil: light, and slightly chalky.
Aspect: full sun is essential.
Propagation: from seed in spring.
Flowering season: late spring to summer.
Type: perennial.

Leucanthemella

see *Chrysanthemum*

Leucanthemum

see *Chrysanthemum*

Leucojum

SNOWFLAKE

Amaryllidaceae

A relatively uncommon plant in gardens, leocojums make an enchanting picture in spring, with their pure white flowers and the tips of their petals tinged with green.

Useful hints

— Bury the bulbs in autumn at a depth of 7.5–10 cm (3–4 in) in ordinary, ideally

slightly heavy soil. Then allow the bulbs to become naturalized, forming clumps of increasing size.

— Divide after five years, just after flowering, and replant immediately, spaced well apart.

Recommended

— Wrongly called the summer snowflake, since it flowers in mid-spring, *Leucojum aestivum* is particularly decorative in large clumps at the water's edge and in cool ground.

— Together with hepatica, *Iris reticulata* and snowdrops, *L. vernum* forms a wonderful carpet in the woods in early spring.

Height: 15–60 cm (6–24 in).
Spacing and planting distance: 15 cm (6 in).
Soil: ordinary, tending towards clay.
Aspect: shade or semi-shade.
Propagation: by separating bulbs after flowering.
Flowering season: spring.
Type: bulb.

Lewisia

LEWISIA

Portulacaceae

Lewisia cotyledon, with its jewel-like flowers, is by no means easy to grow. Its main enemy is moisture in winter. But the flowers provide supreme compensation with their extremely bright colours, particularly among the pinks. The abundance with which the flowers are produced is truly astonishing.

Useful hints

— Plant in spring in an almost vertical crevice between two rocks, or in a pot filled with a mixture of compost and coarse sand. Put some chippings in the bottom of the pot and around the collar to assist drainage. Leave these pots outside until late autumn, then put into a cold frame, setting them at an angle, almost on their sides, to prevent water from stagnating.

— The best method of propagation is to sow seeds in spring in a cold frame. Thin out into pots and make sure to over-winter in a well-insulated cold frame. They will flower for the first time when a year old.

Height: 20–30 cm (8–12 in).
Spacing and planting distance: 25 cm (10 in).
Soil: very well-drained.
Aspect: sun.
Propagation: from seed in spring.
Flowering season: late spring to summer.
Type: perennial.

Liatris

BLAZING STAR, GAYFEATHER

Compositae

The spikes of the liatris have an unusual feature in that the flowers open from the top. With its fine grass-like leaves and tuberous roots, it is difficult to place in the large family of Compositae, particularly since it has abandoned their typical yellow in favour of a gentle violet, pleasantly restful in high summer. It is excellent for cut flowers, which may last for over a week.

Useful hints

— Plant preferably in spring, in rich soil that remains fresh in summer. Put in at least six plants to obtain interesting clumps of flowers from the first year onwards, and leave to establish themselves: avoiding dividing too soon.

— They are best set against plants with broad foliage such as mauve hostas, bergenias or ornamental rhubarb. Their soft colour goes will with that of garden pinks or annual lupins.

Recommended

— *Liatris scariosa* can grow to a height of 90 cm (36 in) and is to be found in white, while *L. spicata*, the most common, is most popular in its 'Kobold' variety, growing to a maximum height of 60 cm (24 in), in an attractive lilac-pink. These species have a white variety known as 'Alba'.

Height: 60–100 cm (24—40 in).
Spacing and planting distance: 20 cm (8 in).
Soil: well-drained, but not dry in summer.
Aspect: sun.
Propagation: by division in spring.
Flowering season: summer to autumn.
Type: perennial.

Libertia

LIBERTIA

Iridaceae

The silhouette of *Libertia formosa* is quite astonishing in mid-winter: its leaves are as green as those of holly. With its compact, neat habit, it is covered in pure white flowers in summer, followed by orange fruits. Combine with plumed foliage, against a background of everlasting shrubs and peonies.

Useful hints

— Plant in spring in a sunny position protected from cold winds. Water regularly and cover the soil with pine bark or dead leaves.

— Divide the clumps only when they have become too densely packed.

Height: 30–60 cm (12–24 in).
Spacing and planting distance: 30 cm (12 in).
Soil: rich and well-drained.
Aspect: full sun essential.
Propagation: by division in spring.
Flowering season: summer.
Type: perennial.

◁ *Liatris spicata*

Ligularia

LEOPARD PLANT

Compositae

Ligularias, which grow exceptionally vigorously in deep, moist soils, are useful for covering large areas. They blend well with ferns, meconopsis, lysimachia and *Lythrum salicaria* to decorate the edges of ponds, etc.

Useful hints

— Plant in autumn or spring after digging the soil to a good depth and mixing in compost and peat to lighten and improve it.

— Protect from slugs by using slug bait, and water regularly over the first summer. Provided the soil remains cool at depth, the plants will thrive as they are easy-going by nature.

Recommended

— *Ligularia dentata* is one of the most modest varieties in terms of size. It forms a dome, 100 cm (40 in) in height. The 'Desdemona' variety has leaves with a purple underside.

— Somewhat taller is *L. przewalskii*, with its amazing denticulate leaves. Its flower spikes tower up to a height of 200 cm (80 in).

— More vigorous still, *L. wilsoniana* is shrub-sized. Its big, rounded leaves show off its large golden yellow flower spikes beautifully.

— *L. japonica* will grow to an impressive size if placed in moist ground. It does, in fact, thrive on water.

— *L. × palmatiloba* needs a lot of space, as it tends to spread.

— *L. tangutica* 'The Rocket' forms elegant clumps. Its slender, brown stems are covered with dense foliage.

Height: 100–200 cm (40–80 in).
Spacing and planting distance: 60–100 cm (24–40 in).
Soil: rich, always moist.
Aspect: sun or semi-shade.
Propagation: by division in spring.
Flowering season: summer to autumn.
Type: perennial.

Ligularia japonica ▷

△ *Libertia formosa*
Ligularia przewalskii ▷

157

Lilium

LILY

Liliaceae

Just a few lilies are all that is needed to give a corner of the garden a welcome touch of refinement. Lovers of soil rich in humus, they will flourish without much attention, provided you choose the more robust varieties.

Useful hints

— Plant preferably in spring, with the exception of the Madonna lily, which has a growing period beginning in autumn and should be planted in summer. Dig to a depth of at least 30 cm (12 in), and mix in plenty of compost. Bury the bulbs at a depth of 15 cm (6 in), and surround with a pocket of sand to prevent rotting and attack by slugs, and also assist their growth.

— Mark the planting site with a tag, as vegetation will only begin to appear in mid-spring. Surround with slug bait, and water regularly. When the stems reach a height of 30 cm (12 in), support them discreetly, either individually or with hazel branches. If any red insects should appear, treat immediately: these are lily beetles, and their larvae are liable to devour the entire foliage of the plant.

— After three years, you may dig up the bulbs in autumn, while the stems are still green. Split off the new bulbs and put into a tray filled with peat in a cold frame. Plant them out in spring. Avoid leaving them in the open air, as they dry out very quickly.

Recommended

— The golden-rayed lily of Japan (*Lilium auratum*) has very large white flowers with brown spots. The flowers open wide, and the petals curl slightly outwards. This is a wonderful variety, but unfortunately one that is highly sensitive to viruses, which kill them off in a matter of just a few years. It should be grown in sandy leaf-mould.

— The Madonna lily (*L. candidum*) is extremely common in old gardens, where it forms large clumps. It flowers early, when its foliage is just beginning to dry out. It is a sun-lover, and likes plenty of heat.

— Relatively little known, *L. hansonii* deserves to be more popular. Its orange-yellow flowers, with their very thick petals, are reminiscent of our turk's-cap lilies. It should be grown in semi-shade to prevent its colour fading.

— One of the giants in the group is

Lilium hybrids △

unquestionably *L. henryi*, whose stem reaches heights of up to 200 cm (80 in). It should be planted deep and carefully staked as its flowers are so numerous that their weight bends down the stem. It is tolerant of lime and can be planted in spaces between spring-flowering shrubs.

— The highly fragrant flowers of *L. longiflorum*, the Easter lily, are well known, taking pride of place in florists' shops. They are best planted in pots.

— The turk's-cap lily (*L. martagon*) originates from mountain regions. Although the flowers have little fragrance, they have an interesting turban shape and a purple-red colour.

— In peaty, moist soil, *L. pardalinum* var. *giganteum*, the leopard lily, will quickly form tangled clumps, as it sends out rhizomes in all directions. It has relatively small but extremely numerous orange flowers dotted with purple and enlivened by a golden heart.

— If you want to be surrounded by fragrance without giving yourself a lot of work, plant some *L. regale*. This is one of the most robust of all lilies, flowering unfailingly year after year. There is a totally white variety ('Album'), but the flowers of the species type are shaded pink on the outside.

— *L. speciosum* does not really deserve the praise that is commonly showered upon it. It is susceptible to viruses and it is slightly out of proportion in view of the exceptional size of its flowers.

— The tiger lily (*L. lancifolium*) is easily increased by simply planting the bulbils

△ *Lilium candidum*

that appear on the stem. They will flower in two years. Their wide open flowers are a virulent orange colour.

— There are numerous hybrid lilies. The most remarkable are 'African Queen', with an orange trumpet; 'Enchantment', nasturtium-red; the Imperial Series with large, widely spread flowers dotted with gold; 'Moonlight', golden yellow; and 'Pink Perfection', a purplish pink which is lighter in the centre.

Height: 30–200 cm (12–80 in).
Spacing and planting distance: 30 cm (12 in).
Soil: rich in humus and sand.
Aspect: mainly semi-shade.
Propagation: by separating new bulbs in autumn.
Flowering season: summer to autumn.
Type: bulb.

Limnanthes

LIMNANTHES, MEADOW FOAM

Limnanthaceae

This plant is particularly popular with English gardeners. Sow it at least once, to enjoy the unique charm of its white flowers with yellow centres, giving rise to its nickname of poached egg flower. Its deeply cut leaves are attractive in themselves, and this plant will reseed itself readily without need for protection. An ideal flower for weekend gardeners.

Useful hints

— Sow the large seeds in their flowering site in spring, and thin out the seedlings after a month, leaving one plant every 20 cm (8 in).

— Water regularly until mid-summer. Flowering will then stop. Cut the foliage at mid height to encourage a second burst of flowers. Apply soluble fertilizer.

— Collect the seeds at the end of the summer and sow at random, without bothering to cover them. Some of them will germinate immediately, and the remainder will do so in the spring.

Height: 15 cm (6 in).
Spacing and planting distance: 20 cm (8 in).
Soil: ordinary.
Aspect: sun.
Propagation: from seed in spring.
Flowering season: summer.
Type: annual.

◁ *Lilium regale*
▽ *Limnanthes douglasii*

Limonium sinuatum △

Limonium

STATICE, SEA LAVENDER

Plumbaginaceae

The distinctive feature of statice flowers is that they are almost dry from the outset. This is why they are so often used in dried flower arrangements. In the garden, the perennial statice is a valuable asset, brightening up beds with its thousands of misty lavender flowers.

Useful hints

— Sow annual statice in mid-spring in a cold frame and in late spring in a corner of the kitchen garden. Hoe regularly and water until in flower.

— Plant perennial statice in spring. It loves watering in summer, and will grow in seaside areas.

Recommended

— *Limonium sinuatum* (grown as an annual) is commonly sold in mixtures for dried flowers. Nowadays it is possible to find *L. suworowii* (syn. *Psylliostachys suworowii*) with long, pale pink spikes.

— The common name for the perennial *L. latifolium* is sea lavender. It is a worthy plant for the edges of rose beds, but its flowers can also be preserved in dried flower arrangements. *L. tataricum* (syn. *Goniolimon tataricum*) is smaller.

Height: 30–60 cm (12–24 in).
Spacing and planting distance: 20 cm (8 in).
Soil: slightly sandy.
Aspect: sun.
Propagation: from seed in spring or by division in early autumn.
Flowering season: summer.
Type: annual, perennial.

Linaria

TOADFLAX, BUTTER-AND-EGGS

Scrophulariaceae

With their miniature antirrhinum-like flowers, linarias add a touch of brightness wherever they grow. They are so frugal that even the tiniest amount of mediocre

△ *Linaria maroccana*
▽ *Linum grandiflorum*

▽ *Linum narbonense*

soil is sufficient for them to flourish. Make good use of them on dry walls, in the rock garden, or in containers.

Useful hints

— Sow linarias in spring. The annual varieties will flower three months later, and the perennials the next year. As the seeds are very fine, mix them with some sand: do not cover with soil. The stems branch out very quickly. Plant the perennial varieties in spring in a pocket of sandy soil.

— Water regularly in hot weather and cut back after flowering to encourage regrowth at the end of the summer.

Recommended

— The annual Moroccan linaria (*Linaria maroccana*) is sold in mixtures such as 'Fairy Bouquet'. Each plant forms an individual clump studded with hundreds of flowers.

— The perennial *L. cymbalaria* (syn. *Cymbalaria muralis*) is frequently found in old walls. It has trailing stems bearing mauve flowers followed by fruits that crackle to the lightest touch. It can sometimes be rather invasive in rock gardens, but it gives an attractive effect on dry stone walls, or on stone steps. A close relative, the perennial alpine linaria (*L. alpina*) forms dense cushions covered with bluish violet flowers with a bright orange centre. It tends to be a biennial rather than a perennial, and again will reseed itself quite readily.

— The purple linaria (*L. purpurea*) is to some extent a purplish blue variation of our common yellow linaria. It should be grown in the garden, in the company of *Euphorbia polychroma*, horned poppies and penstemons.

Height: 5–40 cm (2–16 in).
Spacing and planting distance: 20 cm (8 in).
Soil: ordinary, slightly sandy.
Aspect: sun.
Propagation: from seed or by division of perennials.
Flowering season: summer to autumn.
Type: annual, perennial.

Linum

FLAX, PERENNIAL FLAX

Linaceae

A common feature of all decorative flaxes is a certain elegance of line deriving from their long, thin stems. Their flowers appear to flutter in the air, and move at the slightest wisp of breeze. They are unrivalled in their ability to

brighten up flower beds and give a natural touch to highly sophisticated arrangements. Their only defect is their precarious health, which often causes them to disappear after only a few years, in spite of being classified as perennials. On the other hand, they are easy to propagate from seed.

Useful hints

— Sow in spring. Annual flaxes will flower three months later, while perennial flaxes will take a year to fill out. Shelter in a cold frame over the first winter.

— Combine annual flaxes with nigella, cornflowers and marguerites for a charming rustic combination. Perennial flaxes go well with plants with grey foliage, such as *Senecio greyi* or the medicinal sages, which like the same dry, pebbly soil.

Recommended

— The best of the annual flaxes is *Linum grandiflorum*, of which 'Rubrum' is a stockier improved variety in a lovely bright red. The flax used in textiles (*L. usitatissimum*) has a pale blue flower.

— Of the perennial flaxes, we should mention *L. narbonense* and *L. perenne*, which are bright blue. 'Heavenly Blue' and 'Sapphire' are good varieties. The little *L. flavum*, which is pale yellow, is magnificent in rock gardens, flowering in mid-summer.

Height: 30–60 cm (12–24 in).
Spacing and planting distance: 15 cm (6 in).
Soil: ordinary.
Aspect: sun.
Propagation: from seed in spring.
Flowering season: summer to autumn.
Type: annual, perennial.

Liriope

LILYTURF

Liliaceae

Imagine a giant grape hyacinth that flowers at the end of summer, with striped foliage that is just as decorative as its lilac-mauve flowers, and you have the liriope. Use it in borders, mixed with nerines, colchicums and anaphalis.

Useful hints

— Plant in spring in rather light, non-chalky soil. Water lightly in hot weather. At other times the plants will look after themselves, given their fleshy roots.

— Divide clumps when they become too tight, preferably in spring.

△ *Liriope muscari*

△ *Lithodora diffusa* 'Heavenly Blue'

Recommended

— The best-known is *Liriope muscari*: its long-lasting leaves provide an attractive background for its violet spikes.

— *L. spicata* is slightly larger than this last-named variety but otherwise is quite similar to it. Some plants may produce dark blue flowers, depending on the soil and position.

Height: 40–60 cm (16–24 in).
Spacing and planting distance: 40 cm (16 in).
Soil: ordinary, rather sandy, well-drained in winter.
Aspect: sun and semi-shade.
Propagation: by division in spring.
Flowering season: late summer to autumn.
Type: perennial.

Lithodora (syn. *Lithospermum*)

LITHOSPERMUM, GROMWELL, PUCCOON, INDIAN PAINT

Boraginaceae

Although its name has recently been changed to *Lithodora*, the lithospermum is often still referred to in catalogues by its old name. The best-known cultivar is 'Heavenly Blue'. This is one of the very best rock garden plants for a sunny position and acid soil. The deep blue of its open, funnel-shaped flowers is renewed all summer long, looking equally attractive with helianthemums, broom and the early heathers.

Useful hints

— Plant in spring, in a pocket of acid soil (a mixture of leaf-mould, sand and peat).

— Protect in a cold frame over the winter, as they are liable to be killed by heavy frost.

— Trim the stems hard back after flowering.

Height: 15–20 cm (6–8 in).
Spacing and planting distance: 30 cm (12 in).
Soil: light, acid.
Aspect: full sun.
Propagation: from cuttings in summer.
Flowering season: summer to autumn.
Type: perennial.

◁ *Lobelia cardinalis*   *Lobelia* △
◁ *Lobelia lindblomii*

Lobelia

LOBELIA, CARDINAL FLOWER

Campanulaceae

If we are to judge by the intense blue of the annual variety 'Crystal Palace' or the flaming red of the perennial *Lobelia cardinalis*, lobelias come in bold colours. Use them sparingly next to grey foliage plants and pastel-coloured flowers.

Useful hints

— Sow in the warm, no later than mid-spring as their initial growth is slow. Plant out after the frosts.

— Plant perennial varieties, preferably in spring, in fresh, deep soil. In summer, fork in peat or pine bark. Water regularly, as the plants are very thirsty. In autumn, cover with a layer of straw and a piece of plastic film to protect the roots from the cold and damp.

162

Lobelia erinus △
Lobelia × *gerardii* 'Vedrariensis' ▷

Recommended

— In the **annual** varieties (*L. erinus*): 'Crystal Palace', dwarf, dark blue; 'Sapphire', a bright blue with a white eye.

— In the **perennial** varieties: *L.* 'Queen Victoria', with scarlet flowers and bronze foliage. 'Illumination' has scarlet flowers and dark green foliage. Note also *L. siphilitica*, which is smaller, with soft blue flowers at the end of the summer, and *L.* × *gerardii* 'Vedrariensis', with a violet colour.

— Some fairly hardy and very free-flowering **hybrids** are: 'Bee's Flame' (deep pink with reddish leaves); 'Pink Flamingo' (pink with bronze leaves); 'Russian Princess' (purple flowers and foliage).

Height: 10–90 cm (4–36 in).
Spacing and planting distance: 10–30 cm (4–12 in).
Soil: permanently moist.
Aspect: full sun.
Propagation: from seed in spring, from cuttings, or by division.
Flowering season: summer to autumn.
Type: annual, perennial.

163

Lobularia maritima
(syn. *Alyssum maritimum*)

SWEET ALYSSUM

Cruciferae

Better known by the name *Alyssum maritimum*, *Lobularia maritima* is under-used in gardens. Its fine seeds produce tiny seedlings that initially look rather like weeds before developing into imposing clumps. These are covered in flower heads, at first insignificant, but ultimately covering the entire foliage. With the added benefit of a honey fragrance it is without doubt an excellent plant for growing in borders and containers.

Useful hints

— Sow in late spring in a cold frame after mixing the seeds with fine sand to avoid spreading them too densely. Prick out groups of three or four seedlings one month later, spacing them 20 cm (8 in) apart in all directions.

— Water regularly and hoe the soil. When the first flowering is over, cut back with scissors to prevent fruits from forming, and encourage a further show of flowers one month later.

Recommended

— Beside the classic 'Little Dorrit' and 'Carpet of Snow', in pure white, an even more dense variety, 'Wonderland White', deserves a special mention. The violet varieties 'Royal Carpet' and 'Violet Queen' go well with pastel roses.

Height: 7–15 cm (3–6 in).
Spacing and planting distance: 20 cm (8 in).
Soil: ordinary, even light soil.
Aspect: sun.
Propagation: from seed in spring.
Flowering season: summer to autumn.
Type: annual.

▽ *Lobularia maritima*

Lunaria rediviva △
◁ *Lotus berthelotii*

Lotus

SWEET CLOVER, BIRD'S-FOOT TREFOIL, CORAL GEM

Leguminosae

These are cousins of the yellow sweet clovers that are found in the fields and not of the lotus flower, known to botanists by the name *Nelumbo*. One species is a rock garden plant, the other an unusual container plant, with grey foliage and red flowers of a strange lobster-claw shape.

Useful hints

— Plant yellow *Lotus corniculatus* (sweet clover, bird's-foot trefoil) in any season in a corner of the rock garden or between two stones in a dry stone wall.

— Plant *L. berthelotii* (coral gem) in spring, and bring out only when all risk of frost is over. Water freely, from time to time adding soluble fertilizer. Take cuttings in summer and overwinter the young plants on the verandah or in a cold greenhouse.

Recommended

— *L. corniculatus* is grown mainly for its bright yellow, double form. *L. berthelotii* (Berthelot sweet clover) is becoming increasingly frequently available in catalogues. Try it in hanging baskets, and you will be won over immediately.

Height: 15–30 cm (6–12 in).
Spacing and planting distance: 20 cm (8 in).
Soil: rich, well-drained.
Aspect: sun.
Propagation: from cuttings in summer.
Flowering season: summer to autumn.
Type: perennial.

△ *Lunaria annua*

Lunaria

HONESTY, SILVER DOLLAR

Cruciferae

Everyone knows honesty, a must in dried flower arrangements. We tend to forget that its deep purple flowers are not unattractive either. Plant them in the company of white fleur-de-lys tulips, yellow horned violets or as a carpet at the foot of azaleas or magnolias, as they are tolerant of shade.

Useful hints

— Sow *Lunaria annua* seeds in early summer, in a shady position. Thin out once into pots, then transplant into their flowering site in autumn. They will flower the next spring.

— Allow the fruits to mature on the plant, then cut off the whole stem and dry indoors. Rub each fruit between the fingers to reveal the central pod.

Height: 100 cm (40 in).
Spacing and planting distance: 30 cm (12 in).
Soil: ordinary.
Aspect: sun or semi-shade.
Propagation: from seed in early summer.
Flowering season: spring to summer.
Type: biennial.

Lupinus

LUPIN, LUPINE

Leguminosae

A pleasant green fertilizer in poor, excessively light soil, the annual lupin (*Lupinus subcarnosus*) will readily seed itself in gardens where it feels at home, and will flower prettily in fragrant blue and white spikes at the beginning of the summer, while hybrid perennial lupins and the tree lupin will flower throughout the summer, in a whole range of colours (yellow, white, blue, lilac, pink, red, violet). Lupins are happy in the company of peonies and hollyhocks, producing magnificent flower beds that give no trouble to the gardener.

Useful hints

— Their only weakness: they do not like lime. Don't try: the results are dreadful. They grow well in heavy, clay soils but last longer in light soil.

— Cut off dead flowers to extend the flowering season and propagate by taking cuttings: you will then be certain of your colours.

Recommended

— Of the annual lupins: in addition to *L. subcarnosus* there is the Hartweg lupin, *L. hartwegii*, which reaches a height of 60 cm (24 in) and is enchanting with its flowers in extremely gentle colours.

— Of the perennial lupins: the Russell Hybrids (*L. polyphyllus* hybrids), are well-known. Other varieties include 'The Châtelaine' in pink and white; 'Chandelier' in pale yellow and gold; 'The Page', carmine; 'Blushing Bride', ivory; and 'Thundercloud', deep violet. The Minarette Group has a similar number of variations in a plant that reaches a height of no more than 40 cm (16 in), i.e. half the height of those above. It is also an earlier strain, and flowers practically without fail from the first year if sown early in spring.

— Of the tree lupins: *L. arboreus*, with attractive silvery foliage and slender flower spikes, in gentle colours such as lemon, blue or white. Though short-lived, this species does well in seaside gardens.

Height: 40–80 cm (16–32 in).
Spacing and planting distance: 30 cm (12 in).
Soil: ordinary, not chalky.
Aspect: sun.
Propagation: from seed in spring, from cuttings or by division.
Flowering season: summer.
Type: annual, perennial.

△ *Lupinus* hybrid

△ *Lupinus texensis*
▽ *Lupinus polyphyllus*

△ *Lychnis coronaria*
◁ *Lychnis alpina*
Lychnis chalcedonica ▷
▽ *Lychnis* × *arkwrightii*

Lychnis

CAMPION, CATCHFLY

Caryophyllaceae

The *Lychnis* genus is vast. It contains some plants which remain close to their wild appearance, providing a natural look that is attractive if you are trying to accentuate the 'country' aspect of a particular scene. Lychnis provide a very elegant accompaniment to old roses and aromatic plants.

Useful hints

— Plant preferably in spring, as they do not like the cold if their roots are not well-developed. Give them a well-drained chalky soil and a sunny position.

— You can sow seeds in spring or propagate by dividing the clumps just after flowering. Over-winter young plants in a cold frame for the first year.

Recommended

— *Lychnis alpina* forms a low, tight mat covered with dense clusters of flowers in dark pink.

— The red of *L. chalcedonica* (cross of Jerusalem, or Maltese cross) is so bright that few other colours can stand comparison with it, except for the white of peach-leaved campanula and Madonna lilies.

— *L. coronaria* is a truly magical plant. The harmonious combination of the exceptionally bright magenta-red of its flowers and the silvery velvet of its leaves is perfect. Use in large masses that will remain in flower from summer right through to the first frosts. There is also a highly regarded white variety, although this is a little less vigorous.

— Allow *L. flos-jovis* to become naturalized in the garden, seeding itself spontaneously. It will provide a framework for the garden, and will prosper at the foot of flowering shrubs such as mock orange, lilac and hydrangeas.

— *L. × haageana* is a small hybrid. Its poppy-red flowers are borne on purple-tinted foliage – a combination that not all gardeners find pleasing! *L. × arkwrightii* is even more virulent, if that is possible.

Height: 20–120 cm (8–48 in).
Spacing and planting distance: 20–30 cm (8–12 in).
Soil: chalky, well-drained.
Aspect: sun.
Propagation: from seed in spring or by division.
Flowering season: spring to autumn.
Type: perennial.

△ *Lysichiton americanus*

Lysichiton

LYSICHITON, YELLOW SKUNK CABBAGE

Araceae

It is impossible not to be impressed by the giant arum-like yellow flowers of *Lysichiton americanus*. They appear at the beginning of spring, adding a touch of fantasy by the water's edge where this plant flourishes. Nevertheless, it has to be admitted that its leaves, rather like those of white beet, are not of the most attractive.

Useful hints

— Lysichitons prefer full sun but will tolerate semi-shade.

— These hardy plants will only grow in moist soil. Plant at the water's edge, by the side of a stream or pond. Avoid planting large numbers close to the house, as their flowers give off a slightly unpleasant scent.

— You can sow the many seeds that appear, preferably as soon as they ripen, by simply scattering them about. It will naturalize itself in time. Divide clumps in early autumn.

Recommended

— *L. camtschatcensis* is slightly smaller than *L. americanus* and produces large white spathes.

Height: 100 cm (40 in).
Spacing and planting distance: 60 cm (24 in).
Soil: very moist throughout the year.
Aspect: sun.
Propagation: from seed or by division in early autumn.
Flowering season: spring.
Type: perennial.

167

Lysimachia

LOOSESTRIFE

Primulaceae

Lysimachias are the maids-of-all-work of the garden. Capable of flourishing in moist as well as dry locations, in full sun or in partial shade, less than a finger's

△ *Lysimachia clethroïdes*
▽ *Lysimachia nummularia*

▽ *Lysimachia punctata*

height or growing to 100 cm (40 in), these plants will give you no problems, as they are hardiness incarnate.

Useful hints

— Plant at any time in the season, providing them with deep soil as they have powerful roots. They prefer the cool, but they will be quite happy in soil that is slightly dry in summer. They will simply not grow quite as tall.

— Divide clumps when they begin to flower less abundantly, approximately every three years. By taking action as soon as flowering is over, you will gain a year and the plants will again be attractive the following summer.

— Combine with other flowers that like moist corners of the garden, such as purple loosestrife, marsh mallows, meadowsweet or hostas.

Recommended

— The most curious of the lysimachias is, without question, *Lysimachia clethroïdes*. Its white flower heads bend over, like huge commas. The autumn foliage colours are glorious.

— *L. ephemerum* bears its white spikes above delicate grey-green foliage. In spite of its name, its flowers last for many weeks.

— A dwarf in comparison with the previous varieties, *L. nummularia* forms a very dense carpet sprinkled with hundreds of bright yellow flowers in early summer. Use as ground cover at the foot of conifers. The variety 'Aurea' has yellow-green foliage. It is superb in hanging baskets and containers.

— *L. punctata*, which is recognizable at the first glance, has whorls of yellow flowers in 15–20 cm (6–8 in) spikes. Extremely hardy, this variety will succeed in all types of soil and is even resistant to damage caused by dogs.

— *L. ciliata* makes spectacular though rather unruly clumps. Its leaves, chocolate-coloured in spring, are ablaze with yellow and orange in the autumn.

— *L. barystachys*, with its long slender spikes of tiny white flowers, has a much more restrained habit.

Height: 5–100 cm (2–40 in).
Spacing and planting distance: 30 cm (12 in).
Soil: ordinary, preferably cool.
Aspect: sun or semi-shade.
Propagation: From seed or by division in autumn.
Flowering season: summer.
Type: perennial.

△ *Lythrum salicaria*

Lythrum

PURPLE LOOSESTRIFE

Lythraceae

Lythrum salicaria is a familiar plant, growing in the wild in damp ditches which it populates in the company of golden lysimachia and marsh mallow. Sadly, its pretty rose-red spikes do not last long, but it is an ideal plant for growing in a corner of the garden near a pond or ditch. Alongside rodgersias, macleayas and filipendulas it makes a wonderful show.

Useful hints

— Plant in 20 cm (8 in) deep, wide holes in cool soil treated with compost, in a moist position.

— Divide any overgrown plants every three years.

Recommended

— *L. salicaria* 'Firecandle' has rose-red flowers. *L. virgatum* 'The Rocket' has similar colouring.

Height: 100 cm (40 in).
Spacing and planting distance: 30 cm (12 in).
Soil: moist, ordinary.
Aspect: sun.
Propagation: by division in spring or autumn.
Flowering season: summer to autumn.
Type: perennial.

△ *Macleaya cordata*

Macleaya microcarpa ▷

Macleaya

PLUME POPPY

Papaveraceae

This plant's time of glory was around the year 1900! Nevertheless, it provides an attractive means of decorating wilder corners of the garden, with its tall silhouette and its magnificent white or unusual pink spikes throughout the summer. Like ferns and purple loosestrifes, it likes cool soil. Plant as an accompaniment to rodgersias, gunneras or heracleums and your garden will quickly become spectacular.

Useful hints

— Plant in early spring or autumn, in holes 20–30 cm (8–12 in) wide, filled with well-rotted manure.

— Always plant in deep, cool soil.

— Allow plants to fill out for three years before dividing.

Recommended

— The best-known is *Macleaya cordata* (syn. *Bocconia cordata*), a giant plant with a pinkish white flower.

Height: 150–250 cm (60–100 in).
Spacing and planting distance: 100 cm (40 in).
Soil: ordinary, deep.
Aspect: sun.
Propagation: by division in spring.
Flowering season: summer.
Type: perennial.

△ Malope trifida
▽ Malcolmia maritima

Malcolmia

VIRGINIAN STOCK, VIRGINIA STOCK, MALCOLM STOCK

Cruciferae

In years when there has not been time to sow any annuals in spring, remember *Malcolmia maritima*. Sown in late spring or early summer, it will flower reliably in less than two months. Its flowers

will not last as long as a succession of annuals, but they are more attractive than bare soil. Mix Virginian stocks with clarkias and annual alyssums to give fresh looking borders.

Useful hints

— Sow seeds directly in the flowering site, in crumbled soil enriched with compost. Cover with a mixture of sand and compost. Water every two days. As soon as the seedlings are established, thin the plants out so that they are spaced 20 cm (8 in) apart.

— Mulch the soil with peat. As soon as the main crop of flowers is over, cut the plants back with scissors to encourage a second show. If this is long in coming, resow without waiting.

Height: 20 cm (8 in).
Spacing and planting distance: 20 cm (8 in).
Soil: ordinary.
Aspect: sun.
Propagation: from seed in spring or summer.
Flowering season: 2 months after sowing.
Type: annual.

Malope

MALOPE

Malvaceae

Taller than lavatera, *Malope trifida* provides excellent flowers for summer flower beds. Each clump forms a little shrub that flowers for more than two months. Their rose-purple colouring goes well with white or flesh-coloured old roses. Try them combined with large white antirrhinums, too, or simple marguerites.

Useful hints

— Sow in mid-spring in a cold frame, or in late spring directly in the flowering site. Thin out to a spacing of 30 cm (12 in). Water abundantly during the initial stages and until they flower. Do not over-fertilize, as this often causes excessive foliage development.

— When flowering is over, you can try extending the season by cutting back the dead flower stalks to prevent fruits from forming. Sadly, malope often dies suddenly from a disease caused by a fungus that attacks the stem.

Height: 100 cm (40 in).
Spacing and planting distance: 30 cm (12 in).
Soil: ordinary, not too rich.
Aspect: sun.
Propagation: from seed in spring.
Flowering season: summer to autumn.
Type: annual.

△ Malva moschata

Malva

MALLOW, MUSK MALLOW

Malvaceae

Those who live in the country are bound to have found mallow (*Malva moschata*) flourishing in the wild. It often grows in sunny meadows with clay soil, and is sometimes even found in road gravel. It is an ideal companion to echiums, poppies, corn poppies, helianthemums – to all flowers, in fact, with a predilection for sunny soils.

Useful hints

— You can either sow the seeds (which are greyish brown and are contained in pretty hexagonal plump pillows), plant divided clumps, or take cuttings.

— Seeds can be easily sown in a nursery bed in late spring, but the plants will not then flower until the next spring, so it is quicker to divide the roots.

Recommended

In addition to the mauve-pink type, there is also a white variety, 'Alba', which is extremely graceful but less robust.

— *M. alcea* var. *fastigiata* is more vigorous, with silky pink flowers.

— *M. sylvestris* has reddish purple or blue flowers marked with darker stripes.

— *M. sylvestris* 'Zebrina' is a splendid variety of the above, with striking flowers, pale lilac marked with purple stripes. Height 100–120 cm (40–48 in).

Height: 40–120 cm (16–48 in).
Spacing and planting distance: 30 cm (12 in).
Soil: ordinary.
Aspect: sun.
Propagation: from seed or by division in spring.
Flowering season: summer to autumn.
Type: perennial.

Matthiola incana △

Matteucia

OSTRICH FERN

Woodsiaccae

This could be confused with the male fern, but the fronds of *Matteucia struthiopteris* are of a more delicate texture that catches the light and makes the fronds take on a golden hue. Their tips are attractively curled, like ostrich feathers. They go well with lysimachias, helxines and aquilegias, wherever the garden soil is rich in humus and light, even if it sees little sun.

△ *Matteucia struthiopteris*

Useful hints

— Plant in spring, in well-dug soil, in a semi-shaded position. These ferns dislike full sun, which burns their fronds.

— Space the plants 100 cm (40 in) apart. They need space to develop. Remove faded fronds regularly.

Height: 70 cm (28 in).
Spacing and planting distance: 100 cm (40 in).
Soil: fresh, rich in humus.
Aspect: semi-shade.
Propagation: by division in spring.
Type: perennial.

Matthiola

STOCK, GILLYFLOWER

Cruciferae

Anyone who has not, at least once in his life, smelled a bunch of these stocks could never imagine their powerful, sweet and pleasant fragrance, with a touch of the carnation about it. In the garden, this rather upright plant serves to provide the home with cut flowers.

Useful hints

— Sow in mid-spring in a cold frame, or in late spring directly in rows in the kitchen garden. Cover the seeds with 1 cm (½ in) of sand. Water regularly to prevent attack by insects.

— Certain species may flower earlier, provided that they are sheltered in a greenhouse. They should be sown in summer to flower in early spring.

Recommended

— Stocks in general grow to little more that 30 cm (12 in) but the Ten-week Excelsior stock will grow to more than 120 cm (48 in). It often produces only one stem. The Beauty of Nice stock flowers early in spring and can be forced in a greenhouse. The Ten-week Dwarf large-flowering stocks are compact and are the best for flower beds.

Height: 30–120 cm (12–48 in).
Spacing and planting distance: 20 cm (8 in).
Soil: rather rich and well-drained, with a tendency towards chalkiness.
Aspect: sun.
Propagation: from seed in spring and summer.
Flowering season: spring to autumn, depending when sown.
Type: annual, biennial.

△ *Maurandya scandens*
(syn. *Asarina lophospermum*)
Maurandya erubescens
(syn. *Asarina erubescens*) △

Maurandya (syn. *Asarina*)

MAURANDIA

Scrophulariaceae

It is surprising that maurandya seed is so seldom available when it is one of the most decorative climbing perennials of all. With their splayed, trumpet-shaped, velvet-coated flowers, they are well worth sowing early, in the warm, to be enjoyed all summer through. They are ideal for covering south-facing trellises, not to mention verandahs, which they will turn into a true paradise.

Useful hints

— Sow in the warm, like tomatoes, in spring. Transfer the seedlings into pots, then plant out as soon as all risk of frost is over. Water regularly and apply liquid fertilizer every month.

— Harvest the seeds at the end of the summer so that you always have some available. If you distribute them among your friends and acquaintances, you will make a number of people very happy.

Height: up to 300 cm (120 in).
Spacing and planting distance: 100 cm (40 in).
Soil: rich and cool in summer.
Aspect: full sun.
Propagation: from seed in spring.
Flowering season: summer to autumn.
Type: perennial

Meconopsis

HIMALAYAN POPPY, WELSH POPPY

Papaveraceae

Getting the beautiful blue-flowered species of meconopsis to grow successfully is no easy matter, but the effort is worthwhile when their sky-blue petals begin to unfurl. The yellow and orange *Meconopsis cambrica* is easy to grow.

Useful hints

— Plant in early autumn to give time for their roots to become established before the cold weather. Cover with a cloche to protect from excessive moisture in winter. Treat with slug bait. In spring, fork pine bark or peat into the soil and water regularly.

— Most varieties will die after flowering if flowering has been abundant. As a precautionary measure, prevent one of the stalks from flowering by cutting off the flower stem. Collect the seeds from the others and sow them around the site generally and in a seed tray, which you should expose to the cold in winter. They will begin to sprout the next spring, and the plants will flower a year later.

Recommended

— While still the best-known, *M. betonicifolia* is not the easiest to grow. *M. grandis* is preferable, its flowers being better arranged and of an even more exceptional blue. It is also less likely to die after a year.

— *M. cambrica*, the Welsh poppy, is more like a yellow celandine than its large azure brothers. It often seeds itself spontaneously, and will rapidly colonize all shady areas. This pleasant little pest is in flower virtually all year. There are double and orange-flowered varieties, but the species itself is extremely pretty.

— *M. napaulensis*, a native of Nepal, is grown more for its foliage than for its curious plum-coloured flowers. It develops a rosette of leaves in the first year, then puts out its spike of flowers in late spring. Its hairy leaves, retaining drop-lets of water like pearls of mercury, are exquisitely beautiful.

Height: 30–180 cm (12–72 in).
Spacing and planting distance: 30 cm (12 in).
Soil: acid (leaf-mould and sandy peat).
Aspect: semi-shade.
Propagation: from seed in autumn.
Flowering season: late spring to autumn.
Type: biennial, perennial.

Meconopsis grandis △
Meconopsis × *sheldonii* ▷
Meconopsis betonicifolia ▷
Meconopsis cambrica ▽

Mentzelia

BLAZING STAR

Loasaceae

Originally from America, this plant makes an attractive effect in borders. The flowers have a delightful fragrance.

Useful hints

— Sow *Mentzelia lindleyi* in its flowering location in spring. Sow *M. laevicaulis* at the same time, but in a greenhouse, to be transplanted the following spring.

Recommended

M. lindleyi (syn. *Bartonia aurea*), an annual, has yellow flowers from early to late summer. *M. laevicaulis*, a perennial, has yellow flowers from early to mid-summer.

Height: 40 cm (16 in).
Spacing and planting distance: 20 cm (8 in).
Soil: ordinary.
Aspect: sun.
Propagation: from seed in spring.
Flowering season: summer.
Type: annual, perennial.

▽ *Mentzelia lindleyi*

Mertensia virginica △

Mertensia

VIRGINIAN COWSLIP, VIRGINIA BLUEBELLS, LUNGWORT

Boraginaceae

This North American beauty charms us with both its glaucous luxuriant foliage and its flowers, of a heavenly blue, in gently curving clusters. The two colours, in perfect harmony, are evocative of the cool locations that are the plant's preferred habitat. Combine it with later-flowering plants such as asters, as its foliage dies back from mid-summer onwards leaving nothing but a large, carrot-shaped root, which should under no circumstances be damaged by careless hoeing.

Useful hints

— Plant *Mertensia virginica* in early autumn or very early spring, in well-prepared soil that has been dug over to a good depth and enriched with organic matter (leaf-mould and peat).

— Do not allow the plant to dry out prematurely in spring, and water if the soil is dry. In early spring, treat with 5 cm (2 in) broken pine bark.

Height: 30–50 cm (12–20 in).
Spacing and planting distance: 30 cm (12 in).
Soil: rich in humus.
Aspect: semi-shade.
Propagation: by division in autumn or spring.
Flowering season: spring.
Type: perennial.

173

Mesembryanthemum

(syn. *Dorotheanthus*)

LIVINGSTONE DAISY, ICE PLANT

Aizoaceae

In the 1960s, *Mesembryanthemum crini-florum* (syn. *Dorotheanthus bellidiformis*) was to be found in every garden. Since then it has inexplicably gone out of fashion, even though, delightful and easy to grow, it tirelessly provides us with star-shaped flowers in the very brightest colours from summer to autumn: dazzling pinks and oranges, dark reds and white, often surrounded with a halo of a paler colour.

Useful hints

— Sow in mid-spring under cover in trays filled with compost, and transplant after the frosts are over into their flowering site, in full sun.

— Water well each evening in summer.

— You can also sow them directly *in situ* if the soil is good and the position sunny: these plants will often seed themselves spontaneously.

Height: 15 cm (6 in).
Spacing and planting distance: 20 cm (8 in).
Soil: ordinary.
Aspect: full sun.
Propagation: from seed in spring.
Flowering season: summer to autumn.
Type: annual.

Mimulus cardinalis △ ▷

Mimulus

MONKEY FLOWER, MUSK

Scrophulariaceae

Mimulus, which especially likes damp corners, is to be found in extremely bright colours, with particularly unusual spotted patterns. If the slugs in your garden spare them, they will provide you with some charming flower borders.

Useful hints

— Plant hardy mimulus in spring, in humus-rich soil that remains cool even in summer.

— Annual mimulus should be sown in spring and thinned after a month. They generally produce a spectacular show of flowers and then die. Combine them with marigolds or dwarf china asters to prolong their effect.

— Treat regularly with slug bait or surround with a ring of wood ash, which should be replaced from time to time.

◁ *Mesembryanthemum*

Recommended

— Of the perennial mimulus, *Mimulus cardinalis* has an unusual fragrance and flowers for almost three months in a purple-red shade. It will tolerate relatively dry soil.

— Of the annual varieties, the most remarkable are 'Calypso', with flowers in widely varying colours, and 'Malibu' in a velvety warm orange, almost unequalled in the plant world.

— Once established, *M. luteus* seeds itself from one year to the next.

— *M. ringens*, a perennial with small violet-blue flowers, grows well around a pond.

Height: 30 cm (12 in).
Spacing and planting distance: 20 cm (8 in).
Soil: cool in summer (enrich with peat).
Aspect: sun.
Propagation: from seed in spring.
Flowering season: summer to autumn.
Type: annual, perennial.

Minuartia

SANDWORT

Caryophyllaceae

If you are looking for a robust carpeting plant to cover the bare corners of your rock garden here you have a rare pearl: a single root of *Minuartia laricifolia* will produce a respectable-sized mat in a matter of a few months. It is covered in tiny white flowers that succeed one another in waves for two months at the end of the summer. Combine with spring bulbs, crocuses or botanical tulips.

Useful hints

— Plant early in autumn or spring, in a pocket of loose soil improved with sand.

— Divide clumps every three years and replant immediately. The best time for this is just after flowering, provided that you water regularly, but it can also be carried out in spring.

Height: 10 cm (4 in).
Spacing and planting distance: 30 cm (12 in).
Soil: ordinary, rather light.
Aspect: sun.
Propagation: by division in spring or summer.
Flowering season: spring to summer.
Type: perennial.

Mirabilis

MARVEL OF PERU, FOUR O'CLOCK PLANT, UMBRELLAWORT

Nyctaginaceae

The large black seeds of the marvel of Peru or four o'clock plant grow into vigorous plants giving bushes 100 cm

Mirabilis jalapa △

(40 in) in height that are soon covered in flared, trumpet-shaped flowers. You need to wait until the late afternoon to see them open – hence their common name. And what a sweet fragrance! Make a little space for them at the foot of an east-facing wall and you will spend a large part of the summer season captivated by their charm.

Useful hints

— Soak the seeds of *Mirabilis jalapa* overnight before sowing. They will come up quickly if sown under glass. Otherwise wait till after the frosts are over, and sow directly in the flowering site.

— Water regularly and treat with dilute fertilizer once every three weeks, as this is an extremely voracious plant.

— If you are particularly fond of a given colour, lift the tuberous roots in autumn, in the same way as dahlias, and store in the cellar in a little peat. You can then plant them out in their flowering sites in spring.

Height: 100 cm (40 in).
Spacing and planting distance: 60 cm (24 in).
Soil: rich, remaining cool.
Aspect: east and south-east facing.
Propagation: from seed in spring.
Flowering season: summer to autumn.
Type: perennial.

◁ *Minuartia stellata*

Miscanthus

EULALIA, ZEBRA GRASS

Gramineae

This is a grass that should please the lazy gardener: once it is planted, all you have to do is watch it grow taller and fill out, rustle in the wind and bend in the rain. A plant to accompany bamboo or ferns.

Useful hints

— Sow under cover in mid-spring in trays of compost. Transplant in late spring into garden soil.

— You can also buy plants in pots and plant them out in autumn or spring.

Recommended

Some varieties of *Miscanthus sinensis*, such as 'Zebrinus', have cream-coloured stripes, while others, such as 'Gracillimus', have silvery grey foliage.

— For a screen, it would be difficult to better *M. floridulus*. It grows to 300 cm (120 in) in height.

— *M. sacchariflorus* has a tendency to spread, but its dense, silvery plumes more than make up for this minor vice.

— *M. sinensis*. 'Silberfeder' is the only variety to flourish in all conditions, except in very hot summers. 'Variegatus', which grows to only moderate size, is better suited to the smaller garden.

Height: 60–300 cm (24–120 in).
Spacing and planting distance: 40–60 cm (16–24 in).
Soil: ordinary.
Aspect: sun.
Propagation: by division in spring.
Type: perennial.

▽ **Miscanthus sinensis 'Zebrinus'**

Moluccella laevis △

Moluccella

BELLS OF IRELAND, SHELLFLOWER

Labiatae

Bells of Ireland are often found in dried flower arrangements. The decorative part is the pale green calyx in the form of a shell that surrounds the flower. Grown in rows in the kitchen garden or close together in a separate bed, they can be quite impressive.

Useful hints

— Raising seeds of *Moluccella laevis* can sometimes be a laborious task, particularly if the seeds are past their best. Sow in a cold frame in mid-spring and plant out after the frosts are over, spaced 20 cm (8 in) apart.

— Pick the stems after flowering, at the end of the summer, and dry them, heads down, for three months.

Height: 60 cm (24 in).
Spacing and planting distance: 20 cm (8 in).
Soil: ordinary.
Aspect: sun.
Propagation: from seed in spring.
Flowering season: summer.
Type: annual.

Monarda

BERGAMOT, HORSEMINT, BEE-BALM, OSWEGO TEA

Labiatae

Every part of *Monarda didyma* is aromatic, from its roots to its flowers and the leaves, which give off a strong smell of thyme when crushed. These are excellent plants for flower beds, provided the soil is good and moist in summer, as their leaves transpire a great deal.

Useful hints

— Plant in autumn or spring in well-prepared soil, dug to depth, and improved with peat and leaf-mould. From late spring, mulch with grass cuttings or semi-decomposed compost.

— To propagate, divide clumps in autumn. Monarda soon becomes invasive as it sends out rhizomes in all directions. Combine with polygonums and decorative dahlias with large purple flowers.

Recommended

— There is a whole range of colours to choose from: 'Alba', white; 'Blue Stocking', violet; 'Croftway Pink', pale pink and the most frequently grown; 'Mahogany', bright red, or 'Prairie Night', rich violet.

— The large red flowers of the annual *M. citriodora* are without rival.

— If your soil is not sufficiently moist, try *M. fistulosa*, which will tolerate drier conditions.

Height: 60–120 cm (24–48 in).
Spacing and planting distance: 40 cm (16 in).
Soil: rich, remaining cool in summer.
Aspect: open, but not fierce in sun.
Propagation: by division in autumn.
Flowering season: summer to autumn.
Type: perennial.

Morina longifolia △
◁ *Moraea tricuspidata*

Montbretia

see *Crocosmia*

Moraea

MORAEA, BUTTERFLY IRIS

Iridaceae

Still extremely rare, moraeas are among the jewels of the rich flora of Southern Africa. Although the flowers are only short-lived, like the tigridia, new flowers appear every day. If you look at them closely, you will be unable to resist the charm of their exceptionally fine colours, arranged in rings that appear to have been painted by the most inspired Japanese artist. While the bulbs are still very rare, it is possible to get hold of seeds if you are a member of one of the collectors' associations, or even to order

◁ *Monarda* 'Cambridge Scarlet'

them direct from South Africa, where some nurseries specialize in these remarkable plants.

Useful hints

— Bury the bulbs at a depth of 5 cm (2 in) in soil that is both rich in humus and lightened by mixing with fine gravel. Moraeas will not withstand a normal winter in cool climates, and must be put into pots in a cold frame or greenhouse in winter.

— Stake the stems discreetly to prevent the bulbs from being exposed. Stop watering when the foliage withers of its own accord and allow to rest for several months, until the following spring.

Height: 30–40 cm (12–16 in).
Spacing and planting distance: 10 cm (4 in).
Soil: rich in humus and very well-drained.
Aspect: sun.
Propagation: by separating new bulbs after the foliage has withered.
Flowering season: early summer.
Type: corm.

Morina

WHORLFLOWER

Morinaceae

Morina longifolia could be mistaken for a thistle, but when it comes into flower in the mixed border it will not fail to charm with its trumpet-shaped white and pink flowers. As for the thorns on the leaves, they are not particularly vicious. An excellent plant for gardens with stony soil, with an extremely pleasing silhouette.

Useful hints

— Plant in autumn and cover with a cloche to avoid excessive damp in winter. It is perfectly hardy, but dislikes rot.

— Mulch the soil in early summer, and water generously. The foliage will generally dry out over the summer, partially re-growing again in autumn. You can hide it with marigolds, annual gypsophila or asters.

Height: 70–80 cm (28–32 in).
Spacing and planting distance: 30 cm (12 in).
Soil: rich and well-drained (improved with sand).
Aspect: sun.
Propagation: from seed or by division in spring.
Flowering season: summer.
Type: perennial.

Muehlenbeckia

MUEHLENBECKIA, WIREVINE

Polygonaceae

It is difficult to know how to classify this curious plant – as a climber, or as ground cover. It forms a network of fine stems bearing tiny leathery leaves. If given a trellis, it will act as a climber, otherwise it will trail along the ground, covering everything. Not truly hardy, *Muehlenbeckia complexa* should be grown only in milder climates.

Useful hints

— Plant in spring, in soil enriched with leaf-mould. Water regularly over the first summer, and remove weeds. In subsequent years, it will form such a dense mat that weeding will not be necessary.

— Multiply by dividing clumps of rooted leaves at the ends of the mat in spring.

Height: 10–15 cm (4–6 in).
Spacing and planting distance: 30 cm (12 in).
Soil: rich in humus.
Aspect: sun or semi-shade.
Propagation: by division in spring.
Flowering season: summer.
Type: perennial.

▽ *Muehlenbeckia complexa*

Muscari

GRAPE HYACINTH

Liliaceae

Grape hyacinths are rarely used very successfully. They are at their best in dense masses. Create a blue sea at the foot of bushes, and intersperse with daffodils and wood anemones, or with pink and white tulips, to produce an attractive effect in spring.

Useful hints

— Plant in autumn, burying to a depth of 10 cm (4 in). Arrange in groups of at least twenty, planting them slightly more densely at the centre than at the edges.

— You can also plant them in pots combined with forget-me-nots, *Silene pendula* or wallflowers.

Recommended

— The best-known of the blue grape hyacinths is *Muscari armeniacum*, which naturalizes itself spontaneously, but *M. latifolium* and particularly *M. tubergenianum*, in a very bright blue, are worthy of attention too.

— The little-known yellow-flowered grape hyacinths offer opaline hues: *M. muscarimi* is the prototype, though its flowers are tipped with purple at the top of the spike.

— Quite different from those above, *M. comosum* 'Plumosum' has tufted flowers of a violet-blue. It is also nicknamed the 'feather hyacinth'.

Height: 10–30 cm (4–12 in).
Spacing and planting distance: 5–10 cm (2–4 in).
Soil: ordinary.
Aspect: sun.
Propagation: by separating bulbils after the foliage has withered.
Flowering season: spring.
Type: bulb.

△ *Muscari tubergenianum*
▽ *Muscari armeniacum*

△ *Myosotis sylvatica* 'Ultramarine'

Myosotis

FORGET-ME-NOT, SCORPION GRASS

Boraginaceae

Myosotis sylvatica needs to be planted in the garden only once for its flowers to be enjoyed regularly afterwards, as it seeds itself quite readily. The lovely azure-blue of its flowers is thrilling. It colonizes cool areas, indicating its preference.

Useful hints

— Sow in summer, and plant out into the flowering site in autumn. Keep some in a cold frame in reserve, as it is quite common for rot to kill off some of the plants.

— Combine your forget-me-nots with small-flowered botanical narcissi or lilies and in general with relatively tall plants that will have no difficulty in breaking through the carpet of myosotis.

Recommended

— Many people prefer the dark blue dwarf varieties such as 'Ultramarine', even though this colour tends to jar in spring. Instead, choose the classic myosotis of the Alps with its indigo-blue that you will never tire of, or the variety 'Victoria', which forms very regular cushions that flower for a number of weeks.

— *M. scorpioïdes*, a marshland member of the forget-me-not family, is more than happy to colonize any unoccupied patch of moist ground.

Height: 15–30 cm (6–12 in).
Spacing and planting distance: 15 cm (6 in).
Soil: ordinary, rather light and rich in humus.
Aspect: sun or semi-shade.
Propagation: from seed in summer.
Flowering season: spring.
Type: annual, biennial, perennial.

179

△ *Myrrhis odorata*

Myrrhis

MYRRH, SWEET CICELY

Umbelliferae

Everything about *Myrrhis odorata* is beautiful: its foliage, which is cut like that of ferns, its milky white flowers, similar to those of the wild carrot, and even its elongated fruits, which look like our grandmothers' combs. Add the aniseed fragrance of its foliage and an unbelievable ability to flourish in dark corners, and you have a picture of a highly useful plant. Myrrhis goes well with ferns, foxgloves and peonies.

Useful hints

— Plant in any season in soil that has been dug to depth, as it produces very powerful roots. Water regularly until it flowers. The foliage often tends to dry out afterwards. Cut down to soil level and water from late summer to obtain a further show of leaves.

— Myrrhis will often seed itself. Leave the seedlings to become established, then transplant to their permanent position in autumn.

Height: 100 cm (40 in).
Spacing and planting distance: 30 cm (12 in).
Soil: rich in humus.
Aspect: shade.
Propagation: from seed in spring.
Flowering season: summer.
Type: perennial.

Narcissus

NARCISSUS, DAFFODIL

Amaryllidaceae

There is such a wide range of varieties of narcissus that you can enjoy them for three months in spring without tiring of them for an instant. They become naturalized quite easily, yellow or white, and often give off a gentle perfume. Best grown in large clumps.

Useful hints

— Plant in autumn, leaving time for their roots to develop before the hard frosts.

— Do not cut back the leaves until they have dried out. To prevent your lawn from looking untidy while you wait for this to happen, plant narcissi in groups of twenty, separated by paths that you can mow. In summer, once the leaves have dried out, mow and treat with a little nitrogen fertilizer to restore the grass to an attractive colour.

— Also use dwarf narcissi in pots, which you should keep in a cold frame to speed up the production of their fragrant flowers. Combine them with forget-me-nots or other bulbs, such as scillas.

Recommended

— The best-known are the **trumpet** narcissi. 'Golden Harvest', golden yellow; 'King Alfred', slightly later flowering; 'Mount Hood', white, and 'Mrs R. O. Backhouse', creamy white and apricot-pink, are always effective.

— The **large cup** narcissi are easily recognizable, as they have darker centres. This applies to 'Carlton', yellow and primrose-yellow; 'Flower Record', white and yellow edged with orange; 'Ice Follies', white and ivory; 'Professor Einstein', pale yellow and orange-yellow; and 'Scarlet Elegance', golden yellow and scarlet.

— The **double-flowered** narcissi are a little heavier and are suitable only for elaborate flower beds: 'Texas', an orange-yellow, is the most famous, with 'Mary Copeland', pure white with an orange centre.

— The **small cup** narcissi are marvellous in lawns. The Triandrus narcissi bear two to six pendent flowers on 20 cm (8 in) stems. They are delightful in rock gardens: 'April Tears', yellow, and 'Liberty Bells', pale yellow, are our favourites. Cyclamineus narcissi are little gems in pots. You will be enchanted by 'February Gold', 'Peeping Tom' and 'Tête à Tête', in different yellows.

Narcissus tazetta △
Narcissus hybrids ▷
Narcissus 'Actaea' ▽

△ *Narcissus bulbocodium*

N. jonquilla gives off a delicious fragrance: this also applies to the hybrid 'Trevithian', a pale lemon colour. Excellent cut flowers, Tazetta narcissi tend to be later flowering. 'Geranium' and 'Scarlet Gem' will delight you in spring. The poet's narcissus (*N. poeticus*) is the most fragrant of all. 'Actaea', white and orange edged with red, is delightful.

— We must not forget the **botanical species**, which have succeeded in retaining the charm of wild plants and are very easily naturalized in rock gardens: *N. bulbocodium* (its flowers reduced to a single, widely flared trumpet), *N. tazetta* 'Canaliculatus', *N. juncifolius* and *N. pseudo-narcissus*, the very simple wild daffodil, are among the most attractive.

Height: 15–40 cm (6–16 in).
Spacing and planting distance: 5–15 cm (2–6 in).
Soil: ordinary, rather heavy.
Aspect: sun or semi-shade.
Propagation: by separating new bulbs at the end of summer.
Flowering season: spring.
Type: bulb.

Nelumbo nucifera △

Nelumbo

LOTUS

Nelumbonaceae

For adding an exotic touch to an ordinary duck pond, this is the right plant: the sacred lotus of the Egyptians, *Nelumbo nucifera*. Much hardier than you might think, it produces sumptuous round leaves, quickly covering the entire area available. The flowers slip between them and open in the sun, in pink-tinted white hues that should be contemplated from close at hand. The fruit, too, is quite amazing, punctured with large holes like the rose of a watering can.

Useful hints

— Plant in spring when the water has warmed up a little, in pots of soil enriched with well-rotted manure.

— In cooler climates in winter, remove the rhizomes and protect them in damp sand, in a room that is unheated but above freezing point.

Height: 20–100 cm (8–40 in) depending on the depth of water.
Spacing and planting distance: 200 cm (80 in).
Soil: rich and clay.
Aspect: full sun.
Propagation: by division in spring.
Flowering season: summer.
Type: perennial.

Nemesia

NEMESIA

Scrophulariaceae

The gaiety of their colours is a wonder to behold in the garden, yet nemesias are rarely seen, perhaps because of their relatively short flowering period – three to four weeks. This is an injustice to be remedied, since there are few flowers that offer such innocent freshness in summer. They are as happy in containers as in flower beds.

Useful hints:

— Sow seeds of *Nemesia strumosa* varieties in mid-spring, spacing them several centimetres apart, in an earthenware pot or the corner of a cold frame.

— Transplant the plants after a month, directly to their flowering site if the weather is fine. Pinch out at a height of 10 cm (4 in) to force them to branch.

— Water abundantly when in flower and cut the stems back afterwards, to the level of the leaves. You will then have a further show of flowers three weeks later.

Recommended

The seed stockists offer only a limited number of varieties. The most common is 'Carnival', which reaches a height of 40 cm (16 in) and provides all colours from the palest yellow to pink, through warm browns and velvety oranges.

Height: 20–40 cm (8–16 in).
Spacing and planting distance: 15–30 cm (6–12 in).
Soil: quite rich and light.
Aspect: semi-shade, to prevent the colours from fading in the sun.
Propagation: from seed in spring.
Flowering season: 1 month, at any time between late spring and the first frost.
Type: annual.

▽ *Nemophila menziesii*

▽ *Nemesia strumosa* **variety**

Nemophila

BABY BLUE EYES, FIVE-SPOT

Hydrophyllaceae

This flower's nickname of 'baby blue eyes' derives from the delicate pale blue of *Nemophila menziesii*. While flowering rarely lasts for more than a month, the flowers are borne in abundance. *N. maculata*, which is white, has violet-spotted petals.

Useful hints

— Sow in spring in a cold frame and transplant after a month, or sow directly in the flowering site in autumn. Young plants over-winter well. Thin out the seeds, leaving one plant every 20 cm (8 in).

— When flowering is over, pull up the plants and sow godetias or marigolds which will have time to flower in autumn. Nemophila is particularly attractive when combined with limnanthes.

Height: 20 cm (8 in).
Spacing and planting distance: 20 cm (8 in).
Soil: ordinary.
Aspect: sun or semi-shade.
Propagation: from seed in spring or autumn.
Flowering season: spring to summer.
Type: annual

▷ *Nepeta* (in the centre, *Stachys macrantha*)
▽ *Nemophila maculata*

Nepeta

CATMINT, CATNIP

Labiatae

The gentle blue of *Nepeta × faassenii* reaches its peak in mid-summer, softening the mass of yellow and orange flowers blooming at the time. They are incomparable at the edge of rose beds, hiding the base of the rose, which is often quite ugly.

Useful hints

— Provide them with soil that is not too rich and is well-drained in winter. Plant preferably in spring, so the plants are well-developed before the cold weather.

— Cut back the clumps at the end of the winter to keep them compact. Cats will often sleep on them, as they love the smell of the foliage, hence the nickname of catmint.

Recommended

— The most common is the former *N. mussinii*, nowadays known as *N. × faassenii*. The hybrid 'Six Hills Giant' is the most remarkable, as its blue is brighter and it is less likely to be beaten down by rain. *N. sibirica* 'Souvenir d'André Chaudron' is the tallest. Though flowering more abundantly, it is less hardy than the species.

— *N. govaniana* differs from most nepetas in that it likes damp places and has yellow flowers. It grows to 90 cm (36 in).

— More mat-forming, *N. racemosa* has green leaves and bears violet-blue flowers of a darker hue.

— *N. nervosa* forms stable upright clumps, crowned with brilliant dark blue spikes.

Height: 20–90 cm (8–36 in).
Spacing and planting distance: 30 cm (12 in).
Soil: slightly dry.
Aspect: full sun.
Propagation: by division in spring.
Flowering season: summer to autumn.
Type: perennial.

Nerine bowdenii △

Nerine

NERINE, GUERNSEY LILY

Amaryllidaceae

These relatively uncommon flowers, grown from bulbs, charm us with their delicacy: a bright pink colour, a chiselled form of flower, an elegance of shape and outline, and ribbon-like foliage. *Nerine bowdenii*'s only fault is that it is less than reliably hardy, requiring a particularly well-protected location, and a covering of dead leaves in winter.

Useful hints

— Plant in spring, in soil enriched with sand at the foot of a south-facing wall. Foliage will appear during or just after flowering, in autumn. Allow the clumps to fill out and do not divide too frequently, as they dislike being disturbed and will take several years to flower again.

— To increase the decorative effect, plant in groups (minimum of ten) and combine with artemisias, white asters and pink Japanese anemones.

Height: 60 cm (24 in).
Spacing and planting distance: 15 cm (6 in).
Soil: ordinary, slightly sandy.
Aspect: sun, at the base of a wall, sheltered from cold winds.
Propagation: by separating new bulbs at the end of spring.
Flowering season: autumn.
Type: bulb.

Nicandra physaloides ▷

184

Nicandra

NICANDRA, APPLE OF PERU, SHOO-FLY

Solanaceae

Some plants are instantly evocative of other climes because of their form or their colours. Although *Nicandra physaloides* is by no means dazzling, it is immediately noticeable in flower beds. As the name of the species indicates, it is very similar to the physalis, commonly known as 'Chinese lantern'. Like physalis it forms a beautiful mass of leaves, but its flowers are more freely borne, in a pale blue. It then produces plum-like fruits contained in a calyx of very thin parchment. It is grown as an annual for its fruits, which are used in dried flower arrangements.

Useful hints

— Sow under cover in mid-spring and prick out once before transplanting into the final flowering location after the frosts are over. Water regularly, and apply dilute fertilizer to encourage plump fruits.

— Cut the stems in autumn and dry, heads down. You can then lie them on the soil in a location that gets no rain. The fungi in the soil will attack the cellulose and remove part of the calyx, leaving only the veins.

— If you find any minute white flies hovering around the plants, treat once or twice with a decamethrine-based insecticide.

Height: 80–100 cm (32–40 in).
Spacing and planting distance: 40 cm (16 in).
Soil: rich, well-watered.
Aspect: sun.
Propagation: from seed in spring.
Flowering season: summer.
Type: annual.

Nicotiana

TOBACCO PLANT

Solanaceae

There are few flowers that can claim to be as fragrant as those of the white tobacco plant. In the evening, it gives off a fragrance that is perceptible several metres away.

Useful hints

— Sow under cover in mid-spring and transplant once into pots before planting out into their flowering site after the frosts are over.

— Watch out for invasions of greenfly in summer. Water regularly and apply soluble fertilizer every month, as these are voracious plants. In mild climates, they will often become perennial.

Recommended

— *Nicotiana alata* bears white flowers and will readily exceed 100 cm (40 in) in height. The 'Lime Green' variety, with lime-green flowers, and Sensation Hybrids, in a variety of colours, are becoming increasingly popular and they are magnificent plants for slightly informal flower beds. The Nikki Hybrids are very small, and have no fragrance whatsoever.

Height: 30–200 cm (12–80 in).
Spacing and planting distance: 20–50 cm (8–20 in).
Soil: rich in humus and always cool in summer.
Aspect: semi-shade or non-burning sun.
Propagation: from seed in spring.
Flowering season: summer to first frosts.
Type: annual, biennial.

Nicotiana Nikki Hybrid ▽

Nicotiana sylvestris ▽

Nicotiana alata △
Nigella damascena ▷

Nigella

LOVE-IN-A-MIST, FENNEL FLOWER

Ranunculaceae

A familiar flower in country gardens, nigella will readily seed itself each year, spending winter in plantlet form. It is always delightful in the summer to see its fine parsley-like foliage and its flowers in the hues of old porcelain. Surrounded by a lacy collar, they well deserve their common name of love-in-a-mist.

Combine with late-flowering perennials such as hostas or *Sedum spectabile*. The dried fruits can be used in winter dried flower arrangements, as they are quite spectacular.

Useful hints

— Sow in spring directly in the flowering site, or in a cold frame. Thin out after a month to a spacing of 20 cm (8 in).

— Pinch back the main stems to half height after two months to encourage them to bush out.

Recommended

— The most common are the double-flowered *Nigella damascena* varieties, available in blue, pink or white, the latter being truly magnificent.

Height: 45–60 cm (18–24 in).
Spacing and planting distance: 20 cm (8 in).
Soil: ordinary, even relatively poor.
Aspect: sun or semi-shade.
Propagation: from seed in spring.
Flowering season: summer to autumn.
Type: annual

185

Nymphaea

WATER LILY, WATER NYMPH

Nymphaeaceae

Most people are familiar with the nymphaea, which makes such a spectacular display on lakes and ponds. Fewer people, however, are aware that there are many different varieties, some of which will flourish in very small amounts of water. This puts them in everyone's range, since there is nothing to stop you creating a mini-pond in an ordinary barrel, cut in half.

Useful hints

— Plant in spring, when the water has begun to warm up. Place the crown in a pot filled with heavy soil containing plenty of clay. The depth of planting under the water can be anywhere between 35 and 150 cm (14 and 60 in) or even more for the most vigorous varieties, which should be reserved for large pools.

— If the pond is sufficiently deep, the nymphaeas can be left in position over winter, with no protection. Otherwise keep them in wet sand in a cold room.

Recommended

— There are several hundred! Some of the most readily available are: 'Candidissima', pure white; 'Colonel A. J. Welch', yellow; 'Ellisiana', red, with orange stamens; 'James Brydon', double crimson-pink splashed with maroon; 'Madame Wilfron Gonnère', pure pink; 'Marliacea Carnea', pink, and 'Marliacea Chromatella', yellow; 'Paul Hariot', yellow and copper; 'Sioux', large-flowered copper; the crimson-red 'Froebelii', which will make do with just 20–40 cm (8–16 in) of water; 'Richardsonii', pure white and fragrant.

Height: 20–120 cm (8–48 in) below the water level.
Spacing and planting distance: 30–130 cm (12–50 in).
Soil: heavy and rich.
Aspect: sun.
Propagation: by division in spring.
Flowering season: summer to autumn.
Type: perennial.

◁ *Nymphaea 'Laydekeri Fulgens'*
▽ *Oenothera fruticosa*

Oenothera

EVENING PRIMROSE, SUNDROPS

Onagraceae

There are few perennials that offer such a sparkling yellow as the oenotheras. Their common name, evening primrose, comes from their customary habit of choosing the evening to open. Once their floral display is over, their foliage continues to delight with its interesting autumn tints. They are troubled by few diseases and even fewer insects and so are truly excellent plants for weekend gardeners.

Useful hints

— Plant preferably in spring in small groups of five or six scattered among other fuller plants. They will slip in between them with no need for staking.

— Divide clumps every three years, as they have a tendency to harden over a period of time and to flower less freely. Seeds are generally successful, but they will not come up until after the winter. Try sowing the dwarf varieties, which often die after flowering.

Recommended

— Dwarf oenotheras are wonderful in rock gardens as they flower later than the other alpine plants. This applies to *Oenothera perennis*, which does not exceed 30 cm (12 in) in height and flowers throughout the summer; *O. acaulis*, which has foliage similar to that of the dandelion and very large white flowers that smell delightful; and, of course, the most spectacular of all, *O. macrocarpa*, which forms a mat of foliage strewn with magnificent yellow flowers throughout the summer. It is extremely successful in

▽ *Oenothera macrocarpa*

tubs, where it can accompany conifers, partially concealing the container itself.

— More suitable for flower beds than for rock gardens, the medium-sized oenotheras brighten up our mixed borders at the beginning of summer. The most commonly found is *O. fruticosa*, bright yellow, and its variety 'Fireworks', the buds of which are a surprising waxy red.

— The giant of the group is *O. biennis*. As its name indicates, this is a biennial. A native of North America, it is commonly seen in the company of *O. glazionana*. Its yellow flowers open only in the evening and are borne in succession over a number of weeks, on stems of more than 100 cm (40 in) in height.

— *O. speciosa* 'Rosea', a very bushy species, has pale pink flowers, while those of *O. speciosa* itself, large and particularly fragrant, are white ageing to pink.

— The flowers of *O. stricta* 'Sulphurea' are sulphur-yellow when they open in the evening, turning to salmon-pink as they fade next day.

Height: 15–150 cm (6–60 in).
Spacing and planting distance: 20–50 cm (8–20 in).
Soil: ordinary.
Aspect: full sun.
Propagation: from seed when ripe, or by division in spring.
Flowering season: summer to autumn.
Type: annual, biennial, perennial.

Omphalodes

NAVELWORT, NAVEL-SEED, BLUE-EYED MARY

Boraginaceae

Although the leaves of *Omphalodes verna* are somewhat large, they make a perfect foil for the exquisite delicacy of the flowers, of an entrancing china-blue. This very robust plant will thrive even in dry soil under trees. Combine with wood anemones, daffodils and fritillaries, which will intermingle elegantly with its foliage.

Useful hints

— Plant preferably in autumn, in large groups. This plant will provide excellent ground cover that will compete with ivy and periwinkle. Improve the soil with peat or leaf-mould.

— In late winter, remove dead leaves from the crowns and dress with a little peat or pine bark. The clumps can be divided at the end of summer and replanted immediately.

Omphalodes verna △

Recommended

— *O. cappadocica*, with bright blue, white-eyed flowers, does not produce rhizomes and so will not spread. The variety 'Cherry Ingram' has much larger flowers.

Height: 15–20 cm (6–8 in).
Spacing and planting distance: 20 cm (8 in).
Soil: rich in humus.
Aspect: shade or semi-shade.
Propagation: by division at the end of summer.
Flowering season: spring.
Type: perennial.

Onoclea

SENSITIVE FERN

Dryopteridaceae

A medium-sized hardy plant, this fern is wonderful at the water's edge, in damp corners and at the foot of a north- or west-facing wall. Its fronds, of a beautiful soft green, provide an attractive screen for peonies, lilies and Solomon's seals. Intersperse them among your shrubs to avoid patches of bare earth.

Useful hints

— Plant *Onoclea sensibilis* in spring after improving the soil with peat and leaf-mould. Plant in groups (of at least ten) to create a more natural mass effect.

— Leave the dried foliage on the plants in winter as it protects them from the cold. Cut back in spring, but avoid pulling out roughly. Divide the clumps at around the same time.

— If, as a result of frost, the plants turn brown, don't worry – they will grow up again in the spring.

Height: 50–60 cm (20–24 in).
Spacing and planting distance: 50 cm (20 in).
Soil: rich in humus.
Aspect: shade or semi-shade.
Propagation: by division in spring.
Type: perennial.

Onopordum

SCOTCH THISTLE, COTTON THISTLE

Compositae

A masterly plant for the edge of a border. The distinction between the perennial and biennial plants is not always very clear. This is borne out by the thistle, which appears to some people to last for only two years, while others regard it as a perennial. The explanation of this mystery is due in part to the prodigious ability of *Onopordum bracteatum* to seed itself. The first year, it forms a rosette, close to the ground. It waits until the next spring to display its imposing foliage, so silvery that it looks almost artificial. Flowering continues for so long that the seeds will already have sprouted all around before it finishes.

Useful hints

— Plant one-year-old rosette crowns in autumn. Do not disturb the rootball.

— If you are afraid of this plant becoming invasive, cut off the dead flower heads before the seeds form (wear gloves, as the leaves and stalks can be vicious).

188

— You can replant spontaneously sown seedlings to brighten up areas where nothing else will grow, e.g. at the foot of trees.

Recommended

— As well as *O. bracteatum*, why not try *O. acanthium*, the genuine Scotch thistle? Its broad silver leaves have fine hairs, but beware of the sting. The pale purple flowers come out in summer.

— *O. nervosum* is taller and bears reddish purple flowers, 5 cm (2 in) in diameter, which bloom in summer.

Height: 200 cm (80 in).
Spacing and planting distance: 80 cm (32 in).
Soil: any, even poor.
Aspect: sun or semi-shade.
Propagation: from seed at the end of summer.
Flowering season: summer.
Type: biennial, perennial.

Origanum

OREGANO, SWEET MARJORAM

Labiatae

This is a reliable plant for the inexperienced gardener. Only very wet ground is unsuitable. All species thrive in full sun and do not mind the most prolonged drought. Plant them in the rock garden or, even better, around the edge of your flower beds.

Useful hints

— Plant in the spring or early autumn, in ordinary, well-dug soil. Do not add compost or fertilizer, as these plants do not need it and thrive on a subsistence diet.

Ornithogalum arabicum ▽

— Cut back the flower spikes once the flowers have died off.

— Divide the clumps every three years to keep them fit and healthy.

Recommended

— *Origanum laevigatum* has small, tough, bluish leaves. It forms attractive cushions with a multitude of stiff branching stems, which are covered in flowers in late summer.

— The species you are likely to encounter on country walks is *O. vulgare*, from which are derived the many cultivated varieties beloved of gardeners. 'Compactum' is like the wild form but only 20 cm (8 in) tall. 'Aureum', identical in height, is entirely clothed in yellow leaves. Of a softer yellow are the bushy clumps of 'Thumble's Variety', which persist for several months. All bear their tiny mauve flowers in compact clusters. *O. laevigatum* 'Herrenhausen' has the best qualities of both species.

Height: 20–50 cm (8–20 in).
Spacing and planting distance: 30–50 cm (12–20 in).
Soil: ordinary.
Aspect: full sun.
Propagation: by division.
Flowering period: summer and autumn.
Type: perennial.

Ornithogalum

STAR OF BETHLEHEM, CHINCHERINCHEE

Liliaceae

This genus includes some relatively tender species and others that are extremely hardy. Ornithogalums generally have white flowers and are grown from bulbs.

Onopordum bracteatum ▷
▽ *Ornithogalum umbellatum*

△ *Onoclea sensibilis*

△ *Onopordum nervosum*

Osmunda regalis △

Useful hints

— Plant in autumn and cover with a generous layer of dead leaves. Mark the site with a tag.

— Dig up clumps in summer if you find them too dense after a number of years. Take advantage of doing this to split off the new bulbs, and keep in dry peat until planting.

Recommended

— *Ornithogalum arabicum* must be kept in a cold frame over winter. Its relatively large flowers, marked with a black centre, are long-lasting as cut flowers. It needs a sunny, sheltered position, but does best as a pot plant.

— The largest is *O. magnum*, which grows to a height of more than 60 cm (24 in). Totally hardy, it bears green-striped flowers in summer. It likes chalky or well-drained sandy soils.

— Extremely attractive in the company of ferns and wood tulips, *O. nutans* is easily naturalized in partial shade. It does not exceed a height of 30 cm (12 in).

— An exception among ornithogalums, *O. thyrsoïdes* is planted in spring. It flowers during the summer, and the cut flowers will last for a long time in water.

— *O. umbellatum* flowers for more than a month at the end of spring. It will adapt to any soil.

Height: 20–80 cm (8–32 in).
Spacing and planting distance: 20 cm (8 in).
Soil: sandy.
Aspect: sun or semi-shade.
Propagation: by separating new bulbs after allowing the leaves to dry out.
Flowering season: spring to autumn.
Type: bulb.

Osmunda

ROYAL FERN

Osmundaceae

Osmunda regalis, which reigns majestically over moist sites, well deserves its name 'royal'. Sometimes growing to a height of 300 cm (120 in), when it develops a kind of small trunk, it gives an impression of power and harmony unequalled among indigenous plants. In the wild it is protected, and it would be particularly pointless to dig it up since it is generally difficult to transplant and is easily available from nurseries. Combine osmundas with *Primula florindae*, astilbes and peltiphyllums to produce a luxuriant scene reminiscent of pre-historic times. At the end of the summer, fertile fronds bearing spores appear. Do not remove these, as they too are decorative.

Useful hints

— Plant in spring in humus-rich soil and top dress with more humus each spring.

— Tidy up each autumn by cutting back top growth.

Recommended

— *O. regalis purpurascens* has unusually coloured deep copper-pink fronds.

Height: 100–300 cm (40–120 in).
Spacing and planting distance: 100 cm (40 in).
Soil: rich, cool at all times.
Aspect: sun or semi-shade.
Propagation: by separating secondary crowns appearing around the mother plant in spring.
Flowering season: end of summer.
Type: perennial.

Osteospermum

CAPE MARIGOLD

Compositae

Until recently known as *Dimorphotheca* and only lately renamed *Osteospermum*, these dwarf daisies, true sun-lovers, ought to be found more frequently in gardens, particularly in sun-trap sites. Worthy of their French common name of rain marigolds, they open their flowers as soon as the sun appears and close them again at the slightest cloud.

Useful hints

— Sow seeds either under cover in early spring, transplanting them to their flowering site after a month, or directly at the edge of the flowerbed in mid-spring. Thin out to 20 cm (8 in).

— For perennial varieties, take cuttings in late summer, as for pelargoniums, and harden them off before bringing them out the following spring to decorate your pots.

Recommended

— The best-known are the osteospermum hybrids whose flowers come in a range of colours, such as 'Cannington Roy' (white and pink), 'Buttermilk' (pale yellow), and 'Whirligig' (pale blue). Try the 'Pole Star' variety with white flowers and a blue heart. Your efforts will be rewarded.

△ *Osteospermum* 'Las Vegas'

— Almost hardy in warm and temperate climates, *O. ecklonis* forms a bush, covered with flowers all summer long. It is marvellous in earthenware pots. Bring under cover in winter.

Height: 30–60 cm (12–24 in).
Spacing and planting distance: 20 cm (8 in).
Soil: light and fertile (pots should contain compost and sand).
Aspect: full sun.
Propagation: from seed in spring or cuttings in late summer.
Flowering season: summer to first frosts.
Type: annual, perennial.

Ourisia

OURISIA

Scrophulariaceae

An excellent little plant for moist corners, ourisia will make itself at home in cool places and in some rock gardens.

Useful hints

— Sow seeds in mid-spring and transplant the following spring, or divide clumps at the same time.

Recommended

— *Ourisia coccinea* forms dense mats with tubular red flowers. *O. macrophylla* has tubular white flowers.

◁ *Osteospermum ecklonis*

Height: 20 cm (8 in).
Spacing and planting distance: 50 cm (20 in).
Soil: rich in humus, but well-drained.
Aspect: semi-shade.
Propagation: from seed or by division in spring.
Flowering season: spring to autumn.
Type: perennial.

Oxalis

OXALIS, WOOD SORREL, GOOD LUCK LEAF

Oxalidaceae

This genus contains some real pests, and some interesting flowers. They are best used to produce mats in the rock garden or on a dry stone wall. They can also be used in containers, together with aubrieta or alyssum.

Useful hints

— Plant in autumn in light soil. *Oxalis tetraphylla* can also be planted in spring.

— Lift the clumps two months after flowering to remove bulbils and replant immediately.

Recommended

— *O. adenophylla* is decorative in terms both of its grey foliage, which is folded like a parachute, and its flowers of delicate pink with white hearts.

— Beware of *O. tetraphylla*, also popularly known as the four leaf clover, as it can be extremely invasive. Restrict it to the edges of paths where few plants will grow.

Height: 20 cm (8 in).
Spacing and planting distance: 15 cm (6 in).
Soil: ordinary, preferably chalky.
Aspect: sun or semi-shade.
Propagation: by separating bulbils after flowering.
Flowering season: spring to autumn.
Type: annual, bulb, perennial.

Pachysandra

PACHYSANDRA, SPURGE

Buxaceae

If pachysandras are rather unpopular these days, it is perhaps because we have seen too many of them in public parks, where they are used solely for ground cover, giving them the reputation of being boring. By all means use *Pachysandra terminalis* in these disadvantaged locations, but put them with spring bulbs, hydrangeas and periwinkles to avoid the monotony of just a single type of plant.

Pachysandra terminalis ▷

△ *Oxalis adenophylla*
◁ *Ourisia macrophylla*
Oxalis tetraphylla 'Iron Cross' ▷

Useful hints

— Plants raised in containers can be planted out in any season, while plants with bare roots should be planted out in spring. Cut back the foliage each spring to make the plants more dense. If the soil is of poor quality, apply a dressing of dried blood.

— Every five years, divide the clumps to renew them, preferably in spring or at the start of autumn.

Height: 40 cm (16 in).
Spacing and planting distance: 30 cm (12 in).
Soil: any, although growth will be faster in soil rich in humus.
Aspect: shade or semi-shade.
Propagation: by division in spring or autumn.
Flowering season: spring (insignificant).
Type: perennial.

191

Paeonia

PEONY

Paeoniaceae

Peonies are essential to a garden. Their rounded shape, their abundant foliage in a neutral green and their enormous flowers make them unbeatable in late spring and early summer. For the rest of the season, they serve as a backdrop.

Useful hints

— Plant in autumn, as early as possible. Water abundantly to encourage rooting. Mark the location of the plants, as growth starts late and has little volume the first year. Dress with dried blood to accelerate.

— Support each crown with hazel twigs in late spring, to prevent the weight of the flowers from pulling down the stems. The plants can then be left to their own devices for decades.

Recommended

— *Paeonia officinalis* varieties often have large double flowers, such as 'Alba Plena' (white), 'Rosea Plena' (deep pink), and 'Rubra Plena' (crimson-red).

— Chinese peonies (*P. lactiflora*) are the best-known. Very large, and with an abundance of petals, they are available in every shade, from pure white to dark red, almost black. A selection of colours is given below.

— White: 'Candidissima'; 'Doris Cooper', with just a hint of pink; 'Madame Claude Tain', pinkish white developing to pure white; 'Vogue', tinged with pale pink.

— Pink: 'Albert Crousse', very much a double; 'Blush Queen', tinged with cream; 'Bowl of Beauty', pink with a pale yellow centre; 'Gilbert Barthelot', which produces an unbelievable quantity of flowers; 'Lady Orchid', bright pink; 'Madame Calot', brilliant pink; 'Mariette Vallée', 'Reine Hortense', 'Sarah Bernhardt'.

— Red: 'Chippewa', dark red; 'Felix Crousse', one of the best reds; 'Lord Kitchener', tending towards brown; 'Peter Brandt', burgundy-red.

— Among the botanical species available are: *P. cambessedesii*, pink; *P. mlokosewitschii*, which has sulphur-yellow, globe-shaped flowers; *P. tenuifolia*, whose bright red flowers stand out sharply against the plant's intense green, delicately slashed foliage.

— *P. peregrina* 'Otto Froebel' can be grown in a small space. It has vermilion

△ *Paeonia mlokosewitschii*

flowers with a distinctive bunch of golden yellow stamens in the centre.

— *P. officinalis* has red, pink or white flowers, and a delicious scent.

Height: 100 cm (40 in).
Spacing and planting distance: 100 cm (40 in).
Soil: rich in humus and remaining cool in summer.
Aspect: semi-shade or moderate sun.
Propagation: by division in summer.
Flowering season: late spring to early summer.
Type: perennial.

Papaver

POPPY

Papaveraceae

This genus has both annual and perennial varieties, all of which bear sumptuously coloured flowers with a silky quality. Poppies are at home in both highly sophisticated and country gardens.

Paeonia lactiflora hybrid ▽

Useful hints

— Sow in early spring in the case of annuals and in late spring in the case of perennials. Plant out into small pots while still very young, or directly into their flowering site, as these plants dislike being transplanted once they are older.

— Water annual poppies regularly, and remove the first fruits to prevent them from dying prematurely. Cut back the foliage of perennial species in summer when it is beginning to dry out.

— Plant by the side of asters or china asters to fill in spaces. New foliage will appear in autumn and remain throughout the winter.

Recommended

— The Iceland poppy (*Papaver nudicaule*) is grown as a biennial, i.e. it is sown in summer to flower the next spring. Its flowers are excellent companions to tulips and forget-me-nots. The alpine poppy (*P. alpinum*) is smaller, and varies between yellow and orange.

— One of the annual poppies is the field poppy (*P. rhoeas*). The double varieties are delightful, e.g. the Shirley Poppies. Dot a few plants about your flower beds to give them a touch of gaiety. The opium poppy (*P. somniferum*) bears just a few flowers, as large as peonies. Their flowering can be extended by removing the fruits as they form. 'Paeoniiflorum', with its enormous flowers, is appropriately named.

— The Oriental poppy (*P. orientale*), which is totally hardy, was originally red, but some enchanting selections have now appeared that combine all variations of pink and white with black centres: 'Allegro', dwarf red; 'Black and White', white, black centre; 'Cedric Morris', shell-pink; 'Glowing Embers', orange-red; 'Harvest Moon', deep orange; 'Ladybird', vermilion; 'Mrs Perry', pink.

— *P. atlanticum*, with small orange flowers, is excellent for filling empty spaces.

— There are several varieties of *P. nudicaule*: the dwarf Gartenzwerg Group, which comes in a mixture of colours; 'Matador', with big red flowers; 'Oregon Rainbow', in a mixture of pastel shades.

Height: 15–80 cm (6–32 in).
Spacing and planting distance: 20 cm (8 in).
Soil: any, well-drained in winter.
Aspect: sun.
Propagation: from seed or by division in spring.
Flowering season: spring to autumn.
Type: annual, biennial, perennial.

△ *Papaver somniferum*
◁ *Papaver orientale* hybrid
▽ *Papaver orientale*

193

△ *Paradisea liliastrum*

Paradisea

PARADISE LILY, ST BRUNO'S LILY

Liliaceae

A native of alpine meadows, the bulbous *Paradisea liliastrum* produces a gracious flower spike ending in flowers forming an immaculate white star. It is among the aristocrats of the rock garden.

Useful hints

— Plant in autumn or spring, and mark the site carefully, as the vegetation is visible for only a short period and the plant is likely to be damaged by hoeing.

— Surround with slug bait not only in summer but also in autumn, as black slugs over-winter in the ground close to its tuberous roots.

Height: 60 cm (24 in).
Spacing and planting distance: 15 cm (6 in).
Soil: sandy.
Aspect: sun.
Propagation: by division in autumn.
Flowering season: summer.
Type: bulb.

Pelargonium

GERANIUM, STORKSBILL

Geraniaceae

Everyone knows the garden geranium which is so frequently grown in pots on patios, providing an incomparable display of colour for containers. They are so good-humoured that we simply could not do without them. Although the varieties are rarely named, a number of botanical species are offered, particularly in the major group of fragrant-leaved pelargoniums.

Useful hints

— Plant in mid-spring in warm climates, and in late spring in cool areas. Choose rich, porous soil, based on leaf-mould, peat and sand. Make provision for drainage. Feed with soluble fertilizer every two weeks.

— Pinch out the stems half-way up in late spring to force them to branch out. When the first show of flowers is over, remove dead flower heads and fertilize to encourage a further show.

— In autumn, cut the plants back and bring them under cover in a cool, light room. Cuttings can be taken in summer or in spring.

Recommended

— *Pelargonium × hortorum* (incorrectly known as geraniums) often has leaves marked by a darker, almost reddish area (provided by *P. zonale*, one of the parents). This is the most common of all the pelargoniums. It comes in all colours, from pure white, often damaged by the rain, to the darkest red. 'Irene' has large light red blooms. 'Mauretania' has white flowers with a pink centre. 'Dolly Varden' has red flowers and leaves that are variegated with brown, white and red.

— Ivy-leaved geraniums (*P. peltatum*) have smooth leaves and frequently a supple habit, climbing if provided with a trellis, otherwise trailing. The single-flowered 'Roi des Balcons' is one of the best-known and the most free-flowering. It is available in pink and bright red. 'Elégante' has variegated foliage, with cream margins that sometimes turn pink, and pale mauve semi-double flowers.

— The regal pelargonium, *P. domesticum*, is extremely capricious. Even experienced gardeners are not always successful with it. Its large flowers, sumptuously washed with purple, show up well against its toothed yellowish green leaves. It requires a certain amount of warmth and regular feeding with fertilizer. There are many varieties. 'Purple Emperor' has pink-mauve flowers with a darker centre, while the flowers of 'Manx Maid', smaller than in other varieties, are pink blotched with burgundy.

— Of the fragrant-leaved pelargoniums, the most noteworthy are *P. tomentosum*, with velvety leaves that smell of peppermint, and *P. graveolens*, with highly aromatic, rough, toothed leaves. If you keep an eye open, you will undoubtedly find others on flower stalls.

Pelargonium peltatum △
Pelargonium tomentosum ▷
Pelargonium peltatum ▷
Pelargonium × hortorum ▽

Height: 30–120 cm (12–48 in).
Spacing and planting distance: 30 cm (12 in).
Soil: rich, well-drained.
Aspect: full sun.
Propagation: from cuttings in spring or summer.
Flowering season: all summer.
Type: annual, (perennial in mild climates).

◁ *Peltiphyllum peltatum*

Pennisetum
FOUNTAIN GRASS
Gramineae

This is the most elegant of the gramineae. Ideal for livening up the most ordinary of gardens, these grasses marry perfectly with stone steps, heathers and conifers.

— Combine pennisetums with wild tulips, dierama, ground cover plants such as acaena, or *Sedum spectabile*.

Useful hints

— Plant in any season but preferably in spring, in heavy soil. Improve the soil with sand.

— Hoe carefully for the first year and dress with a little nitrogen fertilizer to encourage growth. Leave dried out leaves *in situ* until spring, as they insulate the crown.

Recommended

— *Pennisetum alopecuroïdes* produces curious plumes that are particularly decorative in dried flower arrangements. There are several garden-worthy varieties including 'Hameln' and 'Woodside', and the form *P.a. viridescens*.

— *P. orientale* grows to little more than 60 cm (24 in) in height. Its leaves turn bronze in autumn.

— *P. setaceum* needs to be resown each year. A graceful addition to border or flower arrangement.

Height: 30–160 cm (12–64 in).
Spacing and planting distance: 30 cm (12 in).
Soil: ordinary.
Aspect: sun.
Propagation: by division in spring.
Flowering season: summer.
Type: perennial.

Peltiphyllum (syn. *Darmera*)
UMBRELLA PLANT
Saxifragaceae

This is a plant that should never be used in small numbers. A well-established patch of *Peltiphyllum peltatum* (syn. *Darmera peltata*) is a rare spectacle, whether in spring when the pink flowers are in bloom, or in autumn when the leaves take on brilliant red hues.

Useful hints

— Plant in spring in well-prepared soil dug deep and enriched with peat to keep it moist in summer. Mulch the soil with pine bark, semi-decomposed compost or grass cuttings. Water regularly in hot weather.

— Leave the foliage in place until the end of winter. Then remove to show off the flowers, which follow shortly afterwards. Combine with lysichitons, which also need moist soil, to create a highly exotic effect.

Height: 60–80 cm (24–32 in).
Spacing and planting distance: 60 cm (24 in).
Soil: permanently moist.
Aspect: sun or semi-shade.
Propagation: by division in autumn.
Flowering season: early spring.
Type: perennial.

▽ *Pennisetum alopecuroïdes*

△ *Penstemon heterophyllus*
Penstemon newberryi △

Penstemon

PENSTEMON, BEARD-TONGUE

Scrophulariaceae

Lovers of dry soil, penstemons are valuable plants as they flower in mid-summer. Their flowers are often of unusual colours, particularly purples and pinks, but also very powerful reds.

Useful hints

— Plant in spring when the worst of the rains are over. Give a well-drained position, with a rich soil. Mulch in summer with pine bark. Water plentifully during the flowering season to keep plants in flower longer.

— In winter, protect the crown from excessive water with a sheet of plastic.

Recommended

— The hardiest is *Penstemon barbatus*, which bears salmon-pink flowers. It has a darker cultivar, 'Coccineus'.

— Of the more prolific species, *P. hirsutus*, violet-blue and white, can be considered the most hardy.

— Of the botanical varieties: *P. heterophyllus* has blue flowers, those of 'Blue Springs' being particularly bright; *P. pinifolius* will form a little shrub in your rock garden. Its flowers are an orangey red, but there is also a yellow-flowered form, 'Mersea Yellow'.

— Of the hybrid penstemons: 'Andenken an Friedrich Hahn', scarlet-red; 'Le Phare' and 'Southgate Gem', bright red; 'Souvenir d'Adrian Régnier', gentle pink. 'Garnet' is one of the best red varieties and will withstand an average winter. 'Sour Grapes' is deep lilac in colour, with a white throat; 'Evelyn' has white and pink flowers.

Height: 15–60 cm (6–24 in).
Spacing and planting distance: 20 cm (8 in).
Soil: rich and well-drained.
Aspect: sun.
Propagation: from cuttings in summer and by division in spring.
Flowering season: summer to autumn.
Type: biennial, perennial.

△ **Penstemon** 'Heavenly Blue'

△ *Petasites japonicus*
▽ *Petasites japonicus* var. *giganteus*

Persicaria

see *Polygonum*

Petasites

SWEET COLTSFOOT, BUTTERBUR

Compositae

When the flowers of coltsfoot appear suddenly like giant dandelions it is always surprising, for their somewhat ordinary-looking foliage resembles that of a weed. The coltsfoot is in fact extremely invasive. Use only in poor sites such as the edges of ditches.

— Combine with snowdrops, peonies, ferns and Solomon's seals.

Useful hints

— Plant *Petasites fragrans* (also known as winter heliotrope) in spring or autumn and ensure that it does not spread beyond the boundaries that you have set for it. It suffers from no particular parasites and needs no particular care but it is worth protecting the crowns with dead leaves as they can be damaged by extremely cold winters.

Height: 50 cm (20 in).
Spacing and planting distance: 30 cm (12 in).
Soil: ordinary, rather rich in humus.
Aspect: semi-shade.
Propagation: by division, any season.
Flowering season: winter.
Type: perennial.

Petunia

PETUNIA

Solanaceae

Great rivals of the pelargonium, petunias beat all records for length of flowering with little attention. Use them either in a mass or interspersed among borders of grey foliage plants such as cerastiums or artemisia.

Useful hints

— Sow *Petunia × hybrida* under cover in early spring and transplant once before moving to their flowering site after the frosts are over. They like rich, well-drained soil. Feed with fertilizer every two weeks to encourage large flowers.

— Remove dead flowers regularly to prevent seeds from forming.

Recommended

— For patios: all medium-sized flower varieties, which are more free-flowering than the large-flowered kinds. The

△ *Petunia* hybrids

Resisto Series is very tolerant of rain. The Cascade Series is often disappointing, as the stems need to be encouraged to trail.

— For flower beds: the compact dwarf single petunias like the Merlin Series are the best, as their flowers are produced in succession over a number of months.

— The cascades of flowers produced by *P. integrifolia* are the most abundant of all.

Height: 20–35 cm (8–14 in).
Spacing and planting distance: 20 cm (8 in).
Soil: rich and well-drained (peaty compost).
Aspect: sun.
Propagation: from seed sown under cover in early spring.
Flowering season: summer to first frosts.
Type: annual.

Phacelia campanularia △

Phacelia

PHACELIA, SCORPION WEED

Hydrophyllaceae

The flowers of phacelia are a beautiful blue, like little upward-pointing bells. If you are looking for an original small annual flower, you should be delighted with *Phacelia campanularia*, although you may have difficulty in finding the seeds. Fortunately, just as pretty, just as blue and just as free-flowering, *P. tanacetifolia*, which flowers on plumed spikes, is very easy to obtain. Phacelias are fragrant and attract bees. Sow in borders, or in the rock garden.

Useful hints

— Like most annual flowers, they are easy to grow. Any good garden soil will suit them, but they need a sunny position to flower freely.

— An easy-going plant, phacelia prefers to be sown directly in the flowering site. Thin the plants out to 15 cm (6 in) in all directions once they appear.

— To extend their flowering season, which is only just over a month, stagger sowing between mid-spring and early summer, and you will then have flowers through to autumn.

— In the kitchen garden, give yourself the pleasure of sowing little strips between rows of vegetables, and you will be rewarded with delightful mats of blue flowers that will be covered with bees and butterflies.

Height: 40 cm (16 in).
Spacing and planting distance: 15 cm (6 in).
Soil: ordinary.
Aspect: sun.
Propagation: from seed in spring.
Flowering season: summer to autumn.
Type: annual.

Phalaris

RIBBON GRASS, CANARY GRASS

Gramineae

If you find your flower beds insufficiently filled in summer, make a little space for Gramineae, particularly *Phalaris arundinaceae* 'Picta' (gardener's garters). With a marking of longitudinal white strips, their foliage provides valuable assistance to poppies, tobacco plants or phlox by acting as an attractive space-filler.

Useful hints

— Plant in spring or autumn in relatively rich soil. Water regularly for the first year.

— Watch the clumps for spreading, as they can become invasive. Leave the foliage intact over winter and cut back only in spring, leaving the new stems *in situ*. These are extremely attractive in fresh Japanese-style bouquets.

Height: 60–80 cm (24–32 in).
Spacing and planting distance: 40 cm (16 in).
Soil: ordinary.
Aspect: sun.
Propagation: by division in spring.
Flowering season: summer (insignificant).
Type: perennial.

▽ *Phalaris arundinacea 'Picta'*

Phlomis

JERUSALEM SAGE

Labiatae

Though not always very hardy, phlomis form attractive shrubby plants where they feel at home. If you combine them with cistus, lavender and salvias you will create a border full of warm colours.

Useful hints

— Plant preferably in spring in the warmest corners of the garden. They are not afraid of the burning sun – indeed, it is precisely in these sites that their foliage is the most attractive.

— Mulch the soil with pine bark in summer. When the first frosts arrive, cover the plant with a sheet of transparent plastic. As a precaution, place a few cuttings taken in summer under shelter.

Recommended

— The true Jerusalem sage is *Phlomis fruticosa*, its foliage covered with grey, slightly dirty-looking down. The yellow flowers are borne in succession throughout the summer. It is an excellent plant for containers on hot sunny patios.

— *P. samia* is better suited than the previous variety to damp climates. Its flowers vary from pale yellow to orange, often ending in pink. They are produced in regular clusters along the length of the stems in early summer.

— The ash-grey foliage of *P. cashmeriana* is a perfect foil to its pink crowns of flowers.

— The pink flower clusters of *P. tuberosa* are borne at intervals along the stems, which grow to almost 200 cm (80 in).

Height: 60–200 cm (24–80 in).
Spacing and planting distance: 50 cm (20 in).
Soil: very well-drained.
Aspect: full sun.
Propagation: from cuttings in summer.
Flowering season: summer to autumn.
Type: perennial.

Phlox

PHLOX

Polemoniaceae

It is difficult to imagine gardens before the phloxes were discovered, all having originated in North America. They are irreplaceable for adding colour and often fragrance to our flower beds, particularly since nature has provided them in all sizes and virtually all colours.

Useful hints

— Sow annual phlox in early spring in a cold frame, or directly in the flowering site in mid- or late spring. To germinate well, seeds should be a year old. Thin out after a month, leaving a plant every 20 cm (8 in). Pinch out the main stalks of tall varieties to encourage them to branch out. *Phlox drummondii* are excellent cut flowers provided that the water is replaced regularly.

— Plant hardy perennial phlox varieties in autumn or spring. A rich soil that remains cool in summer will suit them best. If the foliage becomes wrinkled, this is a sign of attack by nematodes, tiny worms which invade the collar of the plant. Treat preventatively by scattering disulphoton-based granules around the base of the plant. Extend the flowering season by watering regularly and feeding with dilute fertilizer every other watering.

Recommended

— *P. drummondii* are annuals, and are available in dwarf and large varieties. The former are excellent in borders, e.g. 'Twinkle', its flowers marked with a deep eye. The latter provide enchanting cut flower arrangements.

— The most popular of the phlox are without question the perennial varieties, including *P. paniculata*. Of the numerous hybrids, noteworthy reds are: 'A. E. Amos', 'August Fackel', 'Kirchenfurst' and 'Starfire'; the pinks, 'Dodo Hanbury Forbes', 'Early Gem', 'Elisabeth Arden', 'Flamingo', 'Gnom' and 'Tenor'. Among the whites are 'Graf Zeppelin' and 'Jacqueline Maille'. The most surprising of all are the blues: 'Blue Boy', 'Caroline van den Berg', 'Eventide' and 'Parma'; and the salmon-coloured hybrids include 'Orange Perfection' and 'Sommerfreude'. 'Norah Leigh' has variegated leaves.

— Less well-known than those above, and again perennial, *P. maculata* has spotted leaves and flowers arranged in elongated pyramids. 'Alpha', pink, and 'Omega', white, are the most common.

Phlox drummondii △

— Of more modest dimensions than the garden phloxes is *P. carolina* 'Miss Lingard', though it flowers just as freely.

— *P. divaricata* puts on a magnificent springtime show in sparse undergrowth. The hybrid 'Chattahoochee' is more violet in tone, with a striking red eye.

— The carpet-forming *P. stolonifera* thrives in cool, shaded soils. Varieties include 'Ariane', which is white, and 'Blue Ridge.'

— *P. subulata*, which is very small in comparison with those above, resembles a mat of thorns for much of the year until it is covered with a mantle of hundreds of brightly coloured flowers in spring. It is a good match for the botanical tulips. Try 'Betty', pale pink; 'Blue Eyes', mauvish blue; 'Daisy Hill', pink 'Temiskaming', carmine red; and 'White Delight', pure white.

— The varieties of *P. douglasii* are more compact and give denser cover. 'May Snow' has masses of white flowers. The mauve 'Lilac Cloud' or the pink 'Rose Queen' will brighten up your rock garden with their dazzling blooms. The red of 'Crackerjack' is unbelievably strong. Tone it down with the white of thlaspis.

Height: 15–120 cm (6–48 in).
Spacing and planting distance: 15–40 cm (6–16 in).
Soil: rich, remaining cool in summer.
Aspect: full sun.
Propagation: by division in spring, annuals from seed.
Flowering season: spring to autumn.
Type: annual, biennial, perennial.

△ *Phlox paniculata*

▽ *Phlox douglasii*

Phormium
NEW ZEALAND FLAX, FLAX LILY
Agavaceae

Phormium tenax requires a position in the warmest part of the garden, perhaps against a house wall, if it is to come through the winter in cooler climates. Its bold outline provides a focus of attention.

Useful hints

— Plant in spring in a corner which is sheltered from the cold winds and does not get too much water in winter. Lift the crown slightly so that it remains dry during the bad weather.

— Mulch the soil with pine bark from summer onwards and feed regularly with soluble fertilizer as this plant is extremely voracious.

— From autumn onwards, cover the crown with straw or old cardboard and plastic sheeting to protect it against excess water and cold.

Recommended

— *P. tenax.* Less austere and bulky than the parent species, the Purpureum Group, which has a coppery sheen, the dwarf 'Tom Thumb' and various other hybrids offer a wealth of choice. The Rainbow Hybrids combine several colours.

Height: 100–300 cm (40–120 in).
Spacing and planting distance: 150 cm (60 in).
Soil: rich and well-drained in winter.
Aspect: full sun.
Propagation: by division in spring.
Flowering season: summer.
Type: perennial.

Phormium tenax ▽

Phygelius

CAPE FUCHSIA

Scrophulariaceae

Much hardier than is generally realized, phygelius will simply shed the part of the plant above ground if the winter is bad. It will then grow all the more vigorously from spring onwards, and rapidly forms a good-sized clump. You will have to wait until summer to admire its trumpet-shaped red or yellow flowers, but they are worth waiting for.

Useful hints

— Plant in spring in soil that has been dug deep and enriched with leaf-mould. Water regularly and mulch in summer.

— Leave the stems intact in winter, covering only the crown with straw or a good matting of dry leaves.

Recommended

— *Phygelius aequalis* adds a touch of gracefulness to slightly cool corners. Its greenish yellow flowers go well with the shades of ferns and the 'Tricolor' fuchsias. The dense flower heads of *P.a.* 'Yellow Trumpet' add a touch of striking bright colour.

— Its cousin, *P. capensis*, which is a real sun-worshipper, occupies the centre stage for a good three months at the end of summer. It precedes the asters, and goes extremely well with the blue agapanthus.

Height: 60–100 cm (24–40 in).
Spacing and planting distance: 40 cm (16 in).
Soil: rich in humus.
Aspect: sun or semi-shade.
Propagation: from cuttings in summer.
Flowering season: summer to autumn.
Type: perennial.

Phyllitis (syn. *Asplenium*)

HART'S-TONGUE FERN

Aspleniaceae

Hart's-tongues are ferns with elongated, pleated leaves. They often adorn cool, shady locations like the approaches to caves or the insides of wells. They can be used very successfully to edge a path under the trees, where the soil is cool, or north-facing stone steps. The leaves of *Phyllitis scolopendrium* (syn. *Asplenium scolopendrium*) will then serve as a backdrop for bleeding hearts, arum lilies and Solomon's seals.

Useful hints

— Plant at any season if grown in containers, otherwise in spring. Plant in

Phygelius capensis △

rich soil. Water frequently and mulch with light peat in late spring.

— Divide the clumps every three years, in spring.

Recommended

— *P. scolopendrium*. The original forms, such as the Cristatum Group or Undulatum Group, are worthy of a prominent place in a shady part of the rock garden.

Height: 50 cm (20 in).
Spacing and planting distance: 30 cm (12 in).
Soil: rich in humus, enriched with peat.
Aspect: shade.
Propagation: by division in spring.
Type: perennial.

Physalis

CHINESE LANTERN

Solanaceae

When we see the pretty white star-shaped flowers of *Physalis alkekengi* var. *franchetii*, we might guess it to be a cousin of the tomato and potato – although much more graceful! At home in any soil as long as it is in the sun, it will flower freely in summer before revealing its aerial calyces, which change from a tender green to the most beautiful orange in the autumn months. Extremely hardy, it sometimes becomes very invasive. Plant in the company of

robust plants such as tansy, *Stachys byzantina* or cerastium.

Useful hints

— Plant pieces of the fleshy roots (they look rather like a fat bindweed) in autumn or spring, in any good, loose soil, cleared of weeds.

— Position preferably at the edge of a path, to restrict its spread.

— Every three years, dig out and replant.

Recommended

— *P. alkekengi* var. *franchetii*. The less exuberant temperament of 'Pygmaea' makes it more suitable as a bedding plant.

Height: 40 cm (16 in).
Spacing and planting distance: 20 cm (8 in).
Soil: ordinary.
Aspect: sun.
Propagation: by division in spring.
Flowering season: summer.
Type: perennial.

Physostegia

OBEDIENT PLANT, LION'S-HEART, OBEDIENCE

Labiatae

An attractive clump of *Physostegia virginiana* in flower always creates a kind of event in the garden. Not only because it is attractive, but also because the flowers

△ *Physalis alkekengi* var. *franchetii*
◁ *Phytolacca americana*
Physostegia virginiana ▷
▽ *Phyllitis scolopendrium*

have a curious feature: they sit on a type of ball-joint and can be moved into any position, where they will remain. Colours include white and pink.

Useful hints

— Plant in autumn or spring, providing them with soil rich in humus that remains cool in summer. In spite of their vigorous development, these plants do not like competition from weeds. Mulch the soil in summer with grass cuttings.

— Divide clumps as little as possible, no more than every five years. The large white roots are similar to those of bindweed.

Recommended

— *P. virginiana* itself is red-violet but 'Rose Bouquet' and 'Vivid' are pink and a little smaller. 'Alba' is white and slightly earlier flowering (it flowers in mid- rather than late summer.

Height: 50–70 cm (20–28 in).
Spacing and planting distance: 30 cm (12 in).
Soil: rich in humus.
Aspect: sun or semi-shade.
Propagation: by division in spring.
Flowering season: summer to autumn.
Type: perennial.

Phytolacca

POKE, POKEBERRY, POKEWEED

Phytolaccaceae

Known mainly in the tropics where this genus grows as a tree, *Phytolacca americana* is quietly beginning to invade us. It is an amazing plant capable of competing with castor-oil plants for its rate of growth and exotic appearance. If the soil and climate suit it, you will have an extremely vigorous plant reaching more than 200 cm (80 in) in height. The white flowers are followed by violet-red berries which are highly decorative.

Useful hints

— Plant preferably in spring, after breaking up the soil to depth and enriching it with manure.

— Shortly before the cold weather, cover the crown with straw and plastic sheeting. It is not unusual for this plant to seed itself spontaneously.

Height: 150–250 cm (60–100 in).
Spacing and planting distance: 50 cm (12 in).
Soil: very rich and cool in summer.
Aspect: full sun.
Propagation: by division in spring or from ripe seeds in autumn.
Flowering season: summer.
Type: perennial.

Pinguicula grandiflora △

Pilosella

see *Hieracium*

Pinguicula

BUTTERWORT

Lentibulariaceae

Pinguicula grandiflora resembles a violet but is not a violet: it is in fact a strange little carnivorous plant that likes nothing better than the moist atmosphere of damp gardens, as it is a native of the marshes. A hardy plant in regions where winters are relatively mild, it should only be grown by careful gardeners who know the attention that it requires. Beware: like platycodon, it disappears completely in winter. Combine with helxines and maidenhair ferns.

Useful hints

— Plant preferably in spring, in moist soil in semi-shade.

— Mark the site with a twig, such as a stem of holly, to locate your plants.

— It is most effective in a border, or planted in little groups of five or six plants.

Height: 15 cm (6 in).
Spacing and planting distance: 15 cm (6 in).
Soil: rich in humus, moist.
Aspect: semi-shade.

△ *Platycodon grandiflorus*

Propagation: from seed in autumn or by division in spring.
Flowering season: summer.
Type: perennial.

Platycodon

BALLOON FLOWER

Campanulaceae

A delicate blue, due to the diaphanous texture of its petals, or porcelain-white, sometimes pink, platycodon is in fact an attractive campanula that is delightful in carefully tended flower beds in semi-shade. Grow with ferns and hostas.

Useful hints

— Plant preferably in spring, and remember to mark its location with a stick. It disappears completely in winter and often falls victim to the spade.

— Give it good soil, rich and well-drained. In heavy soils it will disappear quite rapidly.

Recommended

— Although there are some double varieties such as 'Plenum', the single varieties with blue flowers are the prettiest, such as *Platycodon grandiflorus mariesii*, or *P. apoyama*, with dark blue flowers.

— *P. grandiflorus* 'Perlmutterschale' ('Mother of Pearl') bears flowers of a delicate mother-of-pearl colour. 'Fuji Pink' is of deeper hue.

Height: 30 cm (12 in).
Spacing and planting distance: 20 cm (8 in).
Soil: rich and well-drained.
Aspect: sun.
Propagation: by division or from seed in spring.
Flowering season: summer.
Type: perennial.

Plumbago auriculata ▽

Plumbago

PLUMBAGO, LEADWORT

Plumbaginaceae

There can be no more attractive decoration for earthenware pots in a warm climate than a *Plumbago auriculata* in flower. The almost unreal blue of its flowers seems to compete with that of the sky. And how robust it is, even in the worst heat. It has just one drawback: its rather unremarkable foliage is slightly sticky where the minute tendrils surround the base of the flowers. Don't forget to bring it inside, to protect it from the cold, in winter. Do not confuse plumbagos, particularly *P. larpentae*, the botanical name of which is now *Cerastostigma plumbaginoïdes*.

Useful hints

— Sow seeds in early spring under cover and continue growing under cover until late spring. The plants will flower abundantly from the first summer. You can also keep cuttings or plants in the conservatory. Pinch out at least twice in spring to encourage them to send out side shoots.

— They like a light but substantial mix best. Where frosts are relatively infrequent, you could try overwintering them protected under a plastic sheet.

— You can train them against a south-facing wall on your terrace. They will then climb to a height of more than 200 cm (80 in).

Height: 50–200 cm (20–80 in).
Spacing and planting distance: 30 cm (12 in).
Soil: rich and well-drained in winter.
Aspect: full sun.
Propagation: from seed or cuttings.
Flowering season: summer to autumn.
Type: annual, perennial in mild climates.

Podophyllum

PODOPHYLLUM, MAY APPLE

Berberidaceae

This plant, which is difficult to find in the catalogues, has a relatively short period of growth, from spring to summer, providing us with a curious spectacle: it begins with elegant denticulate leaves tinged with purple when they first appear. Then the flowers open: they are often large and pale pink, like apple blossom, followed by fruits as large as hen's eggs of a redcurrant colour, which are edible but not particularly tasty. This plant has its place in informal corners of the garden with a cool, acid soil, as under trees.

△ *Podophyllum hexandrum*

Useful hints

— Plant in autumn or spring in deep soil rich in humus. Combine with ferns and meconopsis, which grow in the same conditions.

— Collect the ripe fruits to remove the seeds. Sow in autumn. They will generally come up the following spring, and the young plants can be established the next year.

— Mulch the soil with pine bark at the beginning of spring to show off the beauty of the young foliage at its best.

Height: 50 cm (20 in).
Spacing and planting distance: 30 cm (12 in).
Soil: rich in humus, permanently cool.
Aspect: semi-shade.
Propagation: from seed when ripe or by division at the beginning of spring, before vegetation appears.
Flowering season: spring.
Type: perennial.

△ *Polemonium caeruleum*

Polemonium

JACOB'S LADDER, GREEK VALERIAN

Polemoniaceae

Far more common in the past than it is today, *Polemonium caeruleum* has some of the most handsome foliage to be found in any plant: divided and attractively arched, it makes dense mounds from which the flower spikes protrude upwards. It produces flowers continuously for almost two months at the end of spring, at the same time as the late tulips, oriental poppies and peonies with which it can be combined.

Useful hints

— Plant preferably in autumn or in spring. Mark the site because the foliage disappears in winter. The best position is semi-shade. Polemoniums will therefore flourish at the base of bush roses, particularly old roses.

— The best method of propagation is to sow seeds at the end of spring. Protect young plants in a cold frame and transplant to their flowering locations the following spring.

Recommended

— The species is a soft blue, but there is also 'Sapphire', an intense blue, and 'Album', a very pure white. Lovers of unusual plants should look out for *P. foliosissimum*, which is a little larger, its foliage being more denticulate. It is found in dark blue and white forms.

— *P. carneum* has pink or lilac flowers and finely divided foliage.

— *P. pulcherrimum* has purple-blue flowers with a yellow or white throat.

Height: 30–60 cm (12–24 in).
Spacing and planting distance: 30 cm (12 in).
Soil: ordinary soil, rather well-drained.
Aspect: sun or semi-shade.
Propagation: from seed or by division in spring.
Flowering season: late spring to summer.
Type: perennial.

△ *Polygonatum odoratum*
▽ *Polygonatum × hybridum*

▽ *Polygonum amplexicaule*

Polygonatum

SOLOMON'S SEAL

Liliaceae

Towards late spring, the garden is brightened up by the fresh floral spikes of Solomon's seal, a restful sight that takes over from scillas with their intense blue flowers. Perfect for a shady garden or for under trees, they are very popular with English gardeners. Combine them with magnolias, flowering cherry trees and apple trees. Plant them in the company of Caucasian heracleums and macleayas in an informal corner of the garden. They will flower again reliably, year after year.

Useful hints

— Plant wild species from summer to autumn in fresh soil rich in humus, preferably in partial shade.

— Plant cultivars from autumn onwards. For the plants to flower well, they must be established early in the season.

Recommended

— For preference, choose *Polygonatum × hybridum* or *P. biflorum*, the giant Solomon's seal with spectacular flowers, easily growing to a height of 120 cm (48 in).

— The bell-shaped flowers of *P. odoratum* will fill your shrubbery with their powerful fragrance.

Height: 30–120 cm (12–48 in).
Spacing and planting distance: 30 cm (12 in).
Soil: ordinary, cool.
Aspect: semi-shade.
Propagation: by division and from seed in spring.
Flowering season: late spring to summer.
Type: perennial.

▷ *Polygonum orientale*
▽ *Polygonum affine*

Polygonum (syn. *Persicaria*)

KNOTWEED, FLEECE-FLOWER

Polygonaceae

Knotweeds have an unmistakable family likeness: a certain propensity to spread, leathery green foliage, and spiked flowers, which are often red. In fact there is a certain diversity in flowering season, from summer to autumn, and in the height of the plants, which is extremely variable.

Useful hints

— Plant in spring or autumn in groups (at least six) to create a mass effect.

— Check growth to prevent harm to neighbouring plants. Mulch the soil in summer to keep it cool for longer.

△ *Polygonum campanulatum*

— Divide plants in autumn every three years and replant elsewhere, as they will tend to exhaust the soil.

Recommended

— *Polygonum affine* (syn. *Persicaria affinis*) is excellent at the edges of flower beds, as it forms compact mounds. Its straight leaves turn bronze in autumn and remain for much of the winter. The flowers are dark red in 'Darjeeling Red', salmon-pink in 'Donald Lowndes' and bright pink in 'Superba'.

— Larger than the previous variety, *P. amplexicaule* (syn. *Persicaria amplexicaulis*) grows to a height of 150 cm (60 in). 'Atrosanguineum' is an intense carmine pink, while 'Firetail' is a bright scarlet red.

— An improved cousin of the snakeweed, *P. bistorta* 'Superbum' (syn. *Persicaria bistorta* 'Superba') forms vast colonies producing groups of flowers in the form of luminous pink brushes.

— One of the most attractive knotweeds is without doubt *P. campanulatum* (syn. *Persicaria campanulata*), with deeply veined leaves and pale pink bell flower heads produced in succession throughout late summer and much of autumn.

— Beware of *P. japonicum* (syn. *Persicaria japonica*), the Japanese knotweed, as this is a serious pest. Its stems, reminiscent of bamboo, are propagated at a stupendous rate. Leave them for the roadside and unmanageable slopes.

— Not, unfortunately, reliably hardy, *P. vaccinifolium* (syn. *Persicaria vaccinifolia*) is wonderful in rock gardens, as its pink flowers are produced late, shortly before the change in colour of the foliage. Protect in winter.

— Allow *P. capitatum* (syn. *Persicaria capitata*) the freedom to spread between paving stones or on flights of steps.

— *P. virginianum* (syn. *Persicaria virginiana*) 'Painter's Palette' needs a cool environment in which to put out its yellowish green leaves, with their characteristic coppery V marking.

— In late summer, the bronze-green foliage of *P. weyrichii* disappears beneath a creamy veil of diaphanous flowers.

Height: 15–150 cm (6–60 in).
Spacing and planting distance: 20–50 cm (8–20 in).
Soil: ordinary.
Aspect: sun or semi-shade.
Propagation: by division in autumn or spring.
Flowering season: summer to autumn.
Type: perennial.

△ *Polypodium vulgare*

Polypodium

POLYPODY

Polypodiaceae

Its name is unfailingly evocative of natural science lessons, as this delightful little fern found at the edges of cool, clay areas under trees comes into many a school curriculum. *Polypodium vulgare* has its place in the garden, in a flower bed exposed to partial shade, or to liven up a rather shady corner with a carpeting of dentate fronds. As it is very much at home on slopes, beneath large trees, use it as a border for an informal hedge. It will look highly sophisticated and sculptural, and needs no other work than that of initial planting.

Useful hints

— Try setting up a miniature Japanese garden by planting with all sorts of wood mosses.

— Plant in any garden soil, preferably in spring. It is equally happy in dry or moist soil, sand or clay.

Recommended

— *P. vulgare* The fronds of *P.v.* 'Bifidum' terminate in a curious fork.

Height: 15 cm (6 in).
Spacing and planting distance: 20 cm (8 in).
Soil: ordinary.
Aspect: semi-shade.
Propagation: by division or from seed in spring.
Type: perennial.

Polystichum setiferum △
Pontederia cordata ▷

Polystichum

POLYSTICHUM, CHRISTMAS FERN, HOLLY FERN, SHIELD FERN

Dryopteridaceae

A delicate fern for well-tended gardens, this is at its most effective in flower beds that already contain fuchsias, lysimachias and bicoloured eucomis. You can also grow them under trees, but the area must be well-tended. Unfortunately, certain ferns in this family are only moderately hardy – *Polystichum falcatum* (syn. *Cyrtomium falcatum*), for example.

Useful hints

— Plant in spring, in soil that is very rich in humus. Allow one spadeful of well-rotted compost per plant and mulch the soil as necessary with semi-decomposed compost to lighten and enrich it if at all compacted.

— Grow away from draughts and sun, which would damage its foliage.

Recommended

— *P. falcatum* (syn. *Cyrtomium falcatum*) is the best-known. It will readily grow in pots, but dislikes frost. It is also worth mentioning the evergreen *P. aculeatum* for growing at the water's edge, and *P. setiferum*, which is semi-evergreen, with delicately denticulate fronds. *P. achrostichoides* with its wonderful strong green – which remains throughout the winter – is a good garden plant; it goes well with groups of fuchsias.

— The dense, leathery fronds of *P. polyblepharum* are of a quite unique glossy dark green. *P. setiferum* includes such fascinating varieties as *proliferum* (Acutilobum Group), which produces young plants at intervals along its fronds, the graceful Dahlem Group, and the Plumosum Group, so finely serrated as to appear moss-like.

Height: 60–100 cm (24–40 in).
Spacing and planting distance: 30 cm (12 in).
Soil: rich in humus, cool.
Aspect: semi-shade.
Propagation: from seed or by division in autumn or spring.
Type: perennial.

Pontederia

PONTEDERIA, PICKEREL WEED

Pontederiaceae

A native of Virginia, *Pontederia cordata* is an attractive aquatic plant with heart-shaped leaves borne on long, sheath-like stalks. It flowers in summer with attractive spikes of blue, brightened up by a yellow eye. Totally hardy, it quickly takes over pools and ponds, giving them an almost tropical appearance. Its cousin the water hyacinth (*Eichhornia crassipes*) has to be brought in each winter, for protection.

Useful hints

— Plant in spring when the water has begun to warm up. Set in pots filled with clay soil and arrange at a depth of 30 cm (12 in). If you plant them at the edge of a pond, choose a somewhat peaty soil.

— When the individual crowns begin to impinge upon one another, divide, in spring.

Height: 50 cm (20 in).
Spacing and planting distance: 30 cm (12 in).
Soil: heavy.
Aspect: sun.
Propagation: by division in spring.
Flowering season: summer to autumn.
Type: perennial.

Portulaca

PURSLANE, MOSS ROSE, SUN PLANT

Portulaceae

You will sometimes see these sun plants with silken flowers flourishing in the most unbelievably dry sites. They are succulent plants, and their leaves reveal the fact that they belong to a genus that loves the sun. Indeed, *Portulaca grandiflora* needs the sun for its flowers to open: they close at the first sight of a cloud.

Useful hints

— As the seeds are as fine as dust, mix them with sand before sowing directly in the flowering site in late spring. You can also sow them in a cold frame two weeks earlier and plant them out into containers or directly into the ground after the frosts.

— In spite of their ability to withstand drought, they should be watered from time to time to achieve the best flowers.

Recommended

— *P. grandiflora* 'Sundance' is unique in having semi-double flowers.

Height: 15 cm (6 in).
Spacing and planting distance: 15 cm (6 in).
Soil: ordinary, even dry.
Aspect: full sun.
Propagation: from seed in spring.
Flowering season: summer to autumn.
Type: annual.

Potentilla

CINQUEFOIL, FIVE-FINGER

Rosaceae

This is a family with many species including bushes, such as *Potentilla fruticosa*, woody plants, hybrid cinquefoils and tiny alpine plants like *P. nitida*. Show off their serrated leaves, veined like a strawberry plant's, by planting them amid full foliage like *Stachys byzantina*, senecios and artemisia.

▽ *Portulaca grandiflora*

Potentilla 'Gloire de Nancy' △

Useful hints

— Plant, preferably in spring, in soil which has been dried out well, choosing a sunny spot.

— In heavy soil, dig the planting holes quite deep and let them drain by pouring over 5 cm (2 in) of gravel before filling them with porous soil.

Recommended

— Herbaceous cinquefoils like *P. atrosanguinea* are popular because of their highly coloured, often double flowers. Hybrids include: 'Gloire de Nancy', russet; 'Monsieur Rouillard', tan; 'Yellow Queen', sunshine-yellow.

— *P. alba* forms a greyish green mat spangled with white flowers.

— *P. megalantha* has dense, hairy leaves and large yellow flowers, which open even in semi-shade.

— *P. nepalensis* bears plenty of flowers on well-spread branches. Varieties include 'Helen Jane', pale pink with a darker centre, and 'Roxana', coppery pink with a yellow eye.

— The prostrate branches of *P. × tonguei* grow close to the ground and make it ideal for a rock garden. Its flowers, apricot with a red eye, from a splash of bright colour.

Height: 10–50 cm (4–20 in).
Spacing and planting distance: 15–30 cm (6–12 in).
Soil: ordinary, well-drained.
Aspect: sun.
Propagation: from seed or by division in spring.
Flowering season: summer to autumn.
Type: perennial shrub.

△ *Primula juliae*

△ *Primula palinuri*
▽ *Primula vialii*

△ *Primula bulleyana*
Primula sieboldii alba ▷
▽ *Primula nutans*

▽ *Primula auricula* 'Irish Blue'

Primula

PRIMULA, PRIMROSE

Primulaceae

The primrose family is a vast one, ranging from the tiniest rock garden plants to plants which are almost giant-sized, growing to nearly 100 cm (40 in) in height. There is a similar diversity of habitats and colours, with a definite preference for pastel shades. Both very well-known plants and rarities for collectors are to be found here.

Useful hints

— Plant in spring, preferably, or in early autumn for the early flowering varieties, which must establish themselves well before winter sets in if they are to flower correctly in the first days of spring.

— Mulch with pine bark or peat and water regularly throughout the first summer, as primroses enjoy coolness.

— Divide clumps which have become too large after flowering and replant them immediately.

Recommended

— *Primula vulgaris* and its varieties flower early, some even from autumn onwards. They are ideal companions for tulips and forget-me-nots. Flowering continues for two months.

— *P. alpicola*, whose pale yellow, bell-like flowers exhale a delicious perfume, is a charming addition to the spring garden.

— The bright yellow flowers of *P. helodoxa* are arranged up the stem in five or six successive whorls.

208

△ **Primula florindae**
▽ **Primula waltonii**

△ **Primula denticulata**
Primula japonica ▷
▽ **Primula japonica**

— Other beauties, in brief: *P. denticulata* (drumstick primrose) with its pink, white or lilac flowers clustered in pompons; *P. auricula* and *P. pulverulenta* with fleshy leaves covered in a floury substance; *P. rosea*, which is very compact but with quite large flowers; *P. capitata*, not very hardy, which dazzles with the beauty of its flowers that resemble a blue hyacinth from afar, and give off the same heady scent; and *P. sieboldii*, producing white, pink or purple flowers in early summer. There is a multitude of bright, prolific varieties to choose from, including 'Geisha Girl', pink; 'Snowflake', white; 'Mikado', magenta; 'Seraphim', lavender-blue.

Height: 10–100 cm (4–40 in).
Spacing and planting distance: 10–30 cm (4–12 in).
Soil: cool and rich in humus.
Aspect: semi-shade.
Propagation: from seed or by division in spring.
Flowering season: spring to summer.
Type: perennial.

— Of the candelabra primroses, with flowers arranged in little clusters around the tall stems, *P. beesiana* is lilac-pink while *P. bulleyana* is yellow-orange, colourings which are rare among primroses. Japanese primroses (*P. japonica*) are similar in appearance and love moist corners. The purplish red *P. japonica* 'Miller's Crimson' and *P. j.* 'Postford White', both with a dark eye, are still the best varieties.

— *P. florindae* (giant yellow cowslip) can grow to a height of 100 cm (40 in) and has enchanting pale lemon flowers which are delightfully perfumed. There are also forms with red or copper-coloured flowers.

— There are delights for our rock gardens, too; *P. juliae*, pale pink, is a real gem. 'Verveana' is violet and 'Wanda' purple. *P. vialii* has unusual flowers and needs a great deal of care to thrive.

— With all the appearance of an indoor primrose, *P. polyneura* is one of the best varieties for planting beneath shrubs.

Prunella grandiflora △

Prunella

SELF-HEAL

Labiatae

Common self-heal often happens to take root in shady corners of our gardens, and very few plants can rival it for forming dense ground cover, carpeted with flowers in summer.

Useful hints

— Plant in autumn and mulch from spring onwards. Water regularly to promote rooting. Cut the clumps down at the end of the summer to make them even prettier next year.

— Divide the clumps in spring when they become hollow in the centre.

Recommended

— *Prunella grandiflora* has given birth to a number of varieties including the well-known 'Blue Loveliness', 'Loveliness' with pale lilac flowers, 'Pink Loveliness' and 'White Loveliness'.

Height: 15–20 cm (6–8 in).
Spacing and planting distance: 20 cm (8 in).
Soil: ordinary, preferably rich in humus.
Aspect: shade.
Propagation: by division in spring.
Flowering season: summer to autumn.
Type: perennial.

Psylliostachys

see *Limonium*

Pulmonaria

LUNGWORT, JERUSALEM COWSLIP

Boraginaceae

Why is it that lungworts are not more widely used as ground cover? Their evergreen foliage, spotted with silver, is certainly the equal of supposedly decorative plants like dead nettles or ornamental bramble, for example. When they flower, in mid-spring, they herald the return of spring, even outstripping the primroses and violets.

Useful hints

— Plant in spring or autumn, under shrubs or as ground cover, in semi-shade in good ordinary soil.

— Although they do prefer well-drained soils, lungworts will grow quite easily in moist soils.

Recommended

— As well as *Pulmonaria officinalis* with its red and blue flowers, you can try *P. angustifolia* ssp. *azurea* with its sky-blue flowers and vivid green foliage, and, best of all, *P. saccharata* (Jerusalem cowslip) with flowers of pink through to blue.

— *P. longifolia* has long leaves densely spotted with silver.

— *P. officinalis* 'Sissinghurst White' is the variety with the most striking markings.

— *P. rubra* 'Redstart' is a plain-leaved variety, but has bright red flowers.

— *P.* 'Margery Fish' has larger leaves with broad, overlapping markings.

Height: 20 cm (8 in).
Spacing and planting distance: 20 cm (8 in).
Soil: ordinary.
Aspect: semi-shade.
Propagation: by division in autumn or spring.
Flowering season: spring.
Type: perennial.

△ *Pulmonaria saccharata* 'Mrs Moon'
▽ *Pulmonaria saccharata*

210

Puschkinia scilloïdes △
◁ *Pulsatilla vulgaris*

Puschkinia

STRIPED SQUILL

Liliaceae

When spring comes, *Puschkinia scilloïdes* forms, along with glory of the snow, grape hyacinths, squills and hyacinths, the prettiest borders of all. It thrives quite happily in any position as long as the soil is rich. It can be planted alongside hardy perennials like coral flower or tellima whose foliage, reddened by the cold, blends well with their china-blue flowers. To stop your window-boxes looking sad once the crocuses lose their blooms, mix striped squill with the crocus bulbs when you plant them; they will then bloom in sequence. *P. scilloïdes* has a well-known variety called *libanotica*.

Useful hints

— Plant in autumn, at a depth of 10 cm (4 in) and with 10 cm (4 in) spacing, in all directions, in good soil, rich in humus.

— Plant, preferably, in borders or well-drained, sunny beds; the plants will flourish.

Recommended

— As well as the typical variety with blue flowers, there is a pretty white variety, *libanotica* 'Alba'.

Height: 15 cm (6 in).
Spacing and planting distance: 10 cm (4 in).
Soil: rich in humus.
Aspect: sun or semi-shade.
Propagation: by separating bulbs, after leaves have dried off completely.
Flowering season: spring.
Type: bulb.

Pulsatilla

ANEMONE, PASQUE FLOWER

Ranunculaceae

A real pearl for the rock garden, every spring *Pulsatilla vulgaris* opens out its little bell-shaped flowers of violet-blue, whose petals form perfect stars. The hairy leaves develop as the flowers fade. With foliage as pretty as their flowers, these little plants will be shown off to best advantage set against a miniature landscape to serve as a backdrop for them: a rock garden, of course, but also steps of sunny stones, ferns in the semi-shade. The only requirement is well-drained soil to make them flourish.

Useful hints

— Any good, well-drained soil is suitable for it to fill out quickly. Take care when planting by incorporating half a shovelful of well-rotted compost.

— Plant in autumn or at the beginning of spring.

— Avoid moist soil in winter. If your garden is chalky and quite dry, on the other hand, you will have nothing to fear.

Recommended

— As well as the typical violet-blue, there is a white variety, *Pulsatilla vulgaris alba*, and a red one, *P. v. rubra*.

Height: 20 cm (8 in).
Spacing and planting distance: 15 cm (6 in).
Soil: well-drained.
Aspect: sun.
Propagation: from seed or by division in autumn.
Flowering season: spring.
Type: perennial.

211

△ *Ranunculus asiaticus* hybrid

Ranunculus

BUTTERCUP, CROWFOOT

Ranunculaceae

Do not hesitate to plant these butter-cups with their shimmering colours. They will provide the material for any number of flower arrangements, as they last well in water. Some species are in-vasive and therefore unsuitable.

Useful hints

— *Ranunculus asiaticus*, the Persian buttercup, and its hybrids are planted in autumn in warm climates and in spring elsewhere.

— Plant at a depth of 5 cm (2 in) with the shoot uppermost, spacing the tubers every 20 cm (8 in) as each clump grows very large.

— Water little in winter and more and more in spring, adding some liquid manure from time to time.

— Lift the tubers when the foliage turns yellow.

— Keep the dry tubers in sand or peat, protected against the frost, during winter.

Recommended

— *R. asiaticus* is tuberous-rooted and generally sold as double-flowered vari-eties in a wide range of colours, often referred to as turban ranunculus.

Height: 20–40 cm (8–16 in).
Spacing and planting distance: 20 cm (8 in).
Soil: cool and very rich in humus.
Aspect: sun or semi-shade.
Propagation: by division in autumn.
Flowering season: spring to summer.
Type: perennial.

△ *Ramonda myconi*

Pyrethrum

see *Chrysanthemum*

Ramonda

RAMONDA, ROSETTE-MULLEIN

Gesneriaceae

Although burdened with the reputation of being a difficult plant to grow, *Ramonda myconi* in fact will thrive if given a northerly aspect and will endure the most extreme winters. We know of some plants which have thrived in pots for several years and are now as large as plates. And the flowers are reminiscent of some of the cyclamen. This plant has the feature of being able to dry itself out and then return to life, rather like some mosses.

Useful hints

— Plant in a crack between two rocks in a pocket of sandy soil.

— If you want to enjoy them from closer to hand, plant them in pots which are wider than they are deep, filled with a mixture of peat and sand. Shelter them from the sun by placing them at the foot of a north-facing wall and in winter bring them in under a cold frame.

— Seeds are possible in spring but they take at least a year to give any results.

Height: 20 cm (8 in).
Spacing and planting distance: 20 cm (8 in).
Soil: sandy.
Aspect: north-facing.
Propagation: from seed or by division, and by leaf propagation in spring.
Flowering season: spring.
Type: perennial.

Raoulia

RAOULIA

Compositae

Raoulia australis is a fascinating plant. Originally from New Zealand, it makes a carpet at ground level, following the contours of any slight unevenness in the ground. Its cultivation is not easy, however, as it dislikes excessive dampness in winter.

Useful hints

— Plant in spring, in a well-drained pocket of earth among paving stones. Water regularly during the first summer. As the frosts approach, cover with crushed bark and a plastic film to avoid excessive water.

— At the end of winter, take a small handful of sand and shake it gently over the clump. You can divide it at the same time, too, and let the portions root in sand.

Height: 2 cm (¾ in).
Spacing and planting distance: 20 cm (8 in).
Soil: very sandy.
Aspect: sun.
Propagation: by division in spring.
Flowering season: barely visible, in spring.
Type: perennial.

▽ *Raoulia australis*

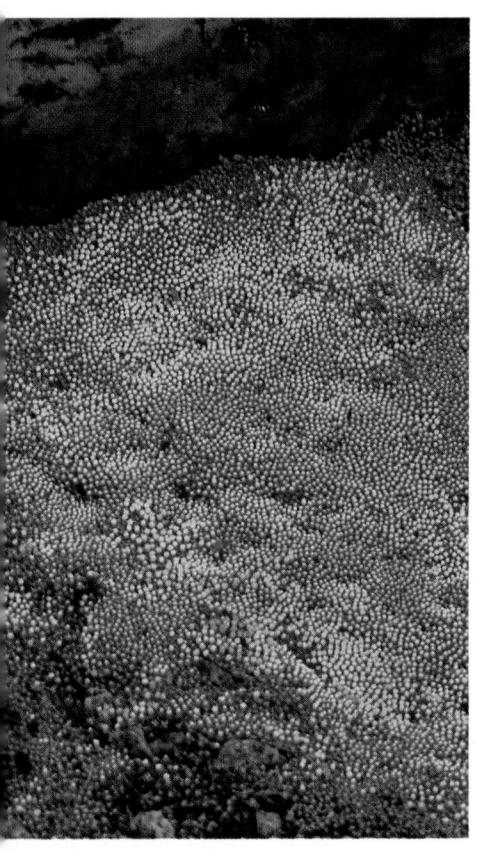

Reseda alba △
Rheum palmatum ▽

Reseda

MIGNONETTE

Resedaceae

The fragrant mignonette (*Reseda odorata*), with its white spears, is well-known in our gardens. Less known, *R. alba* deserves greater attention as it is much more spectacular. With its long thick spears of a milky white, it has its place in beds where, in the company of bellflowers, old roses and delphiniums, it can give a breathtaking display which needs hardly any attention. Although cultivated as an annual, it can survive in warmer climates for two or three years. However, like the snapdragon, it unfortunately tends to lose some of its charm with age.

Useful hints

— Any good ordinary soil, even quite heavy, suits it.

— Loving the light, it enjoys growing in sunny, well-aerated beds.

— As it cannot stand being transplanted, sow it *in situ*, in spring.

Recommended

— As well as *R. alba* you can buy fragrant mignonettes in improved varieties such as 'Goliath'.

Height: 30 cm (12 in).
Spacing and planting distance: 15 cm (6 in).
Soil: ordinary.
Aspect: sun.
Propagation: from seed, at beginning of spring.
Flowering season: summer.
Type: perennial.

Rheum

ORNAMENTAL RHUBARB

Polygonaceae

The sight of *Rheum palmatum* occupying the place of honour in many of the grandest gardens is an inspiring one. It is a truly imposing plant which needs, like its cousin the edible rhubarb, plenty of room to develop. As it is very greedy, give it a good bed and, as bedfellows, sturdy and economical plants such as gaura, tansy, hogweed and loosestrife, which will keep it company while allowing it its pride of place.

Useful hints

— Before planting, in spring, carefully enrich the soil with half a barrowload of well-rotted manure per square metre.

— Always plant it in rich soil which is cool and deep. It is not averse to clay.

— Plant in full sunlight, but do not stint on watering in summer.

— As soon as flowering is over, cut off the dead heads. To maintain the beauty of the plants, one can even prevent them from flowering by cutting off the flower stems as soon as they appear.

Recommended

— The young leaves of *R. palmatum* 'Atrosanguineum' emerge purple and remain reddish on the underside.

Height: 150 cm (60 in).
Spacing and planting distance: 100 cm (40 in).
Soil: cool and deep.
Aspect: sun.
Propagation: by division in autumn.
Flowering season: summer.
Type: perennial.

Rhodanthe manglesii

see *Helipterum manglesii*

△ *Rhodohypoxis baurii*
◁ *Ricinus communis*

Rhodohypoxis

RHODOHYPOXIS

Hypoxidaceae

This plant is really an investment; you pay a fortune for a tiny tuberous root, you cosset it for a few years, and you find yourself the owner of something magnificent and priceless. For it is hard to resist the beauty of these rather waxy flowers, with a purity of colour ranging from white to magenta. The most amazing feature is the length of the flowering season: almost five months, from spring to autumn.

Useful hints

— Plant in spring in a well-drained pot filled with a mixture of compost and sand. Bury the root 5 cm (2 in) down and sprinkle gravel over the soil to prevent it settling.

— Water regularly in summer. Shelter under a cold frame in winter.

Height: 5–10 cm (2–4 in).
Spacing and planting distance: 5 cm (2 in).
Soil: light and rich in humus.
Aspect: sun.
Propagation: by separating offsets at the beginning of spring.
Flowering season: spring to autumn.
Type: perennial.

Ricinus

CASTOR OIL PLANT

Euphorbiaceae

Effortless and spectacular. If you have a corner in your garden which could benefit from the speedy instalment of an imposing and decorative plant, then the castor oil plant could be the answer. With its big palmate leaves, as shiny as an oilcloth, and its crimson fruits, which look like cane apples, it is full of charm. Thanks to its remarkable vitality, *Ricinus communis*, in the space of a few months, presents you with a bush as tall as you are, all from a few large mottled seeds (which are *very poisonous*), which you sowed, in the warm, in the first days of spring. *R. communis* 'Impala' produces scarlet fruits which stand out against the red-brown leaves.

Useful hints

— Sow at 20°C (68°F) after soaking the seeds for twenty-four hours to soften them. Then keep the young plants warm until planting, after the last frosts, in a sunny position.

— Give it a very rich soil if you want it to grow to full size. At the time of planting, give it two handfuls of concentrated fertilizer, in granule form.

— On the coast, beware of winds. Provide support.

Height: 150 cm (60 in).
Spacing and planting distance: 150 cm (60 in).
Soil: very rich.
Aspect: full sun.
Propagation: from seed in spring.
Flowering season: summer.
Type: annual.

Rodgersia

RODGERSIA

Saxifragaceae

Along with gunnera and ornamental rhubarb, rodgersia is one of the most majestic of our garden plants. Planted in cool soils, which they love, they develop imposing foliage, similar to, depending on the particular variety, that of the chestnut, the elder or the lotus. Give them a damp corner alongside astilbes, ferns and Japanese primroses and you will have a stunning effect.

Useful hints

— Plant in spring or in autumn. Break up the soil at depth and improve it with peat so that it stays cool in summer. Mulch the soil with pine bark or peat in summer.

— Slugs can devour part of the young shoots; dissuade them from doing so with bait. In winter, let the frozen foliage protect the clumps from the cold.

Recommended

— *Rodgersia aesculifolia* can really be mistaken for a dwarf horse-chestnut except when the flowers, creamy white

△ *Rodgersia aesculifolia*
Romneya coulteri ▷

spears, appear, reaching more than 100 cm (40 in).

— *R. pinnata* has divided leaves but they are arranged on either side of a central spine. Often the leaves have a bronze sheen. *R. pinnata* 'Elegans' offers a particularly elegant display of pink flower spikes.

— The leaves of *R. podophylla* always have sumptuous bronze or coppery tinges.

— The most spectacular of the rodgersias is undoubtedly *R. tabularis* (syn. *Astilboides tabularis*), the leaves of which are almost circular and grow to 90 cm (36 in) in diameter. Their edge is folded down, giving them the appearance of Chinese ceremonial parasols.

Height: 80–120 cm (32–48 in).
Spacing and planting distance: 60 cm (24 in).
Soil: rich and always cool.
Aspect: semi-shade.
Propagation: by division in spring.
Flowering season: summer.
Type: perennial.

▽ *Rodgersia aesculifolia*

Romneya

TREE POPPY, MATILIJA POPPY

Papaveraceae

This looks like a crêpe-paper flower. Imagine a huge armful of silvery stems, a host of big white flowers, ruffled and crowned with a pompom of golden yellow stamens, and there you have the almost unreal picture of the beauty of *Romneya coulteri*. These plants reach their full splendour in the height of the summer, in wide, rather disorderly strips in the sandy gardens of seaside areas. This fragile beauty is in fact reserved for the most protected southern gardens. Further north only the most careful gardeners are lucky. But if you are successful, you may get hooked – it is worth taking a risk.

Useful hints

— Like most of the poppy family, the tree poppy does not like to be transplanted. Nurserymen sell it in pots, which means it can be planted without disturbing the rootball.

— Loving light soil, it must have lavished upon it two shovels of leaf-mould or peat, to be incorporated into the soil at the time of planting.

— At the onset of winter, cut it back to 15 cm (6 in) from the ground and cover its clump with 20 cm (8 in) of dried-out dead leaves or ferns.

Height: 150–200 cm (60–80 in).
Spacing and planting distance: 150–200 cm (60–80 in).
Soil: light.
Aspect: sheltered and sunny.
Propagation: from seed in spring.
Flowering season: summer.
Type: perennial.

Rudbeckia hirta △
Rudbeckia laciniatus ▽

▽ *Ruta graveolens*
Ruscus aculeatus ▽

Rudbeckia

CONEFLOWER

Compositae

With its strange flowers with a prominent heart, in either black or green, its petals folded back like the ears of a suspicious cat, the coneflower has a look that is all its own. Flowering at the end of summer, at the same time as the inulas, coneflowers make a beautiful end to the season grown with ornamental tobaccos, and will keep the Chinese lanterns company until the first frosts. The warm tones of their flowers are a joy to the eye in autumn.

Useful hints

— Sow annual coneflowers in spring in seed trays, under shelter, then plant out after the frosts are over.

— Plant perennial varieties early, in the spring.

— Any good garden soil suits them well, provided that they are given a sunny position.

Recommended

— From among the annuals choose *Rudbeckia hirta* 'Marmalade', with its warm gold colour. From the perennials, opt for *R. fulgida* var. *deamii* for its orange flowers ringed with yellow, *R. laciniatus* for its foliage and *R. nitida* for its huge yellow flowers topped with a little green cone. 'Goldquelle' produces an abundance of large, bright yellow flowers, while *R. fulgida* var. *sullivantii* 'Goldsturm', with its clusters of well-ordered, upright stalks crowned with large yellow flowers, is most distinctive.

Height: 60–80 cm (24–32 in).
Spacing and planting distance: 30 cm (12 in).
Soil: ordinary.
Aspect: sun.
Propagation: from seed in spring, by division in autumn or in spring.
Flowering season: summer to autumn.
Type: annual, perennial.

Ruscus

BUTCHER'S BROOM, BOX HOLLY

Liliaceae

It is hard to imagine that this little evergreen is a distant relative of the ornamental asparagus. And just like the asparagus, its leaves are in fact flattened stems. It is only at the time of fertilization, which occurs when male and female plants are planted side by side, that the resemblance becomes more striking, as the red berries are almost identical to those of the asparagus (they are also similar to the holly's from a distance). Plant them next to fuchsias, busy lizzies, bleeding hearts and lilies to create informal or formal arrangements.

Useful hints

— Plant *Ruscus aculeatus* in spring, in a shady corner. Water regularly throughout the first year. Growth is very slow at first and the plants only really establish themselves at the end of three years.

— Divide the clumps every five years or else their hearts tend to lose their leaves. The same might also occur after exceptionally hard frosts. The normally evergreen foliage can even disappear quite suddenly. A dose of fertilizer in spring will aid regrowth.

Height: 40–60 cm (16–24 in).
Spacing and planting distance: 30 cm (12 in).
Soil: ordinary, preferably slightly heavy.
Aspect: sun or semi-shade.
Propagation: in autumn, by division, taking cuttings or from seeds.
Flowering season: summer.
Type: perennial.

Ruta

RUE, HERB OF GRACE

Rutaceae

In former times *Ruta graveolens* was cultivated for its medicinal powers but it is now enjoyed largely for its sea-green foliage and acid-yellow flowers. It is an excellent border plant and a good companion for old roses and yellow summer flowers. There is a more compact variety, 'Jackman's Blue', and one with variegated leaves.

Useful hints

— Plant in spring, preferably. Water regularly during the first summer and mulch the soil. In later years rue can survive quite harsh droughts.

— Take cuttings from the ends of the stems in summer and root in a very sandy mixture or sow in spring. These usually take well and produce great quantities of young plants which flourish from the second year.

— Prune them back every spring to half their height to make them bushier.

Height: 100 cm (40 in).
Spacing and planting distance: 30 cm (12 in).
Soil: rich in humus.
Aspect: shade.
Propagation: by division in spring or cuttings in summer.
Flowering season: spring.
Type: perennial.

Sagina

PEARLWORT

Caryophyllaceae

Sagina subulata is one of the favourite plants of those who are interested in Japanese-style gardens because, like helxine, it gives the impression of a newly mown lawn. Moreover, in summer it is covered in tiny white flowers. Sometimes its greenery is used for filling in spaces between the flagstones of a path, and at other times it is used for marking out large geometrical shapes on top of a flagstone base. Unfortunately it is not always as hardy as one would wish. Like other small evergreen plants it is more attractive when grown among other foliage plants, such as hostas or ferns, or when it serves as a foil to a clump of fuchsias. It is also suitable for town gardens where grass doesn't do so well.

Useful hints

— Plant rooted cuttings or divided clumps all year round in well-dug soil completely cleared of weeds.

— Water copiously and regularly during the summer, adding some liquid nitrogen fertilizer to the water once a month.

Height: 5 cm (2 in).
Spacing and planting distance: 10 cm (4 in).
Soil: ordinary.
Aspect: sun.
Propagation: by cuttings or division all year round.
Flowering season: summer.
Type: perennial.

Sagittaria

ARROWHEAD

Alismataceae

Arrowhead is easily recognizable by its leaves which are shaped just like the tips of arrows children draw. It is an aquatic plant native to the edge of rivers and streams. The flowers, white with purple at the centre, grow above the water on strong stems. An excellent plant for small ponds, *Sagittaria sagittifolia* never actually hides the water but rather lends elegance to the setting.

Useful hints

— Plant out in early summer in a rich soil covered by at least 30 cm (12 in) of water. Divide the clumps in spring by separating basal shoots.

— Any leaves growing underwater should be left in place even if they do

△ *Salpiglossis sinuata*
◁ *Sagittaria sagittifolia*
▽ *Sagina subulata*

look more like grass than adult leaves, as they will aid the plant's growth.

Height: 30–80 cm (12–32 in) underwater, 30–60 cm (12–24 in) above.
Spacing and planting distance: 50 cm (20 in).
Soil: rich.
Aspect: sun.
Propagation: by division in spring.
Flowering season: summer.
Type: perennial.

Salpiglossis

SALPIGLOSSIS, PAINTED TONGUE

Solanaceae

Few plants have such a visual impact as this. With its trumpet-shaped blooms, striped or veined in the brightest colours, *Salpiglossis sinuata* creates a really lovely effect. Although the individual flowers are short-lived, they are constantly renewed throughout the summer. You can grow them in large groups or place them in small patches here and there in borders. Since they have only modest foliage, all you will see are the magnificent blooms. You could also try placing them among grey-leaved plants, such as artemisia.

Useful hints

— Sow in spring in a cold frame. Plant out 20 cm (8 in) apart once they are a few centimetres high. They can also be sown direct into their final position, but for this you should wait until after the frosts.

— Keep well watered and remove withered flowers to prolong the flowering period. Pruning the branches in summer will encourage new growth.

Height: 60 cm (24 in).
Spacing and planting distance: 20 cm (8 in).
Soil: ordinary, preferably light.
Aspect: sun.
Propagation: from seed in spring.
Flowering season: summer to autumn.
Type: annual.

Salvia

SAGE, RAMONA

Labiatae

Without salvias, summer would seem quite dull. Not only is there the popular red salvia, sometimes a little too common-place, but there is also a whole host of relatives, more or less perennial, which can put on a splendid show of blues and purples. They reign supreme over sunny, slightly dry places.

Useful hints

— Sow annual salvias in spring, in warm conditions. Harden them off before finally planting them out after the frosts are over, in soil enriched with leaf-mould. Cut back the main stems by half to encourage business. Mulch the soil with peat or semi-decomposed compost. Water every week adding plant food once a month. Trim withered flowers regularly.

— Plant perennial salvias in early autumn or in spring. Lighten the soil with sand and be careful not to over-feed otherwise the plant will become too leafy. Trim withered stems and cut back growth in late summer once the leaves have dried out. New leaves will begin to appear right up until the first frosts.

Recommended

— **Annuals**: Above its leaves, *Salvia viridis* produces stems sporting visible bracts which surround the real, rather small flowers. Available in several colours, from pink to deep purple, they also make good dried flowers.

— *S. splendens* is the famous red salvia seen in so many gardens. Each supplier has his own particular varieties on offer, but they are all in fact very similar. Rather than choosing the super dwarfs, which are really not at all elegant, try going for the medium-tall varieties like 'Bonfire', which although they appear later are more decorative.

— **Perennials**: Best for dampening the blaze of colour caused by the red salvia is *S. farinacea*, which is available in blue, 'Victoria', and white, 'Alba' – a mixture of rare delicacy. They will remain in flower for several weeks.

— Without doubt the loveliest of all is *S. argentea*, with its fabulous silvery leaves. To keep it at its best, protect the clump with sheets of glass throughout the winter months as this plant cannot tolerate the combination of cold and damp.

— The blue sprays of *S. azurea*, which needs protecting in colder climates, come into bloom in late summer.

— *S. officinalis*, the common sage, is well-known for its leaves, which are used in cooking. The flowers together with the violet-tinted silver foliage are a particularly successful combination and they provide a good foil for a range of plants, including roses and carnations. *S. officinalis* 'Grandiflora' bears flowers of a deeper blue. 'Berggarten' stands out by virtue of its broad, almost circular leaves; it flourishes only in warm locations. *S.o.* 'Icterina' has green leaves splashed with yellow variegation. *S.o.* Purpurascens Group is completely purple.

— *S. patens* isn't really hardy but the extravagant blue of its flowers (one of the brightest in nature) makes it well worth the trouble of protecting it in winter with a layer of pine bark. If you

△ *Salvia patens*

△ *Salvia buchananii*
▽ *Salvia viridis*

plant it next to a white tobacco plant, its rather uncertain green leaves will be less in evidence

— The meadow salvia, *S. pratensis*, is an attractive weed found in ditches. The Haematodes Group will astonish you by the amazing mass of flowers they produce.

— The striking *S. sclarea* is another beautiful salvia with a very natural look. Whether the scent of its leaves is pleasant or disagreeable is debatable, but everyone loves the pale blue flowers, which provide some of the best associations for traditional roses. It does very well as a biennial and will quite happily seed itself.

— The most widespread of all the perennial salvias is *S. nemorosa*, noted for its compact shape. There are many varieties to choose from, among which 'Lubecca' is violet and 'Ostfriesland' is even darker.

— Several other species could be mentioned, such as *S. microphylla* var. *microphylla*, *S. uliginosa* or *S. coccinea*, but their hardiness is not always reliable.

Height: 20–150 cm (8–60 in).
Spacing and planting distance: 15–50 cm (6–20 in).
Soil: ordinary, but well-drained.
Aspect: sun.
Propagation: from seed or by division in spring.
Flowering season: summer to autumn.
Type: annual, biennial, perennial.

△ *Salvia sclarea*
◁ *Salvia splendens*
▽ *Salvia sclarea* var. *turkestanica*

Sanguinaria

BLOODROOT, RED PUCCOON

Papaveraceae

Don't go looking for any red in the flowers of *Sanguinaria canadensis*, a relative of the celandine, as it is in fact the root which 'bleeds' when you pull it out. The flowers are as white as snow. The double-flowered variety 'Plena' lasts longer and is considered to boast some of the most beautiful double flowers in existence. They are almost as round and full-bodied as some old-fashioned roses.

Useful hints

— Plant in autumn in a shady corner with a soil rich in peat. Growth is rapid and the plants will burst into flower only a few weeks after the leaves have begun to appear in the spring.

— You can encourage leaf growth by mulching the soil with pine bark or peat.

— It may also be necessary to continue watering right through the summer.

— The rhizomes should be carefully dug up every five years and replanted some distance away with a handful of sand scattered into the soil.

Height: 20 cm (8 in).
Spacing and planting distance: 20 cm (8 in).
Soil: rich in peat.
Aspect: shade.
Propagation: by separating new rhizomes once the leaves have died back.
Flowering season: spring.
Type: perennial.

Sanguisorba

BURNET

Rosaceae

Our good old burnet, with its edible leaves similar in taste to cucumber, has a number of decorative Canadian and Japanese relatives, such as *Sanguisorba obtusa*, which grows to a height of 20 cm (8 in) with pale purple flowers. All the sanguisorbas have in common pretty green, pinnate foliage and flowers borne on long and slender stems. They are ideal for the wild garden and grow well with hellebores and ferns. They can be grown together with spring bulbs which easily acclimatize, such as tulips, the small-flowered narcissi, and *Fritillaria meleagris* (snake's head).

△ *Sanguisorba canadensis*
Sanguisorba obtusa △
◁ *Santolina rosmarinifolia* ssp. *rosmarinifolia*
▽ *Santolina chamaecyparissus*

Useful hints

— Plant in autumn or spring in well-dug soil. Water regularly for the first summer. Thereafter they can be left to their own devices.

— Divide the clumps every three years and replant immediately.

Recommended

— *S. canadensis*. In the 'Multiplex' variety, all the stamens have become petals and form tight clusters.

Height: 20–120 cm (8–48 in).
Spacing and planting distance: 60 cm (24 in).
Soil: rich in humus.
Aspect: sun or semi-shade.
Propagation: by division in spring.
Flowering season: summer.
Type: perennial.

Santolina

COTTON LAVENDER

Compositae

For foliage that stands out, is silver-coloured and has an attractive scent, nothing could be better than santolina. It is a very graceful plant with its grey leaves that are both dense and finely delineated. Bushy, but easy to keep in shape, and with prolific flowers, santolina will fill out gaps in sunny paving and low walls.

Useful hints

— Good garden soil will be sufficient for this plant, but it has a Mediterranean temperament and does best in the sunniest positions. It will be happiest in nooks and crannies of dry stone walls, along with valerian, stonecrop and wallflowers.

— As soon as flowering is over in summer, trim it lightly.

— Avoid planting it in moist or water-logged soil, as this is its worst enemy.

Recommended

— The most popular is *Santolina chamaecyparissus*, but *S. rosmarinifolia* ssp. *rosmarinifolia* is a very pretty delicate green and bears the same yellow pom-pon-shaped flowers as its relative.

Height: 30 cm (12 in).
Spacing and planting distance: 30 cm (12 in).
Soil: ordinary, well-drained.
Aspect: sun.
Propagation: by division in spring.
Flowering season: summer.
Type: perennial.

Saponaria ocymoïdes ▷

Sanvitalia

CREEPING ZINNIA

Compositae

If you are looking for a small plant for a neat border, look no further than *Sanvitalia procumbens*. Sowing in spring will provide you with beautiful neat 'cushions', covered in little yellow flowers with black centres, throughout the summer.

Useful hints

— Sow in the final position in late spring and water every other day until the plant is well established. Thin out the seedlings one month later. At the same time, mulch the soil with grass cuttings.

— Remove all faded flowers once a fortnight and use garden shears to tidy up the border as necessary.

Height: 15 cm (6 in).
Spacing and planting distance: 20 cm (8 in).
Soil: ordinary.
Aspect: sun.
Propagation: from seed in spring.
Flowering season: summer to first frosts.
Type: annual.

Saponaria

SOAPWORT

Caryophyllaceae

The little pink soapwort (*Saponaria ocymoïdes*) grows on dry stone walls, rock gardens and sunny terraces. The pink soapwort will soon make a carpet of flowers, as it seems to have only one aim in life: to spread out as much as possible. Be careful therefore not to cramp it but allow it as much room as possible, for it will happily cover your whole terrace. If you mix it with *Cerastium tomentosum* you will obtain a marvellous pastel-coloured carpet.

Useful hints

— Saponaria is best planted in spring,

△ *Sanvitalia procumbens*

in an ordinary well-drained soil, in a sunny site.

— Water once a week to begin with, to ensure the roots take, and then gradually more sparingly until the plants are well established, when watering will no longer be necessary.

— Divide the clumps every three years.

Recommended

— The bright pink flowers of *S.* 'Bressingham' bloom earlier (late spring to summer) than those of *S. ocymoïdes*.

— The widely spaced clumps of *S.* × *lempergii* will flower continuously for three months.

— *S. officinalis*, the wild soapwort, has a double variety, 'Rosea Plena', which flourishes in colder soils.

Height: 30 cm (12 in).
Spacing and planting distance: 15 cm (6 in).
Soil: ordinary, well-drained.
Aspect: sun.
Propagation: by division in autumn or spring.
Flowering season: summer.
Type: perennial.

△ *Sarracenia flava* 'Maxima'

Sarracenia

PITCHER PLANT

Sarraceniaceae

It's hard to say what is the most striking feature of sarracenias – their brilliantly coloured rolled-up leaves, reminiscent of old-fashioned gentleman's breeches which serve as a trap for insects, or their flowers, which are unique in the plant world. It is well worth allowing these plants a small space, if you can provide the humid spot they need, unless you prefer to grow them in pots, where it is easier to appreciate their strange shape.

Useful hints

— Plant sarracenias in spring, in pockets of peaty soil around a pond or pool. Spread sphagnum moss around the clumps to create a natural environment and combine them with Venus fly-trap or sundew. They will do well in a mild winter, but it's a good idea to cover the crown with peat and plastic film so that the birds cannot disturb them.

— When planting in pots, see that these are wider than their height, and fill with light peat, which should be kept moist. In winter, place the pots under a cold frame or shelter in a very slightly heated greenhouse. In the summer they can be put in a sunny position and should be watered twice weekly.

Height: 30–60 cm (12–24 in).
Spacing and planting distance: 30 cm (12 in).
Soil: peat.
Aspect: sun.
Propagation: by division in spring.
Flowering season: spring.
Type: perennial.

Saxifraga

SAXIFRAGE, ROCKFOIL

Saxifragaceae

Saxifrages are very well-known to rock garden lovers, particularly for their ability to break up rocks. It's certainly true that they do well in crevices. Many of them are sought by collectors, who go to great pains to grow them on flat ground, and others are a boon to the gardener as they will grow in even the densest shade.

Useful hints

— Plant in spring in light and well-drained pockets of soil. Add sand if necessary; they are best suited to a semi-sunny position.

— Before the winter sets in, sprinkle gravel around the neck of the plant so that water won't collect there.

▽ *Sarracenia rubra*

Recommended

— Among the **rosette** saxifrages, *Saxifraga paniculata* forms large silvery rosettes with leaves encrusted with lime secretions. The light, delicate flowers are usually white, but are pink in *S.p. rosea*. *S. cochlearis* is barely taller than 15 cm (6 in) and is white, as are *S. longifolia* and *S. umbrosa* (London pride), the well-known 'painter's despair', thus named because of its very delicate flowers which will move in the slightest breeze. There is also a pink variety and a variety with yellow-variegated leaves.

— Among **clump** saxifrages, the finest have to be *S. cortusifolia*, *S. fortunei* and *S. stolonifera* (syn. *S. sarmentosa*). They flower late, in summer or autumn, and look delightful in the shade and in window-boxes. Their flowers have two petals longer than the others, making them look like little comets. *S. fortunei* is better-known in its red variety, 'Rubrifolia'.

— *S. cotyledon* is one of the largest saxifrages in its group. Its pyramid-shaped spikes contain thousands of individual flowers.

— The **moss** saxifrages have two miniature types which strangely resemble moss: *S. oppositifolia*, a gem in a well-kept rock garden, which is covered in pink flowers in spring. *S. hypnoïdes* or 'Turkish lawn' will grow up to 10 cm (4 in) and has pink flowers. Along with *S. rosacea* this is one of the best plants to choose to fill in the spaces between paving stones.

Height: 10–30 cm (4–12 in).
Spacing and planting distance: 15 cm (6 in).
Soil: rich in humus and well-drained.
Aspect: sun or shade.
Propagation: by separating non-flowering rosettes in spring.
Flowering season: spring to autumn, depending on variety.
Type: perennial.

▽ *Saxifraga × irvingii*

△ *Saxifraga*
Saxifraga 'Rosea' △
Saxifraga 'Tumbling Waters' ▷
▽ *Saxifraga hypnoïdes*

Saxifraga cortusifolia △
Saxifraga crustata ▷

223

Scabiosa

SCABIOUS, PINCUSHION FLOWER

Dipsacaceae

Once very fashionable, scabious have fallen out of favour, possibly because of their sad-looking flowers. The violet and almost black-purple colouring of some is certainly very sombre, but they are as delicate and elegant as many other flowers. Don't hesitate to use them, especially the Caucasian variety which look so pretty with pink carnations.

Useful hints

— Sow annual scabious in spring, under a cold frame, or directly after the frosts are over, in a row in the kitchen garden, for example. Prick them out a month later and nip the stems half-way to make them branch out. Remove withered flowers so that seeds do not form.

— Plant perennial scabious in spring or autumn. Mulch the soil in summer with grass cuttings and divide up clumps every three years to rejuvenate them.

Recommended

— Annual scabious (*Scabiosa atropurpurea*), a large, double, varied type, is the best for bouquets and clumps. Support the plants discreetly, because they can grow up to 90 cm (36 in). *S. caucasica* is perennial and produces lavender-blue

△ *Scabiosa atropurpurea*
▽ *Scabiosa caucasia*

flowers, and also dark blue ones in the variety 'Moerheim Blue'. The perennial *S. ochroleuca* has pale yellow flowers.

— With its grey leaves and blue flowers, *S. graminifolia* flourishes in rock gardens.

— Frost barely interrupts the flowering of the rounded blue clusters of *S.* 'Butterfly Blue'.

Height: 60–90 cm (24–36 in).
Spacing and planting distance: 30 cm (12 in).
Soil: ordinary, preferably chalky and well-drained.
Aspect: sun.
Propagation: from seed and by division in spring.
Flowering season: summer to autumn.
Type: annual, perennial.

Schizanthus

BUTTERFLY FLOWER, POOR MAN'S ORCHID

Solanaceae

Schizanthus flowers are often compared to butterfly wings. They come in a whole range of colours, from the purest white to the darkest violet, and contain yellow markings in their curly flowers. It is a delicate flower which can fill a pot beautifully and could even be used as a border plant in the garden, although its flowering season is sadly limited.

Useful hints

— Sow in autumn and keep under a cold frame for the winter, or wait until spring. Harden off before the final planting. Water regularly and add a little nitrogen fertilizer if the leaves are yellow. This often means that it is too cold for the plant.

— Plant outside after the frosts are over alongside stiffer species, which will serve to prop them up, like cistus or stocks.

Recommended

— *Schizanthus pinnatus* Bouquet Series produces bush plants in a mixture of colours.

Height: 30–40 cm (12–16 in).
Spacing and planting distance: 20 cm (8 in).
Soil: fresh and rich in humus.
Aspect: sun.
Propagation: from seed, in autumn or spring.
Flowering season: summer to autumn.
Type: annual, biennial.

▽ *Schizanthus pinnatus*

Schizostylis

KAFFIR LILY, CRIMSON FLAG

Iridaceae

A smaller relative of croscosmia, *Schizostylis coccinea* shares a preference for well-drained soil near the sea. Its flowers, which range from pink to vermilion, look striking by the seaside. In the right place – next to the shining leaves of pittosporum – the flowers will be shown off to full effect, and if planted near calceolarias will look particularly effective.

Useful hints

— Plant in autumn in pockets of rich compost, spacing the roots out 10 cm (4 in) in all directions and covering with 5 cm (2 in) of soil.

— Protect from frost with a good bedding of leaves.

— Let the clumps fill out for three or four years so that the plants remain in flower.

— In regions where the climate is mild, they can be grown in pots (use five plants per 30 cm (12 in) pot); they will provide a lovely show in your window-boxes throughout the autumn.

Height: 30–50 cm (12–20 in).
Spacing and planting distance: 10 cm (4 in).
Soil: rich in humus.
Aspect: sun.
Propagation: by division in spring.
Flowering season: autumn.
Type: perennial.

▽ *Schizostylis coccinea*

△ *Scilla siberica*

▽ *Scilla campanulata*

Scilla

SQUILL

Liliaceae

From very early spring scillas begin to unfold their flowers; first the Persian scillas (*Scilla mischtschenkoana*), then Siberian scillas (*S. siberica*) and, finally, *S. campanulata* (syn. *Hyacinthoides hispanica*) in spring. These pretty pastel-coloured little flowers make a fine decoration for a wild garden with moist soil.

△ *Scilla peruviana*

Useful hints

— Plant scillas in autumn in large groupings by scattering a handful of about ten bulbs under your spring-flowering shrubs and planting them where they fall.

— Don't mix all the colours together; go for single colour splashes in quite wide areas.

— They will thrive in any kind of good garden soil.

— They can be grown successfully in bowls or pots indoors.

Recommended

— Among *S. campanulata* the loveliest varieties are 'Blue Queen', a bright blue; 'White City', white; 'Queen of the Pinks', pink. Among *S. siberica* the variety 'Spring Beauty' is a Prussian blue. *S. mischtschenkoana* is a milky blue colour and one of the first to flower, often at ground level.

Height: 10–30 cm (4–12 in).
Spacing and planting distance: 15 cm (6 in).
Soil: ordinary, well-drained.
Aspect: sun or semi-shade.
Propagation: by separating bulbs, when foliage is dry.
Flowering season: winter to spring.
Type: bulb.

Scutellaria

SKULLCAP

Labiatae

Scutellarias are widely used to decorate rock gardens. Their relatively late flowering season and mauve colouring provide useful cover for a bare, summer rock garden.

Useful hints

— Sow in spring in pockets of earth lightened with sand. Water regularly until they flower. Each spring add a little leaf compost around clumps to encourage lateral roots which may otherwise detach themselves.

— Watch out for *Scutellaria alpina*; it's very pretty but it tends to take over.

Recommended

— *S. alpina* grows no higher than 20 cm (8 in) but creates a carpet of almost 60 cm (24 in) in diameter. Light-grey leaves encase purplish blue flowers.

— *S. baicalensis* is a perennial species, originating from Siberia, around Lake Baikal. It forms clumps nearly 60 cm (24 in) high and looks a little like some nepetas.

Height: 20–60 cm (8–24 in).
Spacing and planting distance: 30 cm (12 in).
Soil: ordinary, well-drained in winter.
Aspect: sun.
Propagation: from seed or by division in spring.
Flowering season: summer.
Type: perennial.

▽ *Scutellaria baicalensis*

Sedum

STONECROP, ORPINE

Crassulaceae

These plants are a boon to gardens where the soil is thin. Their fleshy leaves, showing their relationship to the large family of succulent plants, are a proof of their durability where water is lacking. The genus is so varied that it contains types which thrive in full sunshine as well as those which will flourish in semi-shade; the latter could even also be grown in the sun if the soil is moist. Use them liberally to fill up all the spaces in your rock garden or the cracks between the stones of a low wall. Pair them with ornamental grasses and grey-leaved plants, which are just as well suited to poor conditions.

Useful hints

— Plant tall stonecrops in containers in autumn, or even in spring if you are worried about heavy rainfall. Cuttings planted directly in the earth at the same time often do very well.

— Once the flowering season is over, cut off withered stalks to encourage new, more abundant ones in the following season. If cobwebs appear on the ends of the stems of *Sedum spectabile*, this in an indication of an invasion by tiny caterpillars. Treat the plants with a suitable insecticide.

— Each spring bank up the crowns a little by adding a few handfuls of compost in the centre.

Recommended

— **Dwarf** stonecrops, which look good in rock gardens or as a border plant:

— *S. aizoon* is a deep yellow and flowers in high summer; it is reminiscent of the well-known fiery stonecrop or wall pepper (*S. acre*) which is used to highlight the tops of walls.

— *S. lydium* is an even smaller species with delightful sea-green or golden foliage, depending on variety 'Glaucum' or 'Aureum'.

— Two other well-known series of rampant stonecrop are *S. spathulifolium* and *S. spurium*. The former creates cushions of rosettes, giving rise to stems bearing bright yellow flowers, while the latter favours white ('Album'), purple ('Atropurpureum'), bright pink ('Coccineum'), or has yellow and pink variegated leaves ('Variegatum').

— **Medium and tall** species, which look best in clumps:

— The best-known is *S. spectabile*, whose pink, bright scarlet ('Brilliant') or deep red ('Meteor') blooms come out in autumn. They make an unforgettable sight with fuchsias and asters. Crossed with *S. telephium*, which grows on embankments, this Chinese species has given birth to the hybrid 'Autumn Joy', which is a lighter plant whose flowers change colour as they open.

— *S. album* is incredibly hardy, and will survive in the thinnest soils.

— The best variety for forming even mats of foliage is called *S. kamtschaticum* var. *floriferum*. Its golden yellow flowers are long-lasting.

— *S. kamtschaticum* itself forms glistening, dark green cushions.

— The slanting stems of *S. reflexum*, with their cylindrical bluish leaves, straighten when bearing their bunches of brilliant yellow flowers.

Height: 15–50 cm (6–20 in).
Spacing and planting distance: 25 cm (10 in).
Soil: ordinary, well-drained.
Aspect: sun or semi-shade.
Propagation: by division in spring.
Flowering season: summer to autumn.
Type: perennial.

△ **Sedum spathulifolium**
◁ **Sedum spectabile**
Sedum spurium ▷
▽ **Sedum acre**

Sempervivum

HOUSELEEK

Crassulaceae

This is another family of small, sparse plants. There is no need to lavish attention on them; you can just pop them in the ground, forget them, and the houseleek will take root! If you have an old thatched roof, or a spare corner in a gloomy low wall, try the houseleek. They are used traditionally to decorate timbers on thatched roofs, just as the iris can be used, and to such an extent that *Sempervivum tectorum* has won the name 'roof houseleek'.

Useful hints

— Plant in any ordinary soil, well-drained and in full sunshine, or between stones in a wall.

— Use in borders, but also in clumps; *S. arachnoïdeum* is particularly decorative, especially when it shows its pink flowers.

Recommended

— There are many species, but two can be particularly recommended – *S. arachnoïdeum*, called 'bride's veil' because of its fleecy veil covering, is decked with pretty pink flowers in summer, and *S. tectorum*, which has bronze-coloured rosettes and garnet flowers, but is unfortunately quite rare. *S. calcareum* is a closely related species, the tips of whose leaves have a pronounced brown tinge.

— The leaves of *S. ciliosum* sometimes take on a brownish colour that makes the minute green hairs around their edges stand out.

— The flat, hairy rosettes of *S. ruthenicum* form a greyish green carpet, decorated occasionally with a touch of brown.

Height: 5–10 cm (2–4 in).
Spacing and planting distance: 10 cm (4 in).
Soil: ordinary, well-drained.
Aspect: full sun.
Propagation: by division in autumn or spring.
Flowering season: summer.
Type: perennial.

Sempervivum tectorum ▽

Senecio maritima △

Senecio
GROUNDSEL
Compositae

The only kinds of senecio we can discuss here are *Senecio greyii* (syn. *Brachyglottis greyii*), which is really a small shrub, and maritime cineraria (*S. cineraria*). The first is widely used to break up monotony and add interest or to provide screens for other plants. Its foliage is such a beautiful silver-grey colour that it blends with just about everything, except perhaps for the yellowish flowers it produces and which you can remove quickly. The latter species fulfils the same functions on a lower level. Put it with red salvias for a brilliant contrast.

Useful hints

— Plant *S. greyii* only in spring, because it does very badly in winter. Add sand and even a few pebbles to lighten the earth. Plant it slightly raised, to protect the plant's neck from too much moisture. As winter draws on, put a handful of rock wool around the base of the plant. If the leaves freeze, the plant will die.

— Sow *S. cineraria* in early spring, in the warm, and harden off before its final planting after the frosts. Pinch the stems so that a good clump will form. Water regularly during the dry days of summer and cut the flowers off as soon as they appear.

Height: 15–150 cm (6–60 in).
Spacing and planting distance: 15–60 cm (6–24 in).
Soil: dry and well-drained.
Aspect: sun.
Propagation: from seed in spring or from cuttings in summer.
Flowering season: end of summer.
Type: annual, perennial, shrub.

Shortia
SHORTIA, FRINGE-BELL
Diapensiaceae

Shortia is a perennial plant for the rock garden. Its leaves have a reddish tint in winter, making a pretty ground covering which could be more widely used.

Useful hints

— Divide the plants in summer and replant immediately with peat.

— Alternatively take cuttings in summer and plant in one-third peat, one-third sand and one-third leaf compost. Grow under glass in winter and plant out in spring.

— Remove dead flowers to prolong flowering.

Recommended

— *Shortia uniflora* has pale pink, waxy flowers with frilled edges in spring. *S. galacifolia* has pale green leaves tinted with red around the edges. Its flowers are white and funnel-shaped.

Height: 10 cm (4 in).
Spacing and planting distance: 30 cm (12 in).
Soil: peat or ordinary soil.
Aspect: semi-shade.
Propagation: by division or from cuttings in summer.
Flowering season: spring.
Type: perennial.

Sidalcea
SIDALCEA, CHECKER MALLOW
Malvaceae

Sidalcea malviflora is much like lavatera. Its slightly stiff carriage and doubtful flowering ability left it somewhat in the shade until good-quality cultivars appeared on the scene. Use large splashes of it with grey-leaved plants – artemisia or stachys, thistles or even lilac scabious.

Useful hints

— Plant in compost and well decomposed manure-rich soil. Mulch the soil in summer with pine bark and water regularly to maintain blooms; add soluble fertilizer with every other watering.

— Divide clumps every five years. You could also try sowing fresh seeds, which generally appear the following spring. But the colours may not be the same as that of the parents.

— Stake with hazel twigs in late spring and put down some slug bait, as the young shoots tend to attract them.

Recommended

— 'Interlaken' is carmine and 'Rose Gem' is bright pink. There is also a white species, which is extremely beautiful and flowers late.

Height: 70–120 cm (28–48 in).
Spacing and planting distance: 30–40 cm (12–16 in).
Soil: rich in humus.
Aspect: sun or semi-shade.
Propagation: from seed when ripe or by division in spring.
Flowering season: summer to autumn.
Type: perennial.

Silene
CAMPION, CATCHFLY
Caryophyllaceae

Carmine-pink is the favourite colour of the *Silene* genus, which includes annuals, biennials and even some perennial species. There are few sunny positions where they will not be happy, from window-boxes to the rock garden and drystone walls.

Useful hints

— Sow *Silene pendula* in spring and move to a nursery bed before final planting in autumn. It will survive the winter without mishap and flower in spring. Pair them with multi-flowered pink tulips and the poet's narcissus.

— Perennial catchfly should be planted in spring in pockets of light, slightly chalky earth. Divide when the blooms become sparse.

Recommended

— *S. pendula*, an annual, comes from Crete, where it tumbles from window-boxes in the springtime in decorative pink or red blocks of colour.

— *S. acaulis* is a very sought-after gem for the rock garden. Rarely taller than just over 2.5 cm (1 in), it provides a thick cushion dotted with flowers. The mountain air is best if you want to see it flower most colourfully.

— *S. schafta* is less capricious, but not everyone likes its very bright pink colour. Its flowers from summer until the frosts set in.

— *S. armeria* is an annual and forms dense pink or purple clusters in summer. This is an excellent bouquet flower, if somewhat sticky to touch. Sow directly in place in spring.

— *S. uniflora* provides marvellous decoration for the paved areas and low walls in which it seeds itself. The flowers of the 'Flore Pleno' variety look like florist's carnations.

Height: 3–60 cm (1–24 in).
Spacing and planting distance: 20 cm (8 in).
Soil: ordinary, preferably light.
Aspect: sun.
Propagation: from seed or by division in spring.
Flowering season: spring to autumn, according to species.
Type: annual, biennial, perennial.

△ **Shortia uniflora**
Sidalcea malviflora ▷
▽ **Silene pendula**

Silybum

MILK THISTLE, HOLY THISTLE

Compositae

This is a striking plant for a wild garden. Annual or biennial, it has pretty leaves, mottled with white veins, in the shape of large, decorative rosettes. The deep violet, lightly perfumed flowers of *Silybum marianum* (Our Lady's milk thistle) bloom at the end of the summer, at the end of long stalks. Perfect companions would be delphiniums or old roses.

Useful hints

— Sow annuals in place in spring or autumn and biennials in early summer. Thin out as soon as the young plants are quite tall.

— Don't spoil them too much. They are quite happy in a poor soil, as long as they can grow in a dry sunny spot.

Height: 100 cm (40 in).
Spacing and planting distance: 50 cm (20 in).
Soil: ordinary.
Aspect: sun.
Propagation: from seed, in spring or autumn for annuals and in early summer for biennials.
Flowering season: summer to autumn.
Type: annual, biennial.

▷ *Sisyrinchium macrocarpum*
▽ *Silybum marianum*

Sisyrinchium striatum △

Sisyrinchium

SISYRINCHIUM, BLUE-EYED GRASS

Iridaceae

With similar foliage to the iris, this plant looks very elegant in a rock garden or a border. It has numerous flowers along the stalk, like pale blue or yellow stars.

Useful hints

— Plant in well-drained soil, enriched with leaf-mould or peat.

— Collect the seeds and sow in seed trays; transplant into pots the following year. Wait three years before the final planting.

— Do not disturb established clumps, except to divide them.

Recommended

— *Sisyrinchium angustifolium* has violet flowers from spring to autumn. There is also a white variety available: *S. angustifolium album.*

230

Sisyrinchium angustifolium △

— *S. striatum* produces abundant creamy yellow flowers from summer onwards. There is a variegated variety, 'Aunt May'.

Height: 40 cm (16 in).
Spacing and planting distance: 20 cm (8 in).
Soil: ordinary, well-drained.
Aspect: sun.
Propagation: from seed in autumn or by division in autumn or spring.
Flowering season: summer.
Type: perennial.

Smilacina racemosa △

Smilacina

FALSE SOLOMON'S SEAL, SPIKENARD

Liliaceae

Smilacina racemosa is happiest in the light shade provided by shrubs. The light green, lanceolate, erect leaves protect a delicate branch of white, scented flowers.

Useful hints

— In autumn, cut down to ground level and mulch with leaves. Don't disturb for three years, as the plants grow slowly but surely.

— Plant from autumn to spring in rich, preferably slightly moist soil.

— Divide clumps every three or four years and replant immediately.

Height: 50 cm (20 in).
Spacing and planting distance: 25 cm (10 in).
Soil: rich, slightly moist.
Aspect: semi-shade.
Propagation: by division in autumn.
Flowering season: early summer.
Type: perennial.

Solanum crispum ▷

Solanum

NIGHTSHADE, FALSE JERUSALEM CHERRY, POTATO VINE

Solanaceae

Solanum capsicastrum is a small shrub and is known as the false Jerusalem cherry. The other species described are climbers and are not all that hardy.

Useful hints

— Sow seeds of *S. capsicastrum* in spring, or take 10 cm (4 in) cuttings in summer and plant in a mixture of sand and peat. When the cuttings have rooted, transplant to pots containing one-third compost, one-third peat and one-third sand. Don't let the soil dry out and see that the temperature does not fall below 13–14°C (57–59°F). Plant out after the frosts are over.

— In colder regions grow the plants in pots under cover in winter; in any case, protect the plants from frost.

— To obtain really fine specimens, pinch out the tops of the young plants when they grow to 10 cm (4 in).

Recommended

— *S. capsicastrum* is usually grown in containers. It is popular for its red fruit and evergreen appearance; it is not very hardy and should be treated as an annual. Misting will encourage it to bear fruit.

— *S. crispum* is practically evergreen and can grow to 250 cm (100 in). Its blue, star-shaped flowers appear from early summer to autumn.

— *S. jasminoïdes* is less hardy than the preceding variety and grows even taller. Its flowers are light blue and bloom from summer to autumn.

Height: 50–250 cm (20–100 in).
Soil: ordinary.
Aspect: sunny but sheltered.
Propagation: from seed in spring or cuttings in summer.
Flowering season: summer.
Type: annual, perennial climber.

231

Soldanella minima △
Solidago canadensis ▷
Soldanella montana ▽

Soldanella

SOLDANELLA, ALPENCLOCK

Primulaceae

Soldanellas provide a pretty mauve carpet between stones or rocks, which echo their natural habitat as they come from mountain regions. Part of their attraction lies in their fringed petals.

Useful hints

— Plant in autumn in peat-enriched soil. Put a handful of coarse sand or gravel around each plant to help it resist rainfall; for the same reason it is a good idea to cover the plants with a 'roof' of glass or transparent plastic film over their heads during the rainy season, which they find hard to survive.

Recommended

— *Soldanella alpina*, with its lavender flowers, does well in rock gardens at the beginning of spring. *S. montana* is a taller and more robust species, a little like the

preceding one, with bell-shaped mauve flowers.

Height: 5–15 cm (2–6 in).
Spacing and planting distance: 30 cm (12 in).
Soil: ordinary, well-drained.
Aspect: sun or semi-shade.
Propagation: by division in summer.
Flowering season: spring.
Type: perennial.

Solidago

GOLDEN ROD

Compositae

This genus is really easy to grow. The golden rod has narrow leaves and tiny flowers, which look like golden feathers. Plant on its own or in beds alongside asters and veronica. An excellent flower

for bouquets, the blooms are also lovely when dried.

Useful hints

— Plant from autumn to spring in any soil, even a chalky one.

— Watch out for mildew on the leaves; as soon as you notice a white powdery substance, treat the whole plant.

— Cut back all the flower stems in autumn.

Recommended

— *Solidago canadensis* will grow to 180 cm (72 in) and flowers in autumn. It forms the origin of many hybrids. Some grow no taller than 50 cm (20 in) and have a small spread, such as 'Golden Dwarf' and 'Goldenmosa'. 'Crown of

and pointed, as in the iris. *Sparaxis tricolor* flowers in early summer and there are varieties in red and yellow, violet and even white, with darker markings. *S. grandiflora* is similar to *S. tricolor*.

Useful hints

— If you want to grow them for cut flowers, plant the corms in autumn 10 cm (4 in) deep. Be sure to keep the ground around them weed-free.

— When the leaves have withered in summer, dig up the bulbs and allow to dry, away from frost and damp, until autumn, when they can be replanted in rich, well-drained soil.

— Sparaxis is a small plant which will suffer from frost, so grow it in a sheltered position. It should be grown in full sun, as the flowers close in cloudy weather.

Height: 40 cm (16 in).
Spacing and planting distance: 10 cm (4 in).
Soil: rich and well-drained.
Aspect: facing south, sheltered from the wind.
Propagation: by separating corms when leaves have withered.
Flowering season: early summer.
Type: corm.

Sprekelia

AZTEC LILY, JACOBEAN LILY

Amaryllidaceae

Grown in either tubs or pots, each stem of *Sprekelia formosissima* bears a scarlet, spectacular, funnel-shaped flower. The genus is of Mexican origin, so the bulbs prefer warmth and are not very hardy in cooler climates. The few long leaves grow as the flowers finish.

Useful hints

— Plant the bulbs in summer in pots or tubs of fresh soil or compost, sheltered from the cold; they will flower three or four years later.

— Do not water before late spring; keep the soil moist thereafter until the leaves have withered.

— Repot every three years in autumn.

Height: 50 cm (20 in).
Spacing and planting distance: 15 cm (6 in).
Soil: mixture of soil, compost and sand.
Aspect: sun.
Propagation: by separating bulbs after foliage has withered in summer.
Flowering season: summer.
Type: bulb.

△ *Sparaxis* hybrid
▽ *Sprekelia formosissima*

Rays' produces deep yellow flowers in dense formation.

Height: 20–180 cm (8–72 in).
Spacing and planting distance: 75 cm (30 in).
Soil: ordinary.
Aspect: sun or semi-shade; does well by the sea.
Propagation: by division at the beginning of winter or spring.
Flowering season: summer to autumn.
Type: perennial.

Sparaxis

AFRICAN HARLEQUIN FLOWER, WANDFLOWER

Iridaceae

The harlequin flower's six petals come in many different colours. Several bloom on the same stem; the foliage is narrow

Stachys

LAMB'S EARS, BETONY

Labiatae

The silvery white leaves of stachys (like a lamb's ears) look woolly. The rather ordinary violet or pale pink flowers nestle along a thick, short stalk. When it forms a border with roses or perennial plants, stachys looks like a velvety carpet.

Useful hints

— Plant in autumn or spring.

— Cut back the leaves in autumn and place a layer of sand at the foot of the plant to protect it from moisture.

Recommended

— *Stachys byzantina* (syn. *S. lanata*), most frequently known as lamb's ears, is an excellent ground cover for a poor, dry soil. You will find it in many catalogues under the names *S. lanata* and *S. olympica*. Of the original variants, *S.b.* 'Primrose Heron', with its yellowish leaves, and *S.b.* 'Silver Cloud', which bears few if any flowers, are particularly noteworthy.

— *S. macrantha* has a truly spectacular variety with very large flowers, called 'Superba'.

— The foliage of *S. macrantha* is greener than the preceding species and it has whorl-shaped violet flowers.

— Known under the common name, betony, *S. officinalis* sports purple flowers, which are tubular-shaped. 'Grandiflora' is one of the most decorative varieties, with pink flowers; it grows to over 60 cm (24 in).

Height: 30–60 cm (12–24 in).
Spacing and planting distance: 20–40 cm (8–15 in).
Soil: ordinary or poor, well-drained.
Aspect: sun or semi-shade.
Propagation: by division in autumn or spring.
Flowering season: summer.
Type: perennial.

⊲ **Stachys byzantina**

Sternbergia

LILY OF THE FIELD

Amaryllidaceae

The brilliant yellow small flowers of sternbergia look a little like the crocus, but they bloom in autumn. It's a good idea to put them with colchicums, as their flowering seasons are complementary. As legend would have it, this little plant is one of the Biblical lilies which grew in the wild on Mediterranean hills.

Useful hints

— Plant in autumn, 10 cm (4 in) deep, in well-drained soil.

— The bulbs should be left undisturbed until they become swollen, then separate them and replant straight away; they will flower either the following year or in two years' time.

Recommended

— The golden yellow flowers of *Sternbergia clusiana* appear at the beginning of autumn and last for two months.

— The brilliant yellow flowers of *S. lutea* open at the same time.

— Unlike its two cousins, the bright yellow *S. fischeriana* flowers in spring.

Height: 10 cm (4 in).
Spacing and planting distance: 10 cm (4 in).
Soil: ordinary, well-drained.
Aspect: sun or semi-shade.
Propagation: by separating bulbs in summer.
Flowering season: autumn, spring for *S. fischeriana.*
Type: bulb.

Stipa

FEATHER GRASS, NEEDLEGRASS

Gramineae

The leaves of stipa are so feathery light that they look like waves when the wind blows over them. They lend a feeling of space and lightness to plants around them. But don't put them with anything which makes too much of a contrast. A carpet of bergenia or sedum with some clumps of feather grass on top would not work at all well. They go much better with meadow daisies, red poppies and Caucasian scabious.

Useful hints

— Plant in spring and fork the soil during the season. Mulch the soil in summer and water regularly during the first summer.

Sternbergia lutea △

Stipa gigantea △
Stipa tenuifolia ▷

— Divide the clumps in spring every three years when they get too thick.

Recommended

— Only size differentiates *Stipa gigantea*, over 200 cm (80 in) tall, and *S. calamagrostis*, 120 cm (48 in). Their feather quills can be used in bouquets of dried flowers, where their violet shades make a lovely complement to copper-coloured perennials.

Height: 120–200 cm (48–80 in).
Spacing and planting distance: 50 cm (20 in).
Soil: ordinary.
Aspect: sun.
Propagation: by division in spring.
Flowering season: summer to autumn.
Type: perennial.

Stokesia laevis △

Stokesia

STOKESIA, STOKES' ASTER

Compositae

The plant is often mistaken for the China aster (*Callistephus*), which has similar flowers. It is quite a rare event to catch a sight of the lovely *Stokesia laevis* in a garden, but this is a hardy border plant none the less, with the fine lines and harmony found among wild flowers. The flowers, which are perfectly set off by its blue-green foliage, range from all shades of white to purple, with a particular predilection for mauve. One word of advice: let the clumps fill out. They are at their most spectacular after three or four years.

Useful hints

— Plant out from pots, preferably in autumn, or in spring if the soil is heavy and sticky in winter.

— Mulch the earth in spring and water properly during the first summer.

— Seeds will give you a variety of colours, often with very interesting results.

Height: 30–50 cm (12–20 in).
Spacing and planting distance: 40 cm (16 in).
Soil: quite rich, moist in summer.
Aspect: sun.
Propagation: by division in autumn, or from seed in spring.
Flowering season: summer to autumn.
Type: perennial.

Symphytum

COMFREY, BONESET

Boraginaceae

This is a most undemanding plant — it is happy in shade or sunshine and will even thrive in moist environments or undergrowth. Its flowers are shaped like little hanging bells. *Symphytum caucasicum* is quite unusual in that the flowers start out pink and then turn a beautiful blue.

Useful hints

— Plant in autumn or at the beginning of spring, in ordinary garden soil.

— To set off the blooms, use hazel twigs to stake the plants.

Recommended

— The clumps of *S. ibericum* join together to form thick mats that give weeds no chance to grow.

— *S. × uplandicum*, often sold under the name *S. peregrinum*, is a hardy hybrid with tubular flowers of reddish blue. 'Variegatum', its leaves splashed with cream variegation, adds a note of colour to ground cover.

— *S. orientale* is a good ground cover under trees; its white flowers blossom in late spring and early summer.

— *S.* 'Rubrum' also flowers at this time, but is a deep red colour and flowers for a longer period.

Height: 60 cm (24 in).
Spacing and planting distance: 40 cm (16 in).
Soil: ordinary.
Aspect: any.
Flowering season: late spring and early summer.
Type: perennial.

▽ *Symphytum caucasicum*

Tagetes erecta △

Tagetes

AFRICAN MARIGOLD, FRENCH MARIGOLD

Compositae

French and African marigolds take the centre stage in a summer garden, although they can be faulted for a slightly unpleasant smell and very strident colouring, somewhere between a lemony yellow and deep orange. They are extremely easy to grow; the seeds simply flourish on their own and the young plants are very vigorous. You can buy them as young plants, which are not costly and will flower after just a few weeks. Whatever you do, don't combine them with red, pink or blue flowers, but use them in small groups surrounded by masses of greenery (rows of kochia, for example, or even nasturtiums), or opt for grey colours like artemisia and stachys.

Useful hints

— Sow under glass in early to mid-spring, in a protected spot a little later or directly in place in late spring. Plant out a month after the shoots appear, or thin out the seeds, leaving one plant every 20 cm (8 in).

— Water until the first flowers appear, then continue to water the base of the plant without touching the blooms, as too much water will kill them.

— Remove withered flowers regularly and you will be rewarded by new ones right until the frosts arrive.

Recommended

— Among the French marigolds (*Tagetes patula*), choose scabious-like flowers such as 'Boy-o-Boy' or 'Bonanza', dwarf forms with large tubular flowers such as 'Honeycomb' or 'Yellow Jacket', and the more compact dwarf varieties 'Lemon Drop', 'Bonita', 'Carmen' and the simple 'Légion d'Honneur' and 'Dainty Marietta'. *T. tenuifolia* makes very dense clumps covered with smaller flowers, golden yellow in 'Golden Gem' and lemony yellow in 'Lemon Gem'.

— The very small African marigolds (*T. erecta*) are not very long-lasting. Preferred varieties are 'Crackerjack' which grows up to 60 cm (24 in), and 'Jubilee Hybrids', 100 cm (40 in).

Height: 20–100 cm (8–40 in).
Spacing and planting distance: 20–40 cm (8–16 in).
Soil: ordinary.
Aspect: full sun.
Propagation: from seed in spring.
Flowering season: summer to first frosts.
Type: annual.

Tanacetum

see *Chrysanthemum*

Tellima

TELLIMA, FRINGECUP

Saxifragaceae

Tellima grandiflora is grown more for its perennial foliage than for its rather ordinary, lightly perfumed yellowish flowers, which bloom in late spring. This is an excellent ground cover plant which is easy to establish but not intrusive. *T. grandiflora* 'Purpurea' is similar in appearance, but boasts very attractive, bronzed green leaves. You can create a very pretty spring tableau by putting tellima with jonquils or tulips.

Useful hints

— Plant in autumn or spring, in any kind of soil.

— Remove withered flowers, unless you want to collect seeds.

Height: 40 cm (16 in).
Spacing and planting distance: 40 cm (16 in).
Soil: any.
Aspect: sun or shade.
Propagation: by division in autumn or spring, or from seed when ripe.
Flowering season: spring.
Type: perennial.

▽ *Tagetes patula*
Tellima grandiflora ▽

▽ *Teucrium scorodonia* 'Crispum'
Teucrium polium ▽

Teucrium

GERMANDER

Labiatae

These plants look quite sober until their flowers appear. They have a long lower lip and sport pastel colours. As the foliage is perennial, they can be used in small borders in place of santolina in colder climates.

Useful hints

— Plant in spring, preferably in soil lightened with sand. Germander loves sunshine but will also do well in slightly shady areas.

— Cut down twice a year, first in spring to shape the border and again in summer to clear clumps of withered flowers.

— Plant spring bulbs between them; ornamental garlic or botanical gladioli are perfect for this.

Recommended

— The best border variety is the small oak germander (*Teucrium chamaedrys*), so called because of the shape of its leaves. There is also *T. scorodonia* 'Crispum Marginatum', with creamy yellow flowers and waxy leaves, a purplish colour in autumn, and *T. polium*, which has nearly white leaves. They are all perennial species and will form small, woody shrubs.

Height: 20–50 cm (8–20 in).
Spacing and planting distance: 30 cm (12 in).
Soil: ordinary, well-drained.
Aspect: sun.
Propagation: from cuttings at the end of summer.
Flowering season: summer to autumn.
Type: perennial.

▽ *Thermopsis montana*

Thalictrum

MEADOW RUE

Ranunculaceae

Meadow rue is grown for its lovely, delicate flowers and slightly blue-grey foliage. The flowers grow as small pink, yellow or mauve tufts at the end of long slender stalks, but unfortunately they are short-lived.

Useful hints

— Plant out in spring in a humus-rich soil.

— Sow seeds in boxes in spring in a compost made up of equal parts of soil, sand and peat, and plant out the following spring.

— Stake before plants reach their maximum height.

— In spring, topdress with a layer of peat and well-rotted manure.

Recommended

— *Thalictrum minus adiantifolium*, 120 cm (48 in) tall, is grown for its silver foliage, as the greenish flowers which appear in mid-summer are not very impressive.

— *T. aquilegiifolium* has pretty silver leaves and mauve flowers (or white in its variety *album*) which come out in mid- to late summer.

— *T. delavayi*, which originates from China, also has mauve flowers, but with prominent bright yellow anthers, in mid- to late summer. The variety 'Hewitt's Double' is generally grown.

— *T. kiusianum* comes from Japan and has silver-green foliage. Its light violet flowers appear in late spring.

— *T. blavum* ssp. *glaucum* bears blue-grey leaves and its bright yellow flowers appear on 20 cm (8 in) long spikes, in mid- to late summer.

Height: 100–150 cm (40–60 in).
Spacing and planting distance: 50 cm (20 in).
Soil: ordinary, preferably rich in humus.
Aspect: sun or semi-shade.
Propagation: from seed or by division in spring.
Flowering season: spring and summer.
Type: perennial.

Thermopsis

THERMOPSIS, FALSE LUPINE

Leguminosae

Stout and tough-rooted, thermopsis looks a little like a lupin with somewhat glaucous foliage. Although easy to grow, its roots spread like wildfire.

△ *Thalictrum aquilegiifolium*

△ *Thalictrum delavayii*

Useful hints

— Plant in autumn or at the beginning of spring in any well-drained soil.

— Cut withered flowers down to 5 cm (2 in) from the ground and you will get a second show.

— It is easy to divide clumps and replant, but the plant only really starts to thrive after two or three years.

Recommended

— *Thermopsis carolinia* has blue-green foliage and spikes of yellow flowers.

— *T. lanceolata* has pretty light yellow flowers along its stalk.

— *T. montana* forms lovely yellow clumps, but its roots need to be carefully controlled.

Height: 80 cm (32 in).
Spacing and planting distance: 50–100 cm (20–40 in) for *T. montana*; 45 cm (18 in) for *T. lanceolata*.
Soil: well-drained.
Aspect: sun.
Propagation: by division in spring.
Flowering season: early summer.
Type: perennial.

Thunbergia

BLACK-EYED SUSAN, CLOCK VINE

Acanthaceae

Climbing thunbergia is an annual, vigorous plant, which will be happy only in a sheltered garden with a mild climate. Flowers grow from a purple tube, expanding into five blue-violet or bright yellow to orange petals, which have a dark, almost black middle. It can grow up to 7 m (21 ft), which makes it ideal for pergolas, where it will climb without needing any support.

Useful hints

— Sow seeds in spring in a fairly warm location (16–18°C/61–64°F). Harden off before final planting after the frosts are over.

— Water generously and regularly during the growing period with a liquid fertilizer, twice monthly through the summer.

Recommended

— *Thunbergia alata* grows to a medium height, roughly 200 cm (80 in). *T. grandiflora* can grow as tall as 7 m (21 ft) and over and bears blue-violet flowers 7 cm (3 in) across.

Height: 2–7 m (6–21 ft).
Spacing and planting distance: 50 cm (20 in).
Soil: ordinary.
Aspect: sunny but sheltered.
Propagation: from seed in pots, in spring.
Flowering season: summer to autumn.
Type: annual.

Thymus

THYME

Labiatae

This is a native of sun-drenched hills and can look very attractive in a rock garden or paving area. Cut back regularly and then allow it to flower to best appreciate its scent and small flowers.

Useful hints

— Plant in autumn or spring in well-drained soil.

— Grow in pots 20 cm (8 in) in diameter and water once a week. Cut back regularly to keep it dense.

— For the rock garden, plant in spring in a well-drained pocket of earth.

Recommended

— *Thymus cilicius* forms a compact clump with lilac tubular flowers.

△ *Thunbergia alata*

— *T. × citriodorus* (lemon-scented thyme) has pale lilac flowers and the leaves have a light lemony smell. It also has a silver variety, 'Argenteus', and a golden variety, 'Golden King'.

— *T. hirsutus* is a mat-forming plant with grey-green leaves and lilac flowers.

— *T. membranaceus* is the most fragrant species, with white tubular flowers and bracts in summer.

— *T. pseudolanuginosus* covers the driest soils with its silvery foliage and pink flowers.

— The grey-green leaves of *T. serpyllum* (wild thyme) are a perfect complement to its pink or purple flowers. Those of the *coccineus* variety are very deep pink, almost red in colour.

Height: 8–15 cm (3–6 in).
Spacing and planting distance: 30 cm (12 in).
Soil: ordinary, well-drained.
Aspect: sun.
Propagation: by division in spring or autumn.
Flowering season: summer.
Type: perennial.

Tiarella

FOAM FLOWER

Saxifragaceae

An excellent ground cover with perennial foliage, tiarella is not a difficult plant to grow. The large leaves provide rapid ground cover, even under trees and shrubs. The plant bears feathery white flowers which grow straight and erect.

Useful hints

— Plant in spring or autumn with a generous handful of peat around the roots.

— Don't let the soil dry out if you want to achieve a dense, very green ground cover.

Recommended

— *Tiarella cordifolia* is an extremely good ground cover with white or pink flowers on 15 cm (6 in) high stalks, which contrast well with its bright or light green foliage.

— *T. wherryi* is a more compact species with smaller leaves which turn russet-brown in autumn. Its flowers appear in abundance from summer to autumn.

— *T. trifoliata* has foliage like the ivy and produces many pinkish white flowers throughout the summer.

Height: 15–50 cm (6–20 in).
Spacing and planting distance: 30 cm (12 in).
Soil: any, except dry.
Aspect: shade or semi-shade.
Propagation: by division in autumn or spring.
Flowering season: summer to autumn.
Type: perennial.

△ *Tiarella wherryi*
▽ *Thymus serpyllum*

Tigridia pavonia △
Tolmiea menziesii ▽

Useful hints

— Plant the bulbs in spring, about 10 cm (4 in) deep, in well-drained soil.

— Do not allow them to dry out, but they appreciate gentle warmth.

— Remove the bulbs before the frosts set in and leave to dry in a heated room. Keep in well-dried sand or peat boxes for the winter.

— Each year you can replant the bulblets and they will flower two years later.

— Bulbs can be left in the soil for the winter in well-protected borders. Remove them and divide them up every two or three years, when the leaves are withered.

Height: 50 cm (20 in).
Spacing and planting distance: 10 cm (4 in).
Soil: ordinary, well-drained.
Aspect: sun.
Propagation: by separating bulbs in spring.
Flowering season: summer to autumn.
Type: bulb.

Tolmiea

MOTHER OF THOUSANDS, PICKABACK PLANT

Saxifragaceae

Because of its peculiar habit of producing young plants directly on the perennial leaves, it has been given a variety of nicknames, such as mother of thousands, youth-on-age or pickaback plant. The tubular flowers appear in summer on long, slender stalks. *Tolmiea menziesii* produces downy leaves and tiny white flowers. An excellent ground cover, this plant can also be grown indoors, but in cool rooms only.

Useful hints

— In autumn or early spring, remove only leaves which have smaller, well-formed plants on them and plant in pots. Water regularly from mid-spring onwards.

— You can plant leaves containing small, new plants directly in a nursery bed, and as soon as they have taken root transfer them to their permanent spot.

Height: 15 cm (6 in).
Spacing and planting distance: 40 cm (16 in).
Soil: rich in humus, well-drained.
Aspect: sun or semi-shade.
Propagation: from leaves with plantlets in spring or autumn.
Flowering season: summer.
Type: perennial.

Tigridia

TIGER FLOWER

Iridaceae

Each shimmering flower lasts only a day, but our consolation is that each tigridia stalk bears six or seven flowers. The leaves are puckered and the flowers have six petals, three large ones separated by three tiny spotted ones. Some gardeners find it resembles the iris, others believe it to be like a tulip. *Tigridia pavonia* has numerous, brightly coloured varieties, in all shades except blue. It flowers between summer and autumn.

△ *Torenia fournieri*

Torenia

WISHBONE FLOWER

Scrophulariaceae

This Asiatic plant is grown as an annual in our climate. The long, serrated foliage is covered in summer with a profusion of flowers. *Torenia fournieri* (wishbone flower) will simply charm you with its tubular, violet, yellow-specked flowers. The variety 'Alba' has white flowers.

Useful hints

— Sow seeds in early spring at a temperature of 18°C (64°F) with just a very light covering of soil. Transplant the young plants under glass before final positioning after the frosts.

— Pinch the top of stems when 8–10 cm (3–4 in) tall, to encourage branching growth.

— Hazel twigs make good supports for the plant.

Height: 30 cm (12 in).
Spacing and planting distance: 15 cm (6 in).
Soil: moist.
Aspect: semi-shade and sheltered.
Propagation: from seed in spring, in the warm.
Flowering season: all summer.
Type: annual.

Tradescantia

SPIDER LILY, SPIDERWORT

Commelinaceae

The three-petalled flowers are accompanied by long, pointed, sad-looking foliage. The flowers last for only a day but are replaced rapidly. Tradescantia is well known as a houseplant, but doesn't belong to the same species that you will find in the garden. These are hardy hybrids of *Tradescantia virginiana* and other species with pink, white, violet or red flowers.

Useful hints

— Sow in spring and transplant when the plants are large enough to handle. Plant out in autumn.

— Don't let the soil dry out in summer.

— Cut back foliage to ground level in autumn.

Recommended

— *T. × andersoniana*. Among the best varieties are the dark blue 'Blue Stone', the pink and white 'Domaine de Courson', the white 'Innocence', the bluish white 'Osprey', the deep pink 'Valour', the pale blue 'J.C. Weguelin' and the red-purple 'Purewell Giant'.

Height: 50 cm (20 in).
Spacing and planting distance: 40 cm (16 in).
Soil: ordinary, well-drained, moist.
Aspect: sun or semi-shade.
Propagation: from seed or by division in spring.
Flowering season: summer to autumn.
Type: perennial.

▽ *Tradescantia* hybrid

Tricyrtis

TOAD LILY

Liliaceae

These unusual plants, which come from Japan, have inhabited our gardens for only a few years. You can guarantee that their spectacular, orchid-like blooms will prompt much admiration from visitors to your garden. Groups of stalks grow from one stem and are topped in the autumn by pretty speckled flowers. Plant next to *Sedum spectabile*, hostas and ferns to cheer up a shady corner.

Useful hints

— Plant in spring in a humus-rich soil, acidified if necessary with the addition of light peat. Don't put them in a spot that is too windy, as their stalks are liable to collapse at the first sign of a storm.

— Put down slug pellets in spring. Divide up clumps after a period of three years, either in autumn or the beginning of spring.

Recommended

— *Tricyrtis hirta*, 75 cm (30 in) tall, has white flowers with a smattering of brown and spreads very well, while *T. macropoda* can grow over 90 cm (36 in) and its creamy white and mauve flowers make it the more decorative of the two.

Height: 40–90 cm (16–36 in).
Spacing and planting distance: 30 cm (12 in).
Soil: rich in humus and moist.
Aspect: semi-shade.
Propagation: by division in autumn or spring.
Flowering season: summer to autumn.
Type: perennial.

Trillium

TRILLIUM, WOOD LILY, WAKE ROBIN

Liliaceae

The foliage, petals and sepals of the trillium all come in groups of three and the feature is common to all varieties. They are most effective when grown in large clumps in a rock garden or border. The marbled, dark green and silvery leaves are punctuated with pointed, twisted, stemless flowers.

Useful hints

— Plant 10 cm (4 in) deep in groups in a wooded location during summer.

— Dig up the rhizomes and divide them as soon as the leaves start to wither, from mid-summer to spring.

Replant straight away in a well-drained soil, without letting them dry out.

— Don't divide up the clumps too often, as the plant takes a long time to establish itself.

— You can also grow them from seeds, but they take up to eighteen months to germinate and it will be several years before you see any flowers.

Recommended

— *Trillium erectum* has purple flowers with groups of three petals reflexed at the tips.

— *T. grandiflorum* is one of the prettiest varieties, sporting white flowers which become flushed with rose-pink, nestling in a group of three leaves.

— The flowers of *T. ovatum* also change colour, but from a pale to a deep pink.

— The leaves of *T. sessile* are marbled grey and green and the maroon stemless flowers appear to be screwed into its cluster of three leaves.

— *T. undulatum* has white flowers with a deep red zone at the base. The petals are more spread out than in other varieties.

Height: 30 cm (12 in).
Spacing and planting distance: 30 cm (12 in).
Soil: moist with plenty of humus.
Aspect: semi-shade or shade.
Propagation: by division when leaves are dry.
Flowering season: spring to summer.
Type: perennial.

Trollius

GLOBEFLOWER

Ranunculaceae

The common feature of the trollius is its globe-shaped flower, ranging from yellow to orange. The bud is slow to open, but they are easy plants to grow provided the roots are kept moist, so it's a good idea to plant them at the margins of streams and ponds.

Useful hints

— Plant preferably in the sun or semi-shade in autumn or spring.

— Cut back flower stems after flowering to achieve a second show.

— Water regularly during high summer, so that the leaves do not dry out.

Recommended

— *Trollius* × *cultorum* hybrids have double flowers and *T. europaeus* has single ones, lemony yellow, orange or golden in early summer. *T. chinensis* has orange flowers which appear in mid-summer. Its sole representative is the orange-yellow 'Golden Queen'.

— *T.* × *cultorum*. With just a few exceptions, garden varieties of the globeflower are hybrids. 'Canary Bird' has canary-yellow and orange flowers, 'Orange Crest', has lemon-yellow and orange flowers and 'Orange Princess', has large orange flowers.

— The orange-yellow flowers of *T. pumilus* can reach a height of 15 cm (6 inches) and are one of the great attractions of rock gardens in late spring.

Height: 30 cm (12 in).
Spacing and planting distance: 40 cm (16 in).
Soil: moist.
Aspect: sun or semi-shade.
Propagation: by division in autumn or early spring.
Flowering season: summer.
Type: perennial.

◁ ***Tricyrtis hirta***

△ ***Trillium ovatum***
▽ ***Trillium sessile***

▽ ***Trollius*** × ***cultorum*** 'Canary Bird'

241

Tropaeolum

NASTURTIUM, BITTER INDIAN

Tropaeolaceae

Both the annual and perennial varieties of nasturtium can climb up to 300 cm (120 in). They enliven pergolas and embankments with their warm red, yellow and orange hues, but some people find their scent unpleasant.

Useful hints

— Sow annuals direct in mid-spring. Thin out as soon as the plants appear overcrowded, so that only the most vigorous are left.

— The tuberous roots of perennial species can be planted in spring but it's preferable to buy them already started in pots.

— Nasturtiums will flower best if the soil is not too rich; fertilizers will encourage leaves to the detriment of flowers.

Recommended

— **Annuals**: *Tropaeolum majus* is used as a climbing and trailing plant, and has red, yellow or orange flowers. Some hybrids have variegated leaves, while others are dwarfs (30–250 cm) (12–100 in).

— *T. peregrinum* (Canary creeper) is a perennial best grown as an annual. It can grow up to 400 cm (160 in) in a year and has blue-green leaves and irregular, yellow flowers from summer to autumn. It grows in shade but prefers sun.

— **Perennials**: *T. polyphyllum* has a good spread (150 cm for 15 cm height) (60 in for 6 in). With its silver-green leaves and yellow flowers which appear in summer, it's a good species for trailing over a stone wall.

— Climbing *T. speciosum* easily reaches 300 cm (120 in) and dies down in winter. From summer to autumn it produces scarlet flowers; it is at home in a moist soil.

— *T. tuberosum* grows up to 300 cm (120 in) with a spread of 100 cm (40 in). Its yellow and red flowers appear from summer to autumn, but it is often cut down by frost and will need protecting in winter. It has grey-green leaves.

Height: 30–400 cm (12–160 in).
Spacing and planting distance: 30–100 cm (12–40 in).
Soil: poor, no fertilizer.
Aspect: sun.
Propagation: from seed or by division in spring.
Flowering season: summer to autumn.
Type: annual, perennial.

△ *Tropaeolum speciosum*
▽ *Tropaeolum majus*

△ *Tropaeolum tuberosum*
◁ *Tropaeolum polyphyllum*
Tropaeolum tricolorum ▷
▽ *Tropaeolum minus*

Tulipa

TULIP

Liliaceae

Everyone knows the tulip, or at least thinks they do, yet it's surprising just how few of the numerous varieties are grown in gardens. They are classified below in order of flowering time, leaving aside botanical types, which are rarely used in beds and tend to appear in rock gardens or window-boxes. Most tulips last about three weeks, so it's best to put them with biennials, such as forget-me-not or stock, so that you are not confronted with an empty space.

Useful hints

— Plant in autumn in soil twice as deep as their diameter: any well-dug soil will do. Never add fresh compost or manure, as the bulbs could well rot on contact. Don't worry if leaves appear very early in spring, as they will withstand frosts, but put down slug pellets.

— After flowering, dead-head them so as not to exhaust the bulbs. Water once a week, adding a soluble fertilizer so that new bulbs will increase in size. Cut back the leaves when they have almost died.

Recommended

— **Kaufmanniana hybrid** tulips will flower almost at ground level in early spring and have brilliant colours. They are suitable for the rock garden, border or window-box.

— 'Heart's Delight', pale pink with red on the outside, has leaves marbled with violet; 'Johann Strauss' is a pure white with external red and yellow; 'Stresa' is a brilliant yellow with red interior, marbled leaves and is one of the finest; 'The First' is a very early variety, ivory on a yellow base with a carmine-washed exterior, a very natural-looking flower despite its large size.

— **Fosteriana hybrids** tend to stand out because of their extremely large flowers. They are usually grown for one year only, as their powerful colouring can be somewhat overpowering. As an alternative to the bright-red 'Madame Lefeber', or pure yellow 'Candela' or 'Golden Emperor', choose lighter colours, such as white 'Purissima' or 'Sweetheart', a lemon-yellow with ivory edges.

— **Single early** tulips flower in early to mid-spring to a height of 40 cm (16 in). The finest are: 'Bellona', pure yellow, often fragrant; 'Generaal de Wet', orange and also fragrant; 'Pink Beauty', deep pink and white; 'Van der Neer', a purplish violet colour.

— Also appearing at this time are the multi-flowered tulips, producing several flowers per bulb. They look delightful in window-boxes, where they outlast other tulips: choose 'Georgette', a yellow bordered with red, or 'Orange Bouquet', a scarlet-orange.

— **Double early** tulips are the amateur's favourite for an even display, as they all grow to the same height (an average of 30 cm (12 in); among them you will find 'William of Orange', an orange variety; 'Mr van der Hoef', golden yellow; 'Peach Blossom', pink and white with a delicate fragrance; 'Triumphator', deep pink. They are often sold in a mixture of colours as Murillo tulips.

— **Mendel** tulips are a kind of cross between single early tulips and the Darwin variety. They are now correctly classified as single early tulips. They flower in mid-spring on 40–50 cm (16–20 in) long stalks. 'Apricot Beauty' is one of the best, with its salmon-pink colour and strong fragrance. 'Pink Trophy', a bright pink, and 'Bestseller', a coppery red, are two excellent varieties.

— **Greigii** hybrids are the last of the large-flowered dwarf species. Their brown-marbled foliage screens warm-coloured flowers. Instead of the very popular 'Red Riding Hood', a brilliant red, try 'Easter Surprise', a bright yellow edged with orange; 'Yellow Dawn', yellow with a pink exterior, or even 'Donna Bella', a creamy-white with red exterior.

— **Triumph** tulips have sturdy stems, making excellent flowers for bouquets. There are hundreds of varieties, including: 'Spring Charm', white edged with deep pink; 'Peerless Pink', smooth pink; 'Pax', pure white with a deep pink base; 'Merry Widow', red edged with white; 'Orange Wonder', brilliant scarlet; 'Dutch Princess', an apricot tinged with mahogany; 'White Virgin', a pure white.

— **Darwin** hybrid tulips are the best-known. Their often long stems, 70 cm (28 in), bear enormous brightly-coloured flowers from their *fosteriana* heritage. Go for something unusual. Instead of the variety 'Apeldoorn', a bright red, and 'Golden Apeldoorn', a hard yellow, opt for 'Big Chief', an antique rose tinged with a hint of orange; 'Elizabeth Arden', a salmon-pink, or even 'Vivex', carmine-pink bordered with yellow and orange.

△ *Tulipa* 'Red Riding Hood'
▽ *Tulipa* 'Electra'

△ *Tulipa* 'Generaal de Wet'
Tulipa 'Attila' ▷
▽ *Tulipa* Darwin Hybrid
Tulipa 'Texas Flame' ▽

◁ *Tulipa clusiana*
Tulipa 'West Point' ▷
▽ *Tulipa* 'Eros'

△ *Tulipa* 'Groenland'
◁ Triumph tulip
▽ Fosteriana tulip

▽ Greigii tulip

▽ *Tulipa* 'Flaming Parrot'
Kaufmanniana tulip ▽

— **Single late** tulips, also known as Cottage tulips, beat all height records, up to 80 cm (32 in)! Their height lends them elegance and they add an old-fashioned charm to the garden. Match them with peonies and pale stocks. Favourites include: 'Aristocrat', a pinkish lilac; 'Dillenburg', deep orange, one of the later varieties; 'Queen of Night', a deep brown; 'Temple of Beauty', light salmon-pink shaded with lilac; 'Queen of Bartigons', light salmon-pink with white markings on the base, or even 'Maya', yellow with strangely fringed petals.

— **Lily-flowered** varieties flower from mid- to late spring. Their very slender petals give them an extremely elegant look. 'China Pink', a pure pink; 'Queen of Sheba', red with orange edges; 'Red Shine', a deep red; 'West Point', acid yellow; and the remarkable 'White Triumphator', a sparkling white, are among the best.

— **Parrot** tulips have fringed edges to their petals. 'Black Parrot' is black-purple; 'Texas Gold', yellow; and 'White parrot', a pure white.

— Finally, there are the **double late** tulips, which flower with azaleas and peonies, creating flowerbeds of true beauty. The loveliest include 'Angelique', a porcelain-pink, 'Mount Tacoma', sporting large white flowers, and 'Rosalia', a pink and slightly earlier variety.

— There are numerous **species** or **botanical** tulips, which are easy to grow and make natural clumps. Examples are: *Tulipa acuminata* (also known as *T. cornuta*) which has straight petals (it gave birth to the lily-flowered tulip); *T. clusiana*, pure white and crimson, nick-named 'straight tulip' (also known as lady tulip); *T. marjolettii*, yellow with red on the exterior, very elegant and flowering only in late spring; the latest of all, *T. sprengeri*, a magnificent variety whose powerful red colour is the perfect complement for white flowers like chervil or rocket; *T. sylvestris*, a yellow and almost round flower which spreads quickly in undergrowth; *T. tarda*, which blooms in late spring and bears white star-shaped flowers with a yellow eye.

Height: 15–80 cm (6–32 in).
Spacing and planting distance: 15 cm (6 in).
Soil: ordinary, preferably deep.
Aspect: full sun.
Propagation: by separating new bulbs when leaves have withered.
Flowering season: spring to summer.
Type: bulb.

Tunica (syn. *Petrorhagia*)

TUNIC FLOWER

Caryophyllaceae

Tunica makes an ideal small plant for rose beds. *Tunica saxifraga* (syn. *Petrorhagia saxifraga*) will create a magnificent carpet in very few years; it is covered in hundreds of minute flowers which are grouped into rose shapes. It has its origins in mountain paths and will do best in an average rather than rich soil. Recommended for the rock garden or for stone walls.

Useful hints

— Plant in spring, preferably in pots that have good drainage, as the young plants do not often survive wet winters in small pots.

— At the beginning of each spring, cut the clumps down to ground level to make them more dense and add a few handfuls of sandy mixture so that new stalks will root.

— Propagate by cuttings in summer or just from seeds, which will do well in spring.

Recommended

— *T. saxifraga* 'Rosette' disappears under hundreds of little pale pink double flowers that cover the small clumps of grasslike grey-green leaves.

Height: 15–20 cm (6–8 in).
Spacing and planting distance: 20 cm (8 in).
Soil: ordinary, stony.
Aspect: sun.
Propagation: from cuttings in summer or by division, or from seed in spring.
Flowering season: summer.
Type: perennial.

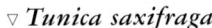

▽ *Tunica saxifraga*

△ *Typha latifolia*

Typha

BULRUSH, REEDMACE, CAT'S TAIL, CAT TAIL

Typhaceae

These dark-looking aquatics are found near ponds and spread wildly on the edges of marshy copses, where they harbour migrating wild birds. Excellent for large garden pools, but be careful they do not invade too much. Like many aquatic or semi-aquatic plants, once they are planted they are extremely difficult to control.

Useful hints

— Plant in spring or autumn in the mud-bank bordering pond or pool.

— Every three years cut the stalks back where they are spreading beyond the limit you have marked out.

— They will make lovely, long-lasting dried bouquets.

Recommended

— The most common, *Typha angustifolia*, easily measures 150 cm (60 in) tall, whereas *T. minima*, a smaller variety, grows no taller than 50 cm (20 in) and is the best one for small pools.

— *T. latifolia* is nothing other than the reed mace that grows along the banks of streams and also deserves a place near water features.

Height: 50–150 cm (20–60 in).
Spacing and planting distance: 30 cm (12 in).
Soil: ordinary, moist.
Aspect: any.
Propagation: by division in spring.
Type: perennial.

Veratrum

FALSE HELLEBORE

Liliaceae

This plant has poisonous, black rhizomes and pleated foliage; numerous, tiny, star-shaped flowers are borne at the end of erect stems.

Useful hints

— Divide the rhizomes and replant in spring or autumn.

— Alternatively, sow ripe seeds at the beginning of autumn under glass. Prick out the seedlings when large enough to handle and grow on in a nursery bed before planting in permanent sites in spring.

— Don't let the soil dry out; it is important to water in spring and summer.

— Cut back the stalks in autumn and mulch in spring with peat.

— Don't worry if you don't see flowers for some time, as it can be three or four years before they appear.

Recommended

— *Veratrum nigrum* bears purple flowers in late summer on long, narrow stems. *V. viride* will grow up to 200 cm (80 in); sprays of yellow-green flowers open in mid-summer on slender branches.

Height: 100–200 cm (40–80 in).
Spacing and planting distance: 40–60 cm (16–24 in).
Soil: light, ordinary.
Aspect: semi-shade.
Propagation: from seed or by dividing rhizomes.
Flowering season: summer.
Type: perennial.

△ **Veratrum album**
◁ **Veratrum viride**
▽ **Verbascum** 'Gainsborough'

Verbascum

MULLEIN

Scrophulariaceae

The mullein has a surprisingly graceful appearance, spreading its large, oval, silvered leaves at random through the garden. The plants grow at an amazing rate, both tall and wide. The stems are peppered with lemony yellow flowers, which look tiny in comparison with this great giant of a plant. It is a real godsend for those awkward slopes, especially when planted alongside stonecrop and valerian.

Useful hints

— Plant in any soil with a favourable situation, preferably in spring if the soil

is heavy, so that plants will not suffer in a damp winter.

Recommended

— *Verbascum bombyciferum*, a biennial, has clusters of yellow flowers, borne like spears. The stems, leaves and buds of *V. b.* 'Polarsommer', which has sulphur-yellow flowers, are completely covered in a silvery white down.

— *V. chaixii*, a perennial species, has yellow flowers with a mauve eye, and looks equally good.

△ *Verbascum phoeniceum*
▽ *Verbascum bombyciferum* 'Polar Bear'

— *V. thapsus*, commonly known as 'White Bubble', is a biennial and has yellow flowers in summer.

— The hybrids grow in graceful clusters: 'Gainsborough' has light yellow flowers, 'Pink Domino' is deep pink and 'Royal Highland' a combination of ochre, salmon-pink and purple. 'Letitia', a small dwarf bush, yellow in colour, should be confined to rock gardens.

— Wild gardens are completely transformed by the presence of *V. olympicum*, a giant variety with divided flower spikes that reach a height of 250 cm (100 in).

— Very easy to obtain from seed, *V. phoeniceum* comes in a whole range of colours, from pure white to purple.

Height: 250 cm (100 in).
Spacing and planting distance: 50 cm (20 in).
Soil: ordinary.
Aspect: sun.
Propagation: from seed in spring.
Flowering season: summer to autumn.
Type: biennial, perennial.

Verbena

VERBENA, VERVAIN

Verbenaceae

The sight of a rich carpet of verbena in a cottage garden in summer is amazing. Most have no fragrance, unlike the lemon-scented verbena, which is not a hardy species, and do not have the medical properties of the true verbena, which is in fact an unsightly weed. But they make a delightful display.

Useful hints

— Buy them as young plants, as they are quite difficult to grow from seed. Plant in late spring in rich soil. Water regularly and add liquid fertilizer once a month. Removed dead flowers in summer, so that the plants are not exhausted and will form new blooms.

— Cover the base of hardy varieties with pine bark in winter and cover with glass to protect from rain.

Recommended

— Among the annuals for summer bedding and containers, everyone has a favourite. 'Showtime' comes in a bright colour range, and 'Blaze' is a compact plant with vivid scarlet flowers. *Verbena rigida* is often grown as an annual; its best colour is purple and it will grow to 40 cm (16 in).

— Perennial species include *V. hastata*, which can grow to 100 cm (40 in) and is

decked with candelabras of small purple flowers. *V. bonariensis* will survive a mild winter. It will cheerfully grow over 100 cm (40 in) high and bears rose-lavender flowers for most of the summer.

–- *V. peruviana* is not particularly hardy, but its abundant, richly coloured flowers make it irreplaceable for summer decoration. The 'Oiseau Bleu' variety has amethyst umbels.

— The hybrids have brilliant shades: 'Aphrodite', crimson and white; 'Silver Anne', salmon-pink and scented; 'Sissinghurst', brilliant pink.

Height: 15 cm–150 cm (6–60 in).
Spacing and planting distance: 20–40 cm (8–16 in).
Soil: rich and well-drained.
Aspect: sun.
Propagation: from seed in spring (but difficult).
Flowering season: early summer to first frosts.
Type: annual, perennial.

△ *Verbena* hybrid
▽ *Verbena rigida*

Veronica

SPEEDWELL, BROOKLIME

Scrophulariaceae

In moist soils, speedwell quickly grows into beautiful clumps with blue spikes. The blues vary from the very pale sky-blue of *Veronica gentianoïdes* to the deep indigo-blue of some *V. longifolia* varieties. Grow them with mauve phlox, bergamot, China asters or scabious.

Useful hints

— Plant in autumn or spring, into soil improved with peat or leaf-mould. If the speedwell's leaves wilt on hot afternoons, it is a sign that the earth is not cool enough and you should mulch the soil with peat and soak the plants before transplanting them next season.

— Divide the clumps once they have begun to produce fewer flowers. If white marks appear, vine-mildew is probably to blame and should be treated with a fungicide.

Recommended

— *V. gentianoïdes* offers smooth and thick foliage with very pale sky-blue spears. It has been crossed with *V. spicata* to produce the deep pink 'Barcarolle'. Using these varieties combined with auricula, you can create very subtle borders.

— *V. spicata* ssp. *incana* is elegant, with its silver leaves and pale blue erect flowers.

— *V. longifolia* has very dark blue flowers and quickly forms into beautiful clumps. It looks at its best beside some of the old roses such as 'Cornelia' or 'Felicia'.

— *V. orientalis* is most suited to sunny rock gardens. Its flowers are pink or blue.

— The commonest type of speedwell is *V. spicata*, which has several

△ *Veronica gentianoïdes*
◁ *Veronica spicata* ssp. *incana*

Veronica longifolia △

Veronica orientalis ▽

varieties: 'Alba', pure white, 'Erika' and 'Heidekind', deep pink; and 'Caerulea', sky blue.

— *V. virginica* (syn. *Veronicastrum virginicum*) grows vigorously and can attain a height of approximately 200 cm (80 in). Its flower spears, however, are relatively short, being only 25 cm (10 in) long. There are blue, light pink and white varieties.

— For borders, use *V. austriaca* ssp. *teucrium* 'Royal Blue', which is gentian-blue, or 'Shirley Blue', which is a similar colour.

— *V. prostrata* favours gravel and paved areas. In addition to the blue variety, there is a mauve one called 'Mrs Holt'.

Height: 20–180 cm (8–72 in).
Spacing and planting distance: 20–40 cm (8–16 in).
Soil: rich and moist.
Aspect: sun or semi-shade.
Propagation: by division in spring.
Flowering season: spring to autumn.
Type: perennial.

△ *Vinca minor*

Vinca

PERIWINKLE

Apocynaceae

This is an ideal plant for ground cover in the most difficult conditions, whether for a sunny bank or a dry meadow, or anywhere trees or hedges are consuming all available moisture. Thanks to periwinkles, however, it is possible to transform these tricky places into carpets of flowers. The greater periwinkle, *Vinca major*, readily grows between the stones of old buildings, apparently quite happily sustaining itself on the mortar walls. If you are growing periwinkles in good soil, try planting a few squill, tulip or narcissus bulbs among them, and you will have some pleasant surprises as the year progresses.

Useful hints

— Plant young stems with roots 15 cm (6 in) long in well-dug soil.

— For ground cover thick enough to walk on, choose the blue- or white-flowered lesser periwinkle, *Vinca minor*, 15 cm (6 in) high.

Recommended

— *V. minor* sometimes bears double flowers, blue on 'Azurea Flore Pleno', otherwise purple. 'Variegata' is never more beautiful than in slightly heavy soils. The flowers of *V. major* ssp. *hirsuta* are divided into tapering lobes.

— *V. rosea* (syn. *Catharanthus roseus*) is not hardy and requires a sheltered spot or to be grown in pots under glass.

Height: 15–40 cm (6–16 in).
Spacing and planting distance: 15 cm (6 in).
Soil: ordinary.
Aspect: any.
Propagation: by division in spring.
Flowering season: spring to winter.
Type: perennial.

Viola

PANSY, VIOLET

Violaceae

The pansy and violet seem less popular than they used to be, which is strange, as they are very easy to grow. Once they are planted they will spread and flower tirelessly for months without needing any further attention. Do as gardeners used to and put them in borders and window-boxes to decorate your windows in spring.

Useful hints

— Sow pansies and violets between mid- and later summer, so they will flower the following summer.

— If you plant them in a humus-rich soil, in a good situation, they will behave like perennials and last for several years. But do note that hybrid pansies with large flowers (*Viola × wittrockiana*) are at their prettiest in their first year and will then tend to wither, especially if allowed to go to seed.

▽ *Viola* hybrid

▽ *Viola sororia*

Recommended

— Hybrid pansies are far too numerous to be listed here, but I would note 'Trimardeau', a very hardy and always pretty old variety with medium-sized flowers. There are also the many pansies from Switzerland.

— Horned violets (*Viola cornuta*) include the well-loved, small-flowered varieties, like 'Bambini', with prettily whiskered faces, as well as white, pink, purple and blue varieties.

— Lovers of the violet will certainly appreciate *V. riviniana* Purpurea Group, with violet flowers and purple leaves, the pretty *V. sororia* 'Freckles', whose flowers are speckled with blue, and *V. odorata*, which flowers in winter and spring.

— The varieties of *V. odorata*, the sweet violet, such as the purplish blue 'Cendrillon' or the purple 'Mrs Pinehurst', flower abundantly but have no fragrance. The double-flowered varieties of *V. suavis*, the Russian violet, such as the lavender-coloured 'Parme de Toulouse' and the pure white 'Reine des Blanches', make the air all around fragrant with their scent.

— Viola hybrids: some of the most famous varieties are 'Jackanapes', which is yellow and blackish brown, 'Molly Sanderson', which is black, and 'Irish Molly', which has large yellow flowers and is extremely free-flowering.

Height: 10–20 cm (4–8 in).
Spacing and planting distance: 15 cm (6 in).
Soil: rich in humus.
Aspect: sun.
Propagation: from seed in summer or by division in spring.
Flowering season: early spring to autumn.
Type: annual, perennial.

▽ *Viola* 'Jackanapes'

△ *Zantedeschia elliottiana*
▽ *Zantedeschia rehmannii*

Viscaria alpina

see *Lychnis alpina*

Vittadinia triloba

see *Erigeron karvinskianus*

Zantedeschia

ARUM LILY, CALLA LILY

Araceae

About twenty years ago the arum lily was the queen of orangery plants, but it seems to have fallen out of flavour for this use. It has reappeared, however, to decorate the margins of pools or lend emphasis to a border in a fresh and slightly wild garden. The white *Zantedeschia aethiopica* is the most popular, no doubt deservedly so, as this is the most elegant species and marries well with Solomon's seal and *Lilium regale*, not to mention ground cover plants like periwinkle or cerastium. Use them to create a bed which will give you a very fine show. The variety 'Crowborough' is hardier.

Useful hints

— Plant in spring or autumn in good garden soil enriched with compost, say one spadeful for every plant.

— Plant deeply in a sunny position, but avoid too much sun.

— If you decide to grow them in pots, water each evening during the summer.

Recommended

— You will be delighted by the yellow *Z. elliottiana*, and a pink one, *Z. rehmannii*, which has white-flecked leaves.

Height: 100 cm (40 in).
Spacing and planting distance: 30 cm (12 in).
Soil: rich and moist.
Aspect: semi-shade.
Propagation: by division in spring.
Flowering season: spring to summer.
Type: bulb.

Zauschneria

CALIFORNIAN FUCHSIA

Onagraceae

Zauschneria californica, with its unpronounceable name, is not exactly a hardy plant. It is one of the last in our alphabetical list, and is one of the last in the garden to flower. It waits until autumn before delighting us with the quite spectacular red of its tubular flowers. The sprays appear on grey-green foliage and, even when dried, still prompt exclamations of admiration. Grow them in sunny window-boxes.

Useful hints

— Plant in spring in a very light mixture (half leaf-mould, half sand). Water regularly until they come into flower so that the leaves do not dry out prematurely.

— Pinch out stalk ends in summer and place in a sheltered spot.

— Complement them with grey-leaved plants, particularly artemisia or *Tanacetum haradjanii*.

Recommended

— *Z. californica* ssp. *latifolia*, with its broad leaves, looks like a fuchsia until its distinctive, long, scarlet, tubular flowers come into bloom.

Height: 50 cm (20 in).
Spacing and planting distance: 30 cm (12 in).
Soil: light.
Aspect: sun.

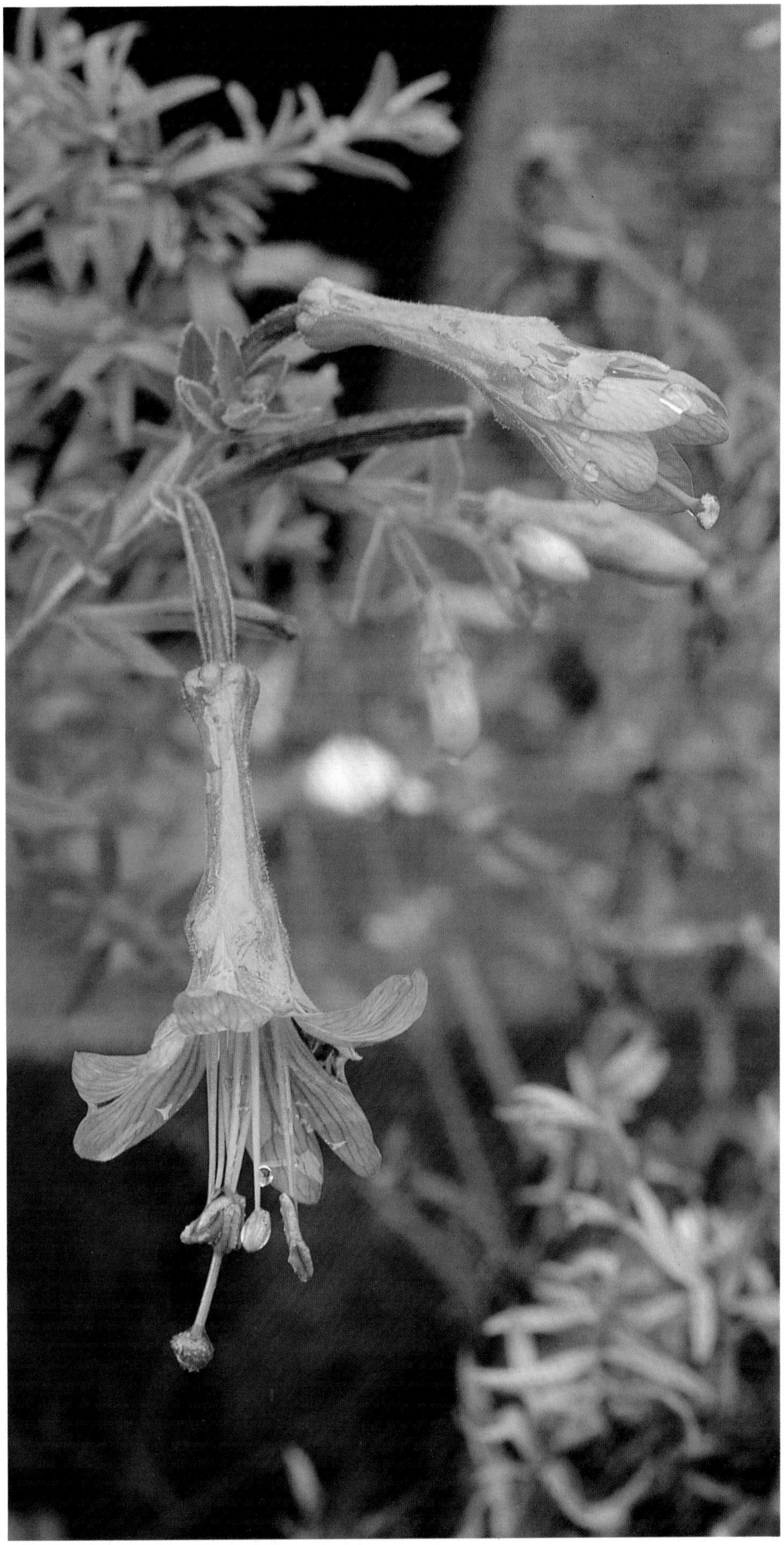

Zinnia elegans △
◁ *Zauschneria californica*

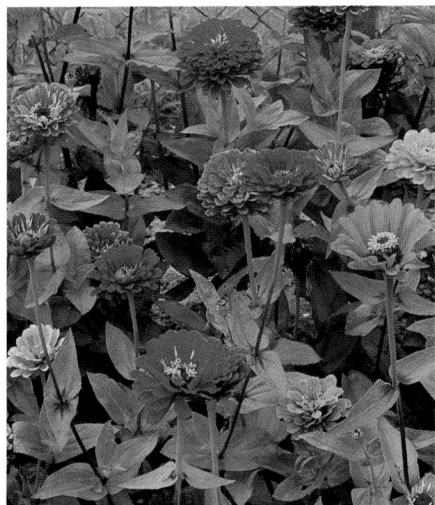

Propagation: from cuttings at the beginning of summer.
Flowering season: autumn.
Type: perennial.

Zinnia

ZINNIA

Compositae

It is no longer fashionable to deck out the summer garden with *Zinnia elegans*, although it hardly deserves a reputation for being difficult to grow. Its huge flowers, with finely arrayed petals and warm colours, ranging from reds and yellows to an unusual cream, make the zinnia appealing. It flowers from mid-summer until the frosts set in. It is a delightful cut flower and smells of beeswax.

Useful hints

— Sow in spring in uncovered seed trays.

— Plant out in beds in a sunny position. Any good garden soil will do, so long as it is well-drained.

— Dead-head plants regularly.

Recommended

— Large varieties include 'Giant Double Mixed', 'Peppermint Stick Mixed', and 'Scabious Flowered'. Well worth growing for cut flowers, even if you have to take a lot of care over staking them.

Height: 60–90 cm (24–36 in).
Spacing and planting distance: 20 cm (8 in).
Soil: ordinary, well-drained.
Aspect: sun.
Propagation: from seed in spring.
Flowering season: summer to autumn.
Type: annual, perennial.

II

TREES
&
SHRUBS

It is not always easy to choose trees and shrubs for a garden. While the surrounding flowers may be renewed each year and different ones will often be planted, trees and shrubs are generally planted once and for all.

They grow year by year and spread out, gaining increasing importance in the overall garden landscape. This is why it is essential, before their permanent planting, that you try to see them from several different views, from all angles of the house and garden, in order to envisage them as they will be when fully grown.

You may wish to plant a tree to give a welcome patch of shade in a sunny garden, or to give privacy. You may be looking for a large tree to hide an unsightly view, or a small shrub suitable for a tiny garden. The choice between evergeen and deciduous may be important.

Whatever your gardening problem, you will find, in the pages that follow, a tree or shrub to meet your needs and satisfy your taste.

Abelia to Zenobia

Abelia

ABELIA

Caprifoliaceae

A small shrub with supple branches, the abelia enjoys an exceptionally long flowering period with a mass of small, scented, pink and white bell-shaped flowers. Its only weakness is that it does not like too harsh a winter: you should therefore shelter it from cold winds and, if necessary, remove any branches scorched by frost in order for it to flourish once again the following spring.

Useful hints

— Plant it either in spring or in early summer, in a sunny spot.

— Water abundantly throughout summer, and provide a mulch of leaf-mould or chipped bark.

— In spring, prune the central branches in order to air the plant and to allow light to filter through.

Recommended

— *Abelia chinensis*, 1–1.5 m (3¼–5 ft), is an elegant little shrub. Its flowers are a delicate pinkish white and its leaves are deciduous.

— *A. × grandiflora*, with pale pink flowers, 1.5–2.5 m (5–8 ft) high. Its foliage is semi-evergreen. 'Francis Mason' does not exceed 1 m (3¼ ft) and flowers continuously from summer to autumn. 'Prostrata', which is even smaller, is suitable for small clumps.

— *A. schumannii* has lilac-pink flowers. It can reach a height of 1.5 m (5 ft).

— *A. triflora* has fragrant white flowers, tinged pink, and grows to 2m (6½ ft).

Height: 1–2.5 m (3¼–8 ft) and more.
Soil: ordinary, not too heavy.
Aspect: sun, protected from cold winds.
Propagation: from cuttings in mid-summer or by layering in spring.
Flowering season: summer to autumn.
Type: semi-deciduous, deciduous or evergreen shrub.

Abies numidica △

▽ *Abelia × grandiflora*

Abies

FIR, SILVER FIR

Pinaceae

The celebrated Christmas tree is actually a picea. As such, it should really be called Christmas picea! There will always be confusion between the genera *Picea* and *Abies* – but there is a simple way to tell the difference between them. Remove a leaf (or a needle, which is the same thing) from the abies: the leaf you have torn off will leave a round and clean mark, while with the picea the leaf will leave a small torn tongue-shape. From a distance you can tell them apart by their cones, erect on the abies and hanging on the picea. Adult trees reach a considerable height.

Useful hints

— Buy only small plants, in pots.

— Take care not to damage the root ball when planting.

— Keep the plants very warm during the first year of planting.

△ *Abies nordmanniana* ssp. *equi-trojani*

Recommended dwarf fir trees

Dwarf firs are particularly suitable for small gardens and rockeries, where their evergreen foliage and cones make for an attractive display, and combine well with alpine plants and heathers.

— *Abies balsamea* f. *hudsonia* (balsam fir) is a small, dense tree with tiny, strongly scented green needles with metallic hues and delicate green young shoots. Its extremely slow growth makes it an invaluable choice for rock gardens; indeed, it takes thirty years for it to grow just 1 m (3¼ ft).

— *A. concolor* 'Compacta' is chosen mainly for its irregular shape and elegant silvery blue foliage. Adult height: 3 m (10 ft).

— *A. lasiocarpa* 'Arizonica Compacta' has an unusual grey-green colour and a slightly conical, globose shape. Adult height: 2–3 m (6½–10 ft).

— *A. procera* 'Glauca Prostrata' is an interesting specimen for a small rock garden because of its dense, compact branches and blue-green foliage. Take care: this small conifer hates chalky soil. It measures little more than 50 cm (20 in).

Recommended tall fir trees

Before making a hasty purchase, you should look into the size these tall conifers can reach as adult trees and try to imagine the shade they will thus create. Many a fir tree has had to be sacrificed to enable a house wall to regain its sunny position.

— *A. alba*. A fast-growing variety, recognizable because of its 20 cm (8 in) long cones, its even, graded shape and its leaves, which are dark green above and marked by silvery bands underneath. It will tolerate any soil but likes to grow in semi-shade and in a damp environment. It can reach a height of 45 m (150 ft).

— *A. cephalonica* (Greek fir) has ample, wide branches which spread out elegantly. Its leaves, a beautiful bright green above with two white stripes on the underside, are arranged in whorls around the branches. These give the tree metallic reflections. The trunk is dark brown. The erect cones measure

◁ *Abies lasiocarpa* 'Compacta'

△ *Abies balsamea* f. *hudsonia*

△ *Abies concolor* 'Compacta'
▽ *Abies procera* 'Glauca Prostrata'

15–20 cm (6–8 in) in length. This fir tree is of great value in arid regions. It can reach a height of 25 m (80 ft).

— *A. concolor* (white fir). Its powerful, dense shape and its unusual rustic quality make this a conifer for large spaces. Its long sea-green leaves give off a strong scent of lemon when rubbed. Both the grey trunk and the large cones are often covered in resin. It can reach a height of 35 m (110 ft).

— *A. concolor* 'Candicans' has a superb silvery sea-green colour. Adult height: 10 m (33 ft).

— *A. grandis* (giant fir, grand fir) is said to grow faster than a poplar and, in the best conditions, can reach a height of 60 m (190 ft) and more. It is certainly true that in fresh, well-drained soil it forms deep roots which enable it to reach a height of 20 m (65 ft) in twenty years. Its leaves are pleasantly tangerine-scented. Be careful: this variety does not like chalky soils but loves humid climates. Medium height: 30–40 m (95–130 ft).

— *A. homolepis* (Nikko fir) is a very beautiful fir tree originating in central Japan, with a wide spread, and a height of 5–10 m (16–33 ft). Its bark is brown with pink glints, its shoots smooth and pink; the purple-brown cones appear even on young specimens: all its features combine to make this an extremely attractive fir. The dense leaves tolerate both drought and pollution.

— *A. koreana* (Korean fir). This pretty little pyramid-shaped fir, which has leaves that are bright green on top and very straight branches, is prized chiefly for the beauty of its cones, which are a very decorative purple-violet. Medium height: 5–6 m (16–20 ft).

— *A. nordmanniana* (Caucasian fir) is a beautiful tree with an even, pyramidal shape, whose lower branches do not lose their leaves. Its foliage is dark green, its buds reddish brown in winter. The cones appear only on the higher branches. It tolerates drought and will thrive equally well in sandy or chalky soil, but it does not do well in cities. Height: 15–20 m (50–65 ft).

— *A. pinsapo* (Spanish fir) is distinguishable above all for its short, thick needles, arranged around the branches like bottle-brushes. Its shape is even, large, pyramidal and impressive. This fir tree likes dry and limy soil and will, indeed, thrive happily anywhere, even on chalk. Its natural habitat is a restricted area around the mountains in southern Spain. Adult height: 15–20 m (50–65 ft). Two interesting cultivars should be noted: *A.p.* 'Glauca', metallic blue (height: 15 m/50 ft) and *A.p.* 'Aurea', with yellow glints. This tree can reach a height of 8 m (26 ft).

— *A. procera* (noble fir) Very narrow and even-shaped, this fir tree boasts very large cones and thrives mainly in deep, acid soil, in a humid climate. It is also very tolerant of cold conditions. In its natural habitat (the mountains in north-western America, from where it originates) it reaches a height of 60 m (190 ft) and more, but when cultivated this tree hardly exceeds 20 m (65 ft).

▽ *Abies nordmanniana* 'Golden Spreader'

Height: varies according to species and variety.
Soil: good-quality, rich in humus.
Aspect: sun, semi-shade.
Propagation: from seed.
Type: evergreen tree.

Acacia

MIMOSA, WATTLE

Leguminosae

This is the popular mimosa. It is not to be confused with those large trees with pinnate leaves that are incorrectly called acacias but which are actually false acacias, whose botanical name is *Robinia*. In botany, trees that are named *Acacia*, and which we discuss here, are known familiarly by the name of mimosa. They originate in Australia, where fossilized traces show that they existed 250 million years ago. A large shrub with many branches or a small, graceful tree, it can reach a height of 8 m (26 ft), but it will not tolerate cold. The evergreen foliage is ferny. The flowers, abundant and shaped like little bright yellow fluffy pompons, are arranged in clusters. They are highly scented and appear in winter or spring.

Useful hints

— Acacias grow successfully only in very mild climates.

— Plant them in acid or alkaline soil and, especially, in a very sunny but sheltered position.

— To slow down the growth of the tree and to strengthen the trunk, water sparingly.

— Take care: mimosas hate wind, as they break easily.

— Generally healthy, they tolerate diseases well but will not live longer than about thirty years.

Recommended

— *Acacia baileyana* is very floriferous. Its golden yellow flowers appear in spring.

— *A. dealbata* (silver wattle). Its silvery green foliage is very delicate and resembles a fern. The clusters of fluffy flowers are highly scented. Some nurserymen still stock some prized old varieties such as 'Gaulois Astier'.

△ *Acacia dealbata*

— *A. longifolia* (Sydney golden wattle) has light yellow flowers gathered in large cylindrical clusters.

— *A. mucronata* is the hardiest: usually, this is a small tree which does not exceed 3.5 m (11½ ft).

— *A. retinodes* reaches a height of 8 m (26 ft). The shoots are smooth, the flowers pale yellow, very scented in spring, blossoming almost all year round. Much cultivated in mild climates, it should be planted in a frost-free position, sheltered by a wall.

Height: 3–8 m (10–26 ft).
Soil: good, not wet.
Aspect: sun, sheltered from wind.
Propagation: from seed or cuttings in autumn.
Flowering season: winter and spring.
Type: evergreen tree.

Acca

See *Feijoa*

Acer

MAPLE

Aceraceae

These are among the most decorative trees of all and they will adapt to any situation. They grow slowly, but their colour, bark and shape are so attractive from a young age that they should be given a special place in the garden or in a container on the verandah or the patio. This is a very well-represented genus, including vigorous trees as well as small trees or large shrubs. All maples originate in the northern hemisphere. The largest ones, with the most spectacular foliage, such as *Acer rubrum* (red maple), come from North America. Maples can be distinguished from other trees because of their palmate leaves, usually composed of five lobes, and their winged fruits, which are scattered in the autumn winds, thus ensuring distribution. The foliage of hybrid varieties offers a wide variety of colours, both in spring and in autumn. Some are interesting because of their prettily marked or coloured bark, which is particularly decorative in winter, and others because of their early flowering. Japanese maples are a perfect choice for smaller gardens.

Useful hints

— The leaves must be protected from the rising sun and from cold winds.

— In spring, remove dead or badly positioned wood.

— Choose a healthy tree or shrub and ensure that the roots are not dried out.

— Watch out for cockchafers and greenfly, which can attack young leaves. Most maples require fertile but well-drained soil, because they do not tolerate excessive moisture.

— If your garden soil is very chalky you should choose *A. campestre*, whose verdant foliage turns coppery gold before falling.

— In very sandy soil, *A.* × *zoeschense* 'Annae' will naturalize very well, as will *A. negundo* (ash-leaved maple). If your garden is by the sea, however, you should note that this species does not tolerate gusts of wind, which can break its branches.

— The enchantment provided by maples during the autumn will depend on where they are planted. For the most part, they are set off to best advantage in an open and sunny position. One exception to this is *A. circinatum* (vine maple), which grows better in semi-shade and takes on red-orange tints which are even more striking in autumn. Japanese maples also benefit from light shade. Full sun is also not recommended for ornamental maples with coloured bark.

Recommended for early flowering

Flowers are not the most important feature of maples. They are fairly unobtrusive, appearing most frequently in late spring, after which they are hidden among the foliage. Nevertheless, some varieties are very early flowering, from the end of winter, which increases their interest.

— *A. circinatum* (vine maple) offers a splendid two-coloured flowering in mid-spring. Its flowers consist of purple sepals and white petals, which form a pleasing contrast.

— *A. rubrum* (red maple) is even more showy. It has beautiful hanging red flower clusters in early spring, before the leaves appear.

— *A. saccharium* (silver maple) reaches a height of 25 m (80 ft). Its leaves are silvery white underneath and its flowers, which are very tiny, appear before the leaves, forming brownish yellow hanging clusters. This variety has the added advantage of rapid growth. In Canada, it grows along river banks.

— *A. saccharum* (sugar maple) produces greenish flowers forming yellowish green clusters in mid-spring before the leaves appear. Americans extract the famous maple syrup from this variety, approximately 3–10 kg (6½–22 lb) per tree.

Recommended for variegated foliage

Variegated leaves, in maples, are a peculiarity of *A. negundo* (ash-leaved maple) and its different cultivars. While the main species has a delicate green, unremarkable foliage, the hybrids have distinctive marbled leaves.

— *A. negundo* 'Flamingo' has variegated pink leaves.

— *A. negundo* 'Variegatum' (or 'Argenteovariegatum') boldly blends green and

△ *Acer griseum*
▽ *Acer palmatum* 'Senkaki'

△ *Acer pseudoplatanus* 'Brillantissimum'

▽ *Acer grosseri*

white. The foliage of *A.n.* 'Aureovarie-gatum' is brightened up by pale yellow. These three varieties reach a height that is below 10 m (33 ft) when adult.

— *A. platanoïdes* 'Drummondii' has green leaves with a wide white border. Adult height: 9 m (30 ft).

— *A. pseudoplatanus* 'Leopoldii' has a very unusual variegation: its green leaves have splotches of ochre and cream. The effect can really only be appreciated by looking at the leaves close up. Take care, however: this variety can reach a height of 15 m (50 ft), so do not plant it too close to the house. Seen from afar, the tree forms a pleasing ochre-green mass.

Recommended for decorative bark

With their attractively marked or coloured bark, some maples are decorative even in the depths of winter, when they are completely bare of leaves and look almost like living sculptures. They should be planted close to the house in order to derive the maximum benefit from them during the winter months.

— *A. campestre.* There are some interesting varieties of this species, such as 'Elsrijk', which is much more compact, or 'Red Shine', with red-stained foliage.

— *A. capillipes* has white stripes on a green-brown trunk.

— *A. davidii* and *A. grosseri* var. *hersii* both have green bark artistically veined with white.

— *A. griseum.* The bark of this species is an attractive cinnamon-brown and peels off in large flakes, like that of the silver maple.

— *A. palmatum* 'Senkaki' (coral-bark maple) provides a good winter show. A small tree or shrub, it derives its common name from the rich coral colouring on its young branches, which is particularly noticeable in cold weather.

— *A. pensylvanicum* (snake-bark maple), from North America, is distinguished by its jade-green bark striped with white.

— *A. rufinerve,* an attractive little Japanese species, has green, white-striped bark.

— *A. saccharinum* has a light grey bark which comes off in large strips or sheets, rather like some eucalyptus trees.

263

△ *Acer cappadocicum* 'Aureum'
▽ *Acer pseudoplatanus*

Recommended for splendid spring colours

Some remarkable maples produce rich spring foliage which is quite different from the summer foliage, which will in turn change again once autumn comes. This means that two, and sometimes three, colours can be seen.

Pinks

— *A. platanoides* 'Drummondii' is a very soft pink when the leaves appear then turns to green and white.

— *A. pseudoplatanus* 'Brillantissimum' is less than 4 m (13 ft) in height. The leaves are a delightful shrimp-pink colour in spring, becoming pale yellowish green before turning a true green.

— *A. pseudoplatanus* 'Leopoldii' has pink foliage, evenly shaded with yellow and ochre. Later it becomes green, speckled with ochre and cream.

— *A. pseudoplatanus* 'Prinz Handjery' is even more unusually coloured: the leaves have a violet underside in spring, with yellow patches on the upper side. Height: 18–20 m (60–65 ft).

Reds

— *A. capillipes* (snake-bark maple). Not only the leaves, but also the branches are red. Height: 9 m (30 ft).

— *A. cappadocicum* 'Rubrum' (Caucasian maple). Its branches and leaves turn green once spring is over, then become an attractive red and gold.

— *A. × zoeschense* 'Annae'. Its foliage, deep red in spring, turns to olive-green or brown-green in summer, before resuming its initial colour in autumn. Height: 15 m (50 ft).

Yellow

— *A. palmatum* 'Aureum'. From a very delicate yellow in spring, its foliage assumes an increasingly golden hue.

Recommended for superb autumn colours

Maples are majestic in spring and summer, and make an attractive decoration in winter with their marked or coloured bark or their early flowering, but it is chiefly in autumn that they surpass themselves with their wonderful colours.

Scarlets

— *A. grosseri* var. *hersii*. Already admirable because of its striped bark, this maple, introduced from China, is one of the most decorative of garden features in autumn, when its foliage acquires magnificent shades of orange-red and yellow. Height: 5–6 m (16–20 ft).

— *A. japonicum* 'Aconitifolium'. This pretty little tree, which comes originally from Japan, has green leaves in summer and in autumn assumes a superb bronze-red tint. Height: 3 m (10 ft).

— *A. palmatum* 'Osakazuki'. This shrub belongs to the Japanese landscape. Its foliage, green during the warm months, turns a splendid scarlet mixed with orange in autumn. It looks particularly effective among rhododendrons. Height: 3–4 m (10–13 ft).

— The leaves of *A. rubrum* (red maple) in summer are deep green above and bluish on the underside, while in autumn they take on vivid and highly spectacular orange-red tints. Height: 20 m (65 ft).

— *A. tataricum* ssp. *ginnala* (Amur maple). Once the foliage of this species has turned light red in autumn the leaves unfortunately do not linger long on the tree. In summer, the leaves are bright green underneath, light green above. The branches are a beautiful vivid red. The Amur maple is very tolerant of pollution and will thrive in poor soil. Height: 5–6 m (16–20 ft).

— *A. × zoeschense* 'Annae' has leaves which start off flame-red, in spring, before changing to olive-green or brown-green in summer. They then turn deep red again in the autumn.

Reds and golds

— The foliage of *A. cappadocicum* 'Rubrum' starts off blood-red in spring, turns green, and then becomes golden in autumn.

— *A. circinatum* (vine maple) is admirable for its two-coloured flowers in spring, and also for its leaves, light green in summer, which in autumn take on magnificent scarlet and orange colours. The branches droop, sometimes to the ground, where they take root. Height: 10 m (33 ft).

— *A. davidii*. This tree, which comes from China, is very spectacular all year round, thanks to its deep green foliage in summer, which contrasts with its vivid red stalks. In autumn, the leaves turn to a superb yellow and purple. Height: 9–10 m (30–33 ft).

— *A. pseudoplatanus* is a giant. Its leaves grow to a size of 25 cm (10 in) and its flowers, arranged in long hanging clusters, appear at the same time as the leaves. This is one of the hardiest trees for a windy position. Height: not less than 30 m (95 ft).

— *A. rufinerve* (snake-bark maple). The large, three-lobed leaves, deep green in summer, turn crimson and vivid yellow in autumn. Height: 9–10 m (30–33 ft).

Yellows

Every shade of yellow is found in acers before the leaves fall.

— *A. campestre*. Its foliage, green during the summer, turns an attractive coppery gold in autumn. Height: 15–20 m (50–65 ft).

— *A. opalus* (Italian maple). This maple, which has leaves like those of the guelder rose, is also called *A. opulifolium*. It seems to be ignored, despite the fact that it is naturally suited to rocky soil.

— *A. palmatum* 'Senkaki' (syn. *A.p.* 'Sangokaku'). Pale green leaves in summer become a very delicate yellow in autumn. Height: 4 m (13 ft).

— *A. pensylvanicum*. A true yellow autumn colouring follows the green of summer. Height: 5–6 m (16–20 ft).

— *A. platanoïdes* (Norway maple) has green leaves during summer, becoming golden yellow in autumn. Height: 20 m (65 ft).

— *A. saccharinum*. The leaves are a beautiful bright green in summer, turning to raw-silk-yellow in autumn.

Recommended purple varieties

These maples remain purple or crimson throughout the summer, striking an unusual note amid the delicate green foliage. This contrast can be emphasized by placing them with trees that have white- or gold-variegated leaves, or that have completely golden foliage such as *Gleditsia triacanthos* 'Sunburst'.

— *A. palmatum* f. *atropurpureum*. This very elegant shrub, 3–5 m (10–16 ft) tall, with supple branches, displays every shade of purple in the course of the year, as does *A.p.* Dissectum Atropurpureum Group, which has elegant foliage and is roughly the same height.

— *A. platanoïdes* 'Crimson King' and 'Schwedleri' reach a height of 10 m (33 ft)

Acer japonicum △
Acer crataegifolium 'Veitchii' ▽

and retain a very vivid black-red tone throughout the summer. Their foliage tends to lighten slightly before falling.

— *A. pseudoplatanus* 'Atropurpureum' is one of the most majestic and most imposing maples, reaching a height of 30 m (95 ft). Its leaves are shaded with lilac-brown.

Height: 2–35 m (6½–110 ft) depending on species and variety.
Soil: ordinary soil which is well-drained, but with one exception: *A. rubrum* prefers an acid soil.
Aspect: sun or semi-shade.
Propagation: from seed, sown in autumn, or by grafting in spring.
Flowering season: spring.
Type: deciduous tree or shrub.

▽ *Acer palmatum* 'Rubrum'

Aesculus × neglecta 'Erythroblastos' △

Aesculus

HORSE CHESTNUT, BUCKEYE

Hippocastanaceae

A large tree for a very spacious garden. It provides a magnificent sight in late spring, when its immense and dense foliage appears to be studded with hundreds of pink, red or white candles. Were it not such a common sight in our parks, we would marvel at so spectacularly ornamental a tree. Adult trees easily reach a height of 18 m (60 ft).

Useful hints

— Give it plenty of room, in a sunny spot.

Recommended

— *Aesculus × carnea* (red horse chestnut)

has rose-pink flowers which appear in late spring.

— *A. × carnea* 'Briotii' has scarlet flowers.

— *A. hippocastanum* (horse chestnut) has

little white candle-like flowers which appear in mid- to late spring. It is the giant among the aesculus. Because it has double flowers, 'Baumannii' does not fruit, which can sometimes be an enormous advantage.

The next two varieties belong to the genus of horse chestnuts that originate in North America. They are regarded as shrubs and do not exceed 4 m (13 ft) in height.

— *A. parviflora* (white buckeye) has white flowers in mid-summer and leaves that colour golden in autumn.

— *A. pavia* (red buckeye) hardly exceeds 2.5 m (8 ft) when cultivated. In summer it has erect clusters of carmine-red flowers spotted with yellow. 'Atrosanguinea' has deep purple flowers.

Height: 2.5–18 m (8–60 ft).
Soil: any.
Aspect: sun.
Propagation: plant chestnuts in spring.
Flowering season: spring.
Type: deciduous tree.

Ailanthus

AILANTHUS, TREE OF HEAVEN

Simaroubaceae

The greatest qualities of this tree are its capacity to grow quickly, its tolerance of pollution, smoke, shade or sun, and its indifference to the soil in which it is planted. It is often used for containing embankments. Its main disadvantage is that it produces suckers that have to be constantly cut away. In addition, its leaves appear late. Despite all this, it is an elegant tree.

Useful hints

— Simply plant it firmly and, above all, keep it away from buildings. Its branches can be damaged by strong winds.

Recommended

— *Ailanthus altissima* (tree of heaven) resembles the walnut tree and reaches a height of 25 m (80 ft). Its composite leaves are extremely long (up to 60 cm/ 24 in) and turn yellow in summer. The greenish flowers, arranged in large panicles, have an unpleasant scent.

◁ *Aesculus parviflora*

— *A. vilmoriniana* is less tall (16 m/54 ft maximum) and tends to spread out widthwise. It can be useful for planting on banks or slopes.

Height: 8–25 m (26–80 ft).
Soil: any, even poor.
Aspect: sun or semi-shade.
Propagation: from suckers or root cuttings.
Flowering season: summer.
Type: deciduous tree.

Albizia

SILK TREE

Leguminosae

A small tree with fine, pinnate foliage similar to that of the mimosa. Its flowers, which appear in summer, are particularly attractive, with clusters of stamens that resemble erect pink bottle-brushes on very straight stems.

Useful hints

— Plant in the sun in a position which is well sheltered from the wind. This is a sensitive tree which will tolerate a little cold, but not prolonged frosts.

— Since albizia does not like being transplanted, it is better to buy a small specimen in a pot.

Recommended

— *Albizia julibrissin* (silk tree). In Japan this is a tree, but elsewhere it is more of a shrub. It is highly scented, and produces panicles of pale pink flowers in summer. 'Ombrella Boubri', a variety with deep red flowers, has only recently come on to the market. It flowers again in autumn.

— *A. julibrissin* var. *rosea* has flowers of a more pronounced shade of pink. This variety is the hardiest.

— *A. lophantha* (syn. *Paraserianthes lophantha*) is a fast-growing, deciduous, spreading shrub which flowers in winter in very mild climates. Its long bottle-brush-like flowers take on a beautiful sulphur-yellow colour.

Height: 2–10 m (6½–33 ft).
Soil: good garden soil.
Aspect: sun, protected from wind.
Propagation: from seed.
Flowering season: summer or winter, depending on species and variety.
Type: deciduous or semi-evergreen tree or shrub.

△ *Ailanthus altissima*
▽ *Albizia julibrissin* 'Rosea'

▽ *Albizia julibrissin*

Alnus

ALDER

Betulaceae

For an alder to reach its maximum height of 30 m (95 ft) and a lifespan of 120 years, it needs a great deal of light and moisture. Like the birch, the alder thrives in poor or moist soil. It is the perfect choice if you want a tree that will grow quickly. In spring, long catkins hang from the branches, soon to be followed by egg-shaped cones. Its wood is hard and durable. Immersed in water, it becomes even harder.

Useful hints

— Plant it in the shade or in sun in moist, even boggy soil. *Alnus cordata* (Italian alder) is the only alder to like well-drained soil.

Recommended

— *A. cordata* (Italian alder) is a very tall species which, in its native Corsica, can reach a height of 25 m (80 ft). When cultivated, it barely reaches 7 m (23 ft). It has a distinctive pyramidal shape and bright deep green heart-shaped leaves.

— *A. glutinosa* 'Aurea' (European alder, common alder) is a dazzling tree, with golden leaves in spring. It rarely exceeds 3 m (10 ft) in height.

— *A. incana* (grey alder). This tree, which reaches a height of 12–15 m (40–50 ft), is recognizable by its silvery grey foliage and bark. The male catkins appear in clusters, in spring. The cones, in groups of three or six, are brown when fully mature. This species thrives in chalky soil or in very moist places.

— *A. maritima*. This large shrub thrives by the sea and may be used to make a hedge. It has yellow catkins 6 cm (2½ in) long.

— *A. rubra* (red alder) is named for the colour of its buds, petioles and the veining on its leaves.

Height: 3–15 m (10–50 ft) on average.
Soil: moist.
Aspect: shade or sun.
Propagation: by layering in spring.
Flowering season: spring.
Type: deciduous tree.

◁ *Alnus cordata*

△ ***Amelanchier canadensis***

Amelanchier

JUNEBERRY, SERVICEBERRY, SHADBUSH

Rosaceae

This is an attractive and decorative shrub or small tree. Its foliage can spread out widely and can reach a height of 5 m (16 ft). In addition, it will change the appearance of the garden by turning colour according to the season: in spring the flowers are a delicate white, as striking as a bride's veil, and the young foliage is pink-bronze, while in autumn its leaves turn flame-red and it carries red berries.

Useful hints

— Plant the amelanchier at the end of summer or in full winter, or even in early spring. It will grow slowly to begin with, but in the second year it will take off.

— It does not need pruning. Simply remove any dead branches.

— In spring, provide a mulch of garden compost or chipped bark.

Recommended

— *Amelanchier alnifolia.* This shrub, 2–4 m (6½–13 ft) tall, is characterized by its very rounded, hairy, whitish leaves and its clusters of creamy white flowers which appear in late spring.

— *A. canadensis* is a small tree, 4–8 m (13–26 ft) in height (but much larger in its natural habitat). It prefers moist conditions. Its flowers are pure white and they are followed by blackish purple fruits.

— *A. laevis* has attractive pure white flowers, gathered in long and abundant scented clusters, which appear in late spring. From spring onwards, the foliage is a rich lilac-bronze colour. The rounded fruits are red.

— *A. lamarckii* 'Rubescens' offers a spectacular springtime display from the mòment the button-shaped flowers open, purplish pink in the beginning, pinkish white as they fade. The copper-coloured foliage turns scarlet in autumn.

△ ***Amelanchier canadensis***

Height: 1.5–8 m (5–26 ft).
Soil: preferably rich and relatively fertile.
Aspect: semi-shade or full sun.
Propagation: from seed or by layering in spring.
Flowering season: spring.
Type: deciduous tree or shrub.

△ *Aralia elata*

Aralia

ARALIA, JAPANESE ANGELICA TREE

Araliaceae

The aralia has a very straight trunk and can grow to 10 m (33 ft). It has attractive pinnate leaves and produces a mass of white flowers in late summer and autumn. It puts out numerous suckers, with sharp spines, that can sometimes be difficult to get rid of. *Aralia cachemirica*, with beautiful white flowers and no spines, can give a dramatic effect when grown in isolation on a lawn. A group of aralias together makes an even more effective picture.

Useful hints

— Plant in good garden soil.

— Protect aralias from the wind because of their delicate foliage, which is deeply lobed.

— Remove the suckers as they appear.

Recommended

— *A. elata* (Japanese angelica tree) has very large leaves, sometimes as long as 1 m (3¼ ft), crowned in late summer and autumn by spectacular bunches of white flowers arranged in large heads.

— *A. elata* 'Aureovariegata'. A very popular shrub, with leaves that are edged with yellow, turning silver at the end of the summer.

— *A. spinosa* (American angelica tree). Sometimes known as devil's rod because of the spines that cover it. In late summer the tiny, whitish flowers open out. Gathered in umbels, they form large, fluffy heads. The hugeness of the leaves, with petioles that are up to 25 cm (10 in) long, gives the plant a stunning subtropical allure.

Height: 10 m (33 ft).
Soil: any.
Aspect: sun or semi-shade, protected from winds.
Propagation: from suckers.
Flowering season: late summer and autumn.
Type: deciduous tree or shrub.

Araucaria

MONKEY PUZZLE

Araucariaceae

Very fashionable in the early twentieth century, this curiously shaped conifer is no longer universally popular. In any climate other than a very moist one, or if exposed to pollution, its branches tend to drop their leaves, giving the tree a slightly ghostly, denuded appearance. Araucarias are either male or female and are frequently planted singly, so it is rare for female trees to be fertilized and therefore produce cones. The cones take two years to reach maturity.

Useful hints

— Give your araucaria plenty of space and plant in deep soil. For a few years it will hardly grow at all, then will grow by 30 cm (12 in) a year.

— Moist, not too cold climates suit it to perfection.

— You can plant it in a conservatory, or keep it indoors until it becomes too tall.

▽ △ *Araucaria araucana*

Recommended

— *Araucaria araucana* (monkey puzzle, Chile pine). Despite its common name, the almost triangular, overlapping and prickly leaves would make it impossible for even monkeys to climb!

— *A. bidwillii.* This tall tree (it grows to 40 m/130 ft in its native Australia) is hardy only in very mild climates. Its cones, the largest in the genus, can reach a length of 30 cm (12 in) and weigh 3 kg (6½ lb) each.

— *A. heterophylla* (Norfolk Island pine). This araucaria, native to Norfolk Island, is one of the most beautiful species of all, with its majestic and highly decorative bearing. Sadly, it is seldom cultivated except in conservatories or as a house-plant.

Height: up to 40 m (130 ft).
Soil: ordinary.
Aspect: sun, but in a very moist atmosphere.
Propagation: from seed.
Type: evergreen tree.

Arbutus

STRAWBERRY TREE, MADROÑA

Ericaceae

This is a large shrub or small tree, some-times growing to 10 m (33 ft) or more in height. The arbutus has evergreen foliage, as thick as leather. Its multiple trunks can, if desired, be cut back to form just one single tree trunk. Clusters of flowers, in the shape of tiny urns, produce fruits that resemble rounded strawberries. The arbutus is frequently seen in mild climates, where it success-fully creates the effect of a natural land-scape, but it also can be grown in cooler regions.

Useful hints

— It thrives by the sea (or in sheltered inland gardens), and tolerates this cli-mate very well, with a good deal of sun.

— Plant it in acid soil.

— Protect it from the wind.

Recommended

— *Arbutus andrachne* (Grecian straw-berry tree) flowers in spring. If it is well protected during the early years after planting, it will acclimatize to cooler conditions.

△ *Arbutus* × *andrachnoïdes*

Arbutus menziesii ▷

— *A.* × *andrachnoides* has peeling, red-dish brown bark and small white flow-ers in autumn. The fruits are orange or red.

— *A. menziesii* (madroña, madroñe). The abundant white flowers of this species, appearing at the end of spring, produce orange-red fruits.

— *A. unedo* (Killarney strawberry tree). With its reddish bark, its tiny leaves that are always green and leathery and its pinkish white flowers, this is a very ornamental tree. Flowers appear in late autumn and winter, when the fruits are ripe. The form *A.u. rubra* has a more compact shape, flowers of a more pro-nounced pink colour and abundant fruits.

Height: at least 10 m (33 ft).
Soil: acid.
Aspect: sunny.
Propagation: from seed, by layering and from cuttings.
Flowering season: spring to winter.
Type: evergreen tree or shrub.

△ *Artemisia absinthium* 'Lambrook Silver'

Artemisia

WORMWOOD

Compositae

These bushy shrubs, which are usually 1 m (3¼ ft) in size with bluish green or grey foliage, and almost always aromatic, are very useful. They thrive best in the most unpromising corners of the garden, in areas that are scorned by other plants. The more gravel and sun wormwood can enjoy, the better it will look. Plant it next to a few shrub roses and you will have a very effective display.

Useful hints

— Artemisias should preferably be planted in spring, adding two handfuls of coarse sand or grit around each stem. At the beginning of winter, cover the base of the stem with a few handfuls of grit. The upper part of the plant may succumb to frost, but in spring, new shoots will appear lower down.

— Prune in summer, cutting away the flowers. These have no visual appeal and will spoil the look of the bush.

— While pruning, take some cuttings which you can root in sand, in the shade, and then protect from the cold during the winter. Note that during this plant's first season after planting, it will make a clump almost 1 m (3¼ ft) in diameter.

Recommended

— *Artemisia absinthium* 'Lambrook Silver' is a shrubby perennial with silvery green foliage and a strong scent of absinthe. Height: 50 cm (20 in).

— *A. arborescens* is a woody-based perennial with very silvery, lacy foliage and a rounded top.

— *A. dracunculus* (tarragon). A well-known perennial plant, this is the popular tarragon herb whose aromatic leaves are used in cooking and to scent the garden.

— *A. schmidtiana* 'Nana', with its fine, delicate silver foliage, is the most beautiful of all.

Height: 20 cm–1 m (8 in–3¼ ft).
A. schmidtiana 'Nana', 5–10 cm (2–4 in).
Soil: light and, most important, well-drained.
Aspect: full sun.
Propagation: from semi-ripe cuttings in summer.
Flowering season: summer.
Type: deciduous shrub.

Arundinaria

BAMBOO

Gramineae

These bamboos are very useful, depending on their size, as windbreaks or for ground cover. All have evergreen, rapidly growing foliage and acclimatize very easily. Take care, though: some spread rapidly and quickly invade the space around them. (This can be an advantage by the waterside or in a large garden.) The strong canes are often used as plant supports.

Useful hints

— Bamboos love humidity and full sun, apart from a few species which will tolerate shade.

— Do not prune them, but at the beginning of autumn cut off dead or damaged canes at the base.

— They can also be grown in containers on a patio or verandah.

Recommended

— *Arundinaria anceps* (syn. *Yushania anceps*) (Anceps bamboo). Vigorous and invasive, this is a good windbreak.

— *A. chino* (syn. *Pleioblastus chino*) reaches a height of 1–2 m (3¼–6½ ft), with leaves that are 2 cm (¾ in) wide.

— *A. fastuosa* (syn. *Semiarundinaria fastuosa*). In the West, this reaches a height of 5–6 m (16–20 ft) but in Japan, its natural habitat, it can climb to a height of 15 m (50 ft). Its magnificent hollow reeds (up to 8 cm/3 in across), are a deep bright green spotted with purple. They

△ ▽ *Arundinaria* species

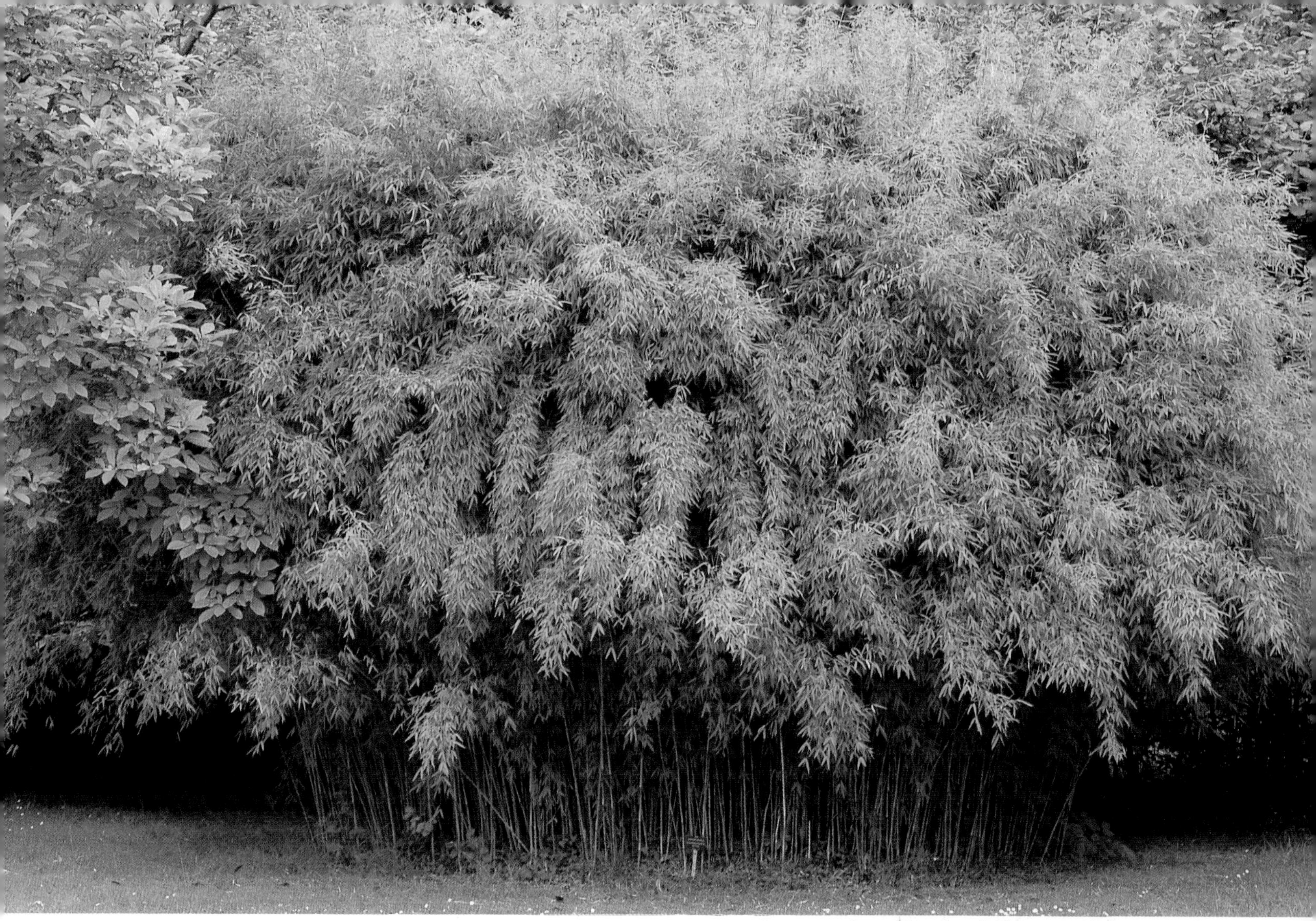

△ ***Arundinaria nitida***
▽ ***Arundinaria viridistriata***

make excellent screens. The very young shoots, 5–10 cm (2–4 in) long, are an edible delicacy.

— *A. graminea* (syn. *Pleioblastus gramineus*) is a good variety for shaded places. The canes are olive-green and the leaves luminous yellow-green. Height: 3 m (10 ft).

— *A. japonica* (syn. *Pseudosasa japonica*) (arrow bamboo) was one of the first Japanese bamboos to be introduced to the West. It is dense and reaches a height of 3–4 m (10–13 ft). Its foliage is bright green and its canes olive-green.

— *A. murieliae* (syn. *Fargesia murieliae*) is an elegant plant with luminous green canes which gradually turn yellow-green as they age. Its shape is slightly drooping, which makes it very attractive as a pot plant for use on the verandah or patio. In addition, it is one of the hardiest bamboo species.

— *A. nitida* (syn. *Fargesia nitida*) is the hardiest of all. Its narrow and delicate foliage dries out and curls up in the cold. Its supple purple canes reach a height of 5–6 m (16–20 ft).

— *A. pumila* (syn. *Pleioblastus humilis* var. *pumilus*). This dwarf bamboo, 50 cm (20 in) high, makes good ground cover.

— *A. variegata* (syn. *Pleioblastus variegatus*) (dwarf white-stripe bamboo). The shoots form an elegant arch shape. The bright green lanceolate leaves are striped with white. Height: 3 m (10 ft).

— *A. viridistriata* (syn. *Pleioblastus auricomus*) is the most beautiful of all, with its lilac stalks rising up to a height of 1–2 m (3¼–6½ ft). Cut out the old stalks at the base in the autumn, and fresh stalks will appear the following spring.

Height: 50 cm–6 m (20 in–20 ft).
Soil: any, provided it is moist.
Aspect: sun.
Propagation: from young shoots cut during spring.
Type: evergreen perennial.

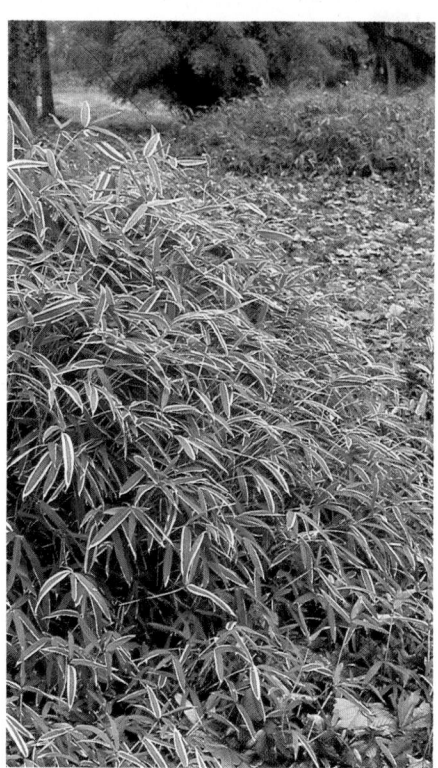

△ *Atriplex halimus*

Atriplex

SALTBUSH, TREE PURSLANE

Chenopodiaceae

There is an annual species of atriplex known as orach that may be eaten as a vegetable. The plant we discuss here is a small shrub which rarely reaches a height of 2 m (6½ ft), whose grey branches and silvery semi-evergreen leaves are highly distinctive. It is found mainly on banks or slopes by the sea, where it is very useful for preventing erosion. It also makes an effective windbreak or hedge, being very resistant to salty spray. It is equally resistant to dust. Flowering is insignificant.

Useful hints

— Plant atriplex in autumn, even in very sandy soil, so long as it is well worked.

— Every two years you can prune the tips of the stems in order to train the plant, which tends to become scrubby, into some sort of shape.

Recommended

— *Atriplex halimus* (tree purslane) will tolerate sandy soil. It reaches a height of 1–2 m (3¼–6½ ft) and produces reddish grey flowers of no interest.

Height: 50 cm–2 m (20 in–6½ ft).
Soil: well-drained.
Aspect: sun.
Propagation: from semi-ripe cuttings in autumn.
Flowering season: summer.
Type: semi-evergreen shrub.

Aucuba

JAPANESE LAUREL

Aucubaceae

This is regarded by some as a rather dismal plant because neglected specimens are often seen in parks. Nevertheless, well planted and cared for, the aucuba can become so decorative that one could happily choose to have it as a houseplant. Throughout the year, its green foliage speckled with yellow and its light green branches bring a fresh note of colour to the garden when many other plants have faded. A robust and persistent shrub, it is also more than able to tolerate city pollution. You can use large groups of it, either to conceal an unsightly corner or to fill the bottom of the garden. A generous quantity of helianthus, 1.5 m (5 ft) in height, blended with the aucubas, with some hypericum as ground cover, will make a splendid display that will brighten the garden all year round.

Useful hints

— Plant aucubas in spring, preferably, or in early autumn.

— Add some fertilizer in spring.

— Site them in semi-shade or in the sun, because they will be less attractive if positioned in full shade, although they will still grow quite happily.

— To obtain berries, you must mix several shrubs of both sexes, because the aucuba is a dioecious plant.

Recommended

— *Aucuba himalaica* reaches a height of 3 m (10 ft). This shrub grows in the Himalayas at an altitude of 2,500 m (8,000 ft). It has spherical berries that are orange in colour.

— *A. japonica* includes more than a dozen varieties recognizable by the oval and dentate shape of their leaves, which are 8–20 cm (3–8 in) long, and by the bright red colour of their berries. 'Rozannie' is small in size but has large leaves with splashes of cream.

— *A. japonica* 'Crotonifolia' has large, glossy, dark green leaves heavily mottled with yellow. Small purplish flowers in mid-spring are followed by bright red berries.

— *A. japonica* 'Gold Dust' has oval, glossy, gold-speckled leaves. The fruits are egg-shaped and bright red.

— *A. japonica* 'Picturata' has a central golden blotch to each leaf.

— *A. japonica* 'Salicifolia', very elegant, can make an excellent screen for potentillas.

— The best-known cultivar is *A. japonica* 'Variegata', with yellow-speckled leaves. It was introduced from Japan during the nineteenth century.

Height: 1.2–3 m (4–10 ft).
Soil: any, so long as it is well-drained.
Aspect: sun or semi-shade.
Propagation: from cuttings in autumn, or from seed as soon as it is mature.
Flowering season: insignificant in spring.
Type: evergreen shrub.

▽ *Aucuba japonica* 'Crotonifolia'

Azara

GOLDSPIRE

Flacourtiaceae

This small evergreen shrub is a little fragile and dislikes the cold. It should be planted against a sheltered south-facing wall. Its pretty arched branches are covered with vanilla-scented flowers, especially at the beginning of spring. This plant may be placed in a container on a verandah or patio, in a sheltered position.

Useful hints

— Provide azara with good soil, adding leaf-mould and sand.

— Protect it in winter with branches or straw.

Recommended

— *Azara integrifolia* is a shrub that reaches a height of 6 m (20 ft). It has yellowish, highly scented flowers in late winter and early spring.

— *A. microphylla* has attractive, bright deep green leaves. Its clusters of flowers with whitish petals and golden yellow stamens appear in the spring. The variety 'Variegata', with variegated foliage, grows very slowly; it can survive quite low temperatures.

— *A. petiolaris* develops large, slightly thick leaves. Tiny scented flowers appear in spring.

Height: 1–10 m (3¼–33 ft).
Soil: ordinary, enriched with humus.
Aspect: sun, protected from the wind.
Propagation: from cuttings in late summer or autumn.
Flowering season: late winter and spring.
Type: evergreen shrub.

△ *Azara lanceolata*

△ *Ballota pseudodictamnus*

Ballota

BALLOTA

Labiatae

This sub-shrub with beautiful, soft, silvery grey and very dense foliage does well in a sun-drenched rock garden. It is an ideal plant for ground cover and for emphasizing flowers with grassy foliage such as dieramas, crocosmias or even some lovely but fragile-looking plants such as penstemons, scabious and *Gladiolus communis byzantinus*, with its brilliant purplish pink flowers.

Useful hints

— Plant ballota in spring, preferably, giving it what it likes best: a thin, stony soil.

— Water it in early summer, then leave it to grow.

— Every spring, tidy up the plant by pruning it, removing any branches damaged by the cold.

— Protect it by taking cuttings in the greenhouse from the tips of the stalks, and planting out in their final position in autumn.

— In early winter, take young plants into a greenhouse or place in a cold frame for the cold months.

Recommended

— *Ballota pseudodictamnus* has woolly foliage and pale pink flowers that open out timidly in summer.

Height: 60–80 cm (24–32 in).
Soil: very light.
Aspect: full sun.
Propagation: from cuttings, in summer.
Flowering season: insignificant, in summer.
Type: evergreen shrub.

△ *Berberis stenophylla*

△ *Berberis thunbergii* 'Harlequin'

Berberis

BARBERRY

Berberidaceae

Berberis associates well with flowers such as crocosmias or hardy geraniums in the summer, poppies in spring. It requires no attention, can grow very tall and does not need any particular kind of soil. Thalictrums and macleayas are a marvellous complement to the more upright berberis. Some varieties are evergreen, some have fragrant flowers, while others bear decorative fruits and colourful foliage. There are even some that make excellent ground cover. Virtually all of them, however, can be trained to grow as hedges, whether clipped or growing freely.

Useful hints

— If the berberis is underdeveloped, give it a little fertilizer just once a year. Otherwise, just let it grow by itself!

— In order to avoid the task of weeding around the base of the shrub, which is always awkward because of its thorns, mulch with plenty of leaf-mould or half-rotted compost.

Recommended

— *Berberis darwinii*, with its splendid dark green foliage, tough and evergreen, is one of the first berberis to flower. Its bright yellow flowers bloom in spring. It will thrive only in very mild climates.

— *B. darwinii* 'Flame' is recommended for making remarkable evergreen barrier hedges. The orange-red flowers, which grow in bunches, are spectacular.

— *B.* × *frikartii*. This includes several hybrids such as 'Amstelveen', which are well-known for the quality of their foliage and their elegant bearing.

— *B.* × *interposita* 'Wallich's Purple' adds colour to the garden throughout the year: coppery in the spring, green or bronze in summer, purple in autumn.

— *B.* × *media* 'Red Jewel' is a dense, semi-evergreen bush, 1 m (3¼ ft) high, that turns purplish red in autumn.

— *B. thunbergii* 'Aurea'. A superb bush, much admired for its golden foliage, which turns pale green in summer. 'Bagatelle' forms a small globe, 40 cm (16 in) in diameter, which is purple in spring and scarlet in autumn.

— *B. vulgaris* easily attains a height of 3 m (10 ft). It is the least demanding species of all, since it tolerates chalky soil, shade and pruning. It is an upright shrub that can be grown as a hedge. In Scandinavia, its berries are used to make a wine-like drink. In Russia, they are used to make jam. The yellow flowers smell of honey.

The best varieties for a rock garden

— *B. darwinii* 'Prostrata', which does not exceed 40 cm (16 in) in height, is a pretty evergreen plant that spreads laterally.

— *B.* × *stenophylla* 'Prostrata' is a dwarf bush with slightly pendulous branches.

— *B. thunbergii* 'Atropurpurea Nana' is an even smaller plant than the preceding one, globular in shape and growing to a height of only 30 cm (12 in) and a diameter of 1 m (3¼ ft).

— *B. thunbergii* 'Rose Glow' is truly delightful; it grows to a height of 1 m (3¼ ft) and has purple leaves splashed with two shades of pink.

Plant a *Geranium macrorrhizum* alongside some berberis and the result will be unexpected, with the geranium threading its way between the branches.

The best varieties to plant in borders or as specimen plants

— *B. prattii* is a dense shrub 2–3 m (6½–10 ft) in height, rather thorny, with yellow flowers in early summer and an abundance of salmon-pink fruit.

— *B. pruinosa* is an upright shrub 2.5–3 m (8–10 ft) tall, with lemon-yellow flowers that bloom in clusters of eight to twenty-five in spring. Its fruits are black and covered with a whitish bloom (giving them a frosted appearance).

— *B.* × *thunbergii* 'Golden Ring' has purple foliage, edged with yellow.

— *B. vulgaris* 'Atropurpurea' has dark purple leaves.

The best varieties for covering banks

— *B.* × *stenophylla*. The long drooping branches of this bush, with its evergreen foliage, form a sort of screen and in spring are covered from top to bottom with orange-yellow flowers that smell sweetly of honey. More modest in its growth, 'Autumnalis' does not exceed 80 cm (32 in) in height, but has an elegant, lighter appearance and flowers again in autumn.

— *B. umbellata* reaches a height of 2 m (6½ ft). The small flowers, clustered in umbels, bloom in early summer; the bush is very dense.

— *B. wilsoniae* is one of the most decorative varieties, despite its deciduous foliage, since its naked branches bear a multitude of small, salmon-pink fruits; the effect is quite superb.

Height: 30 cm–3 m (1–10 ft).
Soil: any.
Aspect: sun or shade.
Propagation: from cuttings in late summer.
Flowering season: spring to summer.
Type: evergreen or deciduous shrub.

Betula

BIRCH

Betulaceae

Birches bring a special note of gaiety to a garden. Their silvery trunks, delicate foliage and supple, graceful bearing mean they can fit into any setting. They are particularly pleasing among conifers, where they lighten a scene that would otherwise be fairly gloomy. They are truly hardy trees, requiring little attention.

Useful hints

— Birches have shallow roots, so saplings have to be staked.

— A nice way of planting them is to arrange them in clusters of two, or even three trees together.

— They need to be watered in the first year of planting.

Recommended

— *Betula albo-sinensis*. The orangey colour of the bark of this species spectacularly enhances the yellow glow of its foliage.

△ *Betula albo-sinensis*
▽ *Betula pendula*

△ *Betula utilis*

— *B. alleghaniensis*, which is better suited to cool soils, is one of the largest varieties, reaching a height of 25 m (80 ft).

— *B. ermanii*. From spring onwards, this variety stands out by virtue of its glossy, dentate leaves. As they fall in autumn, they reveal the orange-brown to cream hues of the bark.

— *B. humilis* is a pretty shrub whose rounded leaves are a dull blue-green on the underside. It hardly exceeds 2 m (6½ ft) in height. The scaly catkins are very small.

— *B. maximowicziana*. Its name is awkward to pronounce, but the tree is very pretty, with its rounded crown and greyish white or orangey bark. The catkins are 10–15 cm (4–6 in) long.

— *B. nana* (dwarf birch) is a bushy shrub, perfect for rock gardens or for terraces in town gardens. It does not exceed 1 m (3¼ ft) in height.

— *B. pendula* (silver birch) is one of the most delightful varieties because of its weeping shape and its silvery bark, easily recognizable even among other birches, which peels off in long thin strips. The branches of 'Fastigiata' grow upwards along the trunk, making a curious profile. 'Purpurea' gleams with a dark purple hue and 'Trost's Dwarf', which is sometimes considered a hybrid, has distinctive jagged leaves and very delicate, pendulous branches.

— *B. pubescens* (white birch/European white birch) is very useful for stabilizing river banks.

— *B. utilis* has creamy white bark and does not grow taller than 20 m (65 ft).

Height: 1–25 m (3¼–80 ft).
Soil: ordinary.
Aspect: sun or semi-shade.
Propagation: from seed under a frame in spring.
Type: deciduous tree or shrub.

Brugmansia

See *Datura*

Buddleja alternifolia △

Bupleurum fruticosum △

Buddleja

BUDDLEJA, BUTTERFLY BUSH

Loganiaceae

The buddleja is known as the 'butterfly bush', because its scent is very attractive to butterflies. This shrub, which can reach a height of 4 m (13 ft), bears long spikes of highly fragrant small flowers, which may be violet, pink or white, depending on the variety. It is very easy to grow and, from early summer to early autumn, forms a high hedge decked with flowers. A good pruning in early spring will ensure a fine display of flowers. Do not be afraid to cut it back to two-thirds of its height.

Useful hints

— Plant buddlejas in autumn or spring.

— Water regularly during the first summer.

— Mulch the soil in early summer with pine bark or lawn clippings.

— If your buddleja has not been pruned for several years, do not be afraid to cut it back drastically, to within 50 cm (20 in) of the ground, and give it a dose of fertilizer in early spring. Better still, fork in a good handful of bonemeal around the roots at the end of winter.

Recommended

— *Buddleja alternifolia*, with its long, supple branches, is extremely decorative even when it is not in flower. When its arched branches are laden with bunches of mauve flowers, it is a very pretty sight.

— *B. davidii* has given rise to a number of cultivars, such as the deep purple 'Black Knight', 'Harlequin', with variegated leaves and purplish red flowers, 'Nanho Blue', a small shrub with silver foliage and purple-blue flowers, and 'Peace', which has large clusters of white flowers.

— *B. fallowiana* 'Lochinch' flowers in late summer if it is cut hard back. Its long, pendulous branches weep downwards, and its purple-blue flowers, with a soft scent of vanilla, reveal an orange bud.

— *B. globosa* is different in appearance from the other species of buddleja because of its flowers, which resemble golden-orange balls, and its evergreen foliage.

— *B. × weyeriana* 'Sungold'. The yellow flowers of this variety, gathered in spherical clusters at the ends of the branches, stand out against the green or greyish green foliage.

Height: 1–4 m (3¼–13 ft).
Soil: ordinary.
Aspect: sun.
Propagation: from cuttings in summer.
Flowering season: from summer to autumn.
Type: deciduous or evergreen shrub.

Bupleurum

HARE'S-EAR

Umbelliferae

This small evergreen shrub is very suitable for planting in seaside gardens. The small, greenish-yellow flowers, clustered in umbels, bloom in summer. Once withered, they remain on the plant for a long time.

Useful hints

— Most important of all, plant bupleurum in a sunny location.

— Prune severely immediately after the flowering season in order to prevent loss of leaves at the base.

Recommended

— *Bupleurum fruticosum* (fruiting hare's-ear). The tough, evergreen leaves of this species are bright green on top and a dull bluish green on the underside. It reaches a height of approximately 2.5 m (8 ft). Take care: this honey-scented shrub is a favourite with wasps.

— *B. longifolium* reaches a height of 2 m (6½ ft) and in early summer bears small yellow flowers. This variety is hardier than *B. fruticosum*, and is probably best classified as a shrub-like perennial rather than a shrub.

Height: 1–2.5 m (3¼–8 ft).
Soil: any.
Aspect: sun.
Propagation: from cuttings or by layering in autumn.
Flowering season: from summer to autumn.
Type: evergreen shrub.

△ *Buxus sempervirens*

△ *Buxus sempervirens*

Buxus

BOX

Buxaceae

One of the commonest and best-known of shrubs, box is often used in formal gardens because of its robustness, its ability to adapt to all soil types and its modest growth rate, which means it does not have to be trimmed too frequently. It requires virtually no attention. Since its foliage naturally grows bushy and dense, it can be clipped to form a decorative feature on either side of a doorway or flight of steps. It can also, of course, be used in borders and the smaller species are often used to make a formal surround for a vegetable garden or potager.

Useful hints

— Plant box in spring, adding peat to lighten the soil. Adding a few handfuls of hoof and horn each spring will help the plants to thrive.

— If the leaves suddenly turn yellow, this is a sign of an attack by the tiny insects that live among the foliage. Treat with a systemic insecticide in early spring.

— For successful cuttings, take them in autumn and let them take root in a mixture of equal parts of peat and sand.

— Plant out the rooted cuttings in late spring in a slightly shady corner and move to their final position the following spring.

Recommended

— *Buxus balearica* (Balearic box) grows into a small tree 5 m (16 ft) or so in height. This variety is most commonly found in the form of small, clipped edgings. It grows slowly, but in time (fifty years) may reach a height of 8 m (26 ft). It thrives in chalky soil and is marvellously easy to trim into round or cone-shaped bushes, or into even more eccentric shapes. 'Elegans' forms a dome-shaped bush 1.5 m (5 ft) high with narrow leaves, cream in colour around the edges and often twisted into distorted shapes.

— *B. microphylla* (small-leaved box) grows to about 1 m (3¼ ft). 'Green Pillow' is a dwarf variety.

— *B. sempervirens* (common box) makes a dense bushy shrub.

— *B. sempervirens* 'Suffruticosa' is the dwarf form of the above, and makes an ideal edging for paths and lawns. It is propagated by dividing the clumps. 'Handsworthensis' is a very compact, more upright variety, a dull bluish green in colour.

— *B. sempervirens* 'Rotundifolia' has oval leaves, which makes it very useful for forming round or cone-shaped bushes; it is also the variety most frequently used for hedges.

Height: 15 cm–8 m (6 in–26 ft).
Soil: ordinary.
Aspect: sun or shade.
Propagation: from cuttings in autumn.
Flowering season: early summer to early autumn, imperceptible.
Type: evergreen shrub.

△ *Caesalpinia gilliesii*

Caesalpinia

CAESALPINIA

Leguminosae

Caesalpinia is a native of the tropics and subtropics. The most important thing for this large shrub or small tree is a well-situated wall to protect it. It is a marvellous plant, with its delicate foliage and spectacular flowers with their scarlet stamens, which look like beautiful dainty butterflies.

Useful hints

— Plant against a warm, sunny wall.

Recommended

— *C. decapetala* var. *japonica*. This is a small, thorny tree that spreads laterally and has large divided leaves that curiously resemble those of the acacia. The canary-yellow flowers, with red stamens, bloom profusely in summer.

— *Caesalpinia gilliesii* is known as the 'Bird of Paradise' and flowers in midsummer. It bears superb sulphur-yellow flowers, with numerous, very long stamens which form purple tufts against a cloud of brilliant green leaves. This delightful tree deserves a place of honour in any garden.

Height: 3–4 m (10–13 feet).
Soil: rich, with plenty of humus.
Aspect: sun and warmth (against a south-facing wall).
Propagation: from seed under glass after the seeds have been soaked in lukewarm water.
Flowering season: summer.
Type: deciduous tree or shrub.

Callicarpa

BEAUTYBERRY

Verbenaceae

One of the most spectacular colours to be seen in a garden is probably that of the fruits of the callicarpa, a delicate violet tinged with lilac, glowing softly in autumn. The chance to admire those fruits in a slightly gloomy season is reason enough to choose this shrub, particularly since it requires no particular care. It can grow to a height of 2.5 m (8 ft), and looks good grown with a carpet of *Stachys byzantina*, which will create a pretty backdrop for the violet berries. You can also plant callicarpas among clumps of *Lysimachia clethroïdes* or hostas, which turn golden in autumn.

Useful hints

— Plant in autumn or spring. If you want to obtain a lot of fruit, plant a number side by side to increase fertilization.

Recommended

— *Callicarpa bodinieri* var. *giraldii*, with its pink flowers, is the one most frequently seen in catalogues. Its leaves are pale green, often tinged with bronze when young. The variety 'Profusion' bears slightly more fruit.

— *C. japonica* 'Leucocarpa' is more compact and has white berries.

Height: 2.5 m (8 ft).
Soil: any.
Aspect: sun.
Propagation: from cuttings in summer.
Flowering season: flowers in summer, berries in autumn.
Type: deciduous shrub.

△ *Callicarpa bodinieri* 'Giraldii'

▽ *Callistemon citrinus*

Callistemon
BOTTLE-BRUSH
Myrtaceae

This ornamental shrub is a native of Australia, with delicately attractive evergreen leaves. Its scarlet flowers, which appear between early spring and midsummer, are superb, but remarkably rare. The callistemon does not tolerate the cold, and only in very mild climates will the dense spikes of large red or yellow flowers, with their protruding brush-like stamens, have a chance to brighten up your garden without you having to give the shrub special attention. One possibility is to pot the plant during the winter and then place it on a verandah or patio as soon as spring arrives.

Useful hints
— Callistemons require light, well-drained soil.

— Do not plant them in a spot where dampness might rot the roots.

— Pruning in early autumn will make the shrub more compact.

Recommended
— *Callistemon citrinus* is a fast-growing shrub that spreads profusely, giving off a delicious lemony scent when crushed between the hands. It bears large spikes of scarlet flowers in summer, and can reach a height of 2.5 m (8 ft).

— *C. rigidus*, with its soft green leaves, flowers very profusely, its deep red bottle-brushes appearing in the spring and early summer.

— *C. salignus* has narrow leaves like those of the willow, and pale yellow flowers. This is the variety most resistant to cold.

— *C. sieberi* has mid-green leaves and small clusters of pale yellow flowers in mid-summer.

— *C. speciosus* (Albany bottle-brush). This callistemon bears spikes of large scarlet flowers in summer.

— The flowers of *C. subulatus* are deep crimson.

Height: up to 2.5 m (8 ft).
Soil: light and well-drained.
Aspect: sun.
Propagation: from seed or from cuttings in spring.
Flowering season: early spring to mid-summer.
Type: evergreen shrub.

△ *Calocedrus decurrens*

Calocedrus

CALOCEDRUS, LIBOCEDRUS

Cupressaceae

Previously known as *Libocedrus*, this conifer has, for reasons of botanical classification, become *Calocedrus*. A native of North America, it is an unusual tree which, while reminiscent of a thuja in its early years, becomes in its maturity a majestic green obelisk with dense foliage. It reaches a maximum height of 40 m (130 ft).

Useful hints

— The calocedrus needs nothing more than deep soil and a certain degree of moisture; it is not harmed by the cold.

— Because of its height and its very upright shape, this is a tree that should be planted in a very large open space, such as a park or a large meadow.

Recommended

— *Calocedrus decurrens*, with its very dark foliage, forms a splendid column of greenery that may reach a height of 40 m (130 ft) and a girth of some 3–6 m (10–20 ft). 'Aureovariegata', with its gold-flecked leaves, stands out among otherwise dark conifers.

Height: 30–40 m (95–130 ft).
Soil: deep and cool.
Aspect: good light.
Propagation: from seed, or from cuttings with hormone powder in mid- to late summer.
Type: evergreen tree.

Calycanthus

SWEET SHRUB

Calycanthaceae

This small shrub is very fragrant. Its flowers may be delicate and unspectacular, but they last virtually all summer. They are brownish red and pleasantly scented. The wood of this shrub is also fragrant, smelling of camphor.

Useful hints

— It is easy to grow, provided you do not plant it in a damp or dark location, since it likes the sun.

— There is no point in cutting it back, but do remove any sickly branches in winter.

Recommended

— *Calycanthus fertilis* 'Purpureus'. The underside of the leaves of this variety are tinged with purple. It flowers throughout the summer.

— *C. floridus* (anemone tree). The whole shrub is fragrant. The large flowers, which never open fully, have a very fruity scent, redolent of strawberries. The leaves, very velvety on the underside, the bark and even the roots smell of camphor.

— *C. occidentalis* (California allspice) has purplish red flowers.

Height: 1.5–4 m (5–13 ft).
Soil: cool and light.
Aspect: sun.
Propagation: by layering.
Flowering season: throughout the summer.
Type: deciduous shrub.

△ *Calycanthus floridus*

Camellia

CAMELLIA

Theaceae

Although camellias are often grown on their own or in pots on terraces for the beauty of their glossy evergreen leaves and their flowers, it is frequently forgotten that in suitable climates (by the sea) they can also be used to form hedges, thus creating a setting for other flowers. This is particularly true of the *Camellia × williamsii* varieties.

Useful hints

— Buy camellias when in flower, and try to select short, dense plants. Shelter them indoors until spring, and plant out once any risk of frost is past. They need an acid, humus-rich soil and a sheltered position. Do not plant them too close to a wall, where the soil is likely to be very dry.

— Each autumn, lay a 20 cm (8 in) thick mulch of leaf-mould that will decompose on the spot and nourish them. Each spring, a little bonemeal or hoof and horn will complete their diet.

— In winter, protect them from snow, which can break their branches.

— Any camellia that has lost leaves at the bottom can be cut right back. The plant will regain its shape in a few years.

Recommended

— The camellias that fit best into a garden are undoubtedly the *C. × williamsii* varieties, which have beautiful dark

△ *Camellia japonica* hybrid

△ *Camellia japonica*

foliage and a slender silhouette. They flower continuously for a good part of the winter and spring. The most beautiful cultivars include 'Anticipation', deep pink and shaped like a peony; the orchid-pink 'Donation'; 'J.C. Williams', which has beautiful single flowers 10 cm (4 in) in diameter, pale pink in colour with crimson highlights; 'November Pink' and 'Saint Ewe', fresh pink in colour and with shiny leaves.

— *C. japonica* was the favourite camellia of Marguerite Gauthier (the Lady of the Camellias) because it has no scent (sweet-smelling flowers made her cough). This species is the most frequently cultivated,

and is said to have given rise to 1,500 cultivars. Among the most interesting are 'Adolphe Audusson', a fast-growing, dense shrub and a prolific flowerer, with bright red, semi-double flowers; 'Alba Plena', with large white double flowers; 'Apple Blossom', pale pink flowers, darker at the edges; and 'Elegans', which spreads more widely and has large, peach-coloured, anemone-shaped flowers. The hybrid 'Leonard Messel' has beautiful pure pink, semi-double flowers.

— *C. sasanqua*, though less majestic than those described above, has other advantages, which is why it is popular. It is hardier and more resistant to cold than

other varieties. It is an early flowerer in mild climates, and its large white flowers are delicately perfumed. Its better cultivars include 'Crimson King', with smaller red flowers, and 'Narumigata', whose large, white, scented flowers have pink-tinged edges.

Height: 1–3 m (3¼–10 feet).
Soil: acid and humus-rich, oak or chestnut leaf-mould and peat.
Aspect: semi-shade.
Propagation: difficult, by grafting or from cuttings under glass with a 'mist system' and hormones.
Flowering season: autumn to spring.
Type: evergreen shrub.

△ *Caragana arborescens*

Caragana

CARAGAN, PEA TREE

Leguminosae

This charming little tree is very hardy, despite its fragile appearance. It is a native of Siberia, which explains its in-difference to cold and dry soil. It grows in semi-shade or in sunny locations, and its delicate flowers look very pleasing against the slender leaves.

Useful hints

— Remove any small dead or dam-aged branches in the spring.

Recommended

— *Caragana arborescens* (Siberian pea tree) will grow on exposed sites. It has clusters of pea-like yellow flowers in late spring. It is used to make thick, sturdy hedges. The variety 'Pendula' has elegant, pendulous branches.

— *C. arborescens* 'Nana', the dwarf form, with twisted branches, is an inter-esting specimen for rock gardens. 'Walker' is a prostrate variety.

— *C. decorticans* is a very thorny shrub whose large yellow flowers also bloom in late spring.

Height: 50 cm–2 m (20 in–6½ ft).
Soil: any, even poor.
Aspect: semi-shade to sun.
Propagation: from seed, sown in spring.
Flowering season: late spring.
Type: deciduous shrub.

Carpenteria

CARPENTERIA

Hydrangaceae

This very beautiful evergreen shrub should be grown in a sunny position against a well-protected wall. The lovely white flowers, with their numerous golden anthers, are 6–8 cm (2½–3 in) in diameter. The bark peels off in strips.

Useful hints

— Carpenteria needs a light soil with some humus.

— Since it is not resistant to wind, frost and damp, plant it in a well-protected place.

— Can be trained.

Recommended

— *Carpenteria californica* reaches a height of 2.5 m (8 ft). The magnificent white flowers, which open out in summer, are scented.

Height: 1.5–2.5 m (5–8 ft).
Soil: light, rich in humus, well-drained.
Aspect: sheltered from winds.
Propagation: by layering or from cuttings in autumn, under plastic sheeting.
Flowering season: mid-summer.
Type: evergreen shrub.

Carpinus

HORNBEAM

Betulaceae

Hornbeams are easily recognized by their ash-grey, fluted trunks, whose bark is similar to that of the beech, and par-ticularly by their pretty, crinkly, oval leaves, which are delicately serrated and ribbed. The hornbeam is monoecious, meaning that the same tree bears both male and female catkins.

Useful hints

— Hornbeams are very easy to grow. In flat, open country they adapt even to the most chalky soils. They live for about 150 years. Although they are deciduous trees, hornbeams retain their leaves for a long time in winter, which means they can be used to make hedges that serve as windbreaks. Hornbeams will not thrive in soil that is either too wet or too dry.

△ *Carpenteria californica*

Recommended

— *Carpinus betulus* (common or Euro-pean hornbeam) reaches a height of 25 m (80 ft); its leaves turn yellow in winter.

— *C. betulus* 'Fastigiata' has a very distinctive flame-like silhouette.

— *C. betulus* 'Pyramidalis' is an orna-mental tree. It can be planted by itself on a lawn or used as a marker when planting a line of trees.

— *C. caroliniana* (American hornbeam) would enhance any garden with its elegant bearing. This small tree, 6–8 m (20–26 ft) in height, turns a magnificent orange-red in autumn.

— *C. cordata*, a native of Asia, has large, heart-shaped leaves. Its maximum height is just 15 m (50 ft).

— *C. orientalis*, which hails from Anato-lia, is the best variety for making hedges that can be clipped. It ranges in height from 5–8 m (16–26 ft).

Height: rarely more than 20 m (65 ft) under cultivation.
Soil: any, even chalky.
Aspect: any.
Propagation: from seed or by grafting.
Type: deciduous tree.

▽△ *Carpinus betulus* 'Pendula'

▽ *Carpinus laxiflora*

285

△ *Caryopteris × clandonensis*

△ *Cassiope lycopodioïdes*

Carya

HICKORY

Juglandaceae

This is a beautiful, fast-growing tree, quite closely related to the walnut. Like the walnut, its fruits are edible nuts. Its trunk, the same grey as elephant hide, is attractive in winter. In autumn it takes on a pretty golden colour. It is a pity that it is so rarely seen in gardens.

Useful hints

— Plant the carya out when very small or, even better, plant a nut. The roots do not like to be disturbed.

— It needs good rich soil in which to develop. It is very tolerant of wet soils.

Recommended

— *Carya aquatica*. As its name suggests, this tree prefers very wet soils. It produces fairly bitter nuts and can reach a height of 10 m (33 ft).

— *C. cordiformis* (bitternut, pignut, swamp hickory). A beautiful tree that reaches a height of over 25 m (80 ft) in its natural habitat, North America. It is easily recognized by its golden yellow buds, clearly visible on the tree in winter. It grows strongly and rapidly.

— *C. glabra* is a spreading tree which grows to a height of 25 m (80 ft). Its dark green leaves turn bright yellow and orange in autumn.

— *C. ovalis* produces astringent nuts. It reaches a height of 25–30 m (80–95 ft).

— *C. ovata* (shagbark hickory, shellbark hickory) is very pretty in autumn. Its nuts are white and sweet, its catkins 15 cm (6 in) long. The tree reaches a height of 30 m (95 ft) or more.

— *C. tomentosa* is a magnificent tree of upright habit, with aromatic leaves that are bright green on top and downy yellow on the underside. The light brown nuts are sweet.

Height: 10–30 m (30–95 ft).
Soil: rich; certain species require moist soil.
Aspect: sun.
Propagation: by planting nuts, in spring.
Flowering season: catkins in spring.
Type: deciduous tree.

Caryopteris

BLUEBEARD

Verbenaceae

Caryopteris blooms in an unusual way, bearing delicate violet flowers the whole length of its dense stalks. Just three shrubs planted together will fill a whole corner of your flower bed. What is more, the great attraction of this shrub is that it flowers in late summer and can therefore take over from plants that have already finished flowering. Positioned in front of a sweet rocket, for example, it will come into bloom when the sweet rocket has stopped flowering. Caryopteris also makes an ideal companion for roses, for when remontant roses flower for the second time in early autumn, the combination of colours is absolutely charming.

Useful hints

— Plant caryopteris in spring, in well-drained soil.

— Even in the first year, a tiny plant will produce a 60 cm (2 ft) clump. Bear this in mind when planting.

— Cutting back to ground level each spring will give you dense, circular clumps each year.

Recommended

— *Caryopteris × clandonensis* 'Heavenly Blue' has slightly silvery foliage and dark blue flowers; however, the fashion will undoubtedly swing towards the new hybrids of *C. incana*, which creep more and are brighter blue in colour, even though they lack the silvery leaves to which the true species owe their charms.

— The bright yellow leaves of the variety *C. × clandonensis* 'Worcester Gold' set off the brilliant blue of its flowers to good effect.

Height: 60 cm–1.2 m (2–4 ft).
Soil: ordinary, not too wet, on the stony side.
Aspect: sun.
Propagation: from cuttings in spring or summer.
Flowering season: late summer to autumn.
Type: deciduous shrub.

Cassia

SENNA

Leguminosae

The cassias originate in the tropics or sub-tropics, so they cannot tolerate severe cold. For this reason, most of the 500 species are still relatively unknown. They flourish in a very mild climate, and are not harmed by drought.

Useful hints

— Give cassias a warm, sunny position, sheltered from cold winter winds.

— Plant them in average, healthy, deep soil. In case of doubt, protect them, at least at the base. If the weather becomes too cold, fold in the stems of bushy kinds in order to make it easier to protect the root-stock.

Recommended

— *Cassia corymbosa* (syn. *Senna corymbosa*), with its evergreen foliage divided into lance-shaped leaflets, grows to a height of up to 3 m (10 ft). Its golden yellow flowers, gathered in clusters at the top of the branches, bloom in late summer.

— *C. fistula*, the false senna, grows sufficiently to become a small tree. Its pinnate leaves reach a length of 50 cm (20 in). It is also grown as a decoration for apartments and verandahs.

— *C. hebecarpa* (syn. *Senna hebecarpa*) should be treated as a perennial even though it is actually a subshrub. Its foliage is reminiscent of the robinia (false acacia).

Height: 2–4 m (6–13 ft).
Soil: ordinary, even dry, and well-drained.
Aspect: sun.
Propagation: from seed and cuttings.
Flowering season: summer.
Type: semi-evergreen and evergreen trees, shrubs or subshrubs.

Cassiope

CASSIOPE

Ericaceae

This is a very curious type of mini-shrub of mountain origin. Cassiopes closely resemble heathers. The small, dense leaves clustered like scales along the branches and the white or pink bell-flowers are so curious and so pretty they are unforgettable. They are carpeting plants, or small shrubs, no more than 30 cm (12 in) in height, well suited to rock gardens or low walls. Ideally, they should be planted where it is possible to see them close to.

Useful hints

— Cassiopes are plants that, because of their mountain origin, tolerate cold very well. What they require above all is good light, so they can be planted in a north-facing position, but never under a tree.

— Their refinement and delicacy place them among the best plants for a rock garden or a well-situated spot, with peat in acidic soil. They can also be used as ground cover in acid soil.

— There is no point in pruning them.

Recommended

It has to be said that there is not a wide choice of cassiopes to be had in garden centres. The selection is usually restricted to the following:

— *Cassiope fastigiata*, which has white-edged leaves and white bell-flowers, grows about 20 cm (8 in) high and is a native of the Himalayas.

— *C. mertensiana* comes from North America and is easier to find. About 25 cm (10 in) in height, its flowers are white and bloom in spring.

— *C. selaginoïdes* grows to 25 cm (10 in) with dark green leaves and white flowers.

— *C. tetragona* has dark green foliage and white flowers that appear in spring.

— *C. wardii* grows to 15 cm (6 in) high and has bell-shaped white flowers. Its dark green leaves cluster thickly along the semi-upright stems.

Height: 10–25 cm (4–10 in).
Soil: acid and wet, heathland or peat.
Aspect: north-facing for preference, but not under trees.
Propagation: by layering or from cuttings in late summer or early autumn.
Flowering season: spring.
Type: evergreen shrub.

Castanea

CHESTNUT

Fagaceae

This deciduous tree can reach a fine height, but may equally possibly not get beyond the bush stage. Everything depends on the soil, the location – and perhaps its goodwill. It develops slowly, but in maturity its magnificent bearing and dense foliage make it a superb tree.

Useful hints

— A moist atmosphere is necessary if the chestnut is to grow properly. If grown in dry soil, it cannot develop and remains a shrub, though one that can be used for ornamental purposes, thanks to its highly decorative flowers.

— The nut can be sown in sandy soil in autumn. The following autumn, transplant the small plant, then wait four or five years before selecting a final location for it. Take care: chestnuts do not prosper in chalky soil. In a suitable

△ *Castanea sativa*

location, the castanea can live for hundreds of years. It will not bear fruit until it is twenty-five years old.

Recommended

— *Castanea sativa* (sweet chestnut) is a fast-growing tree. It can be recognized by its long, narrow, glossy leaves. It has spikes of creamy yellow flowers in summer that are followed by edible fruits in spiky husks.

— *C. sativa* 'Albomarginata' is a variety with glossy, white-edged dark green leaves that turn yellow in autumn. The spikes of creamy yellow flowers appear in summer.

Height: up to 30 m (95 ft).
Soil: fertile and deep, well-drained, no lime.
Aspect: sun or semi-shade.
Propagation: gather chestnuts and sow them in autumn.
Flowering season: catkins in summer.
Type: deciduous tree.

△ *Catalpa bignonioïdes*

Catalpa

CATALPA, BEAN TREE

Bignoniaceae

The catalpa is familiar to all tree-lovers, since its many good qualities – it is decorative, grows rapidly and is not damaged by pollution – have made it a common sight in public gardens and city parks. Its enormous single leaves, light green in colour, would be enough by themselves to attract attention, but it also has a superb appearance, with its extensive crown which spreads out horizontally.

Useful hints

— The catalpas must be planted in soil that is well-drained and not too heavy, and in a spot that is sheltered from winds.

Recommended

— *Catalpa bignonioïdes* (Indian bean tree, southern catalpa). This is the tree found in parks. Not only the leaves but also the clusters of large foxglove-like flowers are highly decorative. They appear in mid- to late summer. The most noteworthy cultivars include 'Aurea', with large, velvety, yellowish leaves. *C.* × *erubescens* 'Purpurea' has purplish black young leaves and shoots that turn dark green with age. The fruits are pods.

— *C. fargesii* has lilac flowers, flecked with rust.

— *C. speciosa* is famous for its large white flowers, flecked with purple.

Height: 30 m (95 ft), *C. bignonioïdes* 'Nana' 4 m (13 ft).

Soil: ordinary, well-drained.

Aspect: sun or semi-shade.

Propagation: from seed, under glass, in spring.

Flowering season: summer.

Type: deciduous tree.

288

Ceanothus

CEANOTHUS, NEW JERSEY TEA, SISOYOU-MAT

Rhamnaceae

Plants of the genus *Ceanothus* provide the most delightful shades of real blue in the garden. When trained to climb, they can reach an impressive height and cover a wall with their flowers, deep blue or sky-blue in colour, depending on the varieties chosen. As a shrub, they form a very dense cover that can completely camouflage a wall. When they come into flower, their leaves disappear under clouds of blue flowers that cluster together in dense bunches.

Useful hints

— Plant in the spring, in soil lightened with a mixture of sand and peat. In the first few years, cut back short each spring in order to obtain compact, well-branched plants. Add a handful of bonemeal when planting.

— Ceanothus thrive wonderfully by the sea. They are set off beautifully by roses and campanulas, with *Veronica incana* planted in the foreground. A bed of lilies makes an elegant combination.

Recommended

— *Ceanothus arboreus* 'Trewithen Blue' grows into a large, irregular, evergreen bush, 2 m (6½ ft) in height and adorned with clusters of lightly scented blue flowers. *C.* 'Burkwoodii' is an even faster-growing hybrid that remains in flower until autumn.

— Of the deciduous ceanothus that flower in mid-summer, *C.* × *delileanus* 'Gloire de Versailles', with its sky-blue flowers, is still one of the most popular.

— *C. impressus.* This evergreen variety, said to be one of the hardiest, thrives by the sea and lends itself marvellously to training.

— *C.* × *pallidus* 'Marie Simon', has palish pink flowers, and *C.* × *delileanus* 'Henri Desfossé' has blue-violet flowers. 'Henri Desfossé' surpasses all others in the intensity of its colour.

— *C. thyrsiflorus* var. *repens* is a creeping variety. In late spring, it is literally covered in mid-blue flowers, forming a mat. Evergreen and fast-growing, it does not require pruning.

△ *Ceanothus delileanus*

△ *Ceanothus delileanus* 'Marie Simon'
Ceanothus thyrsiflorus var. *repens* ▷

— *C.* × *veitchianus* is a vigorous hybrid with deep blue flowers.

— *C.* × *delileanus* 'Topaz', blue-purple in colour, is more compact than those above and flowers in spring. The hybrid 'Cascade' grows to a height of 3 m (10 ft) and has large, dark green, glossy leaves.

Height: 1–3 m (3¼–10 ft).
Soil: rich and light.
Aspect: sun, protected from frost.
Propagation: from cuttings in summer.
Flowering season: from summer to autumn for deciduous varieties; late spring to summer for evergreen varieties.
Type: deciduous or evergreen shrub.

Cedrus

CEDAR

Pinaceae

A majestic native of mountains and forests, the cedar is famous for its size and longevity. It is not suited to small gardens, particularly if they are enclosed. It is a tree that requires open spaces.

Useful hints

— Buy cedars in containers, never with bare roots.

— Plant them in good soil, making sure they have plenty of space to grow in.

— For the first few months after planting, they need to be sprayed during hot weather.

— Take care to inspect them closely, for they are susceptible to fungal diseases.

Recommended

— *C. deodara* (Himalayan cedar) is a graceful tree. Its needles are very delicate and its branches, slightly pendulous at the ends, have a bright green tinge. Its height varies from 30–50 m (95–160 ft), and can be much higher in its native country.

— The variety 'Aurea' (golden Himalayan cedar) has distinctive, very bright, gold-tinged foliage during the summer. Its height at maturity ranges from 3–10 m (10–33 ft). *C. deodara* 'Pendula' is a weeping variety. It grows no higher than 3 m (10 ft), and is 2–4 m (6½–13 ft) in circumference.

— *Cedrus libani* ssp. *atlantica* (Atlas or Atlantic cedar) is a native of the Atlas Mountains of North Africa. Its needles are clustered in greyish green rosettes on the branches. It is pyramidal and even in shape, with large, low branches at the base.

— The cultivar 'Glauca Pendula' (blue weeping cedar) can be recognized by the fullness of its crown, which lies at right angles to the trunk and stretches out to form an immense parasol. It can reach a height of 40 m (130 ft).

— *C. libani* ssp. *libani* (cedar of Lebanon) is difficult to tell apart, when young, from the Himalayan cedar. It is not until it reaches maturity that its crown spreads horizontally in the shape of a table to give the tree its distinctive, elegant silhouette. Its height at maturity is 25 m (80 ft).

△ *Cephalotaxus sinensis*
◁ *Cedrus libani* ssp. *atlantica* 'Glauca Pendula'

◁ *Cedrus libani* ssp. *libani*
▽ *Cedrus libani* ssp. *atlantica* 'Glauca'

▽ *Cedrus libani* ssp. *atlantica* 'Glauca'

The following cultivars are dwarf varieties:

— *C. libani* ssp. *libani* Nana Group, pyramidal in shape, scarcely reaches 2 m (6½ ft) in height.

— *C. libani* ssp. *libani* 'Sargentii' is even smaller and forms a pretty little weeping tree. Its maximum height is 2 m (6½ ft).

Height: varies according to species and variety.
Soil: deep, even dry.
Aspect: any.
Propagation: from seed or cuttings, with hormone powder.
Type: evergreen tree.

Cephalotaxus

COW'S TAIL PINE

Cephalotaxaceae

Closely related to the yews, the genus *Cephalotaxus* is slow-growing, reaching less than 1 m (3¼ ft) in the first ten years. Since the trees are dioecious, the fruits appear only on female plants.

Useful hints

— These are attractive conifers that grow in forest interiors, so plant them in semi-shaded locations and in moist soil alongside rhododendrons and pieris, or even under other conifers.

Recommended

— *Cephalotaxus fortunei* (Chinese plum yew) is a spherical bush that reaches barely 6 m (20 ft) in height under cultivation and has pendulous branches that extend laterally. Its long, scythe-shaped needles are a lustrous deep green in colour.

— *C. harringtonia* 'Fastigiata' is interesting because of its upright silhouette, with its dense branches gathered vertically into the bundles that give it its name (from the Latin *fascis*). It reaches a height of 20 m (65 ft) in maturity.

Height: 3–20 m (10–65 ft), depending on species and variety.
Soil: good garden soil.
Aspect: sun or semi-shade.
Propagation: leave the seed outside through the cold weather.
Type: evergreen tree.

291

△ *Ceratostigma willmottianum*

△ *Cercidiphyllum japonicum*

△ *Cercis siliquastrum*

Ceratostigma

CREEPING PLUMBAGO, CREEPING LEADWORT

Plumbaginaceae

Normally hardy, despite a rumour to the contrary, this magnificent carpeting shrub, with its blue-violet flowers, flowers in early autumn in more northerly latitudes and in summer in warmer climates. Its curious scientific name actually comes from Greek and means 'cone-shaped', perhaps because of the shape of its buds. The bright red autumn foliage is very pretty, particularly in front of shrubs such as *Cornus alba* 'Sibirica' or hamamelis. The plant will happily cover corners of steps, a rock garden or a border. Placed in the foreground, it will blend perfectly with asters that come into flower at the same time and will even take over from *Phlox paniculata* after it has stopped flowering.

Useful hints

— Plant ceratostigma in spring, having first improved the soil with a little peat and leaf-mould.

— Mulch the soil from early summer onwards.

— Water regularly during the first summer.

— In spring, add a little peat to encourage rooting.

— Each clump can remain in place for ten years without being moved, but you can also divide them and replant the separated parts elsewhere.

Recommended

— *Ceratostigma griffithii* has dark blue flowers.

— *C. minus* opens out into slate-blue flowers.

— *C. willmottianum* can reach a height of 60 cm (24 in) if planted in a spot sheltered from the wind.

Height: 15–60 cm (6–24 in).
Soil: ordinary, preferably well-drained.
Aspect: sun.
Propagation: by natural layering or by division in spring.
Flowering season: autumn.
Type: deciduous shrub.

Cercidiphyllum

KATSURA TREE

Cercidiphyllaceae

Cercidiphyllum is a small, elegant tree which requires space if its graceful silhouette and delectably coloured autumn foliage are to be properly admired. Fairly hardy and resistant to disease, it is really harmed only by drought, which causes it to lose its leaves.

Useful hints

— Plant in soil that does not dry out but where the roots are not in danger of becoming water-logged either.

— Since this tree can be damaged by frost, place it in the shelter of trees with light deciduous foliage, in a clearing, for example.

Recommended

— *Cercidiphyllum japonicum* (katsura). The trunk of this little Japanese tree is often divided, from the base upwards, into branches that start off horizontal and then droop slightly. Its bright green leaves turn yellow with splashes of orange-pink in autumn. They give off a scent of burnt sugar.

— *C. japonicum* var. *magnificum* is a rare tree that has golden leaves in autumn.

Height: 15 m (50 ft) in its native Asia, 2 m (6½ ft) in Europe.
Soil: moist, fertile.
Aspect: sun or semi-shade.
Propagation: from seed or cuttings.
Type: deciduous tree.

Cercis

JUDAS TREE, REDBUD

Leguminosae

This is a delightful tree. When it flowers in spring, its height – it doesn't grow above 10 m (30 ft) – and branching habit make it look like a large, compact bouquet of bright mauve-pink flowers. In fact, the tightly packed flowers grow directly on the branches (a phenomenon known as 'cauliflory') and their soft colours provide a striking contrast to the very pronounced dark brown of the bark. Another striking feature is that the flowers appear before the leaves, in the early spring, a characteristic of tropical trees. The Judas tree is a native of the Middle East and is a very old species. It made its appearance in Europe about the time of the Crusades, brought back by pilgrims in the form of seeds and young plants along with its delightful legend. The long flower pods are supposed to represent Christ's tears and their colour the shame of Judas who, after his betrayal, hanged himself from this very tree.

The Judas tree is attractive even in winter, with its beautiful shape, its twisted branches, the irregularities of its trunk and its velvety bark. It can be grown as a tree or a shrub, or even twist and twine against a wall. In autumn, it is ablaze with gold and orange. It is mature after ten years but can live to a hundred.

Useful hints

— Avoid planting the Judas tree in a cold position.

— Allow it to grow naturally. Try pruning when it is about five or ten years old, but this should be the exception rather than the rule. It can also be trained against a wall, but this should be done from a very early age.

Recommended

The many species are distinguished by the colour of their flowers:

— *Cercis canadensis* (Eastern redbud) is crimson or pale pink.

— *C. chinensis* (deep mauve-pink flowers) and *C. occidentalis* (bright pink flowers) do not tolerate temperatures below –5°C.

— *C. racemosa* has pinkish red flowers.

— *C. siliquastrum*, the most common variety in Europe, has dazzling pink flowers. Its white form, 'Alba', is, as yet, not widely found.

Height: 3–10 m (10–33 ft).
Soil: well-drained.
Aspect: sun, protected.
Propagation: from cuttings or seed, sown under glass, in spring.
Flowering season: spring.
Type: deciduous tree.

Chaenomeles

JAPANESE QUINCE, FLOWERING QUINCE

Rosaceae

From early spring, the Japanese quince produces charmingly simple flowers in every shade of red and pink. Its fragrant fruits are used to make preserves. This very spiny shrub prefers to grow against a wall, where it reaches heights of up to 3 m (10 ft) and can be used to support a small-headed clematis such as *C. montana*, as its branches are relatively open. Japanese quinces also make excellent – defensive – hardy hedges. But they do have one major drawback: they are extremely invasive. So keep an eye out for new shoots.

Useful hints

— Plant at any time of the year in carefully turned, humus-rich soil. Weed and water well during their first summer. Encourage flowering, which occurs on the previous year's growth, by pruning the long, straight, new growth after flowering.

— Chaenomeles are very easy to propagate by layering in the spring or summer.

Recommended

— *Chaenomeles cathayensis* has small pink-flushed white flowers which appear from early to mid-spring, and large yellowish green fruit.

— *C. japonica*, the true Japanese quince, is relatively small and produces a profusion of brick-red flowers in spring which turn into tiny yellowish green fruit in autumn.

— *C. speciosa* (syn. *C. lagenaria*) has been used to produce a number of fairly tall varieties which are ideal for background planting. The golden yellow fruit is delicious stewed.

— *C. speciosa* has produced a number of hybrids: the very floriferous 'Moerloosei'; the pure white 'Nivalis' and the smaller, crimson 'Simonii' are among the most beautiful.

— The *C. × superba* varieties are smaller and more compact, forming small, round bushes which are easily incorporated into large beds. 'Crimson and Gold' (crimson with gold stamens), 'Fire Dance' (bright red with a more spreading habit), 'Knap Hill Scarlet' (brilliant red) and 'Rowallane' with its large, deep red flowers are really magnificent. 'Etna' and 'Nicoline' have large scarlet flowers.

Height: 1–3 m (3¼–10 ft).
Soil: ordinary, humus-rich.
Aspect: semi-shade or sun.
Propagation: by layering in spring or summer.
Flowering season: spring.
Type: deciduous shrub.

▽ *Chaenomeles × superba* 'Crimson and Gold'

Chamaecyparis

FALSE CYPRESS

Cupressaceae

Most gardens have a chamaecyparis, simply because there are so many different varieties, ranging from small, rounded shrubs to tall, elegant conifers, and such a wide range of colours – grey, yellow or green foliage. There really is something to suit every taste and every type of garden. They have the added advantage of being extremely tolerant of different soil types and positions, and they are, of course, evergreen.

Useful hints

— These trees are often attacked by rabbits, field mice, insects and a disease which can prove fatal. Keep an eye on young trees.

Recommended

Some varieties are ideal for planting as a specimen in a lawn or at the bottom of the garden as a backdrop for flowering shrubs. Others are suitable for rock gardens or patio containers.

Smaller, more decorative varieties

— *Chamaecyparis lawsoniana* 'Minima Aurea'. This golden yellow, cone-shaped shrub is one of the most attractive varieties. It reaches a height of about 1.5 m (5 ft) after ten years.

— *C. lawsoniana* 'Minima Glauca' is the same as 'Minima Aurea' but has blue foliage. It does not grow above 1 m (3¼ ft).

— *C. lawsoniana* 'Pygmaea Argentea' is very slow-growing. It has an irregular dome-shaped form and cream variegations.

— *C. lawsoniana* 'Wisselii' is an extremely elegant variety with its tall, slender habit and irregular outline (especially when young).

— *C. nootkatensis* 'Aurea' has golden yellow variegations which are more or less pronounced depending on the season.

— *C. obtusa* 'Nana'. This small, flat-topped bush with dark green, shell-like foliage is very decorative on a patio or in a rock garden.

— *C. obtusa* 'Nana Gracilis' has flattened branches arranged in glossy green, shell-like sprays. It is very popular but is often sold as a dwarf conifer, which is

△ *Chamaecyparis obtusa* 'Nana'

wrong, as it grows above 2 m (6½ ft).

— *C. obtusa* 'Pygmaea' is an attractive, low, spreading bush with copper-coloured foliage.

— *C. pisifera* 'Boulevard' has soft, dense, silver-blue foliage. It is often sold as a dwarf variety, wrongly, since it grows to a height of 80 cm (32 in).

— *C. pisifera* 'Filifera Aurea', with its long, shaggy branches, forms a large, attractively coloured, golden cone. Height: 60 cm (24 in).

— *C. pisifera* 'Squarrosa Sulphurea'. Although slow-growing, this can reach a height of 5 m (16 ft). Its sulphur-yellow foliage is more intensely coloured in spring.

— *C. thyoides* 'Red Star' (syn. *C.t.* 'Rubicon') takes a long time to grow to above 1.5 m (5 ft). Its fine grey-green foliage turns purple in autumn.

Specimen varieties

— *C. lawsoniana* (Lawson cypress) can reach heights of 15–20 m (50–65 ft). It makes an excellent windbreak.

— *C. lawsoniana* 'Columnaris' forms a slender column of glaucous foliage. Height: 3–4 m (10–13 ft).

— *C. lawsoniana* 'Ellwoodii' is one of the most well-known varieties, with its erect branches and steel-blue foliage. It grows to a height of 2 m (6½ ft).

— *C. lawsoniana* 'Ellwood's Gold' is a smaller variety and its foliage is yellow-tinged at the tip. It reaches a height of 1 m (3¼ ft) after ten years.

— *C. lawsoniana* 'Fletcheri' is a well-known variety with characteristic, erect branches. Height: 2 m (6½ ft).

— *C. lawsoniana* 'Golden King' is a medium-sized conifer with golden yellow foliage turning to bronze in winter.

△ *Chamaecyparis lawsoniana* 'Lanei'

— *C. lawsoniana* 'Green Hedger' is a beautiful soft green colour.

— *C. lawsoniana* 'Stewartii'. This very well-known conifer is one of the more 'golden' varieties and has an attractive conical habit. Its foliage is almost green in summer, turning darker in autumn. Height: 3.5 m (11½ ft).

— *C. nootkatensis* – a native of North America from the coastal regions of Oregon, Canada – is definitely a hardy variety. It has strong-smelling foliage and an attractive, broadly conical habit. It can reach a height of 15 m (50 ft).

Height: varies according to species and variety.
Soil: any.
Aspect: sun or semi-shade.
Propagation: from seed and by layering.
Type: evergreen tree or shrub.

▷ *Chamaecyparis lawsoniana*

△ *Chimonanthus praecox*

Chamaecytisus

See *Cytisus*

Chimonanthus

WINTERSWEET

Calycanthaceae

It has to be said that this is not a particularly attractive shrub! But it does have saving graces. Its tiny flowers give off a heady perfume which can be smelt from several metres away, in winter. And it tolerates all soil types, even chalk. A green hedge provides an ideal backdrop and sets off its fine, well-spaced branches to the best advantage. Aconites planted generously (at least a dozen plants) around a chimonanthus makes an attractive winter group, especially if you add a few blue crocuses.

Useful hints

— Although chimonanthus doesn't require any particular type of soil, it does require patience as it takes two or three years for it to flower properly.

— Make sure it is protected from winds so that its flowers are not damaged.

— Plant it near a gate or path to get the full benefit of its scent, and you can always pick a few sprigs for the house.

— Chimonanthus doesn't like being pruned. After flowering, thin out by removing any badly positioned twigs or branches.

Recommended

— The most common variety, *Chimonanthus praecox*, has purple-centred flowers ranging from ivory to ochre. There are two varieties: 'Grandiflorus' (darker yellow with red markings) and 'Luteus'

(large, waxy yellow flowers). Both are deliciously scented.

Height: 2.5–4 m (8–13 ft).
Soil: ordinary, well-drained and well-dug.
Aspect: sun, against a south-facing wall.
Propagation: by layering, in summer, or from cuttings, using hormone rooting powder.
Flowering season: winter to spring.
Type: deciduous shrub.

Choisya

MEXICAN ORANGE

Rutaceae

Choisya ternata is a marvellous shrub. It has beautiful, fresh, evergreen leaves and tolerates both sun and shade. It is equally at home in the garden or in a container on the patio. Its common name comes from its membership of the 'orange' family. You only have to rub its leaves to release the characteristic smell of orange peel, and its flowers are just as scented. A happy choisya may even flower twice a year! It makes ideal permanent planting at the back of a border filled with lavatera, cosmos and clumps of foxgloves. Alternatively, plant a choisya under a window, against the wall of the house, or one either side of the front door, where they may well reach a height of 2 m (6½ ft). Try shaping them into a 'ball' – don't worry, you won't stop them flowering!

Useful hints

— Plant in spring, after the last frost, in a south- or west-facing position.

— Water regularly.

— Protect the roots in winter with straw or bracken.

▽ *Choisya ternata*

— If your choisya is in a container, bring it inside in the winter, as plants freeze more easily in pots than in the ground.

— If it is frosted, cut it back and it may shoot from the stem.

Recommended

— *C. ternata* has bright green divided leaves and white flowers in late spring and autumn. 'Sundance' is a golden-leaved variety and is less hardy.

— *C.* 'Aztec Pearl' – a fairly recent hybrid – produces larger flowers, tinged with pink but just as scented.

Height: 1–2 m (3¼–6½ ft).
Soil: humus-rich and well-drained.
Aspect: sun or semi-shade.
Propagation: from cuttings, in summer.
Flowering season: late spring and early summer.
Type: evergreen shrub.

Cistus

ROCK ROSE

Cistaceae

This small evergreen shrub is ideal for very sunny spots and poor, stony soil. And yet it has the most delicate, silky flowers, which are set off beautifully by its dark green foliage. These fragile-looking flowers only last for a day – opening in the morning and disappearing in the evening – but are replaced by new ones the next day. They can be used for background planting – above 1 m (3¼ ft) high – in borders, provided you give them a sheltered position in full sun. Cistus is also ideal for edging pathways or creating large

▽ *Cistus x purpureus*

clumps on a sunny bank, with a border of helianthemums, cotton lavender and dianthus in the foreground.

Useful hints

— Plant in the spring, in very stony ground, where it will be in its element. The soil needs to be well-drained, and not heavy or compacted.

— In winter, surround the stem with bracken or a mulch of leaves.

— In early spring, cut back any branches that you feel spoil the overall shape of the plant.

Recommended

— *Cistus* × *corbariensis*, one of the hardiest varieties, can grow to a height of over 1.5 m (5 ft) with a spread of almost 3 m (10 ft). In summer, the foliage is covered with a mass of white flowers measuring 4 cm (1½ in) across, with yellow markings.

— *C.* × *cyprius* has big, white, saucer-like flowers with brown markings around golden stamens. This shrub can grow to a height of 1.5 m (5 ft).

— *C. incanus* ssp. *creticus* has downy branches spread beneath pale pink, yellow-centred flowers.

— *C. ladanifer* has magnificent large white flowers – 7–10 cm (2¾–4 in) in diameter – with five crimson markings.

— *C.* × *lusitanicus* is a dwarf variety with clusters of white flowers.

— *C. monspeliensis* grows to about 75 cm (30 in), with small white flowers.

— *C. parviflorus* is an attractive, greyish shrub which is not particularly hardy but has magnificent, saucer-shaped, pale pink and white flowers.

— *C.* × *purpureus* produces large, deep purplish pink flowers – up to 12 cm (4½ in) in diameter – in summer. It is one of the hardier species.

— *C.* 'Silver Pink' has unusual, narrow leaves and is covered with tiny, pale pink, white-centred flowers in early summer.

Height: 60 cm –1.5 m (24 in–5 ft).
Soil: poor, stony.
Aspect: full sun.
Propagation: from cuttings or by layering, in summer or autumn.
Flowering season: summer.
Type: evergreen shrub.

△ *Cladrastis lutea*

Cladrastis

YELLOW WOOD

Leguminosae

This slow-growing, ornamental tree has long, pendent panicles of flowers in summer that do not appear until it is ten years old. It is extremely decorative and gives a light shade.

Useful hints

— Plant in full sun, in rich, light soil with added leaf-mould. The branches are fragile, so avoid windy positions.

Recommended

— The rounded, umbrella-shaped

Cladrastis lutea (yellow wood) has long hanging clusters – 30–50 cm (12–20 in) – of scented, wisteria-like white flowers in summer followed by golden autumn foliage.

— *C. sinensis* (Chinese yellow wood) can grow to a height of 30 m (95 ft). Its foliage appears later than that of many trees and shrubs and it has scented, pinkish white flowers.

Height: 6–30 m (20–95 ft).
Soil: humus-rich.
Aspect: full sun.
Propagation: from cuttings.
Flowering season: summer.
Type: deciduous tree.

△ *Clematis florida* 'Sieboldii'
▽ *Clematis* 'Lasurstern'

△ *Clematis armandii*
◁ *Clematis montana*
▽ *Clematis spooneri* (syn. *C. montana* var. *sericea*)

Clematis

OLD MAN'S BEARD, TRAVELLERS' JOY

Ranunculaceae

People always think of clematis as a climbing plant. However, there are several wonderful varieties of shrubby clematis that can be planted in a border among perennials. If you like blue you will love these herbaceous varieties. They look especially good planted with old varieties of roses.

Useful hints

— Clematis are quite demanding. Make sure the soil is fertile and well-prepared with a mixture of leaf-mould, sand and soil. To get them off to a really good start, give them a handful of bonemeal when you plant them, as they like chalky soil. And make sure you protect the base of the plant against sun.

Recommended

— The late-flowering *Clematis heracleifolia* has pale blue, tubular flowers. Height: 60 cm–1 m (2–3¼ ft).

— *C. heracleifolia* 'Wyevale' has strongly scented dark blue flowers.

— *C. integrifolia* produces its beautiful single, deep blue flowers a few weeks before *C. heracleifolia*. It grows to a height of 1 m (3¼ ft).

— *C. recta* grows in vigorous clumps. Its profusion of sweetly scented white flowers is followed by silvery, silky tassels which decorate the plant for the rest of the summer.

Height: 60 cm–1 m (24 in–3¼ ft).
Soil: chalky, lightened with sand and leaf-mould.
Aspect: full sun, roots in shade.
Propagation: by layering.
Flowering season: summer.
Type: deciduous shrub.

Clerodendrum

GLORY-BOWER

Verbenaceae

This very decorative shrub was used during religious ceremonies by the priests of India and Malaysia. Its name in fact comes from the Greek *kleros* meaning 'clergy' and *dendron* meaning 'tree'. There are more than 400 species of clerodendrem worldwide, but only a few of these are hardy. Their foliage, flowers and especially their bright blue berries are really delightful.

Useful hints

— This shrub is quite happy if it is protected from the wind and planted in a normal, well-drained soil, enriched with peat and leaf-mould.

— Cut out any unwanted branches from inside the plant to thin it out, and remove any dead wood.

Recommended

— *Clerodendrum bungei* is not fully hardy, but if frosted it will produce new shoots from the base.

— *C. splendens* grows more quickly in the shade, reaching a height of 1.5 m (5 ft). It produces scarlet flowers in early summer.

— *C. trichotomum* is a bushy-headed shrub which grows to a height of 2 m (6 ft). It produces scented, white flowers in mid-summer which give way, in autumn, to bright blue berries enclosed in maroon calyces.

— *C. trichotomum* var. *fargesii* is a small tree which grows to a height of almost 3 m (10 ft). It is hardier than *C. bungei* and produces beautiful scented flowers in mid-summer.

Height: 1.5–3 m (5–10 ft).
Soil: ordinary, enriched with peat and leaf-mould.
Aspect: semi-shade or sun.
Propagation: from seed and cuttings, and by layering for *C. bungei*.
Flowering season: early to late summer.
Type: deciduous shrub.

Clethra

SUMMERSWEET

Clethraceae

This large, scented bush has long, creamy white and gold flowers scattered attractively against the foliage. Clethras make a delightfully scented hedge, as they grow to a height of 3 m (10 ft) in good, humus-rich soil. If you want a really good show, plant clethras alongside a callicarpa with its striking purple berries. The effect will be stunning.

Useful hints

— Plant in winter, in groups of three, preferably in acid soil.

— Lighten the soil with peat and leaf-mould.

— Give them a leaf-mould mulch every spring.

— Water regularly in summer if the shrub is in a sunny position.

Recommended

— The most commonly found species is *Clethra alnifolia* (sweet pepperbush), which has slender spires of small white scented flowers throughout the summer. In autumn, it turns orange-yellow. 'Rosea' has pink-tinged buds and flowers.

— *C. arborea* (lily of the valley tree) grows to 2.5 m (8 ft), with nodding clusters of bell-shaped white flowers.

— *C. fargesii* is larger, with longer white flowers and bright gold foliage in autumn.

Height: 3 m (10 ft).
Soil: preferably acid and humus-rich.
Aspect: sun, shade or semi-shade.
Propagation: from cuttings, in summer.
Flowering season: summer to autumn.
Type: deciduous shrub.

▽ *Clerodendrum thomsoniae*

▽ *Clerodendrum trichotomum*

△ *Colletia paradoxa*

Colletia

COLLETIA

Rhamnaceae

This unusual shrub is more likely to inspire surprise than admiration. It has a compact, branching habit and its shoots broaden out into thick, rigid, triangular – and extremely pointed – spikes, which make it look more like a piece of metallic sculpture than a plant.

Useful hints

— As a general rule, colletias need a mild climate and will not survive cold winters unless they are moved into an unheated greenhouse. They need a very sunny position to produce a good display of flowers.

— There is no point in pruning them.

Recommended

— *Colletia armata* grows to a height of 2.5 m (8 ft), with rigid, grey-green spines. Pink flower buds open in summer to fragrant, tubular white flowers.

— *C. armata* 'Rosea' has pink flowers which appear in late summer and autumn.

— *C. hystrix* grows to a height of 2 m (6½ ft) and produces a modest display of scented white flowers in summer.

— *C. paradoxa* sometimes exceeds 2 m (6½ ft). Like the prickly pear, it can be used in very mild climates to create an impenetrable, defensive hedge.

Height: 1.5–2.5 m (5–8 ft).
Soil: ordinary.
Aspect: sun.
Propagation: from seed, or cuttings, in summer, in light soil in a cold frame.
Flowering season: very modest display in summer or autumn.
Type: deciduous shrub.

△ *Coriara japonica*

Colutea

BLADDER SENNA

Leguminosae

A fast-growing, summer-flowering shrub with bladder-shaped seed pods (hence the name bladder senna) which children take great delight in bursting.

Useful hints

— An easy shrub to grow, as it tolerates every type of position and soil (even very stony) although it does prefer chalky banks.

— In early spring, cut back the bare branches to half their length.

Recommended

— *Colutea arborescens* (common bladder senna) is a vigorous shrub which can reach a height of 4 m (13 ft) if not pruned regularly. It produces pea-like yellow flowers.

— *C. × media* has silver-grey foliage and bronze-tinged yellow flowers in summer.

— *Colutea × media* 'Copper Beauty' deserves wider recognition for its racemes of flowers ranging from orange to copper-red.

— *C. orientalis* has a more rounded habit, blue-grey leaves and copper-red flowers.

Height: 4 m (13 ft).
Soil: any.
Aspect: any.
Propagation: from cuttings in late summer, or from suckers.
Flowering season: summer.
Type: deciduous shrub.

Cordyline

CORDYLINE

Agavaceae

Originally a tropical plant, the cordyline is unfortunately not very hardy and thrives only in milder climates. In tree form it reaches heights of 8–12 m (26–40 ft). Its large (sometimes divided) trunk is surmounted by long ribbon-like leaves which give it a palm-tree-like appearance. It adds an exotic touch to any garden.

Useful hints

— Plant only in milder regions, in well-drained soil.

— Plant in a sunny position to encourage flowering.

Recommended

— *Cordyline australis* (cabbage tree) is the most widely grown species. It produces long panicles of large, creamy white flowers with golden yellow anthers.

— *C. australis* 'Atropurpurea' has purplish green leaves. White flowers appear in summer. The leaves of 'Veitchii' have red bases and midribs.

— *C. fruticosa* (syn. *C. terminalis*) is known as the good luck plant or ti tree. It has glossy deep green leaves and its flowers are white, purplish or reddish.

— *C. fruticosa* 'Baptisii' has deep green foliage with pink and yellow stripes and spots. The leaves of 'Imperialis' are marked with pink or red.

— *C. indivisa*, with its narrow leaves and more abundant flowers, looks more like a yucca. Its leaves are orange-marked above and blue-grey below.

Height: 8–12 m (26–40 ft).
Soil: light and well-drained.
Aspect: any.
Propagation: from cuttings (stem sections) in summer or suckers in spring.
Flowering season: summer.
Type: evergreen tree.

Coriaria

MYRTLE-LEAVED SUMACH

Coriariaceae

This shrub is found in temperate regions throughout the world, from New Zealand to the Andes of South America and Japan. Some of the species are used in the leather industry. It grows particularly well in milder climates. It rarely exceeds a height of 1 m (3¼ ft), though it grows taller in its native habitat, and has a slightly drooping habit with translucent, green foliage and clusters of greenish flowers. Although its flowers are relatively uninspiring, it has attractive autumn foliage with translucent, gooseberry-like fruits.

Useful hints

— Coriarias cannot survive cold winters and will need protection if there is likely to be hard frost, for example in a green-house or conservatory. However, even if the plant appears to have been frosted, don't despair. The roots have probably survived and will send up new shoots in the spring.

Recommended

— *Coriaria arborea* is known as the tutu by the Maoris of New Zealand. The seeds and shoots are very poisonous.

— *C. angustissima* has the narrowest leaves of the species.

— The arching stems of *C. japonica* make very good ground cover. It is widely grown for its profusion of bright red fruits.

— *C. myrtifolia* (myrtle-leaved sumach) is a native of the south of France. It has extremely poisonous black fruits and a highly developed root system that makes it ideal for planting on banks in warm climates.

— *C. nepalensis* is the largest species, reaching a height of 3 m (10 ft) under good conditions.

— *C. terminalis* has fern-like mid-green leaves that turn red in autumn.

Height: up to 3 m (10 ft).
Soil: any.
Aspect: sun, protected from frost.
Propagation: by layering or from suckers.
Flowering season: late spring.
Type: deciduous shrub.

Cordyline indivisa ▷

△ *Cornus controversa* 'Variegata'

▽ *Cornus mas* 'Variegata'

△ *Cornus alba*

▽ *Cornus florida*

Cornus

CORNEL, DOGWOOD

Cornaceae

Only a few of the cornels are trees, the rest are shrubs. But they are all extremely decorative and unusual in some respect. Some have red or bright yellow bark, which looks wonderful in winter, while others have particularly attractive foliage, flowers or berries. There is room in every garden for a cornus to add a touch of colour.

Useful hints

— Plant at any time of the year in containers, and autumn or spring in open ground.

— Cut the coloured-stemmed kinds hard back in spring, to encourage vigorous, new branches with more brightly coloured bark.

— Plant with helianthus, heleniums, heliopsis or hemerocallis to create a colourful display.

— Cornels like to be near water, and will even tolerate being water-logged from time to time. A few red-barked *Cornus alba* 'Sibirica' and yellow-barked *C. stolonifera* 'Flaviramea', planted behind astilbes in a damp corner of the garden, make a colourful, low-maintenance display.

Recommended

— *C. alba* (red-barked dogwood) is a bushy and vigorous Asiatic shrub which grows to a height of about 2 m (6½ ft). The variegated forms are the most decorative. Cultivars include *C. alba* 'Sibirica', with its beautiful, coral-red branches. The almost black bark of *C.a.* 'Kesselringii' looks striking against its dark purple-green foliage. 'Elegantissima' has white-edged grey-green leaves; 'Gouchaultii' has pink-flushed leaves broadly edged with yellow; 'Spaethii' has green leaves with yellow markings.

— *C. controversa* 'Variegata' (wedding-cake tree) is the only variety which is, botanically speaking, a tree. It grows very slowly to a height of 20 m (65 ft) and is extremely elegant with its spreading branches and light, variegated foliage.

— *C. florida* 'Apple Blossom'. This extremely attractive American native is worth planting for its superb display of spring flowers. A profusion of long, pale pink bracts appears before the leaves develop. 'Welchii' has white bracts, while its leaves are a mixture of green, white and pink, turning red and purple in autumn.

— The bracts of *C. florida* f. *rubra* are tinged with deep pink, while the flowers are red when they open.

— *C. kousa*, a native of Japan, has white bracts, rich crimson autumn foliage and red, strawberry-like fruits.

— In the wild, *C. mas* (cornelian cherry) grows in forests. When cultivated, it produced variegated varieties such as 'Aurea' and 'Elegantissima'. These small, tree-like shrubs produce attractive golden-yellow flowers which appear in early spring before the leaves develop. The scarlet fruits are edible but very bitter-tasting.

— *C. nuttallii* (mountain or Pacific dogwood) produces a profusion of tiny, creamy white flowers which turn to pink. The white bracts of 'North Star' are narrower and its young shoots are purple.

— *C. sanguinea* (common dogwood) is another native species found throughout Europe. It has bright red bark and deep red autumn foliage. The branches of 'Winter Flame' (syn. 'Winter Beauty') are a real eye-catcher in winter: yellow at the base, orange in the centre, turning to red at the tips.

— *C. stolonifera* 'Flaviramea' is a yellow-barked American variety whose spread is greater than its height.

Height: 2–20 m (6–65 ft).
Soil: ordinary, even water-logged in winter.
Aspect: semi-shade or sun.
Propagation: from hardwood cuttings in winter, or by layering.
Flowering season: spring to early summer.
Type: deciduous tree or shrub.

Coronilla

CROWN VETCH

Leguminosae

An eye-catching, low-maintenance shrub which thrives in dry, stony soil and full sun. Its bright yellow flowers are like bursts of sunlight against the evergreen foliage. Coronillas are ideal for softening

△ *Coronilla glauca*

garden steps and low stone walls and are set off beautifully by asphodelines and sun roses.

Useful hints

— Plant coronillas in spring, adding a handful of coarse sand to each hole.

— Water sparingly during their first summer.

— Prune in spring, to clear dead wood.

Recommended

— *Coronilla emerus* has unusual seed pods which are shaped like a scorpion's tail and yellow flowers, frequently red-veined.

— *C. valentina* ssp. *glauca* is the less hardy of the two. It takes its name from its blue-green leaves, which are evergreen. Plant at the foot of a south-facing wall where it will be sheltered but in full sun, and protect the roots in winter with bracken.

Height: 50 cm–2 m (20 in–6½ ft).
Soil: dry and stony.
Aspect: full sun.
Propagation: from cuttings at the end of summer, or by layering.
Flowering season: late spring to early summer, mid-summer to autumn.
Type: deciduous or evergreen shrub.

△ *Corylopsis sinensis*

△ *Corylopsis pauciflora*

Corylopsis

WINTER HAZEL

Hamamelidaceae

Few shrubs are as graceful as the corylopsis. It has a very distinctive habit, erect and then horizontal, with diaphanous leaves which are particularly attractive when young, and small, pendent clusters of primrose-scented yellow flowers which appear before the large, hazel-like leaves. These are several very good reasons to give it the semi-shaded spot and the watering that it needs. It is fully hardy, but late frosts may damage the flowers.

△ *Corylus avellana* 'Contorta'

Useful hints

— Plant corylopsis in winter, in light, acid soil enriched with peat and sand.

— Plant it where it will be sheltered from the hot summer sun. Mulch every autumn with a generous layer of leaf-mould.

— It is a slow-growing shrub, ideal for large containers on the patio. Bring it inside in spring to get the full benefit of its flowering season, and then put it back outside.

— Corylopsis doesn't need pruning, just cut off the dead flowers. Make sure you water it regularly in summer to prevent the leaves wilting.

Recommended

— *Corylopsis pauciflora* is the most common variety, with its little clusters of flowers which open in spring. It doesn't grow above 1.5 m (5 ft).

— *C. sinensis* produces fragrant, yellow flowers in spring.

— *C. sinensis* var. *sinensis* 'Spring Purple' has incredible, plum-purple young stems.

— *C. spicata* has long, drooping clusters of pale yellow flowers.

Height: 1.5–3 m (5–10 ft).
Soil: acid, well-drained.
Aspect: semi-shade.
Propagation: difficult – by layering, in summer.
Flowering season: winter to spring.
Type: deciduous shrub.

Corylus

HAZEL, FILBERT

Corylaceae

Although this little tree is well-known for its fruit (the hazelnut), it is not generally considered as a subject for the garden. As it has a fairly open habit, plant it where it can give some shade to flowers that don't like full sun. Alternatively, including it in a hedge will add a natural touch to the garden.

Useful hints

— Grafting at a height of 2.5 m (8 ft) will produce a more vigorous tree which may grow to 5 m (16 ft).

— Avoid planting hazels in permanently wet soil.

Recommended

— *Corylus avellana* 'Aurea'. This cultivar of the common hazel or cobnut has attractive yellow leaves.

— As well as being extremely decorative, *C. avellana* 'Contorta', with its corkscrew branches, also produces very good nuts. It grows to 3.5 m (11½ ft).

— *C. avellana* 'Pendula' has a weeping habit.

— *C. colurna*, the Turkish hazel, has lobed dark green leaves and yellow catkins. The nuts grow in fringed husks.

— *C. maxima*, the filbert, is vigorous and bushy. It has oval toothed leaves, long yellow catkins in late winter and edible brown nuts.

— *C. maxima* 'Purpurea' (purple-leaved filbert) has remarkable purple-coloured leaves in summer and autumn. The catkins are also purple with yellow anthers.

Height: 5 m (16 ft).
Soil: fertile, cool.
Aspect: any, except very shady.
Propagation: from seed or by layering in summer.
Flowering season: catkins in spring.
Type: deciduous tree or shrub.

△ *Cotinus obovatus*

Cotinus

COTINUS, VENETIAN or WIG SUMACH, SMOKE TREE

Anacardiaceae

This tree is remarkable for its habit, foliage and feathery flowers in summer. The name 'smoke tree' comes from the 'smoky' tones of the flowers towards the end of the summer.

Useful hints

— Plant continus from autumn to spring.

— Water regularly for the first two years.

— It does not need pruning or have any other special requirements.

Recommended

— *Cotinus coggygria* 'Royal Purple'. This cultivar of the Venetian sumach or smoke tree reaches a height of about 4 m (13 ft) and is one of the most beautiful shrubs on the market, both for its translucent, deep purple foliage and its unusual form. Its spreading, trailing branches form a sort of rounded bush which can be as much as 6 m (20 ft) in diameter. This variety does have a tendency to die suddenly for no apparent reason, but you will have time to enjoy it

for at least a few years. Another cultivar, *C. coggygria* 'Flame', has pink flowers and foliage that turns flame-orange in autumn.

— *C. obovatus* is even more vigorous, reaching a height of 6 m (20 ft). It has large oval leaves, bronze-pink when young, which turn orange, red and purple in autumn.

Height: 4–6 m (13–20 ft).
Soil: any.
Aspect: sun.
Propagation: from cuttings or by layering in summer.
Flowering season: summer.
Type: deciduous shrub.

Cotoneaster

COTONEASTER

Rosaceae

Cotoneasters can be badly affected by fireblight. This is a bacterial disease (*Erwinia amylovora*) which can rapidly kill some members of the family Rosaceae. However, the cotoneaster is still the most widely used shrub in our gardens, as there is one to suit every position. It is a shrub with decorative foliage and fruit and attractive autumn foliage colour, as well as being very undemanding.

Useful hints

— Plant cotoneasters from autumn to spring. Mulch the soil in spring and water regularly during hot weather.

— If branches wither for no apparent reason during the summer, cut them back hard to the base of the branch and burn them. Disinfect your secateurs and treat the open wound on the bush with a pruning 'paint'. Keep an eye on the plant. If symptoms recur, this means that it may have fireblight and must be dug up and burned. The disease is incurable and can be transmitted to nearby pear trees.

Recommended dwarf varieties and ramblers

— *Cotoneaster dammeri*, with its shiny, evergreen foliage, is top of the list. Few other prostrate shrubs are so well rooted into the ground and so dense that you can roll on them without doing any damage. There are several cultivars, including 'Eichcholz' with its scarlet berries, the small-leaved var. *radicans* and 'Skogholm', extremely vigorous and one of the best ground covers.

— *C. franchetii* has light, gracefully curving branches with evergreen foliage and long-lasting orange-red berries.

— *C. horizontalis* reaches a height of 2 m (6½ ft). It has elegantly spreading fishbone or fan-shaped branches and very decorative fruits. It has some interesting cultivars, including *C. horizontalis* 'Variegatus', with its small cream leaves marked with red in autumn.

— *C. microphyllus* has dense, shiny, evergreen foliage. *C.m.* var. *thymifolius* is particularly recommended for rock gardens.

— *C. salicifolia* 'Parkteppich' ('Park Carpet') has tiny, elongated leaves. It is widely used for ground cover.

— *C. salicifolius* 'Pendulus' has shiny evergreen foliage and a profusion of red berries. This has the added advantage that it can be trained to form an attractive little tree with a weeping habit.

— *C. splendens*, with its grey-green foliage, is best planted against a wall.

— *Cotoneaster × watereri* has a vigorous, weeping habit, evergreen foliage, white flowers and superb coral-red berries in autumn.

— *C. × watereri* 'Rothschildianus' has distinctive, pale green, evergreen foliage and golden yellow fruits.

Recommended erect varieties

— *C. frigidus* (tree cotoneaster) is a small, vigorous, semi-evergreen tree which grows to a height of 4–5 m (13–16 ft). Its white flower heads (in groups of thirty to forty flowers) appear in summer, followed by large, bright red fruits which hang in decorative clusters.

— *C. frigidus* 'Cornubia' can reach heights of up to 6–8 m (20–26 ft). This superb evergreen tree bears a profusion of spherical, scarlet fruits.

— *C. lacteus* has arching branches and an unusual if somewhat dense habit. The underside of its leaves is covered in silvery down.

— *C. salicifolius* is one of the most vigorous species. It can even be trained over a pergola so that its branches trail down in attractive festoons. It has evergreen foliage and bright red fruits in autumn. It grows to a height of 5 m (16 ft).

Height: 10 cm–8 m (4 in–26 ft).
Soil: ordinary.
Aspect: any, except due north.
Propagation: from cuttings, in summer.
Flowering season: spring to summer.
Type: deciduous or evergreen shrub.

▽ *Cotoneaster splendens*

▽ *Cotoneaster lacteus*

▽ *Cotoneaster salicifolius* 'Pendulus'

▽ *Cotoneaster glaucophyllus*

△ *Crataegus laevigata* 'Rosea Flore Pleno'

Crataegus

HAWTHORN, THORN

Rosaceae

The flowers of the hawthorn appear in spring and bloom well into the summer. The fruits or haws used to be well-known in country areas as 'itching powder'. They stay on the bush throughout the winter, sometimes even until the following spring. Its thorny, untidy-looking branches emphasize the natural appearance of the bush, which grows wild in many parts of Europe. It is particularly useful for growing in polluted urban areas, exposed sites and seaside gardens. It can be grown with other shrubs to form a dense and effective hedge, with the added advantage of a profusion of attractive and delicately perfumed flowers. It can also be grown as a tree,

reaching a height of 7 m (23 ft), by pruning the trunk which, in its natural state, divides at ground level. In the past the haws used to be crushed or ground for culinary use, and its flowers have always made delicious, wholesome infusions.

Useful hints

— Don't plant the hawthorn in soil that is too wet.

— Don't plant it in full shade. Apart from this, it is happy anywhere and is fully hardy (surviving temperatures down to −25°C). Water it regularly in summer.

— To obtain a double hedge, plant in alternate rows, as you would to create densely planted borders.

Recommended

— *Crataegus crus-galli* (cockspur thorn) has a spreading habit and fruits which

can be up to 8 cm (3 in) long. Its Latin and common names were inspired by its formidable, long, curved thorns.

— *C. ellwangeriana* has a spreading habit and toothed dark green leaves. Its flowers are white with pink anthers, and its fruits are crimson.

— *C. flava* (yellow haw) is a small tree which grows to 5 m (16 ft). It has clusters of white flowers and yellow, apple-scented fruits.

— *C.* × *grignonensis* has interesting foliage and fruits which stay on its branches until winter. It is ideal for adding a touch of winter colour.

— *C. laciniata* (syn. *C. orientalis*) is a spreading tree with hairy dark green leaves. The flowers are white and the fruits are red tinged with yellow.

— *C. laevigata*. This simple, attractive shrub has pink flowers, followed by rounded, bright red fruits. This is the hawthorn on our grandmothers' postcards and in children's story books. Grafting produces a small tree which will create a stunning, bouquet-like effect from a distance. Among the more attractive of its many cultivars are 'Rosea Flore Pleno' (double, pink flowers), 'Paul's Scarlet' (double, scarlet), and 'Plena' (double, white). 'Punicea' has crimson flowers and red fruits.

— *C.* × *lavallei* 'Carrierei' has distinctive purple autumn foliage and the berries remain throughout the winter.

— *C. monogyna* (common hawthorn). Grafting produces a beautifully formed, vigorous tree which will grow to a height of 10 m (33 ft). It doesn't need a lot of space and makes an attractive addition to any garden. It also makes a very good barrier hedge.

— *C. pinnatifida* is a very attractive small tree from China. It has beautiful dark green foliage and large fruits.

— *C. tanacetifolia* (tansy-leaved thorn) is an upright, usually thornless tree. It has deeply cut grey-green leaves, clusters of white flowers with red anthers, and yellow fruits.

Height: 5–10 m (16–33 ft).
Soil: any: tolerates very dry conditions.
Aspect: any, but not too shady.
Propagation: from seed; specific varieties are often grafted on to wild root-stock.
Flowering season: spring to summer.
Type: deciduous tree or shrub.

△ *Crinodendron hookerianum*

Crinodendron

CRINODENDRON

Elaeocarpaceae

The crinodendron is an unusual, free-flowering shrub with attractive lantern-shaped flowers. It is a native of Chile and should be grown only in areas where the winters are mild. It only flowers well if it has not suffered from cold during the previous winter.

Useful hints

— This delicate shrub should be grown only in milder climates.

— Plant it in semi-shade, in cool, acid soil, and always give it wall protection.

Recommended

— *Crinodendron hookerianum* (lantern tree). In spring it produces a profusion of long-stalked crimson flowers. It has shiny, evergreen leaves and can reach a height of 7 m (23 ft).

— *C. patagua* has white flowers. It grows quickly but is even more fragile than *C. hookerianum*. Height: 4–7 m (13–23 ft).

Height: 4–7 m (13–23 ft).
Soil: prefers acid soil.
Aspect: sheltered from wind, cold and direct sun.
Propagation: from cuttings in late summer.
Flowering season: spring.
Type: evergreen shrub.

Cryptomeria

JAPANESE CEDAR

Taxodiaceae

Cryptomeria has soft, plume-like foliage tinged with pale green (brown in winter) and a light, open habit. The Japanese cedar is a favourite in Western gardens. In their natural habitat, mature trees grow to a height of 60 m (190 ft), but elsewhere they barely reach 20 m (65 ft).

Useful hints

— Although cryptomerias are generally hardy, like many conifers they don't like snow, which can tend to break their branches. In the event of a heavy snow-fall, protect the branches by tying them up to the trunk.

— In summer, branches can be badly damaged by red spider mite, so keep an eye on the underside of the needles in dry weather.

— Water well in hot weather and spray the foliage of young trees.

— Avoid planting in dry soil.

Recommended

— *Cryptomeria japonica* is a native of the high mountains and central islands of Japan. The ends of the leaves are curved and the soft green foliage usually turns rust-coloured, almost red, in winter. In Europe it can reach a height of 20 m (65 ft), but its cultivars are all smaller than this.

— *C. japonica* 'Araucarioïdes' has an attractive, conical habit, rounded at the top, and fine whorls of foliage on slender branches.

— *C. japonica* 'Bandi-sugi' is a small bush with blue-tinged, moss-like foliage which turns red in autumn and winter. It reaches a height of 2 m (6 ft).

— *C. japonica* 'Cristata' is a conical conifer with twisted, curved shoots and soft, fibrous bark. The bright green foliage becomes brown-tinged with age. It grows to 5 m (16 ft).

— *C. japonica* 'Elegans' is the most popular and most widely grown cultivar. Its soft, feathery foliage is pale green in spring and becomes red-bronze in winter. It maintains a compact, well-balanced habit and grows to a height of 5 m (16 ft). 'Elegans Nana' is a slow-growing, compact shrub which forms an attractive, slightly flattened globe. Its foliage becomes tinged with red in winter. Height: 2 m (6½ ft).

— *C. japonica* 'Globosa Nana' forms a compact dome of blue-green foliage which reaches a height of 1 m (3¼ ft).

— *C. japonica* 'Pyramidata' is narrowly columnar or obelisk-shaped. Its foliage is blue-green when young, maturing to green. It reaches 5 m (16 ft).

— *C. japonica* 'Sekkan-sugi' grows to a height of 4–5 m (13–16 ft) and its young foliage is creamy yellow.

— *C. japonica* 'Vilmoriniana' produces a dense, green globe less than 1 m (3¼ ft) high which turns bronze in autumn.

△ *Cryptomeria japonica* 'Elegans'

△ *Cryptomeria japonica* 'Elegans'
▷ *Cryptomeria japonica*

Height: varies depending on variety.
Soil: acid or deep, humus-rich.
Aspect: sun.
Propagation: from seed, cuttings with hormone rooting powder, or by layering.
Type: evergreen tree or shrub.

× *Cupressocyparis*

LEYLAND CYPRESS

Cupressaceae

About a hundred years ago, two trees from the same family, whose natural habitats were several thousand miles apart, were successfully crossed. They were *Chamaecyparis nootkatensis* from Oregon and *Cupressus macrocarpa* from California, and the operation took place in Wales, in the garden of a certain Mr Leyland. The resulting hybrid, × *Cupressocyparis leylandii*, became extremely popular for several reasons. It is very fast-growing (the fastest-growing conifer, in fact, at a rate of 1 m (3¼ ft) per year), is extremely resistant to pollution and tolerates all types of soil. It can be pruned to form tall hedges and windbreaks. Its grey-green colour and soft foliage are also very popular.

Useful hints

— Plant in well-dug, humus-enriched soil. Although tolerant of all soil types, × *C. leylandii* does not like water-logged soil.

— For hedges, plant the trees at least 1 m (3¼ ft) apart.

— Prune the young trees to strengthen their roots.

Recommended

— × *C. leylandii* 'Castlewellan' has golden yellow foliage in spring, turning to bronze-green in winter. It forms beautifully coloured hedges.

— The foliage of × *C. leylandii* 'Harlequin' (syn. × *Cupressocyparis* 'Variegata') has strange white markings.

— × *C. leylandii* 'Naylor's Blue' has a narrow, columnar habit. Its greyish green foliage becomes glaucous in winter.

— × *C. leylandii* 'Stapehill' is a dense, columnar tree.

Height: 4–6 m (13–20 ft).
Soil: deep.
Aspect: any.
Propagation: by layering or from heel cuttings with hormone rooting powder in autumn.
Type: evergreen tree.

Cupressus

CYPRESS

Cupressaceae

This is not a tree for cold regions. In fact, the most beautiful varieties can be

△ *Cupressus arizonica*

seen in very mild climates. If you want to grow it in a somewhat cooler area, make sure it is well protected from the wind.

Useful hints

— Cypresses should be well staked for the first few years.

— Plant small, container-grown trees and do not disturb them once they have been planted.

Recommended

— *Cupressus arizonica* has a conical habit and grey-green foliage. *C.a.* var. *glabra* has very attractive bright blue-green leaves. Height: 3 m (10 ft). *C.a.* 'Pyramidalis' is a beautiful tree, if somewhat broad at the base, with blue-tinged, dense foliage. It can be used to form impenetrable hedges.

— *C. lusitanica* (Mexican cypress) has graceful foliage and rich brown, peeling bark. As its name suggests, *C.l.* 'Glauca Pendula' has a weeping habit and glaucous foliage.

— *C. macrocarpa* has a fairly broad base. It thrives near the sea and grows to a height of 20 m (65 ft).

— *C. macrocarpa* 'Goldcrest' is a columnar tree with beautiful golden foliage. It is a fairly hardy variety which grows to a height of 12 m (40 ft).

— *C. macrocarpa* 'Golden Pillar' is one of the narrower varieties. Its beautiful

golden foliage looks spectacular in sunlight. It grows to an average height of 10 m (33 ft).

— *C. sempervirens* is a beautiful columnar cypress which evokes Italian gardens. This tree grows to a height of 15 m (50 ft) or more. Its habit is more accentuated in 'Stricta', especially the grafted specimens which are even narrower and more tapered.

— *C. torulosa* 'Cashmeriana' (Kashmir cypress) is draped with silver-grey pendulous branches. It is an attractive specimen and deserves to be carefully positioned in the garden.

Height: 3–20 m (10–65 ft).
Soil: good, not too wet.
Aspect: sun.
Propagation: from seed.
Type: evergreen tree.

Cytisophyllum

see *Cytisus*

▽ × *Cupressocyparis leylandii*

Cytisus

BROOM

Leguminosae

Cytisus is a small to medium-sized free-flowering shrub with a rounded, bushy habit. It adds a welcome splash of colour to flower beds and borders. In some areas, eye-catching clumps of wild broom can still be seen by the roadside. When the bush is in flower, the leaves virtually disappear beneath a mass of golden yellow petals. Nurserymen just couldn't resist the challenge, and there is now a wide range of flamboyantly coloured cultivars.

Useful hints

— Plant cytisus in poor soil. Otherwise they will grow tall and lose their foliage at the base.

— Remove the seed heads each year after flowering. Brooms live for only a short time and have to be replaced every four or five years, but it is well worth the effort, as they are beautiful shrubs.

Recommended

— *Cytisus albus* (syn. *Chamaecytisus albus*) (white broom). Its white flowers go well in any border.

— *C. battandieri*, from Morocco, is a beautifully ornamental shrub. It is extremely vigorous and can reach a height of 5 m (16 ft). It produces a profusion of acid-yellow flowers in summer.

— *C. × beanii* is a dwarf variety, 20–90 cm (8–36 in) high, with bright yellow flowers.

— *C. decumbens* is fairly prostrate, 25 cm (10 in) high, and flowers in spring to summer.

— *C. × kewensis* barely grows above 30 cm (12 in) high but spreads to a diameter of up to 2 m (6½ ft). In spring it is covered with creamy white flowers.

— *C. praecox* 'Warminster' is the earliest flowering variety. In spring it is covered with a mass of pale yellow flowers.

— *C. purpureus* (syn. *Chamaecytisus purpureus*), a small, bushy shrub which reaches a height of barely 50 cm (20 in), is popular for its purple colour. It has several well-known cultivars: 'Albocarneus' (pale pink), 'Albus' (white), and 'Atropurpureus' (an unusual, deep purple).

— *C. scoparius* (common broom) is fully hardy and can reach a height of 2 m (6½ ft). A wide range of colours is now available in this spring to summer flowering variety: f. *andreanus* (golden yellow flowers edged with red); 'Radiance' (brilliant red); 'Killiney Salmon' (salmon-pink); and 'Windlesham Ruby' (large, crimson flowers).

— *C.* 'Burkwoodii' has yellow-edged, scarlet flowers.

— *C. sessilifolius* (syn. *Cytisophyllum sessilifolium*) grows to a height of 1.5 m (5 ft) and produces clusters of yellow flowers in spring.

Height: 20 cm–5 m (8 in–26 ft), depending on species and variety.
Soil: poor, sandy.
Aspect: sunny.
Propagation: from seed in spring, in pots and planted out in spring; for hybrids, cuttings taken in summer under glass.
Flowering season: spring to summer.
Type: deciduous or evergreen shrub.

▽ *Cytisus × beanii*

Daphne

DAPHNE

Thymelaeaceae

This hardy, winter-flowering shrub, with its profusion of richly scented flowers, is a welcome addition to any garden. Its only real disadvantage is that its short branches are rather stiff. However, when the bush is in flower, the tiny bright pink flowers cluster along its fairly thick branches, making it look rather like a flowering candelabra. Its vaguely geometric outline also adds a surprisingly delicate Japanese touch. *Lychnis alpina* and *Penstemon* 'Heavenly Blue' planted near daphnes will create a delightful display of pink and blue.

Useful hints

— Buy daphnes in winter when in flower, but don't plant them until the risk of heavy frosts has passed.

— Evergreen varieties tend to grow away better in autumn, so this is the best time to plant them.

— Don't prune daphnes, except to remove branches which die suddenly as a result of a virus attack (against which there is no remedy).

Recommended

— *Daphne bholua* 'Gurkha' produces strongly scented purple flowers in winter.

— *D. cneorum* (garland flower) is fairly widespread. It is a prostrate, evergreen species which does not grow above 50 cm (20 in) and forms a thick mat on the ground. It is ideal for rock gardens, with strongly scented bright pink flowers that appear in spring. It likes a sunny position and stony, chalky soil.

— *D. genkwa* is an upright shrub growing to 1.5 m (5 ft). It has lilac flowers, faintly scented.

— *D. × hybrida* is a dense, evergreen shrub which grows to a height of 1 m (3¼ ft) and benefits from being staked. It produces strongly scented flowers in spring.

— *D. mezereum* (mezereon) is a well-known deciduous variety. Its candelabra-like branches are covered with deep pink flowers in winter.

— *D. odora* is an evergreen. Its variegated form, 'Aureomarginata', is very elegant and more frost-resistant than other varieties. It is the most strongly scented of the daphnes.

Height: 50 cm–2 m (20 in–6½ ft).
Soil: ordinary, lightened with sand.
Aspect: sun.
Propagation: difficult; cuttings in summer or seed sown in ericaceous compost in shade.
Flowering season: winter to spring.
Type: deciduous or evergreen shrub.

Datura

DATURA, THORN APPLE

Solanaceae

This is not the annual plant, but the shrub form, which is often planted in containers. Its decorative evergreen foliage will look good on your patio but will need protection in winter. It has long, pendent, trumpet-shaped flowers and becomes more free-flowering as it gets older.

Useful hints

— Plant daturas in good, compost-enriched soil, preferably against a pillar or a corner of a wall where they will create the best effect.

— Prune when they have finished flowering to maintain the plants' overall shape.

Recommended

— *Datura arborea* (angel's trumpet) grows to 2.5 m (8 ft) and over. Its strongly scented, white, trumpet-shaped flowers are borne in summer.

— *D. aurea* has white or yellow flowers.

— *D. × candida* 'Grand Marnier' has large, trumpet-shaped flowers whose colour is reminiscent of the liqueur. New strains of seed have produced flowers in other colours such as pink and white.

— *D. cornigera* is the hardiest variety and reaches a height of 1.5 m (5 ft). Its creamy white flowers are at least 20 cm (8 in) long.

— *D. meteloides* has beautiful flowers up to 20 cm (8 in) long in the palest shade of lilac. The fragrance is unforgettable.

— *D. sanguinea* has large, orange-red trumpets and grows to a height of 2.5 m (8 ft).

— *D. suaveolens* is possibly the most attractive variety, with its flannel-like leaves and long, white flowers.

— *D. versicolor*. Its trumpets are narrower and more varied in colour, from pale green to white and yellow to salmon-pink.

Height: 1.5–2.5 m (5–8 ft) and over.
Soil: good, compost-enriched.
Aspect: sun, sheltered.
Propagation: from cuttings or by layering.
Flowering season: summer.
Type: evergreen shrub.

Daphne sericea **Collina Group** ▷

▽ *Daphne mezereum*

▽ *Daphne cneorum* 'Eximia'

▽ *Daphne odora* 'Aureomarginata'   ▽ *Datura sanguinea*

313

314

Davidia

POCKET-HANDKERCHIEF TREE

Nyssaceae/Davidiaceae

First discovered by the French missionary and botanist Père David, *Davidia involucrata* has become a collector's tree although it is in fact easy to grow. Its general outline, and even its pale green leaves and light brown trunk, are reminiscent of the lime. It is at its most spectacular in spring, when it is covered with large, pure white, pendent bracts, about 20 cm (8 in) long, which look like hundreds of pocket handkerchiefs hanging on the tree!

Useful hints

— The davidia is a fully hardy tree which tolerates all types of cool soil and is therefore very easy to grow. It is hard to understand why it should be still be classed as a rare species.

Recommended

— *D. involucrata* (pocket-handkerchief tree, dove tree, ghost tree) has delightful, asymmetrical white flowers which do not appear until the tree is ten years old. In its native China, it grows to a height of 20 m (65 ft).

— *D. involucrata* var. *vilmoriniana* is the same as *D. involucrata* apart from the glaucous underside of its leaves.

Height: 6–20 m (20–65 ft).
Soil: all cool soils.
Aspect: sun or slight shade.
Propagation: very difficult from seed, but possible from cuttings – possibly the explanation for the davidia's rarity.
Flowering season: spring.
Type: deciduous tree.

Desfontainia

DESFONTAINIA

Loganiaceae

The desfontainia, an evergreen shrub from the Andes, looks remarkably like a holly. It has the same glossy, spiky, evergreen leaves and the same erect habit. In fact it can easily be mistaken for a holly outside the flowering season. But in summer it is quite a different matter.

◁ *Davidia involucrata*

△ *Davidia involucrata*

The profusion of long, tubular, red and orange flowers, sometimes marked with yellow, which appear at the base of the leaves are the attractive and unmistakable mark of the desfontainia.

Useful hints

— The desfontainia tolerates both cold and damp, but not severe frost. If you live in a relatively mild region, why not give it a try? Plant it in a sheltered spot and possibly even mulch the roots as a protection.

— Plant in an acid or chalk-free soil (it doesn't like chalky soil).

— Remove damaged branches in spring to tidy up the shrub, but don't prune in the usual manner.

△ *Desfontainia spinosa* 'Harold Comber'

Recommended

— *Desfontainia spinosa* is sometimes found in specialist nurseries. Its scarlet flowers are edged with yellow.

— *D. spinosa* 'Harold Comber' has bright red flowers, 5 cm (2 in) long.

Height: 1.5 m (5 ft).
Soil: acid, chalk-free.
Aspect: semi-shade.
Propagation: from cuttings, in summer.
Flowering season: summer.
Type: evergreen shrub.

△ *Deutzia × rosea*

△ *Deutzia gracilis*
▽ *Deutzia × hybrida* 'Magician'

Deutzia

DEUTZIA

Hydrangaceae

This deciduous shrub from China is very easy to grow. It thrives anywhere, provided it is planted in full sun. Some varieties, such as *Deutzia × magnifica*, have a rigid habit. Others are more arching but still have fairly stiff stems. The clusters of luminous white flowers appear in spring or summer, depending on the variety, and their edges are sometimes tinged with pink or red. It is an ideal shrub for small gardens, as it is very decorative and rarely grows above 2.5 m (8 ft).

Useful hints

— Although deutzias grow in all soil types, they prefer a rich, deep soil. Plant in autumn, with added peat.

— Cut back only when it has finished flowering, as the flowers develop on the previous year's growth. Don't cut back more than 15 cm (6 in).

Recommended

— Among the larger varieties is the hybrid *D. scabra* 'Pride of Rochester', with double flowers tinged with pink on the outside.

— The smaller deutzias, 70 cm–1.5 m (28 in–5 ft), include *D. gracilis*, with pure white flowers, the Lemoine hybrids such as 'Mont Rose', and *D. × rosea* 'Carminea', both with pink flowers.

— *D. × hybrida* 'Perle Rose' is an old variety which is still popular for its soft rose flowers and long flowering season.

— *D. × magnifica* grows to a height of 2 m (6½ ft) and has double white flowers.

— *D. × magnifica* 'Erecta' has an erect habit and panicles of cone-shaped flowers.

— *D. × magnifica* 'Longipetala' has single, long-petalled flowers.

— *D. pulchra*'s racemes of white flowers are like lily of the valley.

— *D. setchuenensis* is an upright shrub with small white flowers and oval, rough dark grey-green leaves.

Height: 70 cm–2.5 m (28 in–8 ft).
Soil: ordinary, well-dug.
Aspect: full sun.
Propagation: from cuttings or by layering.
Flowering season: spring to summer.
Type: deciduous shrub.

△ *Dipelta floribunda*

Dipelta

DIPELTA

Caprifoliaceae

This shrub is a native of China and is grown for its scented, tubular flowers and reddish bark, which peels off in long strips. It can reach a height of 5 m (16 ft), with a spread of 3 m (10 ft).

Useful hints

— Dipeltas are easy to grow. All you have to do is plant them in autumn in well-drained soil, in a sheltered spot and semi-shade.

— When they have finished flowering, cut back the branches that have flowered to ground level. They will flower again the following spring.

Recommended

— *Dipelta floribunda* grows to a height of 3–4 m (10–13 ft) in the West. It has an erect habit that spreads towards the top, and attractive, 'peeling', pale brown bark. Hanging clusters of scented flowers appear in spring. The flowers are pale pink with a yellow throat.

— *D. yunnanensis* rarely grows above 2.5 m (8 ft). It has narrow, glossy green leaves and produces creamy white flowers suffused with orange in spring.

Height: 2–4 m (6½–13 ft).
Soil: ordinary, well-drained.
Aspect: semi-shade or sun.
Propagation: in autumn, take cuttings 20 cm (8 in) long from the current year's growth.
Flowering season: spring.
Type: deciduous shrub.

Drimys

DRIMYS

Winteraceae

These evergreen trees and shrubs should be planted in a protected spot, for example against a wall. In spring they produce clusters of small, fragrant, ivory-coloured flowers. Their bark is also strongly scented and smells of cinnamon.

Useful hints

— Drimys needs a sheltered spot where there is no risk of a prolonged frost. Frosted branches can be cut back if the shrub has not been too badly damaged.

— Plant in moist but well-drained soil.

— Prune long branches to maintain a good shape.

Recommended

— *Drimys aromatica* comes from Tasmania and has white, long-petalled flowers.

— *D. lanceolata* grows to a height of 2 m (6½ ft) and flowers in spring. Every part of the plant is fragrant: leaves, flowers and bark. Even the fruits sometimes smell of pepper. It is a small, elegant shrub which produces ivory-coloured flowers.

— *D. winteri* (Winter's bark) comes from South America and is used as a medicinal plant there. It grows to a height of 3–4 m (10–13 ft) and has large, thick leaves and jasmine-scented flowers.

Height: 2–4 m (6½–13 ft).
Soil: well-drained, lightened with sand.
Aspect: sun, in a sheltered spot.
Propagation: from cuttings in autumn.
Flowering season: spring.
Type: evergreen tree or shrub.

▽ *Drimys winteri*

△ *Elaeagnus pungens* 'Maculata'

Elaeagnus

OLEASTER
Elaeagnaceae

These brightly coloured evergreen or deciduous shrubs are easy to grow, especially near the sea and in light soil. They even tolerate dry soil. *Elaeagnus × ebbingei* makes an attractive feature trained against the front of the house or on a wall. Its dark green foliage is silvery underneath, and its unobtrusive flowers are beautifully scented in autumn. *E. pungens* 'Maculata' has golden foliage marked with green and stands out well in a border with *Lysimachia punctata* or behind heliopsis.

Useful hints

— Plant elaeagnus in spring or autumn, in soil lightened with sand.

— Mulch in spring with forest bark.

— Protect young plants during their first winter with a windbreak and cover their roots with bracken or a thick layer of dead leaves.

Recommended

— *E. angustifolia* (oleaster) has attractive, grey, deciduous or semi-evergreen foliage which is slightly scented.

— The silvery, olive-green foliage of *E. commutata* (silver berry) forms a small, elegant hedge.

— *E. × ebbingei* is a large shrub with evergreen foliage, silvery underneath. It is one of the hardier varieties and is beautifully scented. Trained against a house wall, it makes an unusual permanent feature. The large leaves of 'Gilt Edge' are edged with golden yellow, while 'Limelight' has a central, golden yellow mark.

— *E. pungens* is a spiny shrub which flowers in autumn. It has a number of variegated cultivars: 'Variegata' is marked with white, and 'Maculata' has large central golden yellow markings. Its flowers are silvery white and strongly scented.

— *E. umbellata* is a vigorous, spreading, semi-deciduous shrub. Its leaves have wavy edges and silvery undersides. Its flowers are creamy white and scented.

Height: 3 m (10 ft).
Soil: ordinary to dry.
Aspect: sun and semi-shade.
Propagation: from cuttings in summer and autumn.
Flowering season: autumn.
Type: evergreen or deciduous shrub.

Embothrium

CHILEAN FIRE BUSH
Proteaceae

These trees and shrubs are natives of Australia and South America. Their slender, spreading habit gives them an attractive shape and they produce spectacular scarlet flowers in summer. They are sensitive to cold.

Useful hints

— Plant in deep, acid soil which is moist but well-drained. They also grow in non-alkaline, sandy soil mixed with peat.

— Embothriums are frost hardy but need to be sheltered from cold winds.

— Protect the young plants with leaves or straw in winter.

Recommended

— *Embothrium coccineum* (Chilean fire bush) produces a profusion of spectacular scarlet flowers.

— *E. coccineum* Lanceolatum Group is a more hardy variety, provided it is not planted in an exposed position.

Height: 3–4 m (10–13 ft).
Soil: acid, sandy, well-drained.
Aspect: sun, protected from the cold.
Propagation: from seed in spring.
Flowering season: summer.
Type: evergreen tree or shrub.

Enkianthus

ENKIANTHUS
Ericaceae

This is a shrub of striking contrasts: from the mass of beautiful, fragrant, urn-shaped flowers, delicately suspended at the end of its branches in spring, to its flaming red autumn foliage. To make the best of enkianthus, plant it among pieris and rhododendrons, with hellebores in the foreground. Alternatively, use it to create attractive, fragrant underplanting by combining it with tree peonies, *Lilium regale* and foxgloves against a background of rhododendrons.

Useful hints

— Plant in autumn or spring, in a cool, shady spot.

— Enkianthus likes acid soil, lightened with leaf-mould or peat.

Enkianthus cernuus f. *rubens* ▷

— Mulch every spring with forest bark or peat.

— Water regularly in summer and remove withered leaves (don't leave them on the tree).

Recommended

— *Enkianthus campanulatus* is the best-known species. It has red shoots and dull green leaves. It produces beautiful clusters of pendent, white, urn-shaped flowers in spring and has red and yellow foliage in autumn.

— *E. campanulatus* var. *palibinii* is a rare variety of *E. campanulatus* with red flowers.

— *E. cernuus* f. *rubens* has deep red, urn-shaped flowers. Its denser clusters of dull green leaves turn reddish purple in autumn.

— *E. chinensis* has yellow and red flowers, veined with deep red.

— *E. perulatus* is probably the best-known. It is a slow-growing shrub which produces umbels of pendent white flowers in spring and has bright red autumn foliage. It grows to approximately 1.5 m (5 ft) in height.

Height: 1–2 m (3¼–6½ ft).
Soil: acid, not too wet in winter.
Aspect: semi-shade.
Propagation: difficult; by layering or from cuttings in summer.
Flowering season: spring.
Type: deciduous shrub.

▽ **Embothrium coccineum**

▽ **Enkianthus campanulatus**

▽ **Enkianthus cernuus f. rubens**

319

Erica

HEATHER

Ericaceae

Callunas, daboecias and ericas are all heathers. We have grouped them here according to flowering season, as some flower in spring, some in summer and some in autumn. Some even flower in winter.

They are all evergreens and nearly all like acid soil, also appropriately known as heathland in some areas, but there are a number of varieties that tolerate slightly alkaline soil.

The callunas are very undemanding. In their wild state they grow on heathland and in forests, which means they will tolerate both sun and semi-shade. However, they do require light, sandy, acid soil. On the Scottish moors, *Calluna vulgaris alba*, a white heather, is much sought after as a good-luck charm, rather like a four-leaf clover.

Daboecias also require an acid soil but are not as hardy. They produce red flowers in spring and summer.

Ericas are the hardiest and most varied of the heathers. They flower mainly in spring and summer and come in a wide range of different colours. They all grow well in a good garden soil, some in alkaline soil, with a little peat added.

By combining the three kinds, you can create a garden which has flowering heathers for twelve months of the year! Their different colours also blend beautifully with small conifers, brooms, ferns, potentillas, small hollies, silybum and berberis to create permanent planting combinations. The trees that look best with heathers are conifers, birches and Japanese cedars.

Useful hints

— Plant callunas, daboecias and ericas in autumn or spring, in sandy soil that remains slightly cool during the summer. For chalk-tolerant varieties, improve garden soil with peat.

— Lightly trim off the dead flowers with secateurs or shears as soon as they have finished flowering. This will ensure that the clumps remain dense. New growth will soon appear.

— Weed during the first year or so. Once the heathers are established, they will cover the ground and prevent weeds growing.

Recommended for acid soil

Summer- and autumn-flowering varieties

— *Calluna vulgaris* (common heather). 'Alba Elata' is a free-flowering, bushy plant with white flowers.

— 'Alportii' is a tall, erect bush which produces a mass of crimson flowers against its abundant foliage.

— 'Beechwood Crimson' produces crimson flowers against dark green foliage.

— 'Carole Chapman' has white flowers against lemon-yellow foliage in spring, turning to yellowish green in summer.

— 'County Wicklow' has a mass of double pink flowers against dark green foliage. It has long, branching stems, so pruning is essential.

— 'Elsie Purnell' is a beautiful plant with grey-green foliage and double, lilac-pink flowers borne on long stems.

— 'Flore Pleno' produces double, lilac-pink flowers on long stems. Its elegant habit makes it one of the best varieties.

— 'Gold Haze' has white flowers on beautiful golden foliage.

— 'Hirsuta Albiflora' produces white flowers on grey-green foliage. It makes very good ground cover.

— 'Oxshott Common' is a vigorous plant which produces a mass of mauve flowers. Plant in groups to show off its silver-grey foliage to the best advantage.

— 'Peter Sparkes' produces double, salmon-pink flowers against grey-green foliage. It has a very branching habit.

— 'Ralph Purnell' is a strong-growing plant with lilac-pink flowers.

— 'Summer Orange' has orange foliage in summer, turning darker in winter, and lilac-pink flowers.

— *Erica cinerea* (bell heather) has a long flowering season, throughout summer and autumn. It has a number of attractive cultivars.

— 'Alba Minor' is a dwarf variety and the most compact of the white heathers.

— The bright purple flowers of 'Atro-purpurea' provide a striking contrast against its dark green foliage.

— 'Josephine Ross' makes very good

Erica arborea ▷

ground cover and produces a mass of deep salmon-pink flowers.

— The flowers of 'Miss Waters' are white when they first open, turning to purple during the summer and autumn. It has dark green foliage.

— 'Pink Ice' makes good ground cover. It has clear, pale pink flowers and bronze-green foliage.

— 'Plummer's Seedling' produces a mass of deep red flowers.

— 'P.S. Patrick', with its erect habit and purple flowers, is one of the hardier varieties.

— 'Rosabella' makes ideal ground cover with its attractive purplish red flowers and dark green foliage.

— 'Rose Queen' is a vigorous, bushy plant which produces a profusion of purplish red flowers.

— 'Rosea' has deep purple-red flowers against dark green foliage.

— 'Ruby' is a very free-flowering variety and produces a mass of rose-purple flowers.

— *Erica tetralix* 'Pink Star' is a low bush with star-like pink flowers on soft grey foliage.

Autumn-flowering varieties

— *Calluna vulgaris* 'Autumn Glow' is a beautiful, compact plant which grows to a height of 30 cm (12 in) and produces pink flowers.

— 'Battle of Arnhem' has an erect habit, reaching a height of 60 cm (24 in), and produces purple flowers.

— 'Finale' is a vigorous plant with dark green foliage and pale mauve flowers.

— 'Hibernica' is a low bushy plant with grey-green foliage and mauve flowers.

— 'Hiemalis' has an erect habit and late-blooming, purple flowers which continue well into winter.

Spring-flowering varieties

— *Daboecia × scotica* 'William Buchanan' is a vigorous plant with large deep purple flowers.

— The branches of *Erica × veitchii* 'Exeter', a tree heath, often bend under the weight of its strongly scented, white flowers. It is a very hardy variety.

— 'Pink Joy' has deep pink buds which open into pale pink flowers.

321

Recommended for all soil types and slightly alkaline soil

Spring-flowering varieties

— *Erica arborea* (tree heath). The heathers in this group are among the few which flower throughout the spring and into summer. They are hardy and will tolerate garden soil provided it is not too heavy and has been lightened with sand. In their natural habitat (Spain, for example) the 'tree heath' can reach a height of 4 m (13 ft) and produce a real tree trunk. Elsewhere we have to be satisfied with a height of 1.5 m (5 ft). Prune the upper branches to maintain a uniform length and produce a compact tree.

— *E. arborea* var. *alpina* has slightly scented, white flowers. It is very hardy and one of the best shrub heathers to grow in the garden.

Winter-flowering varieties

— *Erica carnea* 'Snow Queen' grows in small clumps with slightly pendent branches. It has pure white flowers and dark green foliage.

— 'Early Red' produces a mass of deep red flowers in autumn and winter.

— 'King George' has deep pink flowers, turning to crimson as they age, and dark green foliage. It is a hardy plant that will thrive in any climate.

— 'Loughrigg' is a very hardy plant with salmon-pink flowers. Its dark green foliage turns to bronze in winter.

— 'Sunshine Rambler' has clear yellow foliage and pink flowers.

— The slow-growing *Erica* × *darleyensis* 'Jack H. Brummage' is a beautiful plant, especially if planted in rich soil. If planted in acid soil, its deep pink flowers will be fairly insignificant. Its foliage varies with the seasons, from pale yellow to bronze.

Winter- and spring-flowering varieties

— *Erica carnea* 'December Red' produces a mass of rose-red flowers.

— 'March Seedling' has a neat habit and a profusion of rose-purple flowers.

— 'Myretoun Ruby' has dark green foliage and deep purple-red flowers.

— 'Pink Spangles' is a vigorous plant with two-tone (shell-pink and deeper pink), bell-shaped flowers.

— 'Springwood White' is a real gem, with pure white flowers and beautiful apple-green foliage.

— *Erica* × *darleyensis* 'Ghost Hills' is a vigorous, spreading plant with pink flowers.

— 'Arthur Johnson' has small, lilac-pink flowers.

— 'Margaret Porter' is a bushy plant with lilac-pink flowers.

— 'J.W. Porter' has beautiful bright red shoots in spring.

— 'Silberschmelze' spreads vigorously in all directions and produces beautiful white flowers in winter.

— *Erica erigena* 'W.T. Rackliff' is a beautiful plant with an erect habit. It produces white flowers against an abundance of deep green foliage.

Summer- and autumn-flowering varieties

— *Erica vagans* (Cornish heath). 'Birch Glow' has glowing rose-pink flowers.

— 'Carnea' has pale pink flowers.

— 'Cream' is a late-flowering variety with a neat, vigorous habit. It produces long stems of white flowers.

— 'Fiddlestone' has rose-cerise flowers which can become paler pink in colour, depending on growing conditions.

— 'Lyonesse' has dark green foliage and white flowers with brown anthers.

— 'Mrs D.F. Maxwell', with its deep cerise flowers with dark brown stamens, is probably one of the most beautiful cultivars.

— 'Pyrenees Pink' has attractive pink flowers.

— 'St Keverne' has rose-pink flowers, tinged white, and brown anthers and can be used as a hedge.

— 'Viridiflora' has green bracts instead of flowers.

— 'White Pocket' is a vigorous plant with long stems of white flowers.

Height: 20 cm–1.5 m (8 in–5 ft).
Soil: acid or non-acid, depending on species and variety, but always lightened with sand and peat.
Aspect: sun.
Propagation: from cuttings in summer.
Flowering season: varies according to species and variety. Flowering heathers last for a long time indoors and can be used as cut flowers.
Type: evergreen shrub.

Erica carnea ▷

△ *Eriobotrya japonica*

△ *Escallonia* 'Apple Blossom'
◁ *Erythrina crista-galli*

Eriobotrya

LOQUAT

Rosaceae

This slow-growing tree with its spreading, umbrella-shaped habit is a native of the Far East, where it reaches heights of over 6 m (20 ft). Although it doesn't like cold conditions, this rare, exotic-looking tree can be planted in milder regions in the garden or in a container on the patio, as long as it is in a sunny, well-protected position. It has elegant foliage, consisting of large, thick, glossy, oblong leaves, and produces white flowers intermittently from autumn through to spring after a particularly hot summer.

Useful hints

— Plant in ordinary, slightly moist garden soil in full sun and always with wall protection.

— Prune, if necessary, in spring. Feed with bonemeal at the same time, raking it in well around the tree.

Recommended

— *Eriobotrya japonica* (loquat) is an attractive species. Its leaves are veined and glossy on the surface and downy on the underside. It has tiny flowers that smell of bitter almonds, and yellowish orange fruits that look like tiny pears.

Height: 6 m (20 ft).
Soil: ordinary.
Aspect: full sun.
Propagation: from seed in spring, or cuttings in late summer or autumn.
Flowering season: autumn to spring.
Type: evergreen tree.

Erythrina

CORAL TREE

Leguminosae

Outside its native South America, this shrub behaves like a perennial, dying down in winter and sending up new shoots from its woody roots in spring. Its prickly stems grow quickly, producing tough, trifoliolate leaves. Spectacular scarlet flowers are borne on the end of the stems in spring and summer.

Useful hints

— Fortunately, this tropical plant will regenerate from its roots each year provided they are well protected during the winter. Cut it back with the first frosts and cover the roots with straw. In colder regions it may be necessary to treat the plant like a dahlia, i.e. dig up the root-stock and store it indoors. It can be replanted in spring after the last heavy frosts.

— Give it a position in full sun and well protected from the wind.

— Water regularly to ensure a good display of flowers.

Recommended

— *Erythrina bidwilli* has racemes of bright red flowers in summer.

— *E. coralloides* (coral tree) has prickly stems and red pea-like flowers borne before the leaves appear in early spring.

— *E. crista-galli* (cockspur coral tree) can be grown in open ground and produces a spectacular display of crimson flowers, rather like sweet peas.

Height: 1–2 m (3¼–6½ ft).
Soil: humus-rich.
Aspect: full sun, protected.
Propagation: from seed and cuttings.
Flowering season: spring and summer.
Type: deciduous tree.

Escallonia

ESCALLONIA

Escalloniaceae

If you live in a region that doesn't suffer from heavy frosts, escallonia makes a beautiful free-flowering, glossy, evergreen hedge that grows to a height of 1.5 m (5 ft). It does particularly well near the sea, in sunny positions. In other locations it needs to be in a sunny position with wall protection against strong winds. It produces tiny, exotic-looking flowers in the form of purplish pink, white or bright red trumpets. It goes well with *Geranium endressii*.

Useful hints

— Beware of cold winters.

— Plant in spring and prune back hard in the first year to promote vigorous growth.

— Mulch and water well during the summer.

Recommended

— *Escallonia × exoniensis* is the largest variety and grows to a height of 5 m (16 ft). It has pendent branches and pinkish white flowers.

— *E.* 'Iveyi' is a vigorous hybrid with an erect habit. It has glossy, dark green foliage and pure white flowers.

— *E. rubra* var. *macrantha* is the most vigorous variety as well as the most decorative, with its abundance of dark green foliage and bright rose-crimson flowers. It makes a superb hedge.

— *E. rubra* itself has large, aromatic, evergreen leaves (which release their

▽ *Escallonia* hybrid

△ *Eucalyptus pauciflora*

fragrance when crushed) and deep red flowers. It makes an ideal windbreak in coastal regions. The variety 'Crimson Spire' has brilliant red flowers throughout the summer.

— Nurseries now offer many good hybrids, including 'Apple Blossom' (pink and white), 'Donard Beauty' (deep pink), 'Donard Seedling' (white flushed with pale pink), and 'Donard Star' (a large-leaved hybrid with large, pink flowers).

Height: 2–5 m (6½–16 ft).
Soil: ordinary, even slightly chalky, and dry in summer.
Aspect: sun.
Propagation: from cuttings in summer or autumn, but winter them under a cold frame.
Flowering season: summer to autumn.
Type: semi-evergreen or evergreen shrub.

Eucalyptus

EUCALYPTUS, GUM TREE

Myrtaceae

Although the eucalyptus is a native of Australia, some European specimens grow to a height of 50 m (160 ft), with the tallest on record (in 1888) reaching 80 m (260 ft)! Although one of the attractions of these beautiful trees is that they are particularly fast-growing – between 1–1.5 m (3–5 ft) per year – their main charm is their aromatic foliage. They can be cut back hard each year to promote strong foliage growth, but this does not prevent them growing their statutory 1.5 m (5 ft) in the year. Pruning maintains a 'shrubby' shape, but, if left unpruned, they will start to produce tufts of fragrant, white flowers after four years.

△ **Eucalyptus pauciflora** ssp. **niphophila**

▽ **Eucalyptus gunnii**

Useful hints

— Eucalyptus are sensitive to cold and should be grown only in milder regions, where they will thrive. There are some hardy varieties, such as *Eucalyptus gunnii*, but even with these it is advisable to plant them where they are sheltered from the wind.

— If you are growing eucalyptus for its silvery foliage, which is very popular for flower arrangements, prune only in spring, once the risk of frost has passed.

Eucalyptus ▷

326

△ *Eucalyptus gunnii*

△ *Eucryphia* hybrid

variety with a more twisted habit. It has an attractive patchwork bark and silvery white leaves.

Height: 2.5–50 m (8–160 ft) . . . and much taller in their country of origin!
Soil: any.
Aspect: sun.
Propagation: from seed.
Flowering season: winter.
Type: evergreen tree.

Eucryphia

EUCRYPHIA

Eucryphiaceae

This large shrub can make an extremely decorative tree. All euchryphias are evergreen except *Eucryphia glutinosa*. They prefer temperate, frost-free climates. Flowers are produced towards the end of summer.

Useful hints

— Buy a small eucryphia in a container and plant it without disturbing the root ball.

— Plant it at the end of spring, after the last frosts, and protect with a mulch during its first winter.

— Plant it in sun or semi-shade and sheltered from the wind, in fertile, acid soil enriched with peat.

— Remove dead and damaged branches in spring. Your efforts will be rewarded as the eucryphia produces a mass of beautiful white flowers in

Recommended

— *E. coccifera* (Tasmanian snow gum) has white and grey patchwork bark and silver-grey foliage.

— *E. dalrympleana* (mountain gum) has cream, brown and silver bark and bronze-green foliage. It has distinctive, long, pendulous leaves.

— *E. gunnii* (cider gum) is a hardier variety, especially if grown as a shrub. It has small, sage-green leaves, silvery blue when young.

— *E. pauciflora* ssp. *niphophila* (snow gum) is a smaller, relatively slow-growing

summer. It is not suited to cold regions and is difficult to propagate (layering tends to be the best method).

Recommended

— *E. cordifolia* is a vigorous, fast-growing, columnar tree which reaches a height of 3 m (10 ft) if not affected by frost. Large, rose-like, white flowers (up to 6 cm (2½ in) in diameter), with golden anthers, appear from summer to autumn. It can tolerate a slightly chalky soil.

— *E. glutinosa* can grow to a height of 5 m (16 ft). Its evergreen or semi-evergreen foliage has attractive autumn tints. Its hybrid *E.* × *nymansensis* is an autumn-flowering, evergreen variety.

— The best-known cultivar of *E.* × *nymansensis* is 'Nymansay', with its dark green foliage and flowers which are over 5 cm (2 in) in diameter.

— *E.* × *intermedia* 'Rostrevor' produces fragrant, white, yellow-centred flowers on gracefully pendent branches.

— *E. lucida* has glossy dark green leaves and fragrant white flowers in summer. It grows to about 5 m (16 ft).

— *E. milliganii* is an upright shrub, growing to 3 m (10 ft), with small white flowers and bluish-white undersides to the leaves.

Height: 2–5 m (6½–16 ft).
Soil: acid.
Aspect: sun or semi-shade.
Propagation: by layering.
Flowering season: summer to autumn.
Type: deciduous or evergreen shrub or tree.

Euonymus

SPINDLE TREE

Celastraceae

The euonymus is as attractive in winter as it is in summer, and looks just as good on a rock garden as in a border. Although often represented by the evergreens of *Euonymus japonicus*, there are many more besides. There are deciduous species, and species with flamboyant autumn colour or unusually shaped pink or orange fruits. Euonymus spreads vigorously, and it is wise to leave space between it and neighbouring plants.

Useful hints

— Plant in spring and prune immediately to obtain dense shrubs.

— Mulch with forest bark or peat every spring, and water *E. alatus* generously in summer.

— Watch out for cochineal insects on evergreen varieties and treat as appropriate.

Recommended

Deciduous varieties

— *E. alatus* has an open, almost geometric habit. It has corky wings on its branchlets and its broad leaves turn bright red in autumn.

— *E. alatus* 'Compactus' rarely grows above 1.5 m (5 ft).

— *E. europaeus* (spindle) creates a colourful, hardy hedge which reaches a height of 3–4 m (10–13 ft). 'Red Cascade' is literally weighed down with its fruit. It looks best at the back of a border of asters and Japanese anemones.

Evergreen varieties

— *E. fortunei* is a spreading shrub whose branches can be as much as 5 m (16 ft) long! This is why it is so widely used today as ground cover. It has a number of variegated cultivars. 'Emerald 'n' Gold', marked with yellow turning to pink in winter, and the golden carpet of 'Golden Prince' are among the best-known. The extremely compact 'Silver Queen' has white markings on its foliage. The drier the soil, the more purple 'Coloratus' becomes in autumn, although it reverts to green the following spring.

— *E. japonicus* (Japanese spindle) grows to a height of 5–6 m (16–20 ft). It was used as hedging in the early twentieth century as it is very tolerant of shade. It has a number of variegated varieties and thrives in coastal regions. However, as well as being affected by cochineal insect and vine mildew, it freezes at ground level during severe winters. 'Microphyllus Albovariegatus' creates a softer effect in borders.

— *E. phellomanus* is a vigorous variety. It has flamboyant autumn foliage, corky-winged stems and pink fruits.

— *E. planipes* (syn. *E. sachalinensis*) can grow to a height of 5 m (16 ft) and makes a good single specimen, if only for its flamboyant red and orange autumn foliage and abundance of pink or red fruits.

Height: 60 cm–6 m (24 in–20 ft).
Soil: ordinary but well-dug.
Aspect: any.
Propagation: from cuttings in summer.
Flowering season: fragrant, unobtrusive flowers in spring.
Type: deciduous or evergreen shrub.

△ *Euonymus fortunei*
▽ *Euonymus fortunei* 'Variegatus'

Euryops

EURYOPS

Compositae

This attractive evergreen shrub is ideal for containers. Although a native of South Africa, it tolerates European winters quite well if planted in a well-drained, sunny spot. It will thrive in a sheltered corner of a rock garden, where it will produce a mat of greenery dotted with bright yellow, daisy-like flowers in summer. It is set off to advantage by a dark-coloured conifer, such as a yew or a silver pine. Alternatively, plant it among other native African plants such as rhodohypoxis.

▽ *Euonymus europaeus*

Useful hints

— Euryops is best planted in the spring.

— Plant in well-drained soil and cover with a thin layer of gravel to keep the neck of the plant free from damp.

— Every spring, add leaf-mould to the centre of the clump to encourage rooting.

— Cuttings, taken in summer, root well in sand, but should be overwintered in a cold frame.

Recommended

— *Euryops acraeus*, with fine, narrow, silver foliage, produces a mass of canary-yellow daisy-like flowers in early summer.

— *E. pectinatus* produces bright yellow flowers in early summer.

Height: 25 cm (10 in).
Soil: well-drained.
Aspect: sun.
Propagation: from cuttings in summer.
Flowering season: summer.
Type: evergreen shrub.

Exochorda

PEARLBUSH

Rosaceae

The fine, closely packed, soft green foliage of this easily grown shrub is covered with snowflake-like flowers in spring. Although it grows equally well in semi-shade or sun, its flowers last longer if it is planted in a shady corner. Exochorda does not flower for very long, but its flowers are spectacular while they last. It needs room to spread. The genus comes from north-east Asia and contains some of the most beautiful white-flowered shrubs.

Useful hints

— Plant in autumn or spring, in soil which is not too chalky, otherwise its leaves will turn yellow.

— Prune after flowering and remove any weak or badly placed branches.

Recommended

— *Exochorda giraldii* is a widely arching shrub with upright racemes of large white flowers in spring. The leaves are pinkish green when young.

— *E. korolkowii* comes from Turkestan, where it grows at high altitudes, so it is very hardy. Its white flowers are smaller than the other species.

— *E. macrantha* 'The Bride' is a very popular variety which grows well in sun or semi-shade. It makes a dense, arching shrub that forms a mound of branches. It has dark green foliage and large white flowers in spring and early summer.

— *E. racemosa* is a hardy variety which has upright clusters of large, long-stemmed flowers. Its leaves are a blue-green colour.

Height: 2–3 m (6½–10 ft).
Soil: chalk-free, light.
Aspect: preferably shady.
Propagation: from cuttings or by layering in summer, in a cold frame, or from suckers.
Flowering season: spring to summer.
Type: deciduous shrub.

Fabiana

FABIANA

Solanaceae

From a distance it is easy to confuse fabiana with a shrubby heather, as it has the same erect, delicate habit. Its branches are densely covered with slightly sticky evergreen leaves and, in summer, with a mass of tubular, pinkish white flowers which give the plant a plume-like appearance.

Useful hints

— Fabiana thrives in moist, mild climates. It tolerates sea spray so is happy in coastal areas, and does well in gardens near the sea if given a sheltered, south-facing position.

— It prefers a sheltered, sunny site. It can be damaged by frost in hard winters but is relatively hardy in mild ones.

— It grows in all types of soil except very chalky.

— Remove damaged branches when it has finished flowering.

Recommended

— *Fabiana imbricata* is the most popular species. It has tiny, heather-like, deep green leaves and a profusion of tubular white flowers in early summer.

— *F. imbricata* 'Prostrata' is smaller and hardier than the typical form, with pale mauve-tinted flowers borne in profusion in early summer.

— *F. imbricata* 'Violacea' is a variety that is covered with lavender-mauve flowers in spring.

Height: rarely above 2 m (6½ ft).
Soil: chalk-free.
Aspect: sun but a moist climate.
Propagation: cuttings in summer.
Flowering season: spring to early summer.
Type: evergreen shrub.

▽ *Exochorda giraldii* var. *wilsonii*

▽ *Fabiana imbricata*

▽ *Euryops acraeus*

△ *Fagus sylvatica* **Purple Group**

△ *Fagus sylvatica* 'Pendula'

Fagus

BEECH

Fagaceae

The beech is a tall tree with beautiful smooth grey bark and thick deciduous foliage. Its spreading habit gives generous shade. In a forest or woodland environment, it grows straight up towards the light and only starts spreading its branches 2–3 m (6½–10 ft) above the ground. Its pale green foliage becomes tinged with ochre, red and bronze in autumn. Along with the oak and conifers, the beech is one of the most commonly found trees in the forests of Europe. Its beautiful, hard wood is used in carpentry and also makes excellent firewood.

Useful hints

— This impressive tree thrives in any type of soil, although it doesn't like heavy clay or water-logged soil.

— It doesn't like heat and prefers cool climates.

— Although fairly slow-growing, it has the advantage of being able to be pruned into hedges or for the shrubbery. It is very long-lived.

— When planting, don't disturb the root ball.

Recommended

— *Fagus grandifolia* (American beech) reaches a height of 20–30 m (65–95 ft) in its country of origin, where it is grown as an ornamental tree for its fine, blue-grey bark and silky blue-green foliage.

— *F. sylvatica* (common beech), which grows to a height of 35 m (110 ft), is found in the beechwoods and mountains (up to altitudes of 1,900 m/5,600 feet) of Europe. It keeps its leaves for much longer than *F. grandifolia* and has a number of named cultivars:

— The superb habit of *F. sylvatica* Purple Group (purple beech) makes it ideal for planting as a single specimen.

— *F. sylvatica* 'Dawyck' is a tall, columnar tree with rich autumn foliage.

— *F. sylvatica* 'Pendula' (weeping beech) has a weeping habit, and *F. s.* 'Purpurea Pendula' (weeping purple beech) has a weeping habit and magnificent purple leaves.

— *F. sylvatica* 'Red Obelisk' is a tall, columnar tree with purple foliage.

— *F. sylvatica* 'Rohanii' has deeply cut leaves which turn purple in autumn. It doesn't grow above 6 m (20 ft).

— The twisted, contorted branches of *F. sylvatica* f. *tortuosa* are very different from those of the typical form.

— *F. sylvatica* 'Tricolor' is less vigorous, has a spreading habit and grows to a height of 5–6 m (16–20 ft). Its purple leaves are marked with cream and pink-tinged around the rim, especially in spring.

△ ▽ ▷ *Fagus sylvatica*

— *F. sylvatica* var. *heterophylla* 'Aspleni-ifolia' has a broad, branching base.

Height: 20–35 m (65–110 ft).
Soil: any, except heavy clay or marshy soil.
Aspect: sun or semi-shade.
Propagation: from seed in autumn or spring (after storing between layers of soil or sand).
Type: deciduous tree.

Fargesia

see *Arundinaria*

Fatsia

FATSIA

Araliaceae

Much hardier than is generally supposed, this magnificent evergreen shrub is not as popular as it should be. Its wide leaves, which are thick and lobed, and its spherical flowers, which look like large yellowish white pompons, give it a very unusual appearance. Its flowering season is a long one, lasting from early summer to mid-autumn. The black, rounded fruits are also highly decorative.

Useful hints

— The fatsia thrives in fertile, well-drained soil, which should be enriched with leaf-mould.

— Protect the shrub from the wind. While it is young, it is advisable to bring it inside, under cover, during the winter. Later, if the winter is harsh, the stump should be protected with straw or peat. This shrub grows well indoors. From mid-spring, put it out on the verandah or on the patio.

Recommended

— *Fatsia japonica* (Japanese fatsia) has huge palmate leaves that are bright dark green in colour. An excellent choice for a seaside garden.

— *F. japonica* 'Moseri' is hardier, and therefore more suited to inland gardens.
Height: 1.5 m (5 ft).
Soil: fertile, well-drained.
Aspect: semi-shade, in a sheltered spot.
Propagation: from seed, when very ripe, or cuttings in summer.
Flowering season: summer and autumn.
Type: evergreen shrub.

△ *Feijoa sellowiana*

Feijoa (syn. Acca)

FEIJOA

Myrtaceae

The feijoa is an evergreen shrub of great decorative value which ought to be cultivated more often – though being a tropical plant, it will thrive only in very mild climates or in a conservatory. Its pretty pinkish flowers on large sprays of purple stems are exceptionally beautiful, appearing in summer on the previous year's branches.

Useful hints

— Plant the feijoa at the bottom of a wall, in a sheltered, sunny spot. In winter, protect with straw.

— In cooler climates, it should be taken indoors or placed in the greenhouse during the winter.

Recommended

— *Feijoa sellowiana* (syn. *Acca sellowiana*). There are many varieties with large fruits, including 'Coolidge', 'Mammoth' and 'Triumph'.
Height: more than 5 m (16 ft) in its native habitat but elsewhere rarely more than 2 m (6½ ft).
Soil: good garden soil.
Aspect: sun, sheltered position.
Propagation: from cuttings.
Flowering season: early to mid-summer.
Type: evergreen shrub.

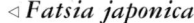
◁ *Fatsia japonica*

Forsythia

FORSYTHIA

Oleaceae

This is the best-known and most frequently planted shrub of all. It is like the first burst of spring sunshine in the garden and appears at the same time as daffodils and jonquils. It should not be planted in isolation, for example on a lawn, because once it has flowered, all that is left is a sad, stunted shrub which is of no decorative value for several months. Site it at the back of a border, as part of a mixed group of plants, or train it against a sunny wall where it will form a golden drape that will brighten up the entire garden.

Useful hints

— Forsythias are virtually foolproof. They may be planted in any season, even during the flowering period, providing they are watered abundantly, especially during early summer. Plant some white narcissi close by. It is even possible to grow a small-flowered variety of clematis among its branches.

— Prune just after flowering, by trimming the secondary branches a few centimetres from the stem. Forsythias with supple and drooping branches flower very well without a lot of pruning being necessary. However, those with very stiff stems should be left to grow, to enable them to lose some of their artificial appearance. Do not cut into the main stem, as this is where the new growth will come from.

Recommended

— *Forsythia × intermedia* is vigorous and bushy. Among its most beautiful cultivars are: 'Beatrix Farrand', erect, with large canary-yellow flowers; 'Karl Sax', with large, deep yellow flowers; 'Lynwood', which flowers all along the stems; 'Spectabilis', one of the most popular varieties because of its intensely dramatic flowering; and 'Spring Glory', which flowers earlier than the others. A new variety, 'Minigold', is interesting because of its large, deep yellow flowers that are lightly veined with green, contrasting effectively against the dark green foliage.

— As a companion to other early shrubs such as *Rhododendron praecox*, with which it will blend well, a good choice is *F. ovata*, which flowers from early spring onwards. It has toothed dark green leaves and bright yellow flowers. Cultivars include 'Ottawa', very upright with abundant flowers, and 'Spring Glory', with bright green leaves and pale yellow flowers.

— *F. suspensa* is a very supple variety, which makes it suitable for training along a trellis. It flowers from early spring.

Height: 1.5–3 m (5–10 ft).
Soil: any.
Aspect: sun or semi-shade.
Propagation: from cuttings in autumn.
Flowering season: early to mid-spring.
Type: deciduous shrub.

◁▽ **Forsythia × intermedia**

△ *Fothergilla gardenii*

Fothergilla

FOTHERGILLA

Hamamelidaceae

This elegant, highly fragrant American shrub is not as popular as it should be. At the very beginning of spring, before the leaves appear, it flowers in yellow or white spikes. The flowers are stiff, oval, light green above and paler green on the underside, with marked veining. They take on very rich colours in the autumn. Fothergilla needs a humus-rich neutral or acid soil and prefers semi-shade to full sun. It thrives best planted on its own, or surrounded by deciduous azaleas.

Useful hints

— Plant fothergilla in semi-shade for preference, or in a sunny spot but avoiding full scorching sunlight. It needs a neutral to acid soil improved by equal parts of sand and peat.

— Do not prune, but remove the branches that crowd the middle of the shrub if necessary.

Recommended

— *Fothergilla gardenii* (witch alder), the smallest of all, barely reaches 60 cm (24 in) in height.

— *F. major* (syn. *F. monticola*) reaches a height of 2 m (6¼ ft). Its dark green foliage turns a shining red and gold in autumn. The white, scented flowers appear in mid-spring, before the leaves.

Height: 60 cm–2 m (24 in–6 ft).
Soil: neutral or acid.
Aspect: semi-shade.
Propagation: from seeds or by layering.
Flowering season: early to mid-spring.
Type: deciduous shrub.

Fraxinus

ASH

Oleaceae

As well as from its rapid growth, this tree has a further advantage in that it is not fussy as to the type of soil it grows in. It makes a cool shade beneath its delicate and deciduous foliage. In nature, the ash can reach a height of 40 m (130 ft) and more (20 m/65 ft when cultivated), and can form a decorative screen at the bottom of a garden or against a dividing garden wall. The best choice for this is a flowering ash, which is also appealing for its fragrance. The ash exudes a sugary substance which used to be used medicinally.

Useful hints

— The ash grows in any soil and is not fussy about climate.

— Prune at the end of winter, in order to achieve the desired shape. Afterwards, any redundant spring shoots in the middle of the tree can be removed.

Recommended

— *Fraxinus americana* (white ash) is a vigorous tree which reaches a height of 30 m (95 ft); its buds appear late and its leaflets, greyish on the underside, are shorter and wider.

— *F. angustifolia* 'Raywood' (narrow-leaved ash) grows quickly; it takes on a lilac tint in the autumn and thrives well in dry or chalky soil.

△ △ *Fraxinus excelsior* 'Pendula'

— *F. excelsior* (common ash) is the best-known ash and the one which is being replanted in European forests. Very robust, it also grows spontaneously in some mountainous regions. Its flowers bloom on the branches before the leaves appear, giving it a very decorative appearance.

— *F. excelsior* 'Diversifolia'. This variety differs from the species by its leaves, which have two leaflets at the base. The leaves of 'Jaspidea' lighten to yellow from summer onwards: in autumn they turn a highly luminous shade of pale yellow; winter shoots are yellow.

— *F. excelsior* 'Pendula' does not exceed 3–5 m (6–16 ft). Its branches become so arched, almost to the ground, that by pruning just a little it is easy to construct a summer shelter under its foliage.

— *F. excelsior* 'Westhof's Glory' grows to a height of 35 m (110 ft), and its leaves have a brown tint before turning a glossy dark green.

— *F. floribunda*, with its panicles of white flowers, is ideal for smaller gardens: it never grows more than 12 m (40 ft).

— *F. ornus* (manna ash) is also a small species. Its abundant, highly scented flowers in late spring and early summer make it a very popular tree, magnificent for decorating the corner of a lawn. It barely exceeds 8 m (26 ft).

— *F. oxycarpa* 'Raywood' (claret ash) is a rigorous and spreading tree. Its dark green leaves turn reddish purple in autumn. It grows to 20 m (65 ft).

Height: 3–20m (10–65 ft) when cultivated; up to 40m (130 ft) in its native habitat.
Soil: any.
Aspect: any.
Propagation: from seed.
Flowering season: late spring to early summer.
Type: deciduous tree.

Fremontodendron

FREMONTIA, FLANNEL BUSH

Sterculiaceae

The fremontodendron is a very interesting and attractive shrub, and one which most collectors will want in their garden at some point. It is semi-evergreen, and can reach a height of 5 m (16 ft). The leaves are trilobate and pale green above. It has yellow flowers throughout the summer. The fremontodendron comes from the USA and was used by early settlers to line footwear – hence its common name of flannel bush.

Useful hints

— The fremontodendron needs a mild climate, where there is little likelihood of severe frost. It likes to be sheltered by a south-facing wall. Protect it with straw during the coldest winter months.

— Fremontodendrons do not last long, but as it is easy to gather their seeds and sow them, the shrub can easily be propagated.

Recommended

— *Fremontodendron californicum* and *F. mexicanum*. The latter is distinguishable from the former by its leaves and its less imposing size. However, the hybrid of these two, 'California Glory', flowers much more abundantly and is hardier, so is the most frequently cultivated.

Height: usually 3 m (10 ft).
Soil: all types of light soil, preferably chalky.
Aspect: sun.
Propagation: from seed, cuttings or by layering.
Flowering season: summer.
Type: semi-evergreen shrub.

◁▽ *Fremontodendron californicum*

Fuchsia

FUCHSIA

Onagraceae

Having rather fallen from favour, fuchsias are now back in fashion. These shrubs are perfect for shaded corners of the garden. Their delicate, intensely coloured flowers, shaped like drop earrings or little bells, stand out particularly effectively either against a background of greenery or as a dense mass on their own. To train as a standard, choose a bushy variety and grow it in a container, removing the small side branches as far as 50 cm (20 in) up the stem as the shoots appear. After this, pinch out the shoots several times until the plant is the required shape.

Useful hints

— In mild climates, wait until midspring before planting fuchsias outside. In colder climates, plant out in late spring. Fuchsias require frequent watering during very hot weather. Put a mulch of some peat or pine bark round the plants in summer.

— Apply liquid fertilizer each month during the summer. If tiny white flies fly up at a gentle touch of the leaves, treat with a systemic insecticide – or take preventive action by spraying the plants before pests are seen, which needs to be done early in the summer.

— When the frosts start, move the fuchsias into a cold greenhouse. Some hardy varieties may be protected where they stand. These should be cut down to ground level, then covered with straw and a sheet of plastic to prevent excessive moisture around the plant.

Recommended

— There is not enough room here to list all the interesting fuchsia hybrids. Nurseries generally offer a wide range of the different fuchsia shapes that are available, some bushy and some pendulous, and can advise on how to display them, in beds or in pots.

— Although not totally hardy, some fuchsia hybrids such as 'Madame Cornelissen' (red and white) or 'Mrs Popple' (red and purple) display a fairly good degree of hardiness. 'Tom Thumb' is a charming dwarf variety suitable for containers.

△ *Fuchsia*

— Among the hardiest is *Fuchsia magellanica* 'Riccartonii' (lady's eardrops). This can form a splendid bush if it is not destroyed by the frost in winter (as a precaution, place straw up to 10 cm (4 in) thick around the plants). They will then grow even better in spring and will soon make bushes more than 1.5 m (5 ft) in height.

— *F. magellanica* var. *gracilis* reaches a height of 2–3 m (6½–10 ft).

— *F. magellanica* var. *gracilis* 'Variegata' has yellow-edged leaves tinged with pink, and small red and purple flowers.

— *F. magellanica* var. *molinae*. Despite its old name of 'Alba', the flowers of this fuchsia are pale pink, not white. With very green and delicate foliage, this is extremely resilient and one of the hardiest fuchsias.

— *F. magellanica* 'Versicolor', an admirable fuchsia with delicate leaves that are variegated with pink and cream, looks like a multi-coloured mist when viewed from a distance. In winter it should be protected with straw around the base. Pruned in spring, it will quickly make new shoots. It looks delightful in the semi-shade, in a corner of a border with gold-coloured flowers.

— *F. parviflora* is a prostrate variety, brightened up by hanging pink flowers, which is hardy only in mild climates.

— *F. procumbens* has the same shape as *F. parviflora*, but it is larger, hardier and has pretty yellow and purple flowers with bright blue pollen. This species suits a rock garden or hanging basket, where it will be encouraged to flower by root restriction.

Height: 20 cm–3 m (8 in–10 ft).
Soil: fresh, humus-rich.
Aspect: semi-shade.
Propagation: from cuttings in summer.
Flowering season: early summer to first frosts.
Type: deciduous shrub.

Fuchsia ▷

△ *Fuchsia magellanica* var. *gracilis*

Garrya

GARRYA, SILK-TASSEL

Garryaceae

Garryas are medium-sized shrubs reaching a height of 2–3 m (6½–10 ft), characterized by their dull green evergreen foliage and by the appearance, in winter and spring, of very long and decorative grey-green male and female catkins.

Useful hints

— Plant garryas either in front of a wall where they will create a handsome effect, or in a northerly or easterly position, in a place where they will not be exposed to gusts of wind. These shrubs are generally hardy in most mild climates.

— Buy plants in pots, at the beginning of spring, and protect them with straw, at least during the first few winters. Hard frosts will damage the catkins.

Recommended

— *Garrya elliptica* is cultivated, the other species not having the same interest.

— *G. elliptica* 'James Roof' has glossy, leathery leaves and grey-green catkins more than 20 cm (8 in) long.

Height: 2–5m (6½–16 ft), rarely more.
Soil: well-drained.
Aspect: northerly or easterly.
Propagation: from cuttings in late summer.
Flowering season: winter to spring.
Type: evergreen tree or shrub.

Gaultheria

WAXBERRY

Ericaceae

With its evergreen, attractive warm tints, this little creeping shrub makes delightful ground cover. The tiny berries are red or black, depending on the variety. The gaultheria is slow to establish itself, but within three years it forms a thick cover which requires no maintenance. Azaleas may be grown near by; gaultheria will blend well with them.

Useful hints

— Plant gaultherias in autumn or spring, in fairly acid light soil, rich in humus.

Recommended

— *Gaultheria cuneata* is a compact shrub with white flowers in summer followed by white berries in autumn.

— *G. procumbens*, the most popular, bends its white or pink flowers to the ground in late spring and summer.

— *G. shallon* reaches a height of 50 cm (20 in), with flowers that are either pink or white, and black-tinged berries.

— *G. tricophylla* has pink bell-shaped flowers in summer and egg-shaped blue berries in autumn.

Height: 15–50 cm (6–20 in).
Soil: humus-rich, acid.
Aspect: semi-shade.
Propagation: by division.
Flowering season: spring and summer.
Type: evergreen shrub.

△ *Garrya elliptica*
▽ *Gaultheria*

△ *Genista cinerea*

Genista

BROOM

Leguminosae

Brooms, all pure yellow in colour, flower in spring and summer and brighten up parts of the garden close to the house. They don't take up much room and their gentle shade enables other plants to live underneath them.

Useful hints

— Plant them in autumn, or in spring, if the garden is in an area where the winters are very cold. Lighten the soil with sand.

— Genistas dislike being pruned, so leave them alone. Gather some seeds and sow them immediately after soaking them in tepid water to soften the hard seed coat.

Recommended

— *Genista aetnensis* (Mount Etna broom) is almost a small tree, approximately 3 m (10 ft) tall, with very light flowering.

— *G. hispanica* (Spanish gorse) is a dwarf, very compact, thorny species producing a spectacular mass of yellow flowers in late spring and early summer.

— *G. lydia* is a prostrate shrub. It has long supple and arched branches, perfect for a rock garden or for containers. It flowers in late spring.

— *G. pilosa* 'Goldilocks'. This is a graceful shrub, tolerant of dry atmospheres and particularly free-flowering. It grows to a height of 60 cm (24 in). The drooping variety 'Vancouver Gold' does not exceed 20 cm (8 in) in height and can be used effectively to decorate large areas.

— *G. tinctoria* (dyers' greenweed) blooms in high summer. The variety 'Royal Gold', an upright shrub with dark green leaves, produces panicles of golden yellow flowers in summer.

Height: 20 cm–3 m (8 in–10 ft).
Soil: light, not too chalky.
Aspect: sun.
Propagation: from cuttings; or better, from seed, in summer.
Flowering season: late spring to summer.
Type: deciduous shrub.

Ginkgo

MAIDENHAIR TREE

Ginkgoaceae

There is only ones species in this genus, a primitive deciduous tree allied to the conifers. It dates from 200 million years ago, and is one of the oldest trees in the world. Its light green foliage turns golden in the winter and its small, rather unpleasant-smelling fruits are also golden. The ginkgo has unusual fan-shaped leaves that are very attractive. A word of warning, however: the tree grows very slowly during the early years.

Useful hints

— The ginkgo can spread out, so allow enough room for this.

— It is tolerant of pollution, which is surprising because it would not have been exposed to it during the 200 million years it has existed.

Recommended

— *Ginkgo biloba* (maidenhair tree). The variety 'Fastigiata' has branches that grow up in a column shape.

— *G. biloba* 'Variegata' has leaves bordered with a band of creamy white.

Height: 14 m (45 ft).
Soil: good, well-drained.
Aspect: any.
Propagation: by grafting or air layering.
Type: deciduous tree.

△ **Ginkgo biloba**

Gleditsia

HONEY LOCUST

Leguminosae

The gleditsia is an even-shaped tree that can reach a height of 5 m (16 ft). Its numerous fine branches and its terrible thorns, which even grow on the trunk, make it easily recognizable, even in deepest winter. Its deciduous foliage is very elegant, with composite, light leaves in an attractive shade of light green. It provides a pleasant shade under which rhododendrons and azaleas thrive. The green, inconspicuous flowers appear in spring. After this the tree produces fruits, large mahogany-coloured pods measuring more than 30 cm (12 in). In autumn the entire foliage takes on a beautiful yellow colour. Their thorns, which can be up to 25 cm (10 in) long, make gleditsias superb as a barrier hedge when kept pruned back.

Useful hints

— A gleditsia should be allowed plenty of room, because it thrives in full light and its elegant outline deserves to be admired from a distance.

— The hardiness of the gleditsia is unaffected by pruning and it is similarly tolerant of pollution, so much so that rows of gleditsias are often planted along city streets. For this, *Gleditsia triacanthos* 'Inermis' is the favoured variety, because it has hardly any thorns.

Recommended

— *G. caspica* (Caspian locust) reaches a height of 10 m (33 ft). The thorns are purple-black. The pods, 20 cm (8 in) long, contain six to eight seeds.

— *G. macracantha*. The top of this species is shaped like a parasol and its thorns are enormous.

— *G. triacanthos* (honey locust) can reach a height of 25 m (80 ft), and much more in its native country. Its trunk is smooth but develops cracks as the tree ages. The yellowish white flowers appear on the previous year's branches. In 'Ruby Lace' the foliage starts off purple then reverts to its normal green shade. 'Moraine' is admired for its steady growth and its large spread, ideal for creating pleasant shaded areas. 'Sunburst' has glossy fern-like foliage which is golden yellow when young; 'Skyline' has golden yellow foliage in autumn.

Height: 10–25 m (33–80 ft).
Soil: any, provided it is not too moist.
Aspect: sun or light shade.
Propagation: from seed, in early spring.
Flowering season: insignificant, in spring.
Type: deciduous tree.

Gleditsia triacanthos 'Sunburst' △
Gleditsia triacanthos 'Elegantissima' ▷
Gleditsia triacanthos ▽

△ *Grevillea banksii*
◁ *Grevillea rosmarinifolia*
▽ *Grevillea rosmarinifolia*

△ *Halesia carolina*

Grevillea

GREVILLEA, SPIDER FLOWER

Proteaceae

The stunning family Proteaceae, to which the grevillea belongs, produces trees in its native Australia with highly unusual flowers. The grevillea's flowers resemble those of the honeysuckle. Arranged in terminal clusters, they are red or yellow depending on the variety.

Useful hints

— Grevilleas thrive in acid soil and in hot countries. They are therefore best reserved for the mildest regions and the most clement climates.

— Plant them in acid, light and well-drained soil, sheltered from the wind and in a very sunny spot. In winter, protect the stump with straw or a layer of leaf-mould.

Recommended

— *Grevillea alpina* is the hardiest of all. It barely exceeds 1 m (3¼ ft) in height, and its evergreen leaves look like steel needles. The flowers are red and yellow.

— *G. juniperina* f. *sulphurea* is rather similar to the callistemon. Its yellow flowers, arranged like bottle-brushes at the tip of the branches, are present throughout summer.

— *G. rosmarinifolia* (meaning with rosemary-like leaves) is a small shrub, barely

2 m (6½ ft) tall, with superb poppy-red flowers which appear in summer.

— *G.* × *semperflorens* is less than 2 m (6½ ft) tall. Its yellow flowers, stained with pink, have a touch of green at the tip; they open out in summer.

Height: no more than 3 m (10 ft).
Soil: must be acid.
Aspect: full sun and protected from frost.
Propagation: from cuttings in summer.
Flowering season: summer.
Type: evergreen tree or shrub.

Griselinia

GRISELINIA

Cornaceae

The griselinia is a rather plain shrub with light green leathery leaves and insignificant flowers. It can be pruned to make a hedge, which makes it invaluable for coastal regions.

Useful hints

— It is not difficult to cultivate this plant in regions that have a mild climate with little likelihood of severe frost. It grows well by the sea: sea breezes and storms have little effect on its supple branches, which have tough, leathery leaves. It grows in any ordinary garden soil, and can be pruned in spring without any problems arising.

Recommended

— *Griselinia littoralis* (broadleaf) is perfect for hedges by the sea. It reaches a height of 3.5 m (11½ ft).

— *G. lucida* 'Variegata', speckled with yellow, is also cultivated. It reaches a height of 2 m (6½ ft).

Height: 2–3.5 m (6½–11½ ft).
Soil: ordinary garden soil.
Aspect: will tolerate wind.
Propagation: from cuttings in summer.
Flowering season: insignificant, in spring.
Type: evergreen shrub.

Halesia

SNOWDROP TREE

Styracaceae

A small, spreading tree or shrub which should be more frequently grown. It has charming pendent bell-shaped flowers, which appear just before the leaves. The flowers look like inverted snowdrops and are very beautiful.

Useful hints

— The halesia's only requirement is soil that is slightly acid and, if possible, sandy. It adapts very well to the cold and can be grown without difficulty in cooler climates.

— Halesias react well to a little shade. They grow well under trees, next to pieris or rhododendrons.

Recommended

— *Halesia carolina* grows to around 5.5 m (18 ft) and produces masses of bell-shaped white flowers which hang from bare shoots in spring. Winged green fruits follow.

— *H. monticola* f. *rosea*, (silver bell, snowdrop tree) is remarkable for the beauty of its white flowers, which are streaked with pink.

— *H. tetraptera*, the largest species, can reach a height of 6 m (20 ft). The flowers, in bunches of five or six, produce winged fruits.

Height: 5–6 m (16–20 ft).
Soil: deep, well-drained, sandy, acid.
Aspect: semi-shade.
Propagation: from cuttings or by layering.
Flowering season: late spring.
Type: deciduous tree or shrub.

Halimium ocymoïdes △
◁ *Halimium lasianthum* ssp. *formosum*

Halimium

HALIMIUM

Cistaceae

The halimiums are small evergreen shrubs up to 90 cm (36 in) high, good for ground cover. They are related to the rock rose. Their soft foliage is delicately silvery and blends well with the vivid flowers, which appear in spring. The petals have brown or purple spots at the base. This is a very good plant for rock gardens and for growing in pots on the verandah or patio.

Useful hints

— Plant halimiums in well-drained soil, in full sun, away from draughts.

— Do not prune other than to remove frost-damaged stems in spring.

Recommended

— *Halimium commutatum* has an erect bearing and is 60–90 cm (24–36 in) in height.

— *H. halimifolium* is a pretty little shrub with narrow grey leaves that are literally covered in bright yellow flowers in the spring; the base of each petal is decorated with a brown spot.

— *H. lasianthum* is slow-growing, with silvery grey foliage In late spring, the golden flowers, which are spotted with a darker colour at the base, open out. This species is less hardy than the previous one.

— *H. umbellatum* is fairly hardy, with white flowers arranged in clusters among a profusion of whitish, velvety leaves.

Height: 20–90 cm (8–36 in).
Soil: poor but well-drained.
Aspect: sun.
Propagation: from seed or by layering.
Flowering season: spring.
Type: evergreen shrub.

Hamamelis mollis △

Hamamelis

WITCH HAZEL

Hamamelidaceae

The hamamelis is a golden shrub with a heady fragrance comparable to that of hyacinths or lilies. In autumn its leaves turn to an ochre colour. More delicate than the forsythia, more slender than the broom, it originates in cold countries and is therefore hardy. It can be grown alongside the broom, because the hamamelis flowers during the winter and the broom in spring and summer and the two plants, happily, require the same slightly acid soil. You will thus enjoy an almost continuous flowering from winter through to summer.

Useful hints

— Plant the hamamelis in a sunny, but not scorching spot.

— Improve the acid soil with equal parts of sand and peat.

— When the flowers appear along the branches, do not prune, but remove any thin, dead branches at the end of the summer.

Recommended

— *H.* × *intermedia* and its varieties have relatively large leaves: 'Diane', with flowers that are nearly red, and 'Jelena', with copper flowers, are the most striking examples. 'Ruby Glow', with copper flowers spotted with red, is exceptional

for its autumn colours. The sulphur-yellow 'Pallida' is very popular.

— *H. japonica* (Japanese witch hazel) grows to 2 m (6½ ft) in height. Its yellow flowers, in small clusters on leafless branches, are pleasantly scented and enhance the tree's appearance from mid-winter to early spring.

— *H. mollis* (Chinese witch hazel) is fairly large and imposing. 'Goldcrest', with golden yellow flowers, lightened with red at the base, is one of the best-known.

— *H. virginiana* is a small tree 3 m (10 ft) high which flowers in early to mid-autumn. Its foliage turns bright yellow and is itself highly decorative.

Height: 1.5–3 m (5–10 ft).
Soil: acid.
Aspect: sun.
Propagation: from seed or cuttings in summer.
Flowering season: autumn to early spring.
Type: deciduous tree or shrub.

◁ *Hamamelis mollis*

345

Hebe

HEBE

Scrophulariaceae

Pretty in rock gardens, or grouped together to pick out a path, these rather stiff-looking plants are very popular. Few shrubs can bring so many colours to the garden so late on in the season. In areas where there is not too much frost, they can make effective evergreen hedges and provide an attractive addition to the border.

Useful hints

— Plant hebes in spring, preferably in soil that is not too heavy. Water regularly during early summer, and add fertilizer, as these are very voracious plants.

— Site them next to silver-leaved shrubs or vivid, brightly-coloured plants, because their purple and lilac colours can be a little sombre.

Recommended

— Some varieties owe their decorative quality chiefly to their foliage. This is the case with *Hebe armstrongii*, with copper-yellow branches that resemble those of the cypress. *H. buxifolia*, which is very compact, is ideal for low hedges. *H. pinguifolia* 'Pagei', a rock garden shrub, has sea-green, glaucous, fleshy leaves that are bluish grey in colour; it combines well with a display of white flowers.

— Other hebe hybrids are cultivated for their flowers, which are arranged in tapering spikes, including:

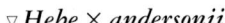

▽ *Hebe* × *andersonii*

△ *Hebe* 'Midsummer Beauty'

— *H.* 'Alicia Amherst' grows fast to 1.2 m (4 ft) and has large spikes of deep purple flowers in late summer and autumn.

— *H.* × *andersonii*, a shrub 2–3 m (6½–10 ft) in height, produces flowers in late summer to early autumn in blue-lilac racemes.

— *H.* 'Autumn Glory' has purplish red shoots and dark green leaves, with purple-blue flowers in autumn.

— *H.* 'Bowles' Hybrid' is not at all hardy, but forms a cushion of mauve flowers from spring to summer.

— *H.* 'Carl Teschner' (syn. *H.* 'Youngii'), a compact globe-shaped shrub, produces white-throated lilac flowers.

— *H. elliptica*, medium-sized, has large fragrant white flowers.

— *H.* × *franciscana* 'Blue Gem' is very tolerant of wind, even of salt breezes. There is also a variegated variety, 'Variegata'.

— *H.* 'Great Orme'. Covered with large lanceolate leaves, this can reach a height of 1 m (3¼ ft) and produces beautiful clusters of pink flowers.

— *H. hulkeana* has loose panicles of pale lilac flowers in spring.

— *H.* 'La Séduisante' has characteristic large glossy leaves and produces large carmine-red spikes in summer.

— *H.* 'Midsummer Beauty', the hardiest hebe, produces superb lilac flowers from early summer to autumn.

— *H. salicifolia*, with white flowers in summer, can reach a height of 1.5 m (5 ft).

Height: 30 cm–3 m (12 in–10 ft).
Soil: ordinary, preferably light.
Aspect: sun.
Propagation: from cuttings of non-flowering shoots in summer or autumn.
Flowering season: spring to mid-autumn.
Type: evergreen shrub.

Helianthemum

ROCK ROSE, SUN ROSE

Cistaceae

Helianthemums are perfect for rock gardens, edges to stone paths, and any areas with a little sunshine and dry, poor soil. The little flowers, red, yellow, white or deep pink depending on the variety, can be seen from a distance because they grow in abundance on this low, bushy evergreen plant and are not concealed by too many leaves. The beauty of these plants will be all the more noticeable if you plant them in company with pinks or, in a border, in front of some galega (goat's rue) or small rose bushes. These small, very low shrubs are equally suitable for growing in containers on the verandah or the patio, together with some lavender cotton. Their name is derived from the Greek *helios*, sun, and *anthemon*, flower.

Useful hints

— Rock roses should be planted in the spring for preference, to enable young plants to be spared winter rain. Plant them in ordinary garden soil, and in a sunny and warm spot, if possible.

— Cut off dead flowers to encourage new ones to appear.

— Divide the bushier clumps every three years.

Recommended

— The varieties are countless, and all are hybrids of the wild species *Helianthemum nummularium*. They include 'Amy Baring', brass-coloured; 'Ben Afflick', delicate orange; 'The Bride', white; 'Wisley Pink', pink with silver foliage, one of the prettiest varieties; 'Wisley Primrose', with silver-green foliage and primrose-coloured flowers; and 'Red Dragon', which has red flowers with a golden throat.

Height: 20–50 cm (8–20 in).
Soil: ordinary, dry.
Aspect: sun.
Propagation: from cuttings, or by division in spring.
Flowering season: early summer to mid-autumn.
Type: evergreen shrub.

Helianthemum nummularium
hybrids ▷

Hibiscus

HIBISCUS, MALLOW

Malvaceae

The most interesting feature of the hibiscus is that it begins to flower in mid-summer, when few other shrubs in the garden are in flower. It can reach a height of 2.5 m (8 ft). Hibiscus are charming because of their lilac or purple flowers, which can be compared to the single flowers of the hollyhock. They have just one drawback: their upright stems give them a somewhat stiff outline. They are, however, unparalleled for creating a medium-sized, well-flowered hedge in summer.

Useful hints

— Plant hibiscus in spring. Do not be surprised if growth does not begin before late spring.

— Prune just after flowering, to avoid the formation of an excessive amount of seed, which would put an unnecessary strain on the plants. However, do not prune systematically in spring or the plant's thin growth will be emphasized without really increasing the number of flowers. It is enough just to remove any overcrowded branches.

Recommended

— *Hibiscus rosa-sinensis* is a rounded shrub with bright crimson flowers and coarsely serrated leaves. The variety 'The President' has pink flowers with magenta centres and yellow stamens.

— *H. sinosyriacus* 'Lilac Queen' produces large pale lilac flowers with red centres from late summer into autumn.

— There is a wide choice among the many hybrids of *H. syriacus*: 'Diana', pure white; 'Red Heart', white flowers with a conspicuous red centre; 'Duc de Brabant', double purple; 'Hamabo', delicate pink and carmine-red; 'Lady Stanley', double white, stained with purple at the base; 'Blue Bird', a large blue flower with a purple throat; and 'Woodbridge', pink with a dark centre.

Height: 1.5–2.5 m (5–8 ft).
Soil: any, slightly chalky.
Aspect: sun.
Propagation: from cuttings in summer and autumn.
Flowering season: summer to early autumn.
Type: deciduous or evergreen shrub.

△ *Hibiscus rosa-sinensis*
▽ *Hibiscus syriacus*

Hippophaë

SEA BUCKTHORN

Elaeagnaceae

A shrub or small tree with deciduous foliage, the hippophaë is widespread throughout milder regions. This charming shrub, with its dense network of roots, fixes itself firmly in the ground, which makes it popular in arid and rocky countries where soil is rare and must be looked after. Requiring little care, and decorative because of its small orange berries, arranged along the stems, the hippophaë is often planted in parks. It tolerates both sea air and drought. It may be pruned as desired in order to form a hedge.

Useful hints

— As it is a dioecious plant, it is necessary to plant a male and several female plants in order to obtain berries. All types of soil will suit it, whether dry, moist, chalky or salty, and any position will do: shade or sun.

Recommended

— *H. rhamnoïdes* (sea buckthorn). The foliage is silver and, unless eaten by the birds, the berries will remain on the tree for several months.

— *H. salicifolia* is a little larger and differs from the previous species by its drooping branches and by its leaves, which are green on one side, brown on the other.

Height: 4 m (13 ft).
Soil: any.
Aspect: any, with a slight preference for sun.
Propagation: by layering or removing suckers.
Flowering season: early to mid-spring, berries in autumn.
Type: deciduous tree or shrub.

Hoheria

LACEBARK, RIBBON-WOOD

Malvaceae

Originating in New Zealand, the hoheria is an altogether splendid shrub. It flowers abundantly at the beginning of summer, the white flowers, in clusters, characterized by their large number of white stamens, which give them an ethereal appearance.

△ *Hippophaë rhamnoïdes*

Useful hints

— Hoherias are unfortunately not hardy in all areas and must therefore be reserved for the mildest climates, where they should be sited in sun or semi-shade. If frost appears to have killed the plant above ground in winter, this does not necessarily mean that all is lost, as it will grow again in spring. It likes to grow on a warm sunny wall.

Recommended

— *H. lyallii* is the hardiest species. Its snow-white flowers appear in early summer. The leaves are deciduous.

— *H. populnea* (lacebark) reaches a height of 6 m (20 ft). The bark on mature trees is frequently flaky, and is pale brown and white. It is an evergreen.

— *H. sexstylosa* (ribbon-wood) is the most striking variety, for the mass of white flowers which totally covers the shrub in mid-summer. It is an evergreen, but grows well only in southern climates.

Height: 3–6 m (10–20 ft).
Soil: light.
Aspect: sun or semi-shade.
Propagation: from cuttings or by division.
Flowering season: summer.
Type: deciduous or evergreen shrub.

Hydrangea

HYDRANGEA

Hydrangaceae

Similar in many ways to the viburnum, hydrangeas mix their fertile flowers, which are usually small, with the sterile ones, which are more developed and highly coloured. White is the favoured colour of the botanical species. However, the blues and lilac-purple colours of the hybrids are just as attractive, and as they age these flowers often take on green tones, stained with a delicate red, at the end of autumn. They make wonderful cut flowers.

Useful hints

— Hydrangeas need soil that is rich in organic matter. They require a lot of leaf-mould or compost when they are planted, and should be mulched each spring with leaf-mould and peat.

— Prune sparingly, but remove dead or stunted branches. In cold areas, protect the stems with dead leaves, surrounded by a sheet of plastic.

— Protect the large terminal buds which contain the future flowers – cut away only the dead flowers, at the end of winter. The cut should be made on the stem, just above a small swelling.

— The most important thing is watering. These plants should not be allowed to dry out.

Recommended

— *Hydrangea arborescens* can grow to 3 m (10 ft) and makes an open bush; its white flowers are arranged in rounded panicles with a diameter not exceeding 30 cm (12 in) in 'Annabelle', the most compact form at less than 2 m (6½ ft).

— *H. aspera* has flat inflorescences composed of tiny fertile blue flowers, surrounded by large white sterile flowers.

— *H. aspera* ssp. *sargentiana*. This looks a little like *H. aspera* itself; its bearing is looser and more spreading.

— The Lacecap hydrangeas, with their fertile flowers in the middle, look like particularly elegant lace bonnets. The most famous include: *H.* 'Blue Wave', pink or blue, depending on the type of soil; 'White Wave', white and blue; and 'Mariesii', with very large flattened clusters in a varying blue.

— The *H. macrophylla* varieties are most frequently sold on the strength of their name. This species, cultivated for centuries, can reach a height of 4 m (13 ft) and spreads out enormously. Here are the most beautiful pink cultivars: 'Altona' and 'Eldorado', pink bordering on red; 'Floralia', very early; 'Maréchal Foch', deep pink often turning gentian-blue; and 'Merveille Rose', with very large flowers. Among the blues: 'Iris' and 'Enziandom', a very even deep blue. Finally, the magnificent, frequently grown 'Soeur Thérèse', an extraordinary shade of white.

— *H. paniculata* is recognizable because of its long pyramid-shaped clusters, almost 25 cm (10 in) in diameter. Its most well-known cultivars include: *H.p.* 'Grandiflora', white mixed with pale pink; 'Kyushu', more compact; 'Praecox', flowering from mid-summer; 'Tardiva', flowering only from mid-autumn.

— *H. quercifolia* (oak-leaved hydrangea) originates in America. It is striking because of the shape of its leaves, which recalls those of the oak, and because of its long panicles of magnificent white flowers.

— *H. serrata* has wide, highly decorative leaves in spring. Its white or blue flowers, in small flat corymbs, are circled with blue or pink round the edges.

— *H. serrata* 'Bluebird'. Its blue panicles are surrounded by sterile white flowers.

— *H. serrata* 'Preziosa' is one of the

△ *Hypericum calycinum*

Hydrangea macrophylla △
Hypericum × *moserianum* 'Tricolor' ▽

most beautiful hydrangeas, with its red stems and salmon-pink flowers which turn a warm shade of red in autumn.

Height: 1–4 m (3¼–13 ft).
Soil: acid for blue flowers, soil rich in organic matter for pink or white flowers.
Aspect: semi-shade; they do well in northerly climates.
Propagation: from cuttings at the end of summer.
Flowering season: mid-summer to late autumn.
Type: deciduous shrub.

Hypericum

ST JOHN'S WORT

Guttiferae

Yet another useful shrub, because of its often evergreen foliage. In past years the yellow flowers were soaked in olive oil to produce a balm that was then applied to plague sores. *Hypericum calycinum* (Aaron's beard, rose of Sharon) may be famed for keeping down weeds, which it suppresses with its leathery foliage, but, having grown tired of its yellow colour all over the garden, it is very difficult to get rid of. It thrives on lawns, along roadsides and in all dry and uncultivated places. The hypericum is a very undemanding plant which is excellent as ground cover to replace a lawn or to brighten up shaded corners.

Useful hints

— Plant hypericums in spring or in autumn, in poor land or in a patch of good soil.

— In the spring of the first year, remove any dead foliage and strengthen the shrub by adding fertilizer.

— Prune any dead or damaged foliage right back and beautiful new leaves will grow.

Recommended

The best choices for a rock garden

— *Hypericum olympicum*, yellow and compact, is a tiny shrub whose branches touch the ground.

— *H. olympicum* f. *minus*, golden yellow with bluish foliage, is the ideal ground cover plant, because it spreads out slowly and never exceeds 15 cm (6 in) in height.

— *H. olympicum* f. *uniflorum* 'Citrinum' is citrus-yellow.

To brighten up a shaded corner

— *H. androsaemum* grows to 80 cm (32 in); its tiny yellow flowers, decorated with long stamens, produce numerous bright red fruits.

— *H.* 'Hidcote' is one of the most beautiful varieties. It forms a shrub that is 1.5 m (5 ft) in height, covered with a mass of golden flowers from mid-summer to mid-autumn.

— *H.* × *inodorum* is one of the strongest and most free-flowering; it produces elongated, salmon-coloured fruits.

— *H. kouytchense* (*H.* 'Sungold'). This has semi-evergreen foliage and abundant flowers. The fruits, initially red, turn to black.

— *H.* × *moserianum* 'Tricolor'. Its flowers are small, but the colour of its foliage is charming, a gradation of pink, cream and green.

— *H.* 'Rowallane' reaches a height of 1.5 m (5 ft) and must be planted against a west-facing wall. It is a splendid shrub, with golden flowers arranged in bright yellow clusters that appear from mid-spring to mid-autumn. It should be cut back to ground level each year.

Height: 15 cm (6 in)–1.5 m (5 ft).
Soil: rather light.
Aspect: sun or semi-shade.
Propagation: by division in spring, or from cuttings.
Flowering season: mid-summer to autumn.
Type: deciduous, semi-evergreen or evergreen shrub.

351

Ilex

HOLLY

Aquifoliaceae

Holly grows slowly, taking years to become a full-sized tree. It is not a difficult plant and does well in shade, though the variegated varieties do need sunshine. An excellent shrub for giving structure to the garden in winter, the holly also bears its cheerful berries at the darkest time of year.

Useful hints

— Plant in autumn or spring. In either case, protect the young plants from searing winds with a canvas windbreak erected on a framework of stakes.

— Each spring, add two or three handfuls of hoof and horn at the base.

— Holly is a good topiary plant, but use secateurs rather than hedge trimmers to avoid cutting the small glossy leaves.

— Plant holly in free-growing hedges, together with deciduous shrubs such as amelanchiers, rowans, elders and medlars.

— As holly is dioecious (either male or female), several specimens should be planted together to be sure of a good display of berries.

Recommended

— *Ilex* × *altaclarensis* withstands urban pollution and grows fairly rapidly. 'Belgica Aurea', a vigorous clone, has large, not very prickly leaves edged with cream or white.

— *I.* × *altaclarensis* 'Camelliifolia' has large, non-prickly leaves. Its elegant pyramidal bearing makes it ideal for tall regular hedges.

— *I.* × *altaclarensis* 'Golden King', with yellow-edged leaves, has won much praise for its beauty. Despite its name, it is a female variety bearing red berries.

— *I. aquifolium* (common holly) has given rise to dozens of hybrids with various types of variegation and even different-coloured berries: brilliant yellow in the case of 'Fructu Luteo' (syn. 'Bacciflava') or red in 'J.C. van Tol', which is the typical colour of holly berries.

— *I. aquifolium* 'Ferox Argentea'. The cream-bordered leaves of this variety are densely edged with prickles, forming

△ *Ilex crenata* 'Mariesii'

a kind of crest on the upper surface.

— *I. aquifolium* 'Golden Queen' (a male variety!) is distinguished by its dark green foliage, marbled with grey and pale green and edged with yellow.

— *I. aquifolium* 'Pyramidalis' is a tall-growing variety with a distinct pyramid shape. It also bears an abundance of berries.

— The prickle-less *I. crenata* eventually grows into a small tree almost 3 m (10 ft) high. It is worth planting in flower beds in the company of perennials. It is also ideal as a hedging plant which will not prick your legs. The only drawback is its rather melancholy black berries.

— *I.* × *koehneana* can grow to over 5 m (16 ft). Its large, chestnut-like leaves never fail to surprise.

— *I. latifolia* has large glossy leaves and bears red berries in abundance.

— *I.* × *meserveae* is one of a group of hybrids hailing from the USA. Many

△ *Ilex aquifolium*

△ *Ilex aquifolium* 'Aurea Marginata'

are known for their hardiness and fine display of berries.

Height: 80 cm–5 m (32 in–16 ft).
Soil: any, as long as it is not too chalky.
Aspect: any, even dense shade.
Propagation: from cuttings, in autumn.
Flowering season: spring (the flowers are insignificant).
Fruiting period: from autumn, throughout the winter.
Type: evergreen tree or shrub.

▽ *Ilex aquifolium* 'Handsworth New Silver'

Illicium

ANISE TREE

Illiciaceae

This is an evergreen aromatic shrub. It has unusual flowers, consisting of thirty or so superimposed petals of different shades – pink, brown and red.

Useful hints

— Plant illiciums in semi-shade, in moist soil mixed with peat.

— These plants are not suited to cold, exposed gardens.

Recommended

— *Illicium anisatum* (star anise) has thick glossy leaves and produces pale yellow, highly fragrant flowers in spring.

— *I. floridanum* is of American origin. It has broad, thick leaves, and large purplish brown flowers in spring.

Height: 1.5–2 m (5–6½ ft).
Soil: moist, mixed with peat.
Aspect: semi-shade, sheltered from winds.
Propagation: from cuttings or by layering.
Flowering season: spring.
Type: evergreen shrub.

Indigofera

INDIGO

Leguminosae

The great virtue of this shrub is the profusion of charming little purple flowers it bears from summer right through to mid-autumn. Its major drawback is that the foliage does not appear until very late in the spring or early summer. On balance, it is well worth turning a blind eye to this defect. Unfortunately, the shrub is not easy to come by. The word *Indigofera* means indigo-bearing, and derives ultimately from *indica*, Indian.

Useful hints

— Plant the indigofera in a free-draining soil in full sun and protect it from strong winds. It does well in dry conditions.

— Plant it against a south-facing wall.

Recommended

— *Indigofera heterantha* grows to 1.5 m (5 ft). It bears a profusion of tiny pea-like

△ *Illicium henryi*

△ *Indigofera heterantha*

flowers and has graceful, pinnate foliage. If the shrub is damaged by hard frosts, cut back the stems to ground level and it will grow again.

— *I. pendula* is a spreading shrub which grows to 2.5 m (8 ft). It makes a superb display, the arching branches bearing long racemes of dark pink flowers in late summer. It has divided leaves which sometimes grow to 20 cm (8 in) long.

— *I. pseudotinctoria* is a subshrub grow-ing to 1 m (3¼ ft). It flowers in summer, with small pink flowers in long dense racemes. This is the shrub from which indigo dye used to be obtained. It comes from the Far East.

Height: 50 cm–2.5 m (20 in–8 ft).
Soil: ordinary.
Aspect: sun.
Propagation: by division or from cuttings.
Flowering season: mid-summer to autumn.
Type: deciduous shrub.

353

Itea

SWEETSPIRE

Grossulariaceae

The glossy toothed leaves, upright bearing and modest height of the itea are reminiscent of holly. Yet its foliage is less rigid and the shrub has a lighter, more graceful air. Summer brings a surprise: thousands of small yellow-green flowers borne in racemes, not unlike the catkins of some species of willow. Another attractive feature is their strong scent.

Useful hints

— The itea is really suited only to areas with a very mild climate. For best results, it should be grown in a light, sandy soil, free of chalk and fairly moist. A mulch of leaf-mould is highly recommended. As the itea does not grow to more than 2 m (6½ ft), it can be grown under trees in open woodland.

Recommended

— *Itea ilicifolia* (holly-leaf sweetspire) is an evergreen shrub. It rarely exceeds 2 m (6½ ft) in height. The greenish flowers hang down in long tails.

— *I. virginica* (Virginia sweetspire) grows to 1.5 m (5 ft). The deciduous foliage turns an attractive red in autumn. It bears white flowers in summer.

Height: up to 2 m (6½ ft).
Soil: light, acid.
Aspect: full sun or semi-shade.
Propagation: from cuttings, by layering, or from seed.
Flowering season: summer.
Type: deciduous or evergreen shrub.

Jovellana

JOVELLANA

Scrophulariaceae

Jovellana is not found often in gardens, but though rarely encountered, it deserves to be more widely adopted. The white or pale violet flowers are spotted with deeper violet or ochre. It blooms in summer.

Useful hints

— Jovellana will do best in regions with a mild climate.

— It can be grown in fairly ordinary soil, provided it is not too alkaline.

△ *Jovellana violacea*

— It thrives in light shade, but will grow in full sunshine in more temperate areas.

— Jovellana will grow well at the foot of a sheltered wall.

— It does not need pruning.

Recommended

— *Jovellana violacea* comes from Chile and is the most widely planted, growing to 1.5 m (5 ft). The mauve flowers are freckled with violet. The leaves are irregularly toothed. Best grown in a sheltered spot.

Height: 50 cm–1.5 m (20 in–5 ft).
Soil: fertile, humus-rich.
Aspect: sun or semi-shade.
Propagation: from cuttings in summer.
Flowering season: summer.
Type: deciduous shrub.

Juniperus

JUNIPER

Cupressaceae

It is not surprising that the genus *Juniperus* is often the best represented at nurseries and garden centres, as it comes in all shapes and sizes: narrow and columnar, conical, compact and prostrate. And for each shape there is a whole range of foliage types and colours, including every shade of silver-blue, golden and green. The common factor is that they all put out needle-like leaves which turn to scales as the plant grows. The juvenile foliage is therefore distinct from the adult. Another advantage is that junipers are easy to grow and will tolerate poor and dry soils. Natives of the northern hemisphere, they thrive in temperate and cold climates.

Useful hints

— Plant junipers in autumn or spring. If you opt for spring planting, water copiously and regularly throughout the first summer, even though most varieties are not particularly thirsty.

— If you decide to plant a number of dwarf specimens as ground cover, space them out sufficiently: they may not grow very tall, but their spread is impressive – up to 4 m (13 ft) across in some cases – so allow at least 4 m (13 ft) between plants. While waiting for them to spread and join up, fill the gaps with heather or other small ground cover plants which can be moved at a later date.

— Junipers will grow in all soil conditions, unless the ground is too acid or too wet. They do well in chalky areas and will withstand the severest winter.

— If you need to prune your juniper, the best time is summer, when the growth rate slows down. Do not cut back later than mid-autumn, or there will be a serious risk of the plant suffering frost damage. In the event of snow, shake the branches to free them of the excess weight.

Recommended

— *Juniperus chinensis* originates from China and Japan. It is sometimes to be found in parks, where it grows to a height of 10–15 m (33–50 ft). It is roughly conical in shape and has dark foliage, but the branches may be somewhat sparse.

△ *Juniperus* × *media* 'Pfitzeriana Glauca'

The pale green leaves may be very close packed, or pointed and spiny. This is a dioecious species, individual trees bearing either male or female flowers. Adult height in cultivation: 10 m (33 ft).

— *J. chinensis* 'Blaauw' has blue-green foliage and a bell-shaped, semi-erect shape.

— *J. communis* grows throughout Europe on chalky, south-facing hillsides. It varies considerably in shape and its cultivars are often directly derived from the wild forms. The foliage consists of sharp needles, white below and green above. Adult height: 5 m (16 ft). Cultivars include:

— *J. communis* 'Compressa', a very slow-growing variety. Planted in a sheltered position, it forms a miniature columnar

◁ *Juniperus horizontalis*
Glauca Group

355

tree. The leaves are darker green on the underside.

— *J. communis* 'Depressa Aurea' is wide-spreading, almost prostrate. The foliage is golden in spring, darkening to green later in the year.

— *J. communis* 'Hornibrookii' is an attractive ground-hugging plant. The green leaves are silvery on the underside.

— *J. horizontalis* (creeping juniper) is ideal as a ground cover plant. It grows to no more than 50 cm (20 in) in height but spreads to a diameter of 4 m (13 ft). The foliage, consisting of both needles and scales, turns a magnificent bronze colour in winter, if the plant occupies a sunny position. It can also be successfully trained against a wall. This species requires fairly damp soil and will not tolerate alkaline conditions. Adult height: 1–3 m (3¼–10 ft). Its cultivars include:

— *J. horizontalis* Glauca Group, whose normally steel-blue foliage takes on splendid winter colours.

— One of the most popular of all conifers is *J. × media* 'Pfitzeriana', which will grow even in shade. The light green foliage is borne on wide-spreading branches, eventually extending to a diameter of 4 m (13 ft).

— *J. × media* 'Gold Coast' is a cultivar which has golden foliage borne on spreading branches.

— *J. × media* 'Mint Julep' has bright green foliage. This conifer is conical in shape.

— *J. oxycedrus* (prickly juniper) is a small twisted shrub which grows in milder climates.

— *J. sabina* is a small, often creeping, shrub, which grows wild in mountainous areas of Europe and the Caucasus. It bears green or grey-green needles and scales, but it is wiser not to touch its attractive foliage: when crushed the leaves give off an unbearable stink. Extremely hardy, the savin, as it is known, will grow in any soil, even limestone or gravel, but it does need a sunny location.

— *J. sabina* 'Hicksii' is a semi-prostrate variety with grey-blue foliage and horizontal branches which dip down at the tips. Adult height: 3 m (10 ft).

— *J. sabina* 'Tamariscifolia' (Spanish juniper) is low-spreading, its green foliage delicately frosted with blue.

△ *Juniperus chinensis*

— *J. scopulorum* (Rock juniper) is a native of the Rocky Mountains and has been much hybridized in the USA. Its foliage is very similar to that of *J. virginiana*, but its silver-green or grey colour has given rise to cultivars that are now very popular in Europe.

— *J. scopulorum* 'Skyrocket' is one of the narrowest conifers on the market. A strikingly elegant variety, it bears blue-grey foliage.

— *J. squamata*, originally from the Himalayas, where it grows at altitudes of up to 5,000 m (16,000 ft), is hardy in the extreme and does well everywhere. A prostrate shrub, it develops very slowly. Its bark is red-brown and flaking and its branches are completely hidden by short, fine needles of an attractive bluish green with an aromatic scent. The cultivars to grow are 'Blue Carpet', with steel-blue foliage, and 'Meyeri', which is semi-erect and has glaucous green leaves.

— *J. virginiana* (Eastern red cedar) often grows to over 10 m (33 ft) and is generally conical in shape. The branches

of young specimens point sharply upwards, but gradually descend to the horizontal with age. The leaves are of two kinds – needle and scale-like – and give off a disagreeable smell when rubbed. The pinkish wood is used in making pencils. Although this species is fairly tolerant of alkaline conditions, it does require a good depth of moisture-retentive soil.

— *J. virginiana* 'Glauca' is a very slender variety with silver-grey foliage.

If you want to choose your junipers according to silhouette – columnar, spreading or prostrate – here is a handy guide:

The best 'columnar' varieties

— *J. chinensis* 'Aurea' is of erect habit. It has golden yellow foliage, which loses some of its brightness in winter. Height at maturity: 4–5 m (13–16 ft).

— *J. chinensis* 'Blue Alps' rises like a silver-blue pyramid to about 1.5 m (5 ft) in height.

— *J. chinensis* 'Kaizuka' is looser-growing but its green foliage responds well to pruning. It may exceed a height of 3 m (10 ft).

— *J. chinensis* 'Keteleeri' is a vigorous clone, column-shaped or narrowly conical, on occasion reaching a height of 10 m (33 ft).

— *J. chinensis* 'Obelisk' has blue-grey foliage. It forms a tree of curious bearing, inclined to both twist and lean. Height at maturity: 3 m (10 ft).

— *J. chinensis* 'Pyramidalis' is very compact, with grey-green foliage. Height at maturity: 2 m (6½ ft).

— *J. communis* 'Compressa' has a fine slender silhouette. It is one of the best varieties for a rock garden. Height at maturity: 1 m (3¼ ft).

— *J. communis* 'Hibernica' (Irish juniper) forms a narrow, grey-green columnar tree, eventually reaching a height of 4 m (13 ft).

— *J. scopulorum* 'Blue Heaven' is perfectly compact and uniformly blue all year round.

— *J. scopulorum* 'Skyrocket' forms a very elegant, narrow column, eventually reaching 5 m (16 ft) in height. Its delicate blue-grey foliage is held very erect in cold regions.

— *J. virginiana* 'Burkii' is very dense and compact and bears both juvenile and adult foliage. It is a greyish blue in summer, steel-blue in winter. Height at maturity: 3 m (10 ft).

— *J. virginiana* 'Glauca' is very slender and compact. Its glaucous green foliage turns a distinctive violet colour in winter. Height at maturity: 6 m (20 ft).

The best spreading varieties

— *J.* 'Blue Cloud' is a vigorous variety which puts out shoots in all directions. Its leaves have a bluish green sheen.

— *J. chinensis* 'Blaauw' is erect and fairly broad in outline. The foliage is a luminous blue-grey. Height at maturity: 1 m (3¼ ft).

— *J.* × *chinensis* 'Kuriwao Gold' is a fairly tall, golden yellow variety. It has a generous, flared shape.

— *J.* × *media* 'Hetzii' is a fine conifer, whose spreading branches form a wide cone shape. It can grow to 3 m (10 ft) in both height and diameter, so it should be given plenty of space. The foliage is a superb silver-blue.

— *J.* × *media* 'Mordigan Gold' is also spreading in habit. The foliage turns from bright yellow to golden.

— *J.* × *media* 'Pfitzeriana' is undoubtedly the most widely planted of all junipers. Renowned for its majestic bearing, it puts out horizontal, wing-like branches with graceful, drooping twigs. Very old specimens may spread out very wide or adopt a pyramid shape. The foliage is light green. This juniper may grow to 4 m (13 ft). It is popular with gardeners, both for ground cover and as a special feature in the middle of a lawn. It also serves to conceal manholes or inspection covers.

— The branches of *J.* × *media* 'Pfitzeriana Aurea' incline more steeply towards the ground. The background foliage is green, but the young shoots are yellow, forming an attractive contrast. This 'Pfitzer' is no less popular than the previous variety.

— *J.* × *media* 'Pfitzeriana Glauca' is slightly less imposing than the type with glaucous green leaves. The 'Pfitzer' varieties are sometimes trained up stakes by nurserymen. In this case they grow taller, but are less elegant.

— *J.* × *media* 'Plumosa Aurea' is a charming juniper of spreading habit. It has soft, feathery golden leaves and grows fairly slowly.

△ *Juniperus sabina*

— *J. procumbens* 'Nana'. Despite its slow growth, this smallest of dwarfs, less than 30 cm (1 ft) high, may eventually form a vast carpet.

— *J. sabina* 'Blue Danube' is another slow grower. Though designated 'blue', the leaves are nearer to green, but there is something particularly graceful about the droop of its branches.

— *J. sabina* 'Tamariscifolia' is one of the finest cultivars of the savin. It eventually forms a fairly tall, flat-topped bush. Used as ground cover on banks or level ground, it reaches 50 cm (20 cm).

— *J. sabina* 'Tripartita' is very similar to *J.* × *media* 'Pfitzeriana' but smaller. Its pale glaucous green foliage turns purple in winter.

— *J. squamata* 'Blue Star' is an attractive little conifer with steel-blue foliage.

— *J. squamata* 'Meyeri' is a charming dwarf of irregular shape and glaucous green foliage.

◁ *Juniperus squamata* 'Meyeri'

357

△ *Juniperus procumbens*

△ *Juniperus horizontalis* 'Douglasii'

— *J. virginiana* 'Grey Owl' (Eastern red cedar) is more of a ground cover plant, growing wider than it is high. It has delicate foliage of a fine grey-blue colour.

The best prostrate varieties

All the junipers described below are perfectly suited to ground cover use or simply to create areas of horizontal evergreen in your garden.

— *J. chinensis* 'Sargentii' is a fine blue-green. Scale-like and needle-shaped leaves appear on the twigs at the same time. They give off a scent of camphor.

— *J. communis* 'Depressa Aurea' is a fine yellow cultivar, whose slightly prickly leaves turn bronze in winter. Like all golden forms, it requires a position in full sun.

— *J. communis* 'Hornibrookii'. This is the most prostrate variety, with grey, slightly frosted foliage.

— *J. communis* 'Repanda' has inoffensive leaves, a good branching habit and bright green foliage.

— *J. horizontalis* 'Bar Harbor' is a rampant, creeping variety (as its name suggests), even though the branches do rise to a height of 50 cm (20 in) off the ground. The grey-green foliage turns mauve in winter. An original feature: the young shoots are an orange colour with mauve spots.

— *J. horizontalis* 'Douglasii' is the most surprising of the prostrate junipers. Normally dark green, it becomes almost chocolate-brown in winter, if it can get enough sunshine.

— *J. horizontalis* Glauca Group is fully prostrate, hugging even the slightest dip in the ground. It has metallic-green foliage. By cutting it back, you can create the impression of a lawn.

— *J. × media* 'Gold Coast', one of the widest-spreading, has golden yellow twigs.

— *J. scopulorum* 'Springbank' is of luminous green appearance, and puts forth delicate, supple shoots.

Height: varies according to species and variety.
Soil: in alkaline soil, plant *J. chinensis*, *J. sabina*, *J. repanda*; in acid soil, plant *J. horizontalis*.
Aspect: sun or semi-shade.
Propagation: from cuttings dipped in a hormone compound or by layering.
Type: evergreen tree or shrub.

Kalmia

CALICO BUSH, MOUNTAIN LAUREL

Ericaceae

If you are looking for an elegant shrub to grow in a patch of acid soil, a kalmia may be the right choice. The clusters of pink, saucer-shaped flowers emerging from the glossy green foliage will add a touch of originality to your flower beds. In areas with a moist, mild climate the shrub grows vigorously, eventually forming dense thickets. The kalmia is also well suited to patios, provided you do not let the soil dry out in the container. A word of warning: the buds and flowers of the kalmia are poisonous.

Useful hints

— Plant in autumn or spring, in an acid soil enriched with peat and leaf-mould so that it will retain plenty of moisture. Mulch with pine bark each spring.

— Plant in semi-shade.

— Do not prune: the flowers are produced in abundance at the ends of the growing shoots. To improve the look of these shrubs, simply remove the dead flowers and any seeds that form. Plant kalmias in the company of azaleas, rhododendrons and heathers, and be careful never to let them dry out.

Recommended

— *Kalmia angustifolia* (sheep laurel). In the USA – its original homeland – it is said that this species is guilty of poisoning sheep. It has handsome green foliage and the blossom is cherry-red.

— *K. angustifolia* 'Rubra', which bears flowers in shades of crimson and deep purple in summer, continues to blossom over a long period.

— *K. latifolia* (mountain laurel) also has attractive foliage. The flowers, borne in clusters 10 cm (4 in) in diameter, are an attractive deep pink. The shrub is spectacular in full bloom.

— *K. latifolia* 'Bullseye' has white flowers, banded purple, while those of 'Clementine Churchill' are deep pink. 'Ostbo Red' bears red buds, but the full-blown flowers are deep pink.

— *K. polifolia* (bog myrtle) has leaves that are narrow and glaucous on the underside. The purplish pink flowers open in summer. This shrub is very well suited to moist soils.

Height: 1–3 m (3¼–10 ft) and more.
Soil: acid.
Aspect: semi-shade.
Propagation: by layering, in summer.
Flowering season: summer.
Type: evergreen shrub.

Kalmia latifolia △
Kerria japonica 'Pleniflora' ▷

Kalmia latifolia 'Clementine Churchill' △

Kerria

JEW'S MALLOW, BACHELOR'S BUTTONS

Rosaceae

At the end of winter, the kerria puts on a cheerful riot of sunny blooms. Suckering with gay abandon, it throws up a multitude of stems, which bend almost horizontal under their weight of bright yellow pompons. Both single and double-blooming varieties are simplicity itself to grow. The kerria can be trained against a wall, where it will attain a spread of 8 m (26 ft). Try planting a mixture of hemerocallis at the base of the shrub.

Useful hints

— Plant in autumn. All you need do is pull up and plant a rooted sucker from a neighbour's garden, and in two or three years you will have a dense clump of your own. Be warned though: it is invasive where other plants are concerned. Take this into account when planting and ensure that its spread is limited by a path or wall.

— Prune after flowering, removing stems from the centre of the thicket to allow plenty of light to penetrate.

Recommended

— The single-flowered *Kerria japonica* may be considered more fashionable, but many people prefer the extravagant show of the double 'Pleniflora'. Lovers of variegated foliage will undoubtedly go for *K. japonica* 'Variegata', a variety with supple stems and leaves edged with white.

Height: 1.5–2 m (5–6½ ft).
Soil: any, even alkaline.
Aspect: sun or semi-shade.
Propagation: from suckers, in autumn.
Flowering season: spring.
Type: deciduous shrub.

△ *Kolkwitzia amabilis*

Kolkwitzia

BEAUTY BUSH

Caprifoliaceae

If not pruned regularly, kolkwitzia may exceed 2 m (6½ ft) in height. In just a few years, this shrub makes a fine symmetrical clump, festooned with white and pink trumpet-shaped flowers in early summer. It is just as much at ease in an informal hedge with other flowering shrubs (snowberry, spiraea) as among border perennials or rose bushes. Kolkwitzia is very undemanding and needs little attention.

Useful hints

— Container-grown specimens can be planted at any time of year, but they are best purchased in late spring, when in full bloom, as some strains have only a meagre display of flowers. Water well during the first summer.

— To propagate, take softwood cuttings in summer and plant them in a cold frame during their first winter.

— Try planting in the company of sweet williams or in a mat of armeria.

Recommended

— *Kolkwitzia amabilis*, a native of China, has pink and white flowers with yellow markings at the throat. 'Pink Cloud', an improved variety, is slightly more profuse, bearing flowers of a more obvious pink.

Height: 1.5–2 m (5–6½ ft).
Soil: ordinary.
Aspect: full sun or semi-shade.
Propagation: from cuttings in early summer.
Flowering season: spring and early summer.
Type: deciduous shrub.

Laburnum

LABURNUM, GOLDEN RAIN

Leguminosae

A small deciduous tree, the laburnum grows to a height of 8 m (26 ft). The graceful foliage casts a dappled shade, while the long pendulous sprays of yellow flowers give the tree its popular name of golden rain. The trunk often divides at the base into two, three or four main branches, increasing the overall volume of the tree. The wood is extremely hard and has been used since ancient times for making musical instruments. Hence the nickname 'false ebony'.

Laburnum × *watereri* ▷

Useful hints

— Laburnum will grow in all types of soil, but has an aversion to wet ground. You will get a better display of flowers in semi-shade, though the tree will in fact do well in almost any location. It has the additional merit of not minding pollution. Laburnum and wisteria go particularly well together: the simultaneous show of yellow and mauve is superb.

— The tree does not need pruning but, if at all possible, remove the seed heads, which otherwise hang down in such unsightly fashion through the long summer months. Take note that all parts of the plant are poisonous.

Recommended

— *Laburnum adamii*, also known as × *Laburnocytisus adamii*, is an interesting novelty: a laburnum/broom hybrid bearing yellow, pink and purple flowers on the same tree.

— *L. alpinum* (Scotch laburnum) is the largest species, growing to heights of 10 m (33 ft). The racemes it bears are also longer than those of other kinds.

— *L. anagyroïdes* 'Aureum' (a variety of the common laburnum) has light yellow foliage.

— Exceptionally for a laburnum, *L. anagyroïdes* 'Autumnale' has a second flowering in autumn.

— *L. × watereri* 'Vossii' differs from the others in the colour of its flowers, which are a dark yellow and very long. This is the most popular variety, magnificent when in bloom.

Height: 8–10 m (26–33 ft).
Soil: any.
Aspect: any, though preferably semi-shade.
Propagation: from seed and cuttings, or by grafting cultivars on to the common laburnum.
Flowering season: early summer; in some cases, autumn.
Type: deciduous tree.

Lagerstroemia

INDIAN LILAC, CRAPE MYRTLE

Lythraceae

The lagerstroemia is of oriental origin and is ravishing when in full bloom, resembling a lilac but not even belonging to the same family. Grown as a shrub, the Indian lilac, *Lagerstroemia indica*, will withstand temperatures as low as –15°C, dying back to the ground but putting out new shoots in spring and flowering again the following summer. It does, however, need prolonged periods of sunshine. Planted on a patio, it is almost bound to win you compliments. In a mild winter, it may not even drop its leaves.

Useful hints

— Spring is the best time to plant the Indian lilac. Mulch and water well in summer. As winter approaches, protect the stem with a blanket of straw or dead

△ *Lagerstroemia indica*

leaves, held in place with plastic sheeting. Remove this protective covering in spring, during a period of mild weather, and cut the stems back to ground level. The plant will respond with vigorous new growth.

— For an attractive, soft-coloured effect, try planting it with *Campanula pyramidalis* and *Salvia sclarea* in a bed against a south-facing wall.

Recommended

— There are a number of hybrids of various colours on offer, ranging from white to deep pink and even violet and red. They bear opulent clusters of flowers. The basic *L. indica* displays its lilac-pink flowers in autumn, while the variety 'Rosea' bears flowers of a rich deep pink.

— *L. speciosa* (Pride of India) needs a warm climate. It has rose pink flowers in autumn, often when the tree is leafless.

Height: 1–2 m (3¼–6½ ft).
Soil: rich, light.
Aspect: full sun.
Propagation: by layering, in summer.
Flowering season: summer and autumn.
Type: deciduous tree or shrub.

△ *Larix decidua*

△ *Larix gmelinii* (syn. *Larix dahurica*)

Larix

LARCH

Pinaceae

The larch is a tall conifer of gracious, symmetrical bearing, whose slim branches curve up at the ends. The soft, thin, needlelike leaves are grouped in whorls, like those of the cedar family. Unlike the vast majority of conifers, the larch drops its leaves in autumn. It shows a distinct preference for moist places. There are few things more beautiful in spring than the sight of this tree, with its delicate light-green foliage, standing out against the darker shades of its neighbours.

Useful hints

— As the larch puts on growth very rapidly, it is preferable to plant a very young specimen so that it will adapt more readily to the soil conditions. The larch is sensitive to pollution, so is best not grown in towns.

Recommended

— *Larix decidua* (European larch). This mountain species, which grows wild in parts of northern Europe, is found in open, sunny locations at altitudes of between 1,000 and 2,500 m (3,250 and 8,000 ft). The new shoots are a lovely tender green, turning a reddish yellow towards the autumn. Its method of reproduction is interesting. In spring, yellow male catkins and their pale reddish brown female counterparts appear on the same tree. The female organs subsequently turn into small light brown cones, which ripen in the tree's first year.

— *L. kaempferi* (Japanese larch) grows spontaneously on the volcanic mountain slopes of one of Japan's islands. It does well in any garden soil. The delicate bluish green foliage turns a pinkish beige in autumn. The scales of its cones are curved rather than straight. It often reaches heights of 30 m (95 ft). 'Pendula' is a fine weeping variety.

Height: 20–30 m (65–95 ft).
Soil: moist.
Aspect: needs an open site.
Propagation: from seed and by grafting.
Flowering season: catkins in spring.
Type: deciduous tree.

362

▽ *Larix kaempferi*

▽ *Larix decidua*

Laurus nobilis △

Laurus

BAY LAUREL, SWEET BAY

Lauraceae

It was the leaves of the bay laurel that the ancient Greeks used to crown their heroes. For them it was a symbol of victory. Since the Middle Ages we have adopted it as the symbol of academic success. The word baccalaureate derives from two Latin words: *bacca* and *laurea*, the berries and leaves of the laurel, placed on the brow of graduating university students. Though severely affected by cold winters, the sweet bay (not to be confused with *Nerium oleander* or *Viburnum tinus*) is still highly prized by gardeners. It combines elegant foliage with ease of cultivation and aromatic leaves. Specimens placed against the south-facing wall of a house can achieve a majestic architectural effect.

Useful hints

— Choose a spot well sheltered from cold winds.

— The sweet bay does well in tubs, provided they are brought in each winter and kept in an unheated greenhouse. It can be pruned to attractive shapes.

— If the shrub is damaged by frost during a severe winter, cut it back to the ground. New shoots will soon appear and the bush will re-establish itself in two or three years.

Recommended

— *Laurus nobilis* will eventually grow to 10 m (33 ft) if not pruned. *L. nobilis* f. *angustifolia* is a variety with narrower, paler leaves. 'Aurea' has distinctive golden yellow foliage. *L.n.* 'Crispa' (syn. *L.n.* 'Undulata'), a variety with undulating foliage, is more hardy.

Height: 2–10 m (6–33 ft) and more.
Soil: rich, free-draining.
Aspect: full sun.
Propagation: from cuttings, in summer or autumn.
Flowering season: spring.
Type: evergreen shrub.

▽ *Lavandula angustifolia* 'Hidcote Blue'

Lavandula

LAVENDER

Labiatae

Lavender, welcome anywhere with its perfume and its power to conjure up southern climes, will grow equally well in more northerly latitudes, provided it is planted in a sunny corner. It will make do with any soil, even the poorest and most stony. However, avoid damp, compacted clays. In return for this minimum of care, it will reward you with dense clumps with which to flank a flight of stone steps or cover a bank. Any brightly coloured flower will benefit from being contrasted with lavender.

Useful hints

— Plant cuttings taken from a large plant in summer, in good, well-drained garden soil.

— Cut the flowers as soon as they begin to fade, so as to maintain a nice rounded shape. Cut back straggly specimens in

spring. They can in fact be pruned very early in the year.

Recommended

— *Lavandula angustifolia* (old English lavender) is the prettiest of all, with its violet-blue flowers and subtle, lingering scent. A good cultivar to try is the lovely violet 'Hidcote'. 'Munstead' has bright green foliage. There is even a pink-flowering lavender, 'Loddon Pink' (albeit a rather insipid colour), and another which blooms white.

— *L. stoechas* (French lavender) has a strange, tousled appearance and tufted purple-coloured flower heads. Its perfume is not so strong as that of *L. angustifolia*.

Height: 30–80 cm (12–32 in).
Soil: ordinary, on the dry side.
Aspect: full sun.
Propagation: from cuttings in summer.
Flowering season: summer.
Type: evergreen shrub.

Lavatera

TREE MALLOW

Malvaceae

The tree mallow is a shrub with grace, charm and colour, and is very easy to grow. It is the perfect answer to a gap in your flower bed: in just three months an insignificant rooted cutting will grow into a sturdy bush 1.5 m (5 ft) tall. It flowers throughout the summer and is a perfect match for perovskia, caryopteris and shrub roses. To complete the picture, try planting some light blue nepetas with them in the border. Lavatera also grows well in a seaside setting.

Useful hints

— Plant the tree mallow in spring. Water regularly, adding some liquid fertilizer to encourage it to flower. In early winter, mulch round the base with leaf-mould as a protection against frost. In spring, cut back the stems to within 10 cm (4 in) of the ground, to stimulate new, healthy growth.

— In autumn, take cuttings from the ends of branches and insert them vertically in a mixture of sand and peat (in equal proportions). They will quickly take root. Keep these cuttings in a sheltered place such as a cold frame to

△ *Lavatera arborea*

replace any adult specimens killed by frost.

Recommended

— There are various cultivars which bear a profusion of flowers to transform the humblest flower bed: 'Ice Cool' (a satiny white), 'Barnsley' (white with a pink centre) and 'Pink Frills'.

— *Lavatera assurgentiflora* is a semi-evergreen shrub with twisted grey stems. The deep cerise flowers are darkly veined, and the leaves are white haired underneath.

— *L. olbia*, though commonly grown in gardens in the past, is not so popular today. A Mediterranean shrub, it bears its large, single, deep pink flowers tightly packed along the whole length of its branches.

— *L. thuringiaca* is a magnificent shrub, wrongly called *L. olbia* until recently. It has downy, slightly greyish shoots, at the ends of which the large, single pink flowers are borne all summer long.

Height: 2 m (6½ ft).
Soil: good garden soil.
Aspect: full sun.
Propagation: from cuttings.
Flowering season: summer.
Type: semi-evergreen shrub.

△ *Leucothoë fontanesiana*

Lespedeza

BUSH CLOVER

Leguminosae

Lespedeza is a strange but attractive shrub. Its large, vigorous branches grow each spring, arch over in summer, and in autumn bear flowers of a ravishing rosy purple. They are not unlike sweet peas. Its cascading habit makes it ideal for decorating a bank. It can also be used as ground cover at the bottom of the garden or to fill the angle of a flight of steps. Just one specimen will end up covering an impressive area. The divided leaves, elegant throughout the summer, form an excellent backdrop for such plants as *Stachys byzantina*, whose soft, silver-grey foliage will set off the purple of its arching branches. Pink Japanese anemones, placed slightly back from it, will come into flower at the same time. Asters also harmonize well with this fine shrub.

Useful hints

— Plant lespedezas in autumn or spring. In spring, cut back all stems to ground level, as it is the current year's branches that bear the greatest profusion of flowers.

— Plant in well-drained soil with plenty of leaf-mould dug in.

— It does not like cold or wet weather.

Recommended

— *Lespedeza bicolor*, a hardier species growing to 2 m (6½ ft), bears purple-pink flowers.

— *L. thunbergii*, classed as a sub-shrub, flowers in autumn. The fine trusses of dark purple flowers are almost 20 cm (8 in) long.

Height: 1.2–2 m (4–6½ ft).
Soil: deeply dug, humus-rich.
Aspect: full sun.
Propagation: from cuttings, in summer.
Flowering season: autumn.
Type: deciduous shrub.

Leucothoë

FETTERBUSH

Ericaceae

Perfect for small gardens in areas with a mild climate, these shrubs grow to 1.5 m (5 ft) and are mainly evergreen. Their bushy habit and extremely dense, arching branches make them ideal for hiding unsightly objects, or they can be planted in front of trees or leggy shrubs. They also make good ground cover on shady banks. White flowers, reminiscent of lily of the valley, are borne in early summer.

Useful hints

— Plant in a shady position, in moist, acid soil mixed with a handful of bone-meal. When the plants are established, remove the old branches to stimulate a growth of young leaves. This will ensure that the shrub maintains a fresh, bushy appearance.

Recommended

— *Leucothoë davisiae* has glossy evergreen foliage and bears white flowers in summer.

— The leaves of *L. fontanesiana* are tinted red in winter. The hanging racemes of white flowers appear in late spring. The cultivar 'Rainbow' has attractive creamy yellow and pink variegated foliage.

— *L.* 'Scarletta' forms a small shrub, much appreciated for its bright red foliage.

Height: 1.5 m (5 ft).
Soil: acid, not likely to dry out.
Aspect: shade or semi-shade.
Propagation: by layering, in summer.
Flowering season: late spring to summer.
Type: mainly evergreen shrub.

Leycesteria

HIMALAYA HONEYSUCKLE

Caprifoliaceae

A native of the Himalayas and now very well-known, *Leycesteria formosa* is one of the best shrubs for decorating a wilder corner of the garden. In summer its long supple stems, which may grow to 2 m (6½ ft), bear long tassels of white flowers surmounted by burgundy-coloured bracts. The purple berries which follow in autumn are a magnet for birds, especially pheasants.

Useful hints

— Plant in spring, burying the root ball 5–8 cm (2–3 in) below ground.

— Protect with a thick mulch of leaf-mould each autumn. Hard frosts may kill off the exposed parts of the plant, but not the roots, and in spring new canes will shoot from the base. In any case, you will get a much better shrub by cutting the stems back to ground level each spring.

— Plant in the company of ferns, hostas, the bright-red 'Fanal' astilbe and filipendulas.

Recommended

— *L. formosa* bears long racemes of white flowers with large purple-red bracts in summer and autumn. It has blue-green shoots, slender, dark green leaves and purple berries.

Height: 1.5–2 m (5–6½ ft).
Soil: humus-rich.
Aspect: sun or semi-shade.
Propagation: by division in autumn, or from seed in spring.
Flowering season: summer and autumn.
Type: deciduous shrub.

Ligustrum

PRIVET

Oleaceae

Privet enjoyed its heyday at the turn of the century, before thuja became widely available. Few shrubs are as easy-going and economical, with the result that privet was often used unimaginatively as a hedging plant. But this shrub has undoubted good qualities and needs rescuing from its present semi-oblivion. A great asset is the scent of its flowers in summer. It also withstands urban pollution and will grow almost anywhere.

Useful hints

— Plant from autumn to spring. Dig the soil deeply and enrich with humus if necessary. Mulch with compost each spring, as privet is very shallow-rooted.

— Prune at least twice a year, in spring and autumn, to give a dense hedge. If your privet is planted in a border, prune only once, and remove a few branches from the centre to let in light and air and give the shrub a fuller shape. If you like the flowers, prune only in mid-summer, when the growing season is over. When grown in a tub and clipped for topiary purposes, privet is not hardy and needs to be kept in the shelter of a greenhouse over winter. It is an extremely hungry shrub, so do not plant flowers or other shrubs in its vicinity as it quickly exhausts the soil.

Recommended

— *Ligustrum japonicum* (Japanese privet) has evergreen foliage similar to that of the camellia. Its flowers are among the largest of their kind. 'Rotundifolium' is slow-growing, with a dense mass of leathery leaves.

— *L. lucidum*, its Chinese cousin, is more erect in habit, with geometrically arranged branches. There are several variegated cultivars, in particular 'Aureo-variegatum' and 'Tricolor', whose leaves are a mixture of green, white and pink. 'Excelsum Superbum' has large, glossy, bright green leaves marked with pale green and with a yellow edge.

— *L. ovalifolium* (California privet) is the most common species and is often used for hedging. Left to itself, it will eventually grow to a height of 4 m (13 ft).

— *L. quihoui* is more like a small tree. It also grows to 4 m (13 ft), and in late summer is covered with a profusion of large, creamy white flower panicles.

▽ *Leycesteria formosa*

Ligustrum japonicum
'Rotundifolium' △

— *L. sinense* is a deciduous or semi-ever-green species with oval, pale green leaves. It has large panicles of white scented flowers in summer, followed by small purple-black berries.

— *L.* 'Vicaryi' is semi-evergreen, with golden yellow leaves and small white flowers in summer.

— *L. vulgare* (European privet) grows wild all over Europe, where it is often to be found in hedges. It does well in alkaline soils. The black berries it bears in autumn are not unattractive, but beware: they are poisonous. This shrub is deciduous.

Height: 1–4 m (3¼ to 13 ft).
Soil: any.
Aspect: sun or semi-shade.
Propagation: from cuttings in summer or autumn.
Flowering season: summer.
Type: deciduous, semi-evergreen or evergreen shrub.

367

◁ △ Liquidambar styraciflua

Liquidambar
SWEET GUM
Hamamelidaceae

The strange name of this tree derives from the Spanish. It was so called by the first Spanish settlers in South America, who observed that an aromatic resin, of a beautiful amber colour, seeped from the trunk of the tree when it was cut or grazed. When the tree was eventually imported to Europe, in the eighteenth century, the resin was used in perfumery and medicine under the name of styrax or gum copal. Knowing its origins, it is easy to understand why the sweet gum is so fond of sun and warmth. It is not a problematic tree, however, withstanding cold and doing well in any kind of soil. Its great assets are its majestic bearing, conical shape and long, straight trunk, which grows to 30 m (95 ft) – even taller in the wild. In autumn, its foliage is a glorious sight as the large, lobed, well-defined leaves turn to incandescent red and purple. Sweet gum is very slow-growing: 5–6 m (16–20 ft) in twenty years. However, at five years old, it is already 4 m (13 ft) high with a spread of 2 m (6½ ft). It will live for eighty years and never needs pruning.

Useful hints
— Sweet gum has just one weakness: it does not transplant well, taking two or three years to recover.

— Transplant with a large root ball.

— Water in well.

Recommended
— *Liquidambar formosa* Monticola Group has very large leaves.

— *L. orientalis* is indigenous to Asia Minor. It has much smaller leaves than the American sweet gum and is of more modest proportions, not exceeding 15–16 m (50–53 ft) in height. Otherwise, it is very similar.

— *L. styraciflua* is the best-known species. 'Aurea' is a cultivar with yellow-splashed leaves. 'Lane Roberts' is a smaller variety. 'Worplesdon' differs in being more pyramid-shaped, and its deep-cut leaves turn a deep red colour in autumn.

Height: 30 m (95 ft), and more in its country of origin.
Soil: moist, cool.
Aspect: sun or semi-shade.
Propagation: by layering or from cuttings in spring.
Type: deciduous tree.

Liriodendron

TULIP TREE

Magnoliaceae

A tall, stately tree, originally from the USA. It is strange to the tips of its leaves, which are as large as they are long, have square-cut ends and dance gracefully in the wind. Also strange are the tulip-shaped flowers which give the tree its name. They are borne in summer but unfortunately do not begin to appear until the tree is at least twenty years old.

Useful hints

— The liriodendron needs a sheltered location, out of the prevailing wind. The ground should be deeply dug before planting.

Recommended

— *Liriodendron tulipifera* flowers in summer and bears its conical fruits in autumn. There are several varieties, including 'Aureomarginatum', which has yellow-edged leaves.

Height: 30 m (95 ft) in Europe, but much taller in its native setting.
Soil: any.
Aspect: sun or semi-shade.
Propagation: by air-layering. Leave for two years before severing the new plant from the parent.
Flowering season: summer.
Type: deciduous tree.

Lumus

see *Myrtus*

Lupinus

TREE LUPIN

Leguminosae

Lupins are common enough plants, but the tree lupin is something of a rarity. On a sandy, well-exposed site, this shrub will produce such a mass of flowers as to completely exhaust itself. Be prudent on its behalf and collect some seeds, or take cuttings, to make sure it survives for future years. It goes well with irises: though very different, their foliage types are complementary. For colour harmonies, plant lupins with *Baptisia australis*, whose soft blue is a pleasant match for the pale yellow, often slightly bluish, shade of the tree lupin.

Useful hints

— Plant in spring, taking care not to damage the tap root, in soil lightened with half a bucket of sand.

— To prevent the plant from exhausting itself, remove all but a few of the seed pods.

— Collect the seeds when mature, nick the very tough seed coat with a knife, and sow in sandy compost straight away.

— The young plants should be kept in a cold frame over the winter and planted out the following spring. You can also take cuttings in summer and plant them in sand.

▽ *Lupinus arboreus*

△ *Liriodendron tulipifera* 'Fastigiatum'

Recommended

— *Lupinus arboreus* (tree lupin) is an evergreen, scented shrub. Of the different varieties, 'Snow Queen' is white, 'Mauve Queen' mauve, and 'Golden Spire' yellow.

Height: 1 m (3¼ ft).
Soil: sandy.
Aspect: full sun.
Propagation: from seed when ripe, or cuttings taken in summer.
Flowering season: summer.
Type: deciduous shrub.

Magnolia

MAGNOLIA

Magnoliaceae

The first magnolia arrived at Nantes, France, at the beginning of the eighteenth century, but a further twenty years were to elapse before it came into flower, giving rise to much surprise and wonderment. The great traveller and botanist Charles Plumier, who discovered the genus, named the tree after Pierre Magnol, then director of the botanical gardens in Montpellier. A large number of species, with a variety of different flowers, were subsequently discovered under cultivation in North America and the Far East. Some are trees, while others are shrubs. The white flowers, which bloom in late spring and early summer, depending on the climate, can be as big as soup plates. Magnolias do not tolerate excessive lime, so they to be regularly mulched with peat or leaf-mould.

Useful hints

— Early spring is the best time for planting. Avoid windy locations – the tree will thrive only in a well-sheltered spot in sun or semi-shade.

— Do not plant the tree too deep, and put plenty of peat into the hole and around the trunk.

— Water generously, particularly during the first year, and avoid planting any other shrubs too close to it. Magnolias do not really need pruning: it should be enough simply to tidy up the branches.

Recommended

— *Magnolia acuminata* (cucumber tree) can reach a height of 20 m (65 ft) in temperate climates. The flowers, which bloom in late spring, have no scent. The green, cucumber-shaped fruits ripen and turn red in autumn.

— *M. campbellii* (Campbell's magnolia), sometimes called the pink tulip tree, produces magnificent blooms, although young trees under twenty years of age do not flower.

— *M. campbellii* ssp. *mollicomata* is said to be hardier and quicker to flower than the species, blooming after ten years.

— *M. delavayi* is a small tree of Chinese origin, about 5–10 m (16–33 ft) in height. Its large, evergreen leaves are thick and leathery. It is less hardy than

△ *Magnolia dawsonia*

▽ *Magnolia hypoleuca*

Magnolia × *soulangeana* △
Magnolia soulrosea 'Newton' ▷
Magnolia fuscata ▽

371

△ *Magnolia × soulangeana*

M. grandiflora and is best suited to mild climates.

— *M. grandiflora* (laurel magnolia, bull bay), an evergreen species, grows very slowly. It can be kept in a tub on a sheltered terrace or supported against a wall. The variety 'Exmouth' flowers for the first time at a much earlier age.

— *M. kobus* has large, star-shaped flowers that appear at the same time as the leaves, in late spring and early summer. This small tree, with its slender, spreading branches, creates a magnificent effect.

— *M. liliiflora* (lily magnolia) is a small tree with spreading branches and very long-petalled flowers. The variety 'Nigra' has enormous, cup-shaped flowers, dark purple on the outside, lighter on the inside.

— *M. × loebneri* 'Leonard Messel' does not exceed the modest height of 4–5 m (13–16 ft). After a few years, it produces an abundance of fragrant pink flowers, with narrow petals. The cultivar 'Merrill' has large, white, highly scented flowers.

— *M. sieboldii* is also suited to modest-sized gardens. Its scented flowers open out in early summer.

— *M. × soulangeana* is a small tree, 2–3 m (6–10 ft) in height. The extremely beautiful bell-mouthed flowers have petals that are white inside with reddish pink tinges on the outside. 'Lennei' is one of the prettiest varieties, with goblet-shaped, purplish red flowers, while 'Rustica Rubra' is a vigorous tree, whose purplish pink flowers bloom in early spring.

— *M. stellata* (star magnolia) is a native shrub of Japan, where it is cultivated. It is ideal for a small garden. Its abundant, star-shaped flowers are pure white in colour and bloom in late spring, before the leaves emerge, giving off a pleasant scent of daffodils. It rarely exceeds 2 m (6½ ft) in height. The cultivar 'Water

△ *Magnolia* × *soulangeana* 'Alexandrina'
▽ *Magnolia cylindrica*

Lily' has even larger, more abundant flowers and is also suited to small gardens.

Height: 1.5–20 m (5–65 ft), depending on variety.
Soil: good garden soil, enriched with peat and leaf-mould.
Aspect: sun or semi-shade.
Propagation: by layering in early summer.
Flowering season: late spring and early summer.
Type: deciduous or evergreen tree.

◁ *Magnolia stellata* 'Royal Star'

373

△ *Mahonia aquifolium*

△ *Mahonia lomariifolia*

△ *Mahonia repens*

Mahonia

MAHONIA, OREGON GRAPE

Berberidaceae

There are virtually no gardens without mahonias, so numerous are their qualities. All of them are evergreen and fragrant and bear yellow flowers; some flower in winter, while others wait until spring to bloom. They are unrivalled as a winter adornment for gardens, particularly since their glossy leaves are often enhanced by a stunningly stylized silhouette. Use them in profusion at the back of beds and in wild hedges, mixed with amelanchiers, elders and viburnums, or even with nandinas, ferns and fritillaries. They will create an unusual and quite surprising atmosphere. The leaves can be used in winter to make very beautiful bouquets, but avoid gathering them when there is a sharp frost.

Useful hints

— Plant mahonias in autumn, or even in early spring. Mulch the soil and water generously during the first summer.

— Do not prune, unless some branches are growing much higher up the stem than the rest, in which case the shrub should be cut back to half its height in early summer.

Recommended

— *Mahonia acanthifolia* is an upright shrub with clusters of enormous leaves at the ends of the branches. The scented yellow flowers resemble those of the mimosa, and bloom in autumn and winter.

— *M. aquifolium* (holly-leaved mahonia) is the best-known species. Its highly scented flowers bloom in small yellow clusters in early spring. Its dark blue

△ *Mahonia × media* 'Charity'

△ *Mahonia lomariifolia*

△ *Mahonia × media* 'Buckland'

berries are very decorative in autumn and can even be used to make some very original jellies. It grows, though only very slowly, in the least favoured locations, in shade and in poor soil. The cultivar 'Apollo' turns bronze in winter.

— *M. aquifolium* 'Smaragd' has larger leaves and is a more prolific flowerer.

— *M. bealei*, a native of China, produces large clusters of lemon-yellow flowers.

— *M. japonica* has beautiful dark green leaves and long bunches of highly scented yellow flowers that last all winter.

— *M. lomariifolia* is very decorative, due to its stately appearance and compound leaves. It flowers in late winter or early spring. Plant it beside a door in order to enjoy its highly scented flowers throughout the winter.

— *M. × media* 'Charity', with its superb dark green leaves, also produces bunches of highly scented, pale yellow flowers that bloom very early, from mid-winter to early spring. *M. × media* 'Lionel Fortescue' is superb, with lovely upright flowers.

— *M. nervosa* is about 50 cm (20 in) in height; it turns red in winter and produces long bunches of flowers and a lot of fruits. It does not suit chalky soils.

— *M. × wagneri* 'Pinnacle' stands out by virtue of its vigorousness and upright bearing, as well as its spectacular bright yellow flowers.

Height: 50cm–3 m (20 in–10 ft).
Soil: any.
Aspect: shade, semi-shade or sun.
Propagation: from cuttings, in autumn.
Flowering season: from late autumn to late spring.
Type: evergreen shrub.

375

△ *Malus* 'Golden Hornet'
▽ *Malus* 'Evereste'

Malus

FLOWERING CRAB APPLE

Rosaceae

This is a deciduous tree cultivated for its flowers or fruits. In spring, it is covered in a profusion of pink flowers, clustered tightly against each other. After the flowering season, the very dense foliage remains pleasantly attractive. The fruits can be yellow, pink, orange or red.

Useful hints

— Although unaffected by the nature of the soil, the tree will be more attractive if fed with a little compost and peat.

— It should be pruned at the end of the winter in order to achieve its pleasing circular shape. Young plants should be staked.

Recommended

— *Malus baccata*, known as the Siberian crab, has scented white flowers and small red or yellow fruits, no bigger than berries (from which it gets its Latin name: *baccata*, 'small-fruited').

— *M.* 'Chilko' has single rose-pink flowers and bright crimson fruits.

— *M. coronaria*, a native of America, is a fast-growing tree that flowers in late spring. The leaves are richly coloured in autumn. The species is known largely by its cultivar 'Charlottae', which has pretty scented flowers, rose-white in colour, and bright red, edible fruits.

△ *Malus transitoria*
▽ *Malus* 'Evereste'

— *M.* 'Evereste'. The white flowers of this variety are unrivalled, and its pollen encourages the fertilization of the large-fruited varieties of apple.

— *M. floribunda* is a pretty little tree, semi-weeping and open in shape. It is a very prolific flowerer, and the deep-pink buds open out into pink flowers that turn white as they develop fully. The little red fruits are about the same size as cherries.

— *M.* 'Golden Hornet' has an upright habit and its cone-shaped fruits are brilliant yellow. They remain on the tree until early winter.

— *M.* × *gloriosa* 'Oekonomierat Echtermeyer' has slightly pendulous branches; the young leaves are purple, its flowers are crimson and its fruits are red.

— *M. hupehensis* is a wide-spreading tree with stiff branches. The highly scented flowers are pink in the bud and white when opened out. This is undoubtedly the species that has helped to produce the prettiest varieties, such as 'John Downie', graceful and slender in appearance, whose pink flowers give way to orange fruits; 'Katherine', which has scented flowers and fruits that can be used to make dessert jellies; 'Profusion', whose young leaves are scarlet-bronze and its scented flowers crimson; the attractive 'Red Jade', with its asymmetrical, pendulous branches; and 'Royalty', graceful and slender in appearance, with lustrous, rich-toned foliage and purple flowers that bloom in summer. The fruits are purplish red.

— *M.* × *purpurea* (purple crab) has reddish young leaves, maturing to green. Single ruby-red flowers are followed by reddish purple fruits.

— *M. tschonoskii*. This is a pyramidal tree with incised leaves. Its white flowers produce yellow fruits, but its main attraction is its incomparable autumn colours.

— *M.* 'Van Eseltine' takes up little space, with its upright habit. Its white, semi-double flowers give way to yellow fruits.

Height: 4–5 m (13–16 ft).
Soil: any, but prefers moist, fertile soils.
Aspect: prefers sun.
Propagation: from seed, by grafting or by air-layering.
Flowering season: spring; fruits in autumn.
Type: deciduous tree.

△ *Metasequoia glyptostroboïdes*

△ ▽ *Metasequoia glyptostroboïdes*

Metasequoia

METASEQUOIA, DAWN REDWOOD

Taxodiaceae

This is a most desirable conifer, well balanced and conical in shape, but with a strange history. Before 1940, it was believed to be extinct. Paleobotanists who had found fossilized remains of it had not hesitated to classify it among the species that had disappeared from the planet. Then a Chinese scientist rediscovered it in a deep valley in the Szechuan region. Although incredulous at first, botanists were sufficiently interested to cultivate a few standing trees from seed in botanical gardens before nursery gardeners also become interested in the discovery.

Useful hints

— Plant young specimens in slightly moist soil and cut the grass below and around them.

— Plant in sun or semi-shade.

Recommended

— *Metesequoia glyptostroboïdes*, a native of China, is a fast-growing tree that can reach a height of 50 m (160 ft). It is conical in shape, with reddish fibrous bark. Its leaves, a pale fresh green in spring, turn gold or brown in autumn, just before the needles drop, since the metesequoia, like the larch, is one of the few deciduous conifers.

Height: 20–50 m (65–160 ft).
Soil: moist.
Aspect: sun or semi-shade.
Propagation: from seed, or cuttings treated with rooting hormones.
Type: deciduous tree.

△ *Morus nigra*

more slowly. However, its leathery leaves have seldom been used as food for silkworms. Its leaves turn yellow in autumn.

Height: from 10–15 m (30–50 ft).
Soil: any.
Aspect: semi-shade or sun.
Propagation: by layering or from cuttings.
Fruiting season: late summer to early autumn.
Type: deciduous tree.

Morus

MULBERRY

Moraceae

This tree is well suited to small gardens in towns, in the country or by the sea. It is the tree on whose leaves silkworms feed. It reaches a maximum height of 15 m (50 ft) and in the right conditions can live for more than a hundred years. Its gnarled, reddish brown trunk is decorative in winter.

Useful hints

— Do not prune, except to remove dead wood.

— Plant in semi-shade or sun.

Recommended

— *Morus alba* (white mulberry). This tree takes its name from the colour of its fruits. It is the species whose cultivation was promoted by Colbert, following the example of Henri IV, in order to provide silkworm food. Although it grows slowly, about 5 m (16 ft) in twenty years, it can live a long time. The 'Pendula' variety has long, pendulous branches that form a veritable curtain.

— *M. nigra* (black mulberry). As the name suggests, this species bears black fruits, which are gathered in late summer and early autumn for making into jam. It reaches the same height as the previous species, lives as long and grows even

Myrtus

MYRTLE

Myrtaceae

The myrtle, an evergreen shrub some 2–3 m (6½–10 ft) in height, was an inspiration to all the poets of antiquity. Its charm and its qualities have made it a symbol of peace and love in numerous civilizations. It is a bush that grows in many regions of Europe, its very simple white flowers perfuming the surrounding air. Its bluish black berries are aromatic and stand out clearly against the leaves, which are small and sharply defined.

Useful hints

— Put the myrtle under glass or bring it indoors for protection in winter.

Recommended

— *Myrtus apiculata* (syn. *Lumus apiculata*) has a pretty trunk, with peeling bark. It flowers in early autumn and its fruits are edible.

— *M. communis* 'Variegata' is a variety with unusual foliage splashed with whitish cream variegation. 'Flore Pleno' has double flowers. The plant is valuable as decoration for a corner of the garden. The subspecies *tarentina* has an upright shape and narrower leaves. Its pink buds produce white flowers.

— *M. nummularia*, with its fragrant leaves, flowers prolifically in spring.

Height: 3 m (10 ft).
Soil: fertile or, preferably, acidic, but well-drained.
Aspect: sun.
Propagation: from cuttings.
Flowering season: spring and autumn.
Type: evergreen shrub.

Nandina

NANDINA, SACRED BAMBOO

Berberidaceae

The stems of nandina are upright at first then veer to the horizontal, and it has evergreen leaves that change colour in winter. These leaves are long, narrow and dark green, and in autumn they turn purple, making them a superb backdrop for the red berries which follow the large bunches of small white flowers that bloom in summer. The nandina is attractive all year round in rock gardens, borders and on terraces. Quite hardy, this shrub is particularly attractive in large numbers. Mix it with tree peonies, rudbeckias or *Spiraea japonica* 'Little Princess', or with *Euphorbia griffithii* 'Fireglow', crocosmias or hemerocallis.

◁ **Myrtus apiculata**

△ **Nandina domestica**

Useful hints

— Nandina is best planted in spring. Water frequently in summer.

— Protect the root-stock from the cold with a thick mulch of leaf-mould. If the stems are killed by frost, cut it back to ground level in early spring.

Recommended

— *Nandina domestica*, known as 'the sacred bamboo', has beautiful green leaves, tinged with red in spring and autumn, and clusters of white flowers in summer. The variety 'Nana Purpurea', more compact than the species, has red-tipped leaves throughout the year. In spring 'Firepower' delights lovers of colour with its coppery hues, which turn to red and orange in autumn.

— *N. domestica* var. *leucocarpa* is a rare and attractive variety of the sacred bamboo, similar to the species but with pure white berries.

Height: 1–1.5 m (3¼–5 ft).
Soil: humus-rich.
Aspect: sun or semi-shade.
Propagation: from cuttings in summer or seed in spring.
Flowering season: mid-summer.
Type: evergreen shrub.

379

△ *Neillia sinensis*

Neillia

NEILLIA

Rosaceae

A native of eastern Asia, this shrub which reaches a height of 2 m (6½ ft) grows anywhere except in very dry soils. The dense, curved branches bear long clusters of small white or pink bell-shaped flowers. Neillia, which is such an undemanding plant, should be used more extensively to fill borders, along-side clumps of astilbes, ferns or hostas, for example.

Useful hints

— Plant in sun or semi-shade and in well-drained soil.

— Cut out some of the older stems after flowering, to encourage the forma-tion of new growth.

Recommended

— *Neillia sinensis*, a laterally spread-ing plant, blooms in late spring, with slender bunches of pale pink flowers that cover the new season's branches. The branches are covered with peeling brown bark.

— *N. thibetica* (syn. *N. racemosa*) produces long, slender branches covered with tubular pink flowers in early summer.

Height: 1.5–3 m (5–10 ft).
Soil: ordinary.
Aspect: sun or semi-shade.
Propagation: from cuttings in spring or from seed when ripe.
Flowering season: late spring and early summer.
Type: deciduous shrub.

Nerium

OLEANDER, ROSE BAY

Apocynaceae

In very mild climates, the oleander reaches a height of 5 m (16 ft). It bears enormous clumps of brightly coloured pink, reddish purple or white flowers. Pruned to shape, it will grow into an upright, robust tree about 3 m (10 ft) in height and will then spread laterally to form a crown of dense foliage adorned with flowers. Its botanical name, *Nerium*, comes from the Greek *nerion*, meaning water, and the oleander does indeed prefer moist soils, which encourage its leaves to grow larger and its flowers to bloom more prolifically. From a distance, the small petals of the perfectly shaped flowers seem to open out in the shape of a star, a feature which is more notice-able in species with single flowers than in those with double.

Useful hints

— Except in very mild climates, olean-ders must be planted in tubs in a mixture of fertile soil and compost. Feed and water frequently.

— In autumn, they should be brought into a conservatory or any other sheltered spot where they will not be damaged by frost. Keep them indoors until late spring. However, avoid overheated houses and excessively dry atmospheres, which will kill them off more rapidly than frost.

— The milky sap is poisonous.

Recommended

— *Nerium oleander* is an evergreen species and has given rise to numerous cultivars with larger, sometimes double flowers, that run the whole gamut of shades of pink, from pinkish white to brilliant red. Among these are 'Album Plenum' (double white); 'Luteum Plenum' (dou-ble creamy yellow); and 'Roseum Plenum' (double pink). 'Variegatum' is a cultivar with cream-margined leaves and pink flowers.

Height: 5 m (16 ft).
Soil: fertile.
Aspect: sun.
Propagation: from cuttings, in warm humid conditions.
Flowering season: early summer to late autumn.
Type: evergreen shrub.

△ *Nerium oleander*

Nothofagus

SOUTHERN BEECH

Fagaceae

This is a fast-growing forest tree, which makes it particularly valuable in large new gardens that look bare. This pretty beech relative, a native of the southern hemisphere, is changeable in character: sometimes tall and powerful, sometimes small and stunted. Under cultivation in temperate climates, it reaches a height of about 12 m (40 ft). Some species have evergreen foliage, while others are deci-duous. The leaves of deciduous species are dense and turn golden in autumn; these species are particularly valuable in winter, since even without leaves the branches and trunks are ornamental. This is something to be borne in mind when choosing trees for a garden.

Useful hints

— Plant the southern beech in deep, well-drained soil; remember to stake young trees, since they are easily damaged by strong winds.

Recommended

— *Nothofagus antarctica* (Antarctic beech) has very small deciduous leaves that take on a kaleidoscopic range of hues in autumn. The gnarled trunk and branches form an interesting winter feature.

— *N. procera* is a fast-growing tree. Its leaves take on a very unusual and very beautiful pinkish tinge in autumn.

— *N. obliqua* is a species whose rapid rate of growth (more than 20 m (65 ft) in

twenty years) makes it a record-breaker. Its slightly weeping branches make it extraordinarily elegant.

— *N. solandri* is an evergreen variety whose branches grow upwards in the shape of a fan.

Height: 10–12 m (33–40 ft) in temperate climates, much more in its native habitat.
Soil: dislikes chalky soil, prefers acidic.
Aspect: sun, sheltered from wind.
Propagation: by air-layering in summer or from seed in spring.
Type: deciduous or evergreen tree.

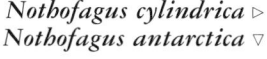

Nothofagus cylindrica ▷
Nothofagus antarctica ▽

Nyssa

TUPELO

Nyssaceae

This tree is planted for its glorious autumn foliage, and is certainly well worth the effort. Some trees or shrubs are prized for their spring flowers, but nyssa is chosen for its leaves, which grow upwards around the trunk in a beautifully symmetrical arrangement and with their autumn colour give the tree the appearance of a giant firework. It can reach a height of 10 m (33 ft) in temperate climates, but grows slowly. Planted on a lawn or in an area of the garden where it will not be hidden, its leaf colour and magnificent shape can be enjoyed throughout the autumn.

Useful hints

— This tree thrives in moist, acidic soil.

— Plant it in semi-shade for preference, though it also tolerates full sun.

Recommended

— *Nyssa sinensis*, 7–20 m (23–65 ft) in height, is still seldom cultivated in temperate climates.

— *N. sylvatica* (tupelo) is a native of eastern North America. In its native country, it reaches a height of 35 m (110 ft), much less elsewhere. Its autumn foliage is among the most beautiful known. 'Jermyn's Flame' is a variety with larger leaves that turn purple, yellow and orange in autumn.

Height: 10–20 m (30–65 ft) in temperate climates.
Soil: prefers acidic.
Aspect: sun or semi-shade.
Propagation: from seed in a cold frame in autumn; protect seedlings until spring.
Type: deciduous tree.

Olea

OLIVE

Oleaceae

The olive does not generally exceed 6–8 m (20–26 ft) in height, but its lateral spread can be equivalent to its height. It is an evergreen tree and has edible fruits. It can live to an extremely old age: some

◁ *Nyssa sinensis*

△ *Olea europaea*

specimens are known to have lived well in excess of 1,000 years. The olive is a beautiful tree in every respect: its grey, gnarled, fluted trunk is like an abstract sculpture, its leaves silvery and glistening. Moreover, it has rendered so many services to humanity, both medicinal and nutritional, that in antiquity it became virtually a sacred tree. It is hardly surprising, therefore, that the olive branch appears in the Old Testament as a symbol of peace.

Useful hints

— The olive has to be planted in regions with a mild dry climate, where temperatures do not fall below −12° C. It requires light and heat and will not grow in moist conditions.

— It prefers fertile soil but will tolerate poor soils.

— Plant in well-dug soil and protect against cold in winter, at least for the first few years.

— Prune just those branches that curve inwards towards the centre. The first olive harvests take place about ten years after the young trees are planted.

Recommended

— *Olea europaea* is the cultivated olive, a common sight throughout the Mediterranean region. It reaches a height of 10 m (33 ft). There are several varieties, including the following:

— *O. europaea* 'Cailletier' produces small black olives that are harvested from mid-winter through to spring.

— *O. europaea* 'Picholine' is resistant to cold. Its fruits are green and are gathered in autumn.

— *O. europaea* 'Tanche' is cultivated for its black fruits, which are gathered in winter.

Height: 6–10 m (20–33 ft).
Soil: any.
Aspect: sun.
Propagation: from seed.
Flowering season: spring to early summer.
Fruiting season: autumn to spring.
Type: evergreen tree.

Olearia

DAISY BUSH

Compositae

Olearias are evergreen shrubs that are used in medium-height hedges, especially by the sea. They are perfectly at home in that difficult environment and their tough foliage sets off their small, white, frequently scented 'daisies'. Cultivating olearias inland is much riskier, since they are not the hardiest of plants; however, if well protected and in a sunny place they will put up a good show. They are very tolerant of urban pollution.

Useful hints

— Plant olearias in spring. Mix with phormium, pittosporum and osmanthus to produce unusual, even exotic-looking hedges of average height.

— Protect the plant each autumn with a few handfuls of leaf-mould. Remove branches killed by the cold at the end of the winter; no other pruning is necessary.

Recommended

— Most flower in late spring or early summer, except for *O. paniculata*, which has olive-green leaves and flowers in late autumn.

— *O. × haastii* is the hardiest. It forms a circular shrub 1.2 m (4 ft) in diameter, with fragrant, white, star-shaped flowers that bloom in mid-summer.

— *O. macrodonta* is more vigorous and gives off a powerful musky odour. Its leaves resemble those of the hollies. The variety 'Major' has silvery leaves. It produces large clusters of flowers in late spring.

— *O. phlogopappa* Splendens Group has pink, blue or lavender flowers, similar to those of the asters, that bloom in late spring.

— *O. × scilloniensis* is more compact, does not exceed 2.5 m (8 ft) in height, and flowers even more prolifically than all the others.

— *O. traversii* is considered the best shrub for making windbreaks by the sea, its round, fleshy leaves tolerating sea-spray well. It grows rapidly.

— *O.* 'Waikariensis' is a graceful shrub with lance-shaped leaves, white on the underside, and has white, bell-shaped flowers.

Height: 1–3 m (3¼–10 ft).
Soil: fairly light, even chalky.
Aspect: full sun.
Propagation: from cuttings in summer or autumn.
Flowering season: late spring to late autumn.
Type: evergreen shrub.

▽ *Olearia macrodonta*

Osmanthus

OSMANTHUS

Oleaceae

This is a 'serious-looking' shrub, with an attractive shape and dense foliage. It can be used to separate more delicate plants such as solidago, malva and asclepias. Sow eschscholzia or plant *Campanula carpatica* in the foreground. The osmanthus has several good qualities: a fine, always elegant silhouette, glossy dark green leaves, and deliciously scented white flowers. It is hardy enough to withstand quite severe winters.

Useful hints

— Plant osmanthus from autumn to early spring. Add some humus in the form of compost if necessary.

— Prune after flowering to give a pleasing shape or simply to make it more compact. This shrub will grow in shade, but does not like windy locations.

Recommended

— *Osmanthus decorus*, a somewhat rambling bush, grows to a maximum height of 2.5 m (8 ft). Its scented white flowers give way to an abundance of purplish fruits.

— *O. delavayi* has tough leaves and highly scented flowers in spring. It reaches a height of 2 m (6½ ft) and gives of its best in well-sheltered locations.

— *O. forrestii* has large glossy leaves, bronze when young, and white flowers.

— *O. fragrans* can grow to become a small tree in temperate climates; its flowers, which bloom in summer, have a delicious scent.

— *O. heterophyllus* has prickly, holly-like leaves and flowers in autumn. It is sometimes used in hedge-making. 'Purpureus' is distinguished from the species by its young shoots and leaves, which are purplish.

▽ *Osmanthus delavayi*

△ *Osmarea burkwoodii*

Height: 80 cm–2.5 m (32 in–8 ft).
Soil: light and humus-rich, not too chalky.
Aspect: sun or semi-shade.
Propagation: from cuttings in summer.
Flowering season: spring to autumn.
Type: evergreen shrub.

Osmarea (syn. *Osmanthus*)

OSMAREA

Oleaceae

This is an elegant shrub no more than 2–3 m (6½–10 ft) in height. The leaves are oval, dark green and lustrous, the branches more or less curved. The tubular, ivory-coloured flowers are highly scented and bloom in late spring. This shrub can be trained, but should preferably be planted in a shady location, where it will thrive. It can also be used to form hedges by planting individual shrubs at intervals of 50 cm (20 in). In this case, they have to be pruned in late spring, before they flower.

Useful hints

— The osmarea is very hardy, thrives in all soil types and is, therefore, easy to grow. The only precaution that needs to be taken is to plant it in an area where it can be protected from direct sunlight.

Recommended

— *Osmarea burkwoodii* (syn. *Osmanthus × burkwoodii*) has dark green leaves and small white flowers. It grows into a dense, rounded shrub.

Height: seldom more than 2–3 m (6½–10ft).
Soil: any.
Aspect: semi-shade.
Propagation: from cuttings.
Flowering season: spring.
Type: evergreen shrub.

Pachysandra

PACHYSANDRA

Buxaceae

The pachysandra, with its small white flowers like brooches set on a cushion of leaves, should be used mainly to close a gap or fill a slightly shady corner. It makes a good ground cover which, once established, spreads without difficulty. However, it will prosper best in acidic soil and likes a little moisture. Plant spring bulbs alongside it. Hydrangeas, which also like shade, will thrive in a carpet of pachysandra.

▽ *Pachysandra terminalis*

Useful hints

— Grow some plants in small containers and then in spring plant them out in the chosen spot.

— Cut them back each spring in order to make the foliage more dense.

— Divide the clumps every five years, preferably in spring.

Recommended

— *Pachysandra terminalis* produces whitish flowers of no great interest in early spring. The variety 'Variegata' has fairly ornamental leaves splashed with white. 'Green Carpet', with deep green, duller foliage, is slower to become established.

Height: 40 cm (16 in).
Soil: any, although growth is more rapid in humus-rich soil.
Aspect: shade or semi-shade.
Propagation: by division in spring.
Flowering season: spring.
Type: evergreen shrub.

Paeonia

TREE PEONY

Paeoniaceae

The tree peonies do not grow quickly, but patience is well rewarded. Very different from herbaceous peonies, they have an undeniable charm. They grow to about 2 m (6½ ft) in height, and their large leaves, their flowers that look like great cups of crumpled paper and the tortuous shape of their branches give them an unusual appearance. Place them alongside plants that flower after the peony blooms have died: phlox or asters, with dahlias for late summer.

Useful hints

— Plant tree peonies in the spring, and do not be afraid to plant the roots deep. Mulch the soil each spring with leaf-mould or bark.

— There is no need to prune them, but if they are damaged by an exceptionally hard frost, cut them back to ground level in spring. New branches will grow within a year and the plants will be restored to their former splendour.

Recommended

— Frequently imported from Japan, tree peonies are usually sold by colour.

— *Paeonia delavayi* has pretty red flowers and is readily available.

— *P. delavayi* var. *lutea* (yellow peony), a fairly dense shrub 1 m (3¼ ft) in height, produces solitary sulphur-yellow flowers.

— *P.* × *lemoinei* 'Chromatella' (sulphur-yellow) and 'Souvenir de Maxime Cornu' (yellow speckled with reddish pink) are still unequalled.

— *P.* 'Satin Rouge' has large ruby-red flowers.

— Among *P. suffruticosa* (moutan), the Japanese varieties have a sublime beauty. They have been cultivated in China for almost 2,000 years, and the flowers may be up to 20 cm (8 in) in diameter. This is the case with 'Rock's Variety', which is worth seeking out, 'Renkaku' (pure white), 'Hana-Kisoi' (cherry-red), 'Higurashi' (crimson) and 'Godaishu' (white and golden).

— Other varieties include *P. suffruticosa* 'Baronne d'Alès', whose large pink flowers have a darker centre; 'Colonel Malcolm', purple-violet; and 'Comtesse de Tudor', which has large salmon-pink flowers with darker edges.

Height: 1–2 m (3¼–6½ ft).
Soil: humus-rich.
Aspect: semi-shade or sun, particularly for *P. suffruticosa*.
Propagation: from seed or cuttings in early spring.
Flowering season: late spring to early summer.
Type: deciduous shrub.

▽ *Paeonia lemoinei* 'Souvenir de Maxime Cornu'

△ *Phoenix canariensis*

▽ *Trachycarpus fortunei*

Palms

PALMS
Palmae

The family Palmae includes numerous genera, and 3–4,000 species, virtually all of them tropical. The choice of tree for any particular location will be determined by its shape. The leaves of some species are fan-shaped, others form clumps, while others have long pendulous stalks. In temperate climates only a few species can be grown permanently out of doors, and these trees have to be planted in a very well-sheltered spot,

protected from northerly winds: in full sun, in a sunny courtyard, for example. They are equally at home in chalky or acidic soil, provided it is well-drained.

Useful hints
— Palms require rich soil.

— Since the terminal bud is the most fragile part of the tree, it should be protected by wrapping the leaves around it in a cold winter, particularly if there is snow. Sheets of matting or dry ferns can also be wrapped around the bound leaves.

— The most important thing is to be patient: it will take several years before the trees start to look attractive.

Recommended
— *Brahea armata* (blue fan palm), with its silver-blue highlights, tolerates the cold well but needs a lot of sun. It grows slowly, particularly when young.

— *Chamaerops humilis* (dwarf fan palm) is a native of southern Europe, where it used to grow wild, being sufficiently hardy to survive the winters there. The species is now fairly widely cultivated and can be seen in other regions of Europe. It grows very slowly and is easily damaged by excessive moisture in either the soil or the air. It has to be protected from rain.

— *Jubaea chilensis* (Chilean wine palm) looks a little like *Phoenix canariensis*, but is bulkier in shape. Moreover, its stem (which is what botanists call the trunk of palm trees) can be up to 1.2 m (4 ft) in diameter. It is a very attractive pearl-grey colour. This imposing tree, 20–25 m (65–80 ft) in height, is equally tolerant of both drought and cold (down to –15°C).

— *Phoenix canariensis* (Canary Island date palm) is the symbol of the Mediterranean region. Yet it is not one of the hardiest palms. It grows rapidly and requires good rich soil, considerable amounts of sunshine and a long, hot summer.

— *Trachycarpus fortunei* (windmill palm) is one of the hardiest of all palms. It will tolerate virtually any soil, but grows most rapidly in clay soils. It grows widely in Europe.

— *Washingtonia filifera* (Californian washingtonia) is a native of Southern California and Mexico. It is accustomed to dry climates and is tolerant of cold. It does not tolerate moist winter air, but when it is happy, its growth is very rapid (ten to fifteen leaves per year). It can reach a height of 5 m (16 ft) and puts out shoots that can be used for propagation. Its flowers, clustered in bunches, produce black berries that American Indians used to pound in order to make flour.

Height: 2–25 m (6½–80 ft).
Soil: rich and well-drained.
Aspect: sun, but sheltered from wind.
Propagation: from seed or shoots.
Type: evergreen tree or shrub.

Parrotia

PERSIAN IRONWOOD

Hamamelidaceae

This tree appears very ordinary in summer but the beauty of its leaves makes it a uniquely striking sight in spring and autumn. From early spring onwards, the greyish branches of the parrotia, still without leaves, are covered in red stamens, clustered up against each other. In autumn, its leaves colour brilliantly to various shades of crimson, yellow, orange and purple. It can reach a height of 10 m (33 ft), but grows slowly. The more sun it receives in summer, the more spectacular it will be in autumn, but it also tolerates semi-shade. It spreads laterally, with branches that tend to grow horizontally.

Useful hints

— The parrotia prefers cool, fertile soil. It is hardy and requires little special care.

Recommended

— *Parrotia persica*, the Persian ironwood, is the only species in the genus. In addition to its spectacular gold and crimson autumn foliage, the flaking bark on the trunk creates a pretty yellow and beige patchwork effect, like that of certain plane trees.

Height: 1–10 m (3¼–30 ft).
Soil: cool and fertile.
Aspect: full sun.
Propagation: layering in spring, or from seed.
Flowering season: early spring.
Type: deciduous tree.

△ ***Parrotia persica***
▽ ***Parrotia persica***

▽ ***Parrotia persica***

△ *Paulownia tomentosa*

Paulownia

PAULOWNIA, FOXGLOVE TREE

Scrophulariaceae

Everything about the paulownia is impressive and exotic. Its enormous leaves form a dense curtain of foliage which, in its natural, unpruned state, begins virtually at ground level, creating a wide skirt around the entire trunk. This foliage becomes increasingly dense, to the point where it becomes a veritable wall of opaque greenery. A superb ornamental tree, which can reach a height of 15 m (50 ft), it is hardly surprising that the paulownia is a frequent sight in public parks and gardens in warmer regions, particularly since it is unaffected by urban pollution.

Useful hints

— If you plant a young specimen of paulownia, cut it back to virtually ground level and you will have a small bush growing to more than 1 m (3¼ ft) in height in the first year.

— Paulownias produce flower buds during late summer and autumn, which are then susceptible to winter frosts.

Recommended

— *Paulownia tomentosa* (empress tree, foxglove tree), a native of China, is a beautiful tree, very similar in shape and foliage to the catalpa. Its leaves, almost 25 cm (10 in) in length, are long-stalked and dark grey-green in colour. The small flowers, clustered at the ends of branches in bunches 20–30 cm (8–12 in) in length, bloom in the middle of spring, just before the leaves emerge. The flowers are blue-purple and fragrant, and resemble those of the foxglove.

Height: 10–15 m (33–50 ft).
Soil: well-drained.
Aspect: sun, sheltered from wind.
Propagation: from seed, sown in autumn in a cold frame, or root cuttings in winter.
Flowering season: spring.
Type: deciduous tree.

Pernettya

PERNETTYA

Ericaceae

This is a shrub that provides interest throughout the year. Now fairly common, the pernettyas should be called the 'pearl shrubs': their bells of white flowers open in early summer and are followed by round berries that vary in colour from white to dark red via a wide range of pinks. Grow it in the foreground of rhododendron beds, alongside kalmias, pieris and enkiathus.

Useful hints

— Plant pernettyas from late autumn to early spring. Add peat if necessary. Plant several shrubs, including one male specimen, to give more berries.

— In summer, remove any branches that spoil the shape of the shrub.

Recommended

— *Pernettya mucronata* has numerous hybrids with berries in a variety of colours; they include 'Crimsonia' (red), 'Mother of Pearl' (pink), 'Mulberry Wine' (magenta, maturing to purple) and 'Wintertime' (white). 'Bell's Seedling' is one of the most common, since it is hermaphrodite and can thus bear fruit even if only a single specimen is planted.

— *P. prostrata* is a spreading species with white flowers and blue-purple fruits.

Height: 60 cm–1 m (2–3¼ ft).
Soil: acidic, staying cool in summer.
Aspect: sun or semi-shade.
Propagation: from cuttings in late summer.
Flowering season: early summer, berries in late summer.
Type: evergreen shrub.

▽ *Pernettya mucronata*

Perovskia

PEROVSKIA

Labiatae

This is undoubtedly one of the most beautiful and useful little shrubs of all. With very aromatic, delicate grey foliage, the perovskia flowers in late summer in ravishing shades of blue which match the season perfectly. Mix with pink phlox, shrubby lavateras and pink shrub roses to give very colourful, maintenance-free beds. Perovskias are set off to equally good advantage by white-flowered shrubs and blue hardy perennials such as aconitum, or against a background of ceanothus and cistus.

Useful hints

— Wait until spring to plant the perovskia, since it is somewhat sensitive to cold in its first year. It does not mind stony soil as long as it is in the sun. Cut back to within 20 cm (8 in) of the ground in spring.

— Taking cuttings in late summer is child's play, and will give you lots of young plants the following spring if they are kept in a cold frame over the winter.

Recommended

— *Perovskia abrotanoides* has grey-green leaves and flowers in late summer to early autumn, a little after *P. atriplicifolia*, with its lavender-blue tubular flowers; the cultivar 'Blue Spire' is an improved form with larger flowers. *P.* 'Hybrida' has very delicate foliage and dark lavender-blue flowers.

Height: 1.5 m (5 ft).
Soil: any, not too moist in winter.
Aspect: full sun.
Propagation: from cuttings in late summer.
Flowering season: late summer to early autumn.
Type: deciduous shrub.

Philadelphus

MOCK ORANGE

Hydrangaceae/Philadelphaceae

The great virtue of this deliciously scented shrub is that it requires little maintenance: plant it in sun or semi-shade, in ordinary or even poor soil. Fine summer evenings would not be the same without the philadelphus adding their own intoxicating scent to those of the roses with which they are inseparably associated. So plant at least one philadelphus in your garden or on your patio. Its hardiness should ensure a long life.

Useful hints

— Plant young containerized plants. Growth is often slow in the first year. If there is no sign of life by late spring, cut the stems back to ground level: shoots will then appear direct from the neck. Then water regularly throughout the first summer.

— Prune after flowering, removing the old wood that has flowered but leaving the green, often very straight, branches intact: these will then bear flowers the following summer.

— Mix mock oranges with old roses, lilies, irises and peonies and have a small, late-flowering clematis, *C. flammula* for example, trailing among their foliage; a few sternbergias will brighten up the scene in early autumn. Mock oranges are completely at home in country hedges, alongside amelanchiers, deutzias, kerrias and mahonias.

Recommended

There are a great many, including some with French names, since the person who produced the most varieties early this century was Victor Lemoine, a famous French nurseryman.

— *Philadelphus* 'Beauclerk' has arching branches with dark green leaves. The large fragrant flowers are produced in summer and are white with a small central pale purple blotch.

— *P.* 'Belle Etoile' is undoubtedly the most beautiful and most prolific flowerer of all, with large, pure white, bell-shaped flowers. Another cultivar, 'Sybille', with a heady scent of orange blossom, has a touch of red.

— *P. coronarius* 'Aureus' is very much at home in dry, chalky soils, and prefers the shade. *P.c.* 'Variegatus' has creamy white flowers and mid-green leaves broadly edged with white.

— *P.* 'Enchantement' has double flowers tightly packed along its branches, while 'Bouquet Blanc', with its tall, supple, graceful branches, has semi-double flowers up to 6 cm (2½ in) in diameter.

△ *Perovskia atriplicifolia*
▽ *Philadelphus coronarius*

— *P. magdalenae* has peeling bark. The white flowers appear in early summer.

— *P.* 'Manteau d'Hermine' is a dwarf shrub with fairly small double flowers.

— *P.* 'Minnesota Snowflake' is the variety most resistant to cold. Ideal for rock gardens or tubs, its flowers are marvellously scented.

— *P.* 'Virginal' is one of the most popular hybrids, tall and vigorous, with large semi-double or double flowers.

Height: 1–3 m (3¼–10 ft).
Soil: ordinary, even fairly chalky.
Aspect: sun or semi-shade.
Propagation: from softwood cuttings in spring, or hardwood cuttings in autumn.
Flowering season: summer.
Type: deciduous shrub.

389

△ *Phillyrea latifolia*

Phillyrea

JASMINE BOX

Oleaceae

Although not particularly ornamental, the phillyrea is a useful evergreen shrub. It forms a dense bush, making a good backdrop for a flower bed. The fragrant white flowers appear in late spring. The fruits which follow are a bluey-black colour.

Useful hints

— Phillyrea can be used for several different purposes. It is a valuable shrub in towns, as it withstands pollution, and elsewhere is equally at home on steepish slopes or under trees.

Recommended

— *Phillyrea angustifolia* easily grows to 3 m (10 ft) and will form a good dense bush.

— *P. latifolia* forms a small tree about 5 m (16 ft) tall. The new season's shoots are covered in a soft down.

Height: 2–5 m (6½–16 ft).
Soil: any.
Aspect: any.
Propagation: from seed or cuttings taken in summer.
Flowering season: late spring.
Type: evergreen tree or shrub.

Phlomis

JERUSALEM SAGE

Labiatae

This is a shrub with a difference: it has velvety evergreen foliage, bears unusual whorls of hooded yellow flowers, and has a rounded, spreading habit. It looks very much at home in the corner of a flower border, mixing well with rock roses, lavender and sage.

Useful hints

— Plant phlomis, preferably in spring, in one of the warmest corners of the garden. It does not mind hot sun – in fact, its foliage looks at its best in such conditions.

— In early summer, mulch the surrounding area with leaf-mould or bark. When the first frosts arrive, allow the vegetation to die down, then protect the plant with conifer branches, straw or transparent plastic sheeting. As a precaution, take a few cuttings in summer and raise them under cover.

Recommended

— *Phlomis fruticosa*, the Jerusalem sage, has furry grey foliage which can look a bit grubby. The yellow flowers are borne in succession throughout the summer. Planted in a tub, this is an excellent plant for a patio which receives the full force of the sun.

— *P.* 'Edward Bowles', a hybrid between *P. fruticosa* and *P. russeliana*, has yellow flowers.

Height: 60–80 cm (24–32 in).
Soil: must be free-draining.
Aspect: full sun.
Propagation: from cuttings in summer.
Flowering season: late spring to early summer.
Type: evergreen shrub.

▽ *Phlomis fruticosa*

△ *Photinia glabra* 'Rubens'

Photinia

PHOTINIA

Rosaceae

Photinia created a sensation in 1955, when the hybrid *Photinia × fraseri* suddenly appeared on the scene. Nurserymen thought they had acquired a hedging shrub with exciting possibilities. It is an evergreen which, in spring, puts out fiery red new growth, followed by white flowers similar to those of hawthorn. Equal in beauty to pieris, photinia is a great deal less fussy about soil quality. However, it has proved something of a disappointment, being prone to fireblight in some areas, but it is still widely grown. In late spring and early summer, any suspect shoot – i.e. a shoot which suddenly withers – should be removed immediately, in case it is fireblight. Let a clematis climb among its branches, and at its feet plant *Geranium sanguineum*. White-flowering shrubs, such as amelanchiers and spiraeas, are most suitable as neighbours.

Useful hints

— Plant photinias in spring, in ordinary well-drained soil.

— Evergreen species are best in acid or neutral soil conditions.

— Photinias do not mind pruning, but wait until the end of summer to avoid harming future flowers. They will not thrive in heavy clay.

Recommended

— *P. × fraseri* 'Red Robin' is the most widely grown variety. Its undeniable vigour makes it one of the best shrubs for an evergreen hedge. The young shoots are a brilliant red, while those of 'Birmingham' are more coppery in colour.

— The leaves of *P. glabra* start off bronze (bright red in the case of 'Rubens') (syn. *P. × fraseri* 'Rubens'), gradually becoming dark green. This species bears white flowers in late spring or early summer, followed by red fruits which turn black as they mature.

— *P. serratifolia* has red shoots when young, maturing to green.

— The leaves of *P. villosa* turn orange-red in autumn.

Height: 2–3 m (6½–10 ft).
Soil: ordinary, but improved with humus, garden compost or leaf-mould.
Aspect: sun, out of the wind.
Propagation: from cuttings in summer.
Flowering season: late spring to early summer.
Type: deciduous or evergreen shrub.

Picea

SPRUCE

Pinaceae

Piceas are conifers of tall, upright habit. The genus includes a large number of species indigenous to the northern hemisphere, where they thrive in supposedly difficult conditions, showing a predilection for cold, moist places and poor soils. It is quite simple to distinguish a spruce (genus *Picea*) from a fir (*Abies*): the cones of a fir point upwards, while those of a spruce hang down. Another method is to pluck a needle from the tree: in the case of a fir, it leaves a tiny round scar on the branch; in that of a spruce, it tears away a small sliver of bark at the base.

Useful hints

— Piceas thrive in moist atmospheric conditions, so young plants should be sprayed frequently with water.

— These conifers should not be planted in an urban environment, as they are highly sensitive to pollution. Their enemies include rabbits and squirrels, which are likely to cause damage, and many types of insect. Keep a close watch and be prepared to treat the tree if it shows signs of distress.

Recommended

— *Picea abies* (syn. *P. excelsa*), the Norway spruce, is the much-loved Christmas tree, which is planted in large numbers for forestry purposes. Its tall silhouette and regularly arranged, slightly curved branches are a familiar sight. In forest plantations, they are often grown too close together and become bare at the base. The dense shade thrown by this tree inhibits the growth of any other type of plant, making a spruce forest a somewhat sinister place. It eventually grows to a height of 30 m (95 ft). *P. abies* has fathered a number of cultivars, including some interesting dwarf varieties.

— *P. abies* 'Acrocona' is a small spruce with drooping branches. It has an unusual characteristic: from a very young age it bears huge, reddish cones at the ends of its branches. At maturity it stands 6–8 m (20–26 ft) tall.

Picea breweriana ▷

— *P. abies* 'Clanbrasiliana' forms a neat, rounded bush. The bright green leaves vary in size and arrangement and, in spring, the new shoots are brown. The shape becomes less regular with age. Its mature height is 1–5 m (3¼–16 ft).

— *P. abies* 'Gregoryana' is a small spruce of unusual appearance: from a distance it looks like a light green sponge with fuzzy edges. It is nevertheless an excellent plant for a rock garden. It grows to 1 m (3¼ ft).

— *P. abies* 'Inversa' is another curious tree, of weeping appearance, the branches forming a cascade of greenery on an upright trunk. Staking is necessary to prevent it falling over. It is 15 m (50 ft) tall when fully grown.

— *P. abies* 'Maxwellii' forms a low, flattened bush which spreads and spreads. It has stiff, blue-green foliage.

— *P. abies* 'Nidiformis' (bird's nest spruce) is well named: this tree resembles nothing so much as a stork's nest with its flat, platform-like top. The young, apple-green shoots make a fine display in spring. A deservedly popular variety, eventually growing to 80 cm (32 in).

— *P. abies* 'Ohlendorfii' forms an attractive conical bush. The spreading branches, which rise and diverge from the trunk, are clothed in yellow-green foliage. It eventually reaches a height of up to 1.5 m (5 ft).

— *P. abies* 'Reflexa', if staked, is similar to 'Inversa'. It is, however, preferable to allow it the freedom to develop into a compact, weeping bush. In spring, it puts out new shoots of a lovely tender green. It does not exceed 40–50 cm (16–20 in).

— *P. breweriana* was discovered in the mountains of California and introduced to Europe a century ago by a Dr Brewer. It is one of the strangest conifers to be found anywhere. The tree is conical in shape. The branches, regularly distributed from top to bottom and held out at a slight upward angle, are clothed in long, pendulous, almost silky branchlets which fall like drapery. It grows to 10–15 m (33–50 ft).

— *P. engelmannii* (Engelmann spruce) is a pyramid-shaped species, with distinctive dense, spreading foliage and stiff, tight-packed needles reminiscent of a bottle

△ *Picea abies*
▽ *Picea glauca*

△ *Picea pungens* 'Koster'
▽ *Picea abies* 'Reflexa'

▽ *Picea abies* 'Gregoryana'

brush. The cones are reddish, turning brown as they mature. When full grown, it reaches 30 m (95 ft).

— *P. engelmannii* 'Glauca' has glaucous green, almost blue foliage. It eventually grows to 12 m (40 ft).

— *P. glauca* (white spruce) is conical in shape, tapering sharply to a point.

The dense foliage consists of fine, thin needles, which have an unpleasant odour. Its grows to an adult height of 20 m (65 ft).

— *P. glauca* var. *albertiana* 'Conica' is the best-known dwarf conifer, compact and excellent as ground cover. The foliage is a most attractive green in spring. It does

Picea pungens △

Picea breweriana △
Picea pungens 'Glauca Prostrata' ▽

curve upwards at the tips. The foliage is dark green, glaucous on the underside, and the cones it bears are a dark violet when the tree is young, becoming brown with age. A majestic, elegant tree when full grown, reaching 30 m (95 ft).

— *P. omorika* 'Nana' is a dwarf form of the same tree. It forms a rounded, compact cone and the foliage has a glint of silver. It does not exceed 1.5 m (5ft).

— *P. orientalis* (Oriental spruce) is a well-proportioned, dark green tree. It has very fine needles which cluster thickly along the branches. The variety 'Aurea' is completely yellow in spring, before reverting to dark green in summer.

— *P. pungens* (Colorado or blue spruce) is not often grown by nurseries, though it is a stately, well-balanced conifer and will grow in practically any soil. Cultivars of the species are occasionally featured in gardens, for example 'Endtz', a tree of regular habit with short branchlets and broad needles which take on a silver-grey sheen in winter. When mature, it is 30 m (95 ft) in height.

— *P. pungens glauca* is the most frequently derived variety. The colour varies from one specimen to another, but the glaucous blue element is very pronounced. The name blue spruce fits this tree very well.

— *P. pungens* 'Globosa' is a dwarf variety which forms a very compact, flattened ball shape. It, too, has fine glaucous foliage.

— *P. pungens* 'Koster' is the most popular variety of blue spruce. It was very fashionable in the 1960s and some are still to be seen, often planted in the middle of a lawn. The young shoots are a lovely pale blue colour, and particularly tender. It grows to 15 m (50 ft).

— *P. sitchensis* is a very tall, spreading spruce. The branches are angled upwards, creating an impression of elegance. This species has been much used for reafforestation purposes in Northern England and Wales. It eventually reaches 40 m (130 ft).

Height: full-sized trees, 6–40 m (20–130 ft); small varieties, 40 cm–5 m (16 in–16 ft).
Soil: ordinary.
Aspect: any.
Propagation: from seed, or from cuttings using a hormone rooting powder.
Type: evergreen tree.

not exceed 80 cm (32 in) in height. A word of warning: it is very susceptible to red spider mite.

— *P. mariana* (black spruce), a native of Canada, is a slow-growing species. The cultivar 'Nana' is an extremely hardy conifer, forming a low bush 50 cm (20 in) in height. Its attractive bluish green foliage makes it a welcome addition to the rock garden.

— *P. omorika* (Serbian spruce) is a native of the Balkans. If you own a park or large garden and want to plant a conifer, this is undoubtedly the tree to go for. A spruce of great beauty and stately bearing, its evenly spaced branches

△ *Pieris formosa* **var.** *forrestii*

Pieris

ANDROMEDA

Ericaceae

Pieris is a superb evergreen shrub, absolutely essential if one has acid soil. It is very slow-growing and the flowers are reminiscent of lily of the valley. There will always be a role for pieris, which can even be grown in a tub sited on a patio in semi-shade. When mixed with rhododendrons, its new foliage, often bright red, lends a touch of colour to the garden in early spring. Try planting it with hellebores and pernettyas.

Useful hints

— Plant pieris in autumn or spring.

— Each spring, treat with three handfuls of dried blood and a thick mulch of leaf-mould or peat.

Recommended

— *Pieris formosa* var. *forrestii* 'Wakehurst', whose tender young foliage is an almost unreal red, has long been a must. It has recently been joined by *P.* 'Forest Flame', a variety less susceptible to frost. Lovers of variegated foliage will find it hard to resist the new varieties from Holland.

— *P. japonica*, a shrub of proven hardiness, forms a dense rounded bush. At the end of winter, it clothes itself in a glorious coppery red.

— Varieties of *P. japonica* include 'Daisen' with bronze leaves maturing to green; 'Dorothy Wyckoff', deep crimson buds; 'Mountain Fire', brilliant red young foliage. 'Variegata' is slow-growing, with small leaves edged with white.

Height: 2–3.5 m (6½–11½ ft).
Soil: acid, not water-logged in winter.
Aspect: semi-shade.
Propagation: by layering in early summer (difficult).
Flowering season: mid-spring.
Type: evergreen shrub.

Pinus

PINE

Pinaceae

Pines are as much a part of the landscape as are oaks and birches. They grow throughout the northern hemisphere, and also in tropical regions at high altitude.

Useful hints

— Although pines are not normally fussy, some are averse to alkaline soils.

— At a nursery, buy only pines that have been grown in a container or that have a good root ball, and plant them immediately, taking care not to disturb the roots. Do not allow grass to grow under the tree, at least during the first year.

Recommended

— *Pinus aristata* (bristlecone pine) is a native of Colorado, where ancient specimens have taken 2,000 years to grow to a height of 15 m (50 ft). In a garden setting, it takes the form of a small tree with resin-spotted needles arranged in groups of five. It is extremely slow-growing, putting on barely 5 cm (2 in) a year. Its height at maturity is 10 m (33 ft).

— *P. cembra* (arolla or Swiss pine) is a mountain species, but it will also grow in a lowland environment, forming a fairly regular cone shape with plenty of growth at the bottom. The needles – dark green on the upper surface, blue on the underside – have an attractive sheen. The upward-pointing cones are violet. When fully grown, it stands 15–20 m (50–65 ft) tall.

— *P. contorta* (stone pine) should not be planted in alkaline soil. It grows well in sand and is often used for stabilizing sand dunes. The needles are arranged in pairs. Its tendency to form odd shapes adds to its charm. It thrives on Atlantic-facing coasts and stands 10 m (33 ft) tall at maturity.

— *P. densiflora* 'Umbraculifera' is an ideal specimen for a rock garden: it has a beautiful full shape and grows extremely slowly, never exceeding a height of 2 m (6½ ft).

— *P. excelsa* (syn. *P. griffithii*) see *P. wallichiana*.

△ *Pinus nigra* **var.** *austriaca* (syn. *P. nigra* ssp. *nigra*)

△ *Pinus tabulaeformis*

— *P. halepensis* (Aleppo pine) is a species from the Mediterranean, where it is sometimes found clinging to masses of fallen limestone rock. The glaucous, somewhat twisted leaves are arranged in pairs. It has reddish brown, deeply furrowed bark. Be warned: this is not a hardy species. Its ultimate height is 20 m (65 ft).

— *P. jeffreyi* (Jeffrey's pine) bears large needles of a bluish green colour. It does well in wet soils, eventually growing to 30 m (95 ft).

— *P. leucodermis* (syn. *P. heldreichii*) has a light grey trunk and dense, dark green foliage, which forms an attractive contrast with its blue cones. It will grow anywhere, even in alkaline soils. It eventually reaches 10 m (33 ft). The dwarf variety 'Compact Gem', which may be rounded or conical, takes years to reach 1.5 m (5 ft).

— *P. montezumae*, from Mexico, is unfortunately not very hardy. It is, however, well worth planting in areas with a mild climate. A magnificent tree, its greyish green foliage consists of extraordinarily long drooping needles. It is a slow grower – 4 m (13 ft) in ten years – reaching 10 m (33 ft) at maturity.

— *P. mugo* (syn. *P. montana*, *P. mughus*) is a native of mountain areas, where it does not grow beyond a shrub or small tree. The young shoots are bright green. The needles, which darken with age, are arranged in pairs. The branches grow upwards. Because its growth is so slow, it makes an excellent specimen for a rock garden. Three dwarf varieties are to be had from nurseries:

— The popular *P. mugo* 'Gnom', which is even slower-growing and more squat.

— *P. mugo* 'Hesse', which forms a dense bush with twisted needles. Tubs and troughs are an ideal setting for this 60 cm (24 in) miniature.

— *P. mugo* var. *pumilio*, a small, bushy, creeping variety, whose foliage has an attractive blue sheen. It eventually grows to 3 m (10 ft).

— *P. pinaster* (maritime pine) is the species much grown in coastal areas with mild climates. It is a slender tree with a powerful trunk, wide crown and long fresh green needles arranged in pairs. The shiny cones have prominent scales. It requires plenty of light and warmth and a fairly humid atmosphere, so does well by the sea and is used for stabilizing sand dunes. It has been densely planted in some forest areas to provide timber. It reaches 30 m (95 ft) at maturity.

— *P. pinea* is the stone pine of coastal areas in southern Europe. It takes fifteen or so years to assume its distinctive shape. The long needles are borne in pairs. The bark is an orange-red, deeply

△ *Pinus pinaster*
▽ *Pinus mugo*

▽ *Pinus bungeana*

furrowed. At the age of about thirty, this species begins to bear cones, which contain delicious edible seeds.

— The giant *P. ponderosa* is found in western coastal areas of the USA, but will also grow in Europe. Its yellowish green foliage and light orange trunk are highly distinctive. It reaches 20 m (65 ft) in Europe, up to 50 m (160 ft) in its native setting.

— *P. radiata* (syn. *P. insignis*), the Monterey pine, originates from California and will do well only in regions with a relatively mild climate. It is a fine conifer, oak-like in appearance when seen from a distance. It grows very rapidly, reaching 15–22 m (50–70 ft) in twenty years. To withstand forest fires in its native region, it has developed a strange form of defence: the cones remain on the tree and open only in the intense heat of a bush fire. To collect its seeds, leave the cones in the oven for half an hour.

— *P. strobus* (Weymouth pine) forms great forests in the eastern parts of the USA. Conical in shape when young, it later opens out so that the lower branches practically touch the ground. The soft, supple needles, arranged in groups of five, are greyish green. Unfortunately it does not like alkaline soils, showing a marked preference for sand. In the right conditions, it will continue to grow for 100 years, reaching a height of 40 m (130 ft), or 60 m (190 ft) in its native America.

— *P. strobus* 'Nana', bearing bluish foliage, is a real dwarf, not exceeding 50 cm (20 in) in height.

— *P. strobus* 'Umbraculifera' is a slow-growing, spreading variety with attractive dark green foliage, eventually forming the characteristic umbrella shape. It takes thirty years to reach a height of 2 m (6½ ft).

— *P. sylvestris* (Scots pine) is an indigenous species, often used in forestry. It adapts to all soils and is extremely hardy. The needles, relatively short and arranged in pairs, are bluish green. The crown of the tree flattens with age. The cones ripen in the autumn of their second year, turning gradually from green to brown. Another feature of the Scots pine is its reddish bark.

— *P. sylvestris* 'Beuvronensis' is one of the best cultivars. Rounded in shape, it bears

▽ ***Pinus pinea***

△ ***Pinus halepensis***

▽ ***Pinus sylvestris* 'Watereri'**

△ **Pinus mugo**

△ **Pinus parviflora**

◁ **Pinus wallichiana**

△ **Pinus pinea**

extremely dense, blue-green foliage. The erect needles put one in mind of a cactus.

— *P. sylvestris* 'Fastigiata', upright and extremely narrow in habit, rather like a cypress, grows to 10 m (33 ft). A valuable conifer for the garden, it has bluish green foliage.

— *P. wallichiana* (syn. *P. griffithii, P. excelsa*),

the Bhutan pine, makes a fine garden specimen. It grows quickly into a majestic tree, and will retain its lower branches. The charm of this species is its long needles, arranged in groups of five, which hang down and give the tree a weeping appearance. The banana-sized pendent cones are covered in resin, and the trunk is clothed in superb greyish bark. The Bhutan pine is also an excellent choice of tree for areas where air

pollution can sometimes be a problem.

Height: varies considerably according to species and variety.
Soil: any, not too chalky.
Aspect: any.
Propagation: from seed. The seeds of some species germinate immediately, others only after a year or two. Some need to undergo a pronounced change of temperature, from hot to cold, before they will grow.
Type: evergreen tree or shrub.

397

Pittosporum

PITTOSPORUM

Pittosporaceae

These evergreen shrubs are easy to grow, provided they are not exposed to very low temperatures. They bear fragrant flowers – white or yellow, according to variety – and the foliage is ideal for flower arrangements. In coastal districts, pittosporum makes an excellent hedge.

Useful hints

— Plant in well-drained soil, out of the wind.

— Remove damaged branches in spring.

Recommended

— *Pittosporum crassifolium* is the hardiest species. It has thick, leathery leaves and bears deep purple, bell-shaped flowers.

— *P.* 'Garnettii' forms a pyramid shape. Its attractive silver-grey foliage is edged with white in summer, pink in winter.

— *P. tenuifolium* grows very slowly but may in time reach a height of 3.5 m (11½ ft). It prunes well and so makes a good hedging plant. The leaves of 'Purpureum' are pale green when they first appear, then gradually turn purple. In the case of 'Warnham Gold', they start yellowish green and progress to a rich gold. The silvery leaves of 'Silver Queen' are edged with white.

— The tiny white flowers borne by *P. tobira* in late spring and early summer give off a delicious fragrance of orange blossom.

Height: 1–3.5 m (3¼–11½ ft).
Soil: any, well-drained.
Aspect: sun or semi-shade.
Propagation: from seed sown in spring, or cuttings in summer.
Flowering season: late spring to early summer.
Type: evergreen shrub.

▽ *Pittosporum tobira*

△ *Platanus orientalis*

Platanus × *acerifolia* ▷

Platanus

PLANE

Platanaceae

Widely planted in urban surroundings, the plane tree is almost universally admired. Its stately bearing, strong boughs, large lobed leaves and the welcome shade it casts make it justly popular. Other great assets are its ability to withstand pollution and resistance to parasites.

Useful hints

— Though very tolerant, plane trees do best in deep, moist alluvial soils. Their chief requirements are plenty of light and space, as their roots will spread over a wide area.

Recommended

— *Platanus* × *acerifolia* (syn. *P. hispanica*), the London plane, is a vigorous species, growing rapidly to 35 m (110 ft) or more. The smooth bark peels off in large strips, exposing areas of whitish trunk below. 'Mirkovec' turns purple in late summer and, being a smaller variety, is not out of place in a garden. 'Suttneri' grows to 20 m (65 ft), with large lobed green leaves blotched with creamy white.

— *P. occidentalis* (American plane) grows to 50 m (160 ft) in its native North America, but not quite so tall elsewhere. The very large leaves are only slightly lobed.

— *P. orientalis* (Oriental plane) is a magnificent tree, reaching 30 m (95 ft) in height. It is indigenous to the Middle East, where it appears to have been cultivated since time immemorial. It grows to be a real giant and is remarkably long-lived. It has large, glossy, pale green leaves.

Height: 20–50 m (65–160 ft).
Soil: any, but prefers moist soils.
Aspect: sun or shade.
Propagation: in late summer, plant 30 cm (12 in) cuttings in light soil under glass. Plant out the following spring.
Type: deciduous tree.

Podocarpus

PLUM YEW, JAPANESE PINE

Podocarpaceae

This is an evergreen tree or shrub which grows in tropical regions. Outside those areas it is usually found only in botanical gardens, and it is a specimen which is well worth looking at.

Useful hints

— Podocarpus may be grown in temperate climates, but it must be planted away from the wind. It grows very slowly, a fact which should be taken into account when planting.

Recommended

— *Podocarpus andinus* (syn. *Prumnopitys andina*), the plum yew. From a distance, this looks like a yew tree. It never grows to more than 6 m (20 ft). Its leaves are dark green above and blue-green underneath. When the leaves move slightly, the glimpse of their blue-green undersides gives the whole tree metallic reflections. Very cold weather can damage this tree. However, it is tolerant of lime-rich soil.

— *P. nivalis* (Alpine totara) is a very compact shrub, with olive-green leaves. Its low, upward-pointing branches are never longer than 1.5 m (5 ft). This conifer is very suitable for adding interest to rock gardens. It may be planted in chalky soil.

— *P. salignus* has long, glossy willow-like leaves and peeling red-brown bark.

Height: 1.5–6 m (5–20 ft).
Soil: lime-rich or chalky.
Aspect: sun.
Propagation: seeds are rare, so propagate from cuttings using hormone powder.
Type: evergreen tree or shrub.

△ *Populus lasiocarpa*

△ *Populus nigra* 'Italica'

Populus

POPLAR

Salicaceae

These ornamental trees, so beautifully slender and elegant, all originate in the cold and temperate areas of the northern hemisphere. Because of this they do well in cold and damp weather. Their only other requirements are light, space and a soil that is deep and moist. They grow quickly and to a great height (about 24 m/77 ft when fully mature), and form drapes of greenery which can splendidly isolate a garden or a house from its immediate surroundings.

Useful hints

— Do not plant poplars next to other trees.

— Prune only in summer.

— Remove the shoots around the trunk at the beginning of spring.

Recommended

— *Populus alba* (abele, white poplar). This tree derives its name from the silvery white felt-like undersides of its leaves. It can reach a height of 35 m (110 ft), but will scarcely last more than 100 years.

— *P. alba* 'Nivea'. This has silver-coloured foliage. It used to be tolerant of drought and salt spray but this is no longer the case.

— *P. × candicans* 'Aurora' (balm of Gilead, Ontario poplar). This tree, which is of North American origin, is very ornamental because of its white-variegated foliage. Its very large leaves, delicately velvety and silvery underneath, are fragrant when young.

coloured tint, before turning purple and falling.

— *P. tremula* 'Pendula'. Its erect branches bear pendulous twigs which give the tree a distinctive shape. It barely exceeds 8 m (26 ft).

Height: 8–35 m (26–110 ft).
Soil: any, but preferably deep and moist.
Aspect: sun or shade.
Propagation: in spring, by digging up the suckers around the trunk and planting them in light soil, kept well watered.
Type: deciduous tree.

Potentilla

SHRUBBY CINQUEFOIL

Rosaceae

An ideal choice to decorate borders and equally suitable for verandahs or patios, this is an indispensable shrub. It is undemanding, easy to grow, and produces flowers from late spring to early autumn. It grows anywhere, with no particular problems or requirements.

Useful hints

— Plant potentillas in well-drained soil.

— Remove any unhealthy or damaged branches in early spring.

— The potentillas grow best in full sun, but cultivars with red, orange and pink flowers will have better colour if they are grown in semi-shade to prevent the sun fading them.

Recommended

— Many varieties are derived from *Potentilla fruticosa*, which has bright yellow flowers. The cultivar 'Abbotswood' produces white flowers and grows to 80 cm (32 in); *P. f.* var. *mandschurica* is creeping, with white flowers and silvery foliage; 'Katherine Dykes' reaches a height of 1 m (3¼ ft) and has yellow flowers; 'Red Ace' has red flowers and reaches a height of 50 cm (20 in) but can have a spread of 2 m (6½ ft).

Height: 30 cm–2 m (1–6½ ft).
Soil: any, preferably well-drained.
Aspect: sun or semi-shade.
Propagation: from seed in autumn or cuttings in summer.
Flowering season: late spring to autumn.
Type: deciduous shrub.

△ *Populus deltoides*

— *P. nigra* 'Italica' (Lombardy poplar) is a narrow columnar tree. It grows very quickly and can reach a height of 13 m (42 ft) in twenty years. After forty years it is a superb, powerful tree. It can last for 200–300 years. Unfortunately, its penetrating roots put a strain on the soil and cause damage to lawns.

— *P. tremula* (aspen). The leaves hang from a very long leaf stalk, which makes them very mobile. Indeed, the characteristic impression of this tree as a whole is one of movement. In autumn the foliage takes on a magnificent straw-

△ *Potentilla fruticosa* 'Elizabeth'
▽ *Potentilla fruticosa* 'Red Ace'

Prunus

CHERRY

Rosaceae

This is a vast genus, including more than 400 species, mainly deciduous. However, two evergreen species are invaluable for establishing hedges or to place at the back of borders: *Prunus lusitanica* (Portugal laurel) and *P. laurocerasus* (cherry laurel). The genus also includes fruit trees such as the cherry, the almond, the apricot and the peach, which blossom spectacularly in the spring, and from which many hybrids, with even more stunning flowers, have been produced. Here, however, we will concentrate on the ornamental species. Plant them in an isolated, sunny spot in order to encourage abundant flowering – by growing several different varieties, it is possible to have trees in flower over a period of several months.

Useful hints

— Ornamental prunus trees are not fussy about the type of soil they are grown in, providing it is well-drained, but they do require a very sunny position in order to flower well. *P. padus*, the bird cherry, will, if necessary, tolerate a position in semi-shade, but prefers a fresh and rich soil in order to thrive.

— For dry, sandy soil a good choice is *P. serotina* (black cherry, wild rum cherry), which will grow rapidly in these conditions, though it will tolerate a moist soil equally well.

— It is best to avoid planting Japanese cherries near water. They may not survive in soil that is not well-drained.

— Evergreen varieties should be pruned to keep them a good shape. Flowering varieties, on the other hand, should never be pruned in winter; simply remove any stunted branches at the end of summer.

— Take care not to plant prunus too deeply. Young trees will need to be staked.

Flowering almond trees

— *P. tenella* is a superb dwarf variety. Its bright pink flowers, which appear in mid-spring, blossom all along the branches. It is less than 1 m (3¼ ft) high.

— *P. triloba*. This fairly common species is admired for its large bright pink pompon-shaped flowers, which appear from early spring. It reaches 3–5 m (10–16 ft), but there is a more compact variety, 'Multiplex', which is 1.5–2 m (5–6½ ft) in height.

Flowering cherry trees

Besides the Japanese cherry trees (see p. 404), which are remarkable for their abundant flowers, flowering cherry trees include numerous species:

— *P.* 'Accolade'. In early spring it transforms itself into a cloud of semi-double pink flowers. A supple and graceful tree, it grows to 7–9 m (23–30 ft.)

— *P. avium*, the well-known wild cherry or gean, reaches a height of 10 m (33 ft), with pretty white flowers that appear in mid-spring. Choose the variety 'Plena' for its rich double flowers, or 'Pendula' for its unusual drooping shape. In addition, all these trees produce pleasantly sour-tasting wild cherries.

— *P.* × *cistena*. When in bloom, in early to mid-spring, the white flowers open out amid wonderful red foliage, providing a stunning colour contrast. It grows to less than 1.5 m (5 ft) in height.

— *P.* 'Hillieri' A small tree (7–9 m/ 23–30 ft) noted for its delicate pink flowers in mid-spring and for the crimson colour of its foliage in autumn. The variety 'Spire' is distinguishable by its conical shape.

— *P. maackii* reaches a height of 12–15 m (40–50 ft) and has attractive brown and honey-coloured bark. In mid-spring it produces small clusters of white flowers. The variety 'Amber Beauty' is even more beautiful than the species itself.

— *P. padus*, the bird cherry, waits until late spring to unveil its exquisite clusters of almond-scented white flowers. This species will tolerate semi-shade and grows to 10–15 m (33–50 ft). The variety 'Watereri' has flower clusters up to 20 cm (8 in) long. 'Colorata' has pale pink flowers and leaves that start off purple then turn to bronze.

— *P. pumila* var. *depressa* (30 cm/12 in) is a creeping variety. Its tiny white flowers bloom in late spring and it takes on attractive tints in autumn.

— *P. sargentii* (Sargent cherry) grows to 12–15 m (40–50 ft) and has delicate pink single flowers in mid-spring. The foliage starts off bronze then turns to orange and crimson in autumn.

— *P. serotina* (black cherry, wild rum cherry). This species produces elegant clusters of white flowers in late spring to early summer. In autumn the foliage turns a pretty russet-yellow colour.

— *P. serrula*. Splendid chiefly because of its mahogany-brown bark, this produces pretty white flowers in mid- to late spring.

— *P. serrulata* (hill cherry). This is a small tree, reaching 3 m (10 ft), originating from the famous Japanese hybrids.

— *P.* × *subhirtella* (Higan cherry, rosebud cherry) has several interesting varieties whose height does not exceed 8–9 m (26–30 ft). Among these are 'Autumnalis', with white flowers, and 'Autumnalis Rosea', with pink flowers, which both blossom between late autumn and early spring, depending on how mild the winter is. 'Fukubana' has scarlet buds, and semi-double bright pink flowers which appear in mid-spring. 'Pendula

▽ *Prunus padus* 'Colorata'

▽ *Prunus maackii*

△ **Prunus serrulata** var. *spontanea*

Rubra' is a small weeping tree with single pale pink flowers in early spring.

— *P.×yedoensis* (Yoshino cherry) is prized for its pleasantly almond-scented pinkish white flowers that appear in early to mid-spring. Its bearing is supple and gracious, with arched branches, and it reaches a height of 12–16 m (40–54 ft). In autumn, the foliage takes on unusual golden yellow and brick-red tints. The variety 'Ivensii' is noted for its weeping shape.

Flowering peach trees

— *P. davidiana* (David's peach). This early-flowering, rather rare species produces single pink flowers from mid-winter (later if the season has been harsh). It should be planted in a spot that is sheltered from the wind. Height 5–10 m (16–33 ft).

Cherry plums and flowering apricot trees

— *P. armeniaca* 'Flora Pleno'. Early flowering, this tree produces double pink, almond-scented flowers from late winter. Height 5–8 m (16–26 ft).

— *P. × blireana* grows to a height of 3–4 m (10–13 ft) and produces abundant bright pink flowers in mid-spring, as well as sumptuous purple foliage with copper reflections.

— *P. cerasifera* (cherry plum, myrobalan) is famous mainly for its variety 'Pissardii', which has pretty, deep purple leaves that start off dark red, and for the abundance of its flowers, pink in bud then white, which appear before the leaves in early to mid-spring. Height 6–8 m (20–26 ft).

— *P. spinosa* 'Purpurea' (blackthorn, sloe) produces pinkish white flowers in early spring, just before the appearance of the leaves, which are red at first and then turn green. Height 3–5m (10–16 ft).

Japanese cherry trees

The prunus listed below are noted mainly for their flowers, and are derived chiefly from two species: *P. speciosa*, which originates in Japan, and *P. serrulata* (hill cherry) which comes from China. They make small trees (5 m / 16 ft for the most vigorous, 'Kanzan' and 'Ukon'), and are particularly suitable for small gardens. They thrive in all types of soil, though if it is poorly drained they will eventually die, so it is best to avoid planting them near water.

— *P.* 'Amanogawa' is admirable for its narrow shape, like a slightly wide-mouthed vase. This tree can reach a height of 5 m (16 ft). Scented, very pale pink flower clusters appear in mid-spring.

— The large double flowers of *P.* 'Fugenzo', which are a distinctive shade of pink and form hanging clusters, do not appear before late spring. The foliage is a beautiful coppery red, and the tree has a spreading shape.

— *P.* 'Jô-nioi' produces single, gorse-scented white flowers in mid-spring amid golden brown foliage. This variety is rare and rather difficult to find.

— *P.* 'Kanzan' is one of the most popular Japanese cherry trees. This vigorous variety has a shuttlecock-shaped crown and flowers in mid-spring. The foliage, which starts off copper, becomes green during the summer before turning orange and bronze in the autumn. The flower buds are scarlet to begin with, and produce large, bright pink double flowers.

— *P.* 'Kiku-shidare-zakura' is a small weeping tree which flowers from early spring, producing large, deep pink double flowers that reach right to the ground. The leaves start bronze-green and then turn bright green.

— *P.* 'Shimizu-zakura' is a variety noted for its clouds of white flowers, on long stalks, which appear in mid-spring. The buds are pink-tinged before the flowers open.

— *P.* 'Shirotae' has pleasantly scented single or semi-double white flowers and a slightly weeping shape.

— The flowers of *P.* 'Ukon' are an unusual colour and appear in mid-spring: semi-double, pale yellow, tinged with green and sometimes pink reflections. It has a spreading shape.

Recommended for decorative bark

— The most famous for its decorative bark is undoubtedly *P. serrula*, with its beautiful mahogany colour. The colouring is further emphasized by the rings around the trunk.

— *P. maackii* is an equally good species for brightening up a garden in winter, thanks to its highly luminous brown and honey-coloured bark, which peels off, like the bark of the silver birch. This feature is particularly noticeable in the variety 'Amber Beauty'.

Recommended for early flowering

If you want blossom in the heart of winter, plant these prunus in a sunny spot that is sheltered from cold winds.

— For early flowering, the best choice is invariably *P. subhirtella* 'Autumnalis' (Higan cherry, rosebud cherry), which produces white blossom between late autumn and early spring, depending on how mild the winter is. For pink blossom, choose the variety 'Autumnalis Rosea'; in a large garden, a group of these trees looks spectacular in flower.

— *P. davidiana* (David's peach) produces single pink flowers from mid-winter. In late winter this is followed by the Japanese apricot tree, *P. armeniaca* 'Flore Pleno', which has fully double pink flowers. Varieties which flower in early spring include *P.* 'Kiku-shidare-zakura', *P.* 'Accolade', *P. triloba* and *P. spinosa* 'Purpurea'.

Recommended for unusual shape

The majority of prunus have a spreading shape, but tapering, weeping, and even creeping varieties can be found.

Creeping varieties

— *P. pumila* var. *depressa* forms a compact ground cover 30 cm (12 in) in height, completely covered with tiny white flowers in late spring. Its beautiful grey-green foliage takes on fire-red colours in autumn, and its twisting branches remain attractive in winter despite the loss of the leaves.

Tapering varieties

— *P.* 'Amanogawa', 5 m (16 ft) in height, grows in the shape of a column.

△ *Prunus laurocerasus*

△ *Prunus lusitanica*

Prunus serrulata △
Prunus 'Accolade' ▷

Prunus triloba △
Prunus laurocerasus ▽

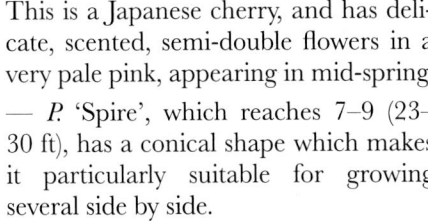

This is a Japanese cherry, and has delicate, scented, semi-double flowers in a very pale pink, appearing in mid-spring.

— *P.* 'Spire', which reaches 7–9 (23–30 ft), has a conical shape which makes it particularly suitable for growing several side by side.

Weeping varieties

— Among the Japanese cherry trees, the variety 'Kiku-shidare-zakura', with deep pink blossom, is a truly 'weeping' variety. 'Shirotae' has only a slightly weeping shape, letting its branches droop like a very large parasol.

— *P. avium* 'Pendula' bows down its long graceful branches, laden from mid-spring with white flowers, towards the ground.

— *P. subhirtella* 'Pendula Rubra', covered in pale pink flowers in early spring, looks almost the shape of a mushroom.

— *P. × yedoensis* 'Ivensii'. The branches of this variety, covered in pinkish white flowers from early spring, start straight and then bow down to the ground. This is one of the most beautiful of all flowering trees.

Recommended for autumn foliage

Some prunus have beautiful autumn foliage – crimson, multi-coloured or yellow.

Crimsons

— Two of the prunus have a rich red autumn colour: P. 'Hillieri' and 'Spire'. P. pumila var. *depressa*, which is a creeper, also turns red.

Multi-colours

— The foliage of P. 'Ukon', a Japanese cherry, starts off bronze, changes to bright green, and provides a riot of rust and purple shades before falling. The foliage of P. *sargentii* is one of the first to change colour in autumn; it starts off bronze in the spring, then turns green, before changing to orange and crimson. P. 'Accolade' also has a mix of orange and bright red foliage in autumn.

Oranges and yellows

— The leaves of P. 'Kanzan', a Japanese cherry, are bright green in summer and turn an impressive deep orange colour in autumn. P. *serotina*, whose summer leaves are a shiny green, has an elegant pale yellow autumn colour.

Cherry trees for small gardens

Here is a selection of prunus of limited growth, suitable for a small garden.

Less than 3 m (10 ft) high

— P. × *blireana* has bright pink blossom in mid-spring.

— P. *spinosa* 'Purpurea' has purple foliage and pinkish white blossom in early spring.

— P. *triloba* has large bright pink double flowers which appear in early spring. A dwarf form of the variety 'Multiplex' scarcely exceeds 1.5 m (5 ft).

Less than 1.5 m (5 ft) high

— P. × *cistena* has white flowers in early to mid-spring, and red foliage.

— P. *tenella* does not exceed 1 m (3¼ ft) in height and produces dense bright pink blossom in mid-spring.

30 cm (12 in) high

— P. *pumila* var. *depressa* is a creeping variety that makes pretty ground cover.

Evergreens

Two species of prunus are evergreen: P. *laurocerasus* and P. *lusitanica*.

— P. *laurocerasus* (cherry laurel) grows to 5–7 m (16–23 ft). It is suitable for all soil types, except chalky ones, and will tolerate all positions, even shade. Its only

406

△ **Prunus × subhirtella 'Pendula'**
▽ **Prunus serrulata**

Prunus avium ▷
Prunus serrulata ▽

▽ *Prunus* 'Shirotae'

weakness is that it does not do well in low temperatures. It has distinctive large, leathery leaves, which are an attractive shade of green, and small clusters of white flowers which appear in the axil of the leaves. In the wild, the cherry laurel grows in Asia Minor in the region north of Iran, where it is found as ground cover in woods. The species has many varieties, which can be adapted to various uses. For hedging, choose large varieties such as 'Caucasica', 'Herbergii' and 'Latifolia', with very large leaves, and 'Rotundifolia', with light green leaves that are rounded at the tip. For low, bushy and thick hedges the compact 'Otto Luyken' is the most striking variety, growing to less than 1.5 m (5 ft). For good ground cover, the variety 'Zabeliana' is best, with elongated leaves that hide the ground.

— *P. laurocerasus* 'Mount Vernon' has a distinctive vase-like shape and gleaming leaves; it does not exceed 1 m (3¼ ft) in height and lends itself extremely well to the decoration of lawns. 'Schipkaensis', extremely robust, flowers abundantly but spreads out in width more than it grows in height.

— *P. lusitanica*, the Portugal laurel, grows to 5–7 m (16–23 ft) in height. It gives best results in chalky soil, and is better able to tolerate intense cold than the previous species. It prefers a sunny position. Its leaves are a gleaming dark green, with red petioles. Clusters of single white flowers appear in mid-summer. Two of its varieties are well-known: *P.l.* ssp. *azorica*, whose young leaves start off red before turning green, and 'Myrtifolia', which does not exceed 5 m (16 ft) in height and has a conical shape and dark green leaves, smaller than those of the species.

Height: depends on variety.
Soil: good, well-drained.
Aspect: sun for deciduous varieties, semi-shade for evergreen varieties.
Propagation: buy small examples in containers.
Flowering season: winter to spring.
Type: mainly deciduous tree or shrub, with two evergreen species.

Prumnopitys

see *Podocarpus*

407

△ *Pseudotsuga menziesii* var. *glauca*

Pseudotsuga menziesii △
Pseudotsuga menziesii ▽

Pseudotsuga
DOUGLAS FIR
Pinaceae

Originating in the Rocky Mountains of the United States, the Douglas fir is a hardy tree, with a straight trunk and conical shape. The highly aromatic foliage, which is a vivid light green, is made up of needles that are about 5 cm (2 in) long. When rubbed, these release a strong scent of citronella. The hanging cones have a kind of bract between the scales. The bark is purplish brown, with wide, deep fissures on older trees. Nowadays, this conifer is frequently used for reafforestation purposes because of its rapid growth. The wood is light, strong and durable. In its native country it reaches 60–70 m (190–210 ft), elsewhere 20–30 m (65–95 ft).

Useful hints

— To grow well, this tree requires space, acid soil and a moist environment. As it has a shallow root system, it does not like rough winds.

Recommended

The species has produced many small-sized cultivars, which are perfect for rockeries or small gardens. These include:

— *Pseudotsuga menziesii* 'Fletcheri', a dwarf shrub, 1–3 m (3¼–10 ft) in height, with a rounded top. It is so compact that all its branches look jumbled up together.

— *P. menziesii* 'Glauca Pendula', a small tree, blue-green in colour at the start of the season and becoming increasingly darker afterwards. It has a twisted shape and all its branches droop almost vertically to the ground.

— *P. menziesii* 'Nana', a dwarf bushy-topped tree which is suitable for the rock garden. It rarely reaches more than 60 cm (24 in) in height.

Height: up to 70 m (210 ft) for the trees, up to 3 m (10 ft) for the small varieties.
Soil: light, not chalky.
Aspect: sun or semi-shade.
Propagation: from seed.
Type: evergreen tree.

△ *Pterocarya × rehderiana*

Pterocarya

WINGNUT

Juglandaceae

This beautiful tree, whose genus is close to that of the walnut, originates in China. It is little known in Europe, which is a pity. Its trunk is attractively striped and it has very large composite leaves that exude a pleasant fragrance. The flowers consist of very long catkins that can reach a length of almost 45 cm (18 in). These catkins give the tree a stylish appearance when they appear in mid-summer.

Useful hints

— Care should be taken with the young shoots that grow from the base, as they can be frost-tender. It is advisable to protect the tree during the early years.

Recommended

— *Pterocarya fraxinifolia* comes from the Caucasus. It is perfect for planting close to water, and reaches a height of 20 m (65 ft).

— *P. rehderiana*. Hardier than the previous species, it tends to produce suckers. It grows well and flowers splendidly.
Height: 15–20 m (50–65 ft).
Soil: ordinary.
Aspect: sun.
Propagation: from seed or suckers.
Flowering season: mid-summer.
Type: deciduous tree.

Punica

POMEGRANATE

Punicaceae

The pomegranate has for a long time been a favoured shrub in warm areas, grown for its flowers and its charm as well as for its fruits. The trunk is twisting, red, very elegant, and the deciduous leaves start off light green, turning red in spring then green again in summer. The tubular red flowers appear in mid-summer. The large round fruits are edible. These shrubs can be planted singly or as hedges and can be grown in containers.

Useful hints

— Plant the pomegranate in full sun. If there is a danger of frost, protect the trunk with straw.

— Position it against a wall, in a sunny spot. The fruit will ripen at the end of the summer.

— For attractive blossom, prune hard in early spring. The flowers will be produced on the current year's shoots.

Recommended

— *Punica granatum*. The orange-red flowers look like small trumpets.

— *P. granatum* 'Nana' is the dwarf form, 60–90 cm (24–36 in) tall. It produces a profusion of flowers at the beginning of autumn.

— *P. granatum* f. *plena* is a form with double flowers.
Height: 60 cm–5 m (2–16 ft).
Soil: good, even dry.
Aspect: full sun.
Propagation: from seed, by layering or by division.
Flowering period: mid-summer to autumn.
Type: deciduous shrub.

Punica granatum 'Nana' ▷

△ *Quercus* × *turneri*

△ **Quercus robur**
▽ **Quercus coccinea** 'Splendens'

Quercus

OAK

Fagaceae

This really is the king of all trees with its imposing stature, ample foliage, enormous branches, massive trunk, and its longevity – specimens of 300 or 400 years old are not at all unusual. In autumn the leaves take on superb colours, depending, as is often the case, on the nature of the soil. The oak is essentially a tree belonging to the northern hemisphere, and it has many cultural and historical links. It used to be honoured by the Druids, and by the Greeks before them. Each species has its

◁ **Quercus** × *hispanica* 'Lucombeana'

own particular requirements, for example the common or English oak needs a lot of light, whereas the Durmast oak, which is essentially a forest tree, does not.

Useful hints

— Allow an oak tree plenty of room to grow. If pruning is necessary in order to improve the shape, this should be carried out in winter.

— It is important to choose the right variety for the soil. This is not difficult, because there are oaks for all soils, even marshy ones.

Recommended

— *Quercus bicolor* (swamp white oak). Originating in North America, this tree thrives in marshy soil. In its native country it reaches a height of 20–30 m (65–95 ft).

— *Q. canariensis* (Algerian oak, Mirbeck's oak). This oak originates in the Canary Islands. It thrives in heavy soil and is tolerant of cold. Height: 30 m (95 ft).

— *Q. cerris* (Turkey oak). This tree derives its common name from its place of origin: it comes from south-eastern Europe and Asia Minor. Its growth is more rapid than that of other oaks. Height: 30 m (95 ft).

— *Q. coccinea* (scarlet oak). This American oak is native to the eastern United States, and derives its name from the superb dark red colour it takes on in autumn. It is very tolerant of drought. Height: 25–30 m (80–95 ft).

— *Q. frainetto* (Hungarian oak). The leaves of this oak have many narrow rounded lobes.

— The evergreen, leathery, gleaming leaves of *Q. ilex*, the holm oak, which resemble those of the holly, make this an ideal hedge tree when pruned. This is a species which is tolerant of heat and drought. Height: 10–15 m (33–50 ft).

— *Q. palustris* (pin oak). This North American oak thrives in marshland and any moist environment.

— *Q. petraea* (Durmast oak, sessile oak). Essentially a forest species, this tree prefers a mild and damp climate, and soil which is light and acid. Height: 30–40 m (95–130 ft).

— The leaves of *Q. petraea* 'Purpurea' can rival the scarlet oak in colour.

— *Q. pubescens* (downy oak). This is the species under which truffles grow in France, and it is known as the white oak in the South and the black oak in the Périgord region. It has a spreading top and a twisting trunk, and loves light and drought. Height: 10–15 m (33–50 ft).

— *Q. robur* (common oak, English oak, pedunculate oak). This oak derives its common name from the length of the stalk to which its acorns are attached. It is the most important oak of all because of the size it can attain. Its longevity is legendary – it has an average lifespan of four centuries, although there are records of specimens having lived for 1,000 years. Height: 35–40 m (110–130 ft).

— *Q. rubra* (red oak). This American oak derives its name from its exceptional autumn colour, ranging from orange through to scarlet.

— *Q. suber* (cork oak). This is a typically Mediterranean species, needing heat, light and a degree of moisture. It greatly dislikes the cold. It is grown for its cork, which is harvested every ten years. Height: maximum 15 m (50 ft).

Height: 10–40 m (33–130 ft), depending on variety.
Soil: differs according to variety.
Aspect: best in full sun.
Propagation: plant a few acorns in autumn.
Type: deciduous tree, with one evergreen species: *Q. ilex*.

Rhaphiolepis

INDIAN HAWTHORN, YEDDA HAWTHORN

Rosaceae

This slow-growing evergreen shrub comes from the Far East. Its vivid, leathery foliage is a perfect foil for the flowers, which appear between winter and summer.

Useful hints

— Plant rhaphiolepis against a sunny wall, in light and well-drained soil, adding some peat.

Recommended

— *Rhaphiolepis* × *delacourii*. The pink flowers, arranged in terminal panicles, appear intermittently between mid-

winter and late summer. This is a hardy shrub. 'Coates' Crimson' is a more carmine-coloured variety. 'Springtime' is covered with pink flowers.

— *R. indica* originates in China. Its pinkish white flowers, which open out between late winter and late summer, must be protected from frost.

— *R. umbellata* is the hardiest species, 2–3 m (6½–10 ft) in height. Its shape is rounded, its foliage dense and dark green. The scented flowers, pure white and arranged in clusters, appear in early summer. The fruits are blackish bronze berries, which remain on the shrub from early autumn to early spring.

Height: 1.5–3 m (5–10 ft).
Soil: light, cool.
Aspect: sun.
Propagation: by grafting on to a quince or hawthorn, or from cuttings.
Flowering season: from early to mid-summer, or intermittently from mid-winter to late summer, depending on variety.
Type: evergreen shrub.

Rhamnus

BUCKTHORN

Rhamnaceae

These are small trees or large, often thorny shrubs. Many of them have beautiful and aromatic evergreen foliage. The flowers are tiny. All the species are easy to grow, and almost all of them have been used medicinally in the past.

Useful hints

— The buckthorns will tolerate all soil types and positions.

▽ *Raphiolepis* × *delacourii*

△ *Rhamnus alaternus*

Recommended

— *Rhamnus alaternus* (Italian buckthorn) forms a dense shrub, with attractive and aromatic foliage. This is a good shrub for both seaside and town gardens. The variety 'Argenteovariegatus' is an evergreen bushy shrub, often used ornamentally. It reaches a height of 2–3 m (6½–10 ft), and will tolerate chalky soil.

— *R. californicus* (2–3 m/6½–10 ft). The young branches are green or reddish, the foliage is evergreen.

— *R. frangula.* Very common throughout Europe, this is a shrub 5–6 m (16–20 ft) tall. It has whitish flowers, and its foliage is deciduous. It grows well in the moist atmosphere of a wood.

— *R. imeritinus* grows well in moist soil. Its foliage turns bronze or purple in autumn. Its flowers are tiny and greenish in colour and appear in late spring. It does not exceed 2.5 m (8 ft).

Height: 2–6 m (6½–20 ft).
Soil: any.
Aspect: any.
Propagation: by layering or from cuttings.
Flowering season: tiny insignificant flowers in mid- to late spring.
Type: deciduous or evergreen tree or shrub.

411

Rhododendron and Azalea

RHODODENDRON, AZALEA

Ericaceae

Almost all gardeners are tempted at some point to plant rhododendrons, and as there are more than 700–800 species throughout the world, which have given rise to thousands of varieties, it is safe to say that there are rhododendrons for all tastes. In addition, because botanists classify azaleas and rhododendrons together, the choice available is greatly increased. Were it not for the fact that they grow naturally in our gardens, it would be tempting to create the environment they love especially for them, because they have so many fine attributes: a great diversity in size, which is unusual in one genus, beautiful, generally evergreen foliage, staggered flowering from early spring through to early summer, and, of course, their wide range of colours. They are hardy, and all are tolerant of shade, poor climate, and city pollution. Rhododendrons are also very convenient to grow, as they require neither pruning nor any particular care and have the added advantage that they can be planted in practically any season of the year.

Useful hints

— Rhododendrons and azaleas require a chalk-free humus-rich soil and sufficient moisture. Their roots, which are not very deep, should never be allowed to dry out and must be protected by a generous bed of leaves. If the soil is not acid and therefore not appropriate for growing rhododendrons, dig a hole 60–80 cm (24–32 in) deep and line it with a sheet of plastic, pierced with holes to allow drainage. Fill the hole with good non-alkaline soil, peat and leaf-mould, a mixture rhododendrons love. Another method, allowing azaleas, alpine rhododendrons and other small-sized species to be grown in any garden, no matter what type of soil it has, involves placing blocks of peat one on top of the other, like brickwork, sloping inward slightly, in order to create a raised terrace in the shade. After watering well, azaleas and rhododendrons can be planted in holes made in the peat. A trench should be made around each plant to facilitate watering and for adding leaf-mould, which retains moisture and discourages weeds.

— Perennials should not be planted near rhododendrons, as they will compete with them for the water these shrubs need.

Planting

— The root ball should not be dug in too deeply (it should barely be covered with soil), and the soil should not be too heavily compacted. If the root ball appears dried out when the plant is taken out of its pot, the roots should be delicately unravelled by hand and the plant then soaked for several hours before planting.

— Rhododendrons and azaleas can provide attractive displays on verandahs or patios, provided they are correctly watered. Sometimes plants that have been forced and purchased in bud refuse to flower once they are in the garden: there is no need to worry about this, as after a year or two they will get rid of their excess fertilizer and adopt a normal flowering rhythm.

Care

— Rather than applying fertilizer, it is preferable to provide rhododendrons with a mulch of leaf-mould or, better still, shredded bark. When this compost rots, it will provide the plants with all the elements they need. In addition, it will retain moisture and will keep the rhododendron roots, which are often very thin and near the surface, cool.

— Should the foliage discolour due to chlorosis, as can happen if the soil is too chalky or the water too hard, an application of iron sulphates, magnesium and manganese should be made once a year using the doses indicated on the packets. In order to lower the pH, some peat should be added.

— Pinch out any withered flowers between thumb and forefinger to improve the appearance of the flower heads.

Recommended: large rhododendrons

— Depending on the variety, these rhododendrons will reach a height of 2–5 m (6½–16 ft), or even more, when fully grown. They should be planted in semi-shade. The following are the best varieties.

△ **Exbury hybrid azaleas**

White

— 'Cunningham's White'. In late spring, the mauve flower buds open to reveal white flowers spotted with green. This very bushy shrub can grow more than 4 m (13 ft) tall.

— *R. fragrantissimum* (syn. *R.* × *sestorianum*). The flowers, lightly flecked with pink and green at the base, have a heady scent and open out in mid- to late spring. The leathery leaves are dark green.

This hybrid, 2–2.5 m (6½–8 ft) in height, is not very hardy and is best reserved for the mildest areas.

— 'Loderi King George' is renowned for its growth, reaching a staggering height of more than 6 m (20 ft). The flowers, which are pink in bud, open out in mid- to late spring.

— 'Mrs A.T. de la Mare' is a vigorous, erect variety which reaches a height of 2.5–3 m (8–10 ft). It flowers in late spring, after a profusion of pink buds. The flowers are spotted with green.

— 'Sappho' produces white flowers, speckled with purple, in late spring. The buds are mauve. This rounded shrub reaches a height of 2.5–3.5 m (8–11½ ft).

Yellow

— 'Golden Wit' is vigorous, reaching over 3 m (10 ft). It has vivid yellow flowers, spotted with red, in late spring.

— *R. macabeanum* is remarkable for the size of its dark green leaves, which have a silvery underside, and for its adult size, which is more than 6 m (20 ft) in height and diameter. The flowers, pale yellow spotted with purple, open out from early or mid-spring. It is recommended for mild areas and soil that is moist in summer.

— 'Margaret Dunn' is a hardy variety that tolerates full sun. The yellow flowers, flecked with a delicate pink, appear in late spring.

— *R. wardii*, a species of medium height (3–3.5 m/10–11½ ft), has light yellow flowers that appear in late spring.

Mauve and purple

— *R. catawbiense* reaches 3 m (10 ft), with lilac-purple flowers in late spring. The cultivar 'Lee's Dark Purple' has deep purple flowers.

— 'Fastuosum Flore Pleno' has a rounded shape and grows to a maximum height of more than 3 m (10 ft). The double flowers have petals with a wavy edge and appear in spring.

— 'Mrs Charles E. Pearson' is a variety which also produces flowers in spring. They are pale mauve. Its height is 2.5–3 m (8–10 ft).

— *R. ponticum*. This species naturalizes in cool undergrowth. Vigorous, it reaches more than 5 m (16 ft) in height. The dark mauve flowers appear in spring and summer. There is a variegated variety, 'Variegatum', with white-edged leaves.

— 'Purple Splendour' has deep purple flowers.

Pink

— 'Anna Rose Whitney' is a late-flowering variety, producing large bright pink flowers in summer. It has a rounded shape and medium height (2–2.5 m/ 6½–8 ft).

— 'Betty Wormald' produces vivid pink flowers, also in spring, and reaches a height of 2.5–3.5 m (8–11½ ft).

— 'Cynthia' is a very hardy and vigorous variety, more than 3 m (10 ft) in height. The carmine-pink flowers appear in spring.

— In spring, the dark pink buds of 'Pink Pearl' blossom into an outstandingly beautiful gentle and luminous pink. This rhododendron exceeds 3 m (10 ft) in height.

Red

— 'Britannia' is a slow-growing variety, reaching 2.5 m (8 ft). The foliage is yellowish green. The scarlet flowers appear in summer and have petals with wavy edges.

— 'Caractacus' is a hybrid of *R. catawbiense* and grows to a height of 3–5 m (10–16 ft). The flowers, purplish red,

lighter in the centre, appear in spring and summer.

— 'Hugh Koster' has ruby-red flowers in spring and reaches a height of 2.5–3 m (8–10 ft).

— 'Lord Roberts' has dark red flowers speckled with black which appear in summer. This shrub reaches a height of more than 3 m (10 ft).

— 'Nova Zembla' produces dark red funnel-shaped flowers in closely set bunches in summer. It does not exceed 2–2.5 m (6½–8 ft).

Recommended: small rhododendrons

These small rhododendrons are suitable for rock gardens or even for planting in containers so long as they are placed in a north- or east-facing position. Unless otherwise stated, they never grow more than 1–1.2 m (3½–4 ft) in height.

White

— 'Percy Wiseman' is a hybrid of *R. yakushimanum*. The cream-coloured flowers, shaded with pink, bloom in spring.

— *R. yakushimanum* is an attractive species with a very compact shape. The leaves, a vivid dark green, are downy on the underside. The flowers, in spring, start off very pale pink and open out to white.

Blue

— 'Bluebird' has violet-blue flowers in spring. This variety does not exceed 60 cm (24 in) in height.

— 'Blue Diamond' produces lavender-blue flowers and vivid foliage in spring. Its maximum height is 90 cm (36 in).

— 'Blue Tit' has superb lavender-blue flowers in spring, but the shrub has a somewhat capricious growth. It reaches 50–90 cm (20–36 in) in height.

Yellow

— 'Chikor' is a dwarf variety which does not exceed 60 cm (24 in) in height. Its yellow flowers appear in spring.

— 'Goldsworth Yellow' can exceed 1.5 m (5 ft). In spring, its apricot-coloured buds open out to yellow flowers that are speckled with green.

— 'Yellow Hammer' produces a bright profusion of yellow flowers in spring.

△ **Knaphill hybrid azalea**

△ *Rhododendron yakushimanum*

Mauve

— 'Moerheim' is a dwarf variety that grows to 50–80 cm (20–32 in) and produces abundant violet flowers in spring.

— 'Praecox' flowers in winter and spring. The foliage, if brushed, releases a powerful fragrance. A compact shrub, it never exceeds 60 cm (24 in) in height.

— 'Saint Breward' has lavender-blue flowers in spring.

Orange

— 'Revlon' is a pretty hybrid with bluish foliage. It flowers in spring and

△ *Rhododendron*

△ *Rhododendron* 'Blue Diamond'

△ *Rhododendron*

△ *Rhododendron* 'Troll'

summer. It can reach a height of 1.5–1.7 m (5–5½ ft).

— 'Trewithen Orange' has dark orange flowers in spring. This shrub exceeds 1.5 m (5 ft) in height when fully grown.

Pink

— 'April Showers' (syn. 'April Glow') is early flowering, with large pale pink flowers.

— 'Bow Bells' has cherry-pink buds that open out into pearly pink flowers in spring. This variety can exceed 1.5 m (5 ft).

— 'Diane' is a hybrid of *R. yakushimanum*, stunning because of its delicate pink flowers in spring.

— *R. moupinense*. Interesting because of its early flowering – from late winter or early spring – this rhododendron is equally attractive because of the fragrance of its flowers, which are pink or white, sometimes tinged with red. Its leaves are dark green above, paler beneath.

— 'Winsome', like 'Bow Bells', can exceed 1.5 m (5 ft). Its dark pink flowers appear in spring.

Red

— 'Baden Baden' has scarlet flowers and dark green foliage. The large brownish red buds appear from the autumn. 'Elizabeth' has geranium-red flowers. This variety is not very hardy and has a spreading shape. 'Scarlet Wonder' has cherry-red flowers and wrinkled leaves. This variety has a very flat shape. These three varieties are hybrids of *R. forrestii* and all flower in spring.

— 'Bambi', a hybrid of *R. yakushimanum*, is stunning for its red flowers, which turn to salmon-pink as they fade.

415

Recommended: deciduous azaleas

These are mostly Mollis and Knaphill hybrids. The first group produce flowers in spring before the leaves appear. Their height varies from 1.2 to 1.8 m (4–6 ft). The second also flower in spring but have a larger growth (1.8–2.5 m/6–8 ft).

White

— 'Ballerina' is a Knaphill hybrid with very large white flowers delicately tinged with orange.

— 'Persil' is also a Knaphill hybrid. Its flowers have a yellow spot.

Yellow

— 'Directeur Moerlands' is a Mollis azalea, with golden yellow flowers that are darker inside.

— 'Golden Sunset', a Knaphill hybrid, has pale yellow flowers that are brightened by orange reflections.

— 'Klondike', also a Knaphill hybrid, has large scented flowers that are orange-yellow tinged with red. The young foliage is leathery.

— *R. luteum* produces fragrant yellow flowers in spring. This shrub reaches a height of 2–3 m (6½–10 ft). Its foliage takes on magnificent colours in autumn.

Orange

— Three Knaphill hybrids: 'Brazil', a vigorous azalea with small orange-red flowers that have curly edges; 'Fireball', with dark orange flowers and leaves that start off copper-red; 'Gibraltar', with orange flowers tinged with yellow.

— Two Mollis azaleas: 'Köningin Emma', with apricot-yellow flowers, and 'Lemonora', with apricot-yellow flowers that are tinged with pink.

Pink

— 'Irène Koster', an Occidentalis hybrid, has scented flowers, pink speckled with yellow, in spring. This shrub reaches a height of 2–2.5 m (6½–8 ft).

— Three Knaphill hybrids: 'Cecile', with large salmon-pink flowers, flecked with yellow; 'Homebush' with semi-double dark pink flowers with paler pink reflections; and 'Silver Slipper', whose flowers are actually white but tinged with pink and spotted with orange. The foliage starts off copper-coloured.

Red

— 'Doctor M. Oosthoek' is a Mollis azalea with orange-red flowers and a dark but striking appearance.

— 'Satan', a Knaphill hybrid, has dark red buds which turn geranium-red when they open.

Recommended: evergreen azaleas

These azaleas flower in spring, most often in late spring. The flowers are so abundant that they completely cover the foliage. Rather squat, they measure 60 cm–1.2 m (24 in–4 ft).

White

— 'Palestrina'. The flowers are flecked with black and the foliage is light green.

Mauve

— 'Beethoven' has lilac flowers that appear in spring.

— 'Blue Danube' has violet-blue flowers.

— 'Hatsugiri' is an early variety, with superb carmine-purple flowers.

Orange and pink

— 'Esmeralda', a dwarf spreading orange-pink azalea.

— 'Kirin' has deep pink flowers with paler reflections.

— 'Odette', a recent hybrid, produces vivid reddish pink flowers in late spring or early summer.

— 'Orange Beauty' is a rather early, spreading azalea with salmon-orange flowers.

Red

— 'Addy Wery' is a compact azalea with blood-red flowers.

— 'Ima-shojo' produces a multitude of bright red hose-in-hose flowers in spring.

— 'John Cairns' has large deep orange-red flowers in spring.

— 'Vuyk's Scarlet', a spreading azalea, produces a profusion of carmine-red flowers in spring.

Height: 20 cm–6 m (8 in–20 ft).
Soil: acid, well-drained but moist.
Aspect: shade and semi-shade.
Propagation: by layering or from cuttings in summer.
Flowering season: late winter, spring or summer, depending on variety.
Type: Deciduous or evergreen shrub.

Rhus

SUMACH

Anacardiaceae

Sumachs are small trees that are best treated as shrubs, interesting for their autumn colours and for their fruits, which look like crimson velvet. In summer the female plant bears conical wine-coloured fruits 15 cm (6 in) long. These plants give light shade, so perennials such as peonies or brunneras can be planted beneath them, to which can be added scillas, snowdrops and daffodils in spring and cyclamen in autumn.

Useful hints

— Sumachs should be planted in spring and watered well during early summer. Avoid damaging the roots while hoeing, otherwise suckers will appear that will eventually become invasive.

— If sumachs are not pruned radically, they thin out at the bottom and grow more like trees than shrubs. To keep a shrubby shape they should be cut

Rhus typhina △

back to 50 cm (20 in) from the ground in winter. If a more tree-like shape is preferred, remove any dead wood from the sumach every three years in autumn. Wear gloves while pruning, as the sap can irritate the skin.

Recommended

— *Rhus coriaria* (Sicilian sumach) is a native of southern Europe and is only recommended for mild climates. It has greenish flower clusters and brownish fruit.

— *R. typhina* (stag's horn sumach), with jagged foliage and flowers arranged in purple cone-shaped clusters, is much more widespread. The variety 'Laciniata' has magnificent foliage which becomes dazzlingly beautiful in autumn, turning to a brilliant orange-red.

Height: 3 m (10 ft).
Soil: ordinary, enriched with humus.
Aspect: sun.
Propagation: from root cuttings in autumn.
Flowering season: summer.
Type: deciduous shrub.

Ribes

CURRANT
Grossulariaceae

Flowering currants rank among the most charming shrubs in the garden in spring and are justly popular because of this. To achieve an unusual effect, plant them in groups of three or four. Their colouring is delicate and their flowers or young leaves have wonderful fragrances, ranging from carnation to blackcurrant. They have the additional advantage of being fast-growing. Grow them in a hedge or behind clumps of perennials.

Useful hints

— Plant flowering currants between autumn and spring. The leaves are often late in appearing in early spring. Plant well down in the soil, so that new branches will then be able to take root directly.

Recommended

— *Ribes alpinum* (alpine currant) has yellow flowers and red berries. It is tolerant of shade. There is also a dwarf form with golden foliage, 'Aureum'.

— *R. odoratum* (buffalo currant) has orange-yellow colours in spring. It has a carnation fragrance which can be noticed a few metres away.

— The best-known flowering currants remain the varieties of *R. sanguineum* (flowering currant): 'King Edward VII', which is a bright red, 'Pulborough Scarlet', which is exactly the same red as the 'Anthony Waterer' spiraea, and 'Red Pimpernel', with deep red flowers.

— Other varieties of *R. sanguineum* include 'Brocklebankii', which has pale yellow leaves and pale pink flowers, and 'Tydeman's White', which has pure white flowers.

— *R. speciosum* (fuchsia-flowered currant) often needs the protection of a sunny wall in order to produce its charming garlands of small red tubular flowers.

Height: 2.5 m (8 ft).
Soil: ordinary.
Aspect: any.
Propagation: from cuttings in winter.
Flowering season: spring.
Type: deciduous shrub.

Ribes sanguineum ▷

△ *Ribes speciosum*

△ *Ribes speciosum*

417

△ *Robinia pseudoacacia*

Robinia

FALSE ACACIA

Leguminosae

The robinia, or false acacia, is a very common sight in public parks and is also very popular in small gardens, with its dense, pale green foliage and its flowers which look like bunches of sweet peas and are pleasantly fragrant in early summer. The tree can reach a height of up to 25 m (80 ft) or more.

Useful hints

— Avoid windy locations, and prune only in summer. The robinia does not like dense or excessively chalky soils. Its virtually rotproof branches are suitable for making fences.

Recommended

— *Robinia* × *ambigua* produces very pretty bunches of pale pink flowers.

— *R. boyntonii*, with its bunches of purplish pink flowers, grows to a height of 3 m (10 ft) and its twisted branches are covered with reddish brown down when young.

— *R. hispida* (rose acacia) is a pretty little tree, 2–3 m (6½–10 ft) in height, with large, bright pink, virtually transparent flowers. The branches are very brittle, but severe pruning after flowering will make them grow stronger and produce a second flowering.

— *R. kelseyi* has weeping branches covered with delicate, greyish green foliage, and small bunches of lilac-pink flowers.

— *R.* × *margaretta* 'Pink Cascade', which sometimes exceeds 6 m (20 ft) in height, has long pendulous bunches of purplish pink flowers.

— *R. pseudoacacia* (false acacia). A native of the eastern United States, this handsome tree, which can reach a height of 30 m (95 ft), is very tolerant of atmospheric pollution. This explains why it is a common sight in towns and cities. Its very delicate foliage and its abundant, strongly scented white flowers, which bloom in early summer, make it a highly valued tree. There are numerous cultivars, for example 'Frisia', which from spring to autumn has spectacular golden-yellow foliage that looks very attractive against a background of dark green conifers and is well suited to the smaller garden.

— Another cultivar, *R. pseudoacacia* 'Bessoniana', has the twin virtues of long-lasting flowers and no thorns.

— *R. pseudoacacia* 'Umbraculifera' (mop-head acacia) has a rounded, dense head but rarely produces flowers.

△ *Robinia pseudoacacia* 'Decaisneana'

— *R.* × *slavinii* 'Hillieri' combines elegance with modest size, and is suitable for gardens in which space is at a premium.

Height: 2–30 m (6½–95 ft).
Soil: any, not too chalky.
Aspect: sun.
Propagation: in autumn, take some of the rooted suckers from around the trunk and plant them under glass.
Flowering season: early summer.
Type: deciduous tree or shrub.

418

Rosa

ROSE

Rosaceae

The problem with roses is that there seem to be far too many varieties to choose from. Each year hundreds of new ones come on to the market, some of which disappear fairly quickly, while others become classics. For this reason, anyone seeking to build up a basic rose garden, whether of old or modern roses, should put their trust in established varieties, known for their hardiness and prolific flowering. In other words, choose roses that are already tried and tested. One of the best ways of making a selection is to visit a rose nursery in early summer, then again in mid-summer and finally in early autumn. This will enable you to see how long the blooms last, and on each visit you can make a note of the roses you like. You will then be able to put in an order in mid-autumn for planting in late autumn.

Each year, competitions are held throughout the world in order to award prizes to the most beautiful and hardiest of the new varieties. Some of the major prizewinners for the years 1990–93 are listed below; any of them would be worthy of a place in your garden.

Rosa 'Centenaire de Lourdes' △

1990

Bagatelle
'Ville du Roeulx'	CFB	Belgium

Belfast
'Malcolm Sargent'	LFB	Harkness
'City of London'	CFB	Hankriee
'Dortmund'	SHR	Ilsink

Glasgow
'Abbeyfield Rose'	LFB	Cocker
'Champagne Cocktail'	CFB	Horner

Le Roeulx
'Pierrette'	SHR	Tantau
Meimoubac	CFB	Meilland

Orléans
'Fragrant Surprise'	LFB	Harkness
Bonica	CFB	Meilland
'Sourire d'Orchidée'	C	Paul Croix

Rome
'Paul Ricard'	LFB	Meilland
'Fry of White'	CFB	Fryer's

1991

Baden Baden
'Climbing Rimosa'	C	Meilland
'Mainaufeuer'	R	Kordes

Bagatelle
'Les Amoureux de Peynet'	LFB	Meilland
'Comtesse Jeanne de Flandres'	FLO	Meilland

Belfast
'Tequila Sunrise'	LFB	Dickson
Cocorico	CFB	Meilland

Courtrai
'Pr Boesman'	LFB	Mlle R.V.S.

The Hague
Meinumid	CFB	Meilland

Le Roeulx
Korbasrem	SHR	Kordes
Poulini	CFB	Poulsen
Lapdiv	LFB	Laperrière

Lyons
'Le Grand Huit'	LFB	Adam
'Paul Ricard'	LFB	Meilland

Madrid
'Frisson Frais'	SHR	Lens

Rome
Dorfuri	LFB	Dorieux
'Sommerwind'	CFB	Kordes

1992

Bagatelle
'Zambra 93'	CFB	Meilland
'Denise Grey'	SHR	Meilland
'Mainaufeuer'	R	Kordes
Korzuri	HT	Kordes
Dicquiet	POL	Dickson
'Doux Parfum'	CFB	Harkness
'Penthouse'	CFB	MacGredy

Geneva
'Impératrice Farah'	LFB	Delbard
Korpinka	CFB	Kordes
Kormalkus	C	Kordes

The Hague
Jacbeau	CFB	Jackson and Perkins
Fryxotic	LFB	Fryer
'Bingo Meillandécor'	SHR	Meilland
'Hurryup'	C	Harkness
'Romanze'	CFB	Tantau
'White Surprise'	SHR	Lens
'Abbeyfield Rose'	HT	Cocker
'Golden Médaillon'	HT	Kordes

Lyons
'Karen Blixen'	LFB	Poulsen

Monza
'Souvenir de Marcel Proust'	LFB	Delbard
Delodive	CFB	Delbard

Rome
'Impératrice Farah'	LFB	Delbard
'Mr JCB'	CFB	Dickson

1993

Bagatelle
'Blühurunder'	CFB	Kordes

Geneva
Adasilli	LFB	Adam
Korsezak	CFB	Kordes
'Shine One'	Min	Dickson
Poulrijk	SHR	Poulsen

Glasgow
'Hello'	CFB	Cocker
'Flower Carpet'	R	Noack

Le Roeulx
Korsarv	SHR	Kordes
Korlamavs	CFB	Kordes

Lyons
'Jacques Prévert'	LFB	Meilland

Orléans
'Ville du Roeulx'	CFB	Belgium
'France Libre'	LFB	Delbard

Key to Abbreviations

C	Climber
CFB	Cluster-flowered bush
FLO	Floribunda
HT	Hybrid tea
LFB	Large-flowered bush
Min	Miniature
POL	Polyantha
R	Rambler
SHR	Shrub

Any names of roses not between inverted commas are the names under which an application for registration as a trademark has been made and are therefore temporary.

Recommended ground cover roses

These will cover tree stumps, slopes and mounds, fill rock gardens, climb over copings or up a corner of a flight of steps and can even make weeding in certain parts of borders a thing of the past. As ground cover these plants barely exceed 60 cm (24 in) in height, but they can spread over more than 2 m (6½ ft).

White

— 'Blanc Meillandécor' is an excellent rambler which bears innumerable pure white double flowers in summer.

— 'Félicité Perpétue'. When trained, its long stems make it an exceptional climber. Left to its own devices it becomes a superb rambler, with delightful small white flowers and purple-tinged buds. Its leaves are semi-evergreen.

— 'Little White Pet' (syn. 'White Pet') produces an avalanche of small white roses from midsummer to autumn.

— 'Paulii' has flat-topped clusters of white flowers that smell of cloves. This is an excellent Rugosa rambler.

— 'Swany' is covered in white flowers throughout the summer. It reaches its best after two years.

— 'Snow Carpet', with its full double flowers, blooms all summer. Height: 90 cm (36 in). Spread: 90 cm (36 in).

Pink

— 'Candy Rose' is a small grower with deep pink semi-double flowers.

— 'Complicata' will produce a great mass of single pink flowers spread over a considerable area.

— 'Max Graf' has pretty pink single flowers, gold-tinged at the centre, set against dense, light green, spreading foliage.

— 'Pink Wave' is a carpeting shrub that has a spread of about 1 m (3¼ ft). It flowers continuously, producing a cascade of delightful pink roses.

— 'Raubritter' has pretty, silvery pink, semi-double flowers with a spicy scent. Flowering season: midsummer. Height: 80 cm (32 in). Spread: 1.8 m (6 ft).

— 'The Fairy', with its multitude of pretty double flowers, is a delightful sight at the front of borders and is in bloom most of the summer. Height: 60 cm (24 in). Spread: 1 m (3¼ ft).

Red

— 'Fiona' produces a multitude of light red roses throughout the summer and has a spread of 2 m (6½ ft).

Recommended miniatures

People are talking more and more about miniature roses, dwarf shrubs that barely exceed 30 cm (12 in) in height. They are delightful plants for pots or tubs and rock gardens.

Yellow

— 'Baby Masquerade' is one of the few remontant (repeat flowering) varieties. The flowers are lemon-yellow and soft pink.

— 'Colibri' is an unusual variety that produces orange-yellow flowers arranged in small clusters.

— 'Rosina' bears fragrant, semi-double, yellow flowers.

— 'Yellow Doll' bears a profusion of pale yellow, scented flowers.

Pink

— *Rosa chinensis* 'Rouletii' has tiny pink flowers, about 1 cm (½ in) in diameter. This variety is the one from which miniature roses are derived.

— 'Mimi' has bright pink, fragrant, double flowers.

— 'Perla de Montserrat'. Only about 15 cm (6 in) in height, this really is a dwarf plant. Its flowers are pink and scented.

Red

— 'Duraft King' has an abundance of bright red double flowers 2 cm (¾ in) in diameter.

— 'Frosty' has flowers that are red when in bud and white once they have opened out. Their scent is reminiscent of honeysuckle.

— 'Meillandina'. These miniature rose varieties produce small flowers of all colours, 3–5 cm (1–2 in) in diameter. They are 25–35 cm (10–14 in) in height.

Roses for making hedges

R. rugosa, the Japanese or Turkestan rose varieties, make particularly good hedging plants, since their height and their thorns serve to form impenetrable barriers. The flowers are often single but are very profuse, and the red fruits make them very attractive in autumn.

△ *Rosa* 'Red Star'

△ *Rosa* 'Penelope'
▽ *Rosa* 'Peace'

△ *Rosa* 'White Queen Elizabeth'

△ *Rosa* 'Madame Isaac Pereire'
▽ *Rosa* 'Catherine Deneuve'

White Rugosa varieties

— 'Alba' flowers throughout the summer and can reach 2 m (6½ ft).

— 'Blanc Double de Coubert' has pure white flowers with delicately crumpled petals and reaches a height of about 2.5 m (8 ft). It has an upright habit.

— 'White Grootendorst' produces large clusters of creamish white flowers.

Pink Rugosa varieties

— 'Belle Poitevine' flowers throughout the summer. The flowers are large, semi-double, flat and a beautiful purplish pink in colour. Height: 1.5 m (5 ft).

— 'Delicata' has very beautiful pink flowers and reaches 2 m (6½ ft).

— 'Fru Dagmar Hastrup' bears decorative fruits that make it an attractive hedging plant. Its foliage is dense and dark green. This rose has a tendency to spread. Height: 1–2 m (3¼–6½ ft).

— 'Hollandina' has very delicate, elegant flowers.

Red Rugosa varieties

— 'Mrs Anthony Waterer' is a superb rose with highly scented flowers. Height: 2 m (6½ ft).

Yellow Rugosa varieties

— 'Agnès' has pastel yellow flowers with petals that mass at the centre. It has a marvellous scent. It reaches 2.5 m (8 ft) and has a spread of 2 m (6½ ft).

Exceptional roses

The choice of roses for beds and borders is so great that it is impossible to mention all the wonderful plants that are available. Some, however, have just the right blend of timeless qualities to make them worthy of a place in any garden. Their flowering season, for some varieties, is long, their scent bewitching. They have good resistance to disease. They are graceful in shape and habit. Some of them are justly celebrated old roses that produce wonderfully scented flowers.

— 'Ballerina' is a slender rose with light green foliage. The pink, five-petalled roses with white centres are arranged in spectacular clusters. It can reach a height of more than 1.5 m (5 ft).

— 'Buff Beauty' bears flowers of a subtle, apricot-pink hue. It is delicate in appearance, very free-flowering, and scented. Height: 1.2 m (4 ft).

— 'Centenaire de Lourdes' is simply covered in flowers throughout the summer and will produce all the more new blooms if those that wither are deadheaded. It is a marvellous sight planted as a single lawn specimen. Height: 1.2 m (4 ft).

— 'Cornelia' is another old rose which is very free-flowering throughout the summer and very beautiful in autumn. The flowers, gathered in clusters, are an unusual peachy pink colour and have a delectable fragrance. It can reach a height of 2 m (6½ ft).

— 'Frühlingsgold' reaches a height of 2.5 m (8 ft) and is covered with marvellously scented, creamy yellow roses.

— 'Golden Wings' can reach a height of 2 m (6½ ft) or more under suitable conditions. Its scented flowers are primrose yellow. Its pliable branches have to be cut back by a third each year. It needs space, and any withered flowers should be dead-headed.

— 'Hansa' is a very robust old rose with crinkled leaves. Its rounded double flowers are mauvish in colour and highly scented. It produces large red hips in autumn. It is perhaps a little difficult to find a suitable location for it – try planting a few specimens together in a rather wild part of the garden.

— 'Louise Odier' is another old rose, with large double flowers reminiscent of camellias, warm pink in colour with a hint of lilac. They have a delectable fragrance. It flowers continuously from early summer to mid-autumn and reaches a height of 1.5 m (5 ft).

— 'Madame Isaac Pereire' is fast-growing and strongly scented, with large, rounded bright pink flowers. It can be grown as either a climber or a shrub and reaches 2 m (6½ ft) in height.

— 'Madame Meilland' produces beautiful large flowers, pinkish yellow in colour. This rose, 1.5 m (5 ft) in height, has an ideal shape and excellent resistance to disease. It flowers throughout the summer.

— 'Marguerite Hilling' can reach a height of 2.5 m (8 ft); its stems are pliable and produce innumerable pale pink flowers. It flowers abundantly in late spring and again in summer.

— 'Nevada', upright in habit, is covered in early summer with pale yellow roses and flowers again in early autumn, though less profusely. Height: 2.2 m (7 ft) or more.

— 'Queen Elizabeth' is familiar to everyone. Upright in habit, with light pink flowers and a perfect shape, it blooms throughout the summer. If it is not pruned too severely, it will grow into a small tree 3 m (10 ft) in height.

— 'Stanwell Perpetual' grows into a bushy shrub covered in pale pink flowers that last until the first frosts. Its scent is intoxicating. Height: 1.5 m (5 ft).

— 'Yves Piaget'. The eighty petals of its flowers are serrated like those of a pale pink carnation, but these enormous, crinkly roses are even more strongly reminiscent of peonies.

Modern floribundas and hybrid teas

These are the rose growers' masterpieces, the fruits of long, patient research, of crosses between varieties in attempts to reproduce some of the qualities of each: the colour of one, the disease resistance of another, the scent of yet another. The supreme goal, however, is a long flowering season. In order to take full advantage of this, it is essential to dead-head flowers as they fade. After a succession of harsh winters, it is advisable to cut back the roses in two stages. In mid-autumn, take about 20 cm (8 in) off all the branches; early the following spring, remove those which are spindly or crossing and those damaged by frost and cut back the remaining stems.

— 'Allgold' has golden yellow flowers that do not fade in the sun and are resistant to disease. It stays in bloom all summer. Height and spread: 80 cm (32 in).

— 'Joseph's Coat', with its semi-double flowers, yellow with reddish tinges and delicately scented, is a rose whose petals change colour with age. It flowers throughout the early summer. It is really a shrub rose. Height: 1.2 m (4 ft). Spread: 1 m (3¼ ft).

— 'Papa Meilland' has highly scented, deep red or even purplish flowers with blue-black highlights and stays in bloom throughout the summer. Height: 60 cm (24 in). Spread: 80 cm (32 in).

— 'Rose Gaujard' bears elegant, scented, semi-double flowers. They are

△ *Rosa* 'Golden Wings'

scarlet in colour with copper striations, silvery white on the underside. Height and spread: 1 m (3¼ ft).

— 'Sylvie Vartan' produces peony-shaped, semi-double, scented flowers. They are deep pink in colour and set against lush foliage. It flowers throughout the summer, abundantly in autumn. Height and spread: 80 cm (32 in).

— 'Virgo' has large, pure white flowers, 12 cm (4½ in) in diameter but rather few in number, and splendid foliage. It flowers all summer. Height and spread: 80 cm (32 in).

Old roses

Many people have a passion for old roses. They are thought to have originated in China and gradually spread west through India and the Middle East. The first known depictions of roses are in frescos in the palace of Knossos, in Crete. In the eighth century, Charlemagne issued a decree ordering that roses be grown in gardens. These roses, the ancestors of our old roses, were used widely in perfumery and confectionery throughout Europe and the Middle East. They remain one of the glories of our gardens.

Alba roses

These are very hardy roses, often with silvery green foliage, and are marvellous trained against a low trellis.

— 'Céleste' is seductive, with its delicate pink, semi-double flowers. It flowers in the earlier part of the summer and grows to a height of 1.5 m (5 ft).

— 'Great Maiden's Blush' has pinkish white flowers and a bewitching scent. It flowers in summer and grows to a height of 1.8 m (6 ft). The only draw-

△ *Rosa* 'Président Léopold Senghor'

△ *Rosa* 'Yolande d'Aragon'
▽ *Rosa* 'Landora'

△ *Rosa* × *floribunda*
▽ *Rosa* 'Gamma'

back is its very short flowering season, 15–20 days at most.

Centifolia roses

These are also very hardy, and can be trained or pruned to form spectacular bushes. Their foliage is a handsome, slightly dark shade of green.

— 'Fantin-Latour' has attractive warm pink flowers with masses of crumpled petals. It has a short flowering season in summer. Height: 1.8 m (6 ft).

Damask roses

These roses (*R. damascena*) have tightly packed, slightly crumpled petals that curve backwards. Their downy leaves have a silvery tinge and the stems are thorny. Most damask roses produce long, slightly hairy fruit in autumn.

— 'Celsiana' is a vigorous plant that bears vivid pink, deliciously scented flowers with bright yellow stamens. It flowers in summer.

— 'Mme Hardy' grows to a height of 1.5 m (5 ft), with a similar spread. The perfectly shaped flowers are pure white with a greenish eye, which is surprising when you see the pink highlights on the buds. It flowers in the earlier part of the summer.

Gallica roses

Grown in France since the fourteenth century, these roses were used mainly for making perfumes and pot-pourris. They are easy to grow and look after, are very tolerant of poor soils and have few thorns. They bear wonderfully scented double flowers in summer.

— 'Belle de Crécy' is a lax bush that requires staking. The highly scented flowers are purplish mauve in colour, with a green eye in the centre of the crumpled petals. It flowers in the earlier part of the summer. Height: about 1.2 m (4 ft). Spread: 80 cm (32 in).

— 'Cardinal de Richelieu' makes a splendid hedge. The flowers turn purplish mauve as they open. It flowers in the earlier part of the summer. Height and spread: 80 cm (32 in).

Hybrid perpetual roses

These usually flower continuously, though sometimes sporadically, throughout the summer until the first frosts.

— 'Frau Karl Druschki' is very pretty, with double, pure white but unscented flowers. It can be grown as a standard – these are coming back into fashion and look very good in borders. It flowers in the earlier part of the summer.

— 'Général Jacqueminot' is a small rose with well-rounded, deep red, sumptuous, heavily scented flowers. Height and spread: 1 m (3¼ ft).

— 'Reine des Violettes' ('Queen of the Violets') is well named, for its purplish mauve flowers contrast delightfully with its grey-tinged foliage. To encourage prolific flowering in summer, prune the branches severely in late winter to within 15–20 cm (6–8 in) of the ground. It flowers in early summer.

— 'Yolande d'Aragon' is an upright bush with abundant foliage and dark pink, double flowers, all of which make it one of the most sumptuous beauties of the garden. Its scented flowers stay in bloom throughout the summer. Height: 1.2 m (4 ft). Spread: 1.5 m (5 ft).

Moss roses

There is a wide variety of roses in this category, but they all have stems and leaf-stalks covered in little hairs that look like moss. These sumptuous roses are scented and resistant to disease.

— 'Gloire des Mousseux' has spindly branches with small, dark leaves. It has dark purple, almost black flowers and golden stamens. It flowers in the earlier part of the summer. Height: 1.5 m (5 ft). Spread: 1 m (3¼ ft).

— 'Mousseline' is a compact rose that can be placed to advantage among perennials in a border. Its small, pretty, globular flowers are a delicate flesh colour and appear in summer. Height and spread: 80 cm (32 in).

— 'Salet' is a free-flowering, strongly scented rose. Its bright pink double flowers remain in bloom virtually all summer. Height: 1.5 m (5 ft). Spread: 1 m (3¼ ft).

Damask Portland roses

These flower fairly early in the summer and then rest until early autumn, when they bloom again, though sparsely. The flowers appear singly or in bunches.

— 'Jacques Cartier' is a vigorous rose that produces semi-double, deep pink flowers with a green centre. It flowers intermittently throughout the summer. Height: 1.2 m (4 ft). Spread: 1 m (3¼ ft).

△ *Rosmarinus officinalis* 'Repens'
▽ *Rubus phoenicolasius*

— 'Madame Knorr' (syn. 'Comte de Chambord') is a slightly stiff shrub. It has sumptuous pink flowers with tightly packed petals that give them a flat appearance, and is strongly scented. It blooms throughout the summer. Height: 1.2 m (4 ft). Spread: 1 m (3¼ ft).

Height: varies according to species and variety.
Soil: good.
Aspect: sun.
Propagation: from cuttings.
Flowering season: late spring to autumn.
Type: deciduous or semi-evergreen shrub.

Rosmarinus
ROSEMARY
Labiatae

This is a pretty shrub, with aromatic evergreen foliage, known mainly for its medicinal properties. It should be used more often in company with roses, cistus or potentilla in areas of dry, stony soil. In spring it produces magnificent soft blue flowers which are an excellent source of nectar for bees and butterflies. In mild climates, rosemary can make excellent hedges up to 1 m (3¼ ft) in height.

Useful hints

— Wait until spring before planting rosemary; the soil should be well-drained even if poor. Protect the base with a few handfuls of straw before the winter.

— Do not prune, but simply remove any branches affected by frost. To create a medium-sized hedge at low cost, take cuttings from the ends of the stems in summer.

Recommended

— *Rosmarinus officinalis* is available in a variety of colours, deep blue in *R.o. angustissimus* 'Corsican Blue', pink in 'Roseus' and even white in var. *albiflorus*. It may be very upright, like the variety 'Fastigiatus', for example, which makes an ideal decoration for a corner of a lawn.

— *R. officinalis* 'Majorca Pink' produces unusual lilac-pink flowers. 'Miss Jessop's Upright' has a very distinctive erect profile.

— The creeping rosemary, *R. officinalis* Prostratus Group, is a good decoration for slopes or banks and is perfect for filling pots, but is less hardy than its cousins.

Height: 30 cm–1.7 m (1–5½ ft).
Soil: light, well-drained in winter.
Aspect: full sun.
Propagation: from cuttings in summer.
Flowering season: spring.
Type: evergreen shrub.

Rubus
RUBUS, ORNAMENTAL BRAMBLE
Rosaceae

There are many species in the genus *Rubus*, some of them familiar to everyone as wild brambles, with their inordinately long, extremely invasive branches. However, few people realize that the genus also includes some extremely elegant shrubs cultivated for their attractive flowers in spring and, in winter, for the beauty of their branches, standing out against a background of bare earth or snow. In general they are pliable; their long branches often have highly coloured bark and some have vicious thorns. The white or pink flowers give way to berries that are much appreciated by birds and, in the case of blackberries or raspberries, by human beings as well!

Useful hints

— Plant rubus between autumn and early spring among other flowers or at the front of shrub borders. The bare branches will stand out against a neutral background, such as a brick wall or a hedge of evergreen shrubs (photinia or holly, for example).

— Prune old branches, identifiable by their crackly bark, right back to ground level each spring. Leave strong branches alone.

Recommended

— *Rubus cockburnianus* produces white flowers, but it is particularly well-known for the very white, waxy bark of its year-old branches, which reach a length of almost 2.5 m (8 ft). Prune it each autumn to remove older wood.

— *R. fruticosus* is none other than the familiar bush that produces blackberries, which can be used to make such delicious jam. The long stems can reach a length of 5–6 m (16–20 ft). The cultivar 'Oregon Thornless' has the advantage of not having any thorns, and has given rise to a multitude of varieties that have few if any thorns, most of which are of American origin.

— *R. henryi* has evergreen foliage which is white on the underside. The flowers, gathered into clusters, are pink and appear in summer, with black berries in autumn. The bush grows to a height of 6 m (20 ft).

— *R. idaeus* (raspberry). This is too well-known to need describing. It grows wild in mountainous regions throughout virtually the whole of the northern hemisphere. It needs well-drained soil and plenty of light. It fruits in late summer.

— *R. nepalensis* is well-suited to rock gardens. It is a small carpeting shrub, with white flowers; its small, orange-red fruits are edible.

— *R. odoratus* grows to a height of 2 m (6½ ft) and produces large clusters of pink flowers from midsummer to early autumn. Its leaves have a soft, velvety texture. It is fast-growing, which makes it best suited to wild corners of the garden.

— *R. pentalobus* (syn. *R. calycinoides*) is an excellent evergreen ground cover plant with branches that root themselves as they go. Its white flowers appear in summer, before giving way to scarlet berries. It is equally happy in sun or shade.

— *R. phoenicolasius* is a deciduous shrub whose branches are covered throughout the year in red down, making it highly decorative. It grows to a height of 3 m (10 ft) and can be trained to grow against a wall or pergola. Its pink flowers bloom in summer and its fruits have a very agreeable flavour.

— *R. spectabilis* is one of the most colourful plants of the genus, with scented magenta-pink flowers that appear in spring. It grows in the shade of tall trees and reaches a height of 2 m (6½ ft).

— *R. thibetanus* throws out clumps of suckers up to 1.5 m (5 ft) in height and bears pink flowers. Its branches are covered with a blue-white bloom and bear silvery, fern-like leaves.

— *R. tricolor* is vigorous and invasive. Its white flowers give way to edible red fruits.

— The most beautiful of the entire genus *Rubus* is undoubtedly the hybrid *R.* 'Tridel' (syn. *R.* 'Benenden'), whose long, thornless stems produce large white flowers in spring.

— *R. ulmifolius* 'Bellidiflorus' is a creeping shrub that bears clusters of pink flowers in midsummer. It makes a perfect companion for roses.

Height: 50 cm–6 m (20 in–20 ft).
Soil: ordinary, preferably humus-rich.
Aspect: semi-shade or sun.
Propagation: by layering, which often happens spontaneously, or from cuttings in summer.
Flowering season: spring to late summer, fruits in autumn.
Type: deciduous or evergreen shrub.

Ruscus

BUTCHER'S BROOM

Liliaceae

This small, evergreen shrub has a wild appearance that makes it a perfect companion for lilies and dicentra. In a shady spot, its pretty, bright green foliage will also provide a splendid setting for the delicate colours of fuchsias and columbine. In winter, its stiff, prickle-tipped leaves are also much appreciated by flower arrangers. If male and female plants are placed side by side, bright red berries will be produced in autumn, attached to what are generally assumed

to be leaves but are in fact flattened green stems.

Useful hints

— Plant in spring in a shady spot. Ruscus requires plenty of watering in the first year. It will take three full years to make large, dense clumps. However, you can encourage the plant's growth by adding fertilizer in spring.

— Divide the clumps every five years, especially after severe frosts.

Recommended

— *Ruscus aculeatus* (butcher's broom), grows to a height of 60 cm (24 in), and although a native of the Mediterranean, will grow in cooler climates. It grows well in shady undergrowth.

— *R. hypoglossum* is a native of Spain but can be grown in cooler climates. It has larger leaves than *R. aculeatus*, and large, red, globular berries.

Height: 60 cm–1 m (2–3¼ ft).
Soil: humus-rich.
Aspect: shade.
Propagation: by division in spring.
Flowering season: early spring, berries in autumn.
Type: evergreen shrub.

Ruta

RUE

Rutaceae

Ruta graveolens was formerly well-known for its medicinal properties. Today it is used as a decorative shrub, largely because of its silvery blue evergreen leaves, which can be easily pruned to produce a roundish shape. The small yellow flowers are insignificant, and it is worthwhile eliminating them. Rues are particularly good companions for old roses and, in spring, for beds of tulips. They can also be used to separate groups of flowers whose vivid colours would otherwise detract from each other.

Useful hints

— Plant rue in spring for preference. It will need plenty of watering in the first summer, and mulching. After the first year, however, it will tolerate very dry conditions, which is an advantage in more southerly climates.

— Take cuttings from the tips of the

△ *Ruscus aculeatus*

△ *Ruta graveolens* 'Jackman's Blue'

stems in autumn and plant them in a very sandy mixture, or sow seeds in spring. This will produce a number of young plants that will flower in their second year.

Recommended

— *R. graveolens* is a hardy plant that becomes woody at the base and grows to a height of 30–70 cm (12–28 in). It has a strong, unpleasant smell. It is often listed in catalogues as a herb.

Height: 40–60 cm (16–24 in).
Soil: ordinary, preferably a little heavy.
Aspect: sun.
Propagation: from cuttings in autumn or from seed.
Flowering season: summer.
Type: evergreen shrub.

△ *Salix* × *sepulcralis* var. *chrysocoma*
◁ *Salix alba*

Salix

WILLOW

Salicaceae

There are at least 300 species of willows, but not all are in cultivation. They are trees or shrubs with all sorts of individual characteristics. Some have brightly coloured bark, others have pendulous branches, yet others have silvery leaves. There are even creeping or dwarf kinds. They have one characteristic in common: they all love water, moist soils and proximity to rivers.

Useful hints

— These trees do not like soils that dry out, and all they require is to be planted in a moist spot with sufficient room to spread out, since they grow rapidly to a considerable size.

— In winter, cut back dead branches or those that need thinning out.

Recommended

— *Salix acutifolia* 'Pendulifolia' has long, pliable branches, that are reddish brown in colour and coated with a silvery blue bloom.

— *S. alba* (white willow) is the largest willow of all, reaching a height of 25 m (80 ft). Its branches have bright yellow or reddish tints. The subspecies *vitellina* has scarlet branches.

— *S. babylonica* (Babylon willow) has become almost too common. A native of Asia, its popularity was given a massive boost by the Romantics of the eighteenth century. Height: 12 m (40 ft).

— *S. lanata* (woolly willow) is a shrub about 80 cm (32 in) high, with pretty, silvery foliage.

— *S. matsudana* 'Tortuosa'. The branches and twigs of this variety, bizarrely twisted into a corkscrew shape, give it a particularly distinctive profile. In order to appreciate it properly, plant it in a prominent location in the garden.

— *S. purpurea* 'Nana' produces bushy clusters of long, slender shoots and makes an excellent decoration for the base of informal hedges.

— *S. repens* (creeping willow) is a very interesting small shrub that does not exceed 80 cm (32 in) in height but can spread up to 1.5 m (5 ft). Silvery catkins appear in spring.

— *S.* × *sepulcralis* var. *chrysocoma*. This is the golden weeping willow, a very beautiful, fast-growing tree, reaching 15 m (50 ft) in twenty years.

Height: 20 cm–25 m (8 in–80 ft).
Soil: moist.
Aspect: sun.
Propagation: from 30 cm (12 in) cuttings in autumn.
Flowering season: spring.
Type: deciduous tree or shrub.

Salvia

SAGE

Labiatae

Without salvias, summers would be singularly lacking in colour. This is not, of course, a reference to the well-known red salvias, which are annuals and perhaps too common a sight in parks and gardens, but to the sages, those marvellous little deciduous or evergreen shrubs that produce such charming blue, yellow and purple flowers. In general, they thrive splendidly in sunny, slightly dry locations.

Useful hints

— Plant salvias in early autumn or spring. Lighten the soil with some sand

△ *Salvia officinalis* 'Tricolor'
▽ *Salvia chamaedryoides*

△ *Salvia microphylla* 'Grahamii'

and do not add too much fertilizer otherwise there will be excessive leaf growth. Cut off any dead stems and cut back the clumps at the end of the summer. New leaves will appear before the first frosts.

Recommended

— The most temperamental salvia of all is undoubtedly the silver sage, *Salvia argentea*, with its fabulous silvery foliage. To produce a truly beautiful shrub, protect the stem during the winter with sheets of glass, because it is very intolerant of winter wet.

— The commonest of all the hardy salvias is *S. nemorosa*, which is compact in habit. There are numerous varieties, including 'Lubecca' with its violet flowers, 'East Friesland', with somewhat darker purple flowers, and 'May Night' with violet-blue flowers.

— *S. officinalis* is well-known for its leaves, which are used to make infusions said to be a very effective aid to digestion, even though they do not taste very good. The flowers are a wonderful match for the silvery leaves, with their purplish tinges, and set off pink roses to perfection. There are purple and variegated forms.

— *S. patens* (Mexican blue sage) is only

semi-hardy, but the extravagant blue of its flowers, one of the brightest in all nature, certainly makes it worth protecting in winter under a layer of pine bark. Combine it with white tobacco plants so that the indeterminate green of its leaves is less evident.

— The imposing *S. sclarea* (clary) is another lovely plant, with a very natural appearance. It can reach a height of 1 m (3¼ ft). The smell of its leaves can be agreeable or disagreeable, depending on time of day and individual opinion, but everybody agrees that its pale blue flowers make it one of the best companions for old roses. It thrives very well as a biennial and seeds itself.

— There are many more species, such as *S. grahamii, S. uliginosa, S. involucrata* 'Bethellii' and *S. coccinea*, but they are often not very hardy. They can be grown in the same way as fuchsias, however, by starting them off in a heated greenhouse.

Height: 20 cm–1.5 m (8 in–5 ft).
Soil: ordinary, but well-drained.
Aspect: sun.
Propagation: from seed or by division in spring.
Flowering season: early summer to autumn.
Type: evergreen or deciduous shrub.

△ *Sambucus racemosa* 'Plumosa Aurea'

Sambucus

ELDER

Caprifoliaceae

Elders can reach a height of 5 m (16 ft), and their foliage looks spectacular at the back of a flower bed, or near a stretch of water. Completely at home in the wilder corners of a garden, elders look superb when their flat clusters of creamy white flowers, which can reach a diameter of almost 50 cm (20 in), are opening out in early summer. Combine them with vigorous plants such as gunnera, ligularia, large ferns and macleaya in order to create an impressive display – though such a combination will require rich, moist soil.

Useful hints

— Plant elders from autumn to early spring, and prune in early spring to give them a vigorous start.

— Prune minor shoots in early spring, to concentrate the sap on the terminal bunches, which will be all the more splendid as a result.

Recommended

— The American elderberry, *Sambucus canadensis*, is particularly spectacular in its variety 'Maxima', with large mid-green leaves and magnificent bunches of flowers giving way to dark red fruit, much loved by birds.

— The common elder, *S. nigra*, has given rise to many varieties, some with differently variegated foliage, some with finely divided, fern-like leaves (f. *laciniata*), and others with golden yellow foliage ('Aurea'). 'Guincho Purple', also known as 'Purpurea', has pink flowers set against purple-flushed leaves. 'Marginata' is enlivened by its creamish variegation.

— The red-berried elder, *S. racemosa*, has divided leaves that resemble a larger version of those of Japanese maples. The variety 'Plumosa' has leaves with finely cut leaflets; 'Plumosa Aurea' is similar but with golden yellow foliage.

Height: 2–5 m (6½–16 ft).
Soil: ordinary.
Aspect: sun or semi-shade.
Propagation: by planting of suckers, in autumn.
Flowering season: early summer.
Type: deciduous shrub.

△ *Santolina virens*

▽ *Santolina chamaecyparissus*

Santolina

SANTOLINA

Compositae

The attraction of this small plant is its scented foliage, which remains silvery throughout the year. In summer, tiny flowers like yellow pastilles appear at the ends of the branches; it is best to eliminate them and trim the plant into a roundish shape. In a dry climate, where box may not be suitable, santolina can be used to make little border hedges. Planted among highly coloured annuals, the soft colours of santolina will add a touch of tranquillity.

Useful hints

— Plant santolina in full sun. It is as well-suited to dry, poor soil as to good, well-drained garden soil. It will also grow in cracks in walls and in rock gardens, alongside valerian, wallflowers and yellow stonecrop.

— As soon as the flowering season is over, in midsummer, prune lightly to improve its appearance.

Recommended

— Although *Santolina chamaecyparissus* (cotton lavender) is the most popular santolina, *S. rosmarinifolia* ssp. *rosmarinifolia*, a delicate green in colour, is very pretty. Its flowers are similar to the yellow pompons of its cousin. 'Primrose Gem' has pale yellow flower heads.

Height: 30 cm (12 in).
Soil: any, dry for preference.
Aspect: sun.
Propagation: from cuttings.
Flowering season: summer.
Type: evergreen shrub.

Sarcococca

SARCOCOCCA, SWEET BOX

Buxaceae

This evergreen shrub grows no higher than 50 cm (20 in) and is bushy in habit. It is useful for planting along the edges of flights of stone steps, along walls or around trees. The leaves are long and sharply pointed, glossy and a handsome green in colour. Even the flowers, tiny but scented, are interesting. They appear in winter, and are followed by black berries.

△ *Sarcococca humilis*

Useful hints

— This shrub tolerates chalky soils but not moist conditions. It prefers shade or semi-shade to sun, and is an ideal plant for a patio, producing a splendid clump of greenery without demanding too much in the way of care.

Recommended

— *Sarcococca confusa*. The dense, sharply pointed leaves spread laterally. The flowers are strongly scented.

— *S. hookeriana* is a species with upright foliage.

— *S. hookeriana* var. *humilis* is a suckering plant. The male flowers have pink anthers. The fruits are black.

— *S. ruscifolia*. This species can reach a height of 1 m (3¼ ft). It bears red fruits. *S.r. chinensis* has narrower leaves.

Height: 50 cm–1 m (20 in–3¼ ft).
Soil: light.
Aspect: shade or semi-shade.
Propagation: from seed or cuttings under glass, or by division.
Flowering season: winter.
Type: evergreen shrub.

Sciadopitys

UMBRELLA PINE

Sciadopityaceae

These pretty, umbrella-shaped conifers are not a common sight. A native of Japan, their small cones are green at first, becoming brown in the second year. The bark separates into thin shreds, revealing new, dark brown bark beneath. Mature height: 30 m (95 ft).

Useful hints

— Sciadopitys can be planted in a slightly shady spot. It does not tolerate chalky soils.

△ *Sciadopitys verticillata*

Recommended

— *Sciadopitys verticillata*. This beautiful pyramidal tree, whose shape always provokes admiration, has some interesting cultivars: 'Pendula', which is a weeping specimen, and 'Variegata', whose foliage is green and yellow. 'Gold Star' has yellow leaves. It is a good subject for planting as a specimen tree in a lawn.

Height: 10 m (33 ft), but much more in its native country.
Soil: acid.
Aspect: sun or semi-shade.
Propagation: from seed, cuttings using hormone powder, or by layering.
Type: evergreen tree.

◁ *Sciadopitys verticillata*

429

Senecio (syn. *Brachyglottis*)

SENECIO

Compositae

The senecio is not hardy in all regions – it does not really tolerate very cold conditions, preferring maritime and mild climates. This shrub, with its beautiful, silver-tinged foliage, can be a useful addition to borders of hardy perennials. Its yellow flowers, reminiscent of small daisies, give it a charming, old-fashioned appearance.

Useful hints

— Plant senecio in full sun and remove damaged or stunted branches in spring.

— Flower heads can be cut for use in bouquets of dried flowers.

Recommended

— *Senecio greyi* and *S. laxifolius* (both now correctly called *Brachyglottis* Dunedin Hybrids Group 'Sunshine'). The flowering season is midsummer. Height and spread are about 80 cm (32 in). The silvery white foliage has a felted appearance. The daisy flowers are yellow.

— *S. monroi* is a bushy, dense shrub with wavy-edged leaves and bright yellow flowers.

Height: 80 cm (32 in).
Soil: any, well-drained.
Aspect: sun.
Propagation: from cuttings in summer.
Flowering season: midsummer.
Type: evergreen shrub.

▽ *Senecio x* **'Monroi'**

Sequoia

SEQUOIA

Taxodiaceae

With sequoias, we enter the world of giant trees, those colossi that can reach a height of more than 100 m (325 ft) in their native environment. Of course, even if you plant these trees today or tomorrow, and even if they grow fast, you will never see them at their peak. However, it may be comforting to know that you are planting them for future generations.

Useful hints

— This tree will not tolerate harsh winters, and may even die during long periods of frost.

Recommended

— *Sequoia sempervirens* (redwood, coast redwood, Californian redwood). In California and Oregon there are whole forests of these trees, some of which are more than 2,000 years old and over 100 m (325 ft) in height. In our climate they will not, unfortunately, reach such stupendous heights. Nevertheless, they are still majestic specimens. Their massive trunks, with very soft, reddish bark, are almost spongy.

— *S. sempervirens* 'Prostrata' is a dwarf form that does not exceed 2 m (6½ ft) in height and can be used in rock gardens.

Height: 40–50 m (130–160 ft) in our climate, more than 100 m (325 ft) in their native country. 'Prostrata' 2 m (6½ ft).
Soil: any, with humus.
Aspect: needs space.
Propagation: from seed.
Type: evergreen tree.

Sequoiadendron

GIANT REDWOOD

Taxodiaceae

Another giant coniferous tree, similar to the sequoia, the sequoiadendron makes an impressive lawn specimen for large gardens and estates. It is a native of California.

Useful hints

— Plant a small specimen, no more than 45 cm (18 in) high, as it will establish better than a larger plant.

△ ▽ ▷ *Sequoiadendron giganteum*

△ ▽ *Skimmia japonica*

Recommended

— *Sequoiadendron giganteum* is a conical tree whose branches can sweep down to the ground. It has red-brown spongy bark, and bright green scale-like leaves. There are several cultivars, including 'Glaucum', with grey-green leaves, and 'Pendulum', with drooping branches and shoots, which is smaller at 35 m (115 ft).

Height: 35–75 m (115–250 ft).
Soil: deep and moisture-retentive.
Aspect: sun, needs space.
Propagation: from seed.
Type: evergreen tree.

Skimmia

SKIMMIA

Rutaceae

Skimmia is a genus of low-growing evergreen shrubs whose white flowers bloom in spring and are soon replaced by brilliant red berries. Male and female specimens should be planted side by side for successful fruiting. These shrubs are perfect for planting in tubs on terraces. They thrive in most soils with slight chalk, but prefer acidic soils. Plant with decorative garlic, lily of the valley, asperula and, for a fine autumn display, Japanese anemone.

Useful hints

— Plant skimmias any time between autumn and early spring. Mulch with pine bark each spring.

— Plant male and female skimmias next to each other.

Recommended

— *Skimmia japonica* has some excellent varieties such as 'Veitchii' (syn. 'Foremanii'), with its very decorative, bright red fruits, 'Nymans', with its relatively large berries, 'Rubella', valued mainly for its buds, which remain red throughout the winter, and Rogersii Group, which provides good ground cover.

— *S. laureola* gives off a pronounced aromatic fragrance when its leaves are rubbed; its scented flowers give way to red fruits.

Height: 60 cm –1.5 m (2–5 ft).
Soil: humus-rich.
Aspect: sun or semi-shade.
Propagation: from cuttings in summer.
Flowering season: spring.
Type: evergreen shrub.

Sophora

SOPHORA

Leguminosae

This is a tree with bushy, pendulous foliage, a handsome dark green in colour. It can reach a height of about 6 m (20 ft), and can be used to form a delightful natural arbour with clusters of drooping leaves. To do this, it is sufficient simply to cut off the lower branches on the inside of the tree but care is needed since they are sometimes thorny.

Useful hints

— Plants purchased in containers should be planted out in spring in a well-protected location.

Recommended

— *Sophora davidii* is the smallest species, reaching a height of only 3 m (10 ft). It is deciduous, and has bluish white flowers. It likes sun and good soil.

— *S. japonica*, known as the Japanese pagoda tree, is the best-known variety.

It has creamy white flowers that bloom fairly late, at the end of the summer or in early autumn. Its cultivar 'Pendula' has stiffly drooping branches.

— *S. macrocarpa* is an evergreen tree that reaches a height of 12 m (40 ft). The leaves are downy on one side. The yellow flowers are 3 cm (1 in) long.

— *S. microphylla* has dense evergreen foliage and pendulous yellow flowers that emerge in late spring.

— *S. secundiflora* is an evergreen tree with purplish blue flowers that smell of violets.

— *S. tetraptera* has spreading or drooping branches. Its very large, tubular, pendulous flowers are a beautiful golden yellow.

Height: 3–12 m (10–40 ft), depending on variety.
Soil: fertile, with no excess of clay or chalk.
Aspect: sun.
Propagation: from seed in spring, after stratification.
Flowering season: late spring to early autumn.
Type: deciduous or evergreen tree.

△ *Sorbaria arborea*

◁ *Sophora microphylla*

Sorbaria

FALSE SPIRAEA

Rosaceae

This is a vigorous plant which becomes a spectacular sight when its large clusters of creamy white flowers appear. This large shrub looks very good near water.

Useful hints

— Plant sorbaria in moist soil and in full sun, since it likes warmth. To keep its handsome shape, the flowering stems need to be cut back to old wood early each spring.

Recommended

— *Sorbaria kirilowii* (syn. *S. arborea*) is a very robust, vigorous shrub. Its flowers are produced at the end of the current year's growths.

— *S. sorbifolia* produces large clusters of more delicate, creamy white flowers.

— *S. tomentosa* var. *angustifolia* (syn. *aitchisonii*) has long spreading branches that are reddish when young. It flowers in the latter part of the summer.

Height: 2–4 m (6½–13 ft).
Soil: moist.
Aspect: sun.
Propagation: from suckers.
Flowering season: late summer.
Type: deciduous shrub.

△ *Sorbus pohuashanensis*

△ *Sorbus aucuparia*

Sorbus

**MOUNTAIN ASH, ROWAN,
SERVICE TREE, WHITEBEAM**

Rosaceae

▽ *Sorbus aria*

The genus *Sorbus* includes many species and varieties, which differ in both size and the colour of their foliage. They can be planted as hedges, as decorative shrubs, or even as single trees that will provide a shady corner. They are charming trees for natural, country settings. They are also valued for their long flowering season. From late spring to midsummer, sorbus are covered with white or cream flowers. These give way to clusters of red, pink or white berries that stand out sharply against the dense foliage and last until late autumn, while the leaves gradually turn golden yellow.

Useful hint

— Sorbus needs only to be well planted in order to thrive.

Recommended

— *Sorbus aria* 'Lutescens' (whitebeam) can reach a height of 10 m (33 ft) and grows into a handsome tree with elegantly spaced branches.

— The *S.* × *arnoldiana* cultivars are valued for their large fruits and exceptional colouring, and include 'Brilliant Yellow' and 'Chamois Glow', which has orange berries tinged with pink.

— *S. aucuparia* is the European mountain ash or rowan, a common sight in the countryside. It can reach a height of 15 m (50 ft). Its brilliant red berries are frequently devoured by birds. The variety 'Asplenifolia' has very elegant foliage faintly reminiscent of fern leaves. This sorbus can be used to form a dense, bushy hedge.

— *S.* × *hybrida* (Finnish whitebeam). A native of Scandinavia, this species is sometimes planted in more southerly climates as an ornamental tree. It produces flowers in early summer.

— *S.* 'Joseph Rock' has yellow berries.

— *S. latifolia* grows well in clearings in woods. This small tree can be up to 10 m (33 ft) in height.

— *S. pygmaea* is a species for small gardens, reaching barely 25 cm (10 in) in height.

— *S. thibetica* 'John Mitchell' is the largest species of all, reaching a height of 15 m (50 ft).

— *S. torminalis* (wild service tree). Its

△ *Spiraea japonica* 'Anthony Waterer'

△ *Spiraea japonica* 'Goldflame'

fruits can be used to make a good liqueur. It can reach a height of 15 m (50 ft) and sometimes lives for more than 200 years.

Height: 25 cm–15 m (10 in–50 ft).
Soil: any.
Aspect: any.
Propagation: from seed sown outside in autumn.
Flowering season: late spring to midsummer, berries in autumn.
Type: deciduous tree or shrub.

Spiraea

SPIRAEA

Rosaceae

Spiraea certainly lives up to its reputation: easy to cultivate, undemanding, producing abundant flowers. It is also fast-growing. Many new varieties have recently become available, giving flowers all summer long. The spring-flowering types are usually white, while those which bloom later in the year tend to be pink or red. *Spiraea japonica* 'Shirobana' bears white, pink and sometimes red flowers on the same plant.

Useful hints

— Plant spiraeas at any time of year. Bear in mind when planting that such varieties as S. 'Arguta', S. × *vanhouttei* and S. × *billiardii* form dense thickets and will reach heights of 2 m (6½ ft).

— Do not prune spring-flowering types. Others should be cut back to within 20 cm (8 in) of the ground.

Recommended

— *Spiraea* 'Arguta' (bridal wreath, foam of May) has supple, arching stems.

— *S. billiardii* bears striking pink flowers in summer. There is also a pinkish tinge to the leaves. 'Triumphans' has bright purplish pink flowers.

— *S. cinerea* 'Grefsheim' is one of the most spectacular white-flowering varieties.

— *S. japonica* 'Goldflame', a compact shrub with golden foliage and small, deep pink flowers, is well suited to moist soil. 'Froebelii' has red flowers which fade to pink, and its new foliage has a purple hue.

— *S. japonica* 'Shirobana' bears an unusual mixture of white and pink flower clusters, while the pale pink 'Little Princess' forms a compact cushion 60 cm (24 in) high.

— *S. nipponica* 'Snowmound' puts on a fine display of small, densely packed flower heads.

— *S. thunbergii* forms a dense, spreading bush, and the stems are completely clothed in clusters of white flowers. This is the first species to flower, and it keeps its leaves for much of the year.

— *S.* × *vanhouttei* is a vigorous shrub bearing a wealth of blossom in early summer. The hybrid 'Pink Ice' forms a more compact bush, splashed all over with cream-coloured blossom.

Height: 50 cm–2 m (20 in–6½ ft).
Soil: ordinary.
Aspect: sun or semi-shade.
Propagation: from cuttings in autumn.
Flowering season: spring, summer.
Type: deciduous shrub.

Stephanandra

STEPHANANDRA, LACE SHRUB

Rosaceae

Stephanandras have a subtle appeal. Their beauty lies not in showy flowers or spectacular fruits but in grace and refinement of shape. The long asymmetrical leaves, arranged on elegant arching stems, turn a beautiful golden colour in autumn. These shrubs are for a gardener with discernment, who will know how to match them with *Hydrangea paniculata* and *Cornus alba*. Planted in large numbers, they also make excellent ground cover, in which case they go well with nandina, spiraea and lythrum.

Useful hints

— Plant stephanandras in early spring. Clumps can be divided in autumn.

— Stephanandras will grow in any soil that is not too dry.

— One year in three, in early spring, prune out stems from the centre of the bush and any that are out of place.

Recommended

— *Stephanandra incisa* has deeply divided leaves and white flowers in early summer. 'Crispa', which has wavy-edged and more deeply lobed leaves, forms a highly decorative dome-shaped shrub.

— In shape, *S. tanakae* is reminiscent of a fountain, with spectacular cascading foliage. The leaves, which turn golden in autumn, are bigger than those of the previous species. In winter, the stems are an attractive warm brown colour.

Height: 1.5–2.5 m (5–8 ft).
Soil: ordinary, fairly moist.
Aspect: sun or semi-shade.
Propagation: by layering or from cuttings, in summer or by division in autumn.
Flowering season: early to mid-summer.
Type: deciduous shrub.

▽ *Stephanandra tanakae*

△ *Stewartia sinensis*

Stewartia

STEWARTIA

Theaceae

There is some controversy as to whether the name of this tree or shrub should be spelt *Stewartia* or *Stuartia*. Both are used. These attractive plants have been too long neglected and are all too rare. And yet there is much to be said for them. They have the advantage of flowering in mid- and late summer, when few other trees are in bloom, though they are not particularly hardy (being natives of Virginia and Florida) and therefore require a well-protected site. A further attraction of stewartias is their autumn foliage.

Useful hints

— They prefer soil that is neither too cold, too moist, nor too alkaline. The ideal is to plant them in a bed of heathers: they thrive in just the same kind of soil. Do not let the soil dry out, and plant them while they are still small, as they will not tolerate too much handling.

— Continue to water them in winter, if the weather is dry.

Recommended

— *Stewartia malacodendron* (silky camellia) is a tall shrub about 4 m (13 ft) in height. It has large white flowers with purple stamens in early and mid-summer.

— *S. ovata* (mountain camellia) is an erect shrub, growing to about 2.5 m (8 ft). Its foliage often has a reddish tint. The white flowers, which can be as much as 10 cm (4 in) across, have attractively scalloped margins to the petals.

— *S. pteropetiolata* var. *koreana* has flat, open flowers of very silky texture. In its native Japan, it may grow to 15–20 m (50–65 ft). Elsewhere it is difficult to predict its ultimate height. The foliage turns red in autumn. It is well worth searching out this delightful little tree.

— *S. sinensis* is a spreading tree with peeling bark. Its leaves turn red in autumn.

Height: 2–20 m (6½–65 ft).
Soil: a mixture of good loam, peat and leaf-mould.
Aspect: a warm location, but in semi-shade, out of direct sun.
Propagation: from seed, sown in sand under a cloche, or from cuttings.
Flowering season: summer.
Type: evergreen or deciduous tree or shrub.

Stranvaesia (syn. *Photinia*)

STRANVAESIA

Rosaceae

From a distance, stranvaesia could be taken for cotoneaster. It has glossy, evergreen leaves. On well-established shrubs the older foliage may turn red in autumn, making a pleasant contrast with the bright green of the younger growth. The white flowers are attractive, if not particularly striking. They appear in early summer, forming flat clusters. Stranvaesia is grown principally for its fruits, which ripen in mid-autumn, by which time they are bright red and the size of peas. The shrub is a magnificent sight when profusely adorned with berries. Note that the berries of stranvaesia are not attractive to birds.

Useful hints

— Despite its complicated name, this shrub is easy to grow, perfectly hardy and happy in all types of soil, provided it is moist and not liable to dry out, and preferably slightly shaded.

Recommended

— *Stranvaesia davidiana* (syn. *Photinia davidiana*) hails originally from China. Its white flowers open out to form large clusters in early summer.

— *S. davidiana* var. *salicifolia* (syn. *Photinia davidiana* Salicifolia Group) has long, narrow, olive-green leaves and bears large white flowers. The berries are orange-red. *S.d.* 'Palette' is a smaller shrub, and has foliage which is mottled with white.

— *S. davidiana* var. *undulata* 'Fructu Luteo' has yellow berries. *S.d.* var. *undulata* 'Prostrata' is a low-growing form, excellent as ground cover.

Height: rarely more than 2.5 m (8 ft).
Soil: any, provided it is moist.
Aspect: semi-shade.
Propagation: from cuttings or seed.
Flowering season: early summer, berries in autumn.
Type: evergreen shrub.

▽ *Stranvaesia davidiana*

△ *Symphoricarpos × chenaultii*

Symphoricarpos

SNOWBERRY

Caprifoliaceae

The snowberry will tolerate sun or shade, a superabundance of water or drought. Its great attraction is the large white or pink berries it bears, reminiscent of marbles, which remain on the shrub well into winter. Snowberry will quickly invade any area in which it is allowed to grow unchecked, thanks to its incredibly vigorous suckers. So limit these all-purpose shrubs to a low hedge, or plant them in an out-of-the-way corner, together with other tough customers such as rubus. They will even flourish under cover of tall conifers and beech trees.

Useful hints

— Plant the snowberry from late autumn to late winter. Mulch around the base and water well during the first summer. Subsequently, all you need do is dig out any suckers which venture too far afield.

— The snowberry will grow in any soil, in sun or semi-shade.

— Prune in early spring if you want to give the shrub a definite shape, though it is better to respect its natural, rounded growth habit.

△ *Symphoricarpos albus*

Recommended

— *Symphoricarpos albus* (common snowberry) is the most widespread garden species. *S.a.* var. *laevigatus* has snow-white berries which are even bigger than those of the standard species.

— *S. × chenaultii* 'Hancock' makes excellent ground cover, rarely growing more than 1 m (3¼ ft) in height. It bears pink and white berries.

— *S. orbiculatus* (Indian currant, coralberry) bears small purplish pink flowers. 'Foliis Variegatus' has leaves marked with yellow. Some of the most common hybrids are *S. × dorenbosii* 'White Hedge', with particularly pure white berries, *S. × d.* 'Mother of Pearl', with big pink fruits, and the more compact *S. × d.* 'Magic Berry', whose fruits are a deep pink, almost red colour.

Height: 60 cm–2 m (2–6½ ft).
Soil: any.
Aspect: any.
Propagation: by removing suckers, in autumn.
Flowering season: mid- and late summer. The flowers are insignificant.
Fruiting season: early autumn to early winter.
Type: deciduous shrub.

△ *Syringa meyeri* 'Palibin'
▽ *Syringa vulgaris*

Syringa

LILAC

Oleaceae

Everyone loves lilac for its magnificent flowers and incomparable fragrance, which make up to some extent for a rather short flowering season. Use it liberally in a flowering hedge, mixed with dog roses, deutzias and snowy mespilus. At the base of the hedge, try planting *Campanula persicifolia*.

Useful hints

— Plant lilac from late autumn to early spring, though not during very cold spells. New foliage is very slow to appear in the first year. To help the shrub get established, take your courage in both hands during its first season and pinch out all the flower buds as they appear. This should ensure a good show of blossom in subsequent years. Mulch and water regularly until early autumn. It is some time before the flower colour stabilizes, so do not blame your nurseryman if the flowers are not as vivid as you expected.

— When the shrub has flowered, remove the fading flower heads, taking care not to damage the new shoots. Every third season, prune more severely to encourage new branches from near ground level. Carefully dig out any suckers; they quickly exhaust the soil at the base of the plant.

Recommended

— Of the single-flowered lilacs, the best-known are hybrids. Among these are 'Charles X', which has vivid purple flowers; the more compact 'Congo', which tends to red; 'Firmament', sky-blue; 'Maréchal Foch', carmine-pink, astounding in its fullness; 'Primrose', one of the first yellow lilacs and still one of the best; 'Souvenir de Louis Spaeth', burgundy-red; and 'Vestale', a prolific shrub bearing pure white blossoms.

— Of the double lilacs, some of the best are the late-flowering 'Charles Joly', deep purple-red; 'General Pershing', more violet-coloured; 'Katherine Havemeyer', bluish mauve and highly fragrant; and the similar but slightly later 'Madame Lemoine'.

— *Syringa* × *josiflexa* 'Bellicent' is well worth seeking out. The drooping flower clusters are like long pink plumes and have a delightful scent. 'Paul Thirion' is one of my favourites, retaining a compact form and bearing light burgundy blossoms. Also deserving of mention are 'Belle de Nancy', satin-pink; 'Duc de Masse', lilac-pink; 'Mrs Edward Harding', light red splashed with pink; and 'Président Poincaré', which has large, pale mauve flowers.

— Also of interest are some of the wild lilac species and their cultivars, such as *S. patula*, a species with attractive foliage which does not grow to more than 1.5 m (5 ft). In late spring and early summer, it bears sprays of pale lilac flowers 10–15 cm (4–6 in) long. A source of wonder is *S. microphylla* 'Superba', which has an unbelievable perfume and bears its pinkish mauve flowers in late summer as well as in spring. Other hybrids worth mentioning are:

— *S. meyeri* 'Palibin', a fragrant shrub for small gardens, which bears lilac-pink flowers with a white throat.

— *S. × prestoniae*, vigorous hybrids, which do not flower until early summer.

— *S. sweginzowii*, an elegant shrub which pours its energy into producing long rose-pink panicles with a fetching scent.

Height: 1.5–4 m (5–13 ft).
Soil: ordinary; does not mind alkaline conditions.
Aspect: sun.
Propagation: from cuttings in summer.
Flowering season: late spring to early summer, and in some cases early autumn.
Type: deciduous tree or shrub.

Tamarix

TAMARISK

Tamaricaceae

This deciduous shrub with delicate, feathery foliage can grow to 8 m (26 ft) in height, but cultivated forms rarely exceed 5–6 m (16–20 ft). The flowers are another attractive feature. When in bloom, the tiny greyish green leaves are completely hidden by abundant plumes of minuscule pink flowers, borne at the ends of the thin, flexible branches. The strengths of the tamarisk are its ability to tolerate any soil and its resistance to both drought and strong winds. Planted in a light, fertile soil, it will put on rapid

△ *Tamarix ramosissima* 'Rubra'

growth to cover a boundary wall or hide an unsightly outlook. It can be clipped to the size and shape you want, whether to form a decorative clump or to provide a hedge.

Useful hints

— The tamarisk does not like being moved, and is best transplanted when young.

— Once established, the tamarisk requires little in the way of care. It does just as well in moist soil by water as in a dry location.

— Pruning should be carried out in winter.

Recommended

— *Tamarix hispida* is the most vigorous species, with stronger, more erect branches than the others.

— *T. parviflora* has purplish brown branches and bears deep pink flower racemes.

— *T. pentandra* has longer, more slender branches than other species, giving it an even more feathery appearance. Its flowers are pink and its leaves are a blue-green colour.

— *T. ramosissima* 'Pink Cascade' puts out great sheaves of glaucous foliage. In summer, it is covered in a cloud of large, luminous pink flowers.

Height: 5–6 m (16–20 ft).
Soil: any.
Aspect: any.
Propagation: easy, from cuttings in autumn.
Flowering season: late spring to late summer, depending on variety and climate.
Type: deciduous shrub.

Taxus

YEW

Taxaceae

This is a very popular conifer for making hedges, and is considered essential to some gardens. It is admired for its tolerance of any soil or situation, the way it lends itself to pruning, its incomparable toughness, and its elegance. The needle-like leaves, arranged herringbone fashion, are dark green above, paler below. Yew is a dioecious species: a male and a female specimen are therefore required if you hope to obtain the poisonous red – or (very rarely) yellow – berries. The seed can be seen at the upper end of the berry, where it lies exposed. There is a vast number of varieties, with shapes and sizes for every location.

Useful hints

— You can plant container-grown or root-balled saplings in any soil, provided it is free-draining. Warn children not to eat the berries: they are highly toxic. One way to avoid this problem is to plant only male specimens, which will not fruit. Also note that golden varieties tend to revert to green if planted in shade.

— Although it grows slowly, the yew is an excellent hedging plant. It does not mind pruning and does not become 'leggy' with age. The supple branches can be trained and pruned to form arches, tunnels and all kinds of shapes.

▽ *Taxus baccata* 'Standishii'

It is therefore excellent for topiary, the art of reproducing animal, human and geometrical forms by 'sculpting' the foliage of trees and shrubs.

Recommended

— *Taxus baccata* is an intensely green shrub with spreading branches. Remarkably tolerant, it is equally at home in sunny and shady locations. When full-grown it becomes a graceful tree with a rounded crown and red-brown bark. It therefore needs plenty of space if it is not to be pruned. If damaged during a particularly severe winter, it recovers well the following spring. It will thrive in any soil, acid or alkaline, provided the ground is not water-logged all winter. It eventually reaches a height of 10–15 m (33–50 ft).

— *T . baccata* f. *adpressa* is a semi-prostrate variety, with spreading branches which turn up slightly at the tips. The small needles are very dark green. It grows to 5 m (16 ft).

— In the case of *T. baccata* 'Adpressa Variegata', the young shoots are a golden yellow colour.

— *T. baccata* 'Dovastoniana' is a very elegant variety, full-skirted with wide-spreading branches. The needles are an attractive golden yellow. Highly decorative, it may spread to a width of 3 m (10 ft).

— *T. baccata* 'Elegantissima' is well-suited to the smaller garden, with upward-pointing, tight-packed branches. The young needles are streaked with pale yellow, which turns white with age, while the leaf edges remain a golden colour. The berries make a striking contrast with the foliage.

— In its native land, *T. baccata* 'Fastigiata' (syn. *T. b.* 'Hibernica'), the Irish yew, is often planted by the roadside, at crossroads or in cemeteries, where it spreads to form a large, many-crowned tree. When young, the Irish yew forms a compact, narrow column of glossy dark green, unsurpassed for elegance.

— *T. baccata* 'Fastigiata Aurea' grows more slowly, as is often the case with golden varieties.

— *T. baccata* 'Semperaurea' has dense-growing, upward-slanting branches and

◁ *Taxus baccata*

△ *Thuja plicata* 'Atrovirens'

△ *Taxus baccata*

forms an attractive bush. The foliage is an attractive golden yellow.

— *T. baccata* 'Repens Aurea' is a low-growing variety. The needles are edged with creamy yellow.

— *T. baccata* 'Standishii' is even more slender and column-like than 'Fastigiata'. The foliage remains golden all year round.

— *T. baccata* 'Washingtonii' often grows wider than it is tall. A bushy specimen, it has almost horizontal branches which droop at the tips. The yellow-edged leaves of this variety turn an 'old bronze' hue in winter.

— *T. cuspidata* 'Strait Hedge' rises in a slender pyramid shape. Relatively quick-growing, it is excellent for making a high-quality hedge.

— *T. × media* 'Hicksii' forms a slim column ending in a sharp point. The ribbed leaves are a very dark shade of green. It can be used for a narrow hedge, but will not grow to more than 1.5 m (5 ft) in height.

Height: 1.5–15 m (5–50 ft), depending on variety.
Soil: any.
Aspect: sun or semi-shade.
Propagation: from seed.
Type: evergreen tree or shrub.

Thuja

THUJA, ARBOR-VITAE

Cupressaceae

Thujas are undoubtedly the most popular of garden conifers. Although they come originally from North America and Eastern Asia, it is difficult to believe they have not always been part of our arboreal environment.

Useful hints

— Thujas thrive in all soils, provided the ground is not too wet. If you are growing them for a hedge, begin pruning them in their second year. Mid-summer is the right time, so that they can put on fresh growth before winter.

— Do not top them at the height you want them to be eventually, but at 20 cm (8 in) shorter. This allows for a little extra growth, and they will not appear to terminate too abruptly. They can also be pruned to form arches, in much the same way as yew.

Recommended

— *Thuja occidentalis* is a native of eastern North America. Old specimens often have multiple trunks, with reddish brown bark. The foliage is bright green on the upper side, paler beneath, and takes on a coppery hue in winter. As with all thujas, the juvenile foliage is needle-like, changing over the years to the green scales which clothe the branches of adult trees. When crushed, the branchlets give off a powerful aromatic scent. *T. occidentalis* is used mainly for hedging. For this purpose, the saplings should be planted at intervals of 80 cm (32 in). This species does less well in alkaline soils. Its height at maturity is 15 m (50 ft).

— *T. occidentalis* 'Danica' forms a small, rounded shrub with compact, bright green foliage. Because of its slow growth habit, it is suitable for planting as part of a patio arrangement.

— *T. occidentalis* 'Holmstrup' is another small variety, perfectly cone-shaped, with dense green foliage which barely changes colour in winter. Another slow grower, it eventually reaches 3–4 m (10–13 ft).

— *T. occidentalis* 'Little Gem' is also conical in shape, but with a flat top. The dense foliage is an attractive pure green. It does not grow beyond 2 m (6½ ft).

— *T. occidentalis* 'Pyramidalis Compacta' is another conical tree, this time with a rounded top. It is useful as a hedging plant, eventually growing to 12 m (40 ft).

— *T. occidentalis* 'Rheingold' is a very popular variety, and rightly so. It forms a slender cone, with delicate foliage which takes on a golden yellow tint in winter. The new season's growth is salmon-pink.

— For many years, *T. orientalis* was not recognized as a thuja. It was given the name 'biota', from the Greek word 'bios', because it was known as the 'tree of life' in its native China. It is conical in shape and grows to 10–12 m (33–40 ft). The feature which distinguishes it from *T. occidentalis* is the vertical arrangement of the branches. The bluish cones are bigger than those of other thujas and have hooked scales. This species will thrive in any soil, provided the ground is not unduly wet.

— *T. orientalis* 'Aurea Nana' is another perfect little conifer for the rock garden. A compact, oval-shaped dwarf, with foliage arranged in vertical planes, it rarely grows to more than 50 cm (20 in).

— *T. orientalis* 'Elegantissima' is columnar in shape. Its most interesting feature is its foliage, which turns from gold in spring, to green in summer, to coppery brown in winter.

— *T. orientalis* 'Juniperoides' is a little on the fragile side, sensitive to cold and snow. It has very fine, silvery juvenile foliage, which turns a reddish ochre colour in winter.

— *T. orientalis* 'Rosedalis' is a charming little oval-shaped tree. Its canary-yellow springtime foliage turns first bluish green, then golden brown with the onset of winter. Despite being somewhat delicate, it makes a perfect specimen for the rock garden, not growing beyond 80 cm (32 in).

— *T. plicata* (Western red cedar), the biggest of the genus, is a magnificent tree, reaching 60 m (190 ft) in its native environment, the forests of the West Coast of America. It is one of the best trees for forming a hedge, but so commonly used as to become rather monotonous. The compact, bright green foliage is borne on slightly curving branches, the lower ones almost touching the ground. Sometimes a tree will reproduce itself spontaneously by layering: the lowest

△ *Thuja plicata*

branches rooting themselves and eventually forming a thicket of new saplings. The brown bark peels away in large strips. In Europe, cultivated varieties grow to around 30 m (95 ft).

— *T. plicata* 'Atrovirens' is cultivated especially as a hedging plant. The glossy, dark green leaves are borne on densely packed branches.

— *T. plicata* 'Rogersii' is cone-shaped when young, forming a pyramid as it matures. The orange-yellow leaves are tinted with bronze – an attractive combination of colours.

— Another pleasing contrast of colours: the green foliage of *T. plicata* 'Zebrina' is irregularly banded with yellow. The tree's ultimate height is 15 m (50 ft).

Height: 3–30 m (10-95 ft). Dwarf forms, 50 cm to 1 m (20 in–3¼ ft).
Soil: *T. occidentalis* requires a moist soil; *T. orientalis* will withstand dry conditions.
Aspect: semi-shade for golden-leaved varieties; full sun for others.
Propagation: from seed, or from cuttings using hormone powder.
Type: evergreen tree or shrub.

441

Thujopsis

THUYOPSIS

Cupressaceae

At first sight, this tree could easily be taken for a thuja: it has the same scale-like leaves and pyramidal habit. But closer examination reveals the new shoots to be much larger in size. It is in fact a quite different species, originating from the mountains of Hondo island, central Japan. The undersides of the large, horizontal leaves are splashed with white. If crushed between thumb and finger, they release a scent of lemon balm.

Useful hints

— Although thujopsis may eventually reach a height of 10–15 m (33–50 ft), it is very slow-growing, particularly in alkaline soil. When used for hedging, the saplings should be spaced at intervals of 80 cm (32 in), possibly alternating with thujas.

Recommended

— The leaves of *Thujopsis dolabrata* are dark green above, silvery below. The tree bears glaucous green cones which turn brown with age.

— *T. dolabrata* 'Aurea', variegated yellow, is the variety most commonly found in nurseries and garden centres.

— *T. dolabrata* 'Nana' is a dwarf bush form, with tender green foliage.

Height: 10–15 m (33–50 ft) in cultivated forms.
Soil: moist but well-drained.
Aspect: semi-shade.
Propagation: from cuttings, using hormone powder.
Type: evergreen tree.

Tilia

LIME, LINDEN

Tiliaceae

The lime is a handsome tree of truly noble stature. Indigenous to practically the whole of Europe, for centuries it has been grown as an ornamental species in parks and gardens. The dense foliage appears in early spring and remains on the tree until the very end of autumn. Among its many assets are the tiny,

△ *Tilia insularis*

deliciously scented flowers, which since ancient times have been used as a remedy against insomnia.

Useful hints

— Prune the tree hard during its early years in order to achieve a good shape.

— Remove any suckers that appear around the trunk.

— Limes are particularly prone to infestation by aphids, which secrete honeydew, a sticky substance which soon turns black. A malathion-based spray, applied in late spring, may prove effective.

Recommended

— *Tilia americana* (American basswood) is badly affected by air pollution. When planted in a suitable environment, it may grow to 40 m (130 ft).

— *T. cordata* (small-leaved lime) is not such a giant, but quickly grows to a size that can dominate a large lawn. This tree lives to a ripe old age: as much as 500 years.

— *T. × euchlora*, a broad-crowned species with elegantly drooping branches, reaches heights of over 20 m (65 ft).

— *T.* 'Petiolaris' (pendent white lime) is

Tsuga canadensis 'Rugg's Washington' ▷

valued as a decorative species for its weeping habit and white-backed leaves on long leaf-stalks, which tremble in the slightest breeze. Its maximum height is around 25 m (80 ft).

— *T. platyphylos* (large-leaved lime) is the most imposing of all: leaves, buds, branches, leaf-sprays, trunk are all of truly monumental proportions. There are specimens several hundred years old with a girth of 3–4 m (10–13 ft). Of its ornamental cultivars, 'Fastigiata' has a tall, column-like shape. In the case of 'Rubra', close pruning encourages the development of bright red shoots.

Height: 20–40 m (65–130 ft).
Soil: moist, but well-drained.
Aspect: any.
Propagation: from rooted suckers. Plant them in a cold frame in autumn and transplant to their final location the following spring.
Type: deciduous tree.

▽ *Tsuga mertensiana*

Tsuga

HEMLOCK

Pinaceae

The hemlocks grown in gardens are small conifers with horizontal, spreading branches. The foliage is similar to that of yew, but more delicate and softer to the touch.

Useful hints

— Hemlock is well-suited to a moist garden with a lot of shade.

Recommended

— *Tsuga canadensis* (Eastern hemlock) is a tree of graceful bearing, with long slender branches and attractive bluish green foliage. It will thrive in a north-facing situation. Its ultimate height is 25 m (80 ft).

— *T. canadensis* 'Aurea' is a more compact, yellow-leaved variety.

— *T. canadensis* 'Jeddeloh' is worth featuring. Dome-shaped, with drooping branches, it will not grow beyond 2 m (6½ ft).

— *T. canadensis* 'Pendula' is another fine variety. It weeps to the point where, if not staked, it will eventually collapse and assume a prostrate habit. When staked, it grows to 1 m (3¼ ft), then cascades downwards. It is perfect for the rock garden.

— *T. heterophylla* (Western hemlock) is of similar growth habit to its eastern cousin. Supple and graceful, it grows rapidly and is perfectly hardy. In its native setting it reaches 30 m (95 ft) at maturity.

Height: 30 m (95 ft) in its native habitat; 1–20 m (3¼–65 ft) in cultivation.
Soil: moist.
Aspect: shade or semi-shade.
Propagation: from seed, or from cuttings using hormone powder.
Type: evergreen tree.

Ulex

GORSE, FURZE

Leguminosae

Gorse is an excellent plant to grow in certain conditions. It thrives in coastal situations and on poor, stony soils. Extremely thorny, these shrubs form a dry scrub which catches fire very easily in a hot, parched summer, so do not plant them too close to the house. In spring, and sometimes in autumn, they bear attractive yellow flowers, somewhat similar to those of the sweet pea, with a fragrance of honey.

Useful hints

— Gorse bushes are averse to being transplanted, so buy container-grown specimens. Do not let the root ball break up when putting them in the ground, and do not plant them in over-rich soil.

— Leggy plants can be cut back very low.

— Prune the branches in autumn.

Recommended

— *Ulex europaeus* flowers in late spring and may continue to bear flowers in succession throughout the summer and into autumn.

— *U. gallii*, a dwarf variety, flowers in the summer and autumn.

Height: 1 m (3¼ ft).
Soil: dry, well-drained, stony.
Aspect: full sun.
Propagation: from cuttings in summer.
Flowering season: late spring, sometimes to summer and autumn.
Type: deciduous shrub.

Ulex ▷

△ *Ulmus glabra*

Ulmus

ELM

Ulmaceae

Elm is a fine deciduous tree, indigenous to western Europe. In parkland and open field, it is valued for its bulky silhouette and the dense shade it gives. The dark green, toothed leaves are small but tightly packed. However, the elm is going through a bad patch: in recent decades elm populations have been decimated by Dutch elm disease, for which no remedy has yet been found. Observe the leaves closely in summer, and if any begin to die off, remove the branch immediately and burn it. Even the burnt wood must not be left lying around, as it may infect the rest of the tree. If the whole tree is affected, there is nothing to be done but

have it cut down and taken away. *Ulmus parvifolia* (Chinese elm) is the species most resistant to disease.

Useful hints

— Buy your sapling small, and plant it with plenty of space for it to grow.

Recommended

— *Ulmus* 'Dicksonii' (Dickson's golden elm) is an ornamental tree with very small golden leaves, from spring into autumn.

— *U. glabra* (wych elm), a mountain species, is found mainly at altitudes of between 600 and 1,400 m (2,000–4,500 ft). It is a substantial tree, growing to a height of 18 m (60 ft).

— *U. glabra* 'Camperdownii', a cultivar of the wych elm, is often grown for

its weeping habit. The branches droop all round the trunk, creating a shady canopy under which to retreat on hot summer days.

— *U. procera* (English elm) has been much used since Renaissance times for creating shady, tree-lined avenues. It is the tallest elm of all, eventually growing to 40 m (130 ft), with a girth of 3 m (6½ ft). One of its cultivars is 'Argenteovariegata', a fine ornamental variety with silvery white striped foliage.

— *U.* 'Sapporo Autumn Gold' is a newcomer. It is vigorous and quick-growing, and appears resistant to Dutch elm disease.

Height: 10–40 m (33–130 ft).
Soil: deep and moist.
Aspect: sun or semi-shade.
Propagation: from seed; the young saplings should be planted out the following spring.
Type: deciduous tree.

Viburnum

VIBURNUM

Caprifoliaceae

Whether you are looking for an elegant, fragrant shrub, a low-spreading shrub to use as ground cover, a hedging plant with a difference, or shrubs for the patio, you will find a viburnum to meet your needs. Diverse in the extreme, and easy to grow, most viburnums have superb autumn foliage and give off a delightful fragrance. Some varieties are evergreen and bear attractive berries. The most strongly perfumed winter flowers are also to be found among the viburnum family.

Useful hints

— Plant viburnums in autumn. A handful of hoof and horn will get the young shrubs off to a good start.

— There is no need to prune. Simply remove any branches which detract from the general shape.

Recommended

Deciduous varieties

— *Viburnum* × *bodnantense* has upright branches. Its pink, pleasantly scented flowers are borne in winter.

— *V. farreri* (syn. *V. fragrans*) is an erect shrub. The abundant white flowers appear before the leaves, from early to late winter.

— *V. × juddii* forms a bell-shaped bush 1.5 m (5 ft) tall, remarkable for its profusion of pink, delicately scented blooms.

— *V. lantana* has dense greyish foliage and will withstand the most unfavourable conditions. Try planting it as an informal hedge.

— *V. opulus* 'Roseum' (snowball bush) is a springtime favourite with its spectacular pompons of white flowers, which sometimes turn pink. Growing to a height of 4 m (13 ft), it occurs in Europe, North Africa and northern parts of Asia.

— *V. plicatum* 'Mariesii' is a shrub of outstanding beauty. Its branches grow in horizontal layers, which in early summer bear large plate-like clusters of white flowers.

— Another variety of *V. plicatum* is 'Pink Beauty', whose flowers start off white. *V.* 'Shasta' is wider-spreading and bears larger flower clusters than any other viburnum.

— *V. plicatum* f. *tomentosum* has attractive burgundy-coloured autumn foliage. The white flowers are followed by red berries, which turn black as autumn advances.

— *V. sargentii* 'Onondaga' has magnificent coppery foliage in spring, turning to red in autumn. The large pink flower clusters gradually become white. The berries are red and spherical.

Evergreen varieties

— *V. × burkwoodii* has glossy green leaves. Its pink buds open to display white flowers in mid- and late winter.

— The white flowers of *V. carlesii*, a semi-evergreen, are some of the most fragrant to be found.

— *V. davidii* has tough leathery leaves with prominent veining. In winter, it bears large clusters of blue, sloe-like fruits.

— *V. rhytidophyllum* is a quick grower, which compensates to some extent for the rather melancholy appearance of its foliage. The leaves are thick and wrinkled like old leather on the upper side, a velvety grey below.

— *V. tinus* (laurustinus) bears pinkish white flowers in winter and black berries from late winter on. It is a good shrub for coastal areas and can be pruned to

△ *Viburnum plicatum* 'Mariesii'

form a hedge. As a fragrant evergreen, it is also suitable for planting on a patio.

— *V. tinus* 'Lucidum', which flowers in late winter, is a variety with larger leaves and flowers. *V. t.* 'Eve Price' is a compact shrub with white flowers and blue fruits; 'Gwenllian' has pale pink flowers.

Height: 2–4 m (6½–13 ft).
Soil: good, humus-rich.
Aspect: sun and semi-shade.
Propagation: by layering in autumn, or from cuttings in summer.
Flowering season: winter to early summer.
Type: deciduous or evergreen shrub.

Vinca

PERIWINKLE

Apocynaceae

Do not be surprised to find periwinkle included in this section. Some authors might not include it as a shrub, but, as well as its charming fresh flowers – straight out of a child's drawing – it has the enormous advantage that it will grow anywhere that shrubs grow – it will thrive among the stones of a rock garden or on steps, or can be used to form a thick mat of ground cover spangled with blue or white flowers. Planted in good soil, perhaps with tulips or daffodils, it will be well established in two or three years. It does not mind shade and does

well when it is planted around the base of trees.

Useful hints

— In spring or autumn, plant young rooted stems 15 cm (6 in) long in well-tilled soil.

Recommended

— *Vinca major*, which grows to 40 cm (16 in), produces flowers throughout the season. *V. minor*, at 15 cm (6 in), is a smaller plant, with blue or white flowers.

Height: 15–40 cm (6–16 in).
Soil: ordinary.
Aspect: sun or shade.
Propagation: by removing rooted suckers in spring.
Flowering season: early spring to mid-winter.
Type: evergreen shrub.

▽ *Vinca major*

△ *Weigela florida*

Weigela

WEIGELA

Caprifoliaceae

Although weigelas are useful border shrubs, the rather dull flowers they display in early summer are reason to use them sparingly. Try planting them with more graceful companions, like galega or variegated cornflowers, to disguise their rather stiff military bearing. They also consort well with bright-coloured thalictrum, *Dictamnus albus*, white sweet rockets and slender flowers generally. Phlox are another good foil for them, flowering when the weigela has finished its display.

Useful hints

— Plant at practically any time of year (they are nearly always sold in containers). In spring, mulch with half-rotted compost and water well throughout the first summer.

— Prune after flowering by removing wood more than two years old to make way for vigorous young stems. Leave these younger branches intact to allow them to arch gracefully. They will flower the following year.

Recommended

— Species weigelas are rarely grown nowadays, apart from *Weigela middendorffiana*, which bears sulphur-yellow flowers in early summer.

— The purple-flushed foliage of *W. florida* 'Foliis Purpureis' makes a lively contrast with that of golden or variegated shrubs.

— *W. florida* 'Variegata' is a much-admired variety.

— There are many hybrids which flower in early summer: 'Ballet', dark red; 'Bristol Ruby', very upright with ruby-coloured flowers; 'Conquête', with large fragrant red blooms spotted yellow in the throat; 'Eva Rathke', crimson-red, a slow grower; 'Fiesta', very profuse, bright red; the paler 'Newport Red'; 'Styriaca', carmine; 'Mont Blanc' and 'Avalanche', both white; 'Abel Carrière', rose-carmine with gold flecks in the throat; and 'Espérance', pale rose-salmon, white on the inside.

— Recently, some new hybrids have appeared, completing the vast range of weigelas with novel colour schemes: 'Briant Rubidor', carmine flowers and golden foliage; 'Carnaval', whose red

buds open to reveal pink and white flowers; and 'Lucifer', with very large scarlet blossoms.

Height: 80 cm–2 m (32 in–6½ ft).
Soil: ordinary.
Aspect: sun.
Propagation: from cuttings, taken after flowering.
Flowering season: early summer to early autumn.
Type: deciduous shrub.

Xanthoceras

YELLOWHORN

Sapindaceae

This charming little shrub, which grows to a maximum height of 3 m (10 ft), is a native of China. Its white flowers are borne at the ends of the branches in upright panicles 15–20 cm (6–8 in) long. They change colour as they open, from yellowish white to pink. The walnut-like seed pods which follow contain large, chestnut-like seeds.

Useful hints

— Plant against a hedge or wall to protect from frost. Yellowhorn is susceptible to fungal infection; remove any affected branches and burn them immediately.

Recommended

— *Xanthoceras sorbifolium* is the only species obtainable. A delightful shrub, it does best in areas where temperatures do not drop below −15°C (5°F).

Height: 2–3 m (6½–10 ft).
Soil: deep, moist.
Aspect: sun.
Propagation: from seed, or from root cuttings in spring.
Flowering season: late spring.
Type: deciduous shrub.

Yucca

YUCCA

Agaraceae

One of the most architectural of plants, the yucca is admirably suited to formal gardens and situations where a tropical effect is desired. Yuccas prefer sun-drenched, dry conditions, and will thrive even in stony ground. The evergreen

△ *Yucca gloriosa*

foliage is a winter bonus, and the flowers, which generally appear two or three years after planting, make an impressive show. After flowering, the plant may die back, but the dead leaves are soon replaced. The plant is unlikely to bloom every season.

Useful hints

— Plant in spring. Free-draining soil is essential.

— Do not prune. Simply remove dead leaves from the base, and the flowers when they fade, being careful of the sharp spikes.

Recommended

— *Yucca filamentosa* is the most impressive species, sometimes reaching 2 m (6½ ft) and forming dense clumps.

— *Y. flaccida*, which flowers somewhat less profusely, comes from the south-eastern states of America. The leaves of 'Golden Sword' have a large yellow central stripe.

— The sword-like leaves of *Y. glauca* grow from a short trunk.

— *Y. gloriosa* is appropriately known as 'Spanish dagger', and has wickedly sharp points to its stiff, rigid leaves. The pendulous white flowers are delicately tinted with red.

— *Y. whipplei* has no trunk. The glaucous leaves form a rosette round the base. The flower stalk, which may grow to 3 m (10 ft), is crowned with large, fragrant, greenish white blooms in late spring and early summer.

Height: 60 cm–2 m (2–6½ ft).
Soil: dry, poor in nutrients.
Aspect: full sun.
Propagation: by transplanting offsets, in spring.
Flowering season: spring to late summer.
Type: evergreen shrub.

Zenobia

ZENOBIA

Ericaceae

Zenobia is a member of the heather family and, as such, prefers acid soils and regions with a damp climate. Though it sometimes grows to 1 m (3¼ ft), the more usual height is 50 cm (20 in). The small, toothed, oval leaves are leathery and covered with a glaucous bloom. In milder regions they are shed at the end of winter; elsewhere they fall in late autumn. The bell-shaped white flowers are strikingly similar to those of lily of the valley, but give off a scent of aniseed. They are borne in late spring and early summer.

Useful hints

— Zenobia thrives in moist, non-alkaline soils, in the shade of trees or, at least, out of direct sunlight. The specimens you buy will be container-grown and should be planted out in the garden in early spring.

Recommended

— *Zenobia pulverulenta* is the only species, and in the past was difficult to get hold of. However, because of its virtues, this shrub is now becoming quite popular and is much easier to obtain.

Height: 50 cm–1 m (20 in–3¼ ft).
Soil: acid.
Aspect: shade or semi-shade.
Propagation: by division or layering; cuttings are more difficult.
Flowering season: late spring to early summer.
Type: deciduous shrub.

▽ *Zenobia pulverulenta*

447

Although you may love plants, the space at your disposal may be strictly limited. But if you at least have a balcony or a wall against which to train plants, a hanging garden is a fascinating possibility.

There are plenty of plants that will take to pergolas, trellises and other supports, and you can also make use of climbing plants of lazier disposition, which would sooner spread out horizontally than reach for the sky.

An attractive setting can be created by letting them trail along the ground: nothing is more romantic than a clematis weaving its way through low shrubs or draping itself casually over heathers. Honeysuckle can also be used as a ground-cover plant, as can all types of ivy.

Be wary of vigorous climbers which become so intertwined and entangled as to form inextricable bundles of stems devoid of foliage and flowers. The only solution in such cases is to cut back the plant to a manageable height. Exceptions to this rule are wisteria and Russian vine, which must be given plenty of room for development.

CLIMBERS & WALL SHRUBS

*A*butilon
to
*W*isteria

△ *Abutilon megapotamicum*
▽ *Abutilon vitifolium*

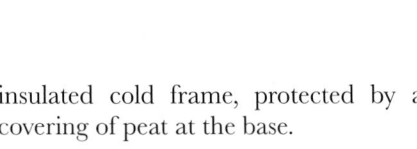

△ *Abutilon megapotamicum*

Abutilon

ABUTILON, FLOWERING MAPLE

Malvaceae

Some varieties of abutilon can be grown only in conservatories. Others are hardier and will make a spectacular show when grown along a wall. They need to be tied to a support, though, as abutilon is a shrubby plant rather than a true climber.

Useful hints

— Plant abutilon against a south-facing wall, in spring, adding sand to the soil if it is too heavy. Water copiously in summer. Before winter sets in, protect the base of the plant with a covering of straw.

— Cut back to ground level each spring, to encourage vigorous new growth to develop.

— Take some cuttings in mid- to late summer and let them take root in sand. In winter, plant them out in a well-insulated cold frame, protected by a covering of peat at the base.

Recommended

— *Abutilon* 'Canary Bird' bears a dazzling array of pure yellow flowers.

— *A. megapotamicum* is hardy when trained against a south-facing wall. It is a good match for ceanothus and *Clematis tangutica*. The cultivar 'Variegatum', splashed with creamy yellow, needs to be grown with more sombre companions.

— *A. vitifolium* is even hardier, and has been known to survive some quite severe winters. The variety *album* has mauve and white flowers, while those of 'Veronica Tennant' are a brighter violet.

Height: 1–2 m (3¼–6½ ft).
Soil: light, well-drained.
Aspect: sun.
Propagation: from cuttings in summer.
Flowering season: summer.
Type: deciduous shrub.

Actinidia

ACTINIDIA, KIWI FRUIT

Actinidiaceae

A feature of one of the actinidia species is its decorative foliage: the tips of the leaves turn pink in summer. It creates an elegant picture when encouraged to climb up the façade of a house or spread along a wall. It can also be used to clothe a pergola, preferably with other climbers such as rambler roses or large-flowered clematis. Or you may prefer to grow the edible kiwi fruit.

Useful hints

— Plant actinidia in spring for preference. Mulch well and water regularly. It has a curious attraction for cats, which use the base of the plant to sharpen their claws! A protective arrangement of wire mesh should keep them at bay.

— If you are hoping for kiwi fruit, you will need to plant two specimens of

△ **Fruits of** *Akebia quinata*

△ *Akebia quinata*

Akebia

AKEBIA, CHOCOLATE VINE

Lardizabalaceae

This vigorous climber is not often grown, though it has many advantages. It is semi-evergreen, with many leaves remaining on the plant over winter, particularly when conditions are mild. It is a good choice for concealing a large tree trunk, and will also make a good job of covering a grille or grating. The fragrant flowers are borne in spindly clusters.

Useful hints

— Plant akebia in full sun or semi-shade.

— The akebia does not like root disturbance, so avoid transplanting.

— Tie the new shoots in to begin with. The plant will then attach itself to its support.

Recommended

— *Akebia quinata* has reddish purple flowers in mid-spring. The fruits which follow look like small greyish purple sausages.

— *A. trifoliata* is not quite so vigorous. Its fruits are a pale violet colour.

Height: 6 m (20 ft).
Soil: ordinary.
Aspect: sun or semi-shade.
Propagation: by layering in spring.
Flowering season: spring.
Type: semi-evergreen climber.

△ *Actinidia kolomikta*

different sex next to each other. Prune in spring, cutting shoots borne on the long creepers back by a third.

— Continue to water regularly in late summer, as this is when new roots are forming, and add some rose fertilizer at this time.

Recommended

— *Actinidia deliciosa* is the species which produces the kiwi fruit, which is rich in vitamin C.

— *A. kolomikta* is hardier and puts on a magnificent display in summer, when the green leaves become marked with splashes of pink and white. The white flowers are borne in summer, male and female on separate plants.

Height: 3–6 m (10–20 ft).
Soil: rich, well-drained.
Aspect: sun, but not too fierce.
Propagation: from cuttings in autumn.
Flowering season: early to mid-summer.
Type: deciduous climber.

△ *Aristolochia durior*

Aristolochia

BIRTHWORT, DUTCHMAN'S PIPE

Aristolochiaceae

This vigorous plant climbs unaided, clinging to and twining around everything in its path. It is ideal for creating shade. Its strange, tubular, yellowish flowers are insignificant and it is grown primarily for its beautiful, dark green, heart-shaped leaves. It looks effective growing up an old tree-trunk, for example.

Useful hints

— Prune unwanted and invasive branches in winter.

— Aristolochias need regular watering, especially when in full growth.

— Spray against red spider and whitefly.

Recommended

— *Aristolochia durior* (syn. *A. macrophylla*) can reach a height of 6 m (20 ft).

Height: 5–6 m (16–20 ft).
Soil: ordinary, humus-rich.
Aspect: sun or semi-shade.
Propagation: by layering.
Flowering season: summer.
Type: deciduous climber.

Bougainvillea

BOUGAINVILLEA

Nyctaginaceae

This well-known evergreen climber was named after the French navigator Louis-Antoine de Bougainville by the botanist who discovered it in Brazil in 1767. It thrives outdoors only in frost-free regions, where its long, brightly coloured floral bracts intertwine to produce a dense curtain of pink, red, yellow, purple or white 'flowers'. It is not the flowers which are coloured but the bracts, the three leaves surrounding the flower proper. The actual flowers are tiny and unremarkable, whereas the bracts are decorative throughout most of the year. If you have the patience, you can graft a white bougainvillea on to a variety with red bracts to obtain both colours on the same plant.

Useful hints

— Bougainvilleas prefer light, fertile soil and a sunny aspect. They grow more quickly and densely if they are watered regularly in summer and fed with fertilizer. Watch out for red spider mite, one of the plant's worst enemies, also for whitefly.

Bougainvillea glabra ▷

452

— Cut back the branches of young plants to promote new growth. Bougainvilleas grow well in containers (plant in a mixture of leaf-mould and compost) and look good against a conservatory wall.

Recommended

— *Bougainvillea glabra* is the best species for containers.

— *B.* 'Sanderiana' is extremely free-flowering.

— *B. spectabilis* is a vigorous species with a number of cultivars, available in white, yellow, deep fuchsia-pink, purple and red.

— There are many excellent hybrids such as 'Mrs Butt' (crimson-magenta), 'Golden Glow' (orange-yellow), 'Scarlet Queen' (scarlet), 'Dania' (deep pink) and 'Miss Manila' (bright pink). The dark green leaves of 'Variegata' are edged with creamy white.

Height: 15–20 m (50–65 ft) under ideal conditions.
Soil: light and fertile.
Aspect: full sun, frost-free.
Propagation: cuttings or layering.
Flowering season: summer.
Type: evergreen climber.

Bougainvillea glabra ▷

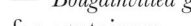

453

Buddleja

BUDDLEJA, BUTTERFLY BUSH

Loganiaceae

Although, generally speaking, buddlejas are ideal shrubs for beds and borders, *Buddleja colvilei* is a particularly attractive species that can be used as a climber or, more accurately, as a wall shrub. It is extremely vigorous, reaching a height of 6 m (20 ft), and has arching branches covered with reddish, woolly hairs. It produces drooping racemes of white-centred, pink or scarlet flowers, 15–20 cm (6–8 in) long, on the previous year's growth.

Useful hints

— Buy a young plant and train it, without attaching it too tightly, against the wall to be covered. A generous helping of leaf-mould when planting will get it away to a good start. It does not need pruning, but cut away any dead and damaged wood.

Recommended

— *Buddleja alternifolia* has easily trained, arching branches which grow to a height of 6 m (20 ft). It produces clusters of lilac or violet-purple flowers in summer.

— *B. colvilei* produces panicles of pink or scarlet flowers, about 20 cm (8 in) long.

Height: 5–6 m (16–20 ft).
Soil: any.
Aspect: sun.
Propagation: from cuttings in summer.
Flowering season: summer.
Type: deciduous shrub (the evergreen buddlejas are not hardy).

Campsis

BIGNONIA, TRUMPET CREEPER, TRUMPET VINE

Bignoniaceae

The common names – trumpet creeper, trumpet vine – of this exotic-looking climber are derived from its distinctive orange or yellow trumpets, with their upturned edges. It is a vigorous plant which reaches a height of 10 m (33 ft) and is ideal for covering house walls, although its aerial roots do need some

◁ *Buddleja alternifolia*

454

Campsis radicans △ ▷

form of support (e.g. wire) to cling on to. It can be grown along a fence or garden wall but needs to be trained.

Useful hints

— Plant campsis in spring or summer, in well-dug soil. Make sure you plant the root ball at least 60 cm (24 in) from a house wall, as its powerful roots can loosen the best foundations.

— Train the stems initially, and cut back any unwanted branches to the trunk in spring. Terminal clusters of flowers will appear on the current year's growth.

— You can create a beautiful contrast in a sunny corner by planting *Sedum spectabile*, hemerocallis or blue agapanthus around the base of a campsis.

Recommended

— *Campsis grandiflora* has narrow, bright orange trumpets.

— The summer- and autumn-flowering *C. radicans* can reach a height of 10 m (33 ft). The form *flava* produces an abundance of yellow trumpets.

— The well-known hybrid *C. × tagliabuana* 'Madam Galen' is extremely popular for its open, salmon-pink trumpets.

Height: 10 m (33 ft).
Soil: rich and cool in summer.
Aspect: sun.
Propagation: cuttings in summer.
Flowering season: summer and autumn.
Type: deciduous climber.

455

△ *Ceanothus* 'Cascade'

Ceanothus

CALIFORNIAN LILAC

Rhamnaceae

This mostly evergreen shrub comes in a remarkable range of blues. If trained as a climber it will reach an impressive height, covering a house wall with deep blue or sky-blue flowers, depending on the variety. *Ceanothus × delileanus* 'Gloire de Versailles', *C. × delileanus* 'Henri Desfossé', C. × *pallidus* 'Perle Rose' and C. × *delileanus* 'Topaz' are deciduous varieties and unsuitable as climbers. They make ideal border shrubs which grow to a height of 1.5–2 m (5–6½ ft).

Useful hints

— Plant in spring, in well-drained soil, lightened with sand and peat. Add a handful of bonemeal when planting.

During the first few years, cut back hard in spring to produce bushy, well-rooted shrubs.

— Ceanothus thrives in coastal regions. It looks particularly good behind shrub roses, *Veronica spicata* ssp. *incana* and groups of lilies.

Recommended

— *C. arboreus* is a tree which reaches a height of 8 m (26 ft) and produces pale blue flowers in spring. It has a spectacular cultivar called 'Trewithen Blue', which has clusters of deep blue, scented flowers.

— Some good hybrids include: 'Cascade', which has large, tightly packed panicles of deep blue flowers in spring; 'Burkwoodii', with long panicles of bright blue flowers during summer and autumn; 'A.T. Johnson', which produces

a wealth of flowers in summer and autumn; and 'Autumnal Blue', a hardy variety which bears pale to mid-blue flowers in summer and autumn.

— The evergreen *C. impressus* grows to a height of 1.5–3 m (5–10 ft). It has tiny leaves and deep blue flowers in spring and summer.

— 'Puget Blue' has dark blue flowers.

— *C. thyrsiflorus* reaches a height of 7 m (23 ft). Its tiny, powder-blue flowers look spectacular against a wall.

Height: 1–8 m (3¼–26 ft).
Soil: rich and light.
Aspect: sun, sheltered from frost.
Propagation: from cuttings in summer.
Flowering season: summer to autumn for deciduous varieties; spring to summer for evergreens.
Type: deciduous or evergreen shrub.

△▽ *Ceanothus impressus*

△ *Cestrum* 'Newellii'

Cestrum

CESTRUM

Solanaceae

The 170 or so species of cestrum are all natives of tropical and subtropical South America. They are not all hardy enough to be planted out in cooler climates, and the more tender kinds need the protection of a cool greenhouse or conservatory. Foliage is evergreen or deciduous depending on the climate, but even if the plant is slightly frosted it will grow away from the base in spring. Its yellow or red flowers are heavily scented at night and are wonderful near an open window in summer.

Useful hints

— Plant in a well-sheltered position, against a wall, and train the branches. Every two or three years, cut one or two of the old branches back to the base.

Recommended

— *Cestrum fasciculatum* is an evergreen species with elegant, arching branches. It climbs to a height of 7–8 m (23–26 ft) and produces salmon-pink flowers.

— *C.* 'Newellii' grows to a height of 4 m (13 ft) with virtually the same spread. It is an evergreen variety which produces beautiful crimson flowers.

Height: 4–8 m (13–26 ft).
Soil: any.
Aspect: sun, sheltered.
Propagation: by layering or from cuttings in summer.
Flowering season: summer.
Type: deciduous or evergreen shrub or climber.

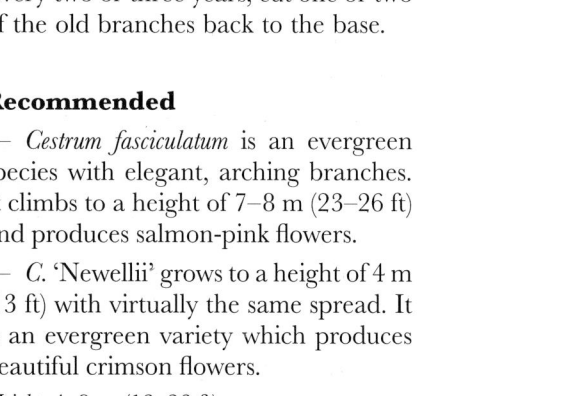

457

Clematis

CLEMATIS, OLD MAN'S BEARD, TRAVELLER'S JOY

Ranunculaceae

Clematis occupies pride of place among the climbers. Although some people maintain that they can't grow them successfully, they are in fact extremely easy plants to grow.

Useful hints

— Plant clematis at an angle, i.e. so that 10 cm (4 in) of the stem is horizontal and covered. This means that the root ball will be about 15–20 cm (6–8 in) from the support or wall that the clematis will climb. They tend to look more spectacular climbing over arches or up a trellis than against a wall. Protect the roots from direct sunlight.

Recommended small-flowered clematis

Clematis can be grouped by colour and flowering season.

White

— *Clematis montana* is one of the most vigorous and free-flowering varieties and ideal for covering large surfaces. It produces white flowers in spring.

— The branches of *C. montana* var. *sericea* (syn. *C. spooneri*) and *C. flammula* are covered in a profusion of small heavily scented white flowers in early summer.

Blue

— *C. alpina* often doesn't grow above 2.5 m (8 ft). It produces lantern-shaped, silky blue flowers in spring.

Yellow

— *C. rehderiana* has attractive, slightly scented, primrose-yellow flowers in early summer.

— The dense foliage of *C. tangutica* is covered in bright yellow, lantern-shaped flowers in summer.

— *C. tibetana* ssp. *vernayi* 'Orange Peel' is one of the hardiest and most vigorous varieties. It can reach a height of 5–6 m (16–20 ft) and produces black-centred yellow flowers in summer.

Mauve

— *C. viticella* does not grow above 3–4 m (10–13 ft) and bears mauve and purple flowers in summer.

Pink

— *C. montana* 'Elizabeth' has scented soft pink flowers.

— *C. montana* var. *rubens* is an early-flowering variety with attractive, bright pink flowers in spring.

— *C. montana* 'Tetrarose' is a very hardy, vigorous variety which is ideal for covering large surfaces or old walls. It produces a profusion of pale pink flowers in spring.

Red

— *C.* 'Gravetye Beauty' has masses of small, tulip-like, single, bright red flowers with brown stamens. 'Duchess of Albany' is similar.

— *C.* 'Madame Julia Correvon' is the most attractive of the small-flowered red clematis. It flowers prolifically throughout summer and autumn.

— The attractive foliage of *C. texensis* sets off its scarlet flowers which appear in early summer.

Recommended large-flowered hybrids

White

— *C.* 'Jackmanii Alba' is a very hardy variety. It has an abundance of decorative foliage and bears magnificent white flowers with cream stamens during late summer and early autumn.

— *C.* 'John Huxtable' is a late-flowering variety with large white flowers with cream stamens.

— *C.* 'Marie Boisselot' (syn. 'Madame Le Coultre') has an abundance of decorative foliage and produces huge white flowers throughout the summer.

Blue

— *C.* 'Haku Ôkan' is a Japanese variety which produces deep violet-blue flowers with large, pale yellow stamens in early summer and again in autumn.

— *C.* 'Lasurstern' is a vigorous plant which produces lavender-blue flowers with cream stamens in early summer and again in autumn.

— *C.* 'Perle d'Azur' bears a profusion of azure-blue flowers with cream stamens in summer.

— *C.* 'Prins Hendrik' is recommended for its cut flowers. It produces beauti-

△ *Clematis tangutica*
▽ *Clematis florida* 'Sieboldii'

▽ *Clematis* 'Bill Mackenzie'

Clematis montana 'Tetrarose' △
Clematis 'The President' ▷
Clematis montana var. rubens ▽

459

△ *Clematis*, large-flowered hybrid

△ *Clematis* 'Trianon'

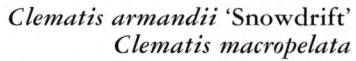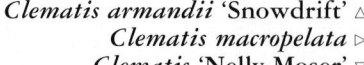

Clematis armandii 'Snowdrift' △
Clematis macropelata ▷
Clematis 'Nelly Moser' ▽

fully formed, lavender-blue flowers during summer and early autumn.

— *C.* 'The President' is the best-known and most popular blue-flowered clematis. It has very decorative foliage and flowers from spring to autumn.

— *C.* 'W.E. Gladstone' is an extremely beautiful, vigorous variety which bears lavender-blue flowers with purple anthers during summer and autumn.

Mauve

— *C.* 'Bees' Jubilee' is an improved version of 'Nelly Moser'. It is a hardy variety which produces an abundance of rose-mauve flowers, with a deep carmine bar on each petal, in early summer and again in autumn.

Pink

— *C.* 'Comtesse de Bouchaud' is a vigorous plant which produces beautiful, pale pink flowers throughout the summer and well into autumn.

— *C.* 'Doctor Ruppel' is a very good variety which produces an abundance of flowers in early summer and again in autumn. Its deep pink petals are marked with a carmine bar.

— *C.* 'Hagley Hybrid' is ideal for the cooler regions of Europe. Its dense foliage sets off the delightful shell-pink flowers with large purple stamens, produced continuously throughout summer and into autumn.

— *C.* 'Nelly Moser' is ideal for training against a north-facing wall, where it will retain its beautiful colours (they fade in strong sunlight). It has attractive pale green foliage and produces a profusion of flowers in early summer and again in autumn.

Red

— *C.* 'Ernest Markham' is one of the best and hardiest red-flowered varieties. It flowers profusely, and continuously, during summer and autumn.

— *C.* 'Niobe' produces masses of rich red flowers throughout the summer.

— *C.* 'Rouge Cardinal' is a plant of average growth. It has extremely decorative dark green foliage and bears a profusion of velvety crimson flowers in summer and autumn.

— *C.* 'Ville de Lyon' is the best-known red clematis because it is both hardy and easily obtainable. It produces an abundance of velvety, carmine-red flowers with yellow stamens during summer and autumn.

Recommended evergreen clematis

— *C. armandii* is a native of China. Its branches can reach a length of 4–5 m (13–16 ft) and bear fragrant white flowers in spring, with a second flowering in autumn.

— The foliage of *C. cirrhosa* var. *balearica*, sometimes referred to as the 'fern-leaf' clematis, turns bronze in winter. Its small, pale yellow, lantern-shaped flowers are marked with purplish red. It flowers in early spring.

— Both the above species are recommended only for milder climates.

Recommended double-flowered clematis

— *C.* 'Countess of Lovelace' has double bluish lilac flowers, with cream stamens, in early summer.

— *C.* 'Duchess of Edinburgh' has dense foliage and magnificent double white flowers during summer and autumn.

— *C.* 'Vyvyan Pennell' is a vigorous plant with decorative dark green foliage. It produces double lavender-blue flowers, in summer and again in autumn, on the current year's growth.

— *C.* 'Yvette Houry' has lavender-blue flowers with white stamens. It is a hardy plant which flowers in early summer and again in autumn.

Height: 60 cm–10 m (2–33 ft).
Soil: humus-rich and fairly light.
Aspect: semi-shade or sun. Protect roots from direct sunlight with a tile or another plant.
Propagation: from cuttings and, especially, by layering, in summer.
Flowering season: spring to autumn.
Type: deciduous or evergreen climber.

461

Clianthus

CLIANTHUS

Leguminosae

This small, evergreen shrub does not grow above 3 m (10 ft). It has tough, dark green leaves and produces an abundance of strange, claw-like, crimson flowers, opening towards the bottom, in spring and early summer. As its branches are very brittle it is best trained against a south-facing wall.

Useful hints

— Clianthus prefers a mild climate and should be given wall protection. It does have a tendency to spread in a rather unsightly manner if it is not trained. Its flowers look better against a wall.

— In cooler regions it is advisable to protect the roots in winter with a 20 cm (8 in) layer of straw.

— Clianthus is a thirsty plant, so don't forget to water it regularly in summer.

▽ *Clianthus puniceus*

Recommended

— *Clianthus formosus* has a prostrate habit. Clusters of brilliant red flowers, marked with black, are borne in spring.

— *C. puniceus* (parrot's bill or lobster's claw) is better adapted to a temperate climate, where if it is happy it will grow into a splendid evergreen shrub and produce drooping clusters of strange-looking red flowers.

Height: up to 3 m (10 ft).
Soil: sandy and humus-rich.
Aspect: full sun.
Propagation: from cuttings or seed.
Flowering season: spring to summer.
Type: evergreen shrub.

Hedera

IVY

Araliaceae

Ivy grows under any conditions and looks good in any position. It is ideal for

▽ *Clianthus puniceus* 'Albus'

filling those shady, empty corners under trees, for trailing over low walls or softening the effect of bare, high walls. And there is no need to worry about its aerial roots and tenacious habit: ivy has preserved more old walls than it has destroyed. Its dense foliage and roots actually protect old rendering from bad weather and hold it together. Bulbs and daffodils planted among covering ivy give a beautiful spring display against its carpet of greenery.

Useful hints

— Tie young branches to train them in the desired direction.

— Water regularly.

— Mulch the soil around the base in autumn, or cover with leaf-mould.

— Grown along a trellis, ivy will also produce a good-sized hedge within three years. Ideal if you are short of space!

Recommended

You are really spoilt for choice!

Algerian ivy

— *Hedera algeriensis* is a large-leaved ivy and has some good cultivars, such as the variegated 'Gloire de Marengo' and the white-edged 'Margino-maculata'.

Canary Island ivy

— *H. canariensis* is a large-leaved species with plain green leaves.

Persian ivy

— *H. colchica* has even larger, oval leaves which are marked with yellow in 'Dentata Variegata' and 'Sulphur Heart'.

Common ivy

— There are many varieties of *H. helix*: 'Buttercup' has golden foliage ageing to pale green; the leaves of 'Goldheart' have a golden centre and green border; 'Arborescens' forms a veritable shrub, 1–2 m (3¼–6½ ft) high; 'Glacier' is rimmed with silver and white; 'Pedata' has grey-green, bird's-foot-shaped leaves.

— *H. helix* 'Chicago' is a vigorous plant whose dark green leaves are often tinged with purple.

— The tiny, long and pointed leaves of *H. helix* 'Doverailensis' (syn. *H. helix* 'Minima') turn bronze in winter. It is

△ *Hedera colchica* 'Dentata Variegata'

▽ *Hedera helix* 'Ivalace'

△ *Hedera helix* cultivar

▽ *Hedera helix* 'Sagittifolia'

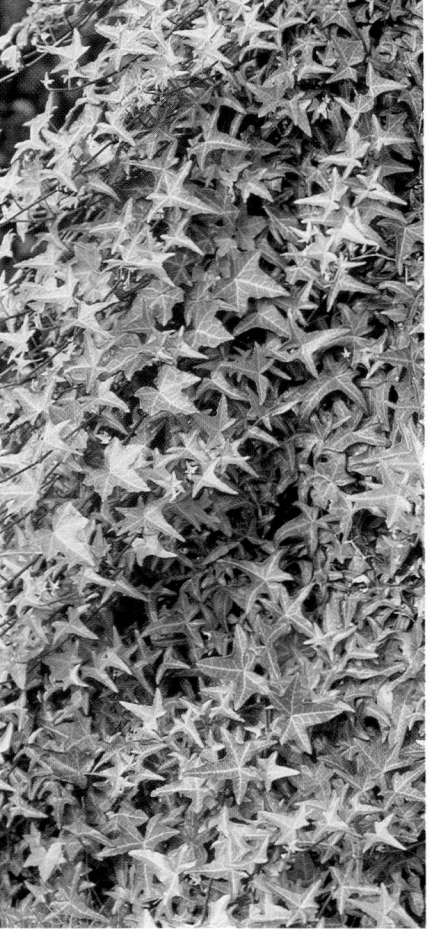

△ *Hedera helix* 'Tricolor'

▽ *Hedera colchica*

a slow-growing variety which is ideal for pots and containers. Many small varieties of ivy can be grown as house plants.

— *H. helix* 'Green Ripple' weaves a dense covering of tough, spiky leaves, veined with cream.

— *H. helix* 'Tricolor' has small, silvery, white-rimmed leaves which become tinged with pink in winter.

— The blue-green foliage of *H. helix* 'Triton' makes good mats with its deeply cut leaves.

— *H. hibernica* (Atlantic ivy) has tough, dark green leaves and makes good ground cover in a shady position.

Height: 30 cm – several metres (12 in – several feet).
Soil: any.
Aspect: shade or semi-shade.
Propagation: by layering or by separating and transplanting shoots in summer.
Type: evergreen climber.

463

Hydrangea

CLIMBING HYDRANGEA

Hydrangeaceae

This extremely versatile native of China and Japan is a climber with a difference. It produces aerial roots and therefore needs no support (it can cling tightly to a wall), but it may take three years before it begins to climb, so don't lose heart. However, once it starts, it goes from strength to strength and produces beautiful white flowers, even in a north-facing, shady position. Hydrangeas are not sun-lovers, so plant in the shade. The flowers on older plants are magnificent and well worth waiting for.

Useful hints

— Plant climbing hydrangeas in light, well-tilled soil enriched with peat and a handful of bonemeal.

— They can also be used as ground cover, where they will form dense bushes. They look good surrounded by fuchsias.

Recommended

— *Hydrangea petiolaris* is a vigorous, summer-flowering climber.

— *H. serratifolia* has dark green foliage and produces small, creamy white flowers in summer.

Height: up to 6 m (20 ft).
Soil: light, well-dug.
Aspect: semi-shade or shade.
Propagation: by layering or from cuttings.
Flowering season: summer.
Type: deciduous climber or shrub.

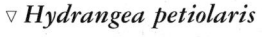

▽ *Hydrangea petiolaris*

Jasminum

JASMINE

Oleaceae

Although most jasmines are not hardy enough to survive in colder regions, there are a few species that will add colour and fragrance to a south-facing house wall for many years. Although they are not true climbers, they can be trained successfully to a height of around 6 m (20 ft). Prune them regularly to prevent an unsightly tangle.

Useful hints

— Plant jasmine in spring for preference, at the foot of a trellis so that its stems can twine around a support.

— Water regularly, adding a soluble feed two or three times during the summer as jasmine exhausts the soil.

— Propagate by bending some stems and covering with soil. Allow them to root during the summer before transplanting.

— Don't plant *Jasminum nudiflorum* against an east-facing wall, as this winter-flowering species doesn't like the early morning sun.

— Plant in a sunny position (preferably south- or west-facing), protected from cold winter winds. Prune the stems once they have flowered.

Recommended

— *J. beesianum* (pink jasmine) grows to a height of 3–4 m (10–13 ft) and bears fragrant, rose-purple flowers.

— *J. humile* (yellow jasmine) is covered with clusters of golden yellow flowers in summer. 'Revolutum' has slightly scented yellow flowers. The branches of this semi-climbing evergreen twine easily around supports up to a height of 3 m (10 ft).

— Although hardy, *J. nudiflorum* (winter jasmine) can be frosted to ground level during hard winters. Its yellow flowers, borne on leafless stems in winter, are unscented.

— *J. officinale* (common jasmine, jessamine), on the other hand, bears deliciously scented white flowers in summer. It is a vigorous species which reaches a height of 10 m (33 ft).

— *J. polyanthum* produces fragrant, pinkish-white flowers and will grow to

△ *Jasminum × stephanense*

△ *Jasminum polyanthum*

a height of over 5 m (16 ft) in a well-protected position.

— *J. primulinum* (syn. *J. mesnyi*) is only half-hardy. It has semi-double pale yellow flowers in spring.

Height: 2–10 m (6½–33 ft).
Soil: rich and light.
Aspect: sun (avoid early morning sun for *J. nudiflorum*, as it will scorch the leaves).
Propagation: by layering in summer.
Flowering season: winter to summer.
Type: deciduous or evergreen shrub or climber.

Lapageria

LAPAGERIA, CHILEAN BELLFLOWER

Liliaceae

Lapageria is an evergreen, twining climber with fairly long, leathery, pure green leaves and large, exotic-looking, tubular red flowers. Its habit (it climbs by twining around its support) and remarkable blooms make it one of the most spectacular climbers available. It is a native of Chile and only grows in mild areas where it is well-sheltered from the wind and not exposed to strong sunlight. In a suitable climate it can be trained along the branches of a tree, where it will thrive in the semi-shade. Otherwise it makes an excellent climber for the conservatory.

Useful hints

— Plant lapageria in a position where it will be well sheltered from cold winds and can climb up a trellis or along the branches of a tree. In regions which

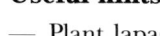
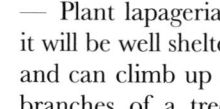
▽ *Lapageria rosea*

have frosts, it does well in a cold or cool greenhouse or conservatory and bears flowers for several months. Always plant it in light, well-drained soil.

— Don't prune unless the leaves have been frosted. In this case, cut back the frosted parts of the plant.

— Slugs are extremely fond of lapageria, so protect the young plants by wrapping strips of cotton-wool around their stems.

Recommended

— *Lapageria rosea* (Chilean bell flower, copihue) is the only species. It can be planted out in an extremely sheltered position, or grown in a greenhouse. Its flowers are a beautiful rose-pink, with deeper pink markings. 'Nash Court' has deeper pink flowers.

Height: 5–6 m (16–20 ft).
Soil: fertile and light, well-drained.
Aspect: protect from direct sunlight.
Propagation: by layering.
Flowering season: late summer to autumn.
Type: evergreen twining climber.

▽ *Lapageria rosea* var. *albiflora*

465

△ *Lonicera periclymenum*

△ *Lonicera × brownii* 'Dropmore Scarlet'

Lonicera

HONEYSUCKLE

Caprifoliaceae

People tend to think of honeysuckle as a climber but, as well as the climbing species, there are also shrubby honeysuckles that can be used as ground cover or to form a hedge. Honeysuckle will thrive in any garden, since this deliciously scented plant tolerates all soil types, all positions (hot sun or semi-shade) and even pollution.

Useful hints

— Honeysuckle can be planted at any time of year if it has been grown in a container (the best way of starting it off). Don't break the root ball, and plant it so that you protect the base of the stem from the cold. Mulch in spring and water regularly in summer to promote new growth.

— Pruning is, generally speaking, of little use except in the case of *Lonicera nitida*, which should be cut back at least three times a year, to maintain a dense

habit. If this species should be frosted, cut it back to ground level and it will produce new growth. It can be pruned to produce spherical, square and other different-shaped shrubs.

Recommended shrubby honeysuckles

— The remarkable fragrance of *L. fragrantissima* compensates for its fairly unattractive habit. Train it against a trellis and plant it with a small-flowered clematis or summer-flowering jasmine to hide its twisted, woody stems. It has semi-evergreen foliage.

— *L. nitida* is widely used to produce low hedges and 'sculpted' shrubs, as it grows quickly and remains very dense, provided it is pruned regularly. It has green or golden foliage – e.g. 'Baggesen's Gold' – and can also be trained as a climber.

— *L. tatarica* is less dense but has beautiful dark green foliage which sets off the pink flowers of 'Arnold's Red' and the cherry-red flowers of 'Hack's Red'. It can reach a height of 2.5 m (8 ft) and flowers in spring or summer.

Recommended climbing honeysuckles

— The distinctive leaves of the summer-flowering *L. caprifolium* (perfoliate honeysuckle) look as if they have been pierced by the stems.

— *L. etrusca* is not completely hardy. It has pale yellow flowers and blue-green leaves.

▽ *Lonicera caprifolium* f. *pauciflora*

— *L. henryi* is a vigorous evergreen climber with long, decorative, spear-shaped leaves which make up for its lack of fragrance.

— *L. hildebrandtiana* (giant Burmese honeysuckle) has large, scented, creamy white flowers, 9–15 cm (3½–6 in) long. However, it is not fully hardy and should be grown only in milder climates.

— Asiatic honeysuckles are often evergreen, e.g. *L. japonica* (Japanese honeysuckle), which has white flowers ageing to yellow. 'Halliana' is an extremely fragrant variety. The foliage of 'Aureoreticulata' has unusual, yellow-veined leaves which look extremely effective grown among lush-leaved perennials such as peonies, acanthus and hellebores.

— *L. japonica* var. *repens* has inherited all the best qualities of the species, with the added advantage of its own beautiful, purple colour.

— The most fragrant varieties lose their leaves in winter. *L. periclymenum* (common honeysuckle or woodbine) grows to a height of 6 m (20 ft) and, although rather invasive, gives a delightful display throughout the summer. It has produced 'Belgica', a more compact, summer-flowering variety, and 'Serotina', whose flowers – bright red on the outside – appear a little later.

— Although *L. sempervirens* (trumpet honeysuckle) has imparted its rich orange colour to many hybrids, they do not have its fragrance. The scarlet blooms of the summer-flowering *L. × brownii* 'Dropmore Scarlet' are totally unscented.

— *Lonicera* × *tellmaniana*, with its copper-coloured flowers, is one of the more unusual varieties, although it does require a very sheltered position.

Height: 1–9 m (3¼–30 ft).
Soil: ordinary, humus-enriched.
Aspect: sun or semi-shade.
Propagation: from cuttings or by layering in autumn.
Flowering season: winter to autumn.
Type: evergreen or deciduous shrub or climber.

Muehlenbeckia

MUEHLENBECKIA

Polygonaceae

Although this is a plant for milder regions, it will grow up every kind of support once established. It can be used to cover unsightly tree trunks, climb up walls or, with the help of a trellis, drape itself between shrubs or cascade attractively over low walls. In short, it will adapt easily to your requirements. Although its small, white flowers are fairly insignificant, they lighten the dense mass of foliage quite effectively.

Useful hints

— Plant muehlenbeckia in spring, in soil enriched with leaf-mould.

— Water regularly during its first summer and pull up any weeds. Once the plant is established, its dense mat of foliage will make weeding unnecessary.

— Propagate in spring, by separating the rooted pieces around the edge of the plant.

Recommended

— *Muehlenbeckia axillaris* has a dense, prostrate habit and tiny, round leaves.

— Given a support, *M. complexa* is a superb climber which reaches a height of 6 m (20 ft).

Height: 10–15 cm (4–6 in) for prostrate varieties; up to 6 m (20 ft) for climbers.
Soil: humus-enriched.
Aspect: sun or semi-shade.
Propagation: by separating rooted pieces, in spring.
Flowering season: summer.
Type: evergreen shrub or climber.

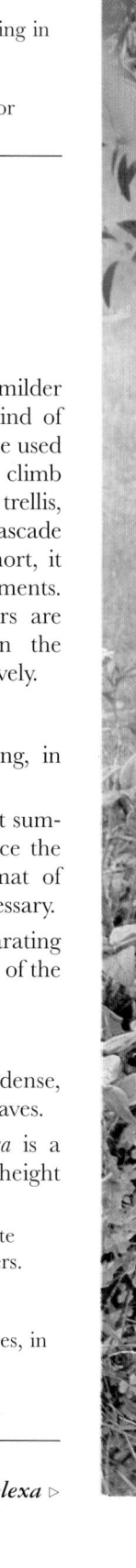

Muehlenbeckia complexa ▷

467

△ *Mutisia ilicifolia*

Mutisia

MUTISIA

Compositae

Mutisia, sometimes referred to as climbing gazania, has large daisy-like flowers in yellow or orange. It is a tendril climber which will climb easily if given a support.

Useful hints

— Mutisia is only fully hardy in milder climates. Allow it to climb up a trellis, against a south-facing wall, or spread through other shrubs.

— It prefers rich, well-drained soil.

Recommended

— *Mutisia clematis* is one of the most beautiful species. It climbs to a height of 5 m (16 ft) and bears large, reddish orange, bell-shaped flowers which appear from early summer onwards.

— *M. decurrens* can reach a height of 3 m (10 ft) and produces red or orange flowers throughout the summer. It can sometimes be propagated from shoots but is difficult to establish.

— *M. ilicifolia* flowers nearly all year and grows to a height of 5 m (16 ft). Its leaves are dark green and holly-like, and its flowers, 5 cm (2 in) across, are pale pink to mauve in colour.

Height: up to 5 m (16 ft).
Soil: fertile, humus-enriched.
Aspect: full sun.
Propagation: from cuttings.
Flowering season: summer.
Type: evergreen climber.

Parthenocissus

VIRGINIA CREEPER

Vitaceae

Parthenocissus looks extremely decorative grown against the wall of a house, where it can reach a height of 15 m (50 ft) and sometimes more. Parthenocissus is characterized by its suckers or aerial roots which enable it to cling to a smooth wall. Bright red autumn foliage and dark blue fruits make the Virginia creeper a particularly attractive plant.

Useful hints

— Plant Virginia creeper in autumn or spring. Train the first shoots against a trellis or wire netting.

— Propagate by bending a branch down and burying two-thirds of it in a

— *P. tricuspidata* 'Robusta' is a fast-growing creeper which covers walls with a drapery of large, glossy leaves. 'Lowii' has small, crinkled leaves with up to seven lobes.

— *P. tricuspidata* 'Veitchii' (syn. *Ampelopsis tricuspidata* 'Veitchii') is a very elegant small-leaved variety with distinctively coloured foliage: purple in spring, turning to a spectacular red-purple in autumn.

Height: 1.5–20 m (5–65 ft).
Soil: any.
Aspect: sun or semi-shade.
Propagation: by layering in summer.
Flowering season: summer, but flowers insignificant.
Type: deciduous climber.

Passiflora

PASSION FLOWER

Passifloraceae

This strange, exotic-looking plant is a native of South America, Asia and Australia, and most of its 500 or so species will not grow outside in cooler climates. The passion flower was named by the Spanish priests of South America, who saw it as a symbol of the Passion of Christ: the ten sepals represent ten apostles, the slightly spiky crown is reminiscent of the crown of thorns, the five stamens symbolize the five wounds of Christ and the three stigma, the three nails. Passion flowers will attach themselves to any support and climb unaided. They produce fruit only if the summer is particularly hot.

Useful hints

— Plant outside only in mild areas, in a well-sheltered position, against a south- or west-facing trellis or wall.

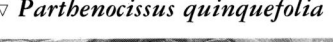
▽ *Parthenocissus quinquefolia*

△ *Passiflora caerulea* 'Constance Elliot'

△ *Passiflora × belotii* 'Impératrice Eugénie'

Recommended

— *Passiflora caerulea* 'Constance Elliot' is a vigorous evergreen climber which can be planted outside in warmer regions. It produces white flowers during summer and autumn.

— *P. edulis* is a vigorous climber with beautiful flowers in white banded with purple. It needs to be planted against a sunny, sheltered wall. It produces edible purple fruit if the summer has been hot enough.

— *P. umbilicata* is a vigorous climber which can reach a height of 8 m (26 ft). It bears amethyst-coloured flowers, 8 cm (3 in) across, during summer and autumn. In its native South America, it grows at altitudes of up to 3,000 m (9,840 ft), and can be grown in our cooler European climates provided it is protected from cold winds.

Height: 4–8 m (13–26 ft).
Soil: well-drained.
Aspect: sun, against a wall.
Propagation: by layering in spring or from cuttings in summer.
Flowering season: summer.
Type: evergreen climber.

(left column, lower)

△ *Parthenocissus tricuspidata* 'Veitchii'

mixture of equal parts of sand and peat. In a few months, the branch will have rooted and can be separated from the parent plant and planted out.

Recommended

— *Parthenocissus henryana* has dark green or bronze-green foliage, with decorative silver veining, which turns red in autumn. This tall creeper – up to 10 m (33 ft) – should be grown in the shade, as its colours fade in direct sunlight.

— The extremely vigorous *P. quinquefolia* (five-leaved ivy or true Virginia creeper) achieves the greatest heights: up to 20 m (65 ft). It has beautiful crimson autumn colour.

— *P. tricuspidata* (Boston ivy or Japanese creeper) is a native of Japan, with magnificent scarlet autumn foliage.

△ *Polygonum baldschuanicum*

Polygonum (syn. *Fallopia*)
RUSSIAN VINE, KNOTWEED
Polygonaceae

Polygonum is an extremely vigorous creeper, growing at a rate of 5 m (16 ft) per year and producing a profusion of creamy white flowers throughout the summer. It is one of the most invasive climbers in existence, and should be grown only in places where you can keep an eye on it and curb its enthusiasm! However, it does have the advantage of being able to cover an unsightly building such as an old garage or shed in only a few years, and grows equally well in sun or shade. It is extremely effective seen from a distance, with its mass of lace-like white flowers cascading down a wall or tree.

Useful hints

— Plant Russian vine at any time of year, in well-dug soil with added manure. To promote growth, feed in spring with three handfuls of garden fertilizer and a good layer of semi-rotted compost.

— Propagate in summer by bending a branch down into the soil, where it will soon take root.

Recommended

— *Polygonum baldschuanicum* (syn. *Fallopia baldschuanica*), the mile-a-minute plant or Russian vine, has pink-tinged flowers.

— *P. multiflorum* is less hardy and more susceptible to cold than the above species. It is a climbing perennial up to 2 m (6 ft) high with white flowers in autumn.

Height: up to 15 m (50 ft) or more.
Soil: ordinary, tending to rich.
Aspect: any.
Propagation: by layering in summer.
Flowering season: summer to autumn.
Type: deciduous climber.

Pyracantha
PYRACANTHA, FIRETHORN
Rosaceae

The pyracantha is popular for its profusion of white flowers in summer and its formidable thorns. Rather than using it to form an impenetrable hedge, try training it against a wall where, with careful pruning, it will produce a beautiful tapestry of brightly coloured berries throughout much of the winter.

Useful hints

— Plant pyracantha in autumn or spring. Mulch every winter with leaf-mould to prevent weeds, as they are difficult to extract from among its thorns. Prune at the end of winter, before the flowering season.

— Be careful if using weedkillers, as some can turn the leaves yellow. Do not use weedkiller near the roots.

Recommended

— *Pyracantha angustifolia* has narrow leaves, grey on the underside, and orange berries throughout winter.

— *P. atalantoïdes* (syn. *P. gibbsii*) looks rather like a small tree and has orange or, in the case of 'Aurea', yellow berries.

— *P. crenulata* is a splendid species for growing on a cold wall, though its berries can sometimes be rather sparse. If grown in full sun it will produce more berries.

— The most numerous pyracanthas are the *P. rogersiana* and *P. coccinea* hybrids. Among the most spectacular are 'Golden Glow' (golden yellow); 'Orange Charmer' (erect habit and bright orange berries); 'Mohave' (vigorous, with orange berries); 'Navajo' (the most disease-resistant); 'Orange Glow' (orange); 'Rosedale' (its bright red berries look superb against a wall); and 'Shawnee' (naturally pyramidal habit). One of the most popular of the hybrids is 'Lalandei', with large orange-red fruits which last all winter.

470

△ *Pyracantha coccinea* 'Lalandei'

△▷ **Pyracantha crenato-serrata**
▽ **Pyracantha rogersiana** f. 'Flava'

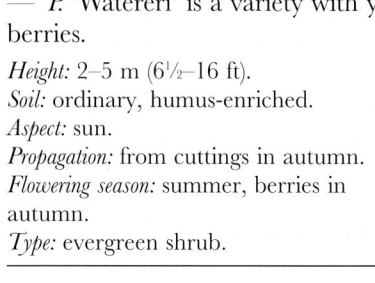

A new development has been the scab-resistant cultivars 'Saphyr Orange' (orange berries) and 'Saphyr Rouge' (red berries).

— *P.* 'Watereri' is a variety with yellow berries.

Height: 2–5 m (6½–16 ft).
Soil: ordinary, humus-enriched.
Aspect: sun.
Propagation: from cuttings in autumn.
Flowering season: summer, berries in autumn.
Type: evergreen shrub.

Rosa

ROSE

Rosaceae

Roses are divided into two groups: first, roses for beds and borders (see pp. 419–24), and second, climbers and ramblers. However, there are subtle variations within this second group, as some larger varieties of shrub roses which are not classified as climbers can in fact be trained as such, while other varieties exist in both shrub and climbing form: for example, the elegant 'Queen Elizabeth' or the subtly fragrant 'Peace'. When buying these, you will need to specify that you want 'Climbing Queen Elizabeth' or 'Climbing Peace'. Other varieties are available in the form of a shrub, a climber, a weeping or a standard rose: for example, 'Centenaire de Lourdes' has shrub, weeping and standard forms. A 'Centenaire de Lourdes' standard rose surrounded by three 'Centenaire de Lourdes' shrub roses creates a stunning display.

Useful hints

— In the first year after planting, prune the branches back to one-third of their height at the end of winter. In subsequent years, remove any dead wood and cut back the branches produced on vigorous wood by a third. This will produce new branches. If you want to use so-called climbing roses as shrubs, cut them back to 50 cm (20 in) during the first two years to produce fine shrubby specimens.

Outstanding varieties

It is difficult to choose the most attractive, the most disease-resistant and the most easily maintained varieties from among the hundreds of climbing roses now available, but here is just a selection.

— 'Albéric Barbier' is a hardy, vigorous rose which produces fragrant flowers in summer. Its small, glossy leaves turn red in autumn and remain on the plant during the first months of winter. Height: 5 m (16 ft).

— 'Alexandre Girault' is a superb rambling rose which will scramble through a tree to a height of 6 m (20 ft). Its beautiful, apple-scented fragrance makes up for the fact that it only flowers once.

— 'American Pillar' is a hardy, vigorous rose with glossy, dark green foliage and clusters of white-centred, pink flowers in summer. Height: 4.5 m (14½ ft).

— 'Ballerina' produces clusters of small, pink-tinged, white-rimmed flowers well into autumn. It can only be trained to a height of 1.2 m (4 ft), as this is its maximum natural height. It is classified as a shrub rose.

— 'Chaplin's Pink Climber' has single flowers with golden stamens and is ideal for a pergola.

— 'Climbing Étoile de Hollande' has a graceful, arching habit and beautiful, fragrant, deep red flowers.

— 'Climbing Iceberg' produces pure white flowers throughout the summer, against attractive, fresh green foliage.

— The reddish green foliage and tea-scented, apricot-coloured flowers of 'Climbing Lady Hillingdon' are ideal against a south-facing wall.

— 'Constance Spry' produces a spectacular display of scented pink flowers in summer.

— 'Félicité Perpétue' produces attractively pink-rimmed, creamy-white flowers throughout the summer. It will climb to a height of over 4 m (13 ft) on a pergola.

— *R. filipes* 'Kiftsgate' is a rampant climber, growing at a rate of over 1 m (3¼ ft) per year and providing hundreds of tiny scented flowers.

— Whether planted in semi-shade or sun, 'Gloire de Dijon' is a celebration of colour, fragrance and form throughout summer and autumn. Each flower is a mass of softly crinkled, buff-pink petals.

— 'Guinée' is an extremely free-flowering variety which produces an abundance of intoxicatingly scented, deep maroon flowers. Height: 5 m (16 ft).

— 'Handel' is a perpetual-flowering variety. Its scented flowers have attractively ruffled, pink-edged petals.

— 'Kew Rambler'. The attractive, grey-green foliage of this tall, summer-flowering rambler sets off its pale pink flowers. It bears tiny orange fruits in autumn. Height: 5.5 m (18 ft). Spread: 3.5 m (11½ ft).

— 'Madame Alfred Carrière' is an extremely vigorous, perpetual-flowering variety which climbs easily to a height

△ *Rosa* 'Climbing Madame Caroline Testout'

△ *Rosa laevigata*

of 6 m (20 ft). It bears a profusion of fragrant, well-rounded, double, ivory-white flowers, tinged with pink, and is a very popular variety.

— Although it flowers only once, 'Madame Grégoire Staechelin' produces an abundance of heavily scented, exquisitely coloured, flesh-pink flowers, shaded darker on the underside. And as if this were not enough, it also flowers on a north-facing wall.

— The large, butter-coloured, single flowers and evergreen foliage of 'Mermaid' look wonderful against a wall, in the sun.

472

Rosa 'American Pillar' ▷
Rosa 'Félicité Perpétue' ▽

— The bright yellow flowers of 'Mrs Pierre S. du Pont' are delightful, even on a dull day.

— 'New Dawn' is a perpetual-flowering variety which produces a profusion of pale pink blooms.

— 'Pink Perpétue' is another perpetual-flowering climber which produces clusters of fresh, pure, deep pink double flowers.

— 'Souvenir du Docteur Jamain' has exquisitely scented, deep crimson – almost black – petals that look as if they are made of velvet. It flowers well into the summer.

473

— The banana-scented 'Wedding Day' looks rather like a 'Kiftsgate' with larger flowers. This summer-flowering climber can reach heights of up to 9 m (30 ft) with a spread of 4.5 m (14½ ft).

Mauve or purple varieties

The purple-flowered climbers tend to be neglected. They are delightful, especially if mixed with clematis, but be warned . . . they clash horribly with red or pink roses.

— 'Amadis' has deep purple, semi-double flowers and can reach a height of 6 m (20 ft). It is at its best when allowed to climb along a hedge, which provides an ideal support for its cascading festoons.

— 'Bleu Magenta' looks like a huge bouquet of deep purplish red flowers.

— 'Rose-Marie Viaud' has rosettes of violet-coloured flowers and is virtually thornless.

— 'Veilchenblau' has clusters of tiny, apple-scented, mauve flowers.

— 'Violette' is a thornless variety. Its apple-scented flowers are purple when they open, ageing to silvery brown.

Recommended climbers for warmer regions: ideal for a wall

White

— 'Aimée Vibert' (syn. 'Bouquet de la Mariée') has a profusion of tiny white, scented flowers and reaches a height of 5–6 m (16–20 ft).

— *R. brunonii* 'La Mortola' has large, strongly scented white flowers and silver-grey foliage. It is extremely vigorous and reaches a record height of 8 m (26 ft): a superb climber for warmer regions, although it only flowers once.

— 'Climbing Sombreuil' is a deliciously scented, ivory-coloured tea rose which flowers into the autumn.

— 'Vicomtesse Pierre du Fou' is a perpetual-flowering variety with heavily scented, white flowers.

Yellow and bronze

— The apricot-yellow buds of 'Alister Stella Gray' open into clusters of scented blooms. It flowers intermittently throughout the summer. Height: 4 m (13 ft).

— *R. banksiae* flowers in spring and seems to beat all records for the number

△ *Rosa* 'Zéphirine Drouhin'
▽ *Rosa* 'Golden Wings'

△ *Rosa* 'Buff Beauty'
▽ *Rosa* 'Iceberg'

△ *Rosa* 'Golden Showers'

△ *Rosa* 'Perpetual Yellow' and
R. 'Neige Rose'

▽ *Rosa* 'Marguerite Hilling'

△ *Rosa* 'Red Parfum'
▽ *Rosa banksiae*

△ *Rosa* 'Smarty'

△ *Rosa* 'Red Flore', *R.* 'Paul's Scarlet Climber' and *R.* 'Veilchenblau'

of flowers on one plant. Old plants can bear as many as 5,000 intoxicatingly fragrant flowers at a time. This rose, introduced from China in 1807, was named after Lady Banks, wife of the then director of Kew Gardens. The variety 'Lutea' has yellow flowers.

— 'Climbing Lady Hillingdon' flowers throughout the summer, up to the first frosts, but doesn't like the cold. It has double, ivory-yellow flowers with apricot-yellow centres.

— 'Gloire de Dijon' has large, double, deliciously scented, crinkled flowers. Their magnificent colour – creamy-buff, orange, tinged with pink – is difficult to describe.

— 'Golden Showers' produces fragrant, pale golden yellow flowers all summer and is an ideal variety for growing up pergolas or walls. It has to be treated against black spot.

— 'Maréchal Niel' is a vigorous, perpetual-flowering variety which grows to a height of 4–5 m (13–16 ft). It produces an abundance of bronze-gold, tea-rose-scented flowers.

— The summer-flowering 'Mermaid' looks more like a wild rose, with its large, canary-yellow flowers full of golden stamens.

— 'Rêve d'Or' has glossy, dark green foliage and flowers during summer and autumn. Its clusters of fragrant, semi-double blooms are bronze-yellow ageing to pale yellow.

▽ *Rosa* 'Toby Tristram'

Pink and red

— The summer-flowering 'Albertine' is ideal on a pergola with its clusters of double, creamy-buff flowers tinged with salmon-pink. It is exquisitely scented but has formidable thorns! Height: 4.5 m (14½ ft).

— 'Belle Portugaise' has grey-green foliage and produces an abundance of deliciously scented, double, salmon-pink flowers in summer.

— 'Coral Dawn' has large coral-pink flowers which are pleasantly scented. It is very free-flowering. Height about 3.5 m (11½ ft).

— 'Lili Marlène' is a delightful, summer-flowering variety. Its small clusters of bright, velvety, peony-like blooms are delicately scented. Height: 3 m (10 ft).

— 'Madame Sancy de Parabère' is a thornless variety which reaches a height of 6 m (20 ft). Its deliciously scented deep pink flowers can measure up to 12 cm (4½ in) across.

— 'Paul's Scarlet Climber' has bright scarlet flowers. Every year, cut back half the branches that have flowered during

476

△ *Rosa* 'Albertine'

△ *Rosa* 'Chaplin's Pink Climber'

▽ *Rosa* 'New Dawn'

▽ *Rosa* 'Dorothy Perkins'

the summer. It occasionally produces a few late flowers in autumn. Height: 3 m (10 ft).

Recommended miniature ramblers or climbers

These roses are, in fact, climbing roses, but they are slow to develop and can be trained directly from containers on a patio or balcony. They can also be used for ground cover in rock gardens.

— The stems – 1–1.5 m (3¼–5 ft) long – of 'Nozomi' are covered in tiny, single, pale pink flowers in summer. Beware of its thorns!

— 'Pink Cameo' or 'Climbing Cameo' has small, attractive flowers, delicately scented.

— 'Pompon de Paris' produces small, double, bright pink flowers in summer. Its branches grow to 1.8 m (6 ft).

Height: varies according to species and variety.

Soil: good.

Aspect: sun.

Propagation: from cuttings.

Flowering season: late spring to autumn.

Type: deciduous or semi-evergreen shrub or climber.

△ *Schisandra rubriflora*
▽ *Solanum species*

Schisandra

SCHISANDRA

Schisandraceae

This is an attractive climber which can be trained up trees or used to cover a fence. The flowers appear on both male and female plants, but only the latter bear berries.

Useful hints

— These plants must be attached to their support once they become established. In spring, a thick layer of leaf-mould should be added after planting. These plants like a well-lit position, but do not tolerate hot sun – a west-facing spot is best.

Recommended

— *Schisandra chinensis* climbs to a height of 6 m (20 ft), with scented pink flowers.

— *S. glaucescens* has slightly thick leaves which are blue-green on the underside. The orange-red blossom, in early summer, is followed by cylindrical scarlet fruits, 8–10 cm (3–4 in) long.

— *S. rubriflora* climbs to a height of 3 m (10 ft). Its flowers are dark red and appear in spring.

Height: 2–6 m (6½–20 ft).
Soil: good, preferably acid.
Aspect: semi-shade.
Propagation: by layering in autumn or from cuttings in summer.
Flowering season: spring to early summer.
Type: deciduous climber.

Solanum

SOLANUM

Solanaceae

This splendid plant with its large clusters of delicate flowers is perfect for a sunny wall that is protected from the wind. The solanum is a shrub with almost evergreen foliage. The flowers, which are mauve-blue or white, have yellow stamens and last for a good part of the year.

Useful hints

— If you protect the shrub in winter with a layer of leaf-mould under a sheet of plastic, the results will be well worth while. In spring, remove any dead or damaged wood.

Recommended

— *Solanum crispum,* known in some countries as the Chilean potato tree, has light lilac-blue flowers that appear in summer and autumn. It is a beautiful plant for covering a wall or shed.

— *S. crispum* 'Glasnevin' is fairly hardy and flowers exuberantly. It is an improved form of the species.

— *S. jasminoïdes* (potato vine) is more delicate, but this depends on the climate. The flowers are pale blue, and there is a white-flowered variety, 'Album', and also a variegated-leaved form.

Height: 2 m (6½ ft).
Soil: good.
Aspect: sun, sheltered.
Propagation: from seed in spring or cuttings in summer.
Flowering season: summer to autumn.
Type: deciduous or evergreen shrub.

Wisteria

WISTERIA

Leguminosae

Wisteria is without question one of the most beautiful climbing plants of all, and one of the easiest to grow. It is impossible not to be captivated by the beauty of a wisteria in full bloom, climbing up a pergola, decorating a house wall, or trained up a support to make a small tree. An elegant display can be achieved by mixing a pale blue Chinese wisteria with an early-flowering yellow rose such as 'Maigold' or even with a white clematis. An unusual effect can also be created by growing a wisteria among the yellow flowers of a laburnum. It is also a good idea to use the same colour on the ground, for example by planting lavender-coloured irises and yellow-flowered lysimachia close by. The combination of these yellow and mauve flowers is stunning.

Useful hints

— Wisteria may be planted in any season, in well-tilled soil with some sand added if it seems heavy. Mulch with straw in spring and water regularly during early summer. If the wisteria grows too quickly it may not flower. If this should happen, add a phosphorus-rich fertilizer and wait patiently for a few years.

Wisteria sinensis △

— Pruning is important in order to achieve good flowers. Cut back the new growth in summer to about 20 cm (8 in) from where it joins the old wood. Prune back further in winter.

Recommended

— The most striking variety is *Wisteria floribunda* 'Multijuga' (syn. *W. f.* 'Macrobotrys'), whose lilac racemes sometimes exceed 1.5 m (5 ft).

— *W. floribunda* 'Rosea' (Japanese wisteria) has pale pink flowers edged with purple.

— *W. floribunda* 'Violacea Plena'. As its name suggests, this has double flowers.

— *W. × formosa* 'Issai' puts out silky shoots and lilac-pink flowers arranged in racemes 25 cm (10 in) long.

— Japanese wisteria (*W. japonica*) has cream or white flowers in spring, but no fragrance.

— The Chinese wisteria (*W. sinensis*) has mauve, white and even double-flowered variations. All are scented.

— *W. venusta* (silky wisteria) is not so well-known. Its strongly scented white flowers, 2–3 cm (¾–1 in) long, are the largest in the genus and are arranged in racemes 15 cm (6 in) long.

Height: up to 10 m (33 ft).
Soil: not chalky.
Aspect: by layering in summer.
Flowering season: spring, and a little in autumn.
Type: deciduous climber.

Wisteria sinensis ▷

479

Every garden should have a few fruit trees or bushes. The flowers in spring are beautiful, and the ripe fruit, later, will be much better than any which can be bought commercially.

Growing and harvesting your own fruit is very satisfying. However, fruit-growing requires a little care and must be approached in the right way. Be guided by what seems to be growing well locally, but do not be afraid to choose uncommon varieties which you may have come across at a flower show or in a friend's garden.

The following section of the book will help you make the right selection.

FRUIT

Actinidia to Vine

△ **Kiwi fruit**

Actinidia deliciosa

CHINESE GOOSEBERRY, KIWI FRUIT

Actinidiaceae

The kiwi fruit, unknown to our grand-parents, has now become quite common. It grows on a strong stem which is able to produce, in one year and in any climate, branches that are 4–10 m (13–33 ft) long. Its large, highly decorative leaves are deciduous: its creamy white flowers, fairly insignificant, appear in summer.

Useful hints

— The plants are male or female, so plants of each sex should be planted side by side, 5–6 m (16–20 ft) apart, except in the case of one new variety which has both types of flowers.

— The actinidia tolerates cold (down to –20°C/–4°F) but dislikes high winds.

— The fruits appear in summer and are picked in autumn (until the first frost), sometimes after the leaves fall.

— They do not last long, except if kept cool (5°C/41°F), but can be bottled or used for making jam. The plant must always have enough water in summer.

Recommended

— 'Hayward', female, has large fruits in autumn; 'Tomuri', male, is a good companion for 'Hayward'.

— 'Jenny', self-fertilizing because both male and female flowers are on the one plant, is very similar to 'Hayward'.

Height: up to 10 m (33 ft).
Soil: not too chalky.
Aspect: semi-shade, cool.
Propagation: by layering.
Type: climber.

Citrus

CITRUS FRUITS

Rutaceae

Citrus dislike the cold – they begin to suffer if the temperature falls below –3°C (25°F) – and can only be grown in the mildest climates. Elsewhere they are best grown in containers, and should be sheltered in a conservatory in winter. In areas where the summers are not very hot, citrus produce very few fruits; they are grown in pots for decoration rather than for their fruit.

Useful hints

— For potted citrus it is advisable to choose small varieties, grafted on to not very vigorous stocks, that will not exceed 1 m (3¼ ft) in height. If possible, select a container that can be taken apart, as this makes changing the soil every two years much easier.

— In summer the containers will need watering frequently, but should be watered very little in winter if they are in a cool place. The fruit ripens in winter, one of the main characteristics of citrus.

— The fruit keeps a long time after being picked, even at room temperature.

Recommended

The citrus recommended are actually different species.

— Calamondin (*Citrus mitis*, syn. *C.* × *citrofortunella microcarpa*) is very good for growing indoors.

— Of the lemons (*C. limon*), the 'Meyer' and 'Villafranca' cultivars are very tolerant of cold. Next to the 'Meyer' in hardiness is the cultivar 'Lisbon'.

— Clementines (*C. reticulata*) can be grafted for indoor cultivation.

— Satsumas (*C. reticulata*) are seedless and tolerant of cold.

— The seedless 'Sallustiana' orange, and 'Washington', which is decorative, are cultivars of *C. sinensis*.

— The 'Star Ruby' pomelo has red pulp.

Height: 1–5 m (3¼–16 ft).
Soil: sandy, well-drained.
Aspect: sun.
Propagation: by grafting.
Type: fruit tree.

△ **Perpetual lemon**

Cobnuts △ ▽

Corylus avellana and C. maxima

COBNUT, HAZELNUT, FILBERT

Betulaceae

Decorative because of their ample green or purple foliage and able either to form enormous shrubby bushes or to be pruned into a hedge, the cobnuts and hazels are easy trees to grow. The female flowers are inconspicuous, whereas the male flowers are arranged in conspicuous catkins in winter and spring. They can grow in all areas and in mountain regions up to an altitude of 1,600 m (4,800 ft).

Useful hints

— Gather the nuts when they fall in autumn to ensure they are perfectly ripe. Shell them, then store in a cool and well-ventilated place for up to a year.

— Remove suckers as they arise.

— This is not a self-fertilizing tree, but its presence in many gardens means that gardeners probably need only plant one tree, as another will be sure to be close by.

Recommended

The pollinating varieties are given in brackets.

— 'A Feuilles Pourpres' will tolerate chalky soil.

— 'Aveline' has round, excellent fruit ('Segorbe', 'Cosford Cob').

— 'Cosford Cob' has an elongated shape ('Merveille de Bollwiller', 'Longue d'Espagne').

— 'Fertile de Coutard' (syn. 'White Filbert') has large fruit, sensitive to frost ('Segorbe', 'Longue d'Espagne').

— 'Imperiale de Trebizonde' has round, excellent fruit.

— 'Longue d'Espagne' is an elongated, quick to fruit variety ('Merveille de Bollwiller', 'Cosford Cob').

— 'Merveille de Bollwiller' is round and tolerant of cold ('Longue d'Espagne').

— 'Segorbe' has large fruit ('Fertile de Coutard', 'Merveille de Bollwiller').

Height: 3–6 m (10–20 ft).
Soil: ordinary.
Aspect: sun or semi-shade.
Propagation: by layering.
Type: fruit tree.

483

△ Strawberry 'Ostara'

Fragaria

STRAWBERRY

Rosaceae

Traditionally grown in the vegetable garden, the strawberry grows everywhere, even at an altitude of up 1,200 m (3,600 ft). It dislikes spring frost but tolerates the winter cold.

Useful hints

— To produce fruit well, the strawberry needs regular applications of fertilizer.

— Pick them every two to three days in order to catch them at the right stage.

— To protect the soil, choose straw, pine needles or black plastic sheeting.

— Because of the viruses that weaken strawberry plants, it is best to renew the supply every five to six years.

Recommended

Varieties ripening in early to mid-summer

— 'Cambridge Vigour' has cone-shaped scarlet fruits of excellent flavour.

— 'Honeoye' has large slightly acid fruits, highly recommended for freezing.

— 'Royal Sovereign' is one of the best-loved strawberries, of excellent flavour, but compared to modern varieties is not a heavy cropper.

— 'Tamella' has well-flavoured fruits and is the heaviest cropping variety once established.

Varieties ripening in mid-summer

— 'Cambridge Favourite' has round or cone-shaped fruits of moderately good flavour.

— 'Cambridge Late Pine' is an old variety with sweet deep crimson fruits.

— 'Elsanta' has large fruits, freely produced and of excellent flavour.

— 'Korona' is a heavy cropper, deep red and of excellent flavour.

— 'Tenira' has cone-shaped, bright red fruits that are good for jam-making.

Varieties ripening in late summer

— 'Domanil' produces heavy crops of of very good flavour.

— 'Kouril', also with very good flavour, has large dark red berries.

— 'Rhapsody' has large cone-shaped fruits of good flavour.

Perpetual or autumn-fruiting varieties

— 'Aromel' has cone- or wedge-shaped fruits of excellent flavour. Replace with young plants every year for best results.

— 'Mara des Bois' has bright red fruits of excellent flavour.

— 'Marastil', a heavy cropper, has fruits of good flavour.

Height: 20 cm (8 in).
Soil: cool, a little acid.
Aspect: semi-shade for perpetual strawberries, otherwise sun.
Propagation: from seed or by division for varieties without runners, otherwise by separating runners.
Type: perennial.

Juglans regia

WALNUT

Juglandaceae

This large tree is grown for its proud bearing, its large composite leaves, its deep cool shade, its wood and its fruit. Only large gardens will have enough room to accommodate it. Walnut trees do not like hot, southerly climates and do not thrive above 600 m (1,800 ft).

Useful hints

— A walnut tree is usually planted not only for the present pleasure it provides, but also to hand down to subsequent generations, because its fruits take a long time to appear. The trees are self-fertilizing.

— Walnuts are picked in autumn, when the green husk surrounding them splits widely, a sign of ripeness. First the green husk is removed, then the nuts are dried as quickly as possible (this maintains their flavour) in the air, but not in the sun, which would desiccate them. Walnuts may be stored in a dry place for three to four months.

Recommended

— 'Franquette' has large fruit reaching

the ripening stage in mid-autumn.

— 'Broadview' has very high-quality nuts, produced at an early age.

— 'Buccaneer' is a heavy cropper, starting when young.

Height: 7–20 m (23–65 ft).
Soil: ordinary, even chalky.
Aspect: plenty of space, preferably west-facing.
Propagation: by grafting.
Type: fruit tree.

◁ △ **Walnuts**

Malus

CRAB APPLE, APPLE

Rosaceae

With clusters of white or pink flowers, crab apples and other apples vie with other trees in terms of beauty. They prefer mild and damp climates, without wide extremes of temperature, but they nevertheless grow easily in all areas (in mountain regions, up to an altitude of 1,200 m/3,600 ft).

Useful hints

— Quite tolerant of pruning, indeed producing larger fruit as a result, these are the ultimate fruit trees, on which all gardeners can practise their skills.

— Summer varieties, picked when ripe, can be stored for a few weeks; later varieties, picked at the end of the season, will ripen in storage and will keep for several months.

Recommended

The choice is vast, and the following list does not include local varieties that are not very well-known. It does, however include those currently sold commercially. Most of the varieties are sufficiently self-fertile, but planting a mixture of varieties can only be beneficial.

— 'Belle de Boskoop' is juicy and best eaten from winter to spring. This can be pollinated by 'Transparente de Croncels'.

— 'Calville Blanc d'Hiver' has excellent fruit, velvety, juicy and sweet. Best eaten from autumn to spring.

— 'Gravenstein' is juicy and best in autumn.

— 'Reinette du Canada', a sour variety, is best used autumn to spring.

— 'Royal Gala', sweet and of good flavour, is best used autumn to winter.

— 'Peasgood Nonsuch', juicy, is best used in autumn.

— 'Transparente de Croncels', juicy, slightly tart, is best used in the autumn.

Ornamental crab apples

There are many ornamental malus which produce crab apples that can be used for making preserves. Often they create a good display with their blossom in the spring, then in the autumn another good show with colourful fruits. They are also good pollinators for other apples. The following are especially recommended:

— 'Chico' has large rounded fruits, vivid crimson in colour, and pink flowers in mid-spring.

— 'Cowichan' has red-purple fruits in abundance, and pink flowers in mid-spring.

— 'Golden Hornet' has golden yellow fruits in abundance, and white flowers in late spring.

— 'John Downie' has orange and red fruits, and white flowers in late spring.

— 'Marshall Oyama' has large red and yellow fruits, and white flowers, flushed with pink, in late spring.

— 'Professor Sprenger' has orange-red fruits, and white flowers from pink buds in late spring.

— *Malus × robusta* has red fruits, and white or pink flowers in late spring.

— 'Veitch's Scarlet' has large deep red fruits, and white flowers in late spring.

Height: 6–10 m (20–33 ft).
Soil: ordinary, but with minimum lime.
Aspect: any (south-easterly with a natural north-easterly shelter is best).
Propagation: by grafting.
Type: fruit tree.

△ **Crab apple 'Astrakan Rouge'**

△ Apricot 'Bergeron'

Prunus armeniaca

APRICOT

Rosaceae

A favourite in warm climates, where it can bask in all the heat it requires, the apricot can nevertheless grow well and produce fruit in cooler areas, provided it is sited in a sheltered corner of the garden, in full sun and away from draughts.

Useful hints

— As it dislikes moist soil, the apricot does not mind drought.

— One single isolated tree can produce fruit, because the varieties are self-fertile.

— The apricot is very tolerant of winter cold, but dislikes spring frost. In cooler climates, it is often recommended that they be covered with a protective awning when they begin to flower.

Recommended

— 'Alfred' has excellent flavour, with juicy orange flesh. It ripens late summer and is an early-flowering cultivar.

— 'Early Moor Park' is similar to 'Moor Park' (see below) but it ripens almost a month earlier in late summer. It is a small grower.

— 'Moor Park' is a very old variety but the most popular cultivar in Britain, with large fruits, sweet red flesh with a rich flavour. It is a reliable cropper, ready for picking late summer, .

— 'New Large Early' has large fruits of excellent flavour ripening mid-summer.

Height: 2–4 m (6½–13 ft).
Soil: sandy, light, chalky; avoid clay, heavy, acid and moist soil.
Aspect: sun (westerly or south-westerly is best).
Propagation: possible from seed, more often by grafting.
Type: fruit tree.

Prunus avium and P. cerasus

CHERRY

Rosaceae

Justly popular because of its beautiful blossom and its fruit, the cherry is more tolerant of winter cold than of intense summer heat. In warmer climates it is planted in a cool place or at an altitude of up to 1,000 m (3,000 ft).

Useful hints

— The cherry detests pruning, and its wood breaks easily. It is important not to climb up it carelessly to pick the cherries, no matter how tempting they may be.

— The fruits are ripe on average forty days after the end of flowering, so the late-fruiting varieties are more tolerant of spring frost.

— It is worth planting two different varieties in the garden, as they will pollinate each other well, most varieties being more or less self-sterile.

Recommended

The most widely grown cherries in Britain are the sweet cherries (*Prunus avium*) and the acid cherries (*Prunus cerasus*). Most sweet cherries are self-sterile, in which case you need to plant two varieties that flower at the same time. Alternatively choose one of the newer self-fertile varieties. Sweet cherries are excellent for dessert and can be eaten uncooked. Most varieties of acid cherry are self-fertile, so only one tree is needed. The fruits are only suitable for cooking and for turning into preserves, as they are very sour.

Sweet cherries

— 'Cherokee' (syn. 'Lapins') is a self-fertile variety, with large deep red fruits of really good flavour, ripening late summer.

— 'Early Rivers' is self-sterile, with large fruits, deep red and of excellent flavour, ripening early summer. It crops heavily and reliably.

— 'Merton Bigarreau' has large black fruits of very good flavour, ready for picking in mid-summer; it crops heavily and regularly and is self-sterile.

— 'Merton Favourite' has large black fruits with superb flavour, ready for picking mid-summer, a reliable and heavy cropper it is self-sterile.

— 'Stella' is self-fertile, with deep red fruits, ready for picking late summer.

— 'Stella Compact' produces deep red juicy fruits in abundance, of excellent flavour, and is self-fertile.

▽ Cherry 'Hâtif Burlat'

Cherry 'Napoléon' ▽

— 'Sunburst', a self-fertile cherry, has large black fruits, ripening late summer.

Acid cherries

— 'Morello', the most popular acid cherry in Britain, is self-fertile, a heavy and regular cropper, producing large dark red fruits, ripening late summer and early autumn.

Height: 5–10 m (16–33 ft) depending on root-stock.
Soil: any, even chalky; but clayey, impermeable, excessively moist soil is best avoided.
Aspect: sheltered from high winds.
Propagation: by grafting.
Type: fruit tree.

Prunus × domestica

PLUM, GAGE

Rosaceae

Very hardy, the plum tree is grown easily in all areas and even at an altitude of up to 1,000 m (3,000 ft). Its flowers and young fruits can tolerate mild frost: –1°C (30°F), –2°C (28°F).

Useful hints

— Only the self-fertile varieties can be planted in isolation; self-sterile varieties have to be fertilized by a nearby tree of another variety.

— If you pick the fruits by shaking the tree, the fruit will be bruised. It will not keep for long, but will nonetheless make excellent preserves.

Recommended

— 'Anna Späth' is a culinary and dessert variety, red, early autumn, self-fertile.

— 'Coe's Golden Drop' is a dessert variety, sweet, early autumn, self-sterile.

— 'Czar' is a culinary variety, deep purple, late summer, self-fertile.

— 'Early Transparent Gage' is a culinary and dessert variety, golden, very sweet, crops reliably, self-fertile.

— 'Imperial Gage' is a dessert variety, very sweet, heavy cropper, ideal for cold areas, self-fertile.

— 'Marjorie's Seedling' is a culinary and dessert variety, purple, early autumn, ideal for cold areas, self-fertile.

— 'Monsieur Hâtif' is a culinary variety, purple, late summer, self-sterile.

— 'Opal' is a dessert variety, superb flavour, mid-summer, self-fertile.

△ Plum 'Anna Späth'

— 'Ouillins Gage' is a dessert variety, yellow, late summer, self-fertile.

— 'Quetsche d'Alsace' (syn. German Prune Group) is a culinary variety, black-purple, early autumn, self-fertile, good raw or dried.

— 'Reine-Claude Dorée' (syn. Green Gage Group) is a culinary and dessert variety, summer.

— 'Thames Cross' is a dessert variety, pinkish yellow, early autumn, self-fertile.

— 'Victoria' is a dessert variety, culinary, purple-red, late summer or early autumn, self-fertile.

Height: 6–8 m (20–26 ft).
Soil: any, except very sandy or acid ones (some lime is necessary).
Aspect: any.
Propagation: by grafting.
Type: fruit tree.

△ Peach 'Amsden June'

Prunus persica

PEACH

Rosaceae

Although it prefers warm climates, the peach tree can be grown successfully in cooler areas, and will produce fruit. In northerly, eastern or mountain areas (up to 600 m/1,800 ft), however, it should be trained on a warm wall. Its flowers are pink, dark pink or pale pink, which is unusual in a fruit tree. The leaves are bright green and lance-shaped.

Useful hints

— The late-flowering varieties require to be watered more generously than the early-flowering ones during the summer months.

— The flowering season does not reflect the ripening of the fruit. Peaches that are picked when ripe (they should come off the stalk quite easily in your hand) are the best.

— Nectarines are varieties of peach. All varieties are self-fertile.

Recommended

Peaches

— 'Amsden June' ripens mid-summer, white flesh, very tolerant of frost.

— 'Bellegarde' has rich flavour, early autumn.

— 'Bonanza' has yellow flesh, summer, a dwarf tree suitable for containers.

— 'Duke of York' has light yellow flesh, good flavour, mid-summer.

— 'Dymond' has white flesh, rich flavour, juicy, early autumn.

— 'Early Rivers' has white flesh, rich flavour, mid-summer.

— 'Garden Lady' has golden flesh, very sweet, summer, forms a small tree.

— 'Hale's Early' has light yellow flesh, good flavour, mid-summer.

— 'Peregrine' has white flesh of excellent flavour, late summer, reliable cropper, very popular variety.

— 'Rochester' has yellow flesh, reasonable flavour, late summer, heavy and reliable cropper, very popular.

Nectarines

— 'Elruge' has green-white flesh, rich flavour, late summer.

— 'Fantasia' has yellow flesh, summer.

— 'John Rivers', mid-summer ripening, is generally considered the earliest.

— 'Lord Napier' has white flesh, rich flavour, heavy cropper, late summer.

— 'Nectared' has yellow flesh, summer, fairly tolerant of spring frost, susceptible to blight.

— 'Nectarella' has yellow flesh, summer, a dwarf tree suitable for growing in containers.

— 'Pineapple' has yellow flesh, excellent flavour, good cropper, late summer.

Height: 2–4 m (6½–13 ft).
Soil: well-drained, neutral (pH 7), not too moist.
Aspect: sun; in cold areas, best sited against a warm wall.
Propagation: possible from seed: most frequently by budding.
Type: fruit tree.

Pyrus communis

PEAR

Rosaceae

The pears have pure white flowers which last for three weeks in early-flowering varieties and only half as long in late-flowering varieties. Highly tolerant of both the cold and the heat, they can be grown successfully in any temperate climate and in mountain areas up to an altitude of 1,200 m (3,600 ft).

Useful hints

— A large tree in nature, the pear adapts itself to any kind of shape it is pruned into. The old wood (even a large trunk) is able to produce young shoots again.

— Grafted varieties adapt better to the soil and are very productive.

— Some varieties are not very self-fertile, in which case at least two varieties should be cultivated side by side that will flower at the same time. 'Williams' Bon Chrétien' will pollinate many varieties.

Recommended

Summer pears are eaten as soon as they are picked, autumn pears should be kept for three to four weeks, and winter pears do not acquire their full flavour until some weeks after they are picked (in autumn). Good pollinators are given in brackets in the following list.

— 'Bergamotte Esperen' is a dessert variety, juicy, tolerant of frost, late autumn to early spring ('Clapp's Favourite').

— 'Beth' is a dessert variety, melts in the mouth, very sweet and rich, early autumn ('Doyenné du Comice').

— 'Beurré Bosc' is a dessert variety, firm flesh, autumn ('Clapp's Favourite').

— 'Beurré Hardy' is a dessert variety with soft flesh, autumn, good for high altitudes ('Conference').

— 'Clapp's Favourite' is a dessert variety with large fruit that melts in the mouth, summer ('Doyenné du Comice').

— 'Concorde' is a dessert variety, flesh firm and of good flavour, can be used early autumn to mid-winter ('Conference').

— 'Conference' is a dessert variety that melts in the mouth, tolerant of spring frost, autumn ripening, ('Doyenné du Comice', 'Beurré Hardy').

— 'Docteur Jules Guyot' is a dessert variety with large juicy fruit, summer to autumn, tolerant of spring frost ('Doyenné du Comice', 'Conference').

— 'Doyenné du Comice' is a dessert variety that melts in the mouth, autumn ('Louise Bonne of Jersey', 'Conference').

— 'Duchesse d'Angoulème' is a dessert variety with large sweet fruit, suitable for dry soil, autumn ('Louise Bonne of Jersey').

— 'Fertility' is a dessert variety with good firm fruit produced from the second year, autumn ('Doyenné du Comice').

— 'Louise Bonne of Jersey' is a sweet dessert variety, autumn ('Seckle').

— 'Onward' is a dessert variety that melts in the mouth ('Beth').

— 'Seckle' is a dessert variety with sweet and juicy flesh, superb flavour, autumn ('Louise Bonne of Jersey').

— 'Williams' Bon Chrétien' is a highly popular dessert variety, sweet and juicy with a musky flavour, early autumn ('Beurré Hardy', 'Conference').

Height: 5–15 m (16–50 ft).
Soil: good, with no lime.
Aspect: any, with plenty of light and space.
Propagation: by grafting.
Type: fruit tree.

Pear 'Fertility' ▷

△ Red currant 'Jonkheer van Tets'

△ Black currant 'Burga'

Ribes rubrum, R.uva-crispa and R. nigrum

RED CURRANT, GOOSEBERRY, BLACK CURRANT

Grossulariaceae

Red currants, black currants and gooseberries are three sister soft fruits. They are not particularly ornamental, unless they are trained as standards, and their greenish flowers pass by unnoticed, but they can occupy a place at the bottom of the garden without causing too much trouble, or can form a small hedge around the vegetable garden, even at an altitude of up to 1,500 m (3,500 ft). These plants need the winter cold in order to produce fruit successfully, and very warm climates do not suit them.

Useful hints

— Watch the fruit in order to pick it at the right time.

490

— The black currant differs from the red currant in that its fruits appear only on very young stalks.

Recommended

Red currant (Ribes rubrum)

All varieties are self-fertile and produce their fruits in the summer.

— 'Jonkheer van Tets' is not too sour, mid-summer, crops heavily.

— 'Laxton No 1' has berries carried on long trusses, ripens early.

— 'Red Lake' has large berries, summer.

— 'Versailles Blanche' ('White Versailles') is a white currant, with juicy berries, ripening in summer.

Gooseberry (R. uva-crispa)

These varieties are all self-fertile and produce their fruits in the summer.

— 'Careless' is very popular in Britain, a culinary variety with whitish green fruits.

— 'Golden Drop' is a dessert variety with yellow fruits.

— 'Greenfinch' is a culinary variety with green berries, needs fertile soil.

— 'Invicta' is a culinary variety, a heavy cropper, pale green berries.

— 'Leveller' is a dessert variety, green-yellow berries, needs fertile soil.

— 'May Duke' is a culinary or dessert variety, red fruits.

— 'Whinham's Industry' is a dessert and culinary variety, red fruits.

Black currant (R. nigrum)

Black currants do not need several varieties for cross-fertilization. Fruits ripen in summer.

— 'Ben Connan' has large berries that ripen early, a small grower.

— 'Ben Lomond' has good flavour, resistant to cold weather, flowers late in the season.

— 'Ben Sarek' has large berries of good flavour, flowers resistant to frost.

— 'Jet' has long strings of berries, flowers late and misses spring frosts.

— 'Seabrook's Black' is an old variety but still popular, reliable, well-flavoured berries.

Height: 1.5m (5 ft).
Soil: ordinary.
Aspect: light, but not in full sun.
Propagation: from cuttings; gooseberries by layering.
Type: fruiting shrubs.

Rubus idaeus and R. fruticosus

BLACKBERRY, RASPBERRY

Rosaceae

Not very ornamental and rather prickly, these cane fruits are well worth growing, for the flavour of their freshly picked fruits far exceeds that of their commercially bought counterparts. They seem to have originated among mountain undergrowth. Blackberries and raspberries have stems which put out new shoots every year, each having a lifespan of only two years. They may be grown anywhere in temperate climates and will tolerate altitudes of up to 1,200 m (3,600 ft).

Useful hints

— Left to their own devices, the very supple branches will bend and take up a great deal of room, so it is advisable to train them, horizontally for blackberries, vertically for raspberries, on a system of posts and horizontal wires.

— These fruits dislike hot summers; they need to be kept in the shade and, in very southerly climates, it is important to give them sufficient water.

— Blackberries produce long trailing stems, whereas raspberries produce clumps of upright stems or canes.

Recommended

Blackberries (Rubus fruitcosus)

These ripen their fruits in summer and

autumn. You only need to plant one variety as they are self-fertile.

— 'Ashton Cross' has rather acid but well-flavoured berries in huge numbers, late summer.

— 'Bedford Giant' has large berries in profusion, rather acid, moderately well flavoured, mid-summer.

— 'Loch Ness' has large well-flavoured fruits, late summer and early autumn.

— 'Oregon Thornless' has rather acid berries, late summer onwards.

— 'Waldo' has large berries with excellent flavour, mid-summer, thornless.

Raspberries *(R. idaeus)*

Most fruit in summer, but there are some autumn varieties available.

— 'Autumn Bliss' has large berries, autumn, heavy cropper.

— 'Glen Moy' has well-flavoured berries, summer, canes free from spines, compact habit.

— 'Glen Prosen' has well-flavoured berries, late summer.

— 'Malling Admiral' has large deep red berries, superb flavour, summer.

— 'Malling Jewel' is a highly popular variety with deep red berries of good flavour, summer.

Height: 1.5–2 m (5–6½ ft).
Soil: ordinary.
Aspect: north-facing or semi-shade.
Propagation: by suckers.
Type: cane fruits.

▽ **Raspberry**

△ **Grape 'Muscat Hamburg'**

Vitis vinifera

VINE

Vitaceae

The vine's toothed leaves in warm autumn colours, and its bunches of fruit, as beautiful as they are delicious, have adorned arbours and walls since time immemorial. The vine grows in most areas, but will not produce fruit in a cool summer unless it is planted against a well-sheltered and sunny wall. It climbs by means of its tendrils and can attach itself to a variety of supports.

Useful hints

— The vine is not a tender plant (it will tolerate a temperature as low as −20°C/ −4°F), and its leaves grow very thickly, so it can give pleasant shade in summer.

— The grapes appear on the current year's shoots, which arise from older branches.

— The bunches of grapes may be kept for many months in a cool place if they are picked, when ripe, leaving a long piece of shoot attached; this should then be put in a jar of water, tilted so that the fruits do not touch it.

Recommended

— 'Madeleine Angevine' is a white grape, grown outdoors in cool climates.

— 'Madeleine Sylvaner' is a white grape, grown outdoors in cool climates.

— 'Müller-Thurgau' (syn. 'Riesling-Silvaner') is a white grape, grown outdoors in cool climates.

— 'Muscat of Alexandria' is a white

△ **Grape 'Muscat of Alexandria'**

grape, best in a greenhouse in cool climates.

— 'Muscat Hamburg' is a black grape, best in a greenhouse in cool climates.

— 'Noir Hâtif de Marseilles' is a black grape with beautiful autumn foliage, the earliest of the muscat grapes; it grows outdoors in cool climates.

— 'Perle de Czaba' is a white grape, suitable for outdoor or greenhouse cultivation in cool climates.

— 'Perlette' is a white grape, a seedless variety which can be dried; it grows outdoors in cool climates.

— 'Seibel' is a black grape which grows outdoors in cool climates.

Height: depends on support.
Soil: ordinary, preferably dry and chalky.
Aspect: sun.
Propagation: from cuttings, by layering and grafting.
Type: climber.

With the right information, anyone can make a garden. Even if you have no previous experience or professional expertise, you can still transform a bare plot into something to be proud of.

This section of the Encyclopedia gives advice on design and gardening techniques that is very easy to follow, and much of it is illustrated.

You will find all the practical advice and technical information you need on how to make a plan of your garden and lay down the basic structure. There is guidance on buying, planting and caring for your plants, and advice on how to use them to maximum decorative effect. Specialist gardens – scree, rock, water gardens – are discussed, and these will inspire you, because this kind of gardening, practical and yet exciting, is within the reach of everyone, even those of you who have always thought you did not have green fingers.

III

GARDENING TECHNIQUES

Contents

First impressions

Your garden gate or entrance is the first thing that greets a visitor and should give a feeling of welcome.

The garden entrance should be in keeping with the style of the house, and can also give a clue to your personality.

Climbing plants can be grown on the front of any house, but you should take into account the character of the area you live in and the amount of time you can spare to look after them.

If you choose evergreen plants, their decorative effect will last all the year round.

Permanence is given to this design by the small conifer hedge and the elegant double row of *Juniperus communis* 'Hibernica' bordering the path. For a cheerful effect in summer, these are interspersed with standard roses, which, because they are grafted at the top of the stem, will never exceed their original height of around 60–80 cm (24–32 in). A metre or so from the front door, a metal arch supports two climbing roses, which could be pink, red, yellow, white or apricot, whichever looks best with the house walls. The brick edging, which works well with a gravel path, could be replaced with cobblestones for a less formal effect.

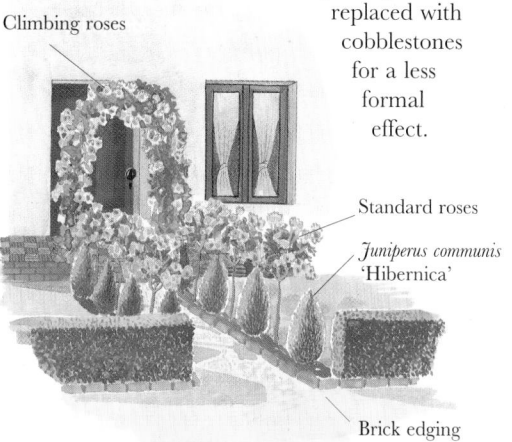

Climbing roses

Standard roses

Juniperus communis 'Hibernica'

Brick edging

Dwarf conifers or evergreens pruned to pyramid shape

Annuals (petunias or pelargoniums)

This design is more suitable for a region with a mild climate, as plants grown in tubs can be adversely affected by frost. The vegetation consists of dwarf conifers or evergreens pruned to a pyramid shape, with annuals planted around the base for a splash of colour. Petunias or pelargoniums will need little attention, apart from watering and the removal of dead flowers. Be careful, though, not to plant over-vigorous shrubs which may eventually have to be transferred to larger tubs.

Clipped ivy

This entrance is very simple, an ideal front garden design for those who have little time to devote to gardening. To achieve this sculptural effect will take several years. The greenery consists of ivy, plain green or variegated according to taste, and is supported on a light wooden framework covered with plaited straw – ivy does not readily take to wire. The slight curve in the hedge gives added interest.

The approach to this front door, sheltered by a tiled roof, has been made most attractive, the gardener's skill transforming what was a very ordinary façade into a charming picture. The wooden pillars can be used as supports for climbing plants: roses, clematis or honeysuckle, depending on the local climate. Steps lead up to a raised verandah in front of the house, the difference in level softened by flower beds 60 cm (24 in) wide on either side.

Flower beds 60 cm (24 in) wide

Climbing plants: roses, clematis or honeysuckle

Designs for small gardens

The majority of gardens could probably be described as 'small', but this need not be limiting in scope. A small garden can be landscaped to include all the attractive features of a much larger plot, on a smaller scale.

Here to prove it are four garden designs, all of equal size, but planned for families with quite different needs.

None of them requires major landscaping work, and all can be laid out on a plot of less than 200 sq. m (230 sq. yd).

A garden for a family with children

This garden includes flower beds and areas of sun and shade, with the children's play area a priority. Instead of a lawn, there is a small orchard, the grass under the trees being left unmown. All parts of the garden can be reached by the grassy path which starts and ends at the patio in front of the house: there are no steps for toddlers to trip over. At the bottom of the garden on the right is a vegetable garden, set somewhat apart.

The large central flower bed is filled with brightly coloured flowers.

The area immediately to the right of the patio has been reserved for soft fruit

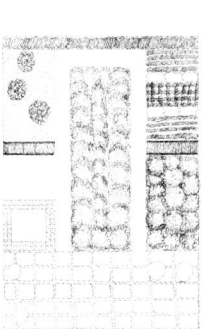

– black currants, gooseberries and raspberries – convenient for the kitchen and at the same time within easy reach of the children's play area.

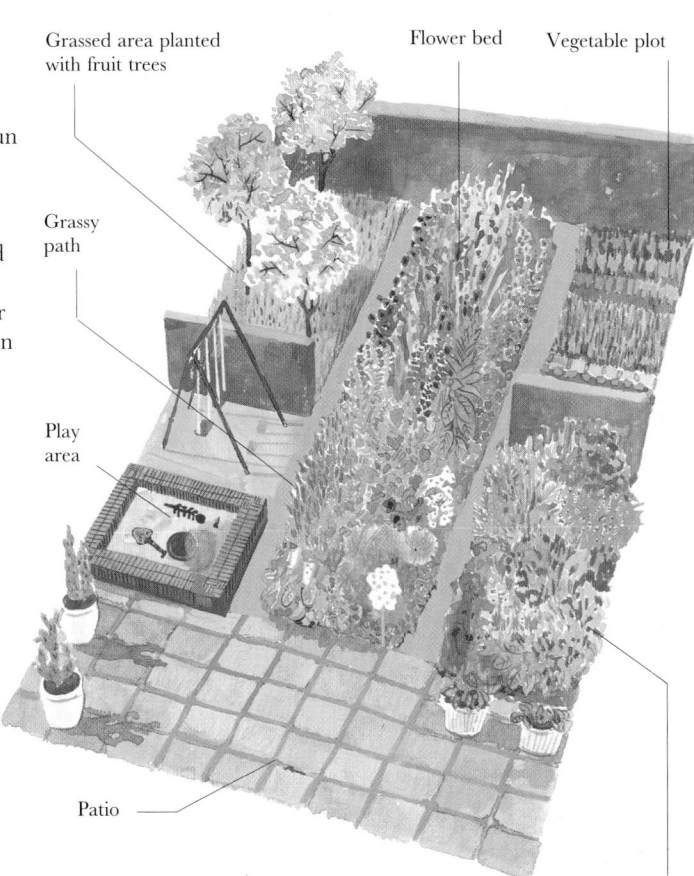

Grassed area planted with fruit trees · Flower bed · Vegetable plot · Grassy path · Play area · Patio · Gooseberry and black currant bushes, and raspberry canes

An easy-to-manage garden

This layout combines the pleasures of growing both vegetables and flowers. The boundary is marked by an informal hedge, and an area of rough grass intersected by mown paths at the far end is shaded by a group of trees. The raised patio is edged with flowering shrubs requiring a minimum of attention. Stepping stones – to keep your feet dry – lead down to a restful arbour shaded by rambler roses.

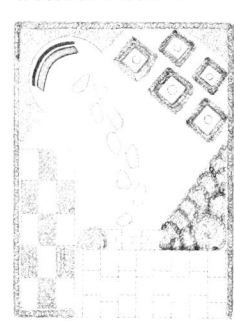

On either side of the arbour an area of grass has been left to grow wild, planted with spring bulbs (daffodils, hyacinths) and sown with a scattering of annual flower seed for summer colour.

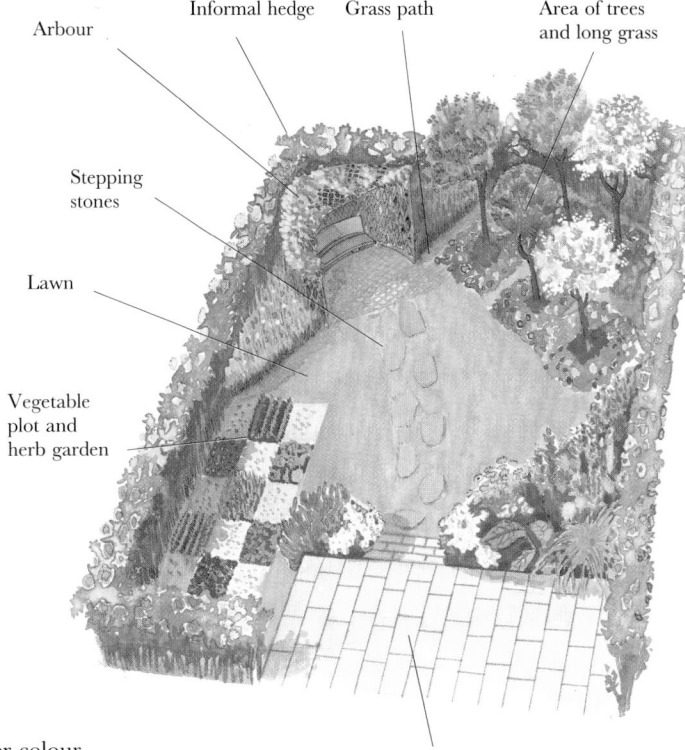

Arbour · Informal hedge · Grass path · Area of trees and long grass · Stepping stones · Lawn · Vegetable plot and herb garden · Patio

A relaxing weekend garden

The aim here has been to achieve a spontaneous, informal setting. The patio, big enough for eating meals out of doors with a few friends, is bordered by an interesting rock garden. The trees and flowering shrubs will fill out in time, ensuring that there is nothing stark or bare about this open-air dining-room.

The irregular design and soft curves of the garden conceal the fact that it was once a very ordinary, symmetrical plot. A pergola occupies an unusual position at the far end, set at an oblique angle to the small group of trees in the corner. The result is an attractive, intimate feature: a small private space flanked by beds of flowers and shrubs which face on to the lawn.

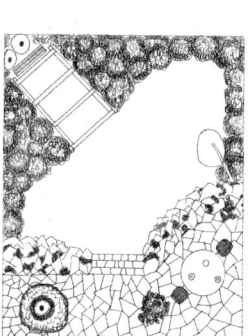

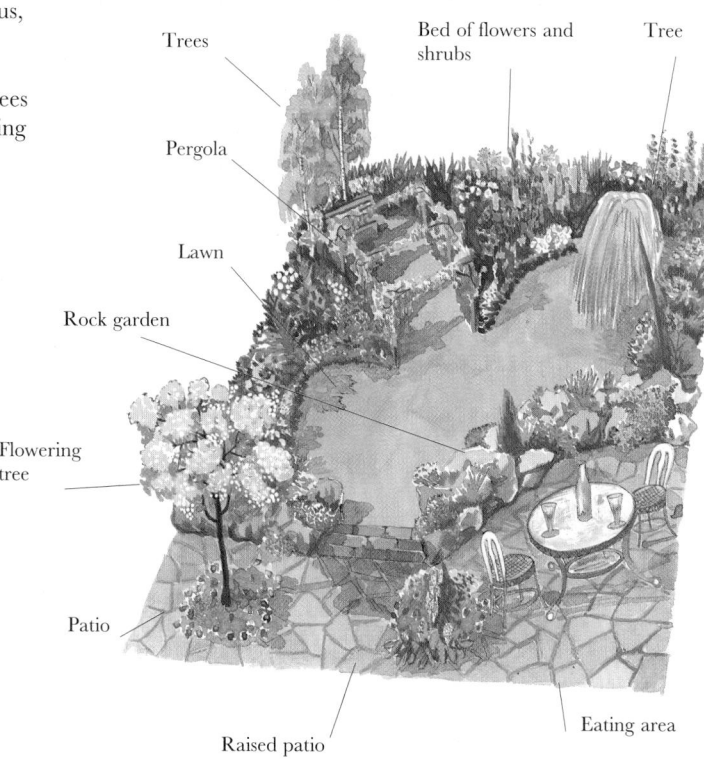

Trees

Bed of flowers and shrubs

Tree

Pergola

Lawn

Rock garden

Flowering tree

Patio

Raised patio

Eating area

A garden for the elderly or handicapped

The interconnecting paths are designed for easy access by a wheelchair. The raised beds, contained by surrounds of split logs, can be tended from a sitting position and are deliberately narrow, so that no plant is out of reach. To create a safe, smooth ground surface, two alternatives are recommended:

• Either dig out 20 cm (8 in) of soil and lay a firm bed of crushed limestone, of the finest grade. It needs to be rolled and watered as each successive layer is put down.

• Or use gravel, which forms a hard but porous surface. At the bottom of the garden, a flower-covered pergola, 2 m (6½ ft) in depth, serves as an open-air sitting area.

The strength of this design is that it is ideally suited both to elderly or handicapped people and to young children: they can ride their bikes to their hearts' content without causing any damage, as the raised beds are well protected by their log surrounds.

Pergola with flowering plants

Raised beds contained by surrounds of split logs

Designs for gardens of different shapes

The shape and layout of your garden may not be ideal, but there are plenty of ways to improve on it by planting and planning.

There are various reasons for wanting to change the original shape of a garden. It may be:

– too square or symmetrical;
– too long and narrow;
– too wide and lacking depth;
– on a steep slope;
– irregular in shape.

It is in fact possible to transform a plot of ground without undertaking major landscaping operations or going to enormous expense. There are two ways to achieve this:

• Using trees and shrubs to create vistas, screens, hedges and sub-divisions which give the necessary structure to the garden (this is the cheaper way).

• Using various materials to construct walls, terraces, paths and pergolas. Your choice will

tend to be dictated by what the garden is to used for. A family with young children, for instance, will not be wanting a large number of flower beds, while a retired couple are unlikely to include a lot of steps and slopes in their garden plans. The less time you have, the more sensible it will be to choose plants requiring only a minimum of care. By choosing evergreens and shrubs which flower at different times of year, you can ensure that the garden is always attractive.

If you intend to carry out the work yourself, you can hire practically all the heavy equipment you will need: mini-digger, rotary cultivator, hole-borer, etc.

Species native to the region can be incorporated into any of the designs suggested here. The flowers, trees and shrubs you choose will play a vital part in the overall result.

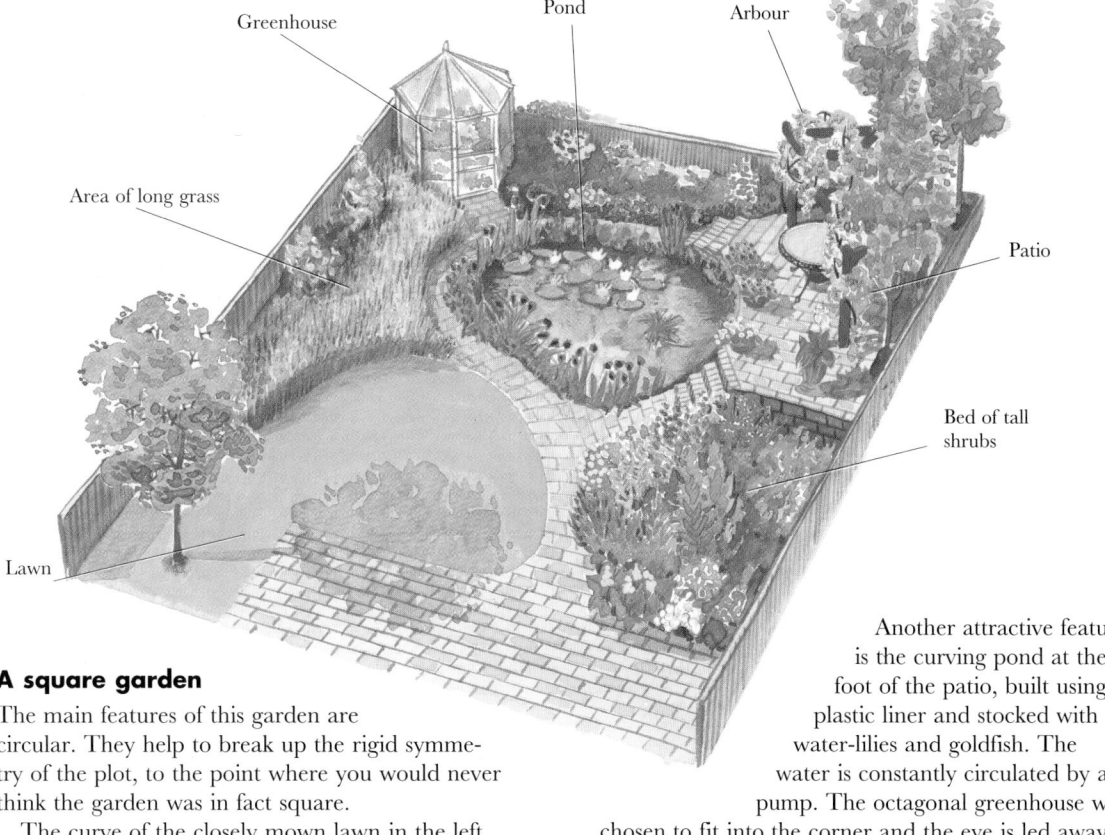

Greenhouse · Pond · Arbour · Patio · Area of long grass · Bed of tall shrubs · Lawn

A square garden

The main features of this garden are circular. They help to break up the rigid symmetry of the plot, to the point where you would never think the garden was in fact square.

The curve of the closely mown lawn in the left foreground is bordered by an area of uncut grass. The raised patio at the far right (used as a dining area) is also asymmetrical in shape. Every detail is designed to destroy the sense of 'squareness', even the round table, which is sheltered from the wind by a triangular arbour and a group of trees with dense foliage.

Another attractive feature is the curving pond at the foot of the patio, built using a plastic liner and stocked with water-lilies and goldfish. The water is constantly circulated by a pump. The octagonal greenhouse was chosen to fit into the corner and the eye is led away from it by the flower border at the bottom of the garden.

A bed of tall shrubs beside the patio is designed to conceal the sudden change in level. The paving is of brick, but stone could equally well have been used. A garden of this kind requires little maintenance.

The garden designs suggested here can be planted with species suited to your own tastes and growing conditions. Flowers, trees and shrubs all have a vital role to play in the garden.

A very wide garden

To create variety and interest, a number of different features have been laid out across the width of this garden. There is a vegetable garden in the top left, with access to an enclosed children's play area. The paved path leading from the patio to the pond, set slightly off centre, is intended to give a sense of depth.

Note the way in which the bins in the bottom right corner have been screened from view.

In the left foreground is a conifer, positioned to cast shade on the children's play area or on the patio, depending on the time of day.

In the top right, an uncultivated area of trees, grasses and wild flowers helps to reduce the apparent width of the plot.

The small rectangular-shaped pond, edged with paving stones, is backed by an informal hedge consisting of various flowering shrubs. A longer hedge would have accentuated the width of the plot.

A small summerhouse, or 'gazebo', completes the illusion: the garden no longer appears disconcertingly wide.

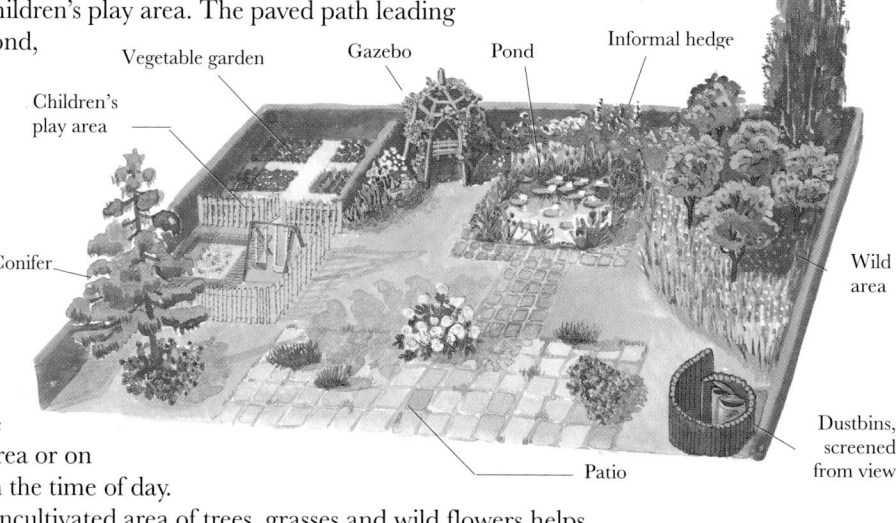

Vegetable garden · Gazebo · Pond · Informal hedge · Children's play area · Conifer · Wild area · Patio · Dustbins, screened from view

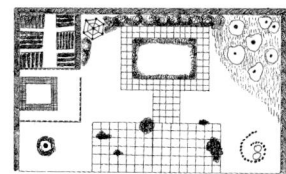

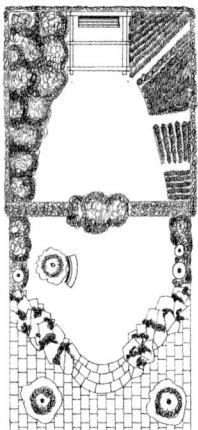

A long narrow garden

For a more balanced, harmonious effect, the plot has been divided into two smaller, rectangular gardens.

The patio, with its trees and semi-circular steps flanked by rock gardens, leads down to a lawn bordered by conifers and beds of evergreen shrubs. The result is a less severe, more rounded effect, and an attractive view from the house at all times of year.

The lawn area is divided by two elegant arches of greenery, joined in the middle by a densely planted flower bed.

The second garden, beyond, is designed with summer in mind. An arbour supporting wisteria and roses projects out into the lawn, helping to make this area seem less long and narrow.

To the right of the pergola is a small herb garden; to the left a herbaceous border backed by a trellis for training climbing roses.

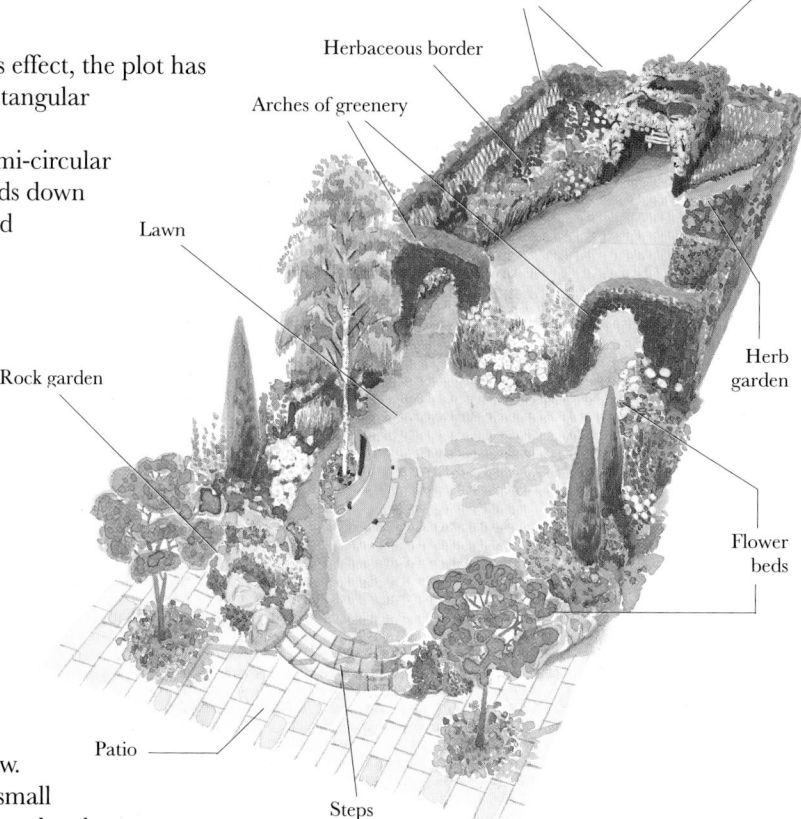

Rose trellis · Arbour · Herbaceous border · Arches of greenery · Lawn · Herb garden · Rock garden · Flower beds · Patio · Steps

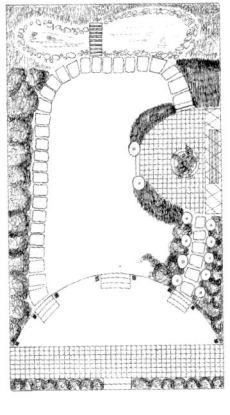

Upper terrace bordered by rose garlands

Patio garden

Herbaceous border

Clipped yews

Flights of steps

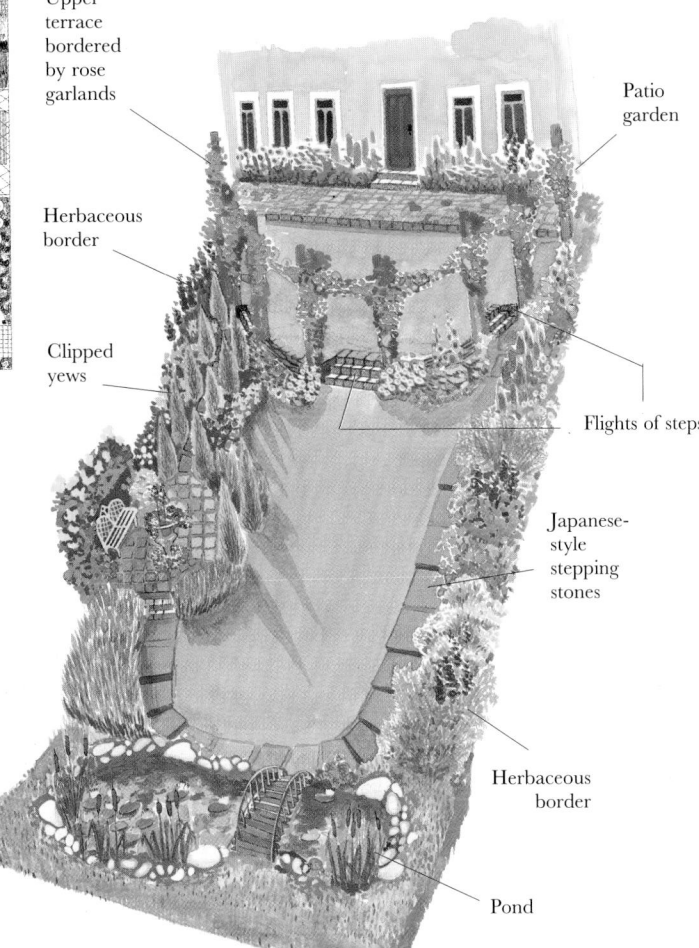

Japanese-style stepping stones

Herbaceous border

Pond

A garden on a slope

If possible, take advantage of surface drainage to make a water garden at the lowest level of the plot. This could be simply a naturally forming pond banked up with clay, or an artificial creation made with a liner and using a pump to recirculate the water.

To break up the slope, we have created a level terrace bordered by roses trained along suspended ropes or chains, with three flights of steps leading down to different garden features.

The central flight leads directly to the sloping lawn. The flight on the right continues as a path of paving stones running alongside a herbaceous border. Given the gentle slope, the paving stones (or slabs) can simply be sunk into the lawn, Japanese-style, with a fall of only a few centimetres between them.

At the bottom of the garden, flat stones have been arranged around the pond to hide the edges of the plastic sheeting used as a liner. Rushes can be planted among them. In the absence of a pump, the pond can be kept relatively clean by stocking it with oxygen-releasing plants and fish.

An irregular-shaped garden

Here the problem is to make the most of the various spaces and odd corners. To the left, adjacent to the patio, is a children's play area with a sand pit and a play house made by tying four conifers together at the top. Next comes an area of grass and wild flowers shaded by trees, a feature intended to create an illusion of space.

To the right of the patio, in full sun and on the same level, is a geometrically arranged vegetable and herb garden.

Three steps framed by a pair of conifers and white 'Iceberg' roses lead down to a lawn. From here we follow a grassy path to a pergola designed to be a place of tranquillity. The roses and clematis trained up its poles are visible from the house. In the awkward corner at the end of the garden is a weeping willow, which will fill out as the years go by. The wire fence surrounding the plot has been successfully hidden by an informal hedge, which helps to blur the outlines of the garden.

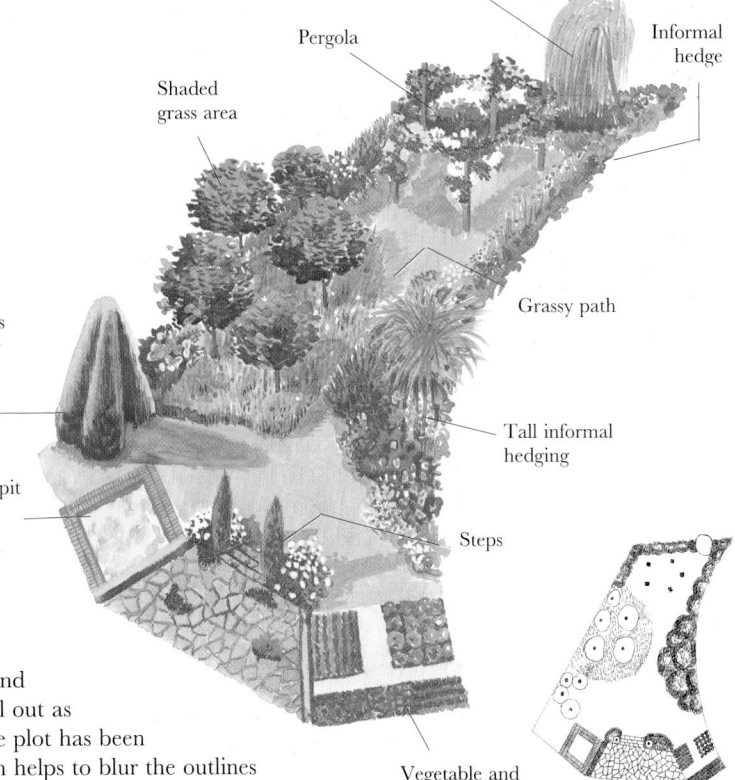

Weeping willow

Pergola

Informal hedge

Shaded grass area

Grassy path

Four conifers tied together to form a play house

Tall informal hedging

Sand pit

Steps

Vegetable and herb garden

Buying plants

An expedition to buy plants is a real treat, but make sure you will not be disappointed when you get them home.

First, buy your plants at the right time of year, when they are in peak condition: autumn and spring for perennials; late autumn to early spring in the case of trees. Nurseries are well stocked at these times, so you have the widest possible choice, though rarer plants may have to be ordered.

If you are buying by post, be sure to read the terms and conditions set out in the catalogue or price list, which provide some guarantee for both buyer and seller. Know what sort of agreement you are entering into. Remember to ask about the size of the plant you are ordering: the 10 cm (4 in) plant you eventually receive will take time to become the 1.5 m (5 ft) flowering shrub shown in the photograph. Always be cautious when buying plants, but without becoming obsessively suspicious.

Catalogues are, by definition, the stuff of dreams. Take what they say with a pinch of salt. When they say 'flowers from late spring until the first frosts', or 'all summer', this means the plant will flower *at some time during* – not *throughout* – the stated period. (Though this is not true of some roses, which flower in succession over several months.)

Disappointment frequently occurs if the buyer is attracted to a plant with a good growth of foliage but does not check the most important element: the part concealed in the pot. Inspect the potting compost carefully, to see that it has not dried out. The fact that plants are often transplanted and moved around from one place to another before they go on sale at the garden centre means they are not always looked after and watered as they should be once they have left the nursery. You should be aware of this, and act accordingly. In particular, be wary of bargains offered by non-specialists, who may have kept the plants in conditions that are too warm or too cold, which will hinder their recovery.

Finally, wherever you buy your plants, be sure to keep your receipt. In this way, you will be able to take them back if they do not come good. The nursery or garden centre should exchange them. Buying at knock-down prices without keeping your receipt is asking for trouble.

Perennials

Perennials are generally sold in pots of 8–11 cm (3–4¼ in) diameter. In the case of smaller plants, you will often do better to grow them from seed yourself, or from cuttings. In this category, prices do tend to vary enormously. Buying the cheapest plants is not necessarily advisable, as the more expensive specimens will often turn out to be stronger and more vigorous. Ask if you can remove the plant carefully from its pot to check that it has a good root system. No nurseryman should take offence at this request provided that you carry out the procedure with care and ask for help if necessary.

Annuals

Annuals can be bought in trays, usually of ten plants, and in pots. After a long winter, plants that will give you an instant show of colour are very tempting. But beware of early morning frosts: these alluring specimens have come straight from a greenhouse (otherwise they would not be in flower), and the shock of being transplanted into the cold soil of your garden may be too much for them. So do not be in a hurry to plant them out, and always choose specimens that are in bud rather than full flower: you will then have the pleasure of seeing them open up in your own garden.

Note: *Check the condition of every plant. When buying a tray of plants, you do not have to accept any that are substandard.*

Buying trees and shrubs

The different forms available

Maiden: The plant, grown from seed or a cutting, or by layering, is at least two years old. It consists of a vertical leader and a number of lateral branches.

Bush form: The plant has at least three strong branches, each growing up from ground level.

Plant branching just above ground level: In this case, the three main stems branch out from the root-stock just above ground level.

Standard: The plant consists of a single bare stem bearing a crown of lateral branches. There are also half- and quarter-standards (mainly in the case of roses).

Roses

Bush roses should have at least three stems. In autumn they are sold bare-rooted; after that they are sold in containers. Here again, it is better to go for quality, even if it means paying more. Roses sold in plastic bags have often spent weeks in the hot, dry atmosphere of a supermarket. Check that the main stem does not have a cracked appearance and has not turned a dark brown, that the branches are smooth and the roots well developed. If you must buy roses after the main selling season, better to buy them in containers. They will cost you more, but are more likely to get off to a good start.

Bare-rooted rose: healthy

Bare-rooted rose: unhealthy

Buying seeds, bulbs, and root-balled, container-grown and bare-rooted plants

Seeds

Selecting seeds is one of the great pleasures of early spring. However, tempting though the flowers shown on the packet may be, there are several points you should check, particularly the 'sow by' date: if kept too long, the seeds may not germinate.

The F1 hybrids deserve to be given priority, even though they are more expensive: they have been carefully selected for vigour and the profusion of flowers they bear. One small drawback: so rigorous is the selection that all the plants will grow to the same height and come into flower together.

For further information, see the advice on seed-sowing on pp. 551–3.

Bulbs and rhizomes

Prices may drop as the season progresses, and it is no bad thing to buy later: you will have a show of flowers when most others have faded.

Dahlias and begonias grow from tubers, irises from rhizomes, fleshy structures with roots on the underside and buds above which produce the new season's stems. Tulips, hyacinths, daffodils and many other flowers grow from bulbs, onion-shaped structures which act as a food store for the plant.

Note: *Check the following:*
– Bulbs, tubers or rhizomes should be firm to the touch and show no sign of damp or mould.
– There should be signs of nascent foliage at the tip of a bulb, proving that it is alive and well.
– Lily bulbs should be firm and compact, and the outer scales should not be withered or curled up, or brown at the edges.

Healthy bulb   Unhealthy bulb

Root-balled shrubs

• The ball of soil protecting the roots is itself wrapped in hessian or netting. Ask if you can open the wrapping and have a look at the soil inside. If it has not been kept watered, there is a danger of it falling apart when you come to plant the shrub.

• Another sign that the plant has dried out is yellowing of the foliage, however slight (especially applicable to conifers).

• The ball of soil may disintegrate completely when unwrapped, indicating that the plant has been hurriedly packaged prior to display and may take a long time to get established.

• Netting is often used instead of hessian for larger specimens.

Root-balled plant in good condition   Root-balled plant in poor condition

Container-grown plants

Container-grown plants can be planted at any time of year, though they establish them-selves better in autumn or early spring. Give the container a tap with your heel to loosen the plant, lift, and check that the soil does not fall away from the roots under its own weight.

Container-grown plant: left, healthy; right, unhealthy

• Lift the container. If it seems very light, it may lack water. Soak it in a bucket of water for a few minutes before removing the plant.

• Carefully tease out the roots and, before planting, cut off some of the tangled root system.

• Roots protruding through the holes in the bottom of the container are often a sign that the plant has become pot-bound. In this case, remove the plant from its container and cut off any tangled roots or the plant will have trouble getting established.

Plant removed from container: left, healthy; right, unhealthy

• Roots growing out of the top of the container are a sign that the plant has been pot-bound too long and the soil has been allowed to dry out.

• Yellowing leaves, or leaves that are reddish on the underside, are often a sign that the plant is suffering from disease or nutrient deficiency.

• Hold the plant at the base of the branches and lift it gently. A plant that comes out of the container very easily is not well established, and is best rejected.

Bare-rooted plants

Purchase these only in autumn and winter. This is an inexpensive way of increasing your stock and has many advantages: you can check the vitality of the plant and ensure that the ratio of rootlets to main roots is at least two to one.

When buying a tree by post, make sure that the catalogue is clear about the size of tree you will be sent. If you are choosing a shrub at a nursery, inspect it carefully and reject any specimens with dried-out roots (a sign that the plant has not been kept in the soil), or branches with rough, cracked bark. Also ensure that the plant has a well-balanced shape.

If you are buying a climber, inspect the stems thoroughly to make sure they are healthy along their whole length. A climber with two or three branches, one of which is dead, is not a good buy. If the plant has been badly pruned, cut the stems back to a suitable bud and remove the last few centimetres of the longer roots. Then give the shrub a treat by soaking the base in water for an hour. When planting, make sure it is buried to the same depth as it was at the nursery (you can tell from the mark left by the soil around the trunk). Last but not least: never expose the roots of a plant to the air while waiting to plant it out; cover them with hessian or polythene sheeting.

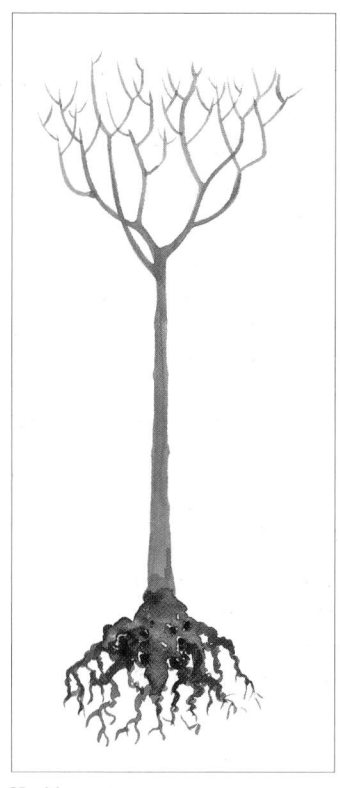

Healthy roots

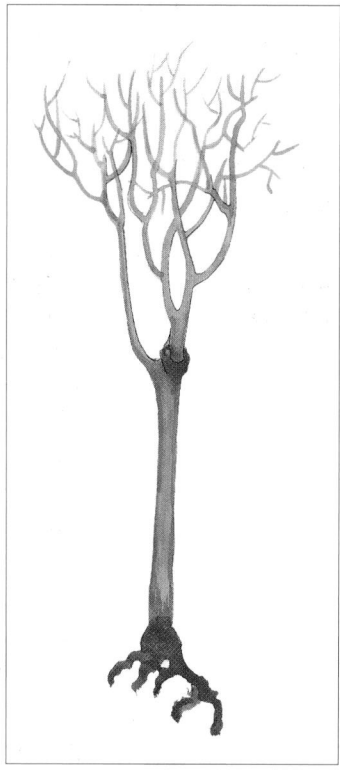

Unhealthy roots

Buying tools

Most tools will have to do heavy duty work: quality is therefore an important consideration.

The best tools have metal handles and will last you a lifetime. Of course, they are more expensive. Tools with wooden handles are quite satisfactory, provided you look after them properly. Here are a few tips. Always wipe wet tools before you put them away. Sharpen the blades of spades and other tools periodically, having first removed any soil and wiped them well. If you follow this advice, they will last for years.

Hang larger tools from a tool rack in a shed or garage, and keep small hand-tools in a trough full of sand, where you can get at them easily.

Trough of sand: adding a few pints of engine oil will prevent your tools from rusting.

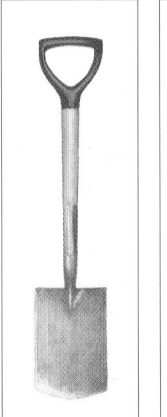

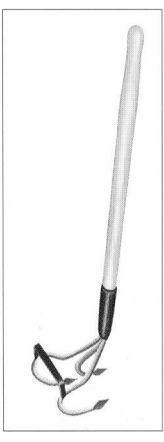

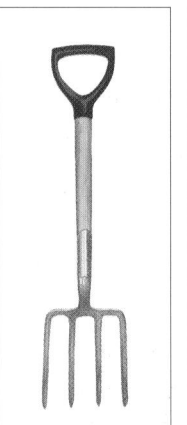

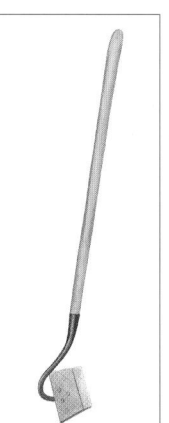

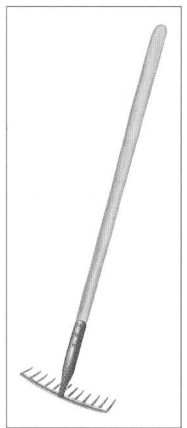

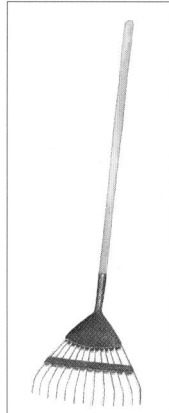

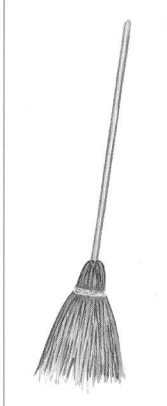

SPADE: essential for digging holes prior to planting.

THREE-PRONGED CULTIVATOR: useful for loosening weeds.

FOUR-PRONGED FORK: for general cultivation, i.e. turning the soil.

DRAW HOE: good for loosening up the soil in flower beds and removing weeds.

GARDEN RAKE: for raking out small stones and twigs, also for levelling the ground in preparation for planting seed.

SPRING-TINE RAKE: has flexible tines, suitable for raking up dead leaves and grass clippings.

BESOM BROOM: useful for sweeping paths; also for lawns that have been treated with sand or a moss killer.

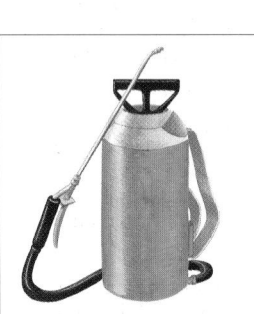

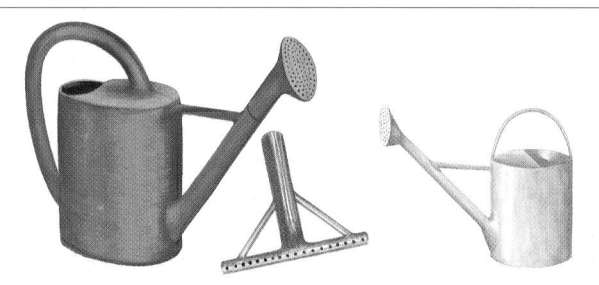

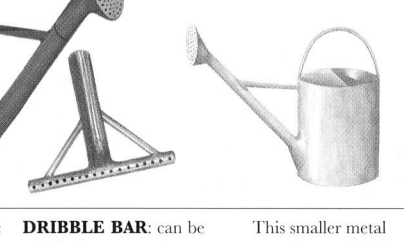

TREE PRUNERS: used for pruning small branches which would otherwise be out of reach. A model with a telescopic pole can be extended to a height of several metres.

SPRAYER: used for treating diseased trees and shrubs. Spray the surrounding soil as well as the plants themselves.

WATERING CAN: plastic type, holding 10 litres (2 gallons), suitable for watering shrubs.

DRIBBLE BAR: can be attached to a watering can or hosepipe for distributing chemical weedkillers on paths and patios.

This smaller metal watering can, holding 3–5 litres (5–9 pints), is better for watering flowers in pots.

GARDEN SHEARS: for trimming hedges, also for shaping shrubs and topiary work.

SECATEURS: for pruning branches and cutting flowers.

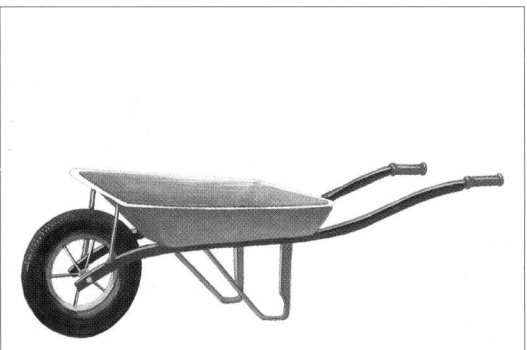

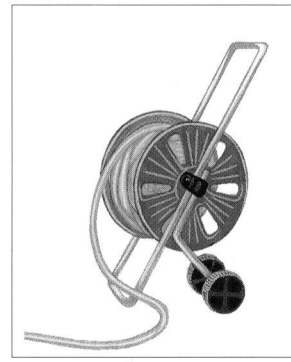

WHEELBARROW: may have one or two wheels, depending on the type of load to be carried. Single-wheeled models are handier but will carry less.

SACK BARROW: an extremely useful item of equipment for transporting heavy or bulky objects, such as sacks of peat or large pieces of stone. Put down planks when you have to run it over the grass.

HOSE REEL: very useful when you have to move hoses about.

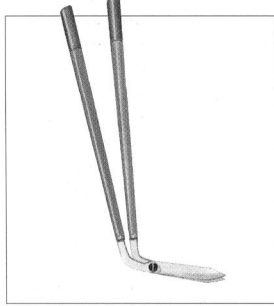

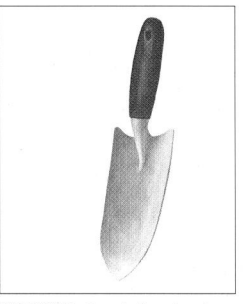

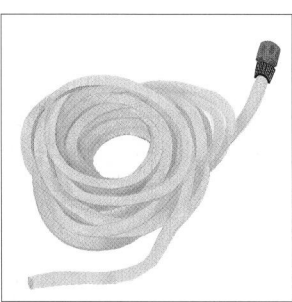

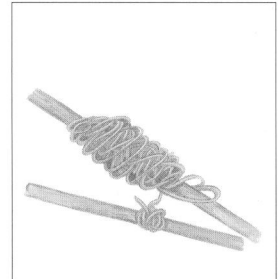

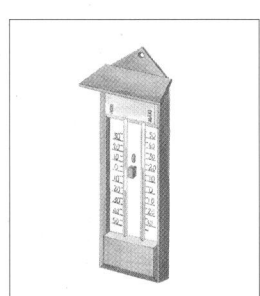

EDGING SHEARS: for manicuring the edge of the lawn without having to bend over. This is a satisfying tool to use.

TROWEL: handy for planting out perennial or annual plants.

HOSEPIPE: an essential piece of equipment once you begin planting.

GARDEN LINE: for marking out a straight line. Can also be used as a guide for cutting a hedge level.

THERMOMETER: maximum/minimum type, should be positioned in a sheltered spot.

Walls and fences

Walls and fences, as well as enclosing a garden and giving privacy, can be decorative features in their own right.

Enclosures are a part of many people's landscape tradition: they like to feel their boundaries are defined. The type of hedge, wall or fence they choose will depend on their individual needs. They may want to:

• avoid being overlooked by the neighbours;

• screen off an unpleasant outlook or cut themselves off from their surroundings generally;

• keep out human intruders or animals;

• create a decorative feature (wall, fence or hedge);

• reduce noise pollution;

• provide shelter from the wind.

Other people seem not to suffer from any of these problems and are quite content with an open lawn surrounding their property. To them, a garden wall would be interpreted as an insult to the neighbours.

One of the fundamental considerations, however, is the cost of achieving privacy. The most expensive choice is a stone or brick wall (breeze-blocks are cheaper).

A wooden fence (made up of panels or feather-edged boards) is a less expensive option. Cheaper still are open fences (post and rail), and right at the bottom of the range are chain-link or stretched-wire fences, or possibly brushwood hurdles.

A fence or wall can also serve as a support for plants, climbers or ordinary shrubs, which can often be used to conceal the rigid lines (or outright ugliness) of certain types of enclosure.

What material and building style you adopt will depend very much on the region. For a country cottage, for instance, you might consider a dry-stone wall, built without cement but skilfully constructed to form a strong barrier. Walls of this type can also be used as decorative features within the garden itself. It is becoming increasingly difficult to find a craftsman skilled in this sort of work but, with patience, it is possible to build a dry-stone wall yourself.

The kind of enclosure most frequently used nowadays is the garden hedge, which combines all the advantages mentioned above and is also attractive to look at.

Before making a final choice, be sure to take into account planning regulations, which may preclude the use of certain materials or structures of more than a certain height.

Walls constructed of brick, rough stone or breeze-blocks, and held together with mortar, need to rest on concrete footings. These should be flush with the ground, or raised slightly above ground level. In the latter case, you will need to use planks and stakes to construct the formwork into which to pour the concrete. Leave it for a few days to harden.

You can then proceed to lay your stones, breeze-blocks or bricks. The bond (or pattern) you choose will depend on the building material, the local style, and the degree of solidity you want to achieve. One of the simplest is English bond (shown here), with successive courses of bricks overlapping lengthways.

If a dry-stone wall is to be solid, the width at the base must be at least 50 cm (20 in) for a height of 2 m (6½ ft). Strip the turf to a depth of 10 cm (4 in) and press the soil down to make a firm base. You can then lay the stones, which should be at least twice as wide as they are thick. By overlapping and marrying them in carefully, a good solid structure can be achieved.

Plants look very attractive growing out of a wall. To achieve this effect, fill the cracks with soil while you are building the wall and make it slightly narrower at the top than at the base, so that it retains rainwater. You can introduce the plants as you build the wall, or plant suitable species once you have finished. It will take two or three years to achieve the desired result. Contrary to conventional wisdom, the plants will strengthen the wall, their long roots helping to bind the stones together.

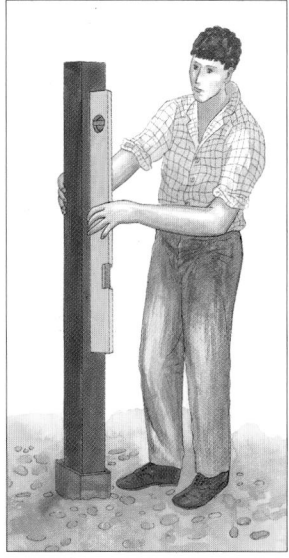

Fencing can now be bought in kit form, and is very easy to erect. Each wooden post fits into a holder on a long metal spike, which you drive into the ground with a sledge-hammer. This system makes it possible to erect posts in any kind of ground without a great deal of labour. The conventional alternative is to dig a hole and use stones to wedge the treated timber post firmly in place, or to use concrete.

Fit the post into the metal holder and check with a spirit level that it is vertical. If it is not, a few taps to the post should do the trick.

Next, assemble the horizontal components (rails, prefabricated fencing panels or trellises). Panels will either slot into mortices already cut into the posts, or can be screwed into the metal brackets provided.

CHEVRON-STYLE FENCING

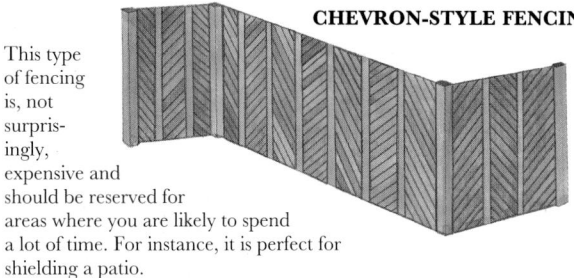

This type of fencing is, not surprisingly, expensive and should be reserved for areas where you are likely to spend a lot of time. For instance, it is perfect for shielding a patio.

BRUSHWOOD HURDLES

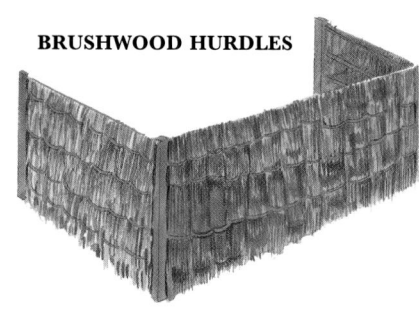

Brushwood hurdles are durable and ensure privacy. As long as the wind is not too strong, they also make an effective windbreak.

CHESTNUT PALINGS

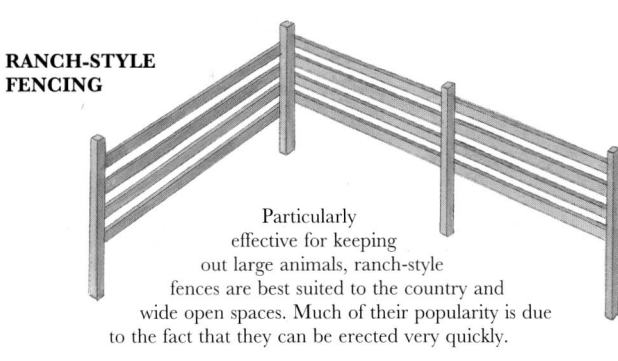

Palings (generally of chestnut) are less expensive than some other types of fencing. They do not ensure complete privacy, but form a good windbreak and afford a fair degree of security. They make an excellent support for climbing plants. They must be attached to a stretched-wire fence.

PLASTIC FENCING

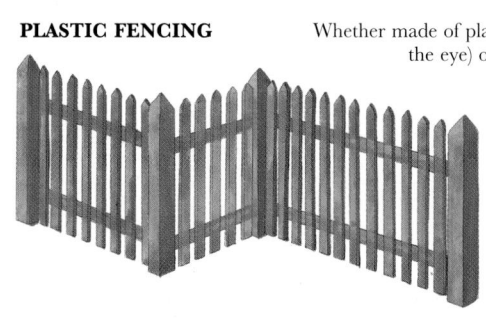

Whether made of plastic (not particularly pleasing to the eye) or wood, a 'traditional fence' consists of upright pickets attached to horizontal rails. This type of fencing can be bought in prefabricated lengths, is easy to assemble and looks attractive in any kind of garden.

RANCH-STYLE FENCING

Particularly effective for keeping out large animals, ranch-style fences are best suited to the country and wide open spaces. Much of their popularity is due to the fact that they can be erected very quickly.

The main purpose of a trellis is as a support for climbing plants. As a barrier, it is largely symbolic. Because of its relative fragility, trelliswork cannot be used to cover long distances, unless of course it is fixed to a wall.

TRELLIS

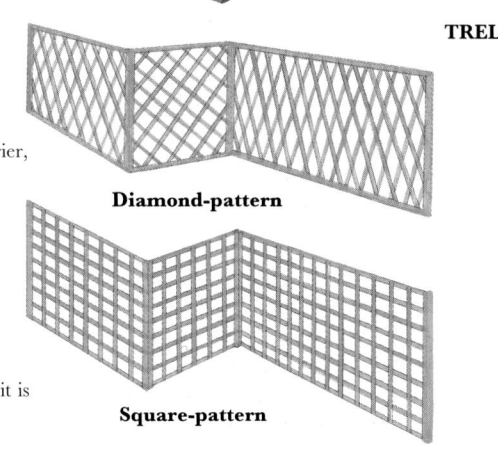

Diamond-pattern

Square-pattern

Paths

Paths are an essential part of garden design, and you should aim to make them both attractive and utilitarian.

Avoid the pitfall of making paths too narrow so that, when going for a stroll with a friend, you have to walk in single file. For comfort, paths should be at least 1 m (3¼ ft) wide. However, in the case of paths laid down for strictly utilitarian purposes (e.g. for wheeling a barrow from the house to the compost heap), a width of 60 cm (24 in) will do.

One important point: all paths should have a slight camber (a 1 per cent fall from the centre to the edges), so that puddles do not form.

How successful and durable your path turns out to be will depend on the preparatory work you put in. Strictly utilitarian paths should be as straight as possible, to minimize the labour involved. At the same time, be careful not to construct a path which divides your garden rigidly down the middle, unless of course you intend to camouflage it with plants.

If you want to make a decorative network of small footpaths, lay them out in a gentle curving pattern: tight curves and sharp angles will make lawn-mowing difficult.

The choice of materials will depend on the style of your house and garden, though some materials go well with almost any kind of architectural style or natural setting. It is all a question of taste. The materials most frequently used nowadays are paving slabs. Whether they are square or rectangular, their tasteful simplicity makes them an asset in almost any garden. Stone may be the most traditional material, but you can achieve much the same effect by using concrete slabs and laying them upside down – rough side uppermost. Appropriate treatment will soon give them an aged appearance. One old trick for making them 'age' quickly is to paint them over with a layer of yoghurt.

When you have decided where the paths should go, consider how much they will be used. A path bearing a lot of traffic needs a solid foundation.

Dig out the topsoil, to a depth of 15 cm (6 in) if the ground is hard, twice as deep if it is soft. Roll or tamp down to give a firm base.

Fill the trench you have dug with good clean hardcore, which should be trodden down and levelled.

Bind the hardcore with a 5 cm (2 in) layer of sharp sand, spreading it well with a rake. Depending on the intended use of the path, you can finish it off with concrete, or lay a thin mix of concrete and use it as a bed for paving slabs, pavers, pea-shingle or bricks.

When laying paving slabs, use a spirit level and tamp the slabs into place with the handle of a club hammer. If the slabs are laid on a bed of mortar (which is relatively impermeable), give the path a 1 per cent camber so that rainwater can get away.

Finish off by brushing dry sand or mortar into the cracks using a yard broom. Water moderately to dampen the joints and harden the mortar. Let the path settle for at least a week before using it.

Stepping stones

Log sections can be used to good effect to create a path in a little-frequented woodland area. In winter, they tend to become damp and slippery. You can get round this problem to some extent by nailing wire netting over the log section before laying it on its bed of sand. Stepping stones proper can be used for crossing a lawn, where a straight path would be inappropriate. Laying the stones is simplicity itself: where each stone is to go, dig out the turf and 10 cm (4 in) of topsoil. Tamp down the base and fill the hole with about 5 cm (2 in) of sand. Then lay the stepping stone on the sand, 2–3 cm (1 in) below the surface of the grass, so that it does not catch the lawn mower.

Paths likely to be used by vehicles

Paths and drives intended to carry wheeled traffic require concrete foundations, or they will soon break up. For convenience, they should be 2 m (6½) wide. Dig out the topsoil to a depth of 15 cm (6 in) if the ground is hard, twice as deep if it is soft. Half fill the site with hardcore and the rest with concrete. Brush the concrete, when it has nearly set, to give it a rough surface: very practical in the case of rain or frost, especially if the path is on a slope.

You can create a more discreet access for vehicles by laying down just two parallel strips of concrete 50–60 cm (20–24 in) wide, with grass in between. Even less visible for a driveway are honeycombed concrete blocks, the holes in which can be sown with grass or plants.

Whichever method you use, do not forget to give the drive or pathway a slight camber, so that rain-water will run off easily. Every 2 m (6½ ft) or so, leave a 1 cm (½ in) expansion joint. Unless there is room for the concrete to expand in hot weather, it will crack, and the continuing action of rain and frost will eventually cause it to break up.

Cobbles

Cobbles can be arranged in geometrical patterns to achieve an interesting textured effect. Set the cobbles by hand in a bed of fresh mortar, then level the whole area using a wooden plank. To achieve a flat, even surface, the plank should be the same width as the path. Even levelled in this way, a path of this kind is not particularly comfortable to walk on.

Crazy paving

A path made of irregularly shaped elements has a characteristic rustic look and is well suited to a country cottage or retreat. The material may be slate or stone and can be bought in a wide range of different colours: white, grey, warm brown or dark red.

Bricks

Bricks can be laid flat or on edge, bedded in mortar or directly on sand. On either side of the path, rows of bricks need to be laid edgeways to create a regular framework for whatever pattern you choose for the path itself. After laying the bricks, brush fine sand over the whole surface to fill in the joints. Modern bricks tend to be colonized by algae and become slippery in winter, but there are products for dealing with this problem.

Paving stones

There are paving stones to match every type of building and garden. Another advantage is that they can be laid without cement on a bed of sand 5–10 cm (2–4 in) deep. When you have laid the stones, fill the joints with a 50/50 sand-and-peat mixture, in which you can sow grass seed if appropriate. If the path is going to carry a lot of traffic, lay the paving stones on a bed of mortar.

Gravel

Gravel is the most commonly used material for paths and is not expensive, but careful preparation is necessary if you are not to end up with a boggy mess in winter and a carpet of weeds in the growing season. The great advantage of gravel is that it enables you to create curves, fill in holes and smooth over irregularities in the terrain.

For best results, dig out 10 cm (4 in) of topsoil and line the trench with plastic sheeting. Spread the gravel or pea-shingle on top of this lining and compress with a garden roller.

Stepping stones should be laid flush with the ground. If the stones are too small, they will tend to sink in. A path of this kind is intended only for occasional use, crossing a lawn or a large flower bed.

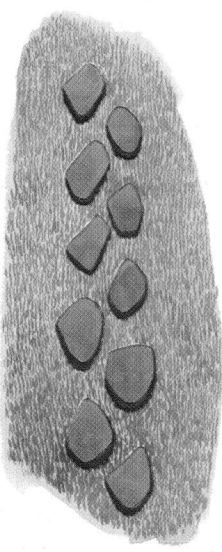

Log sections are also intended only for infrequent use. Sprinkle them regularly with sand so that they do not become slippery in wet weather.

Gravel paths require a layer of plastic or bituminous felt to prevent the gravel being absorbed into the soil. A rigid edging prevents loose gravel from spreading on to lawns and flower beds.

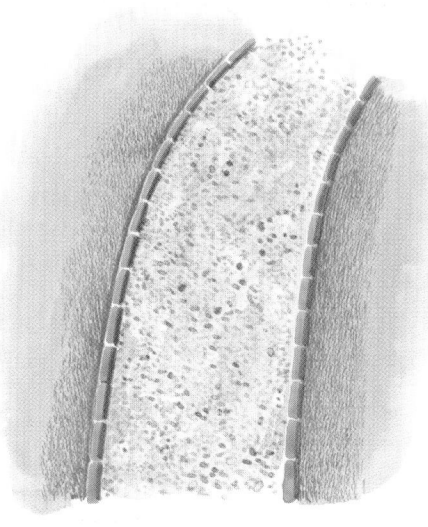

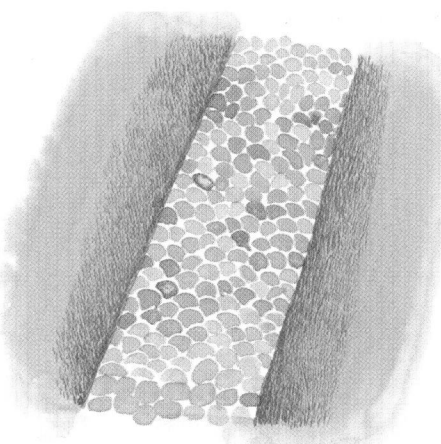

Crazy paving consists of irregularly shaped paving slabs. It has a rustic air, and enables you to make use of broken slabs of varying sizes.

Charming to look at but not very comfortable underfoot, cobbles are only really appropriate in certain regional settings. Lay them on a bed of dry mortar and tamp them down well before watering to make the mortar set.

A path made in a geometrical pattern of rectangular slabs, which may or may not be identical in size, works well with many regional styles of architecture.

Expensive and demanding a lot of hard work, but attractive and extremely durable, real paving stones can be laid on a bed of sand. However, if the path is narrow, or is going to be used as a drive for cars, it is preferable to set them in concrete.

All sorts of different materials are suitable for paths, and you can exercise your ingenuity to create original and unusual effects.

511

Steps and stairways

As well as their obvious usefulness, steps can be an important ornamental feature.

A flight of steps provides an attractive setting for various kinds of plant. You can build them with any of the materials used for paths, or with railway sleepers, which are ideal for the purpose. If these are unobtainable, slabs of timber will do nearly as well.

Great care is needed when constructing a flight of steps, as any difference in the height of the risers could throw someone off balance and lead to an accident.

On ground that slopes, it is better to install a step or two than leave an awkward, sometimes slippery, drop in level.

On gentle slopes, each tread (which can consist simply of turf) should be 50–60 cm (20–24 in) deep from front to back, and in any case never less than 40 cm (16 in). If you are building a steeper flight of steps, the treads should be between 60 and 70 cm (24 and 28 in) deep, with risers of 15 cm (6 in).

Use string and pegs to mark out the sides of your steps and the front of the treads. Dig out the steps, making sure the treads are horizontal. Compact the earth with the back of a spade, taking care not to break down the leading edges. Now try out your steps to see if they feel comfortable.

Begin the building work from the bottom. It is best to lay the first riser on a footing of concrete, particularly if the flight is steep or the soil tends to crumble.

Railway sleepers make ideal risers, being quick and easy to lay in place. Otherwise you can use treated slabs of timber.

Use paving slabs to form the treads. Small slabs should be set in a thin mix of wet concrete, larger ones on the bare earth or a bed of sand. Then fill the joints with mortar.

An elegant flight of steps can be made by setting bricks at right angles to form a parquet pattern. These go well with other brick structures, such as buildings and low walls.

The treads of steps made from old railway sleepers can be filled in with grass or gravel. However, this is not an ideal solution for steps that will see a great deal of use.

Wide, shallow steps built of two different materials blend elegantly into their surroundings and form an attractive setting for luxuriant planting.

Drainage

While some gardeners complain of drought, others have to contend with water-logged or semi-waterlogged ground. In either case, drainage is essential.

Drainage methods will of course depend on the nature of the site and your particular problem.

Draining a flat site

If your garden is flat or very gently sloping, a system of drainage ditches may do the trick. The main ones will run perpendicular to the slope, such as it is, with secondary ditches feeding into them at right angles. The more ditches you dig, the more unobtrusive they can be and vice-versa. How you do it will depend on the way you want your garden to look. On average, they will need to be at least 50–60 cm (20–24 in) deep, and of similar width.

Draining a sloping site

If your garden is sloping, install a system of underground drains, which have the advantage of not spoiling its surface appearance. Rigid clay or concrete land drains are still obtainable, but more common nowadays are flexible plastic drainage pipes, which can be laid to skirt round any obstacle. Cover the whole garden, laying out a herringbone pattern of connecting pipes in the direction of the slope. The principle is simple: the pipes are laid in a trench bedded in gravel, which acts as a sponge. The upper part of each pipe is perforated, while the watertight lower half collects the water which filters through and carries it away – like a gutter. The entire system leads to a main sewer, a cistern, a cesspool or a pond.

Drains of this kind should also be laid around the foundations of buildings, retaining walls and other partially buried structures, otherwise water will accumulate behind them and in time cause serious damage. Areas over drains can be planted with grass or non-vigorous perennials. More vigorous plants should be avoided since the roots of water-seeking trees and shrubs will soon block up the buried pipes.

Lay the drainage system in a herringbone pattern, following the lie of the land. The feeder pipes are all connected to a main drain, which itself discharges into a pond, soakaway or stream.

Each flexible plastic drainage pipe has a perforated upper surface and lies buried in a gravel-filled trench.

If it is not possible to discharge the water into a pool or pond, dig a soakaway and fill it with crushed stone.

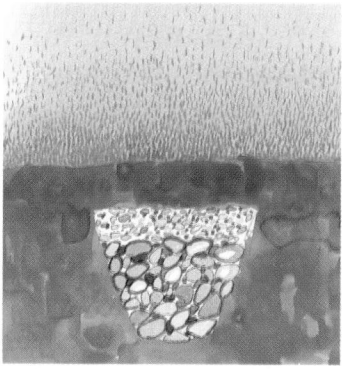

In a limited area where waterlogging is only occasionally a problem, a stone-filled drain may suffice. Dig a trench in the wettest spot, half fill with crushed stone, then cover with gravel and topsoil.

When building retaining walls, lay a drain parallel with the base of the structure. This is to prevent a build-up of water which would damage the footings.

Windbreaks

There is no such thing as a region without wind. Though a light breeze is very pleasant, strong winds wreak havoc on exposed sites, drying out, flattening and deforming shrubs, chilling the gardener and his precious plants, and, in coastal regions, carrying salt spray which kills off vulnerable foliage.

Troublesome though the wind may be, at least it is fairly constant in its direction. Gardens are subject to a 'prevailing' wind, though this may vary from time to time. Your own observations, a neighbour's experience, the information supplied by meteorological stations, will soon give you a good idea of what to expect. First, rid yourself of the firmly entrenched idea that the wind has to be blocked by a solid obstacle. An impermeable barrier (a wall, for instance) will only act as a trampoline, causing the wind to do even worse damage once it has leapfrogged the supposed line of defence. The aim is not to produce absolutely calm conditions, but a tolerable flow of air. Partially permeable barriers, which reduce the force of the gale by between 20 and 50 per cent, will do a far better job. For this purpose, the most natural of garden features is also the most effective: the hedge.

The saplings of deciduous species should be densely planted,

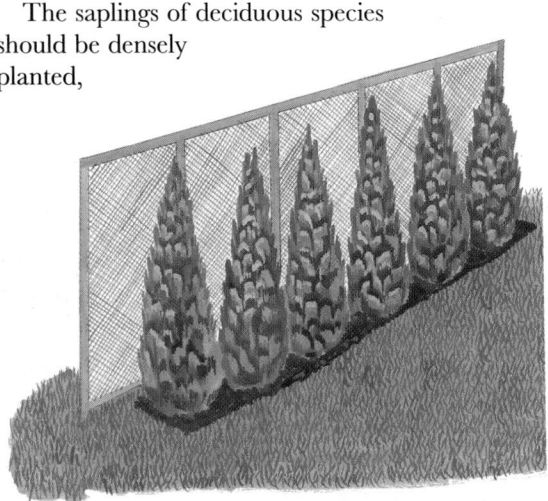

A hedge planted as a windbreak may need to be protected by an artificial windbreak of its own while it is getting established.

Until it is firmly rooted, an individual tree can be protected by a simple screen of plastic material attached to a frame or stretched between three stakes. The stakes will need to be firmly driven into the ground to a depth of at least 50 cm (20 in), with guy ropes to keep them in place.

evergreens more spaced out. The taller the hedge, the greater the area it will shelter in its lee (some twenty times the height of the obstacle). If the wind is only of moderate force, a single row of trees will be sufficient, but in fully exposed areas a double or triple screen of trees is recommended, with smaller shrubs and bushes planted in the gaps to break the air flow at ground level. A zig-zag arrangement is even more effective. You can also buy ready-made windbreaks, which may be rigid (screens, openwork fences) or flexible (netting). These may be suitable if you lack space for planting a natural hedge and your garden is subject to a constant strong wind. One of the best natural windbreaks is the versatile bamboo: unbreakable, permeable, evergreen and quick-growing, it also forms a delightful backdrop for other plants.

Artificial windbreaks

The important thing is to find a material that will filter the wind and reduce its force.

There are several possibilities:

• Hurdles, which consist of woven twigs or bundles of brushwood, are preferable to a rigid wall, as they let some of the airflow through. However, they may not provide sufficient protection, in which case you will have to install something more robust.

• You should also consider local factors. Wattle fencing is fine, but more suitable at the seaside than in a mountain area.

• Not terribly expensive, though less attractive to look at, are screens of plastic mesh firmly attached to a picket fence. This might serve as a temporary expedient, while waiting for a natural windbreak to grow. Mesh of this kind comes in black and green. Artificial screens last seven or eight years, long enough for saplings to get established.

Natural windbreaks

The purpose here is the same, the means different. In this case, the technique is to plant several rows of trees and shrubs to act as a filter. To be effective, a windbreak of this sort will have to consist of three or four ranks, planted in staggered formation, the tallest trees at the back.

Trees planted in rows afford excellent protection, more effective than even the highest wall. Plant the tallest species in the teeth of the wind, with shorter trees in the gaps and even smaller shrubs close to the ground. A utilitarian feature of this kind need not be ugly. Ornamental plants can also be used in its construction.

Space trees at 3–4 m (10–13 ft) intervals, supporting them with sturdy stakes. Shrubs should be planted 75 cm (30 in) apart. Blackberry canes, which have dense foliage and can be trained on a trellis, also make an effective windbreak.

Here are some plants which will withstand salt spray and strong winds

TREES

Acacia dealbata	Mimosa
Acer pseudoplatanus	Sycamore
Carpinus	Hornbeam
Crataegus	Hawthorn
× *Cupressocyparis leylandii*	Leyland cypress
Garrya elliptica	Silk tassel bush
Hippophae	Sea buckthorn
Ilex	Holly
Pinus	Pine
Salix	Willow
Tamarix	Tamarisk

SHRUBS

Cotoneaster	Cotoneaster
Elaeagnus	Oleaster
Euonymus	Spindle
Hydrangea	Hydrangea
Juniperus	Juniper
Phormium	New Zealand flax
Pyracantha	Firethorn
Olearia	Daisy bush
Sambucus nigra	Elder
Sorbus	Mountain ash
Spartium	Spanish broom

OTHER TREES SUITABLE FOR WINDBREAKS

This list includes trees with a double function: their timber can also be used as firewood.

Ash
Beech
Cedar of Lebanon
Chestnut
Lime
Oak
Pine
Plane
Poplar
Rhododendron ponticum (acid soil)
Sequoia
Sycamore
Walnut
Wild cherry

Patios and terraces

Patios and terraces are ideal places to relax and get together with friends and family. They provide a transition between house and garden.

In fine weather, you can put out the deck-chairs, invite your friends round and enjoy an alfresco meal or a drink or two.

When the weather is changeable, a patio or terrace makes an ideal play area for the children, as well as enabling you to make the most of the first and last of the fine weather.

Since a patio or terrace is an outdoor extension of your living space, it is well worth devoting time and thought to its location and design. The ideal position is one which is neither too hot (south-facing) nor too cold (north-facing), but ideal conditions are not always available. Don't build a north-facing patio unless you live in a warm climate. However, there are a number of practical alternatives. For example, you can build a patio against one of the walls of the house, while lightweight, openwork partitions or hedges of ornamental shrubs at either end will create a decorative effect as well as acting as a windbreak.

Always position the patio close to the house; if you have a choice, proximity to the kitchen makes life easier if you eat outside.

Planting using different levels. The ornamental pond in the foreground is set off by low-maintenance seasonal planting.

A very sunny patio or terrace is much more pleasant if it has some form of shade. A lightweight pergola will provide support for such decorative climbers as Russian vine, hops and clematis, or functional plants such as vines and kiwi fruit. Deciduous varieties are better, as they will enable you to enjoy the full benefit of the winter, spring and autumn sun.

If the patio is in a shady position, choose light-coloured materials to create light and warmth. If it is in a very sunny position, you can build an arbour or pergola and grow a deciduous climber which will provide shade in summer and let in sun and light once it has lost its leaves.

Whatever the position, the patio should slope slightly away from the house – 5–6 cm

(2–2½ in) per 4 m (13 ft) – to ensure that rain-water runs off. Mark out the minimum area required, set out your garden furniture, and allow a bit extra before laying the foundations.

Surfacing techniques are the same as for paths and there are a number of different surfacing materials, from bricks and tiles to regularly and irregularly shaped stone or concrete slabs and coloured concrete surfaces.

Raised wooden floors are warm and easy to lay but have the disadvantage of being slippery in wet weather.

Some patios (those by a swimming-pool, for example) are built well away from the house and are becoming increasingly popular in warmer regions. These outdoor living areas are often equipped with shower cubicles and a 'kitchen' area.

A patio is designed to provide open-air living space. But as well as being somewhere to sit and enjoy the sun, it can also double as a dining area. Simple cooking equipment (a barbecue) and a few work surfaces make it extremely user-friendly, while the high proportion of brickwork makes it easy to maintain. Planting is limited to seasonal displays and culinary herbs.

You can create focal points by planting in containers or in round or square beds surrounded by pebbles (make sure their size is appropriate for the dimensions of the patio). The bamboo on the left creates a low-maintenance display.

A raised patio with steps giving access to the garden. Fruit trees can be trained up the trellises on either side and will give the patio a more intimate atmosphere.

The patio itself is positioned partly in the shade, for the afternoon siesta, and partly in the sun, for sunbathing. Avoid building this type of patio near deciduous trees, as they will give you extra work in autumn as well as making the patio surface slippery. However, conifers such as yews and pines are ideal for softening the effect of the large amounts of stonework involved.

Watering

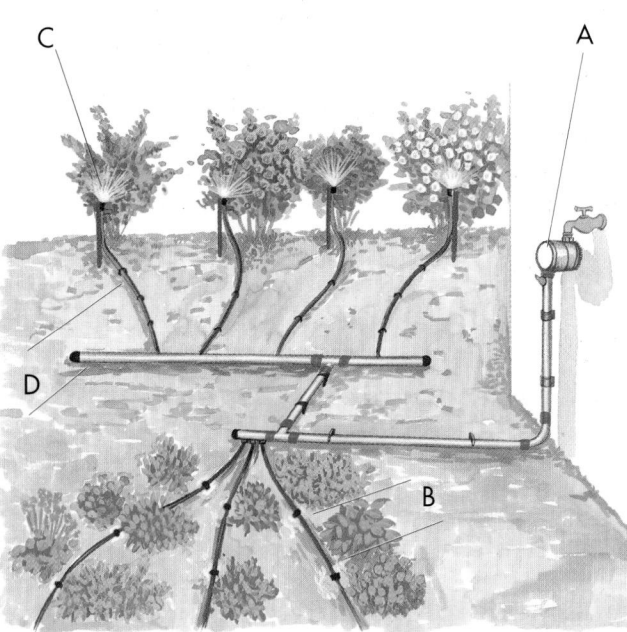

A low-pressure watering system can be linked to an outside water tap and controlled by a meter (A) with a built-in timer, (an electrovalve ensures that the system is switched on at set times). This means your plants can be watered at night and while you are away. Secondary valves enable water to be directed to a particular part or parts of the garden, which is especially useful when the pressure is low. A network of perforated hosepipes (B) running along the surface of the soil maintains trickle watering at the base of the plants. Taller and more permanent plants and densely planted areas (mixed borders) are watered by micro-sprinklers on adjustable posts (C). The feeder pipes (D) can be buried beneath the soil, as can the main distributor pipes. Remember to empty or dismantle the system before winter.

Plants need water as much as they need soil and light. Although these last two commodities are obligingly provided by nature (with the occasional helping hand from the gardener), we know only too well that the natural water supply is extremely erratic. People are often under the misapprehension that a summer shower will do their watering for them, whereas in reality this type of rain doesn't penetrate as far as the roots and, at best, only refreshes the leaves. So the real watering still needs to be done. In fact, plants should be watered regularly from spring through to autumn and sometimes even earlier and later.

Rain-water is best for watering and can be channelled from gutters into storage tanks and water-butts. However, this will obviously not be enough on its own.

Well water can only be used after it has been exposed to fresh air for a long time and should be stored in tanks or butts before use. River water is well aerated and good for watering and stagnant water can also be used. Spring water is extremely cold and should be allowed to warm up before being used.

Equipment

The equipment now available enables us to use a wide range of different watering techniques.

• Watering cans are the oldest and the most traditional piece of watering equipment (they were made in terracotta before galvanized steel was used). Nowadays they are made of light, supple – and inexpensive – plastic. Used without the rose, the spout produces a heavy, localized flow which is ideal for reaching the roots of shrubs without wetting their foliage or flowers. The fineness of the spray produced by the rose can be adjusted by altering the position of the holes. A fine spray is ideal for seeds and seedlings.

• For large-scale watering, the most widely used method is a hose fitted with a rose (with or without a trigger mechanism), gun or adjustable nozzle. Hoses should not be longer than 20 m (65 ft), as anything above this becomes extremely difficult to handle. This tends to happen when taps are a long way – anything up to 40 m (130 ft) – away, or because of obstacles or garden design. The end of a hose can also be fitted with a swivel or rotating spray, ideal for seeds and lawns but not so good for flowers which tend to be flattened, marked and generally damaged by this type of spray. They are better watered using a perforated hosepipe with the holes facing downwards. If you are lucky enough to have access to a natural water supply (a well, pool or spring), you can pump water out. But bear in mind that, at best, you cannot pump from more than 9 m (30 ft) below the level of the surface to be watered. If you have a stream running through your garden, you are entitled to take water from it.

• Complete watering systems (on or below the surface) represent a significant saving in terms of time and energy. They can also be connected to a timer so that the garden is watered at night or while you are away. Although they vary considerably from model to model, the manufacturers' leaflets are very detailed. Nowadays there are also good, automatic watering kits on the market which you can assemble and install yourself.

When to water

The question still remains as to when to water. Some people believe that the evening is the best time, when the plants are at their thirstiest and have all night to refresh themselves. The objection to this method is that the plants are still warm and the cold water comes as a severe shock to their system. The reverse objection is raised against morning watering. The ideal time to water is, in fact, at night, which is one of the many advantages offered by the complete watering system. Failing this, water as late or as early in the day as possible. Whatever you do, avoid watering at midday, especially in summer, to avoid the shock to the plants' system mentioned above, and bearing in mind that droplets of water act like miniature magnifying glasses which burn leaves and flowers. Furthermore, 80 per cent of the water is immediately reabsorbed into the atmosphere, compared with a maximum of 30 per cent at night. Some of our fellow gardeners would be well advised to take note of this fact, especially at a time when water is becoming an extremely valuable commodity.

How to water

The first thing to remember about watering is that it is a time-consuming occupation. It is better to water thoroughly once a week than superficially every day, except in the case of plants with extremely shallow root systems. It is the soil, not the foliage, that needs soaking, but this does not mean turning your hose into a high-pressure water cannon that will tear plants to shreds, expose their roots and furrow the soil . . . without actually watering them! Like most aspects of gardening, watering is a quiet pastime that requires patience. It is also important to remember that, in sunny weather, it is the base of plants and not the foliage that should be watered, while on cloudy days and after sunset, watering should imitate a fine shower of rain which refreshes plants and washes the dust and parasites from their leaves. Some soils require more watering than others. For example, more

water is required to keep a clay soil well watered than a sandy soil. However, because sandy soils absorb water more quickly, they should be watered less generously and more frequently. It has been calculated that 1 cubic m (35.3 cubic ft) of water saturates 1 sq. m (1.2 sq. yd) of sandy soil and 2 sq. m (2.4 sq. yd) of clay soil. Soil rich in peat or leaf-mould can be very acid, and a careful watch should be kept to ensure that it remains moist. Plants grown in this type of soil require a constantly cool subsoil.

You can check whether a soil is well watered by making a small trench, 10 cm (4 in) deep, near the plants. Soil watered superficially causes roots to develop near the surface and the plant becomes more susceptible to frost, wind and heat.

There is no fixed time to stop watering before winter, but there are a few general guidelines you can follow. Reduce or stop watering when plants have lost their leaves, when the hot weather is over, when the air becomes damp and cool or when there is a risk of frost.

Sheds and screens

Garden sheds

Garden sheds are ideal for storing garden equipment: lawn-mowers, wheelbarrows and garden tools.

To replace those ramshackle sheds so often seen in the corners of gardens, looking as though they have been thrown together for next to nothing using any old bits and pieces, a range of reasonably priced garden sheds to suit every need is now available on the market. They come in all shapes and sizes, from self-assembly kits to the more sophisticated models.

You can create an additional feature in the garden by buying a simple shed and covering it with climbing plants.

There are two ways of doing this:

• By using trellis – sold in wood or plastic panels (wood is preferable, as plastic ages badly) – as a support for climbing plants which will cover the shed.

• By planting camouflage plants such as pyracantha at 60 cm (24 in) intervals around the shed and training them up vertical wires. If the roof is flat, cover it with small succulents, planted in 10 cm (4 in) of compost.

Garden camouflage

An offset hedge of laurel, thuja or yew is an ideal way of camouflaging a tank which must also remain easily accessible.

Certain functional and unsightly objects are inevitable in the garden, but can be disguised in much the same way that cupboards are used to hide such items indoors.

A length of flexible garden fencing (available from a garden centre) is ideal for concealing dustbins. Erect it in a spiral, leaving enough room to manoeuvre the bins.

Supporting your plants

Staking, training and bracing are three useful ways of encouraging plants to climb or of supporting plants whose weak or pliant stems can cause them to fall to the ground.

Old branches can be used to form an invisible support for a clump of tall, straight-stemmed perennials.

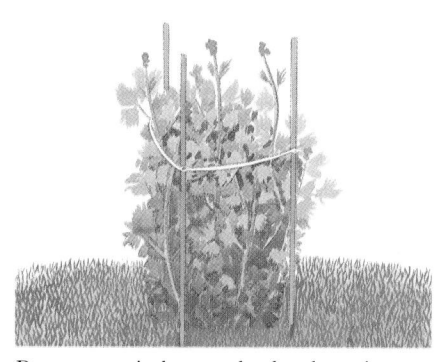

Do not use a single, central stake when tying up perennials. The stems run the risk of being broken. A support of three (or more) stakes joined with a length of garden twine is more effective and looks much better, as the plants soon conceal the support.

Staking

Plants are not staked just to make them look attractive. It is also a way of protecting them against wind damage. Plants blown flat by the wind can damage a lawn and their flowers become spoiled. By using a few old branches to support perennials, even in borders, you will obtain a much better display of flowers. Don't wait for plants to reach their potential 'damage height' before staking, as they will establish themselves between and around the stakes once these are in place.

To obtain a pillar of flowers, use a single stake of a height suited to the vigour of the plant. A 'sleeve' of fine-meshed wire netting around the stake will be virtually invisible and will encourage the plant to climb.

Roses used for ground cover need to be staked to keep them low and to encourage them to cover as wide an area as possible. Drive solid stakes firmly into the ground and tie branches to them as they develop. Keeping them close to the ground also increases the number of flowers produced.

Training

When people think about training plants they generally visualize a wall or fence. Avoid 'pinning' plants against it – they should be trained up wire netting or trellis, in such a way as to remain detached. This makes them easier to prune and treat. There are other ways of training climbing plants as well.

A simple, pyramidal structure in wood or metal is ideal for training rambling plants. Woody plants (honeysuckle, clematis and medium height roses) need only be attached fairly loosely to the framework. To grow annuals such as sweet peas and morning glory, large-meshed netting or trellis between the uprights will encourage them to cover the entire surface.

The various types of wall trellis now available make it easy to cover vertical surfaces (use a strong trellis for larger surfaces). Square mesh is easier to erect yourself, whereas other types may require professional help. The trellis is held in place – slightly away from the wall – by wedges and provides an ideal framework to which branches can be attached. It can be removed for cleaning or restoration.

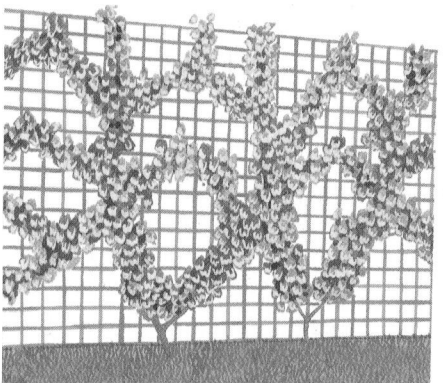

A net stretched between two posts is ideal for training annual climbers and producing an 'instant' flowering hedge or screen. When the flowering season is over, remove the net for cleaning. Woody climbers will require something stronger, e.g. wire netting or trellis.

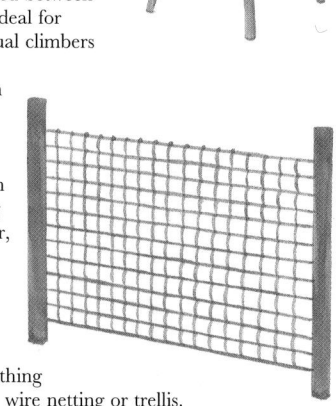

The espalier is a way of training fruit trees to give them the added benefit of wall protection (ideal for the frost-sensitive flowers of peach trees). The young tree is usually trained along regularly spaced wires or rods.

If you don't have a suitable wall, the method can also be used in open ground, with wires stretched between solid posts. Although this type of espalier does not have the benefit of wall protection, the fan shape does have the advantage of producing the maximum number of branches in a relatively small area.

Bracing

All newly planted trees require some form of support to enable their roots to become well established. If not, they run the risk of being blown over or, at least, rocked by the wind, which hinders the rooting process.

Acacia or chestnut wood stakes are best, as they don't rot in the ground. It is important to soak the base of the stakes in a copper sulphate solution. Alternatively, use the simpler, traditional method of burning the base of the stake.

The twin-stake method is strong and reliable, and ideal for all types of trees, although it does require a certain amount of solid wood. A horizontal cross-rail is nailed to two stakes driven firmly into the ground on either side of the tree, and the trunk is attached to the cross-rail, but care should be taken not to tie it too tightly (as this will strangle the tree) and to leave it a little play.

To counter the effect of cross-winds, tie two ropes around the trunk and attach to pegs driven into the ground on opposite sides of the tree. Protect the trunk with a 'cushion' of felt or rubber.

Dominant wind.

On small trees located in windy areas, simply set a stiff stake against the tree opposing the dominant wind.

It can be difficult to place a single stake close enough to the trunk of conifers and certain types of evergreen. In such cases trees can be 'guyed' by attaching ropes to the top of the tree and tying them to pegs hammered firmly into the ground some distance from the base.

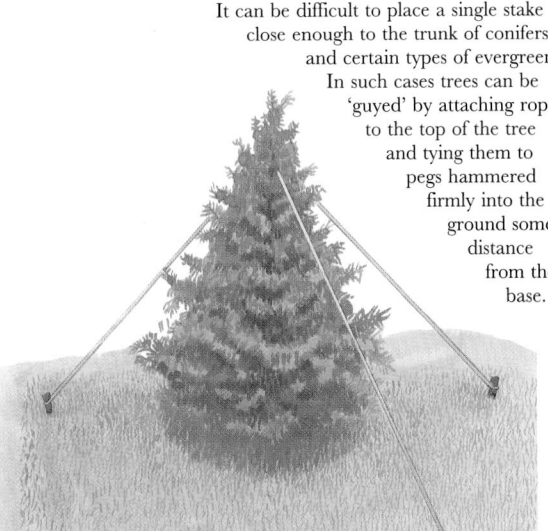

Greenhouses

Greenhouse protection — from the simple cloche to the full-sized greenhouse — gives gardeners a certain amount of control over external climatic conditions. The degree of control varies with the size and sophistication of the structure.

Movable cold frames provide basic protection against heavy frosts and use the 'greenhouse effect' to accumulate heat from the smallest amount of sunshine. There are various types of cold frame available, with movable sections that can be opened to release the build-up of heat, if necessary. Larger frames can be used to sow early seeds a month or two before they are sown in open ground.

Full-sized greenhouses have the obvious advantage that you can move about in them, as well as a significant build-up of heat which represents an even greater difference between internal and external temperatures. Cool greenhouses maintain a temperature just above freezing and are ideal for growing tender plants and over-wintering plants such as fuchsias and pelargoniums. In temperate greenhouses the temperature doesn't fall below 10°C (50°F) and the range of plants that can be grown in them is increased (e.g. semi-tropical plants and a number of orchids), while seeds of tender plants such as begonias and coleus can also be sown in winter. Warm greenhouses (minimum temperature 16°C/61°F) can be used to grow the most demanding tropical plants. However, these are becoming increasingly rare because they consume vast amounts of energy.

As far as possible, always erect your greenhouse in full sun since it is easier to provide shade than light, especially in winter. In any event, make sure it has ventilators which open automatically (there are some very simple systems which are heat activated) to avoid an excessive build-up of heat. Winter heating is provided by a separate system (ask your local dealer or manufacturer) or by extending your domestic heating system (ask your plumber or heating engineer). Except in the case of cool greenhouses where a single (e.g. paraffin) heater is enough, don't try to put a system together yourself, particularly if it is electric: your life may depend upon it! Make sure you have water storage tanks so that water warms up before use, and have at least one tap. Above all, before buying a greenhouse, ask your local dealer if you can see one already *in situ* and preferably in winter. This will enable you to see whether steps have been taken to counter the potential damage caused by condensation. Only use well-established, reputable firms which can offer after-sales service in the event of problems.

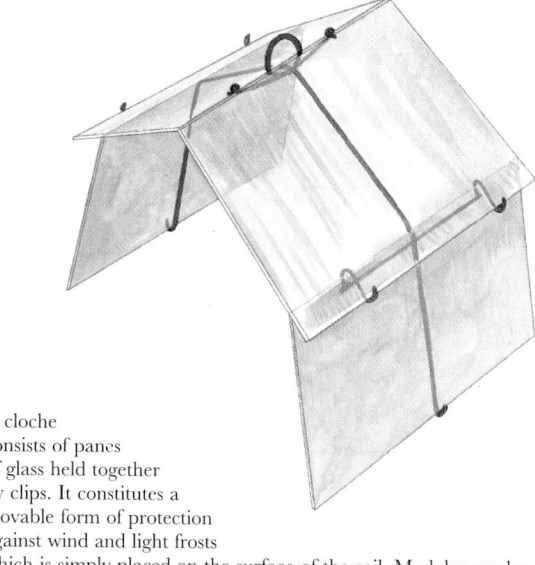

A cloche consists of panes of glass held together by clips. It constitutes a movable form of protection against wind and light frosts which is simply placed on the surface of the soil. Modules can be combined to produce an infinite number of variations, and tend to be most widely used on the vegetable plot or allotment. Nowadays they are more readily available in plastic.

Cold frames provide an outside storage area for tender seedlings or plants which have been in the greenhouse and need to be 'hardened off' before being planted out. They can also be fitted with electric heating cables running beneath the soil, which makes them ideal for propagation.

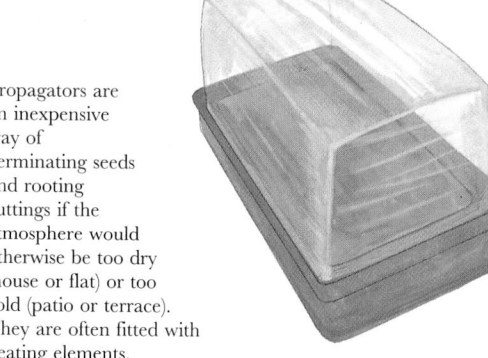

Propagators are an inexpensive way of germinating seeds and rooting cuttings if the atmosphere would otherwise be too dry (house or flat) or too cold (patio or terrace). They are often fitted with heating elements.

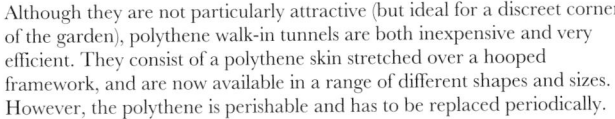

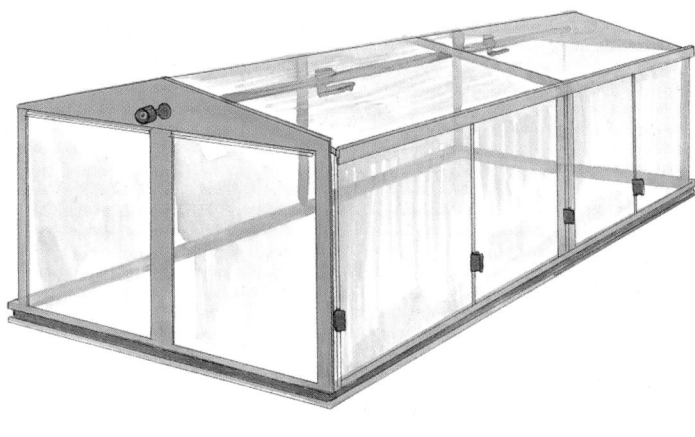

Although they are not particularly attractive (but ideal for a discreet corner of the garden), polythene walk-in tunnels are both inexpensive and very efficient. They consist of a polythene skin stretched over a hooped framework, and are now available in a range of different shapes and sizes. However, the polythene is perishable and has to be replaced periodically.

Movable (plastic, glass or metal) cold frames can be used to house tender plants in regions where the climate is a little too severe or wet. They are particularly popular with collectors of bulbs and alpines and, because they are small, they will fit anywhere in the garden.

A wooden or metal greenhouse built against the wall of a house reduces the amount of materials required as well as taking advantage of the substantial amount of heat given off by the wall. It can be used as a link between two buildings and, as such, makes an ideal winter garden.

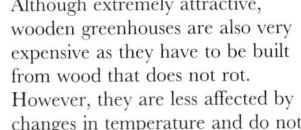

Metal greenhouses with an aluminium framework are available in kit form and can be assembled without the help of a professional. Depending on their size and shape, they can be erected temporarily (for over-wintering, seeds, etc.) or permanently. The type of plants grown depends on the temperature and the amount you want to spend on them.

Although extremely attractive, wooden greenhouses are also very expensive as they have to be built from wood that does not rot. However, they are less affected by changes in temperature and do not result in excessive amounts of condensation.

PLANTING

The soil

Identifying your soil

Plants draw their nourishment from the humus which helps to form the surface layer or topsoil.

Depending on the region, the topsoil varies in depth from a few centimetres to several metres. It is slowly enriched by the plants which grow and die in it. The flowers, fruits, dead leaves and twigs that fall to the ground gradually decompose into an organic matter known as humus, teeming with life. Beneath this nutritious surface layer is a deeper, inert layer devoid of organic matter and unsuitable for sustaining growth.

It is essential to identify your soil type before you start planting so that you know which plants will do well in it and how to improve it.

The four main components of soil are clay, silica (sand), limestone (chalk) and humus (organic matter), and soils are classified as 'clay', 'sandy', 'chalky' or 'humus-rich' depending on which of these components predominates.

Loam is the ideal soil, having a perfectly balanced combination of all four elements.

There are a few simple techniques which will help you identify your soil type.

• Examine your soil.

Take a sample of soil from a spade's depth. The colour and consistency of the soil will give you an initial idea of its type. A brown or black soil which is friable, light and moist and contains fragments of leaves and twigs is a humus-bearing soil. Heathland soil is a very good example of this. A whitish soil indicates the presence of chalk.

If, after a heavy shower, the rain is quickly absorbed by the soil and disappears, it is a sure sign that it contains a high proportion of sand. Another indicator of sand is if the soil is raised in clouds of dust by summer winds.

If you knead and compress the soil in your hand, a sandy soil will disintegrate when you squeeze it, while a clay soil will remain in a firm, shiny compact ball. (Clay also sticks to the soles of your shoes, retains water and forms puddles on the surface in wet weather, and cracks in summer.) If the soil sticks together but disintegrates when you drop it on the ground, it is closer to a well-balanced loam.

• Identify the plants growing naturally in the soil.

Certain plants prefer a particular type of soil, and the presence of these plants in a given area is an indication of the soil type. If wild cherries, hawthorn, elders, poppies and clover grow naturally in your soil, then it is definitely chalky. In warm regions, lavender, cistus, small-flowered gorse and holm-oak are chalk-loving plants found in the wild.

If, however, your garden is invaded by horsetail, wild sorrel, bracken, heathers, primroses and chestnut, you will know that you have a very slightly acid or chalk-free soil.

The tables on pp. 600–683 contain information about the type of soil required by each species mentioned in parts I and II. By consulting the appropriate table you will be able to discover whether a particular plant needs a humus-rich, sandy, chalky or clay soil and whether it requires acid, neutral or alkaline conditions.

• For more detailed information, carry out a chemical analysis of your soil.

It is easy to measure the acidity or alkalinity of your soil by dipping the end of a pH strip (impregnated with a coloured reagent) in a spoonful of soil mixed with an equal amount of distilled water. The strip will change colour, indicating whether the soil is acid (pH below 7), neutral (pH 7) or alkaline (pH above 7).

There are some companies and organizations which offer a complete soil-analysis service, providing detailed information on the nature of the soil, as well as its pH and its chalk, phosphoric acid, potassium and organic matter levels. All you have to do is send a representative sample, taken from several different points in the garden. There are also a number of DIY tester packs, available from garden centres, which enable you to carry out your own soil analysis, but a specialist institute will give you a more detailed, technical analysis, as well as being able to advise you on the nutrient content of your soil.

Levels of acidity or alkalinity can be temporarily adjusted to some degree using the appropriate soil improvers which, although they have no (or at best a very low) nutritive value, do enable you to modify the physical, or chemical, nature of the soil. As far as soil structure is concerned, a humus consisting of well-rotted organic matter (compost, leaf-mould, manure or peat) is the best as it aerates heavy soils and retains water and fertilizer in light soils. Acidity and alkalinity are difficult, but not impossible, to alter long-term. Although a very chalky soil will never be any good for growing rhododendrons, and heathland will never support a flourishing vegetable garden, you can increase the pH level of your soil by one or two points by spreading horticultural lime, for example, while peat, wood shavings and flowers of sulphur will decrease it by the same amount. These adjustments are necessary to bring your soil into line, as far as possible, with the ideal soil type and enable you to grow the widest variety of plants. Various cultivation techniques (e.g. drainage, fertilizers) covered in other sections of this Encyclopedia suggest further methods of adjusting the balance of your soil if it is not the ideal type.

Adjusting and improving your soil

Various mineral improvers (e.g. lime, marl) are available from garden centres and garden suppliers, as are humus improvers, although it is easy enough to make these for yourself.

Humus is organic matter which must be well-rotted before it can be assimilated by plants. It is essential for all soils which support plant growth and can be added in various forms.

Compost for your plants

Compost and mulches are the keys to gardening success. Compost is essential for feeding your plants, while mulches protect them from cold and drought, as well as performing various other functions.

A good, effective compost increases the fertility of the soil and contains the elements that your garden needs.

How to make a good compost heap

Start by separating out your household rubbish. Throw tins, plastic and cardboard containers (which can't be used) into one dustbin and keep another for vegetable peelings, paper, tea leaves and bags and coffee grounds, i.e. the biodegradable waste that can be used to make compost.

In a shady corner of the garden, drive four 1.5 m (5 ft) stakes firmly into the ground and surround them on three sides with wire netting. Place a few logs or small tree trunks on the ground inside the 'cage' and start to pile up your waste, spreading it out evenly each time. When you have a layer about 30 cm (12 in) deep, cover it with a layer of soil and water well.

Continue to build up 30 cm (12 in) layers of compost, sprinkling each layer with two handfuls of garden lime or dolomite (a type of lime containing magnesium). It is advisable to wear gloves while doing this.

Keep adding to the compost heap – remembering to water it from time to time – until it reaches a height of 1 m (3¼ ft). Cover with a final layer of soil and close the fourth side of the 'cage' with wire netting. Cover the heap with a piece of plastic sheeting or, even better, an old blanket. The heap can also be built against a wall.

Some important points about compost-making

For your compost to decompose under optimum conditions, it needs heat, moisture, air and protection. The heap should not be allowed to dry out but, if it does, water well and add a handful of dried blood or bonemeal, a good nitrogen-rich activator, or add a 'compost accelerator', available from garden centres.

Alternatively, try the old gardener's trick (and this is not a joke!) of urinating on the compost heap. This is a very good way of accelerating decomposition and preventing the heap from drying out. If the heap is well constructed, the earthworms will move in and get to work on it for you. After six months, you will have a wonderful pile of compost ready to incorporate into the soil for sowing seeds or planting trees and shrubs. And you needn't worry that your decomposing waste will smell or attract flies: quite the opposite, in fact!

Manure

This excellent, traditional soil improver is becoming increasingly hard to come by. It is a mixture of animal excrement and straw and should be dug in only after being allowed to rot for at least three months. Horse and sheep manure are ideal for clay soil, while cow, pig and poultry manure form large clumps and are better for sandy or chalky soils. In heavy soils, a single addition of about 500 kg (10 cwt) per 100 sq. m (120 sq. yd) will last for 3–4 years of cultivation. In light soils, manure decomposes more rapidly and it is better to add about 15 kg (33 lb) per 10 sq. m (12 sq. yd) every year.

The best time to dig in manure is in the autumn. As well as improving the physical structure of the soil, it also adds several important nutrients.

Peat and substitutes

Peat is formed in marshy valleys from sphagnum and other mosses. It decomposes very slowly and adds little to the soil in the way of nutrients. It is used to lighten heavy soils and retain water in dry soils, but unless you use bags of specially enriched peat (i.e. added nitrates, phosphates and potassium), it is advisable to add a fertilizer at the same time as ordinary peat. Nowadays, peat substitutes such as shredded bark and coconut fibre are replacing peat for soil improvement.

Other ways of adding humus to your soil
Seaweed

Seaweed is rich in potassium and limestone and is a good source of humus. If you collect it yourself, water it well before use to remove the sea salt; ready-to-use seaweed is available from garden suppliers.

Green manure

This is an ideal way of adding organic matter to improve poor soil in a new garden. It involves sowing fast-growing plants which are then dug straight into the soil, where they decompose into humus. For example, leguminous plants (lupins, vetch, crimson or French clover) are rich in nitrogen, cruciferous plants (mustard, turnips, fodder crops and winter rape) are grown for the bulk of their foliage, while grasses (rye and Italian rye grass) and various other plants such as buckwheat or the very decorative phacelia are grown in dry soil. The best time to cut or mow is just before flowering, as the formation of flowers and seeds weakens the plants. Green manure that has been shredded (e.g. by mowing) is assimilated much more easily by the soil. It can be dug in with a garden fork or a cultivator to a depth of 4–5 cm (1½–2 in) below the surface of the soil. The technique can be used on the vegetable plot (remember to rotate the beds) and between the trees in an orchard.

'Home-made' fertilizer

It is possible to produce a very efficient home-made fertilizer without using any chemical products. It has the added advantage that it won't harm your plants if the proportions aren't exact. And because it is slow to release nutrients, it need be added only once a year.

Mix one-third dried blood and bonemeal with two-thirds wood ash and half a bucket of compost. Spread the fertilizer around your plants, rake in lightly and water. You can also use it when planting shrubs and perennials.

Mulching

Mulching is another basic gardening technique which uses waste products to protect your plants from the cold and maintain the moisture levels of the soil in summer. Choose a shady corner of the garden where you can pile up thin layers of grass cuttings and leaves. These can be used, within a relatively short space of time, as a mulch or covering for beds and borders.

When you pick flowers, sweep up dead leaves, cut the grass and pull up weeds, don't throw them away, as you will be depriving your soil of its natural humus. Many gardeners use too much chemical fertilizer when they could simply return to the soil what they have taken from it.

How to make a mulch

All the plants in your garden can be used to make a mulch, although evergreen foliage should be avoided as it takes a long time to rot down. Leaves should be left to decompose for 3–6 months (and should be well turned over) before use.

A mulch produces stronger, more vigorous plants. In winter it protects them from the cold, and in summer it reduces evaporation after watering and keeps the area around the plant cool. It also provides a rich source of food for worms, which they mix into the soil, aerating, lightening and feeding it in the process.

A mulch 10 cm (4 in) deep on borders also helps to keep down the weeds. Weeds need light in order to grow, so all you need do to get rid of them is cut off their light supply. It really is that simple! If the odd weed or two does manage to struggle through the mulch, it is easy to pull them out.

Mulching has many advantages, and tends to be neglected nowadays.

Other types of mulch

Grass cuttings and leaves are not the only materials that can be used as mulches. Small plants that grow in well-drained crevices between rocks don't like the wet, and a layer of coarse river sand or gravel around their necks provides a degree of protection against winter frosts and rain as well as keeping them cool in summer. It is also a good way of keeping down weeds which hinder the growth of small plants.

Although it may seem strange, some gardeners use stones as a mulch. In fact, stones that remain in contact with moisture and soil help to preserve

the soil's nutritive elements. You only have to lift a stone that has lain on the ground for a long time to see just how much activity is going on beneath it. Earthworms and ants are hard at work, moisture levels are maintained and the heat of the sun warms the stone and is transmitted to the soil. Plants also benefit from this type of mulch, which enables them to make the most of the early spring sunshine, while a covering of stones also recreates the native mountain environment of a number of plants (alpines in particular) and makes them feel at home.

Pebbles are highly recommended in warm climates, as they keep roots cool, especially in containers. Composted or chipped bark makes an excellent mulch and has the added advantage of being clean and looking attractive on flower beds.

Peat is another good mulch, and its attractive chocolate colour also looks good on flower beds. Nowadays, peat substitutes such as shredded bark and coconut fibre are replacing peat.

Although shredded straw is the oldest and most reliable type of mulch, modern gardeners are not likely to expend the energy saved in other areas on shredding straw. And straw is also becoming increasingly hard to come by.

When to mulch

The best time to mulch is in the autumn, as it will protect your plants during the winter months.

Working the soil

Digging over

Digging over involves turning the upper layer of soil upside down so as to break it up and aerate it. This makes it easier for the roots of young plants to become established. It is important to remove the roots of any weeds brought to the surface as you dig. If you don't, many of them will grow again and compete with your plants. Digging over also enables you to dig in any soil improvers spread on the surface, as well as adding the appropriate fertilizers. The depth to which you dig is determined by what

you are going to grow in that particular area. For example, it is enough to dig over to a spade's depth to lay a lawn, but you will need to dig to a depth of 60 cm (24 in) – this is known as double digging – to plant a tree. It is best to dig over in autumn to allow the frosts to break down the clumps of earth ready for spring sowing and planting.

Digging over with a spade involves using the cutting edge of the spade to dig out and turn over successive clumps of soil, working along a row. Pile up the clumps from the first row and then dig out the clumps from the next row and turn them upside down in the trench dug for the previous row. Continue in this way until you come to the end of the area you are digging over. Use the soil from the first trench to fill the last trench. For sticky or stony soil use a garden fork rather than a spade, as the prongs make it easier to penetrate the soil.

For large areas, a rotary cultivator – like a small motor-driven plough – will save a great deal of time and physical effort. The blades cut through and turn a strip of soil as you work along each row. In a garden that has been well dug in the past, the soil doesn't need to be turned provided it is well broken down. A simple rotary hoe with vertically rotating blades is ideal for penetrating, breaking up and crumbling the soil. It can also be used to dig in well-rotted, manure-based or humic soil improvers. These tools can be hired very easily.

Raking

Before planting, the clumps of soil must be well broken down. You can do this using a range of hand tools (a claw, a multi-toothed cultivator or an ordinary rake) or, alternatively, you can use a cultivator with a harrow attachment or go over the area a second time with a rotary hoe.

Hoeing

As plants grow, the soil around them tends to harden. Hoeing involves breaking down this 'crust' to aerate the soil and make it more absorbent, as well as to keep it free of weeds. Always hoe when the soil surface is dry. For larger gardens, a cultivator with a hoe attachment or a rotary hoe can be used.

It is important to hoe around vegetables, large clumps of flowers and the base of shrubs several times during the summer. A garden hoed once a week will be virtually weed-free, especially if a mulch is used to protect planted areas.

CLAY SOILS
Clay soils tend to be more or less dark brown in colour, become sticky when wet and harden to something resembling concrete in dry weather. They are usually rich in nutrients and make a good growing medium with added soil improvers, especially organic matter. White chalky clay, however, is an extreme example. It is a very poor soil and presents real problems.

SANDY SOILS
Sandy soils generally have a fine-grained silica base and retain very little in the way of water, fertilizers or nutrients, which means they are extremely poor. Once they have dried out, they are difficult to moisten and can only be revitalized by the addition of organic matter.

CHALKY SOILS
Apart from chalky clay, chalky soils are light brown to white in colour, friable and contain large quantities of variously sized stones which have come direct from the parent rock. As they tend to block trace elements (especially iron), they are extremely poor and require large amounts of soil improvers and regular additions of fertilizers.

HUMUS-RICH SOILS
Humus-rich soils are rich in well-rotted, organic waste. They are dark brown to black in colour, very light and friable, and extremely air- and moisture-retentive. Roots love this type of soil, although it is not particularly rich. Humus-bearing soils are often acid and require a chalk-based soil improver when their pH is below 6.5, except when used for growing acid-loving plants such as rhododendrons and camellias.

Advantages and disadvantages of different soil types

Clay soils

Clay retains water and prevents mineral salts and fertilizers from draining away into the subsoil. However, soils with a high clay content are difficult to work (they stick to your tools when wet and become extremely hard in dry weather) and take a long time to heat up in spring, characteristics which have led to them being described as 'heavy' and 'cold'. Soils with a high clay content can be improved by spreading and digging in coarse sand: 1–2 cubic m (35–70 cubic ft) per 100 sq. m (120 sq. yd). Clay soils lacking in organic matter can be lightened by adding 150–250 kg (3–5 cwt)

of peat, peat substitute, manure or compost to an area 10 m (33 ft) square, while those with a low chalk content can be improved by adding 20–30 kg (44–66 lb) of garden lime per 100 sq. m (120 sq. yd) before they are dug over. More lime can be added to the surface after planting, over a period of 3–4 years. It should be borne in mind that these methods of improving the soil are effective only up to a depth of 30–40 cm (12–16 in). If you want to plant trees and shrubs in a clay soil, it is advisable to choose varieties whose roots are not affected by moist, heavy soil.

Sandy soils

Sandy soils are light and easy to dig, hoe and weed. They warm up rapidly in spring and seeds germinate early. However, they allow water to drain through too quickly, with the result that nutrients tend to be washed away. A very sandy soil can be given body by digging in 2–3 cubic m (70–105 cubic ft) of good clay soil per 100 sq. m (120 sq. yd).

It is essential to add large quantities of humus-forming organic matter (peat, peat substitute, leaf-mould, compost or manure) and to water regularly. In this type of soil, fertilizers should be added several times a year. A sandy soil which is too acid can be improved by adding garden lime as for clay soil. A well-improved sandy soil is ideal for growing vegetables, bulbs and annuals, while a number of conifers also prefer light, sandy soils.

Chalky soils

Although they warm up quickly in spring, chalky soils do not retain water. They dry out in summer and are poor in nutrients. Like sandy soils, they require large amounts of organic manure and balanced fertilizers. Their high alkalinity (pH above 7.5) tends to cause chlorosis in a number of plants; this is a disorder characterized by yellowing of the leaves, while the veining remains green, and

plants lose their leaves and become weak or die.

In such soils it is essential to grow only chalk-tolerant plants, as it is unrealistic to expect to neutralize the effects of the high alkalinity. Vegetables are reasonably chalk-tolerant, as are a number of perennials (for further details see tables, pp. 600–683).

Humus-rich soils

Woodland soils are typical humus-rich soils. They are rich in leaf-mould and, although permeable, soak up water which is in turn absorbed by plants. They warm up quickly in spring and are easy to work. However, they are often extremely acid and suited only to certain types of plants. It is possible

to reduce the acidity by treating with lime and adding phosphorus and potash fertilizers. Plants which grow in heathland soil – hydrangeas, camellias, rhododendrons, azaleas and other acid-loving plants – are ideally suited to this type of soil.

A natural loam soil is every gardener's dream. It consists of a well-balanced mixture of clay, sand and humus and is neutral or very slightly alkaline.

Lawns

What kind of lawn are you going to choose?

This is a fundamental question, and the answer depends on what you are expecting to use the lawn for.

There are some places (marshy or very shady sites) where it would be advisable not to have a lawn at all, but in all other cases, your choice will depend on the use to which the lawn will be put: is it to be an immaculate expanse of close-cropped grass, as smooth as velvet, a flower-scented meadow, a hardwearing utility lawn, or a play lawn for games and sports?

For each of these, experienced professionals have developed mixtures of different kinds of selected seed, from the finest and most delicate to the coarsest and hardiest, depending on the location or type of ground.

A note of caution: the more beautiful a lawn is, the more maintenance it will require. So if you have a second home in the country where you go only occasionally, a tough mixture that will tolerate irregular cutting will be quite adequate.

The choice of seed

To some people there is no more beautiful sight in a garden than a lush, green, well-maintained lawn.

This is one part of the garden that requires the most meticulous preparation and the best aftercare. Grass will actually grow anywhere, but in different ways depending on the quality of the soil. A luxuriant lawn can be produced only on a soil that is suitable for it.

The main question asked by anyone wanting to establish a lawn is 'What kind of seed should I buy?' although the carefully tended appearance of some lawns comes not from the choice of seed but from the choice of mower and its use. There are mixtures available for fine ornamental lawns, but unfortunately such lawns will not tolerate hard use; you should choose a hardwearing mixture containing ryegrass if your lawn is to be used a lot for outdoor living and recreation.

Fine ornamental lawns

Creeping or red fescue – sheep's fescue – bent grasses – fine-leaved perennial ryegrass. These seeds will produce a lawn of excellent appearance and good density. Unfortunately, they are prone to disease, and if this occurs they will need treatment.

Utility lawns for general outdoor living

Perennial ryegrass – smooth-stalked meadow grass – rough-stalked meadow grass – crested dog's-tail – timothy – lesser timothy. Lawns produced from these seed types are easy to establish, have good aesthetic appearance and density, and are resistant to disease and the tramping of feet.

Play lawns for sports and games

Perennial rye-grass – smooth-stalked meadow grass – creeping fescue – timothy.

To create a flower meadow

Mix together the chosen flower seeds in a saucer and scatter them over the grass seed already sown. This will ensure a natural distribution of flowers.

To scare off birds eager to gorge themselves on this feast, attach white plastic bags to sticks so that they flap in the wind.

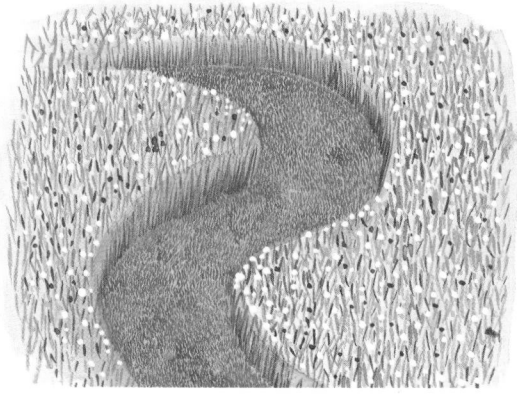

An interesting effect can be created by simply cutting out paths in the meadow with a mower.

Preparing the site

The site of a new lawn must be carefully weeded and dug over and the soil must be broken down, firmed and levelled a long time in advance of sowing. This is absolutely essential, because once the lawn is in place even the best selective herbicides will not get rid of some weeds – couch grass, for example. If the ground is properly levelled, any settlement after the initial sowing will be as gentle as possible and the resultant bumps and hollows will be less likely to upset the mower. Keep obstacles such as benches, statues, beds, trees and so on to a minimum, otherwise you will spend hours dragging the mower round them.

Sowing the grass seed

In theory, grass seed can be sown at any time, but the ideal periods are spring and early autumn. The soil should be moist: it is normal practice to water the site before but not immediately after sowing. Seed can be sown by hand, but a little practice is required to get the distribution even. The seed should be split into two equal portions, one portion being sown down the length of the site, and the other across it. This helps to ensure even distribution. The best method, however, is to buy a seeder, which will be very useful afterwards for spreading fertilizer.

Once sowing is complete, there is no need to bury the seed deeply. For a large area, all you need to do to cover the seed is rake the ground lightly; for a small area, use a piece of wood attached to a handle. To make the edges of the lawn, mark out a small furrow to a depth of about 1 cm (½ in) into which a thin trickle of seed should be sown. You will need 25–35 g per sq. m (1–1¼ oz per sq. yd). If perennial ryegrass is the main seed in the mixture, increase the rate of cover to 35–40 g per sq. m (1¼–1½ oz per sq. yd).

Once the seed has been sown, the enemy will be on the watch for it. No time should be wasted in setting up a system for scaring off the birds (white plastic bags attached to sticks and flapping in the wind should do the trick nicely). The first mowing should not take place until the grass has reached a height of about 5 cm (2 in), with the mower at its highest cutting position. Mow again a week later, lowering the blade a notch.

Maintenance

Once the lawn is established, not only will it require mowing and watering, it will also need feeding, aerating and raking. It will need a fertilizer rich in nitrogen to promote leaf growth. Since it leaches quickly, nitrogen should be applied at peak growth time (in spring and summer). It is possible to buy fertilizer mixtures containing selective herbicides; hormonal in origin, these herbicides act by disrupting the growth of plants other than grasses, which is why they have no effect on couch grass.

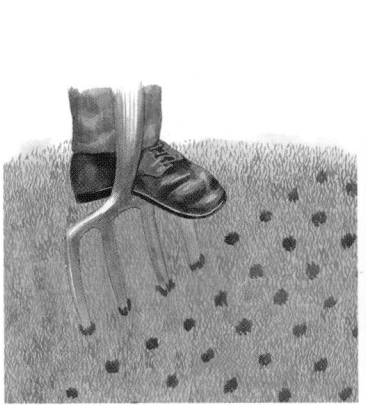

After a few years, the lawn will begin to suffer because of soil compaction. This can be cured by aerating it with a fork or a special aerator.

Fill the holes with coarse sand; this will improve the structure while retaining air and water.

Rolling a lawn helps it take root by forcing the runners of creeping grasses to spread out.

Quick and effective repairs for old lawns

If it is properly planted and well maintained, a lawn will last for years. However, accidents can happen, and if a lawn develops hollows and bumps, or bare patches, it will have to be repaired.

In order to do this, cut out the damaged area, fill it with new, humus-rich soil, sow some grass seed and roll it in. Alternatively, you can fill the gap by laying a piece of turf. Turf can also be used to create a whole lawn more or less instantly, but this method, though relatively effortless, is fairly expensive. In any case, not all seed mixtures are available in turf form.

There is in fact a way of laying a new lawn without having to prepare the site from scratch again. The following operation is best carried out in spring.

• Begin in mid-spring by cutting the grass as close as possible.

• Kill the existing grass with weedkiller.

• Wait a month, then rake the site in order to remove all the dead grass.

• Level the ground if necessary by filling in any hollows with compost.

• If the soil is heavy and dense, apply some sand and work it in with a rake.

• Water and sow the seed.

• Spread a thin layer of compost and roll it in.

The old lawn, rid of its weeds, will provide a basis for the new lawn. Without overwatering, keep the seed moist and protect it from birds.

Turf is normally supplied with each piece rolled for ease of delivery and handling. It can be left for 3–4 days provided it does not dry out.

Unroll the pieces of turf on the prepared and levelled site and simply lay them end to end. There might be a little bit of 'play' at the joints: the grass will fill them in as it grows.

At the edges, roll out a piece of turf and cut it to size with a sharp instrument, without tearing the grass. Unlike fitted carpet, the off-cuts can be easily used elsewhere on the lawn.

Firm the turf with the flat end of a rake in order to make it adhere to the soil and to eliminate air pockets.

In order to repair lawn edges, damaged by tramping feet for example, use a spade to cut out a rectangle of turf around the damaged area.

Turn the piece of turf round so that the damaged area no longer forms the edge, and re-lay. Fill the hole with compost and sow some seed. The damaged area will now be protected and will gradually be restored to good condition.

In order to cut the edges of the turf, use a straight plank as a guide, cutting hard against it with an edging iron or a well-sharpened spade.

Water the lawn thoroughly every day for the next fortnight. This is essential if the grass is to take root properly. Do not mow for 3 weeks.

Choosing a mower

Once the lawn is established, it will need to be mown regularly. This is the most important task in lawn maintenance. The aim of mowing is to keep the lawn at a height of 4–8 cm (1½ in). In temperate climates, mowing should begin in spring and stop in late autumn. In mild climates, start mowing a fortnight earlier and stop a fortnight later. Winter growth is very slight, insufficient to justify mowing, particularly since a lawn should never be cut in frosty weather.

Ideally, the lawn should be mown every 4–5 days between late spring and mid-autumn, and every 8–10 weeks outside that period. Frequent mowings with a good machine mean that the clippings do not have to be removed from the lawn. If mowings are less frequent, remove the clippings to prevent the lawn being smothered.

Standard machines

Most mowers are now motorized. The different types of machine have specific uses and are suitable for particular sizes of lawn.

• Hand-pushed mowers generally have two-stroke engines and are intended for use on small lawns up to about 20 sq. m (24 sq. yd) in area. Using one on a bigger lawn becomes tiresome. However, their small size makes them useful on bigger lawns for cutting round obstacles such as benches and trees. They can be used on fairly sloping ground.

• Miniature tractor-type mowers can be justified only for vast areas of lawn over 1,000 sq. m (1,200 sq. yd). At a price generally running into thousands of pounds, however, these machines enable the operator to play the gentleman gardener.

• Powered rotary mowers are very popular today and are ideal for use on utility lawns. Some also produce a striped effect.

Ancillary and luxury machines

Some machines have particular purposes.

• Mechanical cylinder mowers, which have to be pushed by hand, can only be used on very small lawns on which the grass is already short, because they get clogged by thick grass and require a great deal of effort to push. However, they are useful for finishing touches, such as cutting the grass between the joints of paved pathways.

• An electric nylon-line trimmer is useful for cutting round shrubs, whose bark, in theory, is not damaged by the nylon line. It gives a rough finish, and it really comes into its own for cutting long grass prior to mowing, or in the maintenance of steep, overgrown banks.

• Electric hover mowers have the considerable advantage of working perfectly on steep slopes. They are suitable for short or long grass and for small lawns. It is very important to use a circuit breaker as a safety precaution when using an electric mower, as this will cause the power to cut out if the electric cable is accidentally damaged.

• Petrol-powered cylinder mowers are very expensive, but give the finest cut. These are the machines that give lawns a striped effect. Because of their high price, they are generally used only on golf course greens and high-class ornamental lawns.

When deciding on your choice of mower, go to a reputable dealer and ask him to confirm that after-sales service is guaranteed and that spare parts can be obtained. It is better to pay a little more at the outset in order to buy some peace of mind.

Hedges

Plants for every type of hedge

Hedges are one of the most important items in the garden.

There is hardly a garden that does not have at least one sort of hedge, whether it serves to enclose a plot or acts as a windbreak, partition or purely decorative border. Yet most people have remained very conservative in their choice of

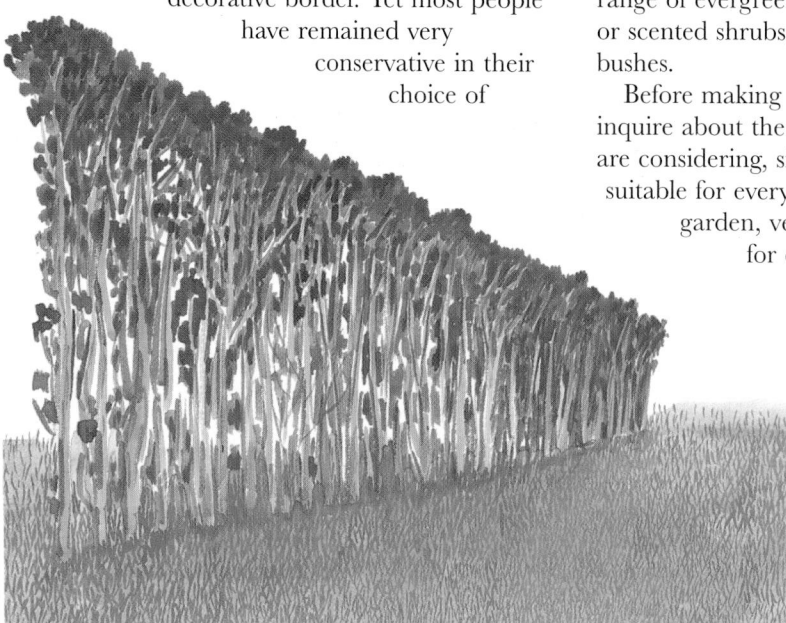

hedging plants. Apart from the eternal conifer, gardeners tend not to be very adventurous, whereas in fact they can choose from a wide range of evergreen or deciduous plants, flowering or scented shrubs, or very thorny defensive bushes.

Before making a final choice, you should inquire about the hardiness of any plants you are considering, since not every variety will be suitable for every situation – a very exposed garden, very dry soil or a high altitude, for example.

Gardeners are always in a hurry to see their hedge reach maturity, which is why they tend to buy large specimens. In fact younger plants have a better chance of developing than older ones, which may grow slowly for a year or two before they become fully acclimatized.

Some distinctive hedging plants

Choisya ternata

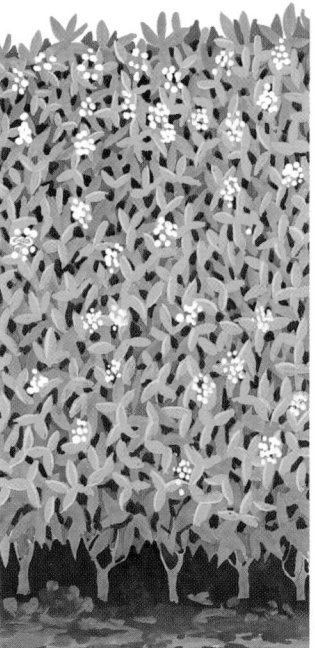

Fagus sylvatica

Ilex

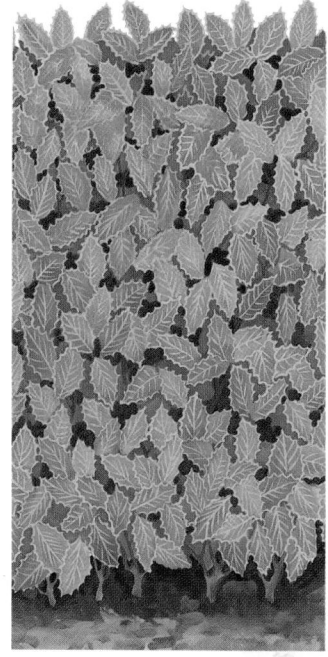

Berberis stenophylla
This has very thorny stems and makes a fearsome hedge, but one that flowers. It can be pruned, although its long, pliable branches look equally attractive if left to grow freely.
Use: Can be planted as part of a mixed hedge, or in combination with other shrubs as a windbreak.

Choisya ternata
This superb plant is not suited to a windy location or to a cold climate. It has shining dark evergreen foliage and the flowers, which sometimes bloom twice a year, are deliciously scented.
Use: Incomparable in a free-growing hedge in warm climates, or as part of a mixed hedge.

× Cupressocyparis leylandii
If you need a high screen of greenery, do not prune Leyland cypresses but just leave them to grow upwards and outwards. They should be planted at intervals of 2 m (6½ ft). This is the fastest-growing conifer.
Use: As a windbreak or in a hedge designed to hide an undesirable view.

Elaeagnus × ebbingei
This shrub can be used in windy locations; its flowers are scented and its leaves are silvery on the underside. It takes well to pruning, but if you start with a plant 50–60 cm (20–24 in) in height, it will need 3–4 years to become fully formed and effective.
Use: As a boundary hedge in seaside locations.

Fagus sylvatica
The common beech can be used to form the most delightful arbour or tree-lined walk that will retain its covering of dead leaves throughout the winter. It can reach a height of 6 m (20 ft).
Use: Ideal for partitioning a garden or bordering walks or driveways.

Ilex
Holly makes an elegant and distinctive hedge, whether its foliage is variegated (*Ilex aquifolium* 'Golden Queen') or just green (*I. aquifolium*).
Use: As a boundary or defensive hedge, or as a windbreak.

Laurus nobilis
This shrub, which can reach a height of 2 m (6½ ft), makes an excellent hedge for a temperate climate.
Use: To divide a garden or enclose a plot.

Ligustrum ovalifolium
This privet has dense foliage and is best pruned with secateurs. Its flowers give off a sweet scent.
Use: The denseness of its foliage makes it invaluable for screening the less attractive parts of the garden. It can also be used as a boundary hedge.

Photinia glabra
This shrub has only recently started to become better known, and to date has hardly ever been used to form hedges. It is a pretty little evergreen tree that has the advantage of growing fast. The tips of its leaves turn scarlet in spring.
Use: As a boundary hedge, to partition a garden, or at the back of a border.

Prunus lusitanica
The large glossy leaves of the Portugal laurel make a broad, dense hedge that produces highly scented flowers.
Use: As a boundary hedge.

Pyracantha
This shrub forms a fearsome, impenetrable hedge. As soon as it is planted, its branches need to be trained along wire. This firethorn, with its handsome evergreen foliage, is particularly striking in autumn, when it bears large clusters of red, yellow or orange berries.
Use: As a boundary hedge, or to hide a less than attractive corner.

Taxus baccata
A row of yews makes the most beautiful and imposing hedge of all. This conifer actually grows more quickly than its reputation would suggest. For best results, buy plants 50 cm (20 in) tall, which will quickly establish themselves.

Thuja
To add some interest to a hedge of thujas, prune it into a rounded shape at the top. Allow the trees at either end to grow, then cut them into a square or circular shape.
Use: As a boundary hedge.

Viburnum tinus
These plants can reach a height of 3 m (10 ft). The foliage is dark green and a little dull, but the flowers are deliciously scented.
Use: As a boundary hedge.

Laurus nobilis

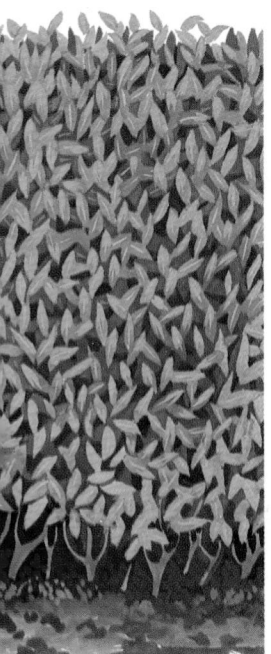

Prunus lusitanica

Pyracantha

Taxus baccata

Some distinctive types of hedge

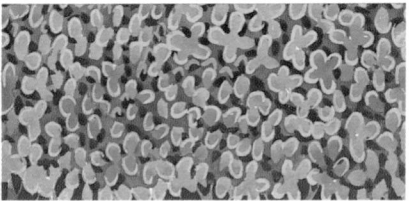

Border hedges

These are low hedges, reaching a maximum height of 40 cm (16 in). The plants used could be euonymus, box, heathers or barberries. In warmer climates, rosemary, santolina (lavender cotton) or lavender could be used; these have the advantage of not requiring too much watering while at the same time tolerating poor, dry soil.

Use: As a border for a flower bed or path.

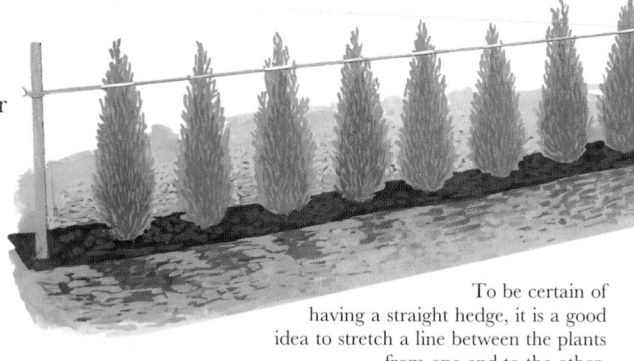

To be certain of having a straight hedge, it is a good idea to stretch a line between the plants from one end to the other.

Mixed hedges

A hedge of this type has many advantages. It will grow without necessarily requiring pruning, and makes a refreshing and colourful change from those dismal curtains of greenery that are an all too common sight.

A mixed hedge is formed from a variety of different plants that develop in different ways. The end result is a screen of different colours, shapes and heights. In order to create a light, delicate effect, intersperse the shrubs in such a way that they form a broken line and plant equal numbers of deciduous and evergreen shrubs. Leave 60 cm–1 m (2–3¼ ft) between the plants, even if the gaps look a little wide at first. After three years' growth, the leaves of the individual shrubs will become entangled.

Use: To enclose a country garden, or to divide up a plot.

Rose hedges

Why don't more gardeners think of planting roses as hedges? A flowering rose hedge can be a spectacular sight from early summer through to autumn. Try to find old roses such as 'Grootendorst', a superb Rugosa rose that in three years will form a thorny, impenetrable hedge 1.5 m (5 ft) high. Rugosa roses, which are hardy, undemanding shrubs with pink, red or white flowers, make splendid hedges. They do not require any particular pruning. The floribunda 'Centenaire de Lourdes' remains in flower throughout the summer until the first frosts arrive. And the elegant floribunda 'Queen Elizabeth' hardly needs any pruning and can easily be grown to a height of 2 m (6½ ft).

Use: As a border for an avenue or driveway or for dividing up a plot.

Planting a hedge

There are two methods of establishing a hedge. The first is to dig a planting hole 50 × 50 cm (20 × 20 in) for each of the shrubs to be planted (this is often done when a beginner starts to plant a hedge without being certain exactly which plants are going to be used, or intends to proceed in stages for reasons of economy). The second method (which is much more convenient, providing that all the shrubs you intend to plant are already on the spot) is to dig a trench approximately 50 cm (20 in) deep and the width of two spade blades across. In both cases, the soil must be well broken down. Add a 10 cm (4 in) layer of leaf-mould generously sprinkled with a slow-acting fertilizer, such as bonemeal. Arrange the shrubs in a straight line, spacing them at intervals of 60–80 cm (24–32 in) depending on the size they will reach at maturity. Fill the trench with soil mixed with peat or leaf-mould in a proportion of 4:1, and finish off the operation by packing down the soil at the base of the plants and watering. Then spread a 10 cm (4 in) layer of peat, pine bark or compost under the plants. This mulch could be replaced by a protective sheet stretched along the ground under the whole length of the hedge (see illustration); this will have the same effect and will also restrict the need for further watering after planting.

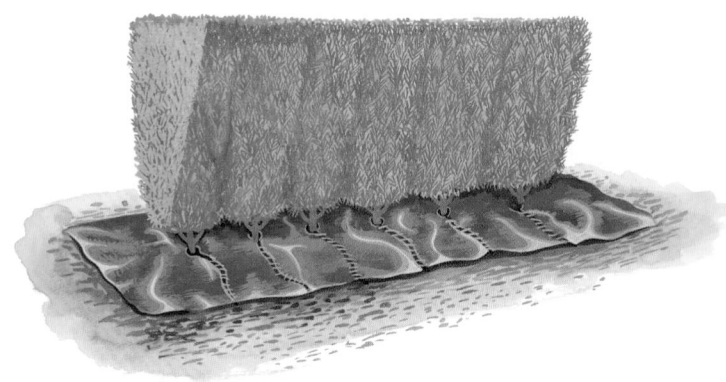

Three settings for flowers: island beds, borders and flower beds

Island beds, borders and flower beds, although similar in their types of planting, differ both in shape and in location. The layout of the garden will often be the deciding factor in the choice of which type to make, but any of the three can provide an attractive setting for a display of flowers and they generally constitute the most colourful and decorative areas of the garden.

Island beds

These are usually cut into a lawn. They can be circular, oval or rectangular in shape, and it must be possible to view them from all sides.

Creating a large island bed

• Unlike those frequently seen in public parks, island beds should not be rounded in the middle. They should be level and set slightly lower than the surrounding lawn; this facilitates water absorption and the spreading of a mulch, which helps to retain moisture in summer and offers protection against frost in winter.

• Taller plants should be placed in the centre, with smaller ones and creepers around the perimeter.

An island bed is relatively easy to establish. The rule is that there are no rules: just give free rein to your imagination. The plants should not be too tightly packed, so that they are all readily visible. Some of the most attractive island beds contain a range of different plants: roses, perennials and shrubs. Others are dedicated to just one type of plant, often roses. They are often bordered by a hedge of box, lavender or santolina.

Creating an island bed in stages

It may not always be possible to establish the large island bed you would like all at once. However, it can be created in stages, by gradually establishing several smaller ones that can then at the appropriate time be joined together to form a single large bed, as follows.

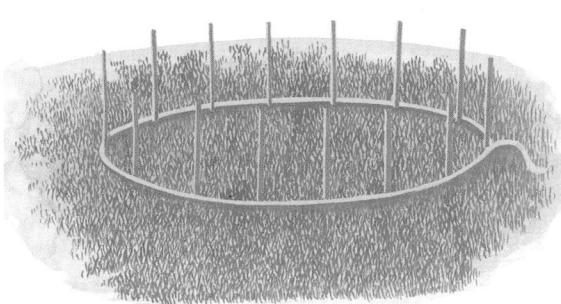

• Mark out the final location of the large bed on the ground (use a hosepipe to do this: any mistakes can be easily rectified).

• Within this 'master' plot, mark out several smaller beds to be established as resources become available. Make a sketch to remind you of what you have planned as you create the individual beds.

• Decide on the bed you are going to start with. Set about establishing that one, leaving the other ones 'on the drawing board' for the time being.

• Once all the beds have been established, the final stage is to fill in the gaps in order to join them up.

Borders and flower beds

Borders

Most borders have one side facing a garden or a path, and the other a wall, a hedge or a building, and are therefore viewed from the front. Like island beds, borders should be level or slope slightly towards the path or garden.

If the border has a hedge on one side, this will absorb a great deal of the rain that falls. Since its roots are likely to interfere with other plants, it is always a good idea to leave a gap of about 50 cm (20 in) between the hedge and the first row of plants; this will also allow access both for tending plants and for cutting the hedge.

A border is the most difficult kind of plot to create. It makes great demands upon the gardener's skills, but success can be yours if you follow the basic rules.

• The border should be at least 2 m (6½ ft) wide.

• It should contain a wide diversity of plants with a variety of different shapes: pointed leaves, jagged leaves, rounded leaves, upright habit, spreading habit etc.

• It is essential to make sure that the plants flower at different times throughout the year.

• The plants that flower first should be positioned in such a way as to be hidden, after their flowering season is over, by plants that flower later.

• Small groups of early-flowering plants, such as bulbs, and late-flowering ones, such as chrysanthemums, dahlias and asters, can be scattered throughout the bed in order to provide colour over a long period.

• Taller plants should be positioned at the back of the bed, with a few groups of tall plants coming forward in sweeps towards the centre to give an impression of movement.

• If you plan to have climbing plants, place them at the back and train them against a wire or wooden framework or against a wall.

Flower beds

A flower bed alongside an avenue or driveway is basically viewed from just one side, i.e. from the driveway.

Beds are created in pretty much the same way as borders, with the relative sizes of the plants always being taken into account, so that taller ones do not block out smaller ones. Generally speaking, flower beds are 1–2 m (3¼–6½ ft) in width and are the favoured location for standard roses and the small, low plants that accompany them: nepetas, lavenders, dianthus and hardy geraniums. However, they can also be designed like borders, overflowing with a multitude of varied plants.

Planting shrubs and flowers in borders and beds

Borders and beds of this kind cannot be simply thrown together; they have to be created either according to a plan or by positioning the various plants on the ground in their containers in order to see the effect they produce. Plan the position of the shrubs first, then the perennials. (For information on choosing plants by height, colour and flowering season, refer to the charts at the end of the book.)

As far as planting proper is concerned, these are the main points to be observed.

• Make sure you leave sufficient space between each of the plants, because in time they will grow to perhaps ten times their current volume.

• The gaps in the first year of planting can be filled in with bulbs or annuals that can be removed as the shrubs become bigger.

• Do not plant shrubs – including roses – in straight lines, and alternate deciduous and evergreen plants, placing species likely to grow tall at the back and leaving wide gaps between them for perennials. Beds and borders can of course be filled solely with shrubs.

• Perennials should be planted in groups of three, five or seven, depending on size, so that the larger ones form clumps or clusters and the medium-sized ones, 40–60 cm (16–24 in) in height, create extended sweeps of colour.

• The smaller plants should be positioned irregularly, with some appearing occasionally among plants of average height.

• It is a good idea to position some plants of average height at the front of borders in order to break up the monotony of a straight line of small plants.

• Avoid positioning your plants in straight rows, and pack the soil down firmly around the stems.

• Bulbs can be used to fill in empty spaces. It is essential to mark their position in some way, in order to avoid the risk of damaging them when planting other plants.

• Annuals are ideal for filling gaps in spring, particularly in the first few years. Plant them from late spring onwards.

• Finally, whenever possible, mark the edge of the border with a row of stones or paving. This will stop the first row of flowers from lying on the lawn.

In the illustration alternate green and grey plants form 'cushions' in the foreground. The next row includes tulips that will flower in spring and can then be replaced by annuals. A series of plants about 60 cm (2 ft) in height comes next, with marguerites and a small tree at the back. These plants will not all bloom at the same time, but as they gradually come into flower they will keep the border full of interest and colour.

Elaborate floral borders of this kind are designed to produce permanent displays; however, you may prefer to use just annuals or perennials, or even just shrubs (which reduces work to the minimum and means you can still plant bulbs). There is a wide choice of evergreen shrubs, but do not take the easy way out by using only small conifers, which would be out of place here.

Planting a floral border for summer
In this floral border alternate greens and greys make up the foreground (hosta, alchemilla, stachys, prunella and sedum). A cluster of tulips has been placed behind them, with artemisias, echinops and peonies. The next row back consists of achilleas, poppies, lupins and delphiniums, and in the background are marguerites, backed by a small tree.

Aspect and soil care

Aspect

Many people believe, wrongly, that all plants need sun, and do their best to find locations in full sun to plant their flowers; however, there are a good many shrubs and perennials that do well in semi-shade (see tables, p. 600). This should be taken into account when deciding where to position plants.

A west-facing aspect is more desirable than an east-facing one, since morning sun can prove very damaging to leaves after night frosts, and north-west is preferable to north-east. A sunny aspect means a wider range of varieties can be planted. That said, however, do not choose a sunny aspect for heathland plants: rhododendrons and azaleas abhor full sun.

Planting time

There are basically two options:

• The first is to plant your shrubs in early spring, after preparing the ground in autumn and then adding the necessary nutrients. In this case, perennials will not be planted out until late spring, and you will have to wait until autumn to plant your spring bulbs. However, you will also be able to plant summer bulbs if you wish.

• The second is to plant shrubs and bulbs in autumn, immediately after preparing the soil, and to plant perennials the following spring so that they do not have to face winter immediately.

Maintenance

After planting beds and borders, mulch with a 5 cm (2 in) layer of peat or bark or a 10 cm (4 in) layer of compost in autumn, in order to protect the young plants during their first winter. In spring, the soil should be raked to cleanse and aerate it.

Trees and shrubs

Choosing trees and shrubs

In both cases, to make a sensible choice you should be guided by the answers to these three questions:

• Is the soil type right for the plant?

• Is the planned location suitable?

• Will the neighbouring plants set it off to good advantage?

A tree is for life

Since any tree you choose as an ornament for your garden will be a permanent feature, it is essential to find out how large it will grow in maturity in order to plant it a reasonable distance from your house and to leave sufficient space between it and any other trees you may plant. A few other small points to bear in mind:

• A single specimen planted on a lawn should be positioned in such a way that you can admire it from the house without it dominating the view too much.

• Beware of trees with a spreading habit: in a few years they may well become too dominant and provide more shade than you had bargained for.

• For small lawns, cone-shaped or even weeping trees are preferable; larger gardens provide a more suitable setting for trees with a spreading habit, even if they are associated with cone or pyramid-shaped trees.

• Finally, you should be aware that a single row of trees planted in a straight line will do nothing to suppress noise (from a road, for example). You need to plant a group of evergreen trees several rows deep in order to reduce noise. The same principle applies to wind.

The importance of shrubs

Shrubs play a major role in gardeners' lives.

There are several reasons for this:

• Shrubs produce immediate results, making a garden look well stocked almost overnight. Relatively few people can employ a gardener these days, and a group of ornamental shrubs that quickly achieve their final shape is infinitely easier to maintain than a border of perennials, a lawn or a bed of annuals.

• It is shrubs that actually give form and structure to borders. Bear this in mind when choosing them.

• Shrubs need only to be planted properly at the outset, and can then be left to their own devices. Of course they need pruning from time to time, and dead branches should be removed, but these tasks require little time.

• Some shrubs described as delicate or unsuited to exposed gardens can be grown successfully when planted against a wall, which will offer them considerable protection against cold and wind.

• Container growing means that shrubs can be planted throughout the year. As a result of this revolution, more varieties from all over the world are constantly coming on to the market: hundreds of different species, some of which flower and give out a fragrance in winter, while others have stems that are as spectacular as their foliage. Even if there are flowers only in spring and summer, a garden can still be a magnificent sight all the year round. It can even be stocked with nothing but shrubs.

A word of warning, however. Most container-grown shrubs are also raised under glass. Planting these shrubs out too early in the season can have fatal consequences, so they should be kept under shelter until the risk of frost has finally passed. There is nothing to be gained by planting them out too early. This applies particularly to magnolias, *Lavatera olbia*, *Choisya ternata* and other shrubs of average hardiness.

How to plant a tree or shrub

The planting of a tree or shrub is of fundamental importance, since it determines its whole future. A badly planted tree, one jammed too tightly into its hole or starved of adequate nutrients, cannot grow properly or develop to its full potential. As a result, some species never reach the heights indicated in the catalogues. What may seem an anomaly can be due to several factors:

• The quality of the soil is not suitable for the plant.

• The plant lacks water or humus.

• Poor planting may have retarded its development.

Planting procedure

The first precaution to take is to ensure that tree roots are not exposed to the air before planting; they should rather be covered with damp cloths, straw or any other protection against sun, wind or simply the drying effects of the air. So even before digging the hole, you should make sure you have everything you will need to hand at the site. You will require:

• A large plastic sheet on which to put the soil removed from the hole. This will be particularly useful if you are planting in a lawn or a flower bed that already contains other plants.

• A watering can full of water.

• One part sand (to lighten the soil if it is heavy and dense).

• One part peat.

• One part leaf-mould.

Bonemeal and dried blood can be purchased at all good garden centres. The taller a tree will eventually grow, the more nutrients it will require in the first years of its life.

Break up the soil on the sides and bottom of the hole so that the roots of the tree can penetrate easily. Spread the mixture of leaf-mould, peat or bark and sand over the bottom of the hole. On top of this mixture, place a 20 cm (8 in) layer of topsoil mixed with 100 g (4 oz) of bonemeal

(the best slow-acting fertilizer there is) and 50 g (2 oz) of dried blood. The tree can now be placed in the hole; care should be taken to ensure that the soil mark at the base of the stem, which indicates the original planting depth, is level with the surface of the soil.

Dealing with delay

There are two options:
• If your shrubs have arrived and you are unable to plant them immediately because of frost, rain or lack of time, lay them in a hole in a shady, draught-free spot and cover the roots with peat or compost. The plants can remain stored like this for several weeks if their growth is not too far advanced. Once mid-spring is past, this strategy becomes risky, particularly for flowering shrubs and roses.
• Given the same circumstances, you could also place bare-rooted shrubs in containers filled with good garden soil; with this approach, there is no risk in waiting for an opportunity to plant them out, as long as you keep the roots well buried in the soil.

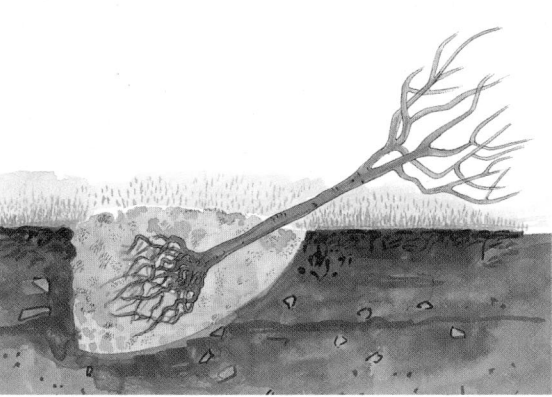

Before planting bare-rooted or root-balled trees and shrubs, cut back any excessively long or broken roots.

It is virtually impossible to plant bare-rooted trees in frosty or very wet weather, but they can be stored temporarily in a hole filled with compost or peat, where the roots will not be damaged by either cold or lack of moisture. They can be kept like this for up to a month.

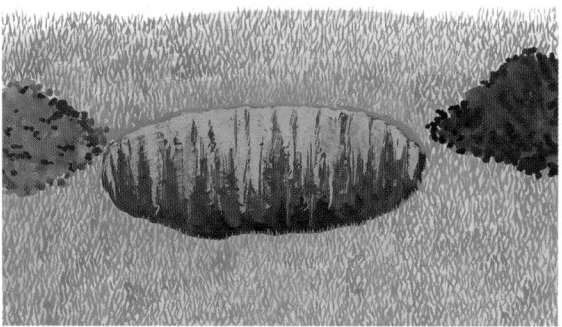

For a tree or shrub of reasonable size, dig a hole some time in advance of planting, separating topsoil from subsoil. Leave the hole open to the air.

When planting, make sure the soil mark at the base of the stem (which indicates the tree's original planting depth) is flush with the surface of the ground. A spade laid across the hole can act as a guide to the level required.

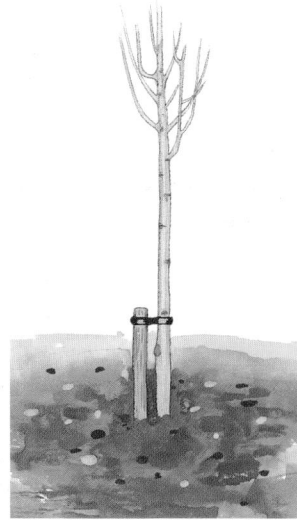

Tie bare-rooted or root-balled trees to a stake immediately after planting. They should be firmly attached, but not too tightly – expert studies show that a tree's roots do not develop unless it can move a little.

Aftercare

The soil should be well firmed around the tree or shrub, which should then be attached to its stake. It is important not to overtighten the ties, however, in order to allow for movement as the tree develops. If you are planting out in autumn, protect the soil with a mulch of leaf-mould, peat or bark, which will enrich the soil at the same time; do not use any chemical fertilizer (this applies to all newly planted trees or shrubs). The tree can be pruned lightly in order to improve its shape and to encourage the onset of growth. This is especially important for deciduous trees and shrubs, but also applies to newly planted hedges and roses.

Protecting a young tree
If rabbits gnaw the bark of a tree, it may die. Deer also have a liking for bark. Plastic guards, like the one shown here wrapped around the base of the trunk (allowing the tree full freedom to grow), can be bought in garden centres.

Some reasons why a tree or shrub might die

• The ground was poorly prepared or the soil not sufficiently broken down. Roots were over-exposed to the air before planting, or had dried out.

• The root ball was broken and the roots damaged.

• A herbicide was used on the site before planting.

• The soil was not sufficiently well firmed around the roots when the plant was put in the ground.

• The roots were smothered in water-logged soil.

• The tree was buried too deeply on planting.

• The tree was attacked by a virus disease.

• The plant was not watered sufficiently during the first year after planting.

• The tree was not suited to the soil.

A gardening revolution: planting under plastic

This new planting technique, much used along motorways and in green spaces where plant maintenance is virtually impossible, can now be adapted for use in gardens. It involves covering the chosen planting area first with a 5 cm (2 in) layer of sand and then with a plastic sheet which will provide sufficient protection for trees and shrubs to develop under optimal conditions. They will not require weeding or watering, because the plastic sheet will protect the roots from bad weather, stop weed growth and maintain a constant level of soil humidity.

The method

• Prepare the ground for planting in the traditional way.

• If the soil is too heavy or too poor, add a mix of sand, peat (or bark) and compost.

• Water generously and rake over the ground in order to level it off.

• Stretch plastic grow sheeting (sold by the metre in garden or do-it-yourself stores) over the whole area.

Mark out the planting area by cutting the desired shape out of the lawn; remove the plants from their containers.

Cover the area in plastic sheeting, splitting it if necessary to make room for existing trees.

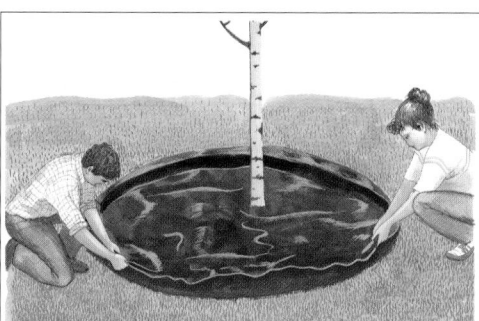

Cut cross-shaped openings in the sheet in the places where you want to plant shrubs or perennials. Plant them, then press the plastic down around the base of the stems.

Finish off with a mulch of gravel, bark or compost, both to secure the plastic and to conceal it. The mulch itself can be hidden under ground cover or rock plants. Water well.

• Secure this protective sheeting either with pegs or by burying the edges 10–15 cm (4–6 in) under the ground.

• Cut cross-shaped openings at the places where you want to plant shrubs or trees, and fold back the corners in order to clear a space for planting.

• Plant your shrubs or trees and press the plastic down around the bases of the stems.

• All that remains to be done is to hide the plastic sheeting under a few centimetres of peat, mulch, gravel or shredded bark.

The advantages The roots will be protected not only against heat, cold and frost but also against invasion by weeds (putting an end to the tedious chores of hoeing and weeding). There will no longer be any need to water either, since the protective sheet locks in moisture. This technique is ideal for planting and maintaining trees, shrubs and hedges.

The disadvantages The method is less suited to seasonal plants (bulbs or annuals). It is possible, nevertheless, to cut out pockets in the plastic sheeting at the places where you want to plant them.

Moving a large shrub

Gardeners are often hesitant about embarking on this procedure, but it may be necessary when plants have grown larger than planned. Both for their well-being and for the general appearance of the garden, it is better to move a large specimen than to allow it to smother its neighbours, particularly since such transplanting is without risk if properly done. It is best to carry out the operation at the end of winter, after the frosts, or in early autumn so that the plant has time to establish itself before the really cold weather sets in. It is evergreens such as rhododendrons, osmanthus and *Viburnum tinus* that require the greatest care; deciduous plants can often be cut back in order to create some space.

The technique

• Lift up the lower branches and tie them so as to leave the bottom of the shrub free.

• Dig a trench all the way round the shrub, about 50 cm (20 in) from the trunk and 50 cm (20 in) deep, cutting the roots where necessary.

• Using a spade as a lever, lift the shrub from its position and slide some sacking (not plastic) under the roots.

• Wrap the roots in this protective sacking and carry the plant straight to its new hole, which will have been prepared and watered in advance. (This part of the operation requires two people.)

• Place the shrub in the hole, taking care not to dislodge the soil around the roots when you open up the sacking. Fill the hole with equal proportions of sand, peat or bark and soil. After planting and watering, spread a 10 cm (4 in) deep mulch all around the plant.

To move a large shrub

Start by tying the branches tightly in order to make handling easier.

With a spade or fork, carefully dig out the root ball.

Tilt the entire plant and, having cut the central roots that stop the root ball from freeing itself, slip a sheet of sacking under the roots.

Tie the sheet around the stem of the shrub and slide a wooden bar through the knot; this will allow the plant to be lifted and carried to its new location.

Place the shrub in its new hole, firm the soil and water generously.

**How to recognize
conifers**

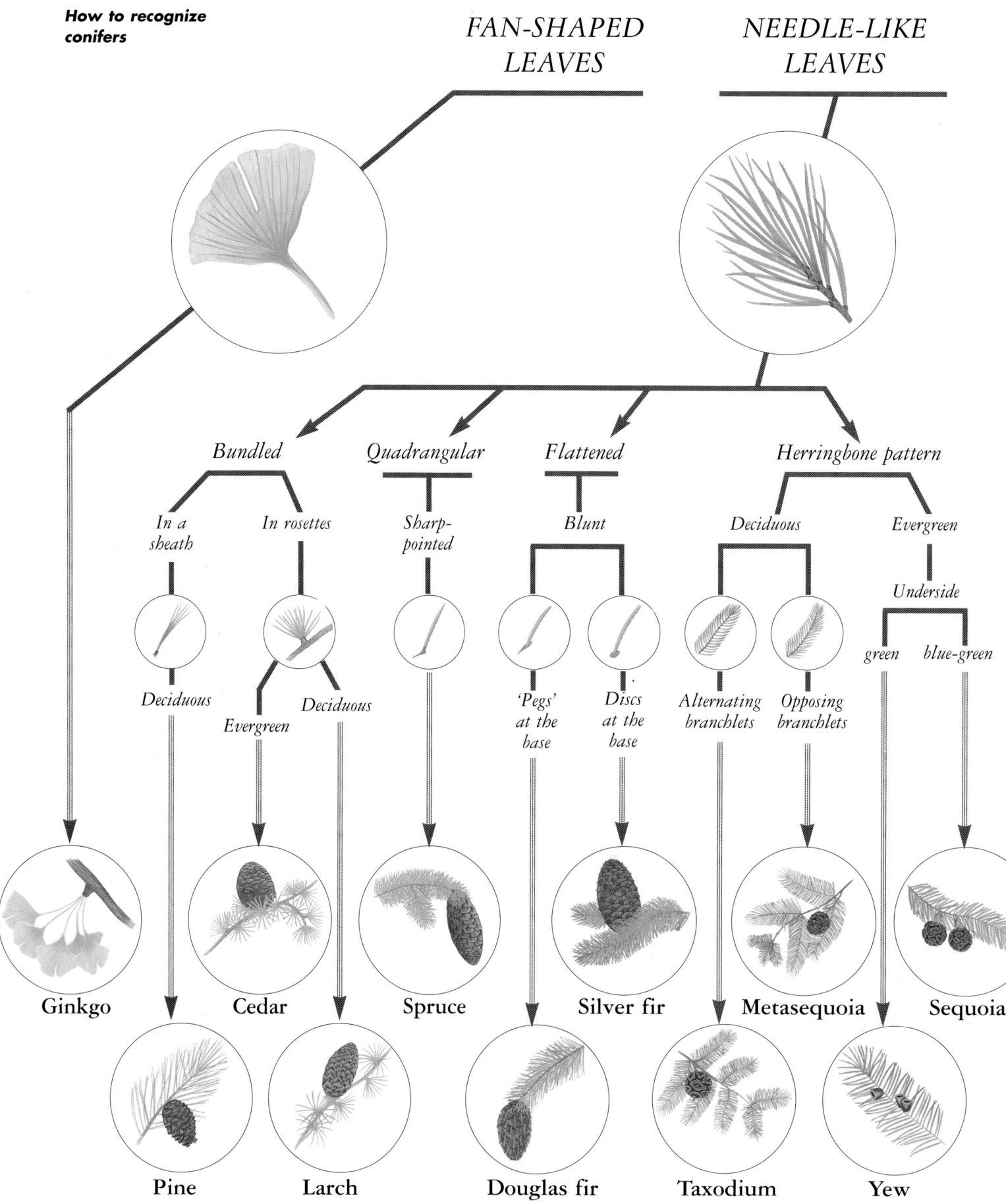

FAN-SHAPED
LEAVES

NEEDLE-LIKE
LEAVES

Bundled

Quadrangular

Flattened

Herringbone pattern

*In a
sheath*

In rosettes

*Sharp-
pointed*

Blunt

Deciduous

Evergreen

Underside

Deciduous

Evergreen

Deciduous

green   *blue-green*

*'Pegs'
at the
base*

*Discs
at the
base*

*Alternating
branchlets*

*Opposing
branchlets*

Ginkgo

Cedar

Spruce

Silver fir

Metasequoia

Sequoia

Pine

Larch

Douglas fir

Taxodium

Yew

SCALE-LIKE LEAVES

Observe closely the needles or scales of conifers (which are actually their leaves) and you will easily be able to tell them apart.

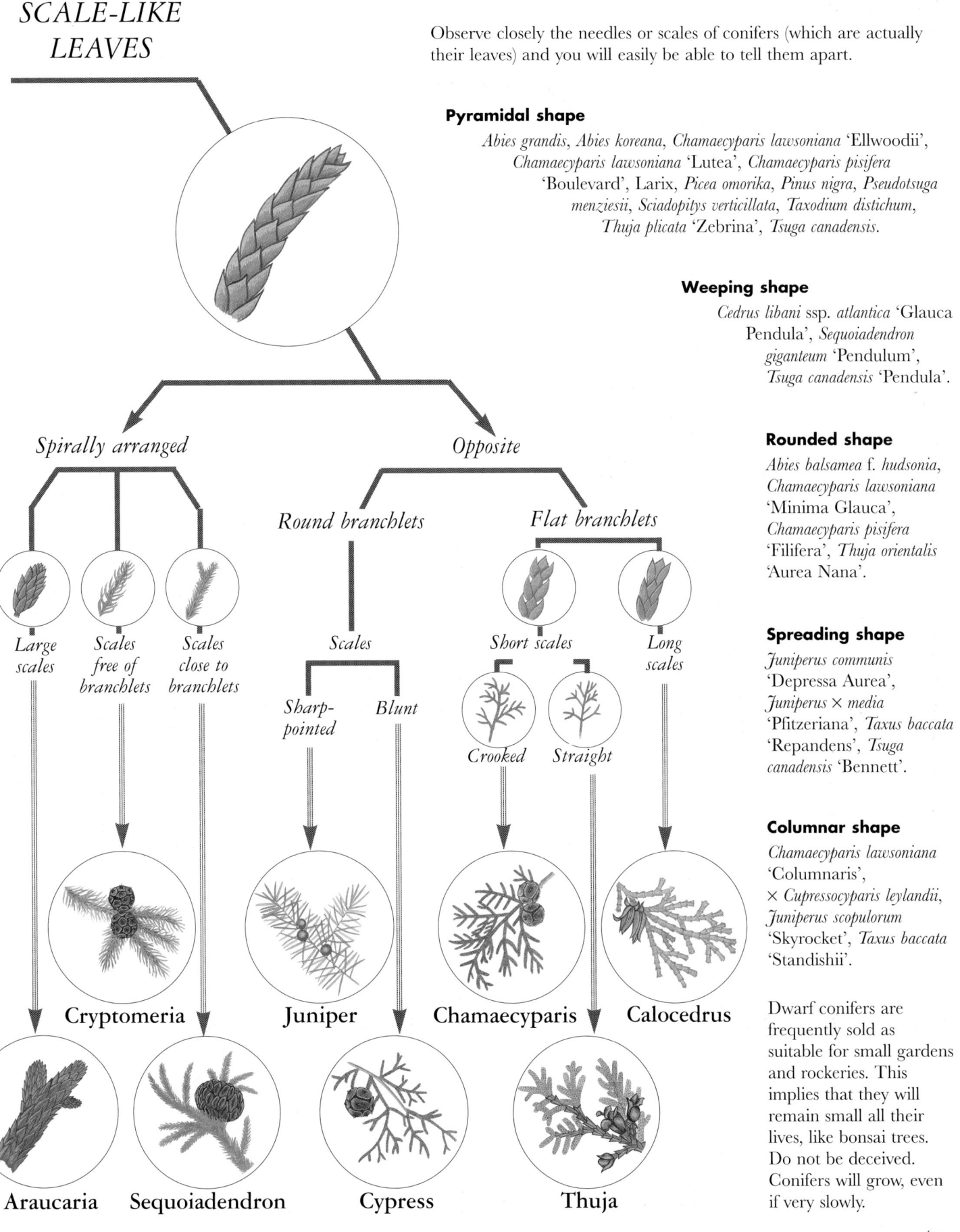

Pyramidal shape

Abies grandis, Abies koreana, Chamaecyparis lawsoniana 'Ellwoodii', *Chamaecyparis lawsoniana* 'Lutea', *Chamaecyparis pisifera* 'Boulevard', *Larix, Picea omorika, Pinus nigra, Pseudotsuga menziesii, Sciadopitys verticillata, Taxodium distichum, Thuja plicata* 'Zebrina', *Tsuga canadensis*.

Weeping shape

Cedrus libani ssp. *atlantica* 'Glauca Pendula', *Sequoiadendron giganteum* 'Pendulum', *Tsuga canadensis* 'Pendula'.

Rounded shape

Abies balsamea f. *hudsonia, Chamaecyparis lawsoniana* 'Minima Glauca', *Chamaecyparis pisifera* 'Filifera', *Thuja orientalis* 'Aurea Nana'.

Spreading shape

Juniperus communis 'Depressa Aurea', *Juniperus × media* 'Pfitzeriana', *Taxus baccata* 'Repandens', *Tsuga canadensis* 'Bennett'.

Columnar shape

Chamaecyparis lawsoniana 'Columnaris', *× Cupressocyparis leylandii, Juniperus scopulorum* 'Skyrocket', *Taxus baccata* 'Standishii'.

Dwarf conifers are frequently sold as suitable for small gardens and rockeries. This implies that they will remain small all their lives, like bonsai trees. Do not be deceived. Conifers will grow, even if very slowly.

Spirally arranged

Opposite

Round branchlets

Flat branchlets

Large scales

Scales free of branchlets

Scales close to branchlets

Scales

Short scales

Long scales

Sharp-pointed

Blunt

Crooked

Straight

Cryptomeria

Juniper

Chamaecyparis

Calocedrus

Araucaria

Sequoiadendron

Cypress

Thuja

Flowers

Annuals and perennials

Annuals are planted in spring and end their growth cycle in summer or autumn, while perennials are planted during either autumn or spring and remain in the ground for a long time, growing larger and sometimes seeding themselves each year.

A well-stocked garden generally includes both annuals and perennials, but it can be useful to know their respective advantages and drawbacks.

Annuals

These last only one summer, but a garden should not be without them because they are very attractive, varied and colourful.

Advantages and drawbacks

• Annuals are rewarding for the amateur gardener, even a novice, because they come in a large variety of species and colours.

• Their flowering period often lasts longer than that of perennials, provided you dead-head them regularly.

• They are inexpensive if you buy them in trays and even cheaper if you sow them yourself.

• You can have a different display each year, as new varieties are always coming on to the market.

• Their major drawback, if you want to grow them yourself from seed (see the table on p. 553), is the long interval (sometimes several months) between sowing the seed and the flowers appearing.

• In addition, the plant dies at the end of the summer and the garden is bare from autumn onwards.

Planting out

Annuals bought in trays or pots are planted out in late spring and early summer, when there is no more danger of frost. To ensure continuous flowering, it is necessary to dead-head them regularly. Only when the autumn frosts start should you dig up the plants.

Perennials

Perennials should last for many years.

Advantages and drawbacks

• Perennials are rewarding because they reappear each year.

• Their propagation is easy: the plants are divided to make more, which can be used in other parts of the garden.

To help container-grown plants to establish themselves quickly, loosen the exterior roots of the root ball as delicately as possible before planting.

To plant perennials, use a hand trowel and loosen the soil well. Take the plant out of its container and plant it gently but firmly, taking care to keep the correct spacing between plants.

• Finally, perennials need far less work than annuals: they need to be divided only every 3–5 years.

• Their major drawback is the fact that they spread: some can even become invasive.

• Once sown, the seeds take longer to germinate, and the flowers to appear, than those of annuals.

A warning on purchasing perennials

Perennials are generally sold in containers and come on to the market from late winter and early spring onwards. It is important to remember that these small plants have been grown in the greenhouse – they are therefore fragile and will be unable to tolerate late frosts. If you wish to plant them out nevertheless, provide some form of protection in case of hard night frost. A simple protective covering will save a few degrees in temperature.

Planting out

Perennials are the easiest of all to plant. However, the results will not always be as you expect unless you allow the correct spacing between plants. Generally speaking, you can take the following as a spacing guide:

• plants under 20 cm (8 in) in height: 10 plants per sq. m (10 sq. ft);

• plants 20–40 cm (8–16 in) in height: 8 per sq. m (10 sq. ft);

• plants 40–70 cm (16–28 in) in height: 6 per sq. m (10 sq. ft);

• plants 70–100 cm (28–40 in) in height: 3 per sq. m (10 sq. ft);

• spectacular plants taller than 100 cm (40 in): 1 per sq. m (10 sq. ft).

Planting is carried out either in spring or in autumn, in watered and well-prepared soil.

The best tool for planting perennials is a trowel. Make a hole at least four times the size of the plant, breaking up the subsoil and the surrounding soil thoroughly, as the roots are fragile.

The bottom of the hole should be filled with compost mixed with approximately one dessert-spoon of hoof and horn, a slow-acting fertilizer. Once planted, the root ball should be covered with a mixture of one-third soil, one-third compost and one-third sand. Take care not to let the soil dry out.

If the plant seems very dry when you remove it from its container, soak it in a bucket of water for a few minutes before planting. This is more effective than overhead watering.

Climbers

There are two kinds of climbers: those that have to be trained and tied in along a support, such as roses, and those that climb naturally, such as pyracantha, ivy, honeysuckle, *Hydrangea petiolaris* and clematis. If you plant them beside a trellis, a tree or a wall, they will establish themselves quickly.

Take care, however, not to let these plants become intertwined; a distance of 2 m (6½ ft) is a minimum. When planting, tilt the root-ball so that the roots face away from the wall or tree.

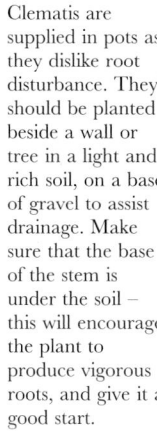

Clematis are supplied in pots as they dislike root disturbance. They should be planted beside a wall or tree in a light and rich soil, on a base of gravel to assist drainage. Make sure that the base of the stem is under the soil – this will encourage the plant to produce vigorous roots, and give it a good start.

Clematis – a particular case

There is an infinite variety of clematis, and they can be in flower from spring through to autumn depending on the varieties selected. They are marvellous plants, adapting well to different situations. They can be very effective in the garden. However, I have often heard people day: 'Clematis just don't work for me.' Here is what you need to know.

• Clematis prefer an alkaline soil.

• They need room for their roots to grow.

• They should be planted a little at an angle, so that 10 cm (4 in) of the stem is under the soil.

• The bottom of the stem should be totally protected from the sun, up to 15 cm (6 in).

Training clematis up a wall is not the only method. You can plant one beside an evergreen shrub; it will grow through the branches and will flower abundantly. Clematis need to be well-watered at the start of the growing season, and they will benefit from a 10 cm (4 in) mulch of grass-cuttings or leaf-mould.

Note: *Like clematis, ivy also needs to be planted at an angle with about 10 cm (4 in) of stem buried in the ground.*

Bulbs

When people talk of bulbs, they generally think of spring flowers such as daffodils, tulips and crocuses. However, there are bulbs that can be planted to flower for all seasons (see the calendar on bulb flowering, p. 549).

Planting techniques

You cannot go wrong when planting bulbs, as long as you plant them at the correct depth. This varies according to bulb size. As a general rule, reckon on planting them at a depth of once or twice their height, in ordinary garden soil. Narcissi, however, are best planted a few centimetres deeper. Spring bulbs are usually planted in autumn, for flowering six months later. (If you delay planting by a month or two, however, you can obtain a later flowering.) It is not advisable to keep fleshy-scaled bulbs, such as lilies and fritillaries, which quickly dry out. They should be planted as soon as you buy them, unless the ground is frozen.

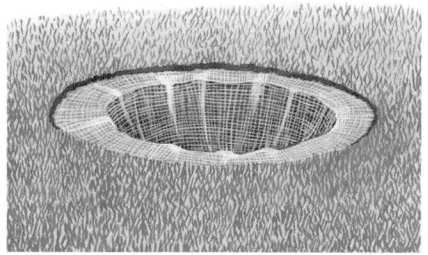

For easy removal of bulbs (tulips, gladioli) from a temporary planting place, line the planting hole with a thin, unbreakable net.

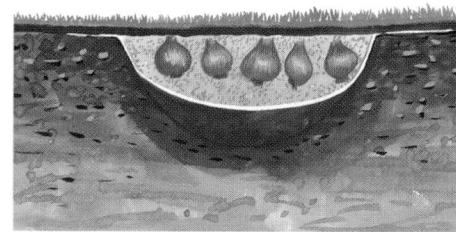

Fill the hole with a mixture of soil and sand and plant the bulbs, covering the hole with grass if you wish.

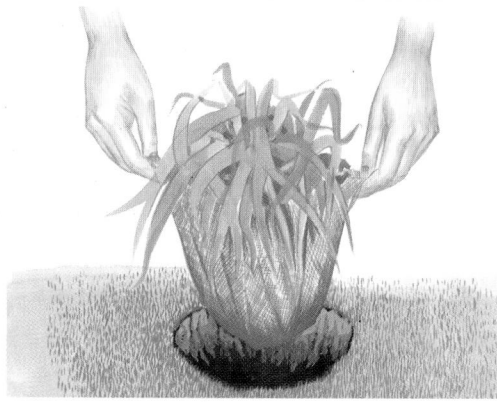

When the foliage has died down after flowering, remove the bulbs by pulling up the net. The hole is then ready for the next batch.

• **Planting out** Use a rounded bulb trowel, with which you can dig a flat-bottomed hole. Place the bulb in the hole, pointed tip upwards, its base in perfect contact with the soil. A traditional trowel is not suitable: its pointed shape allows an air pocket to remain at the bottom of the planting hole. A trowel is practical if you only have a few bulbs to plant or if you are working in stages. Otherwise, the job becomes a long and tiring chore.

• **If you want to group several bulbs together** in order to produce a massed effect, you will have to plant your bulbs differently. Use a spade to dig a fairly large flat-bottomed hole. On the bottom spread a layer of about 5 cm (2 in) of soil mixed with an equal amount of sand. Put your bulbs in place (as above), allowing 5–10 cm (2–4 in) space between them. Cover the bulbs with soil and water them in. Mark their position clearly, so you will not risk damaging them when hoeing or planting above them.

• **To make it easier to take up your bulbs** from a temporary planting place (tulips or gladioli, for example), first line the planting hole with a thin, unbreakable net. Fill the hole with a mixture of soil and sand, place the bulbs in it, and cover with soil. After the bulbs have flowered and their foliage has died down, all you will need to do is pull on the net.

• **All bulbs can stay in the ground** from one year to the next except for frost-tender kinds. Tulips, however, apart from the botanical species, will flower less well if left in the ground.

• **When planting lilies** among large shrubs, particularly rhododendrons, whose roots may damage them, isolate the lily bulbs by first planting a large container, with the base removed, and planting the bulbs inside it.

Different uses for bulbs

Narcissi, tulips, grape hyacinths, fritillaries and crocuses are all bulbs with multiple uses.

• **In the lawn** The bulbs will naturalize and reproduce themselves easily. If you have planted them at random among the grass, take care not to mow the lawn until their foliage has completely died down. If you plant them in specific areas it is easier to protect them by mowing around them.

If you want to plant a large number of bulbs in a particular area of a lawn, first mark out your planting area, and dig out the soil and grass with a spade to a reasonable depth. Break up the soil and add some sand. Put in the bulbs, and cover them with soil to the depth of the soil and grass previously removed.

• **Ground cover** This is the kind of planting bulbs prefer, because the soil has been enriched by falling leaves. Plant hardy bulbs, such as crocuses, eranthis, bluebells and narcissi, in autumn. You can plant cyclamen later, in summer.

• **In beds and borders** Since the soil has been previously prepared you can use a bulb trowel to put the bulbs in, but plant them more deeply than you would if planting in a container or in the lawn. If they are too shallowly planted they may be damaged by hoeing or digging. Mark their position clearly. Plant them close together for an attractive effect. For tulips, avoid too much of a mixture of colours.

• **In a rock garden** This is the ideal place for small bulbs which need to be seen close up. Avoid sophisticated, large-flowered bulbs here. The rock garden is the place where vividly-coloured bulbs planted in small groups of five to six can best be appreciated, and they will thrive happily alongside small conifers and alpine plants.

Note: Bulbs do not require regular watering.

Calendar of flowering bulbs
Winter
Eranthis hyemalis – Galanthus caucasicus – Galanthus nivalis – Iris danfordiae – Iris histrioides – Puschkinia scilloides – Scilla tubergeniana

Early to mid-spring
Anemone blanda – Allium karataviense – Anemone nemorosa – Arum italicum – Chionodoxa luciliae – Colchicum luteum – Corydalis cashmeriana – crocus – cyclamen – erythronium – *Fritillaria camschatcensis – Fritillaria imperialis – Fritillaria meleagris* – hyacinth – *Iris reticulata – Leucojum aestivum – Leucojum vernum* – grape hyacinth – *Narcissus bulbocodium – Narcissus jonquila* – ornithogalum – pleiones – *Scilla sibirica – Tulipa clusiana – Tulipa fosteriana – Tulipa praestans – Tulipa sylvestris*

Late spring to early summer
Allium giganteum – Allium neapolitanum – Allium moly – Anemone × fulgens – Arum creticum – camassia – dierama – *Eremurus bungei – Eremurus himalaicus – Fritillaria persica – Gladiolus communis* – hippeastrum – ixia – *Lilium candidum – Rhodohypoxis baurii – Scilla peruviana – Zantedeschia aethiopica*

Mid- to late summer
begonia – canna – cardiocrinum – crocosmia – *Cyclamen hederifolium – Cyclamen purpurascens* – dahlia – eucomis – freesia – *Gladiolus callianthus – Galtonia candicans – Iris latifolia – Lilium auratum – Lilium canadense – Lilium hansonii – Lilium henryi – Lilium martagon – Ornithogalum arabicum – Oxalis tetraphylla* – ranunculus – *Tigridia pavonia* – tropaeolum – zantedeschia

Early to mid-autumn
Amaryllis belladonna – Arum italicum – Colchicum speciosum – Galanthus nivalis

Late autumn to winter
Cyclamen coum – Nerine bowdenii – Schizostylis coccinea

Planting a rhododendron in unsuitable soil

If you want to have rhododendrons in your garden but your soil is not acid enough for them, you can successfully make a place for them by lining a hole with polythene (with drainage holes at the bottom) and filling it with acid soil.

Do not plant them in full sun. Semi-shade, near trees, suits them very well. Although they do not like excessive moisture, rhododendrons must not be allowed to dry out. A peat or bark mulch will help retain moisture.

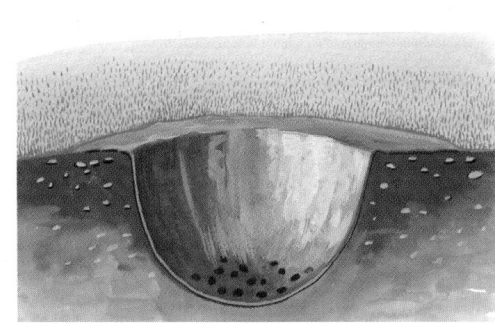

To plant an acid-loving plant in unsuitable soil, dig a hole 1 m (3¼ ft) square by 80 cm (32 in) deep, so that the reserve of soil can last for some years, and line it with plastic sheeting. Prick holes in the bottom for drainage.

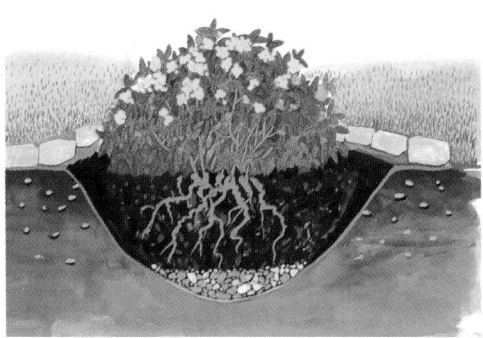

Fill your planting hole with an acid mixture (two-thirds of acid soil, one-third peat), or a proprietary ericaceous compost. Place the plant in this, and disguise the edges of the plastic cover with pebbles or stones.

Roses

It is quite likely that the first flowering shrub many gardeners plant will be a rose.

The longevity and health of a rose will depend on where and how it is planted. It needs a sunny position (a minimum of 50 per cent sunshine each day), sheltered from the wind (its strongest enemy), and a fertile, well-drained soil. Roses are not difficult to grow as far as soil type is concerned.

Planting period

In areas where the winters are harsh, such as North America and northern Europe, roses should preferably be planted at the beginning of spring. In hot climates they should be planted in the middle of winter, and in temperate climates, either in autumn or at the beginning of spring.

Planting

• Never plant a rose in soil where roses have grown previously.

• If you cannot plant roses immediately, keep them in a container or in their packing, in dry conditions, in a place where there is no risk of frost.

• Before planting, make up a mixture of water and soil, add a dose of dry rose fertilizer (available from garden centres), and stand the roses in this mixture for half an hour or so.

• Prepare your planting soil. It should be made up of a mixture of one half good garden soil, one quarter peat, and one quarter coarse sand, with the addition of a handful of bonemeal.

• Dig a hole at least three times the area of the roots in width and depth, and fill it with soil once you have put in the roses.

• If you are planting in spring, you can carry out the first pruning immediately. If you are planting in autumn, wait until spring to prune them.

Lightly cut back the stems and trim the roots, removing all dead or damaged wood. As always when working with thorny branches, arm yourself with thick gloves.

Use a stake, placed horizontally, to place your rose bush correctly in the planting hole, taking care that the budding point (the place where a swelling may be found) is at ground level or just above it. If you bury the budding point, you will encourage suckers to grow.

Budding point

Fill the hole with soil, then water abundantly in order to settle the soil around the roots and remove air pockets. Prune in the usual way the following late winter to spring.

Care

• For early flowering and to keep your roses healthy, give them a handful of proprietary fertilizer at the end of spring or the beginning of summer.

• A mulch of 10 cm (4 in) of compost or bark around the roots at the beginning of spring will help to retain moisture and prevent the growth of weeds, which would be difficult to remove.

• Finally, roses must be dead-headed regularly. All waste material – leaves, dead branches and withered flowers – from roses should be burned to prevent spread of diseases.

Terminology

The term 'remontant' is frequently misunderstood. A rose bush is known as remontant when it flowers again after its first flowering in summer. After a flowerless period which varies in length according to variety, the remontant rose will flower again, sometimes up to the first frosts.

Plants offer the amateur gardener a number of means of propagating them in large quantities: it is fascinating and often easy, and the young plants obtained this way will cost far less than those purchased at a garden centre. The classic method of plant propagation is sowing seed, but it has its disadvantages: not all plants produce seed, some do not reproduce reliably by this means, and it is sometimes a very slow method of reproduction.

You have the further choice between propagation by cuttings, which enables you to obtain a complete plant from small sections; layering, by which roots are encouraged to grow on a stem before this stem is separated from the main plant; grafting, which combines the roots of a plant that is easy to grow with the shoots of a more delicate plant; and division, or the separating of plant roots into sections, each of which rapidly grows into a new plant.

Seeds

Producing your own plants from seed is one of the great joys of gardening. It is the cheapest form of propagation, but is also the method which requires the most care and attention.

Seeds

The seeds you buy in packets should pose no problems if you follow the dates indicated and as long as the packets have been stored in a cool dry place. However, when using seeds from your own garden, since some seeds lose their germinating faculty with age, the best guarantee of success is to sow the seeds soon (a few days or weeks) after collecting them from the plant. Do not be impatient if your seedlings take time to appear: not all seeds germinate in the same way. Some are slower than others. They seem to know themselves when the time is right for germination.

How to sow seeds

• There are several ways of sowing seeds, according to the kind of plant, its habit, or its cultivation. Seeds of hardy plants which will stay in the same place until they flower may be sown directly in the open air, whereas the seeds of plants that are less tolerant of the cold should be sown in containers, pots or seed trays at home or in the greenhouse, to be planted out subsequently in the garden.

• As to the actual sowing method, this also differs depending on the size of the seed, and whether it is to be sown in drifts (a method we have seen for lawns – see p. 531), or in drills. This method, which is ideal for annuals, is explained in detail below.

• Whichever method of sowing is used, whether the seeds are sown in trays, pots or in the soil, one of the most vital conditions of success is that the soil should be well prepared.

Sowing in the soil

Preparing the soil

• To sow directly into the soil, start by digging deeply in autumn, incorporating leaf-mould. Leave the soil for the winter.

• In the spring, break up the clods of soil, weed, rake over in order to obtain a fine tilth, and incorporate a fertilizer. Wait until spring before sowing annuals which will flower in the place they are sown. The weather will guide you: it is important that the soil should have warmed up and that there is no more danger of morning frost. Choose a day when there is no wind.

• Just before sowing, water the soil so that the seeds have moisture to start the germination process. You will not need to do this again.

Sowing in drills

• Make shallow furrows in the soil, using a garden line stretched alone each row to ensure that it is straight.

• If your seeds are very fine, mix them in the hollow of your hand with an equal part of very fine sand.

• Sow your seeds in the furrows and draw some soil over them with the back of a rake.

• When the seedlings have two leaves, this is the time to thin them out, leaving one plant every 5–6 cm (2–2½ in). You will need to thin them out again 10–15 days later, this time leaving a gap of 20 cm (8 in) between plants. After each thinning out, water well to settle the soil.

• If you sow your seeds over only half the soil area, you can use the remaining half to transplant seedlings removed during thinning out.

• To protect your seeds from the birds, use sticks with ribbons of silver foil attached.

Factors which prevent or delay the germination of seeds

• The seeds were poorly stored, in a place that was too hot.

• The seeds were stored in packets that were not properly sealed, thus letting the damp in.

• You chose the wrong time to sow them.

• Poor soil.

• The soil had had chemical treatment.

• The soil was not watered before sowing.

• The seeds were too old.

• The seeds were insufficiently mature (they thus take longer to germinate).

• The temperature did not suit them.

• The seeds were too hot. Plants from temperate climates need to be exposed to a real (or artificial) winter in order to germinate. This is the secret of success with meconopsis (blue poppies), aquilegias (columbine) and many mountain plants. You should store your seeds in a cool but frost-proof place.

• The seeds were too cold. Tropical indoor plants, or hot-climate plants (non-hardy annuals and perennials) such as *Begonia semperflorens* or scarlet salvias, need a temperature of 18–20°C (64–68°F) to germinate well.

Sowing in a seed tray

Fill a tray or box with seed compost, firm it down and level.

Water evenly with a fine watering can spray and leave to drain, before sowing the seeds as evenly as possible. Label.

Treat immediately with a fungicide suitable for the control of the seedling disease, damping off. Repeat this treatment every 8 days.

Cover with a piece of glass or place the tray in a small greenhouse, in the light.

When the seedlings have germinated and begin to crowd each other out, prick them out (a term which means transplanting). Using a stick or a well-sharpened pencil, lift up a group of seedlings.

Remove one seedling at a time, by lifting it up by a leaf. Prick out into another tray or box of seed compost, spacing out well.

Sowing annuals

	Colours	Flowering period	Planting distance in cm	Aspect	Sown under glass at 18°C (64°F)	Sown under glass at 10°C (50°F)	Sown under forcing frame	Sown in place
Ageratum (floss flower)	blue, white, pink	sum to aut	15–20	○ ●			mid-spr	
Alyssum	white, pink, mauve	sum to aut	15–20	○		mid-spr	mid-spr	spr/aut
Antirrhinum (snapdragon)	all colours except blue	sum to aut	25–30	○ ●			early spr	
Begonia	white, pink, red	sum to aut	15–25	○ ● ◗			win	
Calendula (marigold)	cream, yellow, orange	spr to sum	20	○ ●		mid-spr	mid-spr	mid-spr/aut
Callistephus chinensis (China aster)	various	sum to aut	20–35	○ ●		mid-spr	late spr	
Centaurea cyanus (cornflower)	white, blue, pink, red	sum to aut	30–45	○ ●				mid-spr/aut
Chrysanthemum	all colours, mixed	sum to aut	25–35	○ ●		mid-spr	mid-spr	
Convolvulus tricolor	red, purple	spr to aut	25	○ ●			mid-spr	
Cosmos	white, pink, red, orange	sum to aut	30–50	○ ●			mid-spr	
Dahlia	various	sum to aut	30–60	○ ●		mid-spr	mid-spr	
Delphinium	white, pink, red, blue	sum to aut	15–35	○ ●				aut
Dimorphotheca (African daisy, Cape marigold)	white, orange	sum to aut	25	○		mid-spr		late spr
Eschscholzia	yellow, orange, cream	sum to aut	15–25	○				mid-spr/aut
Gaillardia (blanket flower)	various	sum to aut	25	○		mid-spr	mid-spr	
Godetia	white, pink, red	sum	20–25	○ ●				mid-spr/aut
Gypsophila	white, pink, red	sum to aut	5–10	○				mid-spr/aut
Helianthus (sunflower)	yellow, orangeish	sum to aut	60	○ ●				mid-spr
Helichrysum	white, pink, red	sum to aut	20	○	mid-spr		mid-spr	mid-spr
Iberis	white, pink, red, mauve	spr to aut	15–25	○				late spr
Ipomoea purpurea	white, blue, pink, mixed	sum to aut	30	○	mid-spr	mid-spr	mid-spr	
Lathyrus odoratus (sweet pea)	various	sum to aut	20	○	early spr	late spr	mid-spr	mid-spr/aut
Lavatera (tree mallow)	white, pink	sum	30	○ ●				mid-spr
Linum	white, red	sum	15	○ ●				mid-spr
Lobelia	blue, white, mixed	sum to aut	15	○ ●	mid-spr		early spr	
Matthiola (stock)	mixed	sum to aut	20	○	mid-spr		late spr	mid-spr
Mesembryanthemum	yellow, pink, orange	sum to aut	25	○	mid-spr	mid-spr		
Nemesia	pink, white, yellow, red, mixed	sum to aut	15–25	○ ●	mid-spr	mid-spr	mid-spr	
Nicotiana	white, red, mixed	sum to aut	35	○ ●	mid-spr	mid-spr		
Nigella	white, blue, pink, mixed	sum	15–20	○ ●				mid-spr
Papaver (poppy)	white, pink, yellow, orange, red, mixed	sum to aut	20	○				mid-spr
Petunia	various	sum to aut	20	○	mid-spr		mid-spr	
Phlox	various	sum to aut	20	○	mid-spr			
Rudbeckia (coneflower)	gold, brown	sum to aut	25–35	○	mid-spr	mid-spr		
Salvia (sage)	pink, red, violet	sum to aut	25	○	early spr		early spr	
Scabiosa (scabious)	white, blue, violet, mixed	sum to aut	25	○ ●	mid-spr	mid-spr	mid-spr	mid-spr
Tagetes erecta	yellow, orange, brown	sum to aut	20–25	○	mid-spr	mid-spr		late spr
Tropaeolum (nasturtium)	yellow, red, orange, mixed	sum to aut	25	○ ●				late spr
Verbena	various	sum to aut	25	○	mid-spr	mid-spr		
Zinnia	various	sum to aut	25–45	○	mid-spr	mid-spr	mid-spr	

Sowing biennials

	Colours	Flowering period	Planting distance in cm	Aspect	Seeds sheltered	Seeds nursery	Seeds in place
Bellis perennis (daisy)	white, pink, red	spr to sum	15	▲	sum	spr to sum	
Campanula (bellflower)	blue, white, pink, purple	sum	25–30	○ ●	sum	spr to sum	
Cheiranthus cheiri (wallflower)	yellow to brown	spr	25–30	○ ●	sum	spr to sum	sum
Cynoglossum (hound's tongue)	blue	spr to sum	20	○ ●	sum	sum	
Dianthus barbatus (sweet william)	various	sum	20–25	○ ●	sum	sum	sum
Digitalis (foxglove)	various	sum	25–30	○	sum	spr to sum	sum
Lunaria (honesty)	white, purple	spr to sum	15	○ ●	sum	spr to sum	
Matthiola (stock)	various	sum	25	○ ●	sum	sum	
Myosotis (forget-me-not)	blue, pink	spr	15–20	○ ●	sum	spr to sum	sum
Papaver nudicaule (Iceland poppy)	various	sum	25–30	○	sum	sum	
Primula veris (cowslip)	various	spr to sum	15–20	○ ● ◗	spr	spr to sum	spr
Silene (campion, catchfly)	white, pink, red	spr to sum	25–30	○ ●	spr	spr to sum	
Viola cornuta (horned violet)	various	spr to sum	15	○ ●	sum	sum	

Cuttings

Taking cuttings is a popular propagation method and consists in taking a portion of a plant and encouraging it to form roots.

It is best on the whole to take cuttings in the middle of the growing season (spring or summer), so that the plants can derive the maximum benefit from optimal light and warmth and be established before the onset of the cold weather. Root production is cuttings is stimulated by hormones, which act only under particular conditions. They are sometimes present in an insufficient amount in their natural state, and the plant needs a little help in the form of hormone

rooting powder. This can be bought at a garden centre in powder or liquid form and works well.

The easiest plants are those that will take root in water, without any other procedure being necessary: the common oleander (rose laurel) and *Cyperus alternifolius* are the best-known examples, but the African violet, several indoor begonias, datura (angel's trumpets), willow and poplar lend themselves equally well to it. This list is not exhaustive and it is always worth experimenting.

Root cuttings

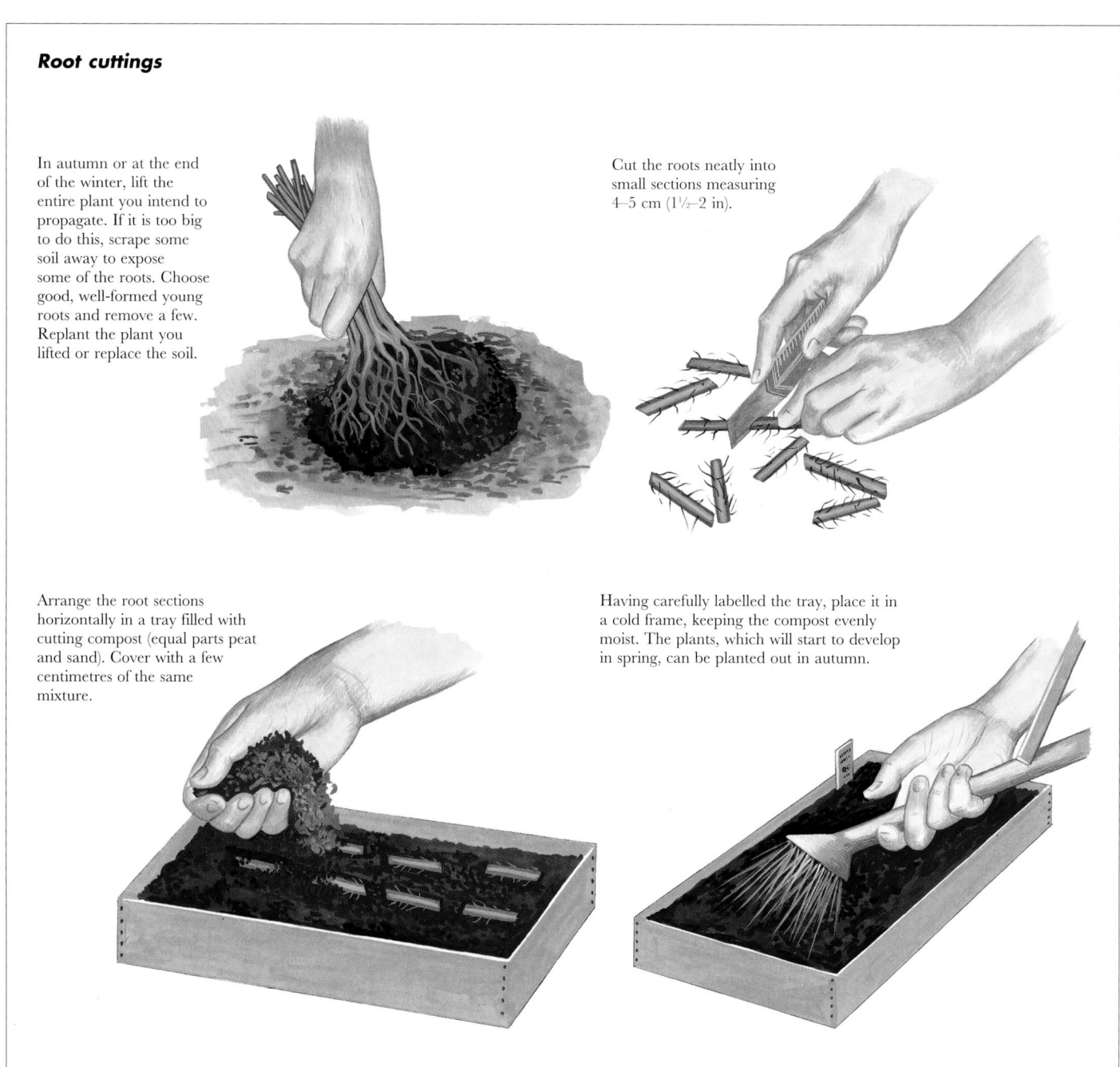

In autumn or at the end of the winter, lift the entire plant you intend to propagate. If it is too big to do this, scrape some soil away to expose some of the roots. Choose good, well-formed young roots and remove a few. Replant the plant you lifted or replace the soil.

Cut the roots neatly into small sections measuring 4–5 cm (1½–2 in).

Arrange the root sections horizontally in a tray filled with cutting compost (equal parts peat and sand). Cover with a few centimetres of the same mixture.

Having carefully labelled the tray, place it in a cold frame, keeping the compost evenly moist. The plants, which will start to develop in spring, can be planted out in autumn.

Division of dahlia tubers

To propagate dahlias, separate the tubers at the end of winter by using a strong paring knife. The number of sections does not matter, but each must have at least one growth bud.

Place the divided tubers immediately in a tray of moist peat, in a heated greenhouse. If you do this during late winter, you will have plants in flower from early summer. Alternatively, carry out the procedure in spring: your plants will flower slightly later in the summer.

You can also propagate dahlias in the autumn. The advantage is that the tubers will be full of water and are soft and easy to divide. First lift the tubers out with a fork.

Having cut the stems hard back, carefully remove any residual soil before it becomes too dry.

You should also remove any rotted or damaged sections and allow the tubers to dry for a few days before dividing. Place your divided tubers in dry peat, where the cuts will quickly heal.

Bulb scale propagation

Several bulbs can be propagated from their scales. Hyacinths and related plants are first cut into quarters, left to dry, then used as illustrated below, but the easiest technique applies to lilies, where the scales are rooted separately.

Lift the plant up carefully during its dormant season.

Separate the outer scales as though unwrapping the leaves of an artichoke, and leave the heart, which you will replant.

Insert the scales halfway into cutting compost (equal parts peat and sand), and protect under a cold frame.

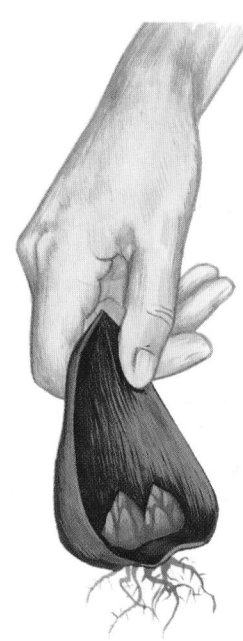

Several bulbils (between one and seven) will form at the base of each scale. You can handle them as soon as their leaves have appeared.

Repot each scale in a container containing the appropriate mixture for the lily you are planting. Plant out within two years.

Stem cuttings Many shrubs can be propagated from cuttings taken in autumn, when the leaves fall. These are known as hardwood cuttings. The technique consists in planting directly into the soil, outside, preferably in semi-shade and under the shelter of a wall, sections of young stems about pencil thickness and 15–30 cm (6–12 in) long, and bearing several buds or 'eyes'. The cut should be made just above and below an eye, the cut being horizontal at the bottom, on the slant at the top.

Using a spade, dig out a V-shaped planting trench half the depth of the cuttings, and spread a mixture of half peat and half sand over the base of the trench. All you have to do next is insert the lower half of the cutting into the hole, the base being in contact with the soil. Fill with soil, firm down well, and water. Allow a year before the roots are sufficiently developed for the shrub to be planted out. Propagation by stem cuttings can also be carried out in a different way much earlier in the season, using leaf-bearing shoots: this is known as propagation by softwood cuttings, explained below.

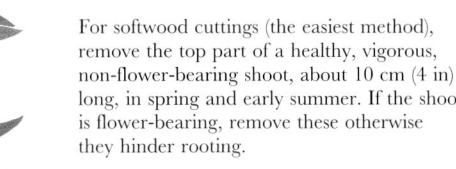

For softwood cuttings (the easiest method), remove the top part of a healthy, vigorous, non-flower-bearing shoot, about 10 cm (4 in) long, in spring and early summer. If the shoot is flower-bearing, remove these otherwise they hinder rooting.

Shrubs that are a little more difficult are propagated by means of half-ripe cuttings (where the shoots are beginning to harden) in summer. Remove a side shoot and prepare it by cutting the base immediately below a leaf joint or node. This is where root-inducing hormones are found.

Remove some of the lower leaves. For large-leaved shrubs (such as hydrangea), you should cut the remaining leaves in half.

Some cuttings can be removed with a heel of older wood attached: simply pull them off the plant and trim the heel.

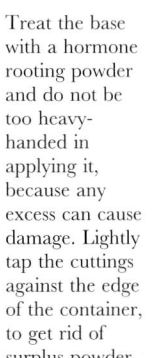

Treat the base with a hormone rooting powder and do not be too heavy-handed in applying it, because any excess can cause damage. Lightly tap the cuttings against the edge of the container, to get rid of surplus powder.

Next insert the cuttings in a cutting compost consisting of half peat and half coarse sand, or any similar materials. Make holes with a pencil or a thin stick.

Place the container under a frame or a bell jar. Failing this, you can make do with a plastic bag, held in place by string or a rubber band. Wait before checking that rooting has taken place. Only pot up cuttings that are really well-rooted. This method is suitable for many shrubs.

Layering

Layering consists in encouraging a part of a plant to root before separating it from the main plant. It offers the double advantage of guaranteed success, even with difficult plants, and of producing plants that are already a good size. Layering usually takes place directly in the soil, but you can also use air-layering for indoor plants or for shrubs and trees that are difficult to bend down to the ground. Layering is useful for propagating a branch that may suddenly display a particularly interesting feature, different from the rest of the plant (variegation, different flowers, etc.)
Always carry out this procedure in spring or early summer.

Layering

Select a branch of the shrub, remove the leaves around the area to be inserted into the soil, and bend it down to the ground.

Make an incision in the middle of this branch, underneath, and, to ensure rooting, dust the cut with hormone rooting powder.

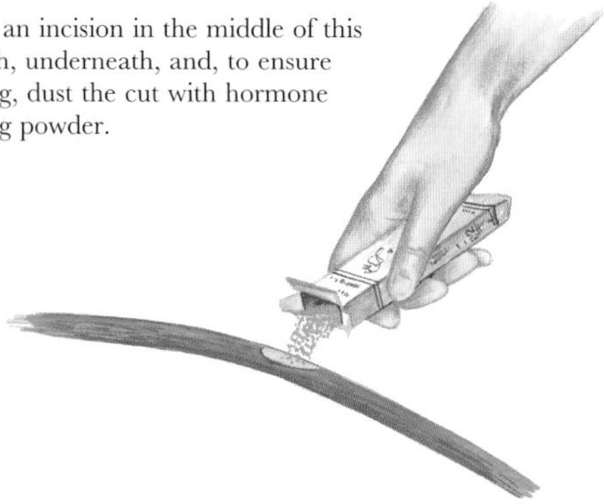

Insert the bare section into the soil, allowing only the tip of the branch to protrude. If necessary weight it down with a heavy stone.

Layering directly into a container ensures a tightly packed root ball which can be transplanted at any time.

Serpentine layering

With this technique several parts of the same stem are inserted into the soil. It is applicable mainly to climbers, which have stems that are both fairly long and supple. This is the technique generally used for wisterias.

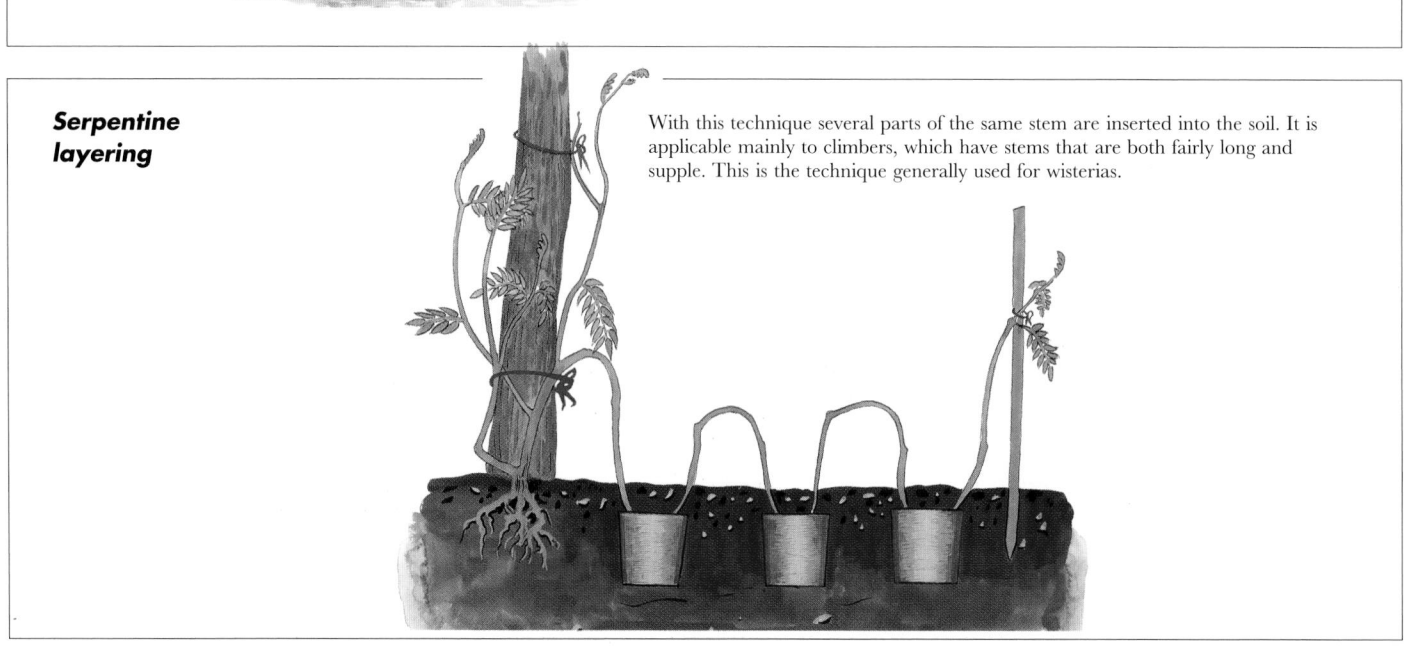

Air-layering

Choose a vigorous young lateral branch and remove the bottom leaves. Cut a tongue in the bare part of the branch.

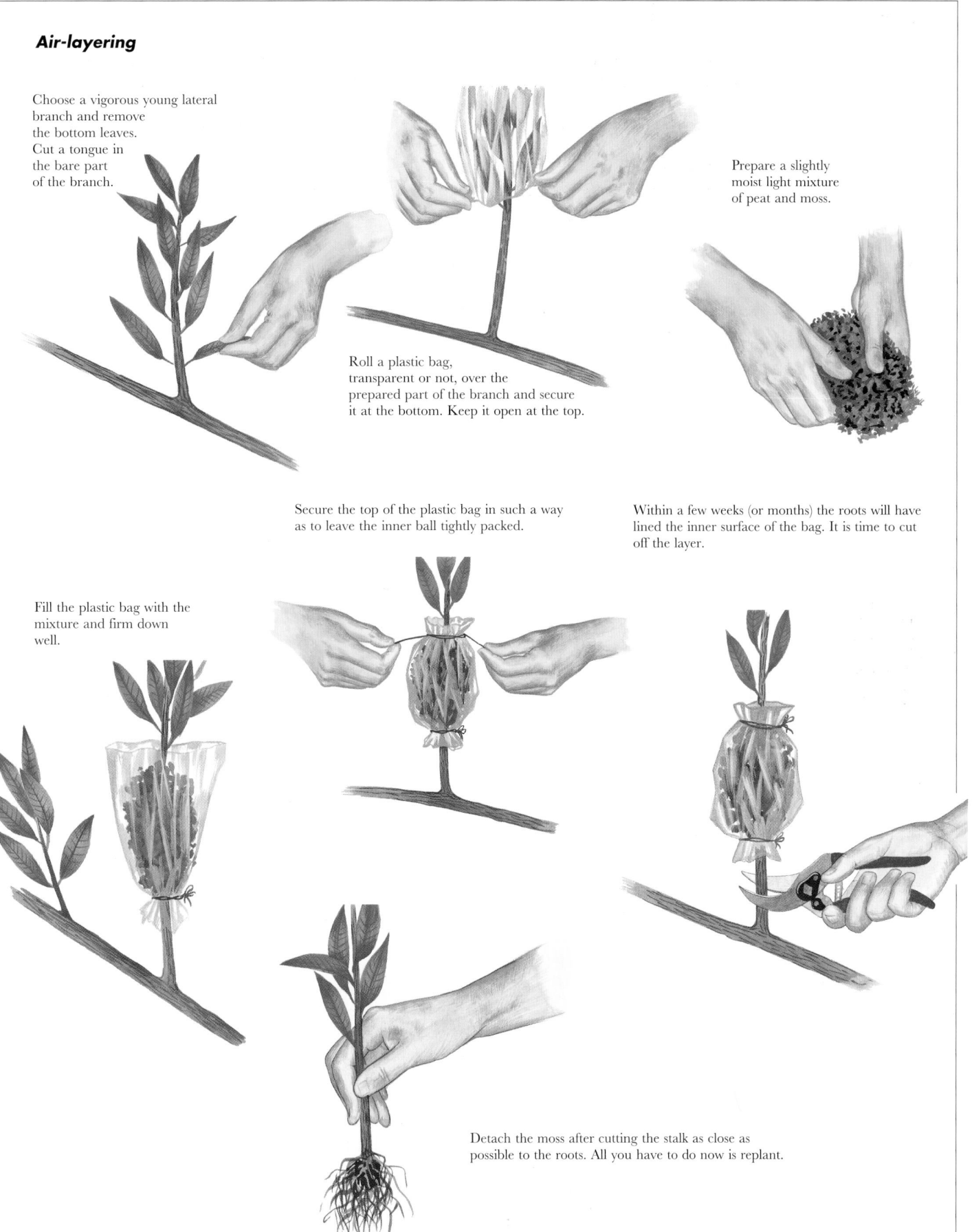

Roll a plastic bag, transparent or not, over the prepared part of the branch and secure it at the bottom. Keep it open at the top.

Prepare a slightly moist light mixture of peat and moss.

Secure the top of the plastic bag in such a way as to leave the inner ball tightly packed.

Within a few weeks (or months) the roots will have lined the inner surface of the bag. It is time to cut off the layer.

Fill the plastic bag with the mixture and firm down well.

Detach the moss after cutting the stalk as close as possible to the roots. All you have to do now is replant.

Propagating heathers

Cut 5–6 cm (2–2½ in) off the plant.

Remove the whole plant, after having watered it.

Insert the plant deeply into a planting hole filled with a mixture of sand and peat, allowing only 5 cm (2 in) of the stems to protrude.

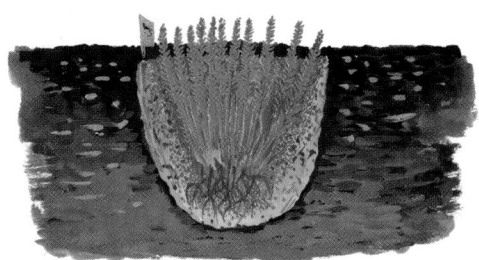

Water. After a year, lift up the heather, remove the tangle of old roots, and plant out the young rooted stems.

Dividing perennials

The most usual technique for propagating perennials is division.

By lifting out clumps from the soil using a spade, it is possible, depending on their size, to divide these into several smaller portions. Do this either by hand or, if the root ball is very tightly packed, with the aid of a sharp knife, a spade or two garden forks.

Sometimes it is best to leave the root ball in a bucket of water for a few minutes to facilitate separation.

Division can be done in the autumn, in warm climates, or at the beginning of spring in areas where the winters are cold.

Division of rhizomatous perennials

To propagate rhizomes, lift up the whole clump during the dormant period (for irises, do this in summer).

Using two forks, separate the rhizomes.

Separate from the circumference of the plant those rhizomes – they are the most vigorous – that have leaves, and shorten them to limit moisture loss.

Insert each division in well-worked soil, spreading out the roots.

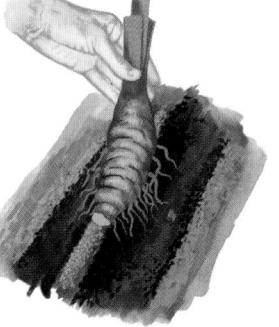

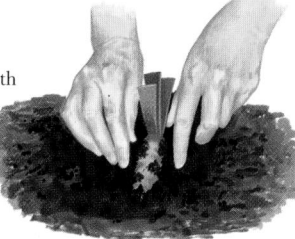

Lightly cover with soil, keeping the rhizomes flush with the ground. Water well.

Note: *Perennials with fibrous roots (asters, for example) can be given the same treatment. Discard the centre of the clump.*

Grafting

Grafting is not one of the most widespread of all propagation techniques for the amateur gardener, and it is the one which is the most off-putting. There is a mystique about it, like the pruning of fruit trees. The truth, however, is that grafting follows a definite logic.

The advantages of grafting are several: with few materials (only the plant you want to obtain), one can obtain a quantity of plants in a short time, thanks to a cheap root-stock. Grafting methods are so numerous that there will certainly be one that is appropriate to your particular case.

For successful grafting, there is no need to be a great scholar: you just need a bit of skill. You have to match – this applies to all types of grafting – the living parts of botanically related plants. The living part of a woody plant is its skin (the bark) and the layer just below it called the cambium. These never cease to grow and nourish the plant. The heart of the plant (the wood) acts only as the frame. The larger parts of plants are therefore not grafted in their entirety, as their union would be uncertain. It is possible, however, to graft young wood on to an old root-stock (but with young bark), which will quickly take on the vigour of the host. Once all the root-stocks have been set up, the delicate part of the operation (and it is the only one) consists in joining the living parts neatly together.

This is the most important thing to bear in mind, and most failures in grafting arise from not doing so. The other mistake often made by the novice gardener is to try to graft in full sap or to remove the branches of a vigorous root-stock too soon. Cleft or wedge grafting, for example, consists in placing young shoots on to a young or adult subject which is much more vigorous. For this method you must choose the period in which the sap is low (autumn or end of the winter), so that the grafting can be achieved before growth resumes. Budding, which is suitable for roses, among other plants, takes place in summer, with a dormant 'eye' (that is, a bud) inserted into a plant in full growth. You should therefore be careful about removing the branches and leaves of the root-stock. If you were to practise the cleft or wedge graft in full sap, or if you removed the root-stock's branches during budding, the violent gush of surplus sap would sweep the grafts away, breaking the poorly established joins.

Choose healthy, well defined root-stocks, tie the graft in carefully to ensure contact, and use grafting wax to fill in the gaps and to act as a waterproof dressing.
Use a very strong, sharp knife, ideally a proper grafting knife. Except for budding, protect the grafted area from the birds, to avoid them perching on the grafts and detaching them.

Different types of graft

Crown grafting (rind grafting)

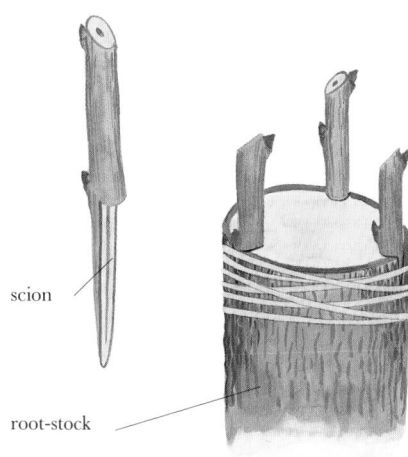

This graft can be carried out rapidly, and enables new branches to form quickly on a fairly large root-stock. Frequently used with fruit trees that are exposed to the wind, or if you want to change the variety, it also encourages the re-shaping of a poorly formed or very damaged tree by cutting back its branches in order to graft neat little branches on to it. Make an incision in the bark in one, two or three places, depending on the thickness of the branch. Slide scions or shoots into this, first making a flat slanting cut at their base. The cut makes it possible to increase the surface area of living wood which is in contact with the root-stock.

Modified crown grafting

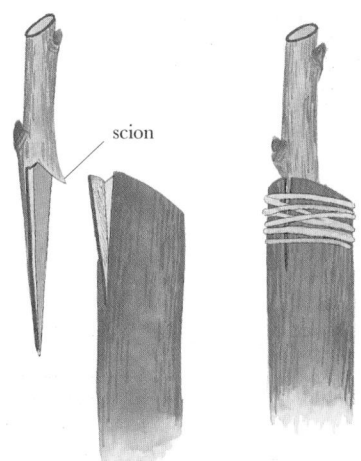

This is used when the bark of the root-stock is very thick. On the cut-back root-stock (cut quite high up), make an incision of a few centimetres in the bark and lift it up on one side only. Prepare scions as above but remove a sliver of bark from one edge of the scion, and place it against the unlifted bark of the root-stock.

Double cleft (or split) grafting

The double cleft or split graft is widespread among fruit growers and suitable for many kinds of fruit. Simply split the ends of the cut-back branches of the root-stock with a pruning knife and a mallet. Keep it open using a wedge, then insert the desired number of scions (usually two), cut to a wedge shape at the base.

After removing the wedge, tie and seal with grafting wax. The advantage is that the grafts are solidly joined together. Make sure the living areas match up.

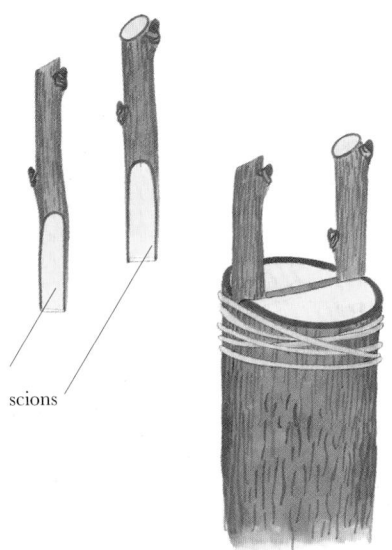

scions

Crown grafting with extra bud

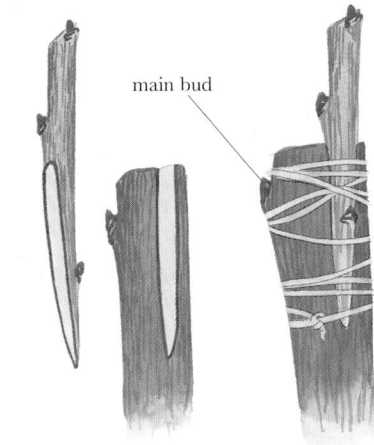

main bud

This is a very simple graft, whose results are always good. The principle consists in taking a normal section with a supplementary 'eye' (bud), which is to be found not above the cut, but against the root-stock. This ensures an excellent circulation of sap (this is the main bud) and prevents any drying out. This technique is useful in windy countries and for rather difficult grafts.

Side cleft grafting

Useful with very hard wood, this method creates a perfect join. The base of the scion is cut on both sides, in order to form a wedge. Make an oblique split in the side of the root-stock, which will enable the barks to line up once the scion is in place. Then just secure with string.

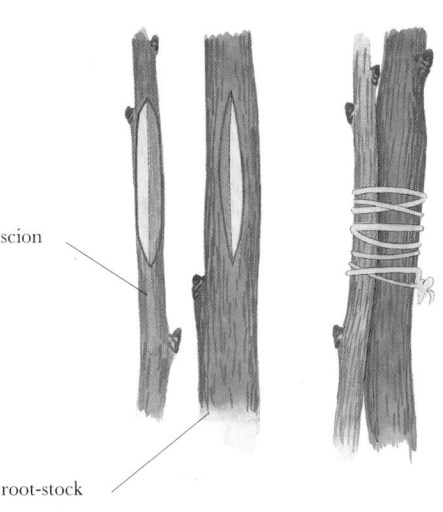

scion

root-stock

Terminal herbaceous cleft or web grafting

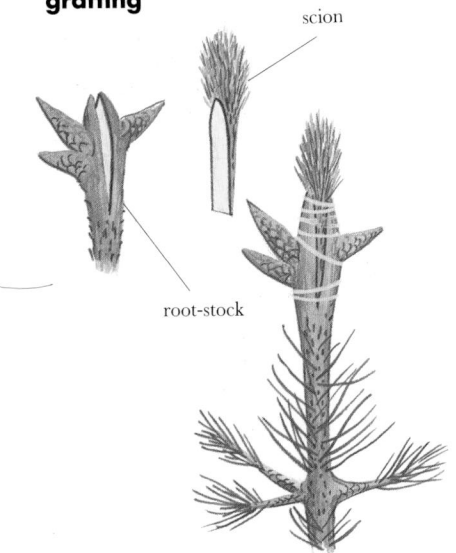

scion

root-stock

This graft is done in spring, on very young subjects, and mainly involves the most delicate plants, with even more tender stems. The scion is a terminal shoot. The root-stock is cut back, split in the middle, then the scion, cut into a wedge shape, is inserted into it. If the scion belongs to a species that flowers earlier than the root-stock, split the stem of the root-stock immediately, without removing the top. As soon as growth resumes, restrict the growth of the buds and remove these the following year.

Approach grafting

For tender trees and shrubs (mimosas, for example), abandon the classic graft in favour of this one, which is a variant of layering. The two shrubs, of which one is in a container, both have roots. Bring the potted shrub close to the shrub in the ground. Remove a long slice of bark from each and join the cuts together. Separate them a few months after growth has resumed.

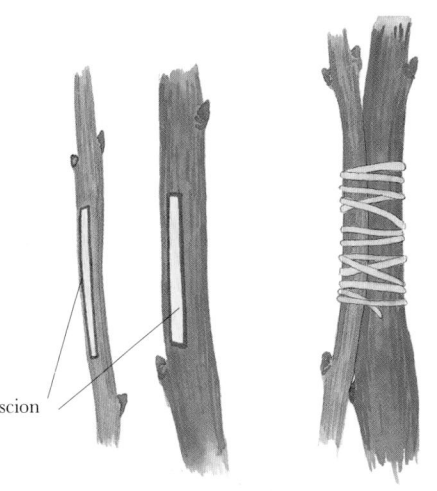

scion

Whip and tongue grafting

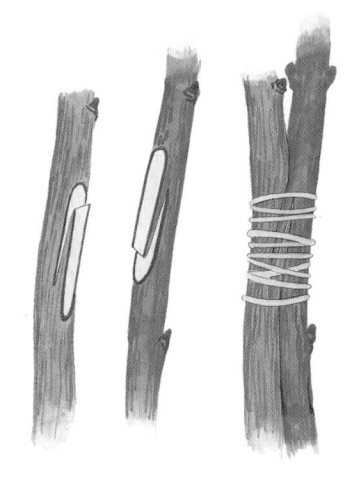

Use root-stocks and scions of the same thickness by making matching cuts in each, complete with tongues, and fit the two tongues together. The join generally remains fairly inconspicuous, but o not practise this technique on wood that is very soft, hollow or with pith.

Spliced side grafting (veneer side grafting)

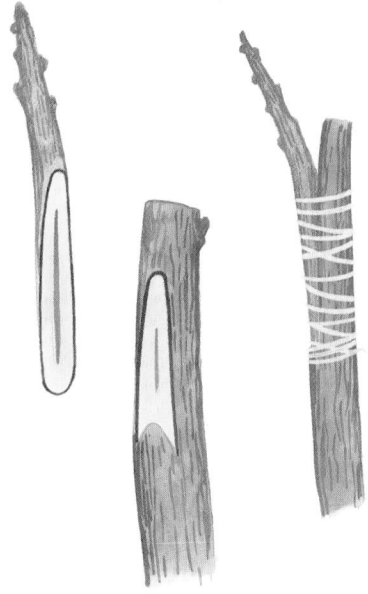

This graft is done on a root-stock that is left whole. Make a short oblique downward cut, then a long cut to meet it in the side of the root-stock. The base of the scion is cut to match. The root-stock is only topped after healing is done, and progressively if the root-stock is less vigorous than the scion.

Veneer grafting

With trees that have soft tissues (poplars, willows, etc.) a deep incision is not necessary. Simply remove a rectangle of bark and fit into it a scion consisting of a rectangle of bark with one or more buds on it. Healing is extremely rapid and any that do not take can be replaced. The binding must be strong.

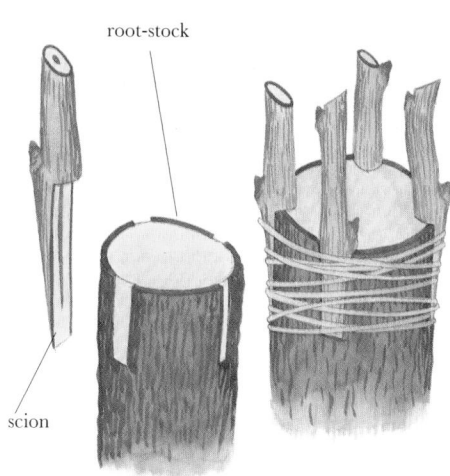

Budding

This well-known graft can be used with a great many trees and shrubs, particularly roses. Its immediate advantage is that you can obtain as many plants as you have buds. You can thus, over three or four years, propagate thousands of examples of unusual or rare plants. Always graft on to young root-stocks either in spring or in summer. The procedure consists in using a pruning knife to remove a bud with a portion of bark attached, avoiding cutting into the old wood. Insert this bud into a T-shaped incision made at the bottom of the root-stock, then tie in, leaving the bud exposed. Leave all the leaves on the root-stock. The bud will remain dormant until the following season. You should then partly cut back the root-stock and cut it completely once the bud has developed into a vigorous stem.

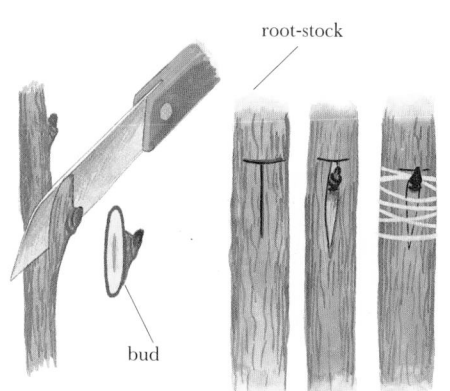

Chip budding

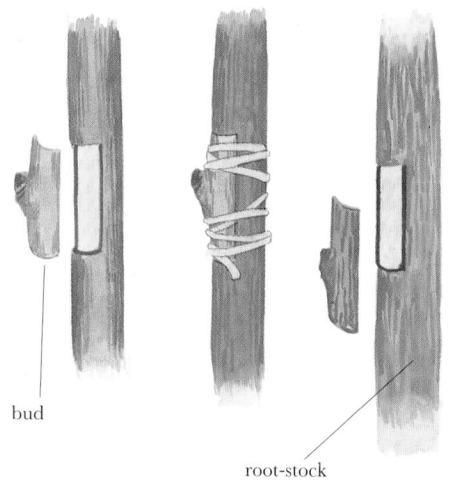

This is an alternative to normal budding. Remove the bud on a rectangular section of bark and cut out an identical rectangle in the root-stock. All you have to do now is fit the two together.

Cleft or split grafting with bud

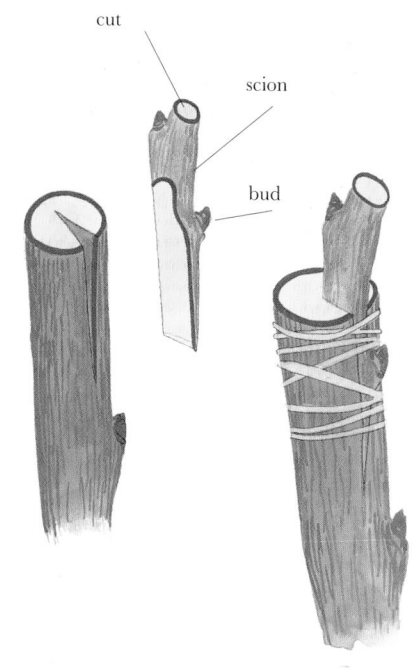

The technique is the same as for the cleft or split graft, in so far as a bud is arranged on the scion, underneath the cut. The branch it produces is more tolerant of the wind, and this technique is thus desirable with breakable wood.

Ordinary cleft or split grafting

Only half the root-stock is split and must be to a reasonable degree larger than the scion (but not too large). If it is very large, opt for the double cleft or split graft. Cut back the root-stock to the desired height, split it by approximately half its diameter, and insert the scion, its base cut into a wedge shape.

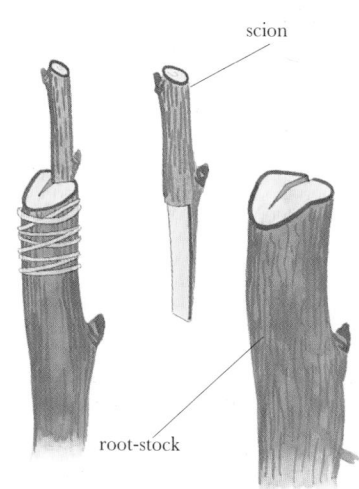

MAINTENANCE

Working the soil

Digging

The purpose of digging is to turn over the soil in order to break it up, lighten it, add any organic matter and weed it at the same time. If you are adopting the traditional method of digging, use a spade or a digging fork. The drawings on these pages show you how to divide up your plot of land by making lines to form sections of about 30 cm (12 in). We shall see why. If you cannot complete the job in one go (it is exhausting work), no matter. Do a little, stop when you begin to feel tired or when you feel the first aches and pains, and continue the following day. Digging is carried out during the plants' dormant season, between autumn and spring. So you have plenty of time in which to do it. Depending on its consistency, the soil may not break down into small lumps. This has no bearing over the end result. If possible, work heavy soils before the onset of winter: the rain and the cold will break it up for you, aided and abetted by the worms.

If the area to be dug is large, manual digging can be replaced by a powered cultivator which will handle clearing and other soil-related jobs, including excavating trenches for the planting of hedges. Rotary cultivators can be hired by the day, and are easy to handle.

Dig out a first trench to one spit (the depth of a spade), and to a spade's width (about 30 cm/12 in), and reserve this soil. Then dig up the area situated on its immediate left. Place the soil of the second trench into the first, turning the soil over as you do so, then the third into the second and so on. Fill the last trench (above left) with the soil from the first.

Whatever the tool used (spade or digging fork), insert it deeply into the soil for best results.

Hoeing and forking

Hoeing consists in breaking up and improving the surface of the soil by means of a light manual tool (a hoe) or a motorized one. The effects are beneficial and multiple:

• preparation of the soil for seed sowing;

• weeding;

• limiting evaporation by creating a protective layer;

• allowing air into the topsoil;

• incorporating fertilizer.

Forking is in effect a deep hoeing process. It consists of digging compressed soil to half a spit. A digging fork is used rather than a spade, both for better penetration and to avoid damaging the roots of trees and shrubs underneath the soil. The effects are the same as for hoeing.

Pruning

Like many horticultural techniques, pruning is part of the mystique of gardening.

Why prune at all? Except by accident, plants in their natural habitat are never pruned and would appear to fare no worse for this. Plants, particularly if they are woody, have two types of stem: flower-producing ones, and woody ones which are covered only in leaves. The first type are a sign of maturity: they produce flowers, then fruit, and sooner or later they die. The second enable the plant to be rejuvenated. With age, the plant will stop producing these and will die completely, after a period that can vary from forty-five years to no less than a few centuries! Human intervention in this pattern helps to effect a harmonious balance between the old and the new wood, since with great foresight, nature has endowed trees and shrubs with well-concealed buds known as

dormant buds. These only awaken if an accident befalls their section of the branch or trunk, in which case they will start to grow to compensate for any shortfall. Every cultivated plant, depending on its horticultural use, undergoes some kind of pruning, which takes into account its function and the use for which it is intended. There are some general rules but if in doubt, do not be too profligate with your secateurs: radical pruning does more harm than good.

There are three rules in pruning, whatever the circumstances:

- Never prune if the weather is frosty.
- Never prune with a blunt tool.
- Prune at the right time of year for each species.

Making a standard shrub

This practice enables the gardener to give a small shrub growing in a shapeless clump the appearance of a neat little tree. This treatment is particularly successful with plants grown in containers, making it possible to create temporary decorations that are extremely elegant.

Many plants are sold both as shrubs and as standards – roses, euonymus, hydrangeas and fuchsias, to name but a few. It is very easy to make a standard yourself. It should be carried out progressively over three or four years, using a plant which has a good central stem.

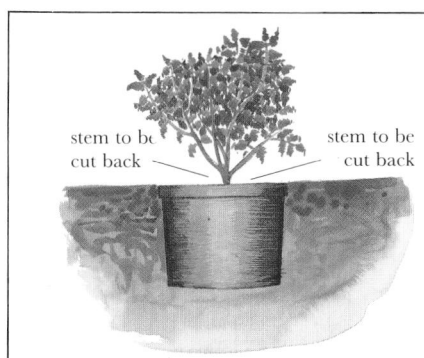

stem to be cut back — stem to be cut back

Choose a bushy shrub and cut off approximately one-third or even half of the stems growing from the base, but no more, to avoid vegetative shock.

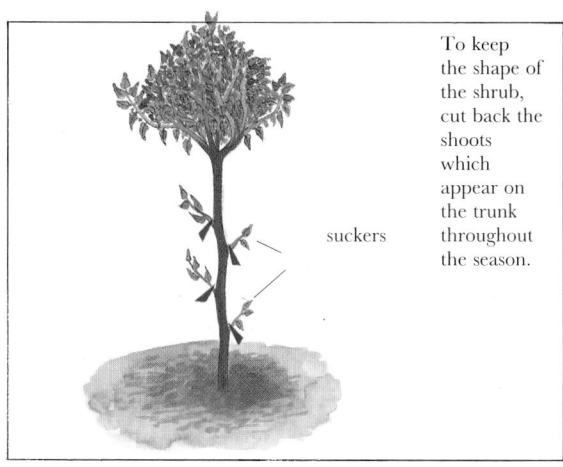

suckers

To keep the shape of the shrub, cut back the shoots which appear on the trunk throughout the season.

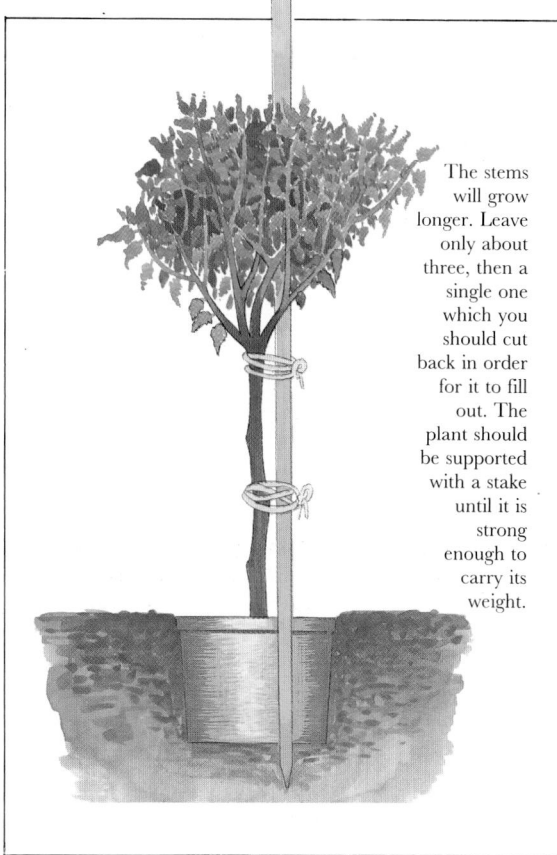

The stems will grow longer. Leave only about three, then a single one which you should cut back in order for it to fill out. The plant should be supported with a stake until it is strong enough to carry its weight.

Pruning roses

Roses are summer-flowering shrubs. As such, they flower on the current year's branches and should therefore be pruned at the end of the winter.

Bush roses, hybrid teas and floribundas are cut back short, depending on the category, for very logical reasons. The least vigorous rose bushes are pruned hard back. This leaves few replacement shoots, but the shrub will be able to nourish them adequately. Vigorous rose bushes, on the other hand, are pruned less harshly (the more vigorous they are the less they are pruned); they are perfectly able to nourish a greater number of branches. By pruning them radically one would also risk having non-flowering branches, the poor shrub trying desperately to make up for the brutal deficit by providing a maximum of leafy branches, yielding good nourishing sap. Bush roses are pruned taking the lower part of the stems as a base. With remontant climbing roses, the master branches are considered as the base for pruning back to and it is the lateral branches that are pruned each year.

No matter what type of rose, always prune following the instructions below. The cut must be clean, about 1 cm (½ in) from the last shoot. Always cut back to outward-facing buds, so that the shoots do not get in each other's way. The cut is slanted to the opposite side of the bud so that water easily runs

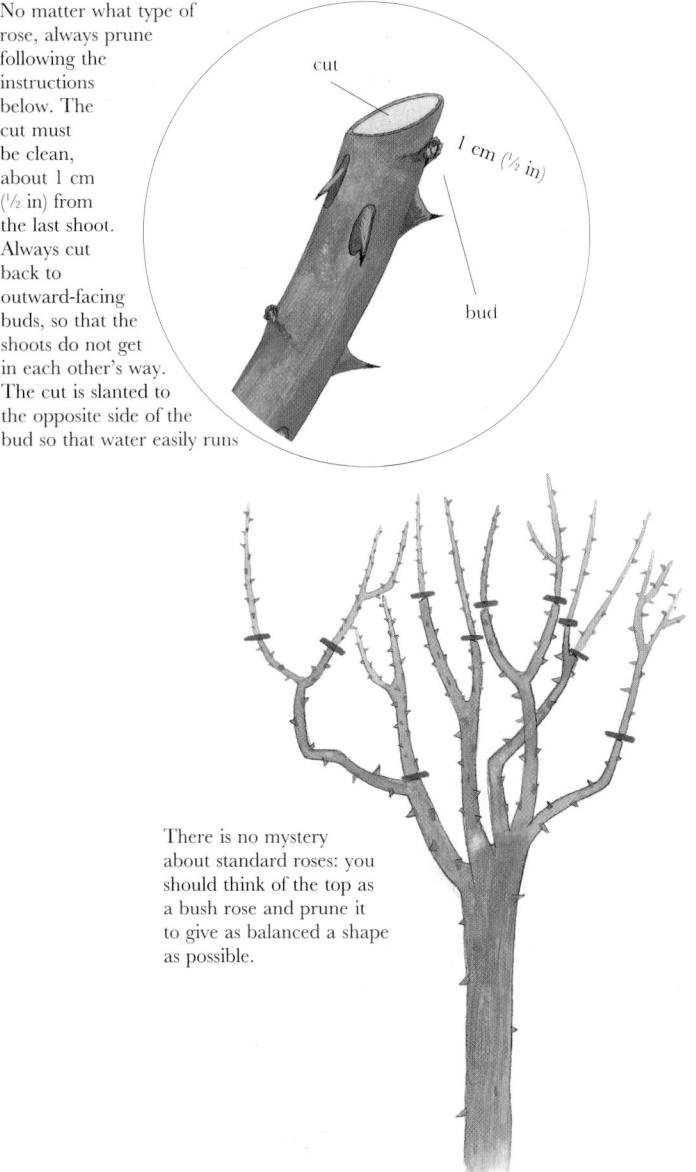

cut

1 cm (½ in)

bud

There is no mystery about standard roses: you should think of the top as a bush rose and prune it to give as balanced a shape as possible.

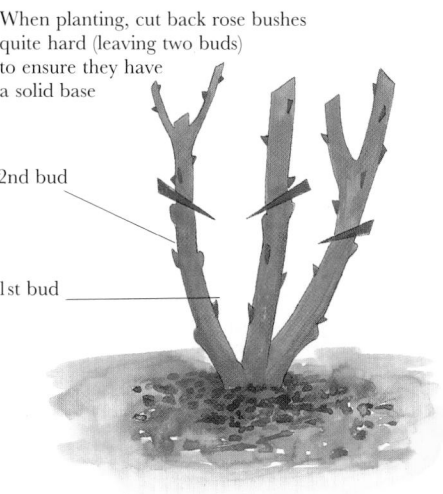

When planting, cut back rose bushes quite hard (leaving two buds) to ensure they have a solid base

2nd bud

1st bud

During the growing season, more branches will form. At the end of the following winter you should remove the weak branches and cut the others back to two or three buds.

Roses that flower in clusters (floribundas) are cut back hard when they are young. More vigorous than other roses, they are subsequently only pruned lightly.

Once a floribunda has taken shape, prune it lightly by removing old, diseased or poorly positioned branches every 2–3 years.

For ground-cover plants, or roses used as such, train the supple branches by spreading them out as evenly as possible. Remove the side branches that have flowered as well as the old branches. The rose will then put out vigorous replacement stems.

Climbing and rambler roses are trained as much as possible into a horizontal shape, on a trellis. They produce abundant flower-bearing stems. Cut back non-remontant varieties at the end of summer, by removing all the branches that have flowered, in order to limit the framework to new vigorous stems. At the end of winter prune remontant climbers by cutting back the lateral shoots to one or two buds.

sucker

It is essential to eliminate suckers from rose bushes. Remove the soil in order to find the point where they join the mother plant, then wrench them out and replace the soil.

**Pruning
trees and
shrubs**

There are several reasons for pruning a tree or a shrub.

Why prune?

• To remove dead wood, which should be cut back to healthy wood.

• To remove small twigs that intersect each other.

• To remove branches that have flowered, giving greater vigour to the new branches that will flower in their turn.

• To remove too strong a concentration of branches in the middle of the plant, preventing air and sunlight from coming through.

• In order to achieve a pleasing shape.

• To encourage the growth of more flower-bearing shoots. Spring-flowering shrubs should be pruned at the end of their flowering period. Summer-flowering shrubs (remontant roses, for example) should be pruned at the end of winter. In practice, pruning cuts away the branches that have flowered, after the shrub's flowering period, at the place where these join another branch.

How to rejuvenate a flowering shrub

Sometimes a shrub has not been pruned and has grown considerably. The centre of the shrub is bushy and the branches are tangled. It is therefore necessary to intervene as soon as the flowering period is over. Remove the older branches (the wood on these is darker), reduce the number of younger branches by half and lightly hoe in a bucketful of compost around the shrub.

Cutting back to the stump

This is radical pruning, which is carried out each year at the end of winter on certain shrubs, to ensure that they will flower the coming season. Buddlejas, caryopteris, deciduous ceanothus, fuchsias, and *Cornus alba* (red-barked dogwood) are all shrubs that need to be totally cut back. Prune the entire plant down to 15 cm (6 in) from the ground. New stems will soon grow on the stump.

To retain the bushiness of evergreen shrubs with fine leaves, such as lavender, trim them every spring, but only the young wood.

Summer-flowering shrubs are cut back at the end of winter just above the new shoots. Do the same for spring-flowering shrubs, but in this case immediately after flowering.

Routine pruning of a shrub, whatever the species, consists in freeing the centre of the plant, removing its weak, dead or badly positioned branches, and in shortening the branches that are too straight, in order to make them branch out.

Pruning climbing plants

Most climbing plants manage quite well without any human intervention at all. Usually the only work they require consists in training them up a support (when necessary) and removing their old branches with secateurs every 4–5 years. Summer-flowering clematis – the only kind in the genus to require pruning – need three different methods, according to purists, depending on their parentage. If you are not sure what this is, opt for a middle course: prune back half the branches very short in early spring one year, and prune the other half the following year. The wisteria, however, a climber in the truest sense and often a devastatingly strong plant, requires more reasoned management.

The wisteria – a special case

After planting, or in the following year if it is a small sapling, remove the shoots at the base in winter, leaving just one stem. You should repeat this procedure every year. Then cut this back by one third.

In the following years, always at the end of winter, prune the side branches by a third or half, as well as the central stem. Young stems should be trained carefully around a support the minute they appear.

Cut back the vigorous young shoots that appear in summer, leaving only three leaves on each.

For a tree-shaped wisteria, train around a parasol-shaped support and prune each branch very short: leave only two buds in winter, and only two leaves in summer.

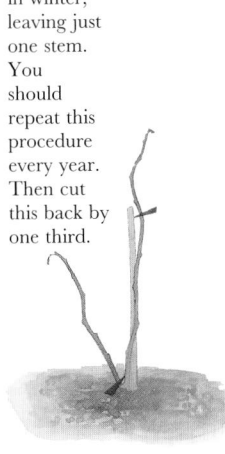
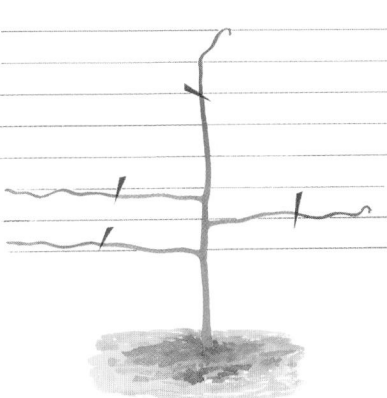

Pruning hedges

Unlike shrubs that are cultivated in isolation, those that make up a hedge have all their shoots pruned back short at the same time, at frequent intervals. The result is quickly visible: instead of putting out long, vigorous, well-spaced-out branches, these plants produce a mass of twigs, all their dormant shoots growing at the same time. The result is dense, compact, and, as one would expect from a hedge, a structure which can form a barrier against the wind, passers-by and noise.

When should hedges be pruned?

Trees and shrubs have different growing periods and habits. To achieve the best results from your hedge, you should know when to prune.

Azalea: after flowering
Elaeagnus: early summer
Euonymus (spindle tree): any time
Ilex (holly): spring, then at the end of summer
Ligustrum (privet): any time
Osmanthus: after flowering
Taxus (yew): end of summer
Thuja: end of spring and end of summer

When pruning a hedge, using a hedge-cutter or hedge-clippers, take care to make the sides slightly tilted, not vertical, the base being a little wider than the top. Two templates, placed at each end and tied with string, will help to get the correct shape.

How to restore a hedge

A hedge made up of yews, even if very old and damaged, can be restored by using methods which are severe but effective.

• Prune all the old branches on one side, at a distance of 25–30 cm (10–12 in) from the trunks.

• Trim the top of the hedge at the required height.

• Remove weeds and hoe lightly.

• Dig in, with a hoe, some nitrogen-based fertilizer and water abundantly.

• The following year, prune the other side of the hedge in the same way.

• In 4–5 years, the hedge will have regained a good appearance. The technique is applicable to most deciduous hedges, for example those made up of hornbeam and beech.

Protection from the elements

Several enemies lie in wait for your plants: wind, rain, cold, hail, drought. How can you protect them? Bear in mind that plants do not all react in the same way.

Plants that feel the cold have few resources to fight it, and are at risk of dying in a harsh winter unless you take the appropriate measures. Do not wait for the thermometer to fall below zero before taking precautions. You should also watch out for morning frosts in spring. Do not plant out until you are certain the frosts are over. Even plants known as hardy, i.e. able to tolerate temperatures of –10°C (14°F) to –15°C (8°F), are liable to succumb if planted in a draught, or if there have been substantial drops in temperature during the winter. The most fragile plants, too, may be those most recently planted, the latest additions to the garden. To protect them, follow this advice.

• Make a protective cover of straw under a sheet of plastic for young grafted trees, bushes and shrubs.

• Place plants that are most sensitive to the cold under a protective plastic covering (tents or tunnels, the latter being useful for protecting both young seedlings and delicate small perennials).

• Wrap trunks (see illustrations) and earth up small mounds of soil covered with straw or peat under a single sheet of plastic, pierced with holes.

• If it snows, shake the branches of shrubs, especially conifers, so that the weight of the snow does not break them.

• Drought is another great enemy of plants. Strangely enough, it should be tackled in the same way as frost, by spreading a straw covering about 10 cm (4 in) deep around the base of the plants. Do this from the beginning of summer.

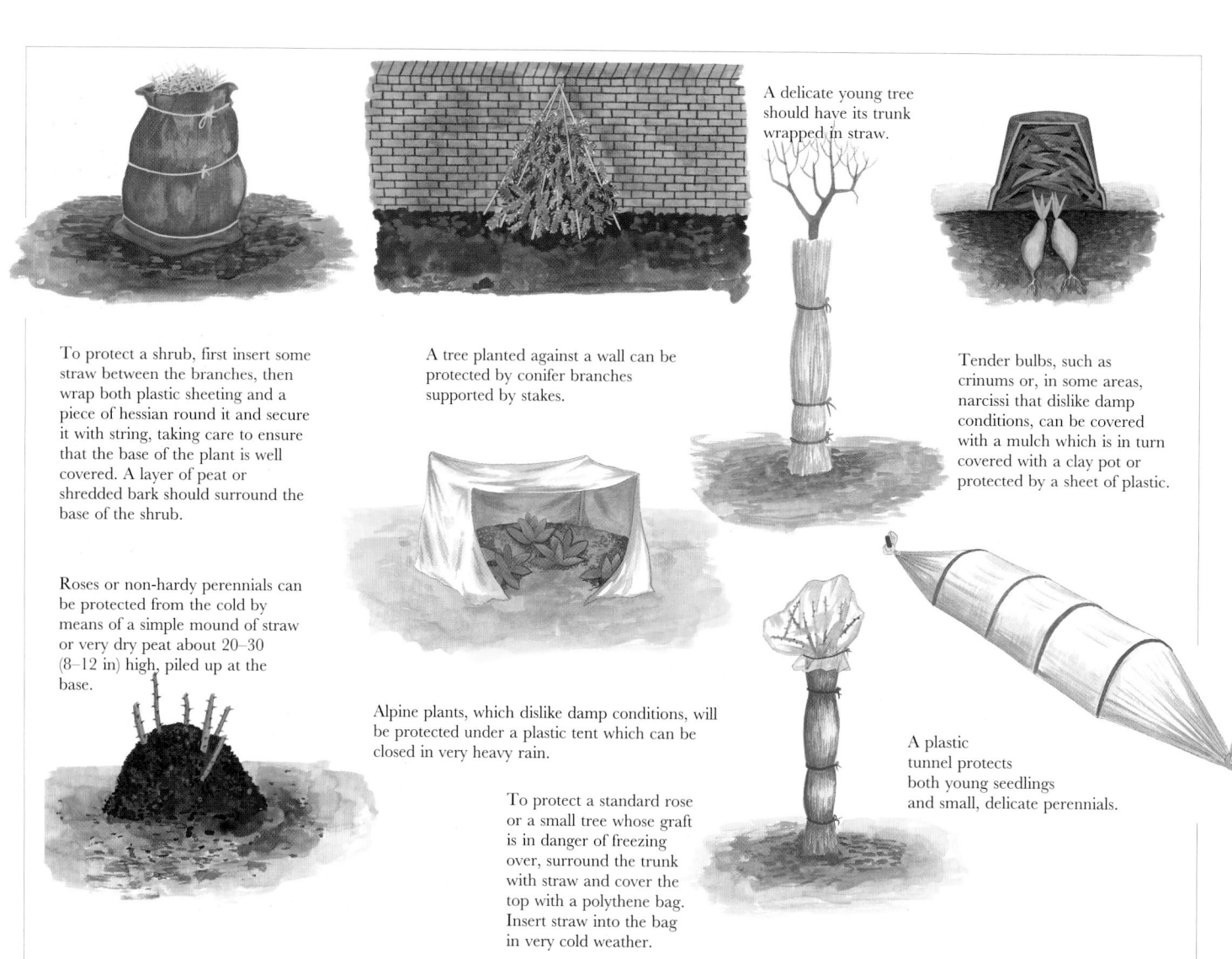

To protect a shrub, first insert some straw between the branches, then wrap both plastic sheeting and a piece of hessian round it and secure it with string, taking care to ensure that the base of the plant is well covered. A layer of peat or shredded bark should surround the base of the shrub.

Roses or non-hardy perennials can be protected from the cold by means of a simple mound of straw or very dry peat about 20–30 (8–12 in) high, piled up at the base.

A tree planted against a wall can be protected by conifer branches supported by stakes.

Alpine plants, which dislike damp conditions, will be protected under a plastic tent which can be closed in very heavy rain.

To protect a standard rose or a small tree whose graft is in danger of freezing over, surround the trunk with straw and cover the top with a polythene bag. Insert straw into the bag in very cold weather.

A delicate young tree should have its trunk wrapped in straw.

Tender bulbs, such as crinums or, in some areas, narcissi that dislike damp conditions, can be covered with a mulch which is in turn covered with a clay pot or protected by a sheet of plastic.

A plastic tunnel protects both young seedlings and small, delicate perennials.

Fertilizers

The soil is supposed to provide everything that plants need, but it is not always ideal and, in addition, its nutrients wear out. A spot of assistance is therefore necessary to help the plants grow, but first it is important to know what they need.

The different types of fertilizer

• The major elements are nitrogen (N), phosphorus (P) and potassium (K), which plants consume in fairly large quantities, in specific, easily assimilated forms. Nitrogen encourages the growth of the green parts of the plant (the leaves), phosphorus works on the woody parts and the roots, and potassium on the flowers and fruit. This is all approximate, however, because these elements in fact all work together. Nevertheless, fertilizers are almost always marketed in the form of a mixture. The numbers indicated, sometimes, on large packages, give the proportions of each of the elements, always following the order N, P, K. For example, a '15, 10, 8' fertilizer will contain 15 parts of nitrogen, 10 of phosphorus and 8 of potassium.

It used to be believed that this was enough. Plants, however, consume equal amounts of calcium, sulphur and magnesium. It is extremely rare, though, for these elements to be missing from the soil or for them to be inaccessible to plants. It can happen sometimes, however, that there will be a deficiency of calcium in a very acid soil, and this must then be treated with lime.

potassium (K)

nitrogen (N)

phosphorus (P)

• Added to these are the minor elements whose role is not very well known, which are necessary in infinitesimal quantities but indispensible. The deficiency of these trace elements leads to serious imbalances, and this is why the compound fertilizers that are marketed nowadays often include them. According to their composition, the form in which they are made up and their proportions in a mixture, different fertilizers are suitable for different plants. If you are a beginner, therefore, you should trust the preparations that are for specific purposes, such as rose fertilizers, tomato fertilizers, flower-garden fertilizers and so on. Know also when to leave well alone; an excess of fertilizer will have the opposite result from the one you are aiming for. Do not be too heavy-handed, and follow the instructions on quantity.

• Organic fertilizers are of animal origin (dried blood, guano, bonemeal, hoof and horn) or vegetable (green manures and compost). The latter provide, above all, humus, but also calcium, trace elements and nitrogen, with a rather slow release of nutrients.

When to add fertilizer?

• Instant fertilizers are spread on to the plant and therefore nourish it immediately. This is the case, for instance, with foliar fertilizers that are immediately absorbed. It is also the case with products that have to be diluted with water and applied to the soil around plants. You should use these instant fertilizers from spring onwards, when the plants are in full growth.

• So-called steady- or slow-release fertilizers release their nutrients slowly over a period of time. They should be applied at the time of planting.

• Instant and steady-release fertilizers should always be used on a previously moistened soil, to avoid burning the roots.

• While small quantities are very practical for indoor use, you should consider buying in larger packages for the garden – these can be shared with friends and they work out much cheaper.

Weedkillers

Weeding is the gardener's scourge, a task which never ends. There are different means (hoeing, digging etc) of getting rid of weeds, of course, but you can never eliminate them all and for some parts of the garden it will be necessary to resort to chemical weedkilling preparations. Different types of weedkiller are available, each having a specific effect.

Non-selective weedkillers

Some of these are spread over the soil, where they are absorbed by the roots and attack the plants by poisoning them. Their effect lasts for a long time (several months), and they decompose into different products that can be easily eliminated. They work on all kinds of plants, without distinction. Non-selective weedkillers are useful mainly for paths and unplanted areas.

Dichlobenil and simazine kill the weeds while they are germinating. They are used among established shrubs and are the best weedkillers to use beneath rose bushes. They are equally suitable for use in the orchard. As their action is not always limited to weeds, it is unwise to use them elsewhere.

Non-selective weedkillers include 'contact' products. These are sprayed on to the leaves and penetrate them by upsetting the cells. There are several types that work only on the plants' green parts, becoming harmless the minute they touch the soil, which enables you to continue planting without too much delay.

Paraquat works on all leaves by burning them, but it is only partially conveyed through the sap stream. It destroys annuals completely, but perennials will grow again.

Dichlobenil and mixtures containing dicamba, MCPA and dichlorprop work on woody plants such as brambles and ivy and on nettles.

Glyphosate, which is almost universal, is systemic (it is absorbed by the plant and circulates in the sap stream) and therefore destroys perennial weeds, even those with very long rhizomes and deep roots. It can be used among woody plants, but do not let it come into contact with them.

Selective weedkillers

These are mainly for lawns, and are well tolerated by the grass, but not by plants with large leaves. Some are included in lawn fertilizers.

Plant ailments

The first thing to understand is why garden plants, especially roses, are subject to disease.

Diseases are caused by two principal factors: animals (essentially insects and molluscs) and pathogenic agents (fungi, viruses, bacteria). Their spread must also be taken into account. Put a child with measles in a class of thirty children, and the result will be inevitable: almost all the children will catch measles. Similarly, the concentration of plants of the same species in the same place makes them more apt to succumb to contagion.

The best way of avoiding diseases as much as possible is to give plants the meticulous care they require: first, plant them spaced well apart so that they can grow easily; next systematically get rid of any debris and rotting material from the flower beds; finally, water adequately so they do not weaken and will thus be less vulnerable to diseases.

Amid the vast selection of products available, the amateur gardener does not know where to turn. When he finds himself in front of the shelves of products, all with scientific names, at his favourite garden centre, the array of choice only complicates the problem. Since the miracle all-in-one product still does not exist, there follows a description of the most common plant diseases, to enable you to recognize them in time. Some minor afflictions are also illustrated because, although they are not threatening, they occur frequently. The treatments suggested give the name of each preparation's basic ingredient. The precise composition of the product will be found on the packet (usually, alas, in small print). Read the packet instructions carefully. Follow exactly the instructions for dosage and for the periods when the product should be used – this is extremely important. You will achieve effective results and will avoid poisoning your plants, useful animals (bees) and indeed yourself. It cannot be said often enough: if you are spraying a product, use the appropriate instrument. Empty it and rinse it out after use. Also, do not trust to luck and mix different treatment products together (for example, a fungicide and an insecticide). If chemically incompatible, these could have a negative and dangerous reaction. Finally, do not worry too much: just like us, plants do not catch all the diseases to which they could be prone and, if they do, in many cases they can be cured very effectively. To help you, remember that fungicides are more effective if applied as a preventive measure (this is more economical and less tiresome); that a 'systemic' product is conveyed through the sap stream of plants and thus protects them all the better; finally, that the level of toxicity of products is always indicated on the packet. Always keep these products under lock and key in a special cupboard, and place on this in case of emergency – conspicuously and in large print – the address and phone number of the nearest hospital able to deal with poisoning cases (check the name of the hospital in advance).

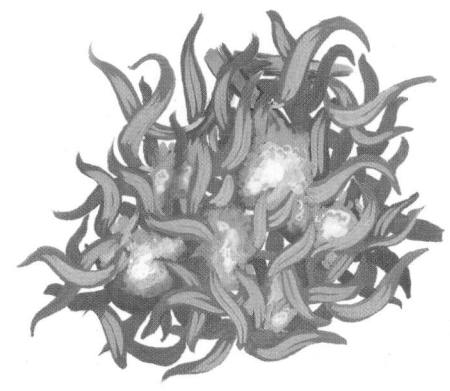

Algae

In conditions of poor aeration and minimum sunlight, sticky, grey or green areas appear on the lawn. Aerate the soil, using a fork, try to let in more light if possible, and treat with dichlorophen.

Blackspot

These are even, round black spots, followed by the leaves dropping off. Treat with carbendazim every 2 weeks. This is a classic rose disease.

Leaf-cutter bee

The edge of the leaves is cut in successive, very characteristic circles. A good contact insecticide usually prevents a recurrence. Leaf-cutter bees also attack woolly leaves (stachys), which they destroy completely, and sometimes lilacs.

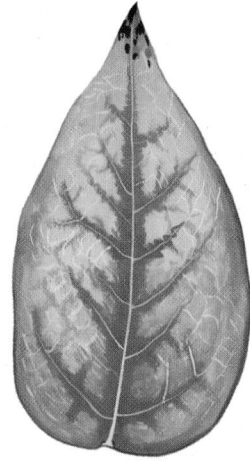

Deficiencies

The absence, or blockage, of certain mineral elements in the soil creates imbalances in plants. The most common deficiency is lime-induced chlorosis, when iron cannot be assimilated, being blocked by lime. The leaves become yellow and fall off. Growth is weak or non-existent. Sequestered iron, applied regularly, will rectify the problem.

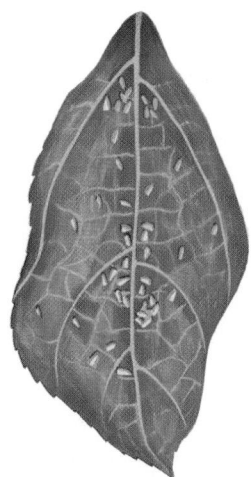

Whitefly

These tiny white flies attach themselves on the underside of the leaves, where their larvae create a lot of damage to the leaves during warm weather. They are not supposed to be able survive the winter outside, and are transmitted through greenhouses. Treat with permethrin four times, with 8 days' interval between doses. In the greenhouse, an integrated attack on them with *Encarsia formosa*, a tiny parasitic wasp, is a good remedy. Tomatoes, fuchsias and lantanas are particularly prone to whitefly infestation.

Honey fungus

Honey-coloured toadstools appear at the base of trees and shrubs and white fungal growths appear under the bark. Eventually the whole plant is killed. There is nothing that can be done about this, unfortunately, because once the toadstools appear the damage is already done. Remove them, nevertheless, so that they do not spread to other hosts. All trees are susceptible to fungal growths of this sort in differing degrees, but, happily, this is only a rare occurrence.

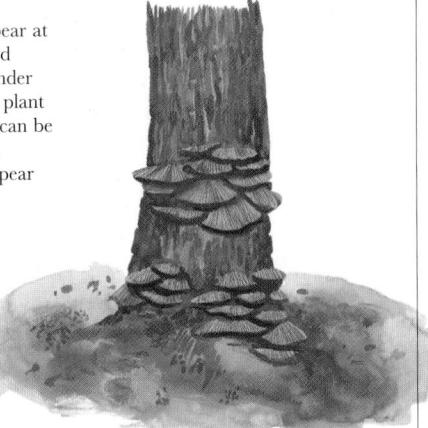

Caterpillars

Butterfly larvae, which have a ferocious appetite, transform plants into lace. The red admiral butterfly has the good grace to make nettles its exclusive target, but the redoubtable cabbage white butterfly enjoys all cruciferous plants, also nasturtiums, and seems to be extending its area of action. Quickly identified, these caterpillars are easily destroyed with the aid of pyrethrum or *Bacillus thuringiensis*, a biological control.

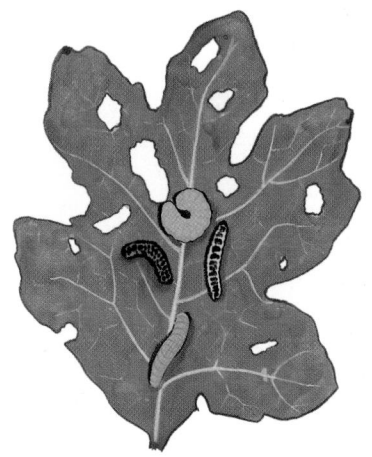

Webber moth caterpillars

The caterpillars of various moths attack different shrubs and trees, often in great numbers. The most spectacular are the juniper webber moth and the brown-tailed moth, which can denude a tree. Other species, however, attack different genera. All shelter in silken webs, of variable size. Spray with pyrethrum, or use *Bacillus thuringiensis*, a biological control.

Lily beetle

Specific to lilies and their relatives the fritillarias, this beetle can defoliate them completely by means of its unappetizing worm-like larvae, which are covered in their own faeces. Treat with permethrin regularly, but with long gaps, (3 weeks) between each treatment.

Fireblight

With fireblight the leaves of trees and shrubs die and turn black without falling off, and the branches die; the disease spreads to the entire tree, which can die. There is no homologous remedy. Destroy and burn all the affected parts. Only plants in the Rosaceae are affected by this disease (apple trees, pear trees, cotoneasters, sorbus trees, etc.).

Flower blight

Often confused by the amateur gardener with damage due to excessive sunlight, this disease, caused by a fungus, appears above all in greenhouse flowers and does not usually have serious consequences. Remove affected flowers and provide good ventilation.

Dollar spot

These are small light yellow patches on lawns, quickly becoming conspicuous in warm and damp weather. Of little importance and of short duration, they should be cured by watering the lawn with carbendazim.

Dead patches in lawns

Whole areas of the lawn can die out after coming in contact with toxic products such as detergents, alcohol, salt, perfume, and dog and cat urine. The infected soil should be dug up, replaced, and re-sown.

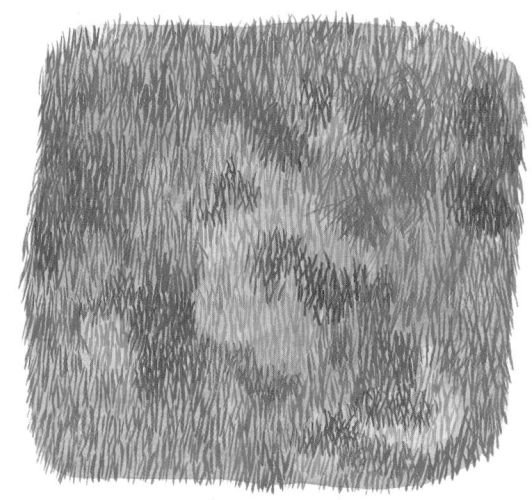

Slugs and snails

Many plants fall victim to these hungry pests, which attack them right in the soil. Leaves and flowers become ragged and disappear. Shiny trails indicate the damage. Different kinds of bait can prove quite effective, in granule or liquid form. Hostas and the shoots of delphiniums are particular targets.

Mildew

This furry white growth, caused by a fungus, appears in dry weather. Spray with a fungicide containing bupirimate and triforine between spring and summer. Many shrubs and trees are affected, such as roses, spindle trees and apple trees, and also some perennials, such as asters and delphiniums.

Leaf miners

Leaf miner larvae make trails through the thickness of the leaves. Contact insecticides are insufficient. Treat with dimethoate. These larvae occur frequently on chrysanthemums, holly and apple trees.

Earwigs

Earwigs attack leaves, but do not often do much damage to them. However, they particularly enjoy the thick, soft flowers of dahlias and chrysanthemums, which they ravage from the outside. Spraying with permethrin will remedy the problem.

Nematodes or eelworms

These microscopic 'worms' invade the plant's tissues, attaching themselves principally to the roots and the leaves, which they deform, preventing the plant's normal nutrition. The only means of control for the amateur is to pick off and burn any affected leaves, or in severe cases dig up and burn the whole plant.

Silver leaf

The leaves discolour, taking on an unpleasant silvery tint, then blacken and fall off. This disease should be tackled by means of prevention: prune only in summer, and remove and burn the affected branches. Several trees and shrubs are prone to silver leaf, above all plum and cherry trees and other members of Rosaceae.

Grey mould (botrytis)

All parts of plants are prone to this fungal disease, which appears in the form of a grey, furry growth. Flowers and fruits (notably red fruits) discolour and die. Bulbs rot. Extremely damp conditions encourage the development of grey mould. Remove all affected parts and spray with carbendazim. Most flowering plants are prone to this.

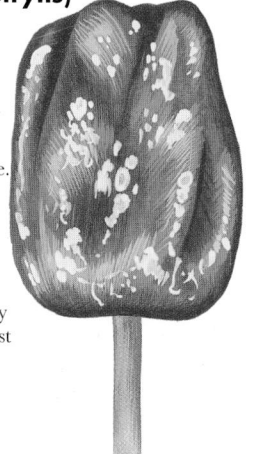

Fairy rings

Several species of mushroom cause this disease, which affects lawns, making them appear burned. Regular circles appear, which spread out wider each year. The growths appear in summer and autumn. There is no chemical cure.

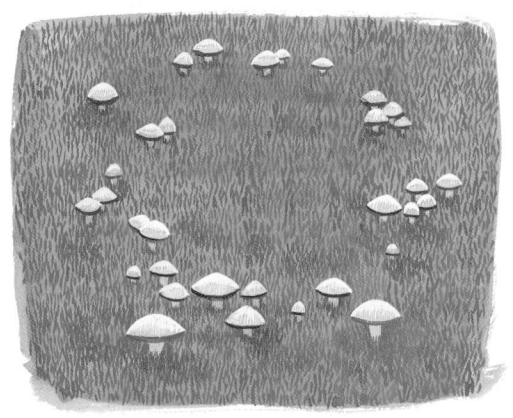

Rust

Different kinds of fungi cause rust, which appears as rust-coloured pinhead spots on the undersides of leaves, which are often yellow above. The importance of rust varies according to the season. Treat with propiconazole or mancozeb. Different species of shrub can be affected.

Woolly aphids

These aphids are covered with a fluffy white growth and they attack apples and some ornamental shrubs. The can cause swelling on the stems. Large trees are impossible to treat, but will tolerate the shock reasonably well. Treat smaller plants with pirimicarb, and take extra precautions at the end of winter or in midsummer.

Fusarium patch

This causes the lawn to discolour, initially in the form of small circles which quickly enlarge during the autumn, to become whole patches. Fight this with carbendazim.

Greenfly and blackfly

These insects appear in dense colonies on the shoots and new leaves of all plants. In great numbers they weaken plants, deforming and sometimes killing the affected parts. They also transmit viruses. Treat with insecticides such as malathion, pyrethrum, rotenone, dimethoate or pirimicarb.

Leaf rolling sawfly

This causes small leaves to roll up like cigarettes. All systemic insecticides easily remedy it. Treat as soon as the leaves have grown. This parasite, which favours roses, appears in waves then disappears just as inexplicably.

To pick fruit at home is the desire of many a gardener, no matter how small the garden. In the countryside it is possible to have a real orchard; in town, where space is limited, fruit trees have to be planted wherever there is space, with some of them being supported against walls.

Before planting, examine the soil or arrange for a soil analysis to be carried out (the quality of the soil will determine in part which kinds of fruit trees you will be able to plant). Once the results are known you can enhance the soil by the following improvements and by adding fertilizer.

• If the soil is sandy, add some manure, peat or compost to give it body and to make it better able to hold water.

• If the soil is clay, add sand, manure and compost to lighten it.

• If the soil is chalky, add sulphur to lower its pH level to 7.

Find out which root-stocks are best for your land. The stronger the root-stock, the larger the tree will be. It will take longer to produce fruit but will last for many years. Weaker root-stocks, used mainly for trained trees, will enable you to have fruit more rapidly but for a shorter period of years.

If your land is too wet, plant your trees on raised mounds at least 50 cm (20 in) high and 2 m (6½ ft) in diameter, and allow the mounds to settle for 1–2 weeks before planting.

Do not forget that, in order to produce beautiful fruit, your trees need plenty of sunshine and an open position.

Do not plant trees too close to one another. A standard needs a space 4–5 m (13–16 ft) in diameter, a goblet-shaped peach tree 2–3 m (6½–10 ft). Trained trees are easier to maintain. Depending on the shape of the tree, allow a space of 60 cm – 2 m (2–6½ ft) between two consecutive trees trained along a wall.

Do not forget to add fertilizer in spring, each year for the first 5 years. Use composite mineral fertilizers, organic fertilizer, or both. Hoe these in.

Watch out for any diseases or parasites so that you can treat the trees immediately and thus avoid having to do so more drastically later. Follow the dosage instructions for fungicides and insecticides.

Mix fruit species and varieties to minimize the risk of diseases, and choose those that are most suitable to the area you live in. They will be less prone to disease.

Above all, do not insist on planting a variety requiring a great deal of heat in a northern climate; conversely, do not place a fruit tree needing cool, moist conditions on a dry south-easterly hillside.

Buying and planting

How to buy fruit trees

Bear in mind your own personal preference and the space you have available. Do not plant ten large standards on land measuring 100 sq. m (900 sq. ft): they would not thrive and would not produce much fruit. Depending on the space available, choose standards or goblets, or trained varieties (espaliers, fans, etc.). You will often need two trees of the same species, but of a different variety, so that they can pollinate each other, because only a few varieties are self-fertilizing.

If you like growing trees and pruning them into shape, buy some young trees that have just been grafted and make a cordon, an espalier, a fan or a goblet. Alternatively, select trees that are already formed. Look at the point where the grafting has been carried out: it should be inconspicuous, a large ridge suggesting a difficult, repeated graft. For preference, buy trees that you can inspect

before buying, from a local nurseryman, and ask him which root-stocks he uses: this is important, depending on the quality of your soil. Do not hesitate to buy trees with bare roots, which is the usual procedure. In containers, they can be planted throughout the year. Water them carefully, to ensure they thrive.

Check that they have a good root system and that they do not turn in on themselves, a sign of poor growing conditions. Do not wait for the end of the season to make your purchases, or you will acquire poor trees, stocked in over-heated shops for weeks, that are not worth having.

The choice of varieties is vast. Be guided by your taste and, preferably, aim for a variety rarely found in greengrocer's shops: it is quality you are looking for in the garden, not quantity.

Planting

The best time to plant is between autumn and spring, during the dormant season. For each tree, dig a hole several days before you plan to plant. If the soil is good, a hole 30 cm (12 in) wide and 40 cm (16 in) deep should be enough. In poor soil, aim for a larger hole (50 cm/20 in square). Add a base layer of manure to the subsoil, plus a general-

purpose fertilizer, mixing them well together so that the roots do not come into direct contact with the fertilizer. Provide wooden stakes for standard trees, a system of wires for trained trees. Shorten the roots of the tree by 5–10 cm (2–4 in), and the branches by a third of their length. Make sure the tree is straight, then fill the hole with soil mixed with two or three parts of compost or well-rotted manure. Firm well, water, and secure the tree to its support. You can plant either a very young tree, making it either into a trained shape (a cordon, espalier or fan) or a half-standard tree (with a trunk of 1.2 m/4 ft), or a standard (with a trunk of 1.8 m/6 ft) or even a shorter shape (goblet, spindle bush).

How to plant a half-standard or standard tree

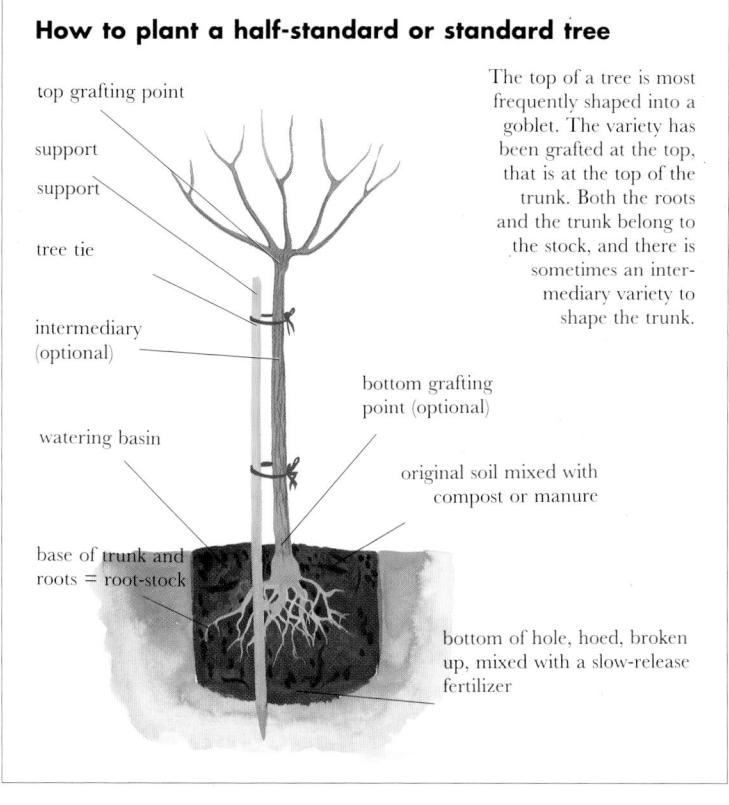

top grafting point

support

support

tree tie

intermediary
(optional)

watering basin

base of trunk and
roots = root-stock

bottom grafting
point (optional)

original soil mixed with
compost or manure

bottom of hole, hoed, broken
up, mixed with a slow-release
fertilizer

The top of a tree is most frequently shaped into a goblet. The variety has been grafted at the top, that is at the top of the trunk. Both the roots and the trunk belong to the stock, and there is sometimes an intermediary variety to shape the trunk.

How to make a goblet shape

(The goblet is suitable for all fruit tree varieties)

                       1st year   2nd year

Basic shape
You do not need to buy a young tree to make this: choose simple shapes. These diagrams show you how to proceed.

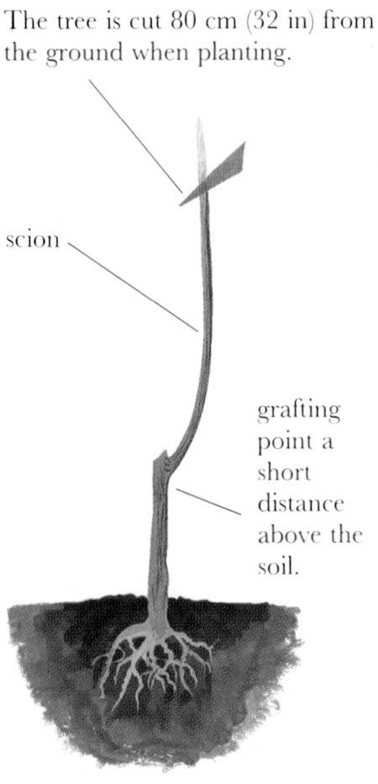

The tree is cut 80 cm (32 in) from the ground when planting.

scion

grafting
point a
short
distance
above the
soil.

Keep three vigorous shoots, evenly spaced out and, if possible, forming an angle of 120 degrees between them, viewed from above.

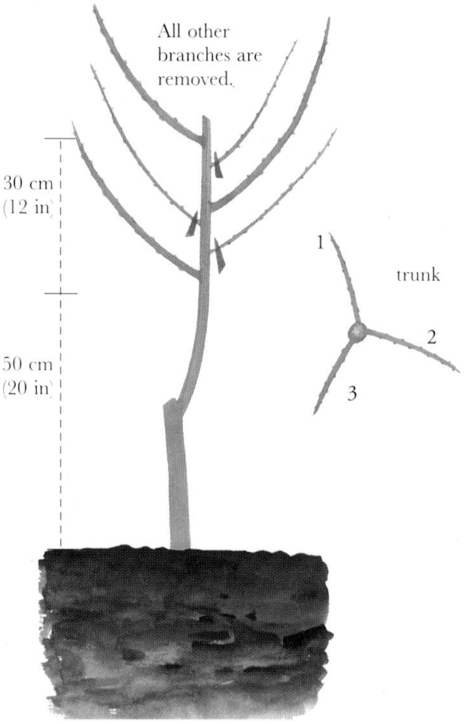

All other
branches are
removed.

30 cm
(12 in)

50 cm
(20 in)

1

trunk

2

3

For each of the three leader branches 1, 2, 3 keep two good shoots, A and B, and eliminate all the others. Also, cut back the growth of 1, 2 and 3 by 25–30cm (10–12 in). You will thus have six main branches on which the fruit-bearing branches will grow.

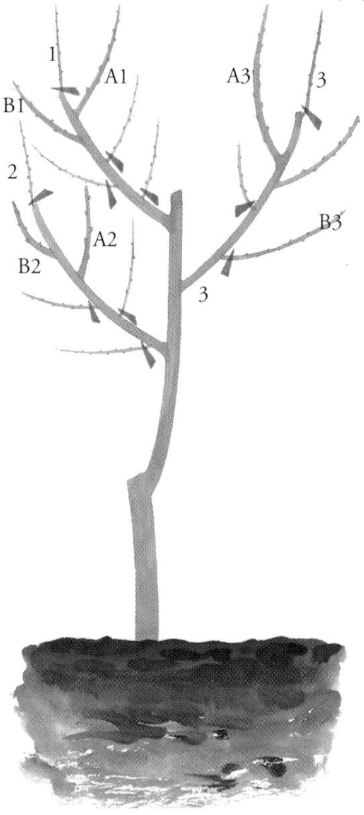

1

A1

B1

A3

3

2

A2

B3

B2

3

How to form a spindle shape
(This shape is particularly suitable for pear trees)

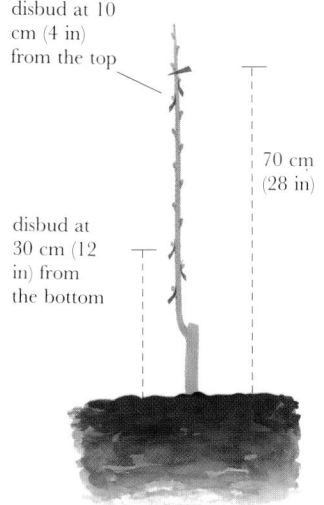

disbud at 10 cm (4 in) from the top

70 cm (28 in)

disbud at 30 cm (12 in) from the bottom

pinch out the shoots that are too vigorous

tree tie securing the young shoot to the remaining part of the main stem, 10 cm (4 in) long

scion

remove the last part of the main stem

30 cm (12 in)

Prune for the first time in the spring following the planting of the tree. Cut the stem 10 cm (4 in) above a bud, at about 70 cm (28 in) from the ground; the bud should be chosen for its apparent vigour. Remove any buds above the one you have chosen and at the bottom of the stem, 30 cm (12 in) from the soil.

In the summer of the same year, pinch out (that is, remove by using your thumb and index finger) the shoots that are too strong. At the same time, attach the central young shoot to the remaining part of the stem, 10 cm (4 in) long, so that it is a good vertical shape.

In the late winter of the following year, remove the last of the main stem and cut off the central branches above an outward-facing bud. Cut the short branches back a little and the long branches back short. In the following years, prolong the central axis by 25–30 cm (10–12 in) and the main lateral branches by the same, or even a little more. The final height should be 3 m (10 ft).

Making a cordon
The stem is bent in the spring and pruned just above a downward-facing bud, which will produce a shoot.

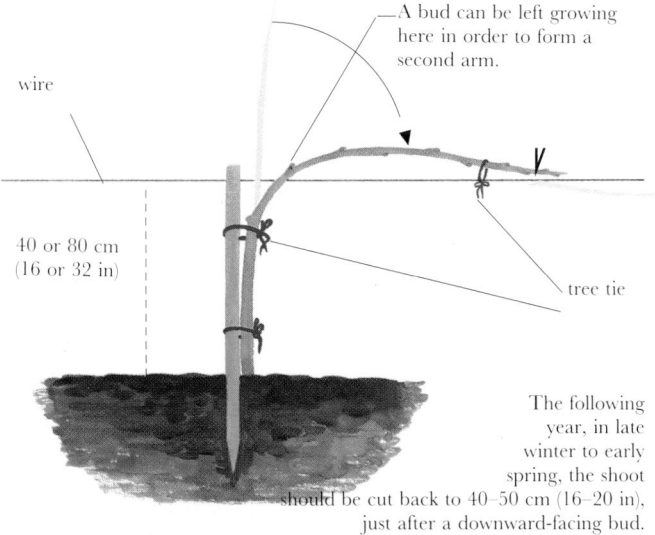

A bud can be left growing here in order to form a second arm.

wire

40 or 80 cm (16 or 32 in)

tree tie

The following year, in late winter to early spring, the shoot should be cut back to 40–50 cm (16–20 in), just after a downward-facing bud.

With two trees, you can form two cordons superimposed one over the other, one at 40 cm (16 in) from the soil, the other at 80 cm (32 in). A cordon can have one or two arms 3 m (10 ft) long, sometimes more. This shape is suitable for apple and pear trees that are not very vigorous (grafted on to root-stocks selected for their poor vigour).

Horizontally branched shape
The branches are trained on a support at irregular intervals, either horizontally, or on a diagonal.

When this branch no longer produces, it should be cut out. The A and B buds begin to grow. The most vigorous should be kept and trained as and when it grows.

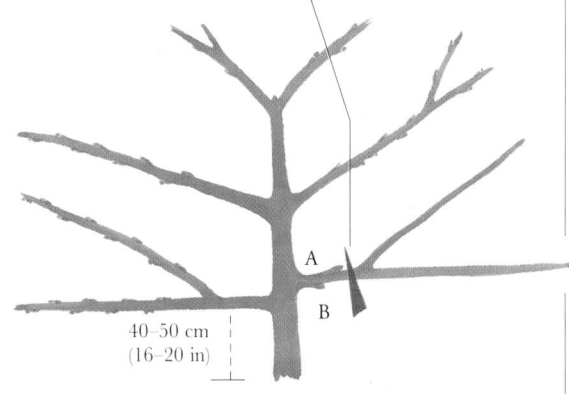

A

B

40–50 cm (16–20 in)

When a leader branch grows old, it should be cut 10–15 cm (4–6 in) from the trunk. It will be replaced by one of the vigorous branches which will grow at the bottom of it. The principle here is just to balance the tree.

Forming the simplest espalier-trained shapes

The tree is planted in the autumn. In spring it should be cut 30 cm (12 in) from the ground, just above the two top buds, A and B, which are kept. All the other buds are removed.

Each bud gives rise to a shoot which should be trained as and when it grows.

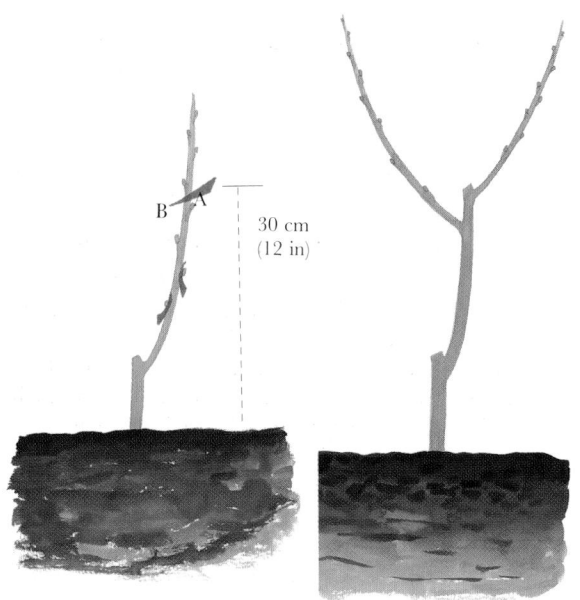

First option: forming crossbars, a type of horizontally branched shape suitable for most varieties. Each branch should be allowed to grow by 30 cm (12 in) each year and should be trained as required.

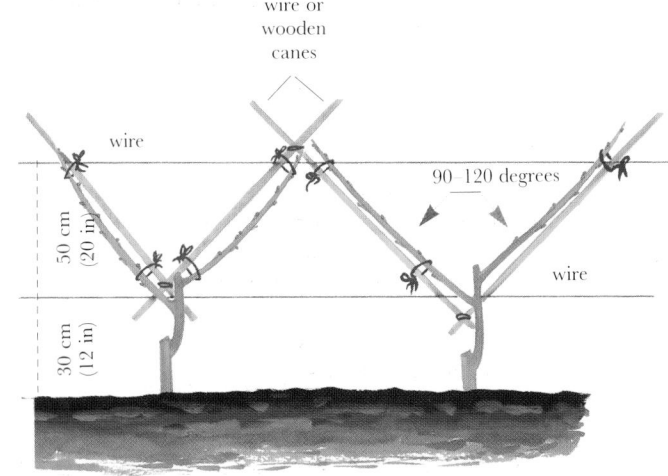

2nd year: cut at 30 cm (12 in) and a bud will grow again.

Second option: forming a simple U-shape

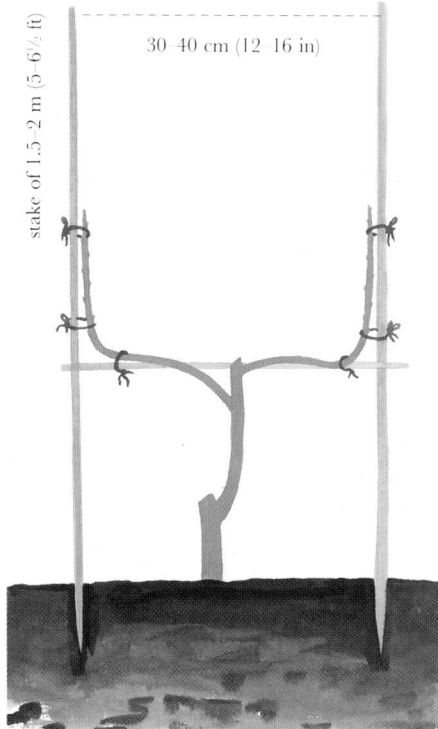

Horizontal training by 15–20 cm (6–8 in), then vertical: this shape is suitable for varieties of apple and pear trees that are not very vigorous. Afterwards, leave each branch of the U to grow by 25–30 cm (10–12 in) each year until a height of 2m (6½ ft) is reached.

Third option: forming a double U-shape (for varieties that are not very vigorous).

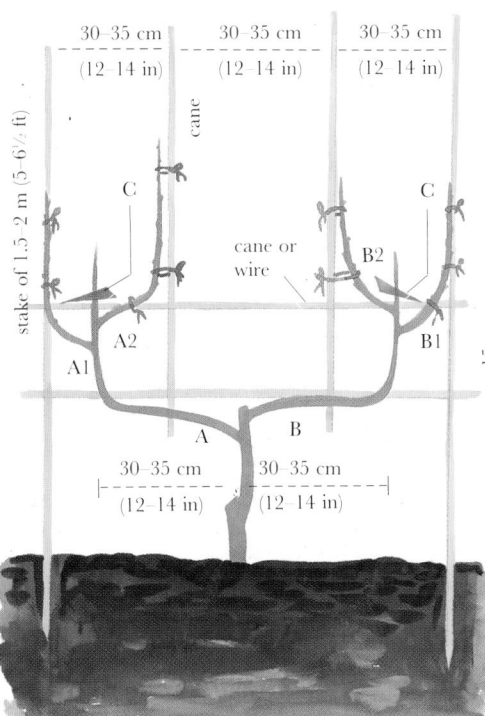

1st year
The two A and B branches should be progressively trained (in summer), horizontally, by 30–35 cm (12–14 in), then vertically.

2nd year
cut in a C-shape, by about 15–20 cm (6–8 in), vertically. Four shoots appear (A1, B1, A2 and B2), which should be trained.

Afterwards the four branches should be allowed to grow by 25–30 cm (10–12 in) every year until a height of 2 m (6½ ft) is reached.

Propagation: grafting and layering

If you want to preserve a fruit tree variety, sowing the stones or pips can be unreliable. It is therefore best to resort either to budding in summer (this consists in sliding a bud, with a little bit of bark attached, from the selected variety under the bark of the root-stock), or to cleft or split grafting, side-grafting, or crown grafting in spring. This process involves sliding under the bark of a large branch or trunk of the root-stock one, two, three or four small shoots of the chosen variety, evenly distributed.

With budding, carried out in summer, the bud does not grow until the following spring.

Some gardeners sometimes carry out an whip and tongue grafting in spring.

The following is the best layering technique for cobnuts, and sometimes for vines and red currant bushes: in late winter, branches kept in position by supports should be driven into the soil; the branches that take root in autumn are then separated from the original plant, and replanted.

Note: *For these grafting and layering techniques, please refer to pp. 561–3, where they are discussed in greater detail.*

Actinidia chinensis
Chinese gooseberry
or kiwi fruit

Planting and propagation

Plant from mid-autumn to mid-spring, in fresh soil which should be kept moist in summer. The Chinese gooseberry, or kiwi, is a climber which needs to be trained around a pergola or an arbour or on a wire stretched over a wall sheltered from high winds and away from direct sunlight. Two plants at least should be planted: one male, the other female. The kiwi is propagated by layering in summer. The branches are divided from the main stalk the following spring.

Pruning for shape and maintenance

Allow a few leader branches to sprout and grow. Then, in winter, cut back all the lateral branches, leaving two buds. In summer, cut back all the fruit-bearing branches, leaving four or five leaves above the fruit. Repeat the operation with the new branches which will grow by nipping them off, leaving two leaves.

Diseases and pests

Rare.

Citrus

Planting and propagation

Plant in spring in well-drained sandy soil. Lime is tolerated in small quantities. (Bear in mind that citrus can only be grown under glass in the UK.) Propagation is carried out by the two budding methods (in spring or autumn). Lemon trees and orange trees are grafted on to Seville orange trees, 25–40 cm (10–16 in) from the ground, clementines on to Poncirus, 10 cm (4 in) from the ground.

Pruning for maintenance

Lighten the branches in spring, by removing the weaker ones.

Diseases and pests

Aphids can be a problem in summer but can be controlled by spraying with malathion or pirimicarb. Control whitefly with permethrin.

Corylus avellana
Cobnut

Planting and propagation

Plant in fresh, light, even chalky soil, rather than in heavy soil, and in a hole not exceeding 25–30 cm (10–12 in) in depth. Afterwards, in spring, the supple branches can be partially buried in the soil, in a trench 15–20 cm (6–8 in) deep, and covered with soil. In summer roots will form on the lower part, and in autumn you will be able to remove these branches in order to replant them.

Pruning for shape and maintenance

No pruning for shape is necessary: the cobnut forms a clump 4–6 m (13–20 ft) tall, from which you should remove dead wood and any branches that are more than ten years old. Plant two different varieties, because they are all more or less self-sterile (unless your next-door neighbour already has a cobnut, in which case you will need only one).

Diseases and pests

Cobnuts are relatively disease-free. The nut weevil may be a problem, but it can be controlled by spraying with HCH two or three times in late spring and early summer. If any winter moth caterpillars are seen, spray in mid-spring with fenitrothion.

Fragaria
Strawberry

Planting and propagation

Strawberry plants need a rich and well-drained soil, lime-free or neutral, enriched with fertilizer every year in spring: 100g (4 oz)/1 sq. m (10 sq. ft) dried manure and 50 g (2 oz) of a compound general-purpose fertilizer. Plant the strawberry plants between mid- and late summer, or else in spring, with a gap of 35–40 cm (14–16 in) between them for varieties with large fruit, 25 cm (10 in) for varieties with small fruit. Mulch the soil with straw. You can increase your stock of strawberry plants by rooting the runners (the long stems bearing a small strawberry plant at the tip).

Pruning for maintenance

Keep a few runners in order to renew and increase your strawberry beds, and remove the others.

Diseases and pests

Treat grey mould with carbendazim fungicide at the beginning and end of the flowering season.

Juglans regia
Walnut

Planting and propagation

Adapting itself to many soil types, even chalky ones, the walnut only dislikes heavy soil and stagnant water. It grows to 15–20 m (50–65 ft) and needs a spacious garden. Cleft or slit grafting on to a hickory in spring, or crown grafting in late spring, makes it possible to obtain smaller trees that produce fruit more quickly but have a shorter lifespan (30 years as opposed to 100).

Pruning for shape and maintenance

A tall or half-standard walnut forms its own framework of branches and needs no thinning out, because it dislikes this just as much as it dislikes routine pruning. If necessary, cut out the branches in autumn and protect the cut with pruning 'paint'.

Diseases and pests

Bacterial diseases cannot be cured. They can be avoided, however, by buying healthy plants.

Malus communis
Crab and other apples

Planting and propagation

The crab apple and other apples tolerate all soils that are not very chalky but do not do well in sandy, excessively dry soil. There are many root-stocks, all of different vigour.

In the UK apples can be obtained on the following rootstocks: M27, which is an extremely dwarfing rootstock, ideal for trained forms; M9, a very dwarfing stock which is widely used by nurserymen for dwarf bush trees and trained forms; M26, a dwarfing stock used for dwarf bush trees and trained forms; MM106, semi-dwarfing and used for bush trees plus trained forms; MM111 and M2, vigorous rootstocks which result in large trees on good soils, but smaller trees on less fertile soils, and can be used for all forms of tree plus trained forms.

Propagation is carried out by means of budding in summer, or either cleft or slit grafting or side grafting in spring. You will find very varied standard trees and espalier forms, as well as cordons. All are planted in autumn.

Pruning for shape and maintenance

The crab apple and others can be trained in many different ways, and if you want to take the trouble to create a cordon, a U-shape or a horizontally branched shape with a young tree as the starting point, this is the tree to use. For trained shapes, this pruning is essential. The most up-to-date is the three-bud cut, which involves cutting the branches to the third bud in late winter. The topmost bud will, in the summer, produce a leaved shoot or woody branch, and the two others will produce leaflets, to be fruit-bearing branches the following year. For trained varieties, cut back the leader branches which have grown the previous summer by 15–20 cm (6–8 in) for the weaker varieties, and up to 40–50 cm (16–20 in) for the more vigorous varieties. Besides, the bending or arching of a branch encourages the production of fruit. In summer, nip out the vigorous branches once in mid-summer and once in late summer, leaving them with only four or five leaves. Finally, thin out the fruit when they are 2 cm ($^3/_4$ in) in diameter in order to leave only one, two or three per cluster.

Diseases or pests

Woolly aphids, which form whitish deposits, drain the sap of the branches and jeopardize the harvest. Trees can be sprayed in winter with a tar-oil winter wash and in spring and summer with pirimicarb. The codling moth is an insect which lays eggs in late spring to early summer. The larvae penetrate into the fruit, making them maggoty. Covering the fruit with bags is a good remedy. However, trees can also be treated with an insecticide containing permethrin in early summer, repeating 3 weeks later. Powdery mildew is a fungus which covers the shoots with white dust. Treat with an insecticide based on bupirimate and triforine.

Three-bud cut (apple and pear trees)

Spring of the 1st year
cut
3 woody buds

Spring of the 2nd year
cut
one-bud cut

Spring of the 3rd year
large round fruit bud
cut
leaflet

Summer of the 1st year
woody branch
two leaflets, small and very pointed

Summer of the second year
woody branch
fruit bud
leaflet

Summer of the 3rd year
fruit

Prunus armenica
Apricot

Planting and propagation

In the autumn plant either a young tree which you can shape into a goblet, or one that has already been formed in the garden centre, or a half-standard or standard tree. The varieties are budded at the top (standard trees) or at the bottom, 50 cm (20 in) from the ground (goblet, spindle) in summer and autumn. Choose a spot with a good deal of light, 5–6 m (16–20 ft) from neighbouring trees, including other apricots. You can plant a fan-trained tree every 2–3 m (6½–10 ft) along a south-facing wall.

Pruning for shape and maintenance

Carry out pruning for shape either in late autumn, so that the cuts can heal before the cold weather, or in early spring because of the danger of gummosis (a sticky oozing fluid). Opt for a simple shape such as the goblet. Afterwards, keep an open shape so that the sun can filter through effectively throughout the tree and in autumn remove the weak branches. Retain the good branches that are growing outwards by cutting the tips of the most vigorous ones. There is no pruning for fruit: it is the branches grown the previous year that bear the fruit. Unless there are exceptional circumstances, there is no point in thinning out the fruit, but the branches must be supported. If a large branch should break, make a clean cut at the point where it has broken off and spread pruning 'paint' over it; if gummosis does not interfere, the tree will make new growth.

Diseases and pests

If the soil is too wet, or if the tree is damaged, gummosis appears, interfering with the healing process and weakening the tree. There is no cure for this. Aphids can bring about deformation of the leaves. Treat with a systemic insecticide. If the fruit is attacked by a grey mould with concentric pustules, this is brown rot, which should be controlled by removing affected fruits and aiming to prevent any damage to the fruits.

Prunus avium
Cherry

Planting and propagation

All soils, even poor and chalky ones, are suitable, provided they are not too wet. Side grafting on to the wild cherry, or slit or cleft grafting in late winter, or budding at the top (never at the bottom), will produce tall trees (8–10 m/26–33 ft). The root-stock Colt will result in less vigorous trees, enabling low goblet shapes (50 cm/20 in from the ground) to be formed, which are much more accessible when picking the fruit. Nevertheless, do not plant a cherry tree less than 4–5 m (13–16 ft) from other trees.

Pruning for shape and thinning out

The first is limited to ensuring a good distribution of the leader branches on the goblets, and the second does not apply because of the danger of gummosis, a sticky fluid which weakens the tree. In case of emergency (a broken or cumbersome branch), take action in autumn and spread pruning 'paint' over the cut.

Diseases and pests

Aphids collect on the leaves in spring. Treat with a tar-oil wash in winter, to destroy the eggs. At least a fortnight before picking the fruit, or after harvesting it, also apply a systemic insecticide based on dimethoate, which is equally effective on cherry fruit moths (these pests are responsible for the worms one finds in the fruit). Gummosis affects diseased or damaged trees in soil that is too damp, and there is no remedy against this.

Prunus domestica
Plum

Planting and propagation

A very undemanding tree, the plum will thrive in all types of soil except very sandy ones, which are too dry for it.

Plant it in autumn, with a gap of 4–5 m (13–16 ft) between each tree, whether a scion, goblet, standard or half-standard. Fan-trained trees are possible.

Varieties may be grafted on to St Julien A root-stock, which is not too vigorous and which will tolerate heavy soil, or even on to a Myrobolan B root-stock, which is more robust and better suited to chalky soils. In spring, graft by the slit or cleft method or by crown grafting, or propagate by budding in summer.

Pruning for shape and maintenance

It is essential to train the tree into the desired shape when it is young – or it will later be susceptible to cutting damage gummosis. Act as soon as the leaves have fallen. Only the goblet shape is recommended. No thinning out is necessary, but the branches that are heavily laden with fruit should be well supported.

Diseases and pests

Aphids should be treated as soon as they appear, to avoid them spreading. A fungus creates brown rot (grey, concentric mouldy patches on the fruit). Pick and destroy the affected fruit: they harbour the disease.

Prunus persica
Peach

Planting and propagation

Plant in autumn, in deep, fertile, well-drained soil that is neither chalky nor acid (pH 7). You can either plant a very young tree or a ready-formed peach tree, both grafted on to a true peach tree that has been produced from seed or more likely St Julien A root-stock. The latter is ideal for moist soils.

Pruning for shape and maintenance

The simplest solution is to give it a shape nearest to the one it should naturally grow into: the goblet. In cold climates, it is possible to train the peach tree along a south- or south-west-facing wall by opting for a fan shape. Only the branches that have grown the previous year bear fruit and they must not be too far from the large branches to avoid breaking. In winter, prune the upward-pointing branches so that the tree is not too bare at the bottom. In spring, when the young fruit is formed, thin it out in order to leave only four or five fruits per branch, and nip out the young shoots which accompany them, leaving three or four leaves. After harvesting, prune the branches that have borne fruit, because they will never bear again, but leave new shoots at the bottom to ensure their replacement.

Diseases and pests

Peach leaf curl reddens and deforms the leaves. It also weakens the tree. Remove affected leaves. Spray trees with a copper-based fungicide in mid- or late winter and repeat a fortnight later.

Pyrus communis
Pear

Planting and propagation

Strongly disliking lime-rich and dry soils, the pear tree needs a deep well-drained loam. Standard trees (planted 4–5 m/13–16 ft apart) may be grafted on to the very vigorous pear rootstock. Smaller forms are grafted on to Quince A or Quince C rootstocks, enabling fruit to be produced more quickly. Propagation is done either by budding, slit or cleft grafting, side grafting, or by crown grafting in the spring.

Pruning for shape and maintenance

The pear tree, like the apple tree, lends itself well to all sorts of shapes, trained or not. Choose a simple one: spindle, goblet or cordon. Pruning for fruit is the same as for the apple tree. It is necessary to thin out in order to keep just one or two fruits per cluster.

Diseases and pests

Scab disease causes brown scabs on the fruits, and brown patches on the leaves which may fall prematurely.

Spray with carbendazim. Gather up the dead leaves and get rid of them because the fungus overwinters there.

If the young shoots are curled, and if the leaves have a burnt appearance, this is undoubtedly the very dangerous fireblight, which has no cure. The only way to deal with it is to burn the diseased branches, or even the whole tree.

Ribes rubrum *Ribes uva-crispa* and *Ribes nigrum*
Red currant, gooseberry and black currant

Planting and propagation
All soil types are suitable, with sandy soils having the edge over the others. Plant bushes you have purchased from your nurseryman from autumn to spring. To propagate, in autumn, cut the current year's shoots into lengths of 20–25 cm (8–10 in) and partially bury them, allowing only two or three buds to show. Plant out the following spring or a year later, leaving a gap of 1 m (3¼ ft) between them.

Pruning for shape and maintenance
Black currants produce fruit on the previous summer's wood, so prune them between early autumn and early spring by removing up to one-third of the oldest wood, leaving as many new shoots as possible. Try if possible to cut back to strong young shoots lower down. Gooseberries and white currants are pruned in early to mid-summer by cutting back all new side shoots to five leaves. Then in winter prune back these shoots further, to two or more buds. Leading shoots are cut back by half their length.

Diseases and pests
Aphids make the leaves shrivel and threaten the plant's growth. Treat from spring onwards, or as soon as the first symptoms are evident, with a dimethoate or pyretheum insecticide.

Rubus idaeus
Raspberry

Planting and propagation
Thriving in all types of soil, even those that are slightly chalky, the raspberry produces more fruit if the soil is rich and moisture-retentive. It is propagated, between autumn and spring, by division of the suckers (the current year's shoots). They should be planted with a gap of 50 cm (20 in) between them, and should be cut back after planting, to 25–30 cm (10–12 in) from the ground.

Pruning for shape and maintenance
The supple stalks are trained on a wire frame. From the second year onwards, prune so as to keep a maximum of only about ten or so stems per clump.

With summer-fruiting varieties, a stem grown during the spring and summer will bear fruit at the top the following year. Then it should be cut out completely, to be replaced by another new stem.

Diseases and pests
There are few problems apart from viruses. It is not possible to propagate your own raspberry bushes indefinitely. Every 10–15 years, it is necessary to plant new ones by purchasing healthy new plants and planting them in a different place. Grubs in the fruits are those of the raspberry beetle. Control by spraying with malathion or dermis as soon as the first fruits start to turn pink, then repeat a fortnight later.

Vitis vinifera
Grape

Planting and propagation
All soils, even chalky and stony ones, will do for the vine, provided there is no stagnant water. Plant in spring, occasionally in autumn. All varieties are grafted on to the American vine, because this is not prone to the vine pest phylloxera. Amateurs can propagate vines from cuttings in the autumn or by layering. A vine can easily cover an entire wall or a pergola.

Pruning for shape and maintenance
It is possible to create a main branch within 3–4 years with strong branches that have been allowed to grow large and which should be trained vertically or horizontally along the support frame. Secondary, fruit-bearing branches (laterals) grow on these long branches. In winter, cut all these laterals back, leaving 2–6 buds. The more vigorous the vine, the less you should prune. In summer, cut back laterals above the last bunch of grapes, leaving two leaves.

Diseases and pests
Phylloxera is an American root louse which attacks the roots and kills vines. Grafting on to resistant American vines is the only effective way to counteract this. Mildew attacks the leaves. It should be treated with a fungicide containing bupirimate and triforine. Botrytis is a fungus responsible for drying the bunches of grapes. It should be controlled with a fungicide containing carbendazim.

DECORATION

Pergolas

A pergola is undoubtedly one of the most attractive features of a garden, but it must be in harmony with its surroundings.

Path, patio or fence

Before choosing the materials and constructing a pergola, think carefully what you are trying to achieve: a sheltered path for getting from A to B; a covered patio, which you can treat as additional living space; or a structure to define the border of your property or divide it in two, which can also be used as a support for flowering shrubs (roses, wisteria) or fruit trees (kiwi, fig, vine).

Building a solid structure

A pergola will have to withstand a certain amount of wind pressure, so the uprights need to be buried at least 50 cm (20 in) into the ground. Greater stability can be achieved by tying in the individual arches to bars running lengthways. This also gives a greater surface area on which to train plants.

Wood, metal, brick or stone

Wood is the material most commonly used, in the form of solid timbers or trellis work. You can also buy metal arches, which are easy to install and ideal for growing roses on. Wooden uprights – treated with horticultural wood preservative – are best for a rustic effect. They should not be taller than 2.5 m (8 ft), nor spaced at intervals of more than 3.5 m (11½ ft).

Pergolas designed to support very vigorous plants, wisteria for example, will require more solid – brick or stonework – pillars of the kind often found in traditional British and American gardens. Remember that the weight of vegetation will increase as the years go by, so your pergola must be strong enough to take the strain. It is therefore sound policy to go for quality materials and ensure that the pergola is solidly constructed.

A pergola with an arched vault is a most elegant structure. It also provides a shaded area for children, who can ride their bikes along the covered path without having to trespass on lawns or flower beds.

Trelliswork arches are an ideal feature for a small garden. Three arches are sufficient for 7 m (23 ft) of path.

Solid timber has been used to make this original pergola, receding elegantly into the distance.
The striking effect is achieved by having the path not more than 2.5 m (8 ft) wide.

Trellises of this kind are ideal for building a light, graceful pergola to mark the boundary of a small garden. They also form an attractive support for clematis and non-vigorous types of rose.

The classic style of pergola, made of strong timbers, requires plenty of space. It is best placed at some distance from the house, where the beauty of the plants will be enhanced by perspective.

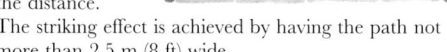

Using stone: scree and rock gardens

The scree garden

If your garden is uneven and covered in rubble, the ground rocky and barren, do not despair. After getting rid of all the weeds, you can create a fascinating garden out of stone. A scree garden is an unusual feature, since not everyone has the material – a pile of rubble, or an area of rocky ground – available.

A garden made of stone

In mountain areas, a naturally occurring area of scree is not necessarily devoid of plant life. A scree garden is best laid out on rough ground, though a really steep slope is un-necessary. It can be planted with alpine plants, and with any other plants requiring good drainage.

Scree is normally a mixture of coarse river sand, rock fragments and loose stones. You can create an area of this kind artificially, but resist the temptation to make it into a rock garden in miniature.

The site

The technique is to take or create a slight slope and cover it with worn-looking, flattish rocks.

• It should be exposed to the full sun, for it is intended as a home for plants which like dry conditions and need good drainage. Another advantage of a scree garden is that, being a 'mineral' environment, the quality of the soil is of absolutely no importance. Rock garden plants will thrive in these surroundings, as will many warm-climate species (provided the temperature in your area does not drop below –10°C).

• In a scree garden, the individual plants have a high profile. They are not hidden away in a flower bed or border, but are dotted here and there among the rocks, which also serve as stepping stones.

Planting

• The plants should be set in pockets filled with equal parts of peat, leaf-mould and sand. After planting, the base of each is covered with 5–10 cm (2–4 in) of gravel and coarse sand. It is best to plant in spring, to give the plants time to get established before winter.

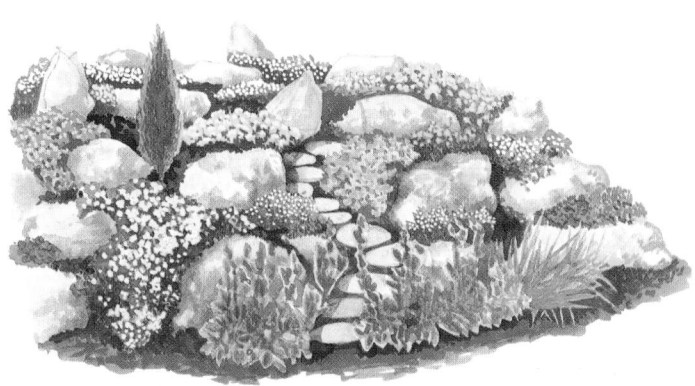

• This mineral environment is also a good setting for dwarf conifers. They lend stability and give the impression that the scree is alive.

Choice of plants

Suitable plants for this kind of terrain are:

• dwarf conifers such as *Chamaecyparis lawsoniana* 'Minima Glauca', with greyish foliage, and *C. obtusa* 'Nana', with attractive green leaves, together with a whole range of junipers;

• heathers, planted in groups of five to seven;

• holly, of various varieties;

• *Lonicera pileata*, an attractive little prostrate shrub;

• rock roses, planted alone or in groups of three, particularly *Cistus laurifolius* and *C.* × *corbariensis*;

• potentillas;

• small spring bulbs and *Iris pumila*, which thrive in well-drained soil;

• creeping perennials such as alyssum, *Phlox subulata* and, flowering from early summer on, *Campanula portenschlagiana* (bellflower), *Aster alpinus* and sedum;

• in mid-summer, *Campanula carpatica* (tussock bellflower), helianthemum and potentilla;

• in autumn, the various species of stonecrop, dwarf asters and plumbago.

The rock garden

A rock garden should be both decorative and useful. Sadly, it is often just a heap of stones, piled up because the owner did not know how to get rid of them.

Its functions

The function of a rock garden is to 'imitate' the terrain of a mountain area. The rocks used to build it should therefore harmonize with the geological structures of the region, assuming that there is a local type of stone. You cannot just build a rock garden in the middle of a flat piece of ground, simply because you have an urge to grow alpine plants. It should fit in with the garden setting.

• A rock garden can be a good solution to a landscaping problem, if you have a steepish slope or an area of uneven ground. But if your garden is really flat, you will have to create some sort of slope otherwise the agglomeration of rocks and stones will appear artificial.

Building the rock garden

To give your rock garden its essential mountain character, choose large rounded rocks with a rugged, weathered appearance, exactly as you would find them in nature. The biggest of these should be used at the base, with more pointed specimens towards the top. To form a good base, you can also use flat stones or broken cement slabs built up in layers. The plants will be rooted in the gaps and cracks.

• To obtain a natural effect, ensure that the width at the base is roughly five times the overall height of the rock garden. When the stones are laid, cover the rocks with a mixture of equal parts of peat, garden soil and coarse gravel. The purpose of this layer is to provide a footing for the plants and to bury the base of the rocks, so that they appear to emerge naturally from the ground. You can add a few flat rocks to use as stepping stones when you need to get on to the rock garden to keep it weed-free and tidy.

• If you cannot get hold of enough large rocks, rather than spread them too thin or reduce the planned area of rock garden, arrange them in groups of three or five and cover the areas in between with broken paving slabs. These can serve as a setting for prostrate shrubs, ground cover species, dwarf conifers and other suitable plants.

Good rock garden plants

• Some shrubs are perfectly at home in the alpine environment of the rock garden, for instance *Abies balsamea*, an attractive bluish green fir of prostrate habit, which grows no taller than 35 cm (14 in), or such junipers as the slim *Juniperus communis* 'Compressa', growing to 40 cm (16 in). A couple of columnar specimens will suffice. Then there are mountain pines which thrive on rocky ground – *Pinus mugo* var. *pumilio* does not grow to more than 1 m (3¼ ft) – and dwarf thujas such as *Thuja occidentalis* 'Danica', with a rounded habit. Turning to deciduous trees, there is the beautiful *Acer palmatum* Dissectum Atropurpureum Group, a tiny Japanese maple with delicately indented purple foliage.

• And if you have acid soil, do not miss the opportunity to plant a few dwarf rhododendrons.

Mistakes to avoid

• building a rock garden against a wall or tree;

• using several different types and colours of stone;

• planting small annual flowers.

The effect of these mistakes will only be to heighten the artificiality of your imitation mountain garden.

A rock garden under a tree

Though lacking the charm of a traditional rock garden, planting flowers and shrubs among stones is a good way of turning a barren area to good account, for instance an area of parched brown grass in the shade of a tree. Nothing will grow in these sort of conditions, because the tree roots absorb all the water available. Using the means at your disposal, you can create a raised area with some of the features of a rock garden.

This is how:

• Dig over the lawn, removing stones and weeds. Water thoroughly and spread a layer of sand 5 cm (2 in) deep.

• Cover the whole area with a layer of plastic, taking care to turn in the edges and fix them to the ground with pegs.

• Cut cross-shapes in the plastic where you intend to install your plants (preferably perennials with a shallow root system) and water them in.

• After planting, bury the plastic under a layer of bark or gravel and arrange the rocks around the plants.

Making your own rocks

If no stone is available in your area, or transport is a problem, here is a way of making your own:

• Mix up 1 part of cement to 2 parts of sand and 2 of peat. Add water until you get a thick paste.

• Pour the mixture into a cardboard box and leave to set.

• Once the concrete has set, tear away the cardboard and break off the corners of your man-made rock to give it a more natural appearance.

Note *Gather all your rocks together on site before you begin. This will make it easier to choose the right rock for each part of your construction.*

Water gardens

A garden benefits enormously from the presence of water, whether a sparkling, fast-running stream or a still, calm pool or pond reflecting the vegetation on its banks.

Modern techniques have made it a whole lot easier and less expensive to make a water garden, and, however small, an area of water gives a sense of relief and vitality. A water garden is a place to stroll, and gives you the opportunity to cultivate some very special plants.

Natural and artificial water gardens

Two types of reservoir

• An area of water may be 'natural', or apparently so, like a pond or small lake.

• Or it may be artificial, with a very definite architecture: a stone basin or fountain with a jet of water supplied by a pump. Structures of this kind can be bought ready-made, or you can have them built by a specialized bricklayer.

It is rare for a garden to contain a natural pond or lake, but there is often water present, not far underground. In this case all you need do is dig down to make your pond. Otherwise, you will have to create the water garden from scratch.

Choosing a site

Whatever you decide to do, choosing a suitable site is fundamental. Do not excavate a pond near trees, or the water will be polluted by their leaves. If possible, locate it at the lowest point of the garden, or at least somewhere near the bottom of the slope, as it would occur in nature.

• Do not be too ambitious, but at the same time avoid something ridiculously small. Aim to make it as natural as possible. If you are short of room, go for a stone container (as in a Japanese garden).

• A simple artificial pool, in harmony with the style of your house, is also an attractive option. Too small a pond is often difficult to maintain, as the water quality quickly deteriorates.

Choice of material

There are various options if you are intending to make your own pond.

• Concrete is always a possibility, though the work will be time-consuming and costly. It needs to be fairly thick to withstand the water pressure and the action of heat and frost.

• Plastic liners are much easier to use, as they adapt to the shape of the terrain. Polythene is the cheapest material, but also the most fragile. PVC is more robust and may last 10 years or more. Butyl rubber is in a class of its own, with a life expectancy of 40–50 years. It comes in various thicknesses, which of course determine its strength. The bigger the pond, the thicker the liner needs to be.

• Finally, you might prefer to buy a preformed mould, made of glass fibre (which is very strong) or a synthetic resin.

Constructing the pond

• Mark out the proposed shape, using string and wooden pegs.

• Excavate the hole. It should be about 1 m (3¼ ft) deep at the centre, a suitable depth for such plants as water-lilies. For safety reasons, and to accommodate plants which grow on the water margins, the periphery should be dug out only to a depth of 30 cm (12 in).

• Line the hole with a layer of sand, felt or fibre-glass loft insulation material, to act as a cushion for the flexible liner and prevent it getting pierced by sharp projections.

• Install the liner. In length it should be equal to the widest distance across the pond plus twice its maximum depth.

• Leave an overlap around the edges.

Filling the pond

• Weight the edges of the liner (with bricks, for instance) and slowly fill with water so that the liner gradually adapts to the contours of the pond. When it is full, conceal the edges of the liner with stones, bricks or clods of earth.

• Spread a layer of soil over the bottom to provide a growing medium for aquatic plants. The soil will also hide the ugly black of the liner.

• Preformed pools should be bedded directly into the soil, in a hole dug to match the contours of the pool as accurately as possible. As they come in very stark colours (white, black or fluorescent blue), paint them dark green or midnight blue before using, to make them look more natural.

• There are various submersible pump systems, which can be installed at any time to oxygenate and purify the water.

Aquatic plants and animals

• Fish are always an asset, but if you are intending to do some planting, let everything settle down for a month before you introduce them. They are useful in getting rid of many kinds of undesirable algae and larvae.

• Marginal plants should be rooted directly on the bottom, where the water is shallow, in about 30 cm (12 in) of soil. They are easy to keep in check, whereas water-lilies tend to be rampant.

• If your pond is small, plant water-lilies in plastic baskets, preferably black, containing a bed of good rich soil.

Excavate carefully, making some areas deeper than others, and smooth down the bottom.

Spread a protective layer of fine sand, fibreglass loft insulation or, as here, felt over the base.

Drape the liner roughly over the hole before filling with water. Leave it to settle for a day or two before trimming the plastic and laying the edging.

If the pond is big enough, you can also spread a layer of good soil over the bottom.

Installing a preformed pool
Mark out and excavate the shape of the pool before installing it.

Use a straight plank and a spirit level to check that the edges are level.

Aquatic plants
Aquatic plants, such as water-lilies, require a fair depth of water in which to grow (60 cm/24 in on average). They are best planted in the deepest part of the pond. For ease of handling and to prevent them spreading too far, plant them in mesh-sided plastic baskets weighed down with stones. Fill the baskets with good soil to provide nourishment for the plants.

Marginal plants
So that your pond will blend in with the rest of the garden, provide a surround of moisture-loving marginal plants. An edging of rocks or flat stones will also contribute to the natural effect you want.

Topiary

Over the centuries, no other style of gardening has aroused such enthusiasm – or antipathy.

Sometimes praised and admired, sometimes decried after a bout of particularly bad taste, the art of sculpting live plants has been popular at various times and places, notably among the ancient Greeks and Romans and in seventeenth- and eighteenth-century England. Gardens in those days were encumbered with assorted collections of monsters and motifs cut out of yew and box, until they were swept away on a wave of public revulsion.

The tradition of clipping shrubs nevertheless continued to be practised in Holland, where horticulturists had to go and relearn the art earlier in this century, when the wind of fashion changed yet again.

These days, topiary has given rise to fewer excesses and the art has made a timid comeback. Current taste is for geometrical forms – balls, pyramids, cones, cubes and spirals – which are easier to create and fit better into the average garden.

The most suitable species

• Various plants lend themselves to topiary. Yew and box are undoubtedly the most common, but there are many others. A hedge of thuja, for instance, is a possible subject, though it needs to be clipped at least twice a year to keep its compact shape.

• Privet was much used in the past, though it needs to be clipped several times each summer and loses its leaves in winter. Its main advantage is that it grows quickly.

• Bay laurel is suitable for topiary in warmer regions. Unwanted growth should be cut back with secateurs, twice over the summer.

• Holly also lends itself to being shaped into compact shapes.

• The evergreen foliage of *Euonymus japonicus* is another potential medium for topiary. It does well in coastal climates and withstands urban pollution.

• Yet another excellent material is the silvery evergreen foliage of *Elaeagnus × ebbengei*. It is a pity it is not often used for topiary, as it grows quickly and makes a bright accent in the prevailing green of the garden.

• Also worth mentioning are the small-leaved Japanese azaleas. They, too, can be transformed into attractive plant sculptures and, contrary to popular belief, clipping does not inhibit them from flowering.

'Cloud' effects

There is an oriental technique which emphasizes the bare trunk and branches of the tree and retains bouquets of greenery only at the extremities. The specimen you wish to sculpt in this way should be chosen for the shape and beauty of its main branches. Juniper is particularly suitable for this exotic treatment.

To create a pyramid, first construct a 'cage' of trelliswork to place over the shrub you intend to shape. Cut back the foliage whenever it begins to grow through the trellis. When the shrub is well trained and clipped, the cage can be removed.

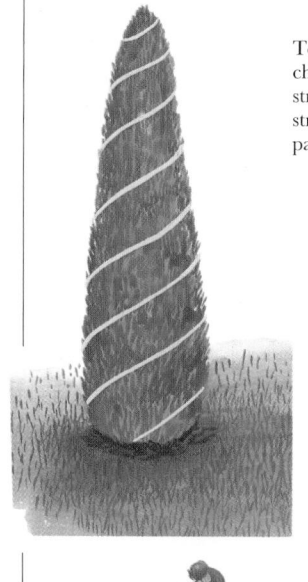

To create a spiral shape, first choose a specimen with a straight main trunk. Use string to mark out a spiral pattern.

Cut into the foliage with secateurs or shears, following the line of the string. You can then remove the string and cut away more of the greenery, until you have almost exposed the trunk.

A guide to the system for naming plants

Most gardeners know that plants have been given botanical names, and sometimes they fight shy of them, saying, 'Why can't we use common names as they are much easier to learn than those difficult Latin names?' It is true that common names are easier, but they are not necessarily known world-wide, and very often are only known locally; botanical names, however, are recognized the world over, so there is no mistaking which plant is being written or talked about, or ordered from nurserymen. Again, there are some plants that simply do not have common names, or several different plants that share the same common name. Sometimes common names are not really applicable. For instance, sun rose. This plant certainly likes the sun, but it is not a rose, it is a cistus. So you can see the possible confusion that common names can cause!

This is why botanical names have been used first and foremost in this Encyclopedia. However, common names are given where possible.

The binomial system is used for naming plants, each plant having two Latin names, and idea that was established by a Swedish botanist, Carl Linnaeus (1707–78). Prior to this, plants were named by means of lengthy descriptions.

In this system the first name is the genus (plural = genera). To go back to our first example, *Cistus* is a generic name. The second name is the specific name, for example, *ladanifer*, a species of cistus. So the full name is *Cistus ladanifer*. There may be many species in a genus, or as few as one.

Genera that are related to each other in respect of the structure of their flowers, fruits and other organs are gathered together into families. Some families contain many genera, such as Rosacea, which includes *Rosa* (roses), *Prunus* (cherries, etc) and *Potentilla*, and the massive daisy family, Compositae, which boasts in excess of 1,000 genera, while other families contain just a few, or even only one genus. Sometimes it is obvious that certain genera are related, for instance those with daisy-like flowers such as *Leucanthemum* and *Rudbeckia* (both in Compositae). But not always. Who would think just by a casual glance that callunas or heathers are related to rhododendrons (both in Ericaceae)?.

When growing in the wild, species can vary. For instance, the effect of local habitats may cause changes in habit of growth or flowering. In this case a variation may be classified as a subspecies, abbreviated ssp. The name would be set out thus: *Rhododendron arboreum* ssp. *delavayi*. If a plant is only

slightly different in botanical structure, it may be classified as a variety, abbreviated car., as in *Rhododendron mucronatum* var. *ripense*. If a plant has only minor variations it may be classified as a form, abbreviated to f., as in *Passiflora edulis* f. *flavicarpa* (passion flower).

As well as variants in the wild, there are many variations in cultivation. They occur in various ways: perhaps as mutations or 'sports' which can then be propagated vegetatively (for example, roses often produce a shoot with a flower of a different colour), or perhaps a plant will produce a shoot with variegated leaves, or a gardener might pick out a particular plant that is different in a group of young plants raised from seed. These are called cultivars (which is short for cultivated varieties. Gardeners often loosely use the word variety to refer to a cultivar (as indeed we have done in this Encyclopedia). Cutivars are given vernacular names (as opposed to Latin names for wild varieties) and when printed are contained in single quotes, thus: *Clematis montana* 'Elizabeth' or *Ribes sanguineum* 'Pulborough Scarlet'. Cultivars usually need to be propagated vegetatively to obtain offspring identical to their parents, although some will come true from specially selected seed.

Hybrids are the result of cross-fertilization between species or genera. In plant naming they are indicated by a multiplication sign. If two genera are crossed the result is known as an inter-generic hybrid. Possibly the best-known example is × *Cupressocyparis*, a conifer resulting from a cross between species of *Chamaecyparis* and *Cupressus*. (Note that the multiplication sign comes first.)

Much more common than intergeneric hybrids are those resulting from the crossing of species in the same genus (known as interspecific hybrids). For example, *Magnolia* × *soulangeana* and *Camellia* × *williamsii* (note that the multiplication sign comes between the names for interspecific hybrids). In turn hybrids are also crossed, particularly by plant breeders, who are forever striving for new colours or habits of growth in plants. Cultivars of hybrids are again given vernacular names, and are listed under the botanical name when this is known, for example, *Camellia* × *williamsii* 'Donation'. However, the generic name only is given, followed by the cultivar name, if the parentage is uncertain or not known, e.g. *Hosta* 'Honeybells'.

There are also hybrid groups, collections of cultivars from hybrid plants that have been extensively hybridized so that it is impossible to assign them to a specific parentage, so they are classified thus: *Viola* Imperial Series (note no quotation marks). However, if some members of such a group are quite distinct they may be given a cultivar name, for example, *Viola* Imperial Series 'Sky Blue'.

There is another type of hybrid produced not by sexual means but vegetatively, by grafting. Sometimes, albeit rarely, a new plant can appear from the graft union where the rootstock and scion are in contact and where the tissues of both have merged. The new plant is known as a graft hybrid or chimaera and is given a name. Probably the best-known example is + *Laburnocytisus adamii*, a graft hybrid of laburnum and cytisus species. Note that a plus sign before the name denotes a graft hybrid.

The study of botanical plant names can be fascinating. You will find out the meanings of names and so plant naming will make more sense to you. A plant name may commemorate somebody; for example, *Davidia* is named in honour of Pere Amand David, a French missionary who collected plants from China in the last century, and *Dahlia* in honour of Andreas Dahl, a Swedish botanist who studied under Carl Linnaeus.

Plants can also be named after the person who introduced them to cultivation: for instance, several plants have been named for the famous plant collector George Forrest, such as *Pieris formosa* var. *forrestii* and *Primula forrestii*.

Names can also tell us where a plant came from such as *Juniperus chinensis* (from China) or *Ulex europaeus* (from Europe).

The specific names often tell us something about the habit of the plant: e.g. flower colour (*alba* = white), habit of growth (*horizontalis* = prostrate, *arboreus* = tree-like), when the plant flowers (*autumnalis* = autumn), foliage characteristics (*variegatus* = variegated), flower form (*flore-pleno* = double-flowered), and so on.

Key to abbreviations

f.	=	form
ssp.	=	subspecies
syn.	=	synonym
var.	=	variety

A seasonal guide to tending your plants

Do not get the idea that the tasks to be done in your garden have to be performed on set dates. Not at all. Weather and temperature will tend to dictate the timing. As you can see, there is plenty of room for flexibility.

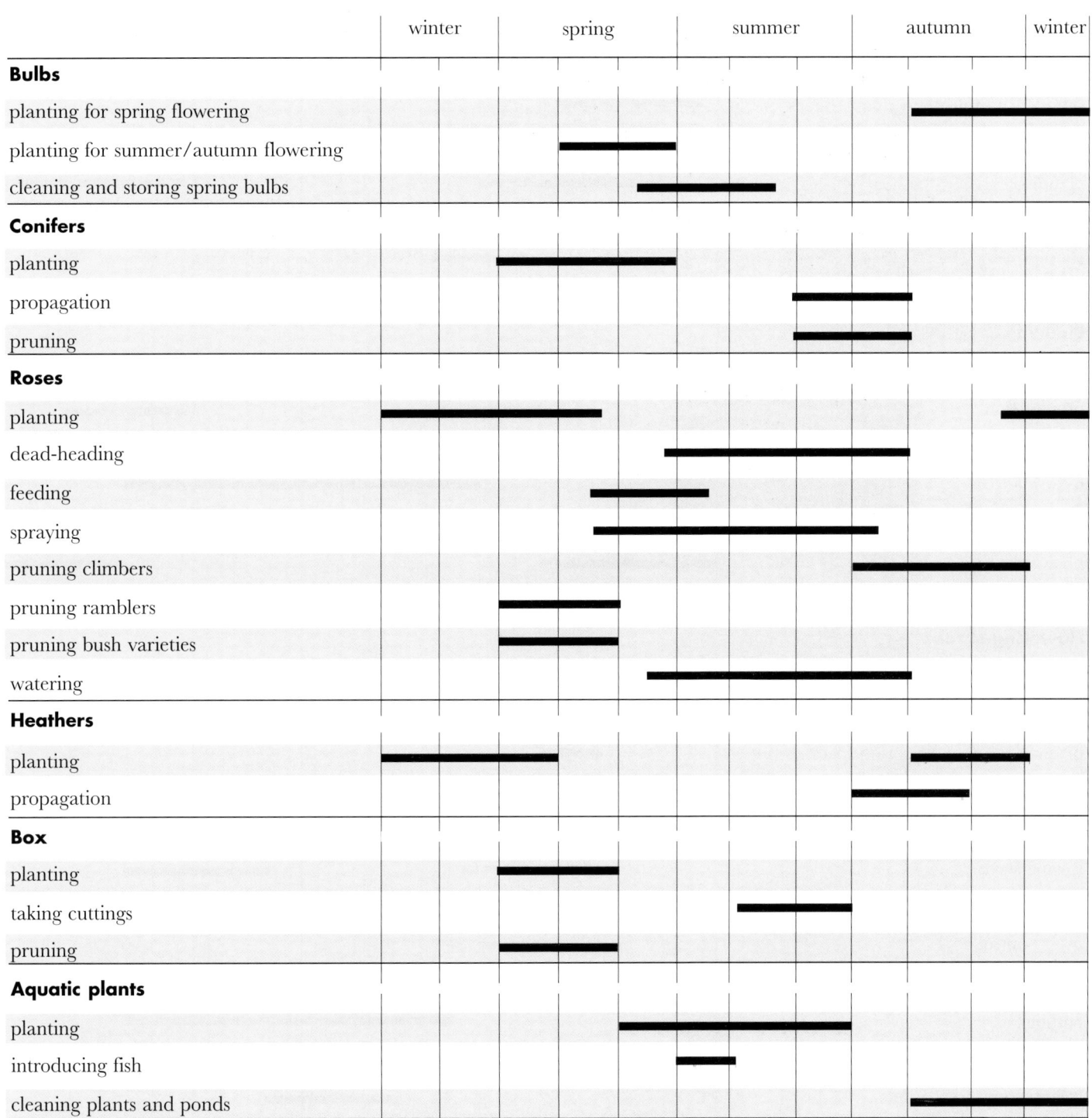

	winter	spring	summer	autumn	winter
Bulbs					
planting for spring flowering				██████	
planting for summer/autumn flowering		███			
cleaning and storing spring bulbs			███		
Conifers					
planting		████			
propagation			███		
pruning			███		
Roses					
planting	████				██
dead-heading			█████		
feeding		██			
spraying		████			
pruning climbers				████	
pruning ramblers		██			
pruning bush varieties		██			
watering			█████		
Heathers					
planting	████			███	
propagation				███	
Box					
planting		██			
taking cuttings			██		
pruning		██			
Aquatic plants					
planting			████		
introducing fish			█		
cleaning plants and ponds				███	

	winter			spring			summer			autumn			winter
Bamboo													
planting					▬▬▬▬	▬▬▬▬	▬▬						
division										▬▬	▬▬▬▬	▬▬▬▬	▬
Clematis													
planting		▬▬	▬▬▬▬	▬▬▬▬	▬▬					▬▬	▬▬▬▬	▬▬	
propagation								▬▬	▬▬▬▬	▬			
pruning vigorous varieties	▬▬												
summer-autumn-flowering varieties	▬▬▬												
Hedges													
planting		▬▬	▬▬▬▬	▬▬▬							▬▬▬▬	▬▬▬▬	▬
watering					▬▬▬▬	▬▬▬▬	▬▬▬▬	▬▬▬▬	▬▬				
clipping					▬▬▬								
feeding					▬▬▬▬	▬							
Biennials													
planting					▬▬▬					▬▬▬			
propagation					▬▬▬					▬▬▬			
sowing				▬▬▬▬	▬								
watering					▬▬▬▬	▬▬▬▬	▬▬▬▬	▬▬▬▬					
Trees													
planting	▬▬▬	▬▬▬	▬									▬▬	▬▬▬
watering saplings						▬▬▬▬	▬▬▬▬						
Flowering shrubs													
planting	▬▬▬	▬▬▬	▬								▬▬	▬▬▬▬	▬
pruning spring-flowering species					▬▬								
pruning summer-flowering species		▬▬											
Lawns													
laying turf				▬▬▬▬	▬▬▬▬	▬▬				▬▬▬	▬▬▬▬		
sowing seed			▬▬	▬▬▬						▬▬	▬▬▬		
feeding established lawns			▬▬	▬▬▬									
moss control				▬▬									
aeration/raking/topdressing		▬▬											
cutting					▬▬▬▬	▬▬▬▬	▬▬▬▬	▬▬▬▬					
watering					▬▬▬▬	▬▬▬▬	▬▬▬▬	▬▬▬▬					
treating with weedkillers						▬▬▬	▬▬						

	winter			spring			summer			autumn			winter	
Wisteria														
planting			■	■	■									
pruning									■	■	■			
propagation									■	■	■			
Dahlias														
planting/planting out seedlings					■	■								
dividing tubers					■	■								
feeding							■	■						
lifting for winter storage											■	■	■	
Annuals														
preparing the ground											■	■	■	■
sowing in nursery bed		■	■	■	■									
sowing in flowering position						■								
Irises														
planting								■	■					
division								■	■					
Perennials														
sowing under cold frame				■	■	■	■							
propagation/establishing cuttings in cold frame									■	■	■			
division									■	■	■			
Lilies														
planting									■	■	■			
division									■	■	■			
spraying					■	■								
Rhododendrons														
planting		■	■								■	■	■	■
layering									■	■	■			
Aromatic herbs														
planting		■	■	■										
harvesting							■	■	■					
Pelargoniums (geraniums)														
taking cuttings									■	■				
repotting		■	■	■										
planting out						■	■							
mulching beds and borders			■	■	■						■	■	■	

Your garden is in shade and the soil is heavy clay . . . You would like to have a display of blue and yellow flowers in summer, attractive foliage in autumn, and some unfussy plants to cover your banks . . . But you have little time to spend in the garden.

You love cyclamen and roses, wisteria and clematis, but you are not sure if they will thrive in the conditions you can offer them.

You are hesitating between strawberry plants whose flowers may not stand spring frosts and a cherry tree which does not like summer heatwaves . . .

Flowers, trees and shrubs, climbers, fruit and roses . . . For each of the botanical species listed in this Encyclopedia, the tables which follow give accurate, user-friendly information about soil conditions, aspect, hardiness, flower colour, flowering season, decorative appeal, special uses and any problems that may arise.

IV

QUICK-REFERENCE PLANT GUIDE

A

Species	Humus-rich	Sandy or dry	Chalky	Moist	Clay	Sun	Shade, semi-shade	Fully hardy[1]	Frost hardy[2]	Half hardy[3]	Tender[4]	Silver, grey	Golden	Variegated	Purple	Deciduous	Evergreen	White, green	Blue, mauve	Yellow, orange	Pink	Red
Acaena adscendens		■				■		■								■		■				
Acaena buchananii		■				■		■				■				■		■				
Acaena microphylla		■				■		■								■		■				
Acanthus mollis			■			■	■	■									■	■				
Acanthus spinosus			■			■	■	■									■	■				
Achillea filipendulina			■			■		■									■			■		
Achillea millefolium		■	■			■		■									■				■	
Achillea ptarmica			■	■		■		■									■	■				
Achillea tomentosa			■			■		■									■			■	■	■
Acidanthera bicolor		■								■								■				
Aconitum carmichaelii	■			■		■	■	■											■			
Aconitum napellus	■			■		■	■	■											■			
Actaea alba	■			■		■	■	■										■				
Actaea rubra	■						■	■										■				
Adiantum pedatum	■						■		■							■						
Adonis amurensis	■	■				■	■													■		
Adonis vernalis			■			■	■													■		
Aethionema grandiflorum		■		■		■		■								■					■	
Agapanthus campanulatus		■				■			■									■	■		■	
Agapanthus umbellatus		■				■				■								■	■			
Agave americana					■	■				■		■			■			■				
Agave victoriae-reginae						■					■											
Ageratum houstonianum										■								■	■			
Ajuga reptans	■			■	■		■							■	■				■			
Alchemilla alpina						■	■	■										■				
Alchemilla conjuncta							■	■										■				
Alchemilla erythropoda				■				■									■	■				
Alchemilla mollis				■	■	■	■													■		
Allium caeruleum		■	■					■											■			
Allium christophii		■	■					■				■							■			■
Allium cirrhosum			■					■														
Allium flavum			■		■	■		■												■		
Allium giganteum		■	■					■							■						■	
Allium karataviense			■					■										■				
Allium moly		■	■					■												■		
Allium neapolitanum		■				■			■									■				
Allium oreophilum		■	■					■													■	
Allium schoenoprasum				■				■													■	
Allium schubertii				■				■													■	
Allium sphaerocephalon		■				■		■										■			■	
Allium ursinum				■			■	■										■				■
Alstroemeria aurea		■							■											■		
Althaea ficifolia																■				■	■	
Althaea rosea		■	■		■			■										■		■	■	■
Alyssum montanum		■	■			■		■							■			■		■		
Alyssum murale		■	■			■		■							■			■		■		
Alyssum saxatile			■			■		■												■		
Amaranthus caudatus						■				■				■						■		■
Amaryllis belladonna		■				■			■									■			■	
Anacyclus pyrethrum var.depressus		■	■						■			■						■			■	
Anagallis monellii		■	■								■								■			

Footnotes
[1] min. – 15°C (5°F), [2] min. –5°C (23°F), [3] min. 0°C (32°F), [4] min. 10°C (50°F)

ANNUALS					FLOWERING SEASON					USES									PROBLEMS				
Scented, aromatic	Sow direct	Sow then plant out	Self-seeding	Long-flowering	Winter	Early-mid spring	Late spr. – early sum.	Mid-late sum.	Autumn	Berry-producing	Ground cover	Walls, rock garden	Borders	Annual	Biennial	Banks	Under shrubs	In or near water	Attracts slugs	Poisonous/allergenic	Thorny	Needs staking	
								■		■	■												Acaena, Sheep's burrs
								■	■	■	■												Acaena, Sheep's burrs
						■			■	■	■												Acaena, Sheep's burrs
								■					■										Bear's breeches
								■					■										Bear's breeches
						■		■					■										Yarrow
						■	■	■					■										Yarrow
						■		■					■										Yarrow
						■		■					■										Yarrow
■							■						■									■	Ethiopian gladiolus, Peacock-orchid
								■					■						■	■		■	Monkshood
								■					■						■	■		■	Monkshood
						■							■				■			■			Baneberry, Cohosh
							■		■								■			■			Baneberry, Cohosh
																	■	■					Maidenhair (fern)
					■						■									■			Pheasant's eye
											■									■			Pheasant's eye
	■		■			■	■				■	■											Stonecress
		■										■											African lily
			■					■															African lily
								■															Century plant
						■																	Century plant
		■	■					■	■														Flossflower
■						■					■	■											Bugle(weed)
			■			■																	Lady's mantle
			■					■								■							Lady's mantle
						■	■				■												Lady's mantle
			■			■					■												Lady's mantle
■			■					■				■											Decorative onion
■		■	■					■			■												Decorative onion
■			■					■															Decorative onion
												■	■										Decorative onion
■			■					■											■				Decorative onion
■			■					■															Decorative onion
■			■					■															Decorative onion
					■																		Decorative onion
■			■					■			■												Decorative onion
■			■					■															Decorative onion
■			■					■															Decorative onion
								■				■											Decorative onion
							■						■			■							Decorative onion
						■												■					Peruvian lily
			■					■					■									■	Hollyhock
		■						■												■		■	Hollyhock
		■				■						■											Rock alyssum, Madwort
		■				■	■					■											Rock alyssum, Madwort
■							■				■	■											Rock alyssum, Madwort
	■	■	■					■															Amaranth, Love-lies-bleeding
■			■					■	■										■				Amaryllis
						■					■												Anacyclus
		■						■	■		■												Anagallis, Scarlet pimpernel

Species	SOIL					ASPECT/HARDINESS						FOLIAGE						FLOWER				
	Humus-rich	Sandy or dry	Chalky	Moist	Clay	Sun	Shade, semi-shade	Fully hardy [1]	Frost hardy [2]	Half hardy [3]	Tender [4]	Silver, grey	Golden	Variegated	Purple	Deciduous	Evergreen	White, green	Blue, mauve	Yellow, orange	Pink	Red
Anaphalis margaritacea		■				■		■								■		■				
Anaphalis triplinervis		■				■		■				■						■	■			
Anchusa azurea								■														
Androsace carnea			■					■				■									■	
Androsace sarmentosa			■					■				■									■	
Anemone blanda	■							■										■	■		■	■
Anemone coronaria	■						■		■									■	■		■	■
Anemone x hybrida			■				■	■								■		■			■	
Anemone hupehensis				■	■		■		■									■	■		■	
Anemone nemorosa	■						■	■										■	■			
Angelica archangelica	■						■	■										■				
Antennaria dioica		■	■			■		■				■						■			■	■
Antennaria dioica var. hyperborea		■	■			■		■				■						■				
Antennaria parvifolia		■	■			■		■				■			■			■				
Anthemis nobilis						■		■							■			■		■		
Anthemis punctata ssp. cupaniana		■	■			■			■			■						■		■		
Anthemis tinctoria		■	■			■		■										■		■		
Anthemis tinctoria hybrids		■	■			■		■								■				■		
Antirrhinum majus			■	■		■				■								■		■	■	
Aponogeton distachyos				■					■									■				
Aquilegia flabellata			■	■	■	■		■										■	■	■	■	
Aquilegia hybrids			■			■		■										■	■	■	■	■
Aquilegia vulgaris			■	■		■		■										■	■	■	■	■
Arabis caucasia			■			■		■				■									■	
Arabis procurrens								■						■				■				
Arctotis x hybrida		■				■				■		■						■			■	■
Arenaria balearica		■				■	■	■									■	■				
Arenaria montana		■						■									■	■				
Argemone mexicana		■	■			■				■		■								■		
Arisaema candidissimum	■						■		■									■	■		■	
Arisaema sikokianum	■			■		■	■		■						■			■				
Armeria maritima		■	■			■		■				■						■			■	■
Artemisia abrotanum		■	■			■		■				■								■		
Artemisia absinthium		■	■			■			■			■								■		
Artemisia armeniaca		■	■			■		■				■				■						
Artemisia dracunculus		■				■			■							■						
Artemisia lactiflora	■		■	■	■		■	■								■		■				
Artemisia ludoviciana		■				■		■				■				■		■				
Artemisia pontica		■	■			■		■				■								■		
Artemisia schmidtiana		■				■			■			■								■		
Artemisia stelleriana		■	■			■		■				■						■		■		
Arum italicum				■	■		■		■					■				■				
Aruncus aethusifolius	■			■	■		■	■								■		■				
Aruncus dioicus	■			■	■			■										■				
Asarum canadense	■						■	■														■
Asarum caudatum	■						■	■								■						■
Asarum europaeum	■						■	■														■
Asclepias curassavica				■	■						■									■	■	■
Asclepias incarnata				■		■		■								■						■
Asclepias syriaca		■				■		■													■	
Asclepias tuberosa		■				■		■												■		

Footnotes
[1] min. – 15°C (5°F), [2] min. –5°C (23°F), [3] min. 0°C (32°F), [4] min. 10°C (50°F)

The following table uses the column groups **ANNUALS**, **FLOWERING SEASON**, **USES** and **PROBLEMS**. A ■ indicates that the attribute applies to the plant in that row.

Common name	Scented, aromatic	Sow direct	Sow then plant out	Self-seeding	Long-flowering	Winter	Early–mid spring	Late spr.–early sum.	Mid–late sum.	Autumn	Berry-producing	Ground cover	Walls, rock garden	Borders	Annual	Biennial	Banks	Under shrubs	In or near water	Attracts slugs	Poisonous/allergenic	Thorny	Needs staking
Pearl(y) everlasting									■	■			■										
Pearl(y) everlasting									■	■		■	■										
Bugloss, Alkanet								■															
Androsace, Rock jasmine								■					■										
Androsace, Rock jasmine								■					■										
Windflower							■						■										
Windflower								■					■							■			■
Windflower					■					■										■			
Windflower					■				■	■				■									
Windflower							■											■		■			
Angelica	■			■				■															
Cat's foot, Pussy-toes								■				■	■										
Cat's foot, Pussy-toes								■				■	■				■						
Cat's foot, Pussy-toes								■				■	■				■						
Anthemis, Chamomile					■			■	■														
Anthemis					■			■				■											
Anthemis								■	■														
Anthemis					■			■	■	■			■										
Snapdragon		■		■																			
Water hawthorn									■										■				
Columbine								■	■														
Columbine					■			■					■										
Columbine								■															
Rock cress	■				■		■	■				■	■										
Rock cress								■		■		■	■										
African daisy								■	■				■			■							
Sandwort							■	■	■			■	■										
Sandwort								■	■				■				■						
Prickly poppy	■	■		■					■														
Jack-in-the-pulpit		■						■										■					
Jack-in-the-pulpit								■										■					
Thrift, Sea pink								■	■			■	■										
Artemisia, Absinthe									■					■									
Artemisia, Absinthe	■							■													■		
Artemisia, Absinthe													■	■									
Tarragon	■								■														
Artemisia, Absinthe									■					■									■
Artemisia, Absinthe	■									■													
Artemisia, Absinthe									■					■									
Artemisia, Absinthe	■											■	■										
Artemisia, Absinthe								■				■	■							■			
Arum, Cuckoo-pint	■										■	■						■		■			
Goatsbeard								■						■				■					
Goatsbeard					■				■									■					
Snakeroot, Wild ginger								■				■	■					■		■			
Snakeroot, Wild ginger			■					■				■	■					■					
Snakeroot, Wild ginger				■				■				■	■					■					
Milkweed, Silkweed	■									■										■			■
Milkweed, Silkweed	■							■	■	■				■									
Milkweed, Silkweed								■	■														
Milkweed, Silkweed								■	■		■												

Group		Humus-rich	Sandy or dry	Chalky	Moist	Clay	Sun	Shade, semi-shade	Fully hardy [1]	Frost hardy [2]	Half hardy [3]	Tender [4]	Silver, grey	Golden	Variegated	Purple	Deciduous	Evergreen	White, green	Blue, mauve	Yellow, orange	Pink	Red
A	Asperula odorata			■	■		■	■	■										■				
	Asphodeline liburnica		■	■			■			■											■		
	Asphodeline lutea		■	■						■			■								■		
	Asplenium adiantum-nigrum	■						■	■									■					
	Asplenium trichomanes				■			■	■									■					
	Aster alpinus								■										■	■		■	■
	Aster amellus								■				■							■			
	Aster cordifolius								■							■				■			
	Aster ericoides								■										■				
	Aster farreri								■											■			
	Aster x frikartii			■			■		■											■			
	Aster novae-angliae					■			■													■	■
	Aster novi-belgii					■			■										■	■		■	■
	Aster tongolensis				■				■											■			
	Aster tradescantii								■										■				
	Astilbe arendsii	■							■										■			■	■
	Astilbe chinensis	■			■			■	■										■				■
	Astilbe thunbergii hybrids	■			■			■	■										■				■
	Astrantia major	■						■	■										■			■	
	Astrantia maxima	■			■	■		■	■										■			■	
	Athyrium filix-femina	■						■	■										■				
	Athyrium nipponicum	■						■		■					■				■				
	Aubrieta x cultorum								■							■			■	■		■	
B	Ballota pseudodictamnus		■						■				■						■				
	Baptisia australis				■				■											■			
	Begonia grandis var. evansiana	■									■								■			■	
	Begonia semperflorens							■								■			■			■	■
	Bellis perennis								■										■			■	■
	Bergenia ciliata							■		■								■				■	
	Bergenia cordifolia				■	■		■	■							■	■					■	
	Bergenia stracheyi							■	■						■	■						■	
	Beta vulgaris				■	■									■	■							
	Bletilla striata				■			■			■											■	
	Borago officinalis		■	■	■				■											■			
	Brachyscome iberidifolia		■	■					■										■	■		■	
	Briza maxima				■				■														
	Briza media		■				■		■									■					
	Browallia speciosa											■							■	■			
	Brunnera macrophylla				■	■		■	■											■			
C	Calamintha alpina			■				■								■				■			
	Calamintha grandiflora			■			■										■						■
	Calamintha nepeta								■														■
	Calandrinia umbellata		■	■							■	■											■
	Calceolaria darwinii	■						■													■		
	Calceolaria herbeo-hybrida	■	■					■				■							■		■	■	
	Calceolaria integrifolia	■	■		■			■		■											■		
	Calendula officinalis			■	■			■													■		
	Callistephus chinensis		■								■								■	■		■	■
	Calluna vulgaris	■	■					■	■					■		■			■	■		■	■
	Caltha palustris				■				■										■		■		
	Caltha palustris var. alba				■	■			■								■		■				

Footnotes
[1] min. – 15°C (5°F), [2] min. –5°C (23°F), [3] min. 0°C (32°F), [4] min. 10°C (50°F)

	ANNUALS				FLOWERING SEASON					USES									PROBLEMS				
Scented, aromatic	Sow direct	Sow then plant out	Self-seeding	Long-flowering	Winter	Early–mid spring	Late spr.–early sum.	Mid-late sum.	Autumn	Berry-producing	Ground cover	Walls, rock garden	Borders	Annual	Biennial	Banks	Under shrubs	In or near water	Attracts slugs	Poisonous/allergenic	Thorny	Needs staking	
■							■				■						■						Asperula, Woodruff
■							■																Asphodeline, Jacob's rod
■							■																Asphodeline, Jacob's rod
																	■						Asplenium, Spleenwort
								■															Asplenium, Spleenwort
								■			■												Michaelmas daisy
								■			■												Michaelmas daisy
								■	■				■									■	Michaelmas daisy
								■														■	Michaelmas daisy
								■															Michaelmas daisy
				■				■	■				■										Michaelmas daisy
									■													■	Michaelmas daisy
									■													■	Michaelmas daisy
								■															Michaelmas daisy
								■															Michaelmas daisy
■				■				■															Astilbe
								■					■			■							Astilbe
								■					■										Astilbe
				■				■								■							Masterwort
								■								■							Masterwort
											■						■	■					Lady fern
			■					■									■	■					Lady fern
■						■					■	■											Aubretia, Purple rock cress
■								■			■												Ballota
■								■															Baptisia, Wild indigo
		■						■								■			■				Begonia
		■						■	■										■				Begonia
				■	■	■					■												Daisy, English daisy
	■		■			■					■	■											Bergenia
				■		■	■				■	■											Bergenia
				■			■				■	■											Bergenia
			■					■								■			■				Swiss chard, Leaf beet
							■									■			■				Bletilla
		■				■	■																Borage, Talewort
■	■		■	■				■	■		■												Brachycome, Swan river daisy
	■	■							■														Quaking grass
							■	■			■	■											Quaking grass
					■																		Browallia, Bush violet
						■											■						Brunnera, Siberian bugloss
								■				■											Calamintha, Calamint
								■	■			■											Calamintha, Calamint
■								■			■												Calamintha, Calamint
								■				■											Calandrinia, Rock purslane
								■															Calceolaria, Slipperwort
		■		■				■															Calceolaria, Slipperwort
		■		■				■															Calceolaria, Slipperwort
	■	■	■																				Calendula
		■		■				■											■		■		China aster
■				■				■	■		■	■											Heather, Ling
						■					■							■		■			Marsh marigold, Kingcup
						■							■					■					Marsh marigold, Kingcup

C

	Humus-rich	Sandy or dry	Chalky	Moist	Clay	Sun	Shade, semi-shade	Fully hardy [1]	Frost hardy [2]	Half hardy [3]	Tender [4]	Silver, grey	Golden	Variegated	Purple	Deciduous	Evergreen	White, green	Blue, mauve	Yellow, orange	Pink	Red
Camassia cusickii				■	■			■										■	■			
Camassia leichtlinii				■	■			■										■	■			
Camassia quamash				■	■			■										■	■			
Campanula alliariifolia								■										■				
Campanula barbata		■				■		■										■				
Campanula carpatica								■										■				
Campanula cochleariifolia								■										■				
Campanula glomerata								■										■				
Campanula lactiflora				■		■		■								■		■	■		■	
Campanula latifolia								■										■				
Campanula medium								■										■			■	
Campanula persicifolia var. sessiliflora				■	■											■		■				
Campanula portenschlagiana						■		■										■	■			
Campanula poscharskiana						■		■										■	■			
Campanula pyramidalis									■									■				
Campanula sarmatica		■	■									■						■	■			
Campanula takesimana			■	■	■	■		■										■			■	
Campanula trachelium								■										■	■			
Canna											■			■	■					■	■	
Cardiocrinum giganteum				■			■		■									■				
Catananche caerulea	■	■	■			■		■				■							■			
Catharanthus roseus				■			■				■	■								■	■	
Celosia	■									■										■	■	■
Centaurea cyanus	■					■		■				■						■	■	■	■	■
Centaurea dealbata	■			■		■		■				■	■								■	
Centaurea hypoleuca	■					■		■													■	
Centaurea macrocephala	■			■		■		■												■		
Centaurea montana	■			■		■		■										■	■			
Centaurea pulcherrima	■					■		■									■				■	
Centranthus ruber			■	■		■		■													■	
Cerastium tomentosum	■	■	■			■		■				■			■			■				
Cerastium tomentosum var. columnae	■	■				■		■				■			■			■				
Ceratostigma plumbaginoides	■					■		■							■				■			
Ceratostigma willmottianum	■	■				■			■									■	■			
Cheiranthus cheiri				■				■				■						■	■	■	■	■
Chelone obliqua							■	■													■	■
Chionodoxa luciliae		■				■	■											■	■			
Chionodoxa sardensis	■					■	■											■	■			
Chrysanthemum arcticum				■		■		■										■			■	
Chrysanthemum carinatum		■				■				■								■	■	■	■	■
Chrysanthemum coccineum		■				■		■										■			■	■
Chrysanthemum coreanum		■				■		■										■		■	■	
Chrysanthemum frutescens		■				■				■								■		■	■	
Chrysanthemum haradjanii		■				■			■			■								■		
Chrysanthemum leucanthemum			■	■				■									■	■				
Chrysanthemum maximum		■				■		■										■			■	
Chrysanthemum multicaule								■												■		
Chrysanthemum paludosum		■				■		■										■				
Chrysanthemum parthenium		■				■				■		■						■		■		
Chrysanthemum uliginosum		■		■		■		■										■				
Cimicifuga dahurica	■						■	■										■				

Footnotes
[1] min. – 15°C (5°F), [2] min. –5°C (23°F), [3] min. 0°C (32°F), [4] min. 10°C (50°F)

Scented, aromatic	Sow direct	Sow then plant out	Self-seeding	Long-flowering	Winter	Early–mid spring	Late spr.–early sum.	Mid–late sum.	Autumn	Berry-producing	Ground cover	Walls, rock garden	Borders	Annual	Biennial	Banks	Under shrubs	In or near water	Attracts slugs	Poisonous/allergenic	Thorny	Needs staking	Name
								■										■					Camassia, Quamash
								■										■					Camassia, Quamash
								■										■					Camassia, Quamash
		■						■															Bellflower, Bluebell
		■						■				■											Bellflower, Bluebell
		■					■			■	■												Bellflower, Bluebell
								■															Bellflower, Bluebell
		■						■			■												Bellflower, Bluebell
				■			■	■				■							■			■	Bellflower, Bluebell
		■						■															Bellflower, Bluebell
	■	■						■															Bellflower, Bluebell
							■	■				■											Bellflower, Bluebell
		■	■					■		■	■												Bellflower, Bluebell
		■	■					■															Bellflower, Bluebell
																					■		Bellflower, Bluebell
							■	■			■	■											Bellflower, Bluebell
							■	■		■		■				■							Bellflower, Bluebell
								■									■						Bellflower, Bluebell
			■					■															Canna (lily), Indian shot
■								■									■	■					Giant lily
			■					■															Catananche, Blue cupidone
			■					■															Madagascar periwinkle
		■	■					■															Celosia, Woolflower
	■	■	■					■															Knapweed, Cornflower
■	■							■															Knapweed, Cornflower
								■					■										Knapweed, Cornflower
								■															Knapweed, Cornflower
							■	■															Knapweed, Cornflower
		■						■	■			■				■							Knapweed, Cornflower
	■		■				■	■			■												Valerian, Jupiter's beard
							■			■	■					■							Mouse-ear chickweed
							■			■	■					■							Mouse-ear chickweed
			■					■	■	■	■												Plumbago, Chinese plumbago
							■		■			■											Plumbago, Chinese plumbago
■	■	■	■		■	■		■		■													Wallflower
							■		■														Turtlehead
					■						■												Chionodoxa, Glory of the snow
					■						■						■						Chionodoxa, Glory of the snow
								■	■				■			■							Chrysanthemum
■			■					■										■					Chrysanthemum
						■		■										■					Chrysanthemum
						■		■										■					Chrysanthemum
								■				■						■					Chrysanthemum
			■					■										■					Chrysanthemum
						■						■						■					Chrysanthemum
								■										■					Shasta daisy
								■						■				■					Chrysanthemum
			■					■										■					Chrysanthemum
			■					■										■					Feverfew
			■				■	■										■					Chrysanthemum
							■	■									■						Bugbane, Rattletop

C

	SOIL					ASPECT/HARDINESS						FOLIAGE						FLOWER				
	Humus-rich	Sandy or dry	Chalky	Moist	Clay	Sun	Shade, semi-shade	Fully hardy [1]	Frost hardy [2]	Half hardy [3]	Tender [4]	Silver, grey	Golden	Variegated	Purple	Deciduous	Evergreen	White, green	Blue, mauve	Yellow, orange	Pink	Red
Cimicifuga racemosa	■						■	■										■				
Cimicifuga simplex	■			■			■	■									■	■				
Clarkia unguiculata		■						■													■	■
Cleome hassleriana		■								■								■			■	
Clivia miniata		■					■			■								■		■		
Cobaea scandens		■								■								■	■			
Codonopsis clematidea	■									■											■	
Colchicum autumnale				■		■		■										■			■	
Colchicum byzantinum				■		■															■	
Colchicum cilicicum				■		■			■												■	
Colchicum luteum				■		■		■												■		
Colchicum speciosum				■		■															■	
Convallaria majalis				■		■												■				
Convolvulus cantabrica		■	■			■		■				■				■					■	
Convolvulus cneorum			■							■		■						■			■	
Convolvulus sabatius		■								■		■						■	■			
Convolvulus tricolor												■						■	■			
Coreopsis basalis	■					■														■		
Coreopsis grandiflora		■		■		■														■		
Coreopsis lanceolata			■			■										■				■		
Coreopsis tinctoria		■		■		■														■		
Coreopsis tripteris			■			■										■				■		
Coreopsis verticillata		■		■		■														■		
Cortaderia selloana			■	■					■									■			■	
Corydalis cashmeriana	■					■	■												■			
Corydalis cheilanthifolia	■			■		■	■								■					■		
Corydalis flexuosa	■			■		■	■									■			■			
Corydalis lutea		■		■		■	■													■		
Corydalis solida		■				■	■	■													■	■
Cosmos atrosanguineus		■	■	■		■				■												■
Cosmos bipinnatus		■	■		■	■				■								■			■	
Cosmos sulphureus		■	■		■	■				■										■		
Crambe cordifolia		■				■												■				
Crepis aurea			■			■														■		
Crepis incana		■				■										■					■	
Crinum x powellii		■		■	■	■			■									■				
Crocosmia x crocosmiiflora		■		■	■	■			■											■	■	■
Crocosmia masonorum		■		■	■	■			■											■		■
Crocus chrysanthus		■	■		■	■												■	■	■		
Crocus ochroleucus						■														■		
Crocus pulchellus						■													■			
Crocus sativus		■				■			■										■		■	
Crocus speciosus		■			■	■								■					■			
Crocus vernus		■	■		■	■												■	■			■
Cucurbita pepo				■						■										■		
Cuphea cyanea										■										■		■
Cuphea ignea				■		■	■				■			■						■		■
Cyclamen cilicium							■		■					■							■	
Cyclamen coum							■		■					■				■			■	
Cyclamen hederifolium				■			■		■					■				■			■	
Cyclamen persicum						■				■							■				■	

608   Footnotes
[1] min. – 15°C (5°F), [2] min. –5°C (23°F), [3] min. 0°C (32°F), [4] min. 10°C (50°F)

Page table — key: ■ = attribute present.

ANNUALS					FLOWERING SEASON					USES									PROBLEMS				Plant
Scented, aromatic	Sow direct	Sow then plant out	Self-seeding	Long-flowering	Winter	Early–mid spring	Late spr.–early sum.	Mid-late sum.	Autumn	Berry-producing	Ground cover	Walls, rock garden	Borders	Annual	Biennial	Banks	Under shrubs	In or near water	Attracts slugs	Poisonous/allergenic	Thorny	Needs staking	
								■	■								■						Bugbane, Rattletop
									■				■				■						Bugbane, Rattletop
	■			■				■															Clarkia, Godetia
		■		■				■															Spider flower
						■	■																Kaffir lily
								■						■									Cobaea, Cup-and-saucer vine
				■				■			■								■				Codonopsis, Bonnet bellflower
									■											■			Colchicum, Autumn crocus
									■											■			Colchicum, Autumn crocus
									■											■			Colchicum, Autumn crocus
									■											■			Colchicum, Autumn crocus
									■											■			Colchicum, Autumn crocus
■								■		■	■						■			■			Lily of the valley
							■	■	■	■	■											■	Bindweed, Morning glory
								■															Bindweed, Morning glory
								■			■												Bindweed, Morning glory
	■							■														■	Morning glory
		■		■				■															Coreopsis, Tickseed
	■	■		■				■															Coreopsis, Tickseed
							■	■	■				■										Coreopsis, Tickseed
	■			■				■															Coreopsis, Tickseed
								■	■				■			■							Coreopsis, Tickseed
				■				■															Coreopsis, Tickseed
						■				■													Pampas grass
				■			■				■												Corydalis, Fumewort
			■				■				■						■						Corydalis, Fumewort
			■	■			■	■			■						■						Corydalis, Fumewort
			■	■			■	■															Corydalis, Fumewort
						■																	Corydalis
■				■				■	■														Cosmea, Cosmos
■	■		■	■				■															Cosmea, Cosmos
■	■			■				■															Cosmea, Cosmos
																							Crambe, Colewort
				■				■			■								■				Hawk's beard
							■	■			■												Hawk's beard
■				■				■											■				Crinum, Spider lily
■				■				■			■										■		Crocosmia, Montbretia
■				■				■			■												Crocosmia, Montbretia
■						■					■												Crocus
									■		■												Crocus
									■		■												Crocus
■									■		■												Crocus
									■		■												Crocus
						■					■												Crocus
										■				■									Ornamental gourd
				■			■																Cuphea, Cigar flower
								■	■		■	■											Cuphea, Cigar flower
■								■															Cyclamen, Sowbread
■					■	■											■						Cyclamen, Sowbread
			■					■									■						Cyclamen, Sowbread
■						■											■						Cyclamen, Sowbread

D

Species	SOIL Humus-rich	Sandy or dry	Chalky	Moist	Clay	ASPECT/HARDINESS Sun	Shade, semi-shade	Fully hardy[1]	Frost hardy[2]	Half hardy[3]	Tender[4]	FOLIAGE Silver, grey	Golden	Variegated	Purple	Deciduous	Evergreen	FLOWER White, green	Blue, mauve	Yellow, orange	Pink	Red
Cyclamen purpurascens							■				■			■					■		■	
Cyclamen repandum	■						■		■													
Cynara cardunculus			■	■					■			■									■	
Cynoglossum nervosum	■						■	■				■									■	
Cyperus eragrostis	■							■														
Cyperus involucratus											■						■	■				
Cyperus longus	■							■													■	
Cypripedium calceolus	■						■	■												■		
Cypripedium reginae	■						■	■										■			■	
Daboecia cantabrica	■	■		■			■		■												■	
Dahlia cactus											■							■	■	■	■	■
Dahlia decorative											■							■		■	■	■
Dahlia double											■							■		■	■	■
Dahlia anemone											■							■		■	■	■
Dahlia single											■							■		■	■	■
Dahlia pompon											■							■		■	■	■
Datura inoxia	■					■					■	■						■				
Datura metel		■									■							■				■
Delphinium cardinale											■							■		■		■
Delphinium grandiflorum						■												■	■			
Delphinium semibarbatum											■							■	■	■		■
Dianthus alpinus			■					■										■			■	
Dianthus arenarius							■	■				■						■				
Dianthus deltoides								■										■			■	■
Dianthus gratianopolitanus								■				■									■	
Dianthus knappii								■				■								■		
Dianthus plumarius								■				■						■	■	■	■	■
Dianthus superbus								■										■	■		■	
Diascia barberae										■											■	
Diascia cordata		■								■											■	
Diascia fetcaniensis				■			■			■						■	■				■	
Diascia rigescens		■				■				■											■	
Diascia vigilis				■		■										■	■				■	
Dicentra eximia	■			■			■	■				■		■							■	
Dicentra formosa	■							■													■	
Dicentra spectabilis		■		■	■		■	■				■						■			■	
Dichelostemma ida-maia		■				■				■												■
Dictamnus albus		■				■				■								■	■		■	
Dierama pendulum		■				■				■								■			■	
Dierama pulcherrimum		■				■				■								■			■	
Dierama pumilum		■				■				■											■	
Digitalis ambigua				■		■	■	■										■		■	■	
Digitalis ferruginea		■		■		■	■	■										■		■	■	■
Digitalis lanata		■	■			■	■	■									■	■				
Digitalis mertonensis		■		■		■	■	■										■			■	■
Digitalis purpurea		■		■		■	■	■										■		■	■	■
Dionaea				■							■							■				
Dodecatheon meadia				■				■													■	
Doronicum pauciflorum				■		■		■												■		
Doronicum orientale				■		■		■												■		
Doronicum plantagineum				■				■												■		

Footnotes
[1] min. – 15°C (5°F), [2] min. –5°C (23°F), [3] min. 0°C (32°F), [4] min. 10°C (50°F)

ANNUALS				FLOWERING SEASON							USES								PROBLEMS				
Scented, aromatic	*Sow direct*	*Sow then plant out*	*Self-seeding*	*Long-flowering*	*Winter*	*Early–mid spring*	*Late spr.–early sum.*	*Mid–late sum.*	*Autumn*	*Berry-producing*	*Ground cover*	*Walls, rock garden*	*Borders*	*Annual*	*Biennial*	*Banks*	*Under shrubs*	*In or near water*	*Attracts slugs*	*Poisonous/allergenic*	*Thorny*	*Needs staking*	
■						■						■											Cyclamen, Sowbread
■						■																	Cyclamen, Sowbread
										■													Cardoon
		■		■				■				■											Hound's tongue
																		■					Papyrus, Galingale
								■															Papyrus, Galingale
								■	■									■					Papyrus, Galingale
								■									■		■				Lady's slipper
								■											■				Lady's slipper
				■				■	■			■											St Dabeoc's heath, Irish heath
				■				■	■										■			■	Dahlia
				■				■	■										■			■	Dahlia
				■				■	■										■			■	Dahlia
				■				■	■										■			■	Dahlia
				■				■	■										■			■	Dahlia
				■				■	■										■			■	Dahlia
■								■						■						■			Datura, Thorn apple
■				■				■												■			Datura, Thorn apple
				■				■											■	■			Delphinium, Larkspur
				■				■											■	■		■	Delphinium, Larkspur
				■				■											■	■			Delphinium, Larkspur
■							■	■				■											Pink, Carnation
■								■				■											Pink, Carnation
■							■	■				■											Pink, Carnation
■							■	■				■											Pink, Carnation
■								■				■											Pink, Carnation
■			■				■	■			■	■											Pink, Carnation
■								■															Pink, Carnation
				■				■				■											Diascia, Twinspur
				■				■				■											Diascia, Twinspur
							■	■	■				■			■							Diascia, Twinspur
								■															Diascia, Twinspur
							■	■					■			■							Diascia, Twinspur
							■	■			■		■				■						Bleeding heart
																	■						Bleeding heart
				■			■	■				■											Bleeding heart
				■								■											Firecracker flower
■								■															Burning bush, Dittany
								■				■											Dierama, Windflower
								■				■											Dierama, Windflower
								■										■					Dierama, Windflower
								■									■			■			Foxglove
								■									■			■			Foxglove
								■					■		■								Foxglove
								■									■			■			Foxglove
								■									■			■			Foxglove
							■											■					Venus's flytrap
							■					■							■				Shooting star, American cowslip
							■												■				Leopard's bane
						■																	Leopard's bane
							■												■				Leopard's bane

E

	SOIL					ASPECT/HARDINESS						FOLIAGE						FLOWER				
	Humus-rich	Sandy or dry	Chalky	Moist	Clay	Sun	Shade, semi-shade	Fully hardy[1]	Frost hardy[2]	Half hardy[3]	Tender[4]	Silver, grey	Golden	Variegated	Purple	Deciduous	Evergreen	White, green	Blue, mauve	Yellow, orange	Pink	Red
Draba aizoides						■		■					■							■		
Dryas octopetala			■					■								■		■				
Dryopteris affinis	■			■		■	■	■									■					
Dryopteris carthusiana	■			■	■	■	■	■									■					
Dryopteris cristata	■					■	■	■														
Dryopteris dilatata	■						■	■														
Dryopteris erythrosora	■			■	■		■			■							■					
Dryopteris filix-mas	■						■	■														
Eccremocarpus scaber			■							■										■		
Echinacea purpurea				■				■													■	■
Echinops bannaticus		■	■			■		■									■		■			
Echinops ritro			■	■		■		■				■							■			
Echinops sphaerocephalus						■		■				■							■			
Echium lycopsis								■										■	■		■	
Echium fastuosum								■										■	■		■	
Echium vulgare			■					■											■			
Epilobium dodonaei		■				■		■									■				■	
Epilobium fleischeri	■		■	■				■									■				■	
Epimedium grandiflorum	■						■	■								■		■	■	■	■	
Epimedium x perralchicum	■		■	■			■	■							■	■				■		
Epimedium rubrum	■						■	■							■	■		■				■
Epimedium versicolor	■						■	■								■					■	
Epimedium x youngianum	■			■			■	■								■					■	
Eranthis hyemalis			■		■			■												■		
Eremurus himalaicus			■						■									■				
Eremurus x isabellinus			■					■														
Eremurus robustus			■						■									■			■	
Eremurus stenophyllus			■					■										■		■		
Erica carnea			■			■	■	■								■	■				■	■
Erica cinerea	■					■	■	■					■				■				■	■
Erica x darleyensis			■			■	■	■									■	■			■	
Erica tetralix	■					■	■	■				■					■	■			■	
Erica vagans						■	■	■									■	■			■	
Erigeron aurantiacus								■												■		
Erigeron karvinskianus									■									■	■	■	■	■
Erigeron leiomerus								■											■			
Erigeron speciosus								■											■			
Erinus alpinus			■			■		■								■		■			■	■
Erodium manescavii			■						■									■			■	
Erodium reichardii										■		■						■			■	
Eryngium agavifolium		■				■			■							■	■	■				
Eryngium alpinum				■		■		■											■			
Eryngium bourgatii			■			■		■				■							■			
Eryngium bromeliifolium				■		■		■											■			
Eryngium maritimum						■		■											■			
Eryngium oliveranum				■		■		■											■			
Eryngium planum		■	■			■		■								■			■			
Eryngium variifolium						■		■											■			
Eryngium yuccifolium		■	■	■		■		■								■	■					
Eryngium x zabelli		■	■			■		■				■							■			
Erysimum hieracifolium			■			■		■									■			■		

Footnotes
[1] min. –15°C (5°F), [2] min. –5°C (23°F), [3] min. 0°C (32°F), [4] min. 10°C (50°F)

Plant	Scented, aromatic	Sow direct	Sow then plant out	Self-seeding	Long-flowering	Winter	Early–mid spring	Late spr.–early sum.	Mid–late sum.	Autumn	Berry-producing	Ground cover	Walls, rock garden	Borders	Annual	Biennial	Banks	Under shrubs	In or near water	Attracts slugs	Poisonous/allergenic	Thorny	Needs staking
Whitlow grass							●					●											
Mountain avens											●	●											
Buckler fern, Shield fern												●	●					●					
Buckler fern, Shield fern												●	●					●					
Buckler fern, Shield fern							●											●					
Buckler fern, Shield fern							●											●					
Buckler fern, Shield fern													●					●					
Buckler fern, Shield fern																		●					
Chilean glory flower				●					●												●		
Coneflower									●														
Globe thistle								●	●				●										
Globe thistle		●			●				●														
Globe thistle		●			●				●														
Viper's bugloss		●			●				●														
Viper's bugloss		●			●				●														
Viper's bugloss	●			●	●				●														
Willowherb, Fireweed								●		●		●											
Willowherb, Fireweed								●	●	●		●											
Barrenwort								●										●					
Barrenwort							●	●			●						●	●					
Barrenwort								●										●					
Barrenwort								●										●					
Barrenwort							●	●				●					●	●					
Winter aconite						●						●								●			
Foxtail lily, Desert candle								●													●		
Foxtail lily, Desert candle								●													●		
Foxtail lily, Desert candle								●	●												●		
Foxtail lily, Desert candle									●												●		
Heather, Heath	●				●	●	●	●				●											
Heather, Heath	●				●				●	●		●											
Heather, Heath	●				●	●	●					●											
Heather, Heath	●				●				●			●											
Heather, Heath					●		●		●	●		●											
Fleabane									●														
Fleabane					●		●					●											
Fleabane									●														
Fleabane									●			●							●				
Fairy foxglove					●			●				●											
Storksbill, Heronsbill								●		●		●											
Storksbill, Heronsbill					●			●		●		●											
Sea holly, Eryngo									●			●											
Sea holly, Eryngo												●											
Sea holly, Eryngo												●											
Sea holly, Eryngo									●														
Sea holly, Eryngo												●											
Sea holly, Eryngo												●											
Sea holly, Eryngo								●	●				●										
Sea holly, Eryngo									●			●											
Sea holly, Eryngo									●				●										
Sea holly, Eryngo									●			●	●									●	
Wallflower							●	●				●	●		●	●							

	SOIL					ASPECT/HARDINESS						FOLIAGE						FLOWER				
	Humus-rich	Sandy or dry	Chalky	Moist	Clay	Sun	Shade, semi-shade	Fully hardy [1]	Frost hardy [2]	Half hardy [3]	Tender [4]	Silver, grey	Golden	Variegated	Purple	Deciduous	Evergreen	White, green	Blue, mauve	Yellow, orange	Pink	Red
E Erythronium dens-canis				■			■	■						■				■		■		
Erythronium revolutum			■				■		■					■				■		■		
Erythronium tuolumnense							■	■												■		
Eschscholzia californica		■	■				■					■						■		■		
Eucomis bicolor		■												■				■		■		
Eucomis comosa		■												■				■				
Eupatorium purpureum				■										■							■	
Eupatorium rugosum								■														
Euphorbia amygdaloides			■				■	■							■	■				■		
Euphorbia characias			■					■									■			■		
Euphorbia characias ssp. wulfenii							■	■									■			■		
Euphorbia cyparissias		■	■			■		■												■		
Euphorbia dulcis		■	■					■						■	■					■		
Euphorbia griffithii								■														■
Euphorbia marginata		■	■				■							■				■				
Euphorbia x martinii		■	■		■			■				■			■					■		
Euphorbia mellifera		■						■									■			■		
Euphorbia myrsinites		■	■						■			■			■					■		
Euphorbia palustris			■	■	■			■								■		■		■		
Euphorbia polychroma								■								■				■		
Euphorbia robbiae		■	■				■										■	■		■		
Euphorbia seguieriana ssp. niciniana		■	■			■			■			■					■			■		
Euryops abrotanifolius		■	■			■						■								■		
Euryops acraeus		■	■									■								■		
F Felicia amelloides		■	■																■			
Festuca glauca			■	■		■						■			■							
Filipendula purpurea	■			■	■		■	■								■						■
Filipendula rubra	■						■	■													■	
Filipendula ulmaria	■						■	■					■					■				
Filipendula vulgaris	■						■											■				
Foeniculum vulgare		■				■									■					■		
Freesia		■								■								■	■	■		■
Fritillaria imperialis							■	■												■	■	
Fritillaria meleagris				■			■	■											■			
Fuchsia boliviana							■			■					■						■	
Fuchsia magellanica							■		■									■			■	■
G Gaillardia aristata		■			■			■												■		■
Gaillardia pulchella		■			■			■												■		
Galanthus elwesii				■	■			■										■				
Galanthus nivalis				■	■			■										■				
Galega officinalis				■	■			■										■	■			
Galtonia candicans		■								■								■				
Gaultheria procumbens	■						■	■							■			■		■		■
Gaultheria shallon	■						■	■							■					■		
Gaura lindheimerii		■	■			■		■										■				
Gazania				■		■				■										■	■	■
Gentiana acaulis								■											■			
Gentiana asclepiadea	■						■	■											■			
Gentiana farreri	■							■											■			
Gentiana lutea	■			■				■												■		
Gentiana septemfida	■						■	■											■			

Footnotes
[1] min. – 15°C (5°F), [2] min. –5°C (23°F), [3] min. 0°C (32°F), [4] min. 10°C (50°F)

ANNUALS				FLOWERING SEASON						USES									PROBLEMS				
Scented, aromatic	Sow direct	Sow then plant out	Self-seeding	Long-flowering	Winter	Early–mid spring	Late spr.–early sum.	Mid–late sum.	Autumn	Berry-producing	Ground cover	Walls, rock garden	Borders	Annual	Biennial	Banks	Under shrubs	In or near water	Attracts slugs	Poisonous/allergenic	Thorny	Needs staking	
						●											●		●				Dog's-tooth violet, Fawn lily
						●											●		●				Dog's-tooth violet, Fawn lily
						●											●		●				Dog's-tooth violet, Fawn lily
	●		●				●				●												California poppy
●			●				●																Pineapple lily
●			●				●																Pineapple lily
●			●					●															Boneset, Joe Pye weed
●			●					●	●														Boneset, Joe Pye weed
				●		●						●				●				●			Euphorbia, Spurge
			●			●	●													●			Euphorbia, Spurge
						●						●								●			Euphorbia, Spurge
						●					●	●			●					●			Euphorbia, Spurge
						●						●	●							●			Euphorbia, Spurge
						●	●													●			Euphorbia, Spurge
●	●		●			●		●												●			Euphorbia, Spurge
				●		●						●	●							●			Euphorbia, Spurge
				●		●					●	●								●			Euphorbia, Spurge
		●		●		●				●	●									●			Euphorbia, Spurge
				●		●						●				●				●			Euphorbia, Spurge
						●				●	●									●			Euphorbia, Spurge
				●		●						●				●				●			Euphorbia, Spurge
						●		●				●								●			Euphorbia, Spurge
						●																●	Euryops
								●				●											Euryops
			●					●			●	●											Felicia, Blue Marguerite
								●				●							●				Festuca, Fescue
								●				●						●					Meadowsweet
●								●															Meadowsweet
●								●															Meadowsweet
								●															Meadowsweet
●								●	●														Fennel
●								●														●	Freesia
●							●																Fritillary, Snake's-head
							●																Fritillary, Snake's-head
●								●															Fuchsia
								●	●														Fuchsia
								●														●	Blanket flower, Firewheel
								●															Blanket flower, Firewheel
●					●														●				Snowdrop
●					●				●										●				Snowdrop
			●				●	●				●											Goat's rue
		●						●										●					Summer hyacinth
										●	●						●						Partridgeberry, Lemonleaf
										●							●						Partridgeberry, Lemonleaf
								●			●												Gaura, White gaura
		●						●		●	●												Gazania, Treasure flower
						●	●																Gentian
			●					●								●							Gentian
									●		●												Gentian
								●															Gentian
			●					●			●												Gentian

G / **H**

	SOIL					ASPECT/HARDINESS						FOLIAGE						FLOWER				
	Humus-rich	Sandy or dry	Chalky	Moist	Clay	Sun	Shade, semi-shade	Fully hardy [1]	Frost hardy [2]	Half hardy [3]	Tender [4]	Silver, grey	Golden	Variegated	Purple	Deciduous	Evergreen	White, green	Blue, mauve	Yellow, orange	Pink	Red
Gentiana sino-ornata	■							■											■			
Gentiana verna		■				■		■									■		■			
Geranium x cantabrigiense			■		■			■								■	■				■	
Geranium cinereum var. subcaulescens		■				■		■									■					■
Geranium dalmaticum			■					■									■				■	
Geranium endressii				■				■									■				■	
Geranium himalayense			■		■			■									■		■			
Geranium ibericum				■				■									■		■			
Geranium macrorrhizum			■					■									■				■	
Geranium maculatum albiflorum								■										■				
Geranium x magnificum					■			■											■			
Geranium nodosum	■		■	■	■	■		■									■		■			
Geranium orientalitibeticum	■	■				■		■									■				■	
Geranium oxonianum			■					■									■				■	
Geranium phaeum	■		■	■	■			■									■					■
Geranium platypetalum								■											■			
Geranium pratense					■			■											■			
Geranium psilostemon								■														■
Geranium pylzowianum				■				■									■				■	
Geranium renardii				■				■				■						■				
Geranium x riversleaianum			■			■		■									■				■	
Geranium sanguineum								■									■					■
Geranium wallichianum		■	■					■									■		■			
Gerbera jamesonii		■							■											■	■	■
Geum chiloense	■						■	■														■
Geum rivale				■	■		■	■								■		■				
Gilia capitata								■											■			
Gilia tricolor								■											■	■		
Gladiolus communis ssp. byzantinus		■						■										■			■	■
Gladiolus colvillei		■							■									■			■	■
Gladiolus primulinus									■									■		■		
Glaucium flavum		■	■			■		■				■								■		
Gloriosa superba										■												■
Godetia amoena		■								■											■	
Gomphrena globosa		■								■								■			■	
Gunnera manicata	■						■		■													
Gypsophila elegans								■										■			■	
Gypsophila paniculata								■										■			■	
Haberlea	■						■	■											■			
Hedysarum coronarium	■							■													■	
Helenium autumnale					■	■		■												■		■
Helenium hoopesii			■	■	■			■												■		
Helianthemum nummularium		■	■		■			■										■		■	■	
Helianthus annuus		■			■			■												■		
Helianthus decapelatus		■			■			■												■		
Helianthus microcephalus			■	■	■			■										■				
Helianthus salicifolius		■						■												■		
Helichrysum bracteatum		■	■			■				■								■			■	■
Helichrysum petiolare		■								■		■						■				
Heliopsis helianthoides								■												■		
Heliotropium arborescens		■								■								■	■			

Footnotes
[1] min. –15°C (5°F), [2] min. –5°C (23°F), [3] min. 0°C (32°F), [4] min. 10°C (50°F)

Scented, aromatic	Sow direct	Sow then plant out	Self-seeding	Long-flowering	Winter	Early–mid spring	Late spr.–early sum.	Mid–late sum.	Autumn	Berry-producing	Ground cover	Walls, rock garden	Borders	Annual	Biennial	Banks	Under shrubs	In or near water	Attracts slugs	Poisonous/allergenic	Thorny	Needs staking	
								■			■												Gentian
				■																			Gentian
						■	■			■		■			■								Geranium
						■	■				■	■			■								Geranium
						■	■			■		■			■								Geranium
							■			■													Geranium
						■	■					■											Geranium
						■	■																Geranium
		■				■	■																Geranium
				■		■																	Geranium
																							Geranium
						■	■			■		■					■						Geranium
						■	■				■	■											Geranium
		■				■	■			■		■											Geranium
						■	■			■		■				■							Geranium
							■			■													Geranium
							■																Geranium
						■	■			■	■					■							Geranium
						■	■																Geranium
			■			■	■				■	■			■								Geranium
			■				■			■													Geranium
			■				■		■		■	■											Geranium
		■					■			■													Gerbera, Barberton daisy
							■		■		■	■											Avens
						■					■	■											Avens
	■	■	■	■			■					■											Gilia
	■		■	■			■					■											Gilia
							■																Gladioli, Sword lily
							■																Gladioli, Sword lily
							■																Gladioli, Sword lily
	■		■				■																Glaucium
			■				■												■			■	Gloriosa, Climbing lily
	■						■																Godetia
		■				■																	Globe amaranth
						■																	Gunnera
	■		■				■																Gypsophila, Baby's breath
							■																Gypsophila, Baby's breath
			■			■					■												Haberlea
		■					■																Sanfoin, Sweet vetch
			■				■		■									■					Helenium, Sneezeweed
							■						■										Helenium, Sneezeweed
			■							■	■												Rock rose, Sun rose
■																				■			Sunflower, Common sunflower
																				■			Sunflower, Common sunflower
			■					■	■			■								■			Sunflower, Common sunflower
								■												■			Sunflower, Common sunflower
	■		■																				Everlasting flower, Strawflower
■			■																				Everlasting flower, Strawflower
								■	■				■				■						Heliopsis, Ox-eye
■		■	■																				Heliotrope, Cherry pie

H

	SOIL					ASPECT/HARDINESS						FOLIAGE						FLOWER				
	Humus-rich	Sandy or dry	Chalky	Moist	Clay	Sun	Shade, semi-shade	Fully hardy [1]	Frost hardy [2]	Half hardy [3]	Tender [4]	Silver, grey	Golden	Variegated	Purple	Deciduous	Evergreen	White, green	Blue, mauve	Yellow, orange	Pink	Red
Helipterum manglesii		■	■							■		■						■			■	■
Helipterum roseum		■				■				■											■	
Helleborus argutifolius		■					■		■									■				
Helleborus atrorubens							■	■											■			
Helleborus foetidus				■	■		■	■										■			■	
Helleborus niger				■	■		■	■										■			■	
Helleborus orientalis				■	■		■	■										■			■	
Helxine soleirolii				■			■								■							
Hemerocallis citrina				■	■		■													■		
Hemerocallis fulva				■	■		■													■	■	■
Hepatica nobilis				■	■		■	■							■			■	■	■		
Heracleum mantegazzianum	■						■	■										■				
Hesperis matronalis		■			■		■	■										■				
Heuchera x brizoides	■						■	■										■			■	■
Heuchera cylindrica	■		■	■				■									■	■				
Heuchera micrantha	■			■				■							■							■
Heuchera sanguinea	■							■							■							■
Hieracium aurantiacum	■							■												■		
Hieracium pilosella	■			■				■												■		
Hosta crispula						■		■	■					■		■						
Hosta fortunei		■		■			■	■				■		■				■	■			
Hosta lancifolia		■		■			■	■											■			
Hosta montana			■	■			■	■										■				
Hosta plantaginea		■		■			■	■							■							
Hosta sieboldiana		■		■			■	■				■		■				■				
Hosta x tardiana			■	■			■											■	■			
Hosta undulata var. univittata			■	■			■	■						■				■	■			
Hosta ventricosa		■		■			■											■	■			
Houstonia caerulea	■						■	■							■			■				
Houttuynia cordata	■						■	■							■			■				
Hyacinthoides hispanica		■			■		■	■										■	■		■	
Hyacinthoides non-scripta		■			■		■	■										■	■		■	
Hyacinthus orientalis		■								■										■	■	■
Hypericum calcycinum		■	■			■	■	■								■				■		
Hypericum olympicum		■				■	■	■								■				■		
Hypericum patulum						■	■									■				■		
Hyssopus officinalis		■	■		■		■												■			

I

Iberis amara				■			■											■			■	■
Iberis sempervirens		■				■	■										■	■				
Iberis umbellata		■	■			■	■									■		■				
Impatiens balfouri			■	■			■			■								■			■	
Impatiens balsamina							■				■							■		■	■	■
Impatiens glandulifera	■						■											■	■		■	
Incarvillea delavayi		■					■														■	
Incarvillea mairei							■														■	
Inula ensifolia				■			■													■		
Inula helenium							■													■		
Inula hookeri				■			■													■		
Inula magnifica				■			■													■		
Inula orientalis							■													■		
Ipheion uniflorum		■								■									■			

Footnotes
[1] min. – 15°C (5°F), [2] min. –5°C (23°F), [3] min. 0°C (32°F), [4] min. 10°C (50°F)

Table of plant characteristics. Marks (●) indicate the presence of a characteristic for each plant.

Scented, aromatic	Sow direct	Sow then plant out	Self-seeding	Long-flowering	Winter	Early–mid spring	Late spr.–early sum.	Mid–late sum.	Autumn	Berry-producing	Ground cover	Walls, rock garden	Borders	Annual	Biennial	Banks	Under shrubs	In or near water	Attracts slugs	Poisonous/allergenic	Thorny	Needs staking	Plant
●								●	●														Everlasting strawflower
								●					●										Everlasting strawflower
		●		●	●																		Hellebore, Christmas rose
						●											●			●			Hellebore, Christmas rose
					●	●											●			●			Hellebore, Christmas rose
			●		●	●											●			●			Hellebore, Christmas rose
						●											●			●			Hellebore, Christmas rose
											●												Mind your own business
●							●	●															Day lily
							●	●															Day lily
						●	●			●	●												Hepatica, Liver leaf
							●													●			Giant hogweed, Cartwheel flower
●		●	●				●																Sweet rocket, Dames' violet
			●				●	●			●												Alum root, Coral bells
							●	●		●		●				●							Alum root, Coral bells
							●	●								●	●						Alum root, Coral bells
							●	●				●				●							Alum root, Coral bells
					●		●																Hawkweed
		●					●																Hawkweed
								●		●			●						●				Plantain lily
●								●		●	●								●				Plantain lily
●								●		●	●						●		●				Plantain lily
							●					●				●			●				Plantain lily
●								●		●	●								●				Plantain lily
●								●		●	●								●				Plantain lily
								●		●		●				●			●				Plantain lily
								●				●				●			●				Plantain lily
						●					●								●				Plantain lily
						●					●												Bluets
●						●		●									●	●					Houttuynia
●						●											●		●				Bluebell
●						●											●		●				Bluebell
●						●														●			Hyacinth
							●	●		●	●												St John's wort
							●			●	●												St John's wort
								●			●												St John's wort
●			●					●															Hyssop
●				●		●		●		●	●												Candytuft
							●				●				●								Candytuft
	●							●			●												Candytuft
	●		●					●															Busy Lizzie, Balsam
		●	●					●															Busy Lizzie, Balsam
●	●		●					●	●								●						Busy Lizzie, Balsam
								●															Incarvillea
								●															Incarvillea
			●					●															Inula
			●					●															Inula
●			●					●															Inula
			●					●															Inula
			●					●															Inula
							●				●												Ipheion, Spring starflower

619

	SOIL					ASPECT/HARDINESS						FOLIAGE						FLOWER				
	Humus-rich	Sandy or dry	Chalky	Moist	Clay	Sun	Shade, semi-shade	Fully hardy[1]	Frost hardy[2]	Half hardy[3]	Tender[4]	Silver, grey	Golden	Variegated	Purple	Deciduous	Evergreen	White, green	Blue, mauve	Yellow, orange	Pink	Red
Ipomoea purpurea		■					■			■									■			
Ipomoea tricolor		■					■			■									■			
Iris bucharica		■						■										■		■		
Iris danfordiae		■						■												■		
Iris ensata	■			■				■										■	■			
Iris foetidissima			■	■	■	■	■	■							■		■					
Iris germanica		■				■	■	■							■		■		■	■		
Iris japonica				■	■		■		■								■	■	■			
Iris kaempferi	■					■		■										■	■		■	
Iris laevigata	■			■				■										■	■			
Iris latifolia	■			■				■										■	■		■	
Iris pseudacorus				■		■		■												■		
Iris reticulata		■						■											■			
Iris sibirica				■				■											■			
Iris spuria				■				■											■			
Iris unguicularis		■	■					■											■			
Iris versicolor				■				■											■			■
Iris xiphium		■						■										■	■	■		
Ixia		■						■		■								■		■		■
Jasione laevis			■					■											■		■	
Kniphofia galpinii		■		■					■									■		■		■
Kochia scoparia		■	■		■	■				■					■							
Lagurus ovatus		■	■																			
Lamium galeobdolon	■					■	■	■												■		
Lamium maculatum	■					■	■	■						■	■			■			■	
Lantana camara		■									■							■		■	■	
Lantana montevidensis		■				■				■						■		■				■
Lathyrus grandiflorus		■		■		■		■										■	■		■	■
Lathyrus latifolius		■				■		■										■			■	■
Lathyrus odoratus		■		■				■										■	■		■	■
Lathyrus vernus	■							■											■		■	■
Lavandula angustifolia		■	■			■		■				■				■			■			
Lavandula x intermedia		■	■			■			■			■			■	■			■			
Lavandula lanata			■			■			■			■						■	■	■		
Lavandula stoechas			■			■			■										■			
Lavatera trimestris				■	■			■										■			■	
Leontopodium alpinum		■	■			■		■				■						■				
Leucojum aestivum				■	■		■	■										■				
Leucojum vernum				■	■		■	■										■				
Lewisia cotyledon			■					■							■					■	■	■
Liatris scariosa						■		■													■	
Liatris spicata						■		■											■		■	
Libertia formosa				■				■										■				
Ligularia dentata	■							■							■					■		
Ligularia x palmatiloba	■			■	■		■	■								■				■		
Ligularia przewalskii	■							■												■		
Ligularia wilsoniana	■						■	■												■		
Lilium auratum	■			■					■											■		
Lilium candidum		■			■				■									■				
Lilium hansonii		■		■	■			■												■		
Lilium henryi		■		■	■				■											■		

Footnotes
[1] min. – 15°C (5°F), [2] min. –5°C (23°F), [3] min. 0°C (32°F), [4] min. 10°C (50°F)

	ANNUALS				FLOWERING SEASON						USES									PROBLEMS				
Scented, aromatic	Sow direct	Sow then plant out	Self-seeding	Long-flowering	Winter	Early–mid spring	Late spr.–early sum.	Mid–late sum.	Autumn	Berry-producing	Ground cover	Walls, rock garden	Borders	Annual	Biennial	Banks	Under shrubs	In or near water	Attracts slugs	Poisonous/allergenic	Thorny	Needs staking	
				■				■										■				■	Morning glory, Blue dawn flower
	■			■				■					■					■				■	Morning glory, Blue dawn flower
							■				■							■					Iris, Flag
■					■	■												■					Iris, Flag
								■										■					Iris, Flag
■									■									■					Iris, Flag
■								■										■					Iris, Flag
							■					■											Iris, Flag
■								■										■					Iris, Flag
																		■					Iris, Flag
				■				■										■					Iris, Flag
						■												■					Iris, Flag
■						■					■							■					Iris, Flag
								■										■					Iris, Flag
						■												■					Iris, Flag
■					■	■					■							■					Iris, Flag
																		■					Iris, Flag
						■					■							■					Iris, Flag
								■			■												Ixia
								■				■											Sheep's bit
			■					■															Torch lily, Red hot poker
	■	■																					False cypress, Summer cypress
	■	■							■														Hare's tail grass
	■							■		■							■						Dead nettle, Henbit
											■						■						Dead nettle, Henbit
■		■		■				■															Lantana, Shrub verbena
■							■	■					■										Lantana, Shrub verbena
				■				■															Sweet pea, Everlasting pea
								■	■											■			Sweet pea, Everlasting pea
■	■		■	■				■												■			Sweet pea, Everlasting pea
				■																■			Sweet pea, Everlasting pea
■							■	■		■		■				■							Lavender
■							■	■		■		■	■										Lavender
■				■							■												Lavender
■				■							■												Lavender
	■			■																			Mallow
						■					■												Edelweiss
■						■					■									■			Snowflake
■					■	■					■									■			Snowflake
						■					■												Lewisia
				■				■										■					Blazing star
								■										■					Blazing star
							■											■					Libertia
■									■									■					Leopard plant
						■		■	■				■				■						Leopard plant
								■															Leopard plant
								■															Leopard plant
■							■	■										■					Lily
■							■					■						■					Lily
■							■											■					Lily
■							■	■										■					Lily

	SOIL					ASPECT/HARDINESS						FOLIAGE						FLOWER				
	Humus-rich	Sandy or dry	Chalky	Moist	Clay	Sun	Shade, semi-shade	Fully hardy[1]	Frost hardy[2]	Half hardy[3]	Tender[4]	Silver, grey	Golden	Variegated	Purple	Deciduous	Evergreen	White, green	Blue, mauve	Yellow, orange	Pink	Red
Lilium longiflorum	■	■				■		■									■	■				
Lilium martagon								■														■
Lilium pardalinum giganteum	■			■		■		■													■	■
Lilium regale		■			■			■										■				
Lilium speciosum	■			■				■										■				
Limnanthes douglasii		■		■				■											■	■		■
Limonium latifolium		■						■											■	■		■
Limonium sinuatum		■								■									■		■	■
Limonium suworowii									■												■	
Limonium tataricum										■									■		■	
Linaria alpina								■											■		■	
Linaria cymbalaria								■											■			
Linaria maroccana		■	■			■		■										■		■		
Linaria purpurea								■											■			
Linum flavum								■											■	■		
Linum grandiflorum								■											■			■
Linum narbonense								■											■			
Linum perenne								■										■	■			
Linum usitatissimum								■										■	■			
Liriope muscari	■						■		■				■		■				■			
Liriope spicata	■						■	■							■				■			
Lithodora diffusa	■	■							■						■				■			
Lobelia cardinalis	■								■			■				■						■
Lobelia erinus		■								■									■			
Lobelia syphilitica	■							■											■			
Lobularia maritima			■	■				■										■				
Lotus berthelottii			■								■	■										■
Lotus corniculatus								■												■		
Lunaria annua		■	■		■		■	■					■						■		■	■
Lunaria rediviva			■	■			■	■								■		■				
Lupinus arboreus									■									■	■	■		■
Lupinus polyphyllus		■		■				■										■	■	■	■	■
Lupinus texensis								■										■	■		■	
Lychnis alpina								■													■	
Lychnis arkwrightii		■				■		■										■				■
Lychnis chalcedonica				■				■										■				■
Lychnis coronaria				■		■		■				■						■			■	■
Lychnis flos-jovis				■				■				■									■	■
Lychnis x haageana		■				■		■													■	■
Lysichiton americanus	■						■	■												■		
Lysichiton camtschatcensis	■			■	■		■	■										■				
Lysimachia barystachys				■	■				■									■				
Lysimachia ciliata				■	■		■							■						■		
Lysimachia clethroides			■				■	■										■				
Lysimachia ephemerum							■					■						■				
Lysimachia nummularia			■	■	■		■	■					■							■		
Lysimachia punctata			■	■	■		■	■												■		
Lythrum salicaria				■	■			■													■	
Macleaya cordata				■	■			■													■	
Macleaya microcarpa				■	■			■				■									■	
Malcolmia maritima			■					■										■	■		■	

Footnotes
[1] min. – 15°C (5°F), [2] min. –5°C (23°F), [3] min. 0°C (32°F), [4] min. 10°C (50°F)

Plant selection chart. Column groups: **ANNUALS**, **FLOWERING SEASON**, **USES**, **PROBLEMS** (with "Scented, aromatic" preceding the groups). A ● indicates the characteristic applies.

Scented, aromatic	Sow direct	Sow then plant out	Self-seeding	Long-flowering	Winter	Early–mid spring	Late spr.–early sum.	Mid–late sum.	Autumn	Berry-producing	Ground cover	Walls, rock garden	Borders	Annual	Biennial	Banks	Under shrubs	In or near water	Attracts slugs	Poisonous/allergenic	Thorny	Needs staking	Plant
●							●						●						●				Lily
●							●												●				Lily
							●												●				Lily
●							●				●								●				Lily
●							●												●				Lily
		●		●			●				●												Limnanthes, Meadow foam
	●	●		●			●				●												Statice, Sea lavender
		●					●				●												Statice, Sea lavender
			●			●		●															Statice, Sea lavender
		●		●			●				●												Statice, Sea lavender
		●					●				●												Toadflax, Butter-and-eggs
		●				●	●	●			●												Toadflax, Butter-and-eggs
	●	●					●				●												Toadflax, Butter-and-eggs
		●					●				●												Toadflax, Butter-and-eggs
								●															Flax, Perennial flax
	●							●															Flax, Perennial flax
						●																	Flax, Perennial flax
			●					●															Flax, Perennial flax
								●															Flax, Perennial flax
				●					●								●						Lilyturf
				●					●								●						Lilyturf
						●		●			●												Lithospermum, Gromwell
				●				●															Lobelia, Cardinal flower
		●		●							●							●					Lobelia, Cardinal flower
								●															Lobelia, Cardinal flower
●	●			●				●		●	●												Sweet alyssum
		●		●			●																Sweet clover, Bird's-foot trefoil
				●			●																Sweet clover, Bird's-foot trefoil
●			●						●														Honesty, Silver dollar
						●	●		●							●							Honesty, Silver dollar
●		●					●												●	●			Lupin(e)
●		●					●												●	●			Lupin(e)
●	●	●					●												●	●			Lupin(e)
											●												Campion, Catchfly
								●															Campion, Catchfly
									●										●				Campion, Catchfly
			●						●														Campion, Catchfly
							●																Campion, Catchfly
							●												●				Campion, Catchfly
●			●			●												●	●				Lysichiton, Yellow skunk cabbage
						●	●						●					●	●				Lysichiton, Yellow skunk cabbage
								●					●										Loosestrife
							●	●															Loosestrife
				●							●												Loosestrife
							●				●												Loosestrife
							●			●	●												Loosestrife
●							●			●	●												Loosestrife
		●	●				●											●					Purple loosestrife
			●				●																Plume poppy
			●				●																Plume poppy
●	●		●				●				●												Virginia(n) stock, Malcolm stock

623

	SOIL					ASPECT/HARDINESS						FOLIAGE						FLOWER				
	Humus-rich	Sandy or dry	Chalky	Moist	Clay	Sun	Shade, semi-shade	Fully hardy [1]	Frost hardy [2]	Half hardy [3]	Tender [4]	Silver, grey	Golden	Variegated	Purple	Deciduous	Evergreen	White, green	Blue, mauve	Yellow, orange	Pink	Red
Malope trifida				■				■										■			■	■
Malva alcea var. fastigiata		■				■		■								■					■	
Malva moschata			■	■	■			■										■			■	
Malva sylvestris								■														■
Matteucia struthiopteris	■						■	■														
Matthiola incana		■	■					■							■			■	■	■	■	
Maurandia erubescens						■				■											■	
Maurandia scandens		■									■					■			■			
Meconopsis betonicifolia	■						■	■										■	■			
Meconopsis cambrica	■						■	■												■	■	
Meconopsis grandis	■						■	■													■	
Meconopsis napaulensis	■						■	■												■	■	
Meconopsis sheldonii	■			■			■	■											■			
Mentzelia laevicaulis								■												■		
Mentzelia lindleyi		■						■												■		
Mertensia virginica	■						■	■				■							■			
Mesembryanthemum criniflorum		■	■			■				■		■						■		■	■	■
Mimulus cardinalis	■									■											■	■
Mimulus luteus	■			■	■				■								■			■		
Mimulus ringens	■			■				■									■		■			
Minuarta stellata								■										■				
Mirabilis jalapa		■	■							■								■		■	■	■
Miscanthus floridulus				■	■			■								■						
Miscanthus sacchariflorus				■	■				■							■						
Miscanthus sinensis				■	■				■							■						
Molucella laevis										■								■				
Monarda citriodora				■		■		■													■	
Monarda didyma				■	■			■										■		■	■	■
Monarda fistulosa		■				■		■													■	
Moraea tricuspidata						■		■											■	■		
Morina longifolia	■								■												■	
Muehlenbeckia complexa								■										■				
Muscari armeniacum		■		■				■											■			
Muscari comosum		■		■				■											■			
Muscari latifolium		■		■				■											■			
Muscari moschatum				■				■											■			
Muscari tubergenianum		■		■				■											■			
Myosotis scorpoides				■				■										■			■	
Myosotis sylvatica	■			■	■		■	■									■	■				
Myrrhis odorata				■				■										■				
Narcissus bulbocodium				■				■										■		■		
Narcissus jonquilla				■				■										■		■		
Narcissus juncifolius				■				■										■				
Narcissus poeticus				■	■			■										■				
Narcissus pseudo-narcissus				■				■										■		■		
Narcissus tazetta		■		■				■										■				
Nelumbo nucifera				■						■								■			■	
Nemesia strumosa		■								■								■			■	
Nemophila maculata		■		■		■	■	■										■				■
Nemophila menziesii		■		■		■	■	■											■			
Nepeta x faassenii		■	■					■										■	■			

Footnotes
[1] min. – 15°C (5°F), [2] min. –5°C (23°F), [3] min. 0°C (32°F), [4] min. 10°C (50°F)

Scented, aromatic	Sow direct	Sow then plant out	Self-seeding	Long-flowering	Winter	Early–mid spring	Late spr.–early sum.	Mid–late sum.	Autumn	Berry-producing	Ground cover	Walls, rock garden	Borders	Annual	Biennial	Banks	Under shrubs	In or near water	Attracts slugs	Poisonous/allergenic	Thorny	Needs staking	
		●						●															Malope
		●				●	●						●										Mallow, Musk mallow
			●				●																Mallow, Musk mallow
		●					●																Mallow, Musk mallow
●																●							Ostrich fern
●			●			●	●				●												Stock, Gillyflower
						●																●	Maurandia
						●	●															●	Maurandia
						●													●	●			Himalayan poppy, Welsh poppy
							●				●									●			Welsh poppy
						●													●	●			Himalayan poppy, Welsh poppy
							●													●			Himalayan poppy
						●																	Himalayan poppy, Welsh poppy
●	●										●												Blazing star
●	●						●				●												Blazing star
						●																	Virginian cowslip
	●		●								●	●											Livingstone daisy, Ice plant
						●	●				●							●					Monkey flower, Musk
		●				●	●	●					●										Monkey flower, Musk
						●	●						●					●					Monkey flower, Musk
						●					●												Sandwort
●	●	●					●	●					●										Marvel of Peru, Four o'clock plant
							●	●					●										Eulalia, Zebra grass
							●	●	●				●										Eulalia, Zebra grass
								●	●				●										Eulalia, Zebra grass
●	●		●	●		●				●													Bells of Ireland, Shellflower
●							●						●	●									Bergamot, Horsemint, Bee-balm
●							●																Bergamot, Horsemint, Bee-balm
●							●	●					●										Bergamot, Horsemint, Bee-balm
							●																Moraea, Butterfly iris
●							●				●												Whorlflower
							●																Muehlenbeckia, Wirevine
●						●						●											Grape hyacinth
●						●						●											Grape hyacinth
●						●						●											Grape hyacinth
●						●						●											Grape hyacinth
●						●						●											Grape hyacinth
●	●		●	●		●				●	●												Forget-me-not
		●	●			●	●	●					●										Forget-me-not
●						●			●											●			Myrrh, Sweet Cicely
●						●						●								●			Narcissus, Daffodil
●						●														●			Narcissus, Daffodil
●						●														●			Narcissus, Daffodil
●						●														●			Narcissus, Daffodil
						●														●			Narcissus, Daffodil
						●																	Narcissus, Daffodil
●							●																Lotus
		●					●																Nemesia
	●		●			●					●								●				Baby blue-eyes, Five-spot
	●		●																●				Baby blue-eyes, Five-spot
●			●				●				●	●											Catmint, Catnip

	SOIL					ASPECT/HARDINESS						FOLIAGE						FLOWER				
	Humus-rich	Sandy or dry	Chalky	Moist	Clay	Sun	Shade, semi-shade	Fully hardy [1]	Frost hardy [2]	Half hardy [3]	Tender [4]	Silver, grey	Golden	Variegated	Purple	Deciduous	Evergreen	White, green	Blue, mauve	Yellow, orange	Pink	Red
Nepeta govaniana				■			■										■			■		
Nepeta mussinii		■	■			■		■									■		■			
Nepeta nervosa		■				■		■									■		■			
Nepeta sibirica		■				■		■									■		■			
Nerine bowdenii		■							■												■	
Nicandra physalodes		■	■		■			■								■			■			
Nicotiana alata				■						■						■					■	■
Nicotiana sylvestris				■							■					■		■				
Nigella damascena		■				■		■								■		■	■		■	■
Nymphaea hybrids								■	■	■						■		■		■	■	■
Oenothera acaulis		■	■			■		■								■				■		
Oenothera biennis								■												■		
Oenothera fruticosa								■												■		
Oenothera glazionana								■												■		
Oenothera macrocarpa			■		■			■								■				■		
Oenothera perennis				■				■												■		
Oenothera speciosa		■	■						■							■					■	
Oenothera stricta								■												■		
Omphalodes cappadocica	■			■		■	■										■		■			
Omphalodes verna	■						■	■											■			
Onoclea sensibilis	■						■	■														
Onopordum acanthium		■				■	■	■														■
Onopordum bracteatum		■	■		■			■				■										
Origanum laevigatum				■					■								■				■	
Origanum vulgare		■	■					■							■		■				■	
Ornithogalum arabicum		■			■					■								■				
Ornithogalum nutans		■		■	■					■								■				
Ornithogalum thyrsoides		■			■					■								■				
Ornithogalum umbellatum		■		■	■			■										■				
Osmunda regalis	■							■														
Osmunda regalis purpurascens	■							■														
Osteospermum ecklonis		■				■				■												
Ourisia coccinea	■							■														■
Ourisia macrophylla	■							■									■					
Oxalis adenophylla	■	■						■				■									■	
Oxalis tetraphylla		■		■					■												■	
Pachysandra terminalis	■						■	■						■			■					
Paeonia cambessedesii									■							■					■	
Paeonia lactiflora		■			■			■								■					■	
Paeonia mlokosewitschii								■								■				■		
Paeonia officinalis		■						■								■						■
Paeonia peregrina								■								■						■
Paeonia tenuifolia								■								■						■
Papaver alpinum								■										■				
Papaver atlanticum						■		■										■		■		
Papaver nudicaule		■						■										■		■	■	■
Papaver orientale		■						■										■		■	■	■
Papaver rhoeas		■	■					■										■			■	■
Papaver somniferum								■							■			■			■	
Paradisea liliastrum								■										■				
Pelargonium domesticum		■				■					■				■						■	

Footnotes
[1] min. – 15°C (5°F), [2] min. –5°C (23°F), [3] min. 0°C (32°F), [4] min. 10°C (50°F)

Scented, aromatic	Sow direct	Sow then plant out	Self-seeding	Long-flowering	Winter	Early–mid spring	Late spr.–early sum.	Mid–late sum.	Autumn	Berry-producing	Ground cover	Walls, rock garden	Borders	Annual	Biennial	Banks	Under shrubs	In or near water	Attracts slugs	Poisonous/allergenic	Thorny	Needs staking	
■							■	■					■										Catmint, Catnip
■				■			■	■	■		■					■							Catmint, Catnip
■							■					■											Catmint, Catnip
■				■				■	■			■											Catmint, Catnip
				■					■		■								■	■			Nerine, Guernsey lily
	■		■					■												■			Nicandra, Apple of Peru
■		■						■												■			Tobacco plant
■		■						■												■			Tobacco plant
■	■		■					■															Love-in-a-mist, Fennel flower
								■										■					Water lily, Water nymph
							■				■	■											Evening primrose, Sundrops
■								■															Evening primrose, Sundrops
								■		■	■												Evening primrose, Sundrops
								■		■													Evening primrose, Sundrops
								■				■											Evening primrose, Sundrops
								■															Evening primrose, Sundrops
■								■		■		■											Evening primrose, Sundrops
								■															Evening primrose, Sundrops
						■	■			■	■				■		■						Navelwort, Navel-seed
						■	■			■	■						■	■					Navelwort, Navel-seed
																			■				Sensitive fern
							■									■							Scotch thistle, Cotton thistle
			■					■															Scotch thistle, Cotton thistle
								■	■		■	■											Oregano, Sweet marjoram
■								■	■		■	■	■			■							Oregano, Sweet marjoram
				■			■			■									■	■			Star of Bethlehem, Chincherinchee
				■		■		■											■	■			Star of Bethlehem, Chincherinchee
				■			■												■				Star of Bethlehem, Chincherinchee
				■			■												■				Star of Bethlehem, Chincherinchee
■							■																Royal fern
								■															Royal fern
■				■			■	■					■										Cape marigold
						■																	Ourisia
											■												Ourisia
						■				■	■												Oxalis, Wood sorrel, Good luck leaf
								■		■	■												Oxalis, Wood sorrel, Good luck leaf
■								■		■						■				■			Pachysandra, Spurge
						■							■										Peony
						■						■								■			Peony
						■	■					■											Peony
■						■						■											Peony
					■		■					■											Peony
					■	■							■										Peony
						■																	Poppy
						■	■			■	■												Poppy
								■															Poppy
			■						■														Poppy
	■		■					■															Poppy
		■	■					■															Poppy
■								■															Paradise lily, St Bruno's lily
						■	■																Geranium, Storksbill

627

	Humus-rich	Sandy or dry	Chalky	Moist	Clay	Sun	Shade, semi-shade	Fully hardy[1]	Frost hardy[2]	Half hardy[3]	Tender[4]	Silver, grey	Golden	Variegated	Purple	Deciduous	Evergreen	White, green	Blue, mauve	Yellow, orange	Pink	Red
Pelargonium graveolens		■	■			■					■							■			■	■
Pelargonium peltatum		■	■			■					■							■			■	■
Pelargonium tomentosum		■	■			■					■							■			■	■
Pelargonium zonale		■	■			■					■							■		■	■	■
Peltiphyllum peltatum				■	■			■													■	
Pennisetum alopecuroides								■														
Pennisetum orientale			■					■														
Pennisetum setaceum		■						■														
Penstemon barbatus						■		■								■					■	■
Penstemon heterophyllus								■											■		■	■
Penstemon hirsutus						■		■									■		■			■
Penstemon pinifolius							■											■		■		
Petasites fragrans				■		■	■															
Petasites japonicus				■			■															
Petunia x hybrida		■	■							■								■	■	■	■	■
Petunia integrifolia						■				■												■
Phacelia campanularia		■		■		■	■					■							■			
Phacelia tanacetifolia				■		■	■					■							■			
Phalaris arundinacea				■			■							■				■				
Phlomis cashmeriana		■				■		■				■					■				■	
Phlomis fruticosa		■						■												■		
Phlomis samia		■	■	■				■												■		
Phlox carolina				■			■											■			■	
Phlox divaricata	■			■		■		■									■		■			
Phlox douglasii							■														■	■
Phlox drummondii										■								■	■	■	■	■
Phlox maculata							■											■			■	■
Phlox paniculata				■			■											■	■		■	■
Phlox stolonifera	■					■	■								■			■	■			
Phlox subulata							■											■			■	
Phormium tenax		■	■						■					■	■							
Phygelius aequalis		■		■		■			■							■	■	■		■		
Phygelius capensis		■	■																			■
Phyllitis scolopendrium			■	■		■	■										■					
Physalis alkekengi var. *franchetii*		■	■	■	■			■														
Physostegia virginiana	■							■										■			■	
Phytolacca americana	■							■									■				■	
Pinguicula grandiflora				■		■	■												■			
Platycodon apoyama								■											■			
Platycodon grandiflorus mariesii		■				■		■										■	■		■	
Plumbago auriculata										■									■			
Podophyllum hexandrum	■					■		■									■				■	
Polemonium coeruleum				■			■												■			
Polemonium foliosissimum				■			■												■			
Polemonium pulcherrimum		■					■									■			■			
Polygonatum biflorum				■		■	■											■				
Polygonatum x hybridum						■	■	■										■				
Polygonatum odoratum							■									■		■				
Polygonum affine				■	■		■									■	■				■	
Polygonum amplexicaule				■	■		■														■	■
Polygonum bistorta				■	■		■														■	

Footnotes
[1] min. – 15°C (5°F), [2] min. –5°C (23°F), [3] min. 0°C (32°F), [4] min. 10°C (50°F)

	ANNUALS				FLOWERING SEASON							USES								PROBLEMS				
Scented, aromatic	Sow direct	Sow then plant out	Self-seeding	Long-flowering	Winter	Early–mid spring	Late spr.– early sum.	Mid–late sum.	Autumn	Berry-producing	Ground cover	Walls, rock garden	Borders	Annual	Biennial	Banks	Under shrubs	In or near water	Attracts slugs	Poisonous/allergenic	Thorny	Needs staking	
■				■				■	■														Geranium, Storksbill
■				■				■	■														Geranium, Storksbill
■				■				■	■														Geranium, Storksbill
■				■				■															Geranium, Storksbill
■								■															Umbrella plant
							■		■		■												Fountain grass
							■		■														Fountain grass
								■					■	■									Fountain grass
							■	■	■				■										Penstemon
								■					■										Penstemon, Beard-tongue
							■	■			■		■										Penstemon, Beard-tongue
								■															Penstemon, Beard-tongue
■								■															Petasites
■						■																	Petasites
■		■						■															Petunia
								■						■									Petunia
	■		■					■			■								■				Phacelia, Scorpion weed
		■	■					■	■			■							■				Phacelia
											■												Ribbon grass, Canary grass
							■		■			■											Jerusalem sage
									■														Jerusalem sage
									■		■												Jerusalem sage
								■					■										Phlox
							■									■							Phlox
						■					■	■											Phlox
			■																				Phlox
								■															Phlox
■				■				■															Phlox
						■	■				■	■				■							Phlox
							■				■	■											Phlox
								■															New Zealand flax, Flax lily
								■	■			■											Cape fuchsia
					■			■															Cape fuchsia
			■																				Hart's-tongue fern
								■															Chinese lantern
			■					■												■			Obedient plant, Lion's-heart
			■					■															Poke, Pokeberry
								■			■												Butterwort
								■	■		■	■											Balloon flower
								■	■		■	■										■	Balloon flower
								■															Plumbago, Leadwort
							■				■												Podophyllum, May apple
								■				■											Jacob's ladder, Greek valerian
							■	■			■												Jacob's ladder, Greek valerian
						■		■					■							■			Jacob's ladder, Greek valerian
									■		■						■			■			Solomon's seal
									■		■						■						Solomon's seal
■						■	■				■						■						Solomon's seal
			■						■		■	■											Knotweed, Fleece-flower
			■					■	■			■											Knotweed, Fleece-flower
								■		■													Knotweed, Fleece-flower

	SOIL					ASPECT/HARDINESS						FOLIAGE						FLOWER				
	Humus-rich	*Sandy or dry*	*Chalky*	*Moist*	*Clay*	*Sun*	*Shade, semi-shade*	*Fully hardy*[1]	*Frost hardy*[2]	*Half hardy*[3]	*Tender*[4]	*Silver, grey*	*Golden*	*Variegated*	*Purple*	*Deciduous*	*Evergreen*	*White, green*	*Blue, mauve*	*Yellow, orange*	*Pink*	*Red*
P																						
Polygonum campanulatum								■										■			■	
Polygonum capitatum				■			■		■					■	■	■					■	
Polygonum vaccinifolium	■							■														
Polygonum virginianum								■														
Polygonum weyrichii				■				■									■	■				
Polypodium vulgare	■						■	■								■						
Polystichum achrostichoides				■			■	■									■					
Polystichum aculeatum	■						■	■									■					
Polystichum falcatum	■						■			■							■					
Polystichum polyblepharum	■						■	■									■					
Polystichum setiferum	■						■	■									■					
Pontederia cordata				■				■											■			
Portulaca grandiflora		■	■								■									■	■	■
Potentilla alba					■			■								■		■				
Potentilla atrosanguinea								■								■					■	■
Potentilla megalantha			■		■	■		■								■				■		
Potentilla nepalensis								■								■			■			
Potentilla nitida						■		■													■	
Potentilla x tonguei		■	■			■		■								■				■		
Primula alpicola	■			■			■	■										■		■		
Primula auricula						■	■	■										■	■	■	■	
Primula beesiana	■						■	■													■	■
Primula bulleyana	■						■	■												■		■
Primula capitata	■						■	■											■			
Primula denticulata	■						■	■										■	■		■	
Primula florindae	■						■	■												■		
Primula helodoxa	■			■			■	■								■				■		
Primula japonica	■						■	■													■	■
Primula juliae	■						■	■													■	■
Primula nutans						■	■	■											■			
Primula palinuri			■			■			■											■		
Primula polyneura	■						■		■							■					■	
Primula pulverulenta	■							■														■
Primula rosea							■	■													■	■
Primula sieboldii	■						■	■										■	■			
Primula vulgaris				■		■	■	■												■	■	
Prunella grandiflora				■	■			■							■			■	■		■	
Pulmonaria angustifolia ssp. *azurea*				■			■	■											■			
Pulmonaria longifolia				■			■	■						■	■				■			
Pulmonaria officinalis				■			■	■				■		■							■	
Pulmonaria rubra				■			■	■								■						■
Pulmonaria saccharata				■			■	■						■							■	
Pulsatilla vulgaris						■		■							■			■	■			
Puschkinia scilloides			■				■	■											■			
R																						
Ramonda myconi				■			■	■										■	■			
Ranunculus asiaticus		■		■						■								■		■	■	
Raoulia australis		■	■	■				■							■					■		■
Reseda alba		■	■					■										■				
Reseda odorata							■	■														
Rheum palmatum		■		■	■			■							■							
Rhodohypoxis baurii		■							■									■			■	■

Footnotes
[1] min. – 15°C (5°F), [2] min. –5°C (23°F), [3] min. 0°C (32°F), [4] min. 10°C (50°F)

	Scented, aromatic	Sow direct	Sow then plant out	Self-seeding	Long-flowering	Winter	Early–mid spring	Late spr.–early sum.	Mid–late sum.	Autumn	Berry-producing	Ground cover	Walls, rock garden	Borders	Annual	Biennial	Banks	Under shrubs	In or near water	Attracts slugs	Poisonous/allergenic	Thorny	Needs staking	
ANNUALS →						FLOWERING SEASON →						USES →								PROBLEMS →				
				●					●	●	●													Knotweed, Fleece-flower
	●								●	●								●						Knotweed, Fleece-flower
									●	●														Knotweed, Fleece-flower
				●					●	●	●													Knotweed, Fleece-flower
									●	●								●						Knotweed, Fleece-flower
	●										●							●						Polypody
	●										●							●						Polystichum, Christmas fern
											●							●						Polystichum, Christmas fern
											●							●						Polystichum, Christmas fern
												●	●					●						Polystichum, Christmas fern
											●							●						Polystichum, Christmas fern
									●										●					Pontederia, Pickerel weed
		●	●		●				●			●												Purslane, Moss rose, Sun plant
							●	●					●			●								Cinquefoil, Five-finger
							●	●				●	●											Cinquefoil, Five-finger
								●					●											Cinquefoil, Five-finger
								●					●											Cinquefoil, Five-finger
								●				●												Cinquefoil, Five-finger
				●		●						●												Cinquefoil, Five-finger
	●						●		●			●												Primula, Primrose
	●						●	●				●												Primula, Primrose
								●				●												Primula, Primrose
								●				●												Primula, Primrose
								●				●												Primula, Primrose
								●				●												Primula, Primrose
	●									●		●												Primula, Primrose
								●					●											Primula, Primrose
			●				●		●			●												Primula, Primrose
							●	●					●											Primula, Primrose
								●					●											Primula, Primrose
								●																Primula, Primrose
								●																Primula, Primrose
												●												Primula, Primrose
							●					●												Primula, Primrose
								●				●												Primula, Primrose
								●										●						Primula, Primrose
			●		●				●		●	●												Self-heal
		●						●			●	●					●							Lungwort
							●	●					●					●						Lungwort
		●						●			●							●						Lungwort
							●	●					●					●						Lungwort
			●					●				●						●			●			Lungwort
									●			●	●											Anemone, Pasque flower
							●					●	●							●				Striped squill
								●				●	●								●			Ramonda, Rosette-mullein
			●					●	●			●							●					Buttercup, Crowfoot
	●							●				●												Raoulia
	●	●		●	●				●	●					●									Mignonette
	●	●		●	●				●	●					●									Mignonette
				●						●									●					Ornamental rhubarb
								●	●			●									●			Rhodohypoxis

631

	SOIL					ASPECT/HARDINESS						FOLIAGE						FLOWERS				
	Humus-rich	Sandy or dry	Chalky	Moist	Clay	Sun	Shade, semi-shade	Fully hardy [1]	Frost hardy [2]	Half hardy [3]	Tender [4]	Silver, grey	Golden	Variegated	Purple	Deciduous	Evergreen	White, green	Blue, mauve	Yellow, orange	Pink	Red, b…
R Ricinus communis		■								■					■							
Rodgersia aesculifolia	■						■	■							■			■				
Rodgersia pinnata	■						■		■						■						■	■
Rodgersia podophylla	■			■	■		■	■							■			■				
Rodgersia tabularis	■						■		■									■				■
Romneya coulteri		■							■									■				■
Rudbeckia fulgida		■			■			■												■		
Rudbeckia hirta		■			■	■		■												■		■
Rudbeckia laciniata		■			■			■												■		■
Rudbeckia nitida		■			■			■												■		■
Ruscus aculeatus					■	■	■	■									■	■				■
Ruta graveolens		■	■	■	■			■			■				■							
S Sagina subulata		■		■				■							■			■				
Sagittaria sagittifolia				■	■			■										■				
Salpiglossis sinuata		■								■								■	■	■	■	■
Salvia argentea		■							■									■				
Salvia azurea		■	■			■										■			■			
Salvia coccinea										■												■
Salvia farinacea		■								■									■			
Salvia guaranitica										■								■				
Salvia involucrata										■											■	
Salvia microphylla							■			■		■				■						
Salvia officinalis			■						■					■	■			■				
Salvia patens			■							■									■			
Salvia sclarea			■					■					■					■				
Salvia sclarea turkestanica							■		■									■	■			
Salvia splendens										■											■	
Salvia nemorosa							■												■			
Salvia uliginosa										■												
Sanguinaria canadensis	■						■	■							■			■				
Sanguisorba canadensis				■		■	■											■				
Sanguisorba obtusa				■	■	■												■			■	
Santolina chamaecyparissus		■	■		■			■				■					■			■		
Santolina rosmarinifolia		■	■					■									■			■		
Sanvitalia procumbens							■													■		
Saponaria x lempergii		■				■										■					■	
Saponaria ocymoides						■															■	
Saponaria officinalis				■	■	■	■									■		■			■	■
Sarracenia flava				■					■						■			■		■		
Saxifraga cochlearis							■	■				■						■				
Saxifraga cortusifolia	■						■	■										■				
Saxifraga cotyledon		■				■												■			■	
Saxifraga crustata							■	■								■		■		■		
Saxifraga fortunei			■	■		■			■							■						■
Saxifraga hypnoides	■						■	■						■				■				
Saxifraga irvingii							■	■										■				
Saxifraga longifolia							■	■										■				
Saxifraga oppositifolia																			■		■	
Saxifraga paniculata			■			■		■										■				■
Saxifraga stolonifera	■						■		■					■				■				
Saxifraga umbrosa	■						■	■							■			■			■	

Footnotes
[1] min. – 15°C (5°F), [2] min. –5°C (23°F), [3] min. 0°C (32°F), [4] min. 10°C (50°F)

Groups: ANNUALS · FLOWERING SEASON · USES · PROBLEMS

Scented, aromatic	Sow direct	Sow then plant out	Self-seeding	Long-flowering	Winter	Early-mid spring	Late spr.–early sum.	Mid-late sum.	Autumn	Berry-producing	Ground cover	Walls, rock garden	Borders	Annual	Biennial	Banks	Under shrubs	In or near water	Attracts slugs	Poisonous/allergenic	Thorny	Needs staking	
	●	●							●														Castor oil plant
●							●																Rodgersia
●							●																Rodgersia
						●	●					●											Rodgersia
●							●																Rodgersia
							●	●															Tree poppy, Matilija poppy
				●					●														Coneflower
				●			●																Coneflower
				●																			Coneflower
				●					●														Butcher's broom, Box holly
●							●				●												Rue, herb of grace
						●				●	●												Pearlwort
							●											●					Arrowhead
	●						●																Salpiglossis, Painted tongue
		●		●						●													Sage, Ramona
				●				●					●										Sage, Ramona
				●			●																Sage, Ramona
				●			●																Sage, Ramona
	●			●			●																Sage, Ramona
				●				●															Sage, Ramona
				●				●															Sage, Ramona
				●							●												Sage, Ramona
				●				●			●												Sage, Ramona
				●			●																Sage, Ramona
●			●	●			●																Sage, Ramona
				●			●																Sage, Ramona
				●			●																Sage, Ramona
			●	●			●				●												Sage, Ramona
							●																Bloodroot, Red puccoon
				●		●											●	●					Burnet
							●																Burnet
●							●			●	●												Cotton lavender
●							●			●	●												Cotton lavender
	●									●													Creeping zinnia
							●																Soapwort
		●				●	●	●			●	●			●								Soapwort
						●				●	●												Soapwort
						●					●												Pitcher plant
						●	●				●												Saxifrage, Rockfoil
						●		●								●							Saxifrage, Rockfoil
						●					●												Saxifrage, Rockfoil
						●					●												Saxifrage, Rockfoil
						●					●												Saxifrage, Rockfoil
						●				●	●												Saxifrage, Rockfoil
						●					●												Saxifrage, Rockfoil
						●					●												Saxifrage, Rockfoil
						●					●												Saxifrage, Rockfoil
						●					●												Saxifrage, Rockfoil
						●					●												Saxifrage, Rockfoil
							●	●		●	●												Saxifrage, Rockfoil

	SOIL					ASPECT/HARDINESS						FOLIAGE						FLOWER				
	Humus-rich	Sandy or dry	Chalky	Moist	Clay	Sun	Shade, semi-shade	Fully hardy[1]	Frost hardy[2]	Half hardy[3]	Tender[4]	Silver, grey	Golden	Variegated	Purple	Deciduous	Evergreen	White, green	Blue, mauve	Yellow, orange	Pink	Red
Scabiosa atropurpurea								■										■	■		■	■
Scabiosa caucasica								■										■	■		■	
Scabiosa graminifolia		■				■			■			■				■			■			
Scabiosa ochroleuca								■												■		
Schizanthus pinnatus		■									■							■		■	■	■
Schizostylis coccinea		■		■					■												■	
Scilla mischtschenkoana						■		■											■			
Scilla peruviana						■													■			
Scilla sibirica		■		■				■											■			
Scilla tubergeniana							■	■										■	■			
Scutellaria alpina								■							■			■	■			
Sedum aizoon								■														
Sedum album		■				■		■						■	■			■				
Sedum floriferum								■							■					■		
Sedum kamtschaticum		■				■		■							■					■		
Sedum lydium								■														
Sedum reflexum		■						■				■						■	■			■
Sedum spathulifolium		■						■				■		■	■							
Sedum spectabile		■					■	■				■									■	■
Sedum spurium		■	■	■	■				■						■		■	■			■	■
Sedum telephium								■														■
Sempervivum arachnoideum			■					■							■		■	■			■	■
Sempervivum calcareum		■	■			■		■						■	■							
Sempervivum ciliosum		■	■					■					■	■						■		
Sempervivum ruthenicum		■	■					■				■			■			■				
Sempervivum tectorum								■							■			■			■	
Senecio cineraria			■					■		■		■			■		■	■	■	■		
Senecio greyii			■					■				■			■					■		
Shortia galicifolia	■						■	■													■	
Shortia uniflora	■						■	■								■		■				
Sidalcea malvaeflora				■				■										■			■	■
Silene acaulis								■													■	■
Silene armeria								■													■	■
Silene malviflora		■						■				■				■		■				
Silene pendula										■								■			■	
Silene schafta								■													■	
Silene uniflora	■					■		■										■				
Silybum marianum		■	■	■				■	■				■								■	
Sisyrinchium angustifolium			■			■		■											■			
Sisyrinchium striatum		■						■				■						■		■		
Smilacina racemosa		■		■			■	■										■				
Solanum capsicastrum		■								■					■					■		
Solanum crispum										■					■				■			
Solanum jasminoides										■					■			■				
Soldanella alpina	■							■											■			
Soldanella minima	■						■	■									■		■			
Soldanella montana	■							■											■			
Solidago canadensis		■			■			■												■		
Sparaxis grandiflora						■				■										■		
Sparaxis tricolor		■								■										■	■	■
Sprekelia formosissima		■								■												■

Footnotes
[1] min. – 15°C (5°F), [2] min. –5°C (23°F), [3] min. 0°C (32°F), [4] min. 10°C (50°F)

ANNUALS				FLOWERING SEASON							USES								PROBLEMS				
Scented, aromatic	Sow direct	Sow then plant out	Self-seeding	Long-flowering	Winter	Early–mid spring	Late spr.–early sum.	Mid–late sum.	Autumn	Berry-producing	Ground cover	Walls, rock garden	Borders	Annual	Biennial	Banks	Under shrubs	In or near water	Attracts slugs	Poisonous/allergenic	Thorny	Needs staking	
■	■							■															Scabious, Pincushion flower
			■				■	■	■		■	■				■							Scabious, Pincushion flower
			■				■	■	■		■	■				■							Scabious, Pincushion flower
■								■															Scabious, Pincushion flower
	■	■		■														■					Butterfly flower, Poor man's orchid
				■							■							■					Kaffir lily, Crimson flag
		■									■							■					Squill
			■					■	■		■							■					Squill
					■						■								■	■			Squill
					■						■								■	■			Squill
						■					■												Skullcap
						■		■		■	■												Stonecrop, Orpine
		■						■			■												Stonecrop, Orpine
						■	■				■				■								Stonecrop, Orpine
		■					■	■	■		■												Stonecrop, Orpine
								■		■	■												Stonecrop, Orpine
		■					■	■			■												Stonecrop, Orpine
■							■			■	■												Stonecrop, Orpine
					■				■	■	■												Stonecrop, Orpine
								■		■	■												Stonecrop, Orpine
									■	■	■												Stonecrop, Orpine
								■			■												Houseleek
								■			■												Houseleek
								■			■												Houseleek
								■			■												Houseleek
								■			■												Houseleek
■		■				■				■	■									■			Groundsel
						■				■	■												Groundsel
						■											■						Shortia
						■	■	■				■											Shortia, Fringe-bell
			■					■															Sidalcea
■			■			■	■				■												Campion, Catchfly
						■	■				■												Campion, Catchfly
		■				■	■	■			■				■								Campion, Catchfly
	■	■	■			■	■	■			■												Campion, Catchfly
		■	■			■			■														Campion, Catchfly
								■															Campion, Catchfly
		■	■					■		■	■												Milk thistle, Holy thistle
						■																	Sisyrinchium, Blue-eyed grass
		■							■		■												Sisyrinchium, Blue-eyed grass
■										■						■							False Solomon's seal, Spikenard
								■												■			Nightshade
								■												■			Nightshade
								■															Nightshade
						■					■							■					Soldanella, Alpenclock
						■					■							■					Soldanella, Alpenclock
						■					■							■					Soldanella, Alpenclock
								■					■										Golden rod
							■		■						■								African harlequin flower
							■				■												African harlequin flower
							■				■												Aztec lily, Jacobean lily

635

Table — genus entries S–T (cultivation/characteristics chart)

Plant	Humus-rich	Sandy or dry	Chalky	Moist	Clay	Sun	Shade, semi-shade	Fully hardy [1]	Frost hardy [2]	Half hardy [3]	Tender [4]	Silver, grey	Golden	Variegated	Purple	Deciduous	Evergreen	White, green	Blue, mauve	Yellow, orange	Pink	Red
S *Stachys byzantina*			■	■	■	■		■				■				■					■	
Stachys macrantha		■		■	■			■									■				■	
Stachys officinalis			■			■		■				■				■					■	
Sternbergia clusiana								■												■		
Sternbergia fischeriana								■												■		
Sternbergia lutea		■		■				■												■		
Stipa calamagrostis		■						■										■		■		
Stipa gigantea		■						■				■			■					■		
Stokesia laevis				■				■											■			
Symphytum caucasicum				■	■	■		■											■			
Symphytum ibericum				■	■	■		■						■						■		
Symphytum orientale							■	■										■				
Symphytum x uplandicum							■	■											■			
T *Tagetes erecta*										■										■		■
Tagetes patula										■										■		■
Tagetes tenuifolia										■										■		■
Tellima grandiflora	■					■	■									■	■	■				
Teucrium chamaedrys								■													■	
Teucrium polium									■			■						■	■			
Teucrium scorodonia									■									■				
Thalictrum adiantifolium	■							■														
Thalictrum aquilegifolium				■				■										■	■		■	
Thalictrum delavayi		■				■	■	■											■			■
Thalictrum kiusianum	■							■														
Thermopsis lanceolata								■												■		
Thermopsis montana		■						■												■		
Thunbergia alata		■								■										■		
Thunbergia grandiflora										■												
Thymus cilicicus			■					■									■				■	
Thymus x citriodorus			■						■								■				■	
Thymus hirsutus			■					■									■				■	
Thymus membranaceus		■	■					■									■				■	
Thymus pseudolanuginosus			■					■									■				■	
Thymus serpyllum			■					■				■					■				■	
Tiarella cordifolia	■						■	■									■	■				
Tiarella trifoliata	■						■	■									■	■				
Tiarella wherryi	■						■	■							■		■	■				
Tigridia pavonia		■								■								■		■	■	■
Tolmiea menziesii	■						■	■										■				
Torenia fournieri		■									■											
Tradescantia x andersoniana	■						■	■										■	■		■	■
Tricyrtis hirta	■							■													■	
Tricyrtis macropoda	■							■													■	
Trillium erectum	■						■	■										■			■	■
Trillium grandiflorum	■						■	■										■			■	
Trillium ovatum	■						■	■										■			■	■
Trillium sessile	■						■	■						■				■			■	■
Trillium undulatum	■						■	■										■			■	
Trollius chinensis	■							■												■		
Trollius x cultorum				■		■	■	■												■		
Trollius europaeus	■							■												■		

Column groups: SOIL · ASPECT/HARDINESS · FOLIAGE · FLOWER

Footnotes
[1] min. – 15°C (5°F), [2] min. –5°C (23°F), [3] min. 0°C (32°F), [4] min. 10°C (50°F)

	ANNUALS					FLOWERING SEASON						USES								PROBLEMS			
Plant	Scented, aromatic	Sow direct	Sow then plant out	Self-seeding	Long-flowering	Winter	Early–mid spring	Late spr.–early sum.	Mid–late sum.	Autumn	Berry-producing	Ground cover	Walls, rock garden	Borders	Annual	Biennial	Banks	Under shrubs	In or near water	Attracts slugs	Poisonous/allergenic	Thorny	Needs staking
Lamb's ears, Betony					●				●		●	●											
Lamb's ears, Betony							●		●				●										
Lamb's ears, Betony					●				●			●											
Lily of the field				●						●		●											
Lily of the field										●			●										
Lily of the field										●			●										
Feather grass, Needlegrass	●								●			●											
Feather grass, Needlegrass										●													
Stokesia, Stokes' aster	●								●			●											
Comfrey, Boneset							●					●											
Comfrey, Boneset					●		●					●		●									
Comfrey, Boneset							●		●			●											
Comfrey, Boneset									●		●								●				
African marigold, French marigold	●	●			●				●											●			
African marigold, French marigold	●	●			●				●				●							●			
African marigold, French marigold	●	●			●				●	●		●											
Tellima, Fringecup				●					●		●						●						
Germander																							
Germander																							
Germander									●												●		
Meadow rue																					●		
Meadow rue							●		●												●		
Meadow rue							●		●												●		
Meadow rue									●														
Thermopsis, False lupine									●														
Thermopsis, False lupine									●														
Black-eyed Susan, Clock vine			●		●				●					●									
Black-eyed Susan, Clock vine									●														
Thyme	●								●		●	●											
Thyme	●								●		●	●											
Thyme	●								●		●	●											
Thyme							●		●				●										
Thyme							●		●				●										
Thyme	●								●		●	●											
Foam flower							●		●	●	●	●											
Foam flower									●		●	●											
Foam flower									●	●	●												
Tiger flower									●				●							●			
Mother of thousands									●									●					
Wishbone flower			●						●											●			
Spider lily, Spiderwort									●					●									
Toad lily						●				●								●		●			
Toad lily						●				●								●		●			
Trillium, Wood lily							●											●		●			
Trillium, Wood lily							●											●		●			
Trillium, Wood lily							●											●		●	●		
Trillium, Wood lily							●											●		●			
Trillium, Wood lily							●											●		●	●		
Globeflower												●											
Globeflower							●					●			●								
Globeflower					●		●							●									

	Humus-rich	Sandy or dry	Chalky	Moist	Clay	Sun	Shade, semi-shade	Fully hardy[1]	Frost hardy[2]	Half hardy[3]	Tender[4]	Silver, grey	Golden	Variegated	Purple	Deciduous	Evergreen	White, green	Blue, mauve	Yellow, orange	Pink	Red
T *Trollius pumilus*	■			■			■	■								■				■		
Tropaeoleum majus		■				■		■											■			
Tropaeoleum peregrinum			■			■		■	■					■						■		
Tropaeolum polyphyllum		■	■			■		■				■								■		
Tropaeolum speciosum	■	■	■	■		■	■	■												■		
Tropaeolum tricolorum		■				■				■										■		■
Tropaeolum tuberosum				■		■				■										■		
Tulipa acuminata			■			■		■										■				■
Tulipa clusiana			■			■		■										■				■
Tulipa Darwin			■			■		■										■	■	■	■	■
Tulipa double early			■			■		■										■		■		■
Tulipa double late			■			■		■										■				■
Tulipa lily-flowered			■			■		■										■				■
Tulipa fosteriana			■			■		■										■		■		■
Tulipa greigii			■			■		■						■				■				■
Tulipa kaufmanniana		■				■		■										■			■	■
Tulipa marjoletti		■				■		■												■	■	
Tulipa Mendel		■				■		■										■				■
Tulipa parrot		■				■		■										■		■	■	■
Tulipa single early		■				■		■										■		■	■	■
Tulipa single late		■				■		■										■		■	■	■
Tulipa sprengeri		■				■		■													■	■
Tulipa sylvestris		■				■		■												■		■
Tulipa tarda		■				■		■										■				
Tulipa Triumph		■				■		■										■	■	■	■	■
Tunica saxifraga						■		■										■			■	
Typha angustifolia				■				■														
Typha latifolia				■	■			■									■					
Typha minima				■				■														
V *Veratrum nigrum*	■							■											■			
Veratrum viride								■										■				
Verbascum bombyciferum		■	■					■				■								■		
Verbascum chaixii		■	■					■				■								■		
Verbascum phoeniceum		■	■					■								■	■				■	■
Verbascum thapsus			■					■												■		
Verbena bonariensis			■						■									■	■		■	
Verbena hastata										■									■		■	■
Verbena peruviana		■					■			■					■	■			■		■	■
Verbena rigida										■								■	■		■	■
Veronica austriaca ssp. *teucrium*		■						■											■			
Veronica gentianoides				■				■											■			
Veronica longifolia								■											■			
Veronica prostrata		■						■									■	■	■		■	
Veronica spicata								■							■			■	■		■	
Veronica virginica	■							■										■	■			
Vinca major	■	■	■	■	■		■	■						■			■		■			
Vinca minor	■						■	■						■			■	■	■		■	
Viola cornuta							■	■										■	■	■		
Viola labradorica	■						■	■							■			■	■			
Viola odorata	■						■	■										■	■			
Viola sororia	■		■		■		■	■									■	■	■			

Footnotes
[1] min. − 15°C (5°F), [2] min. −5°C (23°F), [3] min. 0°C (32°F), [4] min. 10°C (50°F)

Scented, aromatic	Sow direct	Sow then plant out	Self-seeding	Long-flowering	Winter	Early–mid spring	Late spr.–early sum.	Mid–late sum.	Autumn	Berry-producing	Ground cover	Walls, rock garden	Borders	Annual	Biennial	Banks	Under shrubs	In or near water	Attracts slugs	Poisonous/allergenic	Thorny	Needs staking	Name
						■	■				■	■											Globeflower
				■				■												■			Nasturtium, Bitter Indian
	■			■				■					■							■			Nasturtium, Bitter Indian
				■				■					■							■			Nasturtium, Bitter Indian
				■				■												■			Nasturtium, Bitter Indian
				■				■												■			Nasturtium, Bitter Indian
				■				■	■														Nasturtium, Bitter Indian
						■						■	■										Tulip
					■	■						■	■										Tulip
						■							■										Tulip
					■	■							■										Tulip
						■							■										Tulip
						■							■										Tulip
				■		■							■										Tulip
				■		■							■										Tulip
				■		■							■										Tulip
						■							■										Tulip
						■							■										Tulip
						■							■										Tulip
					■								■										Tulip
						■							■										Tulip
						■	■						■										Tulip
■						■							■										Tulip
						■							■										Tulip
						■							■										Tulip
						■							■										Tulip
								■															Tunic flower
									■														Bulrush, Reedmace, Cat('s) tail
							■	■	■									■					Bulrush, Reedmace, Cat('s) tail
									■														Bulrush, Reedmace, Cat('s) tail
								■															False hellebore
							■																False hellebore
				■																			Mullein
						■	■						■										Mullein
						■					■		■										Mullein
			■				■																Mullein
■			■	■				■			■												Verbena, Vervain
											■		■										Verbena, Vervain
											■		■										Verbena, Vervain
■		■	■	■			■	■			■												Verbena, Vervain
						■	■				■		■			■							Speedwell, Brooklime
						■				■	■												Speedwell, Brooklime
				■																			Speedwell, Brooklime
						■					■		■										Speedwell, Brooklime
			■				■																Speedwell, Brooklime
							■																Speedwell, Brooklime
				■		■	■				■						■						Periwinkle
						■	■				■						■						Periwinkle
				■		■	■	■			■	■	■			■							Pansy, Violet
■			■			■	■			■	■					■							Pansy, Violet
■			■		■	■				■	■												Pansy, Violet
			■	■		■					■					■							Pansy, Violet

	SOIL					ASPECT/HARDINESS						FOLIAGE						FLOWER				
VZ	Humus-rich	Sandy or dry	Chalky	Moist	Clay	Sun	Shade, semi-shade	Fully hardy [1]	Frost hardy [2]	Half hardy [3]	Tender [4]	Silver, grey	Golden	Variegated	Purple	Deciduous	Evergreen	White, green	Blue, mauve	Yellow, orange	Pink	Red
Viola suavis							■	■									■	■	■		■	
Viola x wittrockiana							■	■										■	■	■		■
Zantedeschia aethiopica	■									■								■		■		
Zantedeschia elliottiana				■	■						■			■				■		■		
Zantedeschia rehmannii				■	■						■							■			■	
Zauschneria californica		■	■			■				■		■						■				■
Zinnia elegans		■				■				■								■		■	■	■

Footnotes
[1] min. – 15°C (5°F), [2] min. –5°C (23°F), [3] min. 0°C (32°F), [4] min. 10°C (50°F)

	ANNUALS				FLOWERING SEASON						USES									PROBLEMS				
	Scented, aromatic	Sow direct	Sow then plant out	Self-seeding	Long-flowering	Winter	Early–mid spring	Late spr.–early sum.	Mid–late sum.	Autumn	Berry-producing	Ground cover	Walls, rock garden	Borders	Annual	Biennial	Banks	Under shrubs	In or near water	Attracts slugs	Poisonous/allergenic	Thorny	Needs staking	
	■				■		■	■	■			■	■				■							Pansy, Violet
	■		■		■		■	■	■		■									■				Pansy, Violet
	■				■				■															Arum lily, Calla lily
					■				■															Arum lily, Calla lily
					■				■															Arum lily, Calla lily
					■				■	■		■												Californian fuchsia
			■						■	■										■				Zinnia

641

A

	Fast-growing	Large	Small	Banks	Hedging	Specimen	Humus-rich	Sandy or dry	Chalky	Moist	Clay	Sun	Shade, semi-shade	Fully hardy[1]	Frost hardy[2]	Half hardy[3]	Tender[4]	Silver, grey	Golden
Abelia chinensis			■		■							■	■	■					
Abelia × grandiflora			■		■							■		■					
Abelia schumannii			■		■							■		■					
Abelia triflora					■							■		■					
Abies alba		■											■	■					
Abies balsamea f. hudsonia			■			■								■					
Abies cephalonica		■				■	■		■			■		■					
Abies concolor		■				■								■					
Abies grandis	■	■						■	■					■					
Abies homolepis		■				■			■					■					
Abies koreana		■				■								■					
Abies lasiocarpa		■	■			■								■					
Abies nordmanniana	■	■												■					
Abies pinsapo		■	■				■		■					■					
Abies procera		■				■								■					
Acacia baileyana	■						■					■				■			
Acacia dealbata			■	■	■										■			■	
Acacia longifolia	■						■					■			■				
Acacia mucronata			■	■	■							■			■				
Acacia retinodes			■	■	■					■		■			■				
Acer campestre		■		■	■	■	■	■			■			■					
Acer capillipes		■		■		■							■	■					
Acer cappadocicum		■				■	■						■	■					■
Acer circinatum			■			■						■	■	■					
Acer crataegifolium			■			■						■	■	■					
Acer davidii		■				■				■			■	■					
Acer griseum			■			■							■	■					
Acer grosseri			■	■	■	■							■	■					
Acer japonicum			■			■							■	■					
Acer negundo			■		■	■				■			■	■					
Acer opalus			■	■	■	■	■		■			■		■	■				
Acer palmatum			■			■				■			■	■					■
Acer pennsylvanicum			■			■							■	■					
Acer platanoïdes	■	■	■							■				■					
Acer pseudoplatanus	■	■								■	■			■					
Acer rubrum		■											■	■					
Acer rufinerve			■			■							■	■					
Acer saccharinum			■			■		■		■				■					
Acer saccharum		■								■				■					
Acer tataricum ssp. ginnala			■	■	■		■							■					
Acer × zoeschense		■	■			■								■					
Aesculus × carnea		■								■				■					
Aesculus hippocastanum	■	■				■				■				■					
Aesculus × neglecta		■				■	■						■	■					
Aesculus parviflora			■			■							■	■					
Aesculus pavia			■			■							■	■					
Ailanthus altissima	■	■				■	■		■			■	■	■					
Ailanthus vilmoriniana	■	■				■	■		■			■	■	■					
Albizia julibrissin			■			■						■				■			
Albizia lophantha	■		■				■					■		■		■			
Alnus cordata			■	■	■					■	■		■	■					

Footnotes
[1] min. − 15°C (5°F), [2] min. −5°C (23°F), [3] min. 0°C (32°F), [4] min. 10°C (50°F)

		FOLIAGE				FLOWERING SEASON				FLOWERS						MAXIMUM HEIGHT (metres)	PROBLEMS				
Variegated	Purple	Autumn colour	Fast-growing	Deciduous	Evergreen	Spring	Summer	Autumn	Winter	White, green	Blue, mauve	Yellow, orange	Pink	Red, purple	Scented, aromatic		Thorny	Poisonous/allergenic	Intolerant of pollution	Suckering	
				■			■	■					■			1.5					Abelia
							■	■					■			2.5					Abelia
							■	■					■			1.5					Abelia
			■			■				■					■	2					Abelia
					■											45					Fir
					■											1					Balsam fir
					■											25					Greek fir
					■											35					White fir
					■											60					Giant fir, grand fir
					■											10					Nikko fir
					■											6					Korean fir
					■											15					Fir
					■											20					Caucasian fir
					■											20					Spanish fir
					■											25					Noble fir
					■	■			■			■				5					Mimosa, wattle
					■	■			■			■			■	6					Silver wattle
					■	■						■				6					Sydney golden wattle
					■	■			■			■			■	4					Mimosa, wattle
					■	■			■			■			■	8					Mimosa, wattle
		■		■		■										20					Maple
	■			■		■										12					Snake-bark maple
		■		■		■										20					Caucasian maple
		■		■		■				■				■		10					Vine maple
		■		■												10					Maple
		■		■		■										10					Maple
		■		■		■						■				8					Maple
		■		■		■										8					Maple
		■		■		■								■		3					Maple
■		■		■								■				7					Ash-leaved maple
		■		■		■						■				10					Italian maple
	■	■		■										■		5					Maple
		■		■		■										9					Snake-bark maple
■	■	■		■		■						■				25					Norway maple
	■	■		■		■										30					Maple
		■		■		■								■		20					Red maple
		■		■		■										10					Snake-bark maple
		■		■		■						■				25					Maple
		■		■		■						■				25					Sugar maple
		■		■								■				6					Amur maple
		■		■		■										15					Maple
				■		■							■	■		20					Red horse chestnut
				■		■				■						25					Horse chestnut
		■		■												10					Horse chestnut
		■		■			■			■						4					White buckeye
				■			■							■		5					Red buckeye
				■												25				■	Tree of heaven
				■												16				■	Ailanthus
				■			■	■					■	■		10					Silk tree
				■					■			■				6					Silk tree
		■		■		■						■				7					Italian alder

		USES					SOIL					ASPECT & HARDINESS							
	Fast-growing	Large	Small	Banks	Hedging	Specimen	Humus-rich	Sandy or dry	Chalky	Moist	Clay	Sun	Shade, semi-shade	Fully hardy[1]	Frost hardy[2]	Half hardy[3]	Tender[4]	Silver, grey	Golden
A Alnus glutinosa 'Aurea'		■	■		■					■	■	■	■						■
Alnus incana		■						■	■	■	■	■	■						
Alnus maritima			■							■		■	■						
Alnus rubra	■	■		■	■				■			■	■						
Amelanchier alnifolia			■		■					■		■	■						
Amelanchier canadensis			■		■					■		■	■						
Amelanchier laevis			■		■					■		■	■						
Amelanchier lamarckii			■		■	■				■		■	■						
Aralia cachemirica			■			■						■	■						
Aralia elata			■			■			■	■		■	■						
Aralia spinosa			■			■			■	■		■	■						
Araucaria araucana		■				■								■					
Araucaria bidwillii		■				■								■	■				
Araucaria heterophylla													■			■			
Arbutus andrachne			■			■						■			■				
Arbutus × andrachnoïdes						■		■				■			■				
Arbutus menziesii			■			■						■			■				
Arbutus unedo			■		■	■								■					
Artemisia absinthium			■	■				■	■			■		■				■	
Artemisia arborescens			■	■	■	■		■	■			■			■			■	
Artemisia dracunculus			■	■				■				■		■					
Artemisia schmidtiana			■					■	■			■						■	
Arundinaria anceps			■	■	■	■			■	■		■		■					
Arundinaria chino			■	■	■				■	■			■						
Arundinaria fastuosa			■					■				■		■					
Arundinaria graminea						■			■	■			■	■					
Arundinaria japonica			■					■				■		■					
Arundinaria murieliae														■					
Arundinaria nitida			■	■	■				■	■		■		■					
Arundinaria pumila			■	■					■	■				■					
Arundinaria variegata			■	■					■	■		■		■					
Arundinaria viridistriata			■	■								■		■					
Atriplex halimus			■	■	■			■							■			■	
Aucuba japonica			■		■	■		■	■	■	■	■		■					
Azara integrifolia			■			■			■							■			
Azara microphylla			■			■			■						■				
Azara petiolaris			■			■			■					■					
B Ballota pseudodictamnus			■		■			■				■			■			■	
Berberis darwinii			■		■	■				■				■					
Berberis × frikartii			■			■				■				■					
Berberis × interposita			■			■								■					
Berberis × media			■	■		■								■					
Berberis prattii			■	■		■								■					
Berberis pruinosa		■	■	■		■								■					
Berberis × stenophylla		■	■	■		■		■						■					
Berberis thunbergii			■	■		■								■					
Berberis umbellata			■	■		■								■					
Berberis vulgaris			■			■								■					
Berberis wilsoniae			■			■		■						■					
Betula albo-sinensis		■				■		■		■				■					
Betula alleghaniensis		■				■								■					

Footnotes
[1] min. – 15°C (5°F), [2] min. –5°C (23°F), [3] min. 0°C (32°F), [4] min. 10°C (50°F)

	FOLIAGE						FLOWERING SEASON				FLOWERS						MAXIMUM HEIGHT (metres)	PROBLEMS				
Variegated	Purple	Autumn colour	Fast-growing	Deciduous	Evergreen	Spring	Summer	Autumn	Winter	White, green	Blue, mauve	Yellow, orange	Pink	Red, purple	Scented, aromatic		Thorny	Poisonous/allergenic	Intolerant of pollution	Suckering	
		■		■		■						■				25					European alder, common alder
		■		■					■							15					Grey alder
		■		■				■								8					Alder
		■		■		■								■		15					Red alder
		■		■		■				■						4					Juneberry, Serviceberry
		■		■		■				■						8				■	Juneberry, Serviceberry
		■		■		■				■					■	8				■	Juneberry, Serviceberry
		■		■		■				■						8				■	Juneberry, Serviceberry
				■				■		■						4				■	Aralia
				■				■		■						4	■			■	Japanese angelica tree
				■				■		■						6	■			■	American angelica tree
					■											25	■				Monkey puzzle
					■											25	■				Monkey puzzle
					■											30					Norfolk Island pine
					■					■						4					Grecian strawberry tree
					■	■		■	■	■						10					Strawberry tree
					■	■				■						5					Madroña, Madroñe
					■	■				■						6					Killarney strawberry tree
		■			■		■			■						1.2					Wormwood
					■											1.5					Wormwood
					■		■			■						0.4					Tarragon
			■		■		■									0.5					Wormwood
					■											3					Anceps bamboo
					■											3					Bamboo
					■											6					Bamboo
					■											5					Bamboo
					■											5					Arrow bamboo
					■											4					Bamboo
					■											6					Bamboo
					■											0.8					Bamboo
■					■											1					Dwarf white-stripe bamboo
					■											1					Bamboo
			■		■		■					■				2					Tree purslane
■					■	■										3					Japanese laurel
					■			■				■				6					Goldspire
					■	■						■				5					Goldspire
					■				■			■				3					Goldspire
					■		■									0.5					Ballota
					■	■		■				■				1	■				Barberry
					■	■						■				1	■				Barberry
	■				■	■						■				1.5	■				Barberry
		■			■	■						■				1	■				Barberry
	■			■		■		■				■				3	■				Barberry
					■	■						■				3	■				Barberry
					■	■						■				2.5	■				Barberry
	■	■			■	■						■				1.5	■				Barberry
					■	■						■				2	■				Barberry
					■	■						■		■		3	■				Barberry
		■		■		■						■				1.5	■				Barberry
		■		■								■				12					Birch
		■		■		■						■				20					Birch

	USES						SOIL					ASPECT & HARDINESS							
	Fast-growing	Large	Small	Banks	Hedging	Specimen	Humus-rich	Sandy or dry	Chalky	Moist	Clay	Sun	Shade, semi-shade	Fully hardy[1]	Frost hardy[2]	Half hardy[3]	Tender[4]	Silver, grey	Golden
B *Betula ermanii*	■	■				■								■					
Betula humilis			■			■								■					
Betula maximowicziana	■	■				■								■					
Betula nana			■			■				■				■					
Betula pendula		■				■		■						■					
Betula pubescens		■				■				■				■					
Betula utilis		■		■		■								■					
Brahea armata		■							■			■		■	■				
Buddleja alternifolia			■	■	■	■	■	■				■		■					
Buddleja davidii	■		■	■	■	■		■				■		■					
Buddleja fallowiana			■	■	■	■		■				■			■				
Buddleja globosa	■		■	■		■		■				■			■				
Buddleja × *weyeriana*			■	■	■	■				■		■		■					
Bupleurum fruticosum			■	■	■			■				■	■		■				
Bupleurum longifolium			■	■	■							■				■			
Buxus balearica			■	■	■										■				
Buxus microphylla			■						■					■					
Buxus sempervirens			■	■	■	■				■	■			■	■				
C *Caesalpinia decepetala* var. *japonica*			■			■			■		■	■			■				
Caesalpinia gilliesii			■			■			■		■	■			■				
Callicarpa bodinieri var. *giraldii*			■	■		■				■				■					
Callicarpa japonica			■	■	■	■								■					
Callistemon citrinus			■						■			■				■			
Callistemon rigidus			■						■			■			■				
Callistemon salignus			■						■			■			■				
Callistemon sieberi						■			■			■			■				
Callistemon speciosus			■						■			■				■			
Callistemon subulatus						■			■			■			■				
Calluna vulgaris			■	■			■	■				■		■					■
Calocedrus decurrens		■				■				■				■					
Calycanthus fertilis			■	■		■				■		■	■	■					
Calycanthus floridus			■			■				■		■	■	■					
Calycanthus occidentalis			■			■	■			■		■	■	■					
Camellia japonica			■		■	■	■						■		■				
Camellia sasanqua			■			■							■		■				
Camellia × *williamsii*			■			■							■						
Caragana arborescens			■	■	■			■				■	■	■					
Caragana decorticans			■	■	■			■				■	■	■					
Carpenteria californica			■			■						■			■				
Carpinus betulus		■		■	■	■				■	■			■					
Carpinus caroliniana		■		■	■	■				■	■			■					
Carpinus cordata		■		■	■	■								■					
Carpinus laxiflora		■		■	■	■								■					
Carpinus orientalis			■	■	■	■				■				■					
Carya aquatica	■		■			■				■				■					
Carya cordiformis	■	■				■				■				■					
Carya glabra		■				■				■				■					
Carya ovalis		■				■				■				■					
Carya ovata	■	■				■				■				■					
Carya tomentosa	■	■				■				■				■					
Caryopteris × *clandonensis*			■	■	■	■		■	■			■			■			■	

Footnotes
[1] min. – 15°C (5°F), [2] min. –5°C (23°F), [3] min. 0°C (32°F), [4] min. 10°C (50°F)

Columns grouped as: **FOLIAGE** (Variegated, Purple, Autumn colour, Fast-growing, Deciduous, Evergreen) · **FLOWERING SEASON** (Spring, Summer, Autumn, Winter) · **FLOWERS** (White/green, Blue/mauve, Yellow/orange, Pink, Red/purple, Scented/aromatic) · **MAXIMUM HEIGHT (metres)** · **PROBLEMS** (Thorny, Poisonous/allergenic, Intolerant of pollution, Suckering)

Variegated	Purple	Autumn colour	Fast-growing	Deciduous	Evergreen	Spring	Summer	Autumn	Winter	White, green	Blue, mauve	Yellow, orange	Pink	Red, purple	Scented, aromatic	Max. height	Thorny	Poisonous/allergenic	Intolerant of pollution	Suckering	Name
		■		■		■						■				20					Birch
	■	■		■		■						■				2.5					Birch
		■		■		■						■				25					Birch
		■		■		■						■				1					Dwarf birch
	■	■		■		■						■				25					Silver birch
		■		■		■						■				15					White, European white birch
		■		■		■						■				15					Birch
					■		■			■						13					Blue fan palm
				■			■				■				■	3.5					Buddleja
				■			■									4					Buddleja
				■			■			■	■				■	2.5					Buddleja
		■		■			■					■				4					Buddleja
	■			■			■					■			■	3					Buddleja
					■		■					■				2.5					Fruiting hare's ear
					■	■						■				2					Hare's ear
					■											5					Balearic box
					■											1					Small-leaved box
					■											3					Common box
				■			■					■				3	■				Caesalpina
	■						■					■				4					Bird of paradise
							■						■			2.5					Beautyberry
							■						■			1.5					Beautyberry
					■		■							■		2.5					Bottle brush
					■		■							■		2.5					Bottle brush
					■		■					■				2.5					Bottle brush
					■		■					■				1.5					Bottle brush
					■		■							■		2.5					Albany bottle brush
					■		■							■		1.5					Bottle brush
					■		■	■		■			■	■		0.4					Heather
■					■											30					Calocedrus, Libocedrus
				■			■							■		3					Sweet shrub
	■						■							■		3					Anemone tree
	■						■							■		3					California allspice
					■	■			■	■			■	■		3					Camellia
					■			■	■	■			■			3					Camellia
					■	■			■	■			■	■		3					Camellia
						■						■				5					Siberian pea tree
						■						■				4					Caragan
					■		■			■					■	2.5					Carpenteria
		■		■												20					Common hornbeam
		■		■												12					American hornbeam
		■		■												15					Hornbeam
		■		■												20					Hornbeam
		■		■												8					Hornbeam
		■		■												10					Hickory
		■		■												20					Bitternut, Pignut
		■		■												25					Hickory
		■		■												25					Hickory
		■		■												30					Shagbark
		■		■												25					Hickory
				■			■				■					1.2					Bluebeard

	USES						SOIL					ASPECT & HARDINESS							
	Fast-growing	Large	Small	Banks	Hedging	Specimen	Humus-rich	Sandy or dry	Chalky	Moist	Clay	Sun	Shade, semi-shade	Fully hardy[1]	Frost hardy[2]	Half hardy[3]	Tender[4]	Silver, grey	Golden
Caryopteris incana			■	■	■	■		■	■			■		■				■	
Cassia corymbosa			■			■		■				■					■		
Cassia fistula			■			■		■				■					■		
Cassia hebecarpa			■					■				■							
Cassiope fastigiata			■				■			■			■	■					
Cassiope mertensiana			■				■			■			■	■					
Cassiope selaginoïdes			■				■			■			■	■					
Cassiope tetragona			■				■			■			■	■					
Cassiope wardii			■				■			■			■	■					
Castanea sativa		■		■	■								■	■					
Catalpa bignonioïdes	■	■	■			■			■	■				■					■
Catalpa × erubescens		■				■			■	■				■					
Catalpa fargesii		■				■			■	■				■					
Catalpa speciosa	■	■								■				■					
Ceanothus arboreus			■	■		■		■				■		■					
Ceanothus × delileanus			■		■	■						■		■					
Ceanothus impressus			■		■	■						■		■					
Ceanothus × pallidus			■		■	■						■		■					
Ceanothus thyrsiflorus var. *repens*			■	■		■						■		■					
Ceanothus veitchianus						■		■				■		■					
Cedrus deodara	■	■	■			■		■		■				■				■	■
Cedrus libani ssp. *atlantica*	■	■				■								■				■	■
Cedrus libani ssp. *libani*		■	■			■								■					
Cephalotaxus fortunei			■										■	■					
Cephalotaxus harringtonia		■							■				■	■					
Ceratostigma griffithii			■	■		■		■		■		■		■		■			
Ceratostigma minus			■	■		■		■		■		■		■					
Ceratostigma willmottianum			■	■	■	■		■		■		■		■					
Cercidiphyllum japonicum			■			■							■	■					
Cercidiphyllum japonicum magnificum			■			■							■	■					
Cercis canadensis			■			■				■		■		■					
Cercis chinensis			■			■						■							
Cercis occidentalis			■			■		■				■							
Cercis racemosa			■			■						■							
Cercis siliquastrum			■			■		■	■			■		■					
Chaenomeles cathayensis			■	■	■						■	■	■	■					
Chaenomeles japonica			■	■	■						■	■	■	■					
Chaenomeles speciosa			■	■	■						■	■	■	■					
Chaenomeles × superba			■	■	■						■	■	■	■					
Chamaecyparis lawsoniana	■	■	■			■				■				■				■	■
Chamaecyparis nootkatensis		■				■								■					■
Chamaecyparis obtusa			■	■		■							■	■					■
Chamaecyparis pisifera			■	■		■				■				■					■
Chamaecyparis thyoides			■	■						■				■					
Chamaerops humilis			■			■							■			■			
Chimonanthus praecox			■									■		■					
Choisya ternata			■		■	■						■	■	■					
Cistus × corbariensis			■	■	■	■		■				■		■					
Cistus × cyprius			■	■	■	■		■				■		■					
Cistus ladanifer			■	■	■	■		■				■							
Cistus × lusitanicus			■	■	■	■		■				■							

Footnotes
[1] min. − 15°C (5°F), [2] min. −5°C (23°F), [3] min. 0°C (32°F), [4] min. 10°C (50°F)

Variegated	Purple	Autumn colour	Fast-growing	Deciduous	Evergreen	Spring	Summer	Autumn	Winter	White, green	Blue, mauve	Yellow, orange	Pink	Red, purple	Scented, aromatic	MAXIMUM HEIGHT (metres)	Thorny	Poisonous/ allergenic	Intolerant of pollution	Suckering	
				■			■				■					1.5					Bluebeard
					■	■						■				3					Senna
			■		■	■						■				6					False senna
			■		■	■						■				2					Senna
					■	■				■						0.2					Cassiope
					■	■				■						0.3					Cassiope
					■	■				■						0.2					Cassiope
					■	■				■						0.2					Cassiope
					■	■				■						0.2					Cassiope
		■		■			■			■						30					Sweet chestnut
	■			■			■			■						15					Indian bean tree
	■			■			■			■				■		15					Catalpa
				■			■						■			15					Catalpa
				■			■			■						30					Catalpa
					■		■				■					2					Ceanothus
			■				■				■					1.5					Ceanothus
				■		■					■					1.5					Ceanothus
			■				■						■			1.5					Ceanothus
				■		■					■					3					Ceanothus
				■			■				■					3					Ceanothus
					■											25					Himalayan cedar
					■											25					Atlas, Atlantic cedar
					■											25					Cedar of Lebanon
					■											6					Chinese plum yew
					■											20					Cow's tail pine
		■		■			■	■			■					0.8					Creeping plumbago
		■		■			■	■			■					0.6					Creeping plumbago
		■		■			■	■			■					1					Creeping plumbago
		■		■		■										10					Katsura tree
		■		■		■										10					Katsura tree
				■									■			6					Eastern redbud
				■		■							■			4					Judas tree
		■		■									■			4					Judas tree
				■		■							■			6					Judas tree
		■		■		■							■			6					Judas tree
				■		■			■				■			3					Japanese quince
		■		■		■								■		2					Japanese quince
		■		■		■							■	■		3					Japanese quince
		■		■		■							■	■		3					Japanese quince
					■											20					Lawson cypress
■					■											15					False cypress
					■											5					False cypress
					■											5					False cypress
		■			■											1.5					False cypress
					■											5					Dwarf fan palm
	■		■						■			■			■	4					Wintersweet
					■	■	■			■					■	2					Mexican orange
					■		■			■						1					Rock rose
					■		■			■						1.5					Rock rose
					■		■			■						2					Rock rose
					■		■			■						1					Rock rose

	USES						SOIL					ASPECT & HARDINESS							
	Fast-growing	Large	Small	Banks	Hedging	Specimen	Humus-rich	Sandy or dry	Chalky	Moist	Clay	Sun	Shade, semi-shade	Fully hardy [1]	Frost hardy [2]	Half hardy [3]	Tender [4]	Silver, grey	Golden
Cistus monspeliensis								■				■			■				
Cistus parviflorus			■	■	■	■		■				■			■				
Cistus × purpureus			■	■	■	■		■				■			■				
Cladrastis lutea			■			■						■	■						
Cladrastis sinensis			■			■						■	■						
Clematis heracleifolia			■	■		■				■			■	■					
Clematis integrifolia			■	■		■				■		■	■	■					
Clematis recta			■	■						■		■	■	■					
Clerodendrum bungei			■									■	■		■				
Clerodendrum fargesii			■			■				■		■	■		■				
Clerodendrum splendens			■			■						■	■				■		
Clerodendrum thomsoniae							■										■		
Clerodendrum trichotomum			■			■						■	■						
Clethra alnifolia			■			■	■			■		■	■						
Clethra arborea						■	■			■		■				■			
Clethra fargesii			■			■	■			■		■	■						
Colletia armata			■									■			■				
Colletia paradoxa			■		■	■		■				■		■					
Colutea arborescens	■		■	■	■			■	■			■	■	■					
Colutea × media	■		■	■	■			■	■			■	■	■					
Colutea orientalis	■		■	■	■			■	■			■	■	■					
Cordyline australis			■		■							■	■			■			
Cordyline fruticosa						■						■	■				■		
Cordyline indivisa					■							■	■			■			
Coriaria japonica			■					■				■			■				
Coriaria myrtifolia			■					■				■			■				
Coriaria nepalensis			■					■				■			■				
Coriaria terminalis			■					■				■			■				
Cornus alba	■		■	■	■					■	■	■	■						
Cornus controversa			■			■				■		■	■						
Cornus florida			■		■					■		■		■					
Cornus kousa					■							■		■					
Cornus mas			■	■	■	■		■				■	■						
Cornus nuttallii				■	■	■				■		■	■						
Cornus sanguinea			■	■						■	■	■	■						
Cornus stolonifera	■		■	■						■	■	■	■						
Coronilla emerus			■	■				■	■			■			■				
Coronilla glauca			■	■				■	■			■			■				
Corylopsis pauciflora			■			■	■			■		■	■	■					
Corylopsis sinensis			■							■		■	■	■					
Corylopsis spicata			■							■		■	■	■					
Corylus avellana			■	■	■				■			■	■						■
Corylus colurna						■	■	■				■	■						
Corylus maxima			■	■	■	■				■		■	■						
Cotinus coggygria			■			■		■				■	■						
Cotinus obovatus			■			■		■	■			■	■						
Cotoneaster dammeri			■									■	■						
Cotoneaster franchetti			■	■								■	■						
Cotoneaster frigidus	■		■									■	■						
Cotoneaster horizontalis			■	■		■		■	■			■	■						
Cotoneaster lacteus	■		■	■	■	■						■	■						

Footnotes
[1] min. – 15°C (5°F), [2] min. –5°C (23°F), [3] min. 0°C (32°F), [4] min. 10°C (50°F)

Variegated	Purple	Autumn colour	Fast-growing	Deciduous	Evergreen	Spring	Summer	Autumn	Winter	White, green	Blue, mauve	Yellow, orange	Pink	Red, purple	Scented, aromatic	MAXIMUM HEIGHT (metres)	Thorny	Poisonous/allergenic	Intolerant of pollution	Suckering	
					■		■			■						0.6					Rock rose
					■		■						■			1					Rock rose
					■		■						■			1.5					Rock rose
			■	■		■	■			■			■		■	10					Yellow wood
	■			■			■			■			■		■	25					Chinese yellow wood
				■			■				■				■	1					Old man's beard
				■			■				■					1					Old man's beard
	■			■			■			■					■	1					Old man's beard
				■			■	■						■	■	1.5					Glory-bower
				■			■			■					■	3					Glory-bower
				■			■						■		■	1.5					Glory-bower
						■		■			■			■		3					Glory-bower
	■	■		■						■					■	3.5					Glory-bower
	■			■						■					■	2					Summersweet
					■		■	■		■					■	8					Summersweet
■				■						■					■	3					Summersweet
				■			■	■		■					■	2					Colletia
		■		■			■	■		■					■	2.5					Colletia
			■				■					■				3					Common bladder senna
	■						■					■				2.5					Bladder senna
	■			■			■					■				3					Bladder senna
	■															8					Cabbage tree
					■											3					Good luck plant, Ti tree
	■															8					Cordyline
	■			■		■										1.5					Myrtle-leaved sumach
	■			■		■										2					Myrtle-leaved sumach
	■	■		■		■										3					Myrtle-leaved sumach
	■			■						■						1					Myrtle-leaved sumach
■		■		■		■				■						3					Red-barked dogwood
		■		■		■				■						7					Wedding cake tree
		■		■		■	■			■			■			6					Cornel
		■		■			■									6					Cornel
■		■		■					■			■				5					Cornelian cherry
		■		■		■				■						7					Mountain, Pacific dogwood
		■		■		■										4					Common dogwood
		■		■		■				■						2.5					Dogwood
					■	■	■					■				1.5					Crown vetch
					■	■	■	■				■			■	2.5					Crown vetch
		■				■						■			■	1.5					Winter hazel
		■		■								■			■	3					Winter hazel
		■				■						■			■	3					Winter hazel
				■								■				5					Hazel
				■					■			■				20					Turkish hazel
	■	■				■						■				3.5					Filbert
■	■	■		■			■							■		4					Cotinus, Smoke tree
■	■			■			■						■			6					Cotinus
					■		■			■						1					Cotoneaster
					■	■				■						2.5					Cotoneaster
					■	■				■						7					Tree cotoneaster
	■			■		■				■						1					Cotoneaster
					■	■				■						6					Cotoneaster

651

		Fast-growing	Large	Small	Banks	Hedging	Specimen	Humus-rich	Sandy or dry	Chalky	Moist	Clay	Sun	Shade, semi-shade	Fully hardy[1]	Frost hardy[2]	Half hardy[3]	Tender[4]	Silver, grey	Golden
C	Cotoneaster microphyllus			■	■	■	■								■					
	Cotoneaster salicifolius			■	■										■					
	Cotoneaster splendens			■			■								■					
	Cotoneaster × watereri	■		■	■	■	■							■		■				
	Crataegus crus-galli			■	■	■	■			■				■	■					
	Crataegus flava			■	■	■	■								■					
	Crataegus × grignonensis			■	■	■	■								■					
	Crataegus laevigata			■	■	■	■								■					
	Crataegus × lavallei			■	■	■	■								■					
	Crataegus monogyna			■	■	■								■	■					
	Crataegus pinnatifida			■	■	■			■					■	■					
	Crinodendron hookerianum							■								■				
	Crinodendron patagua			■			■	■						■			■			
	Cryptomeria japonica		■	■		■	■							■	■					
	× Cupressocyparis leylandii		■			■									■					■
	Cupressus arizonica		■	■							■				■					
	Cupressus lusitanica		■										■		■					
	Cupressus macrocarpa		■			■	■			■					■					
	Cupressus sempervirens		■			■	■									■				
	Cupressus torulosa						■				■		■		■					
	Cytisus albus			■	■			■		■					■					
	Cytisus battandieri			■	■	■	■	■								■				
	Cytisus × beanii			■	■		■	■							■					
	Cytisus decumbens			■	■								■		■					
	Cytisus × kewensis			■	■			■							■					
	Cytisus praecox			■	■	■	■	■							■					
	Cytisus purpureus			■	■		■	■							■					
	Cytisus scoparius			■	■	■	■	■							■					
D	Daboecia × scotica			■				■			■				■	■				
	Daphne bholua			■			■			■					■	■				
	Daphne cneorum			■			■			■					■	■				
	Daphne × hybrida			■			■			■					■					
	Daphne mezereum			■			■			■				■	■					
	Daphne odora			■			■							■		■				
	Daphne sericea							■					■			■				
	Datura × candida						■						■				■			
	Datura cornigera						■						■				■			
	Datura meteloides						■		■				■				■			
	Datura sanguinea						■						■				■			
	Datura suaveolens						■						■				■			
	Datura versicolor						■						■				■			
	Davidia involucrata		■	■							■			■	■					
	Desfontainia spinosa			■			■						■	■	■					
	Deutzia gracilis			■	■						■				■					
	Deutzia × hybrida			■	■	■	■				■				■					
	Deutzia × magnifica			■	■	■	■				■				■					
	Deutzia pulchra			■	■	■	■				■					■				
	Deutzia × rosea								■				■		■					
	Deutzia scabra			■	■	■	■				■				■					
	Deutzia setchenensis						■		■				■						■	
	Dipelta floribunda			■			■							■	■					

Footnotes
[1] min. −15°C (5°F), [2] min. −5°C (23°F), [3] min. 0°C (32°F), [4] min. 10°C (50°F)

	FOLIAGE					FLOWERING SEASON				FLOWERS						MAXIMUM HEIGHT (metres)	PROBLEMS				
Variegated	Purple	Autumn colour	Fast-growing	Deciduous	Evergreen	Spring	Summer	Autumn	Winter	White, green	Blue, mauve	Yellow, orange	Pink	Red, purple	Scented, aromatic		Thorny	Poisonous/allergenic	Intolerant of pollution	Suckering	
					■	■				■						1					Cotoneaster
					■	■				■						5					Cotoneaster
			■		■	■				■						2					Cotoneaster
					■	■				■						7					Cotoneaster
		■	■	■		■				■						10	■				Cockspur thorn
	■		■	■		■				■						5	■				Yellow haw
	■		■	■		■				■						7	■				Hawthorn
	■		■	■		■							■	■	■	5	■				Hawthorn
	■		■	■		■				■			■			6	■				Hawthorn
	■		■	■		■				■						10	■				Common hawthorn
	■		■	■		■				■						6	■				Hawthorn
					■	■								■		6					Crinodendron
					■	■				■						6					Crinodendron
	■				■											20					Japanese cedar
					■											25					Leyland cypress
					■											15					Cypress
					■											20					Mexican cypress
					■											20					Cypress
					■											20					Cypress
					■											20					Kashmir cypress
			■				■			■						0.6					Broom
			■			■						■				5					Broom
			■			■						■				0.9					Broom
			■			■						■				0.2					Broom
			■			■				■						0.5					Broom
			■			■				■						2					Broom
			■			■						■	■			0.5					Common broom
			■			■					■				■	2.5					Broom
					■	■		■		■			■	■		0.4					Heather
		■							■				■	■	■	0.7					Daphne
					■	■							■	■	■	0.5					Garland flower
					■				■					■	■	1.5					Daphne
		■		■					■				■	■	■	0.7					Mezereon
■					■				■				■		■	1.8					Daphne
					■	■								■	■	0.5					Daphne
					■		■	■		■					■	3					Datura
					■		■			■						1.5					Datura
					■		■			■						1		■			Datura
					■		■					■				2.5					Datura
					■		■			■						3					Datura
					■			■						■		2.5					Datura
		■	■	■		■				■						15					Pocket-handkerchief tree
					■		■					■				1.5					Desfontainia
			■			■				■						0.7					Deutzia
			■			■				■			■			2					Deutzia
			■			■				■						3					Deutzia
			■			■				■						2.5					Deutzia
						■							■			1					Deutzia
			■			■				■						3					Deutzia
			■				■			■						2					Deutzia
		■	■			■							■		■	4					Dipelta

653

Species	Fast-growing	Large	Small	Banks	Hedging	Specimen	Humus-rich	Sandy or dry	Chalky	Moist	Clay	Sun	Shade, semi-shade	Fully hardy[1]	Frost hardy[2]	Half hardy[3]	Tender[4]	Silver, grey	Golden
Dipelta yunnanensis			■			■							■	■					
Drimys aromatica			■			■						■		■					
Drimys lanceolata			■			■						■		■					
Drimys winteri			■			■						■		■					
Eleagnus angustifolia			■	■	■	■		■						■				■	
Eleagnus commutata			■	■	■	■		■						■				■	
Eleagnus × ebbingei			■	■	■	■		■						■					
Eleagnus pungens			■	■	■	■		■						■					
Eleagnus umbellata			■	■	■	■		■						■					
Embothrium coccineum			■			■		■				■		■					
Enkianthus campanulatus			■		■	■	■						■	■					
Enkianthus cernuus f. *rubens*			■		■	■	■						■	■					
Enkianthus chinensis			■		■	■							■	■					
Enkianthus perulatus			■		■	■							■	■					
Erica arborea			■				■								■				
Erica carnea								■	■					■					
Erica cinerea								■						■					
Erica × darleyensis								■	■					■					
Erica erigena						■		■				■		■					
Erica tetralix			■				■			■		■	■	■					
Erica vagans			■					■			■			■					
Erica × veitchii								■				■			■				
Eriobotrya japonica			■		■				■			■			■				
Erythrina crista-galli			■			■		■				■				■			
Escallonia × exoniensis			■	■	■	■			■			■			■				
Escallonia rubra var. *macrantha*	■		■	■	■	■			■						■				
Eucalyptus coccifera			■	■	■	■		■						■				■	
Eucalyptus dalrympleana			■	■	■			■						■		■			
Eucalyptus gunnii		■	■	■	■			■						■		■			
Eucalyptus niphophila			■	■	■			■						■		■			
Eucalyptus pauciflora ssp. *niphophila*						■		■				■			■				
Eucryphia cordifolia			■			■						■	■		■				
Eucryphia glutinosa			■			■						■	■	■					
Eucryphia × intermedia			■			■						■	■		■				
Eucryphia lucida							■		■				■		■				
Eucryphia milliganii							■			■			■		■				
Eucryphia × nymansensis			■			■						■	■		■				
Euonymus alatus			■	■	■	■			■			■	■	■					
Euonymus europaeus			■	■	■					■		■	■	■					
Euonymus fortunei			■	■						■		■	■	■					
Euonymus japonicus			■			■						■	■	■					■
Euonymus phellomanus			■							■		■	■	■					
Euonymus planipes			■	■	■								■	■					
Euryops acraeus			■			■		■				■		■				■	
Euryops pectinatus			■	■				■				■				■			
Exochorda giraldii								■				■		■					
Exochorda macrantha			■	■								■		■					
Exochorda racemosa			■	■								■		■					
Fabiana imbricata			■			■	■					■			■				
Fagus grandifolia		■				■			■	■			■	■					
Fagus sylvatica			■			■			■	■		■		■					

E

F

Footnotes
[1] min. – 15°C (5°F), [2] min. –5°C (23°F), [3] min. 0°C (32°F), [4] min. 10°C (50°F)

FOLIAGE						FLOWERING SEASON				FLOWERS						MAXIMUM HEIGHT (metres)	PROBLEMS				
Variegated	Purple	Autumn colour	Fast-growing	Deciduous	Evergreen	Spring	Summer	Autumn	Winter	White, green	Blue, mauve	Yellow, orange	Pink	Red, purple	Scented, aromatic		Thorny	Poisonous/allergenic	Intolerant of pollution	Suckering	
		■	■			■				■				■		3					Dipelta
					■	■				■						2					Drimys
					■	■				■						2					Drimys
					■	■				■						4					Winter's bark
		■	■			■						■			■	5					Oleaster
			■			■						■			■	3				■	Silver berry
					■	■									■	4					Oleaster
■					■	■									■	1.5					Oleaster
					■	■									■	4					Oleaster
					■	■								■		5				■	Chilean fire bush
		■	■			■				■						2.5					Enkianthus
		■	■			■								■		2					Enkianthus
		■	■			■							■	■		4					Enkianthus
		■	■			■				■						2					Enkianthus
					■	■				■					■	4					Tree heath
					■	■		■		■			■	■		0.2					Heather
					■		■	■		■			■	■		0.3					Heather
					■	■	■	■		■			■	■		0.4					Heather
					■	■		■		■						2.5					Heather
					■	■	■	■		■						0.3					Cross-leaved heath
					■		■	■		■			■	■		0.2					Cornish heath
						■			■	■						2					Tree heath
					■			■	■	■					■	6					Loquat
			■				■							■		2					Cockspur coral tree
		■	■		■					■						5					Escallonia
			■		■								■			3					Escallonia
					■		■	■				■				7					Tasmanian snow gum
					■			■				■				20					Mountain gum
					■			■				■				20					Cider gum
					■											8					Snow gum
					■											10					Snow gum
					■		■			■						5					Eucryphia
		■		■			■			■						7					Eucryphia
					■		■			■					■	6					Eucryphia
					■		■			■						8					Eucryphia
					■		■			■						3					Eucryphia
					■		■	■		■						7					Eucryphia
		■	■			■										2.5					Spindle tree
		■	■			■										5					Spindle tree
■					■	■										0.6					Spindle tree
■					■	■										2.5					Japanese spindle
		■	■			■										3.5					Spindle tree
		■		■		■										4					Spindle tree
					■		■					■				0.3					Euryops
		■	■			■				■						2					Euryops
			■			■				■						3					Pearlbush
		■	■			■				■						3					Pearlbush
					■		■					■				0.8					Pearlbush
			■				■			■						1.5					Fabiana
	■		■			■										20					American beech
■	■		■			■										40					Common beech

	USES						SOIL					ASPECT & HARDINESS							
	Fast-growing	Large	Small	Banks	Hedging	Specimen	Humus-rich	Sandy or dry	Chalky	Moist	Clay	Sun	Shade, semi-shade	Fully hardy[1]	Frost hardy[2]	Half hardy[3]	Tender[4]	Silver, grey	Golden
Fatsia japonica			■			■				■		■	■	■					
Feijoa sellowiana			■			■						■	■	■					
Forsythia × intermedia			■	■	■	■							■	■					
Forsythia ovata			■	■	■	■							■	■					
Forsythia suspensa			■	■	■	■							■	■					
Fothergilla gardenii			■			■	■					■	■						
Fothergilla major			■			■						■	■						
Fraxinus americana	■	■				■			■			■	■	■					
Fraxinus angustifolia	■	■				■				■		■	■	■					
Fraxinus excelsior	■	■	■			■			■			■	■	■					
Fraxinus floribunda			■			■			■			■	■	■					
Fraxinus ornus			■			■		■				■	■	■					
Fremontodendron californicum			■			■			■			■	■		■				
Fremontodendron mexicanum			■			■			■			■	■		■				
Fuchsia magellanica			■		■	■			■	■		■	■	■					
Fuchsia parviflora			■			■			■	■		■	■			■			
Fuchsia procumbens			■			■			■	■		■	■			■			
Garrya elliptica			■			■						■	■		■				
Gaultheria cuneata			■	■		■				■		■		■					
Gaultheria procumbens			■			■						■		■					
Gaultheria shallon			■			■						■		■					
Genista aetnensis			■			■		■				■			■				
Genista hispanica			■	■								■			■				
Genista lydia			■	■				■						■					
Genista pilosa			■	■				■						■					
Genista tinctoria			■											■					
Gingko biloba		■				■				■				■					
Gleditsia caspica			■			■							■	■					
Gleditsia macracantha			■			■			■				■	■					
Gleditsia triacanthos			■			■			■				■	■					
Grevillea alpina			■		■	■						■	■			■			
Grevillea juniperina f. *sulphurea*			■			■										■			
Grevillea rosmarinifolia			■			■										■			
Grevillea × semperflorens			■			■											■		
Griselinia littoralis			■		■	■						■			■				
Halesia carolina			■			■	■					■	■						
Halesia monticola f. *rosea*			■			■	■					■	■						
Halimium commutatum			■			■		■				■			■				
Halimium halimifolium			■			■		■				■			■			■	
Halimium lasianthum			■			■		■				■			■			■	
Halimium umbellatum			■			■		■				■			■			■	
Hamamelis × intermedia			■			■				■				■					
Hamamelis japonica			■			■				■				■					
Hamamelis mollis			■			■				■				■					
Hamamelis virginiana			■			■				■				■					
Hebe × andersonii			■			■			■			■				■			
Hebe buxifolia			■			■		■	■			■		■	■				
Hebe elliptica			■	■		■		■	■			■		■					
Hebe × franciscana			■	■	■			■	■			■			■				
Hebe pinguifolia			■					■	■			■		■				■	
Hebe salicifolia			■		■	■		■	■			■			■				

Footnotes
[1] min. – 15°C (5°F),[2] min. –5°C (23°F), [3] min. 0°C (32°F), [4] min. 10°C (50°F)

Variegated	Purple	Autumn colour	Fast-growing	Deciduous	Evergreen	Spring	Summer	Autumn	Winter	White, green	Blue, mauve	Yellow, orange	Pink	Red, purple	Scented, aromatic	MAXIMUM HEIGHT (metres)	Thorny	Poisonous/allergenic	Intolerant of pollution	Suckering	
					■		■									3					Japanese fatsia
			■				■			■				■		3.5					Feijoa
			■			■						■				3					Forsythia
			■			■						■				1.5					Forsythia
			■			■						■				2.5					Forsythia
		■		■		■									■	0.8					Fothergilla
		■		■		■				■					■	2.5					Fothergilla
		■		■		■										35					White ash
		■		■		■										25					Raywood
		■		■		■										35					Common ash
		■		■		■				■						12					Ash
		■		■		■				■					■	10					Manna ash
					■		■					■				3					Fremontia
			■		■							■				3					Fremontia
				■			■	■						■		3					Fuchsia
				■			■	■					■	■		1.5					Fuchsia
				■			■	■			■					0.2					Fuchsia
					■		■									4					Garrya
							■			■						0.3					Waxberry
	■	■					■			■						0.3					Waxberry
	■						■			■						0.5					Waxberry
				■			■									4					Mount Etna broom
				■		■										0.6	■				Spanish gorse
				■		■						■				0.5					Broom
				■			■					■				0.6					Broom
				■			■					■				1.2					Dyer's greenweed
		■		■												25					Maidenhair tree
	■	■		■												10	■				Caspian locust
	■	■		■												12	■				Honey locust
	■	■		■												25	■				Honey locust
					■		■							■		1					Grevillea
					■		■						■			3					Grevillea
					■		■							■		1.5					Grevillea
					■		■						■			1.5					Grevillea
					■											4					Broadleaf
		■		■		■				■						6					Snowdrop tree
		■		■		■				■						6					Snowdrop tree
					■	■						■				0.6					Halimium
					■	■	■					■				1.2					Halimium
					■	■						■				0.8					Halimium
					■	■				■						0.8					Halimium
	■	■		■					■					■		2					Witch hazel
	■	■		■					■			■			■	2					Japanese witch hazel
	■	■						■				■			■	4					Chinese witch hazel
	■	■						■				■				6					Witch hazel
					■		■							■		1.2					Hebe
					■		■			■						0.4					Hebe
					■		■			■					■	2					Hebe
■					■		■				■					2.5					Hebe
					■		■			■						0.3					Hebe
					■		■			■						1.5					Hebe

	USES						SOIL					ASPECT & HARDINESS							
	Fast-growing	Large	Small	Banks	Hedging	Specimen	Humus-rich	Sandy or dry	Chalky	Moist	Clay	Sun	Shade, semi-shade	Fully hardy[1]	Frost hardy[2]	Half hardy[3]	Tender[4]	Silver, grey	Golden
Helianthemum nummularium			■					■	■				■						
Hibiscus sinosyriacus			■		■	■		■	■				■						
Hippophaë rhamnoïdes			■	■	■	■		■	■				■					■	
Hippophaë salicifolia			■	■	■	■		■	■				■						
Hoheria lyallii			■			■						■		■				■	
Hoheria populnea			■			■						■							
Hoheria sextylosa			■			■						■							
Hydrangea arborescens			■			■				■			■	■					
Hydrangea aspera			■			■			■	■			■	■					
Hydrangea macrophylla			■			■				■			■	■					
Hydrangea paniculata			■			■							■	■					
Hydrangea quercifolia			■			■		■	■				■	■					
Hydrangea serrata			■			■	■						■	■					
Hypericum androsaemum			■	■		■				■	■		■						
Hypericum calycinum			■	■		■				■			■						
Hypericum × inodorum			■	■		■				■			■						
Hypericum kouytchense			■	■		■			■				■						
Hypericum × moserianum			■	■	■	■				■		■			■				
Hypericum olympicum			■	■						■		■							
Ilex × altaclarensis			■		■	■			■				■	■					
Ilex aquifolium			■		■	■			■				■	■					
Ilex crenata				■	■				■				■	■					■
Ilex × koehneana			■		■	■			■				■	■					
Ilex latifolia					■	■			■				■			■			
Ilex × meserveae			■		■				■				■	■					
Illicium anisatum			■			■				■		■	■		■				
Illicium floridanum			■			■				■		■	■			■			
Illicium henryi			■							■			■						
Indigofera pseudotinctoria			■	■		■		■				■		■					
Itea ilicifolia			■			■						■	■	■					
Itea virginica			■			■								■					
Jovellana violacea			■			■										■			
Jubaea chilensis			■			■											■		
Juniperus chinensis	■		■	■		■		■	■		■		■						
Juniperus communis			■	■		■		■	■				■						
Juniperus horizontalis			■	■		■		■	■				■						
Juniperus × media			■	■		■		■	■				■					■	■
Juniperus oxycedrus			■	■		■			■			■	■						
Juniperus procumbens			■	■		■			■			■	■						
Juniperus sabina			■	■		■			■				■					■	
Juniperus scopulorum			■	■		■			■				■					■	
Juniperus squamata			■	■		■			■				■					■	
Juniperus virginiana			■	■		■				■								■	
Kalmia angustifolia			■			■				■			■		■				
Kalmia latifolia			■			■	■			■			■		■				
Kalmia polifolia			■		■	■				■			■	■					
Kerria japonica			■	■		■				■	■			■					
Kolkwitzia amabilis			■	■	■	■								■					
Laburnum adamii			■	■	■	■		■						■					
Laburnum alpinum			■	■	■	■						■		■					
Laburnum anagyroïdes			■	■	■	■		■	■					■					

Footnotes
[1] min. − 15°C (5°F), [2] min. −5°C (23°F), [3] min. 0°C (32°F), [4] min. 10°C (50°F)

Column groups: **FOLIAGE** (Variegated · Purple · Autumn colour · Fast-growing · Deciduous · Evergreen) — **FLOWERING SEASON** (Spring · Summer · Autumn · Winter) — **FLOWERS** (White, green · Blue, mauve · Yellow, orange · Pink · Red, purple · Scented, aromatic) — **MAXIMUM HEIGHT (metres)** — **PROBLEMS** (Thorny · Poisonous/allergenic · Intolerant of pollution · Suckering)

Variegated	Purple	Autumn colour	Fast-growing	Deciduous	Evergreen	Spring	Summer	Autumn	Winter	White, green	Blue, mauve	Yellow, orange	Pink	Red, purple	Scented, aromatic	MAXIMUM HEIGHT (metres)	Thorny	Poisonous/allergenic	Intolerant of pollution	Suckering	Name
					■		■	■				■				0.2					Rock rose
			■				■			■	■		■	■		2.5					Hibiscus
			■			■						■				6	■				Sea buckthorn
			■			■						■				10					Sea buckthorn
			■			■				■						4					Lacebark
			■				■			■						6					Lacebark
					■		■			■						6					Ribbon-wood
			■				■	■		■						2.5					Hydrangea
			■				■	■		■	■					3					Hydrangea
	■		■				■			■			■	■		2					Hydrangea
	■		■				■			■			■			4					Hydrangea
	■		■				■			■	■					2					Hydrangea
			■				■			■	■					1.5					Hydrangea
		■		■			■	■				■				0.8					St John's wort
				■	■		■	■				■				0.4					Aaron's beard, Rose of Sharon
	■			■			■	■				■				1.2					St John's wort
	■			■			■	■				■				0.8					St John's wort
■					■		■	■				■				0.6					St John's wort
					■		■	■				■				0.2					St John's wort
■					■	■					■					5	■				Holly
■					■	■										7	■				Holly
					■	■										4					Holly
					■	■										6					Holly
					■	■										7					Holly
					■	■										4	■				Holly
					■	■					■				■	3					Star anise
					■	■								■		2					Anise tree
					■								■			2					Anise tree
			■				■						■			1.5					Indigo
				■			■			■					■	3					Holly-leaf sweetspire
			■			■				■						2					Virginia sweetspire
			■							■	■					1.5					Jovellana
					■											15					Chilean wine palm
					■											15					Juniper
					■											5					Irish juniper
					■											1					Creeping juniper
■					■											4					Juniper
					■											5					Prickly juniper
					■											0.3					Juniper
					■											1.5					Spanish juniper
					■											6					Rock juniper
					■											3					Juniper
					■											12					Eastern red cedar
					■	■							■	■		1.5					Sheep laurel
					■	■				■				■		3					Mountain laurel
					■	■							■			0.5					Bog myrtle
■			■			■						■				2					Jew's mallow
			■			■							■			3					Beauty bush
				■						■	■	■				5		■			Laburnum
				■		■						■				8		■			Scotch laburnum
				■		■						■			■	7		■			Laburnum

	USES						SOIL					ASPECT & HARDINESS							
	Fast-growing	Large	Small	Banks	Hedging	Specimen	Humus-rich	Sandy or dry	Chalky	Moist	Clay	Sun	Shade, semi-shade	Fully hardy[1]	Frost hardy[2]	Half hardy[3]	Tender[4]	Silver, grey	Golden
Laburnum × watereri			■	■	■	■		■	■					■					
Lagerstroemia indica			■		■	■										■			
Larix decidua		■				■				■				■					
Larix kaempferi		■				■				■				■					
Laurus nobilis			■	■	■	■		■				■			■				
Lavandula angustifolia			■	■	■	■		■				■			■				
Lavandula stoechas			■	■		■		■				■			■				
Lavatera arborea	■							■				■			■				
Lavatera olbia	■							■				■			■				
Lavatera thuringiaca			■	■		■						■			■				
Lespedeza bicolor			■	■				■				■			■				
Lespedeza thunbergii			■	■				■				■			■				
Leucothoë davisiae			■	■	■	■	■			■			■	■					
Leucothoë fontanesiana			■	■	■	■	■						■	■					
Leycesteria formosa			■	■	■								■	■					
Ligustrum japonicum			■	■	■					■	■		■	■					
Ligustrum lucidum			■	■	■					■	■		■	■					
Ligustrum ovalifolium			■	■	■					■	■		■	■					
Ligustrum quihoui			■	■		■		■					■	■					
Ligustrum sinense										■		■	■	■					
Ligustrum vulgare			■	■	■			■			■		■	■					
Liquidambar formosa						■						■			■				
Liquidambar orientalis															■				
Liquidambar styraciflua		■												■					
Liriodendron tulipifera		■				■				■			■	■					
Lupinus arboreus			■			■		■							■				
Magnolia acuminata	■	■				■				■				■					
Magnolia campbellii			■			■				■					■				
Magnolia delavayi			■			■			■	■				■	■				
Magnolia grandiflora		■				■				■		■		■					
Magnolia hypoleuca						■	■	■				■	■	■					
Magnolia kobus			■			■			■	■				■					
Magnolia liliiflora			■			■				■			■	■					
Magnolia × loebneri			■			■			■					■					
Magnolia sieboldii			■			■				■					■				
Magnolia × soulangeana			■			■				■	■			■					
Magnolia stellata			■			■				■				■	■				
Mahonia acanthifolia			■	■	■	■							■		■				
Mahonia aquifolium			■	■						■			■	■					
Mahonia bealei			■							■			■	■					
Mahonia japonica			■	■		■				■	■		■	■					
Mahonia lomariifolia			■			■				■			■		■				
Mahonia × media						■				■			■	■					
Mahonia nervosa			■							■			■	■		■			
Mahonia × wagneri			■	■					■		■		■	■					
Malus baccata			■		■	■						■		■					
Malus coronaria			■		■	■						■		■					
Malus floribunda			■			■						■		■					
Malus hupehensis			■			■						■		■					
Malus × purpurea						■						■		■	■				
Metasequoia glyptostroboïdes		■				■						■		■					

Footnotes
[1] min. –15°C (5°F), [2] min. –5°C (23°F), [3] min. 0°C (32°F), [4] min. 10°C (50°F)

Trees and shrubs selector chart — columns grouped under **FOLIAGE**, **FLOWERING SEASON**, **FLOWERS**, **MAXIMUM HEIGHT (metres)**, and **PROBLEMS**.

Variegated	Purple	Autumn colour	Fast-growing	Deciduous	Evergreen	Spring	Summer	Autumn	Winter	White, green	Blue, mauve	Yellow, orange	Pink	Red, purple	Scented, aromatic	Max height (m)	Thorny	Poisonous/allergenic	Intolerant of pollution	Suckering	Name
				■								■				5		■			Laburnum
				■			■			■	■		■	■		4					Indian lilac
				■												25					European larch
				■												30					Japanese larch
				■												10					Bay laurel, Sweet bay
					■		■			■	■		■		■	1					Old English lavender
					■		■			■	■				■	1					French lavender
				■			■							■		1.5					Tree mallow
					■		■						■			1					Tree mallow
				■						■			■	■		2.5					Tree mallow
				■									■			1.5					Bush clover
				■										■		1.5					Bush clover
	■				■	■				■						1.5					Fetterbush
■	■				■	■				■						1.5					Fetterbush
				■			■	■		■						2					Himalaya honeysuckle
					■		■			■						3		■			Japanese privet
■					■		■			■					■	7		■			Chinese privet
■					■		■			■					■	5		■			California privet
					■		■			■						2.5		■			Privet
					■					■						4					Privet
				■			■			■					■	5		■			European privet
	■			■												12					Sweet gum
	■			■												16					Sweet gum
	■			■												20					Sweet gum
	■			■		■						■				30					Tulip tree
	■		■		■	■				■	■	■			■	2					Tree lupin
				■		■										20					Cucumber tree
				■		■							■			8					Campbell's magnolia
				■			■	■		■					■	8					Magnolia
					■					■					■	20					Laurel magnolia
				■		■				■			■			16					Magnolia
				■		■				■					■	6					Magnolia
				■		■				■				■		4					Lily magnolia
				■						■					■	5					Magnolia
	■			■						■						6					Magnolia
				■		■				■			■	■		8					Magnolia
				■		■				■					■	3					Star magnolia
					■			■	■			■			■	5					Mahonia
	■				■	■						■				1.2					Holly-leaved mahonia
					■			■				■			■	2					Mahonia
					■			■				■			■	2.5					Mahonia
					■			■	■			■				3					Mahonia
					■				■			■				5					Mahonia
	■				■	■						■				0.6					Mahonia
					■	■						■				1.2					Mahonia
	■		■	■		■				■					■	8					Siberian crab
	■		■	■		■							■		■	6					Flowering crab apple
	■		■	■		■										5					Flowering crab apple
	■		■	■		■				■					■	8					Flowering crab apple
■			■	■		■								■		8					Purple crab
	■			■												25					Metasequoia

661

	USES						SOIL					ASPECT & HARDINESS							
	Fast-growing	Large	Small	Banks	Hedging	Specimen	Humus-rich	Sandy or dry	Chalky	Moist	Clay	Sun	Shade, semi-shade	Fully hardy¹	Frost hardy²	Half hardy³	Tender⁴	Silver, grey	Golden
Morus alba	■	■				■				■			■	■					
Morus nigra			■			■				■			■	■					
Myrtus apiculata			■		■	■						■		■					
Myrtus communis			■		■	■						■		■					
Myrtus nummularia			■			■				■		■		■					
Nandina domestica			■			■							■	■					
Neillia sinensis			■			■							■	■					
Neillia thibetica			■			■							■	■					
Nerium oleander			■		■	■				■		■				■			
Nothofagus antarctica		■				■				■				■					
Nothofagus obliqua		■				■				■				■					
Nothofagus procera		■				■				■				■					
Nothofagus solandri			■			■				■				■					
Nyssa sinensis			■			■								■					
Nyssa sylvatica			■			■								■					
Olea europaea												■		■				■	
Olearia × hastii			■	■	■	■		■	■					■					
Olearia lineata			■	■	■	■		■	■					■					
Olearia macrodonta			■	■	■	■		■	■					■					
Olearia paniculata			■	■	■	■			■					■					
Olearia phlogopappa						■			■						■				
Olearia × scillonensis			■			■			■									■	
Olearia traversii	■		■		■	■		■	■					■					
Osmanthus decorus			■		■	■							■	■					
Osmanthus delavayi			■		■	■							■	■					
Osmanthus fragrans			■		■	■							■		■				
Osmanthus heterophyllus			■		■	■							■	■					
Osmarea burkwoodii			■		■	■							■	■					
Pachysandra terminalis			■	■									■	■					
Paeonia delavayi			■			■								■					
Paeonia × lemoinei			■			■								■					
Paeonia suffruticosa			■			■								■					
Parrotia persica						■				■				■					
Paulownia tomentosa	■	■				■				■				■					
Pernettya mucronata			■				■						■						
Perovskia abrotanoides			■	■		■		■				■							■
Perovskia atriplicifolia			■	■		■		■				■							■
Philadelphus coronarius			■		■	■			■					■					
Philadelphus magdalenae			■		■	■			■					■					
Phillyrea angustifolia			■		■	■						■		■					
Phillyrea latifolia			■		■	■						■		■					
Phlomis fruticosa			■	■		■		■				■							
Phoenix canariensis	■		■			■						■				■			
Photinia × fraseri			■		■	■					■			■					
Photinia glabra			■		■	■					■	■		■					
Photinia serratifolia					■	■	■		■			■	■	■					
Photinia villosa					■	■	■		■			■	■	■					
Picea abies		■				■				■				■					
Picea breweriana			■			■				■				■					
Picea engelmannii			■			■				■				■					
Picea glauca		■	■			■								■					

Footnotes
¹ min. – 15°C (5°F), ² min. –5°C (23°F), ³ min. 0°C (32°F), ⁴ min. 10°C (50°F)

Variegated	Purple	Autumn colour	Fast-growing	Deciduous	Evergreen	Spring	Summer	Autumn	Winter	White, green	Blue, mauve	Yellow, orange	Pink	Red, purple	Scented, aromatic	MAXIMUM HEIGHT (metres)	Thorny	Poisonous/allergenic	Intolerant of pollution	Suckering	
		■		■		■										12					White mulberry
	■			■		■										7					Black mulberry
					■		■	■		■						6					Myrtle
■					■		■			■						3					Myrtle
					■	■				■						0.4					Myrtle
		■			■		■			■						1.6					Sacred bamboo
					■	■							■			2					Neillia
					■	■							■			2					Neillia
					■		■	■		■			■	■		5		■			Oleander
		■		■												12					Antarctic beech
				■												12					Southern beech
				■												12					Southern beech
					■											10					Southern beech
		■		■												10					Tupelo
		■		■												10					Tupelo
					■	■						■			■	10					Olive
					■	■	■			■						1.5					Daisy bush
					■		■			■						1.5					Daisy bush
					■	■				■					■	4					Daisy bush
					■			■							■	6					Daisy bush
					■	■				■						2					Daisy bush
					■	■				■						3					Daisy bush
					■		■			■						6					Daisy bush
					■	■				■					■	2.5					Osmanthus
					■	■				■					■	2.5					Osmanthus
					■		■			■					■	5					Osmanthus
					■			■		■					■	3					Osmanthus
					■	■				■					■	3					Osmarea
■					■	■				■						0.3					Pachysandra
			■			■								■		1				■	Tree peony
			■			■						■				1.5					Tree peony
			■										■	■		2.5					Moutan
	■	■		■					■			■				7					Persian ironwood
		■	■			■					■				■	12					Empress tree, Foxglove tree
					■	■	■			■			■			0.6					Pernettya
			■				■				■					1.5					Perovskia
			■					■			■					1.5					Perovskia
			■			■				■					■	3					Mock orange
			■			■				■						4					Mock orange
					■	■						■			■	3					Jasmine box
					■					■		■			■	7					Jasmine box
					■							■				1.2					Jerusalem sage
					■		■			■						20					Canary Island date palm
					■	■				■						3					Photinia
					■	■				■						2.5					Photinia
					■											10					Photinia
		■	■													5					Photinia
					■											40					Norway spruce
					■											15					Spruce
					■											15					Engelmann spruce
					■											15					White spruce

	USES						SOIL					ASPECT & HARDINESS							
	Fast-growing	Large	Small	Banks	Hedging	Specimen	Humus-rich	Sandy or dry	Chalky	Moist	Clay	Sun	Shade, semi-shade	Fully hardy[1]	Frost hardy[2]	Half hardy[3]	Tender[4]	Silver, grey	Golden
Picea mariana		■	■			■								■					
Picea omorika		■				■				■				■					
Picea orientalis		■	■			■								■					■
Picea pungens		■	■			■				■				■					
Picea sitchensis	■	■				■								■					
Pieris formosa			■		■	■	■						■		■				
Pieris japonica			■		■	■	■						■	■					
Pinus aristata			■			■		■				■		■					
Pinus bungeana						■				■		■		■					
Pinus cembra			■			■				■				■					
Pinus contorta		■	■			■		■						■	■				
Pinus densiflora		■	■			■		■						■					
Pinus halapensis		■				■			■			■		■		■			
Pinus jeffreyi		■				■				■				■				■	
Pinus leucodermis			■			■		■	■					■					
Pinus montezumae		■				■						■		■				■	
Pinus mugo			■	■		■		■	■					■					
Pinus nigra								■	■			■							
Pinus parviflora														■		■			
Pinus pinaster		■				■		■				■		■	■				
Pinus pinea		■				■						■		■					
Pinus ponderosa		■				■								■					
Pinus radiata	■	■				■		■						■				■	
Pinus strobus		■	■			■		■		■				■					
Pinus sylvestris	■	■	■			■		■						■				■	
Pinus wallichiana		■				■				■				■				■	
Pittosporum crassifolium			■		■	■						■	■			■			
Pittosporum tenuifolium			■		■	■						■	■			■			
Pittosporum tobira			■			■						■	■			■			
Platanus × acerifolia	■	■				■				■			■	■					
Platanus occidentalis	■	■				■				■			■	■					
Platanus orientalis	■	■				■							■	■					
Podocarpus andinus			■			■					■	■		■					
Podocarpus nivalis			■	■		■				■	■	■		■					
Podocarpus salignus						■				■			■	■					
Populus alba	■	■		■	■	■		■		■	■			■				■	
Populus × candicans	■	■	■			■				■	■		■	■					
Populus nigra	■	■			■	■				■	■		■	■					
Populus tremula		■				■								■					
Potentilla fruticosa			■	■	■	■						■		■					
Prunus avium		■	■		■	■				■				■					
Prunus × blireana			■		■	■				■				■					
Prunus cerasifera			■		■	■				■				■					
Prunus × cistena			■		■	■				■				■					
Prunus davidiana			■		■	■						■		■					
Prunus laurocerasus	■		■	■	■	■				■	■		■			■			
Prunus lusitanica			■	■	■	■			■				■			■			
Prunus maackii			■		■	■				■				■					
Prunus padus		■	■		■	■				■				■					
Prunus pumila			■	■		■			■	■		■		■					
Prunus sargentii			■		■	■				■		■		■					

Footnotes
[1] min. –15°C (5°F), [2] min. –5°C (23°F), [3] min. 0°C (32°F), [4] min. 10°C (50°F)

Variegated	Purple	Autumn colour	Fast-growing	Deciduous	Evergreen	Spring	Summer	Autumn	Winter	White, green	Blue, mauve	Yellow, orange	Pink	Red, purple	Scented, aromatic	MAXIMUM HEIGHT (metres)	Thorny	Poisonous/allergenic	Intolerant of pollution	Suckering	
					●											12					Black spruce
					●											25					Serbian spruce
					●											25					Oriental spruce
					●											15					Colorado, Blue spruce
					●											40					Spruce
					●	●				●					●	2.5					Andromeda
					●	●				●						1.5					Andromeda
					●											8					Bristlecone pine
					●											10					Pine
					●											12					Arolla, Swiss pine
					●											15					Stone pine
					●											18					Pine
					●											20					Aleppo pine
					●											30					Jeffrey's pine
					●											10					Pine
					●											15					Pine
					●											5					Pine
					●											12					Pine
					●											8					Pine
					●											30					Maritime pine
					●											20					Stone pine
					●											20					Pine
					●											25					Monterey pine
					●											30					Weymouth pine
					●											30					Scots pine
					●											30					Bhutan pine
					●	●								●	●	1					Pittosporum
					●	●								●	●	3.5					Pittosporum
						●				●					●	4					Pittosporum
				●												35					London plane
				●												35					American plane
				●												30					Oriental plane
				●												8					Plum yew
				●												1.5					Alpine totara
					●											10					Plum yew
		●	●	●		●										25					Abele, White poplar
●	●		●	●		●										25					Balm of Gilead, Ontario poplar
		●	●			●										30					Lombardy poplar
		●		●				●								25					Aspen
				●						●		●	●	●		1.5					Shrubby cinquefoil
		●		●		●				●						15					Wild cherry, Gean
				●									●			7					Cherry plum
	●	●		●									●			8					Cherry plum, Myrobalan
●	●			●		●										2.5					Flowering cherry
	●			●		●			●	●						8					David's peach
					●	●										7					Cherry laurel
					●		●			●						7					Portugal laurel
	●			●		●				●						7					Flowering cherry
	●			●		●				●					●	15					Bird cherry
	●			●						●						2					Flowering cherry
		●		●		●							●			12					Sargent cherry

	USES						SOIL					ASPECT & HARDINESS							
	Fast-growing	Large	Small	Banks	Hedging	Specimen	Humus-rich	Sandy or dry	Chalky	Moist	Clay	Sun	Shade, semi-shade	Fully hardy[1]	Frost hardy[2]	Half hardy[3]	Tender[4]	Silver, grey	Golden
Prunus serotina		■				■				■		■		■					
Prunus serrula			■		■	■						■		■					
Prunus serrulata			■			■			■			■		■					
Prunus spinosa			■	■	■	■						■		■					
Prunus × subhirtella			■		■	■						■		■					
Prunus tenella			■		■	■								■					
Prunus triloba			■			■								■					
Prunus × yedoensis			■																
Pseudotsuga menziesii	■	■	■	■		■				■			■	■					
Pterocarya fraxinifolia	■	■				■				■	■		■	■					
Pterocarya rehderiana	■	■				■				■	■		■	■					
Punica granatum			■		■	■										■			
Quercus bicolor		■				■				■				■					
Quercus canariensis		■				■		■		■	■			■					
Quercus cerris	■	■				■			■					■					
Quercus coccinea		■				■				■				■					
Quercus frainetto		■				■								■					
Quercus ilex		■				■		■	■	■					■				
Quercus palustris		■				■				■				■					
Quercus petraea		■				■								■					
Quercus pubescens		■				■		■				■		■					
Quercus robur		■				■				■				■					
Quercus rubra		■				■								■					
Quercus suber		■				■						■				■			
Rhamnus alaternus	■		■	■	■							■	■	■				■	
Rhamnus californicus			■															■	
Rhamnus frangula			■	■	■	■	■			■			■	■				■	
Rhamnus imeritinus			■		■	■				■				■	■				
Rhaphiolepis × delacourii			■									■						■	
Rhaphiolepis indica			■									■				■			
Rhaphiolepis umbellata			■									■						■	
Rhododendron catawbiense			■			■	■			■			■	■					
Rhododendron luteum			■			■	■			■			■	■					
Rhododendron macabeanum			■			■	■			■			■		■				
Rhododendron moupiense			■			■	■			■			■		■				
Rhododendron ponticum			■			■				■		■	■	■					
Rhododendron wardii			■			■	■			■		■	■	■					
Rhododendron yakushimanum			■			■	■			■		■		■					
Rhus coriaria			■	■		■				■		■	■	■					
Rhus typhina			■	■		■								■					
Ribes alpinum			■			■						■	■	■					■
Ribes odoratum			■		■	■						■	■	■					
Ribes sanguineum			■		■	■						■	■	■					
Ribes speciosum			■			■				■		■	■		■				
Robinia × ambigua			■			■		■	■				■	■					
Robinia boyntonii			■			■							■	■					
Robinia hispida			■			■						■	■	■					
Robinia kelseyi			■						■					■					
Robinia pseudoacacia		■	■			■						■	■	■					■
Robinia × slavinii			■			■						■	■	■					
Rosmarinus officinalis			■	■	■	■		■	■			■		■				■	

Footnotes
[1] min. – 15°C (5°F), [2] min. –5°C (23°F), [3] min. 0°C (32°F), [4] min. 10°C (50°F)

Variegated	Purple	Autumn colour	Fast-growing	Deciduous	Evergreen	Spring	Summer	Autumn	Winter	White, green	Blue, mauve	Yellow, orange	Pink	Red, purple	Scented, aromatic	MAXIMUM HEIGHT (metres)	Thorny	Poisonous/allergenic	Intolerant of pollution	Suckering	
		■		■		■				■						25					Black cherry, Wild rum cherry
	■			■		■				■						7					Flowering cherry
	■			■		■							■			7					Hill cherry
■	■			■		■							■			5					Blackthorn, Sloe
	■			■		■		■		■						8					Higan cherry, Rosebud cherry
	■			■		■							■			2					Flowering almond
	■			■		■							■			2.5					Flowering almond
	■			■		■				■			■			7					Yoshino cherry
					■											30					Douglas fir
			■	■			■									20					Wingnut
			■	■			■									20					Wingnut
			■	■			■			■				■		5					Pomegranate
	■			■												18					Swamp white oak
			■	■												25					Algerian oak, Mirbeck's oak
			■	■												30					Turkey oak
		■		■												25					Scarlet oak
	■			■												20					Hungarian oak
					■											15					Holm oak
	■			■												20					Pin oak
	■		■	■												30					Durmast oak, Sessile oak
	■			■												15					Downy oak
	■			■												20					Common oak, English oak
	■			■												30					Red oak
					■											1.5			■		Cork oak
■					■	■										3					Italian buckthorn
						■										3					Buckthorn
		■		■		■										6					Buckthorn
	■			■		■										2.5					Buckthorn
					■	■	■						■			1.5					Indian hawthorn
				■	■	■	■			■			■			1.5					Indian hawthorn
				■	■	■	■			■					■	1.5					Indian hawthorn
				■	■	■				■			■	■		5					Rhododendron
	■			■								■			■	3					Azalea
					■	■						■				7					Rhododendron
					■	■			■	■			■	■	■	1.5					Rhododendron
					■	■					■					6					Rhododendron
					■	■						■				3.5					Rhododendron
						■							■			1.5					Rhododendron
	■			■			■									3		■		■	Sicilian sumach
	■	■		■			■									4		■		■	Stag's horn sumach
		■		■		■						■				1.5					Alpine currant
		■		■		■						■			■	2.5					Buffalo currant
		■	■	■		■							■	■		2.5					Flowering currant
				■	■	■								■		1.5					Fuchsia-flowered currant
	■		■	■		■	■						■		■	12					False acacia
	■		■	■		■							■			4					False acacia
	■		■	■		■							■			3					Rose acacia
	■		■	■		■							■			5					False acacia
	■		■	■		■				■					■	30	■				False acacia
		■	■	■		■							■		■	8					False acacia
					■	■	■				■					1.5					Rosemary

S

	USES						SOIL					ASPECT & HARDINESS							
	Fast-growing	Large	Small	Banks	Hedging	Specimen	Humus-rich	Sandy or dry	Chalky	Moist	Clay	Sun	Shade, semi-shade	Fully hardy[1]	Frost hardy[2]	Half hardy[3]	Tender[4]	Silver, grey	Golden
Rubus cockburnianus	■		■		■	■							■	■					
Rubus fruticosus			■					■	■	■		■	■	■					
Rubus henryi			■										■	■					
Rubus idaeus			■							■		■	■	■					
Rubus nepalensis			■									■	■	■					
Rubus odoratus	■		■		■	■				■		■	■	■					
Rubus phaenicolasius			■					■				■		■					
Rubus spectabilis	■		■			■						■	■	■					
Rubus thibetanus			■			■						■	■	■					
Rubus tricolor			■							■		■	■	■					
Rubus ulmifolius			■	■								■	■	■					
Ruscus aculeatus			■	■								■	■	■					
Ruscus hypoglossum			■	■							■	■	■	■		■			
Ruta graveolens			■			■	■					■		■				■	
Salix acutifolia						■				■		■		■				■	
Salix alba		■				■				■		■		■				■	
Salix babylonica		■				■				■		■		■					
Salix lanata			■			■				■		■		■				■	
Salix matsudana			■			■				■		■		■					
Salix purpurea			■	■		■				■		■		■					
Salix repens			■	■		■				■		■		■				■	
Salix × sepulcralis var. *chrysocoma*		■				■				■		■		■					■
Salvia argentea						■		■	■			■		■				■	
Salvia coccinea			■			■						■		■					
Salvia grahamii			■			■						■			■				
Salvia involucrata			■			■						■			■				
Salvia officinalis			■		■					■		■		■				■	■
Salvia patens			■			■			■			■			■				
Salvia uliginosa			■			■				■		■			■				
Sambucus canadensis	■		■			■				■		■	■						
Sambucus nigra			■			■			■			■	■	■				■	
Sambucus racemosa			■			■			■			■	■	■					■
Santolina chamaecyparissus			■	■	■		■		■			■		■				■	
Santolina rosmarinifolia			■	■	■		■		■			■		■	■				
Sarcococca confusa			■	■	■		■					■	■	■					
Sarcococca hookeriana			■	■	■		■			■		■	■	■					
Sarcococca ruscifolia			■	■	■		■			■		■	■		■				
Sciadopitys verticillata			■			■							■	■					
Senecio greyi			■	■		■		■	■			■		■				■	
Senecio laxifolius			■	■		■		■	■			■		■				■	
Senecio monroi			■	■		■		■	■			■		■				■	
Sequoia sempervirens		■	■			■						■		■					
Sequoiadendron giganteum						■						■		■					
Skimmia japonica			■			■	■					■	■	■					
Skimmia laureola			■			■	■		■			■	■	■					
Sophora davidii			■			■						■		■					
Sophora japonica		■				■						■		■					
Sophora macrocarpa			■			■						■			■				
Sophora microphylla			■			■						■				■			
Sophora secundiflora			■			■						■			■				
Sophora tetraptera			■			■								■		■			

Footnotes
1 min. –15°C (5°F), 2 min. –5°C (23°F), 3 min. 0°C (32°F), 4 min. 10°C (50°F)

	FOLIAGE						FLOWERING SEASON				FLOWERS						MAXIMUM HEIGHT (metres)	PROBLEMS				
Variegated	Purple	Autumn colour	Fast-growing	Deciduous	Evergreen	Spring	Summer	Autumn	Winter	White, green	Blue, mauve	Yellow, orange	Pink	Red, purple	Scented, aromatic		Thorny	Poisonous/allergenic	Intolerant of pollution	Suckering	
		■		■		■	■						■			2.5	■				Rubus
			■			■										3					Rubus
					■	■	■						■			6	■				Rubus
			■			■	■									1.5					Raspberry
				■		■				■						0.4					Rubus
				■			■						■	■		2.5					Rubus
		■		■									■			3					Rubus
		■		■									■	■		2					Rubus
					■	■							■			1.5	■				Rubus
	■				■				■	■						0.4					Rubus
		■			■				■				■			1.5					Rubus
					■	■										0.6					Butcher's broom
					■											1					Butcher's broom
					■							■				0.8					Rue
	■			■		■										4					Willow
	■	■		■		■										25					White willow
	■	■		■		■										12					Babylon willow
				■		■										1					Woolly willow
	■	■		■		■										8					Willow
	■	■		■		■										1.5					Willow
	■			■		■										1					Creeping willow
					■											1.5					Golden weeping willow
					■		■			■						0.7					Silver sage
					■		■	■						■		0.6					Sage
					■		■							■		1.2					Sage
					■		■	■						■		1.2					Sage
■	■				■		■				■					0.6					Sage
					■		■				■					0.6					Mexican blue sage
					■		■	■			■					2					Sage
		■		■		■				■				■		2.5					American elderberry
	■	■		■		■				■					■	6					Common elder
		■		■		■				■		■				5					Red-berried elder
					■							■				0.5					Santolina
					■		■					■				0.5					Santolina
					■			■		■					■	1					Sarcococca
					■			■	■	■			■		■	1.5					Sarcococca
					■				■	■					■	1.5					Sarcococca
■					■											10					Umbrella pine
					■		■					■				1					Senecio
					■							■				1					Senecio
					■		■					■				0.6					Senecio
					■											50					Redwood, Coast redwood
					■											30					Giant redwood
					■	■				■					■	0.8					Skimmia
					■								■		■	2					Skimmia
		■				■				■						3					Sophora
	■	■					■			■						20					Japanese pagoda tree
					■	■						■				3					Sophora
						■						■				3					Sophora
					■						■				■	10					Sophora
					■	■						■				3					Sophora

669

	USES						SOIL					ASPECT & HARDINESS							
	Fast-growing	Large	Small	Banks	Hedging	Specimen	Humus-rich	Sandy or dry	Chalky	Moist	Clay	Sun	Shade, semi-shade	Fully hardy[1]	Frost hardy[2]	Half hardy[3]	Tender[4]	Silver, grey	Golden
Sorbaria kirilowii	■		■			■				■		■		■					
Sorbaria sorbifolia			■	■	■	■				■		■		■					
Sorbaria tomentosa			■			■				■		■		■					
Sorbus aria			■		■	■			■					■					
Sorbus aucuparia		■	■		■	■			■					■	■				
Sorbus × hybrida			■		■	■								■					
Sorbus latifolia			■		■	■								■					
Sorbus pygmaea			■			■						■		■					
Sorbus thibetica		■	■		■	■								■				■	
Sorbus torminalis		■			■	■								■					
Spiraea × billiardii			■	■	■				■			■		■					
Spiraea cinerea			■		■	■						■		■					
Spiraea japonica			■									■		■					
Spiraea nipponica			■	■	■							■		■					
Spiraea thunbergii			■	■	■							■		■					
Spiraea × vanhouttei			■	■	■	■						■		■					
Stephanandra incisa			■	■	■							■		■					
Stephanandra tanakae			■	■	■								■	■					
Stewartia malacodendron			■			■	■			■		■	■			■			
Stewartia ovata			■			■	■			■			■						
Stewartia pteropetiolata			■			■	■			■			■						
Stranvaesia davidiana			■		■	■				■									
Symphoricarpos albus			■	■	■	■						■		■					
Symphoricarpos × chenaultii			■	■	■	■						■		■					
Symphoricarpos × doorenbosii			■	■	■	■		■	■			■		■					
Symphoricarpos orbiculatus			■	■	■	■						■		■					
Syringa × josiflexa			■			■						■		■					
Syringa meyeri			■			■							■	■					
Syringa microphylla			■		■	■								■					
Syringa × prestoniae			■			■							■	■					
Syringa sweginzowii			■			■								■					
Syringa vulgaris	■					■						■		■					
Tamarix hoehnackeri			■	■		■		■				■			■				
Tamarix parviflora			■	■		■						■			■				
Tamarix ramosissima			■	■		■		■				■		■					
Taxus baccata		■	■	■	■	■		■	■		■		■	■				■	
Taxus cuspidata								■					■	■					
Taxus × media			■		■	■		■			■		■	■					
Thuja occidentalis	■	■	■		■	■				■	■			■				■	
Thuja orientalis	■	■			■				■	■		■		■					■
Thuja plicata	■	■			■	■				■				■					
Thujopsis dolobrata	■	■				■							■		■				
Tilia americana		■				■								■					
Tilia cordata		■				■			■					■					
Tilia × euchlora		■				■								■					
Tilia petiolaris		■				■				■				■					
Tilia platyphylos	■	■				■				■				■					
Trachycarpus fortunei		■				■				■	■	■					■		
Tsuga canadensis	■	■			■	■				■			■	■				■	
Tsuga heterophylla	■				■	■				■		■	■	■					
Ulex europaeus			■	■	■		■							■					

Footnotes
[1] min. – 15°C (5°F), [2] min. –5°C (23°F), [3] min. 0°C (32°F), [4] min. 10°C (50°F)

	FOLIAGE						FLOWERING SEASON				FLOWERS							PROBLEMS				
Variegated	Purple	Autumn colour	Fast-growing	Deciduous	Evergreen	Spring	Summer	Autumn	Winter	White, green	Blue, mauve	Yellow, orange	Pink	Red, purple	Scented, aromatic	MAXIMUM HEIGHT (metres)	Thorny	Poisonous/allergenic	Intolerant of pollution	Suckering	
		■		■			■			■						4					False spiraea
		■		■			■			■						2					False spiraea
		■		■			■			■						3					False spiraea
		■		■		■				■						10					Whitebeam
		■		■		■				■						12					European mountain ash
		■		■		■				■						10					Finnish whitebeam
		■		■		■				■						10					Mountain ash
		■		■		■							■			2.5					Mountain ash
		■		■		■				■						1					Mountain ash
	■	■		■		■				■						15					Wild service tree
		■		■			■						■			2					Spiraea
		■		■		■				■						1					Spiraea
		■		■			■						■			0.4					Spiraea
		■		■						■						1					Spiraea
		■		■	■											1.5					Spiraea
		■		■	■											2.5					Spiraea
		■		■			■			■						1					Stephanandra
	■	■		■			■			■						2					Stephanandra
		■		■			■			■						4					Silky camellia
		■		■			■			■						2.5					Mountain camellia
		■		■			■			■						10					Stewartia
		■			■	■				■						2.5					Stranvesia
		■		■			■									1.5				■	Snowberry
		■		■			■									1					Snowberry
		■		■												2					Indian currant, Coralberry
		■		■			■									2				■	Indian currant, Coralberry
		■		■		■							■		■	5					Lilac
		■		■		■	■						■		■	1.5					Lilac
		■		■		■			■				■		■	1.2					Lilac
		■		■		■	■				■		■		■	6					Lilac
		■		■		■	■						■		■	5					Lilac
		■		■		■				■				■	■	5				■	Lilac
		■		■			■						■			3					Tamarisk
	■			■		■							■			6					Tamarisk
		■		■			■						■	■		6					Tamarisk
■					■											15		■			Yew
					■											4.5					Yew
					■											4		■			Yew
					■											15					Thuja
					■											12					Thuja
■					■											20					Western red cedar
					■											15					Thujopsis
	■			■												25					American basswood
	■	■		■			■			■					■	30					Small-leaved lime
	■	■		■		■						■				20					Lime
	■	■		■			■					■			■	25					Lime
	■	■		■			■					■			■	30					Large-leaved lime
						■										15				■	Windmill palm
						■										15					Eastern hemlock
						■										30					Western hemlock
					■	■						■				1.5					Gorse

671

	USES						SOIL					ASPECT & HARDINESS							
	Fast-growing	Large	Small	Banks	Hedging	Specimen	Humus-rich	Sandy or dry	Chalky	Moist	Clay	Sun	Shade, semi-shade	Fully hardy[1]	Frost hardy[2]	Half hardy[3]	Tender[4]	Silver, grey	Golden
Ulex gallii			■	■				■						■					
Ulmus glabra		■	■			■				■		■		■					
Ulmus parvifolia		■				■				■		■		■					
Ulmus procera		■				■				■		■		■					
Viburnum × bodnantense			■			■				■		■		■					
Viburnum × burkwoodii			■			■	■					■		■					
Viburnum carlesii			■			■						■		■					
Viburnum davidii			■				■					■		■					
Viburnum farreri			■		■	■				■		■		■					
Viburnum × juddii			■			■				■		■		■					
Viburnum lantana			■	■	■	■		■	■			■		■					
Viburnum opulus			■	■	■	■		■	■	■		■		■					
Viburnum plicatum			■			■	■			■		■		■					
Viburnum rhytidophyllum	■		■		■	■			■			■		■					
Viburnum sargentii			■		■	■				■		■		■					
Viburnum tinus			■		■	■			■			■		■		■			
Vinca major			■	■						■		■	■	■					
Vinca minor			■	■						■			■	■					
Washingtonia filifera			■		■		■					■					■		
Weigela florida			■		■	■				■				■					
Weigela middendorffiana			■		■	■				■				■					
Xanthoceras sorbifolium			■			■				■				■					
Yucca filamentosa			■	■		■		■				■		■					
Yucca flaccida			■			■		■				■		■					
Yucca glauca			■			■		■				■		■					
Yucca gloriosa			■			■			■			■			■				
Yucca whipplei			■			■			■			■			■				
Zenobia pulverulenta			■		■	■	■			■			■	■					

Footnotes
[1] min. – 15°C (5°F), [2] min. –5°C (23°F), [3] min. 0°C (32°F), [4] min. 10°C (50°F)

	Variegated	Purple	Autumn colour	Fast-growing	Deciduous	Evergreen	Spring	Summer	Autumn	Winter	White, green	Blue, mauve	Yellow, orange	Pink	Red, purple	Scented, aromatic	MAXIMUM HEIGHT (metres)	Thorny	Poisonous/allergenic	Intolerant of pollution	Suckering
Gorse						■			■				■				0.6				
Wych elm			■		■												40				
Chinese elm			■		■												12				
English elm			■		■												40				
Viburnum			■							■				■			2				
Viburnum						■				■	■					■	2				
Viburnum			■			■	■				■					■	1.5				
Viburnum						■	■				■						0.5				
Viburnum			■							■	■			■		■	3				
Viburnum			■		■	■	■							■		■	1.5				
Viburnum			■		■		■				■						3				
Snowball bush			■		■		■				■						4				
Viburnum			■		■		■				■						2				
Viburnum						■	■				■						3				
Viburnum			■		■			■			■						4				
Laurustinus						■	■			■	■						3.5				
Periwinkle	■					■	■		■			■					0.6				
Periwinkle	■					■	■	■				■					0.3				
Californian washingtonia						■											10				
Weigela	■			■			■	■						■	■		3				
Weigela							■						■				1.5				
Yellowthorn							■				■			■			3				■
Yucca	■					■		■			■						2				■
Yucca						■		■			■						1.2				■
Yucca						■					■						1.2				■
Spanish dagger						■		■			■						2.5				■
Yucca						■		■			■						3				■
Zenobia			■		■			■			■					■	1.2				

	SOIL			ASPECT			FLOWERING SEASON				FOLIAGE			USES		
	Alkaline	Neutral	Acid	Sun	Semi-shade	Shade	Spring	Summer	Autumn	Winter	Evergreen	Deciduous	Self-clinging	Wall or trellis	Ground cover	Through trees
A *Abutilon megapotamicum*		■	■	■	■			■	■		■		■	■		Abutilon, Flowering maple
Abutilon vitifolium		■	■	■		■		■			■		■			Abutilon, Flowering maple
Actinidia deliciosa		■	■	■	■			■				■		■		Actinidia, Kiwi fruit
Actinidia kolomikta		■	■	■	■			■				■		■		Actinidia, Kiwi fruit
Akebia quinata		■	■	■	■			■				■		■		■ Akebia, Chocolate vine
Akebia trifoliata		■	■	■		■		■				■		■		■ Akebia, Chocolate vine
Aristolochia durior		■	■	■	■			■				■		■		Birthwort, Dutchman's pipe
B *Bougainvillea glabra*		■		■				■			■			■		Bougainvillea
Bougainvillea spectabilis		■		■	■			■			■			■		Bougainvillea
Buddleja alternifolia	■	■	■	■				■				■		■		Buddleja, Butterfly bush
Buddleja colvilei	■	■	■	■				■			■			■		Buddleja, Butterfly bush
C *Campis grandiflora*		■		■				■	■			■		■		Bigonia, Trumpet creeper
Campis radicans		■		■				■				■		■		Bigonia, Trumpet creeper
Campis × tagliabuana		■		■				■				■		■		Bigonia, Trumpet creeper
Ceanothus arboreus		■		■	■		■				■			■		Californian lilac
Ceanothus × delileanus		■		■				■	■			■		■		Californian lilac
Ceanothus impressus		■	■	■			■	■			■			■		Californian lilac
Ceanothus × pallidus		■		■				■	■			■		■		Californian lilac
Ceanothus thyrsiflorus		■		■			■	■			■			■		Californian lilac
Cestrum fasciculatum		■	■	■					■		■	■		■		Cestrum
Clematis alpina		■	■	■	■		■	■				■		■	■	■ Clematis, Old man's beard
Clematis armandii	■	■	■	■	■		■				■			■		Clematis, Old man's beard
Clematis cirrhosa		■	■	■	■					■	■			■		Clematis, Old man's beard
Clematis flammula		■	■	■	■			■	■			■		■	■	Clematis, Old man's beard
Clematis florida	■	■	■	■	■	■		■				■		■		Clematis, Old man's beard
Clematis macropetala	■	■	■	■			■					■		■	■	Clematis, Old man's beard
Clematis montana		■	■	■	■	■	■					■		■	■	Clematis, Old man's beard
Clematis rehderiana		■	■	■	■				■			■		■	■	Clematis, Old man's beard
Clematis tangutica	■	■	■	■				■				■		■	■	Clematis, Old man's beard
Clematis texensis	■	■	■	■			■					■		■		Clematis, Old man's beard
Clematis viticella	■	■	■	■				■	■			■		■	■	Clematis, Old man's beard
Clianthus formosus		■	■	■			■	■			■			■		Clianthus
Clianthus puniceus		■	■	■			■	■				■		■		Parrot's bill, Lobster's claw
H *Hedera canariensis*	■	■	■	■	■	■				■	■		■	■	■	Canary Island ivy
Hedera colchica	■	■	■	■	■	■		■		■	■		■	■	■	Persian ivy
Hedera helix	■	■	■	■	■	■				■	■		■	■	■	Common ivy
Hedera hibernica	■	■	■	■	■	■					■		■		■	Atlantic ivy
Hydrangea petiolaris	■	■	■	■	■			■				■	■	■		Climbing hydrangea
Hydrangea serratifolia		■	■					■	■			■	■	■		Climbing hydrangea
J *Jasminum beesianum*	■	■	■	■	■		■					■		■		Pink jasmine
Jasminum humile		■	■	■				■			■			■		Yellow jasmine
Jasminum nudiflorum	■	■	■	■	■		■			■		■		■		Winter jasmine
Jasminum officinale		■	■	■	■			■				■		■	■	Common jasmine

	SOIL			ASPECT			FLOWERING SEASON				FOLIAGE		USES				
	Alkaline	Neutral	Acid	Sun	Semi-shade	Shade	Spring	Summer	Autumn	Winter	Evergreen	Deciduous	Self-clinging	Wall or trellis	Ground cover	Through trees	
Jasminum polyanthum		■	■	■	■		■				■	■		■			Jasmine
Jasminum primulinum		■	■	■	■		■				■			■			Jasmine
Jasminum × stephanense		■	■	■	■		■				■			■			Jasmine
Lapageria rosea		■			■		■	■			■			■			Chilean bellflower, Copihue
Lonicera × brownii	■	■	■	■	■			■				■		■			Honeysuckle
Lonicera caprifolium	■	■	■	■	■			■				■		■			Perfoliate honeysuckle
Lonicera fragrantissima	■	■	■	■	■					■		■		■			Honeysuckle
Lonicera henryi	■	■	■	■	■			■			■			■		■	Honeysuckle
Lonicera hildebrandtiana	■	■		■	■			■			■	■		■		■	Giant Burmese honeysuckle
Lonicera japonica		■	■	■	■			■			■	■		■			Japanese honeysuckle
Lonicera nitida	■	■	■	■	■	■					■			■			Honeysuckle
Lonicera periclymenum	■	■	■	■	■			■				■		■			Common honeysuckle
Lonicera sempervirens		■	■	■				■				■		■			Trumpet honeysuckle
Lonicera tatarica	■	■	■	■	■			■				■		■			Honeysuckle
Lonicera × tellmaniana	■	■	■	■	■			■				■		■			Honeysuckle
Muehlenbeckia axillaris		■	■	■	■			■			■	■		■			Muehlenbeckia
Muehlenbeckia complexa		■	■	■	■			■			■	■		■			Muehlenbeckia
Mutisia clematis		■	■	■				■			■			■			Mutisia
Mutisia decurrens		■	■	■				■			■			■			Mutisia
Mutisia ilicifolia		■	■	■				■	■		■			■			Mutisia
Parthenocissus henryana	■	■	■	■								■	■	■	■	■	Virginia creeper
Parthenocissus quinquefolia	■	■	■	■	■							■	■	■	■	■	Virginia creeper
Parthenocissus tricuspidata	■	■	■	■	■							■	■	■			Boston ivy, Japanese creeper
Passiflora caerulea		■	■	■	■			■			■			■			Passion flower
Passiflora edulis		■	■	■				■			■			■			Passion flower
Passiflora umbilicata		■	■	■				■			■	■		■			Passion flower
Polygonum baldschuanicum	■	■	■	■	■			■				■		■		■	Russian vine
Polygonum multiflorum	■	■	■	■				■				■		■			Russian vine, Knotweed
Pyracantha angustifolia		■	■	■	■	■					■			■			Pyracantha
Pyracantha atalantoides		■	■	■	■	■					■			■			Pyracantha
Pyracantha coccinea		■	■	■	■	■					■			■			Pyracantha
Pyracantha crenulata		■	■	■	■			■			■			■			Pyracantha
Pyracantha rogersiana		■	■	■	■	■					■			■			Pyracantha
Schisandra chinensis		■	■	■			■					■	■	■		■	Schisandra
Schisandra glaucescens		■	■	■			■					■	■	■		■	Schisandra
Schisandra rubriflora		■	■	■			■					■	■	■		■	Schisandra
Solanum crispum		■	■	■				■			■			■			Solanum, Chilean potato tree
Solanum jasminoides		■	■	■				■			■	■		■			Potato vine
Wisteria floribunda		■	■	■			■					■		■		■	Wisteria
Wisteria × formosa		■	■	■			■					■		■		■	Wisteria
Wisteria japonica		■	■	■			■					■		■		■	Japanese wisteria
Wisteria sinensis		■	■	■			■					■		■		■	Chinese wisteria
Wisteria venusta		■	■	■			■					■		■		■	Silky wisteria

L

M

P

S

W

675

	SOIL				HARDINESS				FLOWERS	FRUIT		
	Chalky	Clay	Sandy	Moist	Fully hardy – down to –15°C (5°F)	Frost hardy – down to –5°C (23°F)	Tender – down to 10°C (50°F)	Flowering season	Ornamental flowers	Fruiting season	Year of first fruiting	Years of fruiting
Actinidia deliciosa	very little	■	■	■		■		early sum.	■	aut.	4	35
Citrus	very little		■	■			■	sum.	■	aut. to early spr.	5 to 8	25 to 40
Corylus avellana	■		■	■	■			early spr.		aut.	7	60
Fragaria		■	■	■	■			spr. to sum.		early sum. to aut.	1	6
Juglans regia	■		■	■	■			early spr.		aut.	15 to 30 [1]	30 to 100
Malus	very little	■	■	■	■			spr.	■ ■	sum.	4 to 10 [1]	30 to 60
Prunus armeniaca	■		■			■		early spr.	■	sum.	4	25
Prunus cerasus	■		■	■	■			mid spr.	■ ■	sum.	6	25
Prunus × domestica	■	■		■	■			spr.	■	sum. to early aut.	5	30
Prunus persica	(possible)			■		■		spr.	■ ■	sum. to early aut.	4	15
Pyrus communis		■		■	■			spr.	■	sum. to aut.	5 to 8 [1]	30 to 60
Ribes rubrum, R. uva-crispum, R. nigrum	■	■	■	■	■			late spr.		mid sum.	3	15 to 20
Rubus idaeus	■	■	■	■	■			late spr. to early aut.		sum. to early aut.	1 or 2	15 to 20
Vitis vinifera	■		■	■	■			early sum.		aut.	4	50

[1] according to form and root-stock

| | PROPAGATION | | | | FORM | | | MAINTENANCE | | |
	Seed	Layering	Cuttings	Budding	Cleft or wedge grafting; crown grafting	Free	Training possible	Training recommended	Fruits must be thinned	Pruning necessary	Pruning unnecessary
Chinese gooseberry, Kiwi fruit		■						■		■	
Citrus fruits				■		■					■
Hazel		■				■					■
Strawberry		■				■					■
Walnut					■	■	■				■
Apple				■	■	■		■	■	■	
Apricot	(possible)			■		■	■				■
Cherry				■	■	■					■
Plum, Gage	■			■	■	■	■				■
Peach, Nectarine	(possible)			■		■	■		■	■	
Pear				■	■	■		■	■	■	
Red currant, Gooseberry, Blackcurrant		■	■			■	■				■
Raspberry		■ (2)				■		■		■	
Vine		■	■		■ (2)			■	■	■	

(2) by taking suckers

ROSES

D = double   Sm = small
SD = semi-double   M = medium
S = single   L = large

	Height	Flower type	APPEARANCE / FLOWER COLOUR — White	Yellow, orange	Pink	Red, purple	FLOWERING SEASON — Late spring	Early summer	Mid-summer	Late summer	Early autumn	Mid-autumn
A ‘Agnes’	2.50m	SD-M		■				■			■	
‘Aimée Vibert’	3m+	D	■						■	■	■	
‘Alba’	2m	S	■					■	■			
‘Albéric Barbier’	5m	SD	■					■				
‘Albertine’	4.50m	D			■			■	■			
‘Alexandre Girault’	5m+	D				■		■	■	■		
‘Alister Stella Gray’	4m	D		■				■	■		■	
‘Allgold’	0.80m			■				■	■	■	■	
‘Amadis’	5m+	SD				■		■	■			
‘American Pillar’	4.50m	S			■			■	■			
B ‘Baby Masquerade’	0.60m			■	■			■	■	■	■	
‘Ballerina’	1.50m	S-Sm			■			■	■	■	■	
‘Banksiae’	5m	S	■				■	■	■	■		
‘Belle de Crécy’	1.20m	D			■	■		■	■			
‘Belle Poitevine’	1.50m	SD-L			■			■	■	■	■	
‘Belle Portugaise’	5m	D-L			■			■				
‘Blanc Double de Coubert’	2.50m	SD-Sm	■			■		■	■	■	■	
‘Blanc Meillandécor’	0.60m	D-Sm	■					■	■	■	■	
‘Bleu Magenta’	5m					■		■	■	■		
‘Buff Beauty’	1m/1.60m	D-M		■		■		■	■		■	■
C ‘Candy Rose’	0.60m	SD			■			■	■	■		
‘Cardinal de Richlieu’	0.80m	D			■	■		■	■			
‘Céleste’	1.50m	SD-M			■			■				
‘Celsiana’	1.50m	SD			■			■		■		
‘Centenaire de Lourdes’	1.20m	D-M			■			■		■		
‘Chaplin’s Pink Climber’	3m	S-M			■			■	■			
‘Climbing Étoile de Hollande’	4m	D-L				■		■	■	■		
‘Climbing Iceberg’	3m+	SD-M	■					■	■	■		
‘Climbing Lady Hillingdon’	7m	D-M		■				■	■	■		
‘Climbing Mme Caroline Testout’	6m	D-L			■			■	■	■		
‘Climbing Sombreuil’	5m	L	■					■	■	■	■	
‘Colibri’	0.30m	D		■				■	■		■	
‘Complicata’	2.50m	S-M				■		■	■			
‘Constance Spry’	3m	M			■			■	■	■		
‘Coral Dawn’	3m	S-L			■			■	■	■		
‘Cornelia’	1m/2m	D-Sm			■			■	■		■	
D ‘Delicata’	2m	S-M			■			■	■	■		
‘Dorothy Perkins’	6m	D-S			■				■	■		
‘Duraft King’	0.50m	D-Sm				■			■	■		
F ‘Fantin Latour’	1.80m				■				■	■		
‘Félicité Perpétue’	4.50m	D-M	■					■	■			
‘Fiona’	1m	SD-Sm				■		■	■		■	
‘Frau Dagmar Hastrup’	1/2m	S-M			■			■	■	■		

	CHARACTERISTICS				USES						
	Exhibition	Remontant	Hips	Scent	Hedging	Island beds (grouped or single)	Borders, containers	Ground cover	Walls, fences	Through trees	
■		■	■		■						'Agnes'
								■	■		'Aimée Vibert'
		■	■		■						'Alba'
		■						■			'Albéric Barbier'
		■						■	■		'Albertine'
		■	■					■	■	■	'Alexandre Girault'
■		■	■					■	■		'Alister Stella Gray'
■											'Allgold'
								■			'Amadis'
								■	■		'American Pillar'
■	■				■		■	■			'Baby Masquerade'
■		■	■	■	■			■			'Ballerina'
		■						■	■		'Banksiae'
		■	■								'Belle de Crécy'
■	■	■	■	■							'Belle Poitevine'
			■					■	■		'Belle Portugaise'
■	■	■	■								'Blanc Double de Coubert'
■		■				■					'Blanc Meillandécor'
■		■						■			'Bleu Magenta'
■		■	■	■	■						'Buff Beauty'
■		■			■	■					'Candy Rose'
		■	■	■							'Cardinal de Richlieu'
									■		'Céleste'
		■	■								'Celsiana'
■		■		■	■						'Centenaire de Lourdes'
■							■				'Chaplin's Pink Climber'
	■		■						■		'Climbing Étoile de Hollande'
■		■						■			'Climbing Iceberg'
■		■						■	■		'Climbing Lady Hillingdon'
									■		'Climbing Mme Caroline Testout'
■		■	■					■	■		'Climbing Sombreuil'
					■	■					'Colibri'
				■		■		■			'Complicata'
		■	■					■			'Constance Spry'
	■	■							■		'Coral Dawn'
■		■	■								'Cornelia'
■				■				■			'Delicata'
								■	■		'Dorothy Perkins'
					■	■					'Duraft King'
		■		■							'Fantin Latour'
		■				■		■	■		'Félicité Perpétue'
			■		■	■					'Fiona'
■	■	■	■	■		■					'Frau Dagmar Hastrup'

D = double   Sm = small
SD = semi-double   M = medium
S = single   L = large

	Name	APPEARANCE		FLOWER COLOUR				FLOWERING SEASON					
		Height	Flower type	White	Yellow, orange	Pink	Red, purple	Late spring	Early summer	Mid-summer	Late summer	Early autumn	Mid-autumn
	'Frau Karl Druschki'	1.50m	D	■					■	■			
	'Frosty'	0.50m		■			■		■	■			
	'Frühlingsgold'	2.50m			■	■	■		■				
G	'General Jacqueminot'	1m					■		■	■	■		
	'Gloire de Dijon'	4m	D-L		■	■			■	■	■	■	
	'Gloire des Mousseux'	1.50m	L-D			■	■		■	■	■		
	'Golden Showers'	2m	L		■				■	■	■	■	■
	'Golden Wings'	1m/2m	S-L		■				■	■	■	■	
	'Great Maiden's Blush'	1.8m	D-M	■		■			■	■		■	
	'Guinée'	5m	D				■		■	■	■		
H	'Handel'	3.50m	SD-L	■		■			■	■	■		
	'Hansa'	1m	D-M				■		■	■		■	
	'Hollandina'	2m	S-M			■			■	■	■		
I J	'Iceberg'	1.50m	D-M	■					■	■	■		
	'Jacques Cartier'	1.20m	SD			■			■	■		■	
	'Joseph's Coat'	1.20m	SD		■	■	■		■	■			
K L	'Kew Rambler'	6m	S-Sm		■				■				
	'Kiftsgate'	8m	S-Sm	■					■				
	'La Mortola'	8m	L	■						■			
	'Lili Marlene'	3m					■		■	■	■		
	'Little White Pet'	0.60m	D-Sm	■					■	■	■	■	
	'Louise Odier'	1.50m	D-L			■			■	■	■	■	■
M	'Maréchal Niel'	4.50m	L		■				■				
	'Marguerite Hilling'	2.50m	S-M			■		■		■	■		
	'Mary Rose'	1.20m	D-L			■	■		■	■		■	■
	'Max Graf'	0.60m	S-Sm			■				■			
	'Meillandina'	0.35m	D-Sm	■			■		■	■			■
	'Mermaid'	8m	S-M		■					■	■	■	■
	'Mimi'	0.60m	D-M			■		■		■			
	'Mme A. Meilland'	1.50m	D-L		■	■			■	■			
	'Mme Alfred Carrière'	6m	D-M	■		■		■	■	■	■		
	'Mme Anthony Waterer'	2m+	S-M				■		■	■			
	'Mme Grégoire Staechlin'	4.50m	SD			■			■	■			
	'Mme Hardy'	1.5m	D-L	■					■	■			
	'Mme Isaac Pereire'	2m	D-L			■			■	■	■	■	
	'Mme Sancy de Parabère'	6m	L			■			■	■			
	'Mousseline'	0.80m	D			■			■	■		■	
N	'Nevada'	2m+	S-L		■			■	■	■		■	
	'New Dawn'	4.50m	SD-M	■		■			■	■	■		■
	'Nozomi'	0.60m	S-Sm			■			■	■			
P	'Papa Meilland'	0.60m					■		■		■	■	
	'Paulii'	1.2m	S-L	■					■	■			
	'Paul's Scarlet Climber'	3m	D				■		■	■			

CHARACTERISTICS				USES						
Exhibition	Remontant	Hips	Scent	Hedging	Island beds (grouped or single)	Borders, containers	Ground cover	Walls, fences	Through trees	
■										'Frau Karl Druschki'
		■	■		■	■				'Frosty'
		■	■	■	■					'Frühlingsgold'
■		■	■							'General Jacqueminot'
■		■					■	■		'Gloire de Dijon'
■		■								'Gloire des Mousseux'
■		■	■				■	■		'Golden Showers'
■		■	■							'Golden Wings'
■		■	■					■		'Great Maiden's Blush'
■		■	■					■		'Guinée'
■		■	■				■			'Handel'
	■	■		■	■					'Hansa'
■		■	■	■						'Hollandina'
■		■	■							'Iceberg'
■		■	■							'Jacques Cartier'
■		■	■							'Joseph's Coat'
	■	■					■	■		'Kew Rambler'
	■	■	■				■	■	■	'Kiftsgate'
		■	■				■	■		'La Mortola'
		■					■	■		'Lili Marlene'
■						■				'Little White Pet'
■		■	■	■	■					'Louise Odier'
■		■					■	■		'Maréchal Niel'
■		■		■	■					'Marguerite Hilling'
■		■								'Mary Rose'
	■					■				'Max Graf'
■						■				'Meillandina'
		■					■	■		'Mermaid'
■		■	■		■	■				'Mimi'
■		■	■	■	■					'Mme A. Meilland'
■		■				■				'Mme Alfred Carrière'
■	■	■	■	■						'Mme Anthony Waterer'
■	■	■				■		■		'Mme Grégoire Staechlin'
		■				■				'Mme Hardy'
■		■	■				■			'Mme Isaac Pereire'
		■	■				■	■		'Mme Sancy de Parabère'
	■	■			■	■				'Mousseline'
■		■	■	■	■					'Nevada'
■	■	■					■			'New Dawn'
						■	■			'Nozomi'
■		■	■		■					'Papa Meilland'
		■					■			'Paulii'
								■		'Paul's Scarlet Climber'

APPEARANCE | **FLOWER COLOUR** | **FLOWERING SEASON**

D = double Sm = small
SD = semi-double M = medium
S = single L = large

Name	Height	Flower type	White	Yellow, orange	Pink	Red, purple	Late spring	Early summer	Mid-summer	Late summer	Early autumn	Mid-autumn
'Peace'	1.2m	D-L	■						■	■	■	
'Penelope'	1.2m	S-D		■				■	■		■	
'Perla de Montserrat'	0.15m	Sm			■			■	■	■		
'Pierre de Ronsard'	3m	D-M			■	■		■	■	■	■	■
'Pink Cameo'	5m	Sm			■			■	■	■		
'Pink Perpetue'	2.8m	D-L			■			■	■	■		
'Pink Wave'	0.60m	D-M			■	■		■	■	■		■
'Pompon de Paris'	1.80m	D-Sm			■				■			
'Queen Elizabeth'	1.80m	SD			■			■		■	■	
'Raubritter'	0.80m	SD-Sm			■			■	■			
'Reines des Violettes'	1.50m					■			■			
'Rêve d'Or'	5m	SD-M		■				■	■		■	
'Rose Gaujard'	1m	SD-M				■		■		■	■	
'Rose Marie Viaud'	5m				■			■	■	■		
'Rosina'	0.30m	SD		■					■			
'Rouletii'	1.50m	D-Sm			■				■	■		
'Rush'	1.50m		■					■	■		■	
'Salet'	1.50m	SD			■			■	■	■		
'Smarty'	1m	S			■				■			
'Snow Carpet'	0.90m	D-Sm	■					■	■	■		
'Sourire d'Orchidée'	0.50m	S-M	■					■	■		■	■
'Souvenir du Doctor Jamain'	5m					■		■		■		
'Stanwell Perpetual'	1.50m	D			■			■	■		■	
'Swany'	0.50m	D	■					■	■	■		
'Sylvie Vartan'	0.80m	SD-M			■			■	■	■		■
'The Fairy'	0.60m	D-Sm			■	■		■	■		■	■
'Toby Tristram'	6m	S-L						■				
'Veilchenblau'	2m	SD-Sm				■			■	■		
'Vicomtesse Pierre du Fou'	5m		■						■	■	■	
'Violette'	5m	D				■			■			
'Virgo'	0.80m	L	■					■	■	■		
'Wedding Day'	9m	S-L	■						■			
'White Grootendorst'	2.50m	S-M	■						■		■	
'White Queen Elizabeth'	1.5m	D	■						■	■	■	
'Yellow Doll'	0.30m			■				■	■			
'Yolande d'Aragon'	1.20m	D			■			■	■		■	
'Yves Piaget'	1m	D-M				■		■	■	■		
'Zéphirine Drouhin'	2.5m	D-L			■				■	■		■

Index letters in left margin: Q R, S, T V, W, Y, Z

682

GENERAL
INDEX